HAY LIBRARY
WESTERN WYOMING COMMUNITY COL

D0575733

Short Story Criticism

809.31 Sh81s 1999
v.34

Short story criticism.

FOR REFERENCE

Do Not Take From This Room

Guide to Gale Literary Criticism Series

For criticism on	Consult these Gale series
Authors now living or who died after December 31, 1959	*CONTEMPORARY LITERARY CRITICISM (CLC)*
Authors who died between 1900 and 1959	*TWENTIETH-CENTURY LITERARY CRITICISM (TCLC)*
Authors who died between 1800 and 1899	*NINETEENTH-CENTURY LITERATURE CRITICISM (NCLC)*
Authors who died between 1400 and 1799	*LITERATURE CRITICISM FROM 1400 TO 1800 (LC)* *SHAKESPEAREAN CRITICISM (SC)*
Authors who died before 1400	*CLASSICAL AND MEDIEVAL LITERATURE CRITICISM (CMLC)*
Authors of books for children and young adults	*CHILDREN'S LITERATURE REVIEW (CLR)*
Dramatists	*DRAMA CRITICISM (DC)*
Poets	*POETRY CRITICISM (PC)*
Short story writers	*SHORT STORY CRITICISM (SSC)*
Black writers of the past two hundred years	*BLACK LITERATURE CRITICISM (BLC)*
Hispanic writers of the late nineteenth and twentieth centuries	*HISPANIC LITERATURE CRITICISM (HLC)*
Native North American writers and orators of the eighteenth, nineteenth, and twentieth centuries	*NATIVE NORTH AMERICAN LITERATURE (NNAL)*
Major authors from the Renaissance to the present	*WORLD LITERATURE CRITICISM, 1500 TO THE PRESENT (WLC)*

ISSN 0895-9439

Volume 34

Short Story Criticism

Criticism of the
Works of Short Fiction Writers

Anna Sheets Nesbitt
Editor

GALE GROUP

Detroit
San Francisco
London
Boston
Woodbridge, CT

STAFF

Anna Sheets Nesbitt, *Editor*

Susan Salas, *Associate Editor*
Shayla Hawkins, Debra A. Wells, *Assistant Editors*

Maria Franklin, *Permissions Manager*
Kimberly F. Smilay, *Permissions Specialist*
Kelly Quin, *Permissions Associate*
Sandy Gore, *Permissions Assistant*

Victoria Cariappa, *Research Manager*
Cheryl Warnock, *Research Specialist*
Patricia T. Ballard, Wendy Festerling, Tamara C. Nott,
Tracie A. Richardson, Corrine Stocker, *Research Associates*
Timothy Lehnerer, Patricia Love, *Research Assistants*

Mary Beth Trimper, *Production Director*
Dorothy Maki, *Manufacturing Manager*
Cindy Range, *Buyer*

Randy Bassett, *Imaging Database Supervisor*
Robert Duncan, Michael Logusz, *Imaging Specialists*
Gary Leach, *Graphic Artist*
Pamela A. Reed, *Imaging Coordinator*

Since this page cannot legibly accommodate all copyright notices, the acknowledgments constitute and extension of the copyright notice.

While every effort has been made to ensure the reliability of the information presented in this publication, The Gale Group neither guarantees the accuracy of the data contained herein nor assumes any responsibility for errors, omissions, or discrepancies. Gale accepts no payment for listing, and inclusion in the publication or any organization, agency, institution, publication, service, or individual does not imply endorsement of the editors or publisher. Errors brought to the attention of the publisher and verified to the satisfaction of the publisher will be corrected in future editions.

The paper used in this publication meets the minimum requirements of American National Standard for Information Sciences—Permanence Paper for Printed Library Materials, ANSI Z39.48-1984.

This publication is a creative work fully protected by all applicable copyright laws, as well as by misappropriation, trade secret, unfair competition, and other applicable laws. The authors and editors of this work have added value to the underlying factual material herein through one or more of the following: unique and original selection, coordination, expression, arrangement, and classification of the information.

All rights to this publication will be vigorously defended.

Copyright © 2000
Gale Group
27500 Drake Rd.
Farmington Hills, MI 48331-3535

All rights reserved, including the right of reproduction in whole or in part in any form.

Library of Congress Catalog Card Number 88-641014
ISBN 0-7876-3080-2
ISSN 0895-9439

Printed in the United States of America

10 9 8 7 6 5 4 3 2 1

Contents

Preface vii

Acknowledgments xi

Preface

A Comprehensive Information Source
on World Short Fiction

Short Story Criticism (SSC) presents significant criticism of the world's greatest short story writers and provides supplementary biographical and bibliographical materials to guide the interested reader to a greater understanding of the authors of short fiction. This series was developed in response to suggestions from librarians serving high school, college, and public library patrons, who had noted a considerable number of requests for critical material on short story writers. Although major short story writers are covered in such Gale series as *Contemporary Literary Criticism (CLC), Twentieth-Century Literary Criticism (TCLC), Nineteenth-Century Literature Criticism (NCLC),* and *Literature Criticism from 1400 to 1800 (LC),* librarians perceived the need for a series devoted solely to writers of the short story genre.

Coverage

SSC is designed to serve as an introduction to major short story writers of all eras and nationalities. Since these authors have inspired a great deal of relevant critical material, *SSC* is necessarily selective, and the editors have chosen the most important published criticism to aid readers and students in their research.

Approximately eight to ten authors are included in each volume, and each entry presents a historical survey of the critical response to that author's work. The length of an entry is intended to reflect the amount of critical attention the author has received from critics writing in English and from foreign critics in translation. Every attempt has been made to identify and include the most significant essays on each author's work. In order to provide these important critical pieces, the editors sometimes reprint essays that have appeared elsewhere in Gale's Literary Criticism Series. Such duplication, however, never exceeds twenty percent of an *SSC* volume.

Organization

An *SSC* author entry consists of the following elements:

- The **Author Heading** cites the name under which the author most commonly wrote, followed by birth and death dates. If the author wrote consistently under a pseudonym, the pseudonym will be listed in the author heading and the author's actual name given in parentheses on the first line of the biographical and critical introduction.

- The **Biographical and Critical Introduction** contains background information designed to introduce a reader to the author and the critical debates surrounding his or her work.

- A **Portrait of the Author** is included when available. Many entries also contain illustrations of materials pertinent to an author's career, including holographs of manuscript pages, title pages, dust jackets, letters, or representations of important people, places, and events in the author's life.

- The list of **Principal Works** is chronological by date of first publication and lists the most important works by the author. The first section comprises short story collections, novellas, and novella collections. The second section gives information on other major works by the author. For foreign authors, the editors have provided original foreign-language publication information and have selected what are considered the best and most complete English-language editions of their works.

- **Criticism** is arranged chronologically in each author entry to provide a useful perspective on changes in critical evaluation over the years. All short story, novella, and collection titles by the author featured in the entry are printed in boldface type to enable a reader to ascertain without difficulty the works discussed. Also for purposes of easier identification, the critic's name and the publication date of the essay are given at the beginning of each piece of criticism. Unsigned criticism is preceded by the title of the journal in which it appeared.

■ Critical essays are prefaced with **Explanatory Notes** as an additional aid to students and readers using SSC. An explanatory note may provide useful information of several types, including: the reputation of the critic, the intent or scope of the critical essay, and the orientation of the criticism (biographical, psychoanalytic, structuralist, etc.).

■ A complete **Bibliographical Citation,** designed to help the interested reader locate the original essay or book, precedes each piece of criticism.

■ The **Further Reading List** appearing at the end of each author entry suggests additional materials on the author. In some cases it includes essays for which the editors could not obtain reprint rights. Boxed material following the further reading list provides references to other biographical and critical sources on the author in series published by Gale.

Beginning with volume six, SSC contains two additional features designed to enhance the reader's understanding of short fiction writers and their works:

■ Each SSC entry now includes, when available, **Comments by the Author** that illuminate his or her own works or the short story genre in general. These statements are set within boxes or bold rules to distinguish them from the criticism.

■ A **Select Bibliography of General Sources on Short Fiction** is included as an appendix. This listing of materials for further research provides readers with a selection of the best available general studies of the short story genre.

Other Features

A **Cumulative Author Index** lists all the authors who have appeared in *SSC, CLC, TCLC, NCLC, LC,* and *Classical and Medieval Literature Criticism (CMLC),* as well as cross-references to other Gale series. Users will welcome this cumulated index as a useful tool for locating an author within the Literary Criticism Series.

A **Cumulative Nationality Index** lists all authors featured in SSC by nationality, followed by the number of the SSC volume in which their entry appears.

A **Cumulative Title Index** lists in alphabetical order all short story, novella, and collection titles contained in the SSC series. Titles of short story collections, separately published novellas, and novella collections are printed in italics, while titles of individual short stories are printed in roman type with quotation marks. Each title is followed by the author's name and corresponding volume and page numbers where commentary on the work is located. English-language translations of original foreign-language titles are cross-referenced to the foreign titles so that all references to discussion of a work are combined in one listing.

Citing Short Story Criticism

When writing papers, students who quote directly from any volume in the Literary Criticism Series may use the following general forms to footnote reprinted criticism. The first example pertains to material drawn from periodicals, the second to material reprinted from books:

¹Henry James, Jr., "Honoré de Balzac," *The Galaxy* 20 (December 1875), 814-36; reprinted in *Short Story Criticism,* Vol. 5, ed. Thomas Votteler (Detroit: The Gale Group, 1990), pp. 8-11.

[2]F. R. Leavis, *D. H. Lawrence: Novelist* (Alfred A. Knopf, 1956); reprinted in *Short Story Criticism,* Vol. 4, ed. Thomas Votteler (Detroit: The Gale Group, 1990), pp. 202-06.

Comments

Readers who wish to suggest authors to appear in future volumes, or who have other suggestions, are invited to contact the editors by writing to The Gale Group, Literary Genres Division, 27500 Drake Rd., Farmington Hills, MI 48331-3535.

Acknowledgments

The editors wish to thank the copyright holders of the excerpted criticism included in this volume and the permissions managers of many book and magazine publishing companies for assisting us in securing reproduction rights. We are also grateful to the staffs of the Detroit Public Library, the Library of Congress, the University of Detroit Mercy Library, Wayne State University Purdy/Kresge Library Complex, and the University of Michigan Libraries for making their resources available to us. Following is a list of the copyright holders who have granted us permission to reproduce material in this volume of *SSC* 34 Every effort has been made to trace copyright, but if omissions have been made, please let us know.

COPYRIGHTED MATERIAL IN *SSC* VOLUME 34, WERE REPRODUCED FROM THE FOLLOWING PERIODICALS:

American Quarterly, v. 16, Winter, 1964. Copyright 1964, American Studies Association. Reproduced by permission of The Johns Hopkins University Press.—*American Transcendental Quarterly,* v. 2, Second Quarter. Copyright 1969 by Kenneth Walter Cameron. Reproduced by permission.—*Bucknell Review,* v. XXXIX, 1995. Copyright (c) Bucknell Review 1995. Reproduced by permission of the publisher.—*The American West,* Fall, 1965. Copyright (c) 1965 by the American West Publishing Company, Tucson, AZ. Reproduced by permission of the author.—*Comparative Literature Studies,* v. 33, 1993. Copyright (c) 1993 by The Pennsylvania State University. Reproduced by permission of The Pennsylvania State University Press.—*Critica Hispánica,* v. 5, Fall, 1983. Reproduced by permission.—*English Language Notes,* v. 7, March, 1970. (c) copyrighted 1970, Regents of the University of Colorado. Reproduced by permission.—*Journal of Modern Literature,* v. XIX, Fall, 1995. (c) Temple University 1995. Reproduced by permission.—*Latin American Literary Review,* v. 3, Spring-Summer, 1975; v. 16, July-December, 1988. Reproduced by permission.—*Luso-Brazilian Review,* v. IV, June, 1967; v. 14, Winter, 1977; v. XXXI, Summer, 1994. All reproduced by permission.—*Mark Twain Journal,* v. XIX, Summer, 1978. Reproduced by permission.—*MELUS: The Journal of Society for the Study of Multi-Ethnic Literature of the United States,* v. 14, Spring, 1987; v. 7, Fall, 1980; v. 19, Winter, 1994. Copyright, *MELUS: The Society for the Study of Multi-Ethnic Literature of the United States,* 1987, 1980, 1994. All reproduced by permission.—*The Mississippi Quarterly: The Journal of Southern Culture,* v. LXIX, Spring, 1996. Copyright 1966 Mississippi State University. Reproduced by permission.—*Modern Philology,* v. 40, February, 1963. (c) 1963 by The University of Chicago. Reproduced by permission of the University of Chicago Press.—*Mosaic,* v.25, Spring, 1992. (c) Mosaic 1992. Acknowledgment of previous publication is herewith made.—*The New York Times Book Review,* October 28, 1923; December 23, 1923. Copyright 1923 by The New York Times Company. Reproduced by permission.—*Nine,* v. 4, Winter, 1953 for "'The Wild Body': A Sanguine of the Enemy" by Geoffrey Wagner. Reproduced by permission.—*Nineteenth-Century Fiction,* v. 19, March, 1965 for "Poe's 'The Tell-Tale Heart'" by E. Arhtur Robinson; v. 28, December, 1973 for "Artemus Ward and Mark Twain's 'Jumping Frog'" by Paul C. Rodgers, Jr.. (c) 1965, 1973 by The Regents of the University of California. Both reproduced by permission of the publisher and the author—*Papers on Language and Literature,* v. 24, Summer, 1988. Copyright (c) 1988 by The Board of Trustees, Southern Illinois University at Edwardsville. Reproduced by permission.—*PMLA,* v, 82, December, 1967. Copyright (c) 1967 by the Modern Language Association of America. Reproduced by permission of the Modern Language Association of America.—*Prismal Cabral,* v. 3, Spring, 1979. Reproduced by permission.—*Revista Canadiense de Estudios Hispánicos,* v. XVIII, Fall, 1992 for "Masking History in Donoso's 'Taratuta'" by Flora González. Reproduced by permission of the publisher and the author.—*Russian Literature,* v. XXIX, 1991 for "'The Enchanted Wanderer': A Parable of National Identity" by R. A. Peace. Reproduced by permission of the publisher and the author.—*Satire Newsletter,* v. 1, Spring, 1964 for "The Infernal Reminiscence: Mythic Patterns in Mark Twain's 'The Celebrated Frog of Calaveras County'" by Paul Smith. Reproduced by permission of the publisher and the author.—*Scando-Slavica,* n. 3, 1957 for "Frame Story and First person Story in N. S. Leskov" by Aleksej B. Ansberg. Reproduced by permission of the author.—*Slavic and East European Journal,* v. 20, 1976. (c) 1976 by AATSEEL of the U.S., Inc. Reproduced by permission.—*Studies in American Fiction,* v. 17, Autumn, 1989; v. 23, Autumn, 1994. Copyright (c) 1989, 1994 Northeastern University. Both reproduced by permission.—*Studies in Short Fiction,* v. 5, Summer, 1968; v. 7, Fall, 1970; v. 8, Winter, 1971; v. 17, Spring, 1980; v. 15, v. 21, Spring, 1984; V. 15, Winter, 1984; v. 22, Fall, 1985; v. 27, Spring, 1990. Copyright 1968, 1970, 1971, 1980.1984, 1985, 1990 by Newberry College. All reproduced by permission.—*Symposium,* v. 38, Winter, 1984-85. Copyright (c) 1984 Helen Dwight Reid Educational Foundation. Reproduced with permission of the Helen Dwight Reid Educational Foundation, published by Heldref Publications, 1319 18th Street, NW, Washington, DC 20036-1802.—*The Slavonic and East European Review,* v. 67, April, 1989. Reproduced by permission.—*The Southern Literary Journal,* v. IX, Spring, 1977 for "The Words for Invisible Things: The Short Stories (1916-1924)" by Julius Rowan Raper. Copyright 1980 by the Department of English, University of North Carolina at Chapel Hill.

Reproduced by permission.—*The Spectator,* v. 139, December 17, 1927. Copyright 1927 by The Spectator. Reproduced by permission of *The Spectator.*—*The Women's Review of Books,* v. VI, July, 1989 for "Windows on a World" by Valerie Matsumoto. Copyright (c) 1989. All rights reserved. Reproduced by permission of the author.—*Western Folklore,* v .22, January, 1963. Reproduced by permission.

COPYRIGHTED MATERIAL IN *SSC* VOLUME 34, WERE REPRODUCED FROM THE FOLLOWING BOOKS:

Bonaparte, Marie. From *The Life and Works of Edgar Allan Poe: A Psycho-Analytic Interpretation.* Imago Publishing Company, 1949. Copyright by Imago Publishing Co. Ltd., 1949.—Branch, Edgar M. From *The Literary Apprenticeship of Mark Twain with Selections from His Apprentice Writing.* University of Illinois Press, 1950. Reproduced by permission. Bynum, Paige Matthey. From "'Observe How Healthily—How Calmly I Can Tell You the Whole Story': Moral Insanity and Edgar Allan Poe's 'The Tell-Tale Heart'" in *Literature and Science as Modes of Expression.* Edited by Frederick Amrine. Kluwer Academic Publishers, 1989. (c) 1989 Kluwer Academic Publishers. All rights reserved. Reproduced by permission with kind permission from Kluwer Academic Publishers.—Callan, Richard J. From "Gaspard de la nuit: Crucial Breakthrough in the Growth of Personality" in *Studies on the Works of José Donoso: An Anthology of Critical Essays.* Edited by Miriam Adelstein. The Edwin Mellen Press, 1990. Copyright (c) 1990 The Edwin Mellen Press. All rights reserved. Reproduced by permission.—Carpenter, Lynette. From *Haunting the House of Fiction: Feminist Perspectives on Ghost Stories by American Women.* Edited by Wendy Kolmar and Lynette Carpenter. University of Tennessee Press, 1991. Copyright (c) 1991 by The University of Tennessee Press. Reproduced by permission of The University of Tennessee Press.—Chapman, Robert T. From *Wyndham Lewis: Fictions and Satires.* Vision Press, 1973. (c) 1973 Vision Press. All rights reserved. Reproduced by permission.—Cheung, King-Kok. From the introduction to *Seventeen Syllables and Other Stories. Kitchen Table: Women of Color, 1988.* Copyright (c) 1988 by Hisaye Yamamoto DeSoto. All rights reserved. Reproduced by permission of the author.—Edgerton, Willliam B. From the introduction to *Satrical Stories of Nikolai Leskov.* Edited by William B. Edgerton. Translated by William B. Edgerton. Pegasus, 1969. Copyright (c) 1969 by Western Publishing Company, Inc. Reproduced with the permission of Macmillan Library Reference USA, a division of Ahsuog, Inc.—Fleak, Kenneth. From *The Chilean Short Story: Writers from the Generation of 1950.* Peter Lang, 1989. (c) Peter Lang Publishing, Inc. All rights reserved. Reproduced by permission.—Fox, C. J. and Robert T. Chapman. From the introduction to *Unlucky For Pringle*: Unpublished and other Stories. By Wyndham Lewis. Edited by C. J. Fox and Robert T. Chapman. Vision, 1973. (c) 1973 Vision Press Limited. All rights reserved. Reproduced by permission. Gerber, John C. From *Mark Twain.* Twayne Publishers, 1988. Copyright 1988 by G. K. Hall & Co. All rights reserved. Reproduced with the permission of Macmillan Library Reference USA, a division of Ahsuog, Inc.—Gordon, Donald K. From "The Dynamics of Psyche in the Existentialism of José Donoso" in *Studies on the Works of José Donoso: An Anthology of Critical Essays.* Edited by Miriam Adelstein. The Edwin Mellen Press, 1990. Copyright (c) 1990 The Edwin Mellen Press. All rights reserved. Reproduced by permission.—Haliburton, David. From *Edgar Alan Poe: A Phenomenolgical View.* Princeton, 1973. Copyright (c) 1973 by Princeton University Press. All rights reserved. Reproduced by permission.—Hoffman, Daniel. From *Poe Poe Poe Poe Poe Poe Poe.* Doubleday and Company, 1972. Also by Louisiana State University Press. 1998. Copyright (c) 1972 by Daniel Hoffman. All rights reserved. Used by permission of the author.—Lafourcade, Bernard. From an afterword to *The Complete Wild Body.* Edited by Bernard Lafourcade. Black Sparrow Press, 1982. Copyright (c) 1982 by the Estate of Mrs. G. A. Wyndham Lewis. Copyright (c) 1982 by Bernard Lafourcade. All rights reserved. Reproduced by permission.—Lantz, K. A. From an introduction to *The Sealed Angel and Other Stories.* Edited and translated by K. A. Lantz. University of Tennessee Press, 1984. Copyright (c) 1984 by The University of Tennessee Press. All rights reserved. Reproduced by permission. Lewis, Wyndham. From a foreword to *Rotting Hill.* Methuen and Co., Ltd., 1951. (c) Wyndham Lewis and the estate of the late Mrs. G.A. Wyndham Lewis by kind permission of the Wyndham Lewis Memorial Trust (aregistered charity).—Lindstrom, Naomi. From *Women's Voice in Latin American Literature.* Lynne Rienner Publishers,1989. (c) Naomi Lindstrom 1989. All rights reserved. Reproduced by permission of the author.—Magnarelli, Sharon. From *Understanding José Donoso.* University of South Carolina Press, 1993. Copyright (c) 1993 University of South Carolina Press. Reproduced by permission.—McDowell, Frederick P. W. From *Ellen Glasgow and the Ironic Art of Fiction.* University of Wisconsin Press, 1960. Copyright (c) 1960 by the Regents of the University of Wisconsin. Reproduced by permission.—McDuff, David. From an introduction to *Lady MacBeth and Mtsensk and Other Stories.* Translated by David McDuff. Penguin Books, 1987. (c) David McDuff 1987. All rights reserved. Reproduced by permission of Penguin Books, Ltd. —McLean, Hugh. From *Nikolai Leskov: The Man and His Art.* Harvard University Press, 1977. Coyright (c) 1977 by the President and Fellows of Harvard College. All rights reserved. Reproduced by permission Harvard University Press.—Meeker, Richard K. From an introduction to *The Collected Stories of Ellen Glasgow.* Edited by Richard K. Meeker. Louisiana State University Press, 1963. Copyright 1963 by Louisiana State University Press. Reproduced by permission.—Michelson, Bruce. From *Mark Twain on the Loose: A Comic Writer and the American Self.* University of Massachusetts Press, 1955. Copyright (c) 1995 by The University of Massachusetts Press. All rights reserved. Reproduced by permission.—Pritchard, William H. From

Wyndham Lewis. Twayne Publishers, 1968. Copyright (c) 1968 by Twayne Publishers, Inc. All rights reserved. Reproduced with the permission of Macmillan Library Reference USA, a division of Ahsuog, Inc.—Pritchett, V. S. From the introduction to *Nikolai Leskov: Selected Tales.* Ttranslated by David Magarshack. Farrar, Struas and Cudahy, 1961. Copyright (c) 1961 by David Magarshack. Reproduced by permission of Farrar, Straus and Cudahy a division of Farrar, Straus & Giroux, Inc—Rainwater, Catherine. From "Ellen Glasgow's Outline of History in 'The Shadowy Third and Other Stories'" in *The Critical Response to H. G. Wells.* Edited by William J. Scheick. Greenwood Press, 1995. Copyright (c) 1995 by William J. Scheick. All rights reserved. Reproduced by permission of Greenwood Publishing Group, Inc., Westport, CT.—Thiébaux, Marcelle. From "Poems and Short Stories" in *Ellen Glasgow.* Frederick Ungar Publishing Co., 1982. Copyright (c) 1982 by Frederick Ungar Publishing Co., Inc. Reproduced by permission.—Wagner, Linda W. From "The Years of the Locust" in *Ellen Glasgow*: Beyond Convention. University of Texas Press, 1982. Copyright (c) 1982 by the University of Texas Press. All rights reserved. Reproduced by permission.

PHOTOGRAPHS AND ILLUSTRATIONS APPEARING IN *SSC* VOLUME 34, WERE RECEIVED FROM THE FOLLOWING SOURCES:

Donoso, José, photograph by Jerry Bauer. (c) Jerry Bauer. Reproduced by permission.
Glasgow, Ellen (hands on right side of face), photograph. Library of Congress.
Lewis, Wyndham, wearing large brimmed hat and smiking a pipe. Archive Photos, Inc. Reproduced by permission.
Poe, Edgar Allen, photograph. The library of Congress.
Twain, Mark, photograph. The Library of Congress.

José Donoso
1924–1996

(Full name José Donoso Yáñez) Chilean novelist, short story writer, essayist, poet, translator, and critic.

INTRODUCTION

One of the leading figures of the Latin American literary phenomenon of the 1960s and 1970s referred to as the "Boom," Donoso is best known for his structurally complex, nightmarish antinovel, *El obsceno pájaro de la noche* (1970; *The Obscene Bird of Night*). While his short stories, written early in his career, are more realistic and conventionally structured than his masterpiece, they exhibit a subtle psychological complexity beneath their apparent naturalism and foreshadow many of the themes found in the later fiction: the moral decay of the haute bourgeois and, particularly, upper-class Chilean society; the spiritual and emotional dissolution of the individual; and the blurred boundaries between truth and hallucination, order and chaos. The novellas, which figure among Donoso's later works, return to a less phantasmagorical world than that of his novels, but in them the ambiguities between fantasy and reality in everyday life are still explored with bold flights of imagination. Donoso's short fiction is also characterized by the use of multiple points of view, unreliable narrators, description of the irrational in rational terms, the use of irony, and a pervasive sense of despair and pessimism at the state of contemporary civilization.

Biographical Information

Donoso was born in Santiago into an upper-middle-class family, a background that acquainted him with the distinct class boundaries within Chilean society. His father was a physician who was as interested in gambling as in his profession, and his mother was the daughter of prominent Chilean aristocrats. When Donoso was seven years old, largely because of his father's inability to hold a job, the family moved into the huge, decaying mansion of Dr. Donoso's three elderly aunts, where he tended to them as a doctor-in-residence. The atmosphere of decrepitude in his great aunts' house was to feature prominently in Donoso's fiction. In the late 1930s the family moved back to their earlier home, and soon thereafter Donoso's maternal grandmother, who was in deteriorating mental health, moved in with them. This difficult period Donoso describes as "one of the episodes that most marked my life," and his insane grandmother was to become one of the protagonists of his first novel, *Coronación* (1957; *Coronation*). Although he was a bookish youth, who in particular loved the works of Henry James, his literary mentor, Donoso acknowledged that it was the experiences with his family and servants that exercised the greatest influence on his work.

Educated by tutors at an exclusive private English school, Donoso dropped out before graduating, spending a year as a shepherd in southern Chile and working as a dockhand in Buenos Aires. In his early twenties he returned to Santiago to resume his education and received a scholarship to study English literature at Princeton University. After completing a bachelors degree, he traveled throughout North America before returning to Chile, where he worked as a teacher and a journalist. After the success of his first volume of short stories in 1956, Donoso moved to Isla Negra off the coast of Chile to complete his first novel, which also enjoyed a favorable reception. In 1958, tired of the oppressive atmosphere of upper-middle-class Chilean society, he set off on a tour of South America; he spent two years in Buenos Aires, where he became acquainted with many important Argentine writers, including Jorge Luis Borges, and met his future wife, María del Pilar Serrano.

In the 1960s, Donoso continued to move beyond the intellectual confines of Chile to become part of a growing community of Latin American writers—major figures of the "Boom" that included his good friend Carlos Fuentes and Gabriel García Márquez. In 1964 Donoso and his wife left Chile to attend a writers' conference in Mexico; they did not return to their homeland for seventeen years, spending the majority of their time in Spain with occasional stints in the United States. Donoso's most celebrated works, including the novels *El obsceno pájaro de la noche, Casa de campo* (1978; *A House in the Country*) and *El jardín de al lado* (1981; *The Garden Next Door*)—which together firmly established his reputation as one of the finest Latin American writers of the twentieth century—were written during this time of self-imposed exile. He returned to Chile in 1981, eight years after General Augusto Pinochet's 1973 military coup overthrew elected Marxist president Salvator Allende. Donoso's 1986 novel, *La desesperanza* (*Curfew*), which tells of life under Pinochet's rule, was praised abroad for its frank depiction of Chile's dispossessed poor and the dispirited political left, but was viewed coolly by Chilean intellectuals because of its lack of a firm political stance. However, Donoso refused to be affected by his critics' censure, pointing out that he was never a crusader nor even a social commentator but a man hurt by the state of affairs in his native land. He wanted change, but asserted that it was not his place to offer yet another misguided explanation of the world. In 1990 Donoso received the Chilean Premio Nacional de Literatura, his country's highest literary honor. He continued to live and write in Chile until his death at age 72 of liver cancer.

Major Works of Short Fiction

Most of Donoso's short stories were written early in his career, but he continued to publish novellas in the 1970s, 1980s, and 1990s. His first published works were two stories written in English while he was a student at Princeton, "The Poisoned Pastries" and "The Blue Woman," which appeared in a literary magazine that he helped establish there. It was not until 1954, when he was nearly thirty, that he wrote his first story in Spanish. A collection of stories, *Veraneo y otros cuentos,* was published the following year at his own expense and with the help of family and friends. These early tales are generally urban in flavor and touch on themes that figure prominently in his more mature work. The title piece, "Veraneo," for example, told from the point of view of a pair of children, depicts the world of the Chilean bourgeoisie and elaborates on the interplay between masters and servants. A second collection, *El charlestón* (*Charleston and Other Stories*), written while he was in Buenos Aires, appeared in 1960. Donoso's interest in the questions of psycho-social identity, marginality, social caste, and the stifling codes of contemporary Chilean society inform these stories, typified by the widely anthologized "Paseo," a narrative about an aged, bourgeois spinster who abandons decorum when she meets a stray dog on the way home from church. Donoso's two volumes of stories plus "Santelices" and his earlier "China" were collected and published as *Los mejores cuentos de Donoso* in 1966, which was reprinted in 1971 simply as *Cuentos.* A trilogy of novellas, *Tres*

novelitas burguesas (1973; *Sacred Families: Three Novellas*), his first published fiction after *El obsceno pájaro de la noche,* treats questions of self-identity in its exploration of fragmented subjectivity, but without the hallucinatory quality that infused the novel. The four novellas in *Cuatro para Delfina* (1982), Donoso's first fiction written after his return to Chile, are marked in style and theme by the author's reencounter with his native country and the Chilean vernacular. The pair of novellas in *Taratuta/Naturaleza muerta con cachimba* (1990; *Taratuta and Still Life with Pipe*), like Donoso's other short fiction, are structured more conventionally than many of the novels, but they are nonetheless complex, cerebral pieces: both are "postmodern" in tone and deal with the power of artistic creation to absorb and transform mundane existence.

Critical Reception

Donoso's first story in Spanish, "China," was written in 1954 for a literary contest and won publication in that year in Enrique Lafourcade's influential *Antologia del nuevo cuento chileno,* the anthology that launched the "Generation of 1950"—a group of middle- and upper-middle-class writers who changed the direction of Chilean fiction by turning away from nativism to cosmopolitanism and a renewed concern with narrative form. Donoso's first, self-published volume of stories was received favorably by critics and won him the 1956 Municipal Prize for Short Stories in Santiago. His collections that appeared in the 1960s were similarly praised for their bitingly satiric portrayals of middle-class Chilean society. However, the seventeen stories, all of which were written between 1950 and 1962, have never received the sustained critical attention that his novels have enjoyed. The stories are not considered those of an artist in full command his literary powers, but in recent years critics have turned their attention to them in part for their inherent merit but also in recognition that they contain in rudimentary form many of the concerns that were to be developed at greater length in the novels. Early critics tended to characterize the stories as primarily realistic, social commentaries on Chilean bourgeois life, ignoring what later critics recognized as the psychologically penetrating analysis of human nature lurking beneath the surface and Donoso's deftly drawn parallels between his characters' mental and physical environments. Donoso's three sets of novellas, *Tres novelitas burguesas, Cuatro para Delfina,* and *Taratuta/Naturaleza muerta con cachimba,* while they are not counted among his major works, have also been praised for being complex but highly readable, showing Donoso at the height of his ability to portray the inexplicable "other side" of reality that lies within the human psyche.

PRINCIPAL WORKS

Short Fiction

Veraneo y otros cuentos 1955

Dos cuentos 1956
El charlestón [*Charleston and Other Stories*] 1960
Los mejores cuentos de Donoso 1966
Cuentos 1971
Tres novelitas burguesas [*Sacred Families: Three Novellas*] (novellas) 1973
Cuatro para Delfina (novellas) 1982
Taratuta/Naturaleza muerta con cachimba [*Taratuta and Still Life with Pipe*] (novellas) 1990

Other Major Works

Coronación [*Coronation*] (novel) 1957
Este Domingo [*This Sunday*] (novel) 1965
El lugar sin límites [*Hell Has No Limits*] (novel) 1966
El obsceno pájaro de la noche [*The Obscene Bird of Night*] (novel) 1970
Historia personal del "boom" [*The "Boom" in Spanish American Literature: A Personal History*] (memoir) 1972
Casa de campo [*A House in the Country*] (novel) 1978
La misteriosa desaparición de la Marquesita de Loria (novel) 1980
El jardín de al lado [*The Garden Next Door*] (novel) 1981
Poemas de un novelista (poems) 1981
La desesperanza [*Curfew*] (novel) 1986
Where Elephants Go to Die (novel) 1995

CRITICISM

Alexander Coleman (essay date 1971)

SOURCE: "Some Thoughts on José Donoso's Traditionalism," *Studies in Short Fiction,* Vol. VIII, No. 1, Winter, 1971, pp. 155-58.

[*In the following essay, Coleman explores the subtle psychological themes that he contends underlie the apparent realism of Donoso's early stories.*]

It is quite interesting that the work of Jose Donoso (b. Santiago de Chile, 1925) has often been described as traditionalist, traditionalist, that is, in the English sense, admiring as he does James and Austen. There has even been mention of the word *costumbrismo,* referring to the genre very much dear to nineteenth-century Spanish writers generally considered to be minor—except Larra, of course. This is confusing, and needlessly so. Such a generally sensible critic as Mario Benedetti, for example, in commenting upon Donoso's first collection of short stories, **El veraneo y otros cuentos** (1955),[1] noted his preoccupation with Chilean reality. Benedetti also underlined the inclusion of many national "types" in these stories, praising the tangible qualities of the very real streets, *barrios,* etc. The stories unquestionably give every evidence of a modest and perfectly calculated kind of realistic literary practice. But to see nothing more than this in the stories is to hide their insidious and quite beautifully disguised thematics.

In the title story, for instance, the whole nightmare of marital infidelity is reflected in a perverse and distorted way through the relationships of the various servants of the triangle, and through the way in which the appropriate children manipulate not only each other, but also the servants in turn. The result is a complicated and perfectly executed depiction of intricate human domination, alleviated only when a realm of feeling between the children cuts through the vertical social structures of hate and authority that the adults have created for their children and which they wish to pass on to them.

And so, too, for the language—apparently odd chatter between servants and children and amongst the children themselves, but in reality a linguistic mask for one of Donoso's nuclear fantasies, the alternance and conflict between Life and Authority. Donoso is able to suggest the variegated power of one over another by the subtlest means—at times it is the power of song, where one child can command the other to laugh or cry according to the tune sung, or at times the barely inferred mystic power of a child with a slingshot.

At times the basic obsession in these early stories is inferred in a more pointed way, as in the echoes of the Quetzalcoatl myth in the story **"El Güero"** from the same collection. Here the elements are perhaps purposefully complicated by Donoso, for it is set in Mexico, with a couple from the (North American) groves of academe who are condemned to spend time in a small village while the husband finishes an erudite volume that will crown his academic career in the United States. The husband, Howland, as depicted by Donoso's narration is dull, hopelessly out of style, and severely circumscribed by the nature of his occupation, a limitation that effects the personal disintegration of the wife.

The counterfigure to this immensely limited couple is their son Mike, who grows in primitive power and audacity as his contact with the local myths and tales becomes deeper and more dominant within himself. He begins to dream, and the natural life takes hold of him until "everything mysterious and everything that vibrates with hidden force came to be his own natural element." As a final dénouement to the implosion of the life force in Mike, he sets off upstream in search of the "blond gods," accompanied by torrential rains, thunder, and lightning, never to be seen again. Beneath the impeccable order and spiritual agony of a marriage in the final throes of its own destruction, the death of the child brings forth a new and higher order of vitalism within the couple. All this is artfully transcribed by a sympathetic narrator as Mrs. Howland returns to the village where all this took place long ago.

Other stories in the collection, such as **"Una señora"** and **"Fiesta en grande,"** are superb set pieces that again are expressive of Donoso's essentially urban sensibility. The polarities of "civilized" and ordered existence finally break down, and man is confronted with an overwhelming sense of the violence of nature and man and consciously throws himself into a maelstrom of unconscious, inhuman, and murderous void.

Any discussion of Donoso's thematics must also take into consideration the tone—violently Romantic in spite of everything—which characterizes the evolution of his characters from constriction to expression. If we take such a definition as that of Henry James, where the romantic stands "for the things that . . . we never can directly know; the things that can reach us only through the beautiful circuit and subterfuge of our thought and our desire,"[2] we are at least at the beginning of an appreciation of the multiple planification of reality that Donoso constantly practices. It is at times a rather brutal fashion, as in his early novel *Coronación,*[3] where the world of the ruined bourgeois as represented by Misiá Elisa Grey de Abalos and her debilitated son Andrés Abalos is counterpoised by the servant class in the old mansion, who apparently serve but actually dominate the exhausted lives of the fading aristocracy.

In two later novels, *El lugar sin límites*[4] and *Este domingo,*[5] both of 1966, this multiple dependence and relationship of class is delineated in a masterful fashion, a portrait of a society in which the etymological meaning of *travesty* is fully explored, a world where all objects are signs to their opposites, a terrifying confusion of doubleness. But in spite of the confusion of identity purposefully practiced by Donoso in his short stories, one is often left with a unique vision of the central character of the story—the old man in **"Ana María,"** hypnotized by the eyes of a three year old child, finally determining to flee with her to a unknown and probably dreadful future; the pathetic Aunt Matilde in **"Paseo,"** who gradually abandons the spinster's role automatically imposed upon her by society and disappears into the Buenos Aires night, never to return; the frustrated bureaucrat Santelices, in **"Santelices,"** convinced that the garden outside his window is populated with fierce animals, throws himself into this imagined hell that is at the center itself of all that is deathly.

Against the rigidities of society, there is an ever-present oceanic sense in Donoso into which his heroes plunge. These pathetic and at times comic figures are pilgrims of their own brand of truth, vague searchers for a freer self and society, constantly at odds with the reality of their own spiritual suffocation. A groping for a sense of transcendence, a whole process that inevitably entails the encounter with the monster that is within them, engendered out of the mathematical rigidities with which societies function in apparent order. As Emir Rodríguez Monegal has pointed out in his brilliant study of Donoso, it is precisely this discovery of violence that is the obsessive and often repeated theme. It has also been pointed out that there are rarely any valid paternal figures in his work—it is very much of a matriarchy, but one in which masculine and feminine roles function nonetheless, all to the detriment of those concerned. And often, too, above all in a few of the early stories, a good story is robbed of its impact by a too obviously psychological explanation in lieu of an ending. Such a story is **"Fiesta en grande,"** where a "Napoleonic" national pistol champion, after having engaged in some tragicomic antics at an office picnic, is lulled to sleep by his ancient mother after she has

rather obviously gone through his jacket to remove the pistol, which is, of course the cause of all the trouble. But such moments are rare in Donoso's short pieces.

But certainly our sensibilities are constantly engaged by Donoso's stories—above all, because of the sheer power of the inarticulate that underlies them all. He is always careful to draw for us a miniature portrait of a society, often from the point of view of a childlike narrator who is sensitized to the significance of every detail. What draws us out as readers is the power of the unspoken in him, the deadly attraction of nothingness. It would seem that his work, glanced at in a cursory fashion, does more than its share of the reader's work, because it is so evidently a refraction of a society, but this aspect can only cloud our vision of this wholly contemporaneous literary achievement. The carefully appointed society with which Donoso began to depict in *Coronación* and in the stories is for us a functioning lie possibly pointing to a truth; the words surround rather than express a reality. If they denote anything, one would have to mention a society that is itself inauthentic and false. Sartre justly observes of Nathalie Sarraute's books that "they are filled with these impressions of terror: people are talking, something is about to explode that will illuminate suddenly the glaucous depths of a soul, and each of us feels the crawling mire of his own. Then, no: the threat is removed, the danger is avoided, and the exchange of commonplaces begins again. Yet sometimes these commonplaces break down and a frightful protoplasmic nudity becomes apparent."[6] In many senses this is the essence of the best of Donoso, too, for daily life has rarely taken on such traumatic resonances as occur so frequently in his stories. As Severo Sarduy states toward the end of his notable analysis of Donoso's *El lugar sin límites,* "The essence (*fondo*) of a work is to be considered as an absence, metaphor as a sign without basis."[7]

Notes

[1] (Santiago: Ed. Universitaria, 1955). I have used the convenient later collection of fourteen stories entitled *Los mejores cuentos de José Donoso* (Santiago de Chile: Editorial Zig-Zag, 1966). The following articles are especially recommended: Emir Rodríguez Monegal, "El mundo de José Donoso," *Mundo Nuevo* (Paris), June 1967. Isaac Goldenberg, "*Coronación* o los límites del aislamiento," *Mundo Nuevo* (Paris), June 1969. Severo Sarduy, "Escritura/travestismo," in *Escrito sobre un cuerpo* (Buenos Aires: Editorial Sudamericana, 1969).

[2] As cited by R. P. Blackmur in his preface to James's *The American* (New York: Dell Publishing Co., 1960), p. 6.

[3] (Santiago de Chile: Editorial Nascimento, 1957).

[4] (México: Joaquín Mortiz, 1966).

[5] (México: Joaquín Mortiz, 1966).

[6] Jean-Paul Sartre, *Situations,* Benita Eisler, trans. (Greenwich, Connecticut: Fawcett Publications, 1966) p. 140.

[7] Sarduy, p. 47.

Alfred A. Knopf has published excellent English translations of two novels by José Donoso: *Coronación* (*Coronation,* translated by Jocasta Goodwin, 1965) and *Este domingo* (*This Sunday,* translated by Lorraine O'Grady Freeman, 1967). The same house is also preparing a translation of Donoso's masterpiece, *El obsceno pájaro de la noche.*

Howard M. Fraser (essay date 1975)

SOURCE: "Witchcraft in Three Stories of José Donoso," *Latin American Literary Review,* Vol. 3, No. 6, Spring/Summer, 1975, pp. 3-8.

[*In the following essay, Fraser asserts that the stories "Veraneo," "Paseo," and "Santelices" exemplify Donoso's technique of combining social and political realism with elements of the occult and supernatural.*]

A paradoxical phenomenon characterizes contemporary Spanish American literature. As Jorge Luis Borges has interpreted this paradox in his essay "The Argentine Writer and Tradition," the tradition of Spanish American literature is that of Europe and the West, all of Western culture, the Universe. For Borges, Spanish American literature is truly national when not defined solely in terms of national traits.[1] Evidence of his contention appears in Gibbon's *Decline and Fall of the Roman Empire.* "Gibbon observes that in the Arabian book *par excellence,* in the Koran, there are no camels." We view illustrations of the paradox in authors such as Julio Cortázar, Octavio Paz, and Borges himself. They all analyze the spiritual essence of their native lands within the context of a profound universalism based on such diverse and esoteric bodies of thought as oriental and primitive religions, Surrealism, and Hebraic mysticism.

Another writer who maintains the paradoxical posture of the traditionalist,[2] whose work also incorporates cosmopolitan, universal systems of thought, is the Chilean José Donoso. Donoso exemplifies the paradoxical nature of contemporary Spanish American literature as Borges explains it. In his short stories a realistic commentary on national "obsessions"[3] collides head-on with an international background of Occultism, magic and witchcraft. At once Donoso merges the modern and ancient. He impresses upon contemporary literature the universal and also profoundly Hispanic traditions of the world of the witches.[4]

Donoso's stories, **"Veraneo"** [**"Summering"**], **"Paseo"** [**"Walk"**], and **"Santelices,"** most clearly exemplify the combination of national themes and magical techniques. In his short fiction Donoso underscores the familiar themes of man's sense of isolation and captivity in the modern world. His characters are pathetic victims of circumstance, trapped in a monotonous existence, who succeed in breaking away from changeless conformity.

In **"Veraneo,"** Donoso explores the world of the seashore summer resort. A deep friendship takes place between two nine-year-old boys. The charismatic and messianic Jaime teaches Raúl the heights of joy and the depths of despair, and thus aids the emotional growth into adulthood of his immature pupil. Matilde, in **"Paseo,"** is liberated from her sterile role as housekeeper and foster mother. A stray dog imparts awareness of her human potential to Matilde who is transformed into a sensitive and loving woman. The title character of **"Santelices"** magically becomes a feline monster as the only alternative to his cloistered existence.

Donoso manipulates the treatment of setting to transform ordinary people and their vulgar way of life into nightmarish experiments in magical realism. For example: the beach as a setting for the summer vacation in **"Veraneo"** symbolizes the conflict of opposing characters as they appear against the stark contrasts of sea and sky. Donoso delineates the two-dimensional quality of the nine-year-old Raúl as he appears in silhouette against the horizon. Donoso utilizes the heat of the beach to fuse Raúl to Jaime, his mentor in the symbolic crucible.[5] The element of setting also represents the theme of the enclosed world in **"Paseo."** Matilde lives in a mansion surrounded by thick walls. Her home is metaphorically described as an immense book which never shows its binding toward the street. The walls of the house's exterior are mirrored within the house by the massive shelves of books and thick doors. Several images reflect Santelices' closed world. Donoso compares his existence with that of caged animals. The pension, Santelices' windowless room, the rigid mealtime schedules and after-dinner program of diversions resemble the controlled atmosphere of the zoo. The protagonist senses this similarity and establishes a spiritual kinship with beasts caged in the zoo. He frequently visits the animals and communes with the instinctive, dangerous creatures. Despite his attraction to kindred souls, Santelices feels his existence is worse by comparison with that of the animals. He observes flies buzzing about the gory maws of the caged cats, but when he returns home he finds only the lifeless specks of his own flies dead from starvation.

Donoso's trapped protagonists manage to escape from their tomb-like enclosure through the intercession of characters who are their mirror opposites. Raúl, Matilde, and Santelices follow the mysterious direction of their mentors: Jaime, the stray dog, and the blonde girl with her house cats. On a symbolic plane, the pairs of characters in these stories interact in a series of occultist experiments. Each teacher, an outsider to the world of the initiate, penetrates the defenses of the naive pupil. As a result of this interaction, the shaman-teachers rescue the trapped protagonists.

Jaime, in the crucible-like heat and light of the beach in **"Veraneo,"** opens a world of emotion for Raúl. Jaime chants the mantras or tones which motivate Raúl to laugh or cry. Raúl learns to imitate Jaime in many ways and finally abandons the childish games of the seashore. During his summer experience Raúl discovers the depth of his emotions, and when Jaime leaves Raúl at the end of the story, his profile resembles that of Jaime, a resemblance which indicates the extent of his spiritual transformation.[6]

Donoso creates characters who lack a sense of their human identity. The opening scenes of **"Veraneo"** present the harsh contrasts of light and dark which make Raúl an insignificant figure on the horizon. In fact, Donoso means to imply that Raúl has not yet begun to exist. Matilde's brothers deny her humanity in **"Paseo"** when they refer to her as "tal cosa debajo de los árboles" ["something underneath the trees"]. (p. 206) Matilde's rigidly scheduled existence befits that of a machine or robot. Matilde herself is a metaphor of the purely rational mother surrogate who lacks the human love her nephew needs. Her life is enclosed by the house and its chores. Her brothers, lacking these touchstones of stability in their lives, maintain their hold on reality by means of billiard games, their symbolic "order" in defense against the "chaos" of life outside the home. (p. 213)

A stray dog violates the ordered space of the household. Matilde recognizes in the *perra* [bitch] a kindred spirit: they both live as marginal members of their worlds, both are ugly, and both feel alone. As soon as the dog manages to climb the high walls around the house, Matilde and the narrator, her nephew, notice a fundamental humanity in the animal, the promise of humanization for Matilde. The narrator refers to the dog as a *payaso* [clown] (p. 221), and when her brothers ask Matilde to throw the animal out, she asks, "¿A quién?" ["Whom?"]. (p. 222) The non-human creature introduces Matilde to the chaotic world of human life just beyond the thick walls. On repeated *paseos* [walks], Matilde grows into a person, learns to share affection with her pet, and finally leaves home forever with the *perra*.[7]

Escape from the artificial order of games is a theme in these stories. As in the adulterous and childish beach games in **"Veraneo,"** and billiards in **"Paseo," "Santelices"** abounds in games. As a symbol of an inhuman, programmed existence, canasta is the after-dinner pastime, with rules changed to suit the landlord. This diversion is juxtaposed to Santelices' own absorbing fantasy of animals. At first Santelices collects animal pictures as a temporary escape from his ordered existence in the pension and from his exacting profession as an archivist. When the landlord protests Santelices' tacking pictures on the wall, and when Bertita, the landlord's daughter, burns the pictures, Santelices creates or recreates the world of the jungle within himself. He interprets the world around him in animal terms and discovers in the *rubia* [blond], who lives five stories below his office window in a penthouse, an object for his animal desires. The sensuous *rubia* and her *gatas* [female cats] transform Santelices from the asexual milquetoast to a brutal macho. He exercises his new-found masculinity by winning at cards and reducing Bertita to tears with the news that he is moving out of the pension. Then, in the most magical metamorphosis in Donoso's stories, Santelices leaps to the aid of the *rubia* and her family as they are about to be menaced by voracious cats. Thus, through the influence of the *rubia,* Santelices transforms himself from a caged, rational being to a free, sexual animal.

For Donoso, the replacement of a sterile, rigid, conformist way of life by the instinctual and fertile is associated with a spiritual magnetism or hypnotic suggestion. In each of these stories the teacher or shaman dominates the spiritual life of the initiate with his eyes. The animalistic or magnetic implications of this hypnotic gesture are apparent in Donoso's metaphoric equation of the shaman's penetrating glance with that of an animal or bird. By means of this magical association Donoso's fiction goes beyond psychological realism to a magical realism which obeys primitive, religious modes of thought.

In **"Veraneo,"** the shaman Jaime captures the visual focus of the story with his striking profile against the horizon. He establishes his hypnotic control of Raúl by means of a penetrating glance: "Sus ojos negros, como dos piedras pesadas, caían sobre todas las cosas, sobre el mar, sobre Raúl, sobre trozos de conchas y guijarros, apoderándose de todo." ["His black eyes, like two heavy stones, weighed on everything, on the sea, on Raúl, on pieces of shell and pebbles, dominating everything."] (pp. 33-4) The comparison of Jaime's eyes with heavy stones reflects his domination of Raúl on another symbolic level. Jaime's glance is compared with that of the *gavilán* [hawk]. Jaime teaches the children to kill *gorriones* [sparrows] with stones thrown from a sling. Thus, the metaphor is complete: Jaime's eyes, symbolic stones, destroy the innocence of youth in Raúl. Once his innocence is lost, Raúl will be able to adopt the emotional and spiritual qualities of his teacher.

The significance of animal imagery in **"Paseo"** has already been discussed, but the manner in which the stray dog and Matilde establish their relationship is treated in a way similar to hypnosis. Matilde meets the dog while walking home from Church. The two participants in the hypnotic experience exchange glances:

> . . . mi tía miró a la perra y los ojos de la perra se cruzaron con su mirada. No vi la expresión de los ojos de mi tía. Sólo vi que la perra la miró, haciendo suya esa mirada, contuviera lo que contuviere, sólo porque se fijaba en ella . . . ¿Tal vez esa mirada que se cruzó entre ellas, de la que yo sólo pude ver lo mecánico—la cabeza de la perra alzada apenas hacia tía Matilde, la cabeza de tía Matilde entornada apenas hacia ella—, contuvo algún compromiso secreto, alguna promesa de lealtad que yo no percibí?

> [. . . my aunt looked at the bitch and the bitch's eyes crossed with her look. I didn't see the expression in my aunt's eyes. I only saw that the bitch looked at her, making that look hers, whatever it held, only because she was gazing at her . . . Perhaps the look that had passed between them of which I saw only the mechanics—the bitch's head raised slightly toward Aunt Matilde, Aunt Matilde's slightly inclined toward the bitch—contained some secret commitment, some promise of loyalty that I did not perceive?] (p. 217)

The rest of the story answers affirmatively the narrator's naive but sensitive question. This initial moment of recognition between two female beings, outcasts of a male world, is at the same time an acknowledgment of a shared "human" condition as well as a reciprocal invitation to a common destiny. Matilde and the *perra* ultimately share their lives together with mutual affection and care.

"Santelices" contains the most violent occurrence of hypnotic attraction and magnetism in Donoso's stories. Santelices' metamorphosis into a beast begins with the meditation upon pictures of animals printed on wrapping paper. He gazes into the fiery eyes of the beasts and experiences fear and repulsion, emotions unknown in his secure world. He is obsessed with the visual images of animals' faces. The wildness of their sharp incisors contrast with the domesticity of his false teeth, more often than not soaking in a glass and not in his mouth. When Bertita burns his pictures, he transforms himself into a beast. Bertita, in a traditional exorcism ritual of burning,[8] frees Santelices from the thralldom to his icons to join the pride of cats on the *rubia*'s penthouse. In the closing pages of the story, he is drawn to the monumental scene of the felines' phosphorescent eyes, gleaming in the night, in the traditional atmosphere of a witches' sabbath.

By means of the interplay of magical and psychological forces in these masterpieces of short fiction, José Donoso joins other writers who have been characterized as cultivators of magical realism. He portrays contemporary society as a closed world which represses the possibility of man's spiritual or emotional growth. As an implication of the extreme difficulty of growing in the modern world, Donoso presents fantastic metamorphoses in which trapped victims of life exchange their threadbare fabric of daily existence for the colorful robes of the supernatural. Their new spiritual condition is symbolic of the new identities they have adopted. In conclusion, Donoso shows, as Dickens, one of his favorite authors, that there is more to man's dreams and hallucinations than an undigested bit of beef, or a crumb of cheese.

Notes

[1] *Labyrinths,* trans. James E. Irby, (New York: New Directions, 1964), pp. 177-185.

[2] See Alexander Coleman, "Some Thoughts on José Donoso's Traditionalism," *Studies in Short Fiction* VIII (1971), 155-158 for a discussion of Donoso's short stories. Coleman concludes that Donoso, while incorporating such traditions in fiction as English realism and the influence of Henry James, explores the nightmarish world of contemporary life combined with an insidious violence masked beneath the appearances of civilization.

[3] Both Coleman (above) and George McMurray refer to Donoso's interest in modern "obsessions." The latter, in "La temática en los cuentos de Jose Donoso" ["Theme in the Short Stories of José Donoso"] *Nueva narrativa hispanoamericana* I (1971), 133-138, discusses the social perspectives in Donoso's short stories. For McMurray, Donoso displays a thorough-going Naturalistic depiction of Chilean society, organized according to antiquated hypocritical conventions.

[4] Julio Caro Baroja, *The World of the Witches,* trans. O. N. V. Glendinning, (Chicago: University of Chicago Press, 1973) evaluates the Hispanic contribution to witchcraft through the centuries.

[5] "Cuando el sol desaparecio, fundiendo el pueblo en vislumbre líquida, . . ." ["when the sun disappeared, fusing the town in a liquid glimmer . . ."], *Cuentos* (Barcelona: Seix Barral/Nueva Narrativa Hispánica, 1973), p. 31. All subsequent citations of Donoso's fiction pertain to this edition.

[6] McMurray (see above) suggests a supernatural interpretation of this relationship: "Este inocente y despreocupado niño, Raúl, cae bajo el hechizo de un robusto joven malévolo llamado Jaime . . . El voluntarioso Jaime encarna una deidad que, después de comunicarle al hombre (Raúl) el concepto del mal, le abonda. La confrontación de Raúl con la realidad sórdida, con su separación de Jaime y su resultante enajenación, reflejan la angustia existencial del hombre moderno en un mundo caótico desprovisto de Dios y de la razón." ["This innocent and carefree child, Raúl, falls under the influence of a robust malevolent youth named Jaime . . . The willful Jaime is the incarnation of a deity who, after passing on to man (Raúl) the concept of evil, abandons him. Raúl's confrontation with sordid reality, with his separation from Jaime, and his resultant alienation reflect the existential anguish of modern man in chaotic world without God and reason."] (p. 134) However, his determination of Jaime as a malevolent figure rests on the fact that he teaches Raúl to kill *gorriones* [sparrows]. I have discussed the metaphorical significance of these birds and their relationship to the immature, vulnerable Raúl whose youthful world must be supplanted by adulthood through the intercession of Jaime the *gavilán* [hawk].

[7] A remarkable parallel to "Paseo" occurs in Edward Albee's *Zoo Story* in which a psychotic city-dweller forms a curious, love-hate relationship with a dog. After he tries to murder the dog, Jerry and the intended victim reach a strange understanding: "I looked more into his face than he looked into mine. I mean, I can concentrate longer at looking into a dog's face than a dog can concentrate at looking into mine, or into anybody else's face, for that matter. But during that twenty seconds or two hours that we looked into each other's face, we made contact. Now, here is what I had wanted to happen: I loved the dog now, and I wanted him to love me. I had tried to love, and I had tried to kill, and both had been unsuccessful by themselves. I hoped . . . and I don't really know why I expected the dog to understand anything, much less my motivations . . . I hoped that the dog would understand. It's just . . . it's just that . . . it's just that if you can't deal with people, you have to make a start somewhere. WITH ANIMALS!" (New York: Signet, 1963), p. 34.

[8] Caro Baroja (above) presents a masterful description of the Sabbath and the rite of exorcism by burning, Chapter 6, pp. 79-98.

Sharon Magnarelli (essay date 1979)

SOURCE: "The Dilemma of Disappearance and Literary Duplicity in José Donoso's *Tres novelitas burguesas,*" *Prismal Cabral,* Vol. 3, Spring, 1979, pp. 29-46.

[*In the following essay, Magnarelli considers the stories in* Tres novelitas burguesas *both realistic socio-economic depictions of modern bourgeois society and self-referential works concerned with the natures of and relationships between truth, reality, art, and language.*]

"il me semble que c'est une pure question de mots . . ."[1]

Literary theory of recent years has focused on the plurality of the literary text—that is, on the capacity of the signifier to evoke two or more different signifieds. In this manner, the literary work is acknowledged to carry a socio-philosophical message as well as a linguistic inquiry, as the text not only refers to the world which surrounds the writer and his interpretation of that world but simultaneously comments on its own existence and mode of being.

Perhaps there is no recent text which demonstrates this duplicity and plurality more overtly than José Donoso's *Tres novelitas burguesas.*[2] Although analyses of the text have centered on the stories as socio-economic portrayals of modern life (portrayals which I do not deny), I shall study the work from other perspectives too and disagree strongly with the critic for the *New York Times Book Review* who refers to the tepidity of the second story and sees the third as mechanically carried out.[3] I shall focus principally on *Atomo verde número cinco* but examine all the *novelitas* in terms of what they say about both themselves and art in general. I hope to show that the text undermines our traditional concept of the relationship between "truth" and art while it centers on the contradictory nature of the artistic creation and the process of naming.

As the title suggests, *Tres novelitas burguesas* is a trilogy of *novelas.* While the protagonists of each story are the secondary characters in the other stories, each segment is autonomous (at least superficially), and there are only peripheral references to the events of the other stories. The text's preoccupation with language and art, however, is underscored from the very beginning by means of the titles of the individual stories. Each title, in itself, refers to another work of art: linguistic, musical or pictorial. *Chattanooga Choochoo,* title of the first story, refers to a North American song of the big band era and, thus, to both a musical and linguistic work of art; *Atomo verde número cinco* is the name given to a painting done by the protagonist of that story; and, *Gaspard de la nuit* refers to the composition by Ravel. Thus, to a greater or lesser extent each composition considers the position and nature of another work of art while it indirectly considers its own creation and being.

The first story, *Chattanooga Choochoo,* recounts some of the events in a week of the life of two Barcelona couples: Ramón Solar, his mate, Sylvia Corday, and their friends, Magdalena and Anselmo Prieto. The action of the story (although not the narrative itself) begins at a social gathering; Sylvia and Magdalena, identically dressed, perform a song and dance number to the tune, *Chattanooga Choochoo.* The story concludes a week later at a similar gathering when Anselmo and Ramón, also identically attired, do that same song and dance number. In between we learn that Sylvia's features are painted on her every day by her husband or Anselmo and that her entire face may be erased at any moment (reducing it to a blank, white ovoid) and re-painted according to the desire of the man at hand. Thus, to this extent her existence, her form, her personality, are entirely dependent upon the whim of another (that other always being male), and her features, individual characteristics, are always repetitions of others' features and, thus, not individual at all. During this same

week, Sylvia teaches Magdalena the technique of dismantling her husband when he becomes vexatious or superfluous. The women also have the ability to store the pieces away in a suitcase until they have need of their husbands and are ready to re-assemble them. Thus, in this story the identity of each individual, each character, is dependent and repetitive.

While the student of naturalism or sociology will be offended by the "unrealistic" dismantling of the characters in this text, he will no doubt attribute it to a *representation* of a Freudian dream of power. On the other hand, we must not neglect the importance of the text as language analyzing itself. In this work, the literary character, a linguistic entity recognized as such, is overtly portrayed as a more or less arbitrary conglomeration of signs—signs, words, elements of meaning which can be joined, separated or erased at will. In many respects this *novela* underscores Sylvia Corday as the literary character *par excellence.* Just as any character can never be more than an arbitrary grouping of nouns, adjectives and verbs, Sylvia is overtly just that. Her creators work with her blank, white face as they use a blank sheet of paper (or in the pictorial arts, perhaps a blank canvas). Her creators write or paint, with other materials, on that blank space and create the character and personality they desire. The text in this manner emphasizes that the literary character is a mere assembly of words and that, contrary to our traditional manner of viewing the character, the group of signs from which each character's signifiers are chosen is finite and shared.[4]

Furthermore, this story in many ways might be seen as self-reading; that is, the text seems to be perusing and interpreting itself as it progresses. Closely related to the detective novel, where the protagonist's main function is to find the clues and "read" or interpret them, *Chattanooga Choochoo* focuses on Anselmo, who, like the detective, repeatedly tries to discover the significance of various events and words of others. He finds as he "reads", however, that the words are not directly related to a single, specific referent and signification; instead, each group of words allows for multiple exegeses. For example, many of the story's beginning pages examine Anselmo's attempts to interpret the words of Sylvia:

> Al pasárselas, Sylvia insistió:
>
> —Y Magdalena tiene tan buen gusto . . .
>
> ¿La había saboreado? Quizá porque pasó la carne junto con decir esas palabras, pensó repentinamente que aludía a ese "sabor" de Magdalena que sólo yo conocía, y esto me hizo replegarme ante la antropófaga Sylvia. Pero se refería, naturalmente, a otra clase de "gusto": al "gusto" que había presidido, como el valor más alto, nuestra visita a las casas durante la tarde, proporcionándonos un idioma común, un "gusto" relacionado con el discernimiento estético determinado por el medio social en que vivíamos (p. 13).

As the story concludes, we discover that Anselmo has encompassed all the major roles in this detective-like story. He has become the narrator as well as the detective or reader of clues while at the same time he is the "murderer" (to the extent that he "erases" Sylvia) and the "murdered" (to the extent that Magdalena disassembles him). Thus, the single signifier—Anselmo—includes all the apparently contradictory referents.

Like **Chattanooga Choochoo,** the second story, **Atomo verde número cinco,** also seems to concentrate on the topics of language and reading. Marta Mora and Roberto Ferrer, an upper-middle class couple without children, have installed themselves in the "definitive" apartment. Roberto, a dentist by profession, paints in his spare time. He and Marta have gone to every expense and effort to surround themselves with perfect and carefully selected objects, which, they feel, reflect their very individual personalities. The irony, of course, is that, as in **Chattanooga Choochoo,** these personalities are not "individual" at all, and even the rooms and objects have been created and combined with considerable influence from others. Just as soon as all but one item in the apartment is finally and definitively located and Roberto is awaiting the "right" moment to begin painting in his empty studio, various items begin to disappear from the apartment, starting with the painting by Roberto, entitled "Atomo verde número cinco." As the objects continue to vanish, Roberto and Marta discover that, after fifteen years of marriage, neither of them any longer possesses anything which belongs to him alone; everything is shared. What they never realize in the course of the narrative is that not only is everything communal property between the two of them, but that, in turn, all (like their very language) is shared with the rest of their society—neither of them has anything which is original and not common to the rest of their group. They suspect everyone, including each other, of stealing their possessions, but Roberto recognizes, enigmatically, that these are not robberies at all—things just disappear. The discovery of a piece of paper on which the name and weight of the painting is written leads them to a wild search in a poor neighborhood, and the text ends, not unlike other Donoso narratives, in a savage, physical, animal-like struggle in the night when language has been replaced by mere guttural sounds.

On one level, then, we might understand this text as a metaphor for art which, lacking just one word, one dot of color, one musical note, becomes invalid and cannot hold itself together in an organic whole (presuming that the disintegration which characterizes the story was effectuated by Roberto's failure to hang that one last painting). But, on another level, the text might be interpreted as a subtle criticism of the social class of material wealth. Here Donoso portrays a pair of characters whose existence is created and defined by means of objects and possessions. It seems that, without such material goods, they would not exist: "enamorado de los objetos, prisionero de ellos, dependiente de ellos" (p. 155). In addition, the frivolity of their lives is emphasized by the fact that the protagonists have nothing better nor more transcendental to do than buy objects and worry about arranging and furnishing the house. As the text notes, the activity of seeking furniture and accessories is not only "una tarea apasionante," but

also "un acto de compromiso" (p. 107). Thus, the story scorns all that is frivolous and idle in a social class which has no higher nor more altruistic aspirations than material wealth and objects to symbolize that affluence. And, perhaps the ultimate problem is one of possession and a realization that the individual may never be truly capable of possessing anything in the very strictest and most exclusive sense, just as in **Chattanooga Choochoo,** where even "personal" features were shared.

Another social problem which arises in the text, and a problem which is perhaps inherent to any social class, is the problem of marriage and possession. The story dramatizes the individual's loss of his or her own personality, identity, in marriage. Marta complains that Roberto has stolen everything that is hers and that she no longer has her own existence or personality: "En sus largos años de convivencia se habían confundido sus fronteras a costa de tanta consideración y de tan abundantes sentimientos positivos, y ya ninguno de los dos tenía nada" (p. 169). The text also states, "Marta recordaba las mil formas en que Roberto la había anulado, sin dejarla tener nada propio," and "era como si, bajo la presión de Roberto, ya hubiera comenzado a desaparecer definitivamente" (p. 170). In other words, the creation of the pair, the unity, the sum of the parts, has resulted in the erasure of the individual; by means of the amalgamation the autonomous part has disappeared in much the same way as the recognition of the plurality of the sign disappears in the text.

On this same "social" level, the story depicts the life of this class in all its orderly arrangement and careful planning. Everything has a determined position within this society, and everything must remain in that place. It is curious and, I believe, revealing that this class (or at least the two protagonists) demonstrate a necessity to feign an ability to confront disorder and the unusual; Roberto dreams of living as a "hippy" and dedicating himself to painting although it is clear to us that he would never be capable of such a "disordered" existence. With the first appearance of fortuitous and unexplainable elements—unplanned happenings which do not already fit perfectly into the schematized outline—such characters become totally unstable and begin to disintegrate.

In this respect, one of the principal topics considered in the narrative is the universal desire for precision and stability. The characters of **Atomo verde número cinco** want to install themselves in "el piso definitivo . . . de manera permanente" (p. 107). They pursue ways to impede the movement and flux of life and retard the endless succession of time. For them, the most frightening and disconcerting is all that is imprecise, ephemeral, transitory and disordered. Thus, their principal activity in the early parts of the *novelita* must be to regularize and systematize all aspects of their life to the extent possible. For this reason, it is very important to them that the flat be definitive and fixed. But, as we all know, such permanence is neither realizable nor to be found, for the world and life are imprecise, imperfect and transitory, and only art fixes and arrests them, as Ortega y Gasset has indicated:

La precisión de las cosas es una idealización de ellas
que el deseo del hombre produce. En su realidad son
imprecisas . . . son sólo aproximadamente ellas mismas,
no terminan en un perfil rigoroso, no tienen superficies
inequívocas y pulidas, sino que flotan en el margen de
imprecisión que es su verdadero ser. La precisión de
las cosas es precisamente lo irreal, lo legendario en
ellas.[5]

Thus, all the efforts to arrange, order and regulate can
only end in the complete opposite, for ironically, the very
attempt to achieve the ultimately mythic harmonic state
inevitably underlines the lack of that same conformity—
that is, the effort to impose homogeneity emphasizes its
absence.

There is little doubt that this endeavor to fix and classify
everything is the primary element in the love Roberto feels
toward painting. For him, a painting signals a world which
is already in harmony, manageable and perfected. This
"world" is in an immutable form and seldom introduces the
gratuitous. It represents a firm, concrete, tangible world.
For this reason, "la pintura confortaba a Roberto—cosa
que no hacía su práctica odontológica, distinguidísima
pero quizá *demasiado vasta*—, como también su cautelosa
colección de grabados: litografías, xilografías, aguafuertes
. . . algún buril . . ." (p. 108, my emphasis). Clearly, the
irony is to be found in the continuation of this citation:
". . . sobre todo, en que lo enamoraba la espontaneidad,
la valiente emoción de la síntesis." Without question,
there is very little in the etching which we could call
undeliberated or spontaneous inasmuch as the etching
quite specifically depends upon precision, intention, careful work, prearrangement and the very finest of lines.

Furthermore, and still on the socio-philosophical level, the
novelita dramatizes the universal nightmare of getting lost
in a strange, unknown place and spending the rest of
eternity trying to find one's way back to the familiar and
known:

> ¿ . . . él y Marta se quedarían dando vueltas y vueltas,
> eternamente, en coche, por las calles de la ciudad,
> buscando el número de una calle donde ellos habían
> instalado su piso definitivo, pero que ahora no existía?
> ¿Buscar y buscar, rodando hasta agotarse, hasta
> envejecer, uno al lado del otro en el asiento del coche,
> decayendo en medio del tiempo que pasaba y de la
> ciudad que crecía y cambiaba, hasta morir sin encontrar
> el número . . . (p. 161).

This quotation points to the vastness and emptiness of
the world of our subconscious and of our nightmares, while
it simultaneously perhaps marks the futility and absurdity
of the endeavors and tasks we assign ourselves throughout
life. As the *novelita* ends with the words, ". . . huir aullando
de terror hasta perderse por el inmenso escenario vacío"
(p. 188), an appropriate termination to an absurd search,
we are reminded not only of the immensity and vacuity of
our world, but also of the notion of Shakespeare and
Calderón, among others, of the world as the great stage of
life with the drama we represent on that stage.[6]

Now, if the text were to stop with these interpretive possibilities, without any other dimension, it would certainly suffice. But, there is still another dimension—the linguistic,
the level on which the text underlines its own existence,
its own formation, and investigates (metaphorically, at
least) the very material of its own creation. In this story,
the self-criticism exists as a concomitant part of the narration. Alicia Borinsky has noted that there are two types
of self-criticism: "la autocrítica incorporada como tema en
la novela y la autocrítica asumida como condición inher-
ente a la narración, sin establecer distancias que permitan
la distinción de momentos en los cuales un narrador privilegiado se desdobla en contemplador de la obra".[7] Clearly,
Atomo verde número cinco pertains to the second group.
It does not take much imagination to apply all that we
have said about painting and other art forms to language
and literature. In the same manner, it is patent that, to a
certain degree, the word functions as art does to adjust,
stabilize and limit "reality". The act of denomination and
classification is a means of confronting the infinite and
fortuitous in the world which surrounds us. To be able to
assign a name to a phenomenon makes it more manageable, more exact, and thus, less threatening. By means of
the word, the chaotic world becomes simplified and cate-
gorized. As Foucault has noted, the word does not function merely as a name, but simultaneously retards and fixes
the process of the action.[8] Literature, then, as a conglomeration of words, usually functions in a manner very similar
to that of painting: it organizes this world by taking a small
segment of the totality, fixing it and presenting us with a
part already controlled and tamed. Often literature demonstrates a causality that we cannot find in the casualness
of life. Thus, the word gives consolation in much the same
sense as painting does. As Roquentin of *La nausée* has
said, "qu'y a-t-il à craindre d'un monde si regulier?" (p. 11).
Also, like the painting, the word seems to present, make
present, that which is already (and always will be) absent.
Such a phenomenon was, of course, already apparent in
El obsceno pájaro de la noche, where we saw that words
not only created a world but also functioned to limit,
regulate and make the "real" world less frightening:

> . . . con mi nombre impreso tantas veces, nadie podía
> dudar de mi existencia . . . .[9]

> . . . cómo alterarlos y perderse dentro de sus existencias
> fluídas, la libertad de no ser nunca lo mismo porque los
> harapos no son fijos, todo improvisándose, fluctuante,
> hoy yo y mañana no me encuentra nadie ni yo mismo
> me encuentra porque uno no es lo que es mientras dura
> el disfraz. A veces, compadezco a la gente como usted,
> Madre Benita, esclava de un rostro y de un nombre y
> de una función y de una categoría, el rostro tenaz del
> que no podrá despojarse nunca, la unidad que la tiene
> encerrada dentro del calabozo de ser siempre la misma
> persona (pp. 155-56).

Nevertheless, I suggest that the clue to the comprehension of **"Atomo verde número cinco"** may be found in the
phrase, things disappear. The disappearance of things
may well be the result of a linguistic process. As long as
one confides naively in a close and immediate relationship
between the thing and the word, and while one accepts as

fact the notion that the word presents, makes present, represents the things (and only one thing), there is no problem and all remains in a very comfortable, if oblivious, state. But, the problem arises with the suspicion or premonition that such a relationship is based on myth, on another creation, and that it does not exist. To say or to write the word in no way presents the thing, the object, the referent. As Derrida has defined it, in fact, writing is "nom courante des signes qui functionnet malgré l'absence totale du sujet".[10] Thus, things disapear, and the text itself underlines and emphasizes the fact that the occurrences are not thievery but disappearances.[11]

Let us remember too, that the entire dilemma of disappearance began when Roberto found himself alone with his possessions or things—at this moment the "robberies" began. Similarly, Roquentin found himself terribly alone with objects and reacted in much the same fashion: "Les choses se sont delivrées de leurs noms. Elles sont là, grotesques, têtues, géantes . . . je suis au milieu des Choses, les innommables. Seul, sans mots, *sans defénses*. . ." (p. 177, my emphasis). It appears, then, that the problem arises with the destruction or demystification of the immediate relation, with the separation or distancing of the word from its referent. As our story progresses, things continue to disappear and distance themselves from the words or signifiers. I suspect that we are to understand that without names, without language which subdues somehow the thing, classifying and limiting it, some of the objects necessarily disappear and vice versa (let us remember the linguistic theories which insist that things exist only when they are named, classified and put into categories), while others lose their definitions and their limits, to expand and become threatening. But again, such a process is not new, but could also be seen in many places, including *Cien años de soledad.*

> Poco a poco, estudiando las infinitas posibilidades del olvido, se dio cuenta de que podía llegar un día en que se reconocieran las cosas por sus inscripciones, pero no se recordara su utilidad. Entonces fue más explicitó. El letrero que colgó en la cerviz de la vaca era una muestra ejemplar de la forma en que los habitantes de Macondo estaban dispuestos a luchar contra el olvido. . . . Así continuaron viviendo en una realidad escurridiza, momentáneamente capturada por las palabras, pero que había de fugarse sin remedio cuando olvidaran los valores de la letra escrita.[12]

Stripped of its affiliation with the thing, the word, too, becomes dangerous. As Foucault has suggested, "je suppose que dans toute société la production du discours est à la fois contrôlée, sélectionnée, organisée et redistribuée par un certain nombre de procédures qui ont pour rôle d'en conjurer les pouvoirs et les dangers, d'en maîtriser l'événement aléatoire, d'en esquiver la lourde, la redoutable matérialité".[13]

The text, thus, centers on the reading of the small piece of paper on which the words, "Atomo verde número cinco Peso 108," are written. The writing is completely misread as the address at which the painting will be found (rather than simply the title and weight of the painting), and it is this misinterpretation of the word which leads to the self-destruction of the conclusion. What becomes clear is that Marta's and Roberto's problem is as much linguistic as social. The couple has failed not only to understand the plurality of any sign, but also to see the arbitrary and ephemeral relationship between the signifier (signifier in both the sense of words and in the sense of objects, possessions which they want to "reflect" their personalities) and the signified. They have simplistically found a one-to-one relationship between the signifier and the signified and have overlooked the fact that the very attempt to capture a single, definitive signified is but the first step in its erasure. Each signifier has a multiplicity of referents, and choosing the correct one at any given moment is the very key to comprehension, communication and signification. Instead, they have buried themselves in the signifiers as the significance has begun to disappear, and they have failed to comprehend that their signs must be the very essence of plurality, insofar as each is shared not only by more than one referent (and vice versa), but also by more than one speaker, writer or reader. In this manner, it is also evident that the words "las cosas desaparecen" may be understood in relation to the linguistic theory of Derrida.[14] One of the bases for his theory is the notion that written words do not function solely as symbols of sounds, that their significance is a result of the supplement and that finally the only thing which remains is the "trace". Similarly, as was noted in *La nausée,* "il ne reste plus que des mots . . . mais ce ne sont plus que des carcasses" (p. 52).

Thus, when things disappear within the text, there are two basic ways to react: one can seek (futilely) the lost origin or referent, or one can pretend not to notice the problem— "No hablar, no elucubrar. Aceptar, nada más" (p. 164)— that is, by means of suppression one can ignore the dilemma completely. And both reactions are dramatized in ***Atomo verde número cinco.*** At first the pair pretends not to notice what occurs, or at least they make an effort not to talk about what is happening. This response, of course, reflects the almost universal credence (subconscious though it may be) that by not pronouncing, not mentioning or verbally expressing the event (by not making it linguistically manifest) it will not exist (again implying that the word itself grants or denies existence). The suggestion is that without articulation, without linguistic recognition and confrontation, things cannot exist and/or disappear (in their previous form, at least).

This tendency not to confront or acknowledge the outside world (external to the subject, that is) is a propensity we find frequently depicted in the works of Donoso. This was the great attraction of the *imbunche* in *El obsceno pájaro*: to have all one's orifices sewn up means not to have to face the world, not to have any contact with that world and, thus, not to be threatened by it:

> aquí adentro se está caliente, no hay necesidad de moverse, no necesito nada, este paquete soy yo entero, reducido, sin depender de nada ni de nadie (p. 525);

> soy este paquete. Estoy guarecido bajo los estratos de sacos en que las viejas me retobaron y por eso mismo

no necesito hacer paquetes, no necesito hacer nada, no
siento, no oigo, no veo nada porque no existe nada más
que este hueco que ocupo . . . Sé que ésta es la única
forma de existencia . . . porque si hubiera otra forma
de existencia tendría que haber también pasado y futuro,
y no recuerdo pasado y no sé de futuro (pp. 537-38).

Similarly, it is important to Roberto and Marta "no hablar,
no enlucubrar. Aceptar, nada más. Darle vuelta la espalda
a los acontecimientos y quizás así, ignorándolos, lograr
conjugarlos" (p. 164).

The other reaction to the disappearances consists of first
recognizing the problem and then trying to encounter the
lost relationship, those presumed ties between the signifier and the signified. But the only possibility that remains
to reconstruct this lost relationship (which is something of
a paradise lost which probably never existed) will be to
seek the origins, the referent, that is, to re-create the
connection. Thus, in a certain sense and in a very dramatic manner, the *novelita* becomes the search for origin; the
protagonists forget the significance of the words and must
re-encounter, re-discover the referent, the significance. The
problem is that they fail to recognize that it is the very
context which gives meaning to things and to words and
that once torn from their context, they change meaning or
lose their significance. As the narrator notes, "era in-
creíble cómo había cambiado ese mueble al arrancarlo del
pesado ambiente burgués de tónica indecisamente post-
modernista de la casa de la madre de Marta, y cómo,
trasladado al contexto *depouille* del piso nuevo, adquiría
un significado estético totalmente contemporáneo" (p. 116).
This search for origins is the motivating factor in much of
Donoso's work; for this reason Mudito, too, sought the
origins of the myth of the *niña-beata* and Inés returned
to the Casa de Ejercicios Espirituales. In a metaphoric
sense, it is for a similar reason that Marta and Roberto go
out in search of the painting at what they thought was an
address, Peso 108: "Con la perspectiva de recobrar algo—
una esperanza de reconstruir todo el edificio de civiliza-
ción y forma que habían perdido . . ." (pp. 171-72). Significantly, "en el vestíbulo soñaron, un instante, en cómo sería
el vestíbulo a su regreso, cuando hubieran recobrado todo
lo perdido, y era como soñar con la paz y el descanso *que
proporciona el lenguaje de los objetos queridos* que sir-
ven como puentes para comunicarse, o como máscaras que
los protegieran de la desnudez hostil que habían estado
viviendo desde hacía tantos días" (p. 172, my emphasis).

In this manner, then, it becomes evident that the act of
simply not confronting or ignoring the world evinces a
reaction that is not completely distinct nor distinguishable
from the act of seeking origins. In both instances there is
ultimately a negation of the fundamental complexity: things
are not to be found in a simple, neat form that art proportions them. To seek the origin or to simply refuse to face
the dilemma are two methods of avoiding the problem of
the relation (or its absence) between things (the world)
and art (linguistic, musical or pictorial). In both cases the
problem results from the acceptance that art creates or
captures presence or essence, while, paradoxically, the
problem is temporarily solved by this same acceptance

(but apparently only temporarily). For this reason the attitude of Roberto and Marta is especially relevant: "Se
quedaron mirando—melancólicamente, impotentemente" (p.
157). They dream of simple presence but are unable to
encounter it, re-introduce it. They realize, although perhaps in an almost unconscious manner, the impossibility
of discovering or witnessing the origins. As for the language and the word, it is the pretext, the delusion that
gives solace; with the recognition that it is only pretense
and that the gratuitous and fortuitous still play a major
role in their lives, Roberto's and Marta's world of possessions must crumble. And so, things disappear or threaten,
and the words become meaningless.

Similarly in the third story of the trilogy, we once again
find the non-uniqueness of identity and possession stressed.
The protagonist of the final *novela,* **Gaspard de la nuit,**
is Mauricio, who has recently come to live with his mother, Sylvia Corday (of the first narrative). Unconcerned
about the things which interest other boys of his age,
Mauricio passes his days whistling "Gaspard de la nuit"
and wandering through the streets trying to entangle others in his tune—"el círculo que trazaba la música de
Mauricio iba a dominarla y a tragársela" (p. 204). The story
concludes after Mauricio meets another boy who looks
and acts exactly like him, but who is poor and in rags. The
two boys exchange clothes and identities, and the poor boy
returns to assume the material affluence of Mauricio's life,
while Mauricio frees himself not only of possessions but
also of name, family and identity to enter a limitless world.

On the surface, **Gaspard de la nuit** would appear to bear
little thematic resemblance to the other two *novelas.* But
as we look more closely, we discover that there are interesting similarities. When Mauricio first arrives in Barcelona, Sylvia struggles to establish a relationship with him,
only to discover that there is something about him which
makes her totally uncomfortable. That "something", in
fact, is that she cannot find the words which label him,
which describe him, and, in turn, which limit and define
him. In a similar manner, Mauricio views her efforts to find
signifiers which are applicable to him and which will define
him as violation, violation which he hates, but which he
simultaneously tries to inflict on others through his music.
In the end, Sylvia is happy with the "new Mauricio"
because he speaks a common language, and she can find
adjectives which are applicable; similarly, the "old Mauricio" is content because he has escaped this naming, this
violation, this limitation.

To this extent, and analogous to the other two stories, we
might see Sylvia in this story as the realistic, naturalistic
writer or reader. She seeks "the right words, to name and
describe events, people, objects, emotions, sensations".[15]
But Mauricio, like Donoso himself, objects to this limitation. Donoso, in fact, has noted his own movement away
from social realism,[16] and Humberto of *El obsceno pájaro*
has criticized those "escritorzuelos" who believe in the
existence of a single reality to be copied.

Thus, while it would unquestionably be easy to understand **Tres novelitas burguesas** as a depiction of bour-

geois society, its dreams and its fantasies, it simultaneously becomes clear that the text is equally concerned with its own existence and its own status. If Donoso were attempting only to portray society, there would be no need to have made the stories so closely interrelated. Ultimately, there can be little doubt that the correspondence of characters in the narratives underscores a linguistic concern. The characters, groups of signifiers, each united by a "proper noun" or name, are repeated in the three *novelas* just as all signifiers, all adjectives, are inevitably repeated, shared and exchangeable.

Concurrently, the format of separating the entire text into three individual stories rather than joining it into one more or less unified novel, emphasizes the isolation of the literary sign. While superficially shared and repeated, like all signs, each character is, nevertheless, isolated and distinct as a result of the context in which he is presented. In the final analysis, The Sylvia of *Chattanooga Choochoo* bears no more resemblance to the Sylvia of *Gaspard de la nuit* than if they were two distinctly named characters placed in similar social milieus. The mask worn (or the face presented) by Sylvia in the first narrative must necessarily be different from that of the last narrative, in spite of the repetition of name and other signifiers, because the context is different—in one, she plays the *femme fatale,* and in the other, the mother.

In conclusion, the texts are not simply descriptions of some external events. Instead, the trilogy is also a self-portrait and a self-analysis. Donoso is not just seeking the right words to describe experience, but trying to analyze experiences which are neither separate nor external, but ultimately a part of the product itself. It is not a question of mere transposition into words, but an analysis of those words and that very transposition. Just as Salvador Elizondo has intricately and inseparably linked the moments of writing, reading and commentary,[17] Donoso, in *Tres novelitas burguesas,* has made the creation and the commentary synchronic, identical and indivisable and has shown that without the word, without art, there is no possibility of possession, and although this artistic, linguistic possession is but a delusion, it is the very basis for the entire bourgeois world.

Notes

[1] Jean Paul Sartre, *La nausée* (Paris: Gallinard, 1938), p. 57.

[2] All page numbers will refer to the Seix Barral edition (Barcelona, 1973).

[3] See Anatole Broyard, "The Exile Who Lost His Tongue", *New York Times Book Review,* 26 June 1977, p. 14. In reference to other Donoso works, see Michael Wood, "Latins in Manhattan," *The New York Review,* 19 April 1973, pp. 35-39.

[4] Without a doubt, all that is said about a literary character here is equally applicable to any artistic entity created by any of the non-verbal mediums.

I discuss *Chatanooga Choochoo* in greater detail in "From *El obsceno pájaro* to *Tres novelitas burguesas:* Development of a

Semiotic Theory in the Works of Donoso" which will appear in *Contemporary Methods of Literary Analysis,* ed. Randolph Pope (New York: Bilingual Press, 1978).

[5] "Introducción a Velázquez-1954," *Obras completas,* Tomo VIII (Madrid: Revista del Occidente, 1965), p. 652.

[6] There are many other apparent links between this *novela* and theater. One must inevitably think of the theater of the absurd in relation to the story as well as Ibsen's *A Doll's House,* among others.

[7] Alicia Borinsky, "Repeticiones y máscaras: *El obsceno pájaro de la noche,*" *Modern Language Notes,* 88 (March 1973), p. 281.

[8] Michel Foucault, *Les mots et les choses* (Mayenne: Gallimard, 1966), p. 302.

[9] I quote from the Seix Barral edition (Barcelona, 1971), p. 150.

[10] Jacques Derrida, *La voix et la phénomène* (Paris: Presses Universitaires, 1972), p. 104.

[11] *To steal* connotes an action mediated by an agent while *to disappear* suggests the lack of such an agent.

[12] Gabriel García Márquez, *Cien años de soledad* (Buenos Aires: Sudamericana, 1971), p. 47.

[13] *L'ordre du discours* (Mayenne: Gallimard, 1971), pp. 10-11.

[14] I refer especially to the thesis expressed in *De la grammatologie* (Paris: Minuit, 1967).

[15] These are the words of Michael Wood, *op. cit.,* p. 35.

[16] Juan Andrés Piña, "José Donoso: Los fantasmas del escritor," *Mensaje* (Santiago), No. 246 (enero-febrero de 1976), p. 51.

[17] See *El grafógrafo* (México: Mortiz, 1972), especially "Futuro imperfecto," p. 77-86.

Guillermo I. Castillo-Feliú (essay date 1980)

SOURCE: "Aesthetic Impetus Versus Reality in Three Stories of José Donoso," *Studies in Short Fiction,* Vol. 17, No. 2, Spring, 1980, pp. 133-39.

[*In the following essay, Castillo-Feliú argues that Donoso's artistic motivation in the stories "China," "Santelices," and "La puerta cerrada" is not purely social, but that his greater concern in the stories is with the stifling effects of reality on the creative self.*]

With the publication of his first story in Spanish titled **"China"** in 1954, José Donoso began a writing career which up to now includes a total of fourteen short stories, five novels and three *novelle.* Although all fourteen short stories appeared between 1954 and 1962, they provide a firm thematic foundation for the longer narratives which have been published between 1957 and 1978. The critic who is familiar with Donoso's prose fiction as a whole is aware that certain themes and character types are consistently treated by the author and that this apparently creative obsession has a logical starting point in the first literary experiments which are those fourteen tales.

Donoso is interested in those characters who most clearly evidence rebellion against the normal canons of society. As a social being, every individual who wishes to be admitted to the nucleus which society is realizes that acceptance of certain norms is required. The process is difficult for it is solely by means of accommodation and discipline that the individual succeeds in overcoming those characteristics which isolate him and accepts the regularity expected by a society which exacts his subordination to the group.

Certain characteristics prevail throughout Donoso's prose fiction. The majority of his characters are children, adolescents or persons who have reached what is commonly referred to as the *âge de retour,* for it is these groups which most clearly evidence man's anarchy before society. In an interview of the author, he explained the basis for this interest this way:

> Esto es una organización estructural y has tocado uno de los puntos más neurálgicos de lo que es toda mi literatura. En ninguna de mis novelas aparece una generación intermedia. . . . Siempre son niños o viejos, o abuelos o nietos. Es la pauta más corriente: lo que me interesa a mí son los estados marginales, los estados anárquicos. La niñez es una anarquía; la neurosis es una anarquá.[1]

The author's interest for marginal states begins to be evidenced with his short narrative. When adults do appear, their lives seem empty and devoid of much interest. On the other hand, Donoso directs his attention to creating beings who exemplify strange, exotic or out-of-the-ordinary characteristics. Progressively, however, these protagonists exhibit a process of mental and creative deterioration which transforms them from positive and imaginative individuals into marginalized, abulic and constricted beings for whom there is no longer a creative outlet for self-expression. Up to the present, much of the criticism of Donoso's narrative has tended to attribute this progressive creative deterioration to the stifling social degeneration of Chile's bourgeois society. In this study, three of the Donoso stories are employed to present findings which at least point toward the plausibility that there exists a more primordial impetus in the author's creative motivation than the rationale commonly presented by present criticism.

Two of the stories treated seem to be especially appropriate for they stand at the beginning and at the end, up to the present, of Donoso's experiments with the short narrative. These are **"China"** and **"Santelices."** The third story, **"La puerta cerrada,"** is certainly his most outstanding example of creative obsession.

"China," written in the first person, tells of a child protagonist who ventures from his home to discover the vast world which exists outside in the hustle and bustle of the large metropolis. His first expedition he undertakes with his mother who has him accompany her through a certain street of the city. An exclamation by his mother provides him with a name for the exotic street which is full of small shops and people scurrying in and out of them and along the sidewalk. He names it **"China."** He tells of his feelings and sensations as he walks, his hand in his mother's: "Yo llevaba los ojos muy abiertos. Hubiera querido no solamente mirar todos los rostros que pasaban junto a mí, sino tocarlos, olerlos, tan maravillosamente distintos me parecían."[2] On subsequent occasions, the protagonist leads his younger brother, Fernando, on odysseys to **"China"** trying to imbue in him the same fascination for the exotic world that he has discovered, but he is unsuccessful. The protagonist's greater sensitivity is incapable of being transmitted to the other child. At the same time, the experience is solely the protagonist's and, thus, **"China"** continues to exist only in his realm of the imagination. As time passes, however, even he finds himself unable to sustain the fantasy of **"China"**: "'China' fue durante largo tiempo como el forro de color brillante en un abrigo oscuro. Solía volver con la imaginación. Pero poco a poco comencé a olvidar, a sentir temor, sin razones, temor de fracasar alli en alguna forma" [*Cuentos,* p. 170].

As the story ends, years have passed and the child is an adult. With his new maturity comes a certain loss which he expresses in the following manner:

> Más tarde salí del país por varios años. Un día, a mi vuelta, pregunté a mi hermano, quien era a la sazón estudiante en la Universidad, dónde se podría adquirir un libro que me interesaba muy particularmente, y que no hallaba en parte alguna. Sonriendo Fernando me respondió: "En 'China'." Y yo no comprendí. [*Cuentos,* p. 171].

In spite of the brevity of this early story, it clearly exhibits the author's predilection for child protagonists. It is they who possess that spirit of creativity which is released by the fertile and as yet untainted imaginative capacity inherent in the child. It is also the first mature literary demonstration of the solitude of the Donosian character; a solitude, maintained by the incomprehensibility of the personal world of each of the children who pass through that stage of life. Although the child exhibits characteristics relatively typical of his age, he already exemplifies those elements which place him within the Donosian frame. As a child, he takes refuge from his surrounding reality, creating for himself one which is more in harmony with his own imagination and circumstances. It is also as adults that these protagonists begin to lose their creative impetus and frame themselves within a stratified and regimented society.

"La puerta cerrada," written in 1959, is the story of an obsession. Sebastián, who lives in a boarding house with his widowed mother, discovers that he truly enjoys sleeping above any other activity. As the years pass, he devotes more and more time to his soporiferous vocation as his aging mother and uncomprehending employer resent and rebuke him for his lack of interest for any other activity. When questioned by don Aquiles Marambio, his superior at work, Sebastián explains his vocation: "Es que se me ocurre que durmiendo, en lo que sueño voy a descubrir algo importante, algo más importante que . . . , bueno, que vivir." Don Aquiles questions him: "Y si te demoras toda la vida en averiguarlo y te mueres antes? Significa que perdiste toda tu vida durmiendo y que no sacaste nada." Sebastián's commitment to his vocations is clear in how he answers don Aquiles: "Se me ocurre que es tan maravilloso lo que voy a encontrar que estoy dispuesto a arriesgarme" [*Cuentos,* p. 108].

Speaking with his mother, Sebastián attempts to transmit to her the depth of his commitment. Referring metaphorically to the impediment he always finds in his search during his dreams as a "closed door," he exhibits his frustration at his inability to cross that threshold in the following way: "Quizás descubra que haber dejado de vivir como los demás fue una equivocación, que tal vez no valía la pena saber lo que ocultaba la puerta. Pero no importa. El hecho de seguir un destino que yo siento auténtico me justifica y le da una razón a toda mi vida" [*Cuentos,* p. 105].

Upon his mother's death, Sebastián leaves his job and wanders from place to place, working just enough to be able to sustain himself during the ever-increasing number of hours which he now devotes to sleeping. Falling asleep, which Sebastián at first had been able to control, now has become a form of narcolepsy. Ultimately, he dies. Don Aquiles, who had broken in disgust with Sebastián, finds him dead at his doorstep. Sebastián's face appears transfigured by such an expression of joy that don Aquiles seems to accept that the dreamer has finally crossed that threshold that he had so earnestly sought.

It is important to note that it is only at the moment of his death that Sebastián is able to realize the object of his vocation. That creative impetus becomes a reality only outside the realm of the reality in which the protagonist lives. The intermittent departure from reality occasioned through his dreams is the only medium within which he can be creative.

"Santelices" is Donoso's last published short story up to the present time. Santelices is a bachelor in his early fifties who lives, like Sebastián, in a boarding house owned by don Eusebio and his old-maidish daughter, la Bertita. She clearly manifests the symptoms brought on by her lonely life style: her sterile life and her sexual frustration; disappointments that she hopes to overcome, at least emotionally, through Santelices. Her pensioner has problems of his own and has no intention of succumbing to her supplications, tenuous and indirect as they are. He has a unique means to effect his escape from the frustration that he feels. His greatest pleasure comes from looking at photographs and drawings of wild animals, a vocation which fuels his imagination and removes him from his sterile and depressing milieu:

> Aquí en las fotografías sensacionales que contemplaba con la nuca fría de emoción, la proximidad de la

amenaza, la crueldad desnuda, parecían acrecentar la belleza, dotarla de eficacia agobiadora, hacerla hervir, llamear, cegar, hasta dejar sus manos transpiradas y sus párpados temblorosos [*Cuentos,* p. 178].

La Bertita, upon discovering this eccentric hobby of her pensioner, accuses him of being abnormal, a devoté of the animals he so admires. She goes so far as to qualify his relationship with the animals as a display of bestiality.

The deception that Santelices subconsciously seeks carries him to the point in which his photographs and drawings slowly cease to satisfy him and he looks for a reality which might involve him more directly and personally. The city's zoological park provides an attraction that is more synesthetic but which, nevertheless, is short-lived in its interest for him.

From the window of his office, Santelices begins to weave a new reality which will allow him to create the world that he yearns for. Five floors below him and for several days, he has been observing a young girl who is playing with some domestic cats. In the beginning, his eyes transmit to him a true and objective vision of a common scene. Slowly, his imagination begins to transport him to a new reality which he has been creating from one day to the next. Expressing his own yearnings and anxieties, Santelices contemplates a scene which becomes savage and violent. The young girl that he has been observing now seems to be surrounded by animals which are advancing and threatening her:

> Las sombras se hundieron, cayendo bloque sobre bloque en el patio exiguo, iluminado por el fulgor de ojos verdes, dorados, rojos, parpadeantes . . . Los animales eran docenas, que circulaban alrededor de la muchacha: ella no era más que una mancha pálida en medio de todos esos ojos que se encendían al mirarla codiciosos [*Cuentos,* p. 190].

The anxiety that he feels becomes an obsession to enter the new world that his imagination is creating. That world he now perceives is more fulfilling and offers him a special place where he will be able to feel that he truly belongs for it is his own. Santelices transports himself completely into the scene that he faces, five floors below, coming not only to see it but to hear it as well:

> Allá estaba la muchacha esperándolo; tal vez gemía; no podía oír su voz en medio del trueno de alaridos, rugidos, gritos, pero tenía que salvarla. Santelices se trepó al alféizar. Sí, allá abajo estaba. De un grito espantó a una fiera de la rama vecina, y, para bajar por ella, dio un salto feroz para alcanzarla [*Cuentos,* p. 193].

George McMurray interprets this final act of the protagonist in the following manner:

> El acto temerario del protagonista enloquecido puede explicarse mediante su identificación con la joven, a quien considera como a una de las víctimas de la vida,

y sobre la cual proyecta sus propios temores, frustraciones y resentimientos. Su salto final representa su último intento desesperado para echarse a un mundo de acción y así salvarse a sí mismo, escapándose de una existencia insoportable.[3]

It seems more plausible and less melodramatic to speculate that by his final actions, Santelices believes that he is escaping into a world which is the product solely of his imagination and, thus, more satisfying. This final act is obviously the end result of his progressive search for a world that is the product of his imagination. It is a world which satisfies him in a way that others' creations (the photographs, drawings) and the living animals (objective reality) cannot. The tragedy, then, lies in the fact that the creation of this new reality is carried out through the psychosis of the protagonist, a psychosis that puts an end to creativity.

The more obvious explanation that the process of marginalization is a direct consequence of the rigidity of a stratified bourgeois society is not one that satisfies. It seems to promote the premise that Donoso's motivation is social and detracts from the author's aesthetic impetus. In response to a query regarding critics' assertions that he is a thesis writer whose motivation is social, the author stated:

> No tengo ninguna visión social. Es un ejercicio interior. No hay ninguna actitud o propósito mío con respecto a la sociedad. Uso dos niveles sociales porque son los que conozco mejor. Parte de la base que yo nunca, o muy raras veces en mis novelas, quiero hacer prototipos; rehuyo de hacerlo. Me parece la negación de la novela de calidad. La novela puede tener reflejos, facetas de ser social.[4]

Alexander Coleman states that Donoso's protagonists are:

> Pathetic and at times comic figures . . . pilgrims of their own brand of truth, vague searchers for a freer self and society, constantly at odds with the reality of their own spiritual suffocation. A groping for a sense of transcendence, a whole process that inevitably entails the encounter with the monster that is within them, engendered out of the mathematical rigidities with which societies function in apparent order.[5]

Coleman's statement penetrates much more deeply into Donoso's creative motivation than McMurray's asseveration that "cuando el rechazo individual de la consagrada ética burguesa se haga general se derrumbará el dique" or these lines from the concluding paragraph of his article titled "La temática en los cuentos de José Donoso": "El rechazo de la realidad banal por parte de la mayoría de los personajes de Donoso y su incapacidad de actuar en una forma positiva sugieren una condenación de la sociedad chilena."[6] The process of marginalization seems to transcend the patently obvious degenerative explanation based on a social struggle premise and emerges more basically as a kind of "sentimiento trágico de la vida." From this standpoint, the creative mind is progressively stifled by the growing realization that the ultimate result of creativity

can be, and as Donoso's characters demonstrate tragically, proves to be, dejection brought on by a personal awareness that a particular instance of creativity does not provide a permanent escape from the real world. Since creativity must be constant and expanding, the creator must repeatedly transcend any plateau which has already been reached.

José Donoso's "sentimiento trágico" is one which is personally his as an individual creative force. Under different social circumstances, the frustration of his characters would perhaps be exposed in different ways but his own reality as a writer would still present him with a set of circumstances which would constantly constrict his realm of possibilities or take him into such unviable solutions as those found by Sebastián and Santelices. It seems not so much to be the bourgeoisie that limits his creativity as it is the constricting pervasiveness of reality itself.

Notes

[1] Guillermo I. Castillo-Feliú, "An Interview of José Donoso," *Hispania,* 54 (December 1971), 958.

[2] José Donoso, *Los mejores cuentos de José Donoso* (Santiago: Zig-Zag, 1965), p. 168. All further references to this work appear in the text.

[3] George McMurray, "La temática en los cuentos de José Donoso," *Nueva Narrativa Hispánica,* 1 (Septiembre 1971) 136.

[4] "An Interview with José Donoso," p. 958.

[5] Alexander Coleman, "Some Thoughts on José Donoso's Traditionalism," *Studies in Short Fiction,* 8 (Winter 1971), 157.

[6] McMurray, "La temática," p. 138.

Richard J. Callan (essay date 1982)

SOURCE: "*Gaspard de la nuit:* Crucial Breakthrough in the Growth of Personality," in *Studies on the Works of José Donoso: An Anthology of Critical Essays,* edited by Miriam Adelstein, The Edwin Mellen Press, 1990, pp. 145-55.

[*In the following essay, which originally appeared in* The Creative Process in the Works of José Donoso, *edited by Guillermo I. Castillo-Feliú (1982), Callan analyzes the novella* Gaspard de la nuit *and emphasizes Donoso's use of Jungian language and symbolism to depict a teenage boy's psychological transformation.*]

Sylvia, the international fashion model, had expected her life to be disrupted when her 16-year old son came from Madrid to spend the summer with her. But far from being a lively teenager, Mauricio is withdrawn and has no normal interests. He likes to roam the streets of Barcelona by himself, whistling a certain music composed by Ravel, and Sylvia finds this behavior disturbing and sometimes exasperating. Mauricio, for his part, is absorbed by inner perplexities and he feels instinctively that whistling Ravel is helping to resolve them. In the end, he experiences a strange exchange of personality with a young beggar who looks like him, and a new Mauricio returns to Sylvia transformed into a normal youth. Such is the plot of *Gaspard de la nuit,* the third of José Donoso's *Tres novelitas burguesas.*[1]

Like the two other narratives in the book, Mauricio's story is surrealistic in parts and lends itself to Jungian analysis, a method that is particularly suitable because Carl Jung's psychology is mentioned several times in the text. From this standpoint, Mauricio is an adolescent seeking personal identity; he must give birth, so to speak, to a potential being that is within him, his new, fuller personality; in short, he must transform and regenerate himself through the symbolic steps of sacrifice, death, and rebirth, which he does.

Although the music of Ravel is only mentioned in the third novelette, the three piano pieces, collectively entitled *Gaspard de la nuit,* and the prose poems that inspired them, contribute significantly to the mood of each of the *Tres novelitas.* In the first piano piece, ONDINE, a water nymph seductively invites a mortal to be her husband in her underwater palace. Interpreted psychologically, this legend evokes the fatal enchantment of the feminine and represents the condition of the male still subject to the instinctive forces of the unconscious, which is to say, he is not his own man. The music of ONDINE therefore sets the mood for the first novelette, *Chattanooga Choo-choo,* where Anselmo feels controlled and dismembered by female figures from his unconscious projected on his wife and her friends.

Ravel's second piece, LE GIBET (the gibbet), renders the dismal feelings provoked by the sight of a man hanging by the neck from a gallows. It sets the mood for Donoso's second story, *Atomo verde,* where the couple, Marta and Roberto, are stripped of their belongings, their dignity, perhaps even of their personality, which is symbolically equivalent to sacrifice and death. In the course of psychological development, a symbolic form of death is necessary for the ego to break away from the mother archetype.

Finally, SCARBO, the third piece of music, is associated with the notion of transformation and rebirth, because in this book it refers to the fabled, self-generating scarab-beetle and to its tremulous, buzzing efforts to emerge from its underground place of origin. The motif of the struggling scarab animates much of the third narrative, just as the droning sound pervades the piano piece, and it equates Mauricio with the sacred beetle as he, too, reaches for the goal of self-renewal.

Still, all three of Ravel's piano pieces correspond in a special way to the story of Mauricio, not solely for the obvious reason that he whistles them, but because it is he who deals with the three phases of psychological development that they represent.

On the Sunday morning this story begins, Mauricio is in the throes of the adolescent transformation process termed the *dragon fight,* because it is patterned on the archetypal confrontation of a hero with a monster, to set free a captive princess. In prosaic language, this refers to the ego's perilous task of confronting the unconscious in its fearsome, devouring aspect in order to redeem from it those elements that are necessary for development. More than a confrontation, it is a conjunction, a coming together of opposites that results in a release of psychic energy: ego-consciousness (the hero) renews itself by contacting its opposite, the unconscious (the dragon). The flow of transpersonal energies into one's personal life is tantamount to a rebirth, and that is what the *dragon fight* is a form of rebirth. The same salutary effect can be achieved through many scenarios other than the *dragon fight,* for example, the archetype of death by hanging from the tree of life. Because wood is a common mother symbol, the tree or gallows represent the mother archetype or the unconscious, thus the man hanging on a gallows is one who returns to the mother's womb for the purpose of rebirth.[2] The hanged man is the form of symbolic sacrifice used in *Gaspard de la nuit.*

Mauricio makes his first appearance when he enters his mother's living room and sees her sitting on her red sofa with her eyes closed. She has been there a long time, attentive to his prolonged, intricate whistling, and it has made her realize that her son is uncommonly solitary. The boy's solitude and unsociability are archetypal, they correspond to the initiate's withdrawal into himself in preparation for the work of transformation. As regards the whistling, which plays a salient and sustained role in this story, it can be an unconscious device for attracting and canalizing psychic energy. This means that whistling, like other rhythmic behavior, is an instinctive way of transferring or redirecting the libido toward creative activity that will strengthen the ego's contact with the world.[3] Mauricio has made a habit of roving through the streets, whistling the three piano pieces of Ravel, sometimes only breathing the music soundlessly to himself, but letting the notes fill his head to the exclusion of everything else (p. 212). He would follow someone surreptitiously and establish a one-sided, semirelationship with him by which he sought to absorb for a few moments some indefinable aspect of that person (pp. 214, 254). All he wanted from these people was to be allowed to be them for a while, and to have his music fill them without their being aware (p. 222).

On the evidence, he must be striving to develop a relationship with the outside world, and looking for a personality, his personality, onto which he may focus his psychic energy, now blocked and impotent.

On that Sunday morning, after leaving his mother's apartment, the first person he followed was a young mother with a baby carriage. He felt pleased with his ability to manipulate her movements by the inaudible strains of ONDINE; but when he started whistling out loud to keep her in line, she became aware of him and the spell was broken (p. 215). This episode shows he has no control over the "mother," meaning, that he is still ruled by the unconscious. Later in a park, as he was directing the music of LE GIBET at a man sitting on a bench, he noted from the corner of his eye that the man was listening to him. Raising the pitch of his whistle, Mauricio then projected the whole musical anecdote of the hanging onto his listener, leading him in his mind up the solemn ladder and into the noose; but the hanged man did not swing: "El aborcado no alcanzó a colgar" (p. 221), because the man on the bench, having other things on his mind, interrupted the music before it was completed. He cheated Mauricio of his power, leaving him vulnerable again, like a little boy. Crestfallen by his failure, Mauricio hurried back to the apartment.

The two attempts to make a mark on reality, the latest of many similar efforts, have been thwarted and the ego takes refuge in the "mother." Although Sylvia prides herself in giving her son total freedom, we must look upon her as Mauricio subconsciously does, as the mother archetype, that is, a personification of the paralyzing, devouring unconscious from whose control he must liberate himself; her every glance or question violates him. When he enters the apartment, he makes for his bedroom, but his mother summons him to the living room to join her and her luncheon guest, Paolo. This man wants to discuss Ravel with him in ways that mean nothing to Mauricio. He feels hounded and trapped by both adults, like a prisoner under interrogation prior to being sentenced to hang: "Era el interrogatorio . . . la violación sistematizada: el culpable antes de ser condenado a la horca, pero que no podía escaparla" (p. 228). Suddenly, he seizes his napkin, knots it around his neck, and drops his head on his chest with his tongue hanging out, mimicking a hanged man. His mother runs to throw her arms around him from behind his chair, and she unties the knot (p. 233).

This dramatic scene is the climax of the psychological plot which can now proceed toward a successful denouement of the boy's conflict, because his symbolic self-sacrifice is the crucial step to regeneration. Sylvia standing behind and embracing him completes the symbol. She, as mother, is the tree of life on which Mauricio has "died," as have died the sacrificed deities of so many religions, for instance, Odin, Attis, Christ.[4] The tableau of Mauricio with his mother represents a union of opposites, which for him means energy redeemed and redirected into higher consciousness. Its importance is emphasized by having been foreshadowed in an episode that also needs to be understood symbolically.

Earlier that day as Sylvia had sat hearing and thinking about her son's whistling, the music felt overpowering to her, as if it would swallow her up: "el círculo que trazaba la música de Mauricio iba a dominarla y a tragársela" (p. 204). A sunbeam crept along the sofa toward her face like a scarab-beetle, and when it struck her eyes, she merely closed them and continued to worry about Mauricio. When she finally looked up, he was standing before her, very tall; he smiled and asked if she'd been sleeping but she had the bothersome feeling that he was dominating her: "que la dominaba" (p. 205). There is an Egyptian myth that tells of Osiris entering his mother's eye, which Jung interprets as the god penetrating into his mother's womb for self-renewal, because the eye stands for the female gen-

itals.[5] While the scarab-beetle is a symbol of the Egyptian sungod, Osiris, in this story it is a form or *alter ego* of Mauricio; it is his partner in the forthcoming travail of rebirth, due to the youngster's total responsiveness to SCARBO, Ravel's third piano piece. Thus, we may say that the scarab-like sunbeam entering Sylvia's eye has the same redemptive meaning for Mauricio as for Osiris, and that it foreshadows the mock hanging scene.

At the luncheon table, Paolo said that Ravel, all through his life, had tried to overpower, to tame the wild beast of romanticism: "domar la fiera salvaje del romanticismo" (p. 229). Mauricio, who through coincidence of names, boasted a kinship with Ravel, was also trying to overpower and tame a wild beast, the devouring unconscious, the instincts.

While finishing lunch, the boy felt inwardly summoned to the woods of Vallvidrera, a slide view of which he has seen in a slot machine. He asked permission to leave, oblivious of the plans that Sylvia and her friend were making for him. Seeing him so unmindful of her solicitude, she let her arms drop; all the tensions within her were loosened as if she'd been disarmed: "se le desanudaron las tensiones, como si la hubieran desarmado" (pp. 233-34). In other words, the "Terrible Mother" has been rendered harmless. She lets go of the ego. She unties the knot (once again). One might even imagine a certain postpartum relief. This also was prefigured earlier that morning, when she felt overpowered at the sight of her son standing over her. At the time, she had thought that she could not concede any power to him without knowing in what it consisted (p. 205). Now things have changed: the Great Mother can be terrible, but she tends to relinquish her control over those who confront her.

Mauricio heads for the Vallvidrera woods, moved by an instinctual drive to develop a fuller and more stable personality. Hitherto, he had wandered through the streets, not aimlessly, but drawn toward a set goal, although the goal was not known to him. Now he perceives this guiding instinct as a gaze (*una mirada*) fixed upon him from out there. It is this gaze that is attracting him to Vallvidrera. Here the text presents appropriate sketches of other phases in the evolution of personality. In the funicular, Mauricio rides with ten little boys on an outing, all greatly excited over the importance of displaying the badge of their hiking club: "diez niños bulliciosos, excitadísimos con la importancia de ostentar la insignia del Club Excursionista Patufet" (p. 236). No identity problem there! The little boys know who *they* are: members of the club, of the outside world; identity with a group is a first break away from the family, the mother. The opposite end of the life span is glimpsed later in the park where, after the family picnic, a decrepit grandfather is collected and packed into the car with the folding furniture: "recogían al abuelo nonagenario . . . lo metían al seiscientos con otros objetos plegables" (p. 245).

The woods are filled with strollers, each anxious to mark the day by the Sunday ritual of having a good time: "iban buscando cualquier cosa que guardar para que este domingo no se muriera sin la dignidad ritual de 'haberse divertido'. . ." (p. 237). This describes the modern-day version of the primordial conception of sacred time. To archaic man, the performance of rituals and other meaningful activities projected him into sacred time, that is, into the same timeless or eternal moment in which the ritual was initially revealed; the rest of his life was spent in profane time, which was meaningless.[6] The Sunday strollers yearn for a snatch of meaningful sacred time at least on weekends. But why is everyday life meaningless, profane for these people? Because they themselves have never transcended the temporal, phenomenal world of limited concerns. They are not in touch with that other world, with the unconscious, and they need psychic transformation through a ritual death and rebirth.

Mauricio is disappointed to find crowds at Vallvidrera. Still, he can blot them out with the help of Ravel, that other Mauricio. He follows a band of youngsters his age to a football match and joins the excitement of the game absent-mindedly because he feels that the gaze rests upon him from across the field. Any formal ball game, a contest between opposites, is a means of transformation, easy to come by though its effect is short-lived because no sacrifice is involved; by sharing a collective stimulation, the individual spectator can forget himself and identify with the crowd, which gives him a heightened sense of life.[7] This exaltation grips his companions, but not Mauricio; he remains there only so that the hidden and meaningful gaze may continue to observe him.

I interpret this gaze as an image of what Jung calls the Self, which is the organizing center of the psyche. It embraces the conscious and the unconscious psyche, and is therefore a personality which we also are.[8] The Self is the source and regulating drive of all psychic growth, and its relation to the ego is well expressed by the idea of a magnetic gaze. As Jung said, "we exist because the sun sees us," and the sun is a common symbol for the Self.[9] The all-seeing eye of God is an associated image, God being another Self-symbol. Mauricio, feeling and desiring this *mirada,* wonders how he can catch hold of it without shattering it: "¿Cómo atraparla—sin aferrarse a ella y sin romperla . . . ?" (p. 244). This would refer to the ego/Self axis, the connecting link between consciousness and the unconscious vital to psychic health. In other words, he hopes to preserve his connection with the Self and to remain ever mindful of its directives.

During the game, the complex music of SCARBO fills Mauricio's mind. He is attentive to the awakening scarab's tremolos rising from the dark, deep earth, its notes still undistinguishable. It is the sound of hidden stirrings and of coming resurgence, for the beetle is an image of the boy's embryonic new personality. Later, walking in the city, Mauricio notices that in its scramble toward the sun, the scarab is obeying the gaze. As the music progresses and he strides along whistling the radiant chords and arpeggios that indicate that the scarab has reached the light, Mauricio hears another whistle, uncertainly imitating his own; he deliberately refrains from looking around lest he spoil the incipient relationship.

Next morning, Monday, the young man returns to the woods, now mercifully deserted. He lies down under the pine trees and gives himself over to Ravel. Soon the defective, echoing whistle reaches him from the left (p. 253, the direction of the unconscious). He corrects its errors and the other responds, accepting the corrections. The training is a long, arduous process, but Mauricio takes pleasure in the eagerness with which the other absorbs everything he has to offer. Then he falls asleep and senses that someone has drawn near and is studying his appearance, as if to assimilate him, but when he opens his eyes, there is nobody there (p. 255). Thus, the scarab, heavy with the symbolism of self-generation, has served its purpose and has turned into a more human entity, the whistle, which Mauricio can train and charge with life-giving libido.

He goes home. Seeing that Sylvia is out and the weather is hot, he takes off his clothes and lies down on her scarlet sofa. The music of Ravel gushes forth from the center of his being, carrying him outside of time; for eight or ten hours he lies there, repeating the musical phrases without seeing or hearing anything else: "se tendió desnudo en el sofá escarlata, repitiendo y repitiendo la música tan sabia . . . uniéndose con su centro mismo de modo que todo él quedó anulado . . . ocho . . . diez horas tendido . . . sin ver ni oír, fuera del tiempo" (p. 256). The spectacle of Mauricio lying naked on *Sylvia's scarlet sofa* suggests that he has become once more a fetus in his *mother's womb,* the place of transformation; or that being outside of time and sensibility, he has figuratively died. Thus, on this the second day of his travail, he is following the archetypal pattern of the "night sea journey," like Jonah in the belly of the whale or Christ in Hades.

When Sylvia finds him in his trance, yet whistling, she is upset and angry. He is a nothing, he has no personality, she cries; it's as if Ravel were his essence, the only feature he has. In response, Mauricio says that Ravel is not his essence, only a means, a way . . . "un camino" (p. 259), but a way to what, that he doesn't know. Making music, like any rhythmic activity is a way to transformation, because it channels the flow of psychic energy.

Tuesday morning he is off to Vallvidrera again, where the other whistle is waiting to finish its apprenticeship. When perfection has at last been attained, Mauricio sits down by the waters and tries to whistle, but he cannot, not even within his head. He has emptied himself of the music and he feels good about it. At a distance, he now notices a young beggar cooking on a fire of twigs. He watches as the fellow eats, stretches out, and goes to sleep. Quietly, he approaches to observe him. He finds that the sleeper is a replica of himself. Mauricio wonders what he is going to do about this being whom he has sought so hard and so long, this body that contains his own: "este cuerpo misterioso que contenía el suyo" (p. 264). Irresistibly, he bends over to touch the other under the chin, and in this instant of physical contact, he discharges into the beggar everything that has been weighing him down. Then he withdraws, careful not to be seen. Without meeting, the two manage to exchange clothing and identities, or rather, the beggar takes over Mauricio's and Mauricio runs off, delighted with the beggar's rags and lack of identification. Now the ex-beggar, the transformed Mauricio, is ready to go to his mother and to dumb-found her by his natural and affectionate bearing; and he does just that.

Mauricio has called forth this other personality from the depths of his introversion. He has redeemed a portion of his unconscious personality by his own active effort, worked on it, and shaped it into a human semblance. Animated by the feminine, life-giving element of his psyche, his labor has been one of true self-generation. It has lasted for the mythical three days, from Sunday to Tuesday. Because he has tamed his fear of the unconscious, he can now relate spontaneously to his mother, who no longer embodies the negative mother archetype for him; he has therefore redeemed his neglected feminine capacity for relatedness and given his ego some stability. In the *dragon fight,* the captive princess symbolizes these qualities of the feminine principle, vitality and feeling. Carl Jung calls her the *anima.* Mauricio's venture into the unconscious is unusual in that he has achieved transformation without any outside incentive. He was not impelled to self-sacrifice by the love of a young woman or by any suprapersonal value, like an exalted cause or a consuming ideal, which normally would carry an adolescent over the threshold to adulthood. Heroism as such is not elicited of him, which is probably appropriate in this era of the anti-hero, and indeed he has turned into the well-adjusted, materialistic youngster his bourgeois mother wants him to be, untouched by any transcendent aspiration.

More symbolic points than can be mentioned here amplify the details of Mauricio's rite of passage, which illustrates the most crucial transition in psychic growth—crucial, because it must be repeated many times in the course of a lifetime, and because failure to make the transition is a common problem for neurotics. The theme turns up in the literature of all periods, but it is found more frequently, expressed with more complexity, in our century. This happens, no doubt, because it is the nature of the literary artist to be, consciously or not, a witness to the needs and reality of his or her times.

Notes

[1] José Donoso (Barcelona: Editorial Seix Barral, 1973).

[2] Carl Jung, *Symbols of Transformation* (Princeton: Princeton University Press, 1976), pp. 219, 263.

[3] Ibid., pp. 94, 154.

[4] Ibid., p. 423f.

[5] Ibid., p. 268.

[6] Mircea Eliade, *Cosmos and History: The Myth of the Eternal Return* (rpt. New York: Harper and Row, 1959), pp. 27-36.

[7] Jung, *The Archetypes and the Collective Unconscious* (Princeton: Princeton University Press, 1969), p. 125.

[8] Jung, *Two Essays on Analytical Psychology* (Princeton: Princeton University Press, 1960), p. 175.

[9] *Symbols,* p. 194n.

Miriam Adelstein (essay date 1983)

SOURCE: "The Insubstantial Country of the Mind: *Cuentos* by José Donoso," *Critica Hispánica,* Vol. 5, No. 2, Fall, 1983, pp. 97-106.

[*In the following essay, Adelstein explores Donoso's preoccupation with the psychological functioning of his characters, which Adelstein contends marks each of the tales in* Cuentos.]

The world of José Donoso: a country of the reflections and dreams of puppets, of their imaginary discourse with others. . . . It is alike Jaynes' world of "unseen visions and heard silences."[1] It is the country of the mind.

The world described by Donoso in *Cuentos*[2] is one that is filled with anxieties, antagonisms and emptiness. The characters are the instruments of those physical/psychological realms which encompass them. They live not only in the physical world which surrounds them, but also in a psychological environment which seems to weigh more heavily on their personalities. The protagonists are Iliadic men, lacking a will of their own, their behaviour directed by inner voices—the clearly discernible voices of friends or authoritative figures; or the anonymous voices representing the expectations of an ordered world. The characters are *told* what to do, how to think, how to feel. They interact passively with the world around them. They are performers in life who disregard the precept of the Delphic oracle: "know thyself."

In *Cuentos,* Donoso devotes an abundance of time and vocabulary to the description of the characters and the world in which they live. He spares no effort in divulging all the details necessary to create a complete picture that shows their interaction with the world around them, as well as the inner workings of their own minds.

Without doubt, Donoso's principal preoccupation is with the psychological functioning of the characters. His interest in the decaying physical environment is only important in its reflection of the character's mental configuration. Donoso's cogent portrayals of the decaying physical environments of his protagonist-victims and of their mental configurations are the mere artifacts of his exploration of human isolation, alienation, loneliness—of the exploration of the void. Indeed, the authenticity of Donoso's conflict-ridden character depictions has its origin in the reflections of many contemporary philosopher-psychologists.

By concentrating on these existential preoccupations, it is possible to examine the multifarious ways in which Donoso's protagonists attempt to rescue their personal identities from total annihilation. If we certainly examine Donoso's works, starting from his first writings, **"The Poisoned Pastries"** and **"Blue Woman"**, we cannot fail to perceive his preoccupation with the individual's anguish before human existence—an anguish that exteriorizes itself in a world of fear, corruption and terror.

One of the themes in the stories in *Cuentos* which is immediately apparent is that of loneliness, social alienation or isolation of the character. From the very first story, **"Veraneo,"** one notes the isolation of the servants. They are not aware of the world which surrounds them, but only exist within their own circle of gossip, boyfriends and dances. Even more important to this theme are the youngsters, Raúl and Jaime. Each boy is alone and apart when the story begins. They experience a period of friendship, but later on, Jaime goes away and Raúl remains intensely alone: even more so than he was before.

The alienation of all of Donoso's principal characters figures in the following stories of the collection as well. In **"Tocayos,"** the protagonists have no friends or family, but live either alone, or with nonrelatives in a large, unfriendly city. Mrs. Howland in **"El güero"** has spent many years of her life not loving her husband, feeling estranged from her family, and finally losing both her child and spouse. The list of unhappy characters goes on with Santelices, the old bachelor who lives in an unfriendly boarding house. The old man in **"Ana María"** finally leaves his wife and home after many years of unhappiness. The young man in **"Una señora"** lives in a world of fantasy totally detached from the real world. In his last story, the narrator describes what he sees: "La hilera de casas bajas se prolongaba a lo largo de la acera: ventana, puerta, ventana, puerta, dos ventanas. . . ." (p. 82) This quote shows the intense void existing within the character as well as his total separation from the world which surrounds him. What he sees has no meaning to him, and seems to be part of a senseless stupor.

The void of loneliness in the works of Donoso extends to all age and social groups. Children are not exempt; old men and young men, as well as women, be they rich or poor, are all plagued by the intense internal despair which characterizes loneliness.

The social structure of the family is not able to survive in Donoso's world. In a great number of the stories, the father is either absent or ineffective, while in **"Paseo,"** the mother is never encountered or even mentioned. Because of this dissolution of the family, the suffering and loneliness are more intensified. In those stories where the father is absent, the mother tries to raise the child on her own, but without exception this attempt always ends in failure.

In **"Veraneo"** Raúl's father is alive but never at home, so the boy does not experience any relationship with his father. The mother tries to do what she thinks is right for her son by forbidding his friendship with Jaime. However, Raúl breaks this interdiction and continues seeing his friend. It is quite possible that in the eyes of Raúl, the tall, older, mysterious and powerful Jaime is a father-figure to

whom he is attached, due to his own lack of a father-presence.

"El güero" is another story in which the child suffers due to the disintegration of the family unit. The father is too involved in scientific research to have time for his son, and the mother imposes restrictions to which the child refuses to adhere. Instead, he takes off on an idealistic boat expedition which inevitably leads to his death.

Perhaps the most classic example of the harm construed by a mother/son relationship can be seen in **"Fiesta en grande."** El Beto is forty-five years old, but in the relationship he has with his mother, he is like a five year old child. Examples of their conversations are:

> "—Albertito, llegó mi hijito?
>
> —Sí, mami. . . ."

Also,

> "—Tranquilo, mi lindo. No te preocupes. ¿Te apago la luz para que te duermas?
>
> —Bueno, viejita. . . .
>
> —Buenas noches, hijo. Descansa bien." (p. 103)

The conversation between mother and son is filled with diminutives and evokes the image of a young mother with her infant child. Emotionally speaking, El Beto has not developed into a man, but rather, he is stunted by the overpowering relationship between his mother and himself.

This suffocating mother/son love is destructive to the character because it renders him incapable of maintaining a relationship with any other woman. Even when he goes to the picnic with La Martita, he compares her to his mother, knowing that "la señora Martita apartaría los mejores sandwiches para él, tal como lo hubiera hecho su madre." (p. 99) Therefore, in the mind of El Beto, there is a confusion between Martita and his mother, to the point where he sees Martita as the embodiment of the two women. Later on in the story, El Beto dreams that he makes love to this Martita/mother figure, symbolically expressed in the dream as a willow tree. What is even more interesting is his desire to destroy the tree, so demonstrating his sense of guilt as well as his frustration with his mother's hold on his life. Killing her in his dream expresses his desire to break away from the ties that hold him to his mother.

This dream, as well as the final episode in the story suggest that El Beto is suffering from an Oedipal complex. He loves his mother, has sexual fantasies about her, and begs her to sleep in his bed with him. When he is with her, he loses all identity as a man and exists only as her "little boy." Obviously, he tries to break this relationship because it denies him an existence separate from his mother. However, at the same time, he returns home to her and remains in the web of her love. He is clearly torn between the options available to him. He wants to break away, but he wants also to remain in the security of this love with which he is familiar. El Beto arrives at an impasse. In the company of his mother he is able to evade responsibility and decision-making; he is able to be "a little boy." This is reminiscent of a passage by Sartre depicting the hero in *The Words*: "Out of cowardice and with a good little boy's timidity [he] had backed away from the risks of a free and open existence, an existence without providential guarantee."[3] El Beto is acting in "bad faith," the term used by Sartre to characterize the "yearning to escape one's liberty and responsibility . . . He who turns to Authority . . . rather than his own self for guidance, [when confronted by a choice, is abdicating his liberty], therefore his authenticity, at the same time, passing on to Others the responsibility of his acts."[4] El Beto is unable to forfeit the security his mother provides, which shelters him from the outside world. As May cautions, "The problem of being prey to someone else's power is reinforced . . . by one's own infantile desires to be taken care of."[5]

This binary opposition of El Beto's character introduces another theme: a theme that expresses another duality. In many of the stories, the characters live in a world of order, rigidity, rules and sterility. Their lives are governed by routine, mundane details that leave no room for aspirations, desires, hopes and dreams. Opposed to this meaningless routine, the characters also live in a world of imaginative fantasy, beauty, satisfaction, love, mystery, and all else that is missing in their everyday lives. The void which they experience every day leads to a deep anxiety and fear which eventually overpower the character, and he is then forced to act.

In **"Paseo,"** Aunt Matilde and the young narrator both experience the void created by their routine existence. The atmosphere in the house is one of sterility and rigidity with no room for impulse or imagination. There is also no show of love between the members of the family. Rather, they all seem to exist in a sort of vacuum, unaffected by each other or by any force outside their existence.

The narrator in the story dreams of the mysterious unknown streets in the city and the exotic ships that go by. For him, these symbols represent a world of adventure, mystery and change.

Tía Matilde also experiences the same anguish as the boy. She too is oppressed by the demanding routine, order and dignity that rule her life. Her initial means of accepting a new life lies in her acceptance and adoption of the white dog. She devotes all her time and stifled love to this dog who reciprocates by loving her in return. Her final act of liberation comes when she leaves the house, never to return. She takes the dog with her: the dog which symbolises love, sexual fantasy, and which is also the symbol of a new beginning for her. The acceptance and adoption of "la perra blanca" by Tía Matilde is contiguous with *her* awakening of consciousness. The dog signals a new beginning. Tía Matilde breaks down her ritualized world: "salió a pasear con la perra después de comida y no volvió más." (p. 230) Tía Matilde's choice is gratifying.

She rejects that which impedes her self-expression and self-actualization and her venture out is a promise to the reader that she is learning to feel, experience and want— that she is becoming a person. The narrator is left speculating "si Tía Matilde, arrastrada por la perra, se perdió en la ciudad, en la muerte, o en una región más misteriosa que ambas." (p. 230) One is left with the impression that this boy too, will one day reject his ordered sterile life for a new, hopeful life, like his aunt has done.

Santelices is another character very much like Tía Matilde. He too is inundated by the senseless, emotionless routine and restrictions which typify his life. He liberates himself by looking at pictures of exotic beasts which represent distant lands and allow him imaginative freedom.

The characters of **Cuentos,** like the hero of Kafka's *Metamorphosis,* live in a world of order, rigidity and sterility, their lives governed by routine. Mrs. Howland in **"El güero"** questions: "¿Conoce usted esa clase de personas que viven según teorías, teorías que estipulan el nombre preciso y el peso exacto de cada cosa, desterrando con eso toda posibilidad de misterio?" (p. 62) Donoso's performers are given scripts, and when so cued, they engage in the dictated acts. In **"Veraneo,"** when it is time to go to the beach, the children do so because "era su hora del deber por cumplir." (p. 38) Similarly, emotion is not generated spontaneously but emitted dutifully; for Tía Matilde and her brothers in **"Paseo,"** "expresar sus afectos era desempeñar perfectamente sus funciones uno respecto a los otros, y, sobre todo, no incomodar, jamás incomodar." (p. 209) Mrs. Howland of **"El güero"** is aware that even thought is directed. But she decides "que este hijo mío iba a ser un gran hombre. Desde temprano debía ser capaz de razonar por sí solo y de actuar según sus inclinaciones, libre de toda oscuridad que entorpeciera lo que habría de ser la más plena de las vidas." (pp. 64-65)

This ordered world requires that an individual know who he is and how he should be. But Donoso's protagonists are dissatisfied with this order and with the rigid channelling of their energies, their potentialities. The order appears to them as hollow, empty. However, Donoso's protagonists are also painfully aware of the profound sense of security that this order provides. The individual is comfortable knowing that he knows what to expect. The protagonist in **"Santelices"** realizes he would never stray from the boarding house which he despises: "Era demasiado difícil comenzar a fabricar una nueva relación con alguien, con cualquiera que fuese . . . Mal que mal, saber que todas las noches podía jugar unas manos de canasta sin sus dientes postizos, estar seguro de que nunca les faltaría un botón a sus camisas, que sus zapatos estarían limpios en la mañana, que se respetaban sus irregularidades estomacales, sus gustos, sus pequeñas manías, era algo tan sólido que sería para él una tragedia abandonarlo." (p. 274) Santelices is the individual who tenaciously and very often paradoxically attempts to safeguard his personal identity from the threat of total annihilation. He appears as a "pathetic" and occasionally a "comic" figure who is tormented by a desire to search for a new order of existence which will allow him to exercise his freedom and consequently achieve a more existentially fulfilling and authentic life. But Santelices is unable to come to terms with the disassociation which he experiences between himself and his empirical world, and he finds it increasingly difficult to live an "authentic" and "human" life.

The love-hate which Donoso's protagonists have towards the order in their worlds in each case provokes inner struggle. Camus in *The Myth of Sisyphus* captures the essence of such order. He writes: "Rising, tram, four hours in the office or factory, meal, tram, four hours of work, meal, sleep, and Monday, Tuesday, Wednesday, Thursday, Friday and Saturday, according to the same rhythm."[6] Camus' narrative is a metaphor of this order. Camus concludes that the order path is followed easily until one day the individual questions *why*.[7] The protagonists in *Cuentos* separately face this *why*.

In questioning *why*, in experiencing the inner struggle, there "can be great joy, but it is as easy to be mangled by the process as to swing with it . . . [for] those who do not know from their own experience what hell this borderline between being and non-being can become [it will require an act of imagination]."[8] El Beto's inner struggle is accompanied by considerable anxiety. He draws back: "Hoy no estaba dispuesto a ponerse a prueba." (p. 100) He turns to his mother: "No se vaya, mami. Acompáñeme hasta que me duerma. Tengo miedo. . . ." (p. 106)

Camus claims that the day the *why* arises, "everything begins in that wariness tinged with amazement."[9] He emphasizes 'beginning': "'Begins'—this is important. Weariness comes at the end of the acts of a mechanical life, but at the same time it inaugurates the impulse of consciousness. It awakens consciousness and provokes what follows. What follows is the gradual return into the chain or it is the definitive awakening."[10]

El Beto in **"Fiesta en grande"** remains in this awakened state only for an instant in a dream during which he brandished a sword and with it impales the willow tree which symbolizes his mother—his keeper. But, in reality his choice is to lapse back into non-being, to remain the infant he has always been.

Like El Beto, Mrs. Howland in **"El güero"** ultimately cannot extricate herself from her rigidly-structured world. She remains a prisoner of that world, even following the deaths of her child and husband, when she is responsible to or for no-one but herself.

Raúl in **"Veraneo"** ultimately rejects his world, breaks from the chain. Raúl chooses self-alienation: "Pasó casi todo el verano sentado en la arena, solo, tarareando algo que nadie conocía. Con el perfil fijo en el horizonte, parecía aguardar a alguien, algo." (p. 44) But Raúl has not "become a person" which entails not only fighting and rejecting that which prevents one from feeling and wanting, but it is also "learning to feel, to experience and to want."[11]

Similarly, this criticism is applicable to both the protagonists in **"Santelices"** and in **"La puerta cerrada"** who do

emancipate themselves from their restrained worlds but consequently compromise life itself. At the peak of his 'awakening,' Santelices jumps to his death—to the fantastic world of "rumores peligrosos . . . cuerpos de andar perfecto, guiños de ojos que al oscurecer fulguraban hasta quemar, olores, bocanadas de aire usado en pulmones poderosos, presencias, roces, calor de pieles tendidas sobre la elegancia de músculos precisos, toda una inervante incitación a participar en una vida candente, a exponerse a ser fauce y sangre, víctima y agresor." (p. 266) With his death, Sebastián attempts to preserve his "selfhood." Ties to an ordered world are broken. This attempt to preserve the "selfhood" in Donoso's fictional world is the embodiment of the conception of authenticity vs. inauthenticity of the philosophy of Heidegger. The individual must not submit to the pressures which arise and operate against him within his society. Camus has expressed that "man is his own end. And he is his only end. If he aims to be something, it is in this life."[12] In **"La puerta cerrada"** Donoso suggests that Sebastián's 'definitive awakening' was sufficient, that this was a 'happy death': "el rostro del muerto [Sebastián] . . . apareció transfigurado por una expresión de tal goce, de tal alegría y embeleso, que María Patricia [a bystander] . . . exclamó: 'Mira, . . . , qué lindo.'" (p. 179)

Without doubt, the rebellion of the characters in *Cuentos* constitute a search or a need within their beings. They are not satisfied with their lives, and recognize that something is missing. The search which they undergo to fulfill their lives is a psychoanalytical study performed by the author, who is deeply concerned with the problems these characters present. He recognizes that their physical lack is essentially the reflection of a psychological need that affects their social behaviour.

In the story **"Fiesta en grande,"** the author is really occupied with an analytic study of the mental state of Alberto. Donoso seeks to find out why this man is irresponsive to others, and particularly to women. After a portrait of Alberto's mother and the relationship that exists between the two, it is quite clear that Alberto finds himself at an impasse. He wants to break lose from his mother's stifling affection, but he is incapable of doing so. This mental frustration is revealed as the principal reason for his insecurity around other people.

Alberto's character shows a personality split which is basic to human nature. Although he wants to liberate himself, he also does not want to, since he begs his mother to stay with him. The agony involved in being on his own also details a responsibility with which he is not prepared to cope. So, even though he wants liberty, he chooses, through fear, to remain imprisoned.

Another character who seeks to liberate himself from the preoccupations of every day existence is Sebastián, the principal character in **"La puerta cerrada."** He can sleep whenever he wishes to, and spends the major part of his life doing so. When questioned by his mother and his boss as to why he sleeps so much, he replies that he is waiting for the closed door of his dreams to open up for him.

Sebastián's mother, Adela, has had a difficult life, bringing up her son on her own, working hard and denying herself any pleasures in life. Sebastían rejects work, order, routine and security because they hold no promise for him. He lives on a level above routine, every day existence; a level which baffles his mother and is totally incomprehensible for her.

One has the impression that Sebastián is seeking to exist on another plane of reality. The closed door is a symbol of the entrance into another life that is more noble, fulfilling and satisfying than this one. So, like Santelices and Tía Matilde, he sacrifices his present life for the promise of a new and better one.

The other characters in the other stories of the collection are all representatives of the basic problems that haunt all of Donoso's characters. They are lonely, isolated, unhappy. They are stifled by an unproductive life and by the lack of inspiration and imagination in their daily routines. For all these characters, existence is characterized by a void, a lack which they cannot identify, but which Donoso probes in psychoanalytic fashion.

Tía Matilde, Sebastián, El Beto, Raúl—through his protagonist pawns, Donoso thrusts his reader-participant into an awareness of "how insubstantial the pageant of external reality can be,"[13] into an exploration of the non-being, the void, the inner apparition that questions the *why* of his cubby-hole existence.

Notes

The idea of this title has been prompted by Julian Jaynes: *The Origin of Consciousness in the Breakdown of the Bicameral Mind,* University of Toronto Press, Toronto, 1976, p. 1.

[1] *Op. cit.,* p. 1.

[2] José Donoso, *Cuentos,* Seix Barral, S.A., Barcelona, 1971. All references from Donoso's short stories are taken from *Cuentos.* Henceforth, references from this edition will be indicated by the page number in parenthesis.

[3] Jean-Paul Sartre, *The Words,* Fawcett Publications, Greenwich, Conn., 1964, p. 124.

[4] Jean-Paul Sartre, *Huis Clos,* Meredith Publishing Company, New York, 1962, p. xii.

[5] Rollo May, *Man's Search for Himself,* W. W. Norton and Company, Inc., New Jersey, 1967, p. 169.

[6] Albert Camus, *The Myth of Sisyphus,* Penguin Books Ltd., Middlesex, England, 1979, p. 19.

[7] Ibid., p. 19.

[8] R. D. Laing, *The Politics of Experience and the Bird of Paradise,* Penguin Books Ltd., Middlesex, England, 1967, p. 36.

[9] Camus, *Op. cit.,* p. 19.

[10] *Op. cit.,* p. 19.

[11] May, *Op. cit.,* p. 103.

[12] Camus, *Op. cit.,* p. 82.

[13] Laing, *Op. cit.,* p. 109.

Carlos J. Alonso (essay date 1984-85)

SOURCE: "Pathetic Falla-City: Donoso's 'Una señora'," *Symposium*, Vol. 38, No. 4, Winter, 1984-85, pp. 267-77.

[*In the following essay, Alonso views the story "Una señora" as an exploration of the tensions between humanity and city life, as well as the postmodern conceit of literature as "a shell that encompasses only itself."*]

The short stories of José Donoso have not received the sustained critical attention that has been accorded his novelistic production. Chronologically, the great majority of them fall in the period immediately preceding the so-called "Boom," if we acquiesce to the received date of 1961 as the unofficial beginning of the surge in modern Latin American letters.[1] Donoso's first collection of short stories, *Veraneo y otros cuentos,* was published in 1955. *El charlestón,* the Chilean writer's other collection of short fiction appeared in print in 1960.[2] This temporal marginality vis-à-vis the "Boom" is symbolic of the way Donoso's short stories are perceived in the context of his literary career. Contrary, for instance, to the case of Gabriel García Márquez the bulk of whose earlier literary production appears to have been recovered and reappraised after the immense success of *Cien años de soledad,* Donoso's stories have benefited little from the universal acclaim received by his *El obsceno pájaro de la noche,* published in 1970 to unanimous critical praise. The reason may lie in the avowed social realism that critics have noted in the stories, to which they oppose the self-referential, multi-layered writing of *El obsceno pájaro de la noche.* Some version of this distinction appears to underlie the following comment taken from the introduction by Ana María Moix to Donoso's collected stories, published in 1971: "Pasados veinticuatro años y juzgando con el distanciamiento que permite el paso del tiempo, puede comprobar el lector que José Donoso no se escapó de pagar su tributo a la moda del realismo social de los años cincuenta."[3] Given its retrospective nature, what the comment quoted above appears to contrast implicitly are two different textual practices: the first, referential and mimetic; the second, the producer of the open, polysemous textual universe of *El obsceno pájaro de la noche,* intent on affirming the rule and play of the signifier.[4] This discrepancy, and the perplexity it elicits in critical circles, are aptly summarized by John Caviglia: "Those who have written on *El obsceno pájaro* do seem near consensus on two points: first, that the work is unique, unprecedented, and somehow, like a monster, sui generis; and second, that its aberrations are doubly puzzling . . . , given the 'traditional' nature of José Donoso's earlier fiction."[5]

This characterization of the signifying practice at work in Donoso's short stories and the subsequent dichotomy perceived by critics with respect to *El obsceno pájaro de la noche* is not entirely unwarranted. The predominantly urban setting and thematics of the stories would appear to lend substance to the characterization of Donoso's early writings as a form of social realism.[6] The understated but evident attention given in these texts to differences in social strata would also seem to evince a conception of literature as social document. More significantly, however, most of Donoso's stories appear to reflect in their dynamics the conception of signification that underlies their production. This can be perceived as a movement in the stories towards meaning and fullness through the achievement of some elusive form of plenitude. **"La puerta cerrada"** and **"Santelices,"** for instance, depict the sense of personal transcendence ultimately achieved by these stories' protagonists. The former narrates the story of a man who finally opens fully in his dreams the door alluded to in the title, whereby he gains access to an unspecified realm of totality. In turn, Santelices, a nondescript and meek public servant becomes the hero of his carefully constructed imaginary apotheosis. By the same token, in **"El charlestón,"** **"Tocayos,"** and **"Ana María,"** this experience of plenitude is arrived at through communion with an Other: through the reaffirmation of a sense of existential solidarity with friends in the first two instances, and by the immersion of an old man in the pre-linguistic universe of a little girl in the third tale.

This desire for a plenum of meaning is incorporated metaphorically in some of Donoso's stories as a longing for communion with the city. Given the generally urban milieu of the stories, the city stands as a sort of extra-textual referent to which the texts allude in the broadest sense of the term. Thus, the city becomes the setting, the emblematic stage for a signifying practice that takes for granted and affirms the necessary nature of the relationship between signifier and signified. This desire for communion with the city, and the fulfillment of that longing which most of the stories purport to depict, can be interpreted as a gesture towards plenitude of signification, towards the perfect concordance of sign and referent. From this perspective then, the stories appear to reflect in their thematics and development the economy of signification that underlies and legitimizes their production.

One can observe quite clearly this mystification of the urban landscape in one of Donoso's tales, **"Paseo."** Here the narrator as a child perceives the city as a distant and mysterious plenitude that he opposes to the safe but suffocating environment of his house: "Yo permanecí en la biblioteca con un vaso de limonada en la mano, mirando el cielo del verano, y escuchando, escuchando ansiosamente algún pitazo lejano de barco, y el rumor de la ciudad desconocida, terrible y también deseada, que se extendía bajo las estrellas."[7] This is the same city through which his Tía Matilde in the end seems to achieve a stage of personal redemption as she ventures out of the house and is finally never heard from again. Significantly, the vantage point for the child as he looks down on the city is the library. Moreover, on two occasions the house is explicitly compared to a book: "Pero nuestra casa está en pie aún, angosta y vertical como un librito apretado entre los gruesos volúmenes de los edificios nuevos" (p. 208). And later: "Los hermanos . . . recorrían los pasillos de aquella casa que, a semejanza de un libro, sólo mostraba la angosta franja de su lomo a la calle" (p. 209). This metaphoric association of building and text should not be unfamiliar to readers of *El obsceno pájaro de la noche.*[8] The fictional space of the novel is organized as a counterpoint between the Casa de Ejercicios Espirituales de la Encarnación de la Chimba and La Rinconada, the museum that houses a collection of teratological specimens. As Sharon Magnarelli has proposed, the text is also characterized by a proliferation of packages, of enclosures within enclosures that allude to the labor of signification enacted by the text. In this scheme, the novel "becomes the very *imbunche* it so frequently portrays. All the exits and entrances to the outside world are closed off. All that remains are packages within packages, signifiers that refer only to other signifiers."[9] If we take this to be an accurate characterization of the signifying practice of *El obsceno pájaro de la noche,* then we must conclude that in the earlier stories we have mentioned there is, at least on the surface, the enactment of an opposite desire. The *casa/libro* of **"Paseo"** is indeed a figure for the text; but if we heed the metaphorical logic described earlier, in the child's longing for the city, for the outside, we can perceive a nostalgia for the signified in its full presence. The same can be stated about **"Una señora,"** where the protagonist sallies forth into the city and encompasses it through his distant relationship with an anonymous older woman.

The concept of the city has served, at various moments in history, as the topos (using the word in both its rhetorical and literal acceptations) of plenitude and fulfillment. It occurs in Plato and Saint Augustine, and it informs the literature of Utopia as well. To furnish an example of a more recent, instance, it appears as an important metaphor in Sartre's *Qu'est-ce que la littérature?* Describing the universe that unites the author and his reader, Sartre proposes that it must project the feeling of being "traversé de part en part et soutenu par une liberté qui a pris pour fin la liberté humaine, et, s'il n'est pas vraiment la cité des fins qu'il doit être, il faut au moins qu'il soit une étape vers elle, en un mot, il faut . . . qu'on le considère et présente toujours . . . du point de vue de son dépassement vers cette cité des fins."[10] In Donoso's stories the recurrent longing for the city suggests the wish to achieve perfect concordance between text and referent, a desire that is systematically thwarted in *El obsceno pájaro de la noche.*

Thus, we seem to have reached in a roundabout fashion the same conclusion as those critics who implicitly establish a chasm between Donoso's stories and his novelistic corpus. However, this gesture towards the outside of the text is accompanied by a simultaneous recognition of the impossibility of signifying anything but the text itself. If I have chosen **"Una señora"** to put in evidence this paradoxical plane, it is simply because it purports to accomplish the most immediate, the most satisfactory incorporation of the extra-textual in the text, as evinced by the cathartic tone with which the story concludes. The same dimension can be unveiled in the other stories as well, although **"Una señora"** is, from this perspective, truly an exemplar.

Donoso's **"Una señora"** is the story of a man's evolving obsession with an anonymous woman he first encounters in a streetcar.[11] Paradoxically, and yet perfectly consistent with the story's overarching concerns, there is nothing that should make her stand out in the crowd. Her nondescript quality is emphasized from the very beginning by the narrator: "Era una señora. Una señora que llevaba un paraguas mojado en la mano y un sombrero funcional en la cabeza. Una de esas señoras cincuentonas, de las que hay por miles en esta ciudad: ni hermosa ni fea, ni pobre ni rica. Sus facciones regulares mostraban los restos de una belleza banal. Sus cejas se juntaban más de lo corriente sobre el arco de la nariz, lo que era el razgo más distintivo de su rostro" (p. 82). And yet, the next morning, the protagonist believes to have seen the same woman once more: "Antes de atravesar una calle divisé una figura que se me antojó familiar, alejándose bajo la oscuridad de las ramas. Me detuve, observándola un instante. Si, era la mujer que iba junto a mí en el tranvía la tarde anterior. Cuando pasó bajo un farol reconocí inmediatamente su impermeable verde. Hay miles de impermeables verdes en esta ciudad, sin embargo no dudé de que se trataba del suyo, recordándola a pesar de haberla visto sólo algunos segundos en que nada de ella me impresionó" (p. 83). Slowly, the woman becomes a fixture, an unavoidable presence in the protagonist's wanderings throughout the city. He makes, however, no attempt to bridge the distance between himself and the unknown woman:

> En adelante comencé a ver a la señora bastante seguido. La encontraba en todas partes y a toda hora. . . . Me asaltó la idea melodramática de que quizás se ocupara en seguirme. Pero la deseché al constatar que ella, al contrario que yo, no me identificaba en medio de la multitud. A mí, en cambio, me gustaba percibir su identidad entre tanto rostro desconocido. Me sentaba en un parque y ella lo cruzaba llevando un bolsón con verduras. Me detenía a comprar cigarrillos, y allí estaba ella pagando los suyos. Iba al cine, y allí estaba la señora, dos butacas más allá. No me miraba, pero yo me entretenía observándola. (p. 83)

The narrator's preoccupation with the woman reaches the point where his inability to come across her causes anguish and obsessive behavior. Finally, one Sunday morning the man awakens with the unshakable certainty that the woman is about to die. The next day, on reading the newspaper, "vi . . . que los deudos de doña Ester de Arancibia anunciaban su muerte, dando la hora de los funerales. ¿Podría ser? . . . Sí. Sin duda era ella. Asistí al cementerio, siguiendo el cortejo lentamente por las avenidas largas, entre personas silenciosas que conocían los rasgos y la voz de la mujer por quien sentían dolor. Después caminé un rato bajo los árboles oscuros, porque esa tarde soleada me trajo una tranquilidad especial" (p. 87).

Even from the sketchy synopsis offered here, it is possible to see that **"Una señora"** is ultimately an exploration of

the confrontation between man and city. The protagonist, through an act of imaginative will, rescues the inconspicuous woman from the sea of anonymous beings that surround him in the city. He manages to establish a powerful link with her that defeats the forces of alienation ruling the urban experience. This is the source for the cathartic dimension projected at the conclusion of the story, the "tranquilidad especial" felt by the narrator as he joined the mourning relatives of the woman. Through his relationship with the woman, the narrator subjectively organizes and appropriates the city. The urban landscape acquires the new meaning engendered by the existence of the two structuring poles—the protagonist and the woman—that the relationship dictates. At the beginning of the story, the narrator's wanderings through the city are random and aimless: "Cuando me aburro de mi pieza y de mis conversaciones habituales, suelo tomar algún tranvía, cuyo recorrido desconozca y pasear así por la ciudad" (p. 81). Once he meets the woman, however, these excursions acquire a purpose and goal: "Poco a poco la comencé a buscar. El día no me parecía completo sin verla" (p. 83). And later on: "A veces tenía tal necesidad de verla, que abandonaba cuanto me tenía atareado para salir en su busca" (p. 84). Moreover, and perhaps more significantly, through his bond with the woman the narrator appears to redeem himself as well from the meaninglessness of city life. We know nothing of him—not even his name—other than those facts that pertain to his developing an affective relationship with the woman. But through her he rescues himself from the tedium of his previous existence and achieves the sense of inner peace with which the story closes. Thus, the text would seem to propose the possibility of immediacy and communication in the context of the supposedly dehumanizing realm of the modern city. If, as proposed earlier, the desire for communion with the city can be interpreted as a commentary on the text's own signifying practice, then **"Una señora"** would appear to suggest the possibility of perfect concordance between signifier and signified. The ensuing analysis will reveal, nevertheless, that this apparently successful overture to the outside of the text is fraught with knowledge of its own problematic nature. This knowledge takes the form of a dimension that underscores the intrinsically literary nature of the text.

To begin with, **"Una señora"** appears to be a catalogue, a compendium of the literature of urban reality. Hardly a motif or topos of that literary tradition is absent from the narrative—no small achievement considering its dimensions: isolation, anonymity, voyeurism, the Other, alienation, etc.[12] What is striking, nevertheless, is that the story seems to call attention to the presence of these topoi in its midst. In the presentation of the protagonist as voyeur, for instance, the description is decidedly self-referential: "El tranvía avanzaba casi vacío. Me senté junto a una ventana, limpiando un boquete en el vaho del vidrio para mirar las calles" (p. 81). This action is restated in the next page as well: "Y volví a mirar la calle por el boquete que limpiara en el vidrio" (p. 82). The literary conventionality of the city experience described in the story becomes quite evident in the triteness of passages like the following: "Una mañana de sol, dos días después, vi a la señora en una calle céntrica. El movimiento de las doce estaba en su apogeo. Las mujeres se detenían en las vidrieras para discutir la posible adquisición de un vestido o de una tela. Los hombres salían de sus oficinas con documentos bajo el brazo" (p. 83). It is hardly surprising, therefore, to find that the text is literally framed by two moments when the narrator comments on the already-seen quality of his experience. The realization is all the more striking since the similar language used in both instances makes of one moment a specular reflection of the other. At the very beginning of the story, the protagonist observes the following: "No recuerdo el momento exacto en que ella se sentó a mi lado. Pero cuando el tranvía hizo alto en una esquina, me invadió aquella sensación tan corriente y, sin embargo, misteriosa, que cuanto veía, el momento justo y sin importancia como era, lo había vivido antes, o tal vez soñado. La escena me pareció la reproducción exacta de otra que me fuera conocida" (p. 81). In the last paragraph of the text, the realization is made once more: "A veces me asalta la idea, en una esquina, por ejemplo, que la escena presente no es más que reproducción de otra" (p. 87). On the surface, the comment would seem to be an allusion to the repeatability of everyday experience in the urban context. The word "reproducción," however, is a most telling sign. Appearing as it does in a fragment that is itself reproduced somewhere else in the story, it points to the already-written quality of the text, its closure with respect to the non-textual. This *mise en abyme* is particularly significant, since the passage purports to describe the immediacy of lived experience, but finds that it can only do so as a function of a previous experience that is, by definition, unreachable.[13]

Placing this repetition in the context of our discussion of the literary conventionality of the story, one can perhaps posit that the two fragments, like two mirrors encasing the text, create a virtual dimension of depth where the history of the city as a literary commonplace—*valga la palabra*—reflects itself. The city in **"Una señora"** is a figure that knows itself to be a literary convention, a repository of all the tropes through which literature has attempted to convey the modern urban experience. The move towards communion with the city as a metaphoric overture to the outside of the text is therefore put in check by the realization that the city, as conceived by the story, is itself a textual construct. Thus, we remain within the realm of the literary, in spite of the story's attempt to project a successful incorporation of the outside, symbolized by the protagonist's subjective appropriation of the city.

Given the density of the literary tradition upon which **"Una señora"** draws, it is not surprising to realize that the germ for Donoso's story was already inscribed in a passage of Baudelaire's *Le Spleen de Paris*. Here, in Baudelaire's own attempt at communion with the city, one finds the following comment in the prose poem entitled "Les Foules": "Ce que les hommes nomment amour est bien petit, bien restreint et bien faible, comparé à cette ineffable orgie, à cette sainte prostitution de l'âme qui se donne tout entière, poésie et charité, à l'imprévu qui se montre, à l'inconnu qui passe."[14] Moreover, one also finds in

Baudelaire the same fascination with the presence of women in the city that characterizes Donoso's text. In poems like "Les Petites Vieilles," "A une passante" and "Les Veuves" Baudelaire proposes the figure of a distant, anonymous woman as propitiatory agent, endowed by the poet with the capacity to turn a chance encounter into a moment of epiphany in the bustling metropolis.[15]

But perhaps the most significant instance of this paradoxical movement in the story is that which describes the moment of the woman's supposed death somewhere in the city. It is here that the affective structure that links man, woman and city has its core:

> [En] alguna parte de la misma ciudad por la que yo caminaba, la señora iba a morir.
>
> Regresé a casa y me instalé en mi cuarto a esperar.
>
> Desde mi ventana vi cimbrarse en la brisa los alambres del alumbrado. La tarde fue madurando lentamente más allá de los techos, y más allá del cerro, la luz fue gastándose más y más. Los alambres seguían vibrando, respirando. . . .
>
> Instantáneamente después, cesaron todos los ruidos al mismo tiempo y se abrió un pozo de silencio en la tarde apacible. Los alambres no vibraban ya. En un barrio desconocido, la señora había muerto. Cierta casa entornaría su puerta esa noche, y arderían cirios en una habitación llena de voces quedas y de consuelos. (p. 86)

It seems clear that what we have here is a repostulation of the rhetorical formula of the pathetic fallacy, with the city becoming a sort of surrogate nature. The city appears to mourn the death of the woman as an echo of the narrator's grief. Thus, the moment of communion with the city, the privileged instance of plenitude in the text, manifests itself in the guise of a rhetorical figure whose literary antecedents are long and well established. Moreover, it is a trope that harks back to the romantic poet's constitution of himself as such. If the pathetic fallacy figured prominently in Ruskin's—and earlier in Peacock's—attacks against the romantics, it was because it alluded directly to the philosophical conceits that underlay the poet's postulation of his literary persona.[16] In this fashion, the movement away from the text in Donoso's work is compromised by the explicitly literary nature of the figure used to convey this privileged moment. We arrive then at identification of a structure similar to the one perceived earlier as the text's closing in on itself, on its literariness, through the postulation of the city as an intrinsically literary referent. In this displacement of literature away from its own specificity, and in the simultaneous assertion of the impossibility of that flight, we see a movement that, according to Paul de Man, is a constitutive element of every literary text. There is in literature the appeal of what de Man calls "modernity," the desire to fulfill itself, to participate in the present, a desire that manifests itself in a recurring attempt to encompass the nonliterary.[17] But since the knowledge that "sign and meaning can never coincide is what is precisely taken for granted in the kind of language we call literary,"[18] this move towards the outside of the text is accompanied by realization of the futility of that gesture. It is precisely this metaphorical trajectory that I have attempted to trace in Donoso's **"Una señora,"** where the attraction of modernity can be perceived as a desire for communion and participation with the immediacy of urban reality. Indeed, the special appeal that the City has held for Modernity determines that the expression "modern city" should carry inescapably pleonastic connotations.[19]

I have endeavored to make problematic the difference that most critics postulate between the supposedly transparent referentiality of Donoso's stories and the disseminatory textual practice of *El obsceno pájaro de la noche.* It seems clear that the difference ultimately is not one of kind but of degree. *El obsceno pájaro de la noche* operates on the far side of the knowledge that **"Una señora"** embodies, namely, that the signifier can never coincide with the signified in a plenitude of meaning. This knowledge is the point of departure, the empty center around which the obscene bird of night of Donoso's novel chatters on and on. It is an insight, however, that was already present in stories like **"Una señora,"** only that it was articulated as the simultaneous assertion and denial of the opposite.

From this perspective, one may perhaps see in **"Una señora"** a prefiguration of *El obsceno pájaro de la noche,* where the solipsistic narrator of the story becomes an earlier avatar of Mudito, and the older woman in the city points towards the role of the old women—*las viejas*—who live in the decrepit monastery. There, in *El obsceno pájaro de la noche,* we find a scene where the narrator and the elusive woman from the earlier text can finally meet as Mudito and Madre Benita respectively, in order to unwrap the packages within packages, the wrappings within packages that one of the other old withces has left after her death. Mudito, the protean authorial figure of the novel speaks here to Madre Benita: "Sé que usted está implorando que este paquete contenga algo más que basura. Le saca el papel café y lo bota. Aparece otro papel, más frágil, arrugado, lo rompe, lo deja caer al suelo. ¿Para qué seguir abriendo y rompiendo envoltorios, éste de tafetán color manzana, debajo un envoltorio de diario . . . si tiene que saber que no va a encontrar nada?"[20] In this conjunction of the two works in an affirmation of the text as a shell that encompasses only itself, we arrive at the founding knowledge of *El obsceno pájaro de la noche,* a knowledge that, contrary to what most critics perceive, was enacted by Donoso's texts from the very beginning.

Notes

[1] 1961 is proposed by various critics as the conventional beginning of the "Boom," since in that year Jorge Luis Borges shared with Samuel Beckett the *Prix Formentor,* the International Publisher's Prize. For a more nuanced view of the last thirty years of Latin American literary production see Emir Rodríguez Monegal's *El "Boom" de la novela latinoamericana* (Caracas: Tiempo Nuevo, 1972). José Donoso offers a candid and intensely personal account of the period in his *Historia personal del "boom"* (Barcelona: Anagrama, 1972).

[2] The only other short story in Spanish not published originally in either of these two collections is "Santelices," which appeared in *Revista de la Universidad de Méjico,* 16 (1962), 13-19.

[3] Ana María Moix, ed., José Donoso, *Cuentos* (Barcelona: Seix Barral, 1971), p. 14. Among the few articles that deal exclusively with Donoso's stories are the following: Miriam Adelstein, "Aislamiento y simbolismo en dos cuentos de José Donoso," *ExTL,* 4 (1975), 157-60; George R. McMurray, "'Santelices' de José Donoso," in *El cuento hispanoamericano ante la crítica,* ed. Enrique Pupo-Walker (Madrid: Castalia, 1973), pp. 215-22, and "La temática en los cuentos de José Donoso," *Nueva Narrativa Hispanoamericana,* 1 (1971), 133-38; Howard M. Fraser, "Witchcraft in Three Stories of José Donoso," *LALR,* 4 (1975), 3-8; Guillermo Castillo-Feliú, "Aesthetic Impetus versus Reality in Three Stories of José Donoso," *SSF,* 17 (1980), 133-39; Mónica Flori, "Las ventanas en 'Paseo' de José Donoso," *Selecta,* 2 (1981), 112-15; Charles M. Tatum, "The Child Point of View in Donoso's Fiction," *Journal of Hispanic Studies Twentieth Century,* 1 (1973), 187-96.

[4] Witness, for instance, the following characterization of the writing of *El obsceno pájaro de la noche:* "Escritura que encarna la polifonía de la descentralización: juego de voces que se enfrentan, se interpenetran, se destruyen y reconstruyen en una dionisíaca fiesta de una infinita sustitución y de un eterno recurrir" (Z. Nelly Martínez, *"El obsceno pájaro de la noche:* la productividad del texto," *RI,* 46 [1980], p. 65).

[5] "Tradition and Monstrosity in *El obsceno pájaro de la noche,"* *PMLA,* 93 (1978), 33-45. In *José Donoso: surrealismo y rebelión de los instintos* (Gerona: Ediciones Aubi, 1972), Hernán Vidal asserts that Donoso's realistic early fiction is marked by social concerns that the author shared with other members of his generation.

[6] "El elemento espacial de los cuentos está por lo general indeterminado, aunque en la mayoría de los relatos podría corresponder a la ciudad de Santiago" (Isis Quinteros, *José Donoso: una insurrección contra la realidad* [Madrid: Hispanova de Ediciones, 1978], p. 39). Although the identification of the city of Donoso's tales with Santiago is somewhat precipitate, Quinteros's comment is indicative of the constant presence of the city in the stories.

[7] José Donoso, Paseo, in *Cuentos,* ed. Ana María Moix, p. 227. All parenthetical page references to Donoso's stories are to this edition.

[8] The motif of the house as representative of the closure of the aristocracy in Donoso is studied succinctly by Estelle E. Quain in "The Image of the House in the Works of José Donoso," in *Essays in Honor of Jorge Guillén on the Occasion of his 85th Year* (Cambridge, MA: Abedul Press, 1977), pp. 85-96. For a compelling examination of the analogies between narrative and architecture, one more attuned to the metaphoric structure described here, see Ellen Eve Frank's *Literary Architecture: Essays Toward a Tradition* (Berkeley: University of California Press, 1979).

[9] Sharon Magnarelli, *"El obsceno pájaro de la noche:* Fiction, Monsters, and Packages," *HR,* 45 (1977), 413-19. See also her "Amidst the Illusory Depths: The First Person Pronoun and *El obsceno pájaro de la noche,"* *MLN,* 93 (1978), 267-84.

[10] *Qu'est-ce que la littérature?* in Jean-Paul Sartre, *Situations, II* (Paris: Gallimard, 1951), p. 110. Another example of this trope is Eugenio Trías' *The Artist and the City* (New York: Columbia

University Press, 1982), where the term 'city' stands for the sphere that encompasses the totality of Western values.

[11] I use the word "obsession" without ascribing to it any pathological connotation. I find unwarranted George R. McMurray's allegation that "'Una señora' . . . presents the Freudian will-to-kill obsession and, simultaneously, exposes the dark side of the psyche" (in his *José Donoso* [Boston: Twayne, 1979], p. 46).

[12] The bibliography on the appropriation of the city by literature is voluminous. I have found particularly useful and challenging the following four works: Lewis Mumford's monumental *The City in History: Its Origins, its Transformations and its Prospects* (New York: Harcourt, Brace & World, 1961); Burton Pike, *The Image of the City in Modern Literature* (Princeton: Princeton University Press, 1981); Raymond Williams, *The Country and the City* (New York: Oxford University Press, 1975); and Elizabeth Lowe, *The City in Brazilian Literature* (East Brunswick, N. J.: Associated University Presses, 1982). See also the following issues of *YFS*: 32, (1964), "Paris in Literature;" and 57 (1979), "Locus: Space, Landscape, Decor in Modern French Fiction."

[13] The term *mise en abyme* is used to describe the literal reproduction, total or partial, of the text within the text. For a detailed study of this technique, consult Lucien Dällenbach's *Le récit spéculaire: Essai sur la mise en abyme* (Paris: Seuil, 1977), and Jean Ricardou's *Problèmes du nouveau roman* (Paris: Seuil, 1967), especially Chapter 4, entitled "Construction," pp. 159-90.

[14] From *Le Spleen de Paris,* in his *Œuvres complètes,* ed. Claude Pichois (Paris: Gallimard, 1975), I, p. 291.

[15] "Les Petites Vieilles" and "A une passante" are included in the section entitled "Tableaux parisiens" of *Les Fleurs du mal* (*O. C.,* I, pp. 89-91, 92-93). "Les Veuves" is from *Le Spleen de Paris* (*O. C.,* I, pp. 292-94).

[16] John Ruskin, "Of the Pathetic Fallacy" and Thomas L. Peacock, "The Four Ages of Poetry," in *Critical Theory since Plato,* ed. Hazard Adams (New York: Harcourt Brace Jovanovich, 1971), pp. 616-23 and pp. 491-97, respectively.

[17] See "Literary History and Literary Modernity," in his *Blindness and Insight: Essays in the Rhetoric of Contemporary Criticism* (New York: Oxford University Press, 1971), pp. 142-65.

[18] Paul de Man, "Criticism and Crisis," in his *Blindness and Insight,* p. 17.

[19] This is one of the corollaries of Marshall Berman's book *All That is Solid Melts into Air: The Experience of Modernity* (New York: Simon and Schuster, 1982).

[20] José Donoso, *El obsceno pájaro de la noche* (Barcelona: Seix Barral, 1972), p. 31.

Kenneth Fleak (essay date 1989)

SOURCE: "José Donoso: The Personality Myth," in *The Chilean Short Story: Writers from the Generation of 1950,* Peter Lang, 1989, pp. 91-114.

[*In the following excerpt, Fleak provides an overview of Donoso's short fiction, noting Donoso's use of psychological realism, existential themes, abstract characterization, and poetic description.*]

Critics see José Donoso's literary world as both traditional and innovative. However, their studies normally concentrate on the traditional aspects. An obvious theme they cite is the decay of the Chilean social structure. Fernando Alegría states that Donoso is "un recio novelista y cuentista preocupado por la decadencia del clan familiar."[2] We find a typical example in the story entitled **"Veraneo,"** from his first collection. Donoso uses the symbol of a deteriorated mansion as a reflection of a social class "that once was": "Estaba en la alto de una duna pequeña. Había sido, quizás a principio de siglo, un gran caserón de madera, con un corredor importante y dos torrecillas en la fachada, frente al mar. Pero de casa le quedaba poco. . . . Era sólo un esqueleto."[3] The same symbol recurs in **"Paseo"**: "Quedaba sólo el respeto como contacto entre los cuatro hermanos silenciosos y aislados que recorrían los pasillos de aquella honda casa que, a semejanza de un libro, sólo mostraba la angosta franja de su lomo a la calle" (p. 209). Donoso himself, however, refuses to accept the role of the author with a social message: "No tengo visión social. Es un ejercicio interior. No hay ninguna actitud o próposito mío respecto a la sociedad."[4]

Donoso's literature is far more complex than the single presence of social themes. Kirsten Nigro accepts Alegría's view only partially in her study of the grotesque in Donoso's fiction. In her view, the repetition of the unifying social theme must be considered in relation to the parallel repression of the natural and instinctive needs of the individual (p. 218).

Other critics have analyzed the predominance of realism and *costumbrismo* in Donoso's prose. Mario Benedetti refers to the emphasis on realistic descriptions when he speaks of Donoso's novels as representative of the "Novela de ciudad" (Nigro, p. 218). In addition, a critic in *Atenea* refers to *Coronación* as a *costumbrista* novel and compares Donoso to Blest Gana.[5] However, these observations are very superficial. Donoso also concentrates on a psychological realism that emphasizes the emotional motivations and repressions of his characters. Because his characters are often presented as abstractions, a poetic background often dominates his stories.

A second story from his *Veraneo* collection entitled **"Tocayos"** gives us an insight into Donoso's poetic descriptions. Here, the mysteriousness and tenderness contained in the word "tocayo" serve as a pretext for Donoso to create a poetic and erotic rendezvous between the characters in a profoundly subdued and ambivalent tone: "Pero lo acarició mientras él indagaba sobre el calor de su vientre y de sus piernas. Repentinamente, el dolor fue feroz, pero se dejó porque si luchaba sería peor. Sería peor y no lo tendría a él. Además, la tenía cargada contra la manilla de la puerta. Juan resoplaba y resoplaba, pero no le decía tocaya. Después se desmoronó sobre el cuerpo de su compañera, que lloriqueaba por sentirse dolorida y húme-

da. Entre sus sensaciones buscaba a cual llamar placer"
(p. 52). In Donoso's fiction, there is frequently an ambiguous tone in the relationship between the animalistic and
the affectionate in the repression and expression of sexual
feelings.

Donoso carefully combines his use of the *costumbrista*
with a psychological portrayal of character relationships.
The *costumbrista* orientation is evident in three areas, the
first, in Donoso's frequent development of stories
around a certain class type. In **"El hombrecito,"** the servant is studied as a separate and peculiar stratum: "Los
'hombrecitos' pertenecían a una raza elusiva, escasa, ter-
riblemente imperfecta, de manera que las crisis eran tan
frecuentes como premiosas" (p. 233). In both **"Paseo"** and
"Ana María," Donoso explores the subject of the elderly
and the retired. Donoso's interest in his main character
as indicative of a social group is also evident in **"Una
señora"**: "Era una señora. Una señora que llevaba un
paraguas majado en la mano y un sombrero funcional en
la cabeza. Una de esas señoras cincuentonas, de las que
hay por miles en esta ciudad: ni hermosa ni fea, ni pobre
ni rica" (p. 82). Juan Acevedo, one of the principal characters in **"Tocayos,"** is interesting in part because of
Donoso's portrayal of the average Chilean in the small
business world.

Secondly, Donoso writes about the traditional customs of
his country. In **"China,"** we witness the enchanting cap-
tivation the Chinese sector of the city holds over the
youthful protagonist. In **"El charlestón,"** the author focuses on traditional dance by the same name. In **"El
Güero,"** Donoso indicates his consistent interest in searching out the traditional or *criollista* elements of reality:
"Aunque no está situado frente al sector más animado de
la plaza, el Café de la Parroquia es lo más criollo que hay
en Veracruz" (p. 58).

And last, Donoso's fiction also incorporates the *costumbrista* style with greater emphasis on external descriptions. He often pauses in the midst of a character portrayal
to accentuate the outstanding characteristics of the landscape or the surroundings. Donoso interrupts a conversation between the two servants in **"Veraneo"** to describe
the setting in detail: "Las siluetas de los niños comen-
zaron a oscurecer frente al cielo y al mar, que no habían
enrojecido aún. Dispersos sobre la arena, grupos de em-
pleadas conversaban y tejían. Pero no perdían de vista a
los niños que corrían por el agua o hacían castillos en la
arena húmeda. Atrás, las casas del balneario familiar y
tranquilo se ocultaban a medias entre los pinos, o lucían
entre cercos de cardenales y buganvillas al remontar la
colina. En el extremo opuesto de la gran playa, a varios
kilómetros de distancia, se divisaban las colinas de otro
balneario, grande, bullicioso y vulgar, coronado por sus
hoteles y torreones de pacotilla" (pp. 28-29). In **"Dinamarquero,"** the narrator seems as profoundly fascinated by
the monotonous landscape as in the conflict in which he
is immersed:

> Eran las cinco. Ensillamos y partimos al galope por la
> huella que conduce a Dinamarquero. Tendríamos luz

hasta llegar, porque en verano el crepúsculo no se
insinúa hasta cerca de las diez. Reflexioné que, siendo
ésta la última vez que hacía el camino, era necesario
que mirara todo muy bien, con el fin de recordarlo más
tarde, en dias y lugares distantes. Pero no había que
mirar. Parecíamos no avanzar, tan monótono era el
paisaje, si puede dársele ese nombre a la nada lisa de
la pampa, a aquella circunferencia en cuyo centro frío
y ventoso permanecíamos a pesar del galope de
nuestros caballos. Sólo el cielo cambiaba. Pasaban nubes
echando charcas de sombras que flotaban o retrocedían
llevadas por el viento, mientras el sol sequía su camino
sin prisa por la inmensa comba del cielo. (pp. 121-22)

In these same stories, Donoso develops a psychological
analysis of the relationship among his characters. For
example, in **"Dinamarquero,"** La Concepción is not merely
the stereotype of a prostitute. While this consideration is
apparent at one level, Donoso also allows us to see the
main characters in their interrelated but independent emotional struggles with the past, and their subsequent disillusionment when its terrifying truths resurface to engulf
them. In **"China,"** Donoso expands on the reflection of
customs in his exploration of the significance of the loss
of adolescence. Here, the protagonist is forced to accept
a haunting and pessimistic realization: "En esa época,
cuando comprendí que no cuidarse mayormente del largo
del cabello era signo de categoría, solía volver a esa calle.
Pero ya no era mi calle. Ya no era 'China', aunque nada
en ella había cambiado" (p. 254).

Existential themes are often apparent in Donoso's stories.
In an analysis of the new sensitivity in Donoso's works,
Mario Rodríguez Fernández comments on the predominance of an interest in "el hombre, su alma, la conciencia
dentro del mundo y éste dentro de ella, interesa la existencia, el 'estar', y la trágica condición de ser. La vida es
hoy día angustiosa, el desamparo existencial es un estado
vital."[6] Two of Donoso's stories are especially good examples of this quality. In **"Una señora,"** neither protagonist
is ever clearly defined; instead, each becomes symbolic of
a character trapped in his own isolation. A man notices a
certain woman in the streets of Santiago, then becomes
anguished because he does not see her again; finally, he
imagines that she is dead. He attends the funeral of a
woman who, he supposes, is this same woman. The main
character is caught between reality and imagination. However, he is eventually lost in the intermediate state of
nothingness. In **"Dos cartas"** the transcendental complexities of human relationships as posed by the problems of
both time and space reach an intense level. Donoso bases
the story on a series of improbabilities that leave both the
characters and the reader with a feeling of emptiness. The
protagonist and his acquaintance were nothing more than
classmates in a Santiago high school; they were never
close friends. In spite of the unlikelihood of their carrying
it out, they decide to write each other from time to time,
as if intending to restart a friendship that never existed.
Although the main characters attempt to bridge the temporal and spatial gap between Chile and Kenya, their
efforts are always frustrated. In the last paragraph the
narrator encompasses the reader in a series of affirmations
and denials that add up to one vast void:

Sólo a veces, en el transcurso de los años, hojeando el periódico en el silencio de su biblioteca o de su club, leía por azar el nombre de Kenya en un artículo. Entonces, durante no más de medio segundo, se paralizaba algo en su interior, y pensaba en ese amigo que ya no era su amigo, que jamás lo había sido y que ya jamás lo sería. Pero era sólo por medio segundo. . . . Después de ese medio segundo, pasaban años, dos o tres, o cuatro, sin que volviera a pensar en Dutfield. Ignoraba que hacía largo tiempo que los vientos africanos habían dispersado sus cenizas por los cielos del mundo. (p. 118)

This obsession with the question of human personality is a central theme in Donoso's short stories. In an interview with Emir Rodríguez Monegal, Donoso states: "Es mi gran obsesión con la no-unidad de la personalidad humana. ¿Por qué me interesan tanto los disfraces? ¿Por qué me interesan los travesti? Es porque estas son maneras de deshacer la unidad del ser humano. Deshacer la unidad psicológica, ese mito horrible que nos hemos inventado."[7] His profound interest in the crisis of identity manifests itself in various ways. The ensuing psychological aberrations frequently lead the main character to an ambiguous existence based on several planes of reality. We have already noted the social background of **"Veraneo."** But, more importantly, the story establishes a pattern of parallels or oppositions in levels of reality. Three such worlds exist for the child protagonist, Raúl. In the family environment, there is little possibility for growth. The implications of marital infidelity and its isolating effects on the child are evident. At the same time, Donoso attaches special importance to the relationship between Raúl and his nursemaid. The presence of the servant character is primary in Donoso's fiction. Ana María Moix observes that Donoso's protagonists "encuentran en las criadas un mundo nuevo, desconocido. En la criada hallan la alianza que no tienen con el universo familiar" (p. 17). In **"Veraneo"** Donoso creates a third possibility through a device that allows Raúl to enter an altogether different world. His existence is altered when he establishes a friendship with Jaime, a mysterious child who teaches him to cry, laugh, sing, look for treasures in the sand, and to use a sling-shot to kill sparrows. This symbolic transformation allows Raúl to experience the true freedom of childhood his parents have denied him. All this occurs in an isolated, marginal existence along the shores of the beach. But when Raúl's parents invade his new world, it is destroyed forever, leaving the child prematurely old and defeated: "Raúl pasó casi todo el resto del verano sentado en la arena, sólo tarareando algo que nadie conocía. Con el perfil fijo en el horizonte, parecía aguardar a alguien, algo" (p. 44).

In four other stories Donoso continues to vary his approach through the incorporation of a subdued magical realism. Howard M. Fraser feels that "by means of this magical association Donoso's fiction goes beyond psychological realism to a magical realism which obeys primitive, religious modes of thought."[8] Donoso affirms that "en muchos personajes míos existe una cualidad casi mágica de ser distintos, como de origen casi divino. Son personajes catalíticos, extraordinarios, locos, fuera de la realidad, fuera de las posibilidades de ser entendidos con los

cánones normales que son los productores de grandes escenas" (Castillo, p. 958). Donoso's characters can free themselves from the rigid social structure only through a lifestyle that stands in direct opposition to it. They must experience a metamorphosis that is magical in nature. In **"El Güero,"** two realities are contrasted: a closed scientific world and a mythic past. As a result of Mike's nightmares, he gradually begins to believe that he belongs to the world of the blond gods who live in the depths of the river. Mike's obsession with the apparent vital force evident in the connection with the Quetzalcoatl myth leads him to enter the river in search of this new and magical past that has now become a significant part of his own reality. Through this mysterious contact, his parents eventually experience an equal renewal of their lives at a new and meaningful level. The symbolic return to the primitive Tlacotlalpan places them near the purity of the past.

In **"Santelices"** Donoso analyzes the split personality. As a victim, Santelices visualizes la Bertita, his landlady, as a missing mother image. As an aggressor, he believes it is his responsibility to save a girl, whom he sees as his lover, from being devoured by the imaginary tigers that surround her. Santelices sees the situation as a means to define his role: "Habia una necesidad, un imperativo que era como el reencuentro de su valor en un triunfo posible, la definición más rica y ambiciosa, pero la única por ser la más difícil. Las ramas se desperjaron allá abajo, en el fondo más lejano. Santelices contuvo la respiración: era ella; sí, elle que le pedía que la rescatara de ese hervidero pavoroso" (p. 283). The protagonist, therefore, symbolically jumps from his office window to the patio below where his confused mind has created an encounter that will allow him to confront and affirm reality. Role reversal is possible through the magical transformation within Santelices. His obsession with wild animal posters reveals itself through the animalistic side of his personality: "Contempló los muros donde poco tiempo atrás campearon una noche sus bestias obedientes, destruidas por la Bertita. No le importabe nada, porque la selva crecía dentro de él ahora, con sus rugidos y calores, con la efusión de la muerte y de la vida" (p. 281). However, the transformation occurs at the expense of Santelices' sanity. In **"La puerta cerrada"** Donoso juxtaposes conscious and subconscious worlds. Because of a mysterious secret that lies behind the closed door of his dreams, Sebastián decides that he must live entirely at a subconscious level in order to unravel the mystery.

It is easy to see Donoso as the outstanding member of the Generation of 1950 because of constant thematic variations and a superior mastery of style. In **"Paseo"** Donoso uses yet another approach to achieve a magical transformation: a non-human element. Aunt Matilde is captive in a world dominated by males. Within this family's house, everything builds up walls against external chaos. The nightly games are symbolic of a controlling ritual in their lives. Howard Fraser sees Matilde as "a metaphor of the purely rational" (p. 5). But when she takes in a stray dog (also female), it introduces her to a new life. Their nightly walks together represent Aunt Matilde's growing ability to feel affection in her life.

Donoso's obsession with the crisis of identity seemingly accounts for his use of the grotesque in two stories. In **"El charlestón,"** which serves as the title story for Donoso's second collection, we find elements of this quality. The three main characters watch a fat man dance until he falls dead: "como un instrumento descompuesto que se independiza de todas las leyes, comenzó a bailar en forma desenfrenada, vertiginosa, agitándose y moviéndose como un loco descontrolado" (p. 147). Donoso's use of the grotesque corresponds to the ambivalent tone of his literature. Philip Thomson states that the present tendency "is to view the grotesque as a fundamentally ambivalent thing, as a violent clash of opposites, and hence, in some of its forms at least, as an appropriate expression of the problematical nature of existence."[9] Through the use of the grotesque, Donoso is able to provoke confused reaction. At first, comedy pervades the scene: "—¡Está hecho un saco de vino!" (p. 147). But almost as quickly tragical implications emerge: "pero me di cuenta de que algo se había roto dentro de ese cuerpo inmenso, dejándolo inconsciente, inconsciente no como un borracho, sino como un cadáver" (p. 148).

Donoso uses yet another facet of the grotesque in **"El hombrecito."** Here he uses the technique to combine a transformation from a magical existence to the depths of social deterioration. A household servant introduces the children to the magical world. At the same time, the rigid order imposed by the family structure forces the servant onto a path of self-destruction. The grotesque is physically manifest as he loses a leg, then sells his orthopedic leg, and, finally, sells his wooden leg. The corporeal abnormalities stand out as Donoso's statement on social decay.

To a large extent Donoso's own background determines the identity of his protagonists, in which there is a predominance of children, old people, and servants. Donoso's own views on his childhood offer us an insight into these choices of characters: "Mi infancia son recuerdos de infinitas decrepitudes, parientes pobretones que venían a hacer la corte a las tías para obtener la herencia, grandes piezas de adobe con olor a brasero, y ropa secándose en el secador de mimbre cuando estaba con sarampión, afuera llovía y me daban sopas de letras para comer. Todo era como muy periclitado. Esos son los recuerdos de mi infancia: no de niños, sino de una infinidad de gente vieja a mi alrededor" (p. 19). Donoso's interest in the encounter between youth and age has its most beautiful and lyric expression in the story entitled **"Ana María."** Together the two main characters achieve the affection that is a necessary part of life.

Even though Donoso suggests that there are possibilities for happiness, we cannot consider him as an optimistic writer. While his attitude does vary considerably from that of other writers in the Generation of 1950, he never leaves us with any certainties. Donoso compares himself to Borges: "Siempre tiendo a una simetría. A mí me gusta mucho lo artificial, tengo una gran pasión por las cosas artificiales y en un sentido, creo que es borgiana: me complacen las simetrías, como diría él, y en mis cuentos, tú ves que todos lo son de alguna manera" (Rodríguez Monegal, pp. 517-536).

The interplay of multi-level realities manifests itself in different ways, and often does not have the effect of affirmation that we see in **"Ana María."** In **"Fiesta en grande"** old age becomes a force antagonistic to the potential of youth. The youthful protagonist falls into a passive role as a victim of his mother's control. A canasta game between them becomes both a symbol of her smothering domination and the attempt to maintain a rigid social order.

Donoso's interest in the child as character includes the use of the narrator-in-retrospect,[10] a possible influence from Henry James. Using this technique, Donoso rarely allows a magical atmosphere to remain unharmed and untouched. Although the adult narrator explains the existence of the magical past as completely as possible, his concluding remarks emphasize its disappearance, and a subsequent division into two realities. In **"El hombrecito,"** we see the way in which time further weakens the magical past: "Pienso buscarlo . . . , no sé para qué. Pero los años pasan. Ahora sólo muy de tarde en tarde llego a preguntarme: '¿Qué será de Juan Vizcarra?'" (p. 246). Time distances the adult protagonist in **"China"** from a magical place that steadily grows more elusive until it disappears altogether: "Más tarde salí del país por varios años. Un día, a mi vuelta, pregunté a mi hermano, quien era a la sazón estudiante en la Universidad, dónde se podía adquirir un libro que me interesaba muy particularmente, y que no hallaba en parte alguna. Sonriendo, Fernando me respondió:—En 'China' . . . Y yo no comprendí" (p. 254).

Hernán Vidal summarizes the levels of opposition in Donoso's fiction as "conflicto instinto - norma social."[11] Occasionally, the individual progresses from a passive to an aggressive expression of his needs. When love and sexual expressions become impervious to social considerations, they become a truly powerful force. But Donoso's marginal realities are never lasting solutions. He constantly varies the relationships among his characters and his techniques to imply that there are no enduring certainties.

In *Tres novelitas burguesas* Donoso returns to the themes and the style of the works written prior to *El obsceno pájaro de la noche.* However, he now turns to Barcelona for the background. Donoso unifies these three short novels through their rebellion against the false values of the bourgeoisie and the repetition of the character double or multiple self.

In *Chattanooga Choochoo* Donoso relates a strange relationship between Anselmo and Magdalena and another couple, Sylvia and Ramón. The title sets the mood: it is a frivolously and aesthetically oriented world in which everything is false and artificial. In his study of the work, Charles M. Tatum refers to the presence of the song as an evocation of an evasive postwar era.[12] Thus, Donoso's characters appropriately surround themselves with the latest styles in order to escape external chaos.

The creation of multiple identities is the most significant aspect of *Chattanooga Choochoo.* We immediately recognize the changing faces of Sylvia: "Parece que la hubieran armado con módulos de plástico como a un maniquí de escaparate. Dicen que no tiene cara. . . . Todas las mañanas se sienta delante del espejo y se inventa la cara";[13] "era como si todo lo que Sylvia sintiera no poseyera una cualidad sustantiva, sino sólo adjetiva, de decoración, parte del ambiente estético que la rodeaba a ella y a Ramón, y si me pareció desagradable fue sólo al principio, ahora no, ya que su artificialidad misma, por último, tenía encanto" (p. 34). Indeed, Sylvia possesses the magical ability to be one or many selves at the same time. Because of this multiplicity, she lacks a unified identity.

Donoso immediately establishes two parallels. When the couples meet, Anselmo quickly observes the relationship between doubles: "Había sido un encuentro muy agradable este encuentro entre Ramón y yo, Sylvia y Magdalena" (p. 32). Anselmo is troubled by the strange affinity between Magdalena and Sylvia. At the same time, he sees Magdalena as almost the mirror opposite of Sylvia: "Me pareció sólo un disparate un poco irritante el hecho de que esa muñeca inconsecuente y decorativa se hermanara con una mujer tan material como Magdalena" (p. 28). Several factors point to the existence of the double in the person of Magdalena. C. F. Keppler sees the combination of both affinity and opposition as necessary elements of the second self.[14] Sylvia herself is the first to recognize her closeness to Magdalena. Ironically, she also observes the contrast: "Yo no soy como mujeres como . . . como Magdalena, digamos, que es siempre la misma . . . Toma este trapo. Sí, ponle Vanishing Cream, no el otro pote . . . Puedo tener mil caras y darle a mi hombre, como le doy a Ramón y ahora a ti, la sensación de que son capaces de enamorar a muchas mujeres, a todas las mujeres" (p. 51). Finally, Anselmo gradually confuses the alternating faces of Sylvia-Magdalena until they become one: "Los dos miramos en silencio, escudriñando fijamente en el espejo el nuevo rostro de Magdalena: sí, era como si hubiera conservado intactas todas sus facciones, y sobre ellas hubieran colocado la máscara de Sylvia, que se fundía con las suyas. . . . Así con Magdalena ahora, que no era Magdalena, sino una mutación del rostro de Sylvia, y Sylvia, a su vez, era todas las variaciones posibles del rostro ovoide de Sylvia" (p. 76).

Doubling also exists between Ramón and Anselmo; it is not coincidental that they dress alike. Anselmo actually refers to Ramón as his double: "Tuve la curiosa sensación de que me estaba desvaneciendo, que me iba borrando, y el hecho de que Ramón, mi doble, desapareciera tragado por el tumulto de la reunión me dejó como sin mi propia imagen en el espejo para poder comprobar mi muy dudosa existencia" (pp. 100-01). In addition, both conceive of the ideal woman as an object. As in other stories from the Generation of 1950, physical dismemberment is a means of reflecting the deterioration of the once stable bourgeoisie. Here, moral and sexual values are distorted until there is no meaning left in an erotic experience. The sexual encounter is always a game in which the partners confront each other motivated by a cruel need for domination and revenge. Ramón possesses the supernatural ability to remove any part of Sylvia's body, erase all of her facial features, and thus return her to an embryonic state. Ansel-

mo later learns this same process from Ramón. Ironically, both lose this sexual freedom and domination through the magical powers that Sylvia and Magdalena acquire: dismembering their husbands' bodies.

Obviously, this ability will result in change in traditional roles. The woman is no longer a sex object; instead she dominates man. Anselmo now sees himself in the way he once saw Sylvia: "Yo un muñeco en las manos de las mujeres" (p. 86). But in spite of the fact that an inversion occurs in the relationship between husband and wife, rebellion continues to be false. Because the role reversal still emphasizes manipulation over affection, it can lead only to the mental fragmentation experienced by Anselmo: "Ella me había quitado lo que hacía gravitar mi unidad como persona, lo que me permitía unirme a Magdalena, y siendo esta unión misma lo que le daba forma a mi trabajo, a mi relación con los demás, con mis hijos, Sylvia había descoyuntado mi vida" (p. 54).

Atomo verde número cinco relates the moments of crisis in a modern marriage that eventually lead to the revelation of an underlying and hidden identity. Charles M. Tatum sees the work as a type of surrealistic journey leading to a mental breakdown, "un viaje dantesco a una zona tenebrosa y laberíntica que simboliza el descenso del matrimonio a su propio infierno para buscar las respuestas evasivas" (p. 14).

Everything appears to be in opposition. Order is a manner of preventing the invasion of the external chaos. Thus, Roberto and María are isolated but secure; their new apartment represents "el piso definitivo" (p. 107) and "una vida definitiva en el edificio definitivo" (p. 120). However, a series of events symbolizes the crisis in which the dehumanization and fragmentation within the bourgeois class intensify. The end result is the emergence of the shadow double: here, the animalistic side of mankind. Donoso always equates order with civilization. Within the esthetically ordered apartment, two things are inappropriate: Roberto's empty room and his painting, "Atomo verde número cinco." Both represent the weak and animalistic side of his personality: "En cuanto encendió la luz del cuarto vacío y vio allí el 'Atomo verde número cinco' dijo no, no; está mal . . . No pertenece a este cuarto vacío que es mi espejo, no corresponde a este cubo puro y sin hollar. Le falta algo. Todo. Todo en el equivocado. Pertenece al mundo de los muebles, no aquí, porque aquí revelaba toda su debilidad, la del cuadro y la suya" (pp. 116-17).

The relationship between physical and emotional aberrations is constant. An absurd situation arises with a series of invasions into the couple's previously secure world. These range from someone's taking the painting, to María's losing her finger; this represents the same gradual loss of a secure identity that we have already observed in *Chattanooga Choochoo*. Donoso shows the mental stagnation of the bourgeoisie in the couple's inability to react. Eventually, the rigid walls of the "piso definitivo" cannot withstand the invasions; inside the apartment, "la basura se estaba pudriendo" (p. 168). Roberto experiences the same integral transformation as Santelices: "Roberto se encerra-

ba en el cuarto vacío, en ese espacio perfecto, aprendién-
doselo de memoria como si temiera que también se fueran
a llevar su proporción y su pureza, tratando de interiorizar-
lo, dejando vacía su mente para que las aristas y la ventana cerrada y el parquet brillante y el portalámparas en
medio del techo se adueñaran de todo su ser y le
pertenecieran" (p. 169). The reversal of roles occurs in the
closing pages. The animal dominates and leads the couple
into catastrophe.

In the three novellas that compose *Tres novelitas burgue-*
sas, Gaspard de la nuit is the only one in which a successful rebellion against the false values of the bourgeoisie does occur. This is possible only because of the significance given to finding a non-identity; in other words,
Mauricio must completely discard his bourgeois self by
exchanging his body with that of a poor child. The transformation will allow Mauricio to free himself of social
classifications, just to be himself. The double is present in
the role of the "Twin Brother," who brings about the
salvation of the original self.

The crisis of identity is a perplexing problem for Mauricio
and his mother, Sylvia Cordey. Donoso characterizes them
as part of "la odiosa comedia madre-hijo" (p. 198). Sylvia's
double role is also evident as model and mother.

Mauricio rejects his mother's attempts to make him conform to what is expected for a youth of his social stratum.
In fact, her desire is to take the present "materia borrosa"
(p. 200) and mold a socially acceptable aristocrat. The
magical realization of the transformations in Donoso's
stories is evident here in his use of the musical title *Gas-*
pard de la nuit. Donoso describes the music Mauricio
whistles as "algo religioso, mágico" (p. 207). It represents
both an attempt to prevent Sylvia's intrusion into Mauricio's freedom as well as his own individual search for a
new identity. The "paseos" remind us of Matilde's symbolic walks in the story entitled **"Paseo."** For Mauricio,
however, liberation is not possible until he realizes that it
can be achieved only through a transformation to a state
of non-identity.

Here, the theme of the double is especially interesting
because it is the first self who initiates the search for the
second. Also, there is absolutely no contact between them
before the moment of metamorphosis. However, we do
find the aspects of affinity and opposition typical of the
doppelganger. Mauricio finds his twin in the body of a
beggar: "su rostro: igual al suyo. . . . Lo importante era que
por fin era él y ya no tendría que seguir inventando
sombras para ahuyentar a los que lo violaban" (p. 263);
and, "ese cuerpo misterioso que contenía el suyo" (p.
264). Mauricio is different from the other characters in
Tres novelitas burguesas because he totally rejects all of
the stifling classifications of his inherited identity. He
learns that to substitute one identity for another would be
a false rebellion. Once again, a unified identity in the
modern world is not possible. Therefore, Mauricio must
choose a beggar with whom to exchange his body. He
defines success in his rebellion as, "Nada. Ni identifi-
cación, ni nombre, no nada que delatara un hábito o una

preferencia: era la hoja en blanco, el pentagrama vacío en
que podía inscribirse" (p. 270).

As a general characteristic of his short fiction, Donoso
combines traditional structures with complex themes. Consequently, his fiction never lies at a simple level of meaning. In Donoso's appreciation of the mythical elusiveness
of personality and the theme of the doppelganger, he
establishes the identity problem as a crisis that haunts him
perhaps more profoundly than any member of his generation. The reader sees Donoso's interest in the servant
class, the elderly, and the deterioration of the middle class
as main concerns which he treats uniquely. Donoso's
obsessions lead him to explore the possibilities of life that
stand in direct contrast to typical life situations, hence the
frequency of magical realism in his fiction. From his early
involvement in the Chilean Generation of 1950, Donoso
has gone on to become one of the most successful writers
in the Latin American short story and novel.

Notes

[1] *A Dictionary of Contemporary Latin American Authors,* David
Foster, ed. (Tempe: Arizona State University, 1975), p. 36.

[2] Kirsten F. Nigro, "From Criollismo to the Grotesque: Approaches
to José Donoso," *Tradition and Renewal: Approaches to José*
Donoso, Merlin Forster, ed. (Urbana: University of Illinois Press,
1975), p. 218.

[3] José Donoso, *Cuentos* (Barcelona: Seix Barral, 1971), p. 35.

[4] Guillermo I. Castillo, "José Donoso y su última novela," *Hispan-*
ia, 54, no. 4 (1971), 957-959.

[5] L. A. M., "*Coronación,* novela, de José Donoso," *Atenea,* 129,
no. 378 (oct.-dic. 1957), 285-286.

[6] Mario Rodríguez Fernández, "Veraneo y otros cuentos, por José
Donoso," *Anales de la Universidad de Chile,* 105 (primer trimestre
de 1957), 272-275.

[7] Emir Rodríguez Monegal, "José Donoso: La novela como 'Happening'," *Revista iberoamericana,* 76-77 (1971), 517-536.

[8] Howard M. Fraser, "Witchcraft in Three Stories of José Donoso,"
Latin American Literary Review, 4, no. 7 (Fall-Winter 1975), 3-8.

[9] Philip Thomson, *The Grotesque* (London: Methuen & Co., 1972), p. 11.

[10] Muriel G. Shile, *The Fictional Children of Henry James* (Chapel
Hill: University of North Carolina Press, 1969), p. 83.

[11] Hernán Vidal, *José Donoso: Surrealismo y rebelión de los*
instintos (Barcelona: Ediciones aubi, 1972), p. 90.

[12] Charles M. Tatum, "Enajenación, desintegración y rebelión en
Tres novelitas burguesas," *The American Hispanist,* 2, no. 16
(March 1977), 12-15.

[13] José Donoso, *Tres novelitas burguesas* (Barcelona: Seix Barral,
1973), p. 19.

[14] C. F. Keppler, *The Literature of the Second Self* (Tucson: University Press, 1972), p. 12.

Donald K. Gordon (essay date 1990)

SOURCE: "The Dynamics of Psyche in the Existentialism of José Donoso," in *Studies on the Works of José Donoso: An Anthology of Critical Essays,* edited by Miriam Adelstein, The Edwin Mellen Press, 1990, pp. 55-75.

[*In the following essay, Gordon evaluates the existential nature of three of Donoso's stories—"Tocayos," "Paseo," and "Santelices".*]

While it is true that the theme which most interests Donoso is the modern bourgeoisie of Chile, and that commentary on his fiction tends to focus on "his preoccupation with Chilean reality,"[1] it is also true that "las obras de Donoso resultan universales como chilenas."[2] Donoso is a social realist, yes, but it is above all the psychological portrayal of his characters which give universal dimension to his narratives.

One may speak of Donoso's existentialism, meaning that he stresses the role of will rather than of reason in confronting problems posed by a hostile universe. In **"Tocayos," "Paseo"** and **"Santelices,"** the reader is introduced to the forces which govern the operation of the human mind; these forces are evident in the process of characters' adjustment to their psychosocial environments.

Donoso's central theme is that of many other twentieth-century writers, e.g., Camus, Sartre, Cortázar, García Márquez, Borges: the quest for identity allied to inner loneliness. There is an external reality which impinges upon, and is interwoven with, the internal anguish of the persona. This existential anguish which is often portrayed as an emptiness stemming from a monotonous routinism, leads to alienation in both senses of the word: estrangement and insanity. In conventional terms, absurdity becomes a feature of behavior. As Zunilda Gertel expresses it, "absurdity and madness are shown to be constants in the daily reality of man."[3] According to Miriam Adelstein, this reality consists of "dos niveles de existencia," the ordinary, run-of-the-mill on the one hand, the imaginative, almost ineffably sensual on the other.[4] There is a superficial life, and another life longed for and dreamed of.

In two of Donoso's most celebrated short stories, **"Paseo"** and **"Santelices,"** psychic dynamics, both within a given individual and between individuals, play a pivotal role. Donoso exhibits a particular interest in unsatisfactory familial relationships. Applicable to both stories is George McMurray's comment on another, **"Veraneo,"** about "the 'false family,' a term Donoso uses to indicate a negation of the archetypal, close-knit family unit, which has been eroded by time, infidelity and hypocrisy."[5]

It would not be far-fetched to presume that Donoso's very own experiences have had at least a tangential bearing on his notion of the "false family." In some autobiographical notes he states that "father had decided to play it safe by taking us to live with his three great-aunts, who were rich, bedridden, widowed, and 'alone in this world' although each was surrounded by her own court of relatives and servants. Father was to be a sort of doctor-in-residence, and mother a sort of glorified housekeeper, or lady-in-waiting."[6] After the deaths of the great-aunts, the Donosos moved back to the home in which the author was born. Here again there was dissonance: "[In 1939] my mother's mother returned from Europe before the war started and she came to live with us. A bachelor uncle, who slept all day and went out at night, also moved in. The overpopulated house began to teem with the usual intrigues, and my grandmother, who for a long time had been going mad (but without anyone's realizing it) made life hell for us."[7]

The theme of madness occurs in both **"Paseo"** and **"Santelices"**. Donoso can empathize with those who, exerting their own individualism, neither think nor conduct themselves in a conventional, rational manner. Donoso's own life experiences have not been unlike those of his Matilde or Santelices. Indeed, the author speaks of having turned to psychoanalysis and psychiatry during periods of intense emotional turmoil. In 1969, after undergoing surgery for an ulcer, and finding that he was not able to tolerate morphine pain killers, Donoso wrote of "[being] mad for a few days, with hallucinations, split personality, paranoia and suicide attempts."[8]

One of Donoso's greatest strengths is his ability to penetrate the mind, so that what comes through to the reader is the very consciousness of the character. He achieves this using diverse narrative techniques: (a) through complete character autonomy as in **"Paseo,"** with its first-person narrator; or (b) via an indirect, yet potent interpretation of the characters' thoughts within a third-person narrative framework as in **"Santelices"**; or (c) through authorial omniscience as in **"Tocayos."**

Although the plot of **"Tocayos"**[9] is simple and straightforward, it is a psychologically penetrating piece, highlighting the psyche, and "the centrality of sexual issues in human existence."[10] As in the other two stories to be analyzed. **"Tocayos"** single-word title serves as an immediate indicator of focal content. The paths of the paronymous pair—Juan and Juana—intersect. Of paramount importance is the inner emotional dynamics which drive each in the quest for achieving specific goals in their existence. Thus, Juan—penniless and unemployed— hopes for a job as a mechanic while awaiting his turn for military service in Chile. But Juan's greatest ambition is to know Buenos Aires: Once a week or so, he visits Mr. Hernández's bakery and this is where he meets 17-year-old Juana, who is employed there as a waitress. Because of the proximity of the bakery to her home, Juana has remained largely shielded from potential disrespect by men. Understandably, she finds Juan Acevedo's mode of speech mesmerizing, and at times stays behind and works late "sólo por el gusto de oír hablar a Juan Acevedo" (75).

Love for Juan grows within Juana, and she longs for the day when she can inform her friend Rosa, that Juan has firmly committed himself to her. Juana has long been desirous of having a "firmeza," of which she could boast to the more experienced Rosa. Juana's interest in Juan increases during his self-imposed two-week absence from the bakery.

When Juan finally secures employment as a mechanic, his self-esteem rises immensely. Employment affords him the means to invite Mr. Hernández, and others in the shop, to premium beers: "¡[E]sta vez convido yo!" (76), he proudly announces.

There emerges an obsessive-like attraction between Juan and Juana. The latter tingles when he calls her "tocaya," "como si la palabra fuera tibia y deliciosa y se hubiera instalado bajo su melena, en la nuca" (75). During Juan's two-week absence, Juana day-dreams of him and of his hands on her body. The eve of his return, Juan speaks to her very little, and—particularly troubling to Juana—he not once calls her "tocaya" that evening. Over the course of the evening she comes to yearn for him more and more. Finally, when Juan abrogates the distance he has deliberately put between them and grabs her thigh under the table, Juana "no sabía si era realidad o si sucedía en su imaginación" (76).

One evening, when Juan wishes rid his system of the beer consumed, and enters the little room in which Juana is washing glasses, she says "pase no más, yo ya me iba" (77), but she does not move. Her response to his approach is diffident and ambivalent: "viendo que un hilillo de luz partía el rostro de Juan como una herida, acarició esa herida. Él, con su mano grande y caliente y engrasada, hurgó en el escote de Juana. Ella lo sintió duro y peligroso apretado contra su cuerpo, y tuvo miedo otra vez" (77). She succeeds in wrenching herself away and returns to the counter. Later, at home in bed, she becomes overwhelmed by mixed feelings—"palpó las desnudeces de su cuerpo, pero sus manos no eran como las manos ásperas y calientes del muchacho" (77).

The denouement occurs one night prior to his imminent departure for military service. Juan waylays Juana on a corner as she is going from work. He takes her to the threshold of a house on a dark street. There, she offers ambivalent resistance to his advances. But finally "se quedaron inmóviles un rato, ambos cansados y doloridos e incómodos" (79).

Psychological warfare escalates. Juan deliberately absents himself for a two-week period from the bakery so that Juana's anxiety to see him grows. After his unsuccessful attempt in the little room in which Juana was washing glasses, Juan's visits to the bakery become less frequent. This change leads its owner to comment that since finding work, Juan seems to prefer "negocios más alegres y concurridos" (78).

But Juan's strategy is clear. He continues to drop into the bakery, but late at night when there are few people around.

But even then, "casi no [mira] a Juana" (77). By the time Juan comes to announce his departure for military service, he hopes to have made Juana more vulnerable to him.

There is little doubt that Juan does succeed in wearing down Juana's defenses. Indeed, one day as Juana observes Juan's big hands as he plays dominoes (a pastime incidentally as important here as billiard-playing is in **"Paseo,"** and card-playing in **"Santelices"**), she begins to imagine Juan's hands on her body. However, she is torn: she also imagines herself fighting to keep those hands off her. Juana simultaneously feels desire and the wish to resist it: "No las quería, y, sin embargo, no hubiera soportado que se fueran esas manos ávidas y mojadas de lluvia que acariciaban la piel tibia de sus senos, sus pezones que iban a estallar" (78).

The story culminates in the coupling of these two birds of a feather upon the realization of their psychic similarity. Ultimately, in his invitation to accompany him to Buenos Aires—"¿No le gustaría ir, tocaya?" (75)—Juan strikes an emotional chord in Juana by underscoring the similarity of their names. This causes her to "sentirse rara" (75). Thereafter he desists from calling her "tocaya"—"No le dijo tocaya" (77)—and she does notice that omission even in the heat of passion: "Juan resoplaba y resoplaba, pero no le decía tocaya" (78). It is she who whispers in his ear "tocayo" and he who laughingly responds, breathing on her neck, "tocaya" (79).

And so, finally, there is mutual joy and fulfillment. By the end of **"Tocayos"** both Juan and Juana achieve cherished goals: He will go to Los Andes for his military service, and at long last, she will be able to tell Rosa that she has a "firmeza." For these "tocayos," will has triumphed.

The triumph of will over reason is also evident in **"Paseo."**[11] This story is told by Matilde's nephew in the first person singular, and we see events from his perspective. The narrator, now an adult, reflects on events that transpired in his childhood. His disclaimer—"puede que mi imaginación y mi recuerdo me traicionen. Después de todo yo no era más que un niño entonces" (171)—in fact, lends great authenticity to his narrative.

The pervading theme of **"Paseo"** is loneliness and of delivery from it. In particular, **"Paseo"** focuses on *Matilde's* peculiar escape from loneliness. The narrator of the story—the now-adult nephew of Matilde—reflects on events that transpired in his childhood. He recalls Matilde's pampering of his father and uncles, all financially successful maritime businessmen. But he also recalls feeling emotionally distant from his aunt, Matilde, from his uncles Gustavo and Armando, and even from Pedro—his own father. And he remembers. The narrator reveals the great chasm, and awful lack of communication within the family, and emphasizes the cramping routine governing the family members' lives. Finally, he relates the story of Matilde's break from this routine existence.

We learn from the narrator that this occurred one day, when Matilde, who disliked dogs, nonetheless resolved to care for and cure a mangy white mutt that had managed (barely) to escape from beneath the wheels of a tram car. The storyteller suggests that, as the affection between Matilde and her adopted pet grew, their after-supper evening walks became longer and longer. Furthermore, he alludes to a gradually developing *physical* relationship between them. We learn that one evening, Matilde and dog never return from their evening walk, and, remarkably, that the three brothers never discuss their sister's disappearance—although individually, they each furtively spy to see if Matilde has returned.

"Paseo" is divided into five sections. The first, structurally linked to the fifth, presents a *fait accompli,* with the brothers spying to see if Matilde will reappear with the dog, and unable to accept her mysterious disappearance. The second delineates the oppressiveness of routine in a cheerless abode in which the child-narrator yearns for his aunt to turn down the covers of his bed at night as she does for her brothers. This section further establishes Matilde's reign over the family and the narrator's virtual insignificance: For example, it is Matilde who dictates whose turn it is at billiards—during the playing of which the narrator is only assigned the role of chalking his father's cue. The third section focuses on the little white dog, which—though injured—narrowly manages to escape from beneath the wheels of a tram. This section is also characterized by Matilde's prescient inquiries about the dog: she repeatedly asks her nephew if the dog is still hovering around the house. A new period— and fourth section—emerges upon Matilde's installation of the pathetic canine in the house—an act achieved much to the discomfiture of her brothers. During this period, Matilde resolutely devotes herself to curing the dog, and understandably, there gradually develops an affinity between Matilde and the animal—an affinity which the men pretend not to notice. The fifth section is characterized by the growing communication between Matilde and the dog which has come to supplant the brothers in importance. Eventually, all that comes to matter to Matilde is the dog. It is during this section that the story reaches its climax: One evening, after seeming suspiciously disheveled ("esa mujer era capaz de todo" (191)), Matilde disappears forever, leaving her brothers to continue living in their isolated and uncommunicative state.

"Paseo" teems with matters psychological; it is a story preoccupied with the play of interrelationships, and a story depicting the ontogenesis of the persona from a primal/ sexual (id-centered) perspective.

Although not explicitly spelled out, there can be little doubt that there was something deviant in the relationship between Matilde and the dog. Matilde's torn skirt and dirty face, the narrator's observation that she was capable of anything, and his going to bed "aterrorizado pensando que era el fin" (191) all suggest his aunt's aberration. Nevertheless, it is clear that in the relationship that others view with repulsion—"con la perra blanca envuelta en sus brazos, su rostro me parecía sorprendentemente joven y perfecto" (191)—Matilde finds happiness.

There are several bits of irony in Matilde's transmutation. While affection does grow between Matilde and her dog— affection which generally renders Matilde less austere ("una gran paz suavizaba su rostro" (187))—she never seeks to bridge the emotional distance placed by her between her nephew, an individual so (self-admittedly) anxious for some touch of simple human affection. Indeed, the nephew laments, "no había lugar para mí . . . yo quedaba afuera" (187). Perhaps, however, the supreme irony is Matilde basically disliked dogs: Before the appearance of the mangy white dog, the narrator recalls Matilde saying, "estos perros, es el colmo que los dejen andar así" (180), and exclaiming, "no quiero tener animales en la casa" (184). Moreover, Matilde considered that particular dog to be of the of the lowest type: "pregonaba toda una genealogía de mesalianzas callejeras, resumen de razas impares" (180). Juxtaposed with this description, and compounding this irony, is the revelation that Matilde has nothing but scorn "por la gente de raza mixta" (180).

These ironies serve to underscore the abysmal desperation Matilde must have been suppressing, namely a desperation to extricate herself from her rigidly-structured life within the confines of a house void of communication and human love, and a house in which she long served as nothing more than an attendant to her brothers' material needs. The surprize is the route that eventually affords her a means of escape: It is through her new-found intimacy with a little white dog, an intimacy which can be described as "the outward expression of sexual inversion,"[12] that Matilde finds a way out. And with what vengeance her suppressed instincts and emotions overwhelm her and burst forth! And how unconventionally—if not aberrantly—are they channeled!

While undoubtedly Donoso's inspiration springs from his native land, and in a sense **"Paseo"** itself can be regarded as a "critical view of the Chilean bourgeoisie . . . of the mannered society of Santiago,"[13] thematically, the story has universal appeal. In **"Paseo,"** Donoso intertwines caricatures of the sterile dominance of routine, of the absence of human warmth and affection, and of impoverished communication.

In **"Paseo,"** Matilde is the mistress of routine; everything was and had to be done, in a set order in accordance with her dictates. The narrator recalls considering the routine sinister. He remembers, as a child, desperately wishing that his father would rebel against Matilde's order; he remembers rejoicing at the addition of the dog to the household, an addition which so clearly represented "un desnivel en lo acostumbrado" (184). The dissolution of established order, "la vida nueva" (188) complete with an unleashing of emotion, is triggered by an incident involving Armando and the dog: The mutt snatches a piece of chalk from Armando, and this evokes irrepressible, laughter from the solemn Matilde. Upon this,

> tío Armando, vejado, abandonó la sala para no presenciar ese desmoronamiento del orden mediante la intrusión de lo absurdo. Tío Gustavo y mi padre prosiguieron el juego; ahora era más importante que

nunca no ver, no ver nada, no comentar, no darse por aludido de los acontecimientos, y así quizás detener algo que avanzaba (186).

In the narrator's words, "algo oscuro la había suscitado" (186).

Also permeating **"Paseo"** are the themes of alienation and isolation, the separation of one human being from another to a degree of insanity. These themes are captured in the narrator's recollections of himself as that little boy, starved for affection, who wishes that he, like the dog, would become gravely ill in order that he might reap the benefit of Matilde's attention and affection. But he notes with a sad touch of humor that "[el] tenía una salud de fierro" (188). Increasingly, the dog becomes the most important entity in Matilde's life, supplanting her own brothers in Matilde's psychic ambit. The brothers become increasingly isolated although they fail to acknowledge what is transpiring. Theirs is a world of pretence. Thus, for example, when the dog appears entering the billiard room with Matilde, the brothers "no hicieron comentario alguno, como si no la hubieran visto" (186). They cling to an intangible psychological need to maintain their routine, and to shut out anything that might upset the status quo—to the extreme that the narrator suggests that any outward rejection of the dog on their part "hubiera sido darle una importancia que para ellos no podía tener" (186). The narrator's boyhood isolation is painfully evident in his recollections of Matilde's bed preparation and pillow fluffing rituals. This is a ritual in which Matilde engaged nightly, but a ritual that extended only to her brothers. We learn that the boy never experienced this luxury (a concrete manifestation of Matilde's affection), or others like it; on the contrary, the boy always had to fend for himself. Nevertheless, we also learn that Matilde eventually ceases to indulge even her brothers with this pillow-fluffing luxury; her nocturnal walks with the dog—walks which the brothers choose to ignore—come to take precedent. But, again, it is the *boy's* isolation which is most painfully captured in **"Paseo."** We learn that from an early age, he boy resorts to building his own dream world. The boy would enter this world through the sounds of whistles from distant and nearby ships, sounds which never failed to evoke for him the mysterious, magical and beautiful— a world of ships quite unlike that sterile nautical world of which Matilde would speak.

Notably absent from **"Paseo"** is evidence of any meaningful communication among its human players, Matilde, the brothers and the boy. Individually, each brother struggles within the rigid confines of his own world. Collectively, the brothers skirt the windows of the house "escondiéndose unos de los otros . . . rostros envejecidos por el sufrimiento" (173). The absence of communication is most conspicuous upon the transmutation and eventual disappearance of Matilde: The brothers never speak to one another about the changes coming over their sister, and when she finally disappeared completely "nadie dijo nada . . . continuaron las esperas mudas . . . todos rondábamos en silencio" (191). Throughout the process of his aunt's metamorphosis, the boy-narrator ardently wishes that each member of the family would "let it all out," that each would release his or her pent-up emotions. The obvious and contrasting irony in the story is that while the brothers become increasingly entrenched in their isolation and noncommunication, the affinity and understanding between Matilde and the dog, grows. In the dog, Matilde finds a soul with which she can communicate, and in the presence of which she can express herself: "Matilde . . . por fin hubiera hallado a su igual, a alguien que hablaba su lenguaje más inconfesado" (187).

The absence of meaningful communication among the human characters of **"Paseo"** is underscored by a symbol which appears at the beginning and at the end of the story: the massive library door behind which the adults conduct their business. Further, that door embodies the emotional distance maintained between the boy-narrator and his family. The repetition of the verb *rondarse* emphasizes circumlocution. The lad "rondaba . . . cerca de la puerta de la biblioteca" (172), the brothers "rondaban las ventanas de la casa" (173), the narrator includes himself in "rondábamos en silencio" (191).

Prior to Matilde's disappearance, the boy suspects how relieved his aunt would feel as a result of any departure from the norm. For example, he suspects this upon perceiving in her eyes a twinkle of joy upon her occasional loss at billiards. The culmination of her breaking-out of the mould of repression is her complete abandonment to her emotional link with the dog "la que mostraba y enseñaba cosas desconocidas a tía Matilde, que se había entregado por completo a su experiencia" (188).

The complete change in Matilde's character is the apex of her quest for an individual identity. Until the appearance of the little dog, Matilde's inner world had been one of anguish, of repressed emotions, although on the exterior, she was a "doer," and a fixer of problems. Accordingly, the narrator notes that "al ver miseria o debilidad en torno suyo tomaba medidas immediatas para remediar lo que, sin duda, eran errores en un mundo que debía, que tenía que ser perfecto" (175). But, from being a hater of animals, she becomes transformed into the lover of a mutt. However, from the first evening Matilde walks the dog, the nephew senses something amiss in his aunt: "tía Matilde . . . agregó algo que me hizo temblar: 'Está tan linda la noche'" (189-190).

Foreshadowing the transformation to be endured by the family is the key phrase, "jamás me gustaron los perros" (179), found at the beginning of the third section of the story, when the narrator asserts that "para . . . [sus] tíos y . . . [sus] padres, los perros, como todo el reino animal, no existían" (179). It is a dog, a lowly mongrel, that ultimately provokes the radical transformation of the family, a family which, in reality, had always been tainted by "falseness." It was a "false family."

There is a precision in the vocabulary of **"Paseo"**'s narrator. His choice of adjectives particularly captures the repression and emotional emptiness of the characters' lives. Thus, he describes how the men would retire "a llenar las efigies vacías de los pijamas" (176). His repetition of a single adjective emphasizes unhealthy suppression: "el amor existía confinado dentro de cada individualidad" (174), "ese círculo de amores confinados . . . no me incluía en su ruedo" (177).

The narrator's evocative descriptions exemplify the visualization of detail so characteristic of Donoso's narratives. A sustained simile is consonant with, and supportive of, the narrow confines in which the family functions. The physical can be equated with the emotional—and each dimension complements the other: "nuestra casa . . . angosta y vertical como un librito apretado . . ." (173); "aquella honda casa que, a semejanza de un libro, sólo mostraba la angosta franja de su lomo a la calle" (174).

The untoward constructions of life and living, and the perilous consequences thereof, are powerfully portrayed in **"Paseo."** The boy-narrator's delineation and assessment of the conduct of all the characters (himself included), illuminate the psychological forces which govern that conduct. Through him, we are led to experience the need for love, and to understand that material well-being is not a sufficient substitute for the warmth of human affection. The three brothers, Pedro, Gustavo, Armando, are representative of sterile routine. Matilde, originally also of that mould, manages to break out of it in the most ironic way—namely, through her alliance with the mangy mutt which she nurses back to good health. Significantly, from the beginning the dog is personified by referral to it with the word the use of "quién" (182, 185). Indeed, the dog, who exchanged with Matilde "cómplices miradas de entendimiento" (188), is elevated to the status of a person: "ahora éramos seis los seres" (188). Like the rejuvenated Matilde of **"Paseo"** who finds her unconventional version of happiness, so does Santelices, in the story bearing his name,[14] find self-fulfillment in an equally unconventional way. In a metaphysical sense, Santelices embodies the crisis of existence faced by so many in an inhospitable world. Because Santelices finds objective reality unsatisfactory and giving his life little purpose, he creates his own subjective reality, and his fertile imagination aids him invaluably in his search for a panacea.

Santelices, an office clerk, is a boarder in the house of don Eusebio, and his daughter la Bertita. Ostensibly, Santelices leads a fairly routine life, including playing canasta with la Bertita and her father. But in the privacy of his own room, Santelices leads another, very different life; he is an avid collector of pictures of wild animals, and lets his imagination run riot. One day, Don Eusebio discovers his boarder's hobby, and the boarder's animal pictures—save for one which she chooses to keep for herself—are subsequently destroyed by Bertita. When, on that same day, Santelices returns to his *sanctum santorum* and finds his pictures destroyed, he is shattered. He immediately returns to his office, and the story ends, when from his office window, Santelices envisions a girl five stories below in a courtyard. He sees the girl surrounded by cats. In Santelices' imagination, the patio becomes a forest teaming with pumas, panthers, ocelots, lynxes, tigers—all about to attack the girl. Santelices leaps from his office window

sill in order to save the imaginary girl: He leaps into his self-created reality—an act perhaps marking the triumph of will over reason. Of course, Santelices commits suicide in the process.

Santelices is essentially a lonely individual. So is la Bertita. As do the characters of **"Paseo,"** these players in **"Santelices"** experience solitude despite the physical presence of other people around them. However, la Bertita, upon meeting her father's new boarder, determines to forge a romantic alliance with him. At first she merely tries to engage his compassion by tearfully describing herself as "una pobre solterona sola" (205). But neither her tears, nor the fact that she had "decked herself out" especially for their meeting, managed to have the desired effect on Santelices. In a subsequent, and final attempt to captivate Santelices, la Bertita resorts to accusing the man of ingratitude, reminding him how after his ulcer operation she had done so much for him: She had not only given him her first floor room and her very bed, but she prepared special meals for him, and stayed by his side throughout his recovery "para que no se aburriera solo" (204). Ironically, and tragically, what Santelices most wanted and looked forward about his operation was recovering upstairs, in his own room, surrounded by his collection of animal pictures.

The graphic quality of **"Santelices"** is remarkable. Donoso has achieved this through a combination of devices: third person authorial narration, vivid dialogue, and an imbuing of character autonomy even in the third person. In **"Santelices,"** Donoso remains the omniscient author, conscious of all his protagonist's activities and thoughts. Meanwhile, Donoso leaves the protagonist forever lost in thought: For example, once Santelices wonders if "era imposible comprender cómo don Eusebio hablaba tanto si los vencidos músculos de su boca desdentada parecían incapaces de producir otra cosa que débiles borbotones y pucheros" (194).

Not only is the story's dialogue vivid (e.g., consider this exchange between Santelices and don Eusebio: "—Claro, pero no eran ni clavos . . . —Clavos, tachuelos, qué sé yo, da lo mismo" (195)), but the dialogue is forceful. Moreover, it is replete with insights into the psychic make-up of each of the characters: Santelices' introspective solitude, la Bertita's lonely spinsterhood, don Eusebio's crotchety lasciviousness.

The story opens upon a very conversational tone, with don Eusebio explaining to his boarder, "porque usted comprenderá, pues, Santelices, que si dejáramos que todos los pensionistas hicieran lo mismo que usted, nos quedaríamos en la calle" (194). The first section consists of a dialogue between Santelices and don Eusebio wherein the landlord upbraids his tenant for having nailed twenty-five pictures of beasts on the walls of his room. Santelices does not manage to get much of a word in to defend himself in light of don Eusebio's accusations: Each time Santelices opens his mouth to speak, don Eusebio interrupts, limiting the boarder to speak only incomplete phrases, e.g., "Muy agradecido, pero . . ." (195), "—Cómo se le ocurre, don Eusebio . . ." (196), "No sé, pero . . ." (196). In the course of the discussion, don Eusebio admits that he would be more understanding "si los cuadros fueran mujeres en traje de baño, o de ésas con un poquitito de ropa interior de encaje negro . . ." (196). This section ends upon the landlord undertaking to have a decorator re-paper the wall (lest la Bertita have a heart attack when she sees it) at Santelices' expense, and taking leave of Santelices with a handful of the man's pictures to serve as evidence of the tenant's perversity.

In the initial part of the second section of the story, Santelices is left among his crumpled pictures, taken down during don Eusebio's harangue, recalling the previous night when he was feeling so anxious to leave the game of canasta that he was playing with don Eusebio and his daughter. Though quite fond of the game itself, Santelices remembers how overwhelming was his desire to go to his room where he could be with his pictures of wild animals. He recalls his disdain for don Eusebio's cheating and making up his own canasta rules, and for la Bertita's spirited defense of her (increasingly "tipsy" and confused) father, who nonetheless end up saying the opposite of what she wants him to say. Finally, Santelices recalls reaching the sanctuary of his room, feeling content having returned to the world of his animals—a world upon which he smilingly reflects, that la Bertita would never understand. There Santelices recalls how his animal fetish began upon seeing the picture of a whelp on a chocolate box, and later, how he discovered other animals in magazines. He recalls how collecting grew into an all-consuming obsession for him, and how he would find a visit to an authentic zoo to be only partially sating. (He preferred the ferocious scenes of beasts in magazines.) In his room that night (the night after canasta), he gave his imagination full rein, pinning up the animals "sintiéndolos adueñarse de su pieza" (202). The following morning was the morning of don Eusebio's unexpected visit, i.e., when the landlord came "obligando a Santelices que arrancara todo eso de la pared inmediatamente" (203); we become aware of the assertion preceding the opening line of **"Santelices"** in which don Eusebio states that they would be penniless if they were to allow all lodgers to do the same as Santelices (194).

That Santelices will have to pay for the re-papering (196) is echoed by la Bertita: "aunque me cueste un millón va a tener que pagar usted" (206). By this time la Bertita is extremely disappointed and disgruntled because she has failed to win Santelices' favour. La Bertita accuses the lodger of ingratitude and exclaims that she will go to see the mess upstairs. At this point, Santelices flees from her for his office, not really caring that he would be late for the first time in sixteen years. From his office, he sees the girl five stories below playing with a cat. Santelices' fear, expressed at the end of the second section—namely, that he would be returning home to nought—comes true in the third section of the story.

That same night subsequent to his confrontation with Bertita, Santelices wanders around the zoo before returning home. He detects the smell of burnt paper upon reaching home, and realizes immediately that his collection has been destroyed. Consequently, Santelices takes refuge in his office from where he can see the girl with the cat. Buoyed by the sight of her and the growing litter of kittens around her, he overcomes his hesitancy to return home. One evening he returns straight home. Santelices returns to find La Bertita to be most accommodating, having made his favorite dish. He also finds that the father and daughter allow him to win easily at canasta and he finds that they begin to flatter him, fearful that he might leave. He borrows don Eusebio's binoculars so he can better see the girl and her cats. That distant affinity with her gives him a feeling of inner security and finds that he is better able to be more aggressive with la Bertita: Indeed, one night, not only does he demand chicken, but, to la Bertita's dismay, he also begins to interrogate la Bertita about his pictures. Each time that Santelices views his mystery girl and her cats, he becomes more courageous, and finds it easier to take greater and greater liberties with la Bertita. Eventually, Santelices falsely informs la Bertita that he has found somewhere else to live—but this falsehood renders it difficult for him to sleep, and in his fertile imagination, he sees the girl about to be devoured. Imagination and reality suddenly become fused when he actually gets out of bed and rushes from the house to his office, ignoring la Bertita's enquiring plea. From his fifth floor office suite, the patio below becomes transformed into a jungle, with exotic animals surrounding the girl. It is then when Santelices fearlessly leaps to save the girl. It is then when he makes his desperate, heroic leap, in the process, achieving ultimate fulfillment of self.

To the rational mind, Santelices' suicide is an irrational act. Yet his delirium may be understood as a cleansing process: a process which enables him to look deeply within himself, and a process which then empowers him, to reach out in a quixotic manner (against all odds), and attempt the impossible. It is a truism that only the thinnest of lines divides sanity from insanity. Striving for the utmost, stretching one's self to the limit, is a commonly inculcated ethic. Valor and folly could be well-nigh synonymous; one's perspective is governed by subjectivity. Santelices in collecting his pictures of animals is making his own order in a chaotic world. Don Eusebio finds his action "un poco raro . . . , como cosa de loco" but hesitates to categorize him as crazy: "usted lo que menos tiene es de loco, pues, Santelices" (195).

Santelices evidences "the non-unity of the human personality".[15] Santelices, like Matilde—and indeed, like most human beings—has more than one face. But, until his leap, Santelices manages to keep his inward self from infringing on his productivity in the outward world, he manages to keep his inward self from compromising his ability to sustain normal outward appearances. This, for example, we learn that inwardly Santelices is utterly devastated by the destruction of his animal pictures; he avoids la Bertita and don Eusebio, and eats so badly that his system acts up again. But "en la oficina era el mismo de siempre: cumplidor, decoroso, ordenado. Nadie notó ningún cambio" (208). Ironically, it is the physical setting of his office that wrings his downfall, however. It is from his office that he becomes fascinated by the girl below playing, at first, with a solitary cat, and soon, with a multiplicity of cats, which, for Santelices, grows into a teeming jungle of animals. The reader, remaining objective, knows that Santelices is delirious: "la selva crecía dentro de él ahora, con sus rugidos y calores" (215), a delirium which culminates in his fearsome, and fearless leap.

Santelices' suicide provides him with a means to exit from his intolerable situation at la Bertita's house. He despised being there after what they had done to him. But schizophrenic-like, he nonetheless found a measure of security and of reassurance there: "sabía que jamás se iría de la casa de la Bertita. Era demasiado difícil comenzar a fabricar una nueva relación con alguien, con cualquiera que fuere" (208). So his threats to move to a boarding house—where he will be the only boarder, and where the widow will be talented and attractive—are in effectively made by him in vain, and designed only to hurt la Bertita.

Clearly, la Bertita, is also afraid of losing Santelices. That is why she is becomes so overly accommodating to him, cooking his favorite chicken dish, "ese que vimos juntos . . . en una revista argentina" (210). Accordingly, she becomes less domineering, and this becomes evident during subsequent canasta games: "ya, pues, Santelices . . . a usted le toca" (198).[16] La Bertita is a frustrated spinster, "cuerpo flojo de virgen vieja" (206), who tries to make herself attractive for Santelices. Undoubtedly, the ambivalence between Santelices and la Bertita underscores the Sartrean view, shared by Donoso, that "conflict constitutes the basis for human associations."[17]

La Bertita and Santelices do share mutual interests, each for individual reasons: she because she would like to attract him sexually, hence her body being "impúdicamente vestido de un camisón transparente" (206), he because he feels a measure of security in that house and recognizes that moving would be most inconvenient: "la idea le dolía. Le causaba una aprensión muy definida" (208).

Notwithstanding their mutual interests, they nonetheless continually find themselves in conflict: she remains characteristically domineering, and he desirous of retreating to his own private world. La Bertita and Santelices both wish for change, each needing to escape from a humdrum routine. It is that need which impels Santelices to create his own fictitious kingdom of wild animals. Indeed, once back in his room after a regular game of canasta he immediately goes to his collection of animals: "nuevos olores, potentes y animales, vencieron los fatigados olores cotidianos" (200). We see that the routine and ordinary cannot suffice for Santelices; so fertile is his imagination that, when he goes to the zoo he is even able to distinguish "entre la turbia multiplicidad de olores los que le eran conocidos" (207).

Interestingly, Santelices is both drawn to and repulsed by the zoo. This ambivalence has a parallel in his relationship with la Bertita: While he has his objections to being in her house, he still finds it difficult to wrench himself away from her. Similarly, though he does not like being at the

zoo, he returns again and again to it. Indeed, at the office he once feigned illness in order to visit the zoo; however, once there, "Santelices huyó" (202). Moreover, once at la Bertita's house, when she had made herself seductive for him, "Santelices abrió la puerta y huyó" (206).

A transformation occurs in Santelices following the misery wrought upon him by la Bertita. He becomes consumed by the desire to seek revenge, by the desire to seek psychological satisfaction for the misery she caused him. Thus, although Santelices really has no intention of moving from the boarding house, he deliberately hurts la Bertita by concocting the story about a (fictitious) charming widow who he claims has offered him alternate lodgings. And he does hurt la Bertita with his invented story: "esto era lo que desde hacía mucho tiempo quería presenciar por sus propios ojos: la Bertita destrozada, llorando sin consuelo por causa suya" (215). Santelices suffers no remorse for the pain he inflicts upon la Bertita with this story. Quite the contrary: in his eyes, he sees this as fitting vengeance. Hence, upon returning to his room "contempló los muros donde poco tiempo atrás campearon una noche sus bestias obedientes, destruidas por la Bertita" (215). Because she destroyed his most cherished possession he destroyed her.

The theme of destruction persists to the end of the story when Santelices is about to be swallowed up in the vortex fired by his fevered imagination. Appropriately, he conjures up animals all around: "se llevó las manos a los oídos para que la marea de ruidos no destruyera sus tímpanos" (216-217). At this point, he even imbues la Bertita with animal-like characteristics: "al cerrar la puerta oyó un gemido como de animal que rajó la noche: - Papá" (216).

The tension between la Bertita and Santelices epitomizes the difficulty of human relationships. La Bertita has physical and emotional needs which she would like Santelices to assuage. Despite her best efforts, she manages to achieve quite the opposite: she alienates Santelices, and thrusts him further into the fantastic world of his imagination. And the psychological interplay of attraction and rejection makes the story powerful. La Bertita pampers Santelices, but also hurts him; Santelices is grateful to la Bertita, but also punishes her severely. In Santelices' eventual suicide, on a mission of fantasy for a cause which seems real to him—the rescue of the girl from a forest of wild animals—he attains a sort of self-fulfillment.

Self-fulfillment, in a most unconventional manner, is also what Matilde achieves through her intimate relationship with the little white dog. Her total reversal of conduct is a symbol of release from repression. In **"Paseo,"** Matilde also finally chooses her own path, non-conformist as it might be, whereas (in contrast), her brothers continue their lives of inner repression, not even communicating with each other about Matilde's disappearance. Matilde chooses, and finds happiness.

So too does Juana, in **"Tocayos,"** choose and find happiness—albeit in a much more conventional manner. Furthermore, Juana's namesake, Juan, also achieves his aim of attaining for himself and Juana satisfaction and contentment.

"Tocayos," "Paseo" and **"Santelices,"** all exemplify the role of will over reason in confronting difficulties. In these stories, Donoso uses his literary artistry to make us intensely aware of the psychological dynamics which permeate interpersonal relationships, and which forcefully mediate individuals' dealings with the challenges of existence.

Notes

[1] John J. Hassett, "The Obscene Bird of Night." In *Review 73*, 27.

[2] Miriam Adelstein, "Aislamiento y simbolismo en dos cuentos de José Donoso." *Explicación de Textos Literarios, IV(2)* (1975-76) (Sacramento: California State University), 157.

[3] Zunilda Gertel, "Metamorphosis as a Metaphor of the World", in *Review 73* (Fall 1973) (New York: Center for Inter-American Relations), 20.

[4] Adelstein, "Aislamiento y simbolismo," 158.

[5] George R. McMurray, *José Donoso* (Boston: Twayne, 1979), 35.

[6] José Donoso, "Chronology." In *Review 73*, 12.

[7] Donoso, "Chronology," 14.

[8] Donoso, "Chronology," 19.

[9] José Donoso, "Tocayos." In Donald A. Yates (Ed.), *Espejos* (New York: Holt, Rinehart and Winston, 1980), 75. Subsequent references to this text are provided in the essay by a page number in parentheses.

[10] McMurray, *José Donoso*, 60.

[11] José Donoso, "Paseo." In Alexander Coleman (Ed.), *Cinco maestros: Cuentos modernos de Hispanoamérica* (New York: Harcourt, Brace and World, Inc., 1969), 171.

[12] Severo Sarduy, "Writing/Transvestism." In *Review 73*, 31.

[13] Alexander Coleman (Ed.), *Cinco maestros: Cuentos modernos de Hispanoamérica* (New York: Harcourt, Brace and World, Inc., 1969), 168.

[14] José Donoso, "Santelices." In Alexander Coleman (Ed.), *Cinco maestros: Cuentos modernos de Hispanoamérica* (New York: Harcourt, Brace and World, Inc., 1969), 194. Subsequent references to this text are provided in the essay by a page number in parentheses.

[15] José Donoso, quoted by Emir Rodríguez Monegal in "The Novel as Happening: an Interview with José Donoso." In *Review 73*, 37.

[16] A domineering attitude towards the male, as a compensatory factor for female frustration (often sexual), is also indicated in Matilde's attitude. Matilde runs the billiard game; la Bertita runs the canasta game.

". . . 'Santelices'—le decía—'a usted le toca.'" (198)

". . . tía Matilde decía:' —'Pedro, tu turno . . .'" (178).

[17] McMurray, *José Donoso*, 120.

Flora González (essay date 1992)

SOURCE: "Masking History in Donoso's *Taratuta*," *Revista Canadiense de Estudios Hispanicos,* Vol. XVII, No. 1, Fall, 1992, pp. 47-62.

[*In the following excerpt, González explores the nature of what she finds to be the fictional and historical discourses that are juxtaposed in Donoso's novella* Taratuta.]

In his recent novella *Taratuta* (1990), José Donoso, as narrator, begins by making us aware of the need to question received versions of history:

> Como tantas cosas relacionadas con el legado Schmidt, este párrafo está lleno de datos que parecen contradecir los que aportaban otros tratadistas . . . Walter favorece la hipótesis de la mala salud del joven industrial, probablemente tísico como varios miembros de su familia. Otro cronista habla de suicidio. Aseguran, también, que la herencia de Nicolás Schmidt se dividió en tres partes. ¿Cuál es la verdad? (11)

As made explicit by this quotation, history purports to arrive at a truth, yet falls into ambiguity and contradiction. Born out of the lack of resolution and consistency in history, Donoso's text examines the nature of both historical and fictional discourses.

Taratuta attempts to retrace the trajectory of the disappearance from Soviet historical records of a marginal character in Lenin's entourage with the pseudonym of Taratuta.[1] In order to effect this "disappearing act," the novella erases the traditional concepts of genealogy, textual authority, beginnings, and endings; it substitutes for them a randomly determined, collectively forged fictional account of history. All these textual strategies highlight the uses and abuses of historical and fictional conventions in order to challenge the cultural and political contexts of those discourses.

In narrative terms, Donoso's novella mirrors the historical character's disappearance by making historical discourse disappear at the same time that alternative fictional languages appear. For example, the descendant of Viktor Taratuta, Horacio Carlos, disappears from the narrator's life at the end of section two. Narrative voice shifts from the historical to the personal at the beginning of section three and suddenly Horacio Carlos reappears as if by magic. The reappearance of the "lost" character coincides with a shift from historical to literary discourse. Thus, within the fabric of the text there are two parallel discourses that are juxtaposed so as to parody each other. On the one hand is fiction; on the other is historical discourse which surfaces as quoted texts from three verifiable sources. The first, and most extensive of the three, is Gerard Walter's biography of Lenin as published in translation by Grijalbo. The quoted passage does not deal with Lenin, but with Nicolás Schmidt, a Russian millionaire, who died in prison and left a good part of his estate to the Bolshevik Revolution. The second is a fragment from the Memoirs of Krupskaya, Lenin's wife, which describes the social life of the Russian immigrants in Paris. The third comprises three fragments of letters by Lenin that speak of Taratuta, the Russian playboy who managed the Schmidt inheritance for the party; Charlie Chaplin, whose irony the Russian leader finds interesting; and the enigmatic smile of the Gioconda, whose meaning seems to escape Lenin. All three sources serve as comic relief in Lenin's letters, which deal mainly with the political foundation of "la plus grande des révolutions que le monde ait connues" (Walter, "Note Préliminaire").

The presence of historical sources within a fictional narrative problematizes the fictionality of that text. Further, since the narrator of the novella is José Donoso himself, are we reading an account of his intellectual curiosity? The narrator clearly distinguishes between this novella and an article he had supposedly published in Spanish and Latin American newspapers entitled "Lenin: Nota a pie de página" (12), a bibliographical search of which proved futile and underlines the basic deceit that characterizes the literary enterprise. "Taratuta," in short, makes a collage of discursive practices and so points to the fluidity of the fictional process. Conversely, by quoting passages that introduce Lenin's interest in extravagant figures like Taratuta and in forms of art that play with sarcasm and irony, Donoso exposes the ironic side of historical discourse and obscures the neat margins between history and fiction.

In addition to the actual quotations that appear in the novella, there are two reworkings of Walter's biography in sections VI-VIII (39-61) and in section XI (77-81). Compilation and summary of the existing data has been consciously transformed into a story because of the contradictory nature of the available record:

> Después de años de ir recogiendo en ecos de textos las astillas dispersas y las versiones trizadas de la historia del legado Schmidt, resulta tan nebulosa, nunca referida de una manera completa por una sola autoridad sino por distintos exégetas y de maneras tan *contradictorias* y llenas de *lagunas,* que no puedo imaginarme cómo logré sintetizar las variantes ni a qué versión de los hechos recurrió mi memoria para improvisar, esa noche en El Viso, algo que puede haber sido más o menos semejante a esta narración. (39, my emphasis)

The narrative that we read is thus a creative improvisation on a faulty, contradictory record. *Taratuta* includes a written transcription of a dialogue between the narrator "José Donoso" and the Argentinian descendant of the Bolshevik Taratuta. Moreover, whenever the narrator assumes the "historical tone," which is markedly more serious than the rest of the novella, he always starts with the premise that he will be relating the Schmidt case, when in fact, the main concern of these particular sections is with the characters of Taratuta, the Bolshevik, and Taratuta, the red-haired Argentinian. There is a movement from Lenin to Schmidt, to Taratuta the Bolshevik, to Taratuta the Argentinian Jew.

The narrator assumes a critical tone whenever he exposes the shortcomings of the historical record. He too, however, sins through the same absentmindedness when he quickly digresses from Schmidt to Taratuta. Furthermore, Donoso is in essence repeating Walter's gesture, who, in his introduction to the biography, confesses to having failed to fill all the gaps left open by twenty years of faulty investigation on the Bolshevik leader:

> Tâche immense, et qui dépasse de beaucoup les moyens dont dispose l'auteur du présent ouvrage. C'est pourquoi le lecteur ne sera pas surpris d'y constater maintes lacunes. On n'éprouve aucune gêne à l'avouer ici en toute franchise: ce livre est insuffisant sous bien des rapports. Mais, aussi, on n'a nul scrupule à déclarer qu'il est, en tout état de cause, moins mauvais que ceux qui, avant lui, avaient traité ce sujet. Et puis, et surtout, on tient à dire hautement que, de la premiére ligne à la dernière, il n'a eu qu'un seul, un constant, un obsédant souci: celui d'écouter la voix de la vérité historique. (Note Préliminaire)

But while Walter's concern is to arrive at the historical truth, Donoso's novelistic interest compels him to digress: "Confieso que no fueron las grandes marejadas de la historia ni el desfile de personajes señeros los que atraparon mi fantasía, sino hechos triviales, personajes secundarios, a veces no más que una alusión al pasar, una sombra, una nota a pie de página relacionada sólo tenuemente con los acontecimientos fundamentales" (9-10). If the purpose of history is to arrive at the truth, and that of fiction to digress, they nevertheless share the obsessive drive to fill in the gaps left by those texts that came before. Moreover, both types of discourse function because of their contradictory nature.

The quotation regarding the contradictory nature of the historical record brings us directly to the literary discourse that underlies the novella and its dialogues with history. This literary discourse is historical in nature as well, for it serves to reevaluate the ironic discourses of the Argentinian masters Borges, Cortázar and Bioy Casares. Although the novella actually refers to "Autopista del Sur" by Cortázar and *Fotógrafo en La Plata* by Bioy Casares, it is with Borges, who is never mentioned in the text, that the novella truly dialogues. From the outset, *Taratuta* sets up a very Borgesian set of relations between historical and fictional texts, the main difference being that in Borges' stories, historical references are in themselves fictional. In Borges' intertextual games, the ironic tone privileges fictional over historical discourse ("Pierre Menard, autor del Quijote"), whereas Donoso at least starts with "true" historical sources embedded in his text. This leads to the question: Is Donoso simply revisiting Borgesian postmodernist games, or is he juxtaposing them against the historical to redefine Latin American literature vis-à-vis contemporary social and political contexts?

Everything about the character of Taratuta smacks of Borges. First of all, the narrator secures knowledge of Lenin's biography through an acquaintance in Moscow. Having read Walter's biography, he corresponds with his friend, referring to specific paragraphs in the text that deal with Taratuta. As expected, the copy that the Russian friend holds does not include the paragraph in question ("Tlön, Uqbar, Orbis Tertius"): "Quedé estupefacto con su respuesta: no sólo jamás había oído hablar del legado Schmidt, y para qué decir de Taratuta, sino que no encontró el párrafo de mi cita en su edición del Walter" (11). While Borges' games with a disappearing imaginary planet lead to a discussion of the nature of language, Donoso's gesture at the disappearance of a historical character serves to point to the presence of censorship in the Soviet Union: "Quedé descontento con mi versión del asunto del legado Schmidt, como si me hubiera aventurado a un ámbito extrañísimo cuya totalidad desconocía y que, por quedar bajo la tutela de guardianes con derecho a arrancar páginas y eliminar párrafos, nunca llegaría a conocer" (12). The reference to censors in such a circular way as "guardianes con derecho a arrancar páginas y eliminar párrafos" underlines the rhetorical devices to which writers must resort in order to evade them. Furthermore, the mention of censorship in the Soviet Union serves as a reminder that matters are not that much better in the Southern Cone. When the narrator travels to Buenos Aires for a book fair, he comments on the situation in Chile: "El distanciamiento por corto tiempo, pone en perspectiva tanto mis problemas personales, como las urgencias políticas y sociales de mi país, y constituye un respiro de la agobiante 'coyuntura' que tiende a ocupar todo nuestro horizonte" (71-72). The word "coyuntura," already set apart by quotation marks, refers to a censored situation that is very much on the minds of all his readers.

Like many of Borges' characters (e.g. the Asian spy in "El jardín de senderos que se bifurcan"), Taratuta stands out because of his marginal aspect: "No lo dije en mi artículo para la Agencia Efe porque entonces no lo sabía, que Taratuta, además de su profesión de terrorista y de su nombre espectacular, poseía una melena y una barba colorada que lo debían hacer blanco fácil para las balas de la policía, que siempre logró evitar" (12). At the beginning of the novella, both Donoso and the Argentinian Taratuta are in the dark as to the character of the Russian ancestor. Moreover, both Taratuta (by wearing a wig to hide his red hair) and the narrator (by not including the information about the red hair in the article), practice the art of self-censorship in order to appear in the public eye.

That which is being hidden is the redness of the ancestor Taratuta, i.e. the fact that he was a Bolshevik. Also obscured, by the unclear genealogy of his name, is the fact that he was Jewish. In fact, there is a question as to the Jewish ancestry of the young Taratuta (Horacio Carlos), who is himself unsure of what he is: "Es discutible el origen judío de la familia: la ausencia de circuncisión en el caso del Taratuta porteño lo prueba, porque, ¿qué padre pudo ser tan atolondrado como para privar a su hijo de un simple rito de iniciación y así hacerlo miembro de su tribu?" (26). The young Taratuta, who was raised by his father alone and was therefore bereft of his Jewish matrilineage, was not circumcised, precisely to protect him. Taratuta's father is known to have disappeared in Buenos Aires during the period of the Dirty Wars. The young Taratuta, however, does not know on which side of the Wars his father fought (18). This complete lack of knowledge leaves Horacio Carlos with an insatiable desire to search for his lost origins. While living in Spain, he reads Donoso's article about the Soviet Taratuta and his voyage to self-identification begins.

Even though Horacio Carlos Taratuta grew up with the insecurity of an invented name, he chose to define himself as Jewish. Yet the fact that he was not circumcised robbed him of his full identity. When he was of school age, his classmates stripped him naked and performed a symbolic circumcision that left him covered with red ink. The red hair and the red ink entitled him to the "privilege" of discrimination: "Tiraron sus pantalones al canal, empolvaron su cara con tiza blanca del pizarrón, y derramaron un frasco de tinta roja sobre su sexo. Lo despacharon chorreando sangre apócrifa de una circuncisión apócrifa, al patio de los grandes, que cayeron en manada sobre él" (17). For Horacio Carlos, self-definition is tied to the writing process: chalk and ink initiate the young man into membership in the desired community. Moreover, it is due to Donoso's published mention of the name "Taratuta" that the Argentinian first becomes aware of his famous ancestor. Placed within a literary frame, the story of the Argentinian Jew follows a melodramatic agenda where a fledgling discovers his aristocratic ancestry and his fight for identity and recognition comes to an end. In melodrama there is an explicit movement from disguise to revelation.[2] Viktor Taratuta had chosen to assume an alias to define himself as a terrorist and protect his Jewish ancestry. Scholars disagree upon his original name: "¿De dónde sacó Walter la autoridad para afirmar que era Lodzinski el apellido de este personaje, y no Taratuta, ni Moskowsky, como aseguran otros, ni Kammerer, que fue el apellido que adoptó al retirarse finalmente a San Remo?" (11). The assumption of the name Taratuta, a name that cannot be associated with any particular nationality, even in a melting pot such as is Argentina, becomes for Horacio Carlos' father a mask that should have insured survival but did not. The orphan, eager to be related to a clan of some kind, identifies himself with those who, like him, historically bear the sign of the outcast. Like all well-kept family secrets, that sign is carried in the unconscious of all members, but is very visible as red hair to all those outside his circle. If the Jewishness is handed down matrilinearly, and Horacio Carlos did not know his mother, the alias, or the capacity to invent one's origins, is transmitted patrilinearly. Even before he knew of the existence of other Taratutas in the world, Horacio Carlos had already invented a name for himself: Tahoca (*Ta*ratuta, *Ho*racio *Ca*rlos). For those who lack origins, self-definition is a function of naming oneself, a writing function.

When the true writer, Donoso, and Horacio Carlos, who is functionally illiterate, meet, the act of self-definition becomes a joint venture:

El papel de mago, de pronto, me apeteció: la arrogancia de un escritor puede hacerlo desafiar dragones y obrar prodigios, y la desorientación de este muchacho condenado a vivir *una historia sin comienzo* me conmovía . . . Desde las páginas expurgadas de la biografía de Lenin de Gerard Walter, una figura había venido postulándose como héroe, yo no sabía héroe de qué, pero esa figura avanzaba hacia nosotros desde antes que yo supiera de las ansiedades de Horacio Carlos. Ahora, sin embargo, con un destello de barbas y melena coloradas, la función de Viktor Taratuta se me aclaró: esta función, lo supe al fin, era la de acoger a Horacio Carlos y decirle: ¡ven! (38, my emphasis)

An arrogant narrator in search of a hero and a nameless outcast in search of an identity meet in the common ground of narrating origins.[3] The implication that narrative life is very much like the real life of the Taratuta ancestry, a life without origins, brings us back to another very Borgesian concern which erases the boundaries between life and literature ("Borges y yo").[4] From the very beginning of the novella, Donoso is concerned with the fact that Taratuta is more like a character than a person, and that, therefore, it will be difficult to write about him: "¿Cómo moverse entre esta gente y manejar estos seres con su aire de haber nacido calzados y barbados y con sus papeles ya asignados, de la mente de otro escritor?" (13). Is Donoso expressing a kind of anxiety about the fact that many of Borges' characters in *Ficciones* are battling with their Jewish origins during the height of the Nazi persecution?[5] More than anxiety about the fact that Borges has said it all and much better, there is a desire to make the Borgesian connection on Donoso's part, so that his reader does not forget that the issue here is that of prejudice against and extermination of dissidents, this time those of Argentina during the Dirty Wars.

Just as Horacio Carlos could not forgive his father for having failed to circumcise him, Donoso, in this novella, berates his literary father for not having spoken out against the Military Junta in the seventies. Even though Borges, in his short stories and essays certainly did attack Nazi fascism in Europe and Argentina during the thirties and forties, he remained silent when faced with a similar situation in his late years.[6] By establishing a literary dialogue with the deceased writer, Donoso corrects Borges' omission and offers a most Borgesian piece to uphold a writer's responsibility toward historical contexts.

Like the history that it is contesting, Donoso's *Taratuta* functions under the sign of contradiction.[7] The novella inscribes within it Borges' intertextual discourse in order to dismantle it and offer an alternative use to metafiction. Although, like Borges, Donoso is ultimately talking about the uses and misuses of literary language, the Chilean novelist consciously plays games of magical substitutions in order to inscribe them in a contemporary historical and social context. Up until the time of the arrival of Horacio Carlos in the text, the reader readily recognizes the parodic dialogue being established with Borges. Upon a first reading, Donoso's novella seems to be taking a step backwards and rehashing old metafictional concerns regarding the loss of power of the narrator and the primacy of fiction

over history. After a careful analysis of the role that historical and fictional discourses play in *Taratuta*, however, it becomes evident that they are made to stand side by side in order to underline the limitations of both. Moreover, with the unexpected arrival of Taratuta's descendant on the scene, the novella rejects a purely bidimensional discourse (fiction vs. history) and welcomes a multiplicity of marginal languages into the fabric of the text:

La segunda circunstancia que después de un tiempo me llevó a involucrarme en la historia del legado Schmidt fue recibir una carta firmada por cierto Horacio Carlos Taratuta Roserman, con remitente en ESTUDIO PARAPSICOLOGICO TAIIOCA, calle de la Escalinata 26, sobreático, Madrid (España). La carta casi se me cayó de las manos al leer el apellido del firmante. (15)

With this poorly handwritten letter, enter two marginal discourses, the epistolary and the parapsychological. It must be noted that, because the young Taratuta is barely literate, his letter does not fall into the nineteenth-century tradition of epistolary literature. Rather, it is reminiscent of other contemporary Latin American writers' use of popular genres (e.g. Manuel Puig in *Boquitas pintadas*) to defend vernacular language and undermine an elitist definition of the artistic. As a consequence of the unexpected letter in Donoso's text, the narrator loses his historian's aplomb. From this moment on, his narrative authority will cease to be singular in nature and will become contaminated with other unexpected voices.

With Horacio Carlos, the thrust of the narrative becomes a drive for self-definition, often propelled by melodramatic impulses: "the indulgence of strong emotionalism; . . . inflated and extravagant expression; dark plottings, suspense, breathtaking peripety" (Brooks 11-12). Up to his contact with Donoso's article in *ABC,* the young Taratuta had turned to the stars in search of his origins. Sections IV-X of the novella constitute Donoso's narration to Horacio Carlos regarding his investigations on Viktor Taratuta, which would inscribe the protagonist within a pseudo-aristocratic lineage. The narrator advises his reader, however, that the story was interrupted by the arrival of Zonga, Haracio Carlos' lover and practitioner of occult arts:

Quiero aclarar que esa noche en El Viso mi narración quedó trunca, no sólo porque es en su esencia fragmentaria, sin más comienzo que el sitio por donde parece posible abordarla, y sin otro final que una serie de conjeturas, sino porque Horacio Carlos desapareció a consecuencia del incidente con la Zonga. Así, Jamás he tenido la ocasión para contar el cuento completo. (40)

Besides being an exposition on the nature of fiction à la Borges, the novella that we read results from the fact that Donoso has not been able to complete an oral narration. Whenever a Taratuta intervenes in history or in a story, a melodramatic tone imposes itself: "Mi olfato de novelista percibió al leer el párrafo de Walter, que esta historia . . . era la maqueta de un folletín portentoso que yo apenas alcanzaba a entrever" (11). Although the expectations of the melodramatic plot are not realized for Horacio Carlos—he never achieves an aristocratic standing—the narrator succeeds in subverting the interest of the reader so that the subject Lenin becomes secondary to the destiny of a marginal character. At the heart of the melodramatic agenda lies an interest in the quotidian rather than the heroic (Brooks 15).

"Taratuta" oscillates between the historically determined discourse of the narrator and the parapsychological interruptions of the character. Soon after Donoso's oral narration begins, Horacio Carlos cuts in so that he may become a participant in the making of his own past:

> —¿Lo nombran en muchos libros?
>
> —Sí . . . tuvo un papel un poco . . .
>
> —¿En qué mes nació?
>
> —No tengo idea.
>
> —Seguro que en julio.
>
> —¿Por qué?
>
> —Debe haber sido Leo.
>
> —¿Por qué?
>
> —Por su don de mando. Los Leo son autoritarios y escalan posiciones de influencia. Por eso Viktor Taratuta llegó a ser un protagonista de la historia, como decía mi profesora . . . (42-43)

Viktor Taratuta was indeed a protagonist of history. According to Donoso, however, he was no more than a Don Juan; but, according to Horacio Carlos, he was "el financista de los bolcheviques" (45). Horacio Carlos' "purely accidental" participation has the effect of stealing the show from Lenin and Viktor Taratuta, so that they are marginalized in Donoso's narration. Horacio Carlos becomes not only its protagonist, but its creative participant as well: "Callé para no contestarle que me parecía embrollado además de poco probable su razonamiento para atribuirse el apellido, la tribu, y el origen. Tampoco quise discutirle las cualidades con que su fantasía adornaba a sus supuestos antepasados" (46). Donoso's silence allows for a much more entertaining, because less historical, narration. If we recall that the first circumstance for the engendering of the novella was an obsession with "la sonrisa de gato oriental de Lenin," we can surmise that Horacio Carlos not only stole the stage from his spectacular predecessor, but also from Lenin himself.

Horacio Carlos' intrusion is the result of a fortuitous meeting between character and narrator. It is true that Donoso writes an article and his character responds with a letter of inquiry. But when Donoso, in spite of his doubts, answers the letter to arrange a meeting in Madrid, where Horacio Carlos now lives, the letter is returned marked "address unknown." When Donoso goes to Madrid in order to meet his literary agent, he accidentally ends up in the coffee shop where Horacio Carlos works. This "accidental" encounter, however, is not quite so accidental. It is tied to the narrator's professional and personal life. He returns to the neighborhood that is coincidentally Horacio Carlos' in order to savor a pastry that had been a favorite of both his and his wife during their exile in Spain:

> Cuando viví en aquel vecindario hace cerca de un cuarto de siglo, sobre todo en invierno antes de ponerme a trabajar, yo hacía rápidas excursiones matinales a comprar esas pastas tiernas para nuestro desayuno porque a mi mujer le encantaban. Cuando vuelvo a Madrid me las arreglo para pasar por esa calle con el propósito de probar una ensaimada perfecta. (21)

Because the taste for pastries is conveniently tied to his personal and professional life, it cues the reader to the connection with Proust, a writer to whom Donoso has confessed a great indebtedness.[8] If Proust uses the famous madeleine to trigger the rescue of a lost memory, Donoso uses the search for his "ensaimada" to usher in a collaborative type of narration.

The second meeting with Horacio Carlos is, likewise, tied to literary pursuits. Two years after the Madrid encounter, Donoso goes to Buenos Aires for a book fair, takes a walk through Palermo talking with an old friend, Josefina Delgado, and they eventually end up in a coffee shop called Yelisavetgrad, named after the originating town of the Taratutas and owned by Horacio Carlos and Zonga. The novella closes with a dialogue between Donoso and "Pepita" (the feminine of Pepe, Donoso's nickname) with the latter constantly challenging Donoso's narrative authority regarding the Taratuta story. This succession of café scenes that underline the collaborative nature of *Taratuta,* also establishes a link between the fictional and the historical. Krupskaya's quoted passage concerns Taratuta's love for the political gatherings at Parisian coffee houses: "Nuestra gente se pasaba el tiempo sentada en los cafés hasta muy tarde por la noche. Taratuta era un gran aficionado a la vida de café y poco a poco los demás rusos que iban llegando fueron adquiriendo sus mismos hábitos" (49). The gathering of political circles in cafés is, of course, not that different from that of literary circles. The narrator's insistence on that fact erases the boundaries between historical and fictional discourses.

Donoso's narrative had begun by attempting to rescue history from its insufficiency at arriving at the truth, and ends with a dialogue that discovers the forgotten characters of that history; characters that appear incognito due to the historical persistence of censorship and oppression in Latin American countries. Because of this political reality, Horacio Carlos' discovery of his origins has resulted in the scarring of his face and in the wearing of a wig in order to conceal his true nature. Having returned to Argentina to reassume his marginal nationality, the immigrant Jew resides in a country that is marginal to the European center, where his ancestors helped forge a revolution. Horacio Carlos and his friend Zonga end up as owners of a coffee shop in a lost neighborhood in Buenos Aires. The wigs they wear make it difficult to be recognized. When Donoso and Pepita, who sit to have a drink at the end of their walk, suggest that their waiter might be Horacio Carlos Taratuta, he recoils, and joins the company of Zonga, the person who had been his center up to the writer's arrival into his life: "La Zonga era la única persona que conocía con la que realmente tuvo una relación y por esto constituía para él un centro" (88).

Horacio Carlos' center is in itself a caricature of a television character. In fact, when the narrator first meets Zonga, he sees her through a window, and the transformations of dress she undergoes (from Morticia to a small town school teacher) are seen as if on a silent television screen:

A poco más de un metro de distancia, al otro lado de los cristales velados por el visillo de encaje, la vi tropezar con todo . . . Una imagen olvidada de la "trivia" de mi adolescencia se interpuso para hacerme entender cual (sic) era la matriz, tal vez inconsciente, que la subyugaba: La Zonga se creía Morticia, de Charles Addams, imagen de lo cómicamente sepulcral . . . Horacio Carlos le estaba gritando algo que el vidrio me impidió oír . . . (65-67)

After losing track of both characters, Donoso confesses that the transforming Zonga was another version of a recurring character in his works: "reconozco en este personaje residuos de otros personajes míos" (71).

More importantly, this character, a symbol of the humorously sepulchral, appears on a silent screen, and functions very much like Charlie Chaplin, whose humorous black and white figure served to bring to millions a whimsical, yet mordant criticism of the fascist figures of Hitler and Mussolini in "The Great Dictator." Horacio Carlos' disoriented character makes him the butt of jokes (e.g. the scene in the Madrid coffee shop where someone trips him when he's holding a tray full of dishes) and mirrors the countless abused outsiders that Charlie Chaplin played during his long career. Donoso quotes one of Lenin's letters regarding Chaplin: "Expresa una actitud escéptica o satírica hacia lo convencional, e intenta dar vuelta al revés todo lo que comunmente (sic) es aceptado, desfigurándolo con el fin de demonstrar la ausencia de lógica en nuestros hábitos diarios. ¡Complicado pero interesante!" (53). Lenin's description of Chaplin's aesthetics is indeed a description of Donoso's own novelistic enterprise. The distancing effect that he practices with the interposing silent screen, the use of historical quotation to describe his own creative process, the transformation of character as symbolized by the assumption of a particular dress, and a prevailing interest in the grotesque, are but a few of the novelistic effects that Donoso has practiced throughout his career. These techniques have the explicit purpose of showing an absence of logic in human behavior and, in this novella's case, specifically of political oppression in Argentina. In *Taratuta,* this appeal to the humorously grotesque so commonly found in mass media serves to honor a creative genius such as Chaplin, who risked his career to convey a political message to the masses. As a

novelist, Donoso is keenly aware of the limitations of his scope and, in effect, is afraid that his intervention may have done little to change his character's destiny. His friend Pepita tells him: "Estás partiendo del supuesto de que tus palabras, esa trade en El Viso, lo conmovieron tan a fondo, que le cambiaron el destino" (89). Donoso is clearly conscious that his extemporaneous contact with Horacio Carlos may have done little to rescue the character from his nameless existence, but his novella does rescue an historical period that was forgotten by Borges. With *Taratuta,* the Chilean novelist performs an ironic inversion of a Borgesian form in order to expose the historical context left silent in the woeks of the Argentinian writer from the seventies on.

The function of the collaborative effort between Donoso and his friend Pepita is to deflate the image of the omniscient narrator. Throughout the novella, the interventions of Horacio Carlos and those of Donoso's commonsensical female interlocutor confront the authorial figure and point to the provisionality of his enterprise: "Claro que lo que te conté no es verdad. ¿No te das cuenta que lo que acabo de contar no es más que un borrador . . . Tengo que limpiarlo, hacerlo coherente, verosímil, elegir, eliminar, desarrollar, y por fin escribir dos, tres, cuatro, siete versiones hasta que quede un elemento esencial de este relato" (90). The essence of Borges' fiction, as described and parodied by Donoso, is its metalinguistic, self-referential nature. *Taratuta* constantly returns to the narrator's preoccupation with his own task. This preoccupation is constantly subverted by the interventions of Horacio Carlos, Zonga, and finally Pepita, who with their direct, more popular interpretation of the historical events at hand, bring the narrator's exaggerated self-importance down to earth. Donoso has, in effect, done a masterful job in replicating Borges' ironic tone, but has managed to subvert it by contaminating the text with the language of the so-called extra-literary: parapsychology, television and film media.

In order to drive home the fact that his novella attempts to go beyond Borges, Donoso makes a habit of postponing the end. *Taratuta* tries to end on page 68 but, after several tries, does not succeed until page 91. In effect, it almost becomes a game when Pepita repeatedly assumes that his friend's narration is now complete, yet Donoso keeps offering other possible conclusions. This game pokes fun at Borges' implicit postponement of the ending in stories such as "La muerte y la brújula," "El milagro secreto," and "El jardín de senderos que se bifurcan." In all of these, the protagonist's death is postponed so that his dramatic story can be told. In all of them, the death of the character neatly coincides with the death of the narrative. In Donoso's *Taratuta,* that is not the case. Not only does Horacio Carlos not die, his life story lacks any dramatic interest and rests, rather, on the quotidian horror of silent repression. The essential element that is to surface in Donoso's novella comes at the end. Pepita and the narrator are about to leave after concluding that the couple they suspect to be Horacio Carlos and Zonga cannot possibly be them. At that moment, they notice the name of the coffee shop. It is Yelisavetgrad, the place of origin for all the Taratutas:

Corrimos a tomar un taxi que pasó por la otra esquina. Le di la dirección de Pepita para pasar a dejarla. Cuando partimos en dirección contraria a la dirección hacia donde se fue la Citroneta, Pepita me preguntó:

—¿Tú crees que importan . . . ?

—¿Qué?

—Los nombres. Yelisavetgrad, por ejemplo.

—Sí. Mucho. En muchos sentidos. (91)

What is in a name? It was originally the outlandish name of Taratuta that propelled Donoso to pursue the story: "Debo confesar que para mí, llamar esta historia LODZIN-SKI o MOSKOVSKY, no TARATUTA, le quitaría gran parte de su encanto. Incluso dudo si hubiera emprendido la tarea de escribirla" (39). In this novella, the narrator bears the name of José Donoso, a gesture which both repeats and subverts Borges' own definition as a writer in "Borges y yo." The name Yelisavetgrad, which at first he could not find on a map because under the Stalinist regime it has been changed, supplies for the protagonist the grounding which he sought all his life. For both Horacio Carlos and Donoso, this novella deals with issues of genealogy in and out of literature. In Donoso's narrative, the name Yelisavetgrad, which was conveniently erased for political reasons, points a finger back at censorship, that hegemonic activity of eradicating names and paragraphs from the face of the earth and from history.

The reinstatement of those names, however forgotten, has become the essential element in Donoso's fiction since his writing of *Casa de campo*. With *El obsceno pájaro de la noche* (1970), the Chilean writer joined other Latin American Boom writers in divorcing language from immediate social, political and historical contexts. In the sixties and early seventies these novels became playgrounds for multiple linguistic manifestations, each always denying the other's claims of definitive authority. But faced with the task of responding to Chile's political tragedy in the seventies and eighties, Donoso wrote three novels that seriously reconsider the role that language plays in his artistic production. With *Casa de campo* (1978), his work takes a tentative step toward a narrative voice clearly conscious of historical transformations (the fall of Allende and the rise of Pinochet). From this allegorical work, Donoso goes on to examine the role of the politically committed artist in *El jardín de al lado* (1981) and *La desesperanza* (1986). In these three novels, by depicting political and personal transformations, Donoso's narrative has shifted from personal to collective concerns. Each novel is now always mindful of the fact that in times of severe oppression and censorship, art becomes the vessel for historical memory. With *Taratuta*, Donoso has opted to outline consciously a poetics of contemporary Latin American literature in an effort to go beyond gratuitous metalinguistic games. Furthermore, its surprisingly serious ending reminds the reader that words do indeed have significant meanings and that literature, and specifically Latin American literature since the seventies, is firmly grounded in a political and historical context that cannot

be ignored (a prime example is Gabriel García Márquez's *La aventura de Miguel Littín, clandestino en Chile,* [1986]). Donoso, like his contemporaries, forges a literature that communicates human concerns in the face of censorship.

To counteract the seriousness of the historical context, *Taratuta* refers to Charlie Chaplin's humor, to Zonga's "sepulchral smile," and to "La Gioconda." The fact that Donoso quotes Lenin as not understanding Gioconda's meaning, presumably that of her smile (53), serves to juxtapose the seriousness of history with that of the multiple enigmatic smiles of literature's face. The perplexing nature of that smile points to a literary tradition of irony in Latin America that hovers above the unresolved contradiction between the discourses of fiction and history. Much contemporary Latin American fiction continues to express that contradiction between truth and deceit, but also expands its scope to encompass the voice of the marginalized. Marginal figures such as Horacio Carlos and Zonga may lack the "literacy" to pursue all the hermeneutic leads in *Taratuta,* but are capable of tapping into the language of mass culture in order to forge their destinies. Donoso's audience for a novella such as *Taratuta* is clearly the literary sophisticate; his message addresses the state of present Latin American literary history. He points to a canon that has transformed itself to go beyond the Borgesian poetics of literary self-consciousness, to encompass the languages of melodrama, oral tradition and mass communication. He goes beyond metafiction by contextualizing it in history: in social, political and literary terms.

Notes

¹ The young, Russian industrialist Schmidt dies in jail and leaves his fortune to the Bolshevik Revolution. He is survived by two sisters whose husbands must also donate their share of the inheritance. One of the two sisters is involved with the anarchist Taratuta at the time of her brother's death and he becomes the financial manager for the Bolsheviks.

² In his book defining the melodramatic imagination, Peter Brooks describes the plot trajectory of melodrama thus: "Yet, typically, the first exchanges of the play, or even the title . . . suggests mysteries or ambiguities hovering over the world, enigmas unresolved. And there swiftly supervenes a threat to virtue, a situation—and most often a person—to cast its very survival into question, obscure its identity, and elicit the process of its fight for recognition" (29). In Donoso's novella this fight for recognition gets played out at the level of characterization, and as we shall see later in this essay, at the discursive level as well.

³ At this time I should remind the reader that in Borges' "El jardín de senderos que se bifurcan" there is a similar encounter between a British researcher of Asian literature who spent his life in the study of one novel, and the descendent of that Asian writer, who before his untimely death comes to understand the significance of being an Asian spying for Nazi Germany.

⁴ With the exception of "Borges y yo," which appears in *Antología personal,* and "Deutsches Requiem" in *El Aleph,* the remainder of the stories mentioned in this essay are found in *Ficciones.*

[5] See "El Milagro Secreto" and "Deutsches Requiem" for the two most obvious parallels. For the definition of literary anxiety of influence see Harold Bloom's book of the same title.

[6] For anti-fascist essays by Borges see *Borges: A Reader*, particularly "A Comment on August 23, 1944" (153-54), "Portrait of the Germanophile" (127-29), and "I, A Jew," (64-65). This last short essay could have been a point of departure for Donoso's novella since in the essay Borges declares his dismay at not being able to find his own Jewish ancestry. Both Borges and Horacio Carlos Taratuta wish to be Jewish and go about defining that identification through a genealogical search. In his article "Borges and Politics," Emir Rodríguez Monegal gives a detailed description of Borges' political involvement through writing in and out of Argentina and starting with World War I. The critic's defense of Borges counteracts the Argentinian writer's unfortunate political support of Franco and Pinochet at a time when he had essentially disengaged from the world of politics due mainly to his increasing blindness and advanced age. Rodríguez Monegal concludes that there is ample evidence of Borges' more progressive ideology in his writings, and points out that critics should not rely on opinion to judge a man's oeuvre: "That is, it would all be acceptable if Borges' critics, so visibly militant on the left of the political spectrum, would actually study the ideology of his texts instead of just adding solemn glosses to his casual opinions. They would find not only that Borges has written more about politics than is usually believed, but that his whole *oeuvre* has a political ideology" (69). Although *Taratuta* is clearly a homage to the Borges that Emir Rodríguez Monegal describes in this article, especially that Borges who rose against the Nazis in the thirties and forties, the novella celebrates a literary practice which manages to transcend an immediate present (Pinochet's Chile and the Military Junta's Argentina), though without neglecting it. Donoso's solution in fact follows Borges' prescription in stories such as "Deutsches Requiem," but actually transcends it by presenting political issues through multiple forms of expression, including history, dialogue, and the language of the mass media, so as to expose fully the complexity of both literary expression during the eighties and nineties and the political contexts it exposes.

[7] In her book on the poetics of postmodernism, Linda Hutcheon posits contradiction as being at the crux of contemporary art: "While all forms of contemporary art and thought offer examples of this kind of postmodernist contradiction, this book (like most others on the subject) will be privileging the novel genre, and one form in particular, a form that I want to call 'historiographic metafiction.' By this I mean those well-known and popular novels which are both intensely self-reflexive and yet paradoxically also lay claim to historical events and personages" (5).

[8] Donoso, *Historia personal del Boom*: "Mis abundantes lecturas de novelas de todas partes, mi estudio con cierta porfundidad de autores como Henry James . . . Marcel Proust, Faulkner, me aportaron entusiasmo y cierta medida de sabiduría técnica, de teoría; pero siempre ejercieron una influencia a nivel de conocimiento, no irrumpieron en mi mundo, hermanándose conmigo para que al competir con ellas tratara de emularlas" (43). See also "El tiempo perdido," a novella published in *Cuatro para Delfina*, which is a bittersweet rendering of the Proustian theme (149-209).

Works Cited

Bloom, Harold. *The Anxiety of Influence: A Theory of Poetry*. New York: Oxford UP, 1973.

Brooks, Peter. *The Melodramatic Imagination: Balzac, Henry James, Melodrama, and the Mode of Excess*. New York: Columbia UP, 1985.

Borges, Jorge Luis. *El Aleph*. Buenos Aires: Emecé, 1957.

————. *Antología personal*. Buenos Aires: Editorial Sur, 1966.

————. *Borges: A Reader: A Selection from the Writings of Jorge Luis Borges*. Eds. Emir Rodríguez Monegal and Alastair Reid. New York: E.P. Dutton, 1981.

————. *Ficciones*. Buenos Aires: Emecé, 1956.

Donoso, José. *Cuatro para Delfina*. Barcelona: Editorial Seix Barral, 1982.

————. *Historia personal del Boom*. Barcelona: Seix Barral, 1983.

————. *Taratuta/Naturaleza muerta con cachimba*. Madrid: Mondadori, 1990.

Hutcheon, Linda. *A Poetics of Postmodernism: History, Theory, Fiction*. New York and London: Routledge, 1988.

Rodriguez Monegal, Emir. "Borges and Politics." *Diacritics* 8.4 (1978): 55-69.

Walter, Gerald. *Lénine*. Paris: René Juillard, 1950.

Sharon Magnarelli (essay date 1993)

SOURCE: "The Short Stories," in *Understanding José Donoso*, University of South Carolina Press, 1993, pp. 14-23.

[*In the following excerpt, Magnarelli interprets Donoso's best known stories—"Paseo" and "Santelices"—as representative of his style and themes.*]

Donoso's short stories mark his earliest incursions into the literary realm. His first story in Spanish, "**'China,'**" was published in 1954 by Zig-Zag in Enrique Lafourcade's *Antología del nuevo cuento chileno* (Anthology of the New Chilean Short Story). His first volume of stories, **Veraneo y otros cuentos** (*Summer Vacation and Other Stories*), appeared in 1955 and included "**Veraneo**" ("**Summertime**"), "**Tocayos**" (Namesakes), "**El güero**" ("**The 'Güero'**"), "**Una señora**" ("**A Lady**"), "**Fiesta en grande**" (A Grand Party), "**Dos cartas**" (Two Letters), and "**Dinamarquero**" ("**The Dane's Place**"). This book won him the Premio Municipal in 1956. His second volume. *El charlestón* (*The Charleston*), included "**El charlestón**" ("**Charleston**"), "**La puerta cerrada**" ("**The Closed Door**"), "**Ana María**" ("**Ana Maria**"), "**Paseo**" ("**The Walk**"), and "**El hombrecito**" (The Handyman), most of which had been published previously in literary magazines. These two volumes of stories plus "**Santelices**" and his earlier "**'China'**" were collected in 1965 and published as *Los mejores cuentos de Donoso* (Donoso's Best Short Stories). That collection was reprinted in 1971 and 1985 and entitled simply **Cuentos** (Stories). An English translation, **Charleston and Other Stories,** includes nine narratives from that group.

In general the stories share a number of characteristics. First, they portray a society that is rigidly structured and leaves little margin for deviance from predetermined behavior patterns. Second, the stories evince a strong sense of inside and outside, both in the spatial sense (inside the house as opposed to outside) and in a sociopsychological sense (inclusion in or exclusion from a group or social class). In turn, this rigidity of structure and space provides the framework for the inevitable rebellion, successful or not. While some characters defy parental authority, others overtly turn their backs on social mores; refuse to play the game, as it were; and disappear. Thus in one form or another almost all Donoso's protagonists rebel against the status quo. In addition, the stories demonstrate a preoccupation with vision and perspective. Stylistically this leads to a technique that centers on point of view and subtly questions the reliability of the narrative voice.[1] Thematically it manifests itself as a concentration on the sense of sight and the eyes and leads to the notion that one perceives what one wishes, what society has deemed appropriate, or what one has words for and can articulate. What one cannot name, one cannot or will not "see."

In spite of the fact that Donoso's short stories have not been frequently analyzed by critics and scholars, they certainly are valuable works in and of themselves and foreshadow the author's later works. Unfortunately, space limitations do not allow a fuller discussion of them here. As perhaps the best known and most representative. **"The Walk"** and **"Santelices"** are the focus of this chapter.

"The Walk"

"The Walk" is one of Donoso's most superbly crafted stories and probably the one most frequently acclaimed by critics. Here the author employs the techniques of the first-person narration and the embedded narrative as he juxtaposes the perspective of a young boy with that of an adult narrator. Reduced to its core, **"The Walk"** is the story of an adult as he remembers and tries to comprehend the circumstances that surrounded the turning point of his childhood: the disappearance of his Aunt Matilde. Before that momentous event but after the death of the boy's mother, his Aunt Matilde and two bachelor uncles had come to live with him and his father so that there would be a woman to care for him. Their home life was characterized by physical comforts and reassuring routines, epitomized in the ritualistic billiard game each evening.[2] Although the family acknowledged the existence of the world outside the confines of their "perfect" home, a world evoked by distant foghorns and lights but always perceived through the filter of a window, that "other" world never infringed upon theirs, where the fortuitous and the unexpected had no place. In fact, heaven is imaged as an exact replica of their house (78/212). In the family's carefully delimited world, screened from the outside by windows, walls, and fences (both physical and psychologi-

cal), misfortunes such as hunger, cold, discomfort, poverty, or weakness were perceived only as "mere errors in a world that ought to be—no, *had* to be—perfect" (76/210; the emphasis is Donoso's). The self-correcting gesture is significant. More important, their "perfect" house is imaged in relation to a book: "narrow and vertical as a book slipped in between the thick shapes of the new buildings" (75/208).[3] However, it was a closed book—"that deep house which, like a book, revealed only its narrow spine to the street" (76/209); it never opened itself up to the threat of the exterior, and it hid as much as it revealed, not unlike "the thick [library] door [that] screened the meaning of the words, allowing [him] to hear only the deep, deliberate counterpoint of their voices" (73/205).

The perfection of this prelapsarian structure was apparently broken by the appearance of a small white dog. To the boy, the dog heralded the beginning of disintegration and chaos: first Matilde stopped playing billiards with the brothers, then she forgot the shooting order, later she laughed (perhaps for the first time), and finally she walked the dog each evening. Those "walks," excursions beyond the confines of their neat, ordered, bookish house into the outside world, eventually led to the final, title "walk" and Matilde's "disappearance."

Although her disappearance is incomprehensible to the narrator, he does define it as the end of the secure, neatly ordered, ritualistic life he had known up to that point: "I went to bed terrified that this would be the end. And I wasn't wrong" (94/230). He was terrified because, as he noted in the preceding sentence, he had realized that his aunt had her whole life before her and was capable of anything. Surely that included turning her back on the established order, opting not to continue caring for the males (narrator, father, and uncles), and leaving them to perpetuate their own structure and order. While there can be no question that they do reinstitute that order, they accomplish it in part by imposing a self-serving blindness and refusing to "see" anything that might threaten it. This blindness and the narrative correcting factor that signals it are apparent throughout the story. For example, although the narrator posits his aunt's disappearance as a major threat to, indeed as the termination of, the status quo, he subsequently negates that concept and assures the reader (or himself), "Life went on in our house as if Aunt Matilde were still living with us" (94/230). His confidence quickly falters, however, and in the next statement he corrects himself by noting that the brothers began to meet regularly behind the closed doors of the library. One of the recurrent elements of the text is this self-correcting tendency that leaves the reader dangling over a void of ignorance paralleling that of the narrator. In fact, the story might be read as the dramatization of order reestablished by means of the act of narration.

Nonetheless, Matilde's disappearance is never labeled as such, for it can be encompassed by none of the terms with which the narrator is familiar. In the story's title it is euphemistically designated by the unthreatening term "walk," and within the text he simply concedes that she "never came back" (94/230). By not naming the event, the narrator silences it (and blinds himself to it) much as the brothers do, in both cases in order to avoid "the useless terror of having to accept that the streets of a city can swallow a human being, annul it, leave it without life or death, suspended in a dimension more threatening than any dimension with a name" (73-74/206)—threatening precisely because it does not have a name.

In this respect it is not so much the streets of the city that "annul" Matilde and leave her suspended in a dimension without a name as it is the narrator himself, for it is he (perhaps along with the brothers) who does not or will not know and cannot or will not name—either as the child who lived the experience or as the adult who has become a mirror image of the brothers and who narrates in an attempt to understand events that have no place in his neatly organized world. When he makes an ineffectual attempt to label the event in the first word of the text, he employs *"Esto,"* "This," an indefinite, neuter, demonstrative pronoun, marked by uncertainty and nonreferentiality. In this way he calls attention to the fact that the event lies outside his frame of reference and cannot be named.[4] Certainly, throughout the story he accentuates his lack of comprehension. At the same time his inability to understand is always linked to the bipolar, antithetical nature of all his perceptions: now/then, before/after, inside/outside the house, inside/outside his aunt's circle of recognition, they/he. Surely his aunt's disappearance falls somewhere between his antitheses. Similarly, throughout the text the narrator highlights his own position as neither inside nor outside (or conversely as both inside and outside): he is part of the family but outside the more intimate circle formed by the siblings; he understands and took part in some of the events but not in all (his role was peripheral, more that of witness). Only in the text he narrates does he overcome his marginality by placing himself at the center. At last he has a role in the family unit: he narrates.

It is significant too that his narration is peppered with desire, with how he wanted things to be (which, like the simile discussed in chapter one, simultaneously evokes how they were not): "I'd rather think" (73/205), "I *wanted* them to be talking" (73/205; emphasis added), "I desperately *wanted* this contained affection to overflow" (76/209; emphasis added), he *wanted* her to turn down his bed (77/210-11), he *prayed* one of the brothers would break the rigid order (79/213), he *wants* her to beckon him with a look (89/224), he *wants* to fall ill so she will pay attention to him (90/226). As a result, one should perhaps conclude that the narrative itself, with its emphasis on the dog's culpability, also represents things as he would have liked them to be. While on the one hand he acknowledges that the changes slowly took place in Matilde even before she started walking the dog, on the other hand he must still blame the dog for dragging her away, in spite of the fact that he portrays her as an active participant, carrying the dog in her arms when she returns at night (93-94/229-30). Does he blame the dog because he "never liked dogs" (80/215) or because he cannot name or does not wish to acknowledge the possibility that Matilde might be subject to such circumstances as love and adventure, "fortuitous" events in which he and the brothers were not central?[5]

Significantly, with the exception of the indirect allusion (in his premonition) that she was capable of anything, the narrator rarely credits Matilde with any will or dynamic force of her own. For him she was more often a passive being, swallowed by the city street or dragged by the dog. Indeed he would prefer to believe her dead than to "torture" himself with questions and the possibility that she had a will and an existence in which they formed no part.

Chronologically the story ends with a renewed attempt to establish order and centrality and thereby mitigate that threatening external, unnameable element. Although the narrator never designates that element, he encloses it within the circularity of the text. For that reason, his final statement must echo his earlier one even as it repeats the brothers' gesture of shutting a door on the event: "The door of the library was too thick, too heavy, and I never knew if Aunt Matilde, dragged along by the white dog, had got lost in the city, or in death, or in a region more mysterious than either" (94/230). The reader will never know either; the limitations of the vision and discursive mastery of the narrator provide as much a barrier as the library door: both contain and retain literary worlds. At the same time, his egocentric need to place himself at the center of the world he portrays blinds him and the reader.

"Santelices"

Santelices's approach to the void or the uncertainties differs from that of the narrator of **"The Walk"** in that Santelices tries to fill the void in his life with art—drawings and photographs of ferocious wild beasts that fascinate him. Like any number of Donoso's other characters, he apparently fails to fill that void and plunges into it, literally and figuratively, in part because he fails to differentiate between art and life, fantasy and reality, inside and outside. Contemporary philosophers and theorists have posited that a perception of difference is essential to both our interaction with our world and our sense of order and stability within that world. That is, one must continually be able to differentiate between X and not X, between self and other, and to recognize the dividing line between the two. To a greater or lesser degree Santelices's demise is the result of an erasure of difference.

Santelices is a middle-aged archivist entrenched in the tedium and inflexible routine of his office and the pension where he boards, the latter run by the also middle-aged, unmarried Bertita and her elderly father, Don Eusebio. Presumably Santelices's office life is filled with the repetitious facts and figures of papers and files while his life at the pension is marked by the nightly canasta games (like the billiard games of **"The Walk,"** games with ritualistic rigidity) and punctuated by weekend excursions to the movies (a projected world of fiction). In sum, Santelices is quiet, neat, punctual, polite, organized, and punctilious—totally "normal" but exceedingly dull.

Nonetheless, normality is only the mask Santelices presents to the world, for he has another, less visible side. The text opens as he has been caught in a flagrant display of this other side, his "perversion": his collection of illustrations and photographs of wild animals. His vice is made public when he decides "to do it" (155/260)—to take the illustrations from the bottom drawer where he has been keeping (hiding) them and hang them on the wall (make them visible to all). From his perspective, this act of assertion or defiance transforms his pension room into a jungle: "New odors, powerful and animal, overcame the tired everyday ones. . . . Animal effusions sullied the air" (158/263-64). Santelices's dual nature and the latent eroticism suggested by the animal pictures are foregrounded in the text's description of his encounter with Bertita the next morning. In a scene marked by grotesque eroticism (she is obese but clad only in a semitransparent nightgown), Bertita reflects Santelices's perhaps unconscious assumption of a mask, for she wraps her eroticism in the guise of maternalism and then projects that eroticism onto him as she calls him a pig who takes advantage of her and accuses him of being a "wolf in sheep's clothing" (164/270).[6] This use of a metaphor based on animals, combined with the implication of a disguise or mask, is neither irrelevant nor totally erroneous, as shall become apparent. Nonetheless, this encounter, followed by his certainty that Bertita has destroyed his pictures, leads him to flee the pension and take refuge in his office and other public locales for several days. He finally returns to the pension and his "old" way of life just long enough to prevaricate by announcing his plans to move in with a widow, thus metaphorically destroying both Bertita and her dream as she had literally destroyed his drawings.

In the meantime, while hiding out in his office, he has been watching the activities of a blonde girl in the patio below his window. His progressively more detailed, sensorial, and dramatic perceptions of what is happening there reflect his increasing alienation from tangible reality and his immersion in a world of sensorial imagination (perhaps also symbolic of latent eroticism) that contrast dramatically with and are punctuated by returns to the prosaic reality of the pension. The evolution and expansion of his perceptions of the girl mirror his earlier "immersion" in the world of his illustrations: his "anxiety . . . grew like a *blinding*, paralyzing vine which left no room for anything but itself" (160/265; emphasis added).

Let us examine the growth of that metaphoric vine. At first, Santelices simply perceives a blonde girl playing in the patio (165/270). In the next paragraph the girl is playing with a cat. A page later the text alludes to the distance that separates them and to the difficulty of perception by noting that she is five stories down. Santelices's fantasy continues to grow, and on the next page, as the girl sews, he begins to imagine how her face (which he cannot see) would look when she plays with her female cat, which he "knows" is female because he has "seen" the litter. By now there are five or six animals around the girl. Curiously, it is his fascination with the birth of those kittens that makes him forget his fears and return to the pension, Bertita, and his former life, for a while at least. In the next reference to the girl (170/277), he sees her through the binoculars he has borrowed and decides she is about seventeen and does not seem to "belong to anybody or anything" (170/278). Now there are eight or nine cats, and the mother cat is enormous. On the next page even more cats have come into the patio, and the reader is told it is a well known fact that they become treacherous at night. Two pages later the patio is lit by the brilliance of animal eyes that greedily watch the unwary girl (172-3/280). At this point Santelices returns once more to the pension and "destroys" Bertita: "this was what he had wanted to *see with his own eyes* for a long time: Bertita destroyed" (174/281; emphasis added). Note, however, that the destruction he "sees" is but metaphoric; she is unhappy but not "destroyed" in the literal sense of the word, a fact that encourages the reader to question all Santelices "sees."

The motif of the eyes is particularly significant here. In his final image of the patio, Santelices perceives the cats, not in their corporeal totality, but only as multicolored eyes; later one of the cats will steal his binoculars. And of course the tale itself brings into doubt one's capacity to see anything that one does not invent or project. What Santelices "sees" does not exist for others. Indeed, the text notes that, like the earlier vine, "the jungle was growing inside him now, with its roars and heat, with its effusions of death and life" (174/281), reinforcing the notion that what he sees is a projection of his own mind. Still, the projection expands to include other sensory perceptions—sounds, temperature. Metaphoric or not, it is becoming all-consuming. Finally the patio teems with beasts that watch him while the jungle grows before his eyes: the trees, which at first do not quite reach his window, moments later are above his vantage point and smother him. What was outside is now inside. He searches for the girl with his eyes. When he locates her down below (note the symbolism: he is above, she below, in the animal, inferior kingdom or hell), where the animals are destroying each other, she is begging him to save her. Since he acknowledges that he cannot hear her, she must be begging him with her eyes, thus suggesting that the projected gaze, his projected vision, has been so well projected that it is perceived as external and returns to him: she and the animals look at him. He is now the viewer *and* the viewed, a status that affords the importance and sense of superiority he had lost when his illustrations were destroyed ("all he needed was this intimate contemplation [of his collection] to feel superior, solid, and proud" [159/264]). His projection and identification are now complete and echo his earlier identification with both the victims and the aggressors of his illustrations. Deprived of them, he feels an imperative and makes "his richest and most ambitious decision" (175/283): he jumps from his window to save her, five stories down, immersing himself in a world of bestiality (and by inference, eroticism) of victim and aggressor. Earlier he had felt "an enervating incitement to . . . risk himself by *becoming . . . victim and aggressor*" (161/266; emphasis added) in "the torturing invitation that for years he himself had prolonged . . . never really taking part except in distant, harmless echoes" (168/275). Now he will forever be a part of the void his illustrations could not fill.

The void (and its danger), first intuited by Eusebio when he discovers the pictures, is dramatically evoked by the tack holes made when Santelices hung the pictures and on which Eusebio focuses in order to avoid the larger blank space, the question mark, the "why." As the text opens, normal order and ritual have already been broken twice: first by the inconsistencies in the card game the night before and then by the hanging of the pictures. The first segment of the story depicts the characters' attempts to reestablish that order through language. Indeed, the first pages are marked by the question of language and the nonconcordance of the two men's language and perspectives. "I'm sure you'll understand," says Eusebio. "It was incomprehensible," responds Santelices mentally, in reference to a different topic. Eusebio calls them nails and insists there are twenty-five; Santelices labels them tacks and corrects the number to twenty-three. The former responds, "It's all the same . . . what's the difference?" His point seems to be that difference is not desirable. Santelices should be like all the other tenants, although admittedly he is not—he is superior. He should put himself in Eusebio's shoes, even though he certainly does not want to "put himself in" his false teeth. Santelices's pictures should be of scantily clad women, like everyone else's, even though that is perverse also. No wonder Santelices is confused; he is receiving contradictory messages here just as he does from Bertita (maternal concern combined with erotic desire). Incapable of distinguishing and deciding between the often undifferentiated antitheses, he slips into the void, the gap of nothingness, the unnameable that lies between the two extremes when his artistic imagination blurs the dividing line between self and other, same and different. Thus he leaps *down* into the primordial void: the metaphoric other, subconsciousness, death, sexuality, animalism, artistic imagination (perhaps the original sin)—all, paradoxically, in order to elude the void, the question mark that, as *Coronation* will suggest, is inevitable and lies within. Difference is erased, and Santelices becomes a part of the question mark, as do so many Donoso characters who follow him.

Notes

[1] A number of critics have noted or analyzed Donoso's use of narrators with limited vision in the style of Henry James.

[2] The game of billiards is noted for its strict order and rigid rules. It is a game that allows nothing unexpected or gratuitous.

[3] The adjectives "narrow" and "vertical" are also intended to evoke the limitation and narrow-mindedness of the family as well as their lofty position.

[4] The opening word. *Esto,* is validly rendered "It" in the English translation, but the indefiniteness of the word is more evident in Spanish, in which the neuter demonstrative pronoun indicates that the narrator does not know the name (or gender) of what he describes.

[5] Matilde's disappearance is also fraught with erotic overtones. Only after the dog enters their lives does she demonstrate characteristics of femininity: she eats bonbons "that came in boxes tied with frivolous bows" (90/225) and chatters with the dog. At the same time, the boy is inexplicably annoyed that the dog's tail is "curled up like a plume, *leaving its hind-quarters shamelessly exposed*" (86/221-22; emphasis added), and Matilde comes home,

one time with her hair disheveled, another time with a tear in her skirt. Perhaps we are to understand that her escapades are of an erotic nature that the young boy can intuit but not articulate.

[6] Although the Spanish original states, "pasarle gato por liebre," which means to swindle or con someone (literally, pass a cat off for a hare), the figure still depends upon animals and suggests deceit, masquerade.

Even earlier the reader is encouraged to view Santelices's reaction to his illustrations in relation to a latent eroticism. His reaction to the sensational photos is described: "he felt the nape of his neck grow cold with emotion . . . until his hands were damp and his eyelids flickered" (159/265).

FURTHER READING

Biography

McMurray, George R. *José Donoso*. Boston: Twayne, 1979, 178 p.
  Important early English-language study of Donoso's life and career, including chapters providing in-depth analyses of the short stories and *Tres novelitas burguesas*.

Criticism

Broyard, Anatole. "The Exile Who Lost His Tongue." *New York Times Book Review* (June 26, 1977): 14.
  In this review of *Sacred Families* and *Charleston and Other Stories*, Broyard offers a generally harsh assessment of Donoso's talent. According to the critic, "Donoso cannot seem to get up much impetus in the space of a short story . . . [and] assumes that every dislocation of the ordinary is extraordinary."

Callan, Richard J. "Animals as Mana Figures in José Donoso's 'Paseo' and 'Santelices'." *Essays in Literature* Vol. 2, No. 1 (Spring 1975): 115-23.
  Discusses the similarities in two stories about humdrum characters whose lives are disrupted when they develop peculiar fascinations with animals.

Fein, John M. "The Genesis of 'Santelices'," in *The Creative Process in the Works of José Donoso,* (Winthrop Studies on Major Modern Writers), edited by Guillermo I. Castillo-Feliú, pp. 89-98. Rock Hill, S.C.: Winthrop College, 1982.
  Discussion of the intense effort and detailed craftsmanship that went into the composition of one of Donoso's most celebrated stories.

Gonzalez Mandri, Flora Maria. *José Donoso's House of Fiction: A Dramatic Construction of Time and Place.* Detroit: Wayne State University Press, 1995, 199 p.
  Comprehensive reading of Donoso's narrative works that draws on the cultural theories of Foucault and Bahktin; includes discussions of the novellas.

Magnarelli, Sharon. "*Sacred Families:* Reading and Writing Power." In *Understanding José Donoso,* pp. 119-32. Columbia: University of South Carolina Press, 1993.

> Study of *Tres novelitas burguesas* in which Magnarelli presents Donoso's stories as self-portraits.

Muñoz, Willy O. "The Past as Source for the Renewal of the Present: Modernity in José Donoso," translated by Robert C. Nocera. *Revista Review Interamericana* 25, Nos. 1-4 (Spring-Winter 1985): 47-60.

> Explains Donoso's short story "El Güero" in mythological terms.

Tatum, Charles M. "The Child's Point of View in Donoso's Fiction." *Journal of Spanish Studies: Twentieth Century* 1 (1973): 187-96.

> Examines Donoso's use of a child's point of view to portray loss of innocence in the novel *Este Domingo* and in the stories "Paseo," "El hombrecito," and "China."

Additional coverage of Donoso's life and career is contained in the following sources published by Gale Group: *Contemporary Authors,* **Vols. 81-84, 155;** *Contemporary Authors New Revision Series,* **Vols. 32, 73;** *Contemporary Literary Criticism,* **Vols. 4, 8, 11, 32, 99;** *DISCovering Authors: Multicultural Authors Module; Dictionary of Literary Biography,* **Vol. 113;** *Hispanic Literature Criticism; Hispanic Writers;* **and** *Major 20th-Century Writers.*

Ellen Glasgow
1874–1945

(Full name Ellen Anderson Gholson Glasgow) American novelist, shory story writer, essayist, and autobiographer.

INTRODUCTION

Considered one of America's leading regional writers, Glasgow was a realist who also employed satire and irony in her depictions of southern society during the period of economic and social transformation after the Civil War. Rebelling against the romanticized portraits of the Old South prevalent in the writings of many of her contemporaries, Glasgow portrayed both realistically and critically what she saw as a decaying civilization clinging to outmoded manners, opinions, and methods in the face of rapid industrialization and a rising middle-class. The place of women in such an environment is a central concern in her fiction, and her short stories in particular explore the difficult relationships between men and women that result from their different sensibilities, social attitudes, and mores. Glasgow's renown is primarily as a novelist, but her twelve short stories also reveal her acuity as an observer of manners who masterfully represents the complexities of the human struggle through her female characters.

Biographical Information

Born into a well-established family in Richmond, Virginia, Glasgow was predominantly self-educated, in part because her health was too delicate for her to attend school regularly. She read widely in the classics from her father's extensive library and was guided in her reading in philosophy and science by her brother-in-law. She began writing with little encouragement, as it was considered inappropriate for young Southern women to have literary ambitions; at age eighteen she secretly wrote and destroyed her first book, and she published her first novel, *The Descendant* (1897), anonymously. After the death of her mother in 1893, Glasgow suffered severe depression as well as partial loss of her hearing, conditions she struggled with the rest of her life. Except for a few years in New York—from 1911 to 1916—and frequent but brief travels, during which she made the acquaintance of other prominent writers, Glasgow lived in the family home in Richmond. She was engaged briefly during her forties to a Southern lawyer, Henry Anderson, whose influence on Glasgow's fiction has been noted by critics. Although the two never married, their friendship lasted until Glasgow's death. Glasgow's autobiography suggests that she faced many of the same dilemmas as those of her fictional female characters: whether or not to marry, whether or not to abandon a career for marriage, whether or not to maintain independence. Glasgow was dealing realistically with these and other "feminist" issues long before women's rights became a subject of national discussion.

Major Works of Short Fiction

Glasgow's first published work was a short story written when she was twenty-two years old, "A Woman of Tomorrow." The theme of a woman's conflict between marriage and a career was to figure prominently in all her fiction. Two other short stories appeared early in her career, but in 1897, after the publication of *The Descendant* and on the advice of her editor, Glasgow halted her work in the short story genre, avowing, "I shall write no more short stories and I shall not divide my power or risk my future reputation. I will become a great novelist or none at all." She did not entirely keep her promise, but she did thereafter concentrate on writing novels. Glasgow published thirteen novels between 1898 and 1922, many of them popular; but only one, the historical work *Virginia* (1913), received serious critical attention. The only collection of short fiction published during her lifetime, *The*

Shadowy Third and Other Stories (1923) was a compilation of seven pieces written mostly between 1916 and 1923. The tales emphasize the supernatural, and in them Glasgow often satirizes men, whom she characterizes as insensitive, insipid, or treacherous, in contrast to her sensitive and independent female characters. Many of the themes addressed and techniques explored in her short fiction were developed most fully in the critically acclaimed novels written during her "high period," the best of which are considered *Barren Ground* (1925), about the emotional and economic survival strategies of a young woman working a depleted farm; *The Sheltered Life* (1932), an exposition of the evasive idealism of the agrarian South; and *Vein of Iron* (1935), which is often cited as one of the best fictional treatments of life during the Depression. The experiments she undertook in the short stories, including exploring the psychological depths of her characters and presenting strong women protagonists, were polished in the subtle portrayals of women in the later novels.

Critical Reception

Glasgow enjoyed a popular following throughout her thirty-year writing career, but never found the serious critical consideration she sought. Five of her twenty novels were bestsellers, and in 1942, essentially in recognition of her considerable literary output, she won a Pulitzer Prize for her novel *In This Our Life* (1941). Although her short stories were almost always favorably received during her lifetime, for many decades after her death even her most sympathetic critics considered them mediocre and unworthy of attention. The first essay to offer an in-depth analysis of her work in this genre was Richard K. Meeker's introduction to *The Collected Stories* (1963). No sustained criticism of the stories appeared again until Julius Rowan Raper's discussion in *The Sunken Garden* in 1980. Since then, appreciation of Glasgow's facility as a writer of short fiction has grown, and, even while she is still considered foremost as a novelist, her stories have been praised for their psychological insight, early feminist sensibility, and bold experimentation as they grapple with themes and ideas that subsequently appear in her novels.

PRINCIPAL WORKS

Short Fiction

The Shadowy Third and Other Stories 1923
The Collected Stories 1963

Other Major Works

The Descendant (novel) 1897
Phases of an Inferior Planet (novel) 1898
The Voice of the People (novel) 1900
The Battle-Ground (novel) 1902
The Freeman and Other Poems (poetry) 1902

The Deliverance (novel) 1904
The Wheel of Life (novel) 1906
The Ancient Law (novel) 1908
The Romance of a Plain Man (novel) 1909
The Miller of Old Church (novel) 1911
Virginia (novel) 1913
Life and Gabriella (novel) 1916
The Builders (novel) 1919
One Man in His Time (novel) 1922
Barren Ground (novel) 1925
The Romantic Comedians (novel) 1926
They Stooped to Folly (novel) 1929
The Sheltered Life (novel) 1932
Vein of Iron (novel) 1935
In This Our Life (novel) 1941
A Certain Measure (essays) 1943
The Woman Within (autobiography) 1954
Letters of Ellen Glasgow (letters) 1958
Beyond Defeat (novel) 1966

CRITICISM

The New York Times Book Review (review date 1923)

SOURCE: A review of *The Shadowy Third*, in *The New York Times Book Review*, October 28, 1923, p. 16.

[*In the following early review of* The Shadowy Third, *the critic finds Glasgow's ghost stories uncommonly believable because of their blend of naturalism and supernaturalism.*]

In these days when perturbed spirits refuse to rest, when they obey that impulse to self-expression even to the point of saying it with flowers, it is pleasant to come upon such well-behaved and considerate spooks as those who people the principal stories of Ellen Glasgow's *The Shadowy Third.* But be it understood that Miss Glasgow refrains from adventuring deliberately into the pseudo-scientific side of psychic phenomena. She merely adopts the device—and in her hands it becomes a highly effective one—of making the dead who continue to live in the memory assume at times a visual form. Miss Glasgow accomplishes the transition so smoothly, and blends the natural with the unnatural so skillfully, that her tales lack entirely the self-consciousness and patent artificiality that one invariably associates with the ghost story. Indeed, the atmosphere and mood in **"Whispering Leaves,"** for instance, or in **"The Past,"** places the reader in such a receptive state of mind that he accepts the shifting or the image from the mental membrane to the retina as nothing glaringly untoward or even very much out of the way.

"The Shadowy Third" possesses all the well-rounded attributes of the deliberate "plot" story, and the interest centres upon the machinations that are of the earth earthy rather upon the ethereal visitor. **"Whispering Leaves,"** on the other hand, shows Miss Glasgow's method developed to its nth power. Here the natural and the unnaturally actually seem to merge. The incident has to do with an imaginative and highly sensitive child. Death deprived him in infancy of his mother's care, and death again, just before the story opens, took from him the negro "mammy" who had filled successfully the mother's place. But so potent is the memory of the old negress in the lad's mind that it is to him as if he really lived, and he feels at all times conscious of her continued care and solicitude. The tale culminates in the assumption that this continued watchfulness from beyond actually saves the boy's life. Proof of the method's success lies in the reader's ready reaction, "Well, why not?"

Not all of Miss Glasgow's stories, by any means, deal with the supernatural. She gives her readers a varied assortment. One, for instance, **"A Point in Morals,"** propounds and proceeds to do its best to solve, the original problem, whether or not, in any circumstances, the saving of a human life may become positively immoral. Another, **"Jordan's End,"** has to do with the attitude toward inherited insanity. But all have at least one point in common. They deal with life at great moments. For Miss Glasgow's characters there is no even tenor. They have no life as calm and unworried members of society. Whether they are "shadowy thirds" who have carried into the next world the traits and feelings that have got the better of them in this, and are obliged to "work them off somewhere," or whether they are flesh and blood mortals tearing at the mesh of circumstances that has caught them, their life's spark burns before us always at white heat. *The Shadowy Third* remains in the memory as a collection of "high moments."

Joseph Collins (review date 1923)

SOURCE: "Gentleman, the Ladies!" in *The New York Times Book Review,* December 23, 1923, p. 23.

[*In the following excerpt from a review of the works of four women writers, Collins praises* The Shadowy Third, *comparing Glasgow's style and technique to that of Guy de Maupassant.*]

[Ellen Glasgow] has told the truth about life as she has observed it and . . . she has done it in pure, chaste, limpid, grammatical English cast in form that constitutes art. She has made herself master of a style that has no superior and few peers among the fiction writers of the day in this country. This distinction of style has been characteristic of all her work since *The Descendant,* but it is particularly true of *The Miller and the Old Church, Virginia,* and *The Shadowy Third.* In addition she knows the value of atmosphere, she is an expert character builder with original ideas and she has learned the value of perspective. Moreover she knows when to let the reader make synopses, inferences, and conclusions. She neither preaches nor predicts, threatens nor moralizes. In the vernacular of the day, her people are "real folks." She knows them, understands them, likes them, sees behind their motives and animations and sympathizes with them. She takes pride in exhibiting them to us, showing us how they surmount

difficulties, resist temptations, throw off handicaps and overcome obstacles. But reporting what she sees and has heard does not encompass her art. She has ideals and a philosophy of life, and she sees man in relation to the whole world as well as to his fellow-man.

. . . . .

Whenever I read Miss Glasgow, I am reminded of Guy de Maupassant. It is not what she says, but the way she says it that recalls his masterpieces. Moreover, I am convinced they mastered their respective languages in a very similar way, viz: by unending effort, by realization that talent is long patience. Miss Glasgow toiled to find the noun to name the thing she wanted to say, the verb to give it motion, the adjective to qualify it, and when she found them she placed them in such juxtaposition that they eye sweeping over them or the lips uttering them found them rhythmical. Her books, and particularly those following *The Romance of a Plain Man,* reveal her conviction that writing is an art which must have form.

The Shadowy Third, Miss Glasgow's last book, is quite different from its predecessors. She has gone from the world of reality into the realm of unreality, from observation and description of the natural to the consideration and depiction of the supernatural. And it is accomplished naturally, adroitly, simply, and convincingly. The titular story, one of crime and retribution, is revealed by suggestion rather than by direct statement. The atmosphere chants the dirge. **"Dare's Gift,"** particularly the second part, shows Miss Glasgow's finest craftsmanship. It has an epic sweep and comprehensiveness that make it a great story. It shows that Miss Glasgow has always in mind that a tale must have a dual theme; a human story and a great problem. She has never done anything that better entitles her to be called artist than **"Dare's Gift."** From consideration of her last volume we readily convince ourselves that she has not yet done her best work.

Louise Collier Willcox (review date 1924)

SOURCE: "Ghosts and Others," in *The Bookman,* Vol. 58, No. 5, January, 1924, pp. 573-74.

[*In this excerpt from a review of four collections of stories about ghosts and the occult, Willcox admires Glasgow's ability to convey convincingly "place and speech" in her writing.*]

Miss Glasgow has four forthright ghost stories and three psychological tales. Her writing retains its customary distinction and freedom from all affectation and use of clichés; such English is a refreshment to mind and spirit, coming as it does from the fine tradition of Addison and Matthew Arnold, unvulgarized by current slang, unvilified by current bad grammar. An environment of long established customs, manners, and traditions has given her what few writers of her day have—both soil and atmosphere; a soil in which her roots are deeply set, and an atmosphere where she is sure of climate, vegetation, human types, manners, customs, and traditions. When she writes of Virginia her touch is as sure, her tone as perfect as was George Eliot's when she wrote of mid-England or Arnold Bennett's when he describes the five towns. **"Dare's Gift"** as well as the grim and terrible **"Jordan's End"** are fine examples of this truth to place and speech. **"The Difference"** is a study of that disastrous breach between the concentrated feminine temperament and the more diffuse masculine instinct, and both **"A Point in Morals"** and **"Jordan's End"** deal with a nice point in morals: is it ever legitimate to take life? Incidentally it seems odd that **"Jordan's End"**, the most powerful of these seven stories, is the only one not to have appeared first in a magazine.

Frederick P. W. McDowell (essay date 1960)

SOURCE: "Fiction of the War Years and After," in *Ellen Glasgow and the Ironic Art of Fiction,* University of Wisconsin Press, 1960, pp. 127-45.

[*In this excerpt from the first book-length study of Glasgow's oeuvre, McDowell dismisses all but two of her short stories as insignificant.*]

Miss Glasgow seems to have needed the leisured form of the novel to develop her characters and situations, so that, as a short story writer, she is not particularly adept.[12] With two exceptions her stories, collected in *The Shadowy Third and Other Stories* (1923), are negligible because in this form she turned primarily to an investigation of the supernatural, an inquiry which did not consort well with her predominantly realistic bent of mind. Most of the stories deal with the occult, but too baldly and literally. The subtlety which frequently distinguished Miss Glasgow's studies of moral conflict and of the manners of the aristocracy is absent from most of these thinly imagined tales.

In **"The Shadowy Third"** a child appears as an apparition to his mother and to the nurse-narrator of the story, although he remains invisible to the father, Dr. Maradick. When his wife insists that she still sees the spirit of her infant son, her husband thinks she is suffering from delusion and has her put in an asylum. After his wife's death, Dr. Maradick plans to marry a shallow woman who had rejected him before his first marriage and who will benefit from the first Mrs. Maradick's money. The child again appears to the nurse, prior to the time the doctor's wedding is to take place. At this point the doctor is killed when he falls downstairs, the result of "an invisible judgment," the nurse is convinced. Why the boy should be visible to the mother and not to the father is never satisfactorily developed, nor are the relations clear between the doctor and the women with whom he is involved. In **"Dare's Gift,"** otherwise a mediocre tale, Miss Glasgow stated the belief which she had also expressed in *One Man in His Time* through Corinna Page, that in Virginia "the personal loyalties have always been esteemed be-

yond the impersonal."[13] Miss Glasgow made clear her views on the psychological nature of time in this story: it is, she has her narrator conclude, "the high moments that make a life, and the flat ones that fill the years" (104). In **"A Point in Morals"** she had concluded in 1899, as she did later in **"Dare's Gift,"** that the highest civilization is the one which places the highest value upon the individual life.[14]

The two best stories in the collection are **"The Difference"** and **"Jordan's End,"** stories of real life rather than the supernatural. In **"The Difference"** Miss Glasgow enlarged upon her familiar theme that women love with their imaginations and whole souls, whereas most men love only with their senses. George Fleming makes light of an affair with Rose Morrison to his wife, Margaret, thus revealing to her his essential triviality. Margaret now sees that she has been too easily satisfied with the second best. She comes, therefore, to despise her husband more than his mistress and actually to feel for her an unconventional bond of affection, originating in "woman's immemorial disillusionment" with man.

In **"Jordan's End"** Miss Glasgow effectively presented a physically decadent aristocratic family, the Jordans. This family has deteriorated because of hereditary insanity deriving, in part, from too much inbreeding. When Miss Judith marries into the family, she is happy with Alan Jordan, her husband, for three years until the hereditary taint shows up in him. At this point, she sees her life stretch out bleakly before her and is overcome by the thought of her physically strong husband miserable for years in an asylum. Three days later the doctor discovers that Alan is dead and that all the opiate he had left behind is gone. In spite of his suspicions, the doctor will never know how the husband died. He cannot question Judith because she is too impersonally removed from her own misfortune: "she was beyond all consolation and all companionship. She was nearer to the bleak sky and the deserted fields than she was to her kind" (291). For once Miss Glasgow wrote with power and discernment about the completely degenerate aspects of the South, and in this short narrative anticipated major works like *The Sound and the Fury.*

Notes

[12] In an interview with Grant Overton (*The Women Who Make Our Novels* [1918], p. 26), Ellen Glasgow declared: "I cannot write short stories. They bore me excruciatingly. The whole technique of the short story and the novel is different. All the best of the short stories must be painfully condensed with slight regard for the evolutionary causes bringing about this or that effect. Everything that I see, I see in the form of a novel—as a large canvas. I want to trace the process of cause and effect; and that is why both *Virginia* and *Gabriella* were a joy in the writing."

[13] *The Shadowy Third and Other Stories* (Garden City, NY: Doubleday, Page, 1923), p. 79. Corinna Page had similarly speculated: "And what was life . . . except a complex and intricate blend of human relations?" (278).

[14] This story first appeared in *Harper's Magazine* for 1899. The

other stories in *The Shadowy Third* first appeared in periodicals from 1916 to 1923.

Richard K. Meeker (essay date 1963)

SOURCE: Introduction to *The Collected Stories of Ellen Glasgow,* edited by Richard K. Meeker, Louisiana State University Press, 1963, pp. 3-23.

[*In the following essay, which is the earliest substantial consideration of Glasgow's short fiction, Meeker argues that the stories mark an important transition in Glasgow's development as a writer.*]

On November 22, 1897, after publishing her first novel, *The Descendant,* Ellen Glasgow wrote to Walter Hines Page, then an editor on the *Atlantic Monthly,* "As regards my work I shall follow your advice in full. I shall write no more short stories and I shall not divide my power or risk my future reputation. I will become a great novelist or none at all."[1] Literary history has already recorded and applauded the eighteen novels which she wrote thereafter; however, history has failed to notice how often Miss Glasgow broke that promise to Page. As a matter of fact, she published eleven short stories by 1925 and left another one in manuscript.[2] Nevertheless, only a few paragraphs have been written about them, and editors of anthologies usually have passed them by for a piece from *The Sheltered Life,* if they have represented her at all.[3] A partial collection, *The Shadowy Third and Other Stories* (1923), has been out of print for over twenty years. It is time to consider whether such neglect of Ellen Glasgow's short stories is justified.

Miss Glasgow's letter to Page calls for further explanation. To begin with, Page, on the inside of the New York publishing world, was perfectly right in asserting that the novel was the thing, and Miss Glasgow was only being prudent in agreeing to his advice. The reading public was still conditioned by the assumption that seriousness required bulk. The literary giants of the late nineteenth century were largely novelists, such as Howells, James, Hardy, Galsworthy, Balzac, and Tolstoy. The short story was still in the hands of the sentimentalists and the local colorists. The best of them—Mary Wilkins Freeman, Sarah Orne Jewett, Margaret Deland, and George Washington Cable—had not yet made the world safe for the realistic short story. Stephen Crane achieved his reputation with a novel, *The Red Badge of Courage,* although he preferred his poetry in *The Black Riders* to any of his fiction. E. A. Robinson, born too soon, had just destroyed the manuscript of his short stories and resolved to be a great poet or nothing.

In short, Page was accurately reflecting the official attitude toward short fiction. But a few weeks later, when he replied to Miss Glasgow's letter, he showed that he was really warning her against spreading herself too thin:

> . . . it is an everyday occurrence that authors of promise scatter the influences that ought to go towards the firm and steady building of a great reputation, by appearing in print here, there, and everywhere. Even if all the minor literature that they put forth be excellent of its kind, the public comes after a very little while to regard the author as a sort of "professional" writer who turns up with poems or short stories, or essays and other things so often as to cause one to regard the writer rather as a "literary operative" than as a person who is bent upon doing only great pieces of work. . . . Of course after a little when you have more firmly established your reputation, you can better afford to amuse yourself with smaller things.[4]

Actually, Ellen Glasgow did follow Page's advice, as much as she followed the advice of any man. She had already written at least two short stories and sent them to her New York literary agent, Paul R. Reynolds, before she promised not to write any more of them. On November 1, 1897, she had suggested that Reynolds offer one of her stories to *McClure's Magazine.* Reynolds apparently sent **"Between Two Shores,"** which was published there in February, 1899. Then, on January 27, 1898, reassured by Page's advice and the successful completion of her second novel, Miss Glasgow announced firmly, "I have decided to write no more short articles—and I wish I could recall them all." Perhaps her decision was reinforced by the fact that another of her stories remained unpublished. She asked Reynolds to return it, but he succeeded in placing **"A Point in Morals"** with *Harper's Magazine* for May, 1899, and made several efforts to sell her poems.

For the next fifteen years Ellen Glasgow concentrated on novels. Her determination was still firm on May 9, 1913, when she wrote to Reynolds, "As for short stories—well, I've tried hard to interest myself in them, but simply can't. The work is so tiresome that I'd rather not have the money they bring than try to write them."[5] Then something happened. On July 1, 1916, she wrote Reynolds that she was working on a story about a haunted house and wondered if there happened to be any particular demand for short fiction just then.

Reynold's reply was encouraging. He said that there was presently a great demand for short stories and that with her reputation she could command a good price for one. He asked to see it as soon as it was ready. This story was undoubtedly **"The Shadowy Third,"** which *Scribner's Magazine* published in December, 1916. During the next eight years Miss Glasgow produced nine more stories and sold all but one.

II

Why did Ellen Glasgow, in the middle of her career as a novelist, just when *Life and Gabriella* had reached fifth place on the *Publisher's Weekly* best-seller list, turn back to writing short stories? An obvious answer, which her correspondence with Reynolds bears out, is that she needed the money. While hardly poor by ordinary standards, Miss Glasgow had large medical bills, traveled extensively, and had to maintain One West Main Street in Richmond after her father's death in 1916. For this reason, she would even sell stories to women's magazines if they paid well, although she did balk at appearing in the *Ladies Home*

Journal. Another answer is that she could afford to follow Page's advice and amuse herself now that she was an established novelist.

The full explanation is more complicated, however. The first hint comes from an interview Miss Glasgow gave in New York in 1916 shortly after the publication of *Life and Gabriella*: "When I began *Virginia* I had in mind three books dealing with the adjustment of human lives to changing conditions. . . . Virginia was the passive and helpless victim of the ideal of feminine self-sacrifice. . . . Gabriella was the product of the same school, but instead of being used by circumstances, she used them to create her own destiny." Then she added, "The third book may never be written. If it should be, it will deal with a woman who faces her world with weapons of indirect influence or subtlety."[6] It is hard to find the prescribed character in *The Builders* of 1919 or *One Man in His Time* of 1922.

There is both biographical and critical evidence that Miss Glasgow faltered between *Life and Gabriella* and *Barren Ground,* that is, between 1916 and 1925. In a letter to Hugh Walpole, dated August 23, 1923, she summarizes her ordeal:

> Ah, I've been through the Slough of Despond about my work. After I wrote *Life and Gabriella* about 8 or 10 years ago, I let go and gave up. I was passing through an experience that seemed to drain everything out of me—vitality, imagination, interest, everything. In that time I lost a great deal, and I slipped somehow, naturally, I suppose, away from what I had won. Now, I have boiled up, I hope, out of those depths, and I am trying to win back what I have lost.[7]

She goes on to describe her plans for *Barren Ground.*

Plainly, Miss Glasgow was struggling to re-orient herself following several disillusionments, public and private, after World War I. But why write short stories during this Slough of Despond? Ironically, the answer may lie in her own deprecation of the short story form during her 1916 interview:

> I cannot write short stories. They bore me excruciatingly. The whole technique of the short story and the novel is different. All the best of the short stories must be painfully condensed with slight regard for the evolutionary causes bringing about this or that effect. Everything I see, I see in the form of a novel— as a large canvas. I want to trace the process of cause and effect.[8]

In other words, the novel calls for a comprehensive view of life, a coherent philosophy to motivate the characters. It is evident that following World War I Miss Glasgow temporarily lost her ability to compose large canvases, that is, lost her sense of evolution. Her writings at this point contain increasing references to a world gone mad, uncivilized barbarians, and ugly deviations from human decency. The modern world began to mystify, even horrify Miss Glasgow. It became increasingly hard for her to write

on a large scale, to trace the causes and effects that had so fascinated her.

Professor Willard Thorp has pointed out to me that Miss Glasgow was preceded by her distinguished rival Henry James in the literary Slough of Despond. James, too, wallowed in frustration during the nineties after a string of successful novels. When he had consolidated his art through writing short stories and plays, he emerged into the "major phase" with *The Ambassadors.* To complete the parallel, we can easily say that Miss Glasgow's major phase began with *Barren Ground,* after she had stabilized herself through short fiction. Like Henry James, Edith Wharton, Willa Cather, and James Branch Cabell, she found the short story a medium perfectly adapted for catching isolated moments in time, when causes are impossible to trace and results are hard to measure. With her talent for epigram, Miss Glasgow found condensation no great strain either.

Furthermore, the short story was rapidly becoming a respectable and profitable literary form in the periodicals. Quality magazines like *Scribner's* and *Harper's* were carrying serious fiction by writers of stature like Mark Twain, Theodore Dreiser, Henry James, and Hamlin Garland. Even the family magazines were competing for stories by established novelists—magazines like *Woman's Home Companion, Good Housekeeping,* and the *Saturday Evening Post.* Ellen Glasgow may have blushed to admit it, but she sold stories to all these magazines. Moreover, she took her stories seriously enough to collect seven of them in 1923 into a volume entitled, after the first story, **The Shadowy Third.** Probably, as Arthur H. Quinn has commented, these seven represent those of which she was proudest. It is significant that all but one of the reprinted stories came from the "quality" magazines, *Harper's* and *Scribner's.*

If Miss Glasgow had had her way, as she usually did with her publishers, **The Shadowy Third** would have been included in the monumental Virginia edition of her works in 1938, but according to Edward Wagenknecht, Scribner's insisted on novels only.[9] Otherwise, we might have had a preface for her short stories, like those collected later in *A Certain Measure.* There Miss Glasgow might have told us where she got the ideas for her stories and what technical problems she encountered. She also might have, characteristically, pointed out the beauties of style and structure, lest we miss them. While we are lacking some useful information, we have also been spared some embarrassment, for Miss Glasgow is inclined to tell us not only how she wrote her stories but what she wants us to think of them. Her prefaces are sometimes like a guided tour in which certain rooms are lingered in too long and other doors kept suspiciously closed. Today, critics like Northrop Frye warn us, "The poet speaking as critic produces not criticism, but documents to be examined by critics."[10]

In addition to those previously quoted, we have only a few brief statements by Miss Glasgow about her short stories. One is contained in a letter she wrote to Mrs. Robert C. Taylor on February 8, 1924: "It makes me happy that you love my Shadowy Third stories. They are very near to my heart, those stories, and I lived in that atmosphere when I was writing them."[11] To Joseph Hergesheimer she wrote on January 7, 1924, "I am sending you the short stories, and I only wish the book could be of the English edition because I was able to correct the proof more thoroughly. Several of these you may like. 'Dare's Gift' is, I think, a perfectly true picture of the closing days of the Confederacy."[12]

III

Every review of *The Shadowy Third* was favorable, and every reviewer pointed out the preponderance of the supernatural in the stories.[13] Ellen Glasgow obviously arranged them to emphasize this effect. The Shadowy Third is the spirit of a dead child who is visible only to sensitive persons; scientifically minded people never see the spirit. Two other stories have spirit characters. In **"The Past"** Vanderbridge's first wife returns to haunt him and his second wife. In **"Whispering Leaves"** Mammy Rhody[14] returns to protect little Pell from harm. These three spirits are all seen by objective narrators with a reputation for reliability. A fourth story, **"Dare's Gift,"** contains a house haunted by the spirit of treachery, which corrupts every inhabitant. These, the first four stories in the book, are plainly intended to dominate it.

No one who has pictured Ellen Glasgow as a sharp-eyed realist can read these four stories without surprise. Ghosts are not fashionable in the twentieth century, least of all visible ones, and yet we are urged to believe in them here, because the narrators all believe in them; all the good people in the story believe in them. Furthermore, the ghosts actually perform; the little girl seems to trip up her father with a jump rope; the second wife sits at the dinner table with the Vanderbridges; Mammy Rhody actually saves little Pell from falling. Why is a Darwinian determinist urging belief in phantoms?

Ellen Glasgow had both personal and ideological reasons for believing in ghosts. She has testified in several places to her frail, sensitive girlhood, where she was protected from harsh realities by the world of her imagination. In an essay she wrote for *I Believe,* she said, "As a very small child I was a believing animal. I believed in fairies; I believed in Souls—not only the souls of men and women and children, but the souls, too, of trees and plants, and winds and clouds."[15] She tells in *The Woman Within* of her happy summers at Jerdone Castle, a farm where the Glasgows lived before moving to Main Street in Richmond. On the farm, accompanied by her Mammy Lizzie, she invented "Little Willie" stories at bedtime, and all of nature came alive for her:

> Every vista in the woods beckoned me; every field held its own secret; every tree near our house had a name of its own and a special identity. This was the beginning of my love for natural things, for earth and sky, for roads and fields and woods, for trees and grass and flowers; a love which has been second only to my sense of an enduring kinship with birds and animals, and all inarticulate creatures. Mammy and I gave every tree on the big blue-grass lawn a baptism. We knew

each one by name, from Godwin, the giant elm, to Charles, the oak, and Alfred, the shivering aspen.[16]

One of her most painful experiences there was the sale of her dog Pat, whom her farther refused to take with them to Main Street.

Out of this period in Miss Glasgow's childhood comes her first written story, **"Only a Daisy,"** which she carefully put on paper when she was either seven or eight years old:[17]

> In a garden full of beautiful flowers there sprung up a little daisy. Everything was bright and cheerful around it, but the daisy was not content. "If I were only one of those roses[,]" it said[,] "then I would be happy, but I am only a little daisy[,]" and the daisy sighed and hung its head.
>
> Days passed and the roses were carried away. There was to be a grand ball in the castle[,] for the you[ng] earl was going away. "If I could only be there but no one would think of taking me[,]" said the daisy when the other flowers were carried away to grace the stands and vases on the night of the ball. "But I am only a little daisy[,]" and it sighed again.
>
> It was the evening before he should go away and the Earl was walking in the garden with a young girl. "Let me give you a flower before you go[,]" she said[,] "for it is the last time I will see you before you go[,]" and she stooped to pluck a tall white lily that grew near, but the young man stopped her[.] "No," he said[,] "I will have this little daisy[.] I will keep it and it will remind me of you[.]" She plucked the daisy and handed it to him. They stood together and talked for a little while and then the girl turned and went into the house. The young [man] stood still a moment[,] pressed the daisy to his lips[,] then hurried away and was soon lost to sight in the darkness. And the little daisy was content at last to be "only a daisy[."]

In this charming little Cinderella myth, there is no mistaking Ellen Glasgow's early sense of being an outcast.

Another story most reminiscent of her childhood is **"Whispering Leaves."** On a visit to an old house of that name, the narrator finds little Pell, a frail, imaginative boy who is ignored by his stepfather, Mr. Blanton, and his stepbrothers and sisters, exactly as Miss Glasgow apparently was by her brothers and sisters. Pell's only companion is the ghost of Mammy Rhody, who, like Ellen's Mammy Lizzie, comforts the child with stories at night. Because of Mammy Rhody's skill at training birds, **"Whispering Leaves"** has gained its name as a bird paradise. Little Pell also has that "enduring kinship with birds and animals" of which Miss Glasgow has spoken. He is actually birdlike in appearance and appetite, and he spends his waking hours outdoors, mostly in the trees. Like Ellen, too, Pell loses his beloved dog through the cruelty of his stepparent. It is not too much to say, then, that in **"Whispering Leaves"** Ellen Glasgow is reliving her childhood at Jerdone Castle.

The other ghost stories would not be so rewarding if interpreted biographically, but no reader can miss the preoccupation with illness, especially nervous illness, in them. In *The Woman Within,* Miss Glasgow tells us about her mother, who, worn out from child-bearing, lived in a state of anxiety that baffled her doctors for years. The autobiography also chronicles the long list of brothers, sisters, and other relatives whom she saw die around her. More specifically, the nurse who narrates **"The Shadowy Third"** and the secretary who narrates **"The Past"** probably derive from Anne. Virginia Bennett, a trained nurse, who was Miss Glasgow's companion and secretary for many years.

Thus Miss Glasgow's personality and childhood experiences would have disposed her to take ghosts and native spirits seriously. But her reading in science and philosophy suggests another rationale. It is significant that the spirits are always manifested through an act of will by one of the characters. Miss Glasgow is plainly suggesting that ideas can be more real than objects, a concept as old as Plato. The reviewer in the Greensboro (North Carolina) *Daily News* explained her system in a way that would have appealed to both Ellen Glasgow and Edgar Allan Poe: ". . . ideas once definitely and strikingly resolved into action do not die, but manifest themselves as still living long after the individual who put his own compelling idea into vivid action has ceased to live. . . ."[18] Primitivism is involved, too, because innocent, young, or uneducated people are the most likely to "see" these ideas. As Miss Glasgow's old friend, Louise Collier Willcox, explained in *The Bookman,* "There may be a stage in training before the mind takes entire control of the nerves, when the *whole* body 'thinks,' and we are aware of more than a densely physical atmosphere."[19]

This is a romantic philosophy, but it is a post-Darwinian romanticism, and it is meant to be taken seriously. The opponents of the believers in spirits are, naturally, scientists—usually doctors. However, it is the specialist—the psychiatrist, the surgeon—not the general practitioner, that Ellen Glasgow attacks in these stories. The famous alienist, Dr. Roland Maradick, in **"The Shadowy Third"** is unable to minister to his own wife, but his young, sympathetic nurse knows intuitively that Mrs. Maradick is not insane, that she is only preserving the memory of her dead daughter. Dr. Drayton, a Washington nerve specialist, can only prescribe a rest in the country for Mrs. Beckwith, but old Dr. Lakeby, a general practitioner from Chericoke Landing, knows immediately that she is under the spell of **"Dare's Gift"** and predicts a speedy recovery once she leaves that contaminated house. Mrs. Vanderbridge in **"The Past"** has had a succession of doctors for her nervous ailment, but Miss Wrenn, her new secretary, soon learns that the spirit of the first Mrs. Vanderbridge is the cause of it. Dr. Estbridge, a psychiatrist in **"The Professional Instinct,"** is unable to meet his wife's needs and ignorant of his own selfish motives until they are revealed to him by a friendly journalist.

Actually, Miss Glasgow was working in a familiar literary tradition. Although she might have been reluctant to ad-

mit it, she was exploring the same psychological vein that Rudyard Kipling and Henry James had explored a decade before. Kipling in "They" and James in such stories as *The Turn of the Screw,* "The Jolly Corner," and "The Beast in the Jungle" were fascinated by the power that ideas, especially fears, have over men's minds. As their stories show, a fear or a wish can be so strong that the object takes on a concrete existence. However, their symbolic ghosts are visible only to the afflicted characters; Miss Glasgow's ghosts are more "real" than that, as I have shown. They take us nearer to modern ghost stories, like Kafka's, where the ghost becomes human and the dream completely displaces reality. For Kipling, James, and Glasgow, ghosts could have either good or bad influences; modern ghosts, supported by Freud and Jung, are consistently frightening because they represent the unconscious levels of the mind.

IV

The first four stories in *The Shadowy Third* have another feature in common: the influence of Edgar Allan Poe. In a letter to Van Wyck Brooks in 1944, Miss Glasgow recognized the unlikely relationship herself: "I have always felt a curious (because improbable) kinship with Poe."[20] This kinship is worth exploring. We might begin by noticing the parallel in plot between Poe's "Ligeia" and Glasgow's **"The Past."** In both stories the first wife tries to destroy the second by supernatural means. The Glasgow approach differs in that the first Mrs. Vanderbridge, who appears in her own body, retires in defeat when the second Mrs. Vanderbridge proves her own moral superiority. However, Poe might well have preferred the first wife.

Whereas "Ligeia" is similar only in plot, "The Fall of the House of Usher" must be admitted as a deep and pervasive influence on all four ghost stories in the Glasgow collection. First, observe that three of the four stories— **"Dare's Gift," "Whispering Leaves,"** and **"Jordan's End"**—are set in symbolic country houses that supply the titles for their stories. All four houses exert a definite moral influence over their inhabitants. The treachery of Sir Roderick Dare in Bacon's Rebellion causes the betrayal of a Union soldier by his Confederate sweetheart and the deception of a corporation lawyer by his wife. Successive acts of treachery have corrupted the very walls of the house. Dr. Lakeby makes this point clear: "Did you ever stop to wonder about the thoughts that must have gathered within walls like these?—to wonder about the impressions that must have lodged in the bricks, in the crevices, in the timber and the masonry? Have you ever stopped to think that these multiplied impressions might create a current of thought—a mental atmosphere—an inscrutable power of suggestion?" This is identical with Roderick Usher's theory of the "sentience of vegetable things." Even the architecture of **"Dare's Gift"** prepares us for the thematic moral decay. The present owners discover, too late ". . . architectural absurdities—wanton excrescences in the modern additions, which had been designed apparently with the purpose of providing space at the least possible cost of materials and labour."

"Whispering Leaves" makes the same point in the same way. The spirit of the first Mrs. Blanton prevails, despite the neglect of the present owners, in the splendid house and flourishing garden, just as the birds remain in their sanctuary after the death of Mammy Rhody. But decadence is inevitable. It is already perceptible in the character of Pelham Blanton, "a tall, relaxed, indolent-looking man of middle age, with grey hair, brilliant dark eyes and an air of pensive resignation. . . ." The narrator concludes, "I had heard, or had formed some vague idea, that the family had 'run to seed', as they say in the South, and my first view of Cousin Pelham helped to fix this impression more firmly in my mind. He looked, I thought, a man who had ceased to desire anything intensely except physical comfort." Cousin Pelham is plainly a cousin to Roderick Usher, too.

By now the analogy with Poe's "Fall of the House of Usher" should be clear. There, too, the decaying house contributed to the decay of Roderick and his sister, just as the Usher family had contributed to the decay of the house itself. The tonal unity achieved by the identification of house and occupants has been one of the most admired features of the Poe story.

The prize demonstration of the House-of-Usher influence is reserved for the last story in *The Shadowy Third* collection, **"Jordan's End."** Even the title bears the same dual symbolism as the Poe story. Jordan's End is simultaneously the name of the crumbling old Virginia plantation and the epitome of the decaying family that inhabits it. The narrator, a young doctor, has been called to treat Alan Jordan, who seems to have fallen prey to the ancestral insanity. Our narrator, like Poe's, arrives at the house as the sun is setting. It is dusk in November, and the doctor pauses at a fork in the road, where there is a dead tree with buzzards roosting in it. Only a sunken, untraveled trail leads to Jordan's End. An old Negro tells him that all the male Jordans have died insane, and now young Alan must be confined and guarded. Carstairs, the famous alienist from Baltimore, is to decide tomorrow whether Alan is, like his ancestors, incurable.

With this information in his mind, the doctor emerges from the gloomy woods.

> The glow in the sky had faded now to a thin yellow-green, and a melancholy twilight pervaded the landscape. In this twilight I looked over the few sheep huddled together on the ragged lawn, and saw the old brick house crumbling beneath its rank growth of ivy. As I drew nearer I had the feeling that the surrounding desolation brooded there like some sinister influence.

But the narrator also recognizes that both the house and its inhabitants once had charm, even distinction. Although the eaves are now falling away, the shutters sagging, the windows broken, and the boards rotting, the house was once of an impressive Georgian design with beautiful details. "A fine old place once, but repulsive now in its abject decay, like some young blood of former days who has grown senile," the doctor muses. Similarly, the Jordan family was once the proudest in the county until the Civil War. "Jest run to seed," Father Peterkin, the old Negro says. Intermarriage is a partial explanation.

But Miss Glasgow uses the House-of-Usher theme to make a point that Poe was unable to make about the South because he was too close to it. The degeneration which the house always symbolizes is brought about by the refusal of the inhabitants to trust more than their senses. The families that go to seed are those that refuse to believe in the intangible. They love material comfort more than beauty; they love tradition more than progress. **"Dare's Gift"** and **"Whispering Leaves,"** Ellen Glasgow's most ambitious stories, show both the necessity and the difficulty of believing in the intangible. The ghosts are only objective correlatives for this idea. We need not believe in them so long as we believe in what they stand for.

The house that destroys its occupants had, we might guess, a real-life parallel in One West Main Street, a house that both attracted and repelled Miss Glasgow because of its burden of memories. Although she left it from 1911 to 1916 and frequently went away during the hot summers after that, it was always her home address, and *The Woman Within* testifies to its powerful impression on her. "The fibers of my personality are interwoven, I feel, with some indestructible element of the place."[21] In 1942 she could say that out of ten children only she and two others remained alive, but still the house stood. Ever since Poe a trademark of Southern literature has been the house that is an image of the family and in turn becomes an image of the society. Ellen Glasgow's character with the vein of iron belongs in a solid gray house like One West Main Street.

V

All four of the ghost stories in *The Shadowy Third* collection have another feature in common: the use of a first-person narrator. Again, the influence of Poe is possible. However, in her preface to *The Romance of a Plain Man* (1909), her only novel told from a first-person point of view, Miss Glasgow testifies to her discomfort: "The question of the proper use of the first person has been frequently discussed in criticism, and either approved or condemned according to the preferences of the critic. For my part, I have always thought that the method contained almost insurmountable disadvantages, even when it was employed by the great masters of prose fiction." Then she adds apologetically, ". . . I think my one and only adventure with the first person singular is likely to have been the sad result of my youthful fondness for the heroes of romance."[22]

Miss Glasgow does not list the disadvantages of the method or the names of the famous practitioners, nor does she mention her short stories. However, one insurmountable disadvantage to her must have been the sacrifice of the godlike, ironic perspective from which she liked to write. It is possible that she would have been an even better artist if she had been able to restrain herself within the limits of the first-person narrator; her love of epigram frequently becomes intrusive editorial comment in fiction.

But why, then, did she deliberately choose an uncomfortable point of view for most of her short stories? She had two distinguished guides in Poe and James, both of whom realized that a first-person viewpoint can plausibly convey the most bizarre details. Because the narrative is told by someone to whom it is actually happening, we are more likely to suspend our disbelief. Where spirits are supposed to be visible, it also helps to have an intelligent, objective eyewitness, such as a secretary, a nurse, a lawyer, or a family doctor.

Poe invariably chose a first-person narrator for his horror stories; James had even better equipment. In his preface to *The Altar of the Dead* (1909) where he collected all his ghost stories except *The Turn of the Screw,* James complained that the sensational white vision at the end of *Arthur Gordon Pym* failed because Poe had made Pym merely the reporter rather than the perceiver of the vision. For James the success of the supernatural depended on its being filtered through the consciousness of a central character. "We want it clear, goodness knows, but we also want it thick, and we get thickness in the human consciousness that entertains and records, that amplifies and interprets it."[23] James used a first-person percipient in *The Turn of the Screw,* but elsewhere he achieved supernatural effects by means of his famous central intelligence viewpoint.

Only one story in *The Shadowy Third,* **"The Difference,"** is narrated from Ellen Glasgow's favorite point of view, the central intelligence. However, James would have found little to praise in her use of it. For example, the viewpoint in **"The Difference"** shifts abruptly from Margaret Fleming to her opponent Rose Morrison so that we can see how Margaret looked to Rose. Four out of the five uncollected stories are also handled from the central intelligence viewpoint, but there is no hint yet of Miss Glasgow's concentrated use of it in *Barren Ground,* or of the multiple viewpoint which she was to use so brilliantly in *They Stooped to Folly, Vein of Iron,* and *The Sheltered Life.*

VI

All five of the uncollected stories and **"The Difference"** from *The Shadowy Third* have as their theme that limitless subject—the relationship between men and women. Although Ellen Glasgow's "social history" of the South appears to have been her main concern, the real focus in all her fiction seems to be the struggle of women for respect in a world dominated by men. Her short stories dramatize a complete cycle of relationships, from the first apprehensive encounter to the last bitter rejection. To a Darwinian, love is apparently a struggle for dominance. Miss Glasgow's women hope that love is something better than that, but they are usually disappointed. Her typical plot sequence runs: girl meets boy; girl is taken advantage of by boy; then girl learns to get along without boys, or, girl gets back at boy.

The cycle begins in Ellen Glasgow's first published story, **"Between Two Shores."** Here fate has placed, on a ship bound for England, a shy, sensitive young widow, Lucy Smith, in a stateroom next to a confident, attentive young man who calls himself Lawrence Smith. Because of the coincidence of names, everyone on the ship considers them married, and "Lawrence Smith" encourages the deception, since he is fleeing from the American police under an alias. Unaware of his past Lucy is alternately frightened and attracted by this strong, impulsive man, who seems devoted to her during her many spells of sickness. In Lawrence she sees ". . . the face of a man of strong will and even stronger passions, who had lived hard and fast. . . . If one were in his power, how quietly he might bend and break mere flesh and bone."

Here the allegory sets in. Lucy has never loved her husband and has never really immersed herself in life. She is obviously ". . . a woman in whom temperamental fires had been smothered rather than extinguished, by the ashes of unfulfillment. To existence, which is a series of rhythmic waves of the commonplace, she offered facial serenity; to life, which is a clash of opposing passions, she turned the wistful eyes of ignorance."

The combination of Lawrence's gentle hands and his passionate nature soon undermines Lucy's restraint, until she confesses, "I should choose to be broken by you to being caressed by any other man—." In fact, when they reach Liverpool Lucy is inspired to protect her "husband" from possible arrest by playing the role of his wife. This symbolic act links her with him and with real life.

"Between Two Shores" means literally a happening between New York and Liverpool, but the title also describes Lucy's state of suspense between repression and indulgence, between ignorance and experience. We might say she began to live at Liverpool. The Freudian critic will see here an ego torn between the id and the superego. Other readers will be reminded of such symbolic works as Conrad's "The Secret Sharer," James's "The Beast in the Jungle," or O'Neill's *The Hairy Ape.*

However, after reading *The Woman Within,* we can see that Miss Glasgow was actually dramatizing her spiritual withdrawal following the death of her mother in 1893. She loved her mother so deeply that she might actually feel widowed after such a loss. She had barely abandoned mourning in June, 1896, when, thanks to the generosity of her brother Arthur, who had become a successful engineer in London, she embarked for a summer in England. She confesses:

> Never before in my life had I felt so suffocated by melancholy as I felt when I sailed, alone, among strangers, to England. I know that I was in a cloud of nervous depression; but it was impossible for me to break through the restraint, or to be natural. . . . I had never looked worse in my life, and I knew that whatever charm I possessed was dimmed by the terror of not hearing strange voices, and of not understanding strange words that were said to me.[24]

Her story dramatizes clearly her need for and fear of emotional commitment. While here she stresses the rewards of such commitment, later she was to concentrate on the dangers.

Four stories constitute a "marriage group," and three of them preach a similar moral: in marriage the woman gives up everything, while the man gains himself a servant. Three husbands are depicted as selfish brutes, ranging from Stanley Kenton in **"Romance and Sally Byrd,"** a philanderer who deceives an innocent kindergarten teacher, to George Fleming, who includes both golf and adultery among his favorite recreations in **"The Difference,"** to Dr. John Estbridge in **"The Professional Instinct,"** who self-righteously decides to abandon his domineering wife. Since these particular stories were written just after Miss Glasgow's unsatisfactory engagement to Colonel Henry W. Anderson, a biographical excursion is tempting here. The self-sacrificing wives in these stories explain well enough why Ellen Glasgow never married. Elsewhere she has celebrated her independence in this way: "I have had much love and more romance than most women, and I have not had to stroke some man the right way to win my bread or the wrong way to win my freedom."[25]

"The Difference" and **"Romance and Sally Byrd"** present the double standard in marriage that irked Miss Glasgow so much. The patient wives endure their husbands' unfaithfulness as if there were no hope for a fairer relationship. Stanley Kenton's wife consoles his latest victim, Sally Byrd: "When your heart is really broken, it lies still and dead like mine. You can't imagine what a relief it is . . . to have your heart break at last." She sits darning a symbolic pair of Stanley's seven-dollar socks as she remarks, "Men are so careless about their things." Margaret Fleming in **"The Difference"** suffers an even worse fate. She loses both her pride in her husband and in herself when she learns, after a visit to his mistress, that he has never loved anybody but himself.

In **"The Professional Instinct"** Miss Glasgow ironically presents the same theme, this time from the point of view of the selfish husband. Dr. Estbridge, a psychoanalyst, is prepared to elope with Judith Campbell, a philosophy professor and author of *Marriage and Individuality,* but when he hears at the last minute of a chance at the chair in physiology at the state university, he leaves Judith waiting at the station. Judith, incidentally, has given up a chance at a college presidency in order to elope with Estbridge. The story fairly bristles with such obvious irony. Like George Fleming, Estbridge loves only his own reflection in women.

"Thinking Makes It So" catches Miss Glasgow in a rare sentimental mood about marriage. Here she describes a romance by correspondence between two middle-aged lovers who have been bruised and worn by life. They still have their dreams, however, and thinking makes them so. The distant echo of **"Only a Daisy"** can be heard here. It is unquestionably the weakest of the Glasgow stories, made up of leftovers from *Life and Gabriella.* Its only interest is biographical.

A more successful attempt to take a comic view of romance is **"The Artless Age,"** which describes a teenage courtship, or rather, two of them. This story is a symbol-hunter's paradise, because the Old-Fashioned Girl, Mary Louise Littleton, and the Modern Girl, Geraldine Plummer, are competing for the affection of the American Boy, Richard Askew. At a costume ball, Mary Louise goes as an angel, Geraldine as a devil. At the end of the story we learn that there is no such thing as an artless age; every age has its own arts. Mary Louise, although protected in a French convent and in the Blue Ridge Mountains, is just as artful as Geraldine, but her wiles are outmoded. The hopeless conflict is well demonstrated by the following dialogue. Mary Louise: "I am so fond of Ruskin." Geraldine: "What's a Ruskin? Do you make it with gin?"

Inevitably, Richard is trapped by the more aggressive Geraldine and led unprotesting to the altar. Poor Mary Louise is sacrificed to the allegory; she marries Geraldine's father, who is an archeologist!

The observant mothers, who play the part of a Greek chorus, deplore Geraldine's tactics, but admit that they are well suited to the modern world. Here and in two novels, *The Romantic Comedians* (1926) and *They Stooped to Folly* (1929), Miss Glasgow managed to take a comic view of the world in the 1920's, but her heart was not really in it. At any rate, in **"The Artless Age,"** her analysis of love has come full circle. In twenty-five years, Lucy Smith has been replaced by Geraldine Plummer.

VII

Two more stories focus on an abstract moral problem— what we now call mercy killing, or euthanasia. Two persons with no reason for living are put out of their misery with the assistance of their fellow men. Is this a crime? There are subtleties in each case which complicate the moral decision. In **"A Point in Morals"** an alienist is asked for a package of opium by a passenger on a train, who has botched his life and wants to commit suicide. The alienist, finally convinced by the young man's story that he has no reason for living and many reasons for dying, leaves the fatal package on the seat when he gets off the train.

Because she has effaced herself completely from the story by means of a dramatic framework, Miss Glasgow makes evaluation of the doctor's act very difficult. The story begins as a dialogue among the five characters around a dinner table on a ship: a journalist, a lawyer, an Englishman, a girl in black, and the doctor. The discussion turns to whether the saving of a human life might become positively immoral. At this point the alienist begins his story, into which he inserts the unhappy man's biography, making a story-within-a-story-within-a-story. The reaction of the audience gives us no clue as to an official interpretation. Each of the characters is ridiculed at some point. Perhaps Miss Glasgow had no stand here but merely wanted to embarrass all these sophisticated observers with a moral problem beyond the reach of science. If we assume that she disliked this alienist as much as those in the other stories, then the doctor must be labeled a monster. We should recall, however, that this is an early story, written before Miss Glasgow had rejected science in favor of philosophy.

An answer may be easier after we consider a parallel situation in the previously discussed **"Jordan's End."** Alan Jordan, incurably insane, dies mysteriously after an overdose of the opiate that the doctor-narrator has prescribed. The doctor knows that Jordan's wife must be to blame, but he cannot bring himself to question her. Jordan's death solves many problems and will cause none, so long as everyone remains silent. The doctor and Mrs. Jordan are described so sympathetically that one is tempted to condone this mercy killing.[26] Taken together, the two stories reflect Ellen Glasgow's early realization that the most serious human problems lie beyond the reach of science. This theme, too, links her with Poe and with the agrarian branch of the Southern literary tradition.

VIII

Two questions remain: what is the relationship of Ellen Glasgow's stories to her novels? And what is the artistic merit of the stories in themselves? The stories are both the causes and the effects of her other fiction. The four stories previously discussed in the "marriage group" may be recognized as pencil sketches for the three full-scale studies of love and marriage: *The Romantic Comedians, They Stooped to Folly,* and *The Sheltered Life.* In George Fleming, Stanley Kenton, and Dr. Estbridge, all fatuous, frustrated, middle-aged husbands, we see trial sketches for Judge Honeywell, Virginius Littlepage, George Birdsong, and even General Archbald, although it would be fairer to call Dr. Lakeby in **"Dare's Gift"** *his* prototype. On the female side, the romantic competition between Mary Louise Littleton and Geraldine Plummer in **"The Artless Age,"** between Margaret Fleming and Rose Morrison in **"The Difference,"** between Sally Byrd and Mrs. Kenton in **"Romance and Sally Byrd,"** and between Mrs. Estbridge and Judith Campbell in **"The Professional Instinct"** reveal simultaneously the male refusal to grow old gracefully and the female refusal to get along without men.

The conflict within as well as between the sexes is enacted on a larger scale in the novels, but with similar results. The conflicts between Annabel Upchurch and Amanda Lightfoot over Judge Honeywell in *The Romantic Comedians,* between Victoria Littlepage and Amy Dalrymple over Virginius Littlepage in *They Stooped to Folly,* and between Jenny Blair Archbald and Eva Birdsong over George Birdsong in *The Sheltered Life,* are all prepared for by romantic triangles of the same kind in the short stories. Mrs. Kenton is the first of many Glasgow women to celebrate the end of her need for sexual love, and, hence, for men. Later, in *Barren Ground,* Dorinda Oakley exults after repulsing Jason Greylock, "Oh, if the women who wanted love could only know the infinite relief of having love over!"[27] Then in *The Romantic Comedians* Edmonia Bredalbane horrifies her twin brother, Judge Honeywell, by asking, "After all the fuss that has been made about marriage, isn't there something more in it than this?"[28] Four husbands have not changed her opinion.

The most complex discussion of the marriage problem is in *The Sheltered Life.* There are no villains here; as in the short stories, there are only weak, selfish people. Jenny Blair and George Birdsong would rather die than bring pain to George's wife, Eva, but their innocent flirtation brings disaster to both of them. Several awkward encounters between Jenny Blair and Eva are anticipated by the climax of **"The Difference,"** where the wife and the "other woman" try to reach an understanding about a man not worth understanding. The exemplary women are held in their places only by a sense of duty; the exemplary men have preserved their status only accidentally. For example, only an accident prevented General Archbald from running off with a married woman in England, but the world knows him as a model husband.

The most substantial transfer of theme and setting from story to novel is from **"Jordan's End"** to *Barren Ground.*[29] The disintegration of Jordan's End prepares us for the deterioration of Five Oaks; there is a difference only in degree. The derangement of all the Jordans is matched by the decadence of all the male Greylocks and the madness of Geneva Greylock. Even the descriptions of the two houses are similar, although there is still hope for Five Oaks: "It was a fairly good house of its period, the brick building, with ivy-encrusted wings, which was preferred by the more prosperous class of Virginia farmers. The foundation of stone had been well laid; the brick walls were stout and solid, and though neglect and decay had overtaken it, the house still preserved, beneath its general air of deterioration, an underlying character of honesty and thrift."

The beginnings of **"Jordan's End"** and *Barren Ground* are almost interchangeable. A doctor in a buggy pulled by a mare approaches a ruined house at sunset in late autumn, after traveling over a mile of rutted track from the Old Stage Road, where a large, dead tree stands. His passenger in one story is Dorinda Oakley, in the other, Father Peterkin.

Judith Yardley Jordan embodies the qualities of both Dorinda Oakley and Geneva Ellegood Greylock. Like Geneva, she was a famous beauty from an adjoining farm before she married into a decadent family. Like Geneva, she drooped under the gloom of the place, but like Dorinda, she found the necessary iron vein when a bold stroke was necessary. Judith's husband, Alan Jordan, is the original of Jason Greylock. Both are the last limbs on a decaying family tree and both succumb to their inheritance.

It would not be too much to say that *Barren Ground* is a continuation of **"Jordan's End"** because Dorinda and Nathan Pedlar reclaim Five Oaks from a state similar to that of Jordan's End as visible proof that the vein of iron can prevail over the temptations of the flesh. In *Barren Ground* Miss Glasgow is celebrating the suppression of sex and of male tyranny. She was thus enabled to take a comic view of human relations in her next two novels; but it is hard to find much comedy in the "evasive idealism" of the "happiness hunters" because the attitudes she mocks are her own discarded ideas.

What makes **"Jordan's End"** and *Barren Ground* such impressive stories is that in both of them Miss Glasgow has tried to dissect the grandeur that was the South. Family pride, refusal to abandon agrarian ways, rutted absorption in the past, inbreeding, sensuality—all are dramatized through plot, character, and setting. **"Jordan's End"** is a tragedy, or the outline of one. *Barren Ground* converts tragic material into tragicomedy. Ironically, another salvation besides the famous iron vein is implicit in a striking scene from **"Jordan's End,"** but Miss Glasgow missed its significance. Two Negroes are sitting beside the fireplace in Alan Jordan's room as the doctor enters. "They had simple, kindly faces, these men; there was a primitive humanity in their features, which might have been modelled out of the dark earth of the fields . . . but the man in the winged chair neither lifted his head nor turned his eyes in our direction. He sat there, lost within the impenetrable wilderness of the insane. . . ."

The short stories not only influenced the novels but they occasionally show the effects of them. *Life and Gabriella* supplied not only the middle-aged romance in **"Thinking Makes It So,"** but the Richmond-to-New York setting of **"Romance and Sally Byrd."** Fiery old Colonel Dare in **"Dare's Gift"** has his original in General Battle from *The Voice of the People* (1900) and in Major Lightfoot from *The Battleground* (1902). The newspaper board meetings in *The Descendant* (1897) and the boarding-house arguments in *Phases of an Inferior Planet* (1898) are models for the dialogue with allegorical characters in **"A Point in Morals."** Even Miss Glasgow's experiment with first-person narration began with *The Romance of a Plain Man* (1909) rather than in the short stories.

But Ellen Glasgow's best stories are those which owe nothing to her novels. They are independent moral and philosophical analyses of the nature of reality and of man's relationship with his fellow man. **"A Point in Morals," "The Difference,"** and **"Jordan's End"** are not so daring today as they once were, but they are the products of a bold mind, and **"Jordan's End,"** at least, escapes being a period piece. The device of making ideas visible in the four "ghost" stories is psychologically sound, if not artistically successful.

It is unfortunate for the artistic stature of her short stories that Miss Glasgow did not continue writing them after 1924. Although she dated *Virginia* (1913) as her first mature work, it is generally agreed that her "major phase" began with *Barren Ground* (1925). This novel, together with *The Sheltered Life* (1932) and *Vein of Iron* (1935), remains unchallenged by anything she wrote in a shorter form. **"Jordan's End"** gives us a hint of what she might have done if she had taken the short story as seriously as she took the novel, if she had not been so obsessed with her "social history of Virginia."

From our perspective today, we can see that Ellen Glasgow kept maturing stylistically, but that her moral and social concepts solidified in the middle of the 1920's. The rebel of the nineties found herself the conservative of the twenties. Nevertheless, the advice of Walter Hines Page and her own iron vein kept her writing fiction even after she had lost faith in her readers, even when she knew she was celebrating lost values. For this she had earned her status as one of America's leading woman novelists.

But her twelve short stories prove that, contrary to what Miss Glasgow believed about herself, her literary talents were not confined to large-scale evolutionary studies. This prejudice she acquired from her early models. She was fundamentally a moralist rather than a historian. Her epigrams reveal a dazzling talent for condensation. Her inclination toward irony and paradox shows up particularly well in a small space. In short, she had all the equipment of a great short story writer, except a respect for the form.

Notes

[1] *Letters of Ellen Glasgow,* ed. Blair Rouse (New York, 1958), 25.

[2] Miss Glasgow began writing poetry before she tried either long or short fiction. The *Atlantic Monthly* published her first poem, "The Freeman," in December, 1897. The following year she had enough poems to make a small volume, which finally appeared in 1902. Although her publisher said that only nine copies were sold, she continued to write occasional verse until about 1920.

[3] One commendable exception is Sculley Bradley, Richard C. Beatty, and E. Hudson Long (eds.), *The American Tradition in Literature* (2 vols.; New York, 1956, 1961), which reprints "Jordan's End." The fullest discussion of the stories is in Frederick McDowell's *Ellen Glasgow and the Ironic Art of Fiction* (Madison, Wis., 1960), 144-45.

[4] Burton J. Hendrick, *The Training of an American: the Earlier Life and Letters of Walter H. Page, 1885-1913* (Boston, 1928), 336-37. The letter is dated December 8, 1897.

[5] The correspondence from Ellen Glasgow to Paul Revere Reynolds has been published, with notes, by James B. Colvert in *Studies in Bibliography,* XIV (1961), 177-96. The two quotations from her letters are taken from that article.

[6] Grant M. Overton, *The Women Who Make Our Novels* (New York, 1918), 32-33.

[7] Rouse (ed.), *Letters of Ellen Glasgow,* 69. This letter and the previous interview recorded by Overton contain no reference to her famous "social history of Virginia." The master plan does not seem to have occurred to her yet, verifying James Branch Cabell's contention that he suggested the idea to her in 1925.

[8] Overton, *The Women Who Make Our Novels,* 26.

[9] Wagenknecht, *Cavalcade of the American Novel* (New York, 1952), 270.

[10] Northrop Frye, *Anatomy of Criticism* (Princeton, 1957), 6.

[11] From a letter pasted in the Taylor copy of *The Shadowy Third* at Alderman Library, University of Virginia.

[12] Rouse (ed.), *Letters of Ellen Glasgow,* 70.

[13] Ellen Glasgow's talent for eliciting favorable reviews has been commented on frequently, especially by James Branch Cabell. Several of these reviews, in *The Bookman* and the Greensboro (N.C.) *Daily News,* for example, have an "inspired" look. They may be said to constitute an official interpretation.

[14] The Negro mammy who brought up Ellen Glasgow's mother was named Mammy Rhoda. There is also a Mammy Rhoda in *The Sheltered Life.*

[15] Clifton Fadiman (ed.), *I Believe* (New York, 1939), 93.

[16] *The Woman Within* (New York, 1954), 27.

[17] The degree of her precocity will probably never be established. A notation in the upper left hand corner of the MS in Miss Glasgow's handwriting says she was seven. In *The Woman Within,* she says she was seven. However, she told her friend, Sara Haardt (later Mrs. H. L. Mencken), that she was eight. One of Miss Glasgow's notebooks says that she was eight. "Only a Daisy" has never before been published. I have supplied essential punctuation and corrected a few obvious mistakes.

[18] Greensboro (N.C.) *Daily News,* December 16, 1923, p. 10. The author was probably Gerald W. Johnson, the associate editor, who knew Miss Glasgow through their mutual interest in *The Reviewer,* a Richmond little magazine, 1921-24.

[19] *The Bookman,* LVIII, No. 5 (January, 1924), 573.

[20] Rouse (ed.), *Letters of Ellen Glasgow,* 352.

[21] *The Woman Within,* 26.

[22] *A Certain Measure,* 70.

[23] R. P. Blackmur (ed.), *The Art of the Novel* (New York, 1953), 256.

[24] *The Woman Within,* 118.

[25] From "Miscellaneous Pungencies," Miss Glasgow's private collection of epigrams in the Alderman Library, University of Virginia.

[26] Professor William W. Kelly suggests that her interest in euthanasia may derive from the long illnesses which her mother and favorite sister Cary suffered before their deaths.

[27] *Barren Ground* (Sagamore Press edition, 1957), 238.

[28] *The Romantic Comedians* (New York, 1926), 36.

[29] The relationship between "Jordan's End" and *Barren Ground* has been pointed out to me by Professors William W. Kelly and Louis D. Rubin, Jr.

Julius Rowan Raper (essay date 1980)

SOURCE: "The Words for Invisible Things: The Short Stories (1916-1924)," in *From the Sunken Garden: The Fiction of Ellen Glasgow, 1916-1945,* Louisiana State University Press, 1980, pp. 53-78.

[*In the first sustained piece of criticism on Glasgow's short stories since Richard K. Meeker's 1963 essay, Raper argues that Glasgow's stories were written during a time of aesthetic and emotional crisis and reflect her search for a new language to express the workings of the deepest reaches of human consciousness.*]

The short stories of Ellen Glasgow have attracted little critical attention, aside from the introduction Richard K. Meeker wrote for **The Collected Stories of Ellen Glasgow.** This neglect exists in large part because the stories do not lend themselves to easy grouping. Glasgow scattered them through thirty years of her career. Some seem to be simple love stories while others are rather transparent ghost stories, and neither approach was typical of her career as a novelist. Nevertheless, there exists one group of stories that played a role in Glasgow's development of far greater significance than they have been accorded. Despite the popular magazine quality of several, this group constitutes a series of experiments in characterization—experiments that opened up essential new realms of behavior for the novelist's later exploration. From discoveries she made here emerged the psychological insight that distinguishes the novels she began to publish with *Barren Ground* in 1925 from those she wrote before 1916.

Of the thirteen short stories Glasgow wrote and preserved, all but three belong to the eight-year period (1916-1924) when her ability to create novels had reached its nadir. Although these ten stories are in general better executed than the novels of the period (*Life and Gabriella, The Builders,* and *One Man in His Time*), they reveal some of the same groping toward a new technique. Editor Meeker divides the ten into two large groups—the ghost stories and those that treat "the relationship between men and women."[1] But seen in relation to the three novels, all the stories are united by a single problem. The character who narrates **"The Past,"** the central story in the group, seems to speak as much for Glasgow as for herself when she says, "My mind has dealt so long with external details that I have almost forgotten the words that express invisible things" (134). Like the three novels, these stories belong to Glasgow's search, during her decade of emotional and aesthetic crisis, for a language to express the invisible world that had very nearly wrecked her life and career. What is most surprising about the stories compared with the novels is the variety and clarity of the languages Glasgow discovered. Whereas the three novels attempt to fill the "hole in reality" with abstractions, the stories reveal a wide range of literary modes that enable a fictionist to grasp and communicate the invisible world inside a character. They thus provide a record of the ways one well-established American novelist came to terms with the psychological knowledge that began, after 1910 or so, to be more and more the central concern of fiction.

Appropriately then, the protagonist of what is probably the earliest of the stories happens to be an "analytical psychologist," a label applied to schools using mainly the introspective method and chosen by Carl Jung to distinguish his type of psychoanalysis from that of Sigmund Freud. Glasgow's Dr. John Estbridge in **"The Professional Instinct"** has, in the last few weeks before the story begins, treated "several cases of changed personalities," "men and women, not far from his own age [he is 'nearing fifty'], who [have] undergone curious psychological . . . crises that brought quite new personalities." Although Dr. Estbridge recognizes "that he [is] in something of the same mental state at this moment," the story shows him powerless to understand, much less to heal, himself (240). Because the "coveted chair of physiology at the University" for which he worked for twenty years has just been awarded to his assistant, he is toying with the thought that he "should cut it for good and begin over again"— by accepting a position in Shanghai. His inner struggle becomes very much tied up with his view of women. As the narrator tells us in the two versions of the text: "Like most men [and all *changed to* according to the] analytical psychologists, he had identified his own dreams with the shape of a woman" (240). This reference is to the anima theory of analytical psychology—according to which men may project the unacknowledged feminine side of their personality, especially the emotions, creativity, and intuition, upon women, who then possess inordinate powers over the men—and explains the dynamics of the story. There are three such women in Estbridge's life.

The first is his wife, Tilly Pratt. Twenty years ago when Estbridge was a youthful reformer, he saw Tilly dressed as the Florentine reformer Savonarola in her graduating play. Even without the theatrical robes and cowl, she "impersonated the militant idealism" of his youth: "For he had loved Tilly, not for herself, but because she had shown him his own image" (240). Although he has kept his own body compact and muscular while his career moved from idealism to prosperity, Tilly has grown "florid, robust, and bristling with activity." Woman as ideal has become the smothering mother figure who ruffles a man's contentment, devours his time, and triumphantly checkmates him. She has become the embodiment of his prosperous failure, even before she tells him that his hold on the chair was sabotaged by her rich uncle at her suggestion (240-43).

The second woman, and the seeming opposite of Tilly, is Judith Campbell, with whom he has previously had a warm friendship. Judith enters the story just after he decides that he will take the post in Shanghai, a solution that brings a "vision of freedom" in which he sees ahead of him ten vigorous years filled with "adventure, accomplishment, and reward" (245). Suddenly Judith seems the perfect complement, if not embodiment, of his new vision. She is the professor of philosophy in a college for women; but she is soft, graceful, gentle, and yielding, "as feminine in appearance as any early Victorian heroine of fiction." For Estbridge she is instantly "everything that his wife was not and could never become"—"the complete and absolute perfection of womanhood." She is what he has wanted since his youth (239, 245-46). In opposition to his judgment, his old ideals, his teaching, and his habits, she is the other pole of his "will to live," an "air of spring" bringing him "the miracle of renewed youth" (246-47).

Most miraculous of all, she is, when he asks, willing to refuse an offer of the presidency of Hartwell College and meet him in one hour at Pennsylvania Station so that they may start cross-country for Shanghai—before they have time to compromise their futures. Estbridge sheds his past self like a husk; for once, destiny moves in obedience to his will (247-49).

Estbridge's third woman, his true mistress, is what he sees when he looks in the mirror: "*Science* had kept him young in return for the *passion he had lavished upon her*. In his bright blue eyes . . . still glistened the eternal enquiring spirit of youth" (242-43, italics added). Because young Tilly was, and Judith is, a mirror in which he sees himself, it is most likely the image of his science—Sophia, the ancients would have called her—he sees reflected in each. This possibility adds poignance to Estbridge's dilemma when, at the end, his assistant dies suddenly in a street accident and Estbridge himself feels "like a man who had died and been born anew"; in an instant he is "living with a different side of his nature—with other impulses." And yet he is a man torn asunder. If he embraces his true mistress (his science) directly, he must remain in New York with domineering Tilly, who will not divorce him (252). If he chooses Judith still waiting for him at the station, he will have only an indirect grasp of his deepest love—what he wants more than he wants any woman, as an old friend Jim Hoadly tells him (252). Speaking as though he were the voice of Estbridge's better judgment, Hoadly underlines the story's theme when he points out, "The only thing you ever loved in any woman was your own reflection" (251). The story ends with the clock ticking slowly on, while Estbridge stands "transfixed, bewildered, brooding," unable to decide between his two selves, between the "absolute perfection" of Judith and the fulfillment of his intellectual ambition. But while Estbridge stews, Glasgow steers the reader to a position of safety by giving us an ironist to identify with. Hoadly, with "the smile of some inscrutable image of wisdom," goads his friend: "It would be a pity to miss that train, wouldn't it?" (253).

Glasgow chose to withhold **"The Professional Instinct"** from publication, perhaps because the reversals, although appropriate to the psychology she sets up, are not appropriate to "realism of the probable and representative," which was the literary mode in which she worked prior to 1916. Or perhaps she withheld the story because it is too much a psychological essay; it too plainly sets forth the salient characteristics of the theory of behavior she was developing. When Hoadly says, "You aren't the first analytical psychologist who has identified the world with himself," he is giving too much away about the way individuals, according to Jungian psychology and more and more in Glasgow's fiction, impose masks of themselves upon the people they know best (251). Perhaps too she was not certain yet how she felt about the theory of psychological homeostasis the story hints she is moving toward: homeostasis, because Estbridge's psyche seems to possess a capacity for restoring its own equilibrium by creating phantasies to compensate for the prosperous failure he has become with Tilly Pratt. Glasgow seems of a divided mind, as she was with Gabriella Carr, whether such phantasies are illusions bred of male vanity or calls to renewed psychic health. Later short stories will throw more light upon these alternatives.

At any rate, the projection of unrecognized dimensions of the self and the spontaneity of compensatory phantasies are both central to analytical or Jungian psychology. Their concurrence in this early story provides a perspective we need to understand Glasgow's later assessment of the effect Jung and Freud had on the modern novel. In her autobiography she wrote:

> It is true that the novel, as a *living force,* if not as a work of art, owes an *incalculable debt* to what we call, mistakenly, the new psychology, to Freud, in his earlier interpretations, and *more truly, I think, to Jung.* These men are to be judged by their own work, not by the excesses of a secondary influence. For my part, though I was never a disciple, I was among the *first, in the South,* to perceive the invigorating effect of this approach to experience. That the recoil went too far does not dishonor its leaders, for it is a law of our nature that every dynamic recoil should spring too far backward. Moderation has never yet engineered an explosion, and it requires an explosion to overturn a mountain of prejudice.[2]

Interestingly, she both stresses Jung and uses his theory of *enantiodromia,* by which things turn into their opposites, to describe the excesses of the movement, as though Jung represented the moderation she preferred. Her claim, that she was "among the first, in the South," to recognize their value, is ambiguous; the books by Freud in her library were published in 1913 and 1914, but those by Jung go back no further than 1936 and 1939.[3] Yet, there exists in *The Wheel of Life* (1906) a very strong parallel to Jung's theory of masks and personality change, though 1906 was probably too early for anyone in America who did not read German to know Jung, unless he or she had associates who kept up on new work in the field. Because *The Wheel of Life* is heavily autobiographic, it is likely that Glasgow's introspection (supported by passages in Carpenter's *Art of Creation* and Maeterlinck's *Wisdom and Destiny*) had led her toward the Jungian position even before she knew of analytical psychology. But her understanding lacked objectivity: in rejecting the phase of her own life described in *The Wheel of Life,* she failed in 1906 to appreciate what she had discovered about her own and, according to Jung, everyman's personality development.

By 1916, if not earlier, she did know someone who read German; had studied in Heidelberg, Vienna, and Munich; and probably kept up with work in the field. The nature and extent of her relationship with Dr. Pearce Bailey of New York are far from clear; he was definitely her suitor, probably her lover and doctor combined. He was also her literary collaborator, at least for the one story **"The Professional Instinct."** His letter to her written March 8, 1916, contains these suggestions: "It seems to me that Estbridge's review of his life should follow the scene with Tilly. Won't you write the scene right in & get it back to me before Wednesday. I think you might go right on from where I stop [illegible]. . . . Have given no thought to the

other stories—want to keep the characters of this one clear in my mind. You will know [illegible] that what I send you is merely dictated & you are free to cut it up [?] or do away with it altogether as you please."[4] The possibilities this note raises are intriguing. Is the story so much the product of Bailey's mind that Glasgow did not feel she could publish it under her own name? Probably not—she did not follow his advice. Is the story part of their affair? Is it Glasgow's reply to the suit of a man who loved her and who, parallel to Estbridge, had been adjunct professor of neurology at Columbia from 1906 to 1910 and cofounder in 1909 of the Neurological Institute of New York? Perhaps—but Bailey's own wife had been dead since about 1912. Is it then Glasgow's view of what had happened in an earlier phase of their relationship? Was it too personal and transparent to publish? Possibly.

The note from Bailey gives clearer answers to another group of questions. It shows that the story of Estbridge was begun by March, 1916, and that this tale belongs with the earliest of the stories included in *The Shadowy Third and Other Stories.* It implies that Bailey would eventually give some thought "to the other stories" Glasgow had underway in 1916—"The Shadowy Third," "Thinking Makes It So," and possibly "Dare's Gift," all three to be in print by March, 1917. It also proves that we should not be surprised if we discover elements of a sophisticated psychological structure beneath the comic or gothic surfaces of any of Glasgow's fictions written around or after March, 1916; for she had by then made solid contact with analytical psychology and, with Bailey's help, had begun to add professional, presumably objective, insight to her own more valuable introspections and intuitions.

All the short stories reflect this new direction. The ghost stories, which seem a little opaque but are probably simpler than the stories of "men and women," will become clearer if we look first at the latter group. Each of these adds subtlety to the psychological discoveries of the prototypic Estbridge pattern.

"Thinking Makes It So" has been dismissed as a childish "example of wishfulfillment" by editor Meeker because the protagonist of this Cinderella phantasy metamorphoses in her forty-third year from a tired, faded, old-fashioned librarian into a woman who is brave, strong, pure, and beautiful—changes apparently because a man she has never met, a railroad builder in far-off Colorado, thinks of her this new way. Meeker's interpretation overlooks the "fairy godmother" of the tale—the process of psychological homeostasis that seeks to balance Margaret French's personality. She is "worn and repressed and overworked" because she has allowed herself to be aged by a "habit of self-effacement": in a "family of commonplace beauties" someone had to be plain and work hard. Margaret, never pretty or young, *chose* the role of the female martyr-saint, suppressed her own drives in the interest of the female selfishness of her sister and nieces, dressed in "colorless and wan and monotonous" clothes, and gave up her poetry to support the others by writing "silly stories" (73-75). The beautiful woman in flaming rose whom the railroad builder John Brown, like Estbridge, dreams into being is partly the product of Brown's Colorado isolation—that is, his projected need for the feminine—but she is also the shadow side of Margaret's personality, the suppressed beauty and energy and youth Margaret distilled into her early poems. In the poems Brown has seen the unconscious half of her which she doesn't believe exists. Even after she chooses this new self and sees someone with "shining eyes," "strangely young and innocent," in her mirror, she remains too critical to accept her own revolt; she considers her choice a lie (78, 81, 82). The chorus figures chant that change is unnatural; the Bible claims, "You can't make yourself over by taking thought" (84). Only one philosophical niece insists that nature has a "way of equalizing things," of "trying not to let you be cheated." The niece thereby confirms Margaret in the contact she has made with "the wealth" of her own nature, "some inexhaustible source of hope and joy," "the very essence of life" she feels in her veins, the woman whom Brown's thought has created (83, 85). In the end Brown's phantasy is transformed into a reality, not because Glasgow has ceased to be critical of evasive idealism, but because she has begun to see that, if imagination is rooted in psychic need, surface reality has no right to tyrannize phantasy. Here there is no ironist for the reader to identify with. Consequently, we are asked to expand our view of reality to allow for abrupt personality changes in which shadow selves come suddenly to the surface.

Glasgow's interest in such dynamics of the personality in part explains why she does better when she deals with the doubleness of adultery than with the single-mindedness of young love, for her married characters generally have suppressed great parts of themselves. In **"The Difference,"** the next of the nonghost stories although it was published six years after the account of Margaret French, Glasgow focuses upon the split within Margaret Fleming, whose conflict chiefly reflects the pull toward opposites in her husband, George. When, after twenty years of happy marriage, Margaret receives a letter from Rose Morrison announcing that she, Rose, is George's mistress, the shock brings with it the strange power of repressed truth suddenly revealed. Margaret feels that "on the surface of her life nothing had changed," but that in "the real Margaret, the vital part of her . . . hidden far away in that deep place where the seeds of mysterious impulses and formless desires lie buried . . . there were unexpressed longings which had never taken shape even in her imagination," "secrets . . . she had never acknowledged in her own thoughts" (167). She begins to think that Rose does the things with her husband that she herself has become too old and "Victorian" to do.

Margaret sees Rose and herself as opposites in a disjunction, of questionable validity, which divides women into those men admire and those men love, women of spirit—herself—and women of "raw flesh"—Rose—Victorian women and modern women (169, 174, 176). When she meets her opposite, she is blinded by "beauty like a lamp." Even when she decides it is no more than the blaze given off by the burning of dead leaves—which she had previously associated with parts of her own life—she is still struck by the security, competence, candor, infallible self-

esteem, and freedom from shame that Rose's youth gives her (173). Rather than embrace her opposite and thereby transform her own life, as well as George's, she retreats to the serene spiritual haven of a role she knows better, the martyred wife who sacrifices herself for her husband's freedom and happiness (177). Even so, Rose has penetrated Margaret's traditional and sternly moral mind enough for the latter to gain some sense that George is "larger, wilder, more adventurous in imagination, than she had dreamed," possessed of "some secret garden of romance where she had never entered" (178). She also recognizes that behind "the marionette" George sees when he looks at her there is her real self. Though silent, the latter longs to tell him that she too is "a creature of romance, of adventure," capable of giving him in marriage "all he sought elsewhere" (180). Despite her timid silence about his longed-for union of opposites, she is irked with George when he rejects her own righteous self-sacrifice by characterizing Rose as a mere "recreation," a girl young enough to be his daughter (181, 182). She finds her tie to Rose, not in the enriching union of opposite traits, but in shared, narrowing qualities: "the bond of woman's immemorial disillusionment" (183). Both women remain mere reflections of a Western man's neurotic split between love and desire. Margaret might have healed this neurosis (which Freud called "The Most Prevalent Form of Degradation in Erotic Life"[5]) if she had insisted upon her own wholeness. Because **"The Difference"** lacks the ironic perspective of **"The Professional Instinct"** and the comic vision of unity and health of **"Thinking Makes It So,"** its tone is chiefly pathetic, if vaguely amusing; its perspective, that of flat realism.

Published in the same year, **"The Artless Age"** shows how a similar view of personalities that are only partially developed can be turned to satiric capital. The contrast here is between Mary Louise Littleton, a "nice girl" who wears the "Victorian aura" although she is just twenty, and Geraldine Plummer, a "modern young girl" who paints her face like a geisha and bobs her hair (185). The older characters have a sense that some sort of synthesis of the two would be desirable; they find each of the extremes as designing and selfish as all youth and figure it "would be good for Geraldine if they could be thrown together" (195, 199). The want of this synthesis produces much of the humor: one-sidedness turns even the virtue of Mary Louise into a vice. These one-dimensional personalities evoke the same response as the character called the "vice" in Roman comedy: we laugh at such divisions of the self to make ourselves whole. We also laugh, with relief, to learn that neither Mary Louise nor Geraldine is as one-sided as she appears: angelic Mary Louise has her duplicities and devilish Geraldine her Victorian female arts. The male characters reveal a similar split between surface and real selves. Richard Askew, a "nice boy" so flawlessly handsome he appears unreal, chooses Geraldine's element of surprise over Mary Louise's static perfection. And Geraldine's father, a "faithful widower" for twenty years, falls, like a dirty old man, for Mary Louise, who is literally young enough to be his daughter. In each of the four characters, the change in conduct brings laughter because it comes as a surprising sign of health.

All the stories discussed thus far share a shortcoming common to much psychological fiction: they are mere fragments. Each either rips the mask off a character or takes a core sample of a character's buried life. They give no hint how such moments of insight might be structured into a full-length novel. If Glasgow had been able to do no more than describe thwarted individuals or tell tales of characters who have brief but revealing adventures, she might have been forced to create catalogs of grotesques like Sherwood Anderson or books of fragments like the novels Thomas Wolfe wrote after *Look Homeward, Angel.* And she probably would have done so without the brilliance of these two and certainly without Faulkner's genius for collage and montage. But she was better trained than any of these in two traditions of the novel: the realist novel of James in which an innocent protagonist becomes lost in a thick web of self-deception only to have his illusions destroyed in a moment of tragic self-discovery and the "evolutionary" novel that traces "the process of cause and effect" and thereby explores the source of the innocence that traps the protagonist in Jamesian realism.[6]

"Romance and Sally Byrd," the last of the stories Glasgow published, provides a bridge from the story as personality exposure to the novel of personality evolution. It does so by combining the psychological theory of the earlier stories with the self-deception and disillusionment of such earlier novels as *Virginia.* But a change has occurred since *Virginia,* for Glasgow now has a different appreciation of the psychological origins of phantasies: she no longer regards them as "mistakes" but as signs pointing the way to health. Because phantasies are necessary and compensatory, they continue to occur, even when "corrected" by reality, until the phantasy maker achieves a more viable compromise between inner and external reality—or resigns himself to defeat. This structure extends the psychological probe of the buried self as well as the Jamesian pattern.

The first quarter of **"Romance and Sally Byrd"** parallels **"Thinking Makes It So."** Sally Byrd's life has suddenly begun to repeat her imagination; there is a name singing "in her mind, as if a thrush were imprisoned there and could not get out" (217, 219). It is the name of Stanley Kenton, whom she met three weeks before by one of those strange chances that occur as though "a beneficent Providence" had intervened "in the chaos of circumstances" (217-18). She has begun to contrast the "fairy ring" of his name in her thought with the "dreary round" of her life before. His name adds the expectation of "something delightful" about to happen where only drabness and poverty and monotony—teaching, eating, caring for her joyless grandparents—had been (217). Bred out of this emptiness, her first phantasy leads her to a sense of community in the joy of living. But it also causes her to pity her family for not escaping, like her, into freedom (220). This illusion collapses when magical Stanley announces he is married—estranged from his wife, but still married. "I thought you knew," he adds, before offering an arrangement slightly different from that Sally had counted on. Although she grows hysterical—the situation suddenly strikes her as absurd—and longs to accept his alternate

offer, her moral instinct survives the shock (222-24). Her second phantasy is that she will let him go but never forget him: she converts this "hopeless love" into a "secret garden" she enters simply by shutting her eyes (225-26). The third phantasy grows out of the second when she hears that Stanley has been injured in an accident and hurries to New York from Richmond because she feels he needs her desperately: a "picture of herself leading Stanley along a crowded street" flashes in her mind as though cast "on a blank white sheet by a magic lantern" (227-28). The light of illusions two and three goes out when Sally finds Stanley's wife already there to nurse him. The fourth phantasy occurs on the train home and takes the person of a "young man with blue eyes," who lives only a few blocks from her house and who happens to be much better looking and much younger than Stanley. He leaves her in the day coach with her fifth phantasy, that—like Stanley's wife, who gave her a lecture on the relief of having your heart break at last and thereby finishing with love—she has finished with romance forever. She sees her "future as a gray, deserted road strewn wth dead leaves." Still there is the "indestructible illusion" that she might any day meet the young man with blue eyes again. Although at the end she enters her house with "withered leaves on the front porch," dramatic irony offsets the imagery; for her final words ("Never again!") are the illusory ones that began the story (236-38). Written during the same period as *Barren Ground,* this story offers in Sally Byrd a preview of the psyche of young, romantic Dorinda Oakley. Perhaps both heroines are by-products of Glasgow's own excursion into triangular love.

After we have grown used to finding the unconscious content of one character projected upon another, in Glasgow's stories of men and women, we should have no difficulty understanding a similar process when we find it in the ghost stories; for the supernatural has been employed as a language for the invisible things of the psyche at least since Book I of *The Iliad.* There Athena, goddess of wisdom, descends to stay the hand of Achilles and thereby keep him from hacking Agamemnon to pieces. Editor Meeker says that Glasgow's ghosts "are only objective correlatives" for an idea, "the necessity and difficulty of believing in the intangible" (14). To put the problem differently, Freud used the mechanics of the nineteenth century for metaphor to reify the intangible needs and fears of man in the "compartments" of the psyche (id, ego, superego); he also described the "energy flow" between these inner "reservoirs." Literature of the supernatural uses the figurative language of religion and superstition to reify the same intangible processes, but in an external form.

Two recent developments may have given ghost stories a type of validity they lacked in Glasgow's generation. Today we know enough about the effects chemical alterations have on consciousness to acknowledge that sane people may sometimes *see things that are not there,* and see them as substantially as though they were there—even when these phenomena exist *only* as chemical changes in the brain. We also know that strong emotions like fear, hatred, guilt, and desire involve significant chemical changes throughout the body—sufficient to color, perhaps even to alter, what we see. This is not to say that Glasgow's ghosts are to be dismissed immediately as figments of disturbed imaginations; to the contrary, the attitude toward the supernatural in these stories covers the full range from the belief of the truly *marvelous,* through the ambiguity of the *fantastic,* to the *uncanny* and merely *exceptional.*[7] Such variety is possible because the narrator in each of the stories is also a character, and the degree of reliability of each narrator determines the reader's response to the supernatural element.

The first-person narrator of **"The Shadowy Third,"** a nurse from Richmond named Margaret Randolph, is—like Margaret French, Sally Byrd, and Caroline Meade (of *The Builders*)—extremely impressionable and receptive to calls to adventure beyond her normal reality. She thinks she is "too emotional." A critical reader might call her romantically hysterical: she accepts her call to care for Dr. Maradick's wife as though it were the "imperative summons" of her "destiny." She is also fey: she frequently knows her fate with a kind of foreknowledge she insists is "beyond any doubt." Endowed with the sympathy and imagination of a novelist, she cannot help putting herself into cases (52-54). Most important, she is telling the story in the past tense—*after* she has been somehow involved in the mysterious death of Dr. Maradick, a man she once hero-worshiped. But because she does not mention this involvement until the penultimate paragraph, we spend the story trying to outwit the narrator (and the author) concerning the motive and conditions for her seeing the ghost of Dr. Maradick's daughter Dorothea.

The first apparition follows a strong suggestion from a superstitious servant and, like the first three appearances, involves some tricky lighting (56, 58, 67). Even Margaret says that she eventually began to persuade herself "that the little figure had been an optical illusion," despite the fact that Mrs. Maradick also sees Dorothea (68). But then Mrs. Maradick seems even more unreliable than Margaret: she is suffering from the fear that Maradick killed Dorothea to get his hands on the large trust her first husband had set up for Dorothea, an arrangement bypassing Mrs. Maradick unless their daughter should die (55). Margaret's doubts about the ghost (after Mrs. Maradick dies in an asylum) tend to reestablish her credibility just before she reports the fourth appearance of the girl, this time skipping rope. Although this apparition is "as clear as day," it comes hard upon the news that Dr. Maradick, now in possession of all his wife's money, is soon to marry again—an announcement that leaves the narrator nervous, "shaken by the suddenness" of his plans. The reader also knows what she doesn't admit: that she now hates the doctor, as much for his choosing a woman other than herself as for whatever he did to Mrs. Maradick. The ghost of Dorothea, especially Margaret's insistence that she saw a child's jump rope on the stairs just before the doctor fell to his death, becomes the phantasy through which Margaret deals with her guilt. The implication is not necessarily that she planned and executed his death, but that she *feels she did* because she wanted revenge and she startled him, enough to cause him to stumble, by

suddenly flipping on the light—to warn him, she tells herself and the reader (71). That Mrs. Maradick may also have had guilt to hide from herself is at least implied by the fact that her first husband chose to bypass her with the trust: was it simply to avoid inheritance tax? Otherwise, for Mrs. Maradick, Dorothea reflects the young goodness the former lost when she realized she had married the sort of doctor all the nurses and patients fall in love with (53-54, 57). In any case, Margaret insists on the ghost to the end, and the reader can choose either the psychological or the marvelous interpretation, an ambiguity that marks literature of the phantastic.[8]

"Dare's Gift," despite the narrator's heavy hints of the incredible and the supernatural, is really little more than uncanny or exceptional, and the choice depends upon how superstitious the reader may be about the effects of place. Dare's Gift is one of those James River plantations like Shirley or Berkeley or Westover but less well-known because it has mainly been associated with treacheries since its first owner betrayed Nathaniel Bacon to Governor Berkeley. Rather than a visible ghost, there is some "spirit of the place" associated with the "thought of the house" and with "the psychic force of its memories," a power that proves too strong for both the neurotic and phlegmatic temperaments of persons who inhabit the place. In the Civil War, Lucy Dare betrayed her Yankee fiancé to Confederate soldiers. More recently, the male private secretary of one owner ran off with embezzled funds, and a caretaker absconded with his own wife's sister (92, 94). The wife of the present owner goes to the opposition with some business secrets her husband, a corporation lawyer, has stumbled across, a scandal that involves the railroad line her husband is employed to defend against charges of illegal rebates (99-101).

Only the Lucy Dare and railroad episodes are developed. The lawyer is the narrator; he is told the tale of Lucy Dare by a long-winded local doctor who had his leg shot off in the Civil War. The relative morality of the two betrayals receives no attention. The emphasis falls instead upon the psychological origins. The Lucy Dare episode becomes an explanation for the southern "sense of place," especially the excessive loyalty and evasive idealism of the region. The Dares, the old doctor claims, had the extreme enthusiasm for the war cause of non-combatants; with no outlet for passion except "thought," they made the idea of the Confederacy into a dream or ideal that ruled them. Lucy had always appeared cold to the men she loved, but during the war her physically starved brain became inflamed, obsessed with the southern cause. Faith in the Lost Cause began as an illusion to compensate for defeat. It was a dangerous illusion, for with Richmond ready to fall in any case, Lucy sacrificed her fiancé to save the Cause (106-109).

Mrs. Beckwith, the lawyer's wife, presents several parallels to Lucy. Her outspoken response to the railroad scandal is compensatory: for ten harmonious years she has been a silent, acquiescent wife, used by her husband as a sounding board for his ideas (95). Probably as a result of this repression, she had the nervous breakdown that led Beckwith to purchase Dare's Gift for a retreat. Her neurosis makes her, like Lucy, susceptible to the isolation of the place, especially to the noises of the country at night. She grows bitter when Beckwith leaves her there to pursue his work in Washington; and after he tells her the details of the scandal, she likely hears the same voices he heard urging him "to something—somewhere—" (99-101). Beckwith's insistence that his wife's behavior was caused by the "invincible spirit of darkness" that hovers about Dare's Gift is simply his way of projecting the guilt he feels for each of her breakdowns. He lacks the objectivity the old doctor brought to the case of Lucy Dare. Were he to achieve that objectivity, he would be forced to reclaim the responsibility he reads into the spirit of the place.

Published in 1920 and the central story in the group, **"The Past"** runs the risk of turning into an allegory—one, as the title implies, about the rather Bergsonian persistence of the spirit of the past—for it is here that Glasgow spells out her ideas about "words that express invisible things" (134). Ghosts are part of the forgotten language. The ghost of the first Mrs. Vanderbridge is simply (the second Mrs. V. tells us) the thought in her husband's mind of his first wife; it is, specifically, his guilt because he married her when she was too young and she died in the first year of the marriage, eight months pregnant (132-33). But beneath this seemingly transparent surface, there are several hidden and therefore intriguing currents. First, Mr. Vanderbridge's subjective reality has become visible without his knowing it: nearly everyone in the story sees the first Mrs. V. sitting with them as they eat. In other words, her ghost embodies a separate fear or other meaning for each person who sees her. She is Mr. V.'s guilt. But because his obsession is destroying not only his mind and health but his second marriage and the health of his new wife—they are all "drugged" by the past—the ghost, selfish and childish, is a visible sign that the new wife feels she may be inadequate to replace the first wife in her husband's affections. The narrator, Miss Wrenn, the present Mrs. V.'s secretary, sees the ghost simply because she is *sympatico*: she comes from Mrs. V.'s background, which gives her the power to step inside the phantastical scenario of the household. The letters Miss Wrenn discovers, written to the first Mrs. V. by her lover *after* her marriage, are suggestive in light of the first wife's early and troubled pregnancy. But they are an effective solution only because they lay the ghost for Mrs. V. by restoring her sense of adequacy compared with the idealized first wife. And her new superiority to the past will better enable her in the future to lay the spirit for her husband. The overt psychologizing reduces the marvelous in this story to the merely uncanny.

The same lack of ambiguity can be charged against the last of the ghost stories, **"Whispering Leaves"** (1923), for its ghost is obviously an embodiment of the maternal instinct. The story is interesting, however, on two counts. First, it is an unexpected story to come from the pen of a woman who insisted the maternal instinct had been left out of her—unless we recognize that the supernatural has traditionally been a mode by which the artist evades censorship, that of his (or her) own psyche as well as of

society.[9] The ghost of the black woman is obviously a substitute mother created by seven-year-old Pell to fill the gap in his emotional life. Not only are his mother and the real Mammy Rhody dead, but Pell is also estranged from his stepmother. He has become a grotesque: birdlike, "ugly and pinched," a nervous, sensitive child with an excitable imagination, though a child not totally lacking in charm (144, 151). Meeker suggests that Pell is a fictional mask of Glasgow's own lonely childhood (10).

Rhody is also visible to Miss Effie, the narrator, *who never saw her alive.* Miss Effie finds "her serene leaf-brown face strangely attractive, almost, oddly enough," she thinks, "as if her mysterious black eyes . . . had penetrated to some secret chamber of my memory. . . . I felt as if I had known her all my life, particularly in some half-forgotten childhood which haunted me like a dream. . . . Stranger still, I felt not only that she recognized me, but that she possessed some secret which she wished to confide to me, that she was charged with a profoundly significant message which, sooner or later, she would find an opportunity to deliver" (147). This language is as close to that of dreams as to the rhetoric of the supernatural, especially since Effie seems to be describing an image from her racial memory—Rhody nursed her mother and grandmother—a figure of the sort that might appear in an especially moving dream.

The second element of special interest is the texture that the setting and the symbols create. Rhody, whose name means *rose* is consistently associated with trees, flowering shrubs, and underbrush in a way which suggests to the animistic mind that, like the birds she tames, she might be a fleeting spirit dwelling in trees (144, 150, 151, 157, 159). But Rhody has a special affinity for the "sunken garden," a flowery space of old fruit trees and shrubs walled off by banks of honey-suckle. Even in this story—where the setting is supposed to appear as though it were part "of a universe painted on air"—the sunken garden seems exceedingly dreamlike (142, 150). Just before the scene in this garden, Effie stands before a "greenish mirror," which reflects her "features in a fog"; her image floats there "like a leaf in a lily pond." Then a "provocative fragrance, the aroma of vanished springs," draws her to the garden, where the moisture of the "low ground by the river . . . released the scents of a hundred springs." "Never," she says, "until that moment had I known what the rapture of smell could be. And the starry profusion of the narcissi! From bank to bank of honeysuckle the garden looked as if the Milky Way had fallen over it and been caught in the high grass" (150). Here in the "enchanted silence" she hears a bell, then sees a light flashing from the house, before she turns to see "the old negress . . . standing motionless under the boughs of a peartree," with the "inarticulate appeal" in her eyes, speaking "in some inaudible language which I did not yet understand" of a message "which, sooner or later, she would find a way to deliver" (150). The mirror and the narcissi offer strong evidence that Rhody's inaudible language is the forgotten one, the word that, when we remember it, carries us past the "primitive wooden stile" to the sunken garden of the mind. In other words, Rhody's ghost here speaks for the deep maternal and fertile and forbidden core of Effie's being. Just how forbidden to Effie—even to her creator—may be suggested by Rhody's race. As the story progresses, Rhody turns out to be a projection of Effie's maternal concern for Pell; and Rhody's secret message, as Pell delivers it, happens to be, "Mammy says you must take me with you when you go away" (160, 163).

Thus far Rhody has been shown to express an obvious need in Pell for maternal "sympathy and understanding" and a secret need in Effie to give him a mother's care (154). If we follow the image clusters of the story, they lead us to a parallel interpenetration of the three identities—Rhody, Pell, and Effie. As we saw, Effie's image in the mirror is like a leaf, but leaves in turn are associated by Effie with birds: "Dreamlike, too, were my own sensations. . . . Feathery branches edged with brighter green brushed my cheeks like the wings of a bird; and though I knew it must be only my fancy, I seemed to hear a hundred jubilant notes in the enchanted gloom of the trees" (147). Birds are compared to ghosts tamed by Rhody and thus seem an avatar or attribute of Rhody; at one point an apparition of Rhody actually dissolves into a scarlet tanager and an ancient crepe myrtle—spirit and body (146, 157). Pell's hand is said to be "like a bird's claw" (152). The three characters thus seem to come together in the leaf and bird imagery. In other stories by Glasgow, especially **"The Difference,"** another of the 1923 stories, leaves represent the past phases of the central character's life (165). As an archetype of dreams and myth, the bird often is an image of spiritual transformation in its flight from the earth to the heavens.

With all these factors taken into account, especially the tightly knit identification of the three main characters, **"Whispering Leaves"** suggests an exceedingly creative and healthy dream by someone—presumably the narrator Effie, otherwise the author—who set out in her phantasy life to rescue the helpless and deprived child in herself from the indifferent stepmother and complacent father to unite that child with the eternally maternal potential of the self. The final image of Effie, now in Rhody's role, taking little Pell—who has just been rescued by a shadowy Rhody from an "old storeroom, which was never opened"—in her arms and holding him there "safe and unharmed" indicates that the integration of the parts of the self has succeeded (163). The fire that destroys **"Whispering Leaves"** suggests that the old self—if not the whole social order—has been left behind.

"Jordan's End" may be another story about setting the self free of its past. Although there is no ghost in the story, it is the most ghostly Glasgow wrote. It could be argued that in **"Whispering Leaves"** Glasgow discovered that the language of dreams provides a more exact tool for expressing invisible things than does the rhetoric of the supernatural, for **"Jordan's End"** is also the most dream-like of the group. As in **"Whispering Leaves,"** the landscape suggests a dream journey, this time through the twilight of a deep tunnel in the November woods to a decaying house—haunted, not by ghosts, but by figures from the past, fates and madmen. There seems to be even

more condensation of identities than in **"Leaves."** This effect is achieved in part by the shadowy quality of the characterization (there is, for example, very little evidence that the narrator is male) and in part by a pairing of characters into sharp alternatives: the narrator is paired, as the new doctor, with Carstairs, the old one; his guide, old man Peterkin, is set off against Peterkin's son Tony; old Mr. Timothy Jordan is mentioned in contrast to his nine-year-old grandson (204-205). Most important, Judith and Alan Jordan are joined, not only by their marriage, but as antithetical parts of a whole. She is tall and thin, with flesh that seems luminous, "as if an inward light pierced the transparent substance"; her beauty is "not of earth, but of triumphant *spirit*"—"perfection" (207). Though "lost within the impenetrable wilderness of the insane," Alan still possesses "the dignity of mere *physical* perfection"; he is at least six feet three, with blue eyes and hair the "color of ripe wheat" (211, italics added). Already in **"Whispering Leaves,"** Glasgow had assigned two sets of twins to little Pell's stepmother but then did not develop that dream motif as she does here (151). Although the logic of day-to-day reality can account for many of the elements in **"Jordan's End,"** only dream logic can account for the meaning concentrated in these pairings of young and old, of spirit and body, and ultimately of the past and the future. In dreams such opposites are halves of a single whole.

Along the same line, all the archetypes of the classic story of the decay of southern culture, from "The Fall of the House of Usher" to *Absalom, Absalom!,* are compacted in this short piece: the big house, the incest, the madness, the burial of the "living dead" (here in padded cells). In addition, the focus falls upon euthanasia, a theme that runs like an unmentionable current through much important writing in the South. It is suggested, for example, by the ending of *Absalom* and by Webber's view of the web of his Joyner past in *The Web and the Rock*; and it is the theme that ties Ike McCaslin's education, in helping to kill the beloved Ben, to his lifework, the dismantling of a cultural order his grandfather created. Since the dream logic of **"Jordan's End"** suggests that, as in **"Whispering Leaves,"** all the characters are attributes of the narrator, it may well be that these stories of euthanasia or beneficent death—a death from which the narrator usually rides away—are actually tales of attempted rescue: the narrator dreams his or her way to the core of his psyche, identifies what is still vital there, rescues it, and allows the dead past to be finally dead. In this case, Judith and Alan are paired at the vital core, but Judith is the viable half that must be delivered. The body has grown unhealthy; it is tainted by its heritage. In addition, the power of the body has become an unspecified threat to the spirit: "Last night something happened. Something happened," Judith repeats. And later: "He is very strong." Again: "We keep two field hands in the room day and night." Finally, when the narrator sees one of the three old crones crocheting an infant's sacque, Judith says, "You know now?" (209-11). Although the narrator answers affirmatively, it is doubtful he knows *all* that Judith has implied. He passes her the opiate, but his ignorance separates him from guilt for the two—or is it three?—acts of euthanasia she will eventually perform.

The narrator has passed through a tunnel of dreams, made contact with his vital center, and delivered her from the impenetrable wilderness of the insane to a lawn where "leaves were piled in long mounds like double graves." He leaves her standing on that neutral ground, "nearer to the bleak sky and the deserted fields than . . . to her kind," her shawl slipping "from her shoulders to the dead leaves" like an old worry or an old self. The narrator then drives "across the field and into the woods" (215-16). Afterward, he "gives up medicine, you know, and [turns] to literature as a safer outlet for a suppressed imagination" (210). Does this not suggest that he senses there is a level of knowledge in the episode that he both fears and lacks the intellectual background to handle? Only the literary tradition preserves the forgotten language he needs to express these invisible things.

With this insight and these stories, Ellen Glasgow transcended the flat realism based on external details that had generally been her métier before 1916 and did so by assimilating many of the insights regarding the unconscious self we usually associate with Freud and, especially in her case, with Jung. Perhaps she preferred Jung because his approach was more literary. The introspection, the supernatural and mythic elements, the waking dreams, the mystic moments, the romantic quests, and the strange personality transformations we find in literature have, as Jung showed, preserved for millennia the forgotten language of man's invisible hemisphere.

Written during the low point of her life, the short stories record the path Glasgow followed from emotional bankruptcy to a level of art she had never before achieved. They are her experiments. In them she masters the technique for revealing a character's unconscious side by projecting it upon other characters, a technique she experimented with, but less successfully, in the three novels between *Virginia* (1913) and *Barren Ground* (1925). In the novels the major characters ultimately believe their needs can be satisfied by unembodied abstractions. In the stories, by contrast, the characters discover their deeply felt emotions—their fears and loves—embodied in one another. In the stories Glasgow also seems to accept something very much like a theory of psychological homeostasis, according to which the psyche tries to achieve inner equilibrium by creating phantasies to guide the individual toward a wholeness of the self. This process can produce abrupt personality changes when the buried self comes suddenly to the surface—an abruptness the realism of William Dean Howells and Henry James would have considered improbable and therefore would have discouraged. But Glasgow could find strong precedents for such strange exceptions in the romances of Edgar Allan Poe or, better because nonromantic, in the psychological realism of Feodor Dostoevsky.[10] All these techniques would be brought to bear when Glasgow sat down to write *Barren Ground*. In addition, the landscape of this important novel would prove to be even more subjective than the sunken garden of **"Whispering Leaves."** The brand of satire that emerges when characters get stuck in one-dimensional roles, as in **"The Artless Age,"** would be brought to perfection when she came to write *The Romantic Comedians*. The combination of com-

pensatory phantasies with the realistic structure of self-recognition and disillusionment that produced **"Romance and Sally Byrd"** would eventually lead to the tragedy of manners that is her finest work, *The Sheltered Life*.

One device she did not carry forward into her major phase was the use of the supernatural in either the phantastic or marvelous modes; even in three of the ghost stories, her ghosts are less ghosts than ideas. In *Barren Ground* her ghosts will further evolve into living people, for there is something exceedingly ghostly about the way, in the second half of that novel, wraithlike Geneva and mummified Jason seem to emerge from Dorinda's mind. Glasgow had obviously decided, by the time she wrote **"Jordan's End,"** that the invisible things which interested her could be better expressed in the dreamlike mode of the merely exceptional than through either flat realism or any variety of the supernatural.

We may safely conclude that without the short stories we would never have known Glasgow's major phase, which begins with *Barren Ground*.

Notes

[1] Richard K. Meeker (ed.), *The Collected Stories of Ellen Glasgow* (Baton Rouge, 1963), 12-16; citations throughout are to this edition and will be given parenthetically.

[2] Ellen Glasgow, *The Woman Within* (New York, 1954), 269, italics added.

[3] Carrington C. Tutwiler, Jr., *A Catalogue of the Library of Ellen Glasgow* (Charlottesville, 1969), 10-13.

[4] Pearce Bailey to Glasgow, in Ellen Glasgow Collection, Alderman Library, University of Virginia; Raper, *Without Shelter*, 104-106, 115, 210-11.

[5] Sigmund Freud, *The Collected Papers of Sigmund Freud*, ed. Ernest Jones (New York, 1959), IV, 203-16.

[6] Quoted by Meeker, *Collected Stories*, 6.

[7] Here I follow the terminology of Tzvetan Todorov, *The Fantastic: A Structural Approach to a Literary Genre*, trans. Richard Howard (Ithaca, N.Y., 1975), 25-33, 36, 46-48.

[8] Todorov, *Fantastic*, 31.

[9] Raper, *Without Shelter*, 60; Todorov, *Fantastic*, 158-62.

[10] Todorov, *Fantastic*, 48.

Marcelle Thiébaux (essay date 1982)

SOURCE: "Poems and Short Stories," in *Ellen Glasgow*, Frederick Ungar Publishing, 1982, pp. 175-88.

[*In the following excerpt, Thiébaux considers the chief interest in Glasgow's stories to be their treatment of themes developed more fully in her novels.*]

Early in Glasgow's career, her editor, Walter Hines Page, urged her to put her best efforts in her novels, and for the most part she followed his advice:

> I shall write no more short stories and I shall not divide my power or risk my future reputation. I will become a great novelist or none at all. For which determination you are in part responsible.[2]

It is true that she liked to explore history, heredity, the long, unfolding causes of things. For this she needed the spaciousness of the novel; the compression the short story demanded was less congenial. After publishing three stories in her early career, she did not publish another for seventeen years. The remaining ten were written or appeared between 1916 and 1924, a period during which her novel writing was at a low ebb. The stories' main interest lies in their treatment of themes that she developed more fully and skillfully in the novels.

The stories are of three general types, with some overlapping. There is the ethical dilemma story **"A Point in Morals."** Eight stories are about the difficult and rarely happy relations between men and women, and four are tales of the uncanny and the supernatural, with a psychic emphasis. These four led reviewers to compare Glasgow to Henry James and Edgar Allan Poe. With Poe, a Richmond writer, Glasgow confessed she felt an affinity.

Possibly the need for money as well as the feeling of creative slump impelled Glasgow to turn to stories once again after renouncing the genre. At any rate, she sold nearly all to women's magazines such as *Good Housekeeping* or to journals of more general literary interest like *Harper's* and *Scribner's*.

STORIES WRITTEN BEFORE 1900

Glasgow's first published story, **"A Woman of Tomorrow"** (*Short Stories: A Magazine of Fact and Fiction,* August, 1895) explores the conflict between work and art that surfaces in three of her novels. The heroine is a young attorney, a Yale honors graduate. She renounces her Virginia lover's pleading to "become a woman for his sake, suffer as other women suffer . . . merge her identity to his." A decade later when she is about to be appointed a Supreme Court justice, she feels suddenly tired. The sight of a nursing mother in the street stirs her emotionally. She returns home to find her old love married, his wife "a small, tired woman in a soiled gown, with a child upon her shrunken breast." The relieved heroine thanks God for her decision and turns her back once and for all on romance.

In **"Between Two Shores"** (*McClure's Magazine,* February, 1899), a young Southern widow, Lucy Smith, meets on shipboard a cynical yet attentive stranger who claims that his name is L. Smith. The other passengers suppose them to be married. They fall in love. At the end of the crossing he confesses that he is hunted for a murder, though it was "a deed of honor." In anguish Lucy sobs alone, "It was so short." Before they disembark to part forever, she al-

lows the deception that he is her husband to continue so that he can temporarily evade pursuers in Liverpool. This story, written after her first trip to Europe in 1896, shows Glasgow toying with the characterization of the sexually vital man who both attracts and menaces. Such alluring males appeared in all three of her novels about the woman artist.

"A Point in Morals" (*Harper's Magazine,* May, 1899) is also a shipboard narrative involving a criminal. A group of ocean passengers converse about topics ranging from civilization to the value of human life. The situation resembles those intellectual discussions at the Gotham Hotel in *Phases of an Inferior Planet.* A doctor then tells his story. He once shared a train ride with a wanted killer who recounted his own harried life story—the women he had loved, the treacherous colleague he had shot. The man, intent upon suicide, possessed only a vial of acid; this would ensure a horrible death. He pleaded with the doctor to leave him a packet of morphine instead so he could die painlessly. The doctor made what he considered a "sincere" and "conscientious" decision: He placed the drug on the seat before getting off the train. The suicide was in the next day's paper. The shipboard hearers of the tale exclaim and comment upon the story, although no real resolution of the moral question is reached. We do not learn the author's opinion. But in later stories she was to create "sincere" physican characters whose egotism or insensitivity are depicted unsympathetically.

LATER STORIES: 1916-1924

Stories about Men and Women

"Thinking Makes It So" (*Good Housekeeping,* February, 1917) tells of a faded, self-effacing librarian of forty-three. Margaret French is also a writer who supports herself, her nieces, and her widowed invalid sister. The sister, who spends her life on the sofa, is a version of the ladylike hypochondriac seen in so many of the novels. When Margaret receives the first of several fan letters from a plain man with a poetic sensibility, her life is transformed. A railroad builder in Colorado, he has read her poetry and loves her from afar. Glasgow here spiritualizes the rugged Western hero of *Life and Gabriella.* Margaret changes her hair, wears a rose-colored dress, and radiates an inner light while the family, grown accustomed to her martyred role, becomes awed and suspicious. When the man insists on coming to meet her, she tremblingly faces him in her own drawing room. So changed is she by his homage that he happily finds her "beautiful . . . just as I dreamed of you."

Aspects of her own experience undoubtedly gave Glasgow the idea for this sugary story. She was herself forty-three. She had recently fallen in love with Henry Anderson. She may have wondered whether the greatest part of her emotional energy was being given to her art. As in some of the earlier novels, she again plays—though more romantically—with the possibility that within a single woman the artist and the beloved might be happily fused.

"The Difference" (*Harper's Magazine,* June, 1923), constructs a favorite triangle, that in which two women compete for a faithless man. Margaret Fleming's husband of twenty years has a young mistress, Rose Morrison. Rose writes to the wife, asking to see her. She proposes that Margaret give up George, the husband, for his sake.

In the interim, a guarded conversation takes place between Margaret and a woman friend in which Glasgow airs some of her views: that "women love with their imagination and men with their senses"; that men are incapable of constancy; and that in the world's malicious eyes a man at forty-five still has plenty of life and adventure ahead of him, while a woman of the same age is through.

Margaret visits Rose, whom she sees as hard, young, and slovenly, her mouth painted "like raw flesh." Rose sees Margaret as Victorian and incapable of understanding George. An artist, Rose believes love is necessary to her "self-development." When Margaret, shocked and sobered, offers George his freedom, she finds he doesn't want it. The affair with Rose is to him only "sort of—recreation." Margaret feels sympathy for Rose, with whom she sees herself "united . . . by the bond of woman's immemorial disillusionment." Written while she was working on *Barren Ground,* the story reflects Glasgow's own disappointment. It also anticipates the conspiracy between those mutual users, the adulterous husband and the sexually liberated girl, that would form an essential element of *The Sheltered Life.* Like many of her fictions, it reveals the man as inferior to the women he betrays.

The Victorian and the modern woman clash again in **"The Artless Age"** (*The Saturday Evening Post,* August, 1923), but here they are both young. Mary Louise is "a nice girl" with "a Victorian aura" who grows roses and plays croquet. Flippant Geraldine is rouged and slangy; she brags about how she sips her dates' whiskey out of a flask at dances. Both girls vie for the well-bred young Richard. But Mary Louise, who feigns an ankle injury so that she can languish charmingly on a sofa, shows herself to be designing. Straightforward Geraldine, however outrageous, wins Richard. Geraldine's correct and elderly widowed father finds Mary Louise exactly to his taste and chooses her. This amusing if obvious tale bears a competent relation to the style of the novels of manners. The same distinction between the prim girl and the flapper is made in *One Man in His Time.*

"Jordan's End," which first appeared in Glasgow's collection *The Shadowy Third and Other Stories* (1923), is one of her three old plantation tales in a Southern Gothic mode. Jordan's End is a crumbling manse set in a tangle of ivy, moss, and boxwood. In it dwell several bizarre members of the Jordan family, particularly a thin, decaying beauty, Miss Judith, and her mad husband. A doctor is summoned to care for the husband. When he returns, he finds that Judith has allowed her husband to take a fatal overdose of a medically prescribed opiate. But the difficulty of proving whether a crime has indeed been committed prevents her being prosecuted.

The motif of the lethal overdose had appeared in the early tale, **"A Point in Morals,"** and the moral dilemma of that tale is faintly echoed here. But two important themes surface that are more pertinent to Glasgow's overarching interest, both concerning the strong woman character. The Southern lady's ability quietly to commit crimes with impunity appears in *The Ancient Law, The Sheltered Life,* and *In This Our Life.* Even more dear to the author's heart is the woman of superior strength who, one way or the other, manages to survive while watching her lover or husband die wretchedly.

"Romance and Sally Byrd" appeared in *The Woman's Home Companion* for December, 1924, and was reprinted in *World's Best Short Stories,* 1925. Sally Byrd has a humdrum life. She agrees to "go away in secret" with a man she loves, only to find that he is already married, although separated. Crushed, she parts from him and will wait for his divorce. Upon learning that he has been in an accident, Sally Byrd lies her way into his luxurious apartment house, pretending to be the nurse. She confronts her lover's middle-aged, graying wife, who is darning his socks and looking like all those other Glasgow women who have "finished with love."

The wife murmurs some cynical truisms: "Marriage for some men, you know, is merely a prop to lean against when they need a support." Sally Byrd goes back to Virginia. She decides that she is through with romance but recovers a little when she meets an attractive man on the train. Another triangular tale like **"The Difference,"** this sprightly specimen of popular fiction shows Glasgow's ability to treat the same topic with humor as well as pathos.

"The Professional Instinct" remained unpublished until 1963.[3] Dr. Estbridge detests his overfed and overbearing wife, who interferes in every aspect of his life, including his profession. He feels himself in revolt "against the whole world of women," feeling they are "victorious over the lives and destinies of men." When he is passed over—through his wife's machinations—for an important promotion, he decides to take a post in the Far East and begin life anew. He romantically asks Judith Campbell, the gentle, yielding woman he loves, to accompany him. Although she has just been offered the presidency of a midwestern college, she throws it over in a moment to go with Estbridge. Despite his elation, the thwarting of his professional hopes still rankles. When, on the same day, the coveted promotion becomes available at the local hospital, the incumbent having died suddenly, ambition gets the better of Estbridge. The story ends with his deep hesitation, even though taking the job would mean betraying the woman who gave up her profession for his sake.

Another sardonic tale of two women and a man, this one also takes up the conflict between work and love that had interested Glasgow in her earliest novels. Here both the man and the woman face the same dilemma; the woman can be counted on to choose love, whereas it appears that the man will choose work. There are obvious flaws. Chiefly, Glasgow has difficulty in making a plausible character of the lovable professional woman, for she had stereotypical ideas of femininity that she considered indispensable. A philosophy professor aiming for a college presidency, Judith is too pliable and Victorian, too full of "delicate graces" to be credible. Nor is it convincing that she would impulsively give up all for the peevish, selfish Estbridge. Glasgow exchanged letters about the story with Dr. Pearce Bailey, a physician friend in New York. If it had any personal allusion to their relationship, this might have been an added reason to avoid publication. The tale's feminist interest lies in its suggestion that Glasgow strove to exorcize the dominant woman by making her a monster and to create an idealized feminine intellectual type.

Stories of the Supernatural

Three of the four supernatural stories also touch on relationships between men and women, a subject central to Glasgow's work as a whole. All are recounted in the first person by a reliable narrator, a technique intended to enhance credibility. The ghosts have a purpose beyond simply inspiring horror. Either they reveal a connection between the past and the present, or they convey some psychological truth about the living characters—those who see the ghost and those who do not.

The first of these tales was **"The Shadowy Third"** (*Scribner's Magazine,* December, 1916); it was the title story in Glasgow's collection of 1923. The narrator, Miss Randolph, is engaged as a private nurse to the nervous wife of a famous surgeon, Dr. Roland Maradick. The surgeon is rich, magnetic, idolized by women. Rumor has it that the marriage is loveless and that the surgeon is only waiting for his wife to die so that he can inherit her fortune and marry another woman. Mrs. Maradick has hallucinations, it seems, of her dead child playing with its toys about the house. She tells the nurse that the doctor had caused the child's death so as to increase his own inheritance. Miss Randolph has, however, already seen the child's ghost, which appears as an elfin little girl in Victorian plaids. The ghost must be believed in. Miss Randolph pleads with Dr. Maradick and a medical colleague of his not to take away the wife, who she believes is sane. But the men of medicine, awesome in their power over their patient, hasten her to an asylum, where she dies.

Miss Randolph stays on as a secretary. One midnight, having dined with his fiancée, Dr. Maradick comes home and ascends the stairs. Summoned down again almost immediately by the telephone, he trips, pitches headlong downstairs, and is instantly killed at the bottom of the flight. In the half-light, the nurse has perceived a child's jump rope coiled in the bend of the stair.

This well-made story is one of Glasgow's best. Her narrator is both sensible and impressionable. She sees the ghost before knowing the child has died. Yet she is also capable of becoming emotionally involved with all the Maradicks: She cherishes the ghost; she sympathizes with Mrs. Maradick; she is both attracted to the surgeon and angry with him. Her resentment is twofold: first for his cruelty to his wife, and secondly for ignoring her, Miss Randolph. There is some hint that she even feels a share

of guilt for his death. She saw the rope an instant before he tripped; she wanted to reach the light switch, to warn him, she says, although the sudden flooding of the light might have startled him into losing his balance. The mingling of the ghost's will with the narrator's own gives this tale a rich psychic dimension.

Encouraged by her success and assured that there was a market for the supernatural, Glasgow went on to write **"Dare's Gift"** (*Harper's Magazine,* February and March, 1917). The title refers to an isolated plantation, its history extending to colonial times. The Virginia owners do not wish to live in it. The narrator is Beckwith, a lawyer who leases the house for himself and his unstable wife. The house feels strange to both. The wife unaccountably betrays her husband by leaking a scandalous business secret of his to the papers. Beckwith is now convinced of her insanity. But an old neighborhood doctor says that the house is responsible. Other sensitive persons have succumbed "to the psychic force of its memories." He recounts tales of treachery associated with the place. The chief story is that of a Southern belle who had allowed her Northern lover to be captured and shot, thinking he had secrets that might save the Confederacy.

The woman who destroys her lover is a familiar type in Glasgow's fiction. Here, however, the motive is impersonal. The obsession with the Confederate cause, even when all is but lost, is seen as a force that might not only unhinge minds (as with Mrs. Blake in *The Deliverance*), but that could and did linger on in the present day. The atmosphere of Dare's Gift, however preternatural, is capable of an almost symbolic interpretation of the way in which the past permeates the present.

"The Past" appeared in *Good Housekeeping* for October, 1920, and was included in *Best Short Stories of 1921.* Events are recounted by Miss Wrenn, secretary to the wealthy Mrs. Vanderbridge. Miss Wrenn feels the mystery of the house, a luxurious dwelling off Fifth Avenue in New York. Both she and her employer are able to see the mist-clad ghost of the first Mrs. Vanderbridge, who joins them at the dining table whenever the husband's thoughts dreamily wander to her. The ghost glides through the rooms as well; its aspect is malignant. Mrs. Vanderbridge's health declines. One day, directed by her employer to clean out a desk that had belonged to the first wife, Miss Wrenn comes upon a cache of love letters, which she turns over to Mrs. Vanderbridge. They discover that the first wife had received them from a lover after her marriage. Should not the letters be shown to the husband, so that the phantom can be exorcized? Then he might see his first wife as she really was. Instead, Mrs. Vanderbridge burns the letters. The phantom reappears in the room, its mien cleared, beneficent. The explanation is offered: "She had changed the thought of the past, in that lay her victory."

Like **"Dare's Gift,"** the story creates a sense of the past so sinister that it infects the present. Both stories suffer from the officious intrusions of the author, who eagerly wishes to rationalize the mystery and turn the ghost fiction into a story of ideas.

"Whispering Leaves" (*Harper's Magazine,* January and February, 1923) is another plantation ghost story. Again there is a reliable narrator, Miss Effie. She comes to visit her distant cousins in the Virginia country house where her mother and several grandmothers were born. She herself has never been in Virginia. The family, it is said, has "run to seed." There are unusual things about the place. The groves are unnaturally full of twittering birds. The black servants won't stay after sundown, nor will they work in the fields close to the house.

Miss Effie observes the pale orphaned boy, Pell, being lovingly tended by a noble-featured black woman in a turban. This is the ghost of his old Mammy Rhody (the name inspired by Glasgow's mother's nurse Rhoda). It is she who tamed the birds. The woman haunts the narrator, as if Rhody had belonged to some "half-forgotten childhood which haunted me like a dream." Had she been her mother's mammy as well? When a fire breaks out in the house, Effie beholds the ghost carrying Pell from the flames. She reaches out her arms and takes the child as the ghost melts away. Effie becomes Pell's guardian, thus fulfilling Pell's directive that she is to take him from Whispering Leaves. As in other of the ghost stories, the supernatural is explained as the legacy of memory.

Glasgow wrote of actual ghosts chiefly in her short stories. An exception is the "haunts' walk" around Jordan's Journey in *The Miller of Old Church.* But "shut in, alone, with the past," Glasgow was at home with the ghosts of sad family memories at 1 West Main. She sometimes thought of them as her only companions. As a child, Glasgow found cemeteries her "favorite haunts"; they were romantic to her then and as an adult. But the real ghost that shadows her writing is the Southern past.

Notes

[2] Letter of November 22, 1897, to Walter Hines Page, *Letters,* p. 23.

[3] Richard K. Meeker, ed., *The Collected Stories of Ellen Glasgow* (Baton Rouge: Louisiana State University Press, 1963), pp. 239-253. The story is edited from the manuscript in the University of Virginia library.

Linda W. Wagner (essay date 1982)

SOURCE: "The Years of the Locust," in *Ellen Glasgow: Beyond Convention,* University of Texas Press, 1982, pp. 50-70.

[*In the following excerpt, Wagner maintains that Glasgow's short stories emphasize characterization—particularly strong women characters—rather than plot development and experiment with ideas subsequently integrated in her novels.*]

For all Glasgow's earlier reticence about focusing on women protagonists, she draws a variety of effective female characters in her stories. As Richard K. Meeker points out in his introduction to the collected stories, many of these women prefigure characters from the later novels.[25] Perhaps more significant at this period of Glasgow's career, the stories gave her a means of drawing numerous different women. Many of these female characters were quite changed from her earlier protagonists, and, accordingly, served as exploration for some characters who might meet the cultural obstacles with those more "indirect" methods of which she had spoken in 1916, those of "indirect influence or subtlety."[26] By this stage in her life, Glasgow had learned that any woman's ability to make successful choices, like that of the artist, was crucial. She had also learned that pleasing herself and pleasing a reading audience was not always possible. If some readers would idealize the Virginias, and feminists demand the Gabriellas, Glasgow knew too well that somewhere between them lived a whole gamut of American women.

In both Glasgow's earliest story, the 1897 **"Between Two Shores,"** and one of her most powerful, the 1917 **"Thinking Makes It So,"** she explores several standard plots for the adventurous turn-of-the-century woman. In **"Between Two Shores,"** Lucy Smith comes to love a shipboard stranger and saves him from arrest for some mysterious past crime. Her "love," consuming and physically powerful, is thus capable of changing lives. The cultural assumption is clear—the best use of *her* life is to save the life of her beloved, a man, and a criminal at that. Margaret French, the forty-three-year-old unmarried poet of **"Thinking Makes It So,"** finds an equally romantic fulfillment. When the unknown John Brown writes to her praising her poems, her physical appearance begins to change; she dresses in an atypical "flaming rose color" and is transformed into a striking woman. This paean to the power of the imagination ends with the meeting of the lovers and gives Glasgow another story in the Cinderella tradition. That Margaret is a middle-aged writer waiting to be brought to life through a man's love suggests Glasgow's personal situation in 1917, when she had just become engaged to Anderson.

Most of Glasgow's stories, however, feature the defiantly strong women protagonists rather than any implementation of conventional plot. In fact, even her four stories billed as "ghost tales"—the ostensible reason for her move into short fiction—are as much character studies of female protagonists as they are suspense stories. Lucy Dare, who betrays her Northern lover to the Confederacy in **"Dare's Gift,"** and Mrs. Vanderbridge, who bests her spirit rival in **"The Past,"** are women who experience spiritual awakening or recognition and act on it: "I had to do it. I would do it again," affirms Lucy Dare.[27] It is most often the women characters who perceive the essential situations. Women characters can apprehend the spirits in the ghost tales because of their uncritical sympathy, their willingness to respond to needs, whether or not human. As Glasgow presents these characters, their clairvoyance is a consistently positive ability. They are not charlatans.

Throughout her stories, Glasgow sets insensitive men against more perceptive women, and what begins as a simple narrative tactic grows into theme. **"The Differ-**

ence" is an effective story about a happily married woman who receives a letter from her husband's mistress. Ready to relinquish him after hearing the impassioned description of their love from Rose Morrison, the wife Margaret is both surprised and disappointed to hear her husband term the affair only "recreation":

> Recreation! The memory of Rose Morrison's extravagant passion smote her sharply. How glorified the incident had appeared in the girl's imagination, how cheap and tawdry it was in reality. A continual compromise with the second best, an inevitable surrender to the average, was this the history of all romantic emotion? For an instant, such is the perversity of fate, it seemed to the wife that she and this strange girl were united by some secret bond which George could not share—by the bond of woman's immemorial disillusionment. (183)

Man's consistent ability to disappoint becomes a pervasive theme in Glasgow's later fiction; not only Corinna Page experiences disillusionment. The dichotomy of woman's moral supremacy and man's ineptness seems to be evinced in more than their sexual roles; Glasgow has defined the differences in the capacity to love as being intimately connected with the imaginative life of the characters. As Margaret's wise friend had said,

> When a man and a woman talk of love they speak two different languages. . . . women love with their imagination and men with their senses. (170)

Once Glasgow had made this statement of **"The Difference"** so forcefully, she concentrated on stories that emphasize the foibles of the self-centered acquisitive male and the women who relate (love, make excuses for, live in deference to, etc.) to him. "Doesn't everything come back to the men?" asks the wry Geraldine Plummer in **"The Artless Age."** She has changed herself chameleon-like to capture and marry Richard Askew. Geraldine is, however, in control; she may have set her ambition too low but her aim is clear. She marries Richard, against incredible odds, but she knows what she has gotten.

Self-understanding is the strength of Mrs. Kenton as well in **"Romance and Sally Byrd."** One of Glasgow's most bitter stories, this one narrates the scene between the faithful wife—whose only role in life is to welcome her philandering husband back after each escapade—and the young, would-be mistress.

> Mrs. Kenton's face softened. "How old are you?"
>
> "Nineteen. Or I was when I came here."
>
> The other smiled. "At nineteen nothing is permanent. You will forget him and be happy."
>
> Sally Byrd shook her head. "I shall forget, but I shall not be happy. It has broken my heart."
>
> A wistful expression crossed the other's face. "No, your heart isn't broken—not so long as it hurts. When

your heart is really broken, it lies still and dead like mine. You can't imagine the relief it is," she added simply, "to have your heart break at last." (233)

Relief it might have been, but by 1924 Glasgow was viewing experience as more necessary to maturity than disillusioning. Most of her attention during the mid-twenties was going to that wisest of her female protagonists, Dorinda Oakley, but she was not above choosing less experienced women as protagonists for her stories.

The pathetic if successful Judith Campbell, for example, in **"The Professional Instinct,"** makes the mistake of believing that Professor John Estbridge can share her self-abnegating passion. When she has been offered a prestigious academic position and is about to leave the area, the married but flirtatious Estbridge asks,

> "Judith, would you give it up if I asked you?"
>
> "If you asked me?"
>
> "Would you stay—would you give it up if I asked you?" The glow in her face seemed to pervade her whole body while she stood before him transfigured.
>
> "I would give up the whole world if you asked me."
>
> "You would sacrifice your ambition—your future?"
>
> A laugh broke from her lips. "I haven't any ambition—any future—except yours." (248)

It is this passion that Glasgow so admires, but it is its misdirection that she so often laments. As William Kelly concludes, these stories show Glasgow in her greatest period of experimentation, working with "ideas which would be incorporated into her best later books."[28] Kelly sees strong parallels between *Barren Ground,* for example, and **"Jordan's End,"** in which the Antigone-like wife murders her husband, defying all convention and creating her own personal bereavement: "Suddenly, without the warning of a sob, a cry of despair went out of her, as if it were torn from her breast. 'He was my life,' she cried, 'and I must go on!'" (215). Woman alone with only land, place, responsibility, sorrow—Judith prefigures Dorinda Oakley's situation, but the more startling parallels between the 1923 story and the 1925 novel are in the way Glasgow describes nature to image character's feelings. Jordan's death is discovered on an "ashen" November day, the somberness of which permeates the entire story.

> In the middle of the lawn, where the trees had been stripped bare in the night, and the leaves were piled in long mounds like double graves, she stopped and looked in my face. The air was so still that the whole place might have been in a trance or asleep. Not a branch moved, not a leaf rustled on the ground, not a sparrow twittered in the ivy; and even the few sheep stood motionless, as if they were under a spell. Farther away, beyond the sea of broomsedge, where no wind stirred, I saw the flat desolation of the landscape. (214-15)

Making description work more intensely as part of both plot and characterization gave Glasgow a powerful method of creating more nuance of personality. Dorinda Oakley, as character, could only benefit from Glasgow's discoveries.

Notes

[25] Richard K. Meeker, Introduction to *The Collected Stories of Ellen Glasgow.* Hereafter cited in text.

[26] Overton, p. 33.

[27] *Collected Stories,* p. 103.

[28] William Kelly, Introduction to "'The Professional Instinct': An Unpublished Short Story by Ellen Glasgow," *Western Humanities Review* 16, no. 4 (Autumn, 1962), p. 302.

Lynette Carpenter (essay date 1984)

SOURCE: "The Daring Gift in Ellen Glasgow's 'Dare's Gift'," in *Studies in Short Fiction,* Vol. 21, No. 2, Spring, 1984, pp. 95-102.

[*In the following analysis of "Dare's Gift," Carpenter sees the story as not merely a tale of the supernatural but as an exploration of one woman's struggle to express her independence and individuality.*]

In addition to her novels, Ellen Glasgow wrote short fiction, including several tales of the supernatural which appear in *The Shadowy Third and Other Stories.* These stories have won little critical scrutiny and less praise; their dismissal by many Glasgow critics suggests consensus with Frederick P. W. McDowell's argument that the stories lack subtlety, that they treat the occult "too baldly and literally."[1] However, a closer look at one of these stories, **"Dare's Gift,"** will reveal a work as complex on a small scale as the epic novels so widely admired.

At first glance, **"Dare's Gift"** may appear to be a straightforward tale of the supernatural: a woman, driven mad by the suggestive atmosphere of a haunted house, betrays her husband. But is the story as straightforward as it first appears? The events of the story are narrated and analyzed for the reader by two professional men, a lawyer and a physician, whose credentials as rational observers would seem impeccable. Indeed, in her recent study of Glasgow, Marcelle Thiébaux writes that the narrators in all of Glasgow's ghost stories are reliable. Similarly, in an earlier essay, when Richard K. Meeker discusses Glasgow's use of the first person in the stories, he accepts the narrator's objectivity in all cases, even though he has linked Glasgow's technique to Poe and James—two masters of the unreliable narrator.[2] A feminist reader might be predisposed to approach the narratives with suspicion, but Glasgow gives all readers cause for doing so by her placement of **"Dare's Gift"** within *The Shadowy Third* collection: the stories which precede and follow it, **"The Shadowy Third"** and **"The Past,"** respectively, are both narrated by sympathetic women who perceive the mental anguish women suffer at the hands of cruel or insensitive husbands.[3] Surely the reader is meant to contemplate how such a narrator might view the events of **"Dare's Gift"** differently.

Part One of **"Dare's Gift"** is narrated by the lawyer-husband of Mildred Beckwith, a woman who suffers from a nervous depression. After her first breakdown, he moves her from Washington to a colonial mansion in Virginia, Dare's Gift, to effect a cure. Unfortunately, important business detains him in town and prevents him from spending a great deal of time with her; he is defending a major railroad against charges of corruption. He notices changes in her at Dare's Gift and fears that her condition is worsening. But he is not prepared for what happens next: after he confesses to her confidentially that he has uncovered proof of the railroad's corruption, she exposes that corruption by informing the press. More importantly, she does not regret her betrayal, thus convincing him that her "mind was unhinged."[4]

When an elderly local doctor arrives, he explains Mildred's "illness" by telling Beckwith the story of Dare's Gift, the narrative of Part Two. During the Civil War, Lucy Dare, a Southerner, had betrayed her Yankee lover, an escaped prisoner of war, to Confederate soldiers. The house is haunted, not by the actual ghost of Lucy Dare, but by the idea of betrayal. According to the doctor, it has been an unlucky house ever since. Mildred's betrayal is neatly dismissed as a kind of temporary madness induced by the atmosphere of the house playing upon her "neurotic temperament" (p. 76).

In Mildred Beckwith, Glasgow describes a classic case of nervous depression, a condition with which she was intimately familiar.[5] Mildred's treatment suggests the now infamous rest cure of Dr. S. Weir Mitchell, perhaps represented in **"Dare's Gift"** by "the great specialist" Drayton (p. 48). Since the cure necessitated the patient's isolation, Beckwith rents Dare's Gift, a house hidden away in the Virginia backwoods, inhabited only by a caretaker's family:

> From the warm red of its brick walls to the pure Colonial lines of its doorway, and its curving wings mantled in roses and ivy, the house stood there splendid and solitary. The rows of darkened windows sucked in without giving back the last flare of daylight; the heavy cedars crowded thick up the short avenue did not stir as the wind blew from the river; and above the carved pineapple on the roof, a lonely bat was wheeling high against the red disc of the sun. (p. 49)

A more isolated place could hardly be imagined; Beckwith tells Mildred after he first sees the house that he has found "just the place" for her (p. 57). Images of enclosure suggest that the house is a prison for Mildred, a substitute asylum: it is "crowded" by "heavy cedars," surrounded by "walls of box" (p. 59), and sealed by "iron gates" (p. 59). On first viewing Dare's Gift, Beckwith reports:

"The Old World charm of the scene held me captive" (p. 49). For Mildred, the captivity is literal, and she first responds to the claustrophobic "box wall" with a dizzy spell (p. 60). Later, she discovers "architectural absurdities—wanton excrescenses in the modern additions" (p. 61) that contradict Beckwith's idyllic portrait of Dare's Gift and contribute to its unsettling effect.[6]

Beckwith adds to Mildred's isolation by escaping to the city, leaving her alone a great deal. He is preoccupied with his lawsuit, about which he says, "I had already thought of it as one of my great cases" (p. 62). And yet, Beckwith seems genuinely concerned about his wife's condition. Theirs is, by his own account, an ideal marriage. While considering Dare's Gift as a potential retreat, he consults with his friend Harrison and then with Mildred:

> "Well, I'll ask Mildred. Of course Mildred must have the final word in the matter."
>
> "As if Mildred's final word would be anything but a repetition of yours!" Harrison laughed slyly—for the perfect harmony in which we lived had been for ten years a pleasant jest among our friends. Harrison had once classified wives as belonging to two distinct groups—the group of those who talked and knew nothing about their husbands' affairs, and the group of those who knew everything and kept silent. Mildred, he had added politely, had chosen to belong to the latter division. . . .
>
> When I told her about my discovery, her charming face sparkled with interest. Never once, not even during her illness, had she failed to share a single one of my enthusiasms; never once, in all the years of our marriage, had there been so much as a shadow between us. (pp. 56-57)

Mildred's illness would seem to challenge her husband's version of matrimonial harmony; he does not attempt to explain her initial breakdown. Perhaps Mildred is paying the emotional price of her silence, of her unflagging good nature, her perpetual sharing in the interests of someone else. Beckwith explains later that he always discussed his cases with her. Of her interests he says nothing, except that she is "happy as a child in her garden" (p. 62), a condescending remark that implies his unwillingness to acknowledge her independent adulthood.

Exhaustion from the effort to sustain enthusiasm can explain why Mildred looks tired when she first sees Dare's Gift (p. 60), and more tired in the weeks that follow; to her husband's inquiry, she replies, "Oh, I've lost sleep, that's all" (p. 63). When Beckwith discusses his case with her, she betrays unaccustomed irritation and distress:

> . . . whenever I paused she questioned me closely, with a flash of irritation as if she were impatient of my slowness or my lack of lucidity. At the end she flared out for a moment into the excitement I had noticed the week before; but at the time I was so engrossed in my own affairs that this scarcely struck me as unnatural.

> Not until the blow fell did I recall the hectic flush in her face and the quivering sound of her voice, as if she were trying not to break down and weep. (p. 65)

Mildred exhibits classic symptoms of depression—insomnia, exhaustion, and a tendency to tears. If, as many contemporary psychologists believe, depression results from repressed or misdirected rage, the true object of her rage is clear. Most modern therapists would consider enforced idle solitude anathema to a depressed client. In the end, Mildred finds a means of expressing her anger by injuring her husband's reputation. Beckwith's introduction of the story as a past "episode" (p. 47), however, suggests that her triumph is short-lived, that she has since resumed her part in sustaining the illusion of domestic tranquility.

Yet Glasgow's story contains a second narrative, Dr. Lakeby's story, which corroborates Beckwith's opinion that his wife is not merely depressed but mad and offers a supernatural explanation for her madness. This story, confirming Beckwith's assertion that his wife's behavior is completely inexplicable and irrational, should serve to lend credibility to Beckwith as narrator. But does it? Having once questioned whether Beckwith is a reliable analyst of the female psyche and female behavior, one should ask the same of Dr. Lakeby.

The doctor himself concedes that there are two possible interpretations of Lucy Dare's act of betrayal, which he calls "her heroic or devilish choice, according to the way one has been educated" (p. 79). A long-winded man, he continues:

> "She missed her time; she is one of the mute inglorious heroines of history; and yet, born in another century, she might have stood side by side with Antigone—" For an instant he paused. "But she has always seemed to me diabolical," he added. (p. 80)

Lucy Dare's sin, according to the doctor, was to esteem the impersonal loyalties beyond the personal (p. 79), a reversal of values that held general sway only once in the history of Virginia: during the days of the Confederacy.[7]

The doctor recreates for Beckwith the Southern obsession with "the idea of the Confederacy" (p. 81), noting, "Like most noncombatants, the Dares were extremists" (p. 84). He recounts how Lucy Dare confided in him about a broken engagement to a Northerner, saying, "My first duty is to my country . . . I could never forget—I can never forgive" (p. 91). She had also confessed that she was then sheltering the young man, an escaped prisoner of war, at Dare's Gift. Shortly afterward, a ragged contingent of Confederate soldiers had arrived, hunting the escaped prisoner. They were desperate; the war was going badly for the South and the prisoner was carrying information that would mean the fall of Richmond if he escaped. Lucy Dare had told them where the young man was hiding, but he had then been shot and killed trying to run. She told the doctor afterward: "'I had to do it . . . I would do it again'" (p. 100), words Mildred speaks to Beckwith after her betrayal (p. 73).

This, then, was Lucy Dare's diabolical act: she had placed her loyalty to a cause and country above personal loyalty to a lover. She had sacrificed a man to save a nation, or so she believed; the clarity of the doctor's hindsight regarding the condition of the Confederacy at the time should not be allowed to obscure her motive.

Why does the doctor resent an action which he himself admits to be heroic? His description of Lucy Dare suggests an answer. He describes her at one point as charming, but adds:

> I knew half a dozen men who would have died for her—and yet she gave them nothing, nothing, barely a smile. She appeared cold. (p. 82)

He cannot decide whether or not she was beautiful, but believes she must have been, "in a way" (p. 82), although he thinks of her as "a woman who was, in the essence of her nature, thin and colourless" (p. 92). He admits, "I cannot recall either her smile or her voice, though both were sweet, no doubt, as the smile and the voice of a Southern woman would be" (p. 92)—a curious assumption, since she "barely" smiled at anyone, by his own earlier account. He asserts:

> In ordinary circumstances Lucy Dare would have been ordinary, submissive, feminine, domestic; she adored children. That she possessed a stronger will than the average Southern girl, brought up in the conventional manner, none of us—least of all I, myself—ever imagined. (pp. 83-84)

Yet a strong-willed girl would hardly be transformed into a submissive girl by "ordinary circumstances," although the doctor has devised a theory that would allow for such a transformation: "to this day I don't know how much of her strangeness was the result of improper nourishment, of too little blood to the brain" (p. 83). Still, the portrait is confusing and inconsistent. Specifically, the doctor confuses his stereotype of ideal Southern femininity with his memory of the actual Lucy Dare. He attempts to invest an assertive, independent woman with the qualities of a flirtatious, docile Southern belle. There is no place in his imagination for the heroic woman:

> I cannot imagine us as a people canonizing a woman who sacrificed the human ties for the superhuman— even for the divine. (p. 78)

A man perhaps, but not a woman.

Beckwith's response to the story indicates that his imagination is similarly constrained; he asks, "So she died of the futility, and her unhappy ghost haunts her house?" (p. 101). The ending of Lucy Dare's story, which is also the ending of **"Dare's Gift,"** is filled with Glasgow's subtle humor: to the last, Lucy Dare obstinately refuses to conform to the romantic stereotypes of the two men. She does not die of a broken heart after a lingering illness, but lives to a comfortable old age. The doctor tells of visiting her in a home for the elderly. He portrays her as decrepit and

senile, an ironic portrayal since he himself must be at least as old as Lucy Dare:

> As we approached her, I saw that her figure was shapeless, and that her eyes, of a faded blue, had the vacant and listless expression of the old who have ceased to think, who have ceased even to wonder or regret. (p. 102)

Moreover she does not sound senile by his own report:

> "'Unfolding the end of the muffler, she held it out to us. 'I have managed to do twenty of these since Christmas. I've promised fifty to the War Relief Association by autumn, and if my fingers don't get stiff I can easily do them.'" (p. 103)

Far from being "vacant and listless," she is an active woman actively committed to a cause. She explains, "It gives me something to do, this work for the Allies" (p. 103). In answer to Beckwith's question, the doctor insists finally that Lucy Dare had long since forgotten her act of treachery, mentioning an illness that followed the incident. But his hesitation suggests that he is unsure; it further suggests that he simply cannot believe that a woman could live so long and contentedly with the memory of a lover betrayed.

What, then, is Lucy Dare's legacy to Mildred Beckwith? The doctor claims that Dare's Gift is haunted by the memory of Lucy's treachery, and there are local stories of other betrayals in the house. Significantly, however, at least one of the stories concerns the first Dare, Sir Roderick, an ancestor of Lucy's (p. 53). In any case, the other stories are not told in detail, so their place in the haunting of Dare's Gift cannot be accurately assessed. The tie that is emphasized is the one between Lucy's betrayal and Mildred's. Indeed, Mildred's treachery also involves the betrayal of personal loyalties for impersonal ones, since the corruption of a large corporation involves the betrayal of a public trust. Mildred sides with the "philanthropic busybody" (p. 62), as Beckwith calls him, who first charges the railroad with corruption. Surely she has good reason to feel angry and upset when her husband proposes to conceal evidence of corporate wrongdoing and build his career on the victory. He himself admits that the issue is "personal honesty" (p. 64). Afterward, she tells him, "I had to do it, Harold . . . I had to tell all I knew" (p. 63). Ironically, Beckwith had speculated earlier: "If I lose— well, I'll be like any other general who has met a better man in the field" (p. 63). It never occurs to him that he might meet a better woman.

Lucy Dare's legacy is one of impersonal responsibility, of female commitment to something beyond personal loyalty. It is also one of individuality, of independence from stereotypes and other constraints on personal expression. Glasgow once defined feminism as "a revolt from pretence of being—it is, at its best and worst, a struggle for the liberation of personality."[8] At Dare's Gift, Mildred has her first opportunity to be herself. Her depression indicates not that she is insane but that she is angry, and she finally acts on her anger under the influence of Lucy Dare's spiritual presence in the house.

Richard P. Meeker has speculated on the reasons for Glasgow's return to short stories during an unproductive period she associated with "the Slough of Despond" and despite her aversion to short fiction, quoting from a 1916 interview:

> I cannot write short stories. They bore me excrutiatingly . . . All the best of the short stories must be painfully condensed with slight regard for the evolutionary causes bringing about this or that effect.[9]

The stories in the *Shadowy Third* collection belie Glasgow's first assertion, and **"Dare's Gift"** demonstrates her skill at condensation. The statement characterizes that process as painful, however—perhaps particularly so when the writer's material is so painfully close to her own experience. After publishing *The Shadowy Third* in 1923, Glasgow never returned to short fiction.

Notes

[1] Frederick P. W. McDowell, *Ellen Glasgow and the Ironic Art of Fiction* (Madison: University of Wisconsin Press, 1960), p. 144.

[2] See Marcelle Thiébaux, *Ellen Glasgow* (New York: Frederick Ungar, 1982), p. 184; and Richard K. Meeker, "The Shadowy Stories of Ellen Glasgow," in *The Dilemma of the Southern Writer* ed. Richard K. Meeker (Farmville, Va.: Longwood College, 1961), pp. 95-117. Linda W. Wagner's comments on "Dare's Gift" in her recent study, *Ellen Glasgow: Beyond Convention* (Austin: University of Texas Press, 1982) would seem to support my reading, although she mentions the story only in passing.

[3] These remarks clearly do not apply to the story as it was first published in *Harper's,* February 1917, pp. 322-330, and March 1917, pp. 515-524, nor to the English edition of the collection.

[4] Ellen Glasgow, *The Shadowy Third and Other Stories* (Garden City, N. Y.: Doubleday, Page, 1923), p. 73. All subsequent references are to this text.

[5] Glasgow, who suffered all her life from nervous depression, would no doubt have heard of Mitchell's "cure." She did not try it, as did her contemporaries Charlotte Perkins Gilman and Edith Wharton.

[6] Glasgow's description of the mansion, like much in the story, may sound familiar to readers of Charlotte Perkins Gilman's "The Yellow Wallpaper." I do not know whether Glasgow had read Gilman.

[7] The story is set in the present of the First World War, or fifty-two years after Lucy Dare's betrayal.

[8] In Josephine Jessup, "The Faith of Our Feminists," *Good Housekeeping,* May 1941, p. 683.

[9] Meeker is quoting from Grant M. Overton, *The Women Who Make Our Novels* (New York: Dodd, Mead, 1918), p. 26.

Lynette Carpenter (essay date 1991)

SOURCE: "Visions of Female Community in Ellen Glasgow's Ghost Stories," in *Haunting the House of Fiction: Feminist Perspectives on Ghost Stories by American Women,* edited by Wendy Kolmar and Lynette Carpenter, University of Tennessee Press, 1991, pp. 117-41.

[*In the following excerpt, Carpenter argues that Glasgow's ghost stories, which are particularly critical of men and sympathetic toward women, showcase her feminist concerns.*]

In 1916, with her father and closest sister recently dead, Ellen Glasgow returned to the family home in Richmond, Virginia, and entered into one of the most difficult periods of her life. She felt keenly the loss of her family, and the war played upon her imagination. Her physical and mental health worsened; she became even more painfully self-conscious about her deafness. She felt herself haunted by the ghosts of dead loved ones, as she described it later in *The Woman Within*: "Ghosts were my only companions. I was shut in, alone, with the past." She added, "This is not rhetoric. This is what I thought or felt or imagined, while I stood there alone, in that empty house" (237).[1]

Yet the house was not always empty. Anne Virginia Bennett, who had nursed Glasgow's father and sister, stayed on in the house as Glasgow's private secretary. A frequent visitor was Henry Anderson, Glasgow's close friend and probable fiance. Anderson's influence on the Glasgow novels from this period, *The Builders* (1919) and *One Man in His Time* (1922), has been noted by critics and biographers, and chronicled by Anderson himself in his correspondence with the author. Rarely discussed are the contemporaneous ghost stories, written, according to Miss Bennett, at her own instigation.[2] The differences between Glasgow's novels and her ghost stories suggest something of the dynamics of her household at the time. More importantly, however, they portray Glasgow's exploration of the alternatives of conventional heterosexual romance and female community. At a time when she was contemplating marriage, Glasgow wrote some of her most radical critiques of marriage in both the novels and the ghost stories, but only the ghost stories envision the possible substitution of relationships between women for the conventional resolution of happy marriage.

Marriage was clearly a subject of preoccupation for Glasgow in these years, for despite her well-documented cynicism about it, by her own admission she was attracted to the prospect of marriage with Anderson, confessing: "It is true that conscience and reason are not inflexible motives" (*Woman Within* 228). A chronology of events in the development of their relationship is difficult to establish (Anderson destroyed all of Glasgow's letters to him following her death), but they were probably engaged when Anderson left for Rumania in 1917 for an administrative post with the Red Cross.[3] Glasgow's own account blames their estrangement on Anderson's infatuation with Queen Marie of Rumania. In any case, the war seems to have effectively ended their engagement, although they may have continued to discuss marriage for years. Glasgow commented: "For seventeen months out of twenty years we were happy together" (*Woman Within* 227). That happiness, however, cannot have seemed secure to one who confessed to "a deep conviction that [she] was unfitted for marriage" (153). Indeed, Anderson's letters to her between 1916 and 1920, dated only by day and not by year, record a troubled relationship punctuated by hurt and humiliation on her part, and misunderstanding on his. Plagued by physical illness and mental depression, she may have felt especially betrayed at a time when she was especially vulnerable. Yet in retrospect, she relates the episode to "the illusion of [her] disillusionment" (215), acknowledging that her disappointment with romance and marriage antedated her experience with Anderson.

More enduring was her relationship with Anne Virginia Bennett, of whom she wrote: "More than anyone else since I lost [my sister] Cary, Anne Virginia has had my interests at heart; and she has shared my compassion for all inarticulate creation, and even turns that compassion upon me" (216). William Godbold writes of other attitudes in common: "They shared a love of dogs and a dislike of men. Ellen liked to think of men as intellectual and social inferiors and unsatisfactory lovers, but she enjoyed teasing them and often sought their company. Anne Virginia hated men almost violently" (196). Godbold observes that Miss Bennett especially disliked Henry Anderson, and Marcelle Thiébaux records that she did not welcome his presence at Glasgow's funeral (22). Like Anderson, Miss Bennett left Glasgow to go abroad with the Red Cross during the war, but unlike Anderson, in Glasgow's view, she returned with her loyalty intact. She did not share Anderson's interest in Glasgow's work; her editorial influence cannot be documented in the way that Anderson's can. Yet she was the most likely prototype for the sympathetic heroines of the ghost stories, who offer an appealing alternative to masculine cruelty and insensitivity.

The ghost stories value sympathy, compassion, and sensitivity, and portray these qualities as a primary source of bonds between women. These are qualities that men neither possess, nor understand, nor value, the stories imply. Glasgow's familiarity with a female tradition in the ghost story is suggested by her personal library holdings at the time of her death: in addition to Bronte's *Wuthering Heights* and Radcliffe's *The Mysteries of Udolpho,* she owned two of Cynthia Asquith's ghost story collections, Edith Wharton's *Tales of Men and Ghosts* (1918) and *Ghosts* (1937), Katherine Fullerton Gerould's *Vain Oblations* (1914), Isak Dinesen's *Seven Gothic Tales* (1934), Virginia Woolf's *A Haunted House and Other Stories* (1944), and miscellaneous collections by Mary Wilkins Freeman, Elizabeth Bowen, Marjorie Bowen, and Vernon Lee. Perhaps most significant among these literary influences was Edith Wharton, whose 1904 story, "The Lady's Maid's Bell," featured a compassionate lady's maid who struggled first to understand and then to help her victimized mistress; if Anne Virginia Bennett was the actual prototype for Glasgow's heroines, Wharton's Hartley was a likely literary model.

In the earliest of the stories, **"The Shadowy Third,"** their counterpart is the narrator, Miss Randolph, a nurse who finds herself siding with her female patient against two powerful professional men. Miss Randolph is flattered when the great surgeon Dr. Maradick chooses her as personal nurse to his wife, vaguely described as a "mental case" (4). Yet she feels an immediate empathy with her new patient, an empathy manifested by their shared vision of Mrs. Maradick's little girl by her first marriage, dead two months previous from pneumonia. Mrs. Maradick accuses her husband of murder, telling Miss Randolph that he had married her for her fortune and killed the child who stood in the way of his inheritance. Questioned by the surgeon, Miss Randolph refuses to confirm his opinion that his wife is insane. Finally, however, she cannot prevent Mrs. Maradick's commitment to an asylum, and she witnesses the tearful farewell between mother and ghostly daughter. She stays on as office nurse to Dr. Maradick, learning of Mrs. Maradick's death and then of his engagement to a wealthy young woman he had known before his marriage. She also learns that Mrs. Maradick's beloved house, the house in which her ghostly daughter lives on, will be torn down upon Dr. Maradick's marriage. On the eve of his second wedding, he is called to the hospital late, but as he starts downstairs, the nurse looks up to see a child's jump rope coiled on a stair in the darkness. He has fallen to his death before she can reach the light.

The story emphasizes sympathetic bonding between women. Nurse Randolph's initial sympathies are with the husband, who is "charming . . . , kind and handsome" (5)—a man, she says, "born to be a hero to women" (6). Even before she is singled out for the attention of the great surgeon, Miss Randolph succumbs to the force of his personality, observing, "But I am not the first nurse to grow love-sick about a doctor who never gave her a thought" (7). The hospital superintendent suspects that she is too sympathetic and imaginative for her own good, and asks, "'Wouldn't you have made a better novelist than a nurse?'" (5). Miss Randolph's first personal encounter with Dr. Maradick leads her to confess: "I felt I would have died for him" (13). By the time Miss Randolph does in fact write her story, however, Dr. Maradick is not its hero but its villain.

When Miss Randolph meets Mrs. Maradick, her sympathies are again besieged, and her loyalties divided. Mrs. Maradick's "sweetest and saddest smile" (16) and her "gentle voice" (17) win over Miss Randolph at once: "There was something about her—I don't know what it was—that made you love her as soon as she looked at you" (18). Despite Mrs. Maradick's accusations of murder against her husband, Miss Randolph concludes, "She was not mad" (20). Understandably, the young nurse has found her first night in the house emotionally draining: "By seven o'clock I was worn out—not from work but from the strain on my sympathy" (21). When next Miss Randolph sees the surgeon and is questioned about his wife's condition, she lies to protect Mrs. Maradick: "How the warning reached me—what invisible waves of sense-perception transmitted the message—I have never known; but while

I stood there, facing the splendour of the doctor's presence, every intuition cautioned me that the time had come when I must take sides in the household. While I stayed there I must stand either with Mrs. Maradick or against her" (26). She may be willing to die for Dr. Maradick, but she is not willing to sacrifice his wife to his convenience. Standing with Mrs. Maradick also means risking her career to contradict the opinion of the nerve specialist, Dr. Brandon.

In actuality, the decision has already been made for Miss Randolph by her cultural background and her gender: she is a Southern woman. She shares with Mrs. Maradick a Southern heritage, since she is from Richmond and her patient's mother was from South Carolina. When she chooses loyalty to the wife over loyalty to the husband, Miss Randolph acts on "intuition," on a message transmitted by "invisible waves of sense perception." The "power of sympathy" (35) that Miss Randolph herself recognizes extends to Mrs. Maradick's attachment to the house in which she was born, the house in which her ghostly daughter lives on.[4] Miss Randolph's own sensitivity to place—an attribute Glasgow frequently portrays as both female and Southern—allows her to see the ghostly child even before she has met Mrs. Maradick, a vision shared only by the black servant. After Mrs. Maradick's death, Miss Randolph does not see the ghost again until she hears that Mrs. Maradick's beloved house is to be torn down (38).

The men in the story are associated with materialism, lack of imagination, and absence of sympathy. Dr. Brandon is the less sinister of the two. Miss Randolph recalls him bitterly: "It wasn't his fault that he lacked red blood in his brain . . . and I hadn't talked to him ten minutes before I knew that he had been educated in Germany, and that he had learned over there to treat every emotion as a pathological manifestation" (24). It is Dr. Brandon who comes to take Mrs. Maradick away at what Miss Randolph describes as the height of her recovery: "Things couldn't have been better with her than they were" (29). Dr. Maradick, despite Miss Randolph's periodic disclaimers, emerges from her narrative as the supreme egotist, determined to gratify his own desires at all costs. Of their first meeting, Miss Randolph says "I have suspected since that he was not entirely unaware of my worship" (14). Later, she is more blunt: "His vanity was incredible in so great a man. I have seen him flush with pleasure when people turned to look at him in the streets" (36). He dines out every evening while his wife is ill. Finally, whatever the narrator claims to believe, the narrative suggests that he allowed his stepdaughter's death and caused her mother's death to acquire the fortune he needed to attract the woman who had once jilted him.

But who causes Maradick's death? Critic Marcelle Thiébaux observes that the ending is ambiguous, implicating Miss Randolph for her failure to light the stairs. Up until the revelation of Dr. Maradick's engagement, Miss Randolph has succeeded, she says, "in . . . acquitting him altogether" (37) and in convincing herself that she had never really seen the ghost. In short, when Mrs. Maradick leaves, she

again falls victim to the force of his personality. With his engagement comes confirmation of his guilt, although Miss Randolph continues to resist the inevitable conclusion. Sensitive to the atmosphere of the house, however, she anticipates—and ultimately aids—its ghostly vengeance. Dr. Maradick's death avenges his mistreatment of mother, child, and Miss Randolph herself, whose adoration of him is rewarded by his engagement to another.

Glasgow had numerous opportunities during this period of her life to compare the intelligence, insight, and skill of doctors and nurses; **"The Shadowy Third"** intimates the extent of her confidence in male doctors to diagnose and treat female illness. From the perspective of **"The Shadowy Third,"** it is difficult to understand why Glasgow critics have been so willing to accept the reliability of the two male narrators of Glasgow's second ghost story, **"Dare's Gift"**—one of them a doctor, the other a lawyer (Anderson's profession).[5] In Part I, the lawyer-husband of Mildred Beckwith recounts the story of their removal to a lonely colonial mansion in Virginia, Dare's Gift, after his wife's first nervous breakdown. Preoccupied with his defense of a railroad against charges of corruption, and mindful of the significance of the case to his career, Beckwith leaves Mildred alone a great deal while he commutes to the city, although he notices that she looks increasingly tired. When he contemplates suppressing incriminating evidence that he has uncovered, Mildred betrays him to the police, saying, "'I had to do it. I would do it again'" (73). Beckwith concludes, "Then it was I knew that Mildred's mind was unhinged" (73). But the elderly local doctor has a different interpretation. He claims that the house is "haunted by treachery" (77), telling the story of Lucy Dare, a staunch Confederate who had once betrayed her former lover, a Yankee, to Confederate soldiers at Dare's Gift. When the young man had been shot and killed, she had said to the doctor, "I had to do it. I would do it again" (100).

The contradictions in both narratives call into question the validity of masculine perception. Beckwith expresses his sincere concern for his wife's condition, but does not explain its cause. Nor does his concern induce him to remain at Dare's Gift and care for her. Mildred's own response to Dare's Gift contradicts his idyllic portrayal. What Beckwith describes as "just the place" for Mildred (69) is in actuality a prison for her, complete with an isolated setting, "walls of box" and "iron gates" (97) reminiscent of the asylum-house in Charlotte Perkins Gilman's "The Yellow Wallpaper." Similarly, the real Mildred emerges only from between the lines of her husband's narrative insensitivity. Once Beckwith has implied a history of mental illness from his reference to Mildred's "first nervous breakdown" (48), the reader must question his description of "the perfect matrimonial harmony in which we lived" (97). The real Mildred seems to be paying a heavy price for maintaining the harmony of which Beckwith is so proud.

Dr. Lakeby's portrayal of Lucy Dare is even more confusing.[6] He calls her "cold," and reflects, "I knew half a dozen men who would have died for her—and yet she gave them nothing, nothing, barely a smile" (92). He describes a recent visit to her in a home for the elderly, but her reported words and actions belie his characterization of her as senile, and she is likely, in any case, to be younger than he is.

Lucy Dare's place in the "haunting" of Dare's Gift is questionable, since at least one of the local betrayal stories involves an ancestor of Lucy's. Yet the men are correct in presuming a relationship between Mildred Beckwith and Lucy Dare, two women victimized by male assumptions about feminine nature. Of Lucy Dare's betrayal, the doctor says, "She has forgotten, but the house has remembered" (104). If the house has remembered anything, however, it has remembered the courage of a woman who placed public commitment above personal commitment, loyalty to a cause above loyalty to a lover. Just as Lucy Dare had believed that her betrayal would save the Confederacy, Mildred Beckwith believed that her betrayal could salvage the public trust. Both women recognize a moral imperative: "'I had to do it. I would do it again.'" Although Beckwith records no ghostly appearance and Lucy Dare is still alive, Mildred may have felt her presence in the same way Miss Randolph feels the tensions present in the Maradick house.

While **"Dare's Gift"** does not portray the deliberate masculine cruelty of **"The Shadowy Third,"** it suggests that masculine insensitivity can be harmful to women. **"The Past"** suggests that insensitivity can be deadly. In a narrative that recalls both **"The Shadowy Third"** and Wharton's "The Lady's Maid's Bell," a secretary, Miss Wrenn, tells her story. Miss Wrenn responds with immediate sympathy to the tragic air of her new employer, the beautiful Mrs. Vanderbridge, and suspects cruelty on the part of her employer's husband. Upon dining with the couple that evening, however, Miss Wrenn is surprised to discover that her host is kindly if preoccupied, and she is astonished when they are joined by another, a graceful, frail young woman to whom no one speaks. The housekeeper afterwards confides that this woman is the "Other One," the first Mrs. Vanderbridge, dead fifteen years. Mrs. Vanderbridge herself first explains that this "Other One" materializes only when Mr. Vanderbridge is thinking of her, that his own feelings of guilt about her death during pregnancy make him imagine her, and make her appear to him, as "hurt and tragic and revengeful" (134). Yet Mrs. Vanderbridge also believes that the apparition appears of her own will, and she has often contemplated an appeal to this ghostly predecessor. Miss Wrenn unwittingly provides the opportunity for such a confrontation when she discovers in a desk old love letters written not by Mr. Vanderbridge but by his adulterous first wife's lover. Miss Wrenn urges Mrs. Vanderbridge to use the letters to break her rival's power over her husband, but instead Mrs. Vanderbridge burns the letters, addressing her nemesis directly for the first time: "'I can't fight you that way. . . . Nothing is mine that I cannot win and keep fairly'" (145). To Miss Wrenn's amazement, the apparition responds to the "great pity, . . . sorrow and sweetness" (145) in that voice with a transformation from "evil" to "blessedness," "just as if a curse had turned into a blessing" (146), and vanishes—presumably for good.

As in **"The Shadowy Third,"** the narrator sees the ghost, first because of her sensitivity to atmosphere, and then because of her sympathy for another woman; she begins her narration, "I had no sooner entered the house than I knew something was wrong" (108). Engaged by Mrs. Vanderbridge, she says, because of "the remarkable similarity of our handwriting" (108), she also shares with her employer a common cultural and educational heritage as a Southern woman educated "at the little academy for young ladies in Fredericksburg" (108). Before she ever sees Mrs. Vanderbridge, then, she observes, "This was a bond of sympathy in my thoughts at least" (108). Overwhelmed by her new employer's beauty, kindness, and air of tragedy, she expresses her devotion at the end of their first meeting: "'I am ready to help you in any way—in any way that I can,' . . . and I was so deeply moved by her appeal that my voice broke in spite of my effort to control it" (III).

Miss Wrenn's sympathy for Mrs. Vanderbridge is encouraged by another woman, the elderly maid, Hopkins. Tearful at their first encounter, Hopkins immediately confides in Miss Wrenn, telling her, "'You look as if you could be trusted'" (115). Her plea is for Mrs. Vanderbridge: "'She needs a real friend—somebody who will stand by her no matter what happens'" (115). Hopkins provides Miss Wrenn with her first information about the ghost's identity; although she has never seen the ghost, she feels its presence and accepts it as only white and black women, black men, and children do in Glasgow's stories: "'I know it is there. I feel it even when I can't see it'" (116). She is the one who tells Miss Wrenn that Mr. Vanderbridge sees neither the ghost nor its effect on his wife.

The ghost herself is an interesting figure, because she too must ultimately become an object of sympathy. When Miss Wrenn first sees the ghost, she compares the young woman to a child: "I was aware, from the moment of her entrance, that she was bristling with animosity, though animosity is too strong a word for the resentful spite, like the jealous rage of a spoiled child, which gleamed now and then in her eyes" (121). As if to further dilute the ghost's malevolence, Glasgow added several lines at this point when editing the original *Scribner's* text for the **Shadowy Third** collection: "I couldn't think of her as wicked any more than I could think of a bad child as wicked. She was merely wilful [sic] and undisciplined and—I hardly know how to convey what I mean—elfish" (121). According to Mrs. Vanderbridge's somewhat illogical theory, Mr. Vanderbridge is at least partly responsible for the ghost's demeanor since she supposedly appears the way *he* thinks of her: "'His thought of her is like that, hurt and tragic and revengeful'" (134). Yet Mrs. Vanderbridge also considers a direct appeal to the ghost, despairing of her husband's capacity to change, or presumably, to understand: "'I've wondered and wondered how I might move her to pity'" (135). Miss Wrenn's depiction of the ghost in the final scene contradicts to some extent her own earlier description; the phantom is now malignant and sinister. Yet as she watches husband, wife, and ghost together, the violence Miss Wrenn advocates is directed not at the ghost but at Mr. Vanderbridge. Concerning the treacherous love letters, she says, "If I had my will, I should have flung them at him with a violence which would have startled him out of his lethargy. Violence, I felt, was what he needed" (144). In Miss Wrenn's view, Mr. Vanderbridge is killing his wife through his neglect, weakness, and insensitivity; he is far more dangerous to her than the ghost.

Instead of violence, Mrs. Vanderbridge chooses feminine weapons: the moral superiority and boundless sympathy of the angel in the house. Turning her sympathy on the ghost, she says, "'The only way, my dear, is the right way'" (145), though whether she is addressing her husband or the ghost here is unclear. Only then can Miss Wrenn see the ghost differently, perhaps because the specter has become a reflection of Mrs. Vanderbridge's thoughts rather than her husband's: "I saw her clearly for a moment—saw her as I had never seen her before—young and gentle and—yes, this is the only word for it—loving" (146). Of Mrs. Vanderbridge, Miss Wrenn concludes: "She had won, not by resisting, but by accepting; not by violence, but by gentleness; not by grasping, but by renouncing" (146). In short, Mrs. Vanderbridge's victory apotheosizes the cardinal feminine virtues of Glasgow's time, an appropriate ending to a drama played out primarily among women, yet indicative of Glasgow's ambivalence as a feminist to a feminine ideal she often criticized.[7]

The vision of female community offered briefly in the final scene of **"The Past"** is at the heart of the last Glasgow ghost story, **"Whispering Leaves."** Appropriately, Glasgow borrowed the ghost of **"Whispering Leaves"** from her own maternal legacy, modeling Mammy Rhody on the Mammy Rhoda who was nursemaid to her mother and sisters. Like three of the four stories, **"Whispering Leaves"** is narrated by a woman; here, it is Effie, who has gone for a visit to her ancestral home, a plantation now owned by an unknown cousin named Blanton. Also in residence, she learns, are Blanton's second wife, her children, the new baby, and a little boy from Blanton's first marriage, Pell. When Effie first encounters Pell, he is courting disaster in a mulberry tree, but when he falls he is caught by "an old negro woman" (73), who disappears as quickly as she has appeared. Effie soon learns that Pell's first nurse, Mammy Rhody, had died several years before, after faithfully fulfilling a promise to his dying mother "that she would never let the child out of her sight" (162). Effie worries about Pell—his pallor, gravity, and shyness seem to her signs of loneliness and parental neglect. As she grows more attached to him, she has several mysterious encounters with the old black woman she had seen the first day. She feels that this silent figure wants something of her, but she does not know what it is. One night, the house catches fire, and Effie is frantic to learn that Pell is trapped inside. When she sees the dark figure emerge carrying Pell, however, she understands at last and steps forward with outstretched arms to claim the child from his ghostly guardian.

The story emphasizes throughout the significance of female history and the strength of female bonding. Effie describes Whispering Leaves as "the house in which my mother and so many of my grandmothers were born" (152).

Female history seems to be the only significant history here, and Effie's sensitivity to the house's female past allows her to see the ghost that no one else can see but Pell. After her first glimpse of the apparition, Effie muses about the woman's place in her own past:

> Though I had had only the briefest glimpse of her, I had found her serene leaf-brown face strangely attractive, almost, I thought oddly enough, as if her mysterious black eyes, under the heavy brows, had penetrated to some secret chamber of my memory. I had never seen her before, and yet I felt as if I had known her all my life, particularly in some half-forgotten childhood which haunted me like a dream. Could it be that she had nursed my mother and my grandmother, and that she saw a resemblance to the children she had trained in her youth? (166)

Before she even learns Mammy Rhody's identity, Effie acknowledges a female bond based on caring, and associates Mammy with her own foremothers.

In fact, she discovers that Mammy Rhody is linked to the female history of Whispering Leaves because Rhody had nursed the first Mrs. Blanton, Clarissa. Effie sees herself as tied to these two other women—her predecessors at Whispering Leaves—by their shared love of nature. Nature is one expression of the house's history which is visible and audible—beautiful, fragrant, and melodious. Effie is warned about the profusion of birds around Whispering Leaves; the black driver tells her, "'Hit seems dat ar place wuz jes made ter drive folks bird crazy'" (155), and the white driver calls them "'the ghosts of Mammy Rhody's pets'" (163), the birds Mammy was said to have tamed for Pell. In one scene, a vision of the red turbaned Mammy Rhody resolves itself into a scarlet tanager (184). But Effie insists, "I liked birds!" (156), and later has a vision of "the bright ghosts of all the birds that had ever sung in this place" (184). The neglected garden that Effie admires is Clarissa's: "Never until that moment had I known what the rapture of smell could be" (184). An observation about the garden elicits from her cousin Pelham, Pell's father, the response, "'That sounds like Clarissa'" (178). Except for Pell, Effie alone seems capable of appreciating the female legacy of Whispering Leaves. Mrs. Maradick's love for her house in **"The Shadowy Third"** is here replaced by the women's love for the garden surrounding the house, and it is the garden that remains when the house burns down.

But the force that most strongly draws the three women together is their love for Pell, who falls out of a tree, behaves like a bird at dinner, and spends his days in his mother's garden. Effie, alive to the feminine past of Whispering Leaves, sees the woman who haunts the garden in order to keep her promise to another woman, and out of love for the two generations of children she nursed. Effie's sympathy for the anguished apparition and her growing love for Pell eventually allow her to translate the "inaudible language" (172) of the ghostly appeal. Pell informs her: "'Mammy says you must take me away with you when you go away'" (191). Yet Effie resists the responsibility; to herself, she says she felt the resistance "as if [she] were disputing with some invisible presence at [her] side" (193). Her love must undergo a literal trial by fire before she fully understands the necessity for her action: "I knew, in that moment of vision, what the message was that she had for me" (197). Effie will continue the female maternal tradition of Whispering Leaves, and will do so unhampered by masculine intervention.

Both parents are insensitive to Pell's suffering, but Glasgow reserves particular contempt for Pell's father, a man of limited interests whom Effie dismisses as "one Pelham Blanton, a man of middle age, who was, as far as we were aware, without a history" (151). To be without a history at Whispering Leaves, where history is so important, is to be utterly insignificant. Effie describes Blanton as "vain, spoiled, selfish, amiable as long as he was given everything he wanted, and still good-looking in an obvious and somewhat flashing style" (176). Her empathy with Clarissa leads her to speculate on the happiness of their marriage: "I wondered how that first wife, Clarissa of the romantic name and the flaming hair, had endured existence in this lonely neighborhood with the companionship of a man who thought of nothing but food or drink. Perhaps he was different then; and yet was it possible for such abnormal egoism to develop in the years since her death?" (176). Her own antipathy for the man is Effie's only basis for presuming an unhappy marriage, yet Mammy Rhody is also clearly unwilling to leave Pell in his hands. Effie accepts the responsibility of motherhood without the burdens of wifehood, and the story suggests that she is better suited for motherhood as a single woman than as a victim of marital misery.

Of all the ghost stories, **"Whispering Leaves"** offers the most radical alternative to conventional romance; building upon the bonds of female sympathy portrayed in **"The Shadowy Third," "The Past,"** and **"Dare's Gift,"** it envisions a sense of female community that exists outside of marriage and transcends heterosexual love. As a whole, the stories constitute a forceful and unflinching critique of heterosexual love and marriage. The contemporaneous novels, however, demonstrate Henry Anderson's influence in their sexual politics as well as in their national and regional politics. Despite their bleak portrayal of marriage, both *The Builders* (1919) and *One Man in His Time* (1922) end with a promise of happy marriage for their heroines.[8]

The conflicts Glasgow experienced during these years— between marriage and singleness, between Henry Anderson and Anne Virginia Bennett, between convention and anomaly—are best illustrated by a comparison of the novels with the ghost stories. The stories, for example, contain no exemplary male characters: at their best, men are unperceptive and insensitive; at their worst, they are malicious and deadly. Nurse Randolph must learn, in **"The Shadowy Third,"** not to confuse a distinguished man's good reputation with the reality. In both *The Builders* and *One Man in His Time,* on the other hand, the heroine must be won over to a man judged harshly by people in general. In the case of David Blackburn, hero of *The Builders,* that judgment is particularly harsh and unjust where women are concerned. *The Builders* allows Blackburn to play a

role Anderson often played in his letters—that of long-suffering victim to female irrationality.

The inaccuracy of the heroines' initial perceptions in the novels disputes the value of female intuition and sympathy. These qualities are under particular attack in *The Builders,* the novel on which Anderson probably collaborated most heavily.[9] When Miss Randolph chooses sides in the Maradick household in **"The Shadowy Third,"** she feels compelled to conceal both her own sympathy and Mrs. Maradick's sensitivity; in a passage quoted earlier, she responds to Dr. Maradick's question concerning his wife's sanity: "Every intuition cautioned me that the time had come when I must take sides in the household. While I stayed there I must stand either with Mrs. Maradick or against her. . . . 'She talked quite rationally,' I replied after a moment" (26).

The Builders, in its portrayal of David Blackburn, values rational intelligence, commitment to a generalized public good, and a strong sense of justice. When nurse-protagonist Caroline Meade praises her female employer's sympathy, she demonstrates her own naivete: "'Her sympathy is wonderful!' Almost in spite of her will, against the severe code of her professional training, she began by taking Mrs. Blackburn's side in the household" (*Builders* 93). In the course of the novel, Miss Meade must come to mistrust her own sympathy, and to recognize that Mrs. Blackburn's is shallow, calculated, false. Presumably, once Miss Meade has learned her lesson, she will return to the "severe code of her professional training"—a phrase recalling Miss Randolph's scornful description of Dr. Brandon's German medical training. Perhaps Anderson hoped that the sympathetic Miss Bennett would follow suit.

In the ghost stories, adherence to rationality prevents white men, and especially professional men, from seeing ghosts. The same quality promotes a generalized insensitivity to atmosphere and environment, and to the feelings of the women around them. It may make them distinguished politicians, but it hardly suits them for matrimony; **"Dare's Gift"** and **"The Shadowy Third"** suggest that it may make them renowned doctors, but it cannot make them good ones. Thus while contemplating marriage and accepting a male collaborator for her work, Glasgow continued her more radically feminist tradition in her ghost stories, choosing a genre she knew to be appropriate to her concerns. Living unhappily in a house she perceived to be haunted, she wrote of other unhappy women and their hauntings. Sensitive to the presence of the past at One West Main Street, she portrayed other houses as texts in a female history available to anyone sensitive enough to read them properly. Dependent upon a female companion for the understanding and sympathy her male lover seemed unable to offer, she celebrated the bond of female friendship as a more fulfilling tie than that of heterosexual romance and marriage.

Notes

[1] A typescript draft of *The Woman Within* in the University of Virginia's Alderman Library records a previous version of this line:

"It is an exact description of my sensations while I stood there in that empty house" (Accession no. 5060, box 5, TS 190).

[2] "Ellen and Anne Virginia were sitting before the fire one night when Anne virginia said: 'Ellen, we need money. Why don't you write a story?' Ellen agreed, and wrote 'The Shadowy Third'" (recounted in Godbold 115). Glasgow's own distaste for short stories has contributed to the critical neglect of the ghost stories. In 1918, she told an interviewer, "I cannot write short stories" (Overton 26). She had published three short stories early in her career but had otherwise devoted herself to novels. That she specifically wrote the ghost stories to earn money is corroborated by Richard Meeker: "While hardly poor by ordinary standards, Miss Glasgow had large medical bills, traveled extensively, and had to maintain One West Main Street in Richmond after her father's death in 1916" (5).

[3] Marjorie Kinnan Rawlings's attempts to document Glasgow's engagement for a projected biography are recorded in E. MacDonald. A primary source of information on this complex relationship, however, is Anderson's correspondence with Glasgow from this period, which is held by the Alderman Library. In addition, Anderson's mother, Laura E. Anderson, wrote Glasgow on 19 November 1918: "Henry . . . told me of the congeniality of feeling existing between you and himself" (Accession no. 5060, box 11). Godbold suggests that "the engagement was abandoned rather than canceled" in the fall of 1919 (124).

[4] Glasgow critic Julius Raper believes that all of the Glasgow ghosts are suspect, merely reflections of their viewers' state of mind. With respect to "The Past," he writes: "We spend the story trying to outwit the narrator (and the author) concerning the motive and conditions for her seeing the ghost of Dr. Maradick's daughter Dorothea. . . . Margaret's [Miss Randolph's] doubts about the ghost (after Mrs. Maradick dies in an asylum) tend to reestablish her credibility just before she reports the fourth appearance of the girl" (68). This is so far from my own experience in reading the story that I question the wisdom of that gender-neutral, generalized "we." Nor would I consider calling Dorothea "Dr. Maradick's daughter," which appears to me to support the doctor's diagnosis of his wife's insanity and paranoia by granting him credibility as a father. Odder to me still is Raper's introduction of the ghost stories with physiological justifications for the supernatural experience: "Today we know enough about the effects chemical alterations have on consciousness to acknowledge that sane people may sometimes *see things that are not there* and see them as substantially as though they were there—even when these phenomena exist *only* as chemical changes in the brain. We also know that strong emotions . . . involve significant chemical changes throughout the body" (67). These explanations recall Miss Randolph's description of the great nerve specialist, Dr. Brandon, through whom, I argue, Glasgow is satirizing the psychological profession.

[5] I include "Dare's Gift" among Glasgow's ghost stories because of the unresolved possibility that it describes some kind of haunting, even though an actual ghost is not likely. For a fuller discussion of the story, see my own essay in *Studies in Short Fiction.*

[6] Again, Raper and I disagree. Whereas Raper argues that Mildred's repression led to her nervous breakdown, and thus that Beckwith is an unreliable narrator, he finds Dr. Lakeby a credible narrator, faulting Beckwith for lacking the "objectivity the old doctor brought to the case of Lucy Dare" (70). I am arguing that objectivity is not a stance valued in the ghost stories.

[7] For a scathing analysis of Glasgow's feminism, see Frazee.

[8] In the case of *The Builders,* although Caroline Meade and David Blackburn cannot marry until his wife dies, the novel ends with an understanding between them, and it is obvious that his wife does not have long to live.

[9] Anderson's letters to Glasgow in the Alderman Library sometimes refer to chapters he has received from her and recommended revisions. Accession no. 5060, box 9.

Works Cited

Anderson, Henry. Letters. Accession no. 5060, box 9. Ellen Glasgow Papers. U of Virginia, Charlottesville.

Anderson, Laura. Letter. Accession no. 5060, box 11. Ellen Glasgow Papers. U of Virginia, Charlottesville.

Carpenter, Lynette. "Lucy's Daring Gift in Ellen Glasgow's 'Dare's Gift.'" *Studies in Short Fiction* 21 (1984): 91-105.

Colvert, James B. "Agent and Author: Ellen Glasgow's Letters to Paul Revere Reynolds." *Studies in Bibliography* 14 (1961), 177-96.

Frazee, Monique Parent. "Ellen Glasgow as a Feminist." *Ellen Glasgow: Centennial Essays.* Ed. M. Thomas Inge. Charlottesville: U of Virginia P, 1976. 167-89.

Glasgow, Ellen. *The Builders.* Garden City, NY: Doubleday, Page, 1919.

———. *One Man in His Time.* Garden City, NY: Doubleday, Page, 1922.

———. *The Shadowy Third and Other Stories.* Garden City, NY: Doubleday, Page, 1923.

———. *The Woman Within.* New York: Harcourt, Brace, 1954.

Godbold, E. Stanly, Jr. *Ellen Glasgow and the Woman Within.* Baton Rouge: Louisiana State UP, 1954.

MacDonald, E. "A Retrospective Henry Anderson and Marjorie Kinnan Rawlings." *Ellen Glasgow Newsletter* 12 (March 1980): 4-16.

Meeker, Richard. Introduction. *The Collected Stories of Ellen Glasgow.* Baton Rouge: Louisiana State UP, 1963. 3-23.

Overton, Grant M. *The Women Who Make Our Novels.* New York: Dodd, Mead, 1918.

Raper, Julius Rowan. *From the Sunken Garden: The Fiction of Ellen Glasgow, 1916-1945.* Baton Rouge: Louisiana State UP, 1980.

Thiébaux, Marcelle. *Ellen Glasgow.* New York: Frederick Ungar, 1982.

Tutwiler, Carrington C., Jr. *A Catalogue of the Library of Ellen Glasgow.* Charlottesville: Bibliographical Society of the U of Virginia, 1969.

Catherine Rainwater (essay date 1995)

SOURCE: "Ellen Glasgow's Outline of History in *The Shadowy Third and Other Stories*," in *The Critical Response to H. G. Wells,* edited by William J. Scheick, Greenwood Press, 1995, pp. 125-38.

[*In the following essay, Rainwater asserts that Glasgow's Gothic stories were influenced by the works of H. G. Wells and Edgar Allan Poe.*]

In several letters in her autobiography, *The Woman Within* (1954), Ellen Glasgow mentions reading the works of Poe and Wells.[1] In contemplating these two authors' works, she joined what has now become a wide network of writers whose art bears complex intertextual connections centering around a mutual literary debt to Poe and, frequently, also to one another.[2] Glasgow admits to feeling a "curious . . . kinship with Poe,"[3] and although she calls Wells's novels "dull" (*WW* 203), she owned at least five of them along with an early edition of *The Outline of History* (1920). Apparently, she found the *Outline* intriguing enough to consult in more than one of its many versions.[4] Glasgow's well-known fascination with Darwin might partly account for her interest in Wells's ideas about history, for *Outline* is firmly rooted in Darwinian evolutionary theory. This same interest in Darwinian concepts and their social and philosophical applications might also partially explain her homage to Poe in several short stories published between 1916 and 1923 and collected as *The Shadowy Third and Other Stories* (1923). Although Poe is a pre-Darwinian writer, his works anticipate important, if not biologically based, questions about human evolution and devolution, and about the existence of primitive, irrational depths beneath the surface of civilized society.

Glasgow wrote these Gothic stories suggesting Poe's and Wells's influence during the years immediately surrounding the end of the first World War—a time when Wells claims that "everyone" was in some way or another "outlining" history in response to global conditions.[5] The tales attest to her efforts to account for the shape of things past and things to come, efforts more typically registered throughout her career in numerous realistic novels. Although Glasgow suffered extreme emotional ups and downs throughout her life, several critics and Glasgow herself have observed that the years between 1910 and 1925 marked a critical period of hesitation, reassessment, and redirection of her artistic energies.[6] She wrote short stories at this time, argues Richard K. Meeker, because she had temporarily lost a sense of a "comprehensive view of life . . . Her writings . . . contain increasing references to a world gone mad, uncivilized barbarians, and ugly deviations from human decency . . . It became increasingly hard for her to write on a large scale, to trace the causes and effects that had so fascinated her" in her earlier works.[7]

Indeed, Glasgow's preface to *Barren Ground* (1925) reports a period of "tragedy" and "defeat" from which she claims to have emerged during the composition of this novel. Dismissing most of her previous work as "thin" and "two-dimensional," Glasgow declares that with *Barren Ground* she has arrived at a "turning point" in her life, and that she can now write as she had always intended to write—"of the South, not sentimentally, as a conquered province, but dispassionately, as a part of the larger world"; and "of human nature" rather than "Southern characteristics." She is sure that "different and better work is ahead."[8] Glasgow's sense of the "large scale" and her "comprehensive view of life" had returned along with renewed confidence in "trac[ing] . . . causes and effects" in history.

Despite this renewed confidence, Glasgow never develops any systematic outline of history (indeed, she seems finally to agree with Wells that progress is the tentative result of "Will feeling about"[9]); however, her ghost stories that address history reveal the characteristically dialectical pattern of her thought as she struggled to attain a sense of a universal pattern grounded upon some reliable authority.[10] Between 1916 and 1923, when most of the pieces in *The Shadowy Third and Other Stories* were written and published, the ideas of Poe and Wells (in *The Outline of History,* at least) apparently served Glasgow as thesis and antithesis in the dialectical development of her own view of historical progress. All of the stories imply Glasgow's internalization of a Poe-esque vision coalescent with her own sense of a mad "world . . . [of] uncivilized barbarians, and ugly deviations from human decency," while the 1923 stories suggest the substantial role that Wells's *Outline* might have played in her development of a "comprehensive view" of it all. Indeed, Poe and Wells might be seen as "opposing angels" that "warred somewhere in the depths of [her] being"[11] for control of Glasgow's sense of historical design.

The stories in *The Shadowy Third* intertextually connect with Poe's in several ways: at least two—**"Dare's Gift"** (1917) and **"Jordan's End"** (1923)—allude overtly to Poe through their use of proper names, and three others strongly suggest Poe's presence in Glasgow's imagination as she wrote. Nearly all exhibit Poe-esque narrative management and, thereby, imply a Poe-inspired worldview with important implications for Glasgow's theory of history. Finally, Glasgow's stories reveal her sympathy with the Southern antebellum ethos of Poe's work, however displaced his regional concerns might be into ostensibly ahistorical contexts.[12] Glasgow seems, on the one hand, to internalize Poe's fearful vision of a dystopian, devolutionary world and, on the other hand, to resist this vision by adopting a typically Wellsian, tentative faith in a better possible future. In fact, we might borrow the trope of a contracting-expanding universe from Poe's *Eureka* (1848) to identify the bipolar phases of Glasgow's thought that are inscribed in the stories comprising *The Shadowy Third.* It is interesting to note that Wells himself went through similar alternating periods of dystopian fears and utopian hopes, and that he transforms this same trope from *Eureka* into his own theory of "systolic" and "diastolic" phases of human development.[13] In her Poe-esque devolutionary, or contractile phase, Glasgow imagines history as a claustrophobic "web" of "destiny," while in her Wellsian, expansive frame of mind, she envisions history as a "spiral" of slow progress.[14]

Though a few other critics have, mostly in passing, remarked Glasgow's literary debt to Poe, none have adequately assessed what Glasgow apparently learned from her predecessor about the subtleties of narrative management and about the worldview that he implies through the dubious claims and judgments of his prototypically unreliable narrators.[15] Glasgow's **"The Shadowy Third"** (1916) is a case in point. Like most of the stories in the collection, it features a first-person narrator whose credibility dwindles in a decidedly Poe-esque fashion as the details of her narrative unfold. Young and infatuated with Roland Maradick, the charming physician who hires her to tend his ailing wife, Glasgow's narrator has a marked "imagination" and admits that she would "have made a better novelist than a nurse" (5). In the Poe tradition of such deluded, vengeful narrators as appear in "The Tell-Tale Heart" (1843) and "A Cask of Amontillado" (1846), Margaret Randolph might in fact be guilty of murdering a man whose sins against her (and others) perhaps exist only in her mind.

Though some evidence in the story suggests that Maradick himself might be a murderer, the Poe-esque unreliability of the narrator precludes the reader's final judgment of him. Subtle hints of the narrator suppressed animosity toward the physician appear early in the tale: "I am not the first nurse to grow love-sick about a doctor who never gave her a thought" (7); and "my worship [of him] . . . was a small thing, heaven knows, to flatter his vanity . . . but to some men no tribute is too insignificant to give pleasure" (14). From the outset, the narrator has mixed motives for believing Mrs. Maradick's story of her husband's evil designs; perhaps the wife's charges are based on fact, or perhaps the narrator decides to believe the story that "nobody [else] believes" (20) because of Dr. Maradick's indifference to her "worship."

Additional clues to the narrator's less than objective state of mind include her self-proclaimed psychic "sensitivity" that she boasts of, then denies in an appeal to the reader's credulity: she claims to see beyond the "web of material fact . . . [to] the spiritual form . . . [Unlike other people's], my vision was not blinded by the clay through which I looked" (35). Yet she contradictorily declares, "I am writing down the things I actually saw, and I repeat that I have never had the slightest twist in the direction of the miraculous" (31). Such direct solicitation of the reader's confidence in a self-incriminating narrator's inconsistent account of events is a favorite technique of Poe, who uses it over and over again in such stories as "The Fall of the House of Usher" (1839), "Ligeia" (1838), and "The Tell-Tale Heart."

Frequently insisting upon her own veracity, the narrator also reveals, "I was conscious of an inner struggle, as if opposing angels warred somewhere in the depths of my being. When at last I made my decision [to defy Dr. Maradick's orders], I was acting less from reason, I knew, than in obedience to the pressure of some secret current of thought" (27). This "secret current of thought" overrides common sense and logic. Recalling the narrator in "The Fall of the House of Usher," who unquestioningly accepts Roderick's bizarre explanation for secretly burying

his twin in the vault, Margaret avoids asking important questions at crucial moments. She seeks no answers to confirm or deny suspicions about what seems to go on in the house, but instead she grows more confident of her "secret" knowledge. Like the narcissistic Mrs. Maradick (who stagnates within the enclosed psychological space of her self, symbolized by her haunted house), the narrator perversely refuses to look beyond her self-validated, intuitive knowledge to the outside world for corroboration of her suspicions.

Indeed, like Poe's "A Cask of Amontillado," Glasgow's story ends with what might be interpreted as a smug confession, a "signature" to an artful act of murder committed by a narcissistic, self-deluded narrator. Margaret tells us that one night as the doctor descended the stairs,

> I distinctly saw—I will swear to this on my deathbed— a child's skipping rope lying loosely coiled, as if it had been dropped from a careless little hand, in the bend of the staircase. With a spring I had reached the electric button, flooding the hall with light; but as I did so, while my arm was still outstretched behind me, I heard the [doctor's] humming voice change to a cry of surprise or terror, and the figure on the staircase tripped heavily and stumbled with groping hands into emptiness . . . Something—it may have been, as the world believes, a misstep in the dimness, or it may have been, as I am ready to bear witness, an invisible judgment—something had killed him at the very moment when he most wanted to live. (43)

This ending leads to at least two possible conclusions, one supernatural and the other natural: (1) the ghost of Maradick's allegedly murdered stepdaughter has left the rope on the stair; or (2) the narrator herself has done it, ostensibly to avenge the murders of the girl and her mother but also to punish the object of her unrequited love, who is soon to marry another woman. Obviously, "the world believes" Dr. Maradick's fall was an accident, while the narrator insists that "an invisible judgment" struck him down. That such judgment might be her own is implied in the "invisible warning" that she receives earlier—"a current of thought . . . beat from the air around into my brain. Though it cost me my career as a nurse and my reputation for sanity, I knew that I must obey that invisible warning" of Dr. Maradick's evil plot against his wife (33).

The narrator's behavior seems even more strange when Mrs. Maradick finally dies; despite her firm belief in the doctor's guilt, the narrator does not leave his house. She stays on to work for him and, eventually, she decides for no apparent reason that he must be completely innocent, after all. Just when he stands "clear and splendid" in her "verdict of him" (37), she learns that he plans to marry a woman who once rejected him because he was poor. Suddenly, all the rumors of Maradick's plot to inherit his dead wife's fortune seem plausible again. Either jealousy or some ultimate revelation of Maradick's true evil sparks the narrator's return to her previous state of mind. She sees the ghost of the little girl again and, eventually, Maradick ends up dead at the foot of the stairs—whether by accident or by design, the reader can never know for sure.

Like most of Poe's own stories, Glasgow's "The Shadowy Third" reveals little if any *overt* concern with history. However, also like many of Poe's works, Glasgow's story supports an allegorical reading of its implications for a view of history. Several critics have observed that Poe's dystopian tales reveal not only his anxiety over national conditions presaging the Civil War, but also his discomfort as an artist and a citizen in a country without a clear sense of national identity rooted in a distinct heritage. "The Fall of the House of Usher," in particular, can be read as a commentary upon the death of a Southern agrarian aristocracy that is out of step with the progressive, urban, industrialized North.

A significant historical context is implied in "The Shadowy Third" in Glasgow's identification of her narrator (Margaret) and Mrs. Maradick with the South, and of Roland Maradick and the setting of the story with the North. The story takes place in New York, but the narrator recently comes from Virginia, and Mrs. Maradick's mother was from South Carolina. The narrator and Maradick's wife are romantic and otherworldly, and both are trapped in the "web" of a dead past. The ailing Mrs. Maradick refuses to leave the house where she was born and where she claims to see the ghost of her dead daughter. Even her fortune constitutes a constraining past; she inherited it from her dead first husband, whose will imposed limits on her disposal of it. The narrator is similarly unable to free herself from the past and appears compelled—like a Poe narrator—to return to it in telling her story.[16] Maradick, on the other hand, is Northern and the controller of both women's "destiny" (6) in the same way that the nation—reconstructed according to terms of the victorious North—controls the destiny as well as the "wealth" of the former Confederacy. As soon as his wife dies, he sells her house to developers who plan to raze it and build modern apartments. The character of Maradick also seems to suggest allegorically the overall evolutionary pattern of human history. In one passage, the narrator describes his "coat of dark fur" (6), a particularly interesting observation given Glasgow's consistent preoccupation with Darwinian evolution. Maradick, wearing the dark coat of an animal, embodies not only the urban industrial future (the "barbarian" aspect of modernity that Glasgow dreaded), but also the bestial evolutionary past. Indeed, the narrator's attraction to him is fundamentally an "animal" attraction to his "shining dark" eyes, the "dusky glow in his face," and the sound of his voice.[17]

This passage resonates with another passage in a later story, "The Difference" (1923), in which the evolutionary past is evoked through a Poe-esque image of the "skeleton of the savage" that lies "beneath the civilization of the ages" (229). Poe's description of Usher's house evokes the archetypal image of a death's head and suggests the nonrational dimensions of mind that rationality masks; the image of the skull-beneath-the-veneer-of-civilization is one that Glasgow doubtless also encountered in her reading of Darwin's *Descent of Man* (1871) as well as in the Darwinian vernacular wisdom of her era.[18] Both "The Shadowy Third" and "The Difference" imply that Glasgow's interest in Poe coalesced with her Darwinian notions of human history.

"Dare's Gift" (1917) is another story with an intertextual relationship to Poe's fiction; furthermore, it is overtly concerned with history, particularly of the South. Richard Meeker has outlined some of the more obviously Poe-esque traits of plot and setting in "Dare's Gift." For example, "Roderick" is the name of the original owner of the ancestral estate. The "house was of great age" (49), and upon close scrutiny, it reveals "architectural absurdities—wanton excrescences . . . The rooms appeared cramped and poorly lighted" (61). The windows appear to be "staring" (63), and a reddish glow surrounds Dare's Gift, recalling the "red litten" windows of Usher's house. Furthermore, a Poe-esque "vegetable sentience" prevails in the house over the rationality and individual will of its inhabitants.

The less obvious features of Glasgow's debt to Poe in this story have gone unremarked, however. Her tale of a haunted mansion implies a claustrophobic view of human history as an unbreakable mold delimiting thought and action. Glasgow's post-Civil-War South is enslaved to a past ideal, according to Dr. Lakeby:

> In every age one ideal enthralls the imagination of mankind; it is in the air; it subjugates the will; it enchants the emotions. Well, in the South fifty years ago this ideal was patriotism; and the passion of patriotism, which bloomed like some red flower, the flower of carnage, over the land, had grown in Lucy Dare's soul into an exotic blossom. (91-92)

Lucy's house, called Dare's Gift, is literally steeped in the history of Virginia. From its first owner's purported betrayal of Nathaniel Bacon (in Bacon's Rebellion), to Lucy Dare's betrayal to the Confederates of her Yankee sweetheart, to Mildred Beckwith's betrayal of her husband (the first narrator) to his legal adversaries, the house exerts a sinister power over its inhabitants, who grow "feverish" and "excited" by their sometimes perverse notions of patriotism the longer they remain on the estate.

Like Roderick Usher, who cannot escape the fate that has befallen his ancestral house, the various descendants of Sir Roderick, such as Lucy Dare and other owners of Dare's Gift, are trapped within an historical pattern that compulsively repeats itself, partially owing to their lack of perspective on the past which the house embodies. Poe's Roderick Usher apparently cannot leave his terrible house; so he summons his analytical friend (from the past) to help him.[19] Instead of helping Roderick, however, the narrator succumbs to the deranging influences of the estate. Like Poe's story, Glasgow's underscores the circularly repetitive and irrational power of the past embodied in a house.

This circularly repetitive historical pattern in "Dare's Gift" is emphasized by Glasgow's narrative structure. She uses a Chinese-box arrangement of stories within stories to suggest that storytelling itself might be one of the ways in which human beings attempt to extricate themselves from historically repetitive patterns. However, Glasgow's narrator resembles Poe's in "The Fall of the House of Usher," who ends up mired in Roderick's history and in need of an audience to listen to his admittedly fantastic tale, presumably to help him, in turn, get some kind of perspective. Glasgow's outermost narrator and latest owner of Dare's Gift, Harold Beckwith, includes old Dr. Lakeby's story within his own in an effort to reach back, through Lakeby's memory, to get a "clear perspective" (47) on his situation. However, nestled inside of Lakeby's narration lies the implacable silence of Lucy Dare, an "ethereal" and "unearthly" (82, 83), Poe-esque woman who no longer remembers her past at Dare's Gift and who, in any case, was "never much of a talker" (103). Ultimately, Beckwith is left with no "clear perspective," but only Lakeby's observation that

> [w]e nibble at the edges of the mystery, and the great Reality—the Incomprehensible—is still untouched, undiscovered. It unfolds hour by hour, day by day, creating, enslaving, killing us, while we painfully gnaw off—what? A crumb or two, a grain from that vastness which envelops us, which remains impenetrable—.(79)[20]

Both **"The Shadowy Third"** and **"Dare's Gift"** end on a note of stagnation, an acceptance of a suffocating, dystopian world of insanity or hollow capitulation to the past. The narrator of **"The Shadowy Third"** needs to tell her story ten years later, perhaps to find the ever-elusive "perspective." Beckwith and Lakeby in **"Dare's Gift,"** who attempt to tell their story, circle about Lucy's silence and the impenetrable mystery of the house. Like the narrator of **"The Shadowy Third,"** the narrator of **"Dare's Gift"** opens with a frustrated remark concerning past events that he has yet to comprehend in full: a "year has passed, and I am beginning to ask myself if the thing actually happened" (47). As compulsively as any of Poe's narrators, he engages in a sort of narrative exorcism, as if reciting the past could relieve him of the burden it constitutes.[21]

In **"The Shadowy Third"** and **"Dare's Gift,"** Glasgow implies that the past is a trap in which we may be caught without comprehension or means of escape. Though she innately resembles both Poe and Wells in her battle with alternating idealism and pessimism,[22] the early stories in Glasgow's collection suggest her particular sensitivity to Poe's dystopian fears (a frame of mind in which, likewise, Wells sometimes found himself.)[23] The stories dated 1923, however, suggest a guardedly optimistic expansion of her thought within the Wellsian frame of reference reflected in *The Outline of History*. These later stories suggest that limited transcendence of ostensibly closed personal spheres—the self, the South—is possible; Glasgow was perhaps affected by Wells's hope for a world synthesis based on tentative notions of will and progress. Indeed, in two of her 1923 stories, the "webs" and "circles" of the early works are replaced with the Wellsian trope of the "spiral" (an image that depicts the overarching pattern of historical evolution that Wells describes in the *Outline*) to represent this idea of tentative progress.[24]

Instead of frustrated efforts to gain an elusive "perspective," Glasgow's 1923 stories conclude with open-ended questions. These questions imply that the present need

not be hopelessly constrained by the past, an idea that Glasgow's story called **"The Past"** (1920) states overtly and that her reading of Wells's *Outline* would certainly have reinforced. (In **"The Past,"** the narrator describes the protagonist's "victory" as a result of "chang[ing] her thought of the past" [146].) As early as 1908, Wells had developed his well-known notion that history is essentially the record of life struggling towards consciousness and of "Will feeling about."[25] In the edition of the *Outline* that Glasgow owned, Wells writes: "[T]he history of our race for the last few thousand years is no more than a history of the development and succession of states of mind and acts arising out of them . . . [T]he world is full of physical evils, but there is this mental awakening to set against them" ([1920] 2:572). He goes on to say that the current era "rises to a crisis in the immense *interrogation* of today [emphasis mine] . . . History is and must always be no more than an account of beginnings . . . Life begins perpetually" (2:579, 594-595).

Wells's evolutionary view of human consciousness and history also stresses the gradual refinement of "free intelligence" as opposed to the atavistic mentality of the primitive past (1:262). This intelligence affords human will the power to modify the apparent designs of destiny. Eventually, according to Wells, all forms of self-serving individualism (greed, nationalism, etc.) will pass away because they are socially maladaptive; Wells's ultimate world synthesis is a secular Nirvana: "The teaching of history, as we are unfolding it in this book, is strictly in accordance with this teaching of Buddha . . . The study of biological progress . . . reveals . . . the merger of the narrow globe of the individual experience in a wider being . . . To forget oneself in greater interests is to escape from a prison" (1:423).

Glasgow's attraction to these and other ideas of Wells registers emphatically in her 1923 stories. **"Whispering Leaves"** and **"Jordan's End,"** in particular, conclude with tentative hope for the future; literally, they end with a Wellsian brand of "interrogation" suggested by the narrators' questions. In **"Whispering Leaves,"** Pelham and the narrator escape the prison of the past as represented by another Poe-esque, haunted family estate. The story ends with two questions inviting the reader to ponder the nature of the "reality" of the past: "Was [the experience with the ghost] a dream, after all? Was the only reality the fact that I held the child safe and unharmed in my arms?" (197). In **"Jordan's End,"** a female protagonist anticipates and even hastens her freedom from the Jordans, her husband's congenitally insane family. This story seems designed deliberately to force the reader to ponder the same questions that the narrator must ask himself for the next thirty years: Did Judith "kill" her husband, and if she did, was it a morally defensible act? Glasgow's third story of 1923, **"The Difference,"** is not literally a ghost story, but it may (like her ghost stories) be read as the record of a character's escape from the tyrannical influence of history. The main character exercises her will and ultimately frees herself of romantic illusions about her husband. Consequently, she is to some extent liberated from the constraining mold of traditional Southern womanhood.[26]

The narrator remarks the "stagnant waters of [the husband's] mind" and observes the wife's gaze pass "from his face" to the freedom implied by the "window beyond" (261).

Like most of the other stories in Glasgow's collection, **"Whispering Leaves"** suggests Poe's influence in its setting (on a remotely located and haunted ancestral mansion which the narrator approaches with some apprehension in the opening of the story) and in its use of the haunted house to represent claustrophobic, enclosed psychological space. However, this story breaks with the Poe tradition in several ways supporting my claim that Glasgow's later stories are marked by Wellsian optimism. First, the ancestral estate is deteriorated and haunted, but it is neither depressing nor frightening to the young female narrator. Indeed, she loves the enchanting songs of birds that she constantly hears, and the old black woman's ghost (Mammy Rhody) appears never to alarm her. Unlike Poe's narrators and unlike the unmoored narrator of **"The Shadowy Third"** and **"Dare's Gift,"** the narrator of **"Whispering Leaves"** is reliable. Though she later wonders whether some part of her experience was "a dream" (197), she never gives the reader any reason to question her sanity or judgment, for she maintains a clear-minded skepticism toward her ghostly "hallucinations." A hardy pragmatist, she concludes her story by saying that whether or not the ghost was a dream, what matters is the "reality" of the empirical evidence of her experience (Pelham's miraculous escape from the fire).

"Whispering Leaves," like the other stories, contains an allegory of history. The house is "primitive" (170, 171), and its inhabitants never use lamps, only candles (181). Old Cousin Pelham remains locked within his primitive world in a state of "abnormal egoism" (176). Mammy, the ghost, represents a Wellsian idea of the past. The ghost bears a "secret" or a "message" (166, 172, 188, 197) for the narrator, just as the past bears its messages for the future; but the past, like Mammy's ghost, must pass away once its messages are imparted. Mammy Rhody, the "past," delivers the "future," little Pelham, into the safekeeping of the "present," the narrator. Pelham thus escapes his destiny as suggested by dilapidated family estate. Moreover, the house burns down in a kind of phoenix-rising-from-flames image at the end of the story and liberates Pell, "an unearthly flower of light," from the literal and figurative "darkness" of his origins (185).

In this story, Glasgow employs a "spiral" image associated with time, memory, and the partial transcendence of history. The narrator remarks her clear memory of the events of fifteen years ago: "I have not forgotten so much as the spiral pattern the Virginia creeper made on the pinkish white of the wall" (167). Moreover, the house has a spiral staircase, and at the end of the story, the ghostly face of Mammy Rhody disperses in "spirals of smoke" (197) as she and the boy, Pelham, are freed from Whispering Leaves. Though the word, "spiral," does not occur in Wells's *Outline,* the pattern of historical progress that he describes is, indeed, a spiral one. Like Wells, Glasgow employs this image in connection not only with the grad-

ual evolution of humanity, but also with collective and individual memory. Glasgow doubtless would have observed in the *Outline* several of Wells's implicit and explicit references to the role of memory in tracing the "great lines upon which our affairs are moving" (2:580). Memory aids in the revision of ideas which, in turn, affect the design of a future that Wells hopes will be marked by selfless thought and action—the opposite of the "egoism" that he and Glasgow so abhor.

In **"Whispering Leaves,"** the "abnormal egoism" of the old proprietor of the estate is implied in the type of flowers he favors—narcissus. By contrast (in what is probably a veiled allusion to Walt Whitman), the narrator tells us she prefers lilacs because they seem to hold "the secret of spring," or of new beginnings (169). Reinforcing the narrator's fondness for such new beginnings, the ending of the story marks a new beginning for everyone. The house has burned, Mammy Rhody's ghost is free, and little Pelham Blanton escapes not only the fire but also his circumscribed life at Whispering Leaves. Apparently, he and the narrator leave Virginia, and perhaps even the South altogether.

In **"Jordan's End,"** another Poe-inspired house with a "sinister influence" (272) represents the tyranny of the past. Like the Ushers, the Jordan family is hereditarily mentally ill, perhaps as a consequence of inbreeding. Recalling Poe's narrator in "Usher," Glasgow's narrator obeys a summons to journey through a depressing landscape to the house of *Alan* Jordan (perhaps named for Poe and certainly a "Roderick Usher" type of character). A chthonic, ancient man called "Father Peterkin" joins the narrator along the road, and explains that the Jordans have "'run to seed'" (269) following the Civil War. Their dilapidated ancestral home reflects this history. As in "The Fall of the House of Usher," house and owner are one.

In contrast to the Jordans, Judith, Alan's wife, is a Poe-esque, "unearthly" beauty. The narrator describes her as "very tall, and so thin that her flesh seemed faintly luminous, as if an inward light pierced the transparent substance. It was the beauty, not of earth, but of . . . spirit" (273). Judith's exercise of what Wells might call "free intelligence" as opposed to blind obedience to traditional morality eventually frees her from the apparent prison into which she has married. She revises her future through an act of mercy killing that alters destiny, both the Jordans' and her own.

Like the house in **"Whispering Leaves,"** the Jordan house has a spiral staircase (275). In a small room at the foot of it sit three old women—wives and widows of other deranged Jordan males. Dressed in black and silently knitting, these old women are an emblem of Fate (278-79). The narrator is appalled that one of the old women knits "an infant's sacque," an image suggesting the inevitable birth of more doomed Jordan descendants in the future, at least until Judith intervenes (282). In another room at the top of the spiral stairs sits Alan. Here in the upstairs room is the scene of Judith's mercy killing that liberates Alan into death and Judith into a future different from that which the old women foretell. Though Judith must ascend and descend these spiral stairs a few more times before the chains of history are completely broken (she has a son), she has changed the future through a carefully considered act that both she and Alan approved.

Because he must live with the knowledge of Judith's action, the narrator becomes the true focus of this story. He knows at the time of Alan's death that Judith administered an overdose of medication, but he chooses to ignore the empty bottle on the nightstand. He also knows that Judith plans one day to help her son, Benjamin, escape his fate in the same way, if necessary. Thirty years later, this narrator has abandoned medicine "for literature" (278); unlike the compulsive narrators of **"The Shadowy Third"** and **"Dare's Gift,"** who narrate the past without "perspective" or comprehension, he tells his story as a complex, ethical "interrogation" of Judith's actions and of his complicity in them. In the end, he is left pondering, and inviting the reader to consider, the very questions that he refused to ask Judith. "I knew that the questions on my lips would never be uttered . . . The thing I feared most, standing there alone with her, was that some accident might solve the [apparent] mystery [of Alan's death] before I could escape" (290).

Together, Judith and the narrator have willed change, but the narrator worries over how and by what means they have intervened in destiny. As a physician-turned-storyteller, he believes he has found a better "outlet" for his "imagination" (278), perhaps in the instructive use of literature to pose questions about the future. The story poses profound ethical questions about the human design of the "new beginnings" that Glasgow contemplates throughout her works and that Wells extols in *The Outline of History* and in many of his novels. Though Glasgow does not necessarily disapprove of euthanasia, her treatment of the subject in **The Shadowy Third** reveals that she shares with Wells an obvious concern with the choices that humanity makes in designing the future. Indeed, she is careful to draw important distinctions between mercy-killing, committed in **"A Point in Morals"** (1899) and **"Jordan's End"** for, arguably, ethical reasons, and murder, committed in **"The Shadowy Third"** for perverse and self-serving ends.

Glasgow's autobiography suggests that she was interested enough in Wells's ideas in the *Outline* to peruse at least one of its post-1920 editions. In *The Woman Within* a quotation from the 1940 edition shows Glasgow returning to a passage in the *Outline* that must certainly have interested her when she read it during the twenties in a slightly different form. The passage concerns Buddhism, a subject that particularly appealed to Glasgow during the years when she wrote her short stories and that continued to interest her throughout her life. Wells's 1920 edition remarks that his evolutionary theory of "history . . . is strictly in accordance with [the] teaching of Buddha," and the 1940 edition powerfully reinforces this notion (1:423). Glasgow quotes the *Outline* of 1940, where Wells "has recently reminded us" that the

fundamental teaching of Gautama, as it is now being made plain to us by the study of original sources, is clear and simple and in the closest harmony with modern ideas. It is beyond all dispute the achievement of one of the most penetrating intelligences the world has ever known . . . For Nirvana does not mean, as many people wrongly believe, extinction, but the extinction of the futile personal aims that necessarily make life base or pitiful or dreadful. Now here, surely, we have the completest analysis of the soul's peace. Every religion that is worth the name, every philosophy, warns us to lose ourselves in something greater than ourselves. 'Whosoever would save his life, shall lose it.' There is exactly the same lesson. (*WW* 174)[27]

In subsequent pages of her autobiography, Glasgow concurs with Wells on the need for historical transcendence of "personality" and individualism. Like Wells, she sees how "human nature" has, so far, impeded evolutionary progress toward an ideal state of being as exemplified by Buddha, Christ, and St. Francis of Assisi. Throughout history, she complains, such "radiance" has been "blotted out by . . . human nature" (175).

Glasgow's characters in her short stories do not transcend human nature, but the stories that suggest Glasgow's Wellsian frame of mind in the 1920's emphasize the possibility of a better future at the end of the expanding "spiral" of human evolution, whereas her earlier, Poe-inspired stories depict people ensnared in the "webs" of their own circumscribed personal interests and histories. Following the example of both Poe and Wells in their different ways, Glasgow apparently looked forward to the loss of the burden of self, including that portion of the burden comprised of delimiting history.

Notes

[1] See *The Woman Within* (New York: Hill and Wang, 1954), pp. 174 and 203; and *Letters of Ellen Glasgow,* ed. Blair Rouse (New York: Harcourt, Brace and Company, 1958), pp. 27, 35, and 352. Glasgow read and marked passages in Wells's *Outline of History,* which she owned. Carrington C. Tutwiler's *A Catalogue of the Library of Ellen Glasgow* (Charlottesville: Bibliographical Society of the University of Virginia, 1969) records her copy as a two-volume, 1921 Macmillan edition. However, the *National Union Catalog* shows no two-volume edition published by Macmillan in 1921. Perhaps Glasgow's copy was, instead, the 1920 edition. Unfortunately, the Alderman Library at the University of Virginia has not preserved the extensive library that Tutwiler (Glasgow's nephew) gave to them, so it is impossible to check the date on her copy. In any case, the parts of *Outline* that I refer to in this article as interesting to Glasgow appear in some form in the 1920 edition as well as in the 1930 and 1940 editions. Thus, it stands to reason that whether her own copy was a 1920 or 1921 version of the much revised *Outline,* it would have contained the ideas and passages to which I refer here.

[2] Twentieth-century writers influenced by Poe are many. They include Wells, G. K. Chesterton, Vladimir Nabokov, Jorge Luis Borges, Paul Bowles, Charlotte Perkins Gilman, Richard Wright, and Theodore Dreiser, to name only a few. Moreover, these writers frequently also read and intertextually refer to one another. Chesterton, Nabokov, and Borges, for example, refer to Wells *and*

Poe in their writings. For a thorough discussion of the Poe tradition, see my *Twentieth-Century Writers in the Poe Tradition: Wells, Nabokov, and Borges* (DAI 1982); my two essays on Poe and Wells reprinted in this volume; and my essay entitled, "'Sinister Overtones,' 'Terrible Phrases': Poe's Influence on Some Works of Paul Bowles," *Essays in Literature,* 11 (1984):253-266.

[3] Rouse, p. 352.

[4] She owned and marked passages in her own edition (see note 1 above), and she quotes directly from p. 395 of the 1940 Macmillan edition of *Outline* in *The Woman Within* (see p. 174).

[5] H. G. Wells, *The Outline of History* (New York: Macmillan 1940), p. 2.

[6] During this time, several family members died, her romantic relationship with Henry Anderson began and ended, and in 1918, she apparently attempted suicide, though the seriousness of the attempt is unclear. Her feelings about her work and her literary competitors (Cather, Wharton) were also a source of stress. On Ellen Glasgow's life, see E. Stanley Godbold, Jr., *Ellen Glasgow and the Woman Within* (Baton Rouge: Louisiana State University Press, 1972) and J. R. Raper, *Without Shelter: The Early Career of Ellen Glasgow* (Baton Rouge: Louisiana State University Press, 1971).

[7] "Introduction," *The Collected Stories of Ellen Glasgow,* ed. Richard K. Meeker (Baton Rouge: Louisiana State University Press, 1963), p. 6. See also Rouse, p. 194, on Glasgow's ideas about the decline of American society.

[8] Ellen Glasgow, *Barren Ground* (San Diego: Harcourt Brace Jovanovich, 1985), pp. vii-viii.

[9] Wells uses this phrase or its equivalent in *Tono-Bungay* (1908), *The Undying Fire* (1919) and the various revised editions of *The Outline of History.*

[10] Glasgow shares Wells's sense of human experience as a search characterized by trial and error. On Glasgow's dialectical thought in this "search," see my "Consciousness, Gender and Animal Signs in Ellen Glasgow's *Barren Ground* and *Vein of Iron,*" in *Ellen Glasgow: New Perspectives* ed. Dorothy Scura, special issue of *Tennessee Studies in Literature,* forthcoming; and "Narration as Pragmatism in Ellen Glasgow's *Barren Ground,*" *American Literature,* 63 (1991):664-682. See also Raper's *Without Shelter,* pp. 2, 10-11; and "Invisible Things: The Short Stories of Ellen Glasgow," *Southern Literary Journal,* 9 (1977): 66-90.

[11] "The Shadowy Third," *The Shadowy Third and Other Stories* (Garden City: Doubleday, Page and Company, 1923), p. 27. Henceforth all references to stories in this volume are noted with page numbers in parentheses.

[12] On Poe's historical consciousness, see Lewis P. Simpson, *The Brazen Face of History: Studies in the Literary Consciousness in America* (Baton Rouge: Louisiana State University Press, 1980), especially pp. 101-102; Louis D. Rubin, *The Edge of the Swamp: A Study of Literature and Society of the Old South* (Baton Rouge: Louisiana State University, 1989), esp. pp. 146-147; and Donald E. Pease, *Visionary Compacts: American Renaissance Writings in*

Cultural Context (Madison: University of Wisconsin Press, 1987). Despite some serious mistakes in factual and bibliographical data concerning Poe, Pease makes some insightful observations about Poe's historical awareness.

[13] See my "Encounters with the 'White Sphinx': The Re-Vision of Poe in Wells's Later Fiction," reprinted in this volume.

[14] Though Poe also uses a version of the spiral image—the vortex or whirlpool—he emphasizes contractile spiral motion to suggest transcendence of history through material destruction, whereas Wells uses an expanding spiral to suggest secular historical development.

[15] Classical discussions of Poe's narrators include Darrel Abel's "A Key to the House of Usher," *University of Toronto Quarterly,* 18 (1949):176-85; James Gargano's "The Question of Poe's Narrators," *College English,* 25 (1963):177-81; and G. R. Thompson's "The Face in the Pool," *Poe Studies,* 5 (1972):16-21.

[16] Wells develops a similarly compulsive set of narrators in *The Croquet Player* (1937), who must keep repeating what they see as a terrifying story. On *The Croquet Player* and narration, see William J. Scheick, *The Splintering Frame: The Later Fiction of H. G. Wells* (Victoria, B. C.: University of Victoria English Literary Studies, 1984). It is also interesting to note that the stories in *The Shadowy Third* and several of Glasgow's novels, such as *Barren Ground,* suggest that she shares with Wells (in *Outline*) the notion that the act of writing is connected with the gradual emergence and liberation of humanity into fuller consciousness.

[17] Glasgow had not yet worked out her equation of animals and men that I explore in my "Consciousness, Gender and Animal Signs."

[18] Both Wells and Glasgow use this skull image, with its source not only in Poe, but also in Darwin's *The Descent of Man, and Selection in Relation to Sex* (New York: A. L. Burt, 1871); especially pp. 191-192. This image occurs throughout Wells's *The Croquet Player* as well as *Mr. Blettsworthy on Rampole Island* (1928).

[19] Many studies of Poe have by now remarked Poe's equation of the narrator with reason, Roderick with irrationality, etc. Many have also observed how the narrator's propensity for rational analysis in the opening of the story diminishes as he succumbs to Roderick's madness. Donald Pease notes in particular how Roderick's summons to the narrator involves a plea not only for rational analysis, but also for an audience to listen to his story and help him get free of the past.

[20] Perhaps by an odd coincidence, this speech by Glasgow's character greatly resembles speeches by Wells's characters in such works as *Tono-Bungay* and *The Undying Fire.* See, for example, Ponderevo's concluding remarks in *Tono-Bungay,* cited in my article on Wells's early works included in this volume.

[21] See Scheick on "exorcising the ghost story" in *The Splintering Frame.*

[22] Indeed, this extreme vacillation between periods of idealism and pessimism seems to be the common characteristic of Poe, Wells, and Glasgow that accounts for the latter two's interest in Poe and

for Glasgow's interest in Wells. On Glasgow's battle with idealism and pessimism, see my "Narration as Pragmatism."

[23] On Wells's dystopian frame of mind, see Bernard Bergonzi, *The Early H. G. Wells* (Manchester, England: Manchester University Press, 1961). Bergonzi argues that Wells's early works reveal a concept of human development that is essentially devolutionary. See also my two other essays on Wells reprinted in this volume.

[24] Poe's, Wells's, and Glasgow's sources of this spiral image are many, including Plato and the Romantics, and (for Wells and Glasgow) the Transcendentalists. Both Poe and Wells would also have served as a source for Glasgow's use of the image.

[25] See note 9 above.

[26] For feminist readings of the stories in *The Shadowy Third and Other Stories,* see "Visions of Female Community in Ellen Glasgow's Ghost Stories," *Haunting the House of Fiction: Feminist Perspectives on Ghost Stories by American Women,* eds. Lynette Carpenter and Wendy Kolmar (Knoxville: University of Tennessee Press, 1991), 117-141.

[27] See Wells's *Outline* (New York: Macmillan, 1920), pp. 422-423; see also the 1940 Macmillan edition, pp. 395-396.

Edgar MacDonald (essay date 1996)

SOURCE: "From Jordan's End to Frenchman's Bend: Ellen Glasgow's Short Stories," in *Mississippi Quarterly: The Journal of Southern Culture. Special Issue: Ellen Glasgow,* Vol. XLIX, No. 2, Spring, 1996, pp. 319-32.

[*In the following essay, MacDonald suggests that Glasgow's uneasy friendship with her one-time fiancé Henry Anderson unconsciously informs the themes of many of her short stories.*]

[1] One of the best things to happen to Ellen Glasgow was Henry Anderson. In her earlier fiction she had juxtaposed the virile self-made man and the effete aristocrat, her heroines usually giving their hearts to the former but marrying the latter. Now here under her minute scrutiny was an exemplar of both fictional males, a well-born man who had not gone to seed but had risen from the ashes of Reconstruction and like a good Virginian had reverted to being an "Englishman," very much as her brother Arthur Glasgow had done. She had fixed her romantic imagination on other males earlier, notably on her brother-in-law, the idealistic Walter McCormack, and on a married man, "Gerald B." She had tried very hard to feel something for the Reverend Mr. Paradise, liking his name. Now on this most auspicious day, Easter of 1916, she was studying a man she knew she would not like; she noted every detail about him; "his skin was burned like his hair, to a deep sand color." She was close to forty-three, no longer young, not yet old. He was not quite three years older.

The two met on equal ground. Recently returned to Richmond from New York, she had won respectable literary recognition as the author of ten serious novels. Early in her career, fatherly Walter Hines Page had warned her away from the lesser genre of the short story, a vehicle for local colorists. Her meeting with a healthy male egotist coincided with her emergence from an artistic malaise. It had to do with reality. Psychiatrists were teaching her there was no one universal perception, *the truth,* and as she had come to realize in her writing, a cataloging of external details constituted nothing more than a surface realism in a work of fiction. It bothered her that *Virginia* (1913), a work from deep within her psyche, had not received the popular recognition of *Life and Gabriella,* her current best-seller but one which did not contain her heart. She had labored over the style of the former, and its early pages capture Virginia's ecstasy, but the later pages of the novel drifted into the earnest, flat realism of earlier work, not conveying the passion the writer had felt as an artist. Unknown to both the lawyer and the lady who met that fateful Easter Sunday, he would become a part of a regeneration of her work, indeed, enter into the fabric. If he was good for her, she was good for him. He liked strong women, she liked strong men. "When I met him, he was drifting in purpose, unsatisfied with his hard-won success in his profession; and much of his sudden interest in public affairs was directly owing to me."[2]

In her confessions, Glasgow observed that she had emerged from a "dark Wood," quoting Dante ("for I had lost the way"), in the early spring of 1916. Arthur Glasgow had handsomely modernized 1 West Main, installing bathrooms and central heat, but with parents dead along with four older siblings, and with brother Frank and brother-in-law Walter McCormack suicides, she saw their ghosts everywhere. As for herself, she was convinced that for the past twenty years she had played in a "comedy of errors." Though also convinced that she and pompous Henry Anderson shared nothing in common, "the kind of person I had always avoided," he might set her "free from remembrance." Thus the two began their comedy. He became "Harold," she became "Vardah." They began collaborating on a novel. She polished his speeches. As befitted their years, their courtship was courtly, intellectual. "For seventeen months out of twenty-one years, we were happy together" (*WW,* p. 227). A remarkably good record, especially considering the contributions Henry Anderson unconsciously made to Ellen Glasgow's maturing artistry.

Another unintentional collaborator had entered the artist's life shortly before her spiritual regenesis. Anne Virginia Bennett, a trained nurse, had cared for Cary, Emily, and Francis Glasgow in their final illnesses. She had been retained to stay on at 1 West Main as Ellen's secretary-housekeeper. Devoid of any interest in literary matters, she too was to make her contributions to the writer's perceptions of reality. Although Ellen enjoyed the income of a small trust set up by Francis Glasgow for his daughters and another set up by her brother Arthur who wanted "no poor relations," she felt financially restricted. Miss Bennett as keeper of accounts suggested she write and sell a short story. She had published none since 1899 when **"A Point of Morals"** and **"Between Two Shores"** had appeared. The genre had returned to respectability, and having proved she was no miniaturist, Ellen set to work; she could think of it as a literary exercise. When **"The Shadowy Third"** was sent off to her agent, she demanded at least a $1,000 for it. She took from Anne Virginia Bennett details of her profession, from the ghosts of 1 West Main, their psychic presence, from herself the allusions to a writer's excitable imagination, and from Henry Anderson character traits bestowed on the male antagonist. In addition, we know that sometime before March 8, 1916, the writer was discussing her work with, perhaps collaborating with, a noted New York psychiatrist. Dr. Pierce Bailey, trained in Germany, "her suitor, probably her lover and doctor combined," according to Raper, enters the **"The Shadowy Third"** as Dr. Maradick. This story was published in *Scribner's Magazine,* December 1916.

It appears obvious that Glasgow had read Henry James's *The Turn of the Screw* before writing a story that parallels it in so many ways. In her safari to meet literary lions in England in 1914, she had encountered "slightly foppish" James. In the Glasgow clone, Margaret Randolph, twenty-two, an inexperienced nurse, travels from Richmond to New York to care for neurotic Mrs. Maradick. Telling her story in the first person and somewhat in the fevered style of the governess in the James story, Margaret too has a girlish crush on her employer. She admits to having a novelist's imagination and wanting to write. Simple Mrs. Gross in *The Turn* has her counterpart in another old housekeeper, housekeepers having no imaginations, being paid to attend to practical matters. Through psychic sympathy with her patient, Margaret sees the ghost child that the mother sees and that the physicians and the insensitive do not. Glasgow deftly leaves the reader in doubt whether Margaret is indeed the passive teller of the tale she claims to be. Just as James's governess becomes the active agent who brings about Miles's death, Margaret Randolph, having fallen out of love with Dr. Maradick ("His vanity was incredible in so great a man"), becomes the avenging force that precipitates his fall. In the Greek dramatic tradition, we see things that protagonists blinded by vanity do not.

Finding she had a newly discovered facility to depict the introspective female consciousness, surely the result of her psychological counseling, Glasgow followed the success of **"The Shadowy Third"** with another ghost story, **"Dare's Gift."** It was published in *Harper's Magazine* in two parts, February-March 1917. The first of three stories bearing names of places, **"Dare's Gift"** will borrow architectural and ownership details from Westover, the home of the Byrds. It is a house imbued with betrayal, and like her other House-of-Usher stories, owes its conception to Poe. Writing Van Wyck Brooks the year before she died, Glasgow observed:

> Of the South you write as if the beauty and the tragedy were in your nerves and in your blood, without that vein of cruelty which seems to me to run through the beauty of all things Southern, wherever that South may be. As for Poe, you might have looked on the shabby splendor of his genius. For the splendor was his own, the shabby cloak was the outward form of his destiny.[3]

Strangely, this story of cavaliers who settle on James River will conclude with *Beyond Defeat,* her very last, flawed effort to impose vision on reality. Prefiguring in miniature the epic canvas of Faulkner, **"Dare's Gift"** encapsulates several generations, incorporating the Civil War (the Yankee soldier betrayed by the Southern Belle), and as Raper points out it conveys a "southern 'sense of place,' especially the excessive loyalty and evasive idealism of the region" (p. 70).

Also in this experimental period based on her analysis, what Raper terms a *homeostasis* (of seeing where she had been and what she had accomplished, counterbalanced with a projection of who she would like to be both as woman and artist), she wrote **"Thinking Makes it So."** It falls into the seventeen-month period of happiness in the company of Anderson, and it reflects that fact significantly. It appeared in *Good Housekeeping,* February 1917, and it would give birth to other works. Glasgow was clearly working with materials and in a state of psychic immersion that could have been only partially apparent to her at the time. Meeker dismissed **"Thinking Makes it So"** as "unquestionably the weakest of the Glasgow stories, made up of leftovers from *Life and Gabriella.* It's only interest is biographical" (Meeker, p. 18). Glasgow herself did not include it in the 1923 collection of her stories; it is certainly biographical, but it points forward rather than backward. Its secondary characters reappear in the "comedies," those novels of manners presumably marking Glasgow's new phase. Raper is kinder to **"Thinking,"** seeing more than simple wish fulfillment. Phantasy (as opposed to fantasy) "is transformed into a reality, not because Glasgow has ceased to be critical of evasive idealism, but because she has begun to see that, if imagination is rooted in psychic need, surface reality has no right to tyrannize phantasy" (p. 61). He also liked the happy, self-ironic tone. That tone marks a growing objectivity on the part of the artist in treating a character that is essentially the artist herself.

Margaret French is the name for her central consciousness in this story, clearly Glasgow herself. She will use the name Margaret in three of her stories of this period; a fourth story has a Miss Wrenn who is clearly a Margaret. Glasgow was given to reciting poetry aloud, she tells us, for it musical qualities in the hope it would infuse her style. Like many of her generation, she was fond of Matthew Arnold's elegiac verses. She too felt suspended,

> Wandering between two worlds, one dead,

> The other powerless to be born. . . .

She empathized with the forsaken merman calling for Margaret, who had grown a soul and moved into the society of humankind. Margaret, "sea-pearl," a woman with a hidden treasure, will be juxtaposed to an alter-ego clothed in rose-colored silk, an alter-ego *named* Rose in **"The Difference."** A rose breathes out its fragrance in a single, transitory night. But in **"Thinking Makes it So,"** Glasgow fuses the two into a single character, suggesting that most women combine both traits. We are reminded that in her confessions she wrote, "At last I recognize my dream for a buried reality" (p. 213)—the pearl within.

Margaret French lives on Franklin Street, Glasgow moving 1 West Main to 1 West Franklin, the Branch house. Margaret is a tired forty-three, precisely Glasgow's age. She has given up writing unremunerative poetry to write "silly stories," denying herself to provide luxuries for a neurotic sister-in-law and pretty, selfish nieces. Neglecting herself, she dresses in gray. Then the letter arrives, a device Glasgow employed with some frequency. A lonely, middle-aged bachelor out West writes "My poet," envisioning her as "rare and pale and all in rose-colored silk." She replies to "Dear lover of my poems." Their letters give them a sense of renewed youth. Margaret blossoms into a rose, just as in real life Henry Anderson had blossomed into a poet for Glasgow, who is now writing the silly stories. Margaret buys the rose-colored silk dress, just as Dorinda in *Barren Ground* will buy the blue to match her eyes. When John Brown, the distant lover, arrives unannounced, a niece will see him as looking "awfully dry and uninteresting," but as Margaret, in the rose silk, crosses the room, John Brown smiles at her. "It is all, she thought to herself afterward, in the way one happens to look at a person."

Early in 1917 Glasgow began writing the novel she and Anderson projected, *The Builders*. If Glasgow was intent on repairing "the hole in reality" while living in a ghost-haunted house, Anderson was intent on self-improvement, a matter for her mingled mirth and admiration. In a sense, he was larger than life, a character destined for an exterior drama. Intellectual interest, as she had illustrated in **"Thinking Makes it So,"** can stimulate the hormones. Ellen wrote in her journal on the evening of Thursday, July 19, 1917, "engaged." On August 3, Harold, with the courtesy title of "Colonel" as head of a relief commission to the Balkans, sailed from Seattle on *The Empress of Russia* for Japan. The commission was composed of a number of prominent Richmonders, including Arthur Glasgow. They crossed Asia via the Trans-Siberian Railroad to Russia. Feted there, they turned south to Rumania, isolated from the Allies, where a glamorous Queen gave them a palace for their mission. Childe Harold's letters became shorter and fewer. In March of 1918 Anne Virginia Bennett left to play in the larger drama of world theatre. Carrie Coleman, a friend, stayed nights at 1 West Main to help ward away the ghosts, but during the day Ellen was alone in the theatre of her mind. With collaborator away and with ambivalence in her heart, *The Builders* went badly.

As the Germans encroached on Rumania the Red Cross Commission left for home in October, but Henry Anderson lingered. On January 1, 1918, he was in Rome, in May in London, in June in New York, and finally home in July. The first night in Richmond he came to see "Vardah" in his resplendent uniform, glittering with decorations.

> "I thought you would like to see me as I looked abroad," he said, with innocent vanity. But at my first glance I saw only the difference; I saw only that nothing would ever be again as it was before he had gone to the Balkans. Something had intervened. I could not give this something a name, nor even a habitation. . . . (*WW*, pp. 234-235)

"The Difference" will be the title of a new short story, "this something" will be described in another short story, **"The Past."** Harold's unheroic welcome home from Vardah placed a powerful chill on their relationship. Ellen Glasgow had not yet become Medea, but neither was she Penelope, nor any other waiting woman of romance. Harold and Vardah quarreled on the evening of July 3, 1918, and the ghosts crowded around. Glasgow would write that she attempted suicide, but as Monique Parent observed, Ellen was too sensitized to barbiturates for a few extra pills to be lethal. She had a few bad dreams and awoke again to a nebulous reality.[4]

Anne Virginia Bennett also returned home from France later that month, commendably exhausted in spirit and with a touch of tuberculosis. She had also suffered from an unrequited crush on one of Richmond's society physicians while in service. The Allies had liberated Rumania, and early in November Childe Harold was on his way back to succor the Circe of the Balkans. With the war over, she was the only enemy Vardah had to fear. Technically still engaged, uneasy Glasgow felt another story welling to the surface. When she and Anderson had dined, she had felt another presence enter the room and seat herself between them. "He could talk of nothing but the Queen." The evil queen was a shadowy third.

In **"The Past"** the Southern girl in New York is a secretary to the second Mrs. Vanderbridge, another Southerner. The secretary is called "Miss Wrenn" throughout, but surely her name is *Margaret*. Through her sympathetic nature she too sees the ghost of the evil first wife that Mrs. Vanderbridge sees. Through the latter's moral force, Miss Wrenn will help banish the intruder from the past. Ellen was still trying to be patient Penelope, not vengeful Medea. Again the first-person narrator speaking in the voice of a character close to Glasgow's own allowed her to achieve a higher degree of artistic control, superior to that of *The Builders*. She can allow herself to exclaim, "Oh I realize that I am telling my story badly!—that I am slurring over the significant interludes! My mind has dwelt so long with external details that I have almost forgotten the words that express invisible things." Meeker links this story with Poe's "Ligea" and notes that the doomed poet might have preferred the ghostly wife (p. 12), **"The Past"** appeared in the October 1920 *Good Housekeeping*. And Harold returned to Richmond that month. Vardah presented him an inscribed copy of *The Builders*, acknowledging his contribution. Harold continued to bring the favored yellow roses when he came to dinner; Vardah provided the favored deep-dish apple pie.

As Anderson became more interested in politics on a local level, the evil queen intruded less frequently, although his house was full of her autographed photographs and her portrait had been commissioned. Glasgow began a new novel. She had treated Virginia politics in *The Voice of the People* (1900), her first truly impressive achievement. When

Henry Anderson became the Republican candidate for Governor of Virginia on July 14, 1921, it was almost as if he had decided to be a character in a Glasgow novel. They were both challengers of the conventional mores, the status quo, the past. She wrote and delivered a speech entitled "The Dynamic Past." The new novel would not succeed as literature, but it would depict the shifting political scene of its time. *One Man in His Time* was published in May of 1922, and while Anderson did not take part in its actual writing, biographical details are everywhere apparent. Widely reviewed, not unfavorably, the consensus was that "Miss Glasgow has it in her to do better work" (Henry Seidel Canby).[5] Raper sees it as an improvement over *The Builders,* its failure owing to a loss of focus or nerve; "propaganda is still not one of the higher literary arts" (p. 51).

While no short stories from Glasgow's pen were published during 1921 and '22, she must have been working on one or more at this time; 1923 saw the publication of four. **"Whispering Leaves"** appeared in the January and February issues of *Harper's.* It is another of Glasgow's House-of-Usher stories, all bearing names of places. "I have always felt a curious (because improbable) kinship with Poe" (*Letters,* p. 352). Just as Forster's *Howard's End* is a metaphor for England and its fate, so too do Glasgow's place stories make their delphic commentaries. Earlier, she had rebelled against her father's Calvinism; now she led the way for others to denounce the sins of Southern patriarchs. In **"Whispering Leaves,"** she delves deeper into her psyche, into her childhood at Jerdone Castle. It reveals a repressed maternal instinct in the writer; oddly the repressed Pell, the bird-like boy, is another alter-ego, the Little Willie of her awakening artistic consciousness. The symbolic sunken garden in the story (from which Raper derived the title of his study) has gone untended by the unworthy inheritors of Whispering Leaves, and the neglected house will end in flames, as will Sutpen's Hundred in Faulkner's *Absalom, Absalom!*

Henry Anderson is nowhere apparent in **"Whispering Leaves,"** but he is very much present in **"The Difference,"** which appeared in the June issue of *Harper's.* Six years after writing the happy **"Thinking Makes it So,"** Glasgow saw there was a better story to be extracted from the materials of the earlier effort. Vardah and Harold had really been a companionable study team, a "marriage of true minds," rather than a dalliance in the garden. **"The Difference"** is perfectly plotted, a series of scenes in which the central character learns something about herself, a novel in miniature.[6] A cataloging of external details is limited to a few poetic images carrying psychological significance. The central intelligence is again named Margaret. "But the real Margaret, the vital part of her, was hidden far away in that deep place where the seeds of mysterious impulses and formless desires lie buried." In this study of the "Margaret" psyche, Glasgow separates the external rose alter-ego of **"Thinking"** into a separate entity named Rose. George, described in Henry Anderson terms, is a faithful-faithless husband, loving Margaret but dallying with Rose, an early sketch for George Birdsong in *The Sheltered Life.* Meeker sees Glasgow returning to

"man's moral inferiority to woman" (p. 183), but surely the story illustrates a more telling truth: the doubleness of male adultery is the counterpart of female ambivalence, the Margaret-Rose syndrome. As one of the secondary characters observes, "When a man and a woman talk of love they speak two different languages. They can never understand each other because women love with their imaginations and men with their senses."

The dramatic structure suggests drawing-room comedy, similar in feeling to James's "The Beast in the Jungle." The series of carefully set scenes is the "outside" of the interior drama, the discovery of multiple selves. "Outside, in the autumn rain, the leaves were falling," doubtless revealing outlines of bare trees. As a tragi-comedy, such as several of her later works will be, living is a series of improvisations. A letter from the other woman arrives. George enters briefly with domestic requests while the letter burns in Margaret's bosom. A visitor intrudes, chatting about a domestic crisis in another household, a parallel that makes Margaret determine to confront the other woman. She leaves the ordered comfort of her in-city home to venture by streetcar to an unfashionable suburban villa. Here Miss Glasgow describes accurately a trip from central Richmond, through the Northern suburbs, to Lakeside, but it is also a symbolic trip, from past security to contemporary transience. Modern, redhaired Rose Morrison is an artist. "Only an artist," Margaret decides, "could be at once so arrogant with destiny and so ignorant of life." Margaret, as a beautiful Victorian, will give up her husband. She clings to "the law of sacrifice, the ideal of self-surrender" (Meeker edition, p. 177). On the ride home in the lurching streetcar, she charitably envisions a "remorseful" George. "What agony of mind he must have endured in these past months, these months they had worked so quietly side by side on his book" (p. 178). Returned home, Margaret is met by a concerned husband. Glasgow handles superbly George's bewilderment over Margaret's taking his little fling so seriously. Raper misses the happily ironic tone of **"Thinking Makes it So"** in **"The Difference,"** but nothing could be more delicious than Margaret swept up in George's protective arms and his telling her she's upset because she's hungry. As Edmonia would shortly make clear in *The Romantic Comedians,* a good appetite is the best remedy for disillusionment; living on duty upsets the digestion. Glasgow is accused of being unfair to males, but her treatment of George, while comic, is not devoid of amused comprehension. Like most males he may have romantic fantasies about other women, but he is realistic enough to admit that he is only one of a series for the Roses of the world and that his basic comforts lie at home with Margaret. As a type George will reappear like a popular film star in later comedies. In this serio-comic curtain-raiser, brief images of leaves, fires, rain, flowers, mirrors are used tellingly, suggesting the four elements and the humors they engender.

"The Artless Age" expands the threesome to a foursome—the perfect lady, the flapper, the fatuous young male, and the fatuous older male. It appeared in *The Saturday Evening Post,* August 25, 1923. Termed by Meeker Glasgow's most frivolous story (p. 202), it can be seen as a continuation of the author's analysis of her own divided anima and as a sketch for *The Romantic Comedians*, explaining why the writer was able to follow up *Barren Ground* so quickly with a sparkling comedy. Glasgow's irony had evinced itself early, notably in *The Deliverance* (1904) with blind Mrs. Blake as the unreconstructed South, as well as in secondary, chorus characters such as Old Adam and Matthew Fairlamb. Like Shakespeare, Glasgow had put her telling truths into the mouths of clowns. By the time she wrote **"The Artless Age,"** however, she was ready to let her protagonists play the fools. Soon, in **"Romance and Sally Byrd,"** she will laugh at herself. Surely Henry Anderson helped her to peer more deeply into the mirror out of which the Lady of 1 West Main spun her fantasies.

> I am wondering if it ever occurred to you that your judgment might be wrong. You judge me so freely and with such apparent sureness that your conclusions are right that it makes me strong in my belief that no human can be capable of judging another. Your judgments seek not only to cover the present but to sweep back over the past. . . . [7]

The happy seventeen months with Harold had sustained Vardah's illusions of romance, but the rest of his nearly thirty-year friendship helped to shape her perceptions of reality.

When *The Shadowy Third and Other Stories* appeared in October of 1923, reviewers were unanimous in their praise. Richmond's own perceptive Hunter Stagg, writing in the *New York Tribune,* averred that it contained some of the best "writing Miss Glasgow has ever done" (*Guide*, p. 62). To six stories previously published in periodicals, she added a seventh, **"Jordan's End."** With this work Glasgow achieved an exemplum that stands with the best of any age. Antigone will bury the dead at Jur'dn's End, just as a cemetery is all that marks the site of Frenchman's Bend. Poe was the seer who foretold the Fall, but the Emily Dickinson of 1 West Main had looked deep into the soul of her South before she had looked into her own. Upon the early death of her grandmother, her maternal grandfather, William Yates Gholson, had moved to Mississippi and sired a second family. Later he would free his slaves and move to Ohio, where he became a Justice of the State Supreme Court. He had children on both sides in the Civil War; William Yates Gholson, Jr., First Lieutenant, Ohio Volunteer Infantry, was killed in Tennessee, at the age of twenty. In failing health, Ellen's mother went to Mississippi to visit her brother Samuel Creed Gholson. Glasgow praised Stark Young's *So Red the Rose* and called him "Cousin." Like a Renaissance Pope, she could have called William Faulkner "Nephew." He too was a seer, a *poietes,* one with an apocalyptic vision of the Cavalier South. Her vision had its genesis in her earliest memories.

At Jerdone Castle, the Glasgow summer retreat in Louisa County, Ellen had known happiness as a child. There she discovered the healing power of nature. Roaming the fields and woods, alone or with her sympathetic siblings Frank and Rebe, she discovered sights, sounds, smells that whispered of myriad forms of life. There she felt the first tentative impulses to record her states of ecstasy. Later, an old spiritual would echo in her consciousness: Deep River, My home is over Jordan (JUR'dn). A deep river separated the woman in middle life from the happy child, from the life forces that had given her an artistic mission. Her studies in Jungian psychology, however, were building a bridge. She knew with increasing conviction that her spiritual home was on the North Anna River, back at Jerdone Castle. Just as nature had healed the child, psychiatry was healing the woman. She was learning to accept human nature for what it was, not necessarily to forgive, but to accept. Laughter was better than tears. In the summer of 1922, Henry Anderson helped her select a new therapist. The psychiatrist is an intimate prober, like a lover. His presence is felt in all her stories of this period, whether "ghost" or character analysis. At the center of everyone is the ghost of self. From the self, one probes into other selves, society, into the past. **"Jordan's End"** represents Ellen Glasgow's deepest understanding of the forces which shaped her as a personality and as an artist.

In *The Battle-Ground* (1902) she had attempted an honest, realistic depiction of the Civil War. *The Deliverance* (1904) had attempted an analysis of the period which followed. While hinting at causes, she was primarily concerned with results, yeoman replacing cavalier, new codes replacing older orders, the homely face of democracy replacing patrician privilege. And always she was concerned to depict how the changes affected women. But with the psychological studies she began to look beyond events to causes, and she was finding the lost words, the symbols, the poetry to convey causes in literature rather than in tracts. As Meeker observes aptly of Poe, he had been too close to causes to see, as Glasgow had been as a child. "The families that go to seed are those that refuse to believe in the intangible. They love material comfort more than beauty; they love tradition more than progress" (p. 14). Still later, Glasgow would come to distrust "progress" in its commercialized forms. She saw that World War II had destroyed society as she knew it. In her very last statement, *Beyond Life,* she will envision a synthesized family, based on love and need. This utopian society will be returned to the lower James, where the concept of cavalier Virginia, the new-world garden, had its beginning. E. M. Forester envisioned a similar future for Howard's End, wherein Mrs. Wilcox, a nature deity, totally unlike her materialistic offspring, leaves the symbolic house to Margaret Schlegel, another protective spirit.

In **"Jordan's End"** and in the next story, **"Romance and Sally Byrd,"** Glasgow says farewell to two aspects of her earlier psyche. Can one doubt that the shawl that slips from the shoulders of Judith Jordan as she reenters the house at the end represents a dead past, or that the narrator has passed through a tunnel of dreams and, as Raper observes, "made contact with his vital center"? (p. 76). Glasgow exorcises the ghosts at 1 West Main and those within, but it takes a ritual "murder." At Jur'dn's End Judith kills her insane lover. "He had gone from life, not old, enfeebled and repulsive, but enveloped still in the romantic illusion of their passion." One last cry of despair escapes Judith: "'He was my life, and I must go on!' So full of agony was the sound that it seemed to pass like a gust of wind over the broomsedge." In relinquishing, she will enshrine. Eva Birdsong in *The Sheltered Life* kills poor George, living up to her marriage vow "Till death do us part." In earlier work, Glasgow's irony frequently undercut her characters; now it was Greek, a medium for universal truths. In a distant past there had been a garden, Jur'dn Castle. In the end all gardens are lost—except in literature. In the work to follow, Dorinda-Glasgow will, with Nathan Pedlar's help, make Five Oaks flourish anew.[8]

Ellen Glasgow published one more biographical short story after the appearance of *The Shadowy Third and Other Stories.* **"Romance and Sally Byrd"** was published in *Woman's Home Companion* in December 1924, just before *Barren Ground* brought her the recognition she felt was hers by right. A bitter-sweet sketch of Dorinda in another guise, **"Sally Byrd"** (of Westover?) is another farewell to the illusions of romance. "Never again!" Sally vows at beginning, middle, and end. But if Glasgow can't believe Sally, can we believe Dorinda when she says she is through with "all that"? That note of ambivalence will be felt in all the works that follow. Sally Byrd echoes Shaw's consummate romantic, Marchbanks in *Candida,* "As long as you have something beautiful to think about, you can't be a beggar." Do we detect Cabell in this spoof of the romantic attitude? Its pervasive irony is disguised by an undertone of lightness. When Sally, ready to nurse the errant, romantic male, visits the neglected wife, the latter is darning a sock, filling in another hole in reality.

Henry Anderson had not been everything Glasgow had half hoped but knew he wouldn't be that Easter Sunday ten years before; he had, however, helped fill in the hole in reality. Their uneasy friendship lasted till death did them part, and his vibrant personality informed her best works, *Barren Ground, Romantic Comedians, They Stooped to Folly, The Sheltered Life,* giving them a vitality that endures to the present. By the age of fifty-two, Ellen Glasgow was giving proof that she had almost come around to Cassius's viewpoint: the fault was not in one's stars; it could, just possibly, lie within.

In *Phases of an Inferior Planet* (1898), Glasgow's heroine had gone to New York to study voice. In the short stories she wrote in mid-career, Ellen Glasgow discovered her own voice. In addition she learned that everyone projected his needs, desires, on an other, and therefore everyone was a creation in someone else's drama. As she might have put it, "Your reality is not my reality—except for brief shared moments." For awhile, seventeen months, she had shared a mirror with Henry Anderson. With understanding came psychic release, artistic control, firmness of purpose. With the achievement of **"Jordan's End,"** not sullied with prior periodical publication, she stands with the best, with James, whom she met, with Conrad, whom she met, with Faulkner, who may have met her. We can regret with Meeker that *Scribner's* did not elect to include the short stories in the Virginia Edition (1938) of her works, for then we would have her commentary concerning their composition. We know she liked them, preferring the English edition because she

had been able to correct it more thoroughly. She did, however, express a thought for us to keep in mind.

> . . . I have tried to leave the inward and the outward steams of experience free to flow in their own channels, and free, too, to construct their own special designs. Analysis, if it comes at all, must come later. (*WW*, p. 227)

Notes

[1] The writer is indebted to the "Introduction," *The Collected Stories of Ellen Glasgow,* edited by Richard K. Meeker (Baton Rouge: Louisiana State University, 1963), and to Julius Rowan Raper, "The Words for Invisible Things," *From the Sunken Garden,* (Baton Rouge: Louisiana State University, 1980). Meeker's collection includes the seven stories published in *The Shadowy Third and Other Stories* (1923), four from magazines not included in that volume, and "The Professional Instinct," not published in Glasgow's lifetime. Professor Meeker's "Introduction" is enlightening, especially his discussion of "post-Darwinian romanticism," and he makes an especially telling case for the influence of Poe on the four "ghost" stories with their first-person narrators. He likewise comments on Glasgow's use of garden imagery and the influence of Henry James and Joseph Conrad. Professor Raper, Glasgow's most sympathetic interpreter, brings deep psychological insight to these products of her mid-life decade of emotional and aethetic crisis. He extends the Poe influence to Faulkner and sees Glasgow as standing "squarely in the doorway through which the tradition of southern writing passes from the often barren past into the fruitful modern period."

[2] Ellen Glasgow, *The Woman Within: An Autobiography* (New York: Harcourt, 1954), p. 299.

[3] Blair Rouse, ed., *Letters of Ellen Glasgow* (New York: Harcourt, Brace, & Co., 1958), p. 352.

[4] Monique Parent, *Ellen Glasgow, Romancière* (Paris: A.G. Nizet, 1960), p. 165.

[5] Cited in Edgar MacDonald and Tonette Bond Inge, *Ellen Glasgow: A Reference Guide* (Boston: G. K. Hall), p. 57.

[6] Ellen Glasgow felt the strictures of the short-story form, aware that only the novel gave her the amplitude "to trace the process of cause and effect" (Meeker, p. 6).

[7] Undated letter quoted in E. Stanly Godbold, Jr., *Ellen Glasgow and the Woman Within* (Baton Rouge: Louisiana State University Press, 1972), p. 125.

[8] In *Barren Ground,* Ellen Glasgow would have Pedlar's Mill on "Whippernock River," Whippernock being the name of Henry Anderson's ancestral acreage in Dinwiddie County.

FURTHER READING

Bibliography

MacDonald, Edgar and Inge, and Tonette Bond. *Ellen Glasgow: A Reference Guide.* Boston: G. K. Hall, 1986, 269 p.

Bibliography of writings by and about Glasgow from 1897-1981.

Biography

Godbold, E. Stanly, Jr. *Ellen Glasgow and the Woman Within.* Baton Rouge: Louisiana State University Press, 1972, 322 p.

Comprehensive biography.

Criticism

Auchincloss, Louis. *Ellen Glasgow.* Minneapolis: University of Minnesota Press, 1964, 48 p.

Lucid, balanced assessment of Glasgow, her work, and her achievements with very brief mention of the short stories.

Branson, Stephanie. "Ripe Fruit: Fantastic Elements in the Short Fiction of Ellen Glasgow, Edith Wharton, and Eudora Welty." In *American Short Story Writers: A Collection of Critical Essays,* pp. 61-71. New York: Garland, 1995.

Compares Glasgow's treatment of the supernatural with that of Wharton and Welty.

Matthews, Pamela R. "Glasgow's Joan of Arc in Context in Ellen Glasgow, 'A Modern Joan of Arc'." *Mississippi Quarterly: The Journal of Southern Culture. Special Issue: Ellen Glasgow* XLIX, No. 2 (Spring 1996): 211-25.

Analysis of an early Glasgow story that was published for the first time in this special issue journal.

Neary, Gwen M. "Glasgow's Ghost Stories and the 'Pattern of Society'." *Ellen Glasgow Newsletter* 36, No. 1 (Spring 1993): 6-8.

Discusses Glasgow's treatment of sex roles in *The Shadowy Third.*

Pannill, Linda. "Ellen Glasgow's Allegory of Life and Death: 'The Greatest Good'." *Resources for American Literary Study* 14, No. 2 (Spring 1984): 161-66.

Initial publication of a Glasgow story written in her youth with critical commentary.

Rouse, Blair. *Ellen Glasgow.* New York: Twayne, 1962, 160 p.

Overview of Glasgow's life and career written by a champion of her work. Very little mention is made of the short stories, which Rouse lists as among Glasgow's "inferior works." Includes a bibliography of previous Glasgow scholarship.

Scheick, William J. "The Narrative Ethos of Glasgow's 'A Point in Morals'." *Ellen Glasgow Newsletter* 36, No. 1 (Spring 1993): 3-4.

Discusses the narrative structure and treatment of will in this story, and discerns the influence of philosopher Arthur Schopenhauer.

Additional coverage of Glasgow's life and career is contained in the following sources published by Gale Group: *Contemporary Authors,* Vols. 104, 164; *Dictionary of Literary Biography,* Vols. 9, 12; and *Twentieth-Century Literary Criticism,* Vols. 2, 7.

Nikolai (Semyonovich) Leskov
1831–1895

(Also transliterated as Nikoli, Nicolai, Nikolay; also Semenovich, Semionovich; also wrote under pseudonym Stebnitsky; also transliterated as Stenickij) Russian short story writer, novelist, and journalist.

INTRODUCTION

One of the masters of the short story in Russian literature, Leskov wrote a prodigious number of tales in a wide variety of genres that realistically portray life at all levels of society in nineteenth-century Russia. Although his considerable literary output included novels, political pamphlets, and drama, he is best remembered for his satires, fairy tales, travelogues, ghost stories, sketches, narratives, and folk-inspired fables. Marked by colorful use of regional vernacular and virtuostic wordplay, Leskov's stories are concerned with the details of real life, especially that of Russia's peasantry. Leskov is praised in particular for his brilliant use of the *skaz,* or frame story, a third-person narrative tale with a first-person account embedded within it. This genre allowed Leskov to combine realism with elements of the ribald, bizarre, and supernatural. His stories also reflect a life-long interest in religion: Leskov was the first author to write about the Russian clergy in realistic—and later, satiric—terms, and some of his most moving tales describe the search for pure spirituality divested of the trappings of orthodox religion. Leskov's political stance made publication of his stories difficult at times, and many of his satires are political indictments disguised as simple fables to escape his censors. Critical recognition of his work during his lifetime was also damaged because of his unpopular views, but writers as distinguished as Leo Tolstoy, Fyodor Dostoevsky, and Maxim Gorky and later critics have admired his storytelling ability, his linguistic facility, and the characteristically Russian flavor of his writing.

Biographical Information

Leskov was born in the District of Orel, in south central Russia, to a family of mixed class, a background that acquainted him with the rich diversity of Russian life. His father held a post in the Russian civil service, his mother was a member of the hereditary landed gentry, one of his grandfathers was a priest, and his grandmother was from the merchant class. Most of Leskov's childhood was spent in the country, where he came to know and developed sympathy for the lot of Russian peasants, both through visits to monasteries with his grandmother and from the tales told to him by his nurses. Leskov attended school in Orel from age ten until the early death of his parents when he was fifteen; these five years constituted his entire formal education. After his parents' death, Leskov joined the civil service and became a junior clerk in the Orel criminal court. In 1849 he obtained a posting to Kiev, where he lived with his uncle, a university professor. Always a voracious reader, Leskov took the opportunity while living with his uncle to further his self-education, making friends with students and professors, reading widely, and engaging in the university's intellectual environment. In 1853 he married Olga Smirnova, the daughter of a merchant, with whom he had two children. The marriage was unhappy from the beginning and lasted only eight years. For three of those eight years, Leskov traveled extensively throughout Russia in his new position as estate manager for a private corporation. During this period, exposed to different regional dialects and customs, Leskov gained even broader experience and knowledge of Russian life and custom, which provided much of the raw material he was to use in his novels and stories. It was also during this time that he discovered his talent for and love of writing, enlivening his business reports with touches of humor and narrative description.

In 1860 Leskov began a career as a journalist in St. Petersburg, where he wrote stories about serfdom, the exploitation of workers, and the oppression of the religious sect the Old Believers. One of his earliest stories, "The Musk Ox," written during this period, is a fictionalized account of an unsuccessful peasant rebellion. An 1862 article Leskov wrote calling for an investigation of the events surrounding an arson attributed to a group of students was misunderstood as a denunciation of revolutionary circles. Consequently, he was labeled as a conservative and shunned by most leading writers and thinkers. This conflict increased after Leskov, out of bitterness and injury, published two novels directed against liberal and radical leaders, *No Way Out* (1864) and *At Daggers Drawn* (1870-71). Because of the animosity between Leskov and members of the Left, many of his short stories, which he began writing in the 1860s, were rejected by the leading periodicals of the day.

In the early 1870s, Leskov made a brief but uneasy alliance with a conservative critic, Mikhail Katkov, whose influential *Russian Messenger* published two of Leskov's first successes, the series of chronicles, *Cathedral Folk* (1872), and the story, "The Sealed Angel" (1874). Because Leskov wrote of his misgivings about the policies of the Right, they soon dismissed him from their ranks, leaving him an outsider to both liberal and conservative camps. However, his sympathetic portrayal of the orthodox Russian clergy in *Cathedral Folk* indirectly led to an appointment to the Ministry of Education, selecting books for schools and public libraries, since the Orthodox Church was closely allied with the Tsarist government. Leskov retained the post until 1883, when it was deemed that his increasingly satirical depictions of orthodoxy were not compatible with his position. His collection of sketches *The Little Things in a Bishop's Life* was banned by the government later that year. Leskov continued his denunciations of the Church, and his later writings are preoccupied with moral and religious themes. These writings include a series of stories set in the early centuries of the Christian world about the lives of "righteous men," who demonstrate true understanding of Christian virtue. In his last years, Leskov found an ally in his compatriot Leo Tolstoy, whose religious beliefs had much in common with his own and whom Leskov admired almost to the point of worship. Tolstoy's influence is apparent in almost all Leskov's writings in the last decade of his life, even though Leskov's preferred form in those years—satire—was a considerable departure from Tolstoy's moralistic tales. Ironically, the satirical works Leskov produced toward the end of his life were deemed too radical for the most liberal journals, and again he had difficulty publishing them. Leskov died in 1895 of heart disease.

Major Works of Short Fiction

Leskov's career as a fiction writer was notably different from that of other Russian writers of his generation, coming as he did from a modest background. With his lack of formal education, Leskov had few literary aspirations as a youth and only started his writing career at age thirty as a journalist. His early tales are told with the realism of a reporter, and indeed his work throughout his life is characterized by his keen narrative sense and the often blurred lines between fact and fiction. Despite his late start, by 1862 Leskov was producing stories that are still counted among his finest, including "The Musk-Ox," "The Mocker," and "Life of a Peasant Martyress." By 1865 he had published his acknowledged masterpiece, the long tale "Lady MacBeth of Mtsensk." In his thirty years as a writer Leskov produced five novels, and those he wrote early in his career; otherwise, he concentrated on short forms. Leskov acknowledged that he had difficulty with structure when it came to novels, which was likely due in part to his composing under pressure of serialization in periodicals. Interestingly, many of his best stories, including "Lady MacBeth" and "The Enchanted Wanderer" (also called "The Enchanted Pilgrim"), are unusually long but do not suffer from structural flaws. Notable, widely anthologized stories among Leskov's considerable output include "The Sealed Angel," a story that reflects his interest in iconography and admiration of the vitality of common Russian people; "Golovan the Immortal," a tale of a "righteous man"; and "On the Edge of the World," a tale of an orthodox clergyman's discovery of spiritual fulfillment in decency and kindness, and not in the rituals of the Church. Perhaps Leskov's best-known short story is the humorous "The Tale of the Crosseyed Lefthander from Tula and the Steal Flea (A Workshop Legend)" (sometimes called "The Lefthander," "Lefty," or "The Steel Flea"), a tale that the critic Hugh McLean regards as the work Russians associate with Leskov in the way that Americans connect *Tom*

Sawyer to Mark Twain. However, Leskov's reputation is not so much tied to particular stories as it is to the *skaz* form, of which he is considered the architect and most accomplished exponent. A typical Leskovian *skaz* employs a realistic frame story in which a credible narrator, often a sophisticated or well-educated person, sets the stage for a second tale to be told in the first person by a less credible, often naive and uneducated, character. The first-person account is generally spoken in dialect and told in humorous terms, with plenty of punning and witty word-play, and often contains touches of the supernatural. As many critics have pointed out, Leskov used the form to considerable aesthetic and practical effect, concealing within these apparently naive tales his biting criticism of the government and clergy. Leskov used the *skaz* form for his very first short story, "A Case That Was Dropped," and continued to use it throughout his career in some of his finest work, including "The Amazon," "The Little Fool," "Vale of Tears," and "The White Eagle."

Critical Reception

Leskov was bitter throughout his writing career at the abuse and neglect he felt he suffered at the hands of critics. After his early break with the Left, the publication of his stories was often in second-rate journals and newspapers, and he was not welcomed into the company of the *literati*. However, Leskov managed to find an enthusiastic reading audience, and in his later years a few of his literary contemporaries praised the quintessentially Russian nature of his work. In 1889-90 his collected novels, stories, and sketches were gathered in ten volumes, a mark of his relative renown, but they never garnered serious consideration by contemporary reviewers. An expanded edition of his collected works was printed posthumously in 1897, and a more comprehensive collection of thirty-six volumes (which still makes up only a fraction of what he wrote) was released in 1902-03. After the 1917 Revolution, because of Leskov's supposed political conservatism and religious bent, his work garnered little press, although he was acknowledged by the Soviets as a writer of distinction. But no serious Russian scholarship on his work appeared until 1945, and it was more than ten years after that when the first Soviet edition of his collected works was published. Common critical complaints against Leskov's work during his life and today are that his stories come too nakedly and with insufficient artistry out of real life; that they are not organized around a central plot but rather made up of anecdotes; and that he carries his tales with florid language at the expense of content. Further, the fact that he did his best work in the "lesser genres," which the great Russian novelists often used as mere exercises, damaged his reputation as a serious artist. Most critics today, however, acknowledge Leskov's mastery of the genres in which he worked, and scholars have remarked on the subtleties in his stories that are often lost on first reading. Even so, while Leskov has finally earned a place in the pantheon of Russian literature, his works are still not well known outside Russia. The first English translation of his work was a small volume of stories published in 1922, and a couple of dozen small collections of his tales have appeared since then. Scholarship on Leskov in English is sparse, but the critics writing in English who review his work agree that Leskov's genius is original and his stories have much to convey, not only about nineteenth-century Russia, but about the wisdom to be gained by experiencing fully the wonders of real life.

PRINCIPAL WORKS

Short Fiction

Meloci arxierejskoj zizni (sketches) 1878-79
Sobranie socinenji. 10 vols. [*Collected Works*] (short stories, novels, and sketches) 1889-90
Polnoe sobranie socinenji. 36 vols. [*Complete Collected Works*] (short stories, novels, and sketches) 1902-03
The Sentry and Other Stories 1922
The Tales of N. S. Leskov: The Musk-Ox and Other Tales 1944
The Enchanted Pilgrim and Other Stories 1946
The Amazon and Other Stories 1949
Sobranie socinenji. 11 vols. [*Collected Works*] (short stories, novels, letters, and sketches) 1956-58
The Enchanted Wanderer and Other Stories 1958
Nikolai Leskov: Selected Tales 1961
Satirical Stories of Nikolai Leskov 1968
Nikolai Leskov: Five Tales 1984
The Sealed Angel and Other Stories 1984
The Enchanted Wanderer: Selected Tales 1987
Lady MacBeth of Mtsensk and Other Stories 1988
On the Edge of the World 1993
Vale of Tears and On Quakerness 1995

Other Major Works

Nekuda [*No Way Out*] (novel) 1864
Rastocitel' [*The Spendthrift*] (drama) 1867
Na nožax [*At Daggers Drawn*] (novel) 1870-71
Soborjane [*Cathedral Folk*] (novel) 1872
Zaxudalyj rod (novel) 1874
Detskie gody (novel) 1875
Evrei v Rossii [*The Jews in Russia*] (pamphlet) 1884

CRITICISM

Aleksej B. Ansberg (essay date 1957)

SOURCE: "Frame Story and First Person Story in N. S. Leskov," in *Scando-Slavica*, No. 3, 1957, pp. 49-73.

[*In the following excerpt, Ansberg discusses Leskov's trademark form, the frame story or* skaz, *and asserts that the author uses it for both aesthetic and practical purposes: to portray intimately subjective points of view and to disguise his sometimes dangerous opinions.*]

The frame story (*Rahmenerzählung*) and the first person story (*Icherzählung*) occupy an important place in Leskov's production. No definite number can be given for either, partly because the 36-volume edition of 1902-3, in spite of its title *Polnoje sobranije sočinenij,*[1] includes less than one fourth of all that Leskov wrote (and there are works by Leskov which have been inaccessible to me), partly because it is sometimes difficult to decide whether a given story is a frame story or not. Some have a definite and well developed frame, e. g. **"Na kraju sveta"**, told apropos during a discussion at a party. Others, like **"Stopal ščik"**, are preceded only by a short and formal introduction. . . .

Of the 94 works included in the 36-vol. ed. about 40 may, with more or less reason, be called frame stories. Furthermore there are about 15 or 16 stories or sketches without a proper frame where the author himself appears, often as a subordinate character, as an eye witness of what happened, as a friend of one of the characters. These may be called authentic first person stories. Typical specimens are **"Tomlen'je duxa"**, **"Judol'"** and **"Po povodu Krejcerovoj sonaty"**, some of them with a subtitle pointing to the biographical character of the story: "Iz otročeskix vospominanij" ("Tomlen'je duxa"). In this connection it is of no importance whether what is told is really authentic—like **"Judol'"**—or not. What interests us is the method, the effect of illusion which is the basis of the narrative.

When we except a group of works which all because of the character of the genre or of the tradition were unsuitable to be presented within a setting or as the authentic experience of the author, viz. *Rastočitel'*—Leskov's only drama, the novels, the three chronicles—*Staryje gody v sele Plodomasove, Sobor'ane* and *Zaxudalyj rod,* the two fairy tales (skazki)—**"Čas voli Božijej"** and **"Malan'ja—golova baran'ja"**, the legends, and a group of non-belletristic works, articles and documentary sketches like "Sosestvije vo ad" and "Vdoxnovennyje brod'agi", there are only six works in the 36-vol. ed. which are presented directly, without any motivation in the form of a frame or the "I" of the author. These are **"Ledi Makbet Mcenskogo ujezda"**, **"Kotin doilec"**, **"Bluždajuščije ogon'ki"**, **"Odnodum"**, **"Staryj genij"** and **"Zimnij den'"**. But even some of these are marked by a certain authentic-documentary character and fixed to a definite place and time by precise place-names and dates. . . .

Further there is in part III of the long novel *Na nožax* an inserted tale, which exploits the possibility for interplay between setting and story, and there are also frame stories not included in the 36-vol. ed., some of them among Leskov's more interesting: **"Železnaja vol'a"**, **"Pod prazdnik obideli"** and **"Zajačij remiz"**; **"Leon, dvoreckij syn"** and **"Christos v gost'ax u mužika"**, both with a sort of introduction by the author; and finally **"Zametki neizvestnogo"**—presented as a manuscript found by the author (*Herausgeberfiktion*).

When the frame story and the authentic first person story between them dominate Leskov's production to that extent, this can be no accident. It is safest to assume when dealing with a distinguished artist that his choice of method is significant. The question of Leskov's choice of method and of his use of that method seems to deserve an investigation. Having only a limited space at our disposal, we cannot explore the question fully. We shall try to elucidate some of the main points and go into more detail when dealing with a few representative examples. This is not an attempt to "prove" anything or to demonstrate cogent reasons for choice of method. This investigation of an author's production in general pretends to be no more than an introduction to the study of the subject in question. In the last analysis every case, every single work, is unique and has to be investigated for itself.

The complex of reasons that governs an author's choice of method ranges from the aesthetically relevant to the aesthetically irrelevant, so one has to believe. Our way is here from the latter to the former.

Originally Leskov had no plans of becoming a writer, and his first belletristic composition—"Pogasšeje delo"—did not appear until 1862, when Leskov was already 31 years of age. . . .

Leskov started his literary career as a journalist, and his articles sprang directly from what he had seen and experienced during the preceding years. They have all a factual character, and they have as their immediate and practical end to discuss and throw light upon questions of the day. . . . His first stories—"Pogasšeje delo" and "Razbojnik", both 1862—were mere sketches. His first serious attempt to emancipate himself from the factual and the documentary came only in 1864, with a *novel—Nekuda*—and accordingly in a genre, that begged for a freer and more artistic treatment.

Even Leskov's later production is marked by certain authentic-documentary traits; he may in an undisguised form tell of his own adventures, he may render what he has heard from others or he may draw on written sources. It is partly the force of habit and of tradition; sometimes he treats a subject in an article, and then he takes it up again in a more poetic form in a work of art. It is also the outcome of his manifold practical interests; he poured out articles all his life; for years he was one of the main contributors to *Istoričeskij Vestnik*. This dependence on the factual is also the result of a limitation of his talent. . . .

It was very natural and easy to present this authentic material in a frame story, or in a first person story, or in a combination of the two. The frame may have been authentic in itself: exactly under these conditions, in such a "setting", Leskov first heard the story told by somebody else. But mostly the frame is arranged and fictitious. The method of presentation is always difficult in fiction, and the frame can be used as a kind of motivation for the narrative; also it conveys an illusion of reality: at a party gathered at Mr. So and so's house a week ago the old officer told us the following story from his battles in the Caucasus . . . Finally, by means of a frame, the author can easily put a question of the day to discussion, after which

the story follows as an illustration or an apropos; compare Leskov's long series of "Rasskazy kstati". V. S. Pritchett writes, having in mind some of Leskov's stories: "They come too unevenly, too amateurishly and only partly digested out of life. They smack sometimes of the reminiscences of a District Commissioner."[2]

There is an extrinsic reason for choosing a combination of frame story and first person story that may seem rather unexpected. Leskov suffered much from the censorship, especially in the eighties and the nineties. The whole of the VIth volume of the first larger edition of his works was withdrawn from sale, and complaints about the censor and speculations on how best to delude him constantly recur in his letters. . . .

Nekrasov developed his Aesopian language to throw the censor off the scent. So did Leskov. He, however, made use also of the frame story for the same purpose; he put a narrator between himself and the readers, created distance and in this way masked dangerous opinions, e.g. in "Polunoščniki"[3] and "Zajačij remiz". . . . Form and style in these two stories were, of course, no innovation in Leskov, and not created only for the purpose of fooling the censor.

The formal building up of a story, the creating of a logical and flawless structure was not Leskov's *forte* as a writer. He was filled with a general dissatisfaction regarding the novel as a narrative form, it seemed to him artificial. Apart from two unfinished attempts Leskov did not return to the novel after 1871. This mistrust in the novel as well as his both shrewd and naive reflections on the genre problems[4] may also be a way of rationalizing his discontent with his own novels, which are rambling and discursive. This, in any case, is part of the background for Leskov's quest for genres and forms where his special talent could better express itself. So we get the whole series of characteristically Leskovian narrative forms, which made him seem such a rare and exotic figure in contemporary, novel-ridden Russian literature, and which embarrassed the critics and prevented them from taking him seriously. . . .

To an author who at bottom was a stranger to the novel as a narrative form, the frame story and the first person story offered obvious advantages. The place of the omniscient author of the novel, he who knows the past and the future as well as the secret thoughts of his characters, is taken by a narrator, who also may make his reflections, comment upon the action and the characters, but whose perspective is limited and *eindeutig,* who can only narrate what he himself has experienced, thought and felt, or what he has heard and read. This simple coherence of a story in the first person, as well as its providing "a ready-made scheme for selection"[5], proved convenient for Leskov. The first person story within a frame became his favourite narrative form, where he created some of his masterpieces. Sometimes the narrator is the main character of his own story—as in "Očarovannyj strannik" and in "Zajačij remiz"—sometimes a minor character like the pious Mark, who in "Zapečatlennyj angel" with awe and pathos tells of the miraculous happenings he has been a witness to, or the slily mischievous and crafty grey head in **"Železna-ja vol´a"**, who with quiet satisfaction describes the collision between the German iron will and the formless Russian dough in the form of the gigantic strife between Gugo Karlovič Pektoralis from Doberan in Mecklenburg-Schwerin and the bibacious Russian artisan Sanfronye.

The frame story is a narrative technique offering wide possibilities and without any particular limitations as regards theme, the attitude of the narrator or the style of the writing. . . .

Leskov, who had so much in common with the poetry of the people (*Volksdichtung*), who more than any of his contemporaries cultivated primitive narrative technique, who utilized both the themes and the forms of pre-Petrine Russian literature, constantly returned to this *Ursituation* and made good use of its potential "primitivism". A look at the first person story in Leskov will make this clear. Historically the epical description in the first person narrative of external adventures and of a broadly painted scene—the picaresque novel—has been superseded by an interest in the happenings within the mind, by psychology. The development has been from a naively narrating "I" to a reflecting and analysing "I". Leskov's "antipsychological" stories, which gave scope to his supreme narrative gift, are, however, nearer to the sources of the epic than, let us say, Dostojevskij and the post-Flaubert novel. A comparison with a work by Dostojevskij, which formally is not far removed from Leskov (Dostojevskij has no proper frame story), will illustrate this radical difference. We choose "Krotkaja" from *Dnevnik pisatel´a,* November 1876. . . . Everything is dissolved into psychology and analysis, and it has rather the character of and anticipates the *monologue intérieur,* the stream of consciousness, that Dujardin and Joyce were to develop further. It would not be correct to say that the interest in psychology is completely absent from the more typical Leskovian first person stories, but it is relegated to the background, subordinated to other elements and takes on other forms. A main trait in Leskov is the rapid action, as well as the typical epic narrator's "Freude an der Buntheit der Welt"[6], which makes him stop before extraordinary situations, out-of-the-way and exotic milieus, and which above all finds its expression in the exuberance of the language. His first person narrators do not analyse themselves; they are made to live through anecdotes, by the situations they are placed into; they are characterized in terms of action and, of course, through their racy language.

In his frame stories and first person stories Leskov was able to put on a "linguistic mask", take up characteristic, individual language and experiment with style.

Leskov, the stylizator, the *pasticheur,* with his Rabelaisian *joie du mot,* apart from sharing the interest in language common to any author, was also somewhat of a philologist. It is not without significance that he counts among his literary ancestors the lexicographer V. I. Dal´ and the stylistic equilibrist A. F. Vel´tman. Leskov was, like Théophile Gautier, another mosaicist, a voracious reader of dictionaries. He collected old books and manuscripts and also picked up words in the field. . . .

Leskov, who in talks with his literary friends never omitted to stress his business and travel background, and who had wide practical interests, knew that words are inseparable from their *realia,* and took a great interest in the language of the different social classes and in the technical language of various professions, from the language of iconography and stone-masonry in **"Zapečatlennyj angel"** to the language of horse-breakers in **"Očarovannyj strannik,"** from jewellers' language in **"Aleksandrit"** to provincial actors' language . . . in **"Tupejnyj xudožnik."** What was more natural for Leskov than to make the representatives of these professions and social classes the narrators of frame stories? In the same way Leskov made use of dialects. His native dialect—that of Or'ol—makes itself felt in a number of his works. He took care to localize Fl'agin, the narrator in **"Očarovannyj strannik."** . . . Ucrainisms abound in **"Figura"** and in **"Zajačij remiz"**—both of them stories with a narrator set within a frame; polonisms occur, and sometimes a certain Hebrew-German jargon; and when Fl'agin tells about his captivity with the Tatars, the language takes on a lexical touch of the eastern steppes. There is a parallel to this in V. I. Dal´, where the frame story sometimes motivates the introduction of dialects or deviating language into a story.

Later, in dealing with **"Očarovannyj strannik,"** we shall see how Leskov utilizes the linguistic contrast between frame and story.

In the *nouvelles* and short stories . . . by Turgenev, the Russian classic who, apart from Leskov, made most frequent use of the frame and the first person, the author in a sense dominates more than in Leskov. In his stories Turgenev himself is all the time in the foreground; he is the medium, the prism, through which all that is told is refracted before it reaches us. As regards a frame story like "Pervaja l´ubov" we know from Turgenev's own words that it is autobiographical. Xarlov, the protagonist in "Stepnoj korol' Lir," has nothing in common with Turgenev, but his story is told as a boy of 15 saw it, and there is little or nothing that distinguishes him from the young Turgenev in "Pervaja l´ubov'". In a first person story like "As'a" the narrator's outlook and attitude are completely identical with Turgenev's, as we know it from stories where he writes in person. They are both penetrated by a feeling of sadness and melancholy, of lost chances; there is the same mildly poetical vagueness of the style and the same use of metaphors and syntactical parallellism. According to the illusion which the introduction intends to create the story of As´a is orally told, but the language is studied and literary. This, then, is the main impression of Turgenev's stories; but of course, there are exceptions.

In the frame stories and the first person stories of the more protean Leskov the author is less of a central character or main reflector, to use the terminology of Henry James. Even if the author himself appears in many of them, there are only a few where the story is told by him throughout, such as **"Vladyčnyj sud"** and **"Tomlen'je duxa"**. The "author-I" may present the frame or appear as one of the characters in it, but then only as the introducer to a story told by somebody else, and the latter is the main narrator; among the examples are **"Voitel´nica"** and **"Tupejnyj xudožnik"**. In many cases the author is completely absent and takes no part in the story at all. What interests us here is not the formal absence of the author himself, but the cases where this absence is accompanied by a change in attitude, in outlook, in point of view.

The main names in any discussion of *point of view*[7] are, of course, Henry James and Percy Lubbock. The former has consciously explored some of its possibilities in his novels and stories, and the latter has given a more systematic exposition of the question in his *Craft of Fiction*.[8]

In Turgenev's stories the author's point of view dominates, in Leskov that of the characters, and so it does in Henry James—but with a difference. James rejected not only the omniscient author (in his later work), but also the use (not always) of the first person narrator. He speaks of the "terrible fluidity of self-revelation that characterizes narratives like *Gil Blas* and *David Copperfield*".[9] James chooses a *reflector,* who permits him to establish an internal point of view, that is, within the novel. In *The Ambassadors,* Strether is the sole reflector, and we see everything in the novel through him; all that we are aware of, is his consciousness of what is going on. His mind is dramatized, as Lubbock would have put it. The same method is used, with less consistency, in *Prestuplenije i nakazanije,* where Raskol'nikov is the main reflector.

What Leskov has in common with the far more subtle James is the extensive use of a point of view different from the author's and also a certain consistency in maintaining it throughout the single work. The difference, however, is great. The method in James' hands is a delicate instrument for psychological analysis. Where James is "modern" Leskov is "primitiv"; where the action in James is dramatic—presented scenically—it is epic in Leskov—presented in retrospect. The time in James' novels is the present; the time in Leskov's stories is the past. James is a writer of fiction; Leskov a writer of narratives, to use Lubbock's terminology once more.

By using the frame story and the first person story (where the "I" was not identical with the author) Leskov was able to motivate a perspective and an outlook that differed from his own, to explore a foreign temperament, including its linguistic manifestations. Some authors put on such a mask without bothering much about the motivation. Examples are Gogol's "Šinel'", as a contrast to "Večera na xutore bliz Dikan'ki", and most of the short stories by Mixail Zoščenko. Such a neglect of motivation is rare in Leskov. In the chronicles and the *skazki* the motivation for the outlook and for the deviating language lies in the genre. . . .

Leskov seems to have felt that some sort of motivation was necessary before taking up a foreign point of view or a deviating language. This, then, should be an indication that here we have one of the main reasons for Leskov's extensive use of the frame story and of the first person story.

We shall examine some frame stories and first person stories with regard to point of view. Leskov has been particularly intent on exploiting the possibilities for creating effects by contrast and irony. He chose a narrator with a limited understanding, horizon or background—a child, a man of the people . . . and played on the contrast between the narrator's more narrow understanding and the author-reader's wider understanding. Apart from the artistic value of irony and indirectness, this may have as practical ends to divert the censor or to drive home the moral.

"Duračok", one of Leskov's most beautiful stories, tells about the serf Pan´ka, who readily takes upon himself the work of others as well as their guilt and sufferings, first as a boy, then as a soldier, and finally in the service of the Tatars, and who, accordingly, is regarded by everybody as a fool.

The story starts with a discursive introduction. . . . After this introduction the story of Pan´ka follows. At the beginning we see him as the author saw him when they were both children. As a boy the author, the "I" of the story, grew up with Pan´ka. Later, when Pan´ka becomes a soldier, the *author-boy* is no longer a person in the story, but turns into a mere voice, reporting to us what Pan´ka's soldier-comrades have to tell about him. Finally that voice turns into the *omniscient author.* Pan´ka is thus seen from a threefold point of view in the story. For some reason this inconsistency does not make itself much felt.

"Duračok" has very much in common with Tolstoj's story "Al´oša Goršok", written 13 years later. Both style and *Ethos* in Leskov's story are in the spirit of the later Tolstoj. The language is more restrained than is usual in Leskov. There is something both of Al´oša Goršok and of Platon Karatajev in the cheerful willingness with which Pan´ka takes all upon himself. The reason why the threefold point of view does not immediately strike the reader is that the tone, the attitude, the style are unchanged throughout. It is the same rapid, easy, maybe somewhat naive way of telling that does not stop at details and that resembles Pan´ka's own way of talking.

"Duračok" is, in any case at the beginning, a first person story. "Al´oša Goršok" is told by the omniscient author. What is the justification for Leskov's method? It must be, that in Leskov the general judgment about the "hero" is more to the foreground than in Tolstoj. Already the title, **"Duračok"**, indicates how people see Pan´ka. A main effect of the story is in the contrast between the general opinion of Pan´ka and the reader's knowledge of the real Pan´ka; this contrast is ironic, that word taken in its widest sense. This irony can best be given relief by the author's letting Pan´ka be seen through eyes that share the general opinion of him. The irony is further stressed by the fact that the Tatars, and not Pan´ka's Christian countrymen, at the end really understand him.

When this is said, it has to be added that Leskov has missed the opportunity of making a good story still better by not keeping to the point of view he started with to the end of the story.

Leskov has a certain fear in common with Turgenev of leaving the judgment to the readers, who are told too much and shown too little. They do not know the full value of objectivity and indirectness. **"Duračok"** would have profited if Leskov to a greater degree had left it to the readers to draw the conclusions.

"Voitel´nica", that is the procuress who, pious and naive, tells the story of her life in St. Petersburg. She feels no qualms of conscience, her view of her own profession is wonderfully uncomplicated, and she does not seem to find it incompatible with her religion. As regards point of view and irony the story has much in common with **"Duračok"**. The author has not resisted the temptation to intrude, to make his commentaries. Bunin's story "Xorošaja žizn´", modelled upon **"Voitel´nica"**, is superior to Leskov's in that the same point of view—that of the unscrupulous woman-narrator—is maintained throughout.

A third Leskov story, **"Polunoščniki"**, is without the hesitation regarding point of view and irony that characterizes the other two stories. The "I" of the frame listens to a nocturnal conversation between two women, where the greater part is occupied by Mar´ja Martynovna's story about the young and beautiful Klavdija, whom she denounces in every respect. Mar´ja Martynovna is the only source of our knowledge of Klavdija, and it should seem that we have nothing to do but to accept her judgment. However, from all Mar´ja says, we understand that her mind is limited, that she is petty and hypocritical and even a potential thief. Indirectly, through her story. Klavdija the Tolstoyan, stands forth as wise, idealistic, self-devoting McLean has well said in his study of the story: "Since Mar´ja Martynovna is the moral opposite of Klavdija, we must learn to place an ideological minus sign before all Mar´ja Martynovna's judgments and attitudes", and further: "After that, if she [Mar´ja Martynovna. A.B.A.] offers us the negation of Tolstoyanism as her positive moral ideal, we are well prepared to negate the negation"[10]. In spite of the consistent maintenance of a single point of view and the ensuing ironic effect, **"Polunoščniki"** is not one of Leskov's best stories. As a whole it is more an interesting than a good story.

The contrast in the preceding stories between the limited intellectual horizon or distorted perspective of the narrators, and the inferences that the readers were able to make builds up an ironical effect. A somewhat different type of aesthetic effect—but also worked by contrast—is aimed at by the use of point of view and outlook in other Leskov stories, among them **"Levša"**.[11]

"Levša" starts directly with the *skaz* narrative, without any motivation. The first edition that was printed in Aksakov's *Rus´* in 1881, had, however, the following subtitle

"Cexovaja legenda" and was provided with a sort of frame in the form of an introduction, where the author speaks. Readers and critics somewhat naively accepted this introduction, and the role of the author was reduced to that of a mere penner. In 1882, in a short notice, Leskov pointed out that the introduction was fictitious, and that the whole story was made up by himself. Later he repeated the same explanation in "Starinnyje psixopaty." The part of the frame that closes the story, written in the same style as the original introduction and radically different from the *skaz,* was retained.

The form of the *skaz* and the frame serve as a motivation for outlook and language in the *skaz* narrative. The core is very simple; it is the anecdote about the left-handed Tula smith who surpassed the ingenious English, in shoeing the steel flea that Aleksandr Pavlovič had received in England, and who died without getting any recognition from his own countrymen. What gives the story life and colour, makes it one of the most original narratives in Russian literature, is, apart from the language, just the use made of the narrator's outlook and attitude (*Erzählhaltung*). The naive attitude, the wild, fantastic ideas about a world that lies beyond the narrator's limited circle of experience, be it foreign countries or the world of the great at home in Russia, the distortions of an unknown milieu, points to a man of the people as the narrator, a *prostol´udin* with a vivid and exuberant imagination and few inhibitions. And, as already stated, the narrator was less anonymous in the first edition.

"Levša" is popular and has been constantly reprinted. The theme—that of a *prostol´udin* telling about a milieu unknown to him—is often repeated in Leskov, and other variations of it are less known. It is at the centre of another story, and for it Leskov wrote an introduction that clearly shows how consciously he utilized the possibilities inherent in the attitude that dominates the story. That is the almost unknown **"Leon, dvoreckij syn"**, like **"Levša"** published in 1881 and not reprinted later. . . .

The narrator's attitude in **"Levša"** is radically different from that of the previously mentioned Leskov stories. It is not, however, without irony. The discreet irony that penetrates the story divided the readers as soon as it was published. Already in his notice about **"Levša"** of 1882 Leskov stated that some found that the people was abased in his story, and others that it was flattered. Even many years later the critic A. L. Volynskij, who in Leskov wanted to see a naive, original, and religious writer, did not understand the irony on Russian patriotism and Russian self-assertion towards foreigners, as it was expressed in **"Levša"**. He took the story seriously. . . .

The same ambivalent attitude runs through a number of Leskov's stories, where the irony is due to the fact that the Russians hold their own towards foreigners not by their best qualities, and where Leskov, as in **"Levša"**, is at a remove from the story, having placed a narrator between himself and the readers. Among the examples are **"Židovskaja kuvyrkollegija"**, **"Železnaja pol´a"** and **"Otbornoje zerno"**.

In one of his stories Leskov employs the first person narrator and in another the frame to play with reality, to mystify the readers and to produce effects akin to romantic irony.

"Dux gospoži žanlis" is a first person story told by Leskov himself (he mentions **"Zapečatlennyj angel"** and the boycott he was subject to), not as the omniscient author, but as a character together with the other characters in the story. In this story Leskov plays on his own personality. . . . He anticipates the development, whets the curiosity of the reader and promises him a *scholastic joke.* The author makes the reader his confidant and discusses with him how the narrative ought to be presented—maybe the satire would have been the ideal form, but it is not within his powers. . . .

In dealing with **"Očarovannyj strannik"** we shall try to explore a wider field and not just the use of frame and first person in the service of point of view.

The enchanted wanderer is Ivan Sever′janyč Fl′agin, who to an audience of fellow-travellers on board a boat on the lake of Ladoga gives an account of his adventurous life, which contains acts of violence and sacrifice, tragedy and comedy, animal vitality and asceticism, which has taken him from the West to the East, from the South to the North, alternately as a "nurse", a judge of horses, a prisoner with the Tatars, an unsuccessful wooer of Gruša, the beautiful gypsy, as a soldier in the Caucasus, an actor in St. Petersburg, until at last he—who had started his grown-up life by killing a monk—is now himself a monk in the Valaam monastery.

We shall stop at a passage in his narrative. Fl′agin has, during his wanderings eastwards, reached the outskirts of the steppes. Here he is the witness to a scene where the Tatars exchange horses between themselves and with the Russians. Fl′agin describes one of these passionate horse-lovers and -judges, Khan Džangar himself, who is inspecting a new horse. . . .

If Fl′agin's narrative primarily is marked by a colloquial style, there is also a definite admixture in it of elements that belong to the high style, and the result is a mixture . . . a mixture which finds its expression partly in morphology and syntax, but above all in vocabulary, with rare words and phrases from Church Slavonic from The Lives of the Saints, and from the liturgy rubbing shoulders with dialectal and genuinely popular words.

The style of the frame is, on the whole, homogeneous. Sometimes it has a faint smell of officialese, sometimes a rhetorical touch with a leaning towards the clerical and unctuous. The common denominator for these small variations is a rather neutral and medium style, somewhat archaic. The whole impression of the frame is of something slightly sated and complacent and also traditional and stereotyped. . . .

Where Fl′agin narrates, the language is neither "correct" nor always wholly in good taste, but the expression is vivid, direct and often unexpected. Fl′agin deals in freshly minted coin, there is no knowing what will follow when he has started a sentence. Everything is freshly seen and sensed, rendered in a style which is unhackneyed, and where all the senses have contributed with their impressions, as in his description of the steppes and salt marshes in Chapter VII.

The contrast between the language of the frame and the language of Fl′agin's narrative should be clear—here a pronouncedly literary style with a leaning towards the old-fashioned and circumstantial, there a narration which is not only oral and colloquial in the usual sense of these words, but which tries to capture even the intonation of the spoken language, the mimetic gestures of the speaker; here a correct and neutral diction, which is homogeneous in structure and vocabulary, there a colourful tale, which does not adhere to the rules, mixing words from different spheres of association, coining new words or giving a new sense to old words; here the greyness and uniformity of official, bourgeois costume, there the bright and gaudy red of the peasant's [dress].

The Formalists used a key term to describe the character of the aesthetic experience . . . 'making it strange'. Viktor Šklovskij, who created the word and developed the theory, to a certain degree, built upon the German aesthetician B. Christiansen's concept *Differenzqualität*[12]. This term, the quality of divergence, covers the immediate impression the reader has when turning from the language of the frame to Fl′agin's narrative, a feeling of contrast, of novelty and of deviation from the norm. Using Formalist parlance, one can see Fl′agin's language as a permanent violation of the automatism of the language in the frame.

Fl′agin's language, as we have described it, has all the characteristics of the language of the *skaz,* as e. g. Boris Ejxenbaum has defined and used the term.

The frame, then, has an important structural function; by its contrast to Fl′agin's narrative it supports our perception of that narrative as *skaz,* i. e. as oral and colloquial, as individualized and deviating and of Fl′agin as the real narrator. . . . The frame not only surrounds Fl′agin's narrative, opening it and closing it. It also repeatedly interrupts the narrative, we return to the frame, the narrative is commented upon there, impressions are summed up; the listeners question Fl′agin, ask for further explanation of obscure and interesting points or urge him to continue his narrative. It is as if Leskov wants to remind us that this is told by Fl′agin and prevent us from becoming imperceptive to the contrast between frame and *skaz.*

The use of the first person in **"Očarovannyj strannik"** must be seen in connection with the whole structure of the narrative. The story of Fl′agin's wanderings has no firmly knit plot. Structurally it is related to the time-honoured story of travels and to the picaresque novel. N. K. Mixajlovskij, the populist writer, complained that there was no centre in **"Očarovannyj strannik"** Every single incident seemed to stand isolated. The sequence of incidents was of no importance; one could without any harm remove an incident and insert another in its place. Mixajlovskij saw formlessness where, after all, there *was* form, even if it was of a character that differed from that of the drama and the dramatic novel.

Like the picaresque novel **"Očarovannyj strannik"** attains a certain unity by the fact that all the incidents in the story are associated with one person (like beads strung on one thread). By his mere presence in the story the hero creates a primitive unity. It is a further step towards unity that **"Očarovannyi strannik"**—also in this respect like the majority of the picaresque novels—is told in the first person. The readers see everything with the narrator's eyes and through his mind. The narrator's personality, the simple fact that he must make a selection from the stream of incidents for his narrative, that he must decide what to stress and what to pass by in silence, how to distribute light and shade—this fact will give his narrative its individual character and form the basis for a unity deeper than the purely mechanical unity afforded by the mere presence of a central hero. In the typical picaresque novel everything is seen by the critical and unsentimental picaro and stamped by his cynical, disillusioned view of life.

There are, however, other and deeper reasons for the use of the first person in **"Očarovannyj strannik"** Among Leskov's narrators many stand more or less outside the story, they are mere eye witnesses and "reporters", so in **"Železnaja vol'a"** and **"Otbornoje zerno."** Leskov has not completely neglected the characterization of these narrators, they have their own individuality and especially a definite attitude, slightly malicious and crafty, but they do not have—and are not meant to have—weight of their own to catch the interest. The colourful persons and incidents they tell about, on the other hand, have that weight.

The narrators are more in the limelight in **"Zapečatlennyj angel"** and **"Čertogon,"** without being the main characters of their narratives. In the course of the stories they undergo a development; they are not just mirrors to a chain of incidents, but these incidents have significance for them and change them. Mark, the narrator in **"Zapečtlennyj angel,"** is spiritually purified. In the course of the story he has passed from the narrowness of his original religious beliefs to tolerance and a wider perception of life. The young narrator in **"Čertogon"** is, at the end of the story, shaken in his disbelief; he has been a witness to phenomena, the existence of which he had never suspected: he has become initiated.

And here we are getting closer to **"Očarovannyj strannik,"** only with the difference that Fl'agin himself is the main subject of his own story. All that is told, is only significant in so far as it is seen by and in relation to Fl'agin, as fragments of his experience, as stages on his way.

In **"Železnaja vol'a"** and **"Otbornoje zerno"**—to keep to the examples already mentioned—the scene exists, so to speak, in its own right, independent of the narrator. The scene there (to use Lubbock's words in another context) holds no dialogue, sustains no interchange with the figure of the narrator. In **"Zapečatlennyj angel,"** on the other hand, in **"Čertogon,"** and still more in **"Na kraju sveta"** (where the narrator is a bishop, who in the course of the story learns to see beyond the boundaries of his church) we continually turn from the scene in the foreground to the narrator, to watch the effect it may produce in him. This is also true of **"Očarovannyj strannik,"** where Fl'agin is the absolute and indisputable protagonist.

This protagonist, in telling about his own life, reads a deeper meaning into it. The artistically gifted, but naive *prostol'udin* Fl'agin is the only one who can tell the story from this point of view. The attitude of the narrator is so intimately bound up with the narrative, that an omniscient author is inconceivable. The narrative demands a naive, simple narrator, marked by the people's religious ideas and feelings.

Fl'agin does not merely relate the facts in his life. He *interprets* his life, so to speak, thereby bringing out a pattern. This interpretation is based upon his naive and simple religiosity. The title itself—**"Očarovannyj strannik"**—is significant. The word "strannik" has a double sense which the translations fail to give. Some choose the wanderer—the English translation—others the pilgrim—**"Le Pèlerin enchanté."** Fl'agin is a wanderer in the literal sense of the word, but as far as his wanderings have a meaning and an end the emphasis is on the pilgrim. This is how Fl'agin sees it, and it is his view, his interpretation, that interests us in this connection.

Fl'agin has special reasons for seeing himself as a wanderer through life, as a pilgrim. He says that he is a "prayer son". . . .

[E]nchantment . . . rules his life. In a vision he later learns from the monk he has killed, that he is also "a promised son" his mother has promised him to God, that he shall become a servant of God in the monastery. His *way,* his *course* of life is, in other words—we keep to Fl'agin's own interpretation—predestined already from birth. Fl'agin interprets his life in such a way that he constantly sees a divine providence intervene. . . .

His sufferings are not without purpose, they are sufferings for an end, Passion, expiation. He suffers for his own transgressions; in a wider sense his sufferings are *sacrificial,* sufferings for others. There is a symbolical scene that seems to illustrate in an almost literal way the notion of Fl'agin as a scapegoat—where he, as an actor clad in goatskin, is beaten in the show-booth theatre on the Admiralty Square.

He takes upon himself lifelong service as a soldier in order that the single son of a poor peasant shall be free and asks to be sent to the Caucasus that he may die for the Faith. When the passengers on the Ladoga meet him, he is on a pilgrimage to the monastery on the Solovetski Islands to save the soul of Gruša, the gypsy. His whole life is now devoted to service and sacrifice. . . .

What Fl'agin reads into his life is an archetypal pattern—vicarious suffering. His life, as he himselfs tells it, has taken the form of a "lived *vita*", of mythical identification.[13]

An interpretation and identification of the same character runs through that other combined frame and first person story—**"Zapečatlennyj angel"**—written in 1873, the same year as **"Očarovannyj strannik"** The narrator Mark is himself a member of the little group of Old Believers, who, living in a hostile world, are persecuted and oppressed. Mark uses expressions which show that the group identifies itself with the Jewish people in its trials in the Old Testament as well as with Christ and the first small Christian communities. Mark fashions his narrative to make it resemble in several places the story of Christ in the New Testament.

Frame story and first person story have been seen to serve different purposes, ranging from the aesthetically irrelevant to the aesthetically relevant—to serve practical, journalistic ends, to disguise dangerous opinions, to motivate deviating language and individual point of view— a subjective interpretation of life. We discern behind this subjective interpretation a whole ideological structure, which has its own aesthetic function in Leskov's creation, and which would, perhaps, merit a separate study.

Notes

[1] All quotations are from this edition, unless otherwise stated. Roman numerals stand for the volume, Arabic numerals for the page quoted.

[2] V. S. Pritchett, *The Living Novel*, 1949, p. 256.

[3] Hugh McLean has written about Leskov and the censorship, especially with reference to *Polunoščniki*, in an article *Leskov and Ioann of Kronstadt, American Slavic and East European Review*, XII, no. I (February, 1953). For censorship and the style of Polunoščniki see also McLean's article *On the Style of a Leskovian Skaz, Harvard Slavic Studies*, vol. II (1954).

[4] E. g. in the introduction to *Bluñdajuščije ogon'ki* (XXXII, 3-4).

[5] Brooks and Warren, *Understanding Fiction*, 1943, p. 592.

[6] W. Kayser, *Das Sprachliche Kunstwerk*, 1951, p. 351.

[7] Brooks and Warren, *op. cit.*, have suggested the less ambiguous term *focus of narration*. We keep to *point of view* because it seems to be generally accepted.

[8] First edition 1921.

[9] Quoted from J. Warren Beach, *The Method of Henry James*, 1918, p. 57.

[10] *On the Style of a Leskovian Skaz, Harvard Slavic Studies*, vol. II (1954), p. 322.

[11] "Levša" is no first person story and, in its present form, no frame story either. We include it because it has so much in common as regards point of view and language with the stories discussed here.

[12] B. Christiansen, *Philosophie der Kunst*, 1909. *Literatura*, 1927, p. 214.

[13] The idea of mythical identification is developed in Thomas Mann's lecture *Freud und die Zukunft*, Vienna 1936.

V. S. Pritchett (essay date 1961)

SOURCE: Introduction to *Nikolai Leskov: Selected Tales*, translated by David Magarshack, Farrar, Straus and Cudahy, 1961, pp. vii-xiii.

[*In the following introduction to a volume of Leskov's stories, Pritchett discusses Leskov's style, his characters' psychological complexity, and some recurring elements in his tales, which Pritchett identifies as the rootedness of the Russian character, the half-dream or vision, and animal symbolism.*]

The sound of the lash has always been heard in Russian literary criticism, the lash of the political fanatic or the intemperate doctrinaire. This sound was as common in Tsarist Russia as it is in the Soviet Union and one can only conclude that the Russians find this savagery stimulating, like a birching after the bath. But there is more than one instance in which the lash has stultified and has blinded judgment. A notorious instance is the ostracism of Leskov by Russian critics during his lifetime. He was generally denounced for political reasons and it was not until the last years of his life that the critics woke up to the fact that Leskov was deeply admired by the Russian people, whose literary taste was surer than their own. Gorki was one of the first to speak of Leskov's greatness.

Leskov was born in 1831 and died in 1895, writing brilliantly until the end. His difficulty was that he did not come to literature by the usual path. If we look at the lives of nearly all the great Russian novelists we find that their beginnings have a standard pattern. The two most important exceptions are Chekhov and Gorki. The rest come of the gentry class; they are brought up by serfs or servants; they go to the university where they absorb French or German ideas and they are at once involved in revolutionary politics, in some degree. They were the *déclassés* of the country house. So marked was the isolation of the intellectuals that guilt at one time assailed them and, during the Populist movement, they "went to the people." Leskov's case was very different. He had a tenuous connection with the gentry in his mother who is described vaguely as "noble," but his grandfather had the humble calling of a priest and his father was a minor civil servant. Leskov was already among "the people" when he was born. Fate made the tie closer, yet at the same time introduced an alien element into his life and one that gives him an almost bizarre link with Western Europe. The boy's parents died when he was sixteen and he was brought up by an English woman, his Aunt Polly, who was also a Quakeress. She had a profound influence on him: the practicality, the moderation, above all the Quaker preoccupation with charity and goodness often appear in his writing. Leskov was sent out to earn his living early. He did not go to the university. (Later on in his life he was sensitive about this and would boil with rage when malicious people said to him: "Aren't you a graduate of the University of Kiev?") He was put to work with an Englishman called Scott who was the steward of the estates of a rich Russian landowner, and his job took him all over Russia. Leskov probably knew Russia better than any other writer of his time. His task was to send back reports to Mr. Scott who was captivated by them. He urged Leskov to go in for journalism.

For Russian journalism in the late fifties and early sixties, Leskov was at a fatal disadvantage. He was not an ideologist. He had not been educated for violent faction. Although a man of the Left, he was religious and unable to attach himself as a partisan. The crisis came when there was a mysterious outbreak of fires in St. Petersburg. The Nihilists were accused of arson. Instead of denouncing the accusation automatically, Leskov asked, in his Quakerish way, for an impartial inquiry. This finished his career as a Left Wing writer; all liberal papers were closed to him and his writings henceforth were ignored and abused. For a time he turned his attention to theology and then began to write his masterly stories out of his vast experience of Russian life. Serious criticism still ignored him, but his tales succeeded instantly with the public. They indeed came directly from the lives of the people, their memories and their folklore; they were written a good deal in popular language, in the rich, pungent tongue packed with local proverbs, phrases, images and even comically made-up words. He caught the people talking among themselves out of their rich store of roguery, poetry, fantasy and inventiveness. No one, we are told and can easily believe, catches so truthfully the diversity of national character in his time. His variety is astonishing.

The first quality of Leskov is that he has both feet in life. He is not, in the least, a literary writer. He appears to burst upon the reader without art in a rambling, wily, diffuse, old-fashioned way. He shambles into his tales without embarrassment, indifferent to technique. The force of his stories would be lost if some editor of the machine-made story started tampering with them. If his story has a plot—see **"The Left-handed Craftsman"**—it is so good that it can stand any amount of raggedness; if it is a wild, heroic, picaresque personal statement like **"The Enchanted Wanderer,"** the epic spirit is lost if the tale is formalized. If one starts checking the detail of characterization one is exposed as a pedant and simpleton. True that in the nineteenth century the Russian novelists excelled in the creation of characters, but they went far beyond the bounds of the social personality, beyond English eccentricity or French analysis. In a sense there is more resemblance between the Russian and American understanding of character than there is between the Russian and the European, although the American becomes rapidly diffused in the preoccupation with what a man or woman might wish ideally to become. The Russian is rooted; his extension is inward. It is an old joke that the Russians have a soul; but Leskov's characters *are* souls as well as being people. They embody imaginations and dreams; they are

always dipping into unexpected layers of consciousness; they are always liable to drop off into the inherited mind of their race.

There are many examples of this faculty in the present selection of Leskov's tales. Take the masterly **"The Left-handed Craftsman."** In this ingenious tale we see the Tsar going off to England to study English craftsmanship because it is the fruit of superior education. He brings back with him a miraculous piece of work, an almost invisible flea made of steel. More wonderful still, it has an even less visible key. You wind up the key and the minute thing dances. The ignorant craftsmen of Tula are challenged to beat *that.* They are in despair; they nearly go mad. They recognize that to make such a flea is beyond them. Nevertheless they shut themselves up and get to work and eventually emerge with something accomplished. The Tsar winds up the flea but it remains still. It cannot jump or dance. They apologize. The trouble is, they say, that they have *shod* the flea and the nails are too heavy! We have no education and no mathematics, they say. They have to get their ideas, they say, in a profoundly Russian sentence, from a book called "the book of half-dreams—those that David left out of the Psalms." We put down the tale realizing that in these craftsmen, wily, boastful, canny, fanatical, who like being familiar or scornful with the boss, Leskov has drawn universal figures, not simply crusty and shrewd old characters. And the book of half-dreams endows them with imagination and a soul.

The half-dream or vision is a recurring element in Leskov's tales; it is related to his religious sensibility. We have the impression of people who move violently back and forth from humility, dishonesty, sin and slavishness to some sort of lyrically heroic vision of themselves. In **"The Enchanted Wanderer"** we have the heroic adventures of a man who might be one of Dostoevsky's great sinners, but without the morbidity. He has been born a man of gigantic physical strength which he misuses because, he says, he has been enchanted or occupied by another's will, a priest whose death he has caused. The hero is powerless in the struggle of conscience and guilt; he simply knows that he is caught by Fate and will experience the knout of retribution. He will even go down on his knees and beg for it. The vision or dream is something that moves into the soul and controls it, against the will; it is what we would call the unconscious, what Dr. Mirsky called "the double"; Leskov catches here something more than a strange man. He catches a people's heroic sense of a self-fluctuating between the extremes of energy and passivity. In the terrible **"Lady Macbeth of Mtsensk,"** we see another kind of possession. The young wife of an elderly merchant is starved for sexual love. She does not understand her state until a lover seizes her. Then wild sensual passion moves into her. She is "occupied" or possessed. It is nothing for her to persuade her lover to commit murder. Drowsing in her bed after her lover has left her, she sees a cat jump on the bed and strokes it. Yet there is no cat; it is a sensual fantasy that has become embodied. Leskov frequently uses a cat in his tales as a symbol of the ungovernable life of the unconscious. We are shown how she experiences the humiliations and jealousies of sexual love and how at last she and her lover are caught and condemned to exile in Siberia. And here, the maker of contrived stories would, no doubt, see the end of the tale. Not so Leskov. He is a writer who rambles on like life to the end. He lives pityingly in the feeling man and woman, drifting along in them through the dragging hours of the day—the hours that do not contribute, one might say, to art, but which contain a life. So, after she and her lover are condemned and are indeed on the awful journey to Siberia, we see her having to face one more horror and to commit one more murder. Her lover has betrayed her with another prisoner. While the prisoners are crossing a river on a raft, she throws herself in, dragging her pretty rival with her. One sees Leskov's mastery of drama in this final scene:

> "A boat hook! Throw them a boat hook!" the convicts on the ferry shouted.
>
> A heavy boat hook attached to a long rope rose in the air and fell to the water. Sonetka disappeared again. Two seconds later, carried away from the ferry by the current, she raised her arms once more, but Katerina broke from another wave, emerging almost to the waist, and threw herself on Sonetka like a strong pike on a soft little perch, and neither appeared again.

A pike, a perch, a cat: these animal symbols are used with visionary effect by Leskov continuously. Yet this terrible woman does not disgust us. We see that it is by misfortune that evil occupied her. In Western literature such characters are commonly hounded down intellectually by their creators as Flaubert hounds Madame Bovary with cold art; or Zola hounds his characters with the logic of melodramatic determinism, theory, or physical nausea in order to enhance a theatrical rather than an occupying, pervading sense of guilt. Their characters are evil or stupid or tragic; but Leskov's are fundamentally good people who have been caught by Fate in a restless, idle hour and he does not condemn them. He exercises the Quaker charity. We feel that in Katerina Lvovna we have met a full and real woman whom we forgive. We are not asked, as we are in Dostoevsky, to see good and evil in the full pride of tremendous spiritual conflict. Leskov's Quaker upbringing had led him to think of goodness as the natural and permanent condition of man; and of passion as the evil, uncalled-for guest of the soul. In his purely ecclesiastical and religious stories—by a bizarre chance he had read Trollope—his instances of goodness appear when pride, and particularly ecclesiastical pride, give place to humility. Abasement in itself is no passport—as it often seems to be in Dostoevsky—abasement is profitable only when it is noble, without sickness and the last step on a lifelong quest for goodness. And in non-religious tales like **"The Sentry,"** a sardonic story about the military bureaucrats, we see the same preoccupation. I recommend to those who are impressed by Leskov in this volume to look out for two long stories, **"The Amazon"** and **"The March Hare."** The first is the long portrait of an old Moscow procuress who is convinced that it is she who is the real victim; and the other a comical yet fiercely satirical portrait of a police officer who has been told to find out not only

what people are thinking, but "what they are going to think." This tale could not be published, for obvious political reasons, until 1917, after Leskov's death. In the Stalinist period its moral acquired new force.

Leskov is a delicate psychologist. He draws women beautifully. He is robustly comical, extravagantly grotesque. His narrative is as vivid as paint but the untidy size of his characters marks them equal to it. He is one of those storytellers who have a deep affection for ignorance for, in its interstices, they know there is a rich residue of strange experience. He recognizes in ignorance a peculiar furniture that encumbers the minds of ordinary people and never disdains them for it. His satire at the expense of the authorities has all the more edge. He is a writer of great vitality who does not suffer from boredom. His voice is the voice of the discoverer and traveler whose stories have the dust and jolts of the journey on them. It is a mistake to think that the sprawling of some of his stories is a sign of incompetence and that he would have been better if he had been as classical in form as Turgenev, as adroit as Maupassant or as sensitive to art itself as Chekhov was. In one of his tales, the narrator begins: "I hope no one will find fault with me if his words and my words get mixed up. . . . I'm afraid it can't be helped." We do not find fault for the man is a so-called lunatic, the victim of officials who are far more lunatic than he, and he conveys precisely that curious mixture of clearheadedness and insinuation which a victim will use to his advantage. Leskov has many manners, but they all weave not only the characters but all the wagging tongues of Russia into the tale. We are made conscious of life outside. We have the impression of a whole society that is like some animal dozing and dreaming on the rug, yelping in its sleep. Leskov was not a preacher. He was, by nature, a modest disciple. (Towards the end of his life he became a Tolstoyan.) His religion was quietist. His natural successor was Gorki whose university was the Russian people and who recognized in Leskov a master.

Walter Benjamin (essay date 1963)

SOURCE: "The Story-Teller: Reflections on the Works of Nicolai Leskov," in *Chicago Review,* No. 16, 1963, pp. 80-101.

[In the following excerpt, Benjamin praises Leskov's craftsmanship and admires what he considers the author's ability to tell a good tale and gently counsel his readers by sharing with them his life experiences.]

"Leskov," writes Gorky, "is the writer most deeply rooted in the people and is completely untouched by any foreign influences." A great story-teller will always be rooted in the people, primarily in the working class. But just as this includes the rural, the maritime, and the urban elements in the many stages of their economic and technical development, there are many gradations in the concepts in which their stores of experience comes down to us. (To say nothing of the by no means insignificant share traders had in the art of story-telling; their task was less to increase its didactic content than to refine the tricks with which the attention of the listener was captivated. They have left deep traces in the narrative cycle of the *Arabian Nights.*) In short, despite the primary role which story-telling plays in the household of humanity, the concepts through which the yield of the stories may be garnered are manifold. What may most readily be contained in the religious in Leskov seems almost automatically to fall into place in the pedagogical perspectives of the Enlightenment in Hebel, appears as hermetic tradition in Poe, finds a last refuge in Kipling in the life of British seamen and colonial soldiers. All great story-tellers have in common the freedom with which they move up and down the rungs of their experience as on a ladder. A ladder extending downward to the interior of the earth and disappearing into the clouds is the image for a collective experience to which even the deepest shock of every individual experience, death, constitutes no impediment or barrier.

"And they lived happily ever after," says the fairy-tale. The fairy-tale, which to this day is the first tutor of children because it was once the first tutor of mankind, secretly lives on in the story. The first true story-teller is, and will continue to be, the teller of fairy-tales. Whenever good counsel was at a premium, the fairy-tale had it, and where the need was greatest, its aid was nearest. This need was the need created by the myth. The fairy-tale tells us of the earliest arrangements that mankind made to shake off the nightmare which the myth had placed upon its chest. . . .

Few story-tellers have displayed as profound a kinship with the spirit of the fairy-tale as did Leskov. This involves tendencies that were promoted by the dogmas of the Greek-Orthodox church. As is well known, Origen's speculations about *apokatastasis*—the entry of all souls into Paradise—which was rejected by the Roman church plays a significant part in these dogmas. Leskov was very much influenced by Origen and planned to translate his work *On First Principles.* In keeping with Russian folk belief he interpreted the Resurrection less as a transfiguration than as a disenchantment, in a sense akin to the fairy-tale. Such an interpretation of Origen is at the bottom of **"The Enchanted Pilgrim."** In this, as in many other of Leskov's tales, a hybrid between fairy-tale and legend is involved, not unlike that hybrid between fairy-tale and legend which Ernst Bloch once mentions in a connection in which he utilizes our division between myth and fairy-tale in his fashion.

"A hybrid between fairy-tale and legend," he says, "contains figuratively mythical elements, mythical elements whose effect is certainly captivating and static, and yet not outside man. 'Mythical' in this sense in the legend are Tao-like figures, especially very old ones. For example, the couple Philemon and Baucis: fabulously escaped, although in a repose like that of Nature. And certainly there is also such a relationship in the far slighter Tao of Gotthelf; in places it deprives the legend of the locality of the spell, saves the light of life, man's own light of life, calmly burning, within as without."

"Fabulously escaped" are the creatures that lead the procession of Leskov's creations: the righteous ones. Pavlin, Figura, the toupet artist, the bear keeper, the helpful sentry—all of them, embodiments of wisdom, kindness, the consolation of the world, crowd about the story-teller. It is unmistakable that they are suffused with the *imago* of his mother.

This is how Leskov describes her: "She was so thoroughly good that she was not capable of harming any man, nor even an animal. She ate neither meat nor fish, because she had such pity for living creatures. Sometimes my father used to reproach her with this. But she answered: 'I have raised the little animals myself, they are like my children to me. I can't eat my own children, can I?' She would not eat meat at a neighbor's house either. 'I have seen them alive,' she would say; 'they are my acquaintances. I can't eat my acquaintances, can I?'"

The righteous man is the advocate for created things and at the same time is their highest embodiment. In Leskov he has a maternal touch which is occasionally intensified into the mythical (and thus, to be sure, endangers the fairy-tale purity). Typical of this is the protagonist of his story **"Kotin the Provider and Platonida."** This figure, a peasant named Pisonski, is a hermaphrodite. For twelve years his mother raised him as a girl. His male and female organs mature simultaneously, and his bisexuality "becomes the symbol of God incarnate."

In Leskov's view, the pinnacle of creation has been attained with this, and at the same time he presumably sees it as a bridge established between this world and the other. For these earthily powerful, maternal male figures which again and again claim Leskov's skill as a story-teller have been removed from obedience to the sexual drive in the bloom of their strength. They do not, however, really embody an ascetic ideal; rather, the continence of these righteous men has so little privative character that it becomes the elemental counterpoise to uncontrolled lust which the story-teller has personified in **"Lady Macbeth of Mzensk."** If the range between a Pavlin and this merchant's wife covers the breadth of the world of created beings, in the hierarchy of his characters Leskov has no less plumbed its depth.

The hierarchy of the world of created things, which has its apex in the righteous man, reaches down into the abyss of the inanimate by many gradations. In this connection one particular has to be noted. This whole created world speaks not so much by the human voice as by what could be called "the voice of Nature" in the title of one of his most significant stories.

This story deals with the petty official Philipp Philippovitch who leaves no stone unturned to get the chance to have as his house guest a field marshal passing through his little town. He manages to do so. The guest, who is at first surprised at the clerk's urgent invitation, gradually comes to believe that he recognizes in him someone he must have met previously. But who is he? He cannot remember. The strange thing is that the host, for his part, is not willing to reveal his identity. Instead, he puts off the high personage from day to day, saying that the "voice of Nature" would not fail to speak distinctly to him one day. This goes on until finally the guest, shortly before continuing on his journey, must grant the host's public request to let the "voice of Nature" resound. Thereupon the host's wife withdraws. She "returned with a big, brightly polished, copper hunting horn which she gave to her husband. He took the horn, put it to his lips, and was at the same instant as though transformed. Hardly had he inflated his cheeks and produced a tone as powerful as the rolling of thunder when the field marshall cried: 'Stop, I've got it now, brother. This makes me recognize you at once! You are the bugler from the regiment of yagers, and because you were so honest I sent you to keep an eye on a crooked supplies supervisor.' 'That's it, Your Excellency,' answered the host. 'I didn't want to remind you of this myself, but wanted to let the voice of Nature speak.'"

The way the profundity of this story is hidden behind its silliness conveys an idea of Leskov's magnificent humor. This humor is confirmed in the same story in an even more cryptic way. We have heard that because of his honesty the official was assigned to watch a crooked supplies supervisor. This is what we are told at the end, in the recognition scene. At the very beginning of the story, however, we learn the following about the host: "All the inhabitants of the town were acquainted with the man, and they knew that he did not hold a high office, for he was neither a state official nor a military man, but a little supervisor at the tiny supply depot, where together with the rats he chewed on the state rusks and boot soles, and in the course of time had chewed himself together a nice little frame house." It is evident that in this story is asserted the traditional sympathy which the story-teller has for rascals and crooks. All farce literature bears witness to it. Nor is it denied on the heights of art; of all Hebel's characters, the Brassenheim Miller, Tinder Frieder, and Red Dieter have been his most faithful companions. And yet for Hebel, too, the righteous man has the main role in the *theatrum mundi*. But because no one is actually up to this role, it wanders from one to the other. Now it is the tramp, now the haggling Jewish pedlar, now the man of limited intelligence who steps in to play this part. In every single case it is a guest role, a moral improvisation. Hebel is a casuist. At no price does he take his stand with any principle, but he does not reject any either, for any principle can at some time become the instrument of the righteous man. Compare this with Leskov's attitude. "I realize," he writes in his story **"À Propos of the Kreutzer Sonata,"** "that my thinking is based much more on a practical view of life than on abstract philosophy or lofty morality; but I am nevertheless used to thinking the way I do." To be sure, the moral catastrophes that appear in Leskov's world are to the moral incidents in Hebel's world as the great, silent flowing of the Volga is to the babbling, rushing little mill stream. Among Leskov's historical tales there are several in which passions are at work as destructively as the wrath of Achilles or the hatred of Hagen. It is astonishing how fearfully the world can darken for this author and with what majesty evil can raise its scepter. Leskov has evidently known moods—and this is probably one of the few characteristics he shares with Dostoievsky—in which he was close to antinomian ethics. The elemental natures in his *Tales from Olden Times* go to the limit in their ruthless passion. But it is precisely the mystics who have been inclined to see this limit as the point at which utter depravity turns into saintliness.

The lower Leskov descends on the scale of created things the more obviously does his way of viewing things approach the mystical. Actually, as will be shown, there is much evidence that in this, too, a characteristic is revealed which is inherent in the nature of the story-teller. To be sure, only few have ventured into the depths of inanimate nature, and in modern narrative literature there is not much in which the voice of the anonymous story-teller, who has primarily been literature, resounds so clearly as it does in Leskov's story **"The Alexandrite."** It deals with a semi-precious stone, the pyrope. The mineral is the lowest stratum of created things. For the story-teller, however, it is directly joined to the highest. To him it is granted to see in this pyrope a natural prophecy of petrified, lifeless nature about the historical world in which he himself lives. This would is the world of Alexander II. The story-teller—or rather, the man to whom he attributes his own knowledge—is a gem engraver named Wenzel who has achieved the greatest conceivable skill in his art. One can juxtapose him with the silversmithy of Tula and say that—in the spirit of Leskov—the perfect artisan has access to the innermost chamber of the realm of created things. He is an incarnation of the pious. About this gem cutter we are told: "He suddenly squeezed my hand on which was the ring with the alexandrite, which is known to sparkle red in artificial light, and cried: 'Look, here it is, the prophetic Russian stone! O crafty Siberian. It was always green as hope and only toward evening was it suffused with blood. It was that way from the beginning of the world, but it concealed itself for a long time, lay hidden in the earth, and permitted itself to be found only on the day when Czar Alexander was declared of age, when a great sorcerer had come to Siberia to find it, the stone, a magician . . .' 'What nonsense are you talking,' I interrupted him, 'this stone wasn't found by a magician at all, it was a scholar named Nordenskiöld!' 'A magician! I tell you, a magician!' screamed Wenzel in a loud voice. 'Just look; what a stone! A green morning is in it and a bloody evening . . . This is fate, the fate of noble Czar Alexander!' With these words old Wenzel turned to the wall, propped his head on his elbows, and . . . began to sob."

One can hardly come any closer to the meaning of this significant story than by some words which Paul Valéry wrote in a very remote connection. "Artistic observation," he says in reflections on a lady artist whose work consists in the silk embroidery of figures, "can attain an almost mystical depth. The objects on which it falls lose their names. Light and shade form very particular systems, present very individual questions which depend upon no knowledge and are derived from no practice, but get their existence and value exclusively from a certain accord of the soul, the eye, and the hand of someone who was born to perceive them and evoke them in his own inner self."

With these words, soul, eye, and hand are brought into connection. Interacting with one another they determine a practice. We are no longer familiar with this practice. The role of the hand in production has become more modest, and the place it filled in story-telling lies waste. (After all, story-telling, in its sensory aspect, is by no means a job for the voice alone. Rather, in genuine story-telling the hand plays a part which supports in a hundred ways what is expressed with its gestures trained by work.) That old coordination of the soul, the eye, and the hand which emerges in Valéry's words is that of the artisan which we encounter in the home of the art of story-telling. In fact, one can go on and ask himself whether the relationship of the story-teller to his material, human life, is not in itself a craftsman's relationship, whether it is not his very task to fashion the raw material of experience, his own and that of others, in a solid, useful, and unique way. It is a matter of a process which may perhaps most adequately be exemplified by the proverb if one thinks of it as an ideogram of a story. A proverb, one might say, is a ruin which stands on the site of an old story and in which a moral clings round a tale like ivy round a wall.

Seen in this way, the story-teller joins the ranks of the teachers and sages. He has counsel—not for a few situations, as to the proverb does, but for many, like the sage. For it is granted to him to reach back to a whole lifetime (a life, incidentally, that comprises not only his own experience but no little of the experience of others; what the story-teller knows from hearsay is added to his own). His gift is the ability to relate his life, his distinction to be able to tell his entire life. The story-teller: he is the man who could let the wick of his life be consumed completely by the gentle flame of his story. This is the basis of the incomparable aura about the story-teller, in Leskov as in Hauff, in Poe as in Stevenson. The story-teller is the figure in which the righteous man encounters himself.

Albert J. Wehrle (essay date 1976)

SOURCE: "Paradigmatic Aspects of Leskov's 'The Enchanted Pilgrim'," in *Slavic and East European Journal,* Vol. 20, No. 4, 1976, pp. 371-78.

[*In the following essay, Wehrle discusses one of Leskov's most popular stories, asserting that it illustrates two original elements in Leskov's works: anecdotism and the weaving together of apparently disparate elements.*]

In his correspondence N. S. Leskov mentioned *Dead Souls, Don Quixote,* and Fénelon's *The Adventures of Telemachus* in connection with his work on "A Telemachus of the Black Earth" ("Černozemnyj Telemak"), which is now known as **"The Enchanted Pilgrim"** (**"Očarovannyj strannik"**) (1873).[1] Each of these works treats a series of adventures connected by the personality of a wandering hero. Leskov's use of this method in **"The Enchanted Pilgrim"** is only one illustration of the dominant principle of his poetics, his "anecdotism." According to Ejxenbaum: "The anecdote (mainly verbal) is the atom, as it were,

in the nature of Leskov's creative work."[2] The influential N. K. Mixajlovskij was outspoken in his criticism of this manner of writing. In 1897 he wrote of **"The Enchanted Pilgrim"**:

> In terms of richness of story this is perhaps Leskov's most remarkable work, but what is most striking about it is its lack of any center whatsoever, so that, in fact, it has no plot, but is a whole series of stories strung together like beads on a thread; and each individual bead could be conveniently removed and replaced by another, while it would also be possible to string any number of additional beads onto the thread.[3]

"Even his longer works," wrote the same critic, "are in fact chains of anecdotes, tied together more or less consecutively, as in 'The Enchanted Pilgrim'. . . . And the anecdote itself, as something fragmentary and accidental, has no real independent meaning."[4]

Mixajlovskij's negative evaluation of Leskov's talent is only of historical interest today, but his is still the classic description of the structure of **"The Enchanted Pilgrim"** and, as such, has been developed further. Leonid Grossman sees "anecdotism" as Leskov's answer to the need for a form capable of reflecting rapid change, "the wide canvas of an agitated and stormy epoch."[5] In the introduction to the 1956-58 edition of Leskov's works Pavel Gromov and Boris Ejxenbaum draw a parallel between the accidental nature (*slučajnost'*) of the pilgrim's fate and the characteristics of his inner world: "Ivan Fljagin's consciousness lacks a focal point, has no thread which might connect the separate manifestations of his personality."[6] Thus, Mixajlovskij's metaphor of randomly-strung beads is provided with extrinsic and intrinsic justification.

But Leskov's novella can be analyzed in another way, in terms of a "vertical" system of relationships between elements of the story. This vertical organization is termed "paradigmatic," as opposed to the linear or "syntagmatic" aspect of the work. Analysis of the paradigmatic system focuses on functional parallels or contrasts between elements. The word "functional" indicates an abstract approach to the material. In the analysis of **"The Enchanted Pilgrim,"** a work marked by exceptional variety on the level of concrete representation, this abstract approach reveals relationships between phenomena which may seem unique and separate. The present analysis of **"The Enchanted Pilgrim"** deals with relationships of parallelism and antithesis. The paradigmatic relationships singled out are central to the meaning of the work as a whole. A complete structural analysis of the novella would require detailed specification of both the paradigmatic and syntagmatic systems.

Leskov consistently uses antithesis to construct the episodes of Ivan Sever'janyč Fljagin's life story. In Chapter 2, for instance, there are two carriage accidents. In one Fljagin is responsible for a monk's death; in the other he saves his count and countess from being killed. He is rewarded for the latter deed with a trivial gift, but harshly punished in the next chapter for maiming the countess's cat. In Chapter 4 the burly cat-maimer finds himself in the incongruous role of babysitter. In Chapter 6 the former gentle babysitter flogs a man to death. He escapes from criminal prosecution into captivity by the Tartars, who hold him prisoner because they like him. The vast expanses of the steppe contrast with his lack of freedom. The desolation of the location contrasts with the poetry of the passages which describe it. After finally returning to Russia, Fljagin meets a "magnetizer," who "cures" him of his drinking problem by forcing him to drink. The magnetizer raises the important antithesis between the beauty of a horse and the beauty that is "nature's perfection," between beauty that can be bought and sold, and beauty that cannot. The latter oppositions are a major theme of subsequent chapters. The juxtaposition of illusion and reality, particularly marked in the magnetizer episode, is a specific case of the dual point of view that pervades the work. Leskov builds this double vision into the narrative by supplying a dramatized audience of educated Russians who listen to and comment on the uneducated Fljagin's "enchanted" tale.

"The Enchanted Pilgrim" opens with an antithesis, the contrast between the desolation of the area around Lake Ladoga and the colorful figure who boards the ship there and begins his remarkable story. Fljagin is not noticed immediately, but turns out to be "an extraordinarily interesting man," and "everyone was amazed that he had not been noticed before" (IV, 386). The terms of this antithesis remind one of the famous passage in *Dead Souls* in which the monotony of the Russian landscape is contrasted to the powerful fascination of its call. The failure of the upper-class, European-ized travelers to notice Fljagin recalls Tjutčev's famous poem in which the "proud foreigner's gaze" does not notice the spiritual richness concealed behind the superficial poverty of Russia's poor villages. This contrast of external appearance to inner (spiritual) reality is more than evidence of mystical nationalism. It is a structural and thematic element of the novella. It immediately reappears in the pilgrim's first story—the story of the humble priest who prays for suicides. The priest is a drunkard, a notoriously weak character. But he also possesses a spiritual power: "He won't renounce the audacity of his calling, but will go on importuning the Creator for them [the suicides], and He will have to forgive them" (IV, 389-90). It is the priest's inner power, revealed to the archbishop in a vision, that saves him from losing his parish. Although the archdeacon's complaint to the archbishop was completely justified by the facts of the matter, external facts and obvious weakness are overruled by spiritual merit.

The primacy of external facts, of external law, is denied once again in the babysitting episode. A burly (and degenerate) civil servant whose wife has left him uses his knowledge of Fljagin's status as a runaway serf to force him to take this incongruous job. The wife soon appears and begs Fljagin for the girl. He refuses because: "If, having defied the law and relig'n [*zakon i relegija*], you have changed your observance [*obrjad*], then you just have to suffer for it" (IV, 412, repeated 413). Fljagin's use of the word *obrjad* ("rite," "ceremony," "observance") is

evidence of legalistic indoctrination; violation of one rule system, in his view, necessarily means the adoption of another fixed set of norms. When the woman and the officer she is living with offer him one thousand rubles for the baby, he throws down the money and thrashes the officer. But when the husband, who is even bigger than the giant Fljagin, appears on the scene, and with a gun, the babysitter changes his mind, gives the mother her daughter, and the four escape the tyrant. In the Gromov-Ejxenbaum article this incident is cited as an example of Fljagin's lack of a consistent moral standard (I, xli-xlii). But, while it is true that the pilgrim acts instinctively here, it can be shown that his instincts follow a definite pattern. One of the terms of this pattern, given in the story of the priest who prays for suicides, is mercy. Like the priest, the woman is externally unworthy. But her love proves more convincing than her husband's threats.

In Chapters 6-9 Leskov develops the external-internal antithesis as satire against the legalistic formalism of the state and organized religion. According to Fljagin's naive understanding of Russian law, only he is guilty of flogging the Tartar to death in the flogging contest. He believes that if the Tartar had killed him there would have been no crime because the law, he thinks, only applies to Christians. While Fljagin's educated listeners act as correctives to his distortions of these legal facts, they are also more aware of the actual tsarist legal inconsistencies that are the real target of Leskov's satire. Fljagin escapes from the Russian authorities, only to be taken captive by the Tartars. He begs some missionaries to help him escape, but they refuse because: "You have to remember that you are a Christian and therefore there's no use our bothering with you any more" (IV, 439). That is, the fact that Fljagin is in a miserable situation is insignificant because the gates of heaven are open to his soul. Fljagin's listeners can relate this principle to the Russian Church's position on social and political issues of the time. Within the system of textual relationships the missionaries contrast with characters willing to take the sufferings of others upon themselves. It should be noted that Fljagin's conscious actions at this time still bear the stamp of legalistic indoctrination. For instance, he does not consider his Tartar children to be his because they are not baptized.

Fljagin's opinion of the missionaries gives an important clue to his development. He says they are unsuccessful among the Tartars because "they preach to them about a meek God. That spoils everything from the start, for without a threat an Asiatic will never respect a meek God and will kill those who preach His gospel" (IV, 440). And yet, Fljagin has already rejected the paradigmatic synonym of a coercive God, the civil servant with his gun. In that episode he instinctively distinguishes between *zakon* and *relegija* on the one hand, and the law of mercy and love on the other. In paradigmatic terms, the story of the drunkard priest connects the law of love with God. In this regard the many parallels that can be drawn between the priest and the magnetizer are most important. The latter begins Fljagin's formal education in the nature of love. Gruša's desperate plea is the existential test of what he has learned:

"Prove to me that you still love me and do what I ask of you in this fatal hour. . . . Take pity on me, my dearest, my dear brother—thrust a knife into my heart! . . . You will live and obtain forgiveness from God for my soul and yours, so do not damn me, do not make me lay hands upon myself." (IV, 496-97.) In doing what Gruša asks Fljagin consciously violates *zakon* and *relegija* and relies upon a God of love to grant him forgiveness.

According to the story of the drunkard priest, even suicides can be forgiven. It will be recalled that Fljagin himself several times is near to taking his own life. As his story closes, however, the pilgrim expresses a different desire: to die for his people (IV, 513). The religious dimension of this wish can be deduced from the fate of those who preach the meek God's gospel of love. Fljagin's desire to lay down his life for others finds a parallel in the magnetizer's "vocation" to take upon himself the sufferings of others. "We, the possessed, suffer so that it shall be easier for the rest," he tells the pilgrim (IV, 460). The fantastic and farcical aspects of Fljagin's adventure with the magnetizer conceal its essential seriousness. "Curing" Fljagin does, in fact, cost the magnetizer his life: "He too had taken a lot upon himself and he couldn't stand it, so, right there in the tavern across from the gypsies' house, he drank so much that he died" (IV, 475). There is little doubt that the same fate awaits the priest who prays for suicides. When Fljagin helps an elderly couple by assuming their only son's name and taking his place in the army, he rehearses taking upon himself the burdens of others. His final wish to suffer for everyone is anticipated by his role as a vaudeville actor, which calls for him to be beaten from noon to midnight to amuse the public. As in the magnetizer episode, the farcical aspects of this role screen its serious implication.

The antithesis between freedom and captivity is important to the novel. The latter element is developed in a series of parallelisms. Fljagin is condemned to kneel in the countess's garden and break rocks. The Tartars sew horse bristles into his heels so he cannot stand. In the monastery he is instructed to kneel because a man's knees are the "first instrument" against the devil: "As soon as you fall on your knees, your soul flies upward right away" (IV, 506). The flying up of the soul from the captive body can serve as a point of entry into the system of parallelisms that have to do with freedom, or, more precisely, the spirit to be free. In the first chapter Fljagin mentions his feeling for the wild horses he saw trained when he was still a boy: "They would always, like birds, be squinting up at the sky, so that pity would come over me when I looked at one of those horses, because you could see that the poor thing would have flown away, if only he had wings . . ." (IV, 397). Later, in one of the poetic descriptions of the desolate steppe, Fljagin watches a little bird fly away: "But you can't even do that, for you have no wings" (IV, 435). The parallel between the "bristled" Fljagin and a hobbled horse is clearly drawn. Bird and horse imagery come together in the first description of Gruša: "Really and truly, what eyelashes! Long, really long, and black, and like they were alive themselves and fluttering like birds." And Fljagin thinks to himself: "The magnetizer was right: it isn't at all like the beauty of a horse, an animal that is bought and sold" (IV, 470). However, Fljagin's employer, a prince, does in fact buy Gruša. When the prince first displays his new acquisition the bird motif appears again, while the description of the action mimes the leading of a horse. "The prince went ahead of her . . . dragging Gruša along, having clasped both her hands in one of his, and she was walking with her head cast down, resisting him and not looking, with only those black eyelashes of hers fluttering along her cheeks like the wings of a bird" (478). Gruša's fate is paralleled by that of the wildest horse Fljagin ever tamed. The horse died because it "was too proud a creature." It "became gentle in its behavior, but couldn't overcome its character" (IV, 393).

In the first chapter Fljagin discloses that he is a "connoisseur," that he possesses the gift of instinctively divining the nature of a horse. In an article on a folklore motif in the novella, M. P. Čerednikova notes that the theme of the "natural gift" is one of the main leitmotifs of the work, and that the taming of the wild horse is of primary significance.[7] Čerednikova focuses on the episode involving the American horse tamer, John Rarey, an historical person who visited Russia in 1857. She discloses that a Frenchman offered Rarey 250,000 francs for his secret, an offer Rarey accepted. In contrast, Fljagin cannot sell his secret to Rarey because it is an instinctive gift. "But he took everything from a 'merican, science point of view, and wouldn't believe me" (IV, 394). In terms of the antithesis discussed previously, scientific explanation can be equated to "external law," the "facts," while Fljagin's "gift" belongs in the group of "internal," spiritual qualities.

The contrast between Rarey and Fljagin anticipates the relationship between Fljagin and the prince who buys Gruša. The initial situation is the same: the prince wants to buy the connoisseur's gift. Although he knows he will not succeed, Fljagin does his best to teach the prince how to perceive the quality of a horse. But the prince is always fooled by the artful deceptions of the horse traders. He cannot see beyond the external; he only sees physical beauty or its illusion. On the basis of this evidence it can be predicted that his infatuation with Gruša will be physical in nature, and that his appreciation of her singing will be superficial, albeit extravagant. Note the importance of the external pose, the picturesque superficiality of the following preparations:

> The prince brought her into the room, took her in his arms, and set her down like a child on a wide, soft divan with her feet in one corner, put a velvet cushion behind her back and another under her right elbow; then he put the [wide scarlet] ribbon of the guitar across her shoulder and placed her fingers on the strings. Then he sat down on the floor beside the divan and leaned his head against her scarlet morocco-leather shoe. (IV, 478-79)

Fljagin, on the other hand, is captivated by Gruša before he even sees her. Outside the gypsies' house he hears her singing a song that is "tender, oh so tender, and so soulful, and the voice that sang it was clear as a bell, so that if it just nipped your soul, it would capture it" (IV, 468). Once he is inside, Fljagin still does not see Gruša as a woman, but rather as a fascinating *figura,* a "serpent" able to "nip" (*ščipat'*) one's soul. That is, his perception follows from the effect of her song, not from her physical presence. Then: "I drank the wine she offered me, while looking at her over the rim of the glass, and I couldn't tell whether her skin was dark or fair, but I could see how underneath her thin skin, as on a plum in sunlight, the color glowed, and how on her lovely temple a vein was beating. . . . 'There it is,' I thought, 'there's real beauty.'" (IV, 470.) The emphasis here is on the internal. Fljagin does not see Gruša's skin, but the light glowing beneath it. The throbbing of the vein is a sign of vital, intense inner life, the passionate spirit that animates her song. Fljagin anticipates the prince in buying Gruša's songs. The fundamental difference between the two purchases is suggested in Fljagin's way of referring to the hundred-ruble notes he throws at Gruša's feet as "swans." Bird imagery has already been associated with freedom. Here, the imagery implies, Fljagin does not so much buy Gruša's songs as give up his freedom to her, surrender his soul to her spirit. The prince, on the other hand, not only buys Gruša's songs, but her body as well. Gruša's pregnancy indicates the physical nature of his attraction and that he imposes his will upon her. It is not surprising, given the prince's shallow appreciation of Gruša's singing, that he abandons her for the most "external" (nonspiritual) of things—money—which he plans to make by selling cheap, gaudy printed cloth to Tartars at fairs. This is the prince's "art." He claims to be an artist, and that Fljagin is an artist too (IV, 477). Fljagin's art is his story, which he tells in his own way as it arises from his instinctive perception of spiritual values.

Tolstoj believed that a true artist creates his own form. He expressed the following opinion more than once: "From Gogol''s *Dead Souls* to to Dostoevskij's *Notes From the House of the Dead,* in the recent period of Russian literature there is not a single prose work rising above mediocrity which fully fits the form of a novel, epic, or novella [*povest'*]."[8] **"The Enchanted Pilgrim"** belongs to this tradition through its original combination of "anecdotism" and a complex paradigmatic system of relationships. Analysis reveals that images, characters, and values are oriented on a fundamental antithesis between spiritual qualities and values which restrict, deny, or are unaware of them. The moral dimension of Fljagin's pilgrimage is another feature of **"The Enchanted Pilgrim"** common to the best works of nineteenth-century Russian literature.

Notes

[1] N. S. Leskov, *Sobranie sočinenij* (11 vols.; M.: GIXL, 1956-58), X, 360; letter to P. K. Ščebal'skij, 4 Jan. 1873.

[2] Boris Ejxenbaum, "'Črezmernyj pisatel'' (k 100-letiju roždenija N. Leskova)," (1930), *O proze* (L.: Xudožestvennaja literatura, 1969), 539.

[3] N. K. Mixajlovskij, "Literatura i žizn'," *Russkoe bogatstvo,* no. 6 (1897), 105.

[4] N. K. Mixajlovskij, *Otkliki. Izdanie redakcii žurnala Russkoe bogatstvo* (SPb., 1904), II, 115; cited in V. Ja. Troickij, *Leskov-xudožnik* (M.: Nauka, 1974), 190.

[5] Leonid Grossman, *N. S. Leskov: Žizn', tvorčestvo, poètika* (M.: Goslitizdat, 1945), 261-62.

[6] Pavel Gromov, Boris Ejxenbaum, "N. S. Leskov (Očerk tvorčestva)" in Leskov, *Sobranie,* I, xxix.

[7] M. P. Čerednikova, "Ob odnom fol'klornom motive v povesti N. S. Leskova *Očarovannyj strannik,*" *Russkaja literatura,* 16, no. 3 (1973), 141.

[8] L. N. Tolstoj, "Neskol'ko slov po povodu knigi *Vojna i mir,*" *Sobranie sočinenij* (20 vols.; M.: GIXL, 1960-65), VII, 382-83.

Hugh McLean (essay date 1977)

SOURCE: "Left, Left, Left," in *Nikolai Leskov: The Man and His Art,* Harvard University Press, 1977, pp. 392-406.

[*In the following excerpt from a full-length study of Leskov's life and career, McLean discusses Leskov's signature story, "The Lefthander," asserting that it expresses leftist social and political leanings more typical of the author's later stories and not right-wing sympathies as many commentators have supposed. McLean also argues that Leskov's linguistic style in this story, which reviewers have faulted as overwrought and unnecessary, serves serious artistic functions.*]

In 1881, at the age of fifty, Leskov wrote his best-known short story, the work Russians associate with his name as we connect *Tom Sawyer* with Mark Twain's: **"The Tale of the Crosseyed Lefthander from Tula and the Steel Flea (A Workshop Legend),"** as it was originally called.[1] In the collected works (1889), the nameless hero's appellation, *Levshá,* "The Lefthander," was established as the main title, the long one becoming a parenthetical subheading.[2] The story will be referred to here as **"The Lefthander."**[3] . . .

"The Lefthander" was far from achieving instant recognition as a classic. Contemporary critics, blind to Leskov's structural subtleties, charged it, quite unjustly, with moral ambiguity. One of the reasons for critics' persistent misunderstanding is the double angle of moral vision in the story. Two sets of judgments are implanted in the text, one immediate and explicit, the other derived and implicit. The first belongs to the narrator, the naive, semieducated, culture-bound gunsmith. The second is that of the "author," who speaks with his own voice only in the concluding chapter, but whose moral presence can be felt. By implication he—and we—condemn behavior the narrator considers normal, such as Platov's pulling out by the roots great gobs of the lefthander's hair.[21] Readers who thought the story a pure transcription of folklore could not acknowledge the double perspective, though they still inconsistently ascribed to Leskov views expressed in the story of which they disapproved. Thus the problem of the story's origin became integrally bound up with the question of moral interpretation.

One moral issue raised by **"The Lefthander"** is our response to the narrator's chauvinism. Although they are somewhat neutralized by the humorous style in which he expresses them, the narrator's ethnic aggressiveness and boastfulness were and are offensive to many readers, including Russians; and some of them, quite wrongly, have imputed these attitudes to the author. Yet anyone even superficially acquainted with Leskov's many stories dealing with confrontations of national types would know that he is anything but a jingoist. Within **"The Lefthander"** it is clear from the linguistic bizarreries alone that the narrator and the author are not to be equated. And apart from style, the outcome of the plot—the tragic fate of the talented Russian artisan in his own country, especially compared with the much more favorable experience of his English friends—hardly sounds like blind insistence on Russian superiority.

Yet there were critics who took Leskov to task for what **"The Lefthander"** does not say. Blinded by their prejudices against the author of *No Way Out* and hostile to anything that had first appeared in Aksakov's Slavophile *Rus',* left-wing ideologues decided that **"The Lefthander"** was just another bought-and-paid-for product of a well-known servant of "patriotic" reaction. "You can't help thinking," *Notes of the Fatherland* wrote with heavy irony, "that if uneducated Russian masters are like this, what would come of them if you taught them from arithmetic the four rules of addition,[22] and you can't help soaring way up high over Europe, singing the praises of Russian talents and patriotic loyalty and chanting 'Ai lvuli, se tre zhuli.'"[23]

In Soviet times, blatant sounding of the national horn no longer evokes the opprobrium it did a century ago. In her analysis of **"The Lefthander,"** Maria Goryachkina praises Leskov (and with just as little justification) for the very chauvinism and xenophobia for which her nineteenth-century predecessors had reprobated him. "The liberal cosmopolites," she writes, "were especially indignant at Les-kov's patriotism, his defense of the national individuality of the Russian people, his celebration of their natural giftedness."[24] Writing in 1963 (and showing some lack of political foresight), Goryachkina triumphantly marshaled in support of her "truly Soviet" appreciation of Leskov's patriotism that distinguished literary critic Nikita Khrushchev, who had once given a pep talk in Tula in which he reminded the "happy descendants of Leskov's lefthander" of the "pride in our people" evoked by the story.[25]

It seems the height of irony to associate Leskov with Khrushchev's shoe-pounding chauvinism. Goryachkina goes further, attributing to Leskov as well an Anglophobia of which he could not have been less guilty. The "profoundly mediocre" English, as Goryachkina calls them,[26] may represent "smugly secure, uninspired practicality and self-satisfaction."[27] But in Leskov's story it is the English who most admire the lefthander's workmanship, so undervalued in his own country, and they offer him not only money, but an English bride as well and urge him to settle

there permanently. Moreover, the lefthander's only defender during his later misfortunes at home is an Englishman, the hard-drinking, Russian-speaking "half-skipper"[28] of the ship that returns the lefthander to his native land.

Left-wing critics in the nineteenth century also disregarded the strong elements of social criticism in **"The Lefthander,"** whereas party-minded Soviet ones reinterpret them to fit their own stereotypes. Conflicting interpretations of the nuclear plot illustrate this point. The dextrous lefthander and his colleagues do show extraordinary skill in putting shoes on the English steel flea. Skillful as it was, however, this feat is not only useless but harmful. The weight of the shoes prevents the flea from doing its dance. The ingenious mechanism is spoiled. When the English point this out to him, attributing the oversight to his insufficient education, the lefthander ruefully acknowledges the justice of their remarks: "There's no argument that we didn't get very far in our studies, but all the same we're truly devoted to our country" (7:50).

However admirable the lefthander's patriotism, the fact of Russian technological backwardness and social injustice thus remains. Leskov symbolically stresses it, though he rightly adds that the backwardness in no way results from the Russians' lack of talent. It is a product of social conditions. Russians as natively gifted as the lefthander are not offered the opportunity to acquire even a rudimentary education; they are therefore not equipped to assimilate, let alone match, the technical achievements of their Western counterparts.

Even worse, Russian society and its rulers show scandalous lack of appreciation for the accomplishments of their talented countryman. Instead of a triumphal return from England the poor lefthander gets a very "Russian" reception, pointedly juxtaposed with the treatment, afforded the English "half-skipper" in the British Embassy. The two friends, Russian and Englishman, reach Petersburg in a state of acute alcoholic poisoning. The Englishman is examined in his embassy by a doctor, given a hot bath and a "gutta-percha pill," laid on a featherbed, covered with a sheepskin coat, and left to sweat out the poison; orders are given that no one in the embassy is allowed to sneeze until he wakes up. By the next morning he is himself again. Even the humorous exaggerations in this account indicate the awareness of Leskov's narrator that among the English, ordinary citizens are treated by their civil "servants" with consideration.

By contrast, the semiconscious lefthander is taken to a Petersburg police station, where he is robbed of his clothes, his watch, and his money, and then sent off in the bitter cold, without blankets, in an unpaid sledge, to any hospital that will take him. However, since General Platov had rushed him off from Tula to Petersburg without giving him time to collect his "tugaments"[29] (identification papers), hospital after hospital refuses to accept him. Finally the lefthander is brought to a hospital where "all those of unknown estate are admitted to die" and dumped on the floor. The next day his English friend finds him in a moribund condition.

The loyal "half-skipper" now rushes from one high Russian official to another, trying to rescue the lefthander, but he is repeatedly rebuffed. He is ushered unceremoniously out of the office of Count Kleinmichel for reminding that dignitary that the lefthander has a human soul.[30] At last a doctor is dispatched to examine the now dying lefthander, and to him the folk hero imparts his testamentary message: Tell the tsar that the army should stop cleaning gun bores with brick dust. This was an English technological advance he wished his country to assimilate, fearing dire military consequences if it failed to do so. The message encounters bureaucratic resistance and never reaches the emperor. The result is the Russian defeat in the Crimean War.

In its picture of the treatment the returning folk hero receives in his beloved fatherland, Leskov's story is the opposite of a rightist panegyric to Russian national superiority. Indeed, **"The Lefthander"** powerfully expresses the leftward leanings of the author's later years. Especially after the assassination of Alexander II, Leskov felt anguish and despair about Russian society—especially the lack of inviolable individual rights and the indifference of its rulers to the fate of their plebeian countrymen. For that reason the second, bitter half of **"The Lefthander"** pleased Leskov particularly. "'The Flea' has been much noticed here [in Petersburg], even by the *literati*," he wrote to Aksakov soon after the issue of *Rus'* containing the story had come out, "but all the same I think the best part is the ending,—the lefthander in England and his tragic demise."[31]

From the opposite camp conservative nineteenth-century critics rebuked Leskov for the excessive pessimism of his image of Russian society,[32] and some Soviet scholars have used the lefthander's fate as a pretext for venting their righteous wrath at the "venal and greedy pack of rulers of autocratic-serf-owning Russia,"[33] who deliberately "destroyed [. . .] talented Russian patriots."[34] (Such writers of course say nothing about how many "talented Russian patriots" have been destroyed by the Soviet regime.) But the most succinct and penetrating appraisal of the ideological significance of **"The Lefthander"** was offered by one of the "liberal cosmopolites" Goryachkina so hotly despises. Alone among his impercipient colleagues, the anonymous reviewer for *Messenger of Europe* understood what Leskov was doing. "The entire tale," he wrote, "appears to be designed to support Mr. Aksakov's theory about the supernatural capacities of our people, who have no need of Western civilization; but at the same time it contains within it a very sharp and malicious satire of that very theory."[35]

From the artistic point of view, the most outstanding feature of **"The Lefthander"** is the "mosaic" of its language, which, as Leskov himself pointed out in letters to a German translator,[36] is impossible to render intact into another tongue. Attempts have been made, of which the best in English is William Edgerton's; but it cannot be said that many of them recapture the sparkle of the original.

Pure linguistic fun is surely one of the artistic aims of this language, perhaps the primary one.[37] Some of Leskov's most successful malapropisms and folk etymologies have become Russian "household words."[38] Despite the resplendence of these verbal fireworks, most nineteenth-century critics and even fellow writers, indoctrinated with the sober canons of realism, expressed disapproval of them, calling them excessive, unnatural, overdone.[39] Perhaps with our modern eclectic capacity to appreciate the most varied styles, including the Baroque, we may be more willing than our great-grandfathers were to enjoy these stunts for their own sake.

But Leskov's verbal tricks actually serve serious and integrating artistic functions. First, they characterize the speaker who uses them and the social milieu from which he sprang. In a programmatic introduction to **"Leon the Butler's Son,"** Leskov laid bare some of these ulterior stylistic motives. The uneducated or semieducated man, when he tries to describe events and personalities drawn from a social world higher than his own, strains to employ language he thinks appropriate to that world. The results are often laughable:

> His language is studded with bizarre deposits of wrongly used words from the most varied milieus. The latter is the result, of course, of too great effort on the part of the originators [of such stories] to reproduce the conversational tone of that social stratum from which they derive the personages represented. Unable to assimilate the true style of such people's colloquial discourse, they think to attain the greatest vividness in transmitting it if they have these persons utter words as quaint and colorful as possible, so as not to resemble ordinary speech. This constitutes a typical feature of *oral popular literature* when it represents persons with a way of life removed from the peasant milieu. (7:61)

Leskov had made good use of this technique in **"The Battle-Axe"** and was to do so again in **"Night Owls"**— in both cases with even more structural effect than in **"The Lefthander,"** since in those stories the narrator is a central figure in her own tale and thus partly characterized through her own speech. In **"The Lefthander,"** the folk narrator, the old Sestroretsk gunsmith—even in the 1881-82 version with the initial frame intact—plays no part in his own story. He therefore need not be depicted as an active participant in events. Yet even as a disembodied voice the folk narrator plays an important structural role in the story. Through his mode of narration—choice of words, selection and arrangement of detail, ordering of events, commentary, evaluation—the narrator projects his "point of view" in both senses of the term—the angle of vision from which he sees the events and his attitude toward them. Since the author distances himself from the narrator's attitude, he creates dynamic tension between the narrator's judgments and his own (which we presumably share).

Furthermore, of the two viewpoints, the author's or final one may contain elements unacceptable to certain readers and especially to censors; they must therefore be insinuated by hint and implication. Bizarre language is thus part of the camouflage beneath which Leskov hoped to slip his subversive message through censorships, official and private, and into his readers' hearts. Unfortunately, the continuing critical confusion indicates that in this aim he failed: readers may have enjoyed the story, but too many of them have misunderstood its moral import.

Notes

[1] "Skaz o tul'skom kosom Levše i o stal'noj bloxe (Cexovaja legenda)," *Rus'*, nos. 49, 50, 51 (Oct. 17, 24, 31, 1881), pp. 20-23, 19-21. A separate edition was published the following year under the title of *Skaz o tul'skom Levše i o stal'noj bloxe (Cexovaja legenda)* (SPb., 1882).

[2] "Levša (Skaz o tul'skom kosom Levše i o stal'noj bloxe)." The question of the final or canonical title of this work, as of its canonical text, is confused by the fact that in 1894, the last year of Leskov's life, the publisher M. M. Stasyulevich brought out a new book edition of the story under yet another title: *Stal'naja bloxa: skaz o tul'skom Levše i o stal'noj bloxe (Cexovaja legenda)* (SPb., 1894). According to accepted principles of textology, this title and text would be considered canonical, since they were the last to appear in the author's lifetime. Except for its title, however, this 1894 edition reproduced exactly the separate edition of 1882, ignoring the changes Leskov had made for the collected works. Since many of those changes had been substantial, incorporating Leskov's efforts to defend himself against critics, it seems inconceivable that in 1894 he would have chosen to ignore these emendations and revert to the 1882 text. The presumption is, therefore, that the use of the 1882 edition was a mistake of Stasyulevich's, that Leskov himself did not supervise the 1894 edition, and that therefore the 1889 text from the collected works should be regarded as the final one. The point is well argued by Boris Bukhshtab in 7:499.

[3] Translators have also been capricious with this title. Variations include: "The Steel Flea" (Hapgood; Deutsch-Yarmolinsky; Edgerton); "The Left-handed Artificer" (Magarshack); "Lefty; Being the Tale of the Cross-eyed Lefty of Tula and the Steel Flea" (Hanna). Apart from the title, the best translation is Edgerton's; Magarshack's and Hapgood's are the least satisfactory.

[21] In the original, magazine version Platov only "grabbed the lefthander by the hair and began to yank him about." In the 1882 text Leskov changed this to "began to yank him this way and that so that tufts went flying." See 7:44, 498.

[22] This is a quotation from the story, an example of the narrator's linguistic oddities. The Russians conventionally referred to the four basic arithmetical processes as *pravila*, "rules." But to speak of the "four rules of *addition*" is nonsense.

[23] *Otečestvennye zapiski*, no. 6 (June 1882), section 2, p. 257; quoted 7:502. The last phrase (7:48) is the ditty sung by the lefthander as he careens drunkenly through Europe, nourished only by vodka. It combines a nonsense, tra-la-la refrain from Russian folk songs with his distortion of *c'est très joli*. The last word is also perhaps contaminated with Russian *žulik*, "crook."

[24] M. S. Gorjačkina, *Satira Leskova* (Moscow, 1963), p. 76.

[25] *Pravda* (Feb. 17, 1959); cited in Gorjačkina, *Satira*, p. 77.

[26] Gorjačkina, *Satira*, p. 75.

[27] Ibid., p. 72.

[28] *Polškiper*, a malapropism for *podškiper*, literally "subskipper," in other words, "first mate." William B. Edgerton's equivalent: "thirst mate."

[29] A folk etymology for *dokumenty*, "documents," contaminated with *tugoj*, "tight, stiff, tough," and perhaps also *pergament*, "parchment."

[30] The original has a quaint rhyming formula: *xot' i šuba ovečkina, tak duša čelovečkina* (7:57), which we might paraphrase, "Though calloused his hands, yet his soul is a man's."

[31] Oct. 26, 1881 (11:252).

[32] For example, "Leskov o russkom narode," *Novoe vremja*, no. 2224 (May 30, 1882); partly quoted 7:502-503.

[33] Gorjačkina, *Satira*, p. 74.

[34] Valentina Gebel', *N. S. Leskov; v tvorčeskoj laboratorii* (Moscow, 1945), p. 36.

[35] *Vestnik Evropy*, no. 7 (July 1882), wrapper; cited 7:503.

[36] "'The Flea' is too Russian and hardly translatable (because of its language)"; Leskov to K. A. Grehwe, Oct. 26, 1888 (11:395). "If you translate The Lefthander,' you'll be the 'foremost magician'"; Leskov to Grehwe, Nov. 29, 1888 (11:400). "It will be hard for you to cope with 'The Lefthander and the Flea.' Here knowledge of colloquial German is not enough. What will you do with the sound effects and the plays on words: 'kleveton' instead of feuilleton [the loanword *fel'eton* contaminated with *kleveta*, "slander"], 'spiral' instead of *spertyi vozdux* ["stuffy air," a folk etymology from *spirat'*, "to crush," confused with *spiral* (coil) and also perhaps with some echo of Latin *spirare*. It is not clear whether this was a genuine folk formation or was invented by Leskov], 'dosaditel'naja ukušetka' [in the story the form is *dosadnaja ukušetka*, the "couch of vexation" on which Platov lies; *couchette* is contaminated with *ukusit'*, "to bite"], etc.? Of course something will come of it, but the general tone of such a piece cannot be conveyed in another language" (Leskov to Grehwe, Dec. 5, 1888 [11:405]).

[37] Some Soviet commentators, for instance, Gebel' (*Leskov*, p. 197), disapprove of such fun for fun's sake.

[38] For example, *melkoskop* for *mikroskop*, "microscope," combining *melkij* "small"; *dolbica* (for *tablica*) *umnoženija*, "multiplication table," combining *dolbit'* "to drill, to learn by rote"; *buremetr* for *barometr*, "barometer," combining *burja*, "storm."

[39] Many of these criticisms are cited or summarized in Gebel' pp. 194-197. Leskov's critics included Dostoevsky and Tolstoy.

K. A. Lantz (essay date 1984)

SOURCE: Introduction to *The Sealed Angel and Other Stories*, edited and translated by K. A. Lantz, University of Tennessee Press, 1984, pp. vii-xiii.

[*In the following excerpt, Lantz notes what he views as Leskov's strengths as a stylist, satirist, and storyteller, and identifies a unique Russian character in Leskov's writings.*]

Although Leskov has earned a sizable niche in the pantheon of Russian literature, there is still some uncertainty about where to locate it. Literary historians most commonly acknowledge him as the foremost practitioner of orally-structured narrative (*skaz*) and place him within a tradition of stylists who were fascinated with the language itself, beginning with the "artistic philologists" (Boris Eikhenbaum's term) such as Vladimir Dal and Alexander Weltmann and continuing into the "ornamental prose" of Alexey Remizov, Andrey Bely, and Evgeny Zamyatin in the twentieth century.

But his significance is not limited to style alone: Leskov is one of Russia's great satirists. His **"Laughter and Grief"** (still untranslated), **"A Will of Iron," "Little Things in Bishops' Lives," "Night Owls," "The Cattle Pen,"** and **"A Winter's Day"** cover the whole spectrum of satire from good-natured ribbing to bitter invective, and expertly puncture some of his countrymen's most cherished illusions about themselves. To sneak his satires past a vigilant censor he developed what he called his "sly manner": an apparently innocuous work aimed at some obvious target heartily condemned by every right-thinking citizen suddenly "ricochets" (another favorite Leskov term) to explode in the faces of those applauding most vigorously.

Leskov is also a great storyteller, an art in which he has few rivals in Russian literature. His well-made plots are full of exciting incident, and his sheer delight in narrative itself has enriched Russian literature and broadened its scope. As Jean-Claude Marcadé has noted, Leskov's innovations in the art of narration (as well as his fascination with linguistic play) anticipate major "modern" trends in twentieth-century literature (Translator's Preface in N. S. Leskov, *Lady Macbeth au village, L'Ange scellé et autres nouvelles* [Paris: Gallimard, 1982], 17).

Leskov expanded the range of Russian literature in yet another way. He probably knew Russia better than any major writer of his day; not merely the Russia of the westernized urban-dweller and the genteel landowner, but the backwoods Russia of the sectarian, the merchant, the soldier, the priest, and the wanderer. This, Leskov would argue, is the real Russia, and he advised young writers to discover it for themselves by leaving St. Petersburg's Nevsky Prospect to work along the Ussuri in Siberia, or on the steppes of the south. His quest for the best and the worst in the Russian character led him to gather both his band of "righteous men" and create his gallery of engaging scoundrels. Perhaps Leskov's greatest achievement is that he captured Russia in the raw by fixing so vividly those persisting traits that define his countrymen for better or for worse.

Variety is another characteristic of Leskov's writings, and it is all but impossible to find a typical work. The five translations here provide a good sampling of the types of stories he wrote and reveal some of his major concerns.

"The Sealed Angel" testifies to Leskov's skill as a storyteller and is also a tribute to the art and the traditions of icon painting; **"A Robbery"** is essentially an anecdote skillfully spun out to create an absorbing story and to evoke a vanished way of life. Both demonstrate one of Leskov's favorite techniques, that of telling a story in the words of a narrator who is a vivid character in his own right and whose very individual and sometimes peculiar point of view is reflected in his distinctive language. **"An Apparition in the Engineers' Castle"** is a Christmas story and a model of its kind; **"The Mountain"** is one of the best of his legends set in the ancient world; and finally **"The Cattle Pen,"** presented, as is often the case with Leskov, as fragments from his autobiography, is typical of the stinging satires of his last years.

Every translator of Leskov should begin with an apology, an apology both to the reader and to the memory of the writer himself, who would not be amused by attempts to tamper with his prose. Putting Leskov into an English which reflects the richness of his style is more than a formidable task, it is probably impossible. Consider **"The Sealed Angel,"** the story in this collection that is most resistant to translation. English has rough parallels for the various elements that make up the narrator's language—the majestically archaic expressions, the pithy colloquialisms, the odd regionalisms that Leskov delighted in rescuing from obscurity. When Leskov puts these diverse strata together the result is a Russian that lives and breathes and soars; when a translator tries to do the same, his English is likely to sound contrived or grotesque. The vivid language of Leskov's narrator brings to life a character whose point of view simply has no equivalent in English. One might make a very distant and far-fetched approximation by imagining, say, a Quaker who has somehow miraculously escaped the influence of twentieth-century media, literature, and education while working as a New York longshoreman. He tells a story in a language derived from the King James Bible, the seventeenth-century English of George Fox, dockworkers' jargon, and a half-dozen other sources. Such an exotic specimen, if one could imagine him at all, would sound impossibly bizarre; but Leskov's Mark Alexandrov is not bizarre in the least: he is a full-blooded and attractive character who speaks with the authentic voice of a culture that was rapidly disappearing in his own day. Through his story he recreates the way of life that existed before Peter the Great's attempts to westernize Russia in the eighteenth century. Mark Alexandrov's story thus evokes a certain nostalgia in the Russian ear, a nostalgia that English speakers, products of a very different tradition, cannot fully share. Such barriers are less formidable in the other stories. Still the greatest difficulty in translating Leskov lies in the fact that he is the most Russian of Russian writers; when we listen to his narrators we come close to hearing the voice of old Russia.

David McDuff (essay date 1987)

SOURCE: Introduction to *Lady Macbeth of Mtsensk and Other Stories,* translated by David McDuff, Penguin Books, 1987, pp. 7-25.

[*In the following excerpt from the introduction to his translation of selected Leskov tales, McDuff presents an overview of the distinctive elements in Leskov's stories, including his dramatic narrative technique, concern with ecclesiastical themes, and Tolstoian influences.*]

Much has been written about the tale, which occupies a unique place in Russian literature and indeed, perhaps, in world literature as a whole, as an example of the highest achievement to which the storyteller's art can aspire. As Walter Benjamin pointed out, Leskov is primarily a teller of stories, a journalist turned fiction-writer. It is often the exceptional, eccentric, tragically self-willed individuals, the Musk-Oxes, the Katerina Lvovnas, who fascinate him, and whose personalities seem to generate a wealth of stylistic nuances and associations through which they are transmuted into the stuff of fables and remain in the memory as legendary, heroic archetypes. The sensual and sexual energy of Katerina Lvovna, her violent thirst for power and freedom, are mirrored in the vivid, almost tactile descriptions of her natural surroundings, and find their sinister and destructive echo in the figure of Sergei, her empty and spiritless lover. The narrative means, almost operatic in their simplicity and dramatic intensity (it is not hard to see why Shostakovich selected the tale for musical development in his *Katerina Izmailova*), are entirely merged with the stormy, passionate nature of the heroine, and the accounts of the murders and their gruesome details are transformed into a quasi-expressionistic death-elegy by the neutral, dispassionate tone of the narration itself. There is nothing of this kind to be found elsewhere in nineteenth-century Russian literature, not even in Dostoyevsky, and it is small wonder that it was not until the twentieth century, after the experience of Symbolism and Russian modernism, that this tale, together with others by Leskov, came to be accepted and understood by readers in the country of its origin.

A work less controversial than **"Lady Macbeth"**, but one that was to prove a success in Leskov's own lifetime (it is nowadays considered a classic of Russian literature), was the 'chronicle of Old Town' which he began in 1866 and finally published in 1872 as the novel *Cathedral Folk (Soboryanye)*. 'Stary Gorod', or 'Old Town', which in the final version of the novel became 'Stargorod' (in imitation of Gogol's 'Mirgorod'), is presented to the reader as a microcosm of Russian society past, present and future. The original title of the chronicle was 'Waiting for the Moving of the Water', a quotation from the Gospel according to St John which refers to the healing by the angel of the 'blind, halt and withered'. The novel in its published form represents only a carefully pruned selection from a vast and formless mass of material on which Leskov worked during these years, which was, in its basic conception, a kind of pot-pourri of chronicles, short stories and novel excerpts which presented a panoply of Russian provincial life, from the struggles of the eighteenth-century Old Believers, through the Katerina Lvovna-like drama of Platonida Deyeva, a young, beautiful woman married to a man twice her age, to a depiction of 'Old Times in the Village of Plodomasovo'. Leskov was unable to carry this project through; *Cathedral Folk* represents those sec-

tions of the material which relate to the Russian clergy. In the characters of Father Savely Tuberozov, whose diary forms one of the book's main stylistic devices, Father Zakhariya Benefaktov and Deacon Akhilla Desnitsyn, the author manages to portray the lived reality of Orthodox belief, seen from the point of view of a sympathetic Protestant outsider, and shows how it concords with a warm and compassionate understanding of human nature. It is contrasted with the nihilistic emptiness of the radicals, such as Prepotensky, Bizyukina and Termosyosov. The language in which the novel—particularly those parts of it which purport to be Tuberozov's 'diary'—is written is a curious blend of nineteenth-century Russian, Old Slavonicisms and ecclesiastical jargon, and is extremely difficult to translate adequately into another tongue.

The same may be said of the linguistic texture of **"The Sealed Angel"** (1873), another literary work by Leskov which deals with ecclesiastical themes and problems, but treats a secular subject—the building of the first suspension bridge across the River Dnieper at Kiev, and the part played in it by a colony of Old Believers. In **"Musk-Ox"**, Leskov had given a negative portrayal of the Old Believers (the outlawed schismatics who did not accept the liturgical reforms introduced by Patriarch Nikon in the mid-seventeenth century) as being cruel and obsessed with the rigid observance of their faith. In 1863, Leskov had accepted a journalistic commission from the Tsarist Ministry of Education to investigate the secret schools of the Old Believers, who ran them illegally in defiance of the state authorities. The Tsarist government was considering a softening of its policy of persecuting the Old Believers, and Leskov was sent to Riga and Pskov to compile a firsthand report on the schools there. In his report, Leskov had pleaded for tolerance, claiming that the schism could only be overcome through education. In **"Waiting for the Moving of the Water"**, he had depicted a mass voluntary conversion of Old Believers to Orthodoxy, and throughout his life he was to return to the subject of their persecution. The plot of **"The Sealed Angel"**, which contains another, similar conversion, represents what is probably his most inspired treatment of the theme, and forms the basis of one of his finest and most gripping tales. As for the conversion itself, Leskov was criticized for this ending to the tale; at the time, many readers (including Fyodor Dostoyevsky, who reviewed the work in his *Diary of a Writer* for 1873) found that it lacked credibility. Yet read today, outside the context of nineteenth-century Russian religious and secular politics, the Old Believers' conversion to Orthodoxy has an undeniable rightness about it: it is Leskov's way of showing how the 'angel', 'the angel in men's hearts' may be revealed, in opposition to the 'aggel', or 'demon' which holds sway over human beings for most of the time.

In addition to a dramatic and exciting plot, **"The Sealed Angel"** also displays a high degree of stylistic ornamentalism. This is mostly associated with the autodidactic specialty around which the action centres—the science of icon-painting. At the time the tale appeared, the study of Russian icons, whose beauty is nowadays universally appreciated, was still in its infancy, and Leskov was in many ways ahead of his time in taking a serious interest in them for their own sake. The studies and treatises which had appeared hitherto, such as the Slavist and folklorist Fyodor Buslayev's *General Concepts of Russian Icon-Painting* (1866), had viewed Russian icons almost solely as an expression of the national religious spirit; in his tale, Leskov writes of them as works of art, and demonstrates their living connection with the environment from which they spring. That he was able to do this was in no small part due to the fact that he had established a friendship with a living icon-painter, Nikita Savostianovich Racheiskov, who had a studio in St Petersburg. The 'isographer Sevastyan' (I have opted to preserve the old Graeco-Russian term *izograf,* meaning 'icon-painter') in **"The Sealed Angel"** derives his character and identity from Racheiskov, who lived entirely from the painting and restoration of icons. In a tribute to Racheiskov, published after the latter's death in 1886, Leskov claimed that 'on the publication of my Christmas story **"The Sealed Angel"** (which was entirely composed in Nikita's hot and stuffy studio), he received many orders for icons of angels'.

"The Sealed Angel" was first published in *The Russian Messenger,* a journal edited by the conservative Russian nationalist and publicist Mikhail Nikiforovich Katkov. Katkov had already published Leskov's long anti-radical novel, *At Daggers Drawn,* and during the years between 1870 and 1875, spurred on by Katkov's encouragement and generosity, Leskov produced a large number of major literary works—in addition to the two already mentioned, they included *Cathedral Folk,* **"The Enchanted Pilgrim"**, **"A Decrepit Clan"** and **"At the Edge of the World"**, and constitute the heart of Leskov's creation—nearly all of which appeared in the *Messenger.* Many of these works make use of the *skaz,* or spoken inner narrative, and their baroquely configured Russian speaks less of 'the individual' and his experience than it does of the mass of highly individual individuals who comprised the Russian people of Leskov's time. It is no exaggeration to say that in Leskov's writings we hear, as almost nowhere else apart from Gogol, the voice of Russia. This ethnocentric quality of Leskov's art seems to have impressed even those who were in charge of Russia's destiny: in 1873, S. E. Kushelev, a prominent statesman and general with influence at the Imperial Court, visited the author to tell him that **"The Sealed Angel"** had been read aloud to the royal family by Boleslav Markevich, and that the Empress Maria Aleksandrovna had expressed a wish to hear the tale read by Leskov himself. In her memoirs, Leskov's granddaughter, Natalya Bakhareva, relates that her mother inherited from her husband a diamond-encrusted gold watch and a gold snuff-box which were gifts from the Empress on the occasion of his reading **"The Sealed Angel"** at court. . . .

Leskov's first meeting with Tolstoy did not take place until 1887. In the twelve years before that time, Leskov had been steadily moving closer to Tolstoy's ideas in life as well as art. Indeed, in several respects Leskov may be said to have anticipated some of Tolstoy's positions. In 1877, he had quietly separated from Katerina Bubnova, and was henceforth to strive towards an ideal of celibacy, even though this ran counter to the strongly sexual component in his nature. For decades, he had regarded Tolstoy with an almost superstitious awe; *War and Peace* and *Anna Karenina* he had experienced not merely as great works of literature, but as spiritual watersheds—they had been a part of his own inner development. By the 1880s, both writers had arrived at a final repudiation of Orthodoxy. Yet while Tolstoy had proceeded to construct his own rationalized, 'Tolstoyan' version of Christianity, Leskov looked back towards the Protestant faith he had encountered at first hand in his childhood in the home of Alexander Scott, where there had been no icons, oil or candles, but only a practical, living desire to serve God and man. Even so, after his meeting with Tolstoy, Leskov became for a time a zealous convert to Tolstoyanism—on occasion his zeal was so strong that the master found it embarrassing.

With the assassination of Tsar Alexander II in 1881, a period of reaction began in Russian public and social life. It was the role played by the Orthodox Church, under the head of its Holy Synod, Konstantin Petrovich Pobedonostsev ('victory-bearer')—Leskov always referred to him as 'Lampadonostsev' ('lampbearer')—in supporting and reinforcing this reaction which finally persuaded Leskov that no good could be expected from the established Church. Before 1881, while turning increasingly towards Protestantism, he had continued to view the Church as a positive force in Russian life, and had hoped that somehow it might yet help to transform society. In a certain sense, it appears that Tolstoy's anti-ritualistic religion, with its intense faith in the Russian people, came to replace Orthodoxy in Leskov's spiritual cosmos; for Tolstoy was no Protestant—indeed, he regarded Protestantism with just as much suspicion and disgust as any other form of established, 'church' religion. Tolstoy appealed to the 'Old Believer' in Leskov—here was a larger-than-life character from one of his own tales, a religious heretic who possessed a demonic angelism which might save the Russian people and return it to the fold of righteousness.

Under Tolstoy's influence, Leskov began to examine the origins of the Christian religion, and its roots in both the Old and the New Testaments. The series of 'Synaxarion' tales on which he worked exclusively between 1886 and 1891 are didactic in the Tolstoyan manner, and look back to the lives of the early Christians. The *Synaxarion,* or *Prolog,* as it is known in Church Slavonic, is a short collection of *exempla*: lives of the early saints, ordered according to the ecclesiastical calendar. The first Slavonic translations of the *Synaxarion* date from the early Middle Ages, and they contain much material of a strange and flavoursome nature. The narrative style in which they are written is a primitive one, consisting to a great extent of long chains of sentences linked by the words 'and then'. These texts were especially cherished by the Old Believers, who did not accept the later editions prepared during the eighteenth and nineteenth centuries by the Holy Synod of the Church of Russia. In turning to them for inspiration, Leskov was also addressing the foundations of Russia's spiritual identity, and the tales he constructed from them must be seen as an attempt to draw the attention of his readers towards a recognition that the

Orthodox Church had distorted the living message of this inheritance.

"Pamphalon the Entertainer" (1887), like the other *Prolog* tales, is set in the oriental world of Palestine, Egypt and Byzantium. This exotic background stimulated Leskov's imagination to many thoroughly un-Tolstoyan flights of imagery, and there are occasions when the reader suspects that, from a stylistic point of view at least, it is the Flaubert of *La Tentation de Saint Antoine* rather than the pedagogue of Yasnaya Polyana whom Leskov is seeking to emulate—as was indeed the case. Leskov had never travelled to the countries he describes in these narratives, and so his fantasy was able to roam freely, untrammelled by memory or fact. The tales are the purest of fictions, and in **"Pamphalon"** Leskov even invented a special form of 'spoken' Russian which is intended to convey the impression that the characters are talking Greek. This effect is almost impossible to bring across in translation, yet the tale deserves to be better known, as it is one of Leskov's liveliest and most succinct statements of his own *art poétique*. The carefree juggler and acrobat Pamphalon is contrasted with the morose, ascetic Hermius; yet through the agency of Christian love, Pamphalon is able to set Hermius's soul free from the bonds of 'self-conceit', and both are finally transformed into weightless spirits, beyond the reach of the earth and its snares.

Leskov's fascination with Tolstoy, though a powerful one, was not sufficient to mitigate the deep sense of anger, sorrow and despair he experienced towards the end of his life, as he saw that the mass of the Russian people were no more developed in a moral sense now than they had been fifty years earlier. **"A Winter's Day"**, written in the last year of his life, gives full vent to his emotions of grief and betrayal, and is one of the bleakest works in Russian literature. In the world that is evoked in this essentially dramatic composition, there is no hope, no redeeming feature to offset the universal panorama of greed, cruelty and stupidity which the author sees around him. Not even Gogol went so far in his denunciation of human nature as Leskov goes here.

Faith Wigzell (essay date 1989)

SOURCE: "Folk Stylization in Leskov's *Ledi Makbet Mtsenskogo uezda*," in *The Slavonic and East European Review*, Vol. 67, No. 2, April, 1989, pp. 169-82.

[*In the following excerpt, Wigzell examines the influence of folklore and other traditional and popular forms in one of Leskov's best-known stories.*]

When Henry Gifford declares that 'Leskov was a writer who loved the pigments of language almost for their own sake,'[1] he is focusing on the facet of Leskov's work most attractive to the contemporary reader: his linguistic virtuosity. As Gifford continues: 'Nearly always he invests himself in a speech disguise; either choosing a narrator, some experienced man with much local and unaccustomed lore whose idiom he can enter; or . . . reflecting the consciousness—and the vocabulary—of his protagonists.'[2] This feel for the linguistic idiom of individuals and groups, whether reflected in the speech of his characters or in a highly distinctive *skaz*, lends a peculiarly Russian flavour to Leskov's writing. Tolstoi was disapproving of the exuberance of Leskov's language, which he felt swamped both message and material, but from the Formalists onwards Leskov's language, particularly in its contribution to an obviously stylized narrative texture, has undergone a reevaluation.[3] Critical attention as a consequence has tended to be directed towards the works with the most colourful *skaz*, at the expense of those works which do not possess a so obviously stylized narrative texture, such as **"Ledi Makbet Mtsenskogo uezda."** And yet, stories such as this also have a pungent Russian flavour, not explicable merely by reference to their provincial Russian setting, and even less to *fabula*. It is unfortunate that emphasis on Leskov's selection of his raw material on the one hand, and the use of a highly coloured narrative style (perhaps within a frame) on the other, has obscured the pervasive presence in his work of elements taken from traditional Russian verbal culture: folklore, popular literature and, less frequently, medieval Russian literature. These may affect not only language and the choice of *fabula*, but, more dramatically, the treatment of the *siuzhet* and presentation of the characters. While the influence of folklore and medieval literature is readily discernable in, for example, **'Ocharovannyi strannik'** or **'Zapechatlennyi angel,'** the importance of folklore for early stories such as **'Ledi Makbet'** has been largely ignored.

Written in 1865, this, the best known of Leskov's early stories, tells of a young provincial woman married to a middle-aged merchant, who forms a liaison with one of her husband's employees. When discovery threatens, she kills first her father-in-law, next her husband, then a potential heir, her lover's new mistress and finally herself. Lacking psychological analysis of the homicidal heroine, the tale might well have been no more than a catalogue of gruesome crimes, were it not for a pervasive but subtle folk stylization conveying the stifling atmosphere of provincial Russia.

Initial choice of subject matter was dictated, however, by other literary factors, the most obvious evidenced in the Shakespearean title. Here Leskov was following Turgenev, whose *Gamlet Shchigrovskogo uezda* had presented a Russian Shakespearean type. Leskov's intention was not to imitate the archetypal portrayal of a woman who murders for political gain, but to express a conviction that Russian provincial life could produce its own examples of tragedy, distinctively Russian, but none the less genuine. This view bore a direct relationship to current controversy over Ostrovskii and Pisemskii, who had both been attacked for sullying literature with pictures of vulgar crime.[4] Pisemskii, like Leskov, had a taste for dramatic stories set in the Russian provinces, featuring realistic characters, while Ostrovskii concentrated on the corrupt world of merchants. In depicting crime in a merchant setting, Leskov was thus expressing his general support for their choice of subject matter.

At the same time, in his choice of name for his heroine, Leskov was disputing the verisimilitude of Ostrovskii's Katerina in *Groza,* which had appeared in printed form six years earlier. Leskov's Katerina is likewise a young girl who has married into a wealthy provincial merchant family, but in other respects is unlike Ostrovskii's heroine, who is endowed with a sensitive and poetic nature and yearns for affection and spiritual freedom. She is hounded to commit suicide by guilt and the censure of her tyrannical mother-in-law. Leskov's Katerina is neither sensitive nor spiritual; rather she is bored, and it is this that makes her respond to the flirtatious attentions of Sergei, her husband's steward. Her habitual lethargy is then swept away by an all-consuming sexual passion, which bears little resemblance to Katerina's and Boris's tender and short-lived affair in *Groza,* not least in the consequences of adultery. Leskov's heroine commits suicide only after four murders, and then not out of penitence, but because she has been jilted. Leskov admired Ostrovskii for his intimate knowledge of Russian merchant life, but felt that in giving his Katerina an honest and sensitive nature, he had idealized her.[5] In his own story he was issuing a corrective, suggesting that reality was much more sombre.

Pisemskii was also interested in the theme of women and extramarital love: in *Boiarshchina,* a novel published in 1858, he depicted an unhappily married woman from the provincial gentry who is ruined by a love affair, and in '**Krasavets,**' a story written about the same time as '**Ledi Makbet,**' he describes a young Russian noblewoman who leaves her husband for a Guards officer, follows him into penal servitude (he has committed murder), and is betrayed by him on their journey east. Unlike Katerina, she recovers and falls in love again. Despite obvious similarities with Leskov, it is inappropriate to talk of influence—'**Krasavets**' and '**Ledi Makbet**' were written at approximately the same time. Where there are parallels, they should be interpreted as a reflection of Leskov's belief that crime was a suitable subject for literary treatment.

Despite the literary allusions and parallels, Leskov himself said that the real impetus for his plot came from an incident that occurred in his youth:

> Once a neighbour, an old man who clung to life despite his more than seventy years, went one summer's day to take a rest beneath a black-currant bush. His impatient daughter-in-law poured boiling sealing-wax into his left ear . . . I remember him being buried, his ear had dropped off . . . Later, on Il'inka (the public square), she was flogged by the hangman. She was young, and everyone was surprised at how white her skin was.[6]

Certainly there are some parallels, most notably in the murder of an elderly man by his daughter-in-law, the public whipping of the criminal and the mention of her lily-white skin.[7] Although the class origins of the family are not described in Leskov's memoirs, the emphasis on skin pallor may suggest that like Katerina she was of merchant origin, since it was merchants who traditionally prized this as an indication of female beauty. However, there are sufficient differences, not least in the motive, to seek other sources. In the story Katerina L′vovna kills her father-in-law to stop him telling her husband of her adultery, not simply as in the memoir because she is 'impatient' for his death presumably because he stands in the way of her husband and his inheritance. Nor does Katerina pour boiling sealing-wax into her father-in-law's ear, although this was precisely the sort of detail to appeal to Leskov. Instead he is poisoned. Nor is her father-in-law decrepit. Old he may be, but energetic still—and determined to expose his daughter-in-law's shameful behaviour; a far cry from the image of the doddery old man snoozing under a black-currant bush.[8]

Thus neither literary debate nor childhood reminiscence explain much about the form of the story, and they certainly do not account for its distinctive Russian flavour. Although the obvious source of this would be Russian folk tradition, little attention has been paid to this aspect. Even N. G. Mikhailova, whose thesis represents the bravest attempt to tackle the complex topic of Leskov and folklore, specifically excludes early works like '**Ledi Makbet**' from her statement that folklore permeates his stories 'in artistically indirect forms, the links being detected through an analysis of the dieas, images, genre, *siuzhet* and style of each work'.[9] The early writing however, she believes, simply reflects the contemporary modish interest in ethnography, which stimulated Leskov to depict customs like matchmaking in "**Zhitie odnoi baby**" (1863).[10] Although she notes *en passant* that in this story the hero and heroine bear similarities to the hero and heroine of the lyric folk song, she does not pursue the matter, devoting her attention almost entirely to the more obviously rewarding of the later stories. In fact what she says is equally valid for '**Ledi Makbet.**' Mikhailova is not alone in paying little attention to folk influence in '**Ledi Makbet.**' Some critics, notably those writing in English, ignore this aspect entirely: even one so knowledgeable as Hugh McLean remarks that there is no folksy language except in the speech of the lower-class characters.[11] Vladimir Semenov is alone in connecting Leskov's characters with the figures of the Russian lyric folk song, where it is commonplace for the young wives of elderly husbands to hanker after dashing young lads.[12] However, Semenov does not point out that lyric songs are expressions of mood about a given situation. Usually presenting the woman's point of view, they here evoke the sorrow of a girl condemned to a loveless marriage, forced to part with her beloved. Alternatively, songs on the same subject may be light-hearted, describing the girl's delight at deceiving her grumpy old husband, but in neither case is there ever any hint of a solution, whether legal or otherwise. As an explanation of the *siuzhet* Semenov repeats, as do other Soviet scholars, Valentina Gebel′'s conclusions, published in a valuable study in 1945. She suggests that there are links with *lubok* literature.[13] These woodcuts and copper engravings, widely popular in the eighteenth and nineteenth centuries, were primarily illustrations of subjects taken from the Bible, saints' lives, translated literature, folklore and history. They might be serious or satirical, moralistic, or comic—even bawdy, and are marked by a distinctive primitivism and bright colours. They were accompanied by texts of varying length, ranging from captions to full-length stories, in which case the illustrations were secondary. *Lubok* pictures and books were immensely popular, though in the latter part of the nineteenth century they were bought mainly by the peasantry,[14] often passing into oral circulation. *Lubok* literature may thus reasonably be said to occupy a half-way position between literature and folklore. Gebel' declares that the *siuzhet* of **'Ledi Makbet'** is based on the popular *lubok* text *O kupecheskoi zhene i prikazchike*.[15] This suggestion has never been subjected to critical scrutiny.

In fact, the similarities between the *lubok* text and Leskov's story are fairly superficial. True, there are the same three main characters from the same social milieu; the merchant with a young wife, who has one eye on his money and the other on his young steward, *ponezhe mlat i soboiu krasnolichen*,[16] but their personalities have nothing in common with those of the trio in **'Ledi Makbet.'** The husband is kind and loving if somewhat naive, and the steward hard-working, honest and chaste. It is the wife who is cunning (*lukavaia*), a standard epithet in medieval literature and later in *lubki* for women who are seen as temptresses. The story, which is set in France, tells how the wife, who has attempted to distract the steward from his work, is piqued to be told that he is busy writing about feminine wiles (*bab'i uvertki*), and determines to give him some practical experience of them. First she entices him into her room while her husband is out hunting. Hearing him return, she hides the steward behind a picture, and then suggests to her husband that he use the picture for target practice. At the last minute she jogs his arm, reproving him for his irresponsible attitude to valuable property. When the husband goes off to see a friend, the shaken steward emerges to a consoling glass of vodka. On the unsuspecting husband's return, she hides the steward in a cupboard, and then lies in bed feigning illness. She begs her worried spouse to fetch her medicine from the cupboard, but just as he is about to comply, she jumps up, kisses him and tells him that she was merely testing his love for her. In the third demonstration of feminine wiles, the steward is persuaded to undress and go into the bath-house with the wife. When her husband arrives home, she invites him in to see what is going on. As he rushes forward angrily, she chucks a tub of cold water over him, telling him she was only joking, and orders a dry kaftan for him. As the husband goes off to get changed, she tells the young man that thanks to her feminine wiles, they can now become lovers, for henceforth her husband will believe anything she tells him. He complies. When the old man dies, they marry, but the steward never forgets his lesson: that his wife is capable of deceiving him at any time.

Despite words like *kaftan,* the work betrays its French origin in its treatment of the characters; the husband and steward are unrealistically virtuous—the sole source of trouble is the coquettish and mischievous wife. The erotic motifs and the element of light-hearted moralizing also point to a foreign origin. What is more relevant for consideration of the story as a source for **'Ledi Makbet'** is that disposal of the husband by violent means is not even

contemplated though, to be fair, the caption to the seventh picture indicates that the Russian illustrator read violence into the text. The steward and wife are shown on the right in the bath-house with the wife, the tub in her hands, advancing on her husband on the left. The caption reads: *zhena kuptsa ublazhaet smert' emu zhelaet.*[17] None the less Leskov's *siuzhet* shares little even with this interpretation of the wife's intentions; Katerina is not scheming but bored. Even so, it is the dashing and cocksure Sergei (who has already had to leave the employ of another merchant for making advances to his wife) who makes all the initial moves. Although Leskov similarly makes Sergei a young steward,[18] he in particular is more closely linked to the *dobroi molodets* who appears with the unhappily married young girl and old husband in the lyric folk song. There are even closer parallels: Semenov notes that the characterization of Sergei goes far beyond the sketchy figure of the songs, owing much more to the bold hired hand, the *batrak* of the folk tale who outwits his master;[19] but, as will be seen, the bold seducer of rich men's wives as well as the adulterous wife are even more fully developed in other folk genres.

Thus, though Leskov might have been acquainted with the *lubok* entitled *O kupecheskoi zhene i prikazchike,* it seems unlikely that he could have taken from it more than the trio of characters, and there were alternative sources for them. The influence of the prose style of the *lubok* novel is, however, felt in Sergei's sentimental and vulgar declarations of love to Katerina:

> This yearning, Katerina L'vovna, is, I swear, so painful for my heart, that I might take it upon myself to cut it out with a knife of tempered steel, and cast it at your feet.'[20]

A much more likely source of the *siuzhet* is in folklore, more specifically in folk ballads. These are narrative songs distinguished from the much better known *byliny* and historical songs both by subject-matter and treatment. Lacking the epic hyperbole of the *byliny,* they tell of the fates of relatively ordinary individuals caught up in a conflict, often of a domestic kind. Unlike *byliny,* they frequently focus on the tragic lot of women, though without any overt sympathy or condemnation, recounting stories of illicit or hopeless love, jealousy, poisonings, suicides, executions and incest, all in a stark style which pares details to the dramatic minimum. Ballads plunge straight into the action, almost entirely without an introduction or any explanation of situation or motivation. Perhaps because of their subject matter, which was closer to the lives of ordinary people than that of *byliny* or historical songs, and their concentrated brevity, which made them easier to commit to memory, ballads were known over a much wider area in the nineteenth century than the other two genres, though they too were very much on the decline.[21]

Among the ballads there is one, 'Zhena muzha zarezala,' that bears a striking resemblance to **'Ledi Makbet Mtsenskogo uezda.'** This ballad was very well known all over central Russia. Leskov might well have learnt it in his youth in Orel province, or on his extensive travels. It seems to have originated on the Volga, possibly in Saratov.[22] As is typical for oral literature, each variant of the story differs. . . .

Parallels with Leskov's story are striking: the husband in both ballad and story is a wealthy merchant, whose wife is young (this is sometimes only implied in the ballad). Katerina kills her husband, just like the wife of the ballad, though the methods differ: stabbing in the ballad, stangulation followed by a heavy blow to the temple with a candlestick in '**Ledi Makbet.**' . . . Though the details of the murder of Katerina's husband are somewhat less gruesome than in the ballad, the accumulation of murders creates a picture no less horrifying. In most versions of the ballad, as in '**Ledi Makbet,**' the body is buried in the cellar. . . . It is not, however, Katerina who buries her husband but, more realistically, Sergei. . . .

Of course there are major differences between the ballad and the story; there is only one murder in the ballad, and three before the criminal is caught in '**Ledi Makbet,**' and there is no figure of a lover. In the ballad the wife, admitting guilt, requests that her head be cut off. This is a stereotyped ending which could not have been used with conviction by Leskov. Instead, he used the contemporary motif of public whipping, taken from the incident recorded in his memoir, continuing the story to cover Sergei's and Katerina's banishment to Siberia. There are no parallels for this part of the story and the folk stylization virtually disappears here.[27] The changes are easily explicable in terms of the literary requirements of the genre and Leskov's aims. He was not, of course, merely rewriting a ballad, but creating a story with a specific purpose in mind, basing it on childhood memory and combining it with a folk ballad on a similar theme. So, whereas in most variants of the ballad, no reason is offered for the wife's actions, Leskov presents them as the natural consequence of an overwhelming passion, building up the tension through the series of murders.[28] To have treated Katerina as a psychological study would have destroyed the folk flavour of the story, which depended upon it being told at a narrative distance without comment or intrusion.

This is why Semenov's parallel between Sergei and the bold and enterprising *batrak* of the folktale is better than with the *dobroi molodets* of the folk song, who is seen through the prism of the singer's emotions. None the less the closest parallel must be with another ballad, the most popular of all the classical (i.e. pre-Petrine) Russian ballads, *Kniaz' Volkonskii i Vania-kliuchnik,* which was frequently published in eighteenth-century songbooks, was known to Pushkin and was even given a literary reworking in the nineteenth century.[29] It depicts the consequences of Prince Volkonskii's discovery that his wife has long been having an affair with his steward (*kliuchnik* is an archaic word similar in meaning to *prikazchik*). Told of his wife's infidelity, Prince Volkonskii interrogates Vania who denies everything. He then bravely submits to torture, taunting the prince before he is hanged. Vania has the same devil-may-care character and sexual allure as Sergei, though the initial denial of guilt and subsequent jibes come not from

him, but from Katerina when she calmly produces him from hiding. His portrait is naturally more complex than that of Vania, but the similarity with this handsome seducer of rich men's wives is too close to ignore.

In one of the variants of this ballad, Vania taunts his master as follows:

> 'It is already the third year that I, my lord, have known the princess. Many the time have I lain on your feather bed, many the time have I clutched her white breasts; oft, my lord, have I cursed your honoured person.'[30]

This passage bears a striking resemblance to the description of the first week of Katerina and Sergei's affair:

> 'On these nights up in Zinovii Borisych's bedroom freely flowed the wine drawn from her father-in-law's cellar, many the time were the lady's sweet lips kissed, and her black curls on the soft pillow teased.'[31]

There is little reason to doubt that Leskov knew these ballads, though it is not possible to establish a precise link with any of the variants cited, since their first publication, though not necessarily their collection, post-dates the story. It is entirely credible that Leskov, as a man with a considerable knowledge of folklore, would have chosen to make artistic use of these popular ballads in his writing.

The quotation above is an example of the use of folk-poetic style, not in the *siuzhet* or characterization of '**Ledi Makbet,**' but in *skaz*. Although Leskov does not give his narrator a clear personality or highly personalized manner of speaking, he makes it clear he is a man from the Mtsensk district, prone to folk expressions as well as provincialisms. Folk-poetic style would be inappropriate in the dialogue, but skilfully used it can and does work effectively in passages of third-person narrative, not surprisingly, mainly in the sections devoted to the idyllic first weeks of Katerina's love. Thus the narrator describes how life continues after the sudden death of Katerina's father-in-law from 'a dish of poisonous mushrooms' (in fact, from a dose of rat poison): 'Meantime Sergei grew strong and tall, and once more boldly swooped around Katerina L'vovna like a living gerfalcon, and once more their sweet life went on'.[32] Folk influence, that of the lyric song, is also strongly felt in the use of the poetic symbol of the apple tree in blossom. In folk songs this is always connected with young girls and usually has implicit sexual connotations. The young maiden traditionally sits beneath the curly-headed apple tree (*pod iablon'iu pod kudriavoiu*) on the green grass (*travka-muravka*) surrounded by blue flowers, awaiting her beloved or lamenting his absence. Here too goes Katerina on a sultry evening, summoning Sergei to her, so that they can laugh and love as night falls and the blossom floats gently down from the tree above them: 'The young white blossom kept falling, falling on them from the curly-headed apple-tree'.[33]

Parallels with the heroine of the lyric song are felt elsewhere, in the twice repeated description of Katerina sitting by the high window (*u sebia na vyshke pod okoshech-kom*) like a folk song heroine (*krasnaia devitsa*) who sits in her *vysok terem* usually by the window (*pod okoshech-kom*) awaiting her beloved.[34] It is clear that, contrary to McLean's view, **'Ledi Makbet'** makes use of folksy language in the *skaz* of the provincial narrator at least in the part of the story up to the departure of Katerina and Sergei into exile. More than this, in wishing to recreate the atmosphere of a merchant milieu in a small provincial town, Leskov, in this story just as in some of his later work, drew extensively on Russian folklore and to a lesser extent, popular literature, not only to flavour the *skaz*, but more particularly in the characterization and details of plot.[35]

Notes

[1] *The Novel in Russia*, London, 1964, p. 75.

[2] Ibid., pp. 77-78.

[3] Notably by B. M. Eikhenbaum, *Literatura. Teoriia. Kritika. Polemika*, Leningrad, 1927, reprinted Russian Study Series no. 66, Chicago, 1969, pp. 210-25.

[4] B. M. Drugov, *N. S. Leskov, Ocherk tvorchestva*, Moscow, 1957, pp. 30-31.

[5] Valentina Gebel', *N. S. Leskov. V tvorcheskoi laboratorii*, Moscow, 1945, p. 20; V. Guminskii, 'Organicheskoe vzaimodeistvie (Ot *Ledi Makbet* k *Soborianam*)', in *V mire Leskova. Sbornik statei*, ed. V. Bogdanov, Moscow, 1983, pp. 243-44.

[6] From the autobiographical reminiscence *Kak ia uchilsia prazd-novat'* quoted by (among others) Leonid Grossman, *N. S. Leskov. Zhizn'—tvorchestvo—poetika*, Moscow, 1945, p. 129, and Gebel', op. cit., p. 86.

[7] 'Ledi Makbet Mtsenskogo uezda,' p. 96 of vol. 1 of N. S. Leskov, *Sobranie sochinenii*, 11 vols, Moscow, 1956-58. Subsequent references to the text are to this edition.

[8] In Britain blackcurrant bushes are much too low to the ground for this, but in countries where they are never pruned, they do grow tall enough to provide space and shade for a pleasant afternoon snooze. In any case, the bush in question is not, as H. McLean, *Nikolai Leskov. The Man and His Art*, Cambridge and London, 1977, p. 147 mistakenly suggests, a blackberry—only a masochist would choose a bramble for a nap!

[9] N. G. Mikhailova, *N. S. Leskov i ustnoe narodnoe tvorchestvo*. Avtoreferat dissertatsii na soiskanie uchenoi stepeni kandidata filologicheskikh nauk, Moscow, 1970, p. 3.

[10] Ibid., p. 4.

[11] McLean, op. cit., p. 146; K. A. Lantz, *Nikolay Leskov*, Boston, MA., 1979 is one who does not discuss this aspect at all.

[12] *Nikolai Leskov. Vremia i knigi*, Moscow, 1981, p. 58. While this article was awaiting publication, a very valuable discussion of folklore in Leskov's writings by A. A. Gorelov appeared (*Russkaia literatura i fol'klor. Konets XIX veka*, ed. A. A. Gorelov, Leningrad,

1987). Gorelov also draws parallels with folk ballads, especially with *Kniaz' Volkonskii i Vania kliuchnik*, in his discussion of *Ledi Makbet*. I have incorporated references to and comments on Gorelov's work into my footnotes whenever they might be useful.

[13] Op. cit., p. 20.

[14] For an account of the distribution and readership of *lubok* literature, especially in the seventy years before the Revolution, see Jeffrey Brooks, *When Russia Learned to Read. Literacy and Popular Literature, 1861-1917*, Princeton, NJ, 1985, pp. 59-108.

[15] Gebel', op. cit., pp. 206-07. For details of the *lubok* story, pictures and captions, see D. Rovinskii, *Russkie narodnye kartinki* (Sbornik ORIaS, 23-27), St Petersburg, 1881, 1, p. 222.

[16] 'For he was young and fair of face'.

[17] 'The wife ministers to the husband but desires his death.'

[18] 1, pp. 112, 118.

[19] Semenov, op. cit., p. 57. Note also that Leskov underlines the links between Sergei and the folk-song hero by repeatedly calling him *krasnyi molodets* in the scene in which he is introduced to Katerina and the reader.

[20] 1, p. 102, quoted by Gebel', p. 207, who cites a number of parallels.

[21] On the evolution and characteristics of folk ballads, see D. M. Balashov's introductory article to his edition of *Narodnye ballady*, Moscow-Leningrad, 1963, pp. 7-40.

[22] Balashov, Narodnye ballady, p. 389. Gorelov, op. cit., p. 157 notes that Pushkin, Kireevskii and P. I. Iakushkin all recorded variants.

[27] Gebel', op. cit., p. 206. Much later in a letter to D. A. Lin'ev, quoted by Grossman, op. cit., p. 129, and Gebel', op. cit., p. 86, Leskov observed that he knew very little about the life of convicts at the time. This is reflected in the style of this section which lacks the confident touch in the rich folk stylization of the first part of the story. However, Gorelov, op. cit., pp. 103-04, is able to point out a few folk parallels.

[28] McLean, op. cit., pp. 147-51, writes graphically on the hypnotic intensity of the story.

[29] Pushkin's variant is published in *Pesni, sobrannye pisateliami, Literaturnoe nasledstvo*, 79, 1968, p. 192. See also Balashov, *Narodnye ballady*, pp. 153-54.

[30] Balashov, *Russkie narodnye ballady*, pp. 265-67 with brief notes on p. 307. Three other variants of the same song are to be found in id., *Narodnye ballady*, pp. 153-56, 354-55. Gorelov, op. cit., p. 99, points out that V. V. Krestovskii, the author of the literary reworking of this ballad (1861), was a friend of Leskov, but that the stylistic links are of course with the folk version.

[31] 1, pp. 103-04.

[32] 1, p. 106, quoted by Gebel', op. cit., p. 206.

[33] 1, p. 112.

[34] 1, pp. 98, 101. Gorelov, op. cit., pp. 100, 157, also notes this parallel, and on pp. 102-03 offers further examples of stylized skaz. He also provides a folk-song parallel to Katerina's obsessive love in a song recorded in 1836 in Mtsensk province (op. cit., p. 103)

[35] It would be inconsistent with the rest of the story if the large grey cat that Katerina L'vovna sees in her dreams were purely the product of Leskov's imagination. In fact, as a symbol, it is taken primarily from Dream Books, where dreaming of cats is a sign of marital breakdown. That the cat is large, grey and male reflects local beliefs from Orel province, where this portends sorrow or disaster. The doubly unlucky symbol partly explains Katerina's sense of supernatural horror. For further details, see F. Wigzell, 'Russian Dream Books and Lady Macbeth's Cat', *Slavonic and East European Review*, 66, 1988, 4, pp. 625-30.

R. A. Peace (essay date 1991)

SOURCE: "'The Enchanted Wanderer': A Parable of National Identity," in *Russian Literature*, Vol. XXIX, No. 4, 1991, pp. 439-54.

[*In the following essay, Peace suggests that in the story "The Enchanted Wanderer," Leskov employs the central figure, Ivan, as a foil to reveal elements of the psychology of the narrator and his audience as much as to convey the personality of the wanderer himself. In this way, Peace asserts, the story presents a complex analysis of the Russian national character.*]

Leskov's **'Očarovannyj strannik'** communicates to the reader a strong sense of a statement on the Russian national character. Gor'kij felt this about Leskov's works in general, and Hugh McLean in his monumental study on the author analyses this story as just such a statement.[1]

From the outset the 'enchanted wanderer' is described in terms of the legendary figure Il'ja Muromec—a *bogatyr'* traditionally identified with the Russian 'folk' and even with Russia herself, exemplifying her sudden shifts of mood and potential for greatness.[2] The 'enchanted wanderer' is *tipičeskij, prostodušnyj dobryj russkij bogatyr'*. Among these epithets *tipičeskij* is particularly striking, and as if to reinforce this emblematic quality, he is Ivan, a name, which, as the story later reveals, is treated by the Tartars as generic for 'Russian'. His patronymic, Sever'janovič, as McLean and others have suggested, hints at *sever,*—'north'; is therefore, in this sense, 'son of the north'.[3]

Ivan Sever'janyč is encountered at the beginning of the story in the Lake Ladoga area to the north of the Russian capital, a primitive, inhospitable region, little frequented by the denizens of that most westernised city, St. Petersburg. From the outset we are aware of the confrontation of two different sets of cultural values—two contrasting modes of consciousness: on the one hand the fatalistic, medieval attitude to life of the enchanted wanderer, and on the other, the more sophisticated, the more 'western' cast of mind of the audience listening to his tale.

Leskov had first submitted the story to Katkov under the title 'Černozemnyj Telemak,' but it was rejected by him in May 1873. The story seemed to Katkov more like raw material than a finished story: the characters were not fully presented and there were many improbabilities. Such objections not only miss the point, they reveal a fundamental misconception of the work. Characters in this tale are presented in a flat one-dimensional way because they are less important as people in their own right than as *phenomena* serving to illustrate the psychology of the narrator himself. The very fact that other protagonists are not seen as full, rounded human beings by the narrator himself, is a *central point* in the exposition of his psychology. In a sense there are only two fully conscious personalities in the story: the narrator and the collective personality of his audience.

This audience is not greatly individualised, but we can identify at least two of its constituents. One is a man *sklonnyj k filosofskim obobščenijam političeskoj šutlivosti,* who is later ironically referred to as the 'philosopher', the other is someone who travels much in this area, a merchant who is *religioznyj i solidnyj* (386).[4] The device of a tale told to an audience is that of a 'frame', but its function is not merely narrational, it is also, and more importantly, a 'frame of reference'. The audience interrupts the tale at key moments, punctuating it with questions, with expressions of surprise and incredulity, and in so doing, articulates the reader's own reactions to the behaviour and attitudes of a psychological outlook totally remote from his own. It is the presence of this listening and articulating consciousness which refocuses a picaresque tale of wandering into a metaphor of psychological exploration in which each bizarre incident of the plot becomes yet another stage in the revelation of character.

The emotional gulf between the narrator and his audience is particularly evident in matters of compassion. Ivan Sever'janyč relates the most cruel and barbaric events without registering anything that his more sophisticated audience can recognise as pity or even deeply felt emotion. One of the first incidents in his tale is his accidental killing of the little monk. As a postillion with the duty of riding one of the leading horses of his master's six-in-hand, he sees a monk asleep on top of a hay cart. Ivan cracks his whip at him and causes the monk to fall to his death. Yet the only reaction recorded is one of mirth: the incident, at first, was seen as funny not only by him, but also by his father and even by the count. Nowhere is there any expression of regret, but there is physical retribution: he is beaten for his fatal prank, though not too hard, as he still has to sit on the count's horse. That appears to be the end of the matter—*tem èto delo i končilos'* (399). However, that night the monk appears to him in a dream. He is weeping, but any suggestion that this is a manifestation of subconscious guilt is quickly dispersed. Ivan greets him with the words: "What do you want from me? Clear off!" (*Čego tebe ot menja nado? Pošel von!*) (399).

He merely accepts the monk's death fatalistically as accomplished fact. The monk, for his part, seems more concerned to reassure Ivan that he is 'saved'—his mother had promised him to God and he is destined: *mnogo raz pogibat' i ni razu ne pogibneš', poka pridet tvoja nastojaščaja pogibel'* (400), then, so he prophesies, Ivan will become a monk.

The monk appears a second night, and although Ivan still seems incapable of regret, the monk himself can express pity for Ivan and what is in store for him; he urges him as soon as possible to beg his master for permission to enter a monastery. Ivan roughly dismisses this suggestion: *Nu dumaju ladno; nado tebe čto-nibud' karkat', kogda ja tebja ubil* (400).

Immediately afterwards the first of his *pogibanija* (near deaths) occurs, when the count's carriage runs away down a precipitous road. Ivan's action saves his master, though he himself is nearly killed. Yet instead of taking advantage of the count's gratitude to request entry into a monastery, as the monk had advised, he merely asks for a concertina which he cannot play and which is stolen the next day.

From then on the catalogue of the many instances of his near destruction begins, and although he suffers without perishing, he brings suffering and destruction to others. Yet at no time does he express remorse or regret, or anything we can recognise as humanitarian feeling, until, that is, he is magnetised into a love for the gipsy girl Gruša. Up to then his one great passion had been for horses, yet he is as brutal with animals as he is with human beings. On one occasion, in order to show a peasant that a gipsy intends to cheat him over a horse, he sticks a pointed awl into the animal's kidneys and it falls down dead. He appears to show tenderness towards the doves he keeps, but he torments the mother by playing with her chick, until finally his rough fondling kills it. When a cat steals his young doves he thoroughly beats it, then cuts off its tail. It is therefore ironic that later, when the Pole entrusts him with his child, he does so on the premiss that if he could take pity on little doves, he is fit to look after his daughter.

Ivan shows no pity for the Pole's estranged wife, when she wishes to take her daughter back, and indignantly refutes the charge that he is made of stone. Yet when the mother's lover seizes one of the child's arms, Ivan seizes the other, and is prepared to engage in a tugging contest to see who will get the larger portion.[5]

A second time he kills a man with a whip, when he engages in a flogging match with the Tartar, Savakirej, over a horse. Ivan's audience is obviously appalled at such a barbaric event. He replies in a "good natured, unemotional" way to their questions, but faced with the horrified and dumbly perplexed glances of his audience, he feels called on to add that it was the Tartar's fault for holding out so long, and that because of this 'fool', he himself nearly ended up in prison. The Russian authorities are not able to look indulgently on his killing an Asiatic, whereas the Tartars themselves are far more accommodating (the whipping contest was, after all, in Ivan's words *ljubovnoe*

delo). They take Ivan off with them to escape Russian justice.

When the audience asks Ivan how he was kept in Tartar captivity, whether he was guarded in a pit, he disparagingly rejects such a suggestion; "the Tartars are kind people" (428), he says, but he then proceeds to tell them of an horrific operation in which horsehair was sewn into his heels, so that he could not walk, let alone escape. He served the Tartars as a herbal doctor, and they gave him wives, by whom he had children, but he showed them no particular affection and did not really consider them his own. At this the finer feelings of his audience are again shocked:

> "How do you mean, you did not consider them as your own? Why was that?"
>
> "Well how could I consider them as mine when they were unbaptised and not anointed with myrrh."
>
> "But what about your parental feelings?"
>
> "What's that, Sir?" (433-434)

Thus we see that his lack of natural feeling has a religious origin: these children cannot be his as they are not baptised, and such apparent callousness is set in stark contrast to the deep emotion Ivan feels for religious values themselves, when almost immediately afterwards he recounts the tears he shed for Holy Russia.

Nevertheless, the authors of the introductory article to the 1957 Soviet collection of Leskov's works, P. Gromov and B. Èjchenbaum, see Ivan Sever'janyč as a man lacking in any inner moral guidelines:

> The internal erosion of the norms of peasant life [*soslovnaja žizn'*] reveals itself here in the absence of moral, indeed of any spiritual criteria.[6]

This is obviously far from being the case: Ivan is a man with strong religious convictions, which shape his attitude to life and to other people. His, of course, is not a modern religious sensibility, the sort which is implied in his audience by the presence of the devout and well-travelled merchant. Nevertheless the religious nature of Ivan is undeniable: we are first introduced to him as a monk (however nominal his attachment to this life might be), moreover his mother had promised him to God, and it was prophesied that he would end up as a monk. He is also identified by the author himself as *strannik,* which has the sense of 'holy wanderer' or 'pilgrim' (indeed the story is also translated as **'The Enchanted Pilgrim'**). The *strannik* had often taken on his pilgrimage as a penance for an ill-spent life. One thinks, for instance, of Nekrasov's poem 'Vlas' depicting such a 'wanderer', and seen by Dostoevskij as a type quintessentially of the Russian folk.[7] Indeed, for all his obvious faults, Ivan Sever'janyč is one of Leskov's *pravednik* figures; his life may have led him into many sins, but he himself sees his tribulations and temptations in the light of a medieval saint:

Only it seems to me that not even in one of the lives of the saints in the Menologia are there such temptations and happenings, as I then endured. (463)[8]

There is, perhaps, too a hint of that stubbornly righteous man Avvakum. Like Avvakum he has been kept a prisoner in a pit in the ground in the north.[9] Indeed the idea of the Lake Ladoga region as a place of exile has been implanted in the reader's mind at the very beginning of the story. The religious values of Ivan Sever'janyč, like a medieval saint, or the seventeenth-century heretic, Avvakum, are those of a simple faith in which form is paramount, and traditional authority unquestioned.

The essential religious nature of Ivan is brought out particularly during his captivity among the Tartars. Although he appears to have taken on their way of life, he is still a Christian. He rejoices at the appearance of Orthodox missionaries in the Tartar camp and, most telling of all, weeps for Holy Russia. He feels constant homesickness, particularly in the heat of summer. He looks at the unending steppe, and has a mental picture of Russia—a Russia which, significantly, is less a geographical than a religious entity:

> You gaze, not knowing yourself where you are gazing, and suddenly out of nowhere a monastery or a shrine comes up before you, and you remember the land of the baptised [lit. *kreščenuju zemlju*] and you weep. (434)

Even when he longs for his native village, his homesickness is essentially a feeling of religious deprivation. Thus he remembers feast days at home and the behaviour of the *dobryj-predobryj staričok,* Father Il'ja, the village priest, and such memories bring home his present situation:

> But I am deprived of all that happiness, and for so many years have not been to confession, and live without the rites of marriage and will die without the rites of burial. (436)

He describes how he becomes seized with homesickness, and when night comes he creeps out beyond the confines of the camp, quietly so that he will not be observed by his wives or his children or any of the infidels (*pogany*) and he begins to pray, to pray so much that sometimes the snow melts beneath his knees, and in the morning grass can be seen where his tears have fallen (436).

He manages to escape from the Tartars, but realising that he has suffered for his sins, he prays to the Virgin Mary and to St. Nicholas to help him convert the Tartars before he leaves them. On his way back to Russia his first encounter is with a Čuvaš tribesman, who offers to let him ride with him, but once again Ivan's first concern is with religious matters: before he will accept the offer, Ivan needs to know whether the Čuvaš has a god. The Čuvaš claims everything is god and is prepared to acknowledge the Virgin Mary and St. Nicholas. Ivan is particularly pleased to learn of his respect for the very Russian saint Nicholas The Wonder-Worker, but soon parts company

from him when he learns that the Čuvaš, in order to preserve his cows in summer, is prepared to sacrifice a bullock to tree spirits, but only give twenty copecks to St. Nicholas (446).

The first Russians he meets—a band of fishermen—also tread on Ivan's religious convictions. Ivan has no passport, and one of them for a joke tells him that, although he can live in Russia without a passport, he cannot die there without one—he cannot be registered for a proper Christian burial. Ivan is so overwhelmed by this news, that he begins to weep and complain, but when they tell him that they are joking, he is hardly consoled (448). He leaves the fishermen in disgust, but further disillusionment awaits him in his native village: for the sin of living with his Tartar wives, he is deprived of the one thing he most desires—he loses the rites of communion for three years.

None of this suggests that Ivan is a man lacking 'inner spiritual criteria', but yet his religious convictions are not those of the modern world. The formalised, ritualistic nature of Ivan's beliefs is perhaps best exemplified in the action he takes to prevent himself succumbing to a drinking bout. He goes to church, prays, and then stops before a mural depicting angels beating the devil in hell with a chain. He prays fervently to the angels, then spits on his fist and pushes it into the devil's face with the words: *Na-ka, mol, tebe kukiš, na nego čto chočeš', to i kupiš'* (457). After this primitive ritual he feels quite reassured that he will be able to resist the demon drink.

Although many aspects of his tale seem to present Ivan as a renegade, he is nevertheless a firm believer in authority. Even though in his later life in the monastery he is something of a rebel, he still acknowledges the need for authority: *čto bol'še povinovat'sja, to čeloveku spokojnee žit'* (504). For the medieval consciousness of Ivan ordinary human values, particularly compassion, appear to be replaced by formal ethical prescriptions, which to a modern sensibility seem largely ritualistic and lacking in real content. Thus, when entrusted with the care of the Pole's daughter, he is deaf to the heart-wringing entreaties of the child's mother, merely countering her demands with formulaic morality: *Esli ty, prezrev zakon i religiju, svoj obrjad izmenila, to dolžna i postradat'* (412): she has transgressed the established religious code; what more can she expect? His one regret in this whole incident is that he has insulted the officer, who is the mother's lover, but this has nothing to do with the officer as a human being, it is a question of an insult offered to formally established authority. As Ivan reasons:

> After all he has taken an oath, and in war he defends the Fatherland with a sabre, and it may be that because of his rank the tsar himself addresses him as *vy,* and I fool that I am, have insulted him like this. (415)

This latter point is of some concern to Ivan and he seeks confirmation from the officer, who tells him that the tsar's document granting him his commission did indeed address him as *vy* and ordered him to be respected and honoured. Hearing this, Ivan can bear his guilt no longer, and to ease his conscience asks the officer to strike him back in return. Thus the whole incident with the Pole's daughter clearly illustrates that Ivan's conscience is vulnerable not to mere human values, but only to those of form and the veneration of authority. Morality is something purely external for Ivan; he is guided by the precepts of the Church and respect for authority. If he transgresses this external code, he feels the need for external punishment—to be physically beaten after insulting the officer, killing the monk, and squandering the prince's money.

Hugh McLean in his analysis of the story has, as he says, "transmuted **'The Enchanted Pilgrim'** into a disquisition on the Russian national character", and he wonders whether this "may be going beyond the bounds of legitimate literary analysis". Obviously this is not a point on which I would wish to take issue, nevertheless his 'disquisition' is concerned with 'universals', which seems to suggest a view of national characteristics as static fixed concepts, whereas the story itself is above all about travel, and travel which is a metaphor for change.[10]

Psychological change, as it is expressed through the anecdotal plotstructure of the story itself, is of two kinds. The first which is relatively superficial, and may be designated as 'change of role', is related to the wandering theme of the title; the second, more fundamental, is connected to that other concept to which the title alludes—enchantment.[11]

The first category seems far more in evidence in the story. As Ivan goes on his wanderings he takes on, at a superficial level, the characteristics of those he meets. When the robber gipsy saves him from suicide, he joins him: *machnul ja rukoju, zaplakal i pošel v razbojniki* (406). From a thief (he has stolen two of his master's best horses) he becomes a male nanny at the suggestion of the Pole, and now has a defined role: *Ja čelovek dolžnostnoj i vernyj; vzjalsja chranit' ditja, i beregu ego* (413). He, therefore, withstands both the mother's entreaties and the officer's attempt to bribe him. But when the Pole approaches firing pistols and ordering him to apprehend his wife and the officer, Ivan rejects this new role: "So that's it, I think to myself, I am supposed to apprehend them for you am I? Let them carry on loving!" (415).

His contact with a military man (the officer who is the wife's lover) has already aroused in Ivan a fighting persona, but once he has thrown his lot in with the officer, he regrets the violence he had shown towards him, and offers up his own face to be beaten in retribution. The officer refuses to oblige him, but Ivan contrives to stand in for him as his substitute in the flogging match with the Tartar, and by killing his opponent wins the officer the horse he prizes. Contact with the Tartars, however, leads him into prolonged captivity, during which he shaves his head, dresses and lives in Tartar fashion, even though his soul is elsewhere. From a deadly fighter he has now taken on the role of healer—he is a herbalist doctor.

After his escape his first contact with his own kind is with the band of Russian fishermen. Obvious signs proclaim

their nationality: *krestjatsja i vodku p'jut,—nu značit, russkie!* (447). Their first gesture is to offer him vodka, and although he has grown unused to alcohol during his prolonged stay with the Tartars, he accepts. It is from this point that he takes on another characteristic, a national one—that of heavy drinker. Ivan Sever'janyč's surname is Fljagin, and as McLean points out:

> "The surname Fljagin comes from *fljaga*, 'flask'—thus symbolizing that passion for drink which ever since the time of St Vladimir has been the favorite national vice.[12]

So far the story of Ivan's wanderings reads almost like an illustration of Čaadaev's pessimistic assessment of the Russian character as rootless, nomadic and uncertain of its role, whose only guideline is the faith of 'miserable Byzantium'—a nation still in its infancy, which has undergone none of the beneficial experiences of the West—notably the Renaissance.[13] Yet this same idea received a more optimistic reevaluation by Gercen, who saw the Russian character as a *tabula rasa* on which great things could still be written. It is in this sense that the Pole seems to define Russianness, when Ivan complains that nature has not endowed him with the physical equipment to act as wet nurse to his child: *Ved'ty russkij čelovek? Russkij čelovek so vsem spravitsja* (408).

Ivan's many changes of role, however, in themselves spring from an 'enchantment'—from the prophecy of the little monk that he would be about to perish many times, a prediction which, coming from the lips of the holy figure he has killed, seems almost like a punishment for original sin, and this is an idea reinforced by the fact that his mother, who dedicated him to God, was actually killed by him at birth because of the size of his head. *Golovan*, 'Big-Head', is a name by which the enchanted wanderer is also known throughout most of the story.[14]

A development which involves perishing many times, yet not ultimately perishing, seems to mirror the history of the Russian nation itself, with its subjugation to the Tartar yoke, its domination by Poland at the Time of the Troubles, its invasion by the French in the early nineteenth century, not to mention more recent catastrophes. Yet if the Russian nation is a *tabula rasa,* the end of its 'enchanted wandering' is clearly written; for according to the prophecy of the little monk Ivan Sever'janyč is ultimately promised to God.

However, the Čaadaevian view of restless, but merely superficial, shifts in the national character does not adequately explain the dramatic changes so noticeable in Russian history. Three years before the appearance of **"The Enchanted Wanderer"** N.Ja. Danilevskij had pointed to this phenomenon in his influential book *Russia and Europe.* He argued that unlike the West, change in Russia had come about not through the clash of parties, but through radical shifts in national consciousness—a process he saw reflected earlier in the lives of the saints, and through which the adultress, Mary the Egyptian, could suddenly become transformed into an ideal of saintliness and chastity.[15] In Leskov's story such radical shifts of consciousness are projected as forms of enchantment; for the prediction of the monk is not the only charm working the wanderer.

To cure himself of his Russian passion for drink Ivan has been 'magnetised', and the enchantment is still working as the following exchange with his audience suggests:

> "And did this magnetism work on you for a long[16] time?"
>
> "How do you mean long? It is perhaps working to this day" (475)

If the enchantment proclaimed by the monk is Orthodox and fatalistic (a working out of the Russian saying *na rodu napisano*) the second enchantment, magnetism, is western magic. Although the 'magnetiser' himself is Russian, he was brought up to pray to God in French (459), and the linguistic formulae of the magnetisation process are themselves, apparently, French.[17] The 'magnetiser' in his turn had undergone a similar change of character; formerly he had been harsh and cruel, now he has no pride left, and can only forget himself in drink . . .

As he is being magnetised Ivan feels that the 'magnetiser' is actually getting inside his head and looking out at the world through Ivan's own eyes, just as though they were panes of glass:[18]

> "Well," I thinks, "Here's a fine thing he's done with me! And where now," I asks, "is my sight?"
>
> "Yours," he says, "no longer exists."
>
> "What sort of nonsense is this," I says, "doesn't exist?"
>
> "That is right," he replies, "With your own sight now you will only see what isn't."
>
> "Here's another parable!" I says, "Well then, let me just make an effort." (466)

Although in the context the word *pritča* (parable) has also the sense of nonsense, there is nevertheless in this whole process the element of a 'parable'. The enchanted wanderer is being made to see with more western eyes, and the change now is not one of 'role' but of character. For the first time the consciousness of Ivan is not far removed from that other consciousness in the story—his audience. The new *persona* he has taken on is that of 'lover';[19] from now on he seems capable of love for his fellow human beings: he is now open to pity. As the 'magnetiser' tells him: "Peasant [. . .] you are a base fellow, if you dare to laugh at the holy feeling of the heart and call it nonsense" (463). Such sentiments are a commonplace of Romanticism, and it is perhaps significant that the theme of 'magnetism' surfaces more than once in the writings of Russia's Romantic period (i.e. in Odoevskij, Vel'tman, Senkovskij, Greč and even Gogol).

Gruša, the gipsy girl, with whom he has fallen madly in love as a direct result of this magnetisation, proves to be unattainable—she has become the mistress of his own employer, the prince. Despite this obstacle Ivan's love for her is still strong; it is like that of a brother for a sister. Gruša is abandoned by the prince, and in her wild desperation, she asks Ivan to show his 'ultimate love' (*poslednjaja ljubov'*) and binds him with a terrible oath. It turns out that she wants him to kill her, so that she herself will not have to bear the unforgiveable sin of suicide.[20] In killing Gruša, he is filled, for the first time, with genuine pangs of remorse, and will suffer a long, and deep-seated feeling of guilt. He had killed people before in his life, but their deaths never evoked even a flicker of remorse—here is something new.

After he has committed this act of 'ultimate love' for her, he is given a lift on a cart by an elderly peasant couple, who are bemoaning the fact that their son is to be sent into the army. Ivan is stirred by human pity and confesses to his audience: *Ja staričkov požalel* (498). He offers to substitute himself for their son.

Thus Ivan out of pity becomes a soldier, and has not only a new role but a new identity. He bears the name of the son, Petr Serdjukov, a name which, although perhaps semantically not connected, seems nevertheless to hint at serdce ('heart') and is thus in opposition to his earlier nickname, *Golovan*.[21] He forgets his former life, and only prays for himself on his real name day, *Ivan Predteča* (St. John the Baptist).[22]

It is on St. John's day that he performs an act of great heroism, by swimming across a mountain river with a rope under Tartar fire. He volunteers for this foolhardy task, when the colonel asks if there is anyone who has a mortal sin on his soul, and in responding to this challenge, Ivan says to himself: "Well, Gruša, my adopted sister, take my blood as exchange for yourself" (500), and as he swims he sees a vision of Gruša as sixteen-year-old girl with huge wings spread out to save him from the Tartar bullets. Thus the two 'enchantments' upon him, linked to two deaths for which he has been responsible, and the two resulting ghosts offering him continuing life, invite obvious comparison. Nevertheless, under the influence of 'magnetism' Ivan has not only acquired a degree of compassion but also a willingness to sacrifice himself for others.

Strangely enough, it is no dramatic sense of perishing which makes him join the monastery, but, once more, compassion for a woman. Working as an actor in a street theatre in St. Petersburg, he begins to take pity on an actress who plays the 'Goddess of Fortune' to his 'Demon'. She is bullied by one of the male members of the troupe, and when Ivan stands up for her, he is dismissed.[23] In return the 'good fairy' gives him food and shelter, but Ivan tells his audience that he felt ashamed (*mne sovestno stalo*) of taking her hospitality as she was so poor and had such a hard life (504). He thought and thought, how he could relieve the situation, and finally came up with the idea of entering a monastery.

The enchanted wanderer now has a new role, and even a new name, Izmail. Yet is this the resolution of the prophecy? No dramatic event has brought him to the monastery, and although he is nominally a monk, he refuses to take the final vows. Indeed, the real appeal of the life appears to be that it allows him to work with horses and makes little demands on his attending services. This is clearly not the end of the road for the enchanted wanderer. He falls foul of the monastic authorities, is placed in a hole in the ground, and while there seeks yet another fundamental change of character.

Contemplating his life, sitting in the pit, he realises what a worthless spirit he has, and how much he has suffered for it. He, therefore, sends a novice to ask a saintly elder, a *starec,* if it is possible to receive another spirit from God: *"Možno li mne u Boga prosit', chot'by drugoj bolee sootvetstvennyj duch polučit'?"* (511). The *starec* sends his reply that he is to pray, so that he might expect, that which cannot be expected. The magic of another potent force, prayer, is thus invoked for yet another radical change in the essential character of the enchanted wanderer.

Izmail, whose name in Hebrew means 'God hears', prays for three nights and reads material provided by another monk: *The Life of St. Tichon of Zadonsk* and current newspapers—the result is that he takes to prophecy. He is struck by a passage in the life of the saint in which St. Paul is supposed to have told Tichon that when there is talk of peace it is a sign of war. This seems to be echoed in the newspapers, which currently talk of nothing but peace. Therefore, concludes the new Izmail, war must be imminent.[24]

For these prophecies he is locked up in a hut with the icon of Blessed Silence and told to pray, but the usual ritualistic means of exorcising the spirit of prophecy proves vain, and after consulting with a doctor, the monastery authorities release him and allow him to wander from one holy place to another. He is still prophesying war and he himself expects to die in the fighting: *mne za narod očen' pomeret' chočetsja* (513). Thus the more compatible spirit (*bolee sootvetstvennyj duch*), for which he has prayed, appears to be not only a spirit of prophecy, but even a warlike one, and he contemplates exchanging his monk's garb for a soldier's uniform. Yet the enchanted wanderer is still wandering, he has not yet found his true end or the *nastojaščaja pogibel'* of the monk's prophecy. Moreover, as we see at the end of the story, Ivan has much in him of the fanatic. Old attitudes die hard, and he can still show a lack of compassion, as for instance when talking of the old Jew, who was identified in the monastery as Judas himself. Nevertheless it is possible for new values to be acquired by one of those sudden, almost demonic shifts of outlook so typical in Russian history, yet whether such new ideas can be fully and properly assimilated is perhaps another question.

There is an obvious polemical intent behind Leskov's treatment of his theme—an implied criticism of authority both temporal and spiritual. The original anecdote told by Ivan Sever'janyč about the little drunken priest who had special dispensation from God to pray for the souls of those who have committed suicide or have died unshriven is a sly attack on a non-humanistic theology which regarded such intercession as a sin. Its purpose is three-fold: it reveals Ivan as a far from conventional monk, with glimmerings of a more humanistic attitude to religion, at the same time it allows Leskov himself the luxury of an oblique attack on the rigid Orthodox values of his pet hate, Metropolitan Filaret,[25] and further suggests that religious revelation is as much the province of the people themselves, as it is of the official church.

If Ivan before his 'magnetisation' shows little concern for basic human values, the representatives of the official church as they are presented in the story are no better than he. The missionaries who turn up at the Tartar camp are delighted at first to think they have made a convert in Ivan, but less than happy when they discover that he is already a baptised Russian. They refuse to help him, merely telling him to put up with his lot:

> You are a slave, and you must suffer what has to be done; for according to St. Paul, it is said, slaves must obey. But you remember that you are a Christian, and there is no point in our concerning ourselves with you, for without our help the gates of heaven are already open for your soul, but these will be in darkness, if we do not convert them, so we must concern ourselves with them. (439)

The missionaries, however, do not fare well at the hands of 'those in darkness'. When Ivan finds the mutilated body of one of them, he gives it Christian burial, but concludes:

> Well, fellow countryman, you did not wish to bother about me, and I judged you for it, but now you have been found worthy of a crown of suffering. Forgive me for Christ's sake. (439)

Again, the *dobryj-predobryj staričok,* Father Il'ja, about whom, in captivity, Ivan has such tender memories, turns out in fact to be anything but an exemplar of Christian compassion: he forbids Ivan communion for three years— the very church rite for which Ivan so longs, and even the police seem less brutal in this respect than Church Law itself, because as Father Il'ja explains:

> I am being merciful in only depriving you of communion, but if you were given correction as is fitting according to the law of the Church Fathers, then you should have had your clothing burned upon you, on your living body, but don't be afraid, because this is not allowed now by police law. (448)

When Ivan is returned to his native village after his Tartar captivity, he is brought before his old master, the count, whose life he had once saved, and who had promised that he would not forget him. But the count has now become very devout, and his first act is to have Ivan beaten, even though he has just been beaten by the police. Then, when the count learns that Ivan has been deprived of the rites of communion, he has him beaten again in public, as an example, and refuses to give him employment. The reception in his homeland of 'Ivan' escaping from hostile captivity seems eerily premonitory of the treatment meted out, also on ideological grounds, to prisoners of war returning to their Soviet homeland.

The end of the story with its prophecy of war is perhaps another polemical sally from the author himself. It is not dissimilar to criticism of the Russian government's preparedness for war, which he would later make through his left-handed blacksmith from Tula.[26] The prophetic phrase: *mnogo raz pogibat' i ni razu ne pogibneš'* may also have a polemical edge. In the story **'Choice Grain' ('Otbornoe zerno')** Leskov refers to a prophetic phrase of Bismarck: that the only thing left for Russia to do was to perish (*pogibnut*).[27]

Whether Bismarck's supposed pronouncement was in Leskov's mind at the time of writing **'The Enchanted Wanderer'** or not, the story does proclaim the ability of the Russian nation to survive, even though many times it has appeared to perish. There is no attempt at a history or even a chronology of major events, but the story hints at the Tartar Yoke, a Polish wardship, and the 'magnetic' influence of western humanism (in whatever distorted form it was received). Ivan the 'Russian', the 'enchanted wanderer' is still moving on from one bizarre episode to another—but will his fate ultimately be religious? Leskov himself does not seem to be entirely sure.

Notes

[1] See Hugh McLean. *Nikolay Leskov: The Man and His Art*. Cambridge, Mass./London, 1977: 241-255.

Gor´kij's view was that "in every tale of Leskov you feel that his basic thought is a thought, not about the fate of a person, but the fate of Russia". M. Gor´kij, *Istorija russkoj literatury*. Moskva 1939: 275-276 (cf. also the introductory article of P. Gromov and B. Èjchenbaum. N.S. Leskov. *Sobranie sočinenij v odinnadcati tomach*. Moskva 1956-1958, Vol. I, LIX).

[2] "The fact is that in the idealised figure of Il'ja Muromec there was fully expressed the historical character of the Russian people." F. A. Brokgauz and I. A. Efron (eds.). *Ènciklopedičeskij slovar'*, St. Peterburg 1895, Vol. 24: 149. Cf. also: "Il'ja Muromec in the eyes of the people appeared as a representative of the peasant class." (ibid.: 151). Critics also point to the fact that Ivan Sever'janyč, like Il'ja Muromec is declared to be invulnerable to death. See: I. V. Stoljarova, *V poiskach ideala: tvorčestvo N. S. Leskova*, Leningrad 1978: 127; M.P. Čerednikova, 'O sjužetnych motivirovkach v povesti N.S. Leskova *Očarovannyj strannik'*. *Russkaja literatura*, 1971, Vol. 14, No. 3: 118.

[3] McLean: 243. The name actually derives from the Latin severus— 'stern'. See: N. A. Petrovskij, *Slovar´ličnych imen*. Moskva 1966: 197.

[4] All page references in brackets are to vol. 4 of the collection of Leskov's works cited above (note 1).

[5] Ivan's own attachment to the child is more a question of 'habit': "i strašno ja stal k nej privykat'" (409). Attachment based on habit seems to recall Gogol''s 'Old World Landowners'. See: R. Peace. *The Enigma of Gogol'*. Cambridge 1981: 40.

[6] Leskov, *Sob. soč.,* vol. 1, XLI. This statement has not gone unchallenged. See: B. Dychanova, *'Zapečatlennyj angel' i 'Očarovanyj strannik' N. S. Leskova*. Moskva 1980: 111. Dychanova, however, bases her objections on the concept of Ivan Sever'janyč as a man of honour.

Russian critics in their eagerness to find good qualities in Ivan stress his artistic nature, picking up the statement of the prince, who later in the story is Ivan's employer, that Ivan is *artist* (i.e. literally a 'performing artist'). See among others: Dychanova: 114; Stoljarova: 129; 148.

[7] Cf. N.A. Nekrasov, *Polnoe sobranie sočinenij i pisem v pjatnadcati tomach*. Leningrad 1981: 152; F. M. Dostoevskij. 'Dnevnik pisatelja za 1873 g.', *Polnoe sobranie sočinenij v tridcati tomach*. Leningrad 1972: 31-41. See also Stoljarova: 138.

[8] In the lives of the saints the birth of a holy man or hero was often a reward to pious parents after a long period of infertility. See: Čerednikova: 116.

[9] Cf. *Žitie protopopa Avvakuma im samim napisannoe i drugie ego sočinenija* (N.K. Gudzij, ed.). Moskva 1960: 108.

For Leskov Avvakum was the "quintessential Russian character", Stoljarova: 118.

[10] McLean: 251. McLean, in fact, appears to be taking up and expanding the view of Gromov and Èjchenbaum that the "internal erosion of norms" spring from the nature of peasant life (*soslovnaja žizn'*). See: note 6 above.

[11] The nature of Ivan's 'enchantment' seems to have caused some confusion among the critics. Volynskij gives it a rather exalted, mystical, religious interpretation (A. L. Volynskij. *N. S. Leskov*. Petrograd 1923: 69). I. V. Stoljarova criticises Volynskij's view and similar interpretations, but herself seems to suggest that the answer may be found in an analogy with folklore and such motifs as Ivan Duračok or the *byliny* figure Il'ja Muromec (Stoljarova: 123-124; 147-149) The Canadian critic K. A. Lanz rather weakly concludes: "Ultimately the 'enchantment' of the pilgrim is the enchantment of life itself." See: K. A. Lanz. *Nikolay Leskov*. Boston 1979: 87.

But the 'enchantment' (*očarovanie*) suggested in the title is surely related to magic (*čary*)—it is a spell cast on the 'wanderer', and it is ironical that he himself is thought of as *čarodej* (magician) because of his skills with horses (450).

[12] McLean: 243.

[13] *Sočinenija i pis'ma P.Ja. Čaadaeva* (M. Geršenzon ed.). Moskva 1913: 78-80; 85.

[14] Another of Leskov's heroes is also called 'Deathless Bighead' (*Bessmertel'nyj golovan*). See also Stoljarova: 127.

[15] N.Ja. Danilevskij. *Rossija i Evropa* (vstupitel'naja stat'ja Ju.

Ivaska), St. Peterburg, 18-, Reprint: New York 1966: 203.

[16] A 'magnetism still working to this day' and involving such a radical shift of perception raises the question of narrational realism; for if Ivan is now a man of greater compassion, how is it that he can still relate incidents from his earlier life, without showing this compassion? Perhaps this is asking too much of the 'realism' of the *skaz* form when used as a vehicle for allegory.

[17] Under this influence Ivan will later attempt 'French' himself: *pti kom p´e* (479)—a phrase used by the 'magnetiser' (465). Volynskij merely sees this scene with the 'magnetiser' as comic (Volynskij: 72-73). Čerednikova points to the association of the 'magnetiser' with the devil (Čerednikova: 124). But cf. the first appearance of Voland in *Masteri Margarita,* which is not only set in a comic key, but, significantly, Voland is taken for an obvious foreigner. M. Bulgakov. *Romany.* Moskva 1973: 426-27.

[18] Leskov seems to have regarded scepticism (i.e. that of Pisemskij) as "ailing sight" (*bolezn´ zrenija*). See: B.M. Drugov. *N. S. Leskov: očerk tvorčestva.* Moskva 1961: 75.

[19] Less flattering Ivan refers to it as 'the devil of philandering' (*bludnyj bes*), but as is obvious from the context the phrase is also related to the theme of wandering (more specifically 'getting lost'—bluždat´, zabludit´sja). "Bluždal, potomu ètot [. . .] magneziter, on p´janogo besa ot menja svel, i bludnogo pri mne postavil" (475) (Cf. *bludnyj syn*—'The Prodigal Son'—a parable not too dissimilar from that of Ivan Sever´janyč himself).

[20] "Ivan Sever´janyč helps her to leave life and this is not a crime, but a noble deed in the name of love. It is precisely at this point that the genuine birth takes place of a hero who assumes all the fullness of responsibility for the sins of another person, who is ruining her own soul." (Dychanova: 145).

[21] Nevertheless, according to Dychanova "Ivan Sever´janyč Fljagin lives predominantly by his heart and not his head" (ibid.: 110).

[22] *Predteča,* however, means 'forerunner', and there is, perhaps, a 'saintly' link between Ivan and the place where his 'enchantment' begins. The editor of vol. 4 of the collected works, I.Z. Serman, identifies the monastery where Ivan kills the monk as *Predtečeva Jaminskaja Pustyn´* (555).

[23] Dychanova comments that in this play the fairy saves the prince from the demon, whereas in actual life it is the other way around (Dychanova: 150). There is, perhaps, also a sense in which the play reflects the 'triangle' of the prince (*knjaz´*), Gruša, and Ivan.

[24] Ivan tells his story as he is sailing to the Valaam Monastery on Lake Ladoga, a place later associated with omens of war. See McLean: 484.

[25] Leskov's son and biographer thought that this was one of the reasons for Katkov's rejection of *"The Enchanted Wanderer."* See: Andrej Leskov, *N. S. Leskov: žizn´—tvorčestvo—poètika.* Moskva 1945: 296.

[26] N. S. Leskov, *Sob. soč.,* Vol. 7: 58.

[27] N. S. Leskov, *Sob. soč.,* Vol. 7: 280.

FURTHER READING

Biography

Lantz, K. A. *Nikolay Leskov.* Boston: Twayne, 1979. 165 p.
  Biographical and critical introduction to Leskov, including four chapters devoted to discussions of his short fiction.

McLean, Hugh. *Nikolai Leskov: The Man and His Art.* Cambridge: Harvard University Press, 1977. 780 p.
  Definitive study in English of Leskov's life and career, including chapters providing in-depth analyses of individual short stories.

Criticism

Amman, Thomas L. "Leskov's First Series of Sketches." *Slavic and East European Journal* XII, No. 4 (Winter 1968): 424-32.
  Discusses two early stories that contain themes, characters, and motifs that Leskov developed more fully in his later works.

Andrews, Larry R. "Hugo's Gilliat and Leskov's Golovan: Two Folk-Epic Heroes." *Comparative Literature* 46, No. 1 (Winter 1996): 65-83.
  Compares the virtuous hero of Leskov's story "Golovan" with the protagonist in a Victor Hugo novel.

Edgerton, William B. Introduction to *Satirical Stories of Nikolai Leskov,* translated and edited by William B. Edgerton, pp. 9-16. Western Publishing Company, 1969.
  Discusses Leskov's various literary styles and themes in the context of his life experiences, in particular his political involvement.

Ingham, Norman W. "The Case of the Unreliable Narrator: Leskov's 'White Eagle'." In *Studies in Russian Literature in Honor of Vsevolod Setchkarev,* edited by Julian W. Connolly and Sonia I. Ketchian, pp. 153-65. Slavica Publishers, 1986.
  Analyzes Leskov's tale 'White Eagle' as a 'puzzle story,' a satire of political corruption in the guise of a simple ghost story.

Jarvin, Janko. "Nikolai Leskov." In *Russian Writers and Their Lives,* pp. 202-15. New York: D. Van Nostrand and Company, 1954.
  Overview of Leskov's work and career, assessing his place in Russian literature and discussing the themes and stylistic features in his most important works.

Lantz, K. A. "Leskov's 'At the Edge of the World': The Search for an Image of Christ." *Slavic and East European Journal* 25, No. 1 (March 1981): 34-43.
  Interprets Leskov's story as one that attacks the dogma of the Russian Orthodox Church but offers hope for the triumph of true piety.

Lottridge, Stephen S. "Nikolay Leskov and the Russian *Prolog* as a Literary Source." *Russian Literature* 3 (1972): 16-39.

Discussion of Leskov's use of the Russian *Prolog,* a collection of traditional didactic tales based on the saints' lives, as a source for his later stories.

————. "Nikolaj Leskov's Moral Vision in the *'Prolog'* Tales." *Slavic and East European Journal* 18, No. 3 (Fall 1974): 252-58.

Analyzes Leskov's later tales as expressing nondenominational, positive Christian virtue.

McLean, Hugh "On the Style of a Leskovian *Skaz.*" *Harvard Slavic Studies* II (1954): 93-108.

An important early essay in Leskov scholarship in English, discussing the linguistic and structural features of Leskov's trademark genre, and asserting that Leskov used the *skaz* form to evade his censors.

Norman, R. Introduction to *The Tales of N. S. Leskov: The Musk-Ox and Other Tales,* translated by R. Norman, pp. vii-xiii. Hyperion Press, 1977.

Introduction to an early volume of Leskov's stories in English translation, in which Norman admires what he considers Leskov's ability to create believable characters of genuine moral virtue.

O'Connor, Katherine Tiernan. "The Specter of Political Corruption: Leskov's 'White Eagle'." *Russian Literature Triquarterly* 9 (August 1974): 393-406.

Demonstrates how Leskov uses the naive, unreliable narrator to present his veiled criticism of Russian bureaucratic institutions.

Additional coverage of Leskov's life and career is contained in the following source published by Gale Group: *Nineteenth-Century Literature Criticism,* **Vol. 25.**

Wyndham Lewis
1882(?)–1957

(Full name Percy Wyndham Lewis) Canadian-born English novelist, essayist, critic, short story writer, editor, poet, autobiographer, and dramatist.

INTRODUCTION

One of the leading and most controversial figures in British literary and artistic circles in the first half of the twentieth century, Lewis has garnered equal measures of praise and censure for his brilliant prose style, startling originality, brash personality, and pro-Fascist political leanings. He was instrumental in establishing the anti-Romantic movement in literature in the early 1900s and the Vorticism movement in art in the years before the First World War; wrote extensively about politics and aesthetics in the 1920s and 1930s; and was the art critic for the *Listener* in the 1950s. A gifted painter, Lewis's writing shows his concern with revealing "external" life using objective, visual techniques, in stark opposition to the "internal" technique of stream-of-consciousness employed by such contemporaries as James Joyce, Gertrude Stein, and Marcel Proust. His short stories, mostly satires, reveal an acerbic sense of the comic and seek to give voice to his complex aesthetic, political, and philosophical theories. Lewis's anti-democratic, elitist political views and satirical attacks on other writers made him an unpopular figure for much of his career, but his talents as a literary stylist were admired by such distinguished writers as T. S. Eliot and W. B. Yeats. Recent critical attention has focused on his skills as a satirist, his portrayals of the suffering artist, his Cartesian philosophical views, and his innovative style.

Biographical Information

Lewis was born aboard a yacht off the coast of Nova Scotia to an American father and English mother, and spent his early years in Canada and Maine before moving with the family to England in 1888. His parents separated shortly thereafter, and Lewis was raised by his mother, to whom he remained very close. After attending a series of day schools in London and then the public school Rugby from 1897 to 1898, Lewis entered the Slade School of Art. Upon completing his formal studies in 1901, he traveled extensively in Europe for seven years, writing, studying, painting, and living the unconventional life of an artist. Lewis returned to London in 1909 to pursue his painting in earnest, soon making a name for himself with his radical post-Impressionist style. He also quickly became acquainted with the literary notables of his day, including Eliot, Ford Madox Ford, Sturge Moore, Ezra Pound, Rebecca

West, and Yeats. In 1909 Ford published Lewis's first short story, "The Pole," in *The English Review,* and in the following years additional short pieces, many of which were written during his stay on the Continent, appeared in other influential literary magazines. During these pre-World War I years, Lewis was also active in organizing the Vorticist group, an abstract art movement that reacted against Futurism and Cubism and which emphasized the use of geometrical lines, impersonality in art, and classical detachment and control. Pound and Lewis together founded a periodical, *Blast,* in which to promote the ideas of the movement, but because of the onset of the war and financial constraints, they managed to publish only two issues. However, with *Blast,* Lewis established his reputation as a brilliant, defiant, and highly original thinker whose anarchic ideas often troubled more conventional critics. A good-looking, brash, and arrogant young man, Lewis also became something of a personality and had a number of mistresses, several of whom bore him children.

In 1916, after completing his novel *Tarr,* which he had been working on since his years in Europe, Lewis enlisted in the army, eventually becoming an officer. *Tarr* was published at the end of the war to excellent reviews but did not sell well, further establishing Lewis's position as an avant-garde writer. In 1920, Lewis's mother died, which had a great effect on him emotionally. Already embittered by the war, he felt that his mother's death was caused by its effects, and in the following decades his writings, many of which were political in nature, were aimed at preventing another such event. He favored right-wing politics, despising liberalism and pacifist democracy—which he considered catered to the weaknesses of the "herd" and encouraged conformity—and advocated a system that promoted a strong, stable authority under which he believed intellectuals and artists could flourish. Lewis's literary output in the 1920s and 1930s was prolific, and included some of his best-known work, including *The Art of Being Ruled* (1926), a rabid critique of politics, art, and society; *Time and Western Man* (1927), an assault on the literary-philosophical positions of the leading writers of his day; *The Wild Body* (1927), a collection of short stories that had been written before the war and were revised to reflect his current aesthetic and political theories; and *The Apes of God* (1930), a venomous portrayal of the members of the literary establishment. The latter work did a great deal to alienate Lewis from critics and other writers, but he never apologized for his unpopular opinions and barbed commentary on what he considered were the shortcomings in others' work. From 1927 to 1929 Lewis edited and wrote for the literary review *The Enemy* (he said he found the literary persona of the "enemy" suitable to his temperament), which was perceived as being sympathetic to Fascism. In his essay *Hitler* (1931), he praised Adolph Hitler's rise to power and expressed approval of National Socialism. Although he retracted these views in his later essays, *The Hitler Cult* and *The Jews, Are They Human?* (1939), Lewis's name was permanently tainted by his earlier, pro-Fascist politics.

Just before the outbreak of World War II, his popularity and reputation in deep decline, Lewis moved to North America with his wife, a woman he had met in 1918, married in 1930, and who stayed with him through his numerous infidelities. The couple lived in virtual poverty for a good part of their stay in the United States, with Lewis earning a little money painting portraits and relying on the goodwill of friends. They enjoyed some stability during Lewis's year-long appointment at a small college in Ontario, Canada, before returning to a life of shortages and rationing in London in 1945. In 1946 Lewis became the art critic for the *Listener,* an influential post he held for five years. His years abroad had softened him somewhat, and in his reviews he offered insightful and generous appraisals of younger artists. Although Lewis was beset by blindness in his last years, he continued to write, in 1954 producing what many consider his finest novel, *Self Condemned,* a tragic story about a self-destructive rationalist living in exile who denies human feelings in his commitment to discovering the truth. Critics consider the work to be based on his humbling experiences in North America. Lewis died in 1957 of a brain tumor.

Major Works of Short Fiction

Lewis wrote in 1935 that "the short story . . . was the first literary form with which I became familiar. . . . The 'short story' was the crystallization of what I had to keep out of my consciousness while painting." Lewis's first literary recognition came from the publication of his short stories in influential literary journals, and early admirers found his work marked by a structural clarity evident in his visual art that announced him as an original talent and thinker. The stories revealed also his anti-Romantic, realist bent and his gift for savagely humorous satire. The 1917 story, "Cantelman's Spring-Mate," considered one of his best, is a fine example of Lewis's controlled, descriptive, hard-edged style. In his 1927 collection, *The Wild Body,* which he called "essays in a new human mathematic," Lewis rewrote some of his early stories and added new ones to form a sequence of satiric tales told by a single comic narrator who recounts his adventures among the peasants of Brittany. Like his other work, the stories explore the contrast between the cultivated intellect and the savage, mechanized body and reveal his low opinion of women. Also included in the collection are two important essays, "Inferior Religions" and "The Meaning of the Wild Body," in which Lewis expresses the aesthetic, philosophic, and comic theories undergirding the stories in the collection. The other volume of stories published during Lewis's lifetime, *Rotting Hill,* is a series of sketches about life in London's Notting Hill after the Second World War and conveys the atmosphere of what he considered the "universal wreckage and decay" of post-war socialist Britain. The tone of this collection is a far cry from the lively satire of the earlier stories, and in this later work Lewis's descriptive realism gives way to the construction of types to make clear his distaste for the social and cultural politics he describes. Before he died, Lewis had intended to publish another book of short fiction, but the project never materialized. *Unlucky for Pringle: Unpublished and Other Stories,* published in 1973, includes unpublished pieces and others written between 1910 and 1956 that were not collected in the two other volumes.

Critical Reception

Lewis never enjoyed popular recognition, in part because his inaccessible style is often underwritten by difficult philosophical or aesthetic theories, but for most of his career he was considered a force in intellectual circles, even when his reputation was at a low ebb. Although Lewis's work was praised highly by some of his literary contemporaries, including Eliot, who called him the greatest prose stylist of the twentieth century, other critics found fault with his pro-Fascist politics, his brutal and unbalanced attacks of other artists' work, and the aggressive theorizing in his non-fiction and fiction alike. Early reviews of singly published stories and his *Wild Body* collection were mixed, with some critics heralding their originality and zest and others characterizing them as brutal, vulgar, and confused. Critical analysis of Lewis's work after his death has been concerned mainly with his novels, essays, and criticism, generally considered his best works, which showcase his incomparable idiosyncratic style and his devastating critical insight. Opinion of his stories in *Rotting Hill* is largely negative, and most critics consider it a tired, unimaginative attack on socialist politics. However, recent studies of the *Wild Body* collection have unanimously praised those stories' brilliant use of satire, strong sense of form, and psychological astuteness. Lewis is a difficult writer whose highly individual style, penetrating eye, and aggressive opinions, critics agree, reveal him to be one of the most fascinating and unsettling figures in modern literature.

PRINCIPAL WORKS

Short Fiction

The Wild Body 1927
Rotting Hill 1944
Unlucky For Pringle: Unpublished and Other Stories 1973

Other Major Works

Tarr (novel) 1918
The Caliph's Design (essay) 1919
The Art of Being Ruled (essays) 1926
The Lion and the Fox: The Role of the Hero in the Plays of Shakespeare (criticism) 1927
Time and Western Man (essays) 1927
The Childermass (novel) 1928
Paleface; The Philosophy of the "Melting Pot" (essays) 1929
The Apes of God (novel) 1930
The Diabolical Principle and the Dithyrambic Spectator (essays) 1931
Hitler (essay) 1931
The Doom of Youth (essays) 1932
Enemy of the Stars (drama) 1932
Snooty Baronet (novel) 1932
One-Way Song (poetry) 1933
Men Without Art (criticism) 1934
Left Wings Over Europe; or How to Make a War about Nothing (essays) 1936
Blasting and Bombardiering (autobiography) 1937
Count Your Dead! They Are Alive!, or, A New War in the Making (essays) 1937
The Revenge for Love (novel) 1937
America, I Presume (essays) 1939
The Hitler Cult (essay) 1939
The Jews, Are They Human? (essay) 1939
Wyndham Lewis the Artist, from "Blast" to Burlington House (essays and criticism) 1939
The Vulgar Streak (novel) 1941
America and Cosmic Man (essays) 1948
Rude Assignment: A Narrative of My Career Up-to-Date (autobiography) 1950

The Writer and the Absolute (essays) 1952
The Demon of Progress in the Arts (criticism) 1954
Self Condemned (novel) 1954
Malign Fiesta (novel) 1955
Monstre Gai (novel) 1955
The Red Priest (novel) 1956
Letters 1962
Wyndham Lewis on Art (criticism) 1969
The Roaring Queen (novel) 1973
Enemy Salvoes (criticism) 1976
Mrs. Duke's Million (novel) 1977

CRITICISM

Rachel Annand Taylor (essay date 1927)

SOURCE: "Some Modern Pessimists," in *The Spectator,* Vol. 139, No. 5. December 17, 1927, p. 863.

[*In the following excerpt from an early review, Taylor finds the "noise and fury" of Lewis's satire in* The Wild Body *distasteful.*]

In **The Wild Body** Mr. Wyndham Lewis finds matter for his savage mirth, his "beast of humour," in the more glaring towns of the Spanish border, and the more brutish spots of Brittany. . . . When he devotes his inordinate vocabulary of scorn to express his Timon-like hatred of mortality by conjuring up the bestial or preposterous figures that give him a painful joy, the noise and fury are too much for me, who fall to thinking with what deadly quietness Swift undertook the assassination of his kind. Mr. Lewis, that hater of the Romantics, here exhibits himself as a Romantic of the worst French kind in his taste for monsters. His Bestre is as much a romantic grotesque as Quasimodo, and obscene as Quasimodo is not. Lashing himself into mirth, Mr. Lewis is a startling spectacle. Since, of course, his is no ordinary mind, one or two of these sketches have a tortured power, like some of the interlinear patterns in his other books that look like scorpions stinging themselves to death.

Conrad Aiken (essay date 1928)

SOURCE: "Wyndham Lewis," in *A Reviewer's ABC: Collected Criticism of Conrad Aiken from 1916 to the Present,* W. H. Allen, 1961, pp. 268-71.

[*In the following review of* The Wild Body, *originally published in the* New York Post *in 1928, Aiken admires what he considers Lewis's first-rate narration in his psychological short stories, but finds that the writer's self-conscious theorizing mars his otherwise brilliant work.*]

Mr. Wyndham Lewis is something of a cornac himself—he is not without curious resemblances to his admirable portrait of a showman in the story called **"The Cornac and His Wife."** In this story we are presented with a melancholy creature who is in a sense a victim of his own audiences. His audience *works* him, just as he, too, in turn works his audience; a queer kind of reciprocal puppetry. The public expects, demands, *extracts* from the sad cornac the kind of humor it wants. His mere presence there, in the ring, provokes the public to a particular appetite: they are unable to look at him without becoming excited; without beginning to desire to see *him* excited. And at the proper moment, when the mutual chemical or psychological influence has reached the right pitch, the cornac goes into action. He and the audience throw themselves into the ritual, which has become inevitable for them, each playing on the other. The cornac thus becomes something which is not exactly himself: a current passes through him, or a string pulls him, and he is drastically changed. He behaves to something outside himself. He is thus two people (at least): a man, and also a man whom an audience has contorted to a particular end.

In his new book Mr. Lewis is very much in that plight. He is on the one hand a very original observer of human nature, a brilliant chronicler of its small beer, with a queer, angular, muscular, awkward and sometimes ungrammatical prose at his command—a prose which despite its lapses is astonishingly effective. He strikes one as being a very independent creature: the kind of fellow who knows exactly why he prefers Latour to Lafitte, who has discovered for himself that salt is good with this and pepper with that, and who measures out the ingredients for a salad with the atomizing eye of a connoisseur. One feels also that he has the power to survey this curious world into which we are born with a very remarkable degree of detachment—a detachment so complete as almost to amount to genius in itself. There is something of the behaviorist in him: he habitually sees emotions as actions, ideas as responses to stimuli, and takes an almost sadistic delight in pursuing a character through rigidly logical sequences of cause and effect. He has, in short, a very keen mind, and a very vigorous imagination, and one can at first discover no good reason why he should not be one of the most brilliant of contemporary writers of fiction.

But there is also, on the other hand, that aspect of Mr. Lewis which makes one think of the cornac being acted upon by his public. One gradually becomes aware, as one reads these delightful and highly idiosyncratic stories, that Mr. Lewis is perpetually adopting a role: he is, in fact, being *forced* into a special part. His awareness, whether vague or definite, of an audience there in the background—an audience waiting to see whether Mr. Lewis is clever or not (and, if so, *how* clever)—is an unresting one and an uneasy one. It gives him a nervous manner, a high degree of self-consciousness; it takes away from him precisely that pure freedom of mind with which he appeared to be starting out. His detachment is swallowed up in this other reaction: he remembers that something unusually dexterous is expected of him, and in his anxiety to produce a startling effect he begins, now and then, when he suspects he is not being too closely observed, to indulge in a questionable sleight or two.

Thus, in the present book [*The Wild Body*], he appears in two lights. He is a first-rate narrator of psychological short stories; and he is also, less fortunately, a theorist with an ax to grind. His ax is the theory, not especially original, of the comic; and throughout his book he is periodically taking this out and giving it a polish, and then burying it again, or simply forgetting it in the pleasure of creation or observation for its own sake. This is the clever side of Mr. Lewis, and one cheerfully enough admits that it *is* clever.

But wouldn't it be a relief to Mr. Lewis, as well as to his audience, if he were told that after all he needn't bother to try to impress us in this fashion? One needn't be a crank to be interesting—and there are moments when one sees Mr. Lewis well along the road to crankiness. There are amusing things in the essay entitled "Inferior Religions"; though one finds some difficulty in seeing it as a work of genius (*cf.* the remarks of Mr. T. S. Eliot on this subject). And one can extract a certain amount of dubious pleasure in watching Mr. Lewis's efforts to project *himself* as a kind of observing character, or recording instrument, in the first of these stories. He informs us that he is large and blond and fiercely humorous, with flashing teeth. Now and again in the later stories he remembers to remind us of this, but for the most part he forgets it. The projection doesn't quite come off. The truth is, it is not good enough. Or perhaps the trouble is that Mr. Lewis could not wholly give himself up to it. Sufficiently sophisticated to see the notion as an engaging one, and the role as amusing and original, he was also *too* sophisticated to be able to carry it out wholeheartedly or simple-mindedly.

So we go back to the stories themselves. And here we are on solid ground. They are brilliant, and they show everywhere a psychological astuteness of a high order. They are at the same time actual and queer. They have that consistence in oddity for which the only convenient word is genius. If only Mr. Lewis would content himself with this admirable tale-bearing as regards the foibles of human behavior and forget for a while that he thinks he has a philosophical mission, one feels certain that he could write fiction that would make any living writer green with envy.

Wyndham Lewis (essay date 1951)

SOURCE: Foreword to *Rotting Hill,* Methuen and Co., Ltd., 1951, pp. vii-xii.

[*In the following essay, the foreword to his volume of stories* Rotting Hill, *Lewis characterizes his work in the collection as showcasing the "universal wreckage and decay" prevalent in politics and social life in post-World War II, socialist Britain.*]

If I write about a hill that is rotting, it is because I deplore rot. For the decay of which I write is not romantic decay. But specific persons or Parties are in no way accountable for the rot. It is either the fault of everybody or of nobody.

If we exist, shabby, ill-fed, loaded with debt (taxed more than any men at any time have ever been), let us recognize that the sole explanation of this is our collective stupidity. If it soothes us to pin the blame upon our masters, past or present, by all means let us do so. The fact remains that this is only a subjective judgement. But who is responsible for ten years of war in a generation? All human groups, whether French, German, Italian, Polish, Korean, Japanese, Chinese, Czecho-Slovak, or any other are like our own a raw material, and are not responsible for the shape they take. I should add that our ostensible masters are raw material too. War is what is immediately responsible for the chaos which afflicts us at the present time. No cause can be assigned for these fearfully destructive disturbances (though of course we account for them in this or that conventional way, in our history books and in our conversation). The most *recent* wars have entirely altered our lives, that is all we can say.

In 1945 we ended a second, a six-year spell of war. We came out of this a ruined society, our economy destroyed, our riches vanished, our empire reduced to a shadow of itself, but our island-population (optimistically built-up to the absurd total of fifty millions) undiminished and requiring just as much food as when we had the money to pay for it. Naturally everybody was dazed. But into this situation burst a handful of jubilant socialists, voted into power, with an overwhelming majority, on the Labour ticket. They were in no way dismayed by the national situation; they proceeded to extract by huge taxation, direct and indirect, the colossal capital needed to stage a honeymoon for the liberated manual-working mass. This of course gave no one any time to despair at the disappearance of national prosperity. The majority of the nation was highly stimulated: and if the landed society was taxed out of existence, the middle class in rapid dissolution, on the whole England became a brighter rather than a darker place. To symbolize this extraordinary paradox the capital city burst into festivities all along the south bank of the Thames; there was whoopee at Battersea, there was the thunder of orchestras in a new national concert-hall, a thousand peep-shows, culminating in a Dome of Discovery lower down the river. This was staged in the ward sanctified by Shakespeare. In the Parliament the lamb lay down with the lion; the Tory bleated softly and snoozed beside the rampant socialist lion: all England seemed to have decided to forget that it had lost everything, and to live philosophically from day to day upon the Dole provided by the United States.

Such is the situation at the moment of writing. In spite of this extremely brilliant, if exceedingly artificial situation, nevertheless decay is everywhere, as might be expected. If an aristocratic society suddenly drops to pieces, after many centuries, and if a mercantile class of enormous power and wealth drops to pieces at the same time, there is inevitably a scene of universal wreckage and decay, as when demolition work is in progress. In a great city like London large areas, until ten years ago expensive and "select", become shabby or even slummish overnight; the food and other shortages make an end of good restaurants, the shortage of power dims the streets, the high

cost of everything turns a well-heeled citizenry into a shoddy, shabby herd, which shuffles round the shops from morning till night in a dense tide.

For the seamy side of socialist splendour the socialists are blamed. Mr. Patricks, the socialist shop-man whose toy-shop you are invited to visit in the ensuing pages, says that his customers even blame the heat and the cold, the rain and the snow and the sleet on the Government. And then, of course, the very bounty of the socialists, their lavish honeymoon spending, militated against the austerity of life and dedication to work which was required to build the New Jerusalem. Decades of ca' canny and the ingrained habit of go-slow, producing a population of the laziest workmen in Europe, has proved the arch-enemy of socialism. So there is a big cancer, a deep rot in the heart of the industry now controlled by the new masters, which it may require a very harsh dictator to eradicate.

I have now supplied you with the credentials of the Rot which is the subject matter of this book of stories. Among the persons gathered between the covers of *Rotting Hill* those who are more or less adult talk a good deal about the situation created by the rapid conversion of England into a Welfare State; the toiling majority naturally do not discuss "Welfare States", merely respond vocally to the pleasant or unpleasant stimuli for which the "high-ups" of whatever political philosophy are responsible. But most of my personnel belong to the disintegrating middle-class, and they naturally discuss the Welfare State since it has a good deal of bearing upon their destinies.

At this point I should perhaps meet the question, to be anticipated after the above delivery of the credentials of the Rot, "Is this a political book?" Not more, it can truthfully be answered than some of Charles Dickens' books, and all by Mr. Shaw, to go no further afield. If my characters are obsessed by politics, it is because today our lives are saturated with them. It is impossible for a work of narrative fiction worth reading to contain less politics than *Rotting Hill.* And those who would contradict me and assert that contemporary fiction can be otherwise than steeped in politics are those who would prefer that you would not have anything to do with books that cause you to use your rational faculty. Best to confine your reading to Detective Stories and to Western Yarns! Nay why read at all, they would argue? Why not save paper so that the Government may have more for its multifarious bureaucratic activities—more than it *already* takes? Just turn on Dick Barton, then take the dog for a nice long tree-crawl and go to bed and dream of next summer's Butlin Camp holiday!

"Socialism" is a word to which we need not pay very much attention. Socialism is merely the name of something which is happening to us, something which could not otherwise than happen, in view of all historical factors present, above all the proliferation of mechanical techniques. If we refrain from looking upon it as a purely *political* phenomenon we shall understand it better. In the present work there is, however, one factor which is especially stressed; namely, socialism seen as a final product of bible-religion.

Conscience is at the root of the principle of Social Justice—without it what would be there? That ethical impulse is of a potency to which no "law of nature" could attain. It is all that remains of Protestant Christianity excepting Christmas Carols, the sacraments of baptism and of marriage, especially in villages where the church is the only public building: and except for burial, of course, since there is nowhere you can dispose of a corpse except the churchyard. But the conscience is almost entire still with some people, though they regard God as quite as Victorian a phenomenon as The Lady of the Lamp and would couple the Bible with Euclid as part of the quaint furniture of childhood.

They would be very surprised indeed to hear they had a conscience. Let me try and show in a few words, how absolutely impossible socialism would have been without the Christian religion. Mr. Attlee and Sir Stafford Cripps as much as Mr. Gladstone are good church-going Christians: and their "socialism" is Mr. Gladstone's "liberalism" taken to its ultimate conclusion. In other words, liberalism was an early stage of socialism. And the nineteenth century of liberalism was demonstrably a product of Christianity: it was at long last the Christian seriously trying to put the New Testament into practice. The culmination of this movement, still using the word "liberal" to describe itself, was Lloyd George's National Insurance Act. That was a most revolutionary measure, far more "advanced" than any adopted in any other country at that time. Finally, the logical conclusion of Gladstone and Morley, and Lloyd George and all their fellow preachers of social fair play, of social justice, was for the classes possessed of money and power to surrender them, and, of course, for England itself as a nation owning a quarter of the globe to surrender everything—as has recently been done in the case of England's greatest possession, India—except this island; and even that must in the end not be looked upon with too possessive an eye.

Now, without the teaching of the New Testament—and we must not forget the Old, and that the Jews were the most moral nation the world has ever seen—or some similar teaching such as Stoicism (and there are exceedingly few teachings of this type), no man gives up anything he has acquired whether it be wealth or land or goods. Why should he? He will fight to defend them with desperation. If you informed him that "Property is a theft" he would laugh at you. Such a saying, in the first instance, to be successful, had to appear with a supernatural sanction. To test the accuracy of what I am saying, you only have to consider whether you would give up anything but a small fraction of your property in order to share it with your less fortunate fellows. There are very few of us who could willingly do so. But a long process of religious conditioning (latterly operating through such words as "decency", "fair play", etc. etc.) has led us to a point at which we empower the State to deprive us of practically everything. This is the work of Jesus.

As I have suggested, it would be absurd to take to task contemporary socialists for carrying to its ultimate conclusions nineteenth-century liberalism. It would be slightly more sensible to criticize the earliest liberals (for, as you would assert, their sentimental and unreal policies), as undoubtedly you would do, were you a catholic or felt no longer, even in "hangover" form, the spell of the Sermon on the Mount. Above I have advocated the discarding of the political approach to contemporary happenings. And I cannot do better than to end this foreword upon a reminder of this earlier counsel. Let me couple with this the advice that you look upon the politician as it is best to look upon a war, as a visitation of the Fiend.

Geoffrey Wagner (essay date 1953)

SOURCE: "*The Wild Body*: A Sanguine of the Enemy," in *Nine*, Vol. 4, No. 1, Winter, 1953, pp. 18-27.

[*In the following essay, Wagner argues that the collection of stories* The Wild Body *embodies Lewis's theory and practice of satire, explaining that his political thinking and comic sense have their roots in the conflict between the savage body and the cultivated intellect, and further that satire is at the heart of Lewis's realism.*]

When Wyndham Lewis defined politcs, in *America and Cosmic Man,* as "a melodrama for teen-aged minds," he was hinting at what he was to elaborate in *Rude Assignment,* namely that "there are no *good* politics." Yet although there can be no "good" politics, he also asserted in *Rotting Hill* that contemporary fiction must be steeped in politics to be a true reflection of reality; this, in short, has been his dilemma. His art was born in war, he has recently written, and his "philosophic criticism", or political "pamphlets" (as he calls a work of over four hundred pages), grew out of his creative work. It is thus consistent that we can find in *The Art of Being Ruled,* which he has called a "key-book", concepts of human nature which subsume his work and in which his earlier satire is embedded.

In *The Art of Being Ruled,* that book of "jujitsu for the governed", Lewis finds that all political thought tends to federate opinion, and that for the politican the true individual must be "an indelicate interloper, a walking lie, a distrubing absurdity". This individual, who is to-day forced into the position of enemy or outlaw, or man who says No, was in classical societies the quintessence of the group and his life accordingly intense. Thus, Lewis proposes, the group or syndicalist ideal, under which head he particularly classes socialism deriving reciprocally from the lust for power and Bible-religion, chiefly thrives when the individual, as to-day, is idle. All these and their related ideas bear strongly on Lewis's satire and especially illuminate *The Wild Body,* answering perhaps the puzzled reviewer of *The Times Literary Supplement* who inquired at the time, "we may ask why we should have to accept Mr. Lewis's emphasis on the body."

The Wild Body, containing work reprinted and revised from *The English Review* of 1909 and *The Tramp* of 1910, embodies a theory and practice of satire from which Lewis has never swerved; indeed, an article in *The London Mercury* of 1934, he wrote on the art of laughter adds little to what we have in his earliest published stories. Yet the concept of "wild" in his satiric terminology derives from subsequently expressed political beliefs, especially from the idea of the "person" and the "thing". In *Paleface,* he put this distinction succinctly:

> "In Rome what constituted 'abnormality' was the being either a slave, a stranger or a minor (of whatever age) within the potestas of some head of a family. A slave and, originally, a stranger, or 'peregrinus', was legally a 'thing'. . . . All animals were naturally 'things'—a lion in the forest or a wild bee was a 'res nullius', but a watch-dog or a slave was not 'wild', so could not be affected to another person than his owner by capture."

With certain reservations, this statement, opposing the Roman "person" to the "thing", or the normal, free, and (for him) formal element in the state to the abnormal, or "wild", is the basis of Lewis's political thinking, and provides the division on which his satire is based. Elsewhere, he advances the distinction as between Goethe's puppets (things) and Natures (persons). In *Count Your Dead: They are Alive!* he simplifies it further.

The "thing", or puppet, in this system, is what is sometimes called the common man. These mass organizations Lewis likens to-day to larvae, or, in another place, to performing mice, "hallucinated automata" produced by stereotyped environment and a standardized education. This element of our society has neither the desire nor the ability to improve; they are the "changeless Many". In this view, and here alone, I think, he approaches his closest to Machiavelli, with whom he has so often been compared. There are two places in Machiavelli's work, Chapter XVIII of *The Prince* and Chapter III of the First Book of the *Discourses,* where he calls men bad, a fundamental tenet of Machiavelli's thought that escapes Mr. Burnham and invalidates his otherwise admirable study. Lewis, however, does not call the mass of the people evil; indeed, he would be likely to agree with Machiavelli's statement that "the aim of the people is more honest than that of the nobility, the latter desiring to oppress, and the former merely to avoid oppression". What he does say is that they passively resist improvement: "Men and women like nothing so much as being 'classified'," and again, "People ask nothing better than to be *types*," and again, "in the mass people wish to be automata." Lewis wrote these phrases in 1926; it took George Orwell about a quarter of a century to learn this and write his dangerous *1984,* dangerous because, as Professor McLuhan of Toronto University has suggested, it projects into the future a world that already exists.[1]

It is, then, the "thing", or puppet, coerced by his environment, who provides the pabulum of satire, rather than the "person", or Nature, who resists the social stereotype, or "group rhythm" as Lewis calls it. This latter, the true individual, free of class, race, sex, or youth prejudice, is what Lewis terms the "Not-Self"; the former is the "wild body" or, as he has put it in another work, the "savage robot".

The wild body, surrendering to the group rhythm, must be the target of laughter, for he lacks "continuity" and falls into the fluxes of his time, becoming like Ratner of *The Apes of God,* "split", in the sense of divided against himself, against that small part of him that still retains traces of the higher "Not-Self". This split, incidentally, is not a Jekyll and Hyde affair, it is what Lewis calls a "longitudinal" cleft existing coevally in the character—this is shown also in illustrative form in the vorticist chapter-head of Part V of *The Apes.* So we read,

> "The more highly developed an individual is, or the more civilized a race, this *discontinuity* tends to disappear. The 'personality' is born. Continuity, in the individual as in the race, is the diagnostic of a civilized condition."

It is the function of the artist, in this system, to maintain our continuity or "differentiation of existence", in a world where personality is equivalent to "person"-ality. In this world, only the "person" is fully free, for only he truly lives. It is the stereotyped "thing" who, owing to his loss of individuality, or life, becomes for Lewis "mechanical" or a "mechanism".

Such, in the most general terms, is the background to the theory to be found in Lewis's earliest satire. It is on the dichotomy between the wild body and the cultivated intellect that he bases his first work—"it is upon that essential separation that the theory of laughter here proposed is based". In the section of the book entitled "The Meaning of the Wild Body" he elaborates this. The mind is to be "the laughing observer", the body simply "the Wild Body". The observer is clearly the showman, Kerr-Orr, "ringmaster of this circus" as he called him in 1950. But we must keep in mind that Kerr-Orr is only an intermediary, not in any sense the heroic "Not-Self". He is simply, as Lewis has so often claimed to be, the detached spectator, or observer of life. When Lewis wrote that his art grew out of war, we must remember that his first contact with war was as an "observer", namely in the Royal Artillery. If we also recall the slight autobiographical association he has made with Tarr, it is only one step to see that Bertha, or "big Bertha" as she indeed is, as the German artillery piece and also as woman representing emotion, makes a natural symbol from which the intellectual and English Tarr would want to disengage himself. If this seems over-subtle, I recommend Part III of *Blasting and Bombardiering.* In passing, one should add that the various *alter ego*'s, which Lewis has assumed in an effort to achieve this necessary detachment, include the Herdsman, Blenner, the Crowd-Master or Cantelman (variously spelt), the Enemy, Ned, Kemp, and Major Corcoran (with a significantly militant eyeglass), but not, however, the Tyro. So we read in *The Wild Body,*

> "The Comic is always strenuous and cruel, like the work. It never flowers. The intermediary, the showman, knows that. He knows the brutal *frisson* in contact

with danger that draws the laughter up from the deepest bowel in a refreshing unearthly gush."

Kerr-Orr is this. So, later, is Tarr. In the first Egoist Ltd. edition, there is a subsequently excised "Prologue" in which we read, "Tarr is the individual in the book, and is at the same time one of the showmen of the author". The rest of the characters in both works are wild bodies, or "things". To say this, however, does not entirely account for Lewis's method of approach to the subject. He tells us that while it is impossible to breach the gap between the two, between flesh and spirit, between not-being and being (and that, in fact, such an effort of self-observation would be disastrous—"Such consciousness must be of the nature of a thunderbolt. Laughter is only summer lightning.") yet "The root of the Comic is to be sought in the sensations resulting from the observations of a *thing* behaving like a person". He gives as an example of this Kantian instance of incongruity, a man running for a train and just catching it in time, the comic effect being produced by the sight of his nicely calculating eye in contrast with his body which is like a sack of potatoes. "His *eye* I decided was the key to the absurdity of the effect."

In other words, the eye, prototype of the intelligence for Lewis, is detached in an anomalous fashion, which is absurd, from the action of the body, and this detachment, one microcosmic of Lewis's political views, too, is the basis of his comedy. "The deepest root of the Comic is to be sought in this anomaly."

Thus, in order to project the wild body, Kerr-Orr, the showman, must, like Tarr, possess a high intelligence quotient. Such is what we find. Kerr-Orr's approach is a detachment, he says, between his "gut-bag" and his "two bright rolling marbles", or "bull's-eyes full of mockery and madness". He confesses to these two "me's" and claims "I hang somewhere in its midst operating it with detachment". This showman, then, may observe and put on the platform for us "puppets", wild bodies, or "Appropriate dummies" (as he called the same element in *One-Way Song*), creatures so elementary they are lifeless machines, gargoyles engaged in a ritual, a ritual resembling the dance of an inferior religion—"All religion has the mechanism of the celestial bodies, has a dance." Kerr-Orr explains that the kind of laughter he represents must be primitive in origin, and is therefore easily located in the peasant communities of Brittany. For the primitive Breton peasant, he tells us, usually designs his laughter to wound. With him the Comic is "always strenuous and cruel" indeed, since for him it is part of fate. That is, he cannot rise above his circumstances and so remains identified, even in laughter, with the often brutal nature of his everyday work. Kerr-Orr here goes on to explain that the civilized man is a greater realist because his philosophic understanding, or imaginative appreciation (as in the artist), enables him to transcend the primitive condition of the peasant who stays "surrounded by signs, not things". "The Cornac" exemplifies this, for the laughter at this clown is torn out of the Breton peasant's own life, and is a means of revenge for the onlookers on this life to which they are so hopelessly subject. This, then, is what "Infe-

rior Religions", the section of the book Lewis tells us explains the title and where T. S. Eliot, in *The Egoist,* saw genius, really means. In his essay, "The Dithyrambic Spectator", there is a passage dealing with religion which substantiates this. In fact, the real meaning of "Inferior Religions" is hinted at when we find Lewis writing to Lord Carlow at the time of the English publication of ***The Wild Body*** as follows:

> The pattern of these 'wild bodies' is all made up out of the shape of living people, into which, as you will see, was introduced the principle of a fanatical obsession, which accounted for the pattern: showing how energetic men attach themselves to an inferior cult, lacking a greater one. Since to-day is the day of Inferior Religions, as you will agree, how very topical these stories are!

In this way "The fascinating imbecility of the creaking men machines . . . involved in a monotonous rhythm from morning till night" gives us the "set narrow intoxication" of someone like the Frenchman of **"A Soldier of Humour"**, enslaved to his desire to become more American than the Americans (a prescient critique, indeed). All these "great comic effigies" (as he called them later) live in "a pattern as circumscribed and complete as a theorem of Euclid". They are "essays in a new human mathematic", "bobbins" or "studies in a savage worship and attraction". They are merely enacting inferior religions, symbols of what Lewis has called our "little age". This idea, of idiotic service to some mechanistic ritual, underlies all Lewis's satire and affects both theme and imagery. Even in the recent ***Rotting Hill*** we find that what he really objects to in contemporary England is the people's "will-to-live as a machine". Only the detaching power of unholy laughter can free us from the spurious philosophies of our day. Introducing his 1921 exhibition at the Leicester Galleries, Lewis defined the Tyro (a periodical of which name he was editing this year) as follows: "An elementary person; an elemental, in short." And he goes on,

> "These immense novices brandish their appetites in their faces, lay bare their teeth in a valedictory, inviting, or merely substantial laugh. . . . This sunny commotion in the face, at the gate of the organism, brings to the surface all the burrowing and interior broods which the individual may harbour."

In short, laughter reveals reality. And although Lewis gives other explanations of his characters (which are obviously not to be ignored), the evidence given in the stories themselves is that the Frenchman is a wild body to the inferior religion of his would-be Americanism, the "Poles" of their "literary political" state of exile and of parasitic and poetic indolence, Carl of his crude appetites, of his "stupid madness, or commonplace wildness", Zoborov of his fight with Mademoiselle Péronette for the Beau Séjour, while "the odious brown person of Bestre" is enslaved to the ritual of his ocular warfare with the painter Rivière. The Cornac, with his wife and "haggard offspring", are slaves of their "implacable grudge" against their public, a "death struggle", as Kerr-Orr describes it, with an audience who long nightly for these clowns to break their necks. In brief, all these puppets are presented as "carefully selected specimens of religious fanaticism".

This juxtaposition of animal-machine, often in a caricature of religious ritual, percolates the whole of Lewis's work. Lord Osmund, in *The Apes,* gives thus "the effect of the jouissant animal—the licking, eating, sniffing, fat-muzzled machine". Lady Fredigonde, seated in her chair which is for her an "elaborate animal dwelling", moves her head "upon the ruined clockwork of her trunk". The magnificently described peasant girl at the opening of *The Revenge For Love* walks with "great clockwork hips", while one of Jack Cruze's secretaries here sways her hips in front of Tristy "in clockwork rhythm". Jack himself is a "love-machine". Coriolanus, we are told in *The Lion and the Fox,* is "congealed into a kind of machine of unintelligent pride". In *The Tyro No. 3* a character called X. defines himself as "an animal", calls his friends Q. and D.T. automata, and has the following exchange with an interlocutor called F.:

"F.—'I feel that my words, as I utter them, are issuing from a machine. I appear to myself a machine, whose destiny it is to ask questions.'"

"X—'The only difference is that I am a machine that is constructed to provide you with answers. I am alive, however. But I am beholden for life to machines that are asleep.'"

This technique is particularly pervasive in **The Wild Body,** for what is it that Kerr-Orr (or "Cairo" as he is also called, hinting at Lewis's interest in Egyptian art, perhaps) learns concerning the pseudo-American Frenchman but "the important secret of this man's entire machine", while, looking at "Father Francis" (or "The Musician" as he appears in manuscript form), he wonders "what emotions had this automaton experienced before he accepted outcast life?" This reverend father's passion is, indeed, "stereotyped into a frenzied machine".

In *The Revenge For Love* this puppetry is taken one stage further and we are faced, I think, with an interesting question. For, with two exceptions, this book is peopled by "machines" or "things"; in fact, it was originally entitled *False Bottoms,* everything in it being a false bottom from the basket taken to Hardcaster at the beginning (food covering seditious material) to the Stamp's car at the end, even to Margot's death over a precipice, another sort of false bottom. These communists live "the machine-life of an hysterical, half-conscious, underworld", they are "sham underdogs". Percy himself is a "shell of the rational man". (Father Francis is first seen as a "shell" by Kerr-Orr.) Yet it is difficult to read this book without feeling some pity for the uncompromising Hardcaster, not so much because of the physical injuries he suffers, as because he realizes the unreality of his companions or realizes, to paraphrase Lewis himself, that politics can never be "good" but we must live in a political world. "Do you suppose that these people are *real?* Do you think they exist?" even Victor asks Margot, whose love of another sort (emotional as

opposed to intellectual) is revenged for equal refusal to conform to the falsification of our world. Yet it is not enough to say that Percy—or Margot—"prolongs his authenticity unpardonably," as the admirably intelligent jacket of the recent Methuen re-issue of this novel puts it. One simply cannot read the last paragraphs of *The Revenge For Love* without pity for Margot, or even without agreeing with Roy Campbell in *Light On a Dark Horse* when he suggests that under "the frozen mask of misanthropy" Lewis can write astonishing lyrical prose when he wishes. Yet we are told, in *Rude Assignment,* to read this work dispassionately. Kreisler, whom he describes as "a *machine* (a 'puppet', not a 'nature')", is "expected to awaken neither sympathy nor repulsion in the reader". Hardcaster is likened to Groucho Marx and *Blasting and Bombardiering* provides the rider that Karl Marx's function in our society was similar to that of the Marx Brothers. The last advice given in "The Code of A Herdsman", in *The Ideal Giant* publication, is "The terrible processions beneath are not of our making, and are without our pity." In this sense, *The Apes of God* may be the nearest to "pure" satire Lewis has written, as he himself has recently suggested, though I would myself put **The Wild Body** up as a close contender for this kind of "pure", dispassionate gift in his canon. But *The Revenge For Love* raises another point.

It is answered, I believe, in two ways; first, that in his comments on his own work Lewis is often thinking of the creator. The creator, for him, must remain totally aloof, free of passion, and register the truth. We, however, as readers, and indeed as "things", may presumably be permitted a moment's pity for puppets like Margot in whom we recognize such as a heartrending account of part of our condition. Secondly, Lewis's satire admittedly treads a hairline with tragedy. "We are tragic beings", he has written in *Rude Assignment.* Exactly. How does *The Childermass* close but with Polemon's acclaimed remarks to the Bailiff, "'Agreed, puppet, and we on our side will treat you as though you were real for the purpose of this examination. So the battle for the reality can be joined for the idea of reality. Who is to be *real*—this hyperbolical puppet or we? Answer, oh destiny!'" When we read that Mr. Patricks, the shopkeeper of **Rotting Hill** who resembles Sartre in looks, "is himself like a wound-up toy", we are reading a tragic statement. For if the majority of human beings today are simply "monuments of dead imperfection", like the "things" of **The Wild Body,** it is scarcely a matter for rejoicing. So we read in this work.

"Laughter is the representative of tragedy when tragedy is away. . . . Laughter is the emotion of tragic delight. . . . Laughter is the female of tragedy."

Again, "'Comedy being always the embryo of Tragedy'", Tarr says to Bertha, "'the director nature weeps'." Introducing his 1937 exhibition, Lewis wrote, "as what we experience in life is not all pleasant, and the most terrible experience, even, is often the most compelling, the result is a tragic picture, as often as not". "There is laughter and laughter, and that of true satire is as it were a *tragic* laughter", he wrote in *Satire and Fiction,* a pamphlet in defence of *The Apes of God.* So Bestre is "a tragic organism", while the Frenchman "was convinced the greater part of the time that he was taking part in a tragedy". In short, what he has called the "tragi-comic" method of his painting is that of his early satire and the comic type is primarily a "thing" failing in intellectual energy in a basically tragic way:

> "A comic type is a failure of a considerable energy, an imitation and standardizing of self, suggesting the existence of a uniform humanity—creating, that is, a little host as like as ninepins."

Such satire, then, plays on an obtuseness to difference—"All difference is energy." Consequently, as it cannot help but be concerned with the reform as well as exposure of vice and folly, it must be strong and militant. Kerr-Orr says, "Violence is of the essence of laughter (as distinguished from smiling wit): it is merely the inversion of failure of *force.*" Kerr-Orr, we note, is a *soldier* of humour; he is to be found "manoeuvring in the heart of the reality", and when he finds life, his inclination is "to make war on it and to cherish it as a lover, at once". His laughter, explicitly, is "reminiscent of war". Again, "Everywhere where formerly I would fly at throats, I now howl with laughter." Bestre combines man's laughter and manslaughter in his formidable eye. So does also an early character called Beresin, in an uncollected short story, **"The War Baby"**. "Smiling wit", however, is what Lewis calls "Humour" rather than "Satire", a distinction he elaborates in the first part of *Rude Assignment.* In association with Kerr-Orr, one should add, "humour" has not taken on this pejorative connotation. In *Blasting and Bombardiering* he wrote that *Blast No. 1* accorded the first "blast" to humour (in the sense of cosy wit of the *Punch* type); actually he was incorrect, humour is assigned the fifth "blast" as "Quack ENGLISH drug.... Arch enemy of REAL". It gets the third "bless" when in the hands of Shakespeare and Swift, and *Blast No. 2* confirms, "The English 'Sense of Humour' is the greatest enemy of England".

It but remains to point out that the method of presenting these puppets is by the manner Lewis calls "fiction from the outside" or "the philosophy of the eye". This only applies to technique, the artistic impulse is by no means necessarily visual—"There can be no pure visual impulses in the art of Letters, I believe." The eye, for Lewis, is life. Ludo, the blind beggar of Rot in **"The Death of the Ankou"**, represents the figure of death, himself dies. (The word Rot conveniently combines for Lewis both a Breton commune and a belch—in *One-Way Song,* he wrote, "I belch. I bawl. I drink.") In ***Rotting Hill,*** Rot is what is affecting, in its many forms, contemporary England, and in the title story, **"The Rot"**, the narrator significantly says No to a representative of this new society. Thus when Rymer enters here with a patch over one eye and eructates, he is halfway to Ludo and ironically reminiscent of his creator who is now himself tragically blind, about the most cruel fate that could have been devised for the author, in *Blast No. 2,* of the statement, "My soul has gone to live in my eyes, and like a bold young lady it lolls in those sunny windows."

In *The Art of Being Ruled* Lewis wrote, "I am an artist, and, through my eye, must confess to a tremendous bias. In my purely literary voyages my eye is always my compass." Blenner, in *Blast No. 2,* has very bright eyes, as opposed to the crowd around him who are blind. In *The Tyro No. 2* Lewis wrote that the eye gives us "an incessant analysis of the objects presented to us for the practical purposes of our lives". This is the method that gives us the caricatures of **The Wild Body.** Whether or not the English art critic, Patrick Heron, is correct in claiming that Lewis, in his graphic work, always finds the outline first, certainly such is his technique in his "fiction from the outside". "The ossature", he wrote in *Satire and Fiction,* "is my favourite part of a living animal organism." "Give me the *outside* of things", he repeated in *Blasting and Bombardiering.* And in that important chapter at the end of *Tarr,* where Anastasya asks Tarr to define art and life, Tarr claims that a statue lives by its external form, by its absence of "*inside*". He says, "this is another condition of art; *to have no inside*", and he goes on, in a paragraph omitted from the revised edition, to explain this:

> "Instead, then, of being something impelled like a machine by a little egoistic fire inside, it lives soullessly and deadly by its frontal lines and masses."

In **The Wild Body** Deborah uses her eyes as weapons against Sigismund, "she threw knives at him sometimes with her eyes", while of course for Bestre the eye is an armament of some consequence. Significantly, Kerr-Orr confesses that he has learnt a lot from Bestre. "He is one of my masters." This militant use of the eye against the surface of things naturally produces machine imagery, especially that of military machinery, like "bombs". Take the word "disc", an object whose shape was meaning much to Lewis in his graphic work of this time: the Frenchman's eyes are found fixed on Kerr-Orr "with the blankness of two metal discs". Bestre's hand is a "pudgy hieratic disc", while in bed Deborah's "flat disc of face lay sideways on the pillow". The vorticist eye of young Will Blood (originally Will Eccles in *The Tyro No. 1*) catches Gladys, "the dreary waitress, in her bored jazz", and,

> "models her with his blue eye into a bomb-like shape at once, associating with this a disc—a marble table— and a few other objects in the neighbourhood".

Before Percy and Jack fight in *The Revenge For Love* their eyes "signalled defiance". Even the fatalistic Kreisler's eyelids are to be found "clapping to like metal shutters".

It will be objected that Lewis is not always consistent, in the rest of his work, with this ideal of "fiction from the outside". It is true that there are notable instances of the interior monologue, or stream of consciousness, such as, to select the most obvious examples, the handling of Lady Fredigonde in *The Apes* or Satters in *The Childermass.* But in *Satire and Fiction* Lewis explains that the interior monologue can be used justifiably in satire either as a parody of the interior monologue (such as in the "Stein-Stutter" sequence in *The Apes* or the skit on Virginia Woolf's style at the start of Part VI of *The Revenge For*

Love) or it can be used, appropriately, to describe the thought-streams of the very young, the very aged, half-wits or animals. It was to these categories that he again confined the technique of the interior monologue in Louise Morgan's interview with him in *Writers at Work.*

Satire, then, such as we have in **The Wild Body,** affords the possibilities of "a great *externalist* art", and indeed, he wrote in 1930, "Satire is in reality nothing else but *the truth*". Exactly twenty years later he wrote, "*where there is truth to life there is satire*". What is truth? He has defined truth, in *The Writer and the Absolute,* as "*what is*". Conversely, Kemp, in *The Ideal Giant,* says, "*Reality* is the 'thing which is not', for the creative artist". That is to say, life as we "futile, grotesque, and sometimes pretty spawn" live it is a sham, a "reality" only. The honest artist can alone provide truth and satire, being closest to "the 'classical' manner of apprehending" can best give us that picture of ourselves which alone will lead to reform. The odd, lively, and picaresque characterizations of **The Wild Body** are not to be thought of as eccentric, but rather as arithmetical equations of life, stereotyped "things". Or, better, in Tarr's words, "The Many they are the eccentric. . . ."

Satire, dealing with men not manners, unconcerned with pleasure ("If you want to be 'happy'," Lewis once advised, "you must not be a man, but a pig.") relying on the least emotional of our senses, can alone truly reform. And by implication the theory of the wild body itself suggests that our tragedy is that we live historically, rather than satirically—"the romantic traditional outlook . . . results in most men living in an historic past", we read in *The Diabolical Principle and The Dithyrambic Spectator.* Satire is the only realism that exists for Lewis, so much so that when I asked him recently in conversation whether a forthcoming work of his we had been discussing was to be a satire, he corrected me by replying, "They *call* my work satire". In *Paleface* he believed that the

> "tragic sloth, and unwillingness to admit anything unpleasant of the Many, is our main difficulty in proposing a change of orientation for our satire, or indeed in proposing a realistic effort of any sort."

We do not satirize, that is, what we are, so much as what we have been; we tend to smile at the foibles of our past and thus fail to progress. Only the laughter, therefore, lives, for only he knows the perpetual present. Only he can be the true realist and the fully civilized man. For only the individual who sees all satirically, externally, and non-romantically, is, in the final analysis, the "person", or Nature, of the political ideal. So Lewis could write, over a quarter of a century ago:

> "What I shall especially neglect is to analyse the artificial character of this puritanical gloom, settling in a dense political smoke-screen about us, gushed from both official and unofficial reservoirs. I shall confine myself to remarking that the person who meets all these sham glooms with an anguished *De Profundis,* in-instead of a laugh (however unpleasant), is scarcely wise, though he may be good."

Notes

[1] The last part of *The Writer of the Absolute* deals with the work of George Orwell, whose language Wyndham Lewis rather naturally finds pedestrian and his ideas insipid. This provoked an attack from the pen of V. S. Prichett in *The New York Times* recently. Interestingly, Orwell is the only writer—with the possible exception of Gertrude Stein—attacked by Wyndham Lewis both for his writing *and* for his influence. It must be remembered that in all his attacks on leading writers of his day Lewis nearly always accords considerable significance and executive skill; *cp.* "Ernest Hemingway is a very considerable artist in prose fiction," Joyce is "a writer of great importance," Lawrence is "one of the most justly celebrated of English novelists." Their work as diagnostic of our civilization is what he criticises. Mr. Grigson does not make this quite clear in his sympathetic little study, *A Master of Our Time.*

Hugh Kenner (essay date 1954)

SOURCE: "Tarr into Cantelman," in *Wyndham Lewis,* New Directions, 1954, pp. 49-57.

[*In the following excerpt, Kenner contends that the protagonist of Lewis's short story "Cantelman's Spring-Mate" is a fusion of two characters, Tarr and Kreisler, from his novel* Tarr, *and embodies Lewis's interest in the interrelated conflicts between mind and body, logic and emotion, intellect and animal nature.*]

Lewis joined the army as a bombardier, shortly after finishing *Tarr,* and took his problems with him to France. Out of the complex experience of the war came two new efforts at focus: a story called **"Cantelman's Spring-Mate"** and an essay, "Inferior Religions."

"Cantelman's Spring-Mate,"[3] the best of his early stories, which Joyce and Pound admired and on account of which, it is now difficult to believe, an issue of the *Little Review* was banned from the mails three years before the more notorious *affaire Bloom,* presents a new Lewis persona, an amalgam of Tarr's detachment and Kreisler's scornful sensuality. This fusion is conveyed by a new mutation of the Lewis prose, a thick suave pigment, marvelously sensuous, yet crisper and more conscious than anything in *Tarr.* The affairs of the body—specifically, sexual affairs—are consigned, Tarr-fashion, to mechanism; they aren't touched by Kreisler's hysterical sense of doom. At least, Cantelman doesn't think they are. he is free, therefore, to indulge in Kreislerian sensualities, and if only because he doesn't fend off the sensual world with an epigram, his human reality is superior to that of Tarr. He notices the redness of a chance girl's cheeks, the animal fulness of the childbearing hips, "with an eye as innocent as the bird or the beast," and laughs "without shame or pleasure."

Cantelman is an infantry officer on leave; hence his urgent compulsion to bring the world into focus as a Dance of Death. He is half conscious, half animal; and it is human consciousness that has brought the War about. "Had it not been for that unmaterial gift that some bungling or wild hand had bestowed, our sisters and brothers would be no worse than dogs or sheep. . . . Should not the sad human amalgam, all it did, all it willed, all it demanded, be thrown over, for the fake and confusion that it was, and should not such as possessed a greater quantity of that wine of reason retire, metaphorically, to the wilderness, and sit forever in a formal and gentle elation, refusing to be disturbed?"

This is the Tarr component of Cantelman talking: Cantelman is a Tarr whom the exigencies of war have pressed into enforced brotherhood with legions of inferior beings. In his Parisian art world, Tarr moved freely enough not to have thoughts about other people forced on him. They were foolish, no doubt, but their foolishness wasn't dragging *him* toward death. Cantelman's "present occupation, the trampling boots on his feet, the belt that crossed his back, was his sacrifice, his compliment to, the animal." No such sacrifice was exacted of Tarr. Kreisler underwent that for him.

The army hasn't even nonanimal compensations. Cantelman regards his brother-officers with "steady gnawing anger at such a concentration of furious foolishness." He shares their uniform but not their fatuous veneration for their own status as officers and gentlemen. Out of disgust with the human ("the newspapers were the things that stank most on earth, and human beings anywhere were the most ugly and offensive of the brutes because of the confusion caused by their consciousness"), he decides, since no rational oasis offers itself, to retreat to "the madness of natural things" and take a casual spring mate; the creatures of nature in spring are busily copulating, and neither copulation nor death is for the bird or the insect anything but a mechanically violent matter of course. Since an animal occupation is exacted of him, he may as well play the part fully.

> In the narrow road where they got away from the village, Cantelman put his arm around Stella's waist and immediately experienced all the sensations that he had been divining in the creatures around him; the horse, the bird, and the pig. The way in which Stella's hips stood out, the solid blood-heated expanse on which his hand lay, had the amplitude and flatness of a mare. Her lips had at once no practical significance, but only the aesthetic embellishment of a bull-like flower.

He immediately discerns that Nature has trapped his antiro-manticism in romance, that his appetites, instead of re-venging him on the merely human, have engaged him with death. Stella is, like all women, he reflects, "contaminated with Nature's hostile power."

> With a treachery worthy of a Hun, Nature tempted him towards her. He was drugged with delicious appetites. Very well! he would hoist the unseen power with his own petard. He would throw back Stella where she was discharged from, (if it were allowable, now, to change her into a bomb) first having relieved

himself of this humiliating gnawing and yearning in his blood.

So on their third meeting, when she enfolds him "with long arms, full of the contradictory and offending fire of spring," Cantelman to the ceaseless tune of a nightingale turns to "the devouring of his mate." "He felt that he was raiding the bowels of Nature, not fecundating the Aspasias of our flimsy flesh, or assuaging, or competing with, the nightingale." He remains convinced that his gesture of contemptuous possession has outwitted Nature; in the trenches he reads gravely through her frequent letters about an expected child without comment, and fails to perceive that the animal world, in so perpetuating itself, has in fact made use of him.

The theme of this story, that one's willed assessment of the emotional texture of things does not in fact liberate one from their logic, is crucial in Lewis's best fiction. That at least is what Lewis would want the commentator to say. In point of fact, a certain critical charity is involved in calling it the theme of **"Cantelman."** One needs to read very closely and sympathetically to see that though Cantelman twice creates his own poetic world, each time under the impression that he is seeing things as they are, he is all the time unawares playing an insignificant part in a real world inaccessible to human notation. A less finicky reading reveals Lewis's prime energy flowing into Illusion No. 1, Cantelman's "tough" identification of himself with the amatory processes of nature, and an imperfect con-trast between this and Illusion No. 2, Cantelman's "unde-ceived" perception that "the miraculous camouflage of Nature" harbors "everywhere gun-pits and 'nests of death.'" The final sentences, where schematically the screw should turn, sound tacked on: "And when he beat a German's brains out, it was with the same impartial malignity that he had displayed in the English night with his spring-mate. Only he considered there, too, that he was in some way outwitting Nature; he had no adequate realization of the extent to which, evidently, the death of a Hun was to the advantage of the animal world."

Animal life thrives on death and is polarized toward it; hence the more animal people are, the more lethal. The paradox that won't quite dissipate is that one doesn't deal with animals but with "the sad human amalgam." Whether you try to deal with it as rational or as animal, the pres-ence of the other component prevents it from seeming quite real. "Inferior Religions" (published in 1917) is an attempt to focus, in a way useful to the artist, this con-viction of human unreality and the contrary conviction of human significance.

Lewis the artist has been intensely interested in people all his working life ("who would paint a tree when he could paint a man?"); it has been an anomalous, trancelike inter-est, however. It is in part professional necessity that underlies this anomalousness. The painter who responds not to a fashionable itch but to a deep creative necessity contemplates people because he wants to do something with them. They are food for his work. The nature of his work requires him to concentrate on their animal integuments; but the emotions behind this work (assuming that he is not painting them because he is paid to), the emotions which he will seek to incarnate in his rendering of this integument, preoccupy him with their saturnine inscrutability; it is difficult to say whether they are emotions engendered in him by creative pressure alone, or by his response to some mystery concealed in his subjects. So what sort of reality underlies this animal form was a subject for Lewisian speculations from the days when the young painter, fresh from two years at Rugby and two more at the Slade School of Art, was working in Paris and Munich and spending summers in Brittany.

In coastal Brittany, his first lunar world, where the peasant language, still Celtic, bristles with angry sibilants, Lewis first cultivated his novelist's eye. "The Atlantic air, the raw rich visual food of the barbaric environment, the squealing of the pipes, the crashing of the ocean, induced a creative torpor. Mine was now a drowsy sun-baked ferment, watching with delight the great comic effigies which erupted beneath my rather saturnine but astonished gaze." The three stories in the 1909 *English Review* are sketches of these comic effigies; "Inferior Religions" was written to preface a fuller collection of them, which for various reasons did not appear until 1927 (*The Wild Body*). The Breton figures are "intricately moving bobbins"; Brotcotnaz for instance, a fisherman who regularly beats his wife, "is fascinated by one object, one at once another vitality. He bangs up against it wildly at regular intervals, blackens it, contemplates it, moves round it and dreams. All such fascination is religious."

But this activity, while comic, is mechanical: the intricate lurching of the carapace. When you see people in that way, you are ignoring whatever warmth and allure human beings put forth. That is precisely why this way of seeing recommended itself to Lewis as an artistic vision. That is also why he discarded the sensuous part of the **"Cantelman"** prose—a rich enough medium for sexual themes to make D. H. Lawrence sound philosophic—and exaggerated its crispness to the point of mechanism. Instead of, Rubens-like, "borrowing the colour of Life's crude blood, tracing the sprawling and surging of its animal hulks," the artist desiderated by him would recognize that human reality lies far below blood and hulks. But since human realities are inaccessible to inspection, he would remain convinced of the essential *unreality* of the "personality" whose gestures he can depict. It is a screen maneuvered in front of the unspeakable, or in front of a void. Hence the most arresting section of the essay:

> The chemistry of personality (subterranean in a sort of cemetery, whose decompositions are our lives) puffs up in frigid balls, soapy Snowmen, arctic carnival-masks, which we can photograph and fix.

> Upwards from the surface of existence a lurid and dramatic scum oozes and accumulates into the characters we see. The real and tenacious poisons, the sharp forces of vitality, do not socially transpire. . . . Capriciously, however, the froth-forms of these darkly-contrived machines twist and puff in the air, in our legitimate and liveried masquerade.

Though this social world, the artist's material, is unreal, we have now discovered its significance. What it signifies is the degree of tension within.

> You may blow away a man-of-bubbles with a burgundian gust of laughter, but that is not a personality, it is an apparition of no importance. But so much correspondence has it with its original that, if the cadaveric travail beneath it is vigorous and bitter, the dummy or mask will be of a more original grotesqueness.

There are duller lives, however, for whom this chemical imagery of ferment and travail would imply too much. They are the robot ready-mades of his next group of novels (1927-32); ". . . a certain category of spirit that is not quite inanimate and yet not very funny. It consists of those who take, at the Clarkson's[4] situated at the opening of our lives, some conventional Pierrot costume. This is intended to assure them a minimum of strain, of course, and so is a capitulation. In order to evade life we must have recourse to these uniforms, but such a choice leaves nothing but the white and ethereal abstraction of the shadow of laughter."

Impressively written as this is, it really brings us back to *Tarr* again. "The travail within" remains private. There is still no formula for envisaging these persons in interaction. Their social machinery interacts, their mechanical bodies interact, and that is all. The essential person—whatever that may be—is enclosed in his private world. What has happened is that Lewis's way of visualizing his characters one at a time has been elevated into a theory about the way the characters exist. And all this—and so all Lewis's fiction—has its germ in the entranced sun-baked torpor with which Lewis, himself congealed, he has confessed, "in a kind of cryptic immaturity," observed on the Breton shingle the primitive antics of an alien race.

Notes

[3] Reprinted 1953 in the *Little Review Anthology*.

[4] Clarkson's: London theatrical costumer's.

William H. Pritchard (essay date 1968)

SOURCE: "Self Condemned: Last Wills and Testaments," in *Wyndham Lewis,* Twayne Publishers, 1968, pp. 136-65.

[*In the following excerpt from a book-length study of Lewis's life and work, Pritchard considers Lewis's collection of stories* Rotting Hill *an artistic failure, noting that the collection's lack of vitality and imagination mirrors the grey austereness of socialist Britain that was the target of Lewis's reproach in the stories.*]

Before his fiction and criticism of the 1950's began to appear, Lewis published *Rude Assignment,* a last enormous effort to explain, justify, qualify, and assert once more various positions he had taken—or had been accused by others of taking. An invaluable document about his past as revealed in the books he wrote, it is perhaps not to be read through or appreciated as an entity so much as to be consulted for the backgrounds and outlines of controversies and misunderstandings. Ideally, *Rude Assignment* was to clear the air and reveal what a considerable writer (and, incidentally, splendid chap) was Mr. Wyndham Lewis. There is no indication that the book accomplished this objective, but with the publication of *Rotting Hill* in the following year Lewis entered a period when, for the first time since the late 1920's, he was accorded some kind of recognition, however embarrassed or grudging it often sounded. But the relative attention he enjoyed did not affect the character of his books—as contrasted with the way a much greater public recognition encouraged Faulkner's self-congratulatory rhetoric during the same period. Mr. Rose is undeniably right when he suggests that the evidence of the letters shows the Enemy to have mellowed, yet no softening of fiber is to be found in the novels and short stories that are explicitly preoccupied with the human condition in an epoch of more bad times than were dreamt of in the 1930's.

Generalizing about the concerns of this fiction must take account of the fact that it varies greatly within itself as to quality: *Rotting Hill,* and even more so *The Red Priest,* are vastly inferior to *Self Condemned* and *The Human Age*; still, the books are united in that none of them displays technique as an object for admiration. It is instructive to compare the austerely highbrow opening of *Tarr* ("Paris hints of sacrifice. But here we deal with that large dusty facet known to indulgent and congruous kind:") with these sentences from the Foreword to *Rotting Hill*: "If I write about a hill that is rotting, it is because I deplore rot. For the decay of which I write is not romantic decay. . . . If we exist, shabby, ill-fed, loaded with debt (taxed more than any men at any time have ever been), let us recognize that the sole explanation of this is our collective stupidity. . . . The most *recent* wars have entirely altered our lives, that is all we can say." This alteration seems to be of such magnitude as to make stylistic inventiveness inappropriate, an anachronistic survival in the age of socialism and the welfare state; and certainly it is true that the stories in this book exhibit a lessened vitality consonant with the low-grade pain that throbs through most of them.

The book's title was suggested, Lewis tells us coyly in a footnote, by "a friend in Washington" who had gleefully penetrated to what truly underlay his Notting Hill address. The friend, residing in Washington in a rather special sense, was Ezra Pound; the "rot" had in fact invaded Lewis' apartment; and in the story of that title he imagines a snarling carpenter addressing him with axe in hand: "You can keep your plaster and your rotten wood, Mr. Lewis! *You* are the dry rot I'm after." Lewis, who is on stage through most of the volume, finds himself harried by plumbers and carpenters, cultivated by a socialist clergyman who wants to buy one of his pictures (**"The Bishop's Fool"**), and plagued by a devotee of spontaneous child art (**"My Disciple"**) or by an up-to-date undergraduate with strong leftist opinions (**"My Fellow-Traveler to Oxford"**).

Clearly it is difficult to generate much dramatic excitement when the author, in *propria persona,* lounges about receiving visitors or dealing with workmen; so the best parts of these often too relaxed narratives are the conversations about England's postwar experiment and attempted recovery. Their thinness as art is evident in that they do not deepen upon rereading; this remark will not sound like carping when we add that *Rotting Hill* is the first of Lewis' fictions about which it could be made.

Although the stories contain a few bright moments of well-being, their prevailing atmosphere is one of failure. It is often assumed, mistakenly, that *Rotting Hill* is simply a document of Lewis' own contempt and hatred for socialist Britian; this reading can be arrived at only by disregarding much of what happens in the stories and by ignoring the biographical note that very obviously enters them. Lewis' letters reveal that he had staked a good deal on his knowledge, even his hope, that the postwar world would be a new era, though he knew also that to be reborn into it might well be a grueling process, especially as old age came on. In a letter to Sturge Moore, previously quoted, the placid world of Hampstead domesticity was looked back on, but not to the obscuring of future necessities: "Whereas the very scale and intensity of the misery that will threaten every nation afterwards will assure heroic measures of public control, which automatically should end the selfish chaos into which our western society had drifted—I hope I am not too sanguine." Whether or not Lewis was sanguine, the stories in *Rotting Hill* testify that even war and exile could not turn the professional satirist into a revolutionary enthusiast. What they did instead was take most of the joy out of the satire, and replace it with a combination of annoyance and self-reproach; it is as if the carpenter had really said to Mr. Lewis that *"You* are the dry rot I'm after."

In only one story, **"Time the Tiger,"** does Lewis manage to objectify his conflicting responses to the new society. It is in the heart of the story's hero, Mark Robins, that the low-grade pain is concentrated; and his heart is in tune with the London morning: "The sky was a constipated mass, yellowed by the fog, suspending over a city awaiting the Deluge." The pain finds ample correlation in the most unpromising of materials for the encouragement of anything but low-grade action: shirts with too small buttonholes, too short shoelaces, vulgarly colored postwar tweeds, uncuttable bread, a tea made by combining "alleged Darjeeling" with "pseudo Ceylon," and, for breakfast, something called Strawberry Jam "recognized by housewives as mainly pectin / or carrot pulp, given appropriate colour of course and flavor to match."

Mark's best friend, Charles Dyat, has decided not to cooperate with the new austerity but to make use of whatever bribes and other shady devices can improve creature comforts. To Charles' cynicism, Mark responds with an earnest defense of the Labour government, and eventually makes the point that he is not a convert to socialism but rather has been reborn a socialist since the world in which he and Charles grew up no longer exists. The seeing of an Existententialist film *Time the Tiger* is the occasion for an extension of the argument about immediate effects and harassments into the philosophic; it is Mark's tendency to replace the image of time as devourer with a less melodramatic one—that of time as a firework fizzling away. And indeed, at dinner with Charles' sister Ida, who is a romantic image of timelessness for Mark, things fizzle away: the Dyats insult Bevan and the socialists; Mark is shocked and annoyed; the dinner and the relationship fall to pieces.

Nothing would have been easier, especially considering what Lewis' fiction has made of previous men of commitment, to expose Mark's naïveté and have him learn something about the incommensurability of politics and the individual. But such an easy score is no longer open to Lewis—at least in this story. The hero's depression is a product of trying to hold the idea of a socialist experiment in his mind while he spoons out strawberry pectin or whatever it may be; as such, the repression cannot be relieved by instant fictional solutions. Or to use another image, the rot is there; and no reason presents itself for its not remaining there in the foreseeable future.

Rotting Hill is the greyest and least artistic of Lewis' fictions because it virtually admits that the imagination is powerless and irrelevant in the new world to which men have been reborn. Yet, and this is the particular fascination and difficulty in dealing with such a work, this collection of stories is in many ways a more admirable and valuable book to have appeared in 1951 than the productions of writers who made the transition from an old world to a new one with effortless smoothness. The limitations of most of these stories are obvious enough; their virtue as a collection consists in the way they unfailingly place us in a material world—England as a recuperating patient who may be doctored to death by well-meaning socialist physicians.

More tentatively, the book is also Lewis' most candid and dispirited questioning of the efficacy of imaginative style in such a world. If the artist is really on the way out, then perhaps this most important of fizzles should be registered by at least one writer. There is a fanciful ending to the final story in the book titled **"The Rot-Camp,"** where the "I," Wyndham Lewis, encounters in a suitably fantastic way first Roy Campbell and his retinue of bullbaiting aficionados, then Augustus John out hunting once more for gypsies, and finally Britannia herself looking shriveled and wasted, begging for alms. The author responds by dropping a lucky three-penny bit into her mug—which appears to contain a phony dollar bill: "In a cracked wheeze she sang 'Land of Hope and Glory.' I must confess that this last apparition, and its vulgar little song, rather depressed me." That Lewis then proceeded to disregard his own prediction of the extinction of art and to transform his depression into something else is the really marvelous story of the novels that follow *Rotting Hill.*

Timothy Materer (essay date 1970)

SOURCE: "The Short Stories of Wyndham Lewis," in *Studies in Short Fiction,* Vol. 7, No. 3, Fall, 1970, pp. 615-24.

[*In the following essay, Materer discusses Lewis's comic theory and sense of irony in* The Wild Body, *arguing that the narrator of the sequence of stories, Ker-Orr, like Lewis, views the world from a detached but not disinterested perspective and sees comedy as springing from the discrepancies between human beings' physical bodies and intellectual aspirations.*]

The short stories of Wyndham Lewis were enthusiastically received by critics like Ezra Pound and T. S. Eliot when they were first published and have earned renewed praise in the past few years. As an editor of *The Little Review,* Pound, supported by Eliot in *The Egoist,* championed Lewis' early writings and welcomed him as a fellow revolutionary.[1] In recent years, V. S. Pritchett and John Holloway in England, as well as Raymond Rosenthal in America, have praised the restrained, sardonic style of Lewis' collection of stories, **The Wild Body**.[2]

Nevertheless, while satires like *The Apes of God,* novels like *Self-Condemned,* and criticism like *Time and Western Man* and *The Lion and the Fox,* are reissued in paperbacks, Lewis' stories appear only as isolated selections.[3] Since his stories suffer more than most short pieces from being read apart from the original collection, the unavailability of **The Wild Body** is doubly unfortunate. Like Joyce's *Dubliners,* Lewis' stories are more a sequence than a collection. Narrated by a single character, the tales develop a richly comic thesis about the peasant life that they explore.

All but one of the stories have a Breton setting. They grow out of Lewis' experiences, a decade before he founded a school of abstract painters in London, as he travelled and painted in Brittany.[4] Like Gauguin some twenty years before, Lewis left his Paris studio to find subjects more spontaneous and colorful among the Breton landscape. The influence of Lewis' painter's eye, we will see, animates every page with visual details.

Though not a painter, Ker-Orr, the narrator of **The Wild Body,** is an adventurous, self-sufficient wanderer like Lewis himself. He is a gay picaro who moves impulsively from inn to inn, where he meets characters as grotesque and vivid as any Henry Fielding found on the London road. Ker-Orr introduces himself, in the words of the title of the first story, as **"A Soldier of Humour."**[5] Though an extremely violent man, he says that he makes one important concession to civilization: "where formerly I would fly at throats, I now howl with laughter": "The result is that I am *never* serious about anything. I simply cannot help converting everything into burlesque patterns. And I admit that I am disposed to forget that people are real—that they are, that is, not subjective patterns belonging specifically to me, in the course of this joke-life." (p. 4)

So obsessive is his comic sense that his own large, unwieldy body seems ridiculous to him: "This forked, strange-scented, blondskinned gut-bag, with its two bright rolling marbles with which it sees, bull's-eyes full of mockery and madness, is my stalking horse. I hang somewhere in its midst operating it with detachment." (p. 5)

This self-description explains what Lewis means by a "wild body." The humor, as well as the pathos, of man's nature is that his body is continually embarrassing his mind. This theory comes from Bergson, whose lectures Lewis attended at the Collège de France. In "Laughter," Bergson asks, "Why do we laugh at a public speaker who sneezes just at the most pathetic moment of his speech?"[6] His answer elucidates much of Lewis' comic technique. If our attention is drawn, Bergson writes, to our physicality, it can make our intellectual or spiritual aspirations seem ridiculous—much as an inappropriate suit of clothes can make our body seem ridiculous. Such an emphasis on our material qualities suggests, he continues, that "the body is no more in our eyes than a heavy and cumbersome vesture, a kind of irksome ballast which holds down to the earth a soul eager to rise aloft. . . . inert matter dumped down upon living energy. The impression of the comic will be produced as soon as we have a clear apprehension of this putting the one on the other."[7]

The influence of this comic theory is increasingly evident in the first three stories of *The Wild Body.* In **"A Soldier of Humour,"** Ker-Orr meets a Frenchman who speaks bad English with, however, a recognizably American accent. Rosenthal describes the story as a "prophetic farce— prophetic of the waves of Americanization which, some decades later, were to inundate Europe. . . ."[8] The Frenchman, Valmore, has the *idée fixe* that he appears to everyone as an authentic American. But when Ker-Orr casually punctures his pretensions to Yankeeism, he makes an influential enemy who is able to turn the whole of a Spanish town, where Ker-Orr hopes to make an extended stay, against him. To the townspeople, Valmore is indeed an American; to them, Americanism is simply a function of Valmore's enormous wealth.

But Valmore's very appearance contradicts his claims to Americanism, which he can never forgive Ker-Orr for noticing. At first, however, his incongruous appearance is a riddle to Ker-Orr:

> He was dressed with sombre floridity. In his dark purple-slate suit with thin crimson lines, in his dark red hat-band, in his rose-buff tie, swarming with cerulean fire-flies, in his stormily flowered waistcoat, you felt that his taste for the violent and sumptuous had everywhere struggled to assert itself, and everywhere been overcome. But by what? That was the important secret of this man's entire machine. . . . Had I been of a superior penetration the cut of his clothes in their awkward amplitude, with their unorthodox shoulders and belling hams, might have given me the key. (pp. 15-16)

The key of course is that he is dressed in his own deluded version of how an affluent American would dress. As in Bergson's theory of laughter, unrealistic pretensions lead to a rigid, mechanical approach to life. The reference to the "secret" (*idée fixe* that causes his rigidity) of Valmore's "entire machine" recalls Bergson's suggestion that "Something mechanical encrusted on the living" is the essence of the ridiculous.[9]

Though his dress provides the clue, his face is the real evidence; it is a standing embarrassment to his attempt to appear as his ideal of a boyish, open-handed American:

> His straw hat served rather as a heavy coffee-colored nimbus—such as some browningesque florentine painter, the worse for drink, might have placed behind the head of his saint. Above his veined and redly sunburnt forehead gushed a ragged volute of dry black hair. His face had the vexed wolfish look of the grimy commercial Midi . . . it had been niggled at and worked all over . . . by a hundred little blows and chisellings of fretful passion. (p. 15)

The story develops leisurely as Lewis shows how Valmore's physical appearance betrays his pretensions.

But **"A Soldier of Humour,"** like most of the stories in *The Wild Body,* avoids the static quality extensive description can produce. The story moves steadily toward an ironic reversal. As Ker-Orr is preparing to leave the town, Valmore has made unlivable for him, he meets three old American friends. Large, loud, vulgar, and wearing the authentically baggy clothes Valmore affects, they are true Americans. Under Ker-Orr's direction, they win the confidence of their "fellow American" and then humiliate him by introducing Ker-Orr as a highly esteemed friend. The irony is that Valmore's rigidity has forced him to accept any American opinion as oracular and thus must welcome the man he most despises. The "soldier of humour" wins his first skirmish.

A similar reversal and concentration on external appearance emerge in the next story, the ironically titled **"Beau Séjour."** The setting of the story might have come from *Joseph Andrews,* but the characters bear the mark of Dostoyevsky (an early work like "The Landlady") as well as of Fielding. The main character is a Russian exile named Zoborov, a morose wandering-student type who has long ago stopped paying rent, thanks to the reluctance of the weak-willed innkeeper, Mademoiselle Péronnette, to throw him out. But Zoborov is an essential peacemaker in the quarrels of Péronnette with Carl, a huge German who became "engaged" to the landlady after she lent him a large sum of money. She is disgusted with Carl because he seduces the maids; Carl is disgusted with her because she will no longer lend him money. Ker-Orr does not see all this at first, but he obtains what he dryly calls an "insight . . . into the inner social workings" of the inn one night when he hears an uproar outside his room, which is across from Mademoiselle Péronnette's. As he looks across to her door, he sees a

> long white black-topped lathe . . . contorted against it. It was [Carl] now quite naked. With his bare arms and shoulders he strained against the wood. . . . His eyes blazed above a black-bearded grin, with clownesque incandescence. He was black and white, dazzling skin and black patches of hair alternating. His thin knees were unsteady . . . his grin of protest wandered in an aimless circle, with me for centre. . . .

The floorboards groaned to the right, a stumpy figure in stocking feet, but otherwise clothed, emerged in assyrian profile, in a wrestling attitude, flat hands extended, rolling with professional hesitation, with factitious rudeness seized the emaciated nudity of the german giant beneath the waist, then disappeared with him bodily down the passage to the left. It was Zoborov in action. (pp. 72-73)

Though he does not pay his board, clearly Zoborov earns his keep.

Ker-Orr takes these goings-on with a droll detachment, as when he strolls into the kitchen one day: "but noticing that Carl was holding Mademoiselle Péronnette by the throat, and was banging her head on the kitchen table, I withdrew" (p. 76). These little domestic tensions explode one night when Péronnette is quietly mending socks, Ker-Orr is reading, and some of the parasitic lodgers, who, like Zoborov, are supposedly penniless Russian exiles, are loitering about. Carl suddenly appears and empties a revolver at Péronnette. Zoborov gets the blame for this shoot-up. The wild firing misses the innkeeper and wounds slightly one of the parasites; when Zoborov tires to help the wounded man, Péronnette denounces him as a troublemaker, and an emotional reconciliation with Carl takes place as they agree to use the peacemaking Russian as a scapegoat. A chaotic party is held to celebrate the new accord and to announce that Carl and Péronnette are now partners in the inn. But still another battle explodes that night. Ker-Orr leaves early next morning to avoid beholding the no doubt absurd outcome of another night of rushing forms in the corridor and wildly slamming doors.

The rebuke Zoborov receives at the hands of the "lovers" is an amusing comment on the thankless role of the peacemaker. But the dénouement of the story gives the tale a further twist. Ker-Orr returns a year later to the town to find Zoborov luxuriously dressed, with obsequious peasants crowding around him. As the Russian ostentatiously orders drinks, he explains that when the new partnership of Péronnette and Carl bankrupted the inn, he—Zoborov—simply bought it. Now, of course, it seems a foolish assumption to think, simply because he did not pay his board, that Zoborov had no money. What, Ker-Orr asks, happened to the other Russian parasites? The affluent Russian owner of a thriving Breton inn replies, "'Oh, I've cleared all that rubbish out! . . . I only have three Russians there now. I kept them on, poor devils. They help me with the work. Two act as valets. I know what Russians are, being one myself, you see! I have no wish to go bankrupt like Mademoiselle Péronnette.'" (pp. 106-107)

Lewis' descriptive prose and painter's eye are at their best in the third story, **"Bestre."** The plot of this story is even less complex than **"A Soldier of Humour."** It merely concerns the way another Breton innkeeper, Bestre, matches insulting grimaces with a Parisian painter. The gaiety and power of the story is in the verbal portraits of Bestre. All these descriptions illustrate the innkeeper's power to intimidate his enemies by the power of his piercing glances, which have an instinctive feeling "for his prey's most morbid spot; for an old wound; for a lurking vanity. . . . On a physical blemish he turns a scornful and careless

rain like a garden hose" (pp. 127-128). Because of this ability, Ker-Orr tells us, "I learnt a great deal from Bestre. He is one of my masters" (p. 129). What Ker-Orr learns is the trick of spotting the revealing details in a person's physical appearance, like Valmore's strange dress and wolfish face, and of using them to reveal his character. Such a satiric technique came naturally to Lewis, who later painted the great character studies of Ezra Pound and Edith Sitwell that now hang in the Tate Gallery.

Ker-Orr satirizes Bestre's petty squabbles by showing how a rigid, mechanized quality characterizes his grimaces. "With a flexible imbrication reminiscent of a shutter-lipped ape, a bud of tongue still showing, he shot the latch of his upper lip down in front of the nether one, and depressed the interior extremities of his eyebrows sharply from their quizzing perch" (p. 115). Mechanical and animal images dehumanize Bestre, making him, as he lumbers about pursuing his petty schemes, a comical grotesque. Yet it is just his grotesque vulgarity that gives his insulting glances their force:

> His very large eyeballs, the small saffron ocellation in their centre, the tiny spot through which light entered the obese wilderness of his body; his bronzed bovine arms, swollen handles for a variety of indolent little ingenuities; his inflated digestive case, lent their combined expressiveness . . . with every tart and biting condiment that eye-fluid, flaunting of fatness . . . could provide. . . . his brown arms were for the moment genitals, snakes in one massive twist beneath his mammillary slabs, gently riding on a pancreatic swell, each hair on his oil-bearing skin contributing its message of porcine affront. (pp. 116-117)

The description is devastating, but it raises the objection that Ker-Orr has descended to Bestre's level. This objection brings us to the one shortcoming in *The Wild Body*. The object of Lewis' satiric descriptions, as well as Ker-Orr's motives, seems too petty to motivate such massive attacks. Of course even a great satire like Pope's *The Dunciad* is open to such an objection. But the problem is a real one here because Ker-Orr satirizes Bestre for the very kind of petty activities that the narrator, as with Valmore, indulges in himself. Ker-Orr even admits, as he meditates on Bestre's activities, that in his descriptions he takes "a human species, as an entomologist would take a Distoma or a Narbonne Lycosa, to study" (p. 120). In a story called **"Franciscan Adventures,"** this cold, pseudo-scientific attitude toward people becomes offensive because it makes Ker-Orr seem haughty and condescending toward the itinerant minstrel he describes. Lewis is aware of this problem, as when he has Ker-Orr admit in a passage quoted earlier, "that I am disposed to forget that people are real. . . ." But the admission implies no guilt, and it does nothing to alter the false note this attitude strikes in **"Bestre,"** nor the chilling, contemptuous tone that spoils **"Franciscan Adventures."**

The three remaining stories fortunately avoid this condescending tone and reveal the range and power of Lewis' irony. V. S. Pritchett (like Rosenthal, impressed with Lewis' "prophetic" qualities) thinks that *The Wild Body* stories are "prophetic of contemporary black comedy. . . ."[10] "Brotcotnaz" best illustrates this sardonic comedy, and another, **"The Cornac and His Wife,"** shows how Lewis anticipated the black humorists. The remaining story, **"The Death of the Ankou,"** demonstrates how smoothly and powerfully Lewis' comic theme modulates into a tragic one.

"The Cornac and His Wife" describes a troup of *saltim-banques,* itinerant circus performers who earn a meager existence by performing pathetic gymnastic and comedy acts before the Breton peasants. This story also reveals a pictorial inspiration; these unfortunate *saltimbanques* recur in a series of pictures Picasso painted around 1905. Like Picasso, Lewis stresses the bewildered suffering of these jugglers and clowns: the supressed ferocity of the father, or "showman," toward the tight-fisted audiences, the bedraggled mother, the mournful children. But Lewis is more interested in how they defy their fate than in how they suffer it.

Their violent sense of humor helps explain the *saltim-banques'* endurance. The showman's comedy routine with the clown, in which he responds with heavy blows to the clown's impertinent witticisms, pleases the rough peasants, whose "laughter is sharp and mirthless and designed usually to wound" (p. 159). As Ker-Orr explained earlier, laughter is an expression of violence. But such violent laughter is also an expression of defiance. The showman understands this: "He knows the brutal *frisson* in contact with danger that draws the laughter up from the deepest bowel in a refreshing unearthly gush. He knows why he and the clown are always black and blue, his children performing dogs. . . . He knows Fate, since he serves it, better than even the peasant." (p. 160)

This conception of a defiant laughter, inspired probably by Nietzsche's Zarathustra, allows Lewis to find humor in perverse and bitterly ironic situations. In **"Brotcotnaz,"** the ironic reversal characteristic of these stories is a violent and even gruesome one. Brotcotnaz's wife, Julie, makes her hard life as a poor fisherman's wife and keeper of a rarely used inn bearable by secret brandy tippling. Despite her attempt to seem prim and respectable, the "many tiny strongholds of eruptive red" in her face betray her secret. Her husband, also a drinker, is suspected of having killed his first wife through a series of beatings, and he seems headed toward the same end with his present wife. But when he drinks, he's violent—that's his character; and her character will not allow her to complain—after all, she is his wife. With this fatalistic detachment, which in Ker-Orr's mind is akin to comic detachment, their relationship thrives: "The morning after a beating—Julie lying seriously battered upon their bed, or sitting rocking herself quietly . . . her head a turban of bandages, he noiselessly attends to her wants, enquires how she feels, and applies remedies. . . . He addresses her on all occasions with a compassionate gentleness. . . . They are resigned, but none the less they remember the cross they have to bear" (pp. 219-220). As things are going, surely one day he will kill her; but at the same time, he will sincerely mourn her. His reactions are too simple to seem sinister. He walks

with "an easy, dainty, and rapid tread, with a coquettishly supple giving of the knees at each step, and a gentle debonair oscillation of the massive head" (p. 214), as if he were a marionette or mechanical man. In other words, he is a "wild body."

The resolution of this conflict comes swiftly. Three weeks after Ker-Orr's initial stop at the inn, he returns to find an unaccustomed stir around it. Julie must have had a last and fatal fight with Brotcotnaz, Ker-Orr assumes. When he enters, he expects to see Brotcotnaz dominating the crowd, grandly receiving condolences, eyeing the available women for a third spouse and a new dowry. Instead, it is Julie, alive, who dominates the crowd, while a crestfallen Brotcotnaz sulks in a dark corner. Julie is displaying the damaged arm and leg she received from a heavy cart. But this dreadful accident is not what depresses Brotcotnaz. Even Julie, in fact, is secretly pleased by this painful misfortune. For Brotcotnaz now realizes that his wife is no longer fair game for his beatings; if she loses her limbs, he "could scarcely proceed to destruction of the trunk only. It was not difficult at least to appreciate the sort of problem that might present itself' (p. 226). Julie immediately grasps the opportunity she now has to dominate her brutal but childish husband. The change is clear already as she accepts the brandy Ker-Orr offers her: "She took the drink I gave her, and raised it almost with fire to her lips. After the removal of her arm, and possibly a foot, I realized that she would be more difficult to get on with than formerly. The bottle of eau-de-vie would remain no doubt in full view, to hand, on the counter, and Brotcotnaz would be unable to lay a finger on her: in all likelihood she meant that arm to come off." (pp. 230-231)

The extreme irony of Brotcotnaz's lament that he can no longer beat his wife, as well as the undertone of violence, supports Pritchett's opinion that Lewis anticipated the Black Humorists. Lewis' tone, however, is far more controlled than that of writers like Heller, Vonnegut, or Pynchon. The black humorists agonize over what they portray; an undertone, not only of violence, but of fear and loathing makes their comedy "black." Lewis' distinction, on the other hand, is that he retains the detached, traditional tone of comedy. Here again he is a follower of Bergson's theories. The "wild bodies" he describes are too innocent to arouse fear, and Ker-Orr's amused appreciation of all he sees controls the reader's reactions. Like the old *saltimbanque,* he knows that what is fated can be accepted with a defiant laugh or an ironic grimace.

But in the final story we will examine, Ker-Orr finds it impossible to laugh. Irony can lead either to laughter or to fear and pity. It leads to the tragic in **"The Death of the Ankou"** because Ker-Orr and, by implication, all of us are brushed too closely by fate. The story begins again in a Pardon, or Breton café, where the book of local folklore Ker-Orr is reading leads him to a startling merger of his imaginative and real life. He reads of the blind Breton death god, or Ankou, and how "the gaunt creature despatched from the country of death traversed at night the Breton region. The peasant, late on the high-road . . . felt around him suddenly the atmosphere of the shades, a strange cold penetrated his tissues, authentic portions of the *Néant* pushed in like icy wedges within the mild air of the fields and isolated him from Earth, while rapid hands seized his shoulders from behind" (p. 166). As he raises his eyes from the book and looks out into the dim, smoky room,

> With revulsed and misty eyes almost in front of me, an imperious figure, apparently armed with a club, was forcing its way insolently forward . . . its head up, an eloquently moving mouth hung in the air. . . . It forced rudely aside everything in its path. . . . He passed my table and I saw a small, highly coloured face . . . the terrible perquisite of the blind was there in the staring, milky eyeballs. . . . Where he had come was compact with an emotional medium emitted by me . . . this overweening intruder might have been marching through my mind with his taunt convulsive step, club in hand. . . . The impression was so strong that I felt for the moment that I had met the death-god. (pp. 172-173)

Ker-Orr gets to know the catalyst of his vision, in reality a blind beggar called Ludo; and he turns to a powerful analysis of how the blind must relate to their unseen world.[11] But even though he is now familiar with Ludo, he tells us, "I still experienced a faint reflection of my first impression, when he was the death-god." (p. 178)

On his final visit to the blind peasant, he finds Ludo ailing. Ker-Orr remarks, "'Perhaps you've met the Ankou.' I said this thoughtlessly, probably because I had intended to ask him if he had ever heard of the Ankou" (p. 180). Ludo behaves like a frightened child when he hears this thoughless but casual remark, cuts off the conversation, and moves back into the cave where he lives. Ker-Orr is puzzled, but reflects that "Perhaps I had put myself in the position of the Ankou . . . unseen as I was, a foreigner, and, so, ultimately dangerous" (p. 182). With this subtle reversal of roles, the story reaches a restrained and ominous climax. The dénouement is contained in the single sentence that concludes the story: "Later that summer the fisherman that I had been with at the Pardon told me that Ludo was dead." (p. 183)

The death-god passed Ker-Orr by and, fixed instead on the object of his original fear. The power of the story lies in what Lewis does not say. No one knows for sure what Ludo dies of. He, like any of us, could have been felled by a random stroke from the death-god; we are as blind to fate as Ludo was to the world around him.

"Brotcotnaz" and **"The Death of the Ankou"** reveal the quality that distinguishes *The Wild Body*: a detached but not disinterested tone. In Ker-Orr, Lewis creates a persona who is interested in everything, but who lets nothing surprise him or throw him off balance. He accepts the world with an ironic laugh or shudder, but sees it always in a clear, cold light.

Notes

[1] See Pound's editorial in *The Little Review*, IV (May 1917), 17-18; Eliot, "Tarr," *The Egoist*, V (September 1918), 106.

[2] Pritchett, "Public Eye," *New Statesman*, LXXIV (1967), 119-120; Holloway, "The Literary Scene," in *The Modern Age*, Boris Ford, ed. (London, 1964), p. 76; Rosenthal, ed., *A Soldier of Humor and Selected Writings* (New York, 1966), pp. 19-21. Lewis first published *The Wild Body* in 1927 (London: Chatto and Windus). The two stories that are printed in a separate section at the end of *The Wild Body* and which do not develop the "wild body" theme are not considered here.

[3] Rosenthal's anthology, *A Soldier of Humor*, reprints two of *The Wild Body* stories, "A Soldier of Humour" and "The Death of the Ankou," as well as the best of Lewis' war stories, "Cantelman's Spring Mate," and two stories from his 1951 collection, *Rotting Hill*. Two of Lewis' war stories are reprinted as an appendix to the new edition of his World War I autobiography, *Blasting and Bombardiering* (Berkeley, California, 1967).

[4] The movement was influenced by Futurism and Cubism and was called (at Pound's suggestion) Vorticism; it was publicized through Lewis' magazine *BLAST* (1914-1915). Though it was basically a school of painters, Vorticism had a literary contingent as well, and both Pound and Eliot published in *BLAST*.

[5] When Lewis first published this story in *The Little Review*, he was actually serving with the British forces during World War I. His experiences at the front lines in France profoundly affected the conception of laughter Lewis develops in his stories. See *Blasting and Bombardiering*.

[6] Henri Bergson, "Laughter," in *Comedy*, Wylie Sypher, ed. (Garden City, New York, 1956), p. 93.

[7] *Ibid.*, pp. 92-93.

[8] *A Soldier of Honor and Selected Writings*, p. 19.

[9] "Laughter," p. 84.

[10] "Public Eye," p. 119.

[11] These speculations on blindness seem especially powerful when one knows that Lewis was to become totally blind in 1951.

C. J. Fox and Robert T. Chapman (essay date 1973)

SOURCE: Introduction to *Unlucky for Pringle: Unpublished and Other Stories*, Vision Press, 1973, pp. 7-17.

[*In the following introduction to a collection of Lewis's short fiction, Fox and Chapman provide an overview of Lewis's work in the genre and touch on some major elements that mark his short stories, including their peculiar sense of dark comedy; rootedness in the politics and culture of the day; unsympathetic portrayal of women; interest in violence; and recurrence of the figure of the Impostor.*]

Recalling the early stages of his career, Wyndham Lewis wrote in 1935 that "the short story, as we call it, was the first literary form with which I became familiar . . . The 'short story' was the crystallization *of what I had to keep out of my consciousness while painting.*"[1] The latter part of this statement would seem to relegate Lewis's short fiction to a disproportionately secondary place in his *œuvre*. For, from the beginning of his 45 years as a visual and literary artist, Lewis was quite prolific as a fiction writer and, with the exception of the later 1920s and the 1930s, the short story figures prominently among his works in this field.

Lewis's first published stories appeared in 1909—a year after Arnold Bennett's *The Old Wives' Tale* and a year before H. G. Wells's *Tono-Bungay*—and the last stories published during his lifetime were contemporary with Kingsley Amis's *Lucky Jim* and Lawrence Durrell's *Justine*. It is not only that the time-span of Lewis's creative life makes it difficult to place him as a writer. The diversity of his fiction is also formidable, ranging as it does from *The Apes of God* (which, he wrote, paid unprecedented attention to "the externals—the *shell,* the *pelt,* the physical behaviour of people"),[2] to *Self Condemned* which, in its intensely subjective analysis of self-destruction, stands comparison as a tragic novel with Malcolm Lowry's *Under the Volcano.* Dostoyevsky, Flaubert, Gogol for the early writing; Dryden, Pope, Smollett, Swift for the satires; the Classics for *The Human Age*—few critics attempting to place Lewis into a literary tradition look to his contemporaries. In one of the earliest reviews of Lewis's writing, Rebecca West suggested Dostoyevsky's influence on *Tarr,* and I. A. Richards, talking about *The Childermass* more than 40 years later, invoked Dante, Plato and Fielding. Like D. H. Lawrence, Lewis had no time for "novels that were copies of other novels," and both writers—in their very different ways—used fiction to embody and explore their predilections. Such formal beauties as *integritas, consonantia, claritas*—preoccupations of Joyce as well as of Stephen Dedalus—were not primary considerations with Lewis. That art is *"about* something" was axiomatic for him and, as he wrote in *Men Without Art* (1934): "Implicit in the serious work of art will be found politics, theology, philosophy—in brief all the great intellectual departments of the human consciousness."[3] Lewis's concept and practice of the fiction of ideas is nearer to the Augustan satirists, in its assertion of positives by the savagely indignant destruction of falsity, than to the varying degrees of Peacockian sophistication in contemporaries such as Norman Douglas, Evelyn Waugh and Aldous Huxley. It is much easier to say which writers Lewis is *not* like than to suggest resemblances and, in literature as well as in painting, it is as a unique phenomenon that he must finally be considered.

The present volume gathers together works of short fiction by Lewis which have remained unpublished or, having been scattered through little magazines between 1910 and 1956, were never collected for purposes of a single book. Naturally of special interest are the previously unpublished stories, most of which were apparently destined for inclusion in a volume to have been entitled *The Two Captains.* The bibliography of E. W. F. Tomlin's British Council pamphlet on Lewis (1955) mentioned an impending book of short fiction, but this book never materialized.

In any event, the stories published here for the first time are part of a 1930s reworking of **"The Crowd Master,"** initially published in *Blast* No. 2 (1915); **"Junior," "The Two Captains"** and **"The Man Who Was Unlucky With Women"** (all from the 1950s); and three tales written by Lewis during his 1940 stay in Sag Harbor, New York— **"The Yachting Cap," "The Weeping Man"** and **"Children of the Great."** Not included in this volume are any of the stories in the two collections of short fiction Lewis published in his lifetime, *The Wild Body* (1927) and *Rotting Hill* (1951).

All of the previously unpublished stories are not of equal literary merit. Nor are they generally on a par with the stories Lewis managed to have published during his lifetime. Yet, when grouped together with other unfamiliar Lewis material, even marginal works by the author of *Tarr* and *The Wild Body* take on added interest sufficient to warrant publication, especially if an effort is made to show how such stories blend with the general corpus of his fiction. Juxtaposed in this way with what turn out to be related works, they also enlarge the understanding of Lewis's literary aims. It should be remembered, however, that Lewis habitually did considerable revision on his writings in the "proof" stage of their production. Since none of the previously-unpublished stories apparently went to press, they lack that extra "finish" characteristic of The Enemy at his proof-slashing best. There have been additional difficulties about the text of at least some of this heretofore-unprinted material. The final typescripts of the stories seemingly to have been published in the 1950s— those of **"The Two Captains," "Junior," "The Weeping Man," "The Yachting Cap," "The Man Who Was Unlucky With Women"** and **"Children of the Great"**—were unavailable. But good carbon copies or other duplicates were found. In the case of **"The Two Captains,"** a holograph mostly in Lewis's hand helped the editors rectify a number of imperfections, mainly dropped commas or simple typographical errors, in the carbon-copy typescript. Any lapse of a more elaborate order is signified accordingly.

The book called *Rotting Hill* was made up partly of sketches from life in the Notting Hill area of London during the post World War II "Crippsean Ice Age" with its pervasive physical and metaphorical "rot." The stories in this present book, on the other hand, are notable for, among other things, the absence of the political preoccupation prevalent in *Rotting Hill.* But obviously there are similarities, quite apart from the drive and sparkle of Lewis's prose at its best. The *Rotting Hill* ambience of the bedraggled Britain of the 1940s obtrudes somewhat in **"The Two Captains,"** and Lewis's life-long fascination with rooms and flats as microcosms is as apparent in **"Unlucky for Pringle"** as it is in the *Rotting Hill* sketch called **"The Rot."** The historian Paul Eldred in another of the *Rotting Hill* tales is as much a "celebrated ruin" exploiting forever afterwards the temporary visitation of a muse as is Thaddeus Trunk in **"Doppelgänger"** (1954), a story included here.

But the stories in this new collection are more closely related to *The Wild Body* than to *Rotting Hill* if only because, as a whole, they are in the category of what might be called pure fiction as opposed to semi-fictional reportage. *The Wild Body,* a modern classic, is a book which, like *Rotting Hill,* brings together works sharing a common theme. In the former collection that theme is the primitive human breed, like "big, obsessed, sun-drunk insects,"[4] which fascinated Lewis as painter and writer in his early years. As such, *The Wild Body*'s inspiration comes closer than that of most of his other books to drawing on themes simultaneously at work in his pictures. Lewis's pre-World War I drawings abound in strange, ritualized figures. But Bestre and Brotcotnaz in *The Wild Body* are as much "executants of a *single* ritual" (the phrase is Walter Michel's) as are the figures in such drawings as "Indian Dance" and "Courtship" (1912). "Their enormous vitality," writes Michel, "is in the service of an obsession."[5] Lewis observed humanity like an anthropologist scrutinizing a newly-discovered species of homunculae, at once unbelieving and delighted by their absurdity. These wild bodies, driven either by demoniacal *idées fixes* or the vagaries of a perverse autonomic system, cavort over the canvases and through the stories of the young Lewis.

In *The Wild Body* Lewis defined his theory of the comic as rooted in "observations of a *thing* behaving like a person."[6] This is an idea to which Lewis adhered throughout his career and it is evident in most of the stories here collected. Polderdick (**"The King of the Trenches"**), for instance, is as mechanical as his "flying pigs," and Kipe in **"The Yachting Cap"** is a tatterdemalion Canute as elemental as the ocean he defies. Similarly, Monsieur Chalaran in **"Unlucky for Pringle,"** with his "animal-like selfishness and self-absorption," is very much in this Lewis tradition and that story as a whole is a tale merely transposed from the French or Spanish settings of the original *Wild Body* universe into an English scheme of things. **"Unlucky for Pringle"** has been chosen as the title story of this collection because, though written while Lewis was still in his twenties, it provides a precocious demonstration of virtually all his gifts and attitudes as a writer. With hindsight, the critic might see in this story an uncannily accurate premonition of the fate that awaited Lewis in the subsequent five decades of Anglo-Saxon literary history.

All of Lewis, it can be said, is in **"Unlucky for Pringle."** There is, for instance, the presence of the rootless connoisseur of rooms from Brittany to Morocco, via frigid Canada, Bayswater and Chelsea; there is the "gusto for the common circumstances of his life," and the ability to infuse the lowliest objects with a bizarre and exciting vitality. But there is also, embodied in Pringle, that "mysterious power of awakening hostility" which Lewis later ascribed to Rousseau in *The Art of Being Ruled* (1926) and which he felt in himself. From his position "outside," Lewis persevered all his life in starkly recording—through his social and literary criticism as well as in his fiction—what in *Self Condemned* (1954) he called "the madhouse of functional character." But like Monsieur Chalaran, this malignantly insane element does not relish the presence of a recording mind. In "Pringle" the crash of a looking-glass, customarily an omen of misfortune, should have warned

the hero of the consequences of his "mystic contentment." Like the ultimate fate held for René Harding by the Hotel Blundell in *Self Condemned* and that reserved by the Anglosaxon cultural establishment for Lewis himself, the destiny of Pringle's lodging house was to "vomit him forth; it could not assimilate him . . . its inhabitants became filled with mysterious hatred for him."

Together with **"Pringle,"** the other writings in the first section of this book give a preliminary display of how Lewis worked from the raw material of life, whether it was the Roland-centred domestic constellation of **"A Breton Innkeeper"** or the fictional presentation of an actual salon event under the shadow of war in the **"Crowd Master"** story. The rest of this collection exemplifies in an even more positive way the main themes evinced in all of Lewis's literary work. It is these themes, to the extent that they manifested themselves in the stories that follow, which determined the form given to this book as a whole.

First there is world war, a twentieth-century fact of life which, in Lewis's case, makes itself powerfully felt not only in the autobiographical *Blasting and Bombardiering* (1937) but also, if more obliquely, in later books such as *Self Condemned* and *The Human Age* (1955). Lewis called the war of 1914-18 "a cyclopean dividing wall in time: a thousand miles high and a thousand miles thick, a greater barrier laid across our life."[7] However, as C. H. Sisson has suggested, Lewis was intellectually steeled, as his Georgian contemporaries were not, to absorb a shock of these proportions. "The Lewisian apocalypse was a pre-war affair," says Sisson. "It was not an excitement borrowed from events but an intellectual performance of his own."[8] Perhaps as a consequence of this, Lewis's most fascinating fictional insight into what the war was doing to Western Man came in a story written prior to his initial taste of military action. In the words of a *Rotting Hill* character created years later, Rob Cairn in **"The French Poodle"** (written 1915) swiftly finds himself "forcibly, violently, reborn" once he becomes a soldier on the western front. This whole story is a subtle analysis of that shell-shocked rebirth and also of the war's wider implications. Even in 1915, when martial enthusiasm on the home front had still not given way to weary disenchantment, Lewis's Cairn, with grim prescience, sees the great conflict as "the beginning of a period, far from being a war-that-will-end-war." In **"The King of the Trenches,"** on the other hand, the focus is on mad Captain Burney Polderdick for his own sake rather than for purposes of any general exploration of the meaning of the war. This is, *par excellence,* a cracking good front-line yarn, although Burney shares some of the characteristics of the hollow-men protagonists found elsewhere in Lewis's fiction, being "a sort of prolongation" of his old self. As monarch of "the terrible narrow Kingdom" of his madness, he merits a prominent place in the galaxy of gargantuan puppets which remain impressive monuments to Lewis's distinctive literary powers.

Unlike Polderdick, however, with his typically modern addiction to mass, mechanized violence as an outlet for pent-up savagery, some of Lewis's characters find their release in metaphysical battles and on another front: against

Woman as personification of "the devil Nature." The fictional Benjamin Richard Wing in Lewis's **"The Code of a Herdsman"** proclaims, for instance, that "women, and the processes for which they exist, are the arch conjuring trick: and they have the cheap mystery and a good deal of the slipperiness, of the conjuror."[9] In most of his literary depictions of women, Lewis fell far short of the ease and grace that typified his portrayal of them in scores of paintings and drawings. In his fiction there is a degree of the deliberately grotesque, but also of genuine awkwardness, about the presentation of his female characters. At the same time, a number of his main male *personae* ridicule their women companions rather in the manner of the "propagandist indictment of the feminine" brilliantly paraphrased by Lewis in *The Art of Being Ruled,* where the female physique is pilloried as a "chocolate-cream trap to catch a rustic fool."[10] Describing the projected theme of *Self Condemned* to a publisher seven years before the book's appearance, Lewis wrote: "Woman has been called 'the eternal enemy of the absolute': so our perfectionist (René Harding) must encounter immediate difficulties when he comes in contact with woman."[11]

The central male characters in **"Cantelman's Spring-Mate," "The War Baby"** and **"Junior"** are by no means perfectionists. Instead—except for John Leslie in **"Junior"**—they are self-styled *übermenschen.* Leslie differs from his two forbears in that he is not aggressively intent on dominating Woman but, like a debased Cantelman figure, flees from an overbearing and over-fecund femininity which he both fears and despises.

Yet there is a strange beauty about some of the very images of derision heaped on characters like the pregnant Tets in **"The War Baby"** who is "softly sculpting a Totem, whereas others had not had that art—or craft." Gestation—"the toad-life at the bottom of the tank"—is a central, indeed menacing fact in all three of these stories just as, along with creation and nativity, it served as an important theme for Lewis's painting during that arduous period of exile, the 1940s. The women portrayed here, however, emerge as anything but defeated parties from the contests into which they are plunged. Tets, for instance, scores a vicarious victory, and a contemptuous Perdita is able to hurl the epithet "insane" at John Leslie in **"Junior."** "Insane" (though also heroic) is the description René Harding too might merit. "She has the effrontery to set herself up as my defender against myself," complains Kell-Imrie in bewailing the machinations of the much-lampooned Val in the novel *Snooty Baronet* (1932).[12] It could be said that this was also the role of Hester in *Self Condemned,* and Lewis had René suffer a living death as the penalty for ascribing to the protective Hester nothing more than an "effrontery" meriting only haughty rejection. In **"Pish-Tush,"** the bluff Lionel Letheridge learns the price of unduly crossing womanhood. His actions arouse the virulence of that "volatile aura" which necessarily is all Constance-the-Spook retains of the redoubtable female life-force, with its "mysterious indomitable will."

As do many of Lewis's stories, **"Pish-Tush"** ends with an eruption of violence. To Lewis, violence was of the essence of human personality. "Within five yards of another man's eyes we are on a little crater, which, if it erupted, would split up as would a cocoa-tin of nitrogen," he wrote in *The Wild Body.* This explosiveness lurks beneath the surface of personality and "the finest humour is the great play-shapes blown up or given off by the tragic corpse of life underneath the world of the camera."[13] Memorable "play-shapes" swarm through Lewis's fiction and elsewhere in his work. He revelled in close-ups of such elephantine grotesques: Bestre and Brotcotnaz in *The Wild Body,* Kreisler in *Tarr,* the Bailiff in *The Human Age,* Jack Cruze in *The Revenge for Love* (1937), Charlie the janitor in *Self Condemned,* Augustine Card in *The Red Priest* (1956), Borzo the hotelkeeper in *Filibusters in Barbary* (1932) and Brandleboyes in *America I Presume* (1940). In the present stories there is "Bob" Allen Crumms racked by the same "convulsions of meaningless mirth" as shook Harding when he pondered the hotel fire and the "absurd" extinction of Affie, the wily but lovable hotel manageress in *Self Condemned.* Or there are the Card-like fighting transports of Dickie Dean in **"The Man Who Was Unlucky With Women,"** or the superb anti-oceanic posturings of Kipe, the bum *à la* Beckett rendered with a flamboyant Lewisian twist in **"The Yachting Cap."**

Finally there is another Lewis speciality represented in the pages that follow. This is The Impostor. The American academic faculty to which René retires at the end of *Self Condemned* was unaware that this celebrated British historian had become by that time "a glacial shell of a man," the authenticity of whose work was by now merely a delusion. Far more deliberate and relentless in his activities as Impostor was Vincent Penhale in *The Vulgar Streak* (1941), whose bourgeois mannerisms were as carefully counterfeited as his false fivers. In the present book, **"The Two Captains"** explores the idea of The Counterfeit not only in its characterization but also, as in *The Vulgar Streak,* in its Social Credit-like ruminations on the subject of money. As for **"Children of the Great,"** it in part is an elaboration of a concept later broached again by René Harding when he remarks: "The children of the great are their deeds. Their biological offspring is generally the dullest or vilest."[14] But, beyond this, **"Children of the Great"** provides another variation on the Impostor theme in the person of Derek Gilchrist, a living "libel upon the great." An authentic reincarnation of the Genius of whom Derek is a cruel parody ultimately takes shape in the story, just as a similar personification of The Real materializes in **"Doppelgänger,"** the third and finest study of an Impostor figure included here. Thaddeus Trunk is a great poet who has been transformed by his clamorous, adoring public into a publicity figure. It is Thad's folly actually to *become* this figment of his fan-club's imagination. As a pioneer student of Publicity—a subject dealt with at length in such books as *Time and Western Man* (1927) and *Doom of Youth* (1932)—Lewis was well qualified to probe the techniques of "image-building" responsible for sundry forms of star status in contemporary western society. "A man's publicity is a caricature of himself," says the narrator of **"Doppelgänger."** "It is really how the public sees 'greatness.'" The destiny of Thaddeus Trunk, majestic word-man consumed by his "publicity scarecrow," has obvious parallels in the real-life world of letters, which—under the logic of twentieth-century civilization—tends to be as dominated by the star system as is show business.

Thus this collection ends with Lewis re-emerging from the realm of fiction and assuming once more his equally characteristic functions as sociologist. His command of this latter genre forms a natural whole with his gifts as fictionist, especially as short-story writer. *The Art of Being Ruled* draws on the same masterly sense of group rhythms as does "A Breton Innkeeper"; or, in the category of travel writing, the account of film-star absurdities in *Filibusters in Barbary*; or, among the novels, the microcosmic goings-on at the Hotel Blundell; or, even in Lewis's painting, the abstract of mob dynamics represented by the great 1914-15 oil, *The Crowd*. In the crowd, yet not *of* the crowd: this is the quintessential Lewisian position. Lewis "manœuvres in the heart of reality," with a voracious eye alert for any new "stylistic anomalies" worthy of satiric note. Lewis called his *Wild Body* stories "essays in a new human mathematic" and spoke of wanting "to compile a book of 40 of these propositions, one deriving from and depending on the other."[15] In a sense, *The Art of Being Ruled* might qualify as that book. In any event, as Geoffrey Grigson once wrote, "all Lewis's work is one work."[16] And it is with this unity in mind that the reader should approach the stories here collected.

Notes

[1] Walter Michel and C. J. Fox, eds., *Wyndham Lewis on Art*. London: Thames and Hudson, 1969, pp. 294-5.

[2] W. K. Rose, ed., *The Letters of Wyndham Lewis*. London: Methuen and Co. Ltd., 1963, p. 191.

[3] Wyndham Lewis, *Men Without Art*. London: Cassell and Co. Ltd., 1934, p. 9.

[4] Lewis, *Rude Assignment*. London: Hutchinson and Co. Ltd., 1950, p. 117.

[5] Walter Michel, *Wyndham Lewis: Paintings and Drawings*. London: Thames and Hudson, 1971, p. 49.

[6] Lewis, *The Wild Body*. London: Chatto and Windus, 1927, p. 246.

[7] Lewis, *The Writer and the Absolute*. London: Methuen, 1952, p. 38.

[8] C. H. Sisson, "The Politics of Wyndham Lewis," *Agenda* (London), Autumn-Winter, 1969-70, p. 109.

[9] Lewis, "Imaginary Letters: The Code of a Herdsman," *The Little Review* (New York), July, 1917, p. 6.

[10] Lewis, *The Art of Being Ruled*. London: Chatto, 1926, p. 276.

[11] *The Letters of Wyndham Lewis*, p. 410.

[12] Lewis, *Snooty Baronet*. London: Cassell, 1932, p. 308.

[13] *The Wild Body*, pp. 238-9.

[14] Lewis, *Self Condemned*. London: Methuen, 1954, p. 261.

[15] *The Wild Body*, p. 233.

[16] Geoffrey Grigson, *A Master of Our Time*. London: Methuen, 1951, p. 18.

Robert T. Chapman (essay date 1973)

SOURCE: "Natures, Puppets and Wars," in *Wyndham Lewis: Fictions and Satires,* Vision Press, 1973, pp. 47-67.

[*In the following essay, Chapman examines the development of Lewis's style and themes in his early stories and their later revision in* The Wild Body, *pointing out that Lewis's early socio-psychological concerns were later abandoned for a greater interest in more abstract philosophical ideas.*]

Looking back on his first published writings, Lewis recalled their genesis in his "long vague periods of indolence" in Brittany:

> The Atlantic air, the raw rich visual food of the barbaric environment, the squealing of the pipes, the crashing of the ocean, induced a creative torpor. Mine was now a drowsy sun-baked ferment, watching with delight the great comic effigies which erupted beneath my rather saturnine but astonished gaze. . . . The characters I chose to celebrate—Bestre, the Cornac and his wife, Brotcotnaz, le père François—were all primitive creatures, immersed in life, as much as birds, or big, obsessed, sun-drunk insects. (*Rude Assignment,* 117)

These primitive creatures were eventually to emerge as "wild bodies" in the 1927 collection of that name, but in their early form these pieces are not, in the accepted sense of the term, short stories. They are plotless travel sketches peopled by Breton "characters" whose idiosyncratic social relationships are the *raison d'être* of the vignettes.

"The Pole" was published in Hueffer's *The English Review* in May 1909; it was, Lewis recalled, "my first success of a practical nature." An exercise in imaginative social psychology, "The Pole" describes the curious phenomenon of permanent Slav boarders at Breton *pensions*. With the analytical eye of the social scientist, Lewis states his proposition at the outset; the remainder of the piece offers illustrative case-histories and inductive generalizations about the type. These early stories, wrote Lewis twenty-five years later, were "the crystallization of what I had to keep out of my consciousness while painting," and although the eye of the *visuel* is very obvious, it is usually subordinate to the polemical design of the whole.

"Some Innkeepers and Bestre," Lewis's second publication, appeared in the following issue of *The English Review* and showed similar preoccupations.

> The truest type of innkeeper is to be found in France. And as these papers deal with some of my experiences

in Brittany last summer it is chiefly with France that I am concerned. (473)

"These papers" suggests that Lewis saw his early publications as imaginative reportage or documentaries rather than fictions, and his tone is often that of the sociologist—of the recorder rather than the creator:

> So the study of the French innkeeper is especially fruitful, for he veritably puts his whole soul into his part, everything in him blossoms prodigiously within the conventional limits of his trade. (479)

The reality that Lewis records, however, is not at all mundane. Delighting in the absurd, the grotesque and the bizarre, the more civilized "I" of the narrative wanders amongst the primitive "sun-drunk insects" assiduously noting their behavioural tics and exploring the tensions between roles and personalities. "So subtle is their method and manner of charming the public that it has an opposite effect," writes Lewis of his "eccentric exponents" of the astonishing art of innkeeping. As if to support his general truth by concrete evidence, Lewis appends—as *exemplum* to *moralitas*—the case-history of Bestre.

In *The English Review* version of the story, rather than seeing Bestre in action, the reader is told *about* his furious and demonic battles of glares. Presentation of character is limited by the exemplary role in which it functions—like the Poles, Bestre is a footnote in Lewis's thesis in social psychology. When these stories were reworked for publication in *The Wild Body* (1927) it was, however, the sociological aspect which was relegated to the footnotes, and the characters, rather than the thesis, become the *raison d'être* of the writing. In turning **"The Pole"** into **"Beau Séjour,"** Lewis is not so insistent in his attempts to "nail things down"; the discursive exposition becomes a short story and, in Lawrence's phrase, the characters "get up and walk away with the nail." From the multiplicity of minor characters in **"The Pole,"** Lewis selects the *ménage* of Mme Peronette, Carl and Zoborov, placing their interrelationship into a formal framework. Picaresque meanderings take on beginning, middle and end; minor characters, if not omitted altogether, are strictly subordinated to the central relationship. Similarly, in the transition from **"Some Innkeepers and Bestre"** to **"Bestre"** (as it appears in *The Wild Body*), the prolegomenous, discursive material—**"Some Innkeepers"**—is filtered out completely, leaving the magnificently grotesque Bestre at the centre of the stage.

Although *The Wild Body* is still very much written to a thesis, this is not expressed in exegetical running commentaries as in the early versions, but stated separately in two essays, "Inferior Religions" and "The Meaning of the Wild Body." These expound the philosophical assumptions which underlie the comic vision of the stories:

> First, to assume the dichotomy of mind and body is necessary here, without arguing it; for it is upon that essential separation that the theory of laughter here proposed is based . . . we have to postulate *two* creatures, one that never enters into life, but that travels about in a vessel to whose destiny it is momentarily attached. That is, of course, the laughing observer, and the other is the Wild Body. . . . There is nothing that is animal (and we as bodies are animals) that is not absurd. This sense of the absurdity, or, if you like, the madness of our life, is at the root of every true philosophy. (243-244)

Reason is the "laughing observer" and the "wild body" is the autonomic physiological system to which it is fettered. Not only can the reflective intellect observe the absurdities of others, but—standing back from the wild body in which it is housed—it can apprehend its own absurdity. In the light of this Cartesian dualism, there is something fundamentally absurd in the very fact of human existence; Kerr-Orr, the narrator, recognizes this in himself as well as in others:

> This forked, strange-scented, blond-skinned gut-bag, with its two bright rolling marbles with which it sees, bull's-eyes full of mockery and madness, is my stalking-horse. I hang somewhere in its midst operating it with detachment. (5)

It is Kerr-Orr's Socratic awareness of his own position which places him above the mechanistic wild bodies. He operates his autonomic system: the wild bodies are operated by theirs. Representing mind over matter, he struts through the Breton countryside searching out bizarre examples of the machine in control of the operator or "the thing" running away with "the person."

Lewis's concept of comedy, of course, derives a great deal from Bergson and, as Geoffrey Wagner has written, "Bergson's *Le Rire* is a primer of Lewisian Satire." The French philosopher's basic point about comedy—that it is "la transformation d'une personne en chose"—becomes the crux of Lewis's definition:

> The root of the Comic is to be sought in the sensations resulting from the observations of a *thing* behaving like a person. But from that point of view all men are necessarily comic: for they are all *things,* or physical bodies, behaving as *persons.* . . . To bring vividly to our mind what we mean by "absurd," let us turn to the plant, and enquire how the plant could be absurd. Suppose you came upon an orchid or a cabbage reading Flaubert's *Salambo,* or Plutarch's *Moralia,* you would be very much surprised. But if you found a man or woman reading it, you would *not* be surprised.
>
> Now in one sense you ought to be just as much surprised at finding a man occupied in this way as if you had found an orchid or a cabbage, or a tom-cat, to include the animal world. There is the same physical anomaly. It is just as absurd externally, that is what I mean.—The deepest root of the Comic is to be sought in this anomaly. (246-247)

Paraded and presented by Kerr-Orr, *The Wild Body* is a collection of such anomalies.

Kerr-Orr is the Lewis-man of these stories, and the *persona* is representative of a type which recurs throughout Lewis's fiction—"the nature." In *The Art of Being Ruled*

(1926), Goethe's distinction between puppets and natures is quoted with approbation. *Homo stultus* is mechanical, puppet-like, ignorant: "Natures," the super-species, are distinguished by self-awareness and control. Even if all men *are* fundamentally absurd, some are less so than others—Kerr-Orr is one of these:

> I know much more about myself than people generally do. For instance I am aware that I am a barbarian. By rights I should be paddling about in a coracle. My body is large, white and savage. But all the fierceness has become transformed into *laughter.* . . . Everywhere where formerly I would fly at throats, I now howl with laughter. . . . My sense of humour in its mature phase has arisen in this very acute consciousness of what is *me.* In playing that off against another hostile *me,* that does not like the smell of mine, probably finds my large teeth, height and so forth abominable, I am in a sense working off my alarm at myself. So I move on a more primitive level than most men, I expose my essential *me* quite coolly, and all men shy a little. . . . I will show you myself in action, manoeuvring in the heart of reality. (3-4, 5, 7)

This physically primitive "soldier of humour" has harnessed his natural violence. As his mind gazes dispassionately upon his own "anomalies" and upon the world's, the fundamental ubiquitous absurdity gives rise to a philosophy of laughter:

> It sprawls into everything. It has become my life. The result is that I am *never* serious about anything. I simply cannot help converting everything into burlesque patterns. (4)

It is as a connoisseur of the grotesque that Kerr-Orr catalogues specimens for his human menagerie. Anxious to catch the slightest comic nuances of behaviour, he installs himself in the midst of his exhibits, often acting as catalyst as well as recorder:

> It was almost as though Fabre could have established himself within the masonries of the bee, and lived on its honey, while investigating for the human species. (120)

The physical closeness of Kerr-Orr's scrutiny—like a gorgonian lens—turns people into things. The description of Ludo, the blind Breton beggar, petrifies the living face into a mask—physiognomy becomes form.

> As I looked at him I realized how the eyes mount guard over the face, as well as look out of it. The faces of the blind are hung there like a dead lantern. Blind people must feel on their skins our eyes upon them: but this sheet of flesh is rashly stuck up in what must appear far outside their control, an object in a foreign world of sight. So in consequence of this divorce, their faces have the appearance of things that have been abandoned by the mind. What is his face to a blind man? Probably nothing more than an organ, an exposed part of the stomach, that is a mouth. (179)

This is what Lewis elsewhere calls "the truth of Natural Science" as opposed to the "truth of Romance": the non-human gaze which plays over the "dry shells and pelts of things," confining itself to the "visible machinery of life" ("Studies in the Art of Laughter").

While action explodes all around, Kerr-Orr, like a ringmaster in a well-organized arena, surveys and controls his charges with consummate ease. He is "the showman to whom the antics and solemn gambols of these wild children are to be a source of strange delight" (232). This is not the Lawrentian fascination with the primitive: Lewis is less interested in the differences between the civilized and the unsophisticated, and more in their similarities. The Breton peasants exhibit, writ large, the "solemn gambols" of all humanity. In laughing at them we are not, like visitors to Elizabethan asylums, laughing at these "carefully selected specimens of religious fanaticism" (234). These grotesques are not on show as curious mutations of nature. Lewis postulates no norm against which his madmen are to be measured, but rather suggests that this "madness" be taken into account in any definition of humanity. Driven by various permutations of *idées fixes,* ruling passions, fetishes and the arbitrary functioning of their autonomic systems, the wild bodies are units in "a new human mathematic," the basic premise of which is that "we have in most lives the spectacle of a pattern as circumscribed and complete as a theorem of Euclid" (233).

One such theorem is the ritual of violence performed by Brotcotnaz on his wife. These beatings are his bloody obeisance to dark gods. Julie, the wife, suffers her perpetual crucifixion in doleful silence:

> Her eyes are black and moist, with the furtive intensity of a rat. They move circumspectly in this bloated shell. She displaces herself also more noiselessly than the carefullest nun, and her hands are generally decussated, drooping upon the ridge of her waist-line, as though fixed there with an emblematic nail, at about the level of the navel. Her stomach is, for her, a kind of exclusive personal "calvary." At its crest hang her two hands, with the orthodox decussation, an elaborate ten-fingered symbol. (208)

The imagery suggests Julie's martyrdom at the hands of Brotcotnaz's "inferior religion": only the rat-like furtiveness of her eyes distances her from the conventional hagiological type. Julie, too, bows the knee to an inferior religion of her own: she secretly drinks, and attempts to pass off her bruises as "erysipelas." Although both "secrets" are widely known to friends and neighbours, Julie pretends, for form's sake, that certain things are true. The neighbours, also for form's sake, are party to the groundrules of their private ritual and the whole affair becomes a complex skein of unspoken assumptions and understanding.

The Brotcotnazs' ceremony of violence is like the formal, highly-patterned dance they perform for Kerr-Orr. The steps are preordained and there is no margin for improvisation. Yet there is no real contact: each partner is aware of what is to come, and the pattern exists independently of themselves:

"Viens donc, Julie! Come then. Let us dance."

Julie sat and sneered through her vinous mask at her fascinating husband. He insisted, standing over her with one toe pointed outward in the first movement of the dance, his hand held for her to take in a courtly attitude.

"Viens donc, Julie! Dansons un peu!"

Shedding shamefaced, pinched, and snuffling grins to right and left as she allowed herself to be drawn into this event, she rose. They danced a sort of minuet for me, advancing and retreating, curtseying and posturing, shuffling rapidly their feet. Julie did her part, it seemed, with understanding. (218)

The dance is a pastiche of reality; attitudes are donned like masks as these two peasants act out a courtly minuet. Just as the minuet exists beyond the dancers, or a Euclidean theorem beyond the page, so the violence of Brotcotnaz is almost impersonal, having its genesis beyond the personalities involved. Running in behavioural grooves seemingly too deeply scored to be changed, their life-style is as mindless a ritual of stimulus-response as that of Pavlovian salivating dogs. However, a near-fatal accident to Julie serves to break the pattern and, like an interrupted dance, things are never the same afterwards. The iconographical fetish of action is smashed, the "inferior religion" falls apart, and Brotcotnaz cannot assimilate the new events into his old ways.

The machinery of habit, the "religious" fascination of people for things, and people for people, all are functions of the wild body. The violent energy which erupts periodically in the brutality of Brotcotnaz is often a feature of these characters—in **"The Cornac and His Wife"** the violence is just as great, but exists beneath the surface, emerging as the performer's hatred of his audience. The Cornac is head of a troupe of itinerant acrobats who scrape a meagre living by giving displays to groups of Breton villagers. He and his wife have an "implacable grudge" against the spectators:

With the man, obsessed by ill-health, the grievance against fortune was associated with the more brutal hatred that almost choked him every time he appeared professionally. . . . These displays involved the insane contortions of an indignant man and his dirty, breathless wife, of whose ugly misery it was required that a daily mournful exhibition should be made of her shrivelled legs, in pantomime hose. She must crucify herself with a scarecrow abandon, this iron and blood automaton, and affect to represent the factor of sex in a geometrical posturing. (136, 137-8)

As with Julie, this life is a self-willed perpetual crucifixion: habit is both torture and palliative; there is no escape from the ritual pattern of existence. The performance witnessed by Kerr-Orr is a ceremonial defiance of the audience. Because a local by-law forbids the appearance of his young daughter, the old man is forced to drag his own weary body through the painful contortions of the act for the pleasure of the audience. A "whistling sneer of hatred" acknowledges the applause; he is aware that they have come to see "the entire family break their necks one after the other" (139). The laughter of the clown and the crowd is another expression of this violence; another primitive response to the latent dangers of the act. "The herd-bellow at the circus is always associated with mock-violent events, however, and (this) true laughter is torn out of a tragic material" (162). The reflex actions that Lewis explores—the nervous laughter in the face of tragedy, the "brutal *frisson*" inspired by danger—are the gut-reactions and mysterious spasms of the human mechanism. As in a Giacometti sculpture, the "civilized" accretions which have gathered around the wild body are pared away, until, in these Breton peasants, "that small, primitive, literally antediluvian vessel in which we set out on our adventures" stands revealed.

Bestre, the finest creation of *The Wild Body,* is, like the Bailiff in *Childermass,* a superb grotesque. The story is very simple: Bestre, a Breton innkeeper, indulges in furious battles of glares with a Parisian artist and his wife. The plot charts the battle and details Bestre's tactics. Kerr-Orr is not interested in the depth-psychology of Bestre's obsession—the ruling passion is a *donnée,* its cause buried in the viscera or the subconscious—but he observes Bestre with such precision that his own activity borders on the obsessive. The prose is thick and glutinous—what Hugh Kenner has called "a species of verbal impasto"—full of biological imagery and verbs of startling action. Bestre emerges:

His tongue stuck out, his lips eructated with the incredible indecorum that appears to be the monopoly of liquids, his brown arms were for the moment genitals, snakes in one massive twist beneath his mamillary slabs, gently riding on a pancreatic swell, each hair on his oil-bearing skin contributing its message of porcine affront. . . . On reaching the door into which he had sunk, plump and slick as into a stage trap, there he was inside—this grease-bred old mammifier—his tufted vertex charging about the plank ceiling—generally ricochetting like a dripping sturgeon in a boat's bottom—arms warm brown, ju-jitsu of his guts, tan canvas shoes and trousers rippling in ribbed planes as he darted about—with a filthy snicker for the scuttling female, and a stark cock of the eye for an unknown figure miles to his right: he filled this short tunnel with clever parabolas and vortices, little neat stutterings of triumph, goggle-eyed hypnotisms, in retrospect, for his hearers. (117-118)

Bestre is not exhibited, like the fat lady in the fair-ground booth, to be mocked as a freak. He is, in a sense, the hidden side of Everyman: if humanity, by definition, is all that humanity has produced, then Lewis, in these stories, is holding up the wild bodies as a mirror to the reader. Bestre's routines are as rigid as those of the donkey turning the water wheel, and his inferior religion is typical of the driving forces behind other *Wild Body* characters: Valmore's *idée fixe* that he is all-American dominates his life ("**A Soldier of Humour**"); Ludo, the blind beggar in **"The Death of the Ankou,"** is hounded by a primitive death-god; Françoise has moulded his personality on the "emotions provoked by the bad, late, topical sentimental songs of Republican France" (**"Franciscan Adventures"**). All are automata: wound up by predilections, they whirr on their giddy way. The right response, according to Kerr-Orr, is a "bark of delight" at the proximity of such absurdities. Yet even in the recognition and enjoyment of the "stylistic anomalies," Kerr-Orr is himself absurd:

> Flinging myself on the bed, my blond poll rolling about in ecstasy upon the pillow, I howled like an exultant wolf. (29)

Observer and observed alike are implicated in the pervasive comic vision. For Lewis, any definition of human life must include this element of the absurd and in his description of "perfect laughter" ("Studies in the Art of Laughter"), he outlines this vision:

> *Perfect laughter* . . . would select as the objects of its mirth as much the antics dependent upon pathologic maladjustments, injury or disease, as the antics of clumsy and imperfectly functioning healthy people. . . . There is no reason at all why we should not burst out laughing at a foetus, for instance. We should after all, only be laughing *at ourselves!*—at ourselves early in our mortal career. (514)

In *Blasting and Bombardiering,* Lewis praised T. E. Hulme for "rubbing everybody's nose . . . in the highly disobliging doctrine" of Original Sin. There are many similarities between Hulme's *Weltanschauung* and Lewis's, and the former's dictum that "Man is in no sense perfect, but a wretched creature who can yet apprehend perfection" (*Speculations*), could well be taken as a definition of the *ethos* underlying much of Lewis's work. An aesthetic which sees satire as a universal "let-down" of the species and a technique of "human defamation" is akin, in many ways, to a notion of Original Sin—a secular Original Sin. This moral vision—implicit in *The Wild Body* and embodied more fully in *The Apes of God*—is voiced discursively in *The Art of Being Ruled*:

> Prostration is our natural position. A worm-like movement from a spot of sunlight to a spot of shade, and back, is the type of movement that is natural to men. As active, erect, and humane creatures they are in a constantly false position, and behaving in an abnormal way. They have to be pushed up into it, and held there, till it has become a habit only to lie down at night; and at the first real opportunity they collapse and are full length once more. (281)

The vision is as profoundly despairing as that embodied in Swift's Struldbruggs or Beckett's Unnamable and *How It Is.* In the light of this philosophy, the wild bodies are representative of the yahoo in all humanity—yet something saves them from the total bleakness of, say, Lady Fredigonde in *The Apes of God*. Lewis, as well as Kerr-Orr, delights in—indeed "celebrates"—their absurdity. The satirical attitude here is ambiguous—as if Swift had, paradoxically, admired the vitality of his yahoos—and it is

this very ambiguity which gives rise to the unique tone of *The Wild Body.* This is the stage prior to *The Apes of God*-attitude where human life is portrayed as "a very bad business indeed": here, it is very absurd indeed, and the artist revels in this absurdity.

Traces of the wild body *ethos* are to be found in a good deal of Lewis's writing outside *The Wild Body* itself. The early story **"Unlucky for Pringle"** which appeared in Douglas Goldring's magazine *The Tramp* (February, 1911), is very much part of this universe, but set in London instead of Brittany. James Pringle is a Kerr-Orr figure with a "gusto for the common circumstances of his life" and an aesthetic appreciation of rooms and their inhabitants as microcosms of an infinitely entertaining reality. Pringle's fastidiousness about the adequacy of rooms as studios has become removed from the realm of necessity to that of fascination. He changes rooms promiscuously, and "Rooms to Let" has a strange, sexual significance for him:

> On the very frequently recurring occasions on which he set out to look for rooms he would savour the particular domestic taste of each new household he entered in the course of his search with the interest of a gourmet. Smiling strangely, as she thought, at the landlady who answered the door, he would at once go to her parlour—come for a debauch that she would never suspect. . . . He had passed like a ghost, in one sense, through a hundred unruffled households. Scores of peaceful landladies, like beautiful women caressed in their sleep by a spirit, had been enjoyed by him. Their drab apartments had served better than any boudoir. (404, 413)

Pringle rents a room from a French couple, the Chalarans, and installs himself in the midst of their life "like a worm in a wall," gradually usurping the indolent, wild-bodied Chalaran as patriarch. Sensing that he is being "enjoyed" by Pringle, Chalaran—in a series of marvellously indirect acts of cognitive dissonance—manages to oust this connoisseur of the ordinary. Chalaran, as much as Bestre or Brotcotnaz, is a wild body, whose frenetic and tangential outbursts are a *locus classicus* of deviations of object and aim:

> . . . in a burst of energy that lasted two afternoons (Chalaran) built a summer-house at the bottom of the garden. The summer-house, no doubt, saved Pringle. But had Pringle grasped then the at once compact and elemental character of these bursts of activity, and his own position as regards Chalaran, he would have shaken in his shoes. For who could say whether the next time a storm of such violence as to build a summer-house might not seize on some more substantial and apposite object. (413)

Similarly, the protagonist of **"Sigismund"** (a short story first published in 1920 and appended to *The Wild Body* collection in 1927) is an idiot son of an idiot tradition who, forever peering into the depths of his aristocratic past with pathological single-mindedness, is a wild body driven by a wild mind. Unlike the corporeal fixation of, say, Brotcotnaz for his wife—which is as physical as pain, hunger or fear—Sigismund's obsession is of the intellect and, in many ways, he is as near to the "Tyro" species as to the wild bodies. His wish to progress backwards is stronger than most people's to progress forwards, and he becomes an embodiment of his pathological studies. In Sigismund's case, and in the Lewisian taxonomy of obsessions generally, the psychological assumptions are closer to those of the seventeenth and eighteenth century than those of early twentieth-century "alienists." Lewis pursues the Bergsonian "thingness" behind the human façade, and his creatures are reduced to their most dominant characteristics. These caricatures of humanity—as in Ben Jonson's comedy of humours or Pope's presentation of "Ruling Passions"—are personifications. There are many similarities between Lewis's reifications and such simplistic moral psychologies, but his "primitive creatures" and "sun-drunk insects" do not function within a morality framework. Representing nothing beyond themselves, they exist to encourage that human bark called laughter which, wrote Lewis, "is *per se* a healthy clatter" ("Studies in the Art of Laughter," 515).

Lewis wrote several stories with World War I as either setting or backcloth, and in these he looks at social phenomena more sophisticated than the primitive group psychology of the wild bodies. In **"The French Poodle"** (*The Egoist,* March, 1916), war is presented as one of the "tragic handicaps" of existence which has been exalted into a way of life in modern society. The ever-present threat of death and the first-hand experience of slaughter create "trench scars" in the mind of Rob Cairn. Suffering from shellshock, Cairn is both physically and emotionally scarred. What man has done to man utterly disgusts him; in place of this inhumanity Cairn postulates "the sanity of direct animal processes." But he has been conditioned to brutality; he kills and is killed; there is no escape from the man-made environment of violence.

In *The Wild Body,* Lewis had focused upon primitive—if complex—individuals in primitive environments; in the war stories he looks at the effects of complex—if, ultimately, uncivilized—environments upon the individual. **"The King of the Trenches"** is the only story of Lewis's to deal directly with life at the Front. It appeared in the second edition of *Blasting and Bombardiering* (1967) and draws on the same experience as is brilliantly recorded in that autobiography. Captain Burney Polderdick is a much-decorated officer in command of a battery of trench mortars, and his exploits are described by Lieutenant Donald Menzies, the Lewis-man of the story. From the outset it is obvious that Polderdick is quite mad—his "eccentricity" having that compulsive power which pushes it beyond acceptable limits. His actions are not always under the control of the rational mind and, in a stressful situation, he becomes a *mélange* of tin-hat and flying limbs. Unlike Cairn, Burney is not viewed as a tragic figure caught in a web of war. He represents, rather, the wild body at war:

> When Polderdick arrived the Line was quiet. A few days afterwards the Trench was constantly shelled. Polderdick was there. They began shelling with shrapnel. At the first patter of the shrapnel Polderdick dived

headlong into a dug-out, but his tin-hat crashed with great force against the tin-hat of an infantry captain who was darting out at the moment. They both disappeared, Polderdick's buttocks revolving as he fell inside. (173)

Polderdick's deranged "Ha! *Ha!*" is yet another category in Lewis's anatomy of laughter: it is the explosion of a mind signalling its unwillingness to adhere to that consensus of opinion called reality. Polderdick's insanity consists of an idiosyncratic restructuring of experience and the creation of a new reality in which he becomes "King of a terrible narrow kingdom."

> "I am the King of the Trenches!" he shouted. "Didn't you know who I was? Yes! I am Burney Polderdick, the king of the Trenches!—Ha! *Ha!*" He flourished his stick, twirled it lightly, lunged forward, and dug the Colonel in the middle of the stomach. (182)

There is a sympathetic attractiveness about Menzies's account of Polderdick, as if he senses that this wild body madness is no more insane, and certainly less dangerous, than the madness of war. Polderdick, however, is transferred to a Training Depot in England, and his demented reign ends in exile.

As *Blasting and Bombardiering* illustrates only too well, war can have the effect of dehumanizing men until they become mere cogs in the great impersonal war-machine. Yet, in the Bergsonian sense of people behaving like things, this dehumanizing can still be seen as comic. Lewis's description of the West Indian sergeant (in *Blasting and Bombardiering*) presents him as a lithe man-machine who returns to his post as automatically and exactly as shells find the breech:

> At our Nieuport position one dark night the negroes were rolling shells up to the guns—very large ones, since the guns were outsize. This operation had to be effected without so much as a match struck, lest the German air patrols should spot us. A negro sergeant I noticed was not only stationary, and peculiarly idle, but actually obstructing the work of the dusky rollers. I spoke to him. He neither looked at me nor answered. I could scarcely see him—it was very dark, and he was dark. I ordered him to do a little rolling. This was a *word of command.* It elicited no response from the dark shape. Whereupon I gave him a violent push. This propelled him through space for a short distance, but he immediately returned to where he had stood before. I gave him a second push. As if made of india-rubber, he once more reintegrated the spot he had just left. After this I accepted him as part of the landscape, and the shells had to be rolled round him, since they could not be rolled *through* him. (152-153)

Soldiers as part of the landscape, the gigantic guns and shells as alive as they—or the soldiers as thing-like as their guns—are features of many of Lewis's war paintings. Caught in mid-action, the soldiers in the background of "A Battery Shelled" (1919) are transfixed in static geometrical positions reminiscent of the figures of Lewis's Vorticist period. These puny metallic shapes, labouring to the massive totemic guns which block out the sky, are sometimes indistinguishable from the ammunition stock-piled beside them. Like the palm of a gigantic hand, the earth is ploughed and furrowed, far more vital than the transmogrified humanity it grasps. The three figures loitering in the foreground of the painting are more realistically portrayed and have an air of authority. Apparently disengaged from the hellish activity continuously grinding on below them, they are more in control, more withdrawn, not so involved in the destructive machine and hence better able to observe its functions. This "outsider" position is everywhere stressed by Lewis, and through his Cantelman *persona* in *Blasting and Bombardiering* he sums it up thus:

> In the first days (after the declaration of war) he experienced nothing but a penetrating interest in all that was taking place. His detachment was complete and his attention was directed everywhere. (77)

In the original Cantelman story, **"Cantelman's Spring-Mate"** which first appeared in *The Little Review* (October 1917), the war is in the background, but casts its shadow over all "ordinary" life. Cantelman is an infantry officer who is on leave, but, about to depart to the Front for the first time, "his thoughts and sensations all had, as a philosophic background, the prospect of death." Played out against this threat of cataclysmic violence, every action has about it a tenseness and a sense of urgency. Like the eponymous hero of *Tarr,* Cantelman is a Kerr-Orr figure who, while all too aware of the limitations of his fellow men, aspires to *übermensch* status—and fails. Perceiving that violence is inherent in all life, that both Nature *and* humanity are red in tooth and claw, Cantelman attempts to defeat life at its own game.

His body feels itself at one with wild Nature and is beguiled by the sensuality of spring; his mind is appalled at the body's grossness and its desire to be part of "the madness of natural things." Cantelman is Cartesian man *par excellence*: combining the traits of both wild body and laughing observer, he observes his own desires in action. "Dissecting his laugh," he compares it to the pig's grunt; without the intellect the wild body would be free to rut with the abandon of pigs, but man is *animal capax rationis* and hence aware of his own absurdity. It is upon Stella, his spring mate and Nature's agent, that Cantelman wreaks his revenge. By humiliating her, he believes, he will be undermining a natural and universal order that is both grotesque and brutal. Stella is a young country girl, quite unaware of the complex reactions she has loosed in her lover. She awakes in him "all the sensations he had been divining in the creatures around him, the horse, the bird and the pig." His relationship with her satisfies both the "gnawing yearning in his blood" and, paradoxically, his wish for revenge upon a Nature which makes him feel such desires. Acting towards Stella "with as much falsity as he could master," his calculated seduction of Nature's "agent" is an attempt to outwit her "hostile power." Remaining "deliberate and aloof," through the medium of Stella, Cantelman feels he is raping Nature:

On the warm earth consent flowed up into her body from all the veins of the landscape. That night he spat out, in gushes of thick delicious rage, all the lust that had gathered in his body. The nightingale sang ceaselessly in the small wood at the top of the field where they lay. He grinned up towards it, and once more turned to the devouring of his mate. He bore down on her as though he wished to mix her body into the soil, and pour his seed into a more methodless matter, the brown phalanges of floury land. As their two bodies shook and melted together, he felt that he was raiding the bowels of Nature. (Reprinted in Calder and Boyars' *Blasting and Bombardiering,* 310)

The complexity of Cantelman's desire for Stella, his hatred for his own weakness, and the ambiguous attractiveness of his revenge, are all allusively conveyed in the violent imagery of intercourse. In his mood of "impartial malignity," Cantelman feels that he has won the laurels in his vendetta with Nature, but the whole tenor of the writing denies this. Far from disrupting the pattern of Nature, he plays an integral part in every stage of the natural progression of copulation, birth and—when beating out a German's brains—death. Cantelman's callous and vicious treatment of Stella is an attempt to defeat Nature on her own amoral terms and thus, by remaining above the processes, avoid the "souillure." But the story reveals the insufficiency of the Nietzschean concept of "Will" in this struggle: it is impossible to remain "indifferent to Nature's threat," even when the essence of this threat is intellectually recognized. To be in life is to be tainted by life; this is the lesson learned by so many of Lewis's Supermen *manqués,* and only Pierpoint in *The Apes of God,* by eremetically withdrawing from life, manages to function successfully as disembodied mind.

Where the early ***Wild Body*** stories presented idiosyncratic characters and conflicts illustrative of human psychology, **"Cantelman's Spring-Mate"** presents conflicts which embody ideas. Published the year after **"Cantelman," "The War Baby"** (*Art and Letters,* Winter 1918), pursues similar concepts against a similar wartime background; but Richard Beresin, the soldier-protagonist, is much more of a buffoon than Cantelman. Beresin's ideals are not the product of strenuous philosophy, but were bred from the "tenacious middle class snobberies" of public school, nurtured by Paris, Huysmans and Nietzsche, and now—tended by a "soldier-servant"—are in full flower. A puppet driven by subjective dreams, Beresin inhabits an idealistic realm cut off from the real world by snobbish illusions. His grandiose vision invades—indeed submerges—reality with the Nietzschean equivalent of Romanticism. Charlie Peace, The Brides in the Bath, Oscar Wilde, Huysmans, together with Nietzsche, all romp promiscuously in Beresin's idiot pantheon, and are responsible for his delusions of grandeur. In the Prologue to the first edition of *Tarr* (1918), Lewis diagnoses the Nietzschean cult which has produced "the ungainliest and strangest aristocratic caste any world could hope to see":

> In Europe Nietzsche's gospel of desperation, the beyond-the-law-man etc., has deeply influenced the Paris apache, the Italian Futuriste *litterateur,* the Russian

revolutionary. Nietzsche's books are full of seductions and sugar-plums. They have made aristocrats of people who would otherwise have been only mild snobs or meddlesome prigs . . . they have made an Over-man of every vulgarly energetic grocer in Europe. (x)

Like Cantelman, Beresin represents a critique of his philosophy. In different ways, both are attempting to live out their ideologies and impose their own patterns upon existence; but once translated into action, ideas lose their purity and become tainted by the imperfections of humanity. In a similar manner, John Porter Kemp, the central character of Lewis's dialectical drama *The Ideal Giant* (1917), propounds a philosophy of extreme action which, however coherently expressed, is shown to be, in practice, totally ludicrous. Kemp's conversations represent his groping towards a satisfactory personal philosophy, and he concludes that conventional behaviour, because mechanical, should be shunned. However, what is intellectually valid and clear-cut can, in action, become chaotic and vague. Philosophy has no law beyond itself, whereas life is hedged in with a multitude of contingencies which blur the edges of ideal forms. When Kemp's "philosophy of action" is put into practice the result is a bizarre emblematic comment upon his original ethic.

Kemp tells Rose that "honesty is a rhythm; it must be broken up," and the important thing is to act positively (instead of merely "playing"):

> "My point is plain. It is entirely a question of whole hogging, and escaping from the dreariness and self-contempt of *play. We play* at everything here—at love, art, winning and losing—don't we? . . . Yet *action,* if you could find the right action, is the 'sovereign cure for our ills'. . . . Any wildly subversive action should be welcomed. *We must escape from the machine in ourselves! Smash it up: renew ourselves.*"

The insistence upon a cataclysmic personal violence beyond the bounds of good and evil is distinctly Nietzschean. Kemp is disgusted with his own puny attempts to break the conventional rhythm of honesty and confound a mundane reality with lies. Similarly, believing that Rose has stolen some spoons as a symbolic act, Kemp tells her that such gesturing is merely playing at desperation:

> "I feel that my lies and your spoons were about as playful as some of the absurdities with which we reproach our art friends. Compared to death on a barricade, or the robber Garnier's Swedish exercises while he was in hiding in the suburbs of Paris, they are slight exploits. The blood that spurts from a tapped proboscis is not enough. A spoon will not thrust you into jail for so long that you forget what the Earth looks like. For the hair to turn white, the heart to turn grey, in an hour, you require the real thing, ma mie."

But, unknown to Kemp, Rose *has* committed herself in the manner set forth by him: she has killed her father. Touched with bloodstained hands, philosophy has become sullied. As a policeman attempts to apprehend Rose, the play ends with a ludicrous scramble of bodies on the floor of the cafe.

In *The Ideal Giant* Lewis treats important themes through a veil of heavy irony. It is as if he finds, like Kerr-Orr who is *"never* serious about anything," that even momentous issues are Janus-faced and are forever pushing forward their absurd aspect. Kemp's philosophizing is, on one level, an attempt to hammer out what Lewis in *The Art of Being Ruled* calls a "working system of thought." Lewis manages to catch that nice balance between recognizing the importance of Kemp's attempt, while, at the same time, satirizing it most savagely. With Rose's arrest Kemp achieves his mock *anagnorosis*; the folly of his *übermensch* idealism is revealed. It is doubly ironical that Kemp should have learned, not through the folly of his own Dostoevskyan extravagance, but through the actions of a female *doppelgänger*. Throughout the play Kemp believes that he is playing Raskolnikov to Rose's Sonia, but finally he discerns that, in fact, the roles have been reversed.

Cantelman, Beresin, Kemp—all are defeated by life. They do assert positives, but the fiction is an embodiment of their inadequacy rather than their validity. Almost as an answer to the *mauvaise foi* of these characters, the fictional Benjamin Richard Wing lays down his premises for the good life in **"The Code of a Herdsman"** (*The Little Review,* July 1917). Just as the first versions of the **Wild Body** stories showed Lewis exalting argument above design, so **"The Code"** represents a fictional presentation of ideas without plot or character. In the form of a letter, this epistolary dramatic monologue is a short but comprehensive set of rules for the avoidance of "the obscenities of existence" and the type of social contacts which dogged the other failed "Natures." Wing is quite dogmatic in his assertions: Mankind and the Exceptional Man cannot coexist and so the only answer is a rigidly divisive Olympian life-style for the "Herdsmen" or "Mountain people." The deliberately extravagant irony of the piece does not mask the seriousness of intent: **"The Code"** contains the seeds of the Manichean vision of *The Art of Being Ruled,* Pierpoint's Encyclicals in *The Apes of God,* and Lewis's own "Enemy" *persona.* The *sine qua non* of Wing's argument rests upon the assumption that humanity can be divided, on the one hand, into "Herd" and, on the other, into "Mountain people" or "Herdsmen." It is also understood that any trafficking with the "Yahooesque and rotten herd" must be distasteful in the extreme:

> Spend some of your spare time every day in hunting your weaknesses, caught from commerce with the herd, as methodically, solemnly and vindictively as a monkey uses with his fleas. You will find yourself swarming with them while you are surrounded by humanity. But you must not bring them up onto the mountain. . . . Do not play with political notions, aristocratisms or the reverse, for that is a compromise with the herd. Do not allow yourself to imagine "a fine herd, though still a herd." There is no *fine herd.* The cattle that call themselves "gentlemen" you will observe to be a little cleaner. It is merely cunning and produced with a product of combined soda and fats. But you will find no serious difference between them and those vast dismal herds they avoid.

The basis of this elitism is ontological not social and, like Plato's exaltation of the Philosopher-King, proceeds from an unquestioned acceptance of the primacy of the intellect. The arrogant Mosaic tone of the piece is brilliantly sustained throughout, and much of the sardonic humour derives from the straightfaced precision with which the allegory is pursued:

> *There are very stringent regulations* about the herd keeping off the sides of the mountain. In fact your chief function is to prevent this happening. Some in moments of boredom, or vindictiveness, are apt to make rushes for the higher regions. Their instinct always fortunately keeps them in crowds or bands, and their trespassing is soon noticed.

The inhumanity of the attitude lies in the deliberate confusion of image and reality: "herd" gradually loses its metaphorical sense and the "Yahoos of the plain" are spoken of, quite literally, as animals. "The terrible processions beneath," writes Wing from the heights, "are not of our making, and are without our pity." This superb egotism reduces others to mere functions of the self, and one is reminded of Kerr-Orr's confession in *The Wild Body*:

> I admit that I am disposed to forget that people are real—that they are, that is, not subjective patterns belonging specifically to me, in the course of this joke-life, which indeed has for its very principle a denial of the accepted actual. (4)

Wing looks upon humanity with all the indifference that Joyce characterized as central to the aesthetic attitude. Paring his fingernails, Wing does not "forget" the reality of others—he *denies* it. Yet, apart from Pierpoint, Lewis's characters never long endure the rarified air of the Mountain (even Wing has "a pipe below sometimes"), and a recurrent theme throughout the fiction is just this conflict between the concepts of the Mountain and the exigencies of the Plain.

Bernard Lafourcade (essay date 1982)

SOURCE: Afterword, to *The Complete Wild Body,* Black Sparrow Press, 1982, pp. 403-14.

[*In the following afterword to a collection of Lewis's stories, Lafourcade, following Lewis's own example, catalogues the six basic "attributes" of the* Wild Body *stories, which are "a real presence," "fascination," "comedy," "tragedy," "the grotesque," and "the absurd."*]

To get some idea of the present status and sweeping magnitude of this remarkable collection of stories—Wyndham Lewis's great initial outburst and constant source of reference for what was to prove most actively vital in his vision—imagine a population of Easter Island monoliths lying face down, half buried in the dust. This spectral host must sooner or later be recovered from oblivion as one of the great exhumations of Modernism, and the object of this book is to promote a long overdue

recognition by presenting the procession of these stories complete for the first time.

Pondered and elaborated by Lewis over a period of nearly twenty years, the early intuitions of 1909 eventually yielded a collection of stories, *The Wild Body* of 1927—a landmark in the history of English short fiction as significant as *Dubliners,* but which, for a variety of reasons, has remained largely ignored. The final product, with the exception of a second meagre impression in 1932, was not reissued during the author's lifetime, though Methuen planned a reprint in the early fifties—and since Lewis's death, only one facsimile reprint has been made available. Moreover none of the constitutive monoliths of *The Wild Body* was ever included in any of the numerous anthologies of the modern short story—which in the course of half a century is surprising, to say the least, unless it is realized that these objects must have been perceived from the start as disturbingly alien, not to say incomprehensible, thus confirming Hugh Kenner's diagnosis of Lewis as "a one-man alternative avant-garde."[1] Surely, as was so often the case with Lewis, and still is, the pundits felt that, rather than grappling with complex nonconformity, it would be simpler to ignore the whole thing altogether. Thus "the alternative" remained in the cupboard.

So, these sketches, essays and stories sank into oblivion outside the narrow circle of Lewis's critics. But even the latter bear some responsibility for this neglect. Though the early reviewers of 1927-1928 had often proved enthusiastic and sometimes highly perceptive, the recent commentators have not approached Lewis's uncouth tribe systematically. Unanimous in asserting the importance of *The Wild Body* in the shaping of the author's *Weltanschauung,* but often at variance about the value of the stories, they usually contented themselves with a few random samples before moving on to the study of the more accessible and homogeneous novels, which means that a number of the "bodies" have hardly been anatomized, and some of them not at all. The most obvious idiosyncrasies of these "little dead totems" have been discussed, but the organization of their clan, its genesis and growth, its changing philosophy, its collective unconscious and structural obsessions must still be ascertained. An overall vista is needed—the cliché of Lewis the man springing from nowhere being still too often used as a smoke screen. True enough, there are signs that a more attentive attitude is appearing, but this comprehensive spectrum of the work of Lewis *jeune* is still likely to come as a revelation to many.

A saga no doubt, but no mere Ur-Lewis for the delight of experts alone. The evolution from the earlier texts to the final *Wild Body*—or, to cut a long story short, from groping vitalism to rigid formalism—was considerable. But from the start the central Lewisian gap between creator and creation was there. The earlier, almost Lawrentian, observation of reality was already undermined by phantasmic parody. The documentary accidentalness of the travelogue was in fact selective of aspects of reality which were both haunted and haunting. As to the more polished and fictional final products, they were to perpetuate this initial tension by "a verbal impasto" thanks to which, according to Hugh Kenner, Lewis "exalted his vices into a style,"[2] downgrading reality to present it as an artificial mechanism. A diagnosis confirmed by Jean-Jacques Mayoux who, when analysing the rationale behind Lewis's style and vision, remarks that "no sooner has subjectivity been kicked out than it bursts in through the window."[3] However brief the expulsion, it leaves its mark, turning interiority into a sort of collage. This may well constitute the essence of the Lewisian "alternative," and suggests a "post-modernism" before the hour.[4]

The prolonged distillation of such paradoxes is probably responsible for the most salient feature of *The Wild Body*. It stands as one of these rare collections of stories which, though elusive, are felt to be intensely controlled by "a logical pattern," "an inherent design," or "a strong sense of form," as John Gawsworth[5] recognized fifty years ago. In the final version of "Inferior Religions," Lewis saw his characters as a colony of "theorems," and one is tempted to evoke here—though they have with them little in common apart from some pivotal concern with the body—such collections as Roussel's or Kafka's "machines célibataires"[6], Joyce's *Dubliners*, Hemingway's "Nick" sketches and Sartre's *Le Mur*. There must be a few more, but not many, of these systematic "Diaboliques," and on all counts *The Wild Body* and its characters belong to that party of sublime extremists.

Such comparisons may at least shed some light on the practice of the Lewisian "alternative." Lewis's "bodies" are not submitted to a crucial test—epiphany, fracture or execution. Half-document, half-fiction, these "stories" generally present a gang of active paralytics prone to mock aggressions, by means of which they project a primitive tottering shadow for the benefit of an ambiguous observer or *agent provocateur*. A world of degraded myths inviting the reader to recognize some ancestral grimace filtering through our existential routine. Not characters facing a liberating crisis, but "shells," congealed in rituals, whose very human, though degenerate, gestures told Beckettian "Stories and Texts for Nothing," long before the hour. Lewis did with Descartes, Goethe, Dostoevsky and Bergson what Beckett was to do with Dante, Geulincx, Proust and Joyce.

A late but characteristic postscript to this manipulation of the real is offered in the opening pages of *Snooty Baronet* (1932), when Kell-Imrie (first named Carr-Orr, which suggests that this novel was initially conceived as a sort of sequel to *The Wild Body*) defines himself in these terms:

> I am not a narrative writer. As to being a "fiction" writer, I could not bring myself to write down that I am not *that*. I may never I hope be called upon to repudiate an imputation of that order. But the art of narrative, that is a different matter to "fiction." To Defoe I take off my hat. Then there was Goldsmith. I should prefer to make it clear at once at all events that I occupy myself only with scientific research. Such claim as I may have to be a man-of-letters reposes only upon the fact that my investigations into the nature of the human being have led me to employ the arts of the myth-maker, in order the better to present (for the purposes of popular study) my human specimens. Henri Fabre dramatized his insects in that way . . .

Lewis's reverence for Defoe is suggestive: the forefather of the English novel only began his literary career (shuffling reporting and forgery) when he found himself hopelessly entangled in the "fictions" of a treble *agent double*. Such contamination is typical of *The Wild Body*. It explains why these stories are only animated by the ghost of an action—the "narrative" vector becoming a "fictional" vortex, with no compensatory introspection being allowed in. These are severe limitations, and one may wonder what is left to fill up the stories. An answer may be sketched by doing what Lewis did for "Laughter" in "Inferior Religions," when he decided to "catalogue (its) attributes." We can name six basic "attributes" of *The Wild Body*: 1) a real presence, 2) fascination, 3) and 4) comedy and tragedy, 5) the grotesque, and 6) the absurd. At least implicitly, all these elements were present from the start, but it is only progressively that they came to be recognized as such—and this in the above order, just as in a monogram the intertwined letters are to be read in a given succession. Elucidating these took Lewis twenty years—a highly significant process paralleled by the similar rewriting or repeating of the rest of his early creative production (the two *Tarrs* and the two *Enemy of the Stars*, **"The War Baby"** duplicating **"Cantelman's Spring-Mate"**).

1) A REAL PRESENCE. The prerequisite for any of these stories is a casual meeting with a "body" or group of "bodies" perceived as foreign, strange, and alien. Such presence is "given"—apparently imposed from the outside on the anonymous witness. It is not invented and organized by an author as will be the case later with sophisticated productions like "Sigismund." Often presented as an illustration of some sociological or cultural observation, the documentary vignettes exploit the picturesque and the picaresque, as if Baedeker and Dickens were joining hands to caricature national types—provocative, yet essentially flat. Some of Ker-Orr's poses smack of a typically English superiority complex towards foreigners. Yet, ascribing strange physical aspects or behaviours to a national mould was not the original object, as Lewis's elimination of capital letters for adjectives of nationality will soon prove. The nation—like games and sports (see "Our Wild Body")—was recognized as one more "opium du peuple"—an inferior religion. In fact the characters of the early stories all tend to overdo their foreignness by their being so marginal, eccentric or primitive—a multistoreyed alienation culminating in Monsieur de Valmore, this French pseudo-American operating in Spain. What it must have meant for young Lewis was that French mechanical Cartesianism, the Slav soul feeding on Dostoevskian contradictions, and the baroque austerity of the Spaniards combined to infect the dreamy imagination of a slow-developing Briton. There "the alternative" found its first expression—in a reality, which, being selected by an obscure emotion, could not be properly focused, could not yield a clear message.

2) FASCINATION. A coherence, which is compulsive and disquieting, gives the travelogue another dimension—magnetic, ontological, and problematic—and herein lie the difficulty and significance of *The Wild Body.* Irreducible yet split, it acquires an existence less touristic than Berkeleyan, being inseparable from that other presence, the beholder's. The only mode of perception allowed by its gesticulating opaqueness is fascination. Bestre, the "eye-man," became Lewis's "enfant chéri," because he was the archfascinator of the tribe; le Père François exists only in so far as his disjointed utterances turn reality into a mesmerizing patchwork full of holes; whereas Ludo shut in an opaque body by his blindness is killed by a reflected otherness he embodies. According to Maurice-Jean Lefevre[7], "the awareness of a fissure in reality," making it appear "super-real," constitutes the essence of fascination. This applies very well to what is constantly happening in *The Wild Body.* An author may handle his material so as to make it appear fascinating, but fascination here is rooted in an uncertainty involving both subject and object. The puzzled observer is as paralyzed as the object of his perception—and perception always seems to imply a dangerous frontier and cruel no-man's-land. This was not obvious at first because the author-narrator remained impersonal, but **"A Breton Journal,"** which embodied the first apprehensions of The Wild Body, was animated by such "fissures" suggested by static characters exuding a "super-reality" of sorts (a "sub-reality" might be a better word in view of the future "*Inferior* Religions"). Postures suspend time, and the body becomes "a tableau vivant."

The Wild Body and its "fissures" offer an approach to an understanding of Lewis's dual genius. In "Beginnings" we learn how, when he started writing in Brittany, Lewis kept drawing and story-telling in tight compartments—the story feeding on what was left over after the drawing had been completed. Yet the literary Lewis remained manifestly visual. A prisoner of his fascination? This suggests an unresolved tension, the enduring effects of which probably determined—to name only two significant developments contemporary with the long story of *The Wild Body*—the adoption of the Vortex (an archetype of fascination with its centripetal immobility), and the defence of space and fixity as expressed in *Time and Western Man.* That the prolonged rumination of *The Wild Body* was not accidentally due to World War I but was more fundamentally personal, solipsistic and Berkeleyan seems confirmed by the way its saga came to its conclusion. Lewis redoubled the duplication by endowing his "eye" with a distinct personality and body—that of a showman with a full name and a family background secretly and ironically modelled on his own (see **"A Soldier of Humour"**). Ker-Orr, acting as a screen, reduced the effect of fascination and enabled the paralyzed observer to complete his saga and eventually emerge as The Enemy[8].

Then, retrospectively, fascination could be seen as corresponding with the repressed recognition of an intimate trauma. But here the *Zeitgeist* should not be ignored. Lewis belonged to a generation of exiles repelled by the debilitating respectability of the Victorian scene and attracted by the artistic ebullience of the Continent. The two

most conspicuous "anti-Lewises," Joyce and Lawrence, are obvious names here, but also the more transitional Forster with such contemporary novels as *Where Angels Fear to Tread.* All these writers specialized in "fascinating fissures" of one sort or another—and all suffered from a parental deficit, on the father's side. Let us concentrate on a so far unexplored comparison with J. M. Synge, whose formative years—not long before Lewis's—greatly resemble those which saw the incubation of *The Wild Body.* Like Lewis, who, by his own admission, was "congealed in a kind of cryptic immaturity" (see "How One Begins," a diagnosis confirmed by Augustus John in his memoirs), Synge squandered years of his life in that Mecca of the arts, Paris, gripped by an inertia redolent of "fin de siècle" *ennui,* before, suddenly, on his homecoming, erupting into creativity with the discovery of a liberating primitivism. Synge's Connemara played a part strikingly similar to Lewis's Brittany and the Playboy is a wild body par excellence. Synge's Parisian exile and subsequent primitivist explosion can be reasonably linked to a parental "fissure" (his father died when he was very young) which the Oedipal explosions of *The Playboy of the Western World* can be seen to perpetuate by an extraordinary jargon akin to that of the final **"Bestre"** for instance—this in an atmosphere of comedy both exacerbating and bridging the abysmal paralyzing absence.

Bridging impossible existential gaps is precisely what—for structural anthropology—seems to be the *raison d'être* of mythic thought. Lewis's "saurian" immersion in the Breton summer and his somnambulic approach to his "bodies" may well have reflected the circumstances of his early life—his family romance—and an "indigestion of reality" which later Pringle obscurely recognized. Let us recall that Lewis's parents separated when their son was eleven, and that the "fissure" was spatially intensified by his father being American and his mother British.[9] As time passed his mother asserted herself as protectress, confidante and money-lender while the father (who had eloped with the maid) receded into the role of an absentee. Much could be made out of this to explain aspects of Lewis's future behaviour, but such approaches are irritating in that they seem amateurishly to oversimplify things, yet it may also be that such an easy geometry recaptures something of the original fascination—and it must be recognized, at least, that this is the sort of explanation Lewis himself succumbed to later when he wrote:

> My mother's and father's principal way of spending their time at the period of my birth was the same as mine now: my mother painting pictures of the farmhouse where we lived, my father writing books inside it . . . For a person like myself to both write and paint is being bi-lingual.[10]

This is a reconstruction on the author's part, but nonetheless telling. This idyllic vignette, rather reminiscent of Lewis's Breton scenes, constitutes an attempt at bridging the gap and going back to the Golden Age home—and Lewis's dual genius, as defined here, appears as an indirect effort to reunify the separated (and now dead) parents. That this sketch should not have been included in

Rude Assignment is all the more revealing—it was probably thought too intimately limpid.

Seen in this light the basic fictional ingredients of *The Wild Body* take on "a family likeness" confirming the secret coherence of these stories, and the lasting effects of the fascination.

Settings: foreign inns and hotels, cafés and boarding houses—rooms, opposing their ambiguous privacy to the bleak openness of public places, mostly streets and squares. Clearly a frontier world of doors and windows for this decadent version of the Romantic Wanderer, the then fashionable Tramp (see Augustus John, W. H. Davies and Douglas Goldring). One telling exception, the only "private house" is the Ankou's—and it is a cave, a troglodytic tomb to which the narrator is refused admission.

Actions: no plot, but all the grotesqueries of hotel life—the violent enticing of customers, invasion and trespass, parasitism and voyeurism, escape and expulsion.

Characters: vagrants and guardians, all specialists in hospitality or inhospitality—with even the Saltimbanques offering the brief shelter of their tent and benches.

Couples: young lovers are rare and aggressive—"amours ancillaires" exclusively (again, Charles Lewis had eloped with the maid). Married couples are bitter, destructive and generally childless—the Saltimbanques exhibiting their "gytes" only to make the world more fundamentally gloomy. The only happily united family (that of the painter in **"A Spanish Household"**) is comically mechanical.

Children: unexpectedly, from what has just been said, a very active group, with the true children, such as the laughing apocalyptist of **"Les Saltimbanques,"** the Picasso-esque shadows of **"A Breton Journal,"** and the Soutine-esque dull groom stunned by Roland in **"A Breton Innkeeper,"** but above all the permanently infantile characters who contaminate the adult world, such as the child-man persecuted by brats in the final snapshot of **"The 'Pole.'"** Ultimately all the inmates of *The Wild Body* will be defined as "wild children" in "Inferior Religions."

Showmanship: the author-narrator may be suspected of being the arch-child of the whole system—and to pass from the impersonal narrator of 1909, through Pringle (the devouring "child" and uncertain lover), to the aggressive showman of 1927, is to pass from the foundling to the bastard of the Freudian family romance,[11] an evolution confirmed by that of the rather meek Isoblitsky of **"The 'Pole'"** into the enigmatic Zoborov who, like a hermit crab, usurps the erotic shell of **"Beau Séjour."**

Parental figures: if the conquest of a home can be seen as the mainspring of these stories, then the childless fascinating "bodies" animating them should be susceptible to interpretation as father and mother images. Madame Brotcotnaz (curiously associated through heavy drinking with Ker-Orr's absent mother), or Madame Chalaran, or the Cornac's wife seem to present various facets of the moth-

er seen from the son's point of view (a victim of male brutality, a money guardian, a charming companion, etc.). Treated in sympathetic half-tones, they are definitely less prominent than the father images. The isolation of these may stand for the father's absence—and they are brutally dealt with. Wrecks and invalids (Monsieur Jules Montort, Ludo, le Père François, Monsieur Chalaran), or else unstable giants (Monsieur Brobdingnag, Monsieur de Valmore), all are manipulated, humiliated or killed by fate, or the "son's" aggressiveness. To this, two exceptions: **"Beau Séjour,"** in which various "sons" compete in the absence of any parent—and Bestre, first taken as a model reconciling life and art, but eventually discarded, though dearly loved (a typical ambivalence), as a degenerate impotent exhibitionist.

The body: why is it a "body" and why is it "wild"? Here is the central question. An answer should now be less tentative. The body prevailed over the person, because full identity had been denied it by the parental split—the home disappearing and leaving it as the only remaining "shell." Its wildness is therefore inseparable from the absence of a hospitable family nucleus. It is condemned to an exile during which layer upon layer of externality is built up to make up for the lost identity and protect the inner void—see the image of the Russian doll in *Tarr* or Turgenev's "Six Unknown" in **"The Code of a Herdsman."** This process of aggressive reappropriation is nowhere so obvious as in Ker-Orr's triumphant big gnashing teeth which, in his victory over Monsieur de Valmore, confirm him both as an American and as an Enemy.

Recrossing these tempestuous thresholds after the war, and the death of his parents, Lewis—in all likelihood thanks to his recent acquaintance with Freud[12]—probably came to an understanding of what had animated the Breton fascination. This did not lead him to exorcism but allowed him to use laughter as a smoke-screen for sex. *The Wild Body* had acted as a sort of rite of passage for this slow-developer. A rite of passage—is this not a primitive equivalent of the *Bildüngsroman?*

3) and 4) COMEDY and TRAGEDY. The other basic constituents of *The Wild Body* are easier to assess because they translate a subliminally perceived existential anguish into clear formal patterns. The obscure fascination exerted by the actors of *The Wild Body*—which Lewis was unable or reluctant to understand—had to be tamed, given a reassuring vestment making the story communicable and lively while preserving its secret message. Comedy provided this great cloak—all the more easily as its eruptive gaiety harmonized with Lewis's release from his long Continental inertia. Like Synge, Lewis, quite naturally, opted for forms of comedy closely associated with the body—farce, horseplay, practical jokes and the burlesque—wrongly considered as "low" forms, whereas they are in fact more profound than intellectual wit through being—as with Jonson or Swift—near to sheer physical reality, or the unconscious. Just as in *The Playboy of the Western World* the parricidal mood arouses a collective explosion of joyful physical liberatio, the Lewisian vortex of fascination is strategically counterbalanced by the bumping acceleration of the fête surrounding it.

Alan Munton, who shrewdly investigated this aspect, rightly relates it to the celebrations of Carnival and the *commedia dell'arte* deriving from it—and surely from Paris to Munich, from balls to travelling circuses, Lewis explored a festive Europe. This leads Munton to draw a convincing contrast between the vitalistic celebrations of the early stories and the sour intellectual satires of Lewis's post-World War I period. It is true that the feast is no longer to be found in **"Sigismund"** or **"You Broke my Dream."** But this does not mean that the early *Wild Body* was just "good fun," and Munton makes it clear that not only comedy but satire originates in the Carnival impulse, which is intensely concerned with the body, its dark contradictory functions and revitalizing dismemberment. As R. C. Elliott's studies of satire and utopia[13] confirm, the topsy-turvidom of The Feast of Fools allows the mixing of *genres* so typical of *The Wild Body.* Degenerate rites, inferior myths, apocalyptism (so very close to utopia), sordidness, decay and death are just as active in these stories as the enjoyment of the ludicrous, or the cultivation of black humour (see Timothy Materer's analysis), or the pursuit of an "idée fixe" (see Robert Chapman's study).[14] Laughter has its shadow—and in tragi-comedy even the killing of Death reasserts the "fissure" over which "it is impossible for logic to throw any bridge."[15]

Such dualism marks the limits of Lewis's primitivism when compared with D. H. Lawrence's "polarity." Lawrence, when he perceives the "fissure" (in "Snake" or "Medlars and Sorb-Apples") makes a rush for it to merge the conflicting poles of his fascination down there in the darkness. Lewis, on the contrary, explodes out of it—volcanically. Just compare—for the final confrontation of the body and its impending fate—the Orphic torches of Lawrence's "Bavarian Gentians" with the high voltage bulb Lewis lights in "The Sea Mists of the Winter" as a defence against blindness. Jean-Jacques Mayoux is certainly right when he defines Lawrence as "the last of the great anti-absurdists."[16] With Lewis—inseparable from an intense lucidity—the paradox went on asserting itself, as can be seen in the neo-Nietzschean aphoristic definitions of "Inferior Religions" where comedy systematically collides with tragedy, thus belittling the mythopoeic vision. By 1917, sure enough, the Carnival had become "arctic"—frozen.

5) THE GROTESQUE. The effort to dominate the still obscure fascination by associating its "fissure" with the clash of comedy and tragedy in the mixing of *genres* led to the growth of a strained, bombastic, out of the way style. In the early sketches, the behaviour of the characters was definitely grotesque, but not the style and viewpoint communicating them—and their fascination remained encapsulated in the objectiveness of the travelogue. With **"Unlucky for Pringle,"** fiction and reality begin to overlap in exploding combinations—the plea for a healthy physical communication advocated in "Our Wild Body" being systematically flouted. On the one hand Lewis pays lip service to fictional verisimilitude by introducing dialogues and an apparently realistic two-storeyed narration. But the commentary corrupts this to exalt voyeurism and the tortuous paradoxes of body and home, digestion and excretion. We find such sentences as "the unwearied

optimism of these inanimate objects, how they occupied stolidly room after room, was appalling," or "Monsieur Chalaran had shown his displeasure and discomfort by eating everything within reach," or towards the end of the story "the house *would* vomit him; it could not assimilate him." Formal sophistication and stylistic amplification marked the first **"Soldier of Humour,"** and, under the influence of the Vortex and the War, blew up in the exuberant imagery of "Inferior Religions." Thereafter it was caught up in the extreme "impasto" of the 1922 **"Bestre"** which paved the way for the final systematic exploitation of the grotesque in the general rewriting of 1927. It was then only that Ker-Orr spoke of "stylistic anomaly" and "grotesque realism."

The grotesque shows a remarkable structural similarity to fascination, in that it stylistically expresses an "unresolved clash of incompatibles."[17] Here is the "fissure" again, with this difference perhaps that the grotesque seems to be essentially a gesticulation whereas fascination paralyzes the beholder. Besides, grotesque exaggeration turns reality into a collage, and this is why grotesque characters are necessarily "flat," to use E. M. Forster's distinction. It is appropriate here to note that this grotesque flatness has been linked with "Oedipal arrest."[18] The obsessions of *The Wild Body,* as well as the cryptic disclosure of Ker-Orr's family backdrop, do not contradict such ascription. The "fissure" of laughter was superimposed onto that of sex, and the resulting wildness—which may well be a tongue-in-cheek sublimation—nonetheless perpetuates the rich initial incomprehensibility by a perverse gibberish. It is not surprising therefore that such a pioneer in noncommunication and mind-"massaging" nonsense should have turned out to be one of Marshall McLuhan's mentors.

6) THE ABSURD. The aphorisms of the 1917 "Inferior Religions" made it clear that Lewis was in search of a philosophy to replace the superficial vitalism of "Our Wild Body," and fit his new turbulent style in which each word made grimaces at its neighbours. Philip Thomson comes to the conclusion that the "consistent perception of the grotesque, or the perception of grotesqueness on a grand scale, can lead to the notion of universal absurdity."[19] This was the road followed by Lewis, and it led to the apparently illuminating discovery of the concept of the absurd in the final act of *The Wild Body*—"The Meaning of the *Wild Body*"—in which the word "absurd" occurs no less than seven times in seven pages. Lewis seems to have been the first to use this word systematically as a formal critical concept. The Lewisian "alternative"—this intuition of post-modernism—is closely associated with this exaltation of the absurd, which in many ways prefigured not only existentialism (see *Self Condemned* and *The Writer and the Absolute*) but the formalist distortions of The Theatre of the Absurd and the Dark Humourists, as well as the geometric expressionism of the "Nouveau Roman."

The part played by the absurd in *The Wild Body* has been sufficiently analysed by Robert Chapman and myself to make all but attention to a few essential points unnecessary here. The final exaltation of the absurd does not mean that it was absent from the earliest work (see the antics of the Farceur in **"The 'Pole'"**), but it is only later that Lewis came to perceive its universality. For surely there is not one literary work which, at one stage or another, does not make use of absurdity, but this universalizing—a complete reduction—is compulsory for a work to be "a work of the absurd." In the case of Lewis, this discovery coincided with the 1914-1918 war, and also probably with the death of his parents—the old personal fascination of the Breton summer was superseded by a general theoretical vision of the absurd, whose structure is in fact similar to that of both fascination and the grotesque ("the chasm lying between being and non-being"). It operates however on the level of logic, for it takes a logical man to perceive the absurd—a situation congenial to the mechanical paradoxes of Lewis's dualism. The elimination of personal involvement and the use of a systematic reduction separate the two post-war stories (**"Sigismund"** and **"You Broke my Dream"**) from the main stream of The Wild Body; yet they were included in the final *Wild Body* because reduction and irreducibility are twins after all.

The final organization of *The Wild Body,* with its core of seven stories, its accompanying essays, and its comet tail—and all its talk about "theorems" and "propositions"—constitutes the stringent demonstration of "a system of feeling." This suggests what is the specific, and indeed unique and paradoxical, nature of the Lewisian absurd—its energy. Vitalism expelled, there remained the sheer energy of the Vortex—the Eye.

The Wild Body has an origin, but no message, outside the turbulence which surrounds its fixity.

Notes

[1] Preface to the Black Sparrow Press bibliography of Lewis, page 11.

[2] *Wyndham Lewis,* page 92.

[3] "Wyndham Lewis ou la puissance du sensible," *La Quinzaine Littéraire,* XVI, no. 347 (1-15 May 1981), page 24.

[4] See Fredric Jameson's important study, *Fables of Aggression: Wyndham Lewis, the Modernist as Fascist,* 1979.

[5] *Apes, Japes and Hitlerism: A Study and Bibliography of Wyndham Lewis,* 1932.

[6] To use Michel Carrouges' seminal metaphor. See *Les Machines Célibataires,* Paris, Arcanes, 1954—and the ensuing recent exhibition of the same title at the Centre Pompidou.

[7] *L'image fascinante et le surréel,* Paris, Plon, 1965, page 267.

[8] A liberation comparable, perhaps, to Conrad's who, when "blocked" in the writing of the intensely autobiographical *Lord Jim,* hit on the idea of Marlow, the mediator.

[9] His having been born on a yacht—his father's yacht—may also contribute to explain Lewis's "quartered" vision of space.

[10] "The Vita of Wyndham Lewis," an unpublished biographical sketch written in 1949, Cornell University.

[11] See Marthe Robert's *Roman des Origines, Origines du Roman,* Paris, Grasset, 1972.

[12] See the introduction of the word "libido" in the 1922 "Bestre," Ker-Orr's family background in the 1927 "Soldier of Humour," the deletion of "succès d'hystérie" in the final "Inferior Religions," Zoborov's "inferiority complex," and what Lewis said on Freud in *Time and Western Man.* See also my "Off to Budapest with Freud."

[13] *The Power of Satire,* Princeton University Press, 1960. *The Shape of Utopia,* The University of Chicago Press, 1970.

[14] *Wyndham Lewis the Novelist,* 1976. *Wyndham Lewis: Fictions and Satires,* 1973.

[15] "The Meaning of the Wild Body."

[16] *D. H. Lawrence. Poèmes,* Paris, Aubier, 1977 page 64.

[17] Philip Thomson. *The Grotesque,* 1972, page 27.

[18] See Mark Spilka's *Dickens and Kafka,* 1963.

[19] *The Grotesque,* page 32.

Kelly Anspaugh (essay date 1995)

SOURCE: "Getting Even with Uncle Ez: Wyndham Lewis's 'Doppelgänger'," in *Journal of Modern Literature,* Vol. XIX, No. 2, Fall, 1995, pp. 235-43.

[*In the following excerpt, Anspaugh argues that the protagonist of Lewis's story "The Doppelgänger" can be seen to represent Lewis's friend Ezra Pound, while the "Stranger" who in the tale proves to be the protagonist's alter ego and superior as a poet, scholar, and man, is a symbol for Lewis himself.*]

The protagonist of **"Doppelgänger,"** Lewis' Gothic *récit a clef,*[33] is named Thaddeus Trunk or "Uncle Thad" (thereby conflating Pound's self-given "Uncle Ez" and the name of Pound's grandfather, Thaddeus Coleman Pound, who appears as "T.C.P." in the *Cantos*).[34] Trunk is a poet and scholar, "a snuffly old *passéiste,* digging about among musty old manuscripts" (p. 25). Here Lewis' text recalls his earlier representation of Pound in *Time and Western Man* as a "man in love with the past." Trunk has for health reasons retreated with his wife to a mountain-top cabin in Vermont and is there surrounded by a host of sycophants. "He may be regarded," observes Lewis' narrator, "as a victim of the Public. Those who, like myself, know what he can do away from men, where he can be a great poet, and hold up his head among the Gods, have lamented at what we saw" (p. 27). Again we hear echoes of Lewis' representation of Ezra in *Time* as a "crowd," as well as of his complaint that Pound has abandoned his true vocation of Poet.

Enter on the scene a mysterious "Stranger," claiming to be a distant relative. Thaddeus invites the Stranger to stay, and the latter proves himself to be—to borrow Lewis' earlier description of Pound—a most gentlemanly, discriminating parasite. In a series of uncanny incidents, the Stranger proves himself Trunk's better as scholar, poet, and man. Trunk's hostility towards this figure builds, and the story climaxes, as most of Lewis' narratives do, in a violent physical confrontation: "But the next minute the Stranger was battering at [Trunk's] face, and then delivering a haymaker, as the youthful audience later described it, in the center of the bulging beard, which sent him reeling down upon the floor, where he lay at full length, completely still" (p. 32). The Stranger departs, taking Trunk's wife with him, and the narrator comments: "to state briefly what has happened, a second Thaddeus, whom Stella recognized as the real Thaddeus had made his appearance, and Stella, very simply, changed Thaddeuses" (pp. 32-3).

In his brief commentary on this story, Timothy Materer claims that Lewis "is so fearful of seeming unfair to his old friend that the begins the story with a fictional preface in which the author of '**Doppelgänger**' tells his editor that he does not wish to 'debunk' Pound."[35] This preface, in fact, echoes the opening chapter to *Blasting & Bombardiering,* in which Lewis explains that his intention is to save all his fellow "Men of 1914" (and himself) from biography of the sort perpetrated by Lytton Strachey: "I would rescue a few people I respect, and who are, for their sins, objects like myself, of great popular curiosity and liable to continue so, from the obloquy and misrepresentation which must be their unenviable lot."[36] In the **"Doppelgänger"** preface, Lewis assures his editor (and by extension his reader) that he is debunking not Pound but rather what he calls his "publicity figure": "For a man's publicity is a caricature of himself; it is really how the public sees 'greatness.' Now it was this heroic publicity scarecrow which you had in mind when you spoke of *debunking,* was it not?" (p. 24). Thus Lewis represents his story as yet another effort on his part to save Pound, both from himself and from malicious others.

Once again, though, it appears that the Enemy may be protesting too much. To begin with, one wonders about Lewis' translation of St. Elizabeth's Hospital into a sort of New England Parnassus—or, at the very least, magic mountain. Given that Lewis may have felt it necessary to disguise the setting in order not to offend the American authorities, such a translation is not likely to win Pound a reader's sympathy (to "soften the heart of the world," as Lewis put it in his letter to Paige). Rather, it works to underscore Pound's egotism and elitism. Lewis' Trunk clearly is a pompous ass and, although highly comic, not especially lovable. He is a type of *Miles Gloriosus,* and the reader enjoys seeing him flattened. Finally, although Lewis tells us that his Stranger is meant to represent the true Thaddeus (that is, the true Pound), one cannot help but see the *doppelgänger* as Lewis' double, or rather as Lewis himself projected into his story. Once this identification is made, **"Doppelgänger"** resolves into a piece of wish fulfillment or fantasy, in which the author invades his rival's space, proves himself *il miglior fabbro* and walks away with the girl. The Stranger's question to Trunk after having beaten him, "Was I to remain passive, under your

filthy abuse?" (p. 32), might well be read as the paranoid Lewis' response to Pound, who once accused him of writing "like . . . a God damn fool."[37] In short, **"Doppelgänger"** can be seen as a sort of neo-Gothic allegory of revenge, or what Fredric Jameson, in his analysis of Lewis' narrative technique, terms a "fable of aggression."[38]

Yet there is one final turn of the screw to be taken into account. **"Doppelgänger"** concludes with Thaddeus Trunk lorn and lonely on the mountain-top, a mere "shell" of the man he once was (p. 33). Lewis' metaphor recalls the final chapter of his autobiographical novel *Self Condemned,* published in the same year as his story. In "The Cemetery of Shells," Lewis presents his protagonist Rene Harding—who is indeed self-condemned, having ruined his life through reckless acts of pride—as an Eliotic hollow man, as a "glacial shell of a man."[39] That Lewis should employ the same metaphor in the same year for himself and Pound is highly suggestive, for Pound and Lewis were, in a sense, doubles in their shared catastrophe. That Pound may have sensed his own presence in *Self Condemned* and been greatly moved is suggested by his letter to Lewis of 6 December 1954: "to confirm HIGH opinion of "Self-Cndd" / it and Rot-Hill [**Rotting Hill,** a collection of stories that Lewis published in 1951[40]] all post 2nd / hell lit / yet discovered among ruins of Albion. Shd / git yu the Nobble [Nobel Prize]."[41]

Any psychoanalytic reading of the Lewis/Pound relationship would please neither of the principals, for both were openly hostile to Freud and his work.[42] My interpretive paradigm, however, is not Freud's—or Harold Bloom's—Oedipal one, with Son rebelling against Father. Rather, when considering the case of Lewis and Pound, one is reminded of Cain and Abel: the eternal story of sibling rivalry. Joyce recognized the appropriateness of this paradigm when he cast both Lewis and Pound as his agonistic brothers—Shauns to his Shem—in *Finnegans Wake.* Brothers, it seems, will always be loving and hating one another, and Lewis was always loving and hating Pound. The latter, having a kind heart, overlooked the hate. "I am FOR Mr. Lewis, even when he is wrong" Pound once proclaimed, and offered as justification for his position: "I believe that all large mammals shd. be preserved."[43] Perhaps contemporary critics should follow Uncle Ez's lead.

Notes

[33] Wyndham Lewis, "Doppelgänger," Encounter, IV (1954), pp. 23-33; hereafter cited parenthetically within the text.

[34] That Lewis was indeed aware of Pound's grandfather and his personal history is suggested by a passage in *Blasting & Bombardiering* in which Lewis echoes an English anti-Semite's accusation that Pound was of the "diaspora of Wisconsin" (p. 274). T. C. Pound was once lieutenant governor of Wisconsin. Other parallels between Pound and Trunk are pointed out by Timothy Matere in his introduction to *Pound/Lewis The Letters of Ezra Pound and Wyndham Lewis* (New Directions, 1985), pp. xv-xvi.

[35] *Pound/Lewis,* p. xv.

[36] *Blasting and Bombardiering* (1937; Calder, 1982), p. 13.

[37] *Pound/Lewis*, p. 152.

[38] Fredric Jameson, *Fables of Aggression: Wyndham Lewis, the Modernist as Fascist* (University of California Press, 1979).

[39] *Self Condemned* (1954; Black Sparrow, 1983), p. 407.

[40] *Rotting Hill*, ed. Paul Edwards (1951; Black Sparrow, 1986). The title is taken from Pound's comic corruption of the name of the London area Notting Hill, where Pound had lived while in England and where Lewis lived during his last days.

[41] *Pound/Lewis*, p. 283.

[42] Lewis rejects Freud as "a sort of mephistophelian Dr. Caligari" in *Time and Western Man* (p. 310) and caricatures him as "Dr. Frumpfsusan" in Part II of *The Apes of God* (1930; Black Sparrow, 1981). In a letter to Lewis of 11 August 1952, Pound remarks of psychoanalysis: "as for the Viennese sewage/ 40 years and not produced ONE interesting work. In fact hoax for paralyzing the will . . ." (*Pound/Lewis*, p. 269).

[43] "On Wyndham Lewis," *Shenandoah*, IV (1953), p. 17.

FURTHER READING

Biography

Meyers, Jeffrey. *The Enemy: A Biography of Wyndham Lewis.* London: Routledge and Kegan Paul, 1980, 391 p.

> Major, well-documented biography of Lewis, including extensive coverage of his childhood years.

Wagner, Geoffrey. *A Portrait of the Artist as the Enemy.* New Haven: Yale University Press, 1957, 363 p.

> Early biography paying more attention to the details of Lewis's life and work and less on critical assessment; includes an extensive bibliography.

Criticism

Beatty, Michael. "The Earliest Fiction of Wyndham Lewis and *The Wild Body.*" *Theoria* 48, No. 1 (1977): 37-45.

> Discussion of Lewis's early stories that were later revised and included in *The Wild Body.*

Duncan, Ian. "Towards a Modernist Poetic: Wyndham Lewis's Early Fiction." In *Wyndham Lewis: Letteratura/Pittura*, pp. 67-85. Selerio editore, 1982.

> Argues that a "redefinition of sensibility" can be detected by examining the differing aesthetic and theoretical concerns in Lewis's early stories and their revised forms in *The Wild Body.*

Meyers, Jeffrey. *Wyndam Lewis: A Reevaluation; New Essays.* Montreal: McGill University Press, 1980, 276 p.

> Studies of various aspects of Lewis's work.

Munton, Alan. "Wyndham Lewis: The Transformations of Carnival." In *Wyndham Lewis: Litteratura/Pittura*, a cura di Giovanni Cianci, pp. 141-57. Palermo: Sellerio editore, 1982.

> Discussion centrally concerned with *The Wild Body.*

Soons, Allan. "Sigismundo, Delbora and Wyndham Lewis's 'Sigismund'." *Arcadia* 19, No. 3 (1984): 170-74.

> Examines the Spanish source of Lewis's short story "Sigismund."

Additional coverage of Lewis's life and career is contained in the following sources published by Gale Group: *Contemporary Authors*, Vols. 104, 157; *Dictionary of Literary Biography*, Vol. 15; and *Twentieth-Century Literary Criticism*, Vols. 2, 9.

Clarice Lispector
1920–1977

Ukrainian-born Brazilian novelist, short story writer, journalist, essayist, children's book author, and translator.

INTRODUCTION

One of the preeminent Latin American writers of the twentieth century and a revolutionizing force in Brazilian literature, Lispector has been hailed as a brilliantly original prose stylist whose modernist narratives moved away from the regional interests of her predecessors to take up universal themes deeply rooted in the psychological drama of everyday existence. While her novels and non-fiction have enjoyed critical acclaim, it is generally agreed that Lispector's short stories are her most accessible works, and in them are found the purest expression of her major concerns: human suffering and failure; the interrelation of language, life, and identity; the effect of social constraints on individuals; the place of women in male-dominated society; and the subjective nature of reality. Like her longer works, her philosophically oriented stories are told in a stream-of-consciousness or interior-monologue style, with plot subordinated to the inner experiences of her solitary, sensitive characters. The use of paradox also characterizes her fiction, and often in her tales the quotidian and the realm of the fantastic merge, realistic observation is coupled with poetic description, and minor events give rise to extraordinary insight. Her prose style in her short works in particular shows a poet's concern with linguistic nuance and the use of symbolism and metaphor. In addition, Lispector is celebrated as an early practitioner of poststructural and feminist writing because of her interest in the problems of language and existence, gender roles, and sexuality.

Biographical Information

Lispector was reluctant to divulge information about her background to critics, so the details surrounding her birth are difficult to ascertain. Most likely she was born in the Ukraine in 1920, shortly before her family, of Jewish origin, immigrated to the Americas. She spent her early childhood in economically depressed Alagoas and Recife in northeastern Brazil before moving to Rio de Janeiro. Her mother died when Lispector was nine, and she and her sisters were raised by their father, a man of modest means but with a love of books and music. Lispector took advantage of the cultural and educational opportunities available to her in Rio de Janeiro, reading widely in Brazilian and foreign works, expressing a particular fondness for the fiction of Katherine Mansfield, Virginia Woolf, Herman Hesse, and Fyodor Dostoevsky. She decided early that she would become a writer, and her earliest efforts from her teenage years, some of which were published posthumously in *A bela e a fera* (1979), show considerable maturity.

In 1943 Lispector married Mauro Gurgel Valente, a fellow law student at the National Faculty of Law in Rio de Janeiro. After graduating with a law degree, she began working for the Rio de Janeiro newspaper, *A noite*. In 1944 she published her first novel, *Perto do coração selvagem.* Immediately it was applauded for its lyrical language and insightful treatment of the external events in a woman's life seen from an internal perspective. The novel was groundbreaking also because it marked a shift away from the realism and regionalism of traditional Brazilian literature to a modern aesthetic with universal and psychological concerns. Her next two novels, *O lustre* (1946) and *A cidade sitiada* (1948) were written while she lived in Europe, where her husband, then a diplomat, was posted. The couple and their two young boys moved to the United States in 1952. That year, Lispector's first collection of stories, *Alguns contos,* was published to little critical or commercial response.

Lispector separated from her husband in 1959 and resettled in Brazil with her two children. In 1960 she gained widespread recognition for *Laços de família,* an expanded version of her 1952 short story collection. The publication of the novel *A maçã no escuro* in 1961 confirmed her reputation as a major figure in Latin American letters. This was followed with several other well-received novels, including the widely read *A paixão segundo G. H.* (1964), a first-person narrative with biblical overtones. Told by a bourgeois woman, the novel centers on the strange events that lead to her existential awakening. From 1967 to 1973 Lispector wrote short weekly pieces for the *Jornal do Brasil* on a range of subjects, from interviews with other writers to short "chronicles" with fictional qualities. She remarked that her success during this period made her feel as though she was forced to play the role of the "Great Lady of Brazilian Letters," which went against her nature as an intensely private woman. In the 1970s, facing financial difficulties, she reissued many of her earlier works in new anthologies and translated works by Jack London, Walter Scott, Jules Verne, Edgar Allan Poe, Oscar Wilde, and Henry Fielding. With her last novel, *A hora da estrela* (1977), Lispector reached a broader audience as she touched on the theme of social oppression, an element some critics found wanting in her earlier works. She was diagnosed with cancer in the fall of 1977 and died a few weeks later.

Major Works of Short Fiction

Throughout her career, Lispector constantly revised her works, reissuing old stories under new titles, modifying pieces and publishing them under the original titles, and incorporating shorter pieces into longer ones. The six stories in the 1952 collection, *Alguns contos,* appeared eight years later in *Laços de família,* together with other stories written and published while she was living abroad. The reissue of these stories in 1960 immediately captured the imagination of critics, and they continue to be regarded as the reason Lispector is considered a genius of the short story genre. Most of her best-known stories, acknowledged classics of modern Latin American literature, are included in this volume. Many of the protagonists of these tales are females, young and old, who experience epiphanies regarding their identities: in "Amor," for example, a young woman's encounter with a blind man on a tram forces her to question her regimented existence. Several stories deal with the "ties" of family and community that serve to bind and repress, as in "Feliz aniversário," a sad tale about the strained family relationships made clear during an old woman's eighty-ninth birthday party. Animals also figure prominently in these tales; for example, in "O búfalo" a woman goes to the zoo in order to experience the purity of emotion that animals enjoy, and in "O crime do professor de matemática," a man discovers his humanity when he buries a stray dog.

Lispector's third volume of stories, *A legião estrangeira,* also deals with characters awakening to their own consciousness and the reality of the external world. Another recurring theme of these stories, which are almost all told with interior voices, is human beings' isolation from one another. The most anthologized story from this volume, "A mengasem," which describes the coming-of-age of two teenagers, is a commentary on a society that does not allow individuals to choose their own identities but rigidly imposes gender roles on both men and women.

Two collections of stories from the early 1970s, *Felicidade clandestina* and *Onde estivestes de noite?,* are marked by a highly metaphorical, abstract, and self-referential style. Lispector's aesthetic sensibilities saw further development in *A via crucis do corpo,* the last volume of her stories published while she was alive. Lispector herself called these stories potentially dangerous and subversive because they deal frankly with various aspects of sexual behavior considered taboo by conventional society, including masturbation, homosexuality, bisexuality, and geriatric sex. For example, in "Ruído de passos," an eighty-one-year-old woman, too old to take a lover but whose desire for sexual pleasure has never ceased, relies on the guilt-ridden practice of masturbation to relieve her torment and frustration. In "Miss Algrave," a repressed English woman finds freedom and authenticity through her sexuality after being seduced by an extra terrestrial. Gender roles in these stories are often questioned and reversed, as in "Praça Mauá," in which a transvestite who adopts and cares for a child proves to be a better mother than his married female friend.

The stories in a posthumous collection, *A bela e a fera,* comprise Lispector's earliest work, written in the early 1940s, as well as two stories penned during the last year of her life. The emphasis of these stories makes clear that pressing concerns throughout Lispector's writing career were women's issues, the irrationality of human life, and the repression of identity through societal conventions.

Critical Reception

Lispector's potential as a major writer was recognized by Brazilian reviewers with the publication of her first novel in 1944, and critics offered immediate praise for her extraordinary flair for poetic language, intensity of expression, and the psychological complexity of her protagonists, features critics continued to admire in her later works. Lispector's reputation was established with her short story collection *Laços de família,* whose translation into English in 1972 made her one of the most respected writers of short fiction in the late twentieth century. English-language criticism of her short stories has tended to concentrate on this volume, with earlier commentators remarking on the tales' existential concerns and later critics noting the stories' use of myth, religious symbolism, animal imagery, social parody, and feminist thematics. These elements, it has been pointed out, are echoed in all her stories, and even her earliest tales reveal a young writer concerned with the problems of sexual and social identity, gender roles, and the nature of androgynous existence.

It is generally agreed that Lispector's 1974 collection, *A via crucis do corpo,* marks a transition in her development as a writer. As several critics have noted, the stories in this volume depart from her earlier works in their overtly sexual nature; their lack of focus on characters' inner being; their use of colloquial language; the presence of lower-middle-class characters; and their emphasis on the reader's role in conferring meaning to text. Initial reception to the stories was mixed. Many of Lispector's admirers believed the stories marked a decline in the quality of her work. However, others have noted that the stories use a new deconstructivist/postmodern aesthetic model to express in artful form many of her most important concerns, including sexual independence, authenticity, absurdity, male/female relationships, consciousness, and self-determination.

PRINCIPAL WORKS

Short Fiction

Alguns contos   [*Some Stories*] 1952
Laços de família   [*Family Ties*] 1960
A legião estrangeira [*The Foreign Legion*] (stories and essays) 1964
Felicidade clandestina [*Secret Happiness*] 1971
A imitação da rosa [*The Imitation of the Rose*] 1973
Onde estivestes de noite? [*Where Were You That Night?*] 1974
A via crucis do corpo [*The Via Crucis of the Body*] 1974
A bela e a fera [*Beauty and the Beast*] 1979
Soulstorm: Stories 1989

Other Major Works

Perto do coração selvagem [*Near to the Wild Heart*]
  (novel) 1944

O lustre [*The Chandelier*] (novel) 1946

A cidade sitiada [*The Besieged City*] (novel) 1948

Agua viva [*The Stream of Life*] (mixed-genre work) 1960

A maçã no escuro [*The Apple in the Dark*] (novel) 1961

A paixão segundo G. H. [*The Passion According to G. H.*]
  (novel) 1964

O misterio do coelho pensante [*The Mystery of the Thinking Rabbit*] (children's fiction) 1967

A mulher que matou os peixes [*The Woman Who Killed
  the Fishes*] (children's fiction) 1968

Uma aprendizagem; ou, O livro dos prazeres [*An Apprenticeship; or, The Book of Pleasures*] (novel) 1969

A vida intima de Laura [*The Private Life of Laura*]
  (children's fiction) 1974

Visão do esplendor: impressoes leves [*Visions of Splen-
  dor: Slight Impressions*] (essays and sketches) 1974

A hora da estrela [*The Hour of the Star*] (novel) 1977

Um sopro de vida: pulsações [*A Breath of Life: Pulsations*] (mixed-genre work) 1978

A descoberta do mundo [*Discovering the World*] (journalistic essays) 1984

CRITICISM

Rita Herman (essay date 1967)

SOURCE: "Existence in *Laços de família*," in *Luso-Brazilian
Review,* Vol. IV, No. 1, June, 1967, pp. 69-74.

[*In the following essay, Herman analyzes five stories in*
Laços de família, *comparing Lispector's pessimistic out-
look with that of French existentialist thinkers Jean-
Paul Sartre and Albert Camus.*]

Laços de Família, a collection of short stories by Clarice
Lispector, constitutes a personal interpretation of some of
the most pressing psychological problems of man in the
contemporary western world. Liberty, despair, solitude,
the incapacity to communicate, are the main themes that
unite the separate stories into a definite configuration of
the author's pessimistic perception of life. Lispector presents a series of characters, "víctimas agónicas," as Miguel
de Unamuno would say, who find themselves trying desperately to maintain an equilibrium between "reality" and
their own powerful imaginations. Imagination, and by implication solitude, is represented as a double-edged dag-
ger, since on the one hand deviation from the norms that
society erects leads to rejection, unhappiness, and alienation, and on the other, to retreat into a personal fantasy
world, no more than a cowardly escape mechanism.

The existential struggle, for the author, consists in a series
of paradoxes with no solution. How does one establish a
balance between the need to conform and the pulsating
inner life that demands expression? If one is in constant

fear of revealing oneself, how can one interact with others
on an authentic level? The main characters in **Laços de
Família,** nevertheless, are fully conscious that true communication is impossible: society is an artificial barrier that
must not be transcended. Yet their essential problem, as
might be expected, is not to find a meaning for their
senseless lives, but to run from the meaning they have
already acknowledged within themselves and cannot accept. In order to feel themselves part of humanity, in so
far as they are able, they force themselves to cover up
their deepest feelings with the mechanized actions expected of them, thus perpetuating their own isolation. The
outside world, or other human beings, constitute an ever-
present threat to the precarious balance necessary in order to avoid the total disintegration of their own personality vis-à-vis the accepted patterns. The word "laços,"
therefore, has a double significance: the chains of
outward conformity that bind each person to others by
means of a false set of values, and the ties that bind each
one to the other, "sans le savoir," by the total aloneness
that they possess in common. Each character lives in his
own little world, estranged from the rest of humanity,
unable to be free, unable to give, unable to be, and unable
to feel solidarity with the universe. Caught in critical
moments of their existence, they prefer anything rather
than the responsibility of being what they really are—
human beings.

As can be seen from this brief introduction, Lispector's
mentality, rather than Brazilian, comes very close to the
existentialist thought of Albert Camus and Jean-Paul Sartre. Her orientation, however, tends towards a more pessimistic outlook on humanity. Whereas both Camus and
Sartre propose positive solutions within this pessimistic
framework (the former, that of enjoying life to its fullest
and bettering social and economic conditions; the latter
with his theory of "engagement"), Lispector offers no
redemption for her tortured characters. The psychological
anguish from which they suffer ultimately destroys them
and their only hope of salvation. It should be mentioned
here that in the various stories, nothing of importance
really occurs; the emphasis remains on a psychological
level; the action is interior rather than exterior. The tension
is maintained by use of a coherent and logical stream of
consciousness method.

The main characters are living in their own particular Hell.
To the "enfer bourgeois" in *La Chute* by Camus and the
Hell created by oneself and others in *Huis Clos* by Sartre,
Lispector adds a new dimension. None of her characters
are able to assume responsibility for the mere fact that
they are human. If being a "person" implies the ability to
give, receive, feel, and be an individual, not one of the
terrified protagonists in **Laços de Família** has the courage to accept life as it is and live it. Guilt-ridden, confused,
seeking to expiate for an uncommitted crime, they can
neither enjoy life nor escape from it. "Reality" has only
negative connotations and idealism is an excess or a sinful
pleasure which must be avoided at all costs. Saints, mar-
tyrs, poets and mystics are taboo. One must simply be a
person, but how many times does the author repeat that
this is the hardest thing in the world!

If we examine this question further, we can see why the problem that anguishes Lispector is that of being *real.* One of the methods that the author employs to clarify this point is the use of animals in contrast to human beings. In **"O Búfalo,"** the main character goes to the Zoo, not to enjoy herself watching the animals, but to find what she, as a human being, cannot experience—pure hate. Only an animal can feel pure emotions, in view of the fact that its experiences are not colored by the contradictions inherent in human nature. An animal is born, lives without being able to form judgments about its existence, as exemplified in **"Uma Galinha,"** and then dies, totally unaware of any significance or lack of it in the universe. An animal, as has been stated many times before, is no more than a prolongation of the physical world, unable to distinguish between the environment and itself. Thus, it "hates" when denied, "loves" when satisfied. The complexities of human nature, however, vary to such a degree that love and hate are often confused, meaningless actions become meaningful and vice-versa, emotions are distorted, impressions change rapidly, nothing is black and white, and existence offers no easy solutions. It is much easier to be an animal, according to Lispector, since an animal lives on a purely elementary level, while human beings are by nature chaotic and confused. In some of the stories, therefore, the protagonists envy animals, because they are not presented with the difficulties that arise from the necessity to make sense out of a senseless world.

Here, in fact, we have arrived at the essential paradox in Clarice Lispector's stories. In spite of the fact that existence is viewed as totally negative, conditioned by meaningless social patterns from the outside and characterized by interior disunity, according to the author, this very situation must be maintained in order for one to be a human being. If the chains that bind men together are absurd, false, and based on self-denial, these are the very values which must be upheld. Just as in *The Myth of Sisyphus,* in which the desire for meaning and the realization that the world is irrational does not impede man from repeating the same action over and over again, in *Laços de Família,* the characters, fully aware of their own useless efforts, know that they must stop themselves from making any sort of metaphysical leap. On the contrary, all their psychic energy is utilized towards perpetuating absurdity.

Lispector, in a cruel and unequivocal manner, closes off all avenues of escape from the "ananké" that for her is essential to humanity. Man must keep alive his own ridiculous plight in order to be man. Intense beauty is a sensual damnation, perfection, the door to insanity, and the imitation of Christ an easy way out. For the author, these are false positions, because they do not involve contradictions. How much easier it is to give oneself totally to an ideal, an idea, or a passion, than to be human. As Lispector states, "Cristo era a pior tentação." In **"A Imitação da Rosa,"** Laura, seeking to escape from the disintegration of her obsessive-compulsive personality, does not choose, but falls into the temptation of loving perfection, and thus leaves the world of humanity. Instead of playing the role that is expected of her—that is, a normal, problematic

woman and wife—she is dragged into fantasy, tempted by the perfect beauty of the roses that she has purchased, not because she wanted to, but because the vendor insisted. She is, therefore, a failure, because she has been unable to resist her desire to transcend her foolish life. In **"O Crime do Professor de Matemática,"** the main character wishes to expiate his sin—the sin of abandoning his dog, who only asked of him that he be a human being. The act of burying a strange dog, however, does not save him from the realization that he is precisely trying to escape the fact that he is human. He still will try to remain aloof, untouched by those around him, and thus perpetuate *ad infinitum* the sin of desiring perfection, the sin of avoiding his responsibility as a man, the sin of wishing to be a Christ figure. From these few examples, it can be seen that for Lispector, the greatest infamy is both the search for perfection and the idea of perfection as a positive value. Ideals, if obtained, represent the dishumanization of man— the road to a sort of ecstatic slavery (how easy it is to be a slave, how difficult to be free), the denial of the dreadful facts implicit in *la condition humaine.*

In one of the short stories, **"Amor,"** the aforementioned problems are delineated with a strong emotional appeal as well as a profound psychological impact. Lispector, by means of an interior monologue, conveys the existential duality of "to be or not to be," in the main character, Ana. At the beginning of the story, Ana is fully conscious of the paradox she herself has set up. At the same time that she is the perfect mother, wife, housekeeper, she realizes that these roles are nothing more than parts she fulfills expertly in order to reject her own inner reality. The only way in which Ana can replace her own lack of solidity or the inner disorder of her thoughts and emotions, is by losing herself completely in the mechanical and routine tasks she must do. But she is quite aware that the slightest disturbance can change her whole existence. As she comments to herself, "certa hora da tarde era mais perigosa," referring to those few moments during the day, when, without specific duties to perform, she finds existence itself seeming to laugh at her and her useless efforts to organize it into recognizable patterns. Even the trees laugh at her, because she has made the fatal compromise, and exchanged beauty, happiness, and disorder for maturity. Beauty and happiness are too intense to bear, demand total surrender, and have no logical roots. The only way, therefore, in which Ana can justify her lack of courage and her own vicarious existence is by giving of herself (not herself) entirely to that which needs her: her husband, her children, her house, her things. She has rejected the intensity that real living demands for an ordered life. She has simulated real meaning and adheres only to outside demands. In this, however, lies her strength as a real human being.

Her equivocal position, nevertheless, is destroyed by a simple yet profound incident. In a bus, Ana sees a blind man chewing gum and "o mal estava feito." Ana's carefully organized life gives way to fear, hate, and love, to an intensity of emotion so powerful that its beauty is destructive. What does the blind man represent? In the first place, he is a man who cannot see, carrying out a mechanical function—chewing gum. In this action, we can see the identification of the heroine with the blind man, whose life approached her own symbolically, except that she has purposely closed her eyes and continued *acting* instead of living. Ana has refused to acknowledge her life for what it is, and, locked up in her own shell of solitude, has perpetuated her senseless existence. Secondly, the blind man arouses two conflicting emotions in Ana, love and hate: love because of the sympathy for his plight; hate because of her inability to resolve his problem. Because of his physical defect, Ana realizes that not everyone is as fortunate as she. Not everyone has the opportunity to arrange his life in neat little blocks, shutting out suffering, struggle, and pain. The blind man reminds Ana that her world between four safe walls is not the only possible world, that existence takes many strange forms and many different roads. Everyone has the potential to be blind, or lame, or anything. In the manner of Jean-Paul Sartre, Ana reflects upon the "ausência de lei" in the universe. A human being is always in danger: the equilibrium can always crash in one sudden moment of revelation. One cannot help but think again of Sartre, and his marvellous scene in *La Nausée,* where Roquentin, seated on a bench in the park, suddenly realizes that all existence is a possibility of being anything, that nothing is safe or sure, and that the classification of the world is only man's way of trying to impart a false solidity that reality lacks. Equally, each person, within his own little world, chooses his own system of values and rejects those which do not agree with his needs. Reality, on the other hand, retains the potentiality of transforming itself suddenly into strange and unknown forms. Ana goes through the same spiritual metamorphosis as Roquentin. She realizes that she has excluded blind men from her world, pity, hate, all the human emotions that one lives with intensity. Just as Roquentin experiences nausea at the moment of revelation, Ana, at the crisis, feels herself in "uma vida cheia de nausea doce."

Absorbed in her thoughts, Ana forgets to get off the bus. When she finally realizes that she has missed her stop and descends, she discovers that she is lost. She notices that she is near the Botanical Gardens and goes inside. Again, sitting on a bench, she observes the truth about reality; the plants, animals and trees take on strange new forms and colors. The intensity of the emotions that this discovery imparts brings on the same suffocating feeling of nausea that she had experienced upon seeing the blind man. And the intense beauty of existence brings on a reaction of fear. "O jardim era tão bonito que ela teve mêdo do Inferno." Ana has perceived the diabolic quality of existence in all its possibilities and of the infernal nature of beauty. She runs from the garden physically and runs from her own thoughts.

When she finally returns home, she is unable, for a moment, to understand the strange world of order and accepted values that she encounters. But, due to the fact that her husband and children need her, she slowly returns to the life she has so carefully built up—the life of lies, of roles, of certainty, of lack of feeling, And, in another moment of revelation, she realizes that "era mais fácil

ser um santo que uma pessoa." It would have been easier for her to have followed the path that the blind man indicated. If she could have followed the truth, she would have been truly happy. Why? While for a saint there is no duality, on the other hand, for a human being, life consists of constant conflict, cross currents of emotions, uncertainty, and doubt. The hardest task is that of just living as a human being, without convictions, without being able to obtain a oneness or an integrated personality. Ana knows that she cannot follow the easy road—to truth, beauty and perfection. She must continue to act and not to be. Ana permits her husband and children to save her from herself, from her own desire to live.

> Ela continuou sem força nos seus braços. Hoje de tarde alguma coisa tranqüila se rebentara, e na casa toda havia um tom humorístico, triste. É hora de dormir, disse êle, é tarde. Num gesto que não era seu, mas que pareceu natural, segurou a mão da mulher, levando-a consigo sem olhar para trás, afastando-a do perigo de viver.

In destroying her inner reality, Ana has returned to contradiction, to duplicity, to failure—a failure that for Clarice Lispector signifies success. By leaving the world of truth, of all possible combinations, of total liberty, Ana faces only a meaningless system that is unreal because she knows that there is no meaning in the universe—only a useless attempt to order the inexplicable.

Massaud Moises (essay date 1971)

SOURCE: "Clarice Lispector: Fiction and Cosmic Vision," in *Studies in Short Fiction,* Vol. 8, No. 1, Winter, 1971, pp. 268-81.

[*In the following essay, Moises discusses Lispector's use of epiphany or "privileged moments," the relation of her characters to animals, and the influence of existentialism and phenomenology in* Laços de família *and* A legião estrangeira. *Moises contends that the two collections are united by a despairing "cosmic vision" whose only hope of escape is found in art.*]

At the very beginning, let us agree that an essay on the short stories of Clarice Lispector (born 1925), to be complete and satisfactory, should require an all-encompassing examination of her fiction, including both novels and "crônicas."[1] It is indeed true that such a necessity imposes itself whenever we deal with writers skilled in more than one form of literary genre; the examination of each of the various facets sheds light on the others and receives in turn indispensable illumination from them. However, Clarice Lispector's short narratives, far from constituting mere exercises for her novels, conform perfectly to the mold of the short story. The similarity between the two manifestations of her literary craft does not infer that her short narratives escape being short stories but simply that certain of their virtualities are only fully developed in the physical space allowed by the novel form. One may say that the full utilization of the intuitions of this fiction writer occur in her novels without doing damage to the remarkable qualities of her short stories. Because of this condition, it becomes clear that quite a few of the problems that arise in examining her short stories will remain untreated or treated only partially, awaiting related research in the novels and "crônicas."

Conforming to the fundamental structure of the short story, those of Clarice Lispector gravitate around a dramatic unity, that is to say, a unique episode in which either the conflict between two or more characters attains its climax or the protagonist experiences a decisive event in his life which is to mark him indelibly forever. However, her short stories differ from this model, respected for better or worse by the cultivators of the genre since its appearance, in that dramatic unity is not observed through external action, progressively accelerated until the crisis, but by an internal action.[2]

In reality, the existential moment on which the characters stake their destinies is not revealed by action or exuberant clashes of personality, but rather by a sudden profoundly psychological revelation which lasts a fleeting second, like the flashing light of a beacon in the dark, and thus escapes being captured in words.

If the verbalization of this brief lapse of time in which the character's intuition breaks through is a radical impossibility, how can we describe it and judge it? In order to organize the answer, I believe that it is wisest to establish the method by which the writer operates and later venture an interpretation.

The writer *knows* that when the moment of this seizure of primordial vision takes place, it is as if suddenly the character were returning to the *Beginning.* But she knows also that she is allowed only to *represent,* by means of metaphors, the essential discovery, as in the following examples:

> It was at that instant that she went deaf: she was missing one of her senses. . . . It was at that moment that she (he?) looked at the man pausing at the bus stop. . . . Then unexpectedly, he perceived with horror that the room and the woman were calm and unhurried. . . . It was at that instant that the explorer, for the first time since he had known her, instead of feeling curiosity, exaltation, victory or scientific interest, fell ill at ease. . . . But abruptly, came that visceral flight, that pause in the heartbeat that is surprised in mid-flight. . . . (*Laços de Família,* pp. 19, 25, 61, 86, 156.) Only at that moment of sweetness and light did I discover how I would heal anyone who loved me. I would cure in this way anyone who suffered because of me. . . . And abruptly, my heart was responding very coldly: But that is not sweetness, that is death. . . . It was precisely at lunchtime that it occurred. . . . It was at that instant that I saw Ophelia again. And at that instant, I remembered that I had been an observer of a little girl. (*A Legião Estrangeira,* pp. 27, 52, 81, 110.)

One must note that the "privileged moment"[3] is like a sudden awareness or an instant in which the sensory perceptions of the character are keenest. He *sees,* for the first time, reality gaping before him. The liminal vision occurs exactly at the privileged moment, which is, in the final analysis, the entire narrative: the occurence in a banal life that surpasses the limitations of the everyday. Thus, "life surrounds the character with comfort, the security of his day-to-day life domesticates the aggressive potential of the world. The unforseen is virtually absent from this world. But suddenly, in spite of this circle of security, through an unexpected breach, surges into the existence of the characters, an unanticipated sensation, a dangerous contact. The impact of what exists reaches those who, only shortly before, were protected."[4]

Thus becoming deaf, the character of the short story **"Devaneio,"** from *Laços de Família,* awakens and defines herself dull and predictable.[5] The capacity of her existence becomes obvious. The great climax of her life is trivial, mute, but as important dramatically as any climax of tragic connotation: the incident, to be her privileged moment, need not be exceptional or shocking. Suffice that it be revealing, singular and determining. In describing such a moment, Clarice Lispector has made her own precisely that which any fiction writer, especially a short story writer, seeks—a moment of complete lucidity during which the character unveils the intimate reality of things and himself: "Any destiny, however vast or complicated it may be, consists in reality of *one lone moment*: the moment at which a man knows forevermore who he is."[6] "Cualquier destino, por largo y complicado que sea, consta en realidad *de un solo momento*: el momento en que el hombre sable para siempre quién es."

But not only does fiction seek to capture the privileged moment. Philosophical thought, especially in the area of phenomenology and Existentialism, to which the Brazilian short story writer Clarice Lispector is indebted, is concerned with characterizing it: "The meeting of time and eternity" ["Rencontre du temps et de l'éternité"], in the words of Kierkegaard, or "the moment when, by the decision that we have made, we *take stock of ourselves* and, joining the past and the 'projet,' take responsibility for what we are"[7] ["le moment où dans la décision résolue nous nous prenons nous-mêmes sur nous-même et, joignant l'origine et le projet, prenons la responsabilité de ce que nous sommes"] or Husserl's "Vision of essences." (*Wesensschau*)[8]

The privileged moment, with which philosophical inquiry as well as literary intuition concerns itself, presents the intricate problem of the concept of truth and its criteria of judgment. As the analysis of this problem would obscure the thesis of this essay, suffice it to remember that we are dealing with a cultural area in which "truth is subjectivity,"[9] without giving, however, a pejorative connotation to the word *subjectivity.* Strictly speaking, the "subjective" encounter of the privileged moment has validity and "objectivity" as long as it is attached necessarily to the real world: "An essence is possible because an 'essence' is in the object and it is there that we see it."[10] By the word *object,* we must understand, in a philosophical sense in which the affirmation is possible, and in a literary sense in which the cosmic vision of Clarice Lispector is situated,—the "other" (= the non-I) represented by humans, nonrational creatures, and things. Indeed, exterior reality appears to this Brazilian writer as a territory to be discovered, to be deciphered: it is toward the "other" that her regard is anxiously directed "in search of the meaning of life, to penetrate the mystery that surrounds man."[11] This is true to such an extent that she builds an entire narrative, **"A Mensagem"** from *A Legião Estrangeira,* around the friction between the existential "project" of the characters and "others."

In a fashion coherent with her existential vision, Clarice Lispector chooses her subjects, human and animal, from the world which she contemplates and investigates. It is they which constitute the mirror in which "I" is reflected and revealed, for the impossibility of a "pure I", as Phenomenology teaches us, leads to the verification that, although there is no "necessity of the world in order to exist,"[12] the "I" is radically linked to it.

Hence, the privileged moment, upon which Clarice Lispector bases her cosmic vision, consists, in her short stories, of the character's realization of what is happening in his immediate "circumstance" (excluding only plants) and, at the same time, in the "I" itself and vice versa. The character, upon his liberation from the mystery that inhabits his circumstance, discloses to himself the surrounding world. This sudden insight unveils both the inhabited Cosmos and the microcosm that surrounds the character. Forming a true "phenomenological reduction," the "I" and the universe meet as if for the first time, framed in a halo of original "purity," causing the mutual discovery to become suspended in time, a vision of the most intimate part of reality, without the deformation of thought or prejudice. To discover is thus to return to the Beginning, but only for a brief instant, as clairvoyance would destroy itself were it to last. Endowed with this "ingenuous" vision, the person comprehends his own secret and that of the universe, but must return immediately to his previous (un)consciousness, which allows him to live without major anxiety. He is granted single insight into the most hidden part of man and things and nothing more, as mental blindness is indispensable for him to continue living and surviving.

People (= characters) and animals make up the "other," the suddenly discovered reality. As for the characters, they are submerged in an existential milieu[13] like aquatic creatures in their natural element, static, deprived of metaphysical imagination or even of profound inner life. They are aware only of their daily existence, expecting nothing, going nowhere. Undifferentiated as people, "they are constantly reflecting upon what they feel"[14] and they cherish an inner dialogue which, for them, is reduced to the mentalization of their senses' messages from the different stimuli of the outer world. Hypnotized by the contemplation of a spectacle that doesn't vary but occasionally presents surprises; they let themselves drift without aim or anxiety. Withdrawn into themselves, they question nothing save their own "I," the profound secret of their being: "Oh, how good it was to be back, truly back, she

smiled with satisfaction. . . . Oh, how good it was to be tired again. . . . She, who aspired to be nothing more than someone's wife, returned gratefully to her daily imperfect role. With closed eyes, she sighed thankfully. How long had it been since she had last rested?" (*Laços de Família,* p. 46)

For this reason, the dialogues between characters become absurd games, devoid of communication to the point that there is finally no continuity between questions and answers. Each utterance becomes complete in itself, an affirmation without reply, a true monologue addressed to an interlocutor, likewise more interested in his own dialogue than in listening to that of the "other." And if any revelation of self results from this incessant self-explanation, it is not because the other answered or listened but because he was present at the moment when the "I" of the character vocalized his own inner functioning. This explains the obvious similarity between the interior monologues and the dialogues in the fiction of Clarice Lispector: we are always dealing with a monologue of the "I" adversed to itself, apparently addressed to an "other" who, in turn, concentrates on enunciating his own existential drama. For example, in the short story **"Amor,"** from *Laços de Família,* the irremediable separation between the married couple is shown in a dialogue charged with mortal silence and total lack of communication. "I don't want anything to happen to you ever," she said. "At least, let the oven explode," he answered smiling. (*Laços de Família,* p. 33)

In spite of the profound discord between the characters, their only recourse as a manifestation of their essences is language. "Language is the house of Being."[15] Its existential "projet," to the extent that it implies inevitably the attempt that a being undertakes in the direction of the "other," in search of self-knowledge and *ipso facto,* knowledge of the world,—is a linguistic "projet." Man's essence creates itself through a constant flux based on the verbal image that he makes of himself: his self-creation is equal to his self expression or, in other words, the essence of each individual simultaneously reveals itself and creates itself by means of words. Nevertheless, upon reflecting that this vital process, self-creation by means of language, is connected to the notion of irreversible finitude of time, man becomes conscious of moving toward death and existential nothingness. This is what occurs to the characters of Clarice Lispector.

The least that can be said of this short story writer is that she records the tragic density present in the daily existence of defenseless creatures, unconscious of what is occurring around them; she *sees* the microscopic details of creatures who are drowned in the quotidian but who do not understand that they cannot see. For this reason, their introspection constitutes an operation of the writer and not of their own characters she created. The latter are more symbols, personifications, or even archetypes than individuals or types. They appear "always alike," "they can be summed up in only one character,"[16] they are more life-styles or paradigm-situations of man in the world than fictional representations of people in the real world.

Such life-styles take the form of "dialy existence in all its banality" ("la existencia cotidiana en su banalidad"); that is to say, "that manner of human existence by which the subject of action and speech is not oneself but the impersonal conditions in which we live under the dictatorship of the 'ifs' of mediocrity" ("aquella manera de ser del hombre en la cual el sujeto del obrar y del decir no soy yo, sino que es el impersonal, en que nosotros vivimos bajo la dictadura del 'se' que representa la medianía")[17] one sees in Clarice Lispector's verisimilitude her representation of isolated beings but of groups of beings, collective "I's," city—"I" 's, humanity—"I" 's. Although the characters are few and generally of the female sex, they symbolize all or almost all of mankind: to attain the archetype, the desired universalization, Clarice Lispector does not need to set in motion diversified characters, as ten or even one hundred of them would result in an identical index of mediocrity and banality.

"To be is to be with"[18] postulates the existential doctrine to which is linked unavoidably the fiction of Clarice Lispector. We saw that the "other" may be a character thrust "into situation," in a dialogue without communication or with communication established only indirectly. But the "other" may also be an animal. It makes no difference in the fictional world of Clarice Lispector if the encounter of the "I" occurs with another "I," or with irrational creatures as the result is the same. The zoological creature even presents an advantage in that his silence or lack of verbal expression "responds" precisely to what the character is seeking. Thus, animals, without assuming the rigorous function of protagonists, often appear opposite humans, distracted or absorbed in their existential games: word-puzzles through which the essence of their being reveals itself, presents itself, and transforms itself into existence.

For this very reason, animals, besides being numerous and even providing the title for several stories (**"Uma Galinha"** and **"O Búfalo"** from *Laços de Família* and **"Macacos" "O Ovo e a Galinha"** from *A Legião Estrangeira.*) "constitute, in the work of Clarice Lispector, a symbolism of Being" and "acquire ontological relevance."[19] They acquire this relevance as projections of the characters; the latter, situated at a threshold situation in their existence, lend to the objects, human and sub-human, that surround them the ontological ecstasy in which they themselves are submerged.[20] The stress remains upon the "I" of the protagonist and only by reflection seems to transfer to the occasional interlocutor, of any level of the zoological kingdom, anywhere from a cockroach (**"A Quinta História"** from *A Legião Estrangeira*) to a monkey.

Thus, it is not the hen who is significant in the story that bears her name but the human being, notably the woman who confronts her; and if we speak of the "metaphysics" of the fowl, it is simply because the author attributes an interior dimension to the hen that is exclusive to the human species. Likewise, the modern fable **"O Crime do Professor de Matemática"** comments upon the hero of the story and not the dog: the animal is simply a scapegoat or mythical pretext that reflects and defines the existence of the professor, the perpetual prisoner of his own moral compromise and dubious past. Again likewise, the egg itself in **"O Ovo e a Galinha"** functions like an oval-shaped mirror where the character is reflected: "But the egg? This is one of its subterfuges: while I was talking about the egg, I forgot the egg. "Speak, speak," they instructed me. . . . Out of loyalty to the egg, I forgot it. My necessary forgetfulness." (*A Legião Estrangeira,* pp. 65-66).

It is not by chance that such an ontological transference takes place between humans and animals: eventually, a double exchange occurs, so that there is the anthropomorphization of animals and the animalization, vegetablization or mineralization of humans. In the description of the hen, the story writer discovers that she "is a person" (**"A Galinha"** from *Laços de Família,* p. 38) and "has a rich inner life" (**"O Ovo e a Galinha,"** *A Legião Estrangeira,* p. 59). Similarly, the character who visits the zoo realizes that "the eyes of the buffalo, his eyes were looking into her eyes. and a paleness so deep was exchanged, that the woman grew numb, drowsy. Standing erect yet in a deep sleep. Small red eyes were looking at her. The eyes of the buffalo." (*Laços de Família,* p. 161)

Everything happens as if, with the wink of an eye, the character were discovering a planet populated by myths incorporated in animals. And it is in the journey between the human and the supernatural that even objects take on life as if they also were participating in the general process of universal ontologicalization: "A certain time of the afternoon was more dangerous. At a certain afternoon hour, the trees that she had planted laughed at her . . . that glass of milk that finally acquired secret powers, that had in each swallow the near taste of a word and started giving her strong pats on the back again . . . and as if it were the room that had napped and not she." (*Laços de Família,* pp. 23, 45, 51)

In the reverse transference, the character becomes fossilized, due to the gradual deprivation of his humanity through the projection of the "other," or becomes an animal in an ontological exchange with animals. A perfect example of the first process, which occurs throughout the fiction of Clarice Lispector, is found in the short story **"Feliz Aniversário"**: "The muscles in the face of the birthday celebrator told them nothing, so that nobody could tell if she was happy. She was seated at the head of the table. She was a tall thin old lady, imposing and dark-complexioned. She looked hollow." (*Laços de Família,* p. 67)

An example of the animalization of the human is found in **"O Crime do Professor de Matemática,"** where the anthropomorphization of the animal is also well illustrated: "We understood each other too well, you with the human name that I gave you, I with the name that you gave me and that you never pronounced except with an insistent look," the man thought fondly, free now to reminisce unhindered. (*Laços de Família,* p. 146) In both cases, a danger is stalking the character, that of his downfall.

Similar to that expressed by Fernando Pessoa in the poem "Ela Canta, Pobre Ceifeira," the characters of Clarice Lispector are searching for "happy unconsciousness," the happiness of not understanding, of not knowing (*A Legião Estrangeira,* pp. 51, 65) because they suspect that danger lurks in self realization, understanding, knowledge. In other words, the unveiling of the self, the *aletheia* of Heidegger,[21] is what opens the abyss at the feet of the being who questions his condition and the enigma of the surrounding world. The unveiling or revelation of the self implies a previous stage in which the self was concealed and occult. Thus, it would be fitting of the self, inherent in its irreductible nature, to be concealed or occult. And the priviledged moment around which gravitates the cosmic vision of Clarice Lispector, as expressed in *Laços de Família* and in *A Legião Estrangeira,* would correspond exactly to the revelation of self. However, it is not that easy a process; for, if it were the essence of human nature to want to be occult, the privileged moment would constitute an instant in which the character discovers or reveals his own occultness. He would become conscious that being is by nature occult or unveils the occult that characterizes being. Thus, rather than finding out that being is not occult, he discovers precisely its essential occultness. Unparadoxically, he uncovers the occultness of existence. Or, in other words, at a determined moment, an unexpected intuition reveals the character to himself, making him affirm that "He also, a man, believed as she did, in grand lies." (*A Legião Estrangeira,* p. 25)

And given that "The essence of the commonplace is the lie, that which consists of lying to oneself,"[22] to expose the self is synonymous with victory over the lie and, therefore, with the establishment of truth on the perimeter where life's dominance carries on: "Once a man was accused of being what he was and he was called That Man. It was not a lie; he was. But to this day, we have not recovered. The general law of our survival: one may say, "a pretty face" but whoever says "the face" will die for having exhausted the subject." (*A Legião Estrangeira,* p. 57)

In the analogy concealment = lie, revelation = truth, is implied an entire ethical code or morality in that the person is always confronted with a choice between these two poles of reality. However, in the daily flux of life, sooner or later, the moment comes when truth unavoidably imposes itself and the person "takes control of his essence." (*"prendo charge de son essence"*). Futhermore, "To take control of a thing or person in its essence is to love it, desire it."[23] ("prendre charge d'une chose on d'une personne dans leur essence, c'est les aimer, les desirer.") In the short story **"O Búfalo,"** the unveiling occurs with the confrontation of the character and the animal: "The buffalo turned around, became imobile and considered her from a distance. "I love you", she said, full of hate, to the man whose great unpunishable crime was not to love her. "I hate you", she said, begging for love from the buffalo" (*Laços de Família,* p. 161). Both love and desire lead compellingly into a dangerous adventure, as simply living implies unconsciousness and respect for the occult of a person's essence that "leads to death," truly existing corresponds to the consciousness of the concealment and of the relativity of the self. (*A Legião Estrangeira,* pp. 57

ff.) The hen, a frequent presence in the fictional world of Clarice Lispector, constitutes one of the most persuasive symbols of the concealment of self: contact with the essence of the hen takes place directly, without words which, if uttered, would protect the ontological mystery or postpone its unveiling. "And the egg remains completely protected by so many words." (*A Legião Estrangeira,* p. 66)

Choosing being or consciousness, the unveiling of the self, truth, or liberty, the character knows the danger. He runs risks and commits errors when he perceives the reality that accompanies the stripping of the self. Knowledge is temptation and sin; awareness is failure, risk and folly. But knowledge and awareness of what? Love, goodness, beauty, pity, enchantment, innocence, hope: "Seeing hope terrified me, seeing life upset my stomach." (*A Legião Estrangeira,* p. 23)

To sum up: imperfection resides in becoming aware, in unveiling the self, in abandoning anonymity and the mental stagnation which maintains reality intact, in order to gain the condition of being a person, to display the essence of the self, distinct from the rest of humanity:

> Because, upon seeing, she risked for a moment becoming an individual, and they also. It was as she had been warned: as long as she lived out the ideals of the classical world, as long as she was impersonal, she would be the daughter of the gods, and aided by what she had been taught was proper to do. But, having seen that which eyes diminish upon sight, she risked becoming her true self which tradition would not protect. For an instant, she hesitated, completely lost. But it was too late to draw back. It would not be too late if she would just run. . . . And even when one runs, they chase behind: everybody knows that. (*Laços de Família,* pp. 105, 106)

Nevertheless, this consciousness that metamorphoses the character so completely has its roots in an impossibility: that of the person recognizing himself as existing as that which exists, as the existent "dissipates when we observe it."[24] However, the cognizant person is not the same after he becomes self-aware, however ephemeral his instant of lucidity; the unveiling of the self endures a fleeting moment but alters substantially him who experiences it. This rapid existential enlightenment not only allows the character to overcome a type of brutality or animal torpor in order to take on life but also awakens him to a great danger, risk and perdition: the day-to-day vacuum around him.

The diabolical insight of Clarice Lispector into the constant fragmentation or dilution of reality presupposes awareness, on her part and on that of the protagonists, of confronting a decadent and closed-in world abandoned to its fate although with a certain "nostalgia of religiosity."[25] And this world is inhabited by people who, not knowing the reason for life, commit endless gratuitous acts, fail to communicate among themselves, are impermeable to the "other" and are condemned to an irremediable solitude.[26] The certain result is anguish and its opposite, apathy, or in other words, existential nausea, the discovery of existence as an absolute irreducible fact . . . "the discovery that this fact is contingent, totally gratuitous, reduced to the Absurd that no reason, no motive can eliminate."[27] The character Ana in the short story **"Amor,"** from *Laços de Família,* seems to personify the nausea in which the characters that inhabit the esthetic world of Clarice Lispector founder: "And through compassion, a life full of sweet nausea rose in Ana's throat . . . it was fascinating, the woman was nauseous and it was fascinating" (*Laços de Família,* pp. 27, 29). And the narrator of **"O Jantar,"** from the same collection, confesses: "I am seized by the palpitating ecstasy of nausea. Everything seems imposing and dangerous to me." (*Laços de Família,* p. 94)

In turn, Sofia, the protagonist of the first short story of *A Legião Estrangeira* recalls: "And my stomach filled with the water of nausea." (*A Legião Estrangeira,* p. 22)

Although the remaining characters fail to become completely aware of the tragedy that is suffocating them, their natural state is that of nausea, Sartrean and existential nausea. From there to Nothingness, which has become one of the most important themes of modern art and philosophy,[28] is a short step: "She did not look at them for her face remained turned serenely toward nothingness . . . the victorious fury with which the bench hurled her into nothingness. . . . But as if she had swallowed the vacuum, with surprised heart." (*Laços de Família,* pp. 107, 156, 157)

Is there any salvation for such nihilism, the "being unto death" of Heidegger, the end game of Beckett, in which the characters of Clarice Lispector are enveloped? Confined to the "here and now," they glimpse a precarious escape through "the desire to kill" and the hate that sustains this desire (*Laços de Família,* p. 157), through Kierkegaardian "singularity." They seek liberation and purification that finally lead them to symbolically mystical attitudes, expressed in the above-mentioned "nostalgia of religiosity"[29] In **"A Repartição dos Pães,"** the narrator perceives the reverse of the negative privileged moment when he describes the vital moment in which the self is integrated into his condition, into Nature and into the comfort of God. ("Never was God so seized by what he is," *A Legião Estrangeira,* p. 33), defining thus his place in the Cosmos as that of an irrational animal (= the being unaware of himself and of the world), forever at one with his primary instincts, facing a totality that he does not know or see.[30] The biblical tone[31] of this story characterizes admirably the *manner* of Clarice Lispector, which, in the remaining stories, is present only obliquely like background music. **"O Crime do Professor de Matemática"** is an exception also. It is permeated with the atmosphere of a modern fable or a revived primitive myth and given the tone of a strange and metaphysical transcendental torture marked by the act of killing and burying a dog. It is invested with a naivité that predates Logos, revealed in the most total absence of gestures.

Both the active response of hate and the contemplative intuition of the supernatural are inadequate roads to salvation; an impasse remains in the life and conscience of

each of Clarice Lispector's characters, because his dilemma exemplifies the conflict of man himself, condemned to be "in situation," hesitating between a consciousness that loses and an unconsciousness that angers and nullifies. Elevated to the level of the best modern fiction that probes this existential labyrinth, the fiction of Miss Lispector conceives life as a chaos in which only by chance is an appeasing lyricism occasionally present to relieve the sensation of the human being caught between two equally inauspicious alternatives. Her fictional probing does not interpret the world of today, but reflects it, in her descriptions of the phenomenological appearance that it presents to her penetrating regard and in her descriptions of the psychological depths which her creative imagination sounds. Participating in the so-called Magic realism movement, she sustains a despairing cosmic vision. Looking out on a cultural horizon without myths, she sees no escape except perhaps in Art itself. Her fiction exposes, with the verisimilitude of the enchanted world that she elaborates, the perplexity of a declining civilization, where life itself, besieged by alienation, seems to have lost its meaning: "The possibility of alienation exists whenever social and political progress creates feelings of anxiety and despair, rootlessness and insecurity, isolation and apathy. Life is innately tragic and a profound art always begins with this assumption."[32]

This is precisely the characteristic that, in the framework of contemporary Brazilian literature, Clarice Lispector's fiction and cosmic vision reveal. Clarice Lispector shows us the occult facets of the self and reveals the greatest danger that stalks us in the recesses of alienation. Finally, she offers to guide us, through Art, back to the right path. In this way, attaining the highest goal of art, she teaches us to see and to understand the world and those around us.

Notes

[1] Contos: *Alguns Contos.* Rio de Janeiro: Ministério da Educação e Cultura, 1952; *Laços de Família.* São Paulo: Liv. Francisco Alves, 1960; *A Legião Estrangeira* (inclus crônicas). Rio de Janeiro: Ed. do Autor, 1964; romances: *Perto do Coracão Selvagem.* Rio de Janeiro: Ed. A Noite, 1944; *O Lustre.* Rio de Janeiro: Agir, 1946; *A Cidade Sitiada.* Rio de Janeiro; Ed. A Noite, 1949; *A Maçã no Escuro.* São Paulo: Liv. Francisce Alves, 1961; *A Paixão segundo G.H.* Rio de Janeiro; Ed. do Autor, 1964; *Uma Aprendizagem ou O Livro dos Prazeres.* Rio de Janeiro: Ed. Sabiá, 1969.

[2] Assis Brasil notou-o bem: "O drama psicológico, ou a ação interna, forma a nuclearidade das peças" [*Clarice Lispector* (Rio de Janeiro: Organização Simões Ed., 1969), p. 23]

[3] Benedito Nunes, "O Mundo Imaginário de Clarice Lispector," in *O Dorso do Tigre* (São Paulo: Perspectiva, 1969), p. 122.

[4] Luiz Costa Lima, "A Mística ao Revés de Clarice Lispector," in *Por Que Literatura* (Petrópolis: Vozes, 1966), p. 100.

[5] "Reality, too, reveals itself to the artist . . . as etc. opaque, dense, concrete, and in the end inexplicable. At the limits of reason one comes face to face with the meaningless and the artist today shows

us the absurd, the inexplicable, the meaningless in our daily life." [William Barrett, *Irrational Man: A Study in Existential Philosophy* (New York Doubleday Anchor Books, 1962), p. 64.]

A anciã do conto "Feliz Aniversário" pensa: "como tendo sido tão forte pudera dar à luz aquêles les sêres opacos, com braços moles e rostos ansiosos?" (***Laços de Família,*** à 71).

6 Jorge Luis Borges, *El Aleph* (Buenos Aires: Emecé Ed., 1962), p. 66.

7 Jean Wahl, *Les Philosophies de l'Existence* (Paris: Armand Colin, 1954), p. 53.

8 J. F. Lyotard, *A Fenomenologia,* Braz. tr. (São Paulo: Difusão Européia do Liven, 1967), p. 16.

9 Jean Wahl, p. 126.

10 Vergílio Ferreira, Prefácio a *O Existencialismo é um Humanismo,* de Sartre (Lisboa: Ed. Presença, 1962), p. 23.

11 Antônio Cândido, *Brigada Ligeira* (São Paulo: Martins, s.d.), p. 105.

12 J.F. Lyotard, p. 27.

13 Heidegger, *Lettre sur l'Humanisme,* French trans. (Paris: Aubier, 1964), p. 61.

14 Benedito Nunes, p. 117.

15 Heidegger, p. 27. V. ainda pp. 29, 65, 165.

16 Benedito Nunes, p. 116.

17 Norberto Bobbio, *El Existencialismo,* Mexican trans. (México: Fondo de Cultura Económica, 1958), p. 57. "Our novels are increasingly concerned with the figure of the faceless and anonymous hero, who is at once everyman and nobody." *William Barrett,* p. 61.

18 Jean Wahl, p. 119.

19 Benedito Nunes, pp. 124, 125.

20 Wayne Shumaker, *Literature and the Irrational. A Study in Anthropological Backgrounds* (New York: Washington Square Press, 1966), pp. 150-151.

21 Heidegger, p. 185; *Que é Metafísica?,* Brazilian ed. (São Paulo: Liv. Duas Cidades, 1969), p. 62; *O Problema do Ser,* Brazilian trans. (São Paulo; Liv. Duas Cidades, 1969), p. 51; Jean Wahl, pp. 127-128.

22 Norberto Bobbio, p. 58.

23 Heidegger, *Lettre sur l'Humanisme,* p. 35.

24 Jean Wahl, 44.

25 *Ibid.,* p. 154.

26 Norberto Bobbio, pp. 86 ff.

27 Benedito Nunes, p. 97.

28 William Barrett, pp. 62 ff.

29 Norberto Bobbio, pp. 31, 39 ff.

30 Herbert Read, *Arte e Alienação,* Brazilian trans. (Rio de Janeiro: Zahar, 1968), p. 170.

31 Embora Semelhe paradoxal á primeira vista, tem-se a impressão que o pensamento Zen cruza a narrativa. Humberto Eco, *Obra Aberta,* Brazilian trans. (São Paulo: Perspectiva, 1968), pp. 203 ff.

32 Herbert Read, p. 18.

Giovanni Pontiero (essay date 1971)

SOURCE: "The Drama of Existence in *Laços de família,"* in *Studies in Short Fiction,* Vol. 8, No. 1, Winter, 1971, pp. 256-67.

[*In the following essay, Pontiero maintains that the characters in Lispector's stories in* Laços de família *experience what Albert Camus calls the absurdity of existence, and points out that Lispector draws readers into the private, subconscious worlds of her protagonists without ever losing touch with the drama of real life.*]

Although Clarice Lispector has written a number of successful novels in her somewhat hermetic style, her critics generally agree that her true outlet lies in the shorter forms of prose fiction. The stories of ***Laços de Família*** give a comprehensive picture of her private world with its deep psychological complexities. Directly influenced by Existentialist writers, she shows an obsessive preoccupation with the themes of human suffering and failure, the disconcerting implications of man's nature and existence, of solitude and anguish and the terror that fall upon a man when he recognises the essential Nothingness. Man, for her, is surrounded and trapped in the world of nature by hostile forces and his feeling of alienation is as inevitable as his need to try to overcome it.

In his careful analysis of the philosophical thought in Miss Lispector's writing, Benedito Nunes finds echoes of Kierkegaard, who spoke of Man's anguish in the face of freedom; Heidegger, who considered anguish as the apprehension of Nothingness; and most profoundly of all, Sartre and Camus.[1] Her debt to Sartre's version of Existentialist theory is obvious. Like Sartre, Clarice Lispector emphasises an opposition between "sincerity" and "Bad Faith," but her conclusions are invariably more pessimistic than his. "Bad Faith, according to Sartre, consists in pretending to ourselves and to others that things could not be otherwise, that we are bound to our way of life and could not escape it even if we wanted to. We see most appeals, therefore, to duty and most of our strong beliefs as instances of Bad Faith, since we are free to choose to do all these things and we need not do them."[2]

A similar dilemma produces the violent emotional crises that haunt and finally crush the characters in the stories of *Laços de Família.* This freedom, which brings anguish, springs from Man's recognition of the essential Nothingness. Anguish comes when a man faces up to the gulf between himself and his possibilities, when he must choose between them and suffer the consequences of that choice. Like the "sincere" man described by Sartre in *La Nausée,* Miss Lispector's characters experience nausea when faced with the recognition of Nothingness; and, like Sartre's hero, Roquentin, they come to accept that this nausea is part of themselves, indeed that it is themselves, in relation to other people and things.

Clarice Lispector explores the tortured ambiguity of our existence, that privilege which is also a curse of being human, of recognising both our freedom and the world's indifference, the condition Camus has labelled Absurdity. Her treatment of situations and the dramatic individual response to them is entirely consistent with the examples of Absurdity offered by Camus in *Le Mythe de Sisyphe.* Camus writes:—

> "It happens that the *décor* of our daily life crumbles. Dress, tramway, office, factory, meal, tramway, the daily timetable and routine. Only one day the *Why* appears and everything begins in a weariness tinged with surprise. . . . If we do not sink back into our routine and go back to sleep again, we start to look about us with new eyes and we are launched upon a perilous adventure."[3]

In almost every story in *Laços de Família* characters express this malaise of the modern sensibility. Nearly all the characters in these stories experience that feeling of Absurdity that can strike any man in the face at any street corner, and Clarice Lispector adheres to the four possible ways described by Camus in which this feeling can arrive.

1. The mechanical nature of many people's lives may lead them to question the value and purpose of their existence and this is an intimation of absurdity. As Camus comments in his essay on Sartre's *La Nausée:* "In the best ordered of lives, a moment always comes when the background collapses. Why this and that, this woman, this job and this appetite for a future? The man who likes to dig right down into ideas finds that if he looks directly at this idea his life becomes impossible. And to live knowing that life is pointless is what gives rise to anguish. And if you live against the stream the whole of your being is seized with disgust and revolt."[4]

2. An acute sense of time passing and the recognition that time is a destructive force. Also linked to this experience is an awareness of the inevitable and intransigent character of death.

3. The sense of being in an alien world. An alienation felt in varying degrees when man is confronted by the contingent and arbitrary nature of our existence or produced by that intense feeling of what Camus has called "l'hostilité primitive du monde."

4. A sense of isolation from other beings. According to Camus human beings have a capacity for exuding a kind of inhuman essence, even of self-induced alienation as if seeing a familiar and yet disquieting brother (who is ourself) in a mirror or a photograph. The world reveals itself as bleak, hostile and unknowable and we do not recognise ourselves in the looking-glass.[5]

The message of these experiences, in brief, is that life is Absurd, and there can be no final justification for what we do. Everyone is *de trop* and everything is dispensable. In *Laços de Família* this belief is central, namely that "for human beings, existence precedes essence: there is no essential human nature, given in advance. Men are stuck down in this world, and they become whatever they choose to become by doing and feeling, what they choose to do and feel. . . . We find ourselves in a world peopled by demands, and life is fraught with dangers between the level of reflection and the level of action."[6]

"Amor" is perhaps the most representative of the thirteen stories that comprise *Laços de Família* since this story combines all the recurring patterns of thought and sensibility and fully illustrates the author's wide range of moods. The sole character is Ana, whose shopping expedition unexpectedly develops into a mysterious and disconcerting adventure. When the narrative opens we find Ana wrapped up in her thoughts, seated on a tram, satisfied and relaxed as she quietly reflects on her domestic situation, on her role as a mother and wife, on the security of her home and the responsibilities to her family that provide her with roots and a *raison d'être.* Her calm, however, is abruptly interrupted when she sees a blind man waiting to board the tram, a blind man chewing gum at the tram stop. Her sudden confusion is both puzzling and unexpected, and the disgust that wells up inside her defies any clear explanation. The effect of this sudden confrontation is extreme, her eyes glued to this uncomfortable apparition of a blind man with open eyes 'chewing gum in his darkness,' appearing to smile one moment, appearing to be serious the next; a sight that fills Ana with repugnance, fear, even anger.

Laura's situation in **"A Imitação da Rosa"** is comparable with that of Ana's, but in some ways more delicate and extreme. The story concerns a woman recovering from a nervous breakdown. She is preparing for her first outing to dine with friends since her illness. Laura's interior monologue develops a cautious and apprehensive confrontation with the test before her—a victory over self which she feels she owes to her husband Armando on the one hand and to herself on the other.

The emphasis upon the nausea of existence is further explored in another ambiguous narrative, **"O Jantar."** It is wholly taken up with the obsessed and anguished observation of an elderly man eating in a public restaurant. The narration is in the first person by an unidentified witness who is initially struck by the powerful presence and authority of the new arrival. Interest soon gives way to fascination as the narrator becomes absorbed by the man's behaviour, by the strength and potential violence of this venerable giant: "a luz aureolava a cabeça robusta de Plutão" (p. 74) seated in his ample proportions like some God . . . Patriarch . . . child-eater . . . This image strikes terror in the heart of the silent witness, who experiences sudden revulsion as he watches the old man eat with avid greed, resentful of that figure of unnerving strength and impassiveness, cold and commanding with the servile waiter; superior, indifferent, and oblivious to the presence of the other people in the restaurant. "Eu é que já comia devagar, um pouco nauseado sem saber por quê, partic- ipando também não sabia de quê." (p. 73)

Equally ambiguous, but even more imaginative in treat- ment are two stories that defy any strict classification within the collection itself. These are **"Devaneio e Em- briaguez duma Rapariga"** and **"A Menor Mulher do Mundo."**

"Devaneio e Embriaguez duma Rapariga" is probably the most complex and elusive of the narratives in the book. Moving between a woman's fanciful image of herself and the reality of her situation, the monologue shifts from the brooding sensualtiy of the coquettish role she acts to the more factual role of being a housewife and mother. In this interplay of reality as seen by a slightly drunk woman and reality as it really exists, boredom is the great trial. It is boredom that drives the woman to surrender to the impu- rity of life with all its dark and incongruous fantasies.

"A Menor Mulher do Mundo" has the same dark humour. The narrative develops from the surprise discovery made by a French explorer in the African jungle of the smallest woman in the world: "Escura como um macaco" (p. 64). Like a true explorer he proceeds scientifically to come to grips with this unnexpected find. He makes a systematic classification, carefully listing the relevant statistics and data, and the whole procedure is quite straightforward until the explorer begins to sense the strange nature of this tiny human creature at his feet: "a coisa humana menor que existe," (p. 66) which he timidly christens Pe- quena Flor. When a photograph of Pequena Flor appears in the colour supplement of a Sunday newspaper, the news of this unique discovery reaches civilisation. Differ- ent responses are registered in a number of homes: amuse- ment, disgust, compassion, longing, lust, hatred and fas- cination, when each reader is confronted by this sudden and unexpected phenomenon—a full-scale picture of Pe- quena Flor in her pregnant state. The various reactions provoked by her portrait reveal man's cruel necessity of love, the malignity of man's desire for happiness, the fierceness with which he craves the game of love . . . and the number of times man kills for love.

Some of the more subtle and sensitive writing in *Laços de Família* is to be found in the stories that deal with the theme of adolescence. The author shows a deep under- standing of this difficult stage in life when young people become conscious of existence and its meaning. Here al- legory plays an important part, and the rituals of initiation are elevated to the solemnity of classical and sacred rites. Clarice Lispector treats the mystery of adolescence in poetic mood in **"Mistério em São Christóvão,"** where the

entire narrative is tinged with magic. Largely descriptive, the action of the story takes place from dusk until dawn on a glorious night of May.

"Preciosidade," by contrast, offers a much more dramatic and turbulent account of adolescence, with its penetrating analysis of the dark, tortured recesses of a girl's mind during the difficult time of puberty. One deft paragraph in the narrative sums up everything: "Tinha quinze anos e não era bonita. Mas por dentro da magreza, a vastidão quase majestosa em que se movia como dentro de uma meditação. E dentro da nebulosidade algo precioso. Que não se espreguiçava, não se comprometia, não se contam- inava. Que era intenso como uma jóia. Ela." (p. 78)

The third story on the theme of adolescence deals, on a more factual note, with the adolescent problems of a boy. **"Começos de Uma Fortuna"** is less interested, however, in the onset of puberty and its problems than in the ambig- uous question of independence. The question is probed on several planes; independence from parental control, independence from one's friends, from emotional attach- ments and obligations, and yet linked by Artur's central preoccupation—namely, never having enough money. Faced with the need to contract debts and, consequently, to contract obligations, Artur resents the loss of indepen- dence involved. This causes him to review the whole father-versus-mother-versus-child relationship on the one hand, and boy-versus-boy and boy-versus-girl relation- ships on the other. One see the material aspects of life, depressingly enough, to be inextricably tied to feelings that bind one human being to another.

Two stories in the collection deal more specifically (or at any rate more directly) with family relationships. **"Os Laços de Família,"** the title-story, explores the delicate relation- ships between daughter and mother, between husband and wife, between husband and mother-in-law, between mother and child, initially with a note of malicious humour as it touches on that well-worked triangle, and ultimately in much more dramatic terms as Miss Lispector probes further into human attitudes. On this deeper level, she reveals a much more disconcerting interplay of responses, the truths we avoid recognising even in the closest rela- tionships of blood and marriage. The conflict arises be- tween what duty calls for and what we really feel, ha- rassed as humans are by boredom, resentment, disgust, mutual distrust and even hostility.

The second of the two stories is undoubtedly one of Clarice Lispector's most successful. **"Feliz Aniversário"** is based on a birthday party to celebrate an old lady's eighty-ninth birthday. The story is confined in time to a few hours from the moment the first guests arrive until they all make their noisy exit as darkness falls. But by the time the solitary candle has been blown out on the cake, the last crumbs consumed and the last empty platitudes exchanged between relatives who loathe each other, we have learned a great deal about this old woman's children and their children, her disappointments and failure forbid- dingly expressed by her resolute silence and stoic impas- siveness, her bitterness and hostility summed up in one defiant act of spitting on the floor before the assembled guests. Fate, through the eyes of this old woman approaching death, is seen as a cruel reversal of one's hopes and efforts: "O tronco fôra bom. Mas dera aquêles azedos e infelizes frutos, sem capacidade sequer para uma boa alegria. Como pudera ela dar à luz aquêles sêres risonhos, fracos, sem austeridade? O rancor roncava no seu peito vazio. . . . Pareciam ratos se acotovelando, a sua família" (pp. 56-57). The consolations of old age have eluded her, yet in her defeat she towers over those quarrelsome, resentful, and unhappy members of her family. Her silent presence at the head of the table is for some a rebuke, for others a painful confrontation; and for the anguished Cordelia, experiencing some dangerous moment, an impassive oracle withholding any guidance or sign of hope.

"Feliz Aniversário" most forcefully of all stresses the double significance of the word *Laços* (ties)—referring on the one hand to the chains of conformity with social conventions that link each human to his fellow men; on the other hand to the bonds of solitude and alienation inherent in our humanity.

The last three stories to be considered from the collection can be conveniently grouped together because all three explore an important confrontation between man and the animal world. Critics have already noted the exceptional vigour and precision with which Clarice Lispector has described these animals in her stories, and, they are clearly there to define the vital links between man and primitive life.

"Uma Galinha" is an engaging little story about a hen bought for the Sunday lunch that suddenly escapes onto a roof until eventually recaptured by the master of the house. An exceptional sympathy for the chicken's plight is drawn from her unexpected, because uncharacteristic, courage in the face of danger. The hen herself is bewildered by her own bravura: "Estúpida, tímida e livre. Não vitoriosa como seria um galo em fuga" (p. 27), and the limited resources open to this fragile creature arouse the most passionate feelings in that startled household. Exhausted after her adventure, the hen lays an egg in her agitation; and her captors, confronted by this miracle of creation, feel unable to kill her. From this moment the chicken's position is dramatically changed and she unwittingly becomes the queen of the household. Her defence in these new surroundings consists of two main attributes—her apathy and her fear. The chicken's existence is finally swallowed up by the passage of time, and the day finally arrives when she is killed and eaten. The details, however, of this little tale are less important than the actual assertion of the chicken's existence, however fragile and vulnerable: "A galinha é um ser. . . . Esquentando seu filho, esta não era nem suava nem arisca, nem alegre nem triste, não era nada, era uma galinha" (pp. 27-28). Her species is repeatable in an identical form: "Sua única vantagem é que havia tantas galinhas que morrendo uma surgiria no mesmo instante outra tão igual como se fôra a mesma" (p. 27), and that species, however ephemeral, has been with us since the beginning of time: "Na fuga, no descanso, quando den à luz ou bicando milho—era uma

cabeça da galinha, a mesma que fôra desenhada no comêço, dos séculos" (p. 29). And this is the chicken's real and unassailable triumph that cannot be measured in human terms.

Finally, we come to two of the most intense stories in the collection. In **"O Crime do Professor de Matemática"** a man experiences a profound feeling of guilt after abandoning his dog, and in order to expiate his crime he decides to bury a dead dog which he has found on a street corner. 'Quando com um choque descobrira o cão morto numa esquina, a idéia de enterrá-lo tornara seu coração tão pesado e surpreendido que êle nem sequer tivera olhos para aquêle focinho duro e de baba sêca. Era um cão estranho e objetivo.' (pp. 116-117)

The collection ends with **"O Búfalo,"** which describes an anguished pursuit of hatred and violence in a zoological garden. The only character is a woman who has come to the end of a love affair and, finding herself spurned and humiliated, is intent upon revenge. But it is spring and all the woman can discover as she stumbles in her grief from cage to cage, is love, companionship, innocence and compassion: 'O mundo de primavera, o mundo das bêstas que na primavera se cristianizam em patas que arranham mas não dói . . .' (p. 127). The giraffe, the hippopotamus, the monkeys, the elephant, all fail her—even the lions playing in their cage where: 'só o cheiro quente lembrava a carnificina que ela viera buscar.' *ibid.*

What happens in these stories evolves from something which is quite trivial, from some momentary or minor experience apparently without much significance. Action, as such, is virtually non-existent and the intensity of the stories is created and maintained by the use of stream-of-consciousness techniques and interior monologues narrated by one central character. The strength and compelling power of these "meditations" bring Clarice Lispector to the very heart of the complex and varied experiences she is writing about. Stories like **"Devaneio e Embriaguez duma Rapariga,"** **"Amor,"** and **"Os Laços de Família"** create a special world compounded of feminine intuition and feminine fancy; and if this intensely personal style of writing can sometimes give the impression of being laboured and excessive in her novels, it is most effective in her short stories, where brilliant flashes of insight are less likely to repeat themselves. In the stories of *Laços de Família* commonplace situations and dream fantasies meet and merge, and highly poetic prose mingles with realistic observation. Obvious examples are **"A Imitação da Rosa,"** **"Preciosidade,"** and, best of all, **"Mistério em São Cristóvão,"** where the reader is drawn into the nebulous regions of the subconscious without ever losing touch with the real world.

The characters created by Clarice Lispector also defy straightforward definition. They cannot be described as "types" even in a psychological context. Indeed, they could be seen more appropriately as images of different states of mind. This is true of her settings as well: the gardens and parks in **"Amor"** and **"O Búfalo,"** the urban scenes in **"Preciosidade,"** and the jungle in **"A Menor**

Mulher do Mundo," all exist outside of time and space. As with her characters, anything that is particular, personal or subjective reflects the profounder reality that is impersonal and transcendental. From this we can see that Clarice Lispector as a writer is interested not in the individual, his passions and his contexts but in the passions that dominate and defeat him. Nevertheless, there is nothing ghostly about her men and women, nor about her landscapes. These "real" characters in real situations are moved by a desire to exist, a desire that is the source of their worldly ambitions and their ultimate failure. Thus human anguish and the idea of existence are linked together. Like Camus and Sartre, Clarice Lispector believes that acts alone are important, and that isolation and violence become the two crucial features of human experience.

Alarmed by the dangers of existing, the protagonists in these stories face crises the full significance of which they cannot grasp. In **"Amor"** we are close to Kafka's vision of the world that is full of signs we cannot understand; but in **"O Búfalo"** we are nearer the world of Camus, who saw the human predicament as stemming from the absence of such signs . . . Suddenly conscious of an absolute freedom, Clarice Lispector's characters, like Roquentin in *La Nausée,* find themselves unable to ignore or transcend this discovery. Powerless to act, they witness the metamorphosis of people and places as emotion transforms the world. The Botanical Gardens in **"Amor,"** the streets in **"Preciosidade"** and the garden in **"Mistério em São Cristóvão"** become places of secret activity, haunted by strange presences and disturbed by the sudden removal of law and order. The world is possessed by a rarefield atmosphere. There is a dangerous calm, alertness, luminosity, and metallic transparency that puts the nerves of the characters on edge. As at Bouville, there is "the sudden feeling that something unpleasant is about to happen . . . people appearing to be play-acting . . . something like a breath of cruelty passing over us."[7]

Clarice Lispector also exploits the existentialist image of the universe as a great machine whose movements are hidden and beyond our control, but which creates life and death. Nature is seen as the pure act of being, the state of being-in-itself. As in Sartre's "half-way house between non-existence and rapturous abundance, existence to the point of mildew, blisters, obscenity."[8] Nature in Clarice Lispector's stories is represented as a mass of sickening objects, viscous, cloying, richness bordering on putrefaction; here, too, we find those uncomfortable associations of flesh, shape and colour, nausea produced by spoiled meat or fresh blood and man's disgust at the viscosity of things: the simultaneous fascination and horror of a viscosity that is neither solid nor liquid, and which when touched is ready to engulf its victim.

Finally, there is the important question of style. Her complex probing and poetic attitude to man's existence has led Clarice Lispector to forge a highly unusual style among contemporary writers in Brazil. It is a style that is particularly effective when she creates the image and atmosphere of the world bordering on the realm of phenomenology. Like her characters, the reader is invited to exam-

ine experience from inside. Thus her prose style comes close to achieving that "fertility and fluency" of expression discussed by Virginia Woolf in *Writer's Diary* (1953). Like the English novelist, Clarice Lispector also appears to be learning her craft under the most fierce conditions: now confronted by the brutality and wildness of the world, now overcome by the poetry of life. In this "dialogue of the soul with the soul," Clarice Lispector, too, is intent upon capturing the inexpressible in her narrative, using a technique that Benedito Nunes has described as "uma técnica de desgaste . . . um efeito mágico de refluxo da linguagem que deixa à mostra o *aquilo,* o inexpressado."[9] This is achieved by means of unorthodox syntax and a consistent note of ambiguity both of atmosphere—"na nova palidez da escuridão"—and emotion: "uma bondade perigosa." Clarice Lispector also uses constantly, and impressively, staccato rhythms and the obsessive repetition of certain words and phrases that take on a strange and exalted significance, words like "*devaneio, cansaço, silêncio, advertência, vigorosa, vago*" etc. She also uses terms of negation, destruction, and defeat insistently: "*desabrochamento, desopressão, desprendido, desmoronável, desmanchar, desarrumar, deslocar*", and so forth, which contribute to the general effect of lyricism and dramatic tension.

In *Laços de Família* the conflict between interior and external worlds, between existence and thought is thus extended to a conflict between existence and the linguistic expression of existence. Like Sartre, Clarice Lispector recognises the intimate relationship between the failures of existence and those of language. As men and women, we are not content merely to live. We need to know who we are, to understand our nature and express it. Her vision of reality in these stories seeks to impose an identity on Being and Nothingness and satisfy the need "to speak of that which obliges us to be silent."

All the page references of extracts from Laços de Família refer to the 3rd edition published in Rio, 1965.

Notes

[1] Benedito Nunes, *O Mundo de Clarice Lispector* (Manaus, 1966).

[2] Mary Warnock, *The Philosophy of Sartre* (London, 1966), p. 53.

[3] Germaine Brée, *Camus* (New Brunswick, New Jersey, 1959), Chapter 20, "Vies Absurdes."

[4] Albert Camus, *Lyrical and Critical Essays,* selected and translation from the French by Philip Thody (London, 1963), p. 146.

[5] John Cruikshank, *Albert Camus and the Literature of Revolt* (London, 1959). Chapter 3.

[6] Warnock, pp. 53-54.

[7] Baldick, p. 232.

[8] *Ibid.,* p. 183.

[9] Nunes, *Debates,* pp. 137-138.

Dennis Seniff (essay date 1977)

SOURCE: "Self Doubt in Clarice Lispector's *Laços de família*," in *Luso-Brazilian Review,* Vol. 14, No. 2, Winter, 1977, pp. 161-73.

[*In the following essay, Seniff questions the emphasis on philosophical and existential concerns asserted by early critics of* Laços de família, *analyzing instead the psychological "thematics" and "stylistics" of self-doubt—the "mortal perception of reality"—and noting the pattern of equilibrium-disequilibrium-equilibrium in seven stories.*]

Clarice Lispector's collection of short stories, *Laços de Família,* yields an intimate and subjective exposition of the psychological trauma that frequently accompanies mortal perception of reality: self-doubt. Criticism of the work during the last decade has, however, tended to avoid analysis of this predilect concern of many of the *contos,* preferring instead to emphasize considerations that are often more philosophical than literary. The designation of Clarice's characters as Existentialist/Unamunian "'víctimas agónicas'" by one critic[1] is symptomatic of interpretations that have looked more to the works of Camus and Sartre than the text of *Laços* itself.

The philosophic perspective on Clarice's work, while intriguing, fails to emphasize that its primary concern is not the problem of "being in itself" per se, which is the major preoccupation of ontological philosophy, but the *acceptance* of a particular state of existence after a period of self-doubt has occurred. Clarice crystallizes these moments of self-examination; her characters emerge either rehabilitated (although this may be a temporary condition) or shattered, self-doubt serving as a psychological force that is now nutritive, now destructive.

What each story of *Laços* depicts, then, is a tense emotional drama in which a basic progression is generally observed: a) the protagonist experiences—the term "enjoys" may sometimes be employed—a particular social and psychological equilibrium; b) an external disruption occurs to this state, which may be of the nature of emotional anguish or illness (e.g., the broken love affair in **"O búfalo"** or Laura's nervous breakdown in **"A imitação da rosa"**), or have a basis in the contemplation of a scene, person, or event (as in the case of Ana and the blind man who chews gum in **"Amor"**); c) the disruption is usually followed by a period of disgust, revulsion, or hatred which, although cathartic, is at best a short-term solution for one's problems: at this time psychological anguish is exteriorized through the hurling of insults (**"Feliz aniversário"**) or an expiatory act (i.e., the burial and disinterment of the dog in **"O crime do professor de Matemática"**); d) the protagonist undergoes a period of resolution and recovery. It is during this last phase that one of three things happens: the original psychological status quo is reaffirmed, a state that must necessarily exist as a dynamic equilibrium (e.g., the cases of Ana and the Portuguese *rapariga* of **"Devaneio e embriaguez duma rapariga,"** who accept again their rôles of wife and mother); the equilibrium of self-understanding is elevated to a

higher plane (as in the example of the adolescent school girl of **"Preciosidade"** who becomes aware of her physical maturity and the existence of a world beyond the walls of academe); or psychological disaster occurs, which is manifested in the form of a debilitating, often chronic, neurosis (e.g., Laura's relapse in **"A imitação da rosa"** and the Professor's identity crisis in **"O crime"**).

As such, this progression of equilibrium-disequilibrium-equilibrium is guided largely by the element of self-doubt, which prompts the protagonist either to continue with his or her present life style or to alter this mode of existence. Self-doubt signals that it is time for reaffirmation or abandonment of one's current psychological state, a time for the Socratic "knowing of the self."

THEMATICS OF SELF-DOUBT

Let us now consider in more detail some thematic expressions of the vital moment of self-doubt in *Laços de Família.* The use of the term "self-doubt" in this study, it should be noted, carries no philosophical connotation; self-doubt is a characteristic of the human psyche that Clarice explores and manipulates for esthetic, literary purposes. Self-doubt, as used herein, does not correspond to the *nausée* of the life lived under the circumstances of Existentialist "bad faith," an existence that is conducted in philosophical silent desperation.[2]

The problem of "bad faith," at best a tangential consideration, could arise only after a period of self-doubt has been experienced, and only then if the particular protagonist in question deems as valid his or her existence *and* psychological state when superior alternatives are actually available. This philosophical "bad faith," if it is going to be considered at all, must necessarily be seen as posterior to the moment of self-doubt; yet it is to this psychological moment, one of candid honesty with the self, that we will limit our analysis of Clarice's *contos.*

"Devaneio e embriaguez duma rapariga"

In this story keen insight into feminine psychology is demonstrated in the presentation of some moments in the life of a nameless Portuguese *rapariga,* a coquettish but dedicated mother and wife. The external disturbance to her domestic existence occurs in a manner that is pleasant enough: she becomes inebriated on a Saturday night while dining out with her husband and his business associate. It is a convenient means of escaping her daily existence: "No sábado à noite a alma diária perdida, e que bom perdêla . . ." (p. 10).[3] To the lady comes a moment of revelation, of nausea, of contempt for others and for herself. The Latin *in vino veritas* [*est*] applies to her condition: "Um holofote enquanto se dorme que percorre a madrugada—tal era a sua embriaguez errando lenta pelas alturas" (p. 11).

She mentally vents her spleen on a stylish female patron in the establishment, degrading her biological potential: ". . . vai ver que não era capaz de parir-lhe, ao seu homem, um filho" (p. 12). Her disgust increases, but her anger, in reality, is rapidly deflated: "Na sua sagrada cólera, estendeu com dificuldade a mão e tomou um palito" (p. 13). Righteous indignation, after several drinks, can only be asserted with a toothpick.

The disturbing force, the inebriation, takes its toll the following morning: she is overcome by fear and nausea; the tedium of life bears down on her. At first this sensation is attributed to the plan of Divine Providence: "Aborrecimento, aborrecimento, ai que chatura. . . . Enfim, ai de mim, seja lá o que Deus bem quiser. . . . Enfim, seja lá bem o que Deus quiser" (p. 14). The repetition is ironic, for she has no one to blame but herself for this life-style she suffers; when she later states "Ai que cousa que se me dá!" a terse omniscient response further exteriorizes this doubt and melancholy: "Era a tristeza" (pp. 15-16).

The *rapariga*'s comprehension of her wretched existence becomes perfectly clear to her now, evoked through a crescendo-climax of adjectival accumulation: ". . . desiludida, resignada, empanturrada, casada, contente, a vaga náusea. Foi nesse instante que ficou surda: faltou-lhe um sentido . . . : pois encheu-se-lhe o ouvido de um rumor de elevador, a vida de repente sonora e aumentada nos menores movimentos" (p. 15).

The lady fears and doubts; the slightest sounds become exaggerated, overwhelming. But the recollection of the preceding evening's events awaken the realization of the need for stability in her life. The liberty that the dinner host, her husband's business associate, had taken with her; the fly that had alighted on her bosom: these small, but significant, incidents bring the *rapariga* back to an acceptance of a domestic status quo not unlike the one she longed to abandon. For she realizes that some aspects of the domestic state are, in fact, good because they *are* almost nauseating: the aforementioned noise of the elevator; her family. Things that vitiate her self-doubt and reaffirm her existence as an optimum one. She has returned to a state of psychological equilibrium; she accepts her domestic tranquility.

Tomorrow the house would be cleaned once again. Better to maintain a status quo of secure domesticity than to risk any chaotic alternatives. The *rapariga*: a domesticated *hausfrau*; a stereotype of contentment. Self-doubt, playing the rôle of the preserver Vishnu in Hindu cosmology, maintains the protagonist's psychological state by coaxing a return to the same; it is a positive force in this story.

"Amor"

Self-doubt has a fairly positive function in **"Amor"** as well. The protagonist Ana, like the Portuguese *rapariga*, is a housewife and mother who leads a mechanical, domestic life. Yet she comprehends more fully than does her counterpart in **"Devaneio"** the deadliness of this existence, one that is defined strictly in terms of the relationship to her family—her *laços de família*. It is apparent that Ana's contentment with this life style, "sua corrente de vida" (p. 18), has been in jeopardy for some time as the omniscient narrator, commenting on her innermost thoughts, notes that "Certa hora da tarde era mais perigosa. Certa hora da tarde as árvores que plantara riam dela" (p. 18). Ana's activities, it is implied, are merely exercises in futility.

Just as her family life is based on a rigid schedule, so is her daily moment of self-doubt. On this particular day, the moment would be expanded to an entire extraordinary afternoon of distraction, temptation, and return to her little world of domestic order and perfection; an afternoon that is prompted by several small but crucial incidents.

Ana, riding on a local tram, contemplates a blind man chewing gum: it is a sobering experience, one that fills her with the conflicting emotions of compassion, love, revulsion, and nausea. In the course of this anxious moment her parcel of eggs is crushed, symbolic of the rupture within her world, one of compartmentalized perfection; a world that until now has been hermetically sealed. Ana, at the center of a momentary commotion, briefly attracts the blind man's attention, as is poignantly described: "O cego interrompera a mastigação e avançava as mãos inseguras, tentando inutilmente pegar o que acontecia" (p. 21).

But there would be no contact between the two; only the trauma of self-doubt would remain. Clarice's references to Ana's emotional "end of innocence" are numerous: ". . . o mal estava feito" (p. 21); "O que chamava de crise viera afinal" (p. 22); "Ela apaziguara tão bem a vida, cuidara tanto para que esta não explodisse. . . . E um cego mascando goma despedaçava tudo isso." Ana is now filled with the "náusea doce" (p. 22) of her life style; of the manner in which she, up to this moment, has contemplated life in general.

Ana is baffled, disoriented. Descending from the tram, she enters the Botanical Garden, a world of odiferous, luxuriant and exotic plant life; a world of exuberance and chaos that verges on the surrealistic. The garden symbolically exteriorizes her present self-doubt: a paradoxical world of beauty and decomposition, it is at once sensuously attractive and repulsive. "As árvores estavam carregadas, o mundo era tão rico que apodrecia. Quando Ana pensou que havia crianças e homens grandes com fome, a náusea subiu-lhe à garganta, como se ela estivesse grávida e abandonada. . . . O Jardim era tão bonito que ela teve medo do Inferno. . . . Sob os pés a terra estava fofa, Ana aspirava-a com delícia. Era fascinante, e ela sentia nojo" (pp. 24-25).

Her life up to now has been too regimented, too strict; she has not indulged herself enough. The ugly and grotesque aspects of life have been excluded from her world, but so have its glorious and exuberant qualities. The thought of her children reminds her of domestic bondage; torn between the two worlds of personal freedom and responsibility to her family, she is on the "razor's edge" that distinguishes self-domination from emotional chaos.

Ana's life has become a series of love-hate relationships. Clarice presents this development in the form of paradoxes, paradoxes in crescendo: "A piedade pelo cego era tão violenta . . ." (p. 25); "Ela . . . amava o que fora criado—amava com nojo" (p. 26); ". . . e que nome se deveria dar à sua misericórdia violenta?" (p. 27); "[sua piedade:] uma piedade de leão" (p. 27). Her entire life has become a paradox, a sea of turbulent self-doubt. The "call of the wild" beckons; she fantasizes a passion for the blind man that tends toward the erotic: "A vida do Jardim Botânico chamava-a como um lobisomem é chamado pelo luar. Oh! mas ela amava o cego! pensou com os olhos molhados. No entanto não era com este sentimento que se iria a uma igreja" (p. 27). Again another paradox: the repulsive, the erotic, the sublime and the divine all appeal to Ana in varying degrees.

Uncertainty and doubt govern Ana's existence: fear, serving as a psychological defense mechanism, now governs her actions. All her senses are honed to a fine edge: sounds, tactile sensations, and sight are now intensified in their respective capacities. The distant ringing of a school-bell, the seeing of dust and a spider, and the touching of a flower are all loathsome to her. The death of an ant; the wretched summer beetles. "O pequeno assassinato da formiga. . . . Os besouros de verão. O horror dos besouros inexpressivos. Ao redor havia uma vida silenciosa, lenta, insistente. Horror, horror" (p. 28). Clarice then presents a cryptic paradox: "A fé a quebrantava, o calor do forno ardia nos seus olhos" (p. 28). Interior psychological discord and physical discomfort: two forces that symbolize a small Hell for her, reminiscent of the Inferno that she feared while in the Botanical Garden.

The trauma—the self-doubt—now begins to subside: a cool summer's evening breeze, the animated chatter of visiting relatives, and the security of her husband's arms soon provide a psychological release of tension for Ana; a refuge from her self-doubt. From her level of initial equilibrium, Ana had descended into a trough of fear, self-doubt, and despondency on considering the alternative life-style inspired by exotic wanderlust. Yet this disruption served only to frighten her, jolting a renewal of faith in her prior mode of existence.

In Existentialist terms, the Kierkegaardian "leap" would be a backward one for Ana; love/hate, self-indulgence, and a sense of domestic responsibility are factors in the elimination of her self-doubt and making the decision to return to her family. Self-doubt has revitalized Ana for her life-style: "E, se atravessara o amor e o seu inferno, penteava-se agora diante do espelho, por um instante sem nenhum mendo no coração" (p. 30). That Ana lacks any "special" world is irrelevant to her, for she is now back home.

The danger has passed, at least for the time being. Her existence will continue to be defined in terms of a mechanical routine—until the "lobisomem" within her once again longs for release, an indication of her life being led in terms of Existentialist "bad faith." In **"Amor,"** we see a fairly positive, regenerative function exercised by self-doubt; yet this function could have just as well been a negative, destructive one. Ana might not have returned home that evening.

"A imitação da rosa"

In this intriguing story the rôle of self-doubt is expressed in clinical terms. Laura suffers from the megalomania of perfection: clinically, she is a neurotic. Hers is the classic case of self-doubt carried to an extreme level of emotional instability. Self-doubt no longer implies a mere feeling of nausea or fear that results from a momentary disruption to a routine, as in the cases of the Portuguese *rapariga* and Ana.

All of Laura's activities since her childhood have been defined in terms of the pursuit of perfection. We are told that she was, for example, the only student in her class to complete the "Imitação de Cristo." With the reference to this particular religious work, Clarice provides an ironic commentary on those who long to achieve perfection upon this earth (recall, too, the comment of Ana in **"Amor"**, "era mais fácil ser um santo que uma pessoa" [p. 27]). Perfection is an admirable goal, but it is not necessary to destory one's perspective on life in the pursuit of insignificant details as Laura has done.

As a married adult, Laura's mania for perfection in every small thing that she does has been carried to its logical conclusion: her extreme self-doubt and lack of confidence in herself her general inability to make the smallest decisions—have forced her to a nervous breakdown. We see her about to attend the first social engagement since her recent return from the hospital, a dinner with some friends. Laura wishes to provide her hostess with some beautiful roses in advance of her arrival with her husband.

The near perfection of the flowers inspires an intense psychological debate in Laura, indicative of the exaggerated self-doubt that rules her life. The roses are nearly perfect: part of her believes that she should keep them, while another part implores her to send them to the hostess. Laura's old neurosis has returned; she is as she was before.

Let us consider Laura's plight of extreme self-doubt in comparison to the situation of Ana. Unlike the latter, who temporarily flees from her mechanical existence, Laura forces herself to return to a state of chronic self-doubt; such a state is the norm rather than the exception for her. Laura's sojourn in the hospital is but a momentary respite from her life-style of self-doubt, from her neurotic insecurity.

To make a value judgment, Ana's routine is at least a nutritive one; she has borne children, whereas Laura is childless. Laura has not fulfilled her biological potential; her energies are devoted to useless affectation and ornamentation. The implication is that Laura is psychologically an incomplete woman, and that it is this deficiency which causes her life to be filled with self-doubt.

Clarice deftly notes this problem: "Por acaso alguém veria . . . nesse mínimo ponto ofendido [no fundo de seus olhos] a falta dos filhos que ela nunca tivera?" (p. 36). The writer emphasizes the absurd pathos of Laura's existence by means of enumeration of her activities, step-by-step:

"Ela não precisasse fazer mais nada, senão 1.E) calmamente vestirse; 2.E) esperar Armando já pronta; 3.E) o terceiro o que era? Pois é" (pp. 36-37). Such enumeration is, moreover, reminiscent of the ordered, deliberate instructions that a mental patient would receive from a doctor.

Laura's mind is now regimented by mechanical, repetitive actions; she is practically an automaton. Her life has constantly been defined in terms of mechanical perfection and based on models; when the latter are removed, she falls into despair and becomes a non-entity. "E as rosas faziamlhe falta. Haviam deixado um lugar claro dentro dela. Tira-se de uma mesa limpa um objeto e pela marca mais limpa que ficou então se vê que ao redor havia poeira. As rosas haviam deixado um lugar sem poeira e sem sono dentro dela. No seu coração, aquela rosa que ao menos poderia ter tirado para si sem prejudicar ninguém no mundo, faltava. Como uma falta maior" (p. 54).

Laura informs her husband that "it" has returned. Clarice's laconic observation of the unfortunate victim, neurotic in her self-doubt but nevertheless tranquil, provides a memorable ending: "Da porta aberta [o homem] via sua mulher que estava sentada no sofá sem apoiar as costas, de novo alerta e tranqüila como num trem. Que já partira" (p. 58). We see that in Laura's case the problem of extreme self-doubt, other considerations apart, can create a psychological void. The mere mechanical actions that she has performed have not been sufficient to eliminate—or satiate—this void, with the result that a debilitating neurosis has developed. Self-doubt, constructive in the situations of Ana and the Portuguese woman, is in Laura's case carried to a devastating end.

"Feliz aniversário"

The title of this story, like that of **"Amor,"** is ironic. The *aniversário* is certainly not *feliz.* The old woman who is celebrating her eighty-ninth birthday does not regret her own actions or mode of existence—having married the man she did or living the life she has—but those of her children and grandchildren. The disruption is her birthday, the occasion of the family's annual reunion with her. As she dislikes these people from afar, the old woman certainly does not relish their immediate presence. None of them, we are told, mean anything to her except Cordélia and her son Rodrigo, her daughter-in-law and grandson. The rest of the family pay lip-service to the *materfamilias,* communicating with her on only the shallowest of planes. It is Cordélia alone who perceives the doubt-turned-hatred of the old woman: "Cordélia olhou-a espantada. O punho mudo e severo sobre a mesa dizia para a infeliz nora que sem remédio amava talvez pela última vez: É preciso que se saiba. . . . Que a vida é curta" (p. 71).

Cordélia sees and comprehends the old woman's clenched fist and bitterness, realizing that this sensation is experienced when life slips away from one's hands; when one longs to clench life tightly. Cordélia doubts herself, then tries to understand. For she, too, will be old one day, possibly experiencing nausea and revulsion as she contemplates her own progeny. Perhaps she also will doubt

until death, at which time mysteries are solved; as "a morte era o . . . mistério" (p. 75) of the *aniversariante,* so might it be for Cordélia.

"A menor mulher do mundo"

This little tale emphasizes the self-doubt that can be experienced when the disturbance to one's life-style or comprehension of existence is a phenomenological one. Marcel Pretre, French explorer, announces to the world that he has discovered the smallest woman alive. For the explorer himself and the world at large the question is posed: what does she represent? Pequena Flor, as she is named by the explorer, makes him ill at ease. "É que a menor mulher do mundo estava rindo. . . . Esse riso, o explorador constrangido não conseguiu classificar. . . . O explorador estava atrapalhado" (p. 84). And later: "Marcel Pretre teve vários momentos difíceis consigo mesmo" (p. 86).

For Pequena Flor represents a new manner of love and—what is for her virtually the same thing—existence. What Pequena Flor symbolizes, the pure essence of existing and not being devoured, is incomprehensible to the explorer and the rest of the "civilized" world. Pequena Flor violates accepted physical and social laws, filling many people with self-doubt. She is a curiosity and a pariah in a world that would be equally alien to her.

We are told that one woman longs for Pequena Flor in an erotic manner; the woman becomes disconcerted, knowing that this cannot be realized. In another house a little girl is baffled by the possibility of an adult who is actually smaller than herself, a child. Nonetheless, Pequena Flor *lives* while the rest of the world is disoriented by this existence. Her existence instills shock and unrest. Self-doubt is herein utilized in an "open-ended" but basically negative thematic manner.

"Preciosidade"

Clarice's sensitivity to the problem of self-doubt at the adolescent stage is evident in this story. Like the Portuguese *rapariga* in **"Devaneio . . . ,"** the Spanish protagonist of this narrative is also nameless. From the outset, the negative, rutinary existence of the school-girl is emphasized. Clarice informs us of her appearance in a terse, negative fashion: "Tinha quinze anos e não era bonita" (p. 95).

The moment of disruption to this existence is one of self-awareness—a moment of *preciosidade.* She is led to this through an early-morning encounter with two youths. This is a nutritive experience, for it makes her doubt and comprehend: she is elevated above her prior level of self-realization to a higher plane. "Depois amanheceu. . . . Quando [ela] se abaixou para recolhê-lo [seu caderno], viu a letra redonda e graúda que até esta manhã fora sua" (p. 106). The symbolic sunrise and the handwriting that had until recently been hers: something has happened to her. Arriving at school, she confronts herself in a mirror. Before, she was insignificant; now, a transformation has occurred: ". . . ela era tão feia. Ela possuía tão pouco, e eles haviam tocado. Ela era tão feia e preciosa. . . . 'Preciso cuidar mais de mim,' pensou" (p. 107). Her later sentiments and actions reflect the tension between feelings of inadequacy and the need for self-assertion: "'Uma pessoa não é nada.' . . . 'Uma pessoa é alguma coisa,' disse por gentileza." Self-assertion, as manifested by material adornment, triumphs: "E ela ganhou os sapatos novos" (p. 108).

A formative, dialectic synthesis: from self-doubt, a negative condition, an affirmative perspective develops in response. The result is the achievement of a higher level of self-comprehension and maturity. In **"Preciosidade,"** self-doubt provides the fertile atmosphere that is necessary for a metamorphosis to occur, it has a very positive function herein.

"O crime do professor de Matemática"

This curious tale of expiation explores a case of self-doubt which is not unlike that of Laura in **"A imitação da rosa."** The disruption herein: the mathematics professor, on moving, has had to abandon his dog. As the dog had become a veritable extension of the man himself, its loss creates a tremendous psychological deficiency in him: he begins to suffer a minor identity crisis. The only punishment that he can inflict upon himself is to perform an act of expiation, the burial of another dog. He imagines his former dog, now free of its master and roaming the streets; he cannot, however, conceive of himself as being free of his former pet. "Pôs-se então a pensar com dificuldade no verdadeiro cão como se tentasse pensar com dificuldade na sua verdadeira vida . . . [1] 'Enquanto eu te fazia à minha imagem, tu me fazias à tua,' pensou então com auxílio da saudade" (p. 143).

The rôles of master and animal are exchanged: the professor, always doubting himself, believes that the dog has forced *him* into playing the rôle of being a man. He states "'De ti mesmo, exigias que fosses um cão. De mim, exigias que eu fosse um homem. . . . Agora estou bem certo de que não fui eu quem teve um cão. Foste tu que tiveste uma pessoa'" (p. 147).

He now disinters the buried dog, desiring that his "crime" be exposed. The self-doubt of the mathematics professor has plunged him into a state of utter insecurity. Since he believes that he has entrusted his pet dog, now abandoned, with the perception of his own existence, he now asserts that he must suffer eternally for the crime of self-abandonment. Self-doubt, as is evident, serves as a destructive force in this story.

"O búfalo"

The background of this episode in the context of its action is paradoxical. It is Spring, a time for the assertion of existence and love: two positive quantities. But in the midst of the biological accord of the Zoological Gardens, the story's setting, the dominant human sentiments are of self-doubt and hatred. We experience the anguish of a young woman whose affections have recently been spurned; the disruption in her life-style equilibrium is the rejection by her lover. She, who has until now known only love, must be stimulated to hate.

Yet she knows that she is unable to hate, unable to exteriorize the psychological anguish that she is experiencing. But she realizes that it is necessary to find a partner in hate, just as she has had one in love. She asks: "'Oh Deus, quem será meu par neste mundo?," (p. 152), which echoes her earlier invocation of "'Deus, me ensine somente a odiar'" (p. 151). Clarice creates a paradox by inverting the biological urge to create life by associating the womb with death: "Então, nascida do ventre, de novo subiu, implorante, em onda vagarosa a vontade de matar . . . um tormento como de amor, a vontade de ódio . . ." (p. 155).

Encountering the buffalo, the woman believes that her goal of finding a hate-object is achieved. But what in fact occurs is a psychological dialectic: she loves and hates simultaneously, having found an object that can exteriorize her pain. The buffalo allows her to destroy her lover mentally, yet she also longs for *its* destruction and that of herself: ". . . a mulher meneava a cabeça espantada com o ódio com que a búfalo, tranqüilo de ódio, a olhava" (p. 160).

A mutual assassination has occurred: she has destroyed the beast by hatred and it—having taught her to hate—has destroyed her as well. Just as love had once been a regenerative force in her life, the self-doubt and insecurity generated by the absence of love now force her temporary psychological self-destruction. In response to the mental anguish that has reached a climax within her, she swoons: it is a period of catharsis, a temporary release from her tormented state.

Her existence seems wretched; self-doubt leads her to challenge it. As such, this psychological defense-mechanism becomes a two-edged sword in **"O búfalo"**: it causes anguish, but in this anguish are planted the seeds of release and psychological rejuvenation.

STYLISTICS OF SELF-DOUBT

Certain aspects of Clarice Lispector's literary style have been mentioned in connection with the above thematic expositions of the stories of *Laços de Família*. Let us now consider her stylistics of self-doubt in more detail.

Impressionistic negation

In the utilization of impressionistic bits of data to elicit and reveal the hermetic worlds of the protagonists of *Laços de Família,* Clarice demonstrates considerable stylistic virtuosity. These impressions slowly but surely contribute to a negative and/or depressed depiction of the protagonists and their circumstances. Such is the case of Laura and her neurotic history in **"A imitação da rosa,"** the scene of the contemplation of the roses: "Quando [ela] reuniu as rosinhas úmidas em buquê, afastou a mão que as segurava. . . . E quando olhou-as, viu as rosas. . . . Um segundo depois, muito suave ainda, o pensamento ficou levemente mais intenso, quase tentador: não dê, elas são suas. Laura espantou-se um pouco: porque as coisas nunca eram dela" (p. 49).

In other stories we are quickly confronted with the protagonist's "negative" world, which serves to reflect some degree of lack of confidence in appearance and/or ability. In **"Preciosidade"** we become acquainted with the Spanish girl's lack of self-assurance almost immediately: "Tinha quinze anos e não era bonita" (p. 95). The techniques of impressionistic negation crystallize the element of self-doubt in the psychology of Clarice's protagonists throughout *Laços de família.*

Paradox and irony

These two stylistic aspects have been cited on several occasions in the above thematic analyses; they play vital rôles in the reinforcement of self-doubt in the stories. Titles themselves may be ironic: **"Amor," "Feliz aniversário."** Paradox may lend special emphasis to the theme of self-doubt if used in a staccato progression, as in the anguished eroticism of Ana described in **"Amor."** Not unrelated to the concept of irony in the stories is that of antithesis: we recall Ana's state of mind on returning to her domestic situation after a few precious—but tormented—moments in the Botanical Gardens, wherein the *decomposição* of a luxuriant nature intermingles with fragrance *perfumada.*

Accumulation and Repetition

The classic example of the former stylistic device is the enumeration of Laura's perfunctory activities in **"A imitação da rosa."** That the lady can keep no more than two thoughts in her mind at once is a statement on the clinical neurosis from which she suffers, a neurosis induced by insecurity: self-doubt. Such an accumulative description becomes all the more tragic—bitterly ironic—given that a mind has been destroyed by a lifetime of continuous dwelling upon useless and petty detail.

Repetition may symbolize the futility of a life-style, as with the Portuguese *rapariga* in **"Devaneio"** whose resignation before an accepted Providential Ordering becomes an ironic justification for her boredom with life: ". . . seja lá o que Deus bem quiser . . . seja lá o que Deus quiser" (p. 14). Ana, of **"Amor,"** resigns herself before the consequences of mortal existence while riding in a tram: "Criara em troca algo enfim compreensível, uma vida de adulto. Assim ela o quisera e escolhera. . . . E alimentava anônimamente a vida. Estava bom assim. Assim ela o quisera e escolhera" (p. 19). An attempt to reassure herself of the validity of her life-style—an attempt that is futile, as is later seen in that story.

Symbolism

Symbols play crucial rôles in *Laços de Família* by exteriorizing uncertainty and self-doubt. In **"Amor,"** the breaking of the parcel of eggs foretells Ana's state of psychological trauma. The nauseating luxuriance of the Botanical Gardens reflects her longing for the sordid, the sensuous. In **"A imitação da rosa"** the roses, connoting perfection,

are the agents of Laura's relapse to her neurotic state that is attributable to her own pursuit of perfection. In **"O crime do professor de Matemática"** and **"O búfalo,"** the buried dog and the buffalo serve as agents of psychological self-inflicted torment and catharsis for the protagonists of the respective stories.

In conclusion, it can be said that the element of self-doubt is a major thematic concern in many of the psychological dramas of *Laços de Família.* The exposition of this element ranges from the superficial uneasiness of the *rapariga* in **"Devaneio . . ."** to the neurosis of Laura in **"A imitação da rosa"** and the persecution/identity complex of the professor in **"O crime. . . ."** The stylistic art of Clarice Lispector in the elucidation of these thematic concerns is also evident in the stories: the psychological tension that her characters experience becomes intensified or dispelled through the employment of irony, paradox, accumulation, antithesis, and symbolism. In short, the *contos* of *Laços de Família* are both disturbing and gratifying as studies in psychological perception; as psychological expositions on the literary plane.

Notes

[1] Rita Hamilton, "Existence in *Laços de Família," Luso-Brazilian Review,* 4, no. 1 (June, 1967), p. 69. Other critics putting particular emphasis on Existentialist philosophical interpretations of this collection are Benedito Nunes (*O Mundo de Clarice Lispector* [Manaus:1966]); Giovanni Pontiero ("The Drama of Existence in *Laços de Família," Studies in Short Fiction,* 8 [1971], pp. 256-67); and Massaud Moises ("Clarice Lispector: Fiction and Cosmic Vision," trans. Sara M. McCabe, *Studies in Short Fiction,* 8 [1971], pp. 268-81).

[2] Robert G. Olson (*A Short Introduction to Philosophy* [New York: 1967], p. 134), in his comment on Existentialist philosophy, notes that most men would prefer ". . . the dignity of a free being . . . but cannot face up to the dreadful responsibility that goes with it [and,] therefore, live out their lives in bad faith." Self-doubt, when initially experienced, is an indicator of the need for some modification in one's current psychological equilibrium, i.e., the alteration of one's activities or life-style. If self-doubt persists after changes in the *modus vivendi* have been effected, it may be assumed that one's existence is being carried out in "bad faith."

[3] All citations from stories of *Laços de Família* are accompanied by page references of the sixth edition published by Livraria José Olympio, Rio de Janeiro, 1974.

Works Cited

Lispector, Clarice. *Laços de Família.* Rio de Janeiro: Livraria José Olympio Editora, 1974.

Olson, Robert G. *A Short Introduction to Philosophy.* New York: Harcourt, Brace and World, Inc., 1967.

Works Consulted

Herman, Rita. "Existence in *Laços de Família," Luso-Brazilian Review* 4, no. 1 (June 1967), 69-74.

Lispector, Clarice. *Seleta de Clarice Lispector,* seleção e texto-montagem do Prof. Renato Cordeiro Gomes; estudos e notas do Prof. Amarilcs Guimarães Hill. Brasília: Instituto Nac. do Livro/ Ministério da Educação e Cultura, 1975.

Moisés, Massaud. "Clarice Lispector: Fiction and Cosmic Vision," *Studies in Short Fiction* 7, no. 1 (Winter, 1971), pp. 268-281.

Nunes, Benedito. *O Mundo de Clarice Lispector.* Manaus, 1966.

Pontiero, Giovanni. "The Drama of Existence in *Laços de Família,*" *Studies in Short Fiction* 7, no. 1 (Winter, 1971), pp. 256-267.

Nelson H. Vieira (essay date 1984)

SOURCE: "*The Stations of the Body,* Clarice Lispector's *Abertura* and Renewal," in *Studies in Short Fiction,* Vol. 15, No. 1, Winter, 1984, pp. 55-69.

[*In the following essay, Vieira examines the textual and thematic structure of* A via crucis do corpo, *asserting that the main theme of this collection of sexually explicit tales is the sufferings of the female with regard to the body. Vieira goes on to argue that, with these stories, Lispector reaches out to a wider readership but still addresses the issues of her earlier stories: self-determination, sexual independence, authenticy, absurdity, male/female relationships, bad faith, oppression, and rebellion.*]

Clarice Lispector is recognized as one of Brazil's master short story writers. Her figurative narratives are known for their evocative and suggestive moods, sensitive insights and sparks of awareness about the human condition, rather than for their actual storytelling in the conventional, mimetic and realist sense. Associated with those writers of the lyrical novel and their extensive use of metaphor, symbol and stream-of-consciousness for purposes of portraying introspection and perception, Clarice Lispector's short fiction as well as her earlier novels, for the most part, attempts to recreate the process of reflection—that inner world of feelings and emotions difficult to express and conceptualize. For the reader, the effect is one of experiencing through suggestive words and their images the psychic states of her protagonists and narrators, most of whom are women grappling with forces that frequently alienate them from society's norms. Ergo, the creation of narratives which dwell upon and intimate obliquely the feelings and thoughts of characters struggling to come to grips with emotions they do not fully comprehend. Due to her sensory use of metaphorical language which often captures an intuitive sense germane to experience or un-conscious and preconscious states, her writings in form and content have been labeled hermetic, intimate, expres-sionistic, and figurative, reflecting more human contempla-tion than specific, dramatic action. Affonso Romano de Sant' Anna refers to Clarice Lispector's aesthetics in this manner: "Sua literatura não é *realista,* mas simbólica, na medida em que o texto é o instaurador de seus próprios referentes e não se interessa em refletir o mundo exterior de um trabalho mimético."[1] (Her literature is not *realist,*

but symbolic in the sense that the text is the fount for its very own referents and thus has no interest in mirroring the exterior world of a mimetic work.)

Owing to her relentless search for a hidden truth—a gleam-ing "apple in the darkness" of human tribulations and transgressions, the eternal *maçã no escuro*—Clarice Lispec-tor has placed less attention upon such narrative compo-nents as action and plot, locale and space, elements which would inhibit her fluid style of expressive, thought-pro-voking odysseys through states of mind and emotion. In this vein, her voyages inward frequently evoke a solitary quest for existential perception as well as an explanation of the connections between human angst, God and the drama of existence. As a result, her language becomes a *vehicle* for consciousness-raising about such concepts as being and nothingness. In a 1975 interview with Celso Arnaldo Araújo, she characterizes the function of her narratives in the following manner: "Qualquer pessoa pode entender a seu modo. Basta um mínimo de sensibilidade. Eu não trago mensagem, só uma forma."[2] (Anybody can understand in his own way. All one needs is a bit of sensitivity. I don't bring a message, just the means.)

In terms of consistency, Clarice Lispector's work has al-ways reflected this focus. Nevertheless, several critics have noted a change in her narrative, particularly in the '70's, during the last years of her life. For example, Hélio Pólvora believes the collection, *A Via Crucis do Corpo* (1974), to be an "abertura" in her career, a kind of renewal and "opening up" foreshadowed in the collection, *Onde estivestes de noite?* (1974), and the novel, *Uma Apren-dizagem ou o livro dos prazeres* (1969).[3] In his cogent, book-length study, *Clarice Lispector* (1985), Earl E. Fitz refers to the *Via Crucis* collection as ". . . notable for presenting at times a Clarice Lispector very different from the one the readers had come to know."[4] In reference to her last novel, *A Hora da Estrela,* published in 1977, the year of her death, Samuel Rawet in the *Suplemento Literário Minas Gerais* stated: "Devemos falar de uma nova Clarice Lispector, exterior e explícita, *o coração selvagem* compro-metido nordestinamente com o projecto brasileiro."[5] (We ought to be talking about a new Clarice Lispector, exterior and explicit, the savage heart Northeasternly aligned with Brazilian progress.) The overt, sociological concerns drama-tized in this novel have led critics to recognize new themes and approaches. At the time of Lispector's death, Cristina Miguez, in homage to the author's literary legacy, wrote:

> A partir de 1974, com *A Via Crucis do Corpo,* Clarice abre novo horizonte em sua prosa. O bom criador não se contenta, como disse Hemingway, em tirar sempre o mesmo suco da mesma garrafa. . . . Clarice Lispector decidiu-se a atacar mais de frente a realidade, num processo, talvez, de impregnação naturalista.[6]

> (From 1974 on, with *The Stations of the Body,* Clarice sets a new horizon in her prose. The fine artist is not content, as Hemingway once said, in drawing the same juice from the same bottle. . . . Clarice Lispector decided to attack reality more directly, via a process filled with, perhaps, naturalist tendencies.)

In light of the above comments, this study will point more specifically to those elements which manifest a change in Lispector's craft, particularly those which emerge in *A Via Crucis do Corpo.* Although critics have alluded to this collection as a manifestation of a shift in her narrative approach, there has been little attempt to examine these stories closely, from a technical and thematic standpoint, in order to define the "newness" in her narrative voice. The scant commentaries on these stories dwell upon the obvious—their direct treatment of sex and their openness in dealing with such themes as rape, nymphomania, prostitution, masturbation, and lesbianism. In other words, an expansion of the sensorial to areas that had remained in the past somewhat dormant, elusive or at best suggestive. Malcolm Silverman offers the following explanation for her former ambivalent or evasive attitude toward the portrayal of sex in literature:

> . . . ambivalência de Lispector, até aqui bloqueada embora há muito incubada, em relação ao papel do sexo instintivo no contexto da sua tese. Possivelmente inibida pela tradicional dominação masculina dos valores sociais brasileiros, mas ultimamente instigada pela ascensão do feminismo, ela lhe deu um tratamento direto, começando com a publicação em 1969 de *Uma Aprendizagem ou O Livro de Prazeres,* e concretizando-o em *A Via Crucis do Corpo,* sua mais recente coleção de contos (1974).[7]

> (. . . although dormant for some time, Lispector's ambivalence in relation to the role of spontaneous sex within the context of her work has up until now been stifled. Possibly inhibited by the traditional male supremacy in Brazilian social values, but ultimately provoked by the rise of feminism, she treated it more directly, beginning in 1969 with the publication of *An Apprenticeship or the Book of Pleasures,* and rendering it concretely in *The Stations of the Body,* her most recent collection of short stories [1974].)

The preoccupation with sex as a central theme appears forthrightly in the volume's foreword, entitled "Explicação." Here, while discussing the book's genesis and sexual tone, Clarice states: "E era assunto perigoso."[8] ("And it was a dangerous subject.") In the same piece, she refers to criticism aimed at the collection's sexual focus:

> Uma pessoa leu meus contos e disse que aquilo não era literatura, era lixo. Concordo. Mas há hora para tudo. Há tambem a hora do lixo. Este livro é um pouco triste porque eu descobri, como criança boba, que este é um mundo-cão. (8)

> (Someone read my stories and said that that wasn't literature, it was filth. I agree. But there's a time for everything. There's also a time for filth. This book is a little sad because I discovered, like some dumb child, that this is a beastly world.)

In her 1975 interview with *Manchete* she makes a similar pronouncement: "Um crítico disse que o livro era um lixo, sujo, indigno de mim. Mas meus filhos gostaram e esse é o julgamento que mais me interessa."[9] (Some critic said that the book was filthy, dirty, unworthy of me. But my children liked it and that's the judgment which interests me more.)

With the above statements, it is understandable why *Via Crucis* represents a departure, i.e., at least a thematic one in terms of its sexual frankness, one that undoubtedly was pulsating in earlier narratives where an undercurrent of suggestive images hinted at Clarice Lispector's sensual and provocative nature and prose. However, owing to her consistent integration of form and content, it is not surprising to find in these stories a harmonious coordination of theme and technique. In tune with this keen sense of form and content, her use of narrative points of view, internalized dialogue and colloquial language will be examined with the aim of better understanding her aesthetic *abertura* in this collection. Moreover, since *Via Crucis* has been afforded little in-depth treatment, it will be important to study these seemingly simple, concrete and realistic short stories for traces of the thematic complexity apparent in her earlier collections and novels. Along with the above concerns, attention will be placed upon Clarice Lispector's feminine perspective, one which gains new strength within this volume's scope. Interestingly, the feminine stance, couched in her earlier work as a dependent/independent dialectic of female versus male, becomes in this volume one conveying the theme of repression and liberation—a theme congenial with those surfacing in Brazilian socio-political literature of the seventies. Professor Marilena Chauí in her book, *Repressão Sexual* (1984), refers to one of the stories in this collection to illustrate the repressive and hypocritical demands made upon female morality in contemporary Brazilian society.[10]

Taking a cue from its title, this collection specifically portrays the sacrifice and hardships women undergo in dealing with the carnal aspects of their identity. Their saga is dramatized here as a *via sacra* or way of the cross/body,—tableaux of the various stations of the body, depicting different ordeals or sufferings stemming from society's identification of their bodies as objects for sexual gratification and child-bearing as well as models for family morality. In this manner, the reader may interpret the whole collection as a painful exposé, striving for a liberating awareness, consciousness or response which may emerge from the actual reading process, just as the faithful pray and make the way of the Cross or the Stations in order to gain grace or plenary indulgences.

The religious parallels not only stem from the title, the biblical references and the repeated question of God in many of the stories, but also from the volume's very structure: "É um livro de treze histórias. Mas podia ser de quatorze. Eu não quero" (8). (It's a book of thirteen stories. But it could have been one of fourteen. I don't want it to be.) While refusing to establish a possible equation between the fourteen Stations of the Cross and the number of stories in the collection, Clarice Lispector nonetheless provides fourteen narratives if one were to include the "Explicação," her foreword, which for all purposes could represent her "story" of how the collection came to be—that is, her being commissioned to write three of the stories on a Friday and her having completed them and most of the others by the following Monday, May 12 being Sunday, Mother's Day, and the 13th, the date commemorating the liberation of slaves in Brazil. The juxtaposition of, and allusion to, these dates are hardly gratuitous when one considers the volume's feminine bent.

Although one may draw direct parallels between specific stories and the symbolism in the respective Stations of the Cross, Clarice Lispector did not wish to create such a rigid framework. However, the reference to the body, a woman's body, is the underlying thematic thread through all of these narratives and it is via this motif where she makes some of her strongest statements about women's roles in society. The related themes of carnal and divine passion, as well as one's Calvary or death, bestow upon these very short stories a Via Dolorosaesque ambience, a symbolic pilgrimage where the very brief, quick nature of each narrative propels the reader on to the next. As an uninterrupted exercise in meditation, these stories, as the fourteen Stations of the Cross, engage the reader to proceed from one to the other until the volume is completed. The stress upon the forward movement envelops the collection as a whole and in turn influences the rhythmic flow of each individual story.

In the parlance of short story criticism, the terms "mimetic" and "lyric" have been coined to characterize, respectively, narratives which, on the one hand, display an "inconspicuous language of prose realism," and, on the other, the "figured language of poems."[11] Since Clarice Lispector's kinship to lyrical prose has already been mentioned, a theoretical classification of lyric versus mimetic will serve well in accounting for the formal differences in her later writings. In the insightful study, *Coming to Terms With the Short Story* (1983), Susan Lohafer discusses much of the pertinent scholarship related to the short story and its poetics. While presenting an overview of poetic fiction and the theses of such critics as Charles May, *Short Story Theories* (1970), and Ralph Freedman, *The Lyric Novel* (1963), Lohafer champions the work of Eileen Baldeshwiler and her studies on the lyric short story where she identifies the poetic elements in contrast to those narratives which have a more mimetic base.[12] For our purposes, this classification will lead to a more clear definition of Lispector's narrative techniques in the *Via Crucis* collection which adheres less to the lyric mode and more to the mimetic. As a contrasting theoretical base, consideration shall be given to the four elements Baldeshwiler includes in her classification of *poetic* fiction: (1) marked deviation from sequenced chronological action; (2) exploitation of such resources as tone and imagery; (3) a concentration upon increased awareness rather than upon completed action; and (4) a high degree of suggestiveness, emotional intensity, achieved with a minimum of means.[13] As described, the above points quickly call to mind such famous Lispector stories as **"Amor"** and **"A Imitação da Rosa,"** stories which reflect via minimal action a more poetic vision of a psychological state or reality. Although it would be unfair to regard this volume as deprived of the poetic, it does appear that this mode is less pronounced

in this particular collection. In other words, sequenced chronological action, less figurative language and imagery, emphasis upon completed action and the use of the "inconspicuous language of prose realism" are the predominant elements in these stories.

In terms of narrative point of view, the third person omniscient voice is used to describe the forward movement of the action or plot. But plot development can also be found in the considerable use of interior monologue, both direct (internalized dialogue) and indirect. However, in this case, the viewpoints are articulated in a most colloquial style, conveying to the reader a telluric and immediate picture of the central characters and their telling the story via their thoughts. Due to the colloquial or conversational style of the language, there is an emphasis upon noun/object and verb/action icons with minimal use of adjectives. The effect is a very approachable text, via accessible language, commensurate with the empathetic and easily identifiable plights of middle to lower-middle class women and personages. This effect is enhanced even more in the few stories told intimately in the first-person and complemented with dialogue. To these formal devices, dramatic irony is added, that is, circumstances which at any given point in the story force the reader to ponder over their puzzling or conflictual role in the story. This element, above all, accounts for most of the thematic insights distilled in the narrative process.

As stated above, the stories as a whole represent diverse aspects of the same themes—the sufferings or plight of the female with regard to her body. The strong identification with the body, positive or negative, stems from an image of oppressive male authoritarian figures, such as God and patriarchs, who impose their carnal views and moral codes upon women. In the first story, the heroine, **"Miss Algrave,"** a puritanical, serious and religious English virgin, living in London, negates the existence of her flesh by adopting a strict moral code which accounts for her loneliness and unhappiness. Shocked by the lack of shame in the world, she vows never to have someone touch her: "E lamentava muito ter nascido da incontinência de seu pai e de sua mãe. Sentia pudor deles nâo terem tido pudor" (16). (And she lamented very much having been born from her father and mother's incontinence. She felt ashamed of them for their not having had shame.) However, Miss Algrave does in fact discover carnal pleasure, even with fervor, via her seduction by an extraterrestrial, Ixtlan from the planet Saturn. Ironically, the vibrant yet tender awakening of her sexuality betrays both a spiritual as well as a passionate quality that only the E. T. can embody and symbolize. Her dealings with terrestrial men, as she slips into a life of prostitution for sexual gratification and livelihood, convince her that they are vile beings to be used and denigrated—a decidedly ironic result of her newly discovered sexual nature. Her anger, in the form of vengeance, after so many years of neglect and socio-economic abuse, also stems from her past virginal behaviour, a consequence of society's rigid morality for women. In an imagined scene of internalized dialogue, she directs her rebellion and self-assertion at her stingy and insensitive boss:

Chega de datilografia! Você que não me venha com uma de sonso! Quer saber de uma coisa? Deite-se comigo na cama, seu desgraçado! e tem mais: me pague um salário alto por mês, seu sovina! (22) (Enough of typing! Don't come around here with your wily ways! You want to know something? Come to bed with me, you bastard! and there's more: pay me a high salary each month, you skinflint!)

Narrated from her point of view, the story shifts frequently from indirect to direct interior monologue in order to capture, in her own words, her thoughts and actions. But instead of long paragraphs of interior monologues interspersed with an omniscient narrator, a clipped style of short paragraphs, many two to three sentences in length, narrates Miss Algrave's adventures from prim, proper and repressed secretary to extra-terrestrial sex and then to self-realization as a whore. The narration cultivates a quick-paced, immediate, almost first-person colloquial directness which finds its outlet in the direct discourse at the story's center, her dialogue with Ixtlan, the E. T. Furthermore, while she develops an awareness about herself, this is illustrated by occasional images that are very concrete:

Ela nunca tinha sentido o que sentiu. Era bom demais. Tinha medo que acabasse. Era como se um aleijado jogasse no ar o seu cajado. (18)

(She had never felt what she then felt. It was too good. She was afraid it would end. It was as if a cripple had thrown his crutch up in the air.)

In this way, the story imparts a realist tone, in spite of the fantastic and ironic element of the E. T. Narrated in a very conventional manner with beginning, middle and end, the story leaves the reader with a sense of completed action:

E quando chegasse a lua cheia—tomaria um banho purificador de todos os homens para estar pronta para o festim com Ixtlan. (22)

(And when the moon was full—she would take a bath purifying her from all the men in order to be prepared for the feast with Ixtlan.)

Here one senses Miss Algrave's unsympathetic view (tone set by her name) of terrestrial love and men, her own sexual nature being a combination of a religious and carnal sense of love: "Ela pensava: aceitai-me! Ou então: 'Eu me vos oferto.' Era o domínio do 'aqui e agora'" (18). (She would think: accept me! Or else: "I offer myself to you." It was the dominion of the "here and now.") But the ironic conflict raised between her terrestrial and extraterrestrial experiences provides an insight into her ambivalence—this insight or perception being similar to the effect of awareness instilled in the readers of Lispector's earlier work. The insertion of a fantastic, dramatically ironic component in an otherwise mimetic story accounts in part for Clarice Lispector's new narrative approach, that is, her way of achieving Poe's famous "single effect" of perception through the use of conflict or contradiction. Moreover, thematically, the female protagonist's joy of sex affirms the joy of self-realization as a woman. However, the moral/immoral and saint/sinner dialectic related to her body still looms over her and undercuts her joy: ". . . será que vou ter que pagar um preço muito caro pela minha felicidade?" (20). (. . . am I going to have to pay a high price for my happiness?)

The emphasis upon male as well as female sexuality is central to the second story, **"O Corpo,"** where it becomes clear that Xavier is a voraciously sexual animal who displays no consideration or sensitivity toward the two, supposedly non-jealous, women with whom he jointly lives and sleeps: "Na noite em que viu *O último tango em Paris,* foram os três para a cama: Xavier, Carmen e Beatriz. Todo o mundo sabia que Xavier era bígamo: vivia com duas mulheres" (23). (The night he saw *The Last Tango in Paris,* the three of them went to bed: Xavier, Carmen and Beatrice. Everybody knew that Xavier was a bigamist: he lived with two women.) Through simple language, the omniscient narrator indirectly establishes, from the start, sympathy for the two women:

Foi ver *O último tango em Paris* e excitou-se terrivelmente. Não compreendeu o filme: achava que se tratava de filme de sexo. Não descobriu que aquela era a história de um homem desesperado. (23)

(He went to see *The Last Tango in Paris* and got himself terribly excited. He didn't understand the film: he thought it was a film about sex. He didn't know that that was the story of a desperate man.)

As in the first story, the narrative tells the tale, in simple, straightforward fashion, of Xavier's insatiability, his adulterous adventures with a whore; his "wives" indignation; their lesbian explorations; his proclivity toward exhibitionist sex; their subsequent, brutal stabbing of Xavier as he sleeps like a baby; their burying him in the garden; their eventual confession and their unexpected, last-minute release by the police. This story, a reversed crime-of-passion, mocks the usual events in a situation where a man righteously kills the woman to salvage his honor and then is miraculously absolved. The enslaved women, already submitted to an unnatural situation, are forced to endure the humiliation of Xavier's dalliance with a prostitute. The following passage exemplifies the shifting, ambiguous, interior monologue from direct to indirect to omniscient narrator, disclosing the brief and unobtrusive shift from clips of thought to descriptive narration of the action:

Como é que começou o desejo de vingança? As duas cada vez mais amigas e desprezando-o. Ele não cumpriu a promessa e procurou a prostituta. (27)

(How did the desire for vengeance begin? The two of them each day closer friends and despising him. He didn't keep his promise and went out looking for the prostitute.)

The shockingly savage murder reveals their strong compulsion for vengeance as well as the women's physical and willful strength:

O rico sangue de Xavier escorria pela cama, pelo chão, um desperdício.

Carmen e Beatriz sentaram-se junto à mesa da sala de jantar, sob a luz amarela da lâmpada nua, estavam exaustos. Matar requer força. Força humana. Força divina. As duas estavam suadas, mudas, abatidas. Se tivessem podido, não teriam matado o seu grande amor. (29)

(Xavier's rich blood ran all over the bed, the floor, a waste.

Carmen and Beatrice sat down next to the dining room table, beneath the yellow light of the naked light bulb, they were exhausted. Killing takes strength. The two of them were sweaty, silent, spent. If they could have, they wouldn't have killed their greatest love.)

The power and brutality springing forth from these two women surprise and terrify the policemen. Moreover, when Carmen insists on their being placed in the same cell, the policemen are disgusted and want to avoid any scandal:

—Olhe, disse um dos policiais diante do secretário atônito, o melhor é fingir que nada aconteceu senão vai dar muito barulho, muito papel escrito, muita falação. (32)

("Look," said one of the policemen in front of the astonished secretary, "the best thing is to pretend that nothing happened, because otherwise there's going to be a lot of noise, a lot of paperwork, a lot of talk.")

As if their actions and lesbian relationship would corrupt or shatter social and sexual morality, Carmen and Beatriz are allowed to go free and live in Montevidéu. The implications concerning society's reactions in this story, as in the first, translate into Clarice Lispector's strategies for conveying indirect sociological criticism about social repression and the potential rebelliousness in women. Reacting herself to statements about her lack of socio-political commitment, Clarice Lispector in 1975 responded in this manner:

Não existe escritor, pintor, ou qualquer artista, que não reflita sua época. A meu modo, estou participando. Eu falo sobre angústias, alegrias, sentimentos humanos. Há algo mais participante do que isso?[14]

(There isn't a writer, painter, or artist whatever, who doesn't mirror his times. In my way, I am doing my share. I talk about anguish, joys, human feelings. Is there anything more committed than that?)

Other stories in the collection transmit a sociological consciousness, not customarily associated with Lispector's prose. In the story, **"Praça Mauá,"** most reminiscent of Dalton Trevisan's underworld of "inferninhos" and hypocritical souls, Lispector unmasks the dual side of the petty bourgeoisie:

Carla era dançarina no "Erótica." Era casada com Joaquim que se matava de trabalbar como carpinteiro.

E Carla "trabalhava" de dois modos: Dançando meio nua e enganando o marido. (69)

(Carla was a dancer in the club "Erotica." She was married to Joachim who killed himself working as a carpenter. Carla "worked" in two ways: Dancing around half-naked and by being unfaithful to her husband.)

As a possible parody of a Trevisan story, familiar phrases and expressions are repeated here to invoke the false, parasitical, vampiresque demi monde of Carla and her homosexual friend Celsinho: "E o nome de guerra de Luísa era Carla" (69). (And Luisa's pseudonym was Carla.) "O nome de guerra de Celsinho era Moleirão" (71). (Celsinho's pseudonym was Softy.) Their double life is narrated in a series of adventures, sprinkled with such socioeconomic commentary as: "O 'Erótica!' estava cheio de homens e de mulheres. Muita mãe de família ia lá para se divertir e ganhar um dinheirinho" (73). (The club 'Erotica!' was filled with men and women. Many a mother would go there to have a good time and to earn a little extra cash.) The dramatic irony in this story revolves around the expected roles normally identified with gender. Here Celsinho, the *bicha* (fag), manifests more maternal instincts than Carla and, in addition, exudes more sexual attraction vis-à-vis their shared male suitors. A further irony surfaces here with the fact that men still dominate or gain the upper hand even when they are role-playing as women.

The structural device that accompanies the corporeal thesis in all these stories is the introduction of the "unexpected" through dramatic irony which in effect serves to undermine the predictable or the foreseeable in narratives which, on the surface, are conventional and mimetic. Consequently, the reader faces a series of stories which do indeed "épater le bourgeois" in their portrayal of the feelings and roles of women in society. For example: an eighty-one-year-old woman who still desires sexual gratification; the sexually repressed nun who rebels against family and Church in order to marry; women who can't be maternal; women who kill as opposed to being killed (homicide instead of uxoricide), etc. As the embodiments of the theme of female sexuality, these narratives subvert the patriarchal, homocentric, male-deity supremacy, authoritarian figures rampant in society. But the challenge that is set forth also aims to underscore general human suffering as well, not solely female. Perhaps the story that best captures the essence of this more human perspective is **"Via Crucis"** where the prototypical Maria das Dores becomes a latter-day Virgin Mary with her impotent husband as a modern St. Joseph. In parodic fashion, the awaiting of the Messiah's birth and the self-sacrifice cultivated to protect him only serve to diminish the sanctity of Maria's and Jesus' roles:

—Maria das Dores, mas que destino privilegiado você tem!

—Privilegiado, sim, suspirou Maria das Dores. Mas que posso fazer para que meu filho não siga a via crucis? (34-35)

("Oh Mary of Sorrows, but what a privileged fate you have!"

"Privileged, yes," sighed Mary of Sorrows. "But what can I do so that my son doesn't end up going the way of the Cross?")

The legendary and holy story told in modern, simple, colloquial prose, with allusions to Brazilian *espiritismo* (spiritualism) *curandeiras* (folk healers), mocks this "privileged" mother and child:

> De manhã bem cedo ia espiar as vacas no estábulo. As vacas mugiam. Maria das Dores sorria-lhes. Todos humildes: Vacas e mulher. (37)

> (Early in the morning she would go and take a peep at the cows in the stable. The cows mooed. Mary of Sorrows smiled at them. All so humble: Cows and woman.)

By sabotaging the sanctified aura usually afforded this tale, Lispector subverts the male Christian ethic and its insidious teachings. The story's concluding statements—mundane, realistic, and very *terre a terre*—reinforce Clarice Lispector's vision for both female and male:

> São José cortou o cordão umbilical. E a mãe sorria. A tia chorava.

> Não se sabe se essa criança teve que passar pela via crucis. Todos passam. (38)

> (St. Joseph cut the umbilical cord. And the mother smiled. The aunt cried.

> It is not known if this child had to go the way of the cross. Everybody does.)

While the mimetic qualities of these stories are enhanced by more naturalist, frank, concrete, blunt, even kitschy circumstances and settings, the collection acquires a veritable "real," historical quality with the four stories using first-person narration. Besides their imparting a more immediate proximity with the dramatized narrator as she tells her tales, there exists a conscious attempt to flavor these narratives with an autobiographical tone—the voice being that of Clarice Lispector herself. In each of these four stories, the narrator is a writer who lives alone in a Rio apartment where most of the action or storytelling takes place. These four stories are remarkable for their direct, face-to-face, up-front, honest quality in discussing such themes as motherhood, alienation, literary image, sexuality, and death. Maintaining the *via crucis* tone, these stories nevertheless stress the importance and value of life, despite its disappointments, tragedies and scabrous sides. The two stories which appear to be the most autobiographical are at the actual center, the veritable core of the collection. They make reference to that weekend when the stories were purportedly written. The palpable, *à flor da pele* (close to the skin) nature of the stories provides keen insights into the Lispector temperament. Stylistically simple and colloquial as the other stories, regardless of their self-questioning, introspective orientation, frequently captured via internalized dialogue, these two narratives

are perhaps, for this collection, the most revelatory about the author. In this sense, they convey a mimetic quality about her character and personality. The intimacy and inherent verisimilitude of the first-person voice are also enhanced by Lispector's actual reference to titles of some of the other stories in the book:

> —Já pedi licença a meu filho, disse-lhe que não lesse meu livro. Eu lhe contei um pouco as histórias que havia escrito. Ele ouviu e disse: está bem. Contei-lhe que meu primeiro conto se chamava "Miss Algrave." Ele disse: "'grave' é túmulo." (58)

> (I already asked my son's forgiveness, I told him not to read my book. I told him a little about the stories I had written. He listened and said: Fine. I also told him that my first story was called "Miss Algrave." He said: "'grave' means tomb!")

One of these two stories, **"Por Enquanto,"** speaks to the author's loneliness, the tiny deaths we go through in daily life, the down-and-out sensation of emptiness—all characteristic of her existential heroes and heroines. She also speaks to the transitory nature of the carnal and the melancholy which may be overcome by resisting and keeping oneself busy:

> A questão é saber aguentar. Pois a coisa é assim mesmo. Às vezes não se tem nada a fazer e então se faz pipi. (. . .)

> Quando a gente começa a se perguntar: para quê? então as coisas não vão bem. E eu estou me perguntando para quê. Mas bem sei que é apenas "por enquanto!" (54-55)

> (The thing to do is to know how to withstand it all. Because that's what it's all about. Sometimes one hasn't got a thing to do and so one pees. (. . .)

> When people begin to ask: What for? Then things don't go very well. So I am asking what for. But I know only too well that it's only "for the time being!")

The concrete *mundo-cão* that surfaces in these stories becomes directly linked to Clarice Lispector's aesthetic sense of creation. Her identification with this world and its evocative power stems from her curiosity, imagination, disgust as well as her empathy. In other words, her social consciousness as a woman and a writer evolves from the linguistic link between her real emotions and the tangible nature of the stories she tells:

> Ele, o pai da moça, vestido com terno verde e camisa cor-de-rosa de listrinhas. Como é que sei? Ora, simplesmente sabendo, como a gente faz com a advinhação imaginadora. Eu sei, e pronto. (. . .)

> Não sei que fim levaram essas pessoas, não soube mais notícias. Desagregaram-se? pois é história antiga e talvez já tenha havido mortes entres elas, as pessoas. A escura, escura morte. Eu não quero morrer. (67-68)

(He, the girl's father, was dressed in a green suit and a striped pink shirt. How do I know? Well, by simply knowing, just as one does when one guesses out-of-the-blue. I know, and that's it. (. . .)

I don't know how these people ended up, I didn't get any more news. Did they separate? Well it's an old story and maybe there've been a few deaths among them. Dark, dark death. I don't want to die.)

Besides pointing to her preoccupation with death and the lives of her suffering protagonists, this story, **"Antes da Ponte Rio-Niterói,"** describes Clarice's simultaneous fascination and disgust with human transgressions as a veritable resource for her storytelling:

O que fazer dessa história que se passou quando a ponte Rio-Niterói não passava de um sonho? Também não sei, dou-a de presente a quem quiser, pois estou enjoada dela. Demais até. Ás vezes me dá enjôo de gente. Depois passa e fico de novo toda curiosa e atenta.

E é só. (68)

(What to do with this story which happened when the Rio-Niterói bridge was only a dream? I too don't know, I give it as a present to anyone who wants it, cause I'm sick of it. Much too much. Sometimes I get sick of people. After, this passes and I again become very curious and attentive.

And that's about it.)

The desire to portray feelings about her life and its tribulations and to connect them with the people she knows and observes is only new in its no longer requiring an elaborate, figurative mask to recreate an inner reality. Due to the unpredictable, ironic situations in each story, an inner response on the part of the reader emerges, forcing one to speculate and ponder over the implications of the sudden shift in action or in the narrative change from fiction to history.

As a conclusion, the story **"O Homem Que Apareceu"** is a fine illustration of Lispector's new approach. Composed mainly of dialogue between her and a desperate, failed poet who visits her apartment, the first-person narrator serves as contrast to the I in the dialogue, the I and the sense of the "other" being the formal and thematic dialectic for self-examination—a being and a being seen. In the simple plot, the burnt-out poet appears to be seeking some solace from the established woman writer, as if being a woman were also synonymous with her being maternal to everyone:

Eu estava muito triste. E sem saber o que fazer para ajudá-lo. É uma terrível impotência, essa de não saber como ajudar. (43)

(I was very sad. Not knowing what to do to help him. It's a terrible weakness, not knowing how to help.)

Her inability to provide him with tea and sympathy leads to her feeling of helplessness and his indirect accusation:

—Você tem mania de oferecer café e coca-cola.

—É porque não tenho mais nada para oferecer. (44)

("You have the habit of offering coffee and coca-cola."

"That's because I have nothing else to offer.")

His sense of failure and desperate declaration about possibly killing someone someday remind her of the film, *They Shoot Horses, Don't They?*, translated into Portuguese as *A Noite dos Desesperados*. His painful angst has touched her and in one way has snuffed out her *joie de vivre,* even if momentarily, or "por enquanto":

Isso foi ontem, sábado. Hoje é domingo, 12 de maio, Dia das Mães. Como é que posso ser mãe para este homem? perguntou-me e não há resposta.

Não há resposta para nada.

Fui me deitar. Eu tinha morrido. (45)

(This was yesterday, Saturday. Today is Sunday, May 12, Mother's Day. How can I be a mother to this man? I asked myself and there is no answer.

There is no answer to anything.

I went to bed. I had died.)

By allowing herself through more mimetic, colloquial fiction to describe how she has been touched by others, Clarice Lispector reaches out to a wider readership in this collection. In so doing, she nonetheless addresses those social issues and philosophical concepts which she has always developed in her earlier work—self-determination, sexual independence, authenticity, the absurdity of life, male/female relationships, bad faith, being and nothingness, oppression and rebellion. All these themes are embedded in this collection but are couched in everyday language or discourse, direct or internalized, and proceed from external, ironic action and description toward internal questioning, expression and consciousness. The emphasis upon the physical world of objects and actions becomes the springboard for the world of feelings and moods. Earl E. Fitz in his study of Clarice's last novel, *A Hora da Estrela,* compares this less elusive approach to T. S. Eliot's understanding of the "objective correlative"—"the vehicle by means of which emotion can be expressed in the objectivity of the art form, the only way the author can conjure up and express the proper emotional response."[15]

In *Via Crucis do Corpo,* the reader responds to the intense dramas, sexual entanglements and ordeals affecting characters who, despite their moments of anguish and suffering, recognize in the face of death the value of living: "Viva eu! que ainda estou viva" (61). ("Hooray for me! I who am still alive.") In *Hora da Estrela,* her last book, the spark of life in the heroine's barren existence is celebrated symbolically in the novel's title. In a similar manner, *A Via Crucis do Corpo,* with its mimetic orientation of female sexual strife and abuse, leads to a kind of carnal knowledge—an *Hora do Lixo*—that ultimately celebrates the value of living through a heightened awareness of our natures as imperfect, suffering beings.

As Benedito Nunes states at the conclusion of his book *Leitura de Clarice Lispector* (1973), literature for Clarice was her vehicle for self knowledge:

> Narrar é narrar-se: tentativa apaixonada para chegar ao esvaziamento, ao Eu sem máscara, tendo como horizonte—existencial e místico mas não mítico—a identificação entre o ser e o dizer, entre o signo escrito e a vivência da coisa, indízivel e silenciosa.[16]

> (To narrate is to narrate about oneself: a passionate attempt at reaching the emptying, the maskless I, having as a horizon—existential and mystical but not mythical—the identification between being and saying, between the written sign and the experience of life, indescribable and silent.)

Notes

[1] Affonso Romano de Sant'Anna. *Análise Estrutural de Romances Brasileiros,* 2nd ed. (Petrópolis: Editora Vozes Ltda., 1974), p. 184. (All translations in this paper from the original Portuguese into English are by the author of this study.)

[2] Celso Arnaldo Araújo, "Clarice Lispector: Uma Escritora no Escuro" in *Manchete,* No. 1202, May, 1975, pp. 48-49.

[3] Clarice Lispector. *A Via Crucis do Corpo,* 2nd ed. (Riode Janeiro: Nova Fronteira, 1984), inside jacket.

[4] Earl E. Fitz. *Clarice Lispector* (Boston: Twayne Publisher, 1985), p. 114.

[5] Samuel Rawet, "A Hora da Estrela ou As Frutas do Frota, ou um Ensaio de Crítica Literária Policial" in *Suplemento Literário, Minas Gerais,* No. 648, March 3, 1979, p. 8.

[6] Cristina Miguez, "A Morte de Clarice Lispector" in *Folha de São Paulo,* December 10, 1977, p. 29.

[7] Malcolm Silverman. *Moderna Ficção Brasileira,* trad. João Guilherme Linke (Riode Janeiro: Civilização Brasileira; BraÑilia: INL, 1978), p. 82.

[8] Lispector. *A Via Crucis,* p. 7 (all quotes from this text will subsequently be followed by the page numbers in parenthesis).

[9] Araújo, pp. 48-49.

[10] Marilena Chauí. *Repressão Sexual: Essa Nossa (Des) Conhecida,* 3rd ed. (São Paulo: Editora Brasiliense, 1984), pp. 196-197.

[11] Susan Lohafer. *Coming to Terms with the Short Story* (Baton Rouge and London: Louisiana State University Press, 1983), p. 21.

[12] Lohafer, pp. 18-20.

[13] Lohafer, pp. 19-20.

[14] Araújo, p. 49.

[15] Earl E. Fitz, "Point of View in Clarice Lispector's *A Hora da Estrela"* in *Luso-Brazilian Review,* 19 (1982), 195-196.

[16] Benedito Nunes. *Leitura de Clarice Lispector* (São Paulo: Edições Quíron, 1973), p. 155.

Earl E. Fitz (essay date 1988)

SOURCE: "A Writer in Transition: Clarice Lispector and *A via crucis do corpo,"* in *Latin American Literary Review,* Vol. 16, No. 32, July-December, 1988, pp. 41-52.

[In the following essay, Fitz analyzes the themes, style, and role of the reader in A via crucis do corpo. *He then compares the collection with Lispector's earlier fiction, and claims the stories are transitional because of Lispector's overt concern with sexuality and self-consciousness but adds that they also contain elements and preoccupations that characterize her best work.]*

Although it is often overlooked by scholars interested in her fiction, Clarice Lispector's *The via crucis do corpo* [1974; *The Via Crucis of the Flesh*] ranks as a singular achievement. This collection of thirteen short stories (plus an "explanatory" note by Lispector herself) is not what a reader accustomed to Lispector's fiction would expect, however. Indeed, four features make it stand out from her earlier work: there is an unusually high degree of textual self-consciousness, there is a strong note of sexuality present in the stories; there is much less emphasis placed on protagonal moments of self-realization; and, finally, there is a new style here, one starkly simple and shorn of much of the lyricism that had become a benchmark of Lispector's narratives. *The Via Crucis of the Flesh,* then, offers much that shows us a new and different Clarice Lispector, yet without abandoning those technical and thematic features that, by 1974, had come to characterize Lispector's best work. Still prominent are her preoccupation with language, reality, and consciousness, her sense of how isolation, failure, and solitude define the human condition, and her singular ability to focus on a character's silent, inner drama.

One of the most conspicuous new features present in *The Via Crucis of the Flesh* is the number of pieces that are openly ironic and self-referential, that call upon the reader to participate actively in what Jonathan Culler describes as the "deconstruction" of the text.[1] The extent to which this narrative self-consciousness is employed marks an important technical development in Lispector's evolution as a fiction writer. As such, it anticipates the more sustained efforts at writing metafictional prose undertaken in the widely acclaimed novels, *The Hour of the Star* (1977; Eng. trans., Giovanni Pontiero, 1985) and *Um sopro de vida* [1978; *A Breath of Life*]. Seen from this historical perspective, some of the stories of *The Via Crucis of the Flesh* can be read as experimental precursors of a major development in Lispector's later fiction—her utilization of the self-conscious and unreliable narrator. Stories like, **"Dia após dia"** [**"Day after Day"**], **"Antes da ponte Rio-Niterói"** [**"In Front of the Rio-Niterói Bridge"**], **"A língua do 'p'"** [**"Pig Latin"**], and "Mas vai chover" [**"But it's Going to Rain"**] all show Lispector involving the reader more directly than she had ever done before in the creation and interpretation of a text's "meaning." Retaining the famous ambiguity of her earlier work, these laconic, often pathetic tales engage the reader in ways new to Lispector's pre-1974 work. As the narrative voice in the partially autobiographic **"Day after Day"** says, for example:

> If this book is published with "bad luck," I'm lost. But people are lost anyway. There's no escape. We all suffer from battle fatigue.[2]

By converting the "I" of the narrative into a "we," Lispector subtly draws the reader into a state of if not complicity, then certainly sympathy with the text's narrator. The effect is to establish a sense of empathy and trust between the teller of the tale and the person experiencing it. Echoing sentiments that to some degree Lispector herself held about her fame as a writer and the value of literature, the narrative voice then continues its critically self-conscious discussion:

> How would I know if this book is going to add something to my work. My work be damned. I don't know why people give so much importance to literature. And what about my name? It can be damned, too. I've got more to think about (**"Day after Day,"** 65).

The self-deprecating tone of the narrative voice here parallels many of Lispector's public pronouncements about her fame.[3] More importantly, however, the postmodernist sentiments expressed in this passage by the narrative voice openly challenge the very concept of literature as something epistemologically worthwhile. Ironically, though, the more our narrator calls the value of literature into question, the more positively we respond to the "truths" being illuminated by the narrator's discourse. Lispector is really working in these stories with one of her most fundamental issues, the shifting relationship between language, reality, and human consciousness. What is new here is Lispector's handling of the problem, her development of the tension that exists between the text's narrator, its narratee and the reader. In her earlier work, like *Family Ties* (1960), *The Apple in the Dark* (1961; Eng. trans., Gregory Rabassa, 1967), and *A paixão segundo G. H.* [*The Passion According to G. H.,* 1964], Lispector relied on the epiphany, on depicting the evanescent inter-relationships between objects in the world and the ways a single human consciousness perceived them. Because of this particular thematic inclination, Lispector's fictions were always dynamically phenomenological, that is, they structured themselves around recurring patterns of outer stimulation and inner response rather than on the resolution of an externally occurring conflict.

In many of these tales, however, Lispector changes her approach to the issue of human condition, an issue that is fundamental to her work. Very often in *The Via Crucis of the Flesh* Lispector allows her self-conscious narrators to step out of their story and speak directly to the reader about the "validity" or "worth" of the text itself. By converting the text from the mechanism by which the story is presented into the subject matter of the story itself, Lispector forces the reader to confront in a startling way one of her most recognizable themes—the mysterious relationship between words and reality.[4] In *The Via Crucis of the Flesh,* then, Lispector deals in a technically new way with one of her most basic concerns, the role language plays in the process of human self-perception and awareness.

Of the several pieces that involve the reader's direct response to the text, the darkly violent and sexually charged **"In Front of the Rio-Niterói Bridge"** is perhaps the most exemplary. The unnamed narrator (a woman) begins the tale by saying, "Pois é" ("All right"). She follows this enigmatic opening with some thematically complex third-person description. Then, unexpectedly, the voice changes to a self-conscious first-person, one that calls its own efficacy into question:

> Either I'm confusing myself completely or it's the case that it's (the text) so tangled that I'll untangle it only if I'm able. Its realities are invented. I beg your pardon because besides telling the facts I also guess things, and what I guess I write down here, happenstance recorder that I am. I guess at what reality is. But this story isn't my subject matter. It's the product of someone more capable than me, humble as I am. (**"Antes da ponte Rio-Niterói,"** 73).

Calling attention to the nature of "reality" as "invented" by means of language and inviting anyone "more capable" than the author (that is, the narrator) to imbue her words with their "proper" significance, the narrative voice here typifies the kind of complex interaction between text and reader that Gerald Prince, Roland Barthes, Tzvetan Todorov and others discuss in their essays on the nature and function of the narratee.[5] The narrator continues in an archly self-conscious but fallible mode, saying, "I think I got lost gain, since everything is a little confused, but what can I do?" (**"In Front of the Rio-Niterói Bridge,"** 75). This fluid and uncertain relationship between the narrative voice, the reality constructed by the text, and the reader's role in its signification is maintained to the story's uncertain conclusion. As the narrator says:

> What can you do with a story that took place when the Rio-Niterói bridge was no more than a dream? I don't know either . . . I'll give it as a present to anyone who wants it, since I'm sick of it. Really fed up. At times it makes me disgusted with people. Later only this feeling passes and I once again feel curious and attentive.
>
> And that's all.

> (**"Antes da ponte Rio-Niterói,"** 77).

A second conspicuous feature of *The Via Crucis of the Flesh* is the number of stories that feature themes, scenes, and conflicts of an overtly sexual nature. Although eroticism and sensuality are not new to Lispector's work,[6] the candor and frankness with which they appear in this collection of stories is a strikingly new development. No fewer than ten[7] of the pieces deal with such issues as heterosexuality, homosexuality, transvestism, rape, bondage, degradation, prostitution, voyeurism, group sex, masturbation and sexual frustration.

The sexuality of these stories is of a very specific kind, however. Never anatomically explicit, in the sense that graphic scenes fill the pages of erotic or pornographic literature, Clarice Lispector's sexuality is both sensual and clinically objective. Presented succinctly and with a minimum of eros-inducing commentary, the sexually-oriented scenes of *The Via Crucis of the Flesh* link a character's sexuality with the same character's sense of identity, the latter issue being another of Lispector's most venerable themes. The role sexuality plays in the development of a person's self-perception is an old one in Lispector's fiction.

It can, for example, be traced to her first novel, *Perto do coração selvagem* [1944; *Close to the Savage Heart*] and the chapter "O banho," ["The Bath"], in which the protagonist begins, physically and psychologically, to discover herself. But though the linkage of human identity and sexuality may be omnipresent in Lispector's work, nowhere is it as candidly established as in *The Via Crucis of the Flesh*.

Of the ten selections that involve sexual issues, three can be taken as typical of Lispector's treatment of this subject. The first of these stories, **"Miss Algrave,"** is a droll tale about a sexually repressed spinster, Ruth Algrave, who creates a new identity for herself (she quits her job as a typist and becomes a prostitute) after experiencing an exhilarating and transforming sexual adventure with an extraterrestrial being. Taking pains to describe her in objectively realistic yet sensuous terms, the narrative voice observes:

> She was red-haired, wearing it rolled up in a tight knot on the nape of her neck. She was very freckled and had skin so clear and fine that it seemed to be white silk. Even her eyelashes were red. She was an attractive woman.

> She took a great deal of pride in her body; she was tall and full-bodied. But no one had ever touched her breasts. (**"Miss Algrave,"** 16).

After her erotic experience the woman begins to grow psychologically stronger, to establish a new identity for herself, one that includes a new sense of her sexual vitality and freedom as well as a new sense of her soci-political power. No longer sexually repressed after her unexpected encounter with Ixtlan (a creature from Saturn), she will masturbate without feeling guilty when her lover is not present to satisfy her new openly-acknowledged carnal urges. She also resolves to use her newly-won sexual potency to achieve a better economic situation at work. Imagining what she will order her boss to do, she declares:

> I've had it with being a typist! Don't you come on to me with your wily ways! Do you want to know something? Get into bed with me, you creep! And something else . . . Pay me a real monthly wage, you skinflint! (**"Miss Algrave,"** 24-25).

The story then ends abruptly with the protagonist deciding to take a bath in order to purify herself "of all men" (". . . de todos os homens. . . .") in order to be properly prepared for her non-human lover, Ixtlan. Feminist in tone and combining the raw power of sex with the subtleties of psychological and cultural emancipation, **"Miss Algrave"** is one of Lispector's most overlooked short stories.

A second piece in this same vein if **"O corpo"** [**"The Body"**], another sardonically humorous tale that concerns a violent and oppressive man, Xavier and two lonely, vulnerable women, Carmem and Beatriz. Involving voyeurism, transvestism, group sex, lesbianism and bondage, **"The Body"** tells how Beatriz and Carmem, after being routinely humiliated by Xavier, conspire to murder their tormentor. When this deed is discovered, the police, not wanting to do the paperwork such a case would involve, decide to tell the two women to go to Montevideo and never come back.

In terms of its sexuality, **"The Body,"** can be taken as the prototype of Lispector's work in this mode. Although Carmem and Beatriz are portrayed as pathetic victims of a man and a culture, Xavier is also shown to be a victim. This theme of socio-sexual victimization, like the quest for sexual and psychological identity, is endemic to Lispector's fiction. It appears as a major theme in early works like *O Lustre* [1946; *The Chandelier*] as well as in later ones like *The Hour of the Star* in which Olímpico, unaware of how he has been victimized by a feudalistic social and economic structure, presumes to dominate Mecabéa, a *nordestina* waif who is struggling to better her lot in life. A key scene in **"The Body"** suggests how part of Xavier's tyrannical control over the two women derives from his inability to perceive how deplorable his own socio-sexual situation is. He is "terribly excited" by the film "The Last Tango in Paris,"but, believing it is a "sex film" and not about the agony of a desperate man, he fails, in a moment of dramatic irony, to appreciate its primary message.

The reader is told that at times the two lonely women would go to bed together and make "sad love." Upon learning this, Xavier becomes very aroused and insists that they make love in front of him. But since they are now being forced to do what they did earlier of their own volition, Carmem and Beatriz cannot (or will not) perform, and Xavier becomes enraged with them. This decisive scene, one electrified with a subtly eroticism yet rendered politically potent by its depiction of Xavier's total domination of the women, is very matter-of-factly presented to the reader:

At times the two women would go to bed together. The day was long. And, in spite of not being homosexuals, they would excite each other and make love. Sad love.

One day they told this fact to Xavier. Xavier quivered. And that night he wanted the two of them to make love in front of him. But, ordered to do it like that, nothing happened. The two women cried and Xavier became crazy with anger. (**"The Body,"** 30).

Later, in the turning point of the story, Xavier finally succeeds in forcing Carmem and Beatriz to do what he wants, to make love in front of him. But while Xavier watches them, the reader learns (in a line that suggests how selfish and exploitive Xavier really is) that, ". . . envy gnawed him to pieces," (**"O corpo,"** 32). Having gotten what he wanted, Xavier then fails to keep a simple promise (that he find a "third woman" to do the cooking for them) he had made to Carmem and Beatriz. Disregarding them utterly and reducing to ever lower levels of sexual chattel, Xavier's conduct leads the women to plot to murder him, which they do.

By describing the murder in a macabre yet lyrical fashion, Lispector gives a new twist to another of her most fundamental concerns—the simultaneously constructive and destructive effects of "love." She shows us in **"The Body"** not just an unhappy and ill-fated ménage à trois but how easily bloody violence can erupt from a relationship based on sexual and emotional enslavement. Yet Lispector does not stop here. Entwining her newly developed interest in action with yet another of her traditional concerns, the nature of the psychological and social repression that so often permeates and debases relationships between men and women, she created some radically new kinds of characters in *The Via Crucis of the Flesh,* men and women whose sense of identity is powerfully tied to their sexuality. This concern over the sexual nature of her characters appears in several of Lispector's other works, *Close to the Savage Heart,* many of the stories in *Family Ties* and *An Apprenticeship or the Book of Delights* (Eng. trans., by Richard A. Mazzara and Lorri A. Parris, 1985) for example, but only in *The Via Crucis of the Flesh* does it play such a pronounced role.

A third outstanding selection from this anthology to handle sexual issues is **"Ruído de passos,"** in which Lispector merges another of her basic concerns, the problems of old age, with the issue of sexual desire. The protagonist of this very short, very unhappy story is Dona Cândida Raposo, an eighty-one year old woman who, ". . . had the giddiness of life . . . ," a woman for whom the sexual, ". . . desire for pleasure had never ceased" (**"Ruído de passos,"** 69-70). Alone and with no chance to take a lover, Dona Cândida comes to rely on the solitary and, for her, guilt-ridden practice of masturbation to relieve the frustration that torments her. Speaking obliquely to a doctor, she asks:

And . . . and if I took care of myself alone? Do you understand what I mean?

"Sure," said the doctor. "That could be one remedy." (**"Ruído de passos,"** 70).

Then, in a conclusion that typifies the poignantly human sense of irony, isolation, failure, and dissatisfaction that pervades most of these stories, the reader learns:

On that same night, she found a way and, alone, satisfied herself. Mute fireworks . . . Afterwords, she cried. She felt ashamed. From then on, she would use the same process. Always sad. That's life, Senhora Raposo, that's life. Until the blessing of death.

Death.

It seemed to her that she could hear the sound of footsteps. The footsteps of her husband, Antenor Raposo. (**"Ruído de passos,"** 70-71).

With the line, "That's life, Senhora Raposo, that's life. Until the blessing of death," reflecting a change in the narrative voice, possibly to that of Lispector herself, the essential sadness of this story underscores the idea advanced in the collection's title-story, **"Via crucis"**: that in this life of pain, frustration and solitude, we all walk the way of the cross, that to be alive, to be a sentient human being is to experience a kind of daily crucifixion, that, ironically, only in the ". . . blessing of death" can we expect to find the satisfaction we seek in life.

Readers familiar with Lispector's fiction know that structurally it is built on the lyrical depiction of epiphany-like moments of self-awareness and vision. The renowned compilation of stories, *Family Ties* (1960) offers many outstanding examples of how skillful Lispector could be at creating this kind of intense, metaphoric, and deeply private experience. Less sharply focused than her brilliantly done short narratives, Lispector's novels, build along similar lines, are basically concatenations and expansions of these moments of inner vision and awareness. Yet in the best tradition of her short stories *The Via Crucis of the Flesh* offers the reader something different in regard to how these protagonal "moments" are portrayed. The main difference is that now these "moments" are externalized and action-oriented rather than being internalized and psychologically oriented, as had been the norm for so long in Lispector's fiction.

This shift in treatment does not mean these "moments" are devoid of psychological significance for the characters, however, for this is definitely not the case. As with the "open" texts and sexual emphasis of *The Via Crucis of the Flesh,* Lispector succeeds here in handling a long-standing concern of hers (how to depict the moment of self-realization and awareness) in a way that generates the new social significance, one that reinforces and in some cases amplifies the ontological importance it had always held for her.[8] Thus, what is "new" in these stories is once again an unusual and unexpected expansion of "old" material.

In **"Miss Algrave,"** to cite one outstanding example, the essential personality of the protagonist is established in terms of her being sexually repressed, isolated in her solitude, and painfully discontent with a superficial and inauthentic existence. Suddenly the unanticipated even happens and her sense of being is irrevocably altered. As the narrative voice structures it:

> There she was, in bed with her solitude. Like that.

> It was then that it happened. (**"Miss Algrave,"** 19).

Reflecting later on what had transpired, the protagonist's sense of having been transformed by an erotic experience makes her reminiscent of characters like Joana, G. H., Lóri and the voice of *Agua viva*:

> She took off her camisole. The moon was enormous in her room. Ixtlan was white and small. He lay down alongside her in the iron bed. And he passed his hands over her breasts. Black roses. She had never felt what she felt at that moment. It was too good to believe. She was afraid it would end. It was as if a cripple had thrown away his crutch. (**"Miss Algrave,"** 20-21).

The remainder of the story is devoted to showing the "new" Ruth Algrave, a woman whose suddenly germinating inner reality (her freedom) is paralleled by her sexually and socially aggressive behavior in the external world.

The main distinction between this 1974 story and Lispector's earlier work is that here the internal experience itself is not the structural and thematic focal point of the story. In stories like **"Miss Algrave,"** it is the protagonist's psychological inner condition that is established by the narrative voice, not the epiphanal experience that momentarily suspends time and generates the flow of consciousness. Here, however, as in the luminous tales of *Family Ties,* it is the unforeseen incident that causes the change. As in her pre-1974 fiction, then, Lispector relies in these stories on the disruptive force of the unplanned-for event to elicit a response from her frustrated, discontented characters. Sometimes, as with Ana (**"Love,"** *Family Ties*), the response demands a personal freedom and responsibility that become too great a burden for the character to bear, and the character retreats into what Sartre called the "bad faith" of "inauthentic" modes of being. Other times, as we see in the case of Ruth Algrave, the response to the unexpected event projects the character into a new and vital existence, one in which the character accepts full responsibility for the freedom that he or she has attained. In her earlier efforts Lispector chose to play out her narratives within the minds of her character, to render their anxieties overwhelmingly internalized, private, and psychical. In *The Via Crucis of the Flesh,* by way of contrast, she connects what Georges Poulet calls the frustrated "interiority" of her characters to action, to what they do or plan to do in the social world.[9] In a sense, the "action" of the narratives in *The Via Crucis of the Flesh* begins where the psychological "portraits" of the characters in *Family Ties* end. The characters of both books are essentially the same; what has changed in the later work is the perspective from which the reader sees them. Both works, however, share the structural device of the unanticipated

occurrence, the catalyst that, controlled or not, disrupts the established order of things. The contextual dimension in which we see the characters responding makes the two collections different, yet fascinatingly complimentary.

Essentially, what happens in **"The Body"** follows this same plan. After Xavier breaks his promise to Carmem and Beatriz and begins to humiliate them even more egregiously than before, the text indicated that unforeseen events are about to take place:

> He did not keep his promise and procured a prostitute. She excited him because she used a lot of dirty words. And she called him a son of a bitch. He accepted everything.

> Until one certain day came along. (**"The Body,"** 32).

As in **"Miss Algrave,"** the remainder of the story is given over to a presentation of the two women in action, though only after they have resolved to murder Xavier. Nevertheless, the psychic transformation wrought by the decision to take action in the external world is not as striking in **"The Body"** as it is in **"Miss Algrave."** Even after they commit the murder, Carmem and Beatriz are more passive than Ruth Algrave following the actions stemming from her unexpected moment, her movement of "love." But though Beatriz and Carmem are much less aggressive in their behavior, the reader responds to them not through the silent and hermetically sealed ebb and flow of their minds, as was typically the case in *Family Ties,* and in novels like *O lustre, The Passion According to G. H.,* and *The Apple in the Dark,* but through their spoken words, their actions, and their sense of identity as beings in a certain social context. And since they had been portrayed as social, sexual, and psychological victims, their passivity is actually in keeping with the true nature of their characters, with their timorous and stunted sense of self.

A fourth distinctive feature of *The Via Crucis of the Flesh* has to do with its style. Long recognized as one of Lispector's most singular narrative attributes, style is an aspect of her work that is integrally linked to the themes she writes about. Among these, the symbiotic and constantly evolving relationship between language and our sense of being can be said to be the subject that most interested her, the raw material that gave form and substance to her work. A review of Lispector's fiction shows clearly that from the beginning her imagistic and fluid style was close linked to her depiction of the quicksilver workings of the human mind. The essential lyricism of Lispector's voice was first noted by Alvaro Lins in 1944,[10] and with one major exception, it continued unabated to the end of her career. The lone exception is *The Via Crucis of the Flesh,* a work that does not eliminate Lispector's lyricism as much as it modifies it, paring it down and making it both reflect and express not the flux of an inner consciousness in the process of becoming but the flat, static, and objectified prose of three-dimensional reality. The poetic quality of works like *O lustre* (1949), *Family Ties* (1960), *The Apple in the Dark* (1961), *The Passion According to G. H.* (1964), and *Agua viva* (1973) stands in sharp contrast to the stark simplicity of *The Via Crucis of the Flesh,* a work which, as we have seen, tends to concentrate on action and conflict in the external world. Just as the thematic focus of this late-appearing 1974 story collection shifts to what characters do and say to one another in the social realm, so, too, does Lispector's style change. To write as she did in her earlier work about the ever-changing nances of the mind in its quest for self-awareness and self-expression, Lispector relied on an intensely poetic prose, one rich with symbolism, metaphors, paradox and ambiguity. To write as she does in *The Via Crucis of the Flesh,* however, about the surface appearance of things, requires a different style, one that is comparatively free of imagery, syntactically uncomplicated, and prosaic in its linear representation of corporeal reality.

Although the language of Lispector's fiction has always been simple, in stories like **"The Man Who Appeared,"** **"He Drank Me," "For the Time Being"** and **"Better than to Burn"** it becomes cipher-like in its brevity and concision. The diction and syntax of **"Por enquanto,"** for example, are elemental in their quotidian portrayal of very ordinary men, women, and things:

> But a person has a smoke and feels better right away. It's five till seven. If I become careless, I die. It's very easy. It's a question of stopping the clock. It's three minutes to seven. Should I turn on the television or not? But it's so boring to watch television alone. (**"Por enquanto,"** 62).

The word "chato" ("boring," or "flat") is of special importance here because it accurately describes the style that characterizes these stories. Basically paratatic in their composition, the sentences of *The Via Crucis of the Flesh* are semantically cryptic rather than poetically polysemous, as they are in most of Lispector's other work. In general, only *The Hour of the Star,* with its unlettered and unsophisticated protagonist, is similar to *The Via Crucis of the Flesh* in the severely abrupt, non-metaphoric nature of its style. Offering an outstanding example of how a skilled writer integrates theme and style, *The Via Crucis of the Flesh* involves the reader both denotatively and connotatively in the decoding of its text. The message that the reader takes from a story like **"Better than to Burn,"** for example, does not involve merely the literal meaning of the words used. It also elicits varying textual and contextual responses in the reader's consciousness, responses which, as Stanley Fish says, derive "affectively" from the ways in which the ostensibly "clear" and "unambiguous" messages are received by the reader.[11] So although Lispector's style in these stories is noticeably different, it nevertheless continues to express another of her most definitive beliefs: that since language not only names reality but creates and shapes it as well, it is never as "simple" or as "reliable" as we think it is. In Lispector's fictional universe the unstable relationship between language, reality, and human consciousness is of central importance, and *The Via Crucis of the Flesh* is not an exception to this rule. What has changed in this collection is the style, the manner in which the characters and the problems are presented. Developed here in terms of their external existence, the men and women of *The Via Crucis of the Flesh* use and are described by a language that both parallels and gives substance to their one-dimensional, materialistic, and unimaginative lives. Absent here is the densely figurative, strongly rhythmic, and syntactically-arresting style that we have long associated with Lispector's fiction.

Yet even when she writes in this stripped-down and abbreviated style, Lispector still succeeds in demonstrating the essential ambiguity that marks her best work. At the end of **"Praça Mauá,"** for example, we see how by unobtrusively gliding from within the mind of the protagonist and back out again, Lispector succeeds in imbuing the conclusion of the story with a mysterious sense of uncertainty about exactly what the main character thinks has really happened to her:

> She remained on her feet, dressed in black, in Mauá Square, at three o'clock in the morning. Like the most vagrant of prostitutes. Alone. Helpless. It was true: she didn't even know how to fry an egg. And Celsinho was more of a woman than she was.

> The square was in darkness. And Luísa sighed deeply. She looked at the pillars. The square was empty.

> And in the sky there were stars. (**"Praça Mauá,"** 84).

Extremely simple in its diction and syntax and virtually devoid of repetition, imagistic language, and elaborate rhythm patterns, Lispector's style in **"Praça Mauá"** does not fail to remind the reader that one never sees all there is to reality. Integrally related to the nature of the language system that creates and describes it, reality remains an enigma to us and to the characters of Lispector's fictive world.

Striking a new balance between theme and style, the stories of *The Via Crucis of the Flesh* show us a Clarice Lispector who has changed a great deal but without abandoning those essential features of her work that had made her one of Latin America's most respected post-World War II narrativists. Because *The Via Crucis of the Flesh* offers so much that is vintage Clarice Lispector while at the same time presenting us with the emergence of a new and challenging writer, it is appropriate to read *The Via Crucis of the Flesh* as a transitional work, a work that reflects Lispector herself in the process of change, of aesthetic growth. Giving the lie to those critics who believed Lispector to be monotonously one-dimensional author, the stories of *The Via Crucis of the Flesh* show her dealing with old problems in radically new ways, ways that amount to a new kind of writing for her. With their deconstructivist self-consciousness, their sexual power, their focus on the social world of action and event, and their startlingly spare style, the stories of *The Via Crucis of the Flesh* rank second only to those of the justly famous *Family Ties* in terms of artistic merit. Too often passed over by readers interested in Lispector's art, the surprising tales of *The Via Crucis of the Flesh* deserve much more attention.

Notes

[1] Jonathan Culler, *On Deconstruction* (Ithaca: Cornell University Press, 1982), pp. 137-39; 200-05; 214-15; 240; 243-47.

[2] Clarice Lispector, *The Via Crucis of the Flesh* (Rio de Janeiro: Editora Artenova, 1974), p. 65. All further references to the stories in this collection will be included parenthetically in the text. Unless otherwise indicated, the translations are by Earl E. Fitz. Three of the stories have been translated into English by Alexis Levitin. They are "Pig Latin" ("A língua do 'P'"), *Ms.,* July 1984, pp. 68-69; "The Man Who Appeared" ("O homem que apareceu") *Latin American Literature Today,* ed. Anne Fremantle (New York: Mentor Books, 1977), pp. 165-169; and "Better Than to Burn" ("Melhor do que order"), *Latin American Literature Today,* pp. 169-171.

[3] See, "The Passion According to Clarice Lispector: Elizabeth Lowe Interviews Clarice Lispector," *Review 24,* 1979, pp. 34-37, and "From the Chronicles of *The Foreign Legion*" (trans. and with an introduction by Giovanni Pontiero), *Review 24,* 1979, pp. 37-43. See also "Explicação Para Quem Talvez Não Entenda," *Visão do esplendor* (Rio de Janeiro: Francisco Alves, 1975), pp. 63-65.

[4] Elizabeth Lowe, "The Passion According to Clarice Lispector," p. 34.

[5] Gerald Prince, "Introduction to the Study of the Narratee." *Reader Response Criticism,* ed., Jane P. Tompkins (Baltimore: John Hopkins University Press, 1980), pp. 7-25; Roland Barthes, "Introduction à l'Analyse structurale des récits," *Communications 8* (1966), 18-19 and Tzvetan Todorov, "Les catégories du récit littéraire," *Communications 8* (1966), 146-47. Hélène Cixous's studies on the twin questions of feminism and feminine voice in Lispector's fiction are also very important in this regard. See her "L'approche de Clarice Lispector: Se laisser lire (por) Clarice Lispector—*A paixão segundo G. H.*" *Poetique,* Vol. 40, Nov. 1979; 408-419, her "The Laugh of the Medusa," trans. by Keith Cohen and Paula Cohen, *Signs: Journal of Women in Culture and Society,* I (1976), pp. 875-893, and *Vivre L'orange* (1979). Also of interest in this regard are Gina Michelle Collins's, "Translating a Feminine Discourse: Clarice Lispector's *Agua viva,*" *Translation Perspectives* (Binghamton, N.Y.: SUNY-Binghamton, 1984), pp. 119-124, Naomi Lindstrom's, "A Feminist Discourse of a Drunken Housewife," *Latin American Literary Review,* Vol. IX, No. 19 (Fall/Winter 1981), pp. 7-16, and Earl Fitz's, "Freedom and Self-Realization: Feminist Characterization the Fiction of Clarice Lispector," *Modern Language Studies,* Vol. 10, No. 3, 1980.

[6] Emir Rodríguez Monegal has commented on this seldom noticed but very significant aspect of Lispector's work. See his "Clarice Lispector en sus libros y en mi recuerdo," *Revista Iberoamericana,* Núm. 126, Enero-Marzo, 1984, pp. 231-238.

[7] They are: "Miss Algrave," "O corpo" ["The Body"], "Via crucis," "Ele me bebeu" ["He Drank me"], "Ruído de passos" ["Noise of Footsteps"], "Antes da ponte Rio-Niterói" ["In front of the Rio-Niterói Bridge"], "Praça Mauá" ["Mauá Square"], "A língua do 'P'" ["Pig Latin"], "Melhor do que order" ["Better Than to Burn"], and "Mas vai chover" ["But it's going to Rain"].

[8] David Bleich, "Epistemological Assumptions in the Study of Response," *Reader Response Criticism,* ed. Jane P. Tompkins (Baltimore: John Hopkins University Press, 1980), pp. 134-163.

[9] Georges Poulet, "Criticism and the Experience of Interiority," *Reader Response Criticism,* ed. Jane P. Tompkins (Baltimore: John Hopkins University Press, 1980), pp. 41-49.

[10] Alvaro Lins, *Os Mortos de sobrecasaca,* (Rio de Janeiro: Editora Civilizaçao Brasilera, 1963), pp. 189-191.

[11] Stanley Fish, "Literature in the Reader: Affective Stylistics," *Reader Response Criticism,* ed. Jane P. Tompkins (Baltimore: John Hopkins University Press, 1980), pp. 164-184.

Naomi Lindstrom (essay date 1989)

SOURCE: "Clarice Lispector: Articulating Women's Experience," in *Women's Voice in Latin American Literature,* Lynne Rienner Publishers, 1989, pp. 23-45.

[*In the following essay, a revised version of an article originally published in* Chasqui: Revista de Literatura Latinoamericana *in 1978, Lindstrom argues that while Lispector's philosophical debt is often ascribed to the male French existentialists, her emphasis on women's diminished existential possibilities in the stories "Amor," "Devaneio e embriaguez duma rapariga," and "Preciosidade" shows a greater affinity with the theories of feminist existential thinker Simone de Beauvoir.*]

I

Looking at the critical commentary on the fiction of Clarice Lispector, one immediately notes how much attention has been given to the existential themes that run through her work. Benedito Nunes and others have studied Lispector's writings as the literary elaboration of a set of philosophical concerns: the human being's need to make choices and take responsibility; the terror of contemplating nothingness and meaninglessness; the evasions with which people avoid consideration of such terrifying phenomena. Criticism that focuses on these issues has established Lispector as an artistic explorer of the human condition, an "existential writer" comparable to Jean-Paul Sartre and Albert Camus.[1]

A second feature of Lispector's work has drawn the attention of literary analysts with a more structural approach. The Brazilian writer shows great inventiveness in her handling of narrative voice or fictional point of view. Maria Luisa Nunes, for instance, studies the many narrative strategies employed in the short stories of *Lacos de familia* (1960; English translation, *Family Ties,* 1972). She finds this multiplicity of techniques exceptionally efficacious in providing access to the characters' consciousness.[2] Silvio Castro, too, makes the variegated treatment of the narration the point of departure for his study. In his analysis, the very fact that so many techniques are used in conjunction is a significant break with traditional fiction. The fusion of "discurso indireto radical, monólogo interior como fonte de revelação da ficção (radical indirect discourse, interior monologue as the source of fictional exposition)" as part of the innovation that "permitirá a Clarice Lispector uma nova linguagem (allows Clarice Lispector [to develop] a new language)." In Castro's analysis, the use of swiftly varying narrative techniques structures "uma montagem psicológica, montagem que se realiza antes do recolhimento do material a ser montado (a psychological montage, a montage that is set up before acquiring the matter to be placed in it)."[3] Bella Jozef discusses the meta-literary implications of the "estructura polifónica (polyphonic structure)" of the fiction, which presents a "diálogo de varios discursos (dialogue of several discourses)."[4] These discussants underline the functionality of such patterning in conveying the inner upheaval occasioned by sudden insights into the nature of one's existence. Owen Kellerman's formal typological study again reveals the complex multiplicity characteristic of this aspect of Lispector's writings.[5]

This study takes as its point of departure these already-established features of Lispector's work: her existential questioning and her shifting-about of narrative control. I propose to show how these two aspects of her work function jointly in the generation of a commentary upon the condition of being female. The "femininity" of the Brazilian's work has often attracted notice. For instance, Maria Ester Gilio calls Lispector's fiction "esencialmente femenina (essentially feminine),"[6] while Dennis Seniff praises her "keen insight into feminine psychology."[7] Rosario Castellanos made the Brazilian one of the subjects of an inquiry into the literary manifestations of feminine consciousness. In her 1973 *Mujer que sabe latin . . . (A Woman Who Knows Latin . . .),* the Mexican feminist critic shows the implicit examination of the female role that runs through Lispector's writings.[8] Moreover, one of Clarice Lispector's early literary models and a writer with whom she is often compared is Virginia Woolf, perhaps the literary feminist *par excellence.*[9]

At first, it might seem an eccentric displacement to seek an examination of societally-determined sex roles in writings so focused on the individual's existence. Bella Jozef, to cite one critic, states that Lispector "no busca un explicatión social, al nivel ideológico (does not look for a social explanation, at the ideological level)."[10] Yet, Jozef's analysis ably reveals Lispector's abrasive irony intended to "desmitificar la sociedad (demythify society)," whose "padrones y normas sociales ya consagrados (pre-sanctified social norms and patterns)" force people into "formas cristalizadas de comportamiento (rigidly fixed forms of behavior)."[11] Social factors enter this fictional world insofar as they constrict the characters, stifle awareness, and prevent the emergence of fully existent humanity. Since this constraining effect is most severe for those in a too-circumscribed role, it is significant that in **Laços de família,** considered the best working-out of the author's existential subject-matter, several protagonists are found living in very delimited, traditional-housewife roles. Among these are the heroines of two of the stories to be examined here, **"Amor (Love)"** and **"Devaneio e embriaguez duma rapariga (Daydreams of a Drunken Woman)."** The adolescent heroine of the third story under discussion, **"Preciosidade (Preciousness)"** also finds herself troubled and confused by society's notions of femininity and the female role.[12]

For a perspective on women's diminished existential possibilities, one should refer to Simone de Beauvoir's *Le Deuxième Sexe (The Second Sex,* 1949). Beauvoir's complaint about women's role is, precisely, that woman is not treated as one capable of becoming "an autonomous existent."[13] Under the current social arrangement, men are led to believe that women, unlike themselves, do not confront doubt, decision, nothingness and absurdity and hence are not fully human:

> Appearing as the Other, woman appears at the same time as an abundance of being in contrast to that existence, the nothingness of which man senses in himself; the Other, being regarded as the object in the eyes of the subject, is regarded as *en soi;* therefore as a being. In woman is incarnated in positive form the lack that the existent carries in his heart, and it is in seeking to be made whole through her that man hopes to attain self-realization.[14]

In Beauvoir's judgement, this view of women is not peculiar to men, nor are men the only ones to derive gratification from it. Women, too, come to believe that they cannot be other than they are, that their female nature freezes them into established patterns and obviates the human need to create oneself continually anew. Diffused throughout the culture, this tenet becomes both an oppressive constraint and an excuse for women not to take a voice in determining their own actions.

Beauvoir does not, of course, claim that all males enjoy optimum conditions for realizing an authentic and responsible existence. A life lived by Sartrean standards of "good faith" is massively demanding for any member of modern Western society. Nor is the feeling of having "no say" in the running of one's affairs an experience exclusive to women. Nonetheless, women are more vulnerable to this apparently voiceless, stagnant plight. This is because society maintains them in a restrictive role and discourages them from articulating life choices. At the same time, at least as a social ideal, "man is defined as a being who is not fixed, who makes himself what he is," and who can assert his will.[15] Of particular importance in Beauvoir's analysis, is the fact that women are discouraged from formulating, either inwardly or in overt speech and writing, the alternatives to their present pattern of life. Rather, the social arrangement pushes women toward a trivial, limited manner of thought and verbal expression that tends to preserve their narrowly-defined role.

Before applying these concepts in the analysis of three short stories, I should reemphasize that I am using *voice* in the sense of efficacy in discourse activities. The issue of narrative voice or narrative point of view is important as the technical device that helps lay bare patterns of discourse. In analyzing shifts in point of view. I am looking for structures that reveal women's difficulty in achieving an efficacious inner and outer voice.

II

The female malaise Beauvoir describes finds a fictional representative in Ana, the housewifely protagonist of the short story **"Amor."** When the reader first meets Ana, she has spent years in a muted and suppressed form of life, as far removed as possible from the anxieties of freedom. Her unwillingness to address herself to any but routine domestic matters results in a virtual silencing of her most vital self. Ana's evasive tactic is, notably, an exaggerated compliance with the socially-prescribed wife-and-mother role. For instance, the narrator explains Ana's habitual strategy for warding off the stirrings of existential terror: "Mas na sua vida não havia lugar para que sentisse ternura pelo seu espanto—ela o abafava com a mesma habilidade que as lides em casa lhe haviam transmitido. Saia então para fazer compras ou levar objetos para consertar, cuidando do lar e da família á revelia dêles. Quando voltasse era o fim da tarde e as crianças vindas do colégio exigiam-na. Assim chegaria a noite, com sua tranqüila vibração (But in her life there was no opportunity to cherish her fears—she suppressed them with that same ingenuity she had acquired from domestic struggles. Then she would go out shopping or take things to be mended, unobtrusively looking after her home and her family. When she returned it would already be late afternoon and the children back from school would absorb her attention. And so the evening desended with its quiet excitement)."[16] The event upon which **"Amor"** turns is a dramatic attitudinal upheaval in which Ana comes to see her fixed, rigid housewifeliness as "um modo moralmente louco de viver (a morally crazy way to live: p. 26)."

Maria Luisa Nunes has identified a multiplicity of narrative strategies within this one story: narrated monologue (or indirect interior monologue), internal analysis of the character by a third-person narrator, as well as direct quotation from Ana's mental processes (to use Nunes' terminology).[17] For Nunes, the interest of these various structures is their efficacy in the vivid rendering of consciousness.

In terms of the present study, the very fact that there should be so much intervention on the narrator's part and that the mediation should vary so greatly in degree is highly significant. The text has as its foremost task to communicate the mechanical quality of Ana's life in the years preceding her crisis and to narrate her crisis and its aftermath. It effects this labor through, on the one hand, the narrator's reportage, editorializing and summary and, on the other, the direct and indirect transmission of Ana's perception, formulation and attempted communication of this same subject-matter. By comparing passages in which the narrator's skillful elaboration is apparent with passages in which Ana's thoughts and speech are salient, the reader receives a commentary on the heroine's relatively poor powers of articulation. This becomes a commentary on her womanly role.

An example of matter treated twice, once with much editorial participation by the narrator and once with very little, is how Ana has avoided all contemplation of the drama of existence. The first account appears before the "plot," such as it is, begins. The narrator provides a preliminary summation of Ana, supplementing the character's limited vision with wit, eloquence, insight, and mastery of metaphorical and abstract language:

No fundo, Ana sempre tivera necessidade de sentir a raiz firme das coisas. E isso um lar perplexamente lhe dera. Por caminhos tortos, viera a cair num destino de mulher, com a surprêsa de nêle caber como se o tivesse inventado. O homem com quem casara era um homem verdadeiro, os filhos que tivera eram filhos verdadeiros. . . . Havia . . . emergido para des cobrir que também sem a felicidade se vivia: abolindo-a, encontrara uma legião de pessoas, antes invisíveis, que viviam como quem trabalha. . . . O que sucedera a Ana antes de ter o lar estava para sempre fora de seu alcance: uma exaltação perturbada que tantas vezes se confundira com felicidade insuportável.

Deep down, Ana had always found it necessary to feel the firm roots of things. And this is what a home had surprisingly provided. Through tortuous paths, she had achieved a woman's destiny, with the surprise of conforming to it almost as if she had invented that destiny herself. The man whom she had married was a real man, the children she mothered were real children. . . . She had . . . emerged to discover that life could be lived without happiness; by abolishing it she had found a legion of persons, previously invisible, who lived as one works. . . . What had happened to Ana before possessing a home of her own stood forever beyond her reach: that disturbing exaltation she had often confused with unbearable happiness (pp. 18-19).

Four pages later, one finds a second elaboration of the same subjectmatter. This time, the topic appears as part of Ana's ongoing thoughts during her crisis, which is now fully underway. The language of narration is assimilated to that of Ana herself. There is still a mediator interposed between heroine and reader, relaying Ana's thoughts, but the narrator refrains from tampering with the material. Maria Luisa Nunes describes such passages in *Laços* as a reporting of the character's consciously formalized thoughts. Nunes finds that, essentially, only the verb forms have been changed and the pronouns transferred from first to third person; everything else is the character's "own."[18] Here, then, is Ana's retrospective look at her lost, precrisis life:

Ela apaziguara tão bem a vida, cuidara tanto para que esta não explodisse. Mantinha tudo em serena compreensão, separava uma pessoa das outras, as roupas eram claramente feitas para serem usadas e podia-se escolher pelo jornal o filme da noite—tudo feito de modo a que um dia se seguisse ao outro.

She had skillfully pacified life; she had taken so much care to avoid upheavals. She had cultivated an atmosphere of serene understanding. separating each person from the others. Her clothes were clearly designed to be practical, and she could choose the evening's film from the newspaper—and everything was done in such a manner that each day should smoothly succeed the previous one (p. 22).

What immediately differentiates the two summaries is the homely, pedestrian quality of the second: the references to quotidian things, the absence of complex, thought-demanding figures such as appear in the first version (e.g., "a legion of persons, previously invisible . . ."), the comparatively low level of abstraction. It is now possible to see, by comparing the two accounts, signs of Ana's weak ability to register experience fully and structure coherent thoughts about it.

The first indication of her problem is the tremendous amount of upheaval she must experience before she is able to assemble this portrait of her life. In this connection, the four pages that elapse between the two versions are important. When one first reads of Ana's mechanical housewife routine, she is still immersed in it, incapable of standing outside it. The narrator points out that up until she takes a seat on a trolley, she has had no free moment for observation or reflection, being occupied with errands. Indeed, she clings to unreflective habits of mind to the last possible moment; even as she enters her crisis of doubt, "Ana ainda teve tempo de pensar por um segundo que os irmãos viriam jantar (Ana still had time to reflect for a second that her brothers were coming to dinner: p. 20)."

Because Ana has forbidden herself to formulate thoughts on the nature of existence, she finds it difficult to explain to herself what is happening to her. Her first reactions are nonverbal and inchoate: allowing her shopping bag to drop to the floor, letting out a shriek, paling, staring at the blind man who has somehow triggered her turmoil. She then registers perceptions that metaphorically express her discomfort in her role. Especially prominent is her net shopping bag, emblematic of her neatly-contained, tied-in domesticity: "A rêde de tricô era áspera entre os dedos, não intima como quando a tricotara (The string bag felt rough between her fingers, not soft and familiar as when she had knitted it; p. 21)." Not only is the confining network now chafing and oppressive, but its contents are no longer held intact: "Vários anos ruíam, as gemas amarelas escorriam (Several years fell away, the yellow yolks trickled: p. 21)."

As Ana's awareness of her situation grows, these metaphorical displacements finally lead to a recognition that the discomfort and rupture are not in her shopping bag or eggs, but within her being: "O que chamava de crise viera afinal (What she called a crisis had come at last; p. 22)." With this sentence the narrator emphasizes that Ana has reached the point where she can now use words to confront and pattern her turbulent experience. Only after Ana has reached this level of aware articulation is she able to produce a summary of her previous unreflective life.

However, Ana's review of her past is still not as fully elaborated as the one in which the narrator editorializes. Looking at the two versions, one notes that the narrator has laid bare the connection between Ana's exaggerated female role and her existential absurdity. In the first version, *home, husband* and *children* figure saliently; it is clear that forming a home was Ana's pretext for rejecting the dangerous part of her human condition. Ana's version completely omits what the narrator stresses, her hyperbolic "cair num destino de mulher ([having] achieved a woman's destiny; p. 18)," The woman also fails to account for another aspect of her ultradomesticity: the fact that it obliges her to live "sem a felicidad (without happiness; p. 18)," as the narrator puts it, closed to the stimulation of a more widely-lived existence. In short, Ana's self-accounting is good in comparison with her previous inarticulate condition, but poor compared with the narrator's richer elaboration. She has attained an inner voice, but an incomplete one.

III

In the second part of **"Amor,"** these mediated renderings of Ana's consciousness are supplemented with direct quotations, including actual utterances addressed to other characters. The first of these direct manifestations occurs when Ana attempts to communicate her new-found insights to another person. Upon arriving home after her crisis, the woman faces an evening of discourse tasks: greetings, dinner-table conversation. These verbal transactions require a good deal of social skill, but none of them can possibly be accommodated to her new and urgent concerns. Her wife-and-hostess role is so patterned as to leave no room for the critical discussion of such questions as life's ultimate meaning.

Because of this inadequacy in her normal speech opportunities, Ana steps entirely outside the rules and improvises a strange interchange with her small son. This event is intended to create a conduit for her "unspeakable" existential concerns: "Abraçou o filho, quase a ponto de machucá-lo . . . A vida é horrivel, disse-lhe baixo, faminta (She embraced her son, almost hurting him . . . 'Life is horrible,' she said to him in a low voice, as if famished; p. 26)." Here Ana has no trouble verbalizing her discovery in a way that is accurate and conscious. However, she has not taken into account the character and probable reaction of her intended confidant. When she adds to this first statement "Tenho mêdo (I am afraid)," the child bursts into frightened weeping. The encounter degenerates still further when the mother instructs the child: "Não deixe mamãe te esquecer (Don't let Mummy forget you; p. 26)." The transaction becomes so weird that the chosen recipient of Ana's new vision flees, directing at her "o pior olhar que jamais recebera (the worst look that she had ever received; p. 26)."

Ana's remarkably inept handling of this encounter indicates that she has no verbal skills—no "voice"—suitable to the overt questioning and criticism of basic assumptions. Here one sees the fictional laying-bare of a problem that has much interested feminist linguists. As Robin Lakoff observes in her 1975 *Language and Women's Voice,* even women who are fluent in the discussion of routine topics may be virtually voiceless concerning crucial or potentially threatening issues. Lakoff specifies that this silencing is not primarily the result of overt repressive measures, such as forbidding women to speak. Rather, the socialization of girl children into the female role provides an insufficient apprenticeship in the verbal questioning of certain highly sensitive matters. Moreover, when women do attempt to speak out on these charged subjects, they may be returned to a more harmless form of discourse through a variety of covert, often unconscious strategies.[19]

The displacement of discourse from disturbing questions to housewifely ones becomes evident in an exchange between Ana and her husband. Ana expresses what appears to her husband to be a disproportionate amount of anxiety. However, he resolves the matter by attributing all of her distress to excessive concern over the malfunctioning kitchen stove. Thus when Ana proclaims sweepingly, "Não quero que lhe aconteca nada, nunca! (I don't want anything ever to happen to you!)," her husband narrows that statement in scope by replying: "Deixe que pelo menos me aconteça o fogão dar um estouro (You can't prevent the stove from having its little explosions; p. 29)." His wry humor and smile succeed in reducing Ana's terror at the instability of existence to a womanly case of over-apprehension about trifles, which he can dissipate with an embrace and soothing utterance.

This brief verbal transaction illustrates Lispector's satisfyingly complex critique of social roles. It would be ridiculous to blame Ana's husband for exhibiting a condescending attitude toward his wife or for circumscribing her horizons. The husband is only trying to bring an inexplicable, threatening situation back within the bounds of an exchange between damsel-in-distress and manly protector. The "villain" here is neither masculine nor feminine, but abstract. The rigidity of structuring in socialized discourse prevents Ana from making manifest the source of her terror. In turn, her inability to share her vision of absurdity leads to the rapid dimming of that vision. After this conversation, with its trivializing and neutralizing effect, the narrator describes Ana's husband as "afastando-a do perigo de viver (removing her from the danger of living; p. 30)."

Most telling, in this respect, is the fact that the narrator assigns no names to those with whom Ana speaks; they remain the husband, the child, the brothers, the maid. This manner of reference suggests that the conversational partners are playing their socially assigned parts around Ana, nudging her back into her own proper role as wife, mother and hostess. Ana possesses not only a name but, through her special awareness, an individuality highly incompatible with the performance of her prescribed womanly functions.

IV

During the second half of the story, the narrator begins to signal that there is now a more direct transmission of the "utterances" of Ana's inner voice. This is the case, for example, when the heroine becomes aware of her deviant reaction to the stranger she saw on the trolley: "Oh! mas ela amava o cego! pensou com os olhos molhados. No entanto não era com êste sentimento que se iria a uma igreja ('Oh! but she loved the blond man,' she thought with tears in her eyes. Meanwhile it was not with this sentiment that one would go to church: p. 27)."

Here Ana makes perhaps her most direct confession of deep-seated aberrance. Yet, her self-characterization falls short of being overt, either in what is admitted or in the form that admission takes. Impressively, although the

narrator's *she thought* signals a direct quotation from Ana's mental processes, the third-person, past-tense statement does not look like anything Ana could actually think. Jozef sees Ana's presentation as a form of duplication in which the woman's fragmented self allows her to be both the commentator and commented-upon: "El comportamiento artistico se caracteriza por el desdoblamiento del yo que se ve en el acto de producción, actor y espectador de si mismo, sujeto del espectáculo y objeto del juego, captando una conciencia en fraccionamiento por la disociación del yo (The artistic procedure is characterized by a duplication of the *I* which is seen in the act of production, actor and spectator of itself, the subject of the spectacle and the object of the game, capturing a consciousness that has been fragmented by the tearing-asunder of the *I*)."[20] Whether or not the form of Ana's self-characterization reflects such a divided self, its ambiguity is purposely troubling. Its equivocal character is yet another sign of Ana's extreme difficulty in formalizing insights not proper to her official, housewifely sense of self.

A further ambiguity appears when the reader attempts to attribute the second assertion ("Meanwhile . . .") either to the narrator or to Ana. This statement, with its implications of unruly eroticism, may be too upsetting for the heroine to voice, even to herself. In that case, the narrator is once again supplementing Ana's incomplete elaboration and, in so doing, revealing its limited, censored character. Alternatively, the sentence may be a continuation of the quotation from Ana's mind marked by *she thought*; both statements are in the third person and past tense. Sharing Ana's disorientation to some extent, the reader is unable to ascertain what the woman really knows, admits, and formalizes in her unspoken verbal material.

V

Throughout the greater part of the story, one observes Ana's painful coming to consciousness. From an unreflective immersion in household routine, she progresses to a chaotic flow of disconcerting perceptions that metaphorically correspond to her plight and moves on to a partial articulation of her human problem. As Ana gains awareness, the narrator entrusts a greater burden of the story to her, calling upon her inner and even her spoken voice to tell the reader where she stands.

The last paragraphs, however, present a swift change. Ana's new insight has come to an end, as the narrator explicitly announces. Now nothing of Ana's voice is heard as the third-person narrator does all the work of explaining how her husband calms her supposedly stove-related fears and the couple retires for the night.

The handling of narrative voice in this story gives an artistic representation to a phenomenon frequently explored in the social essays of feminists.[21] Ana is voiceless largely through acquiescence to her wife-and-mother role. Nonetheless, the reader sees her acquire the beginnings of a voice when, for example, she correctly identifies the nature of her problem by saying "Life is horrible (p. 26)." Here is the implication that even the most suppressed individual can yet generate a voice capable of speaking out and questioning. The acquisition of this voice is painful; early attempts at articulation may be disastrous. If the new voice finds no support from the social environment, it may disappear, and the individual may resume the predictable patterns of socialized discourse.

For this reason, the narrator's intervention and stepping-back give an index to Ana's varying progress in being her own spokeswoman. The reader sees how much of Ana's situation cannot be stated by the woman herself and, hence, falls to the narrator. Woman here epitomizes the human being silenced in a narrow role. The shifting pattern of voices shows how such an individual must develop in order to become able to enunciate life decisions and vital awareness—in sum, to become fully existent.

VI

The heroine of **"Devaneio e embriaguez duma rapariga (The Daydreams of a Drunken Woman),"** another short story included in the same volume, differs superficially from the verbally stifled Ana. The nameless *rapariga* provides plentiful outpourings from both her inner and outer voices. Large portions of the text represent her rambling interior monologues. These passages are patently marked as the character's "own" by their adherence to a Lusitanian standard of speech proper of the heroine's Portuguese origin.[22] There is no reason for the narrator's occasional summaries and intercalated remarks to assume this notably European form. Thus, one can see that the overt editorial presence and participation is relatively slight; often the narrator's only task is to pass on to the reader what the heroine thought or said. Apart from her interior soliloquies, the heroine gives audible voice to a wide, rather random variety of material. She bursts into song, recites ritualized verbal formulae and talks to herself, her husband and imaginary conversation partners.

Moreover, the *rapariga* considers her skill as a conversationalist to be one of her accomplishments in life. Early in the story she is heard rehearsing, in front of a mirror, coquettish repartee. Later, immersed in a social occasion, she secretly glories in her participation: "Naturalmente que ela palestrava. Pois que lhe não faltavam os assuntos nem as capacidades (Naturally she talked, since she lacked neither the ability to converse nor topics to discuss; p. 10)." In her judgment, her fluent production of sociable "palestras (conversation)" proves that "ela não era nenhuma parola d'aldeia (she was no provincial ninny; p. 9)." Indeed, her narcissistic obsession with her imagined verbal prowess becomes a recurring topic in the text. Repeatedly, she defines herself as a woman who has a voice and knows how to use it smoothly and efficaciously. This insistence, however, is one of the text's ironic strategies. The reader cannot possibly concur with the *rapariga*'s self-assessment. From the outset of the story signs of conflict, uncertainty and inadequacy are manifest in the woman's habits of speech and thought.

The *rapariga* first appears at a moment when the demands of her mothering role have suddenly diminished. With her children away, she lacks her routine patterning and cannot manage to structure her own time. In an empty house with an empty day ahead, she fills time with lengthy sleeping, priming and reflection.

During this first part of the story, the narrator's presence is more evident than it will be subsequently. Authorial presence is visible in occasional summaries of the heroine's thoughts and actions and in verbs of declarandi following quotations from her uttered and unuttered speech. As in **"Amor,"** the narrator's burden of telling the story is greatest before the heroine enters the crisis that brings her inner turbulence to a conscious level. Once agitation forces her to begin formalizing her existential terrors, her direct and indirect interior monologues can become the substance of the narration. However, even before she achieves this involuntary eloquence, the *rapariga* formulates a good many telling phrases without being aware of their significance.

Her early formulations lay bare a deep-seated conflict in her view of herself and her life situation. She harbors within her mind two mutually contradictory voices. One, cheerful and given to romanticizing, insists she is a langorous belle luxuriating in a stretch of leisure. Indirect interior monologue reports such thoughts as "Ai, ai, vinha da rua como uma borboleta (Oh my!—she would come fluttering in from the street like a butterfly; p. 6)." A darker voice, though, hints that she is beginning to face nothingness and meaninglessness: "que chatura (how boring; p. 6)." The omniscient narrator's remarks favor this latter view, for they describe the heroine as "colérica (irritated)" and "com leve rancor (slightly annoyed; p. 6)." Nonetheless, it remains uncertain whether or not one should consider matters to be seriously amiss.

The next segment resolves the ambiguity of the woman's behavior. Her wildly inappropriate responses to her homecoming husband reveal that crisis, not delightful leisure, is her true state, and that her self-lyricizing contains an element of self-misrepresentation. In this scene, each of the woman's unusual behaviors represents a further rupture with her normally-defined wife-and-mother role. Her patterning of her life has already been thrown into question by the removal of her child-care duties. Now she refuses to make any of the expected wifely responses to her husband: she fails to greet him, to care about his food, clothing or activities and finally she rejects, with impressive crudity, his sexual overtures.

The *rapariga*'s lack of insight into her inchoate rebellion is reflected in the fact that her thoughts on the issue are not heard. The implication is that her notions are not yet sufficiently formed to appear represented even as unuttered speech. It falls to the narrator to describe the chaos of this household in which the wife refuses to play the part of wife. The heroine remains opaque even when the narrator speaks of her mental processes, for one only learns what she is not thinking: "O marido apareceu-lhe já trajado e ela nem sabia o que o homem fizera para o seu pequeno-almôço, e nem olhou-lhe o fato, se estava ou não por escovar, pouco se lhe importava se hoje era dia dele tratar os negócios na cidade (Her husband appeared before her, having already dressed, and she did not even know what he had prepared for his breakfast. She avoided examining his suit to see whether it needed brushing . . . little did she care if this was his day for attending to his business in the city; p. 7)." All that is heard from her overt voice is two harsh rebuffs to her husband; she seems unwilling to recognize or comment upon her obvious disturbance. The husband does offer an interpretation that brings his wife's baffling unwifeliness back within the bounds of normal actions: "estás doente (you're ill; p. 7)." Despite the lack of any somatic disturbance, the heroine accepts this soothing normalization, further delaying recognition of or confrontation with her life crisis.

This scene of household interaction precedes two segments that highlight the heroine's mental processes. These two explorations of consciousness employ, again, a variety of techniques to provide a mass of verbal material documenting what the heroine was saying to herself. The two stand in marked opposition to one another. In the first, the *rapariga* stands outside her everyday housewife persona and thinks in an extraordinary "voice." In the second, she has abruptly returned to her old self and to her routine habits of organizing her world.

As her aberrant, nonwifely self, the woman imagines her life as one open to all possibilities. The real-world constraints on her choices—the result of her family circumstance—now disappear. What replaces them is a vision of freedom and availability to new experience, this vision being strongly colored by an element of Bovarization: "Ela amava. . . . Estava previamente a amar o homem que um dia ela ia amar. Quem sabe lá, isso às vêzes acontecia, e sem culpas nem danos para nenhum dos dois (She was in love. . . . She was anticipating her love for the man whom she would love one day. Who knows, this sometimes happened, and without guilt and injury for either partner; p. 8)."

After these timeless, unfettered imaginings, one is startled to hear the down-to-earth housewife's voice suddenly reassert itself. The woman reminds herself of "as batatas por descascar, os miúdos que voltariam à tarde das titias ai que até me faltei ao respeito!, dia de lavar roupa e serzir as peúgas . . . (the potatoes waiting to be peeled, the kids expected home that same evening from their visit to the country. God, I've lost my self-respect, I have! My day for washing and darning socks . . . ; p. 8)."

What is interesting here is that, in all her ramblings, the heroine avoids referring to the issues underlying her crisis. Indeed, she seeks to mask her turmoil through a euphemistic subterfuge. Scolding herself, she transmutes her conflicted rejection of her role into a simple case of neglectful housekeeping. The notion that she is "vagabunda (lazy; p. 8)," like her husband's assertion that she is unwell, gives an incomprehensible situation the features of recognizability and quotidian verisimilitude.

Nonetheless, in the juxtaposition of her two identities, one can see implicit the matters that generate her trouble.

Simone de Beauvoir's characterization of the housewife is descriptive of the *rapariga*'s problem:

> The tragedy of marriage is not that it fails to assure woman the promised happiness—there is no such thing as assurance in regard to happiness—but that it mutilates her; it dooms her to repetition and routine. The first twenty years of a woman's life are extraordinarily rich, as we have seen; she discovers the world and her destiny. At twenty or thereabouts, mistress of a home, bound permanently to a man, a child in her arms, she stands with her life virtually finished forever. Real activities, real work are the prerogative of her man; she has mere things to occupy her which are sometimes tiring but never fully satisfying.[23]

VII

The next segment of the story moves the heroine out of her housebound langour and into the city's nightlife. Accompanied by her husband and his employer, she makes a display of coquettish charm and drinks massive quantities of wine. The wine, along with the turmoil she already harbors, produces a state of almost transcendent excitation.

This section offers copious documentation of the thoughts the woman formulates to herself. These inner reflections reveal still further her inability to take one coherent stance toward the topic, which nonetheless becomes the repeated focus of her anxiety. On the one hand, she reviles her housewife self as a banal and trivialized one from which she has now escaped: "No sábado à noite a alma diária perdida, e que bom perdê-la, e como lembrança dos outros dias apenas as mãos pequenas tão maltratadas (Saturday night, her every-day soul lost, and how satisfying to lose it, and to remind her of former days, only her small, ill-kempt hands; p. 10)." Contradictorily, she glories in the respectability that her matronly status confers upon her. She reassures herself that she can afford to be drunk in public, because she is "protegida pela posição que alcançara na vida (protected by the position she had attained in life; p. 11)." The fact that the woman can tell herself such patently opposed things reflects the contradictions that Beauvoir diagnoses in the traditionally-defined female. In Beauvoir's analysis, when women chafe under the restraints imposed upon them, they "simultaneously demand and detest their feminine condition; they live through it in a state of resentment."[24]

This resentment finally finds a suitable object in the person of a blonde woman seated in the same restaurant with the *rapariga*. In a seizure of anxiety, the *rapariga* inwardly constructs a miscellany of accusations against the stranger. At first the list of complaints appears as a random babble, since the strange woman is accused both of licentiousness and of excessive piety and prudery. What confers unity upon the accusations is the *rapariga*'s continuing obsession with the female role. Lithe, elegant, wearing a beautiful hat, the rival represents a woman not yet fettered by domesticity. To counter the jealousy she feels, the *rapariga* seeks to magnify the importance of her own wife-and-mother status. The untrammeled blonde lacks these essential attributes of womanhood: "vai ver que nem casada era (Bet you anything she isn't even married)," "vai ver que não era capaz de parir-lhe, ao seu homem, um filho (I'll bet she couldn't even bear her man a child; p. 12)." She succeeds in elaborating a scheme in which all the blonde woman's attractive features become indices of a reprehensible deviation from the proper role.

The climax of this scene occurs when the *rapariga* appoints herself as the voice of well-regulated womanhood and, in direct but unuttered allocution, reprimands the aberrant and incomplete female: "Bem sei o que te falta, fidalguita, e ao teu homem amarelo! E se pensas que t' invejo e ao teu peito chato, fica a saber que me ralo, que bem me ralo de teus chapéus. A patifas sem brio como tu, a se fazerem de rogadas eu lhes encho de sopapos (I know what you need, my beauty, you and your sallow boyfriend! And if you think I envy you with your flat chest, let me assure you that I don't give a damn for you and your hats. Shameless sluts like you are asking for a good hard slap on the face; p. 13)."

Maria Luisa Nunes, noting the directness of address in the scolding and the absence of a mediating narrator, correlates this directness to the heroine's extreme, overwrought state.[25] One may also say that this direct "stating her case" shows that the *rapariga,* after wandering about amid contradictory and half-formulated thoughts, has finally developed a point of view that she can voice. Her defense of traditional wifely behavior is firm and programmatic, capable of being preached to the sinful. Although this voice is assertive, few readers will find it a satisfactory instrument for resolving the heroine's tumult. Rather, it is a falsifying voice, another evasive displacement. Its essential inefficacy is revealed when the heroine, lying on her bed later that night, finds her inner turbulence still in force.

VIII

The next section, the drunken reverie of the story's title, finally breaks with the preceding pattern of vague perturbation, attitudinal upheaval and successful evasion of the root problem. The *rapariga* comes face to face with her domesticated persona and with her disaffection from that role. She abandons her defensive strategy of constructing authoritative-sounding statements to neutralize her puzzling new sense of existential terror.

Direct quotation from the woman's ongoing mental processes reveals a self-examination which is neither distorted by romanticizing nor by a rigid model of proper womanhood. She makes an anguished attempt to identify those features of her existence that now seem distressingly absurd: "Aborrecimento, aborrecimento, ai que chatura. Que maçada . . . Que é que se havia de fazer. Ai, è uma tal coisa que se me dà que nem bem sei dizer (Boredom . . . Such awful boredom . . . How sickening! . . . What was one to do? How can I describe this thing inside me? p. 14)." The struggle culminates in the production of a synthesizing self-description: "desiludida, resignada, empanturrada, casada, contente, a vaga náusea (disenchanted, resigned, satiated, married, content, vaguely nauseated; p.

15)." Throughout the course of the story, she has elaborated numerous self-characterizations: the belle, the fragile lily, the woman with a housekeeping problem, the sparkling conversationalist. Now, for the first time, she has worked out an image that the reader can accept as an accurate one.

Following this breakthrough, the woman has considerably greater success in dealing with her crisis. Having admitted that her household life is somewhat absurd and meaningless, she convinces herself that this status is, paradoxically, good and comforting. She refers frankly to her husband and children as the "cousas   nauseantes (nauseating . . . things; p. 15)" that will enable her to go on living after her crisis of insight.

Although the heroine here achieves her most authentic voice, her powers of articulation still lag considerably behind her desire for self-knowledge. She herself bewails her insufficiency, while the omniscient narrator emphasizes it by ironically "helping her along." The heroine gropes for an adequate description of her new revelations: "Ai que cousa que se me dá! (Heavens above! What *is* wrong with me?)" The narrator emerges from a period of silence to provide, in omniscient fashion, the answer: "Era a tristeza (It was unhappiness; pp. 15-16)."

The incomplete, but authentic, articulation of her life situation frees the *rapariga* from the anxiety that has plagued her up to this point. The story's ending reveals her planning a reaccommodation into her newly-conceptualized role, beginning with a massive housecleaning: a notably partial triumph.

The *rapariga*'s problem is emblematic of a more generalized difficulty affecting women. To achieve a valid and effective voice, women need more than the simple ability to make statements. Here, the heroine has cultivated a markedly feminine set of verbal skills. These capacities serve her well for such functions as socializing, flirtation, scolding, moralizing and the fabrication of a princess persona for herself.

The heroine's serious difficulties arise when she tries to apply these hyperfeminine strategies to her existential crisis. The radical self-questioning she needs to enunciate cannot find its adequate expression. The *rapariga* avoids taking a responsible look at her life situation by producing a barrage of frivolous or self-righteous verbiage. To assume a conscious hold on the issue at stake, she must find a new "voice" altogether.

The narrator reveals this struggle by withdrawing when the woman faces the possibility of speaking to her true problem. On each of these crucial occasions, the woman makes an attempt to address the issues of her life, but only at the story's end has she achieved a satisfactory statement.

IX

Compared to these housewives who formalize so little of their insight into overt utterance, the adolescent heroine of **"Preciosidade (Preciousness)"** presents an impressive picture of verbalization. After her crisis of self-reappraisal, she not only voices her new perception but shouts it out, albeit in solitude. Moreover, unlike the older heroines, she does not allow her circumstance to remain unchanged after her great moment of introspection. She demands a small, but figuratively important, alteration in the world's treatment of her. This novel speech act, a startling self-assertion, is successful in obtaining the desired results. Before she can effect this successful articulation, though, the heroine must emerge from a rigid and self-stifling life pattern that leaves no room for such communication.

In this story, as in the previous two, the heroine has mastered a complex set of strategies to suppress awareness of her status as human being. Instead of obsessive conformity, though, she relies on deviance as her chief protection. She conceives of herself as an exceptional being unaffected by the incompleteness and instability that afflict existents. Variously, she is "um centauro (a centaur; p. 99)," "impessoal . . . filha dos deuses (impersonal . . . the daughter of the gods; p. 103)" and "a princesa do mistério intacto (the princess of that intact mystery; p. 101)." The outward manifestation of this pretension to a special *être en soi* is a massive avoidance of human contact. Discourse tasks, insofar as they confirm the uniform humanity of the participants, pose a threat to her privileged status. The narrator details the girl's tactics for evading verbal transactions. For example, here is her behavior at school: "Atravessava o corredor interminável como a um silêncio de trincheira, e no seu rosto havia algo tão feroz—e soberbo também, por causa de sua sombra—que ninguém lhe dizia nada. Proibitiva, ela os impedia de pensar (She crossed the corridor, which seemed as interminable as the silence in a trench and in her expression there was something so ferocious—and proud too because of her shadow—that no one said a word to her. Prohibitive, she forbade them to think; p. 98)." The intensity of her horror of verbal contact becomes even more manifest through the structuring of narrative voice. The narrator very rarely quotes directly from the girl's inner voice during the first part of the story. The two longest citations from her conscious formulations refer directly to her continual fear that others "dissessem alguma coisa (might say something [to her]; p. 96)." Here, the narrator carries the burden of explanation for the girl's rejection of human contact; she herself cannot look at her behavior and interpret it. In the narrator's analysis, the heroine dreads even the most mundane speech acts because they may call into question her specialness: "era obrigada a ser venerada (she was obliged to be venerated; p. 96)," not humanized.

When discourse cannot be suppressed, it can be frozen into a private ceremony, again reducing the possibilities of human contamination. A dominant reliance on ritual format is evident in the girl's relations with the family maid. Because the heroine's schedule is unlike that of other family members, she spends several hours each day alone in the house except for the company of the servant. These hours have their own routine. Breakfast is served in silence. Upon coming home from school, the girl initiates

speech, but only to direct a unilateral verbal aggression against the maid: "gritava com a empregada que nem sequer lhe respondia (she shouted at the maid who did not even answer; p. 99)." As the maid serves lunch, the ceremony of stylized hostility becomes a reciprocal exchange:

—Magrinha, mas como devora, dizia a empregada esperta.

—Pro diabo, gritava-lhe sombria.

"Skinny, but you can eat all right," the quick-witted maid was saying.

"Go to blazes," she shouted at her sullenly. (p. 99)

Fear of human contact, though, must be weighed against the girl's equal horror of solitude. When she is not in a definable role in relation to others, she suffers intimations of nothingness. By setting herself back within the established context of conventionalized relations she can feel secure, "poder se tornar com alivio uma filha (become to her relief a daughter; p. 100)." The girl's solution to this dilemma is to cultivate a form of discourse with the maid that still maintains the necessary distance: "conversando, evitava a conversa (conversing, she avoided conversation; p. 100)."

None of this "nonconversational" conversation appears transcribed in the text. However, the narrator gives several clues to its functioning. The girl conceives the interaction as a rite in which the maid is an "antiga sacerdotisa (ancient priestess; p. 100)." The goal of the conversation is to forestall the transfer of information. The maid is the possessor of worldly knowledge with which she may try to contaminate the heroine. Again, the heroine's actions evade exposure to the more problematic aspects of the human condition. Although she cannot bear literal solitude, she cannot let the maid impinge on her spiritual solitude. As an index to the intensity of her concern, her own formulation of it appears in a direct quotation from her consciousness: referring to the worldly maid, the girl thinks "Ela imagina que na minha idade devo saber mais do que sei e é capaz de me ensinar alguma coisa (She imagines that at my age I must know more than I do, and she is capable of teaching me something; p. 100)."

X

The detailing of the girl's strategems has an ironic edge. The most notable feature of her postures, apart from their Byzantine intricacy, is their inadequacy. The girl is troubled by a dim awareness that she is acting in bad faith, shirking her human responsibility. The signs of this awareness are the words the narrator applies to her, presumably reflecting something the heroine feels but cannot quite formalize. Displaying aloofness in the hall, the girl dreads penetration of "o seu disfarce (her disguise; p. 98)." Exhibiting scholarship in the classroom, she becomes "a grande fingida (the great pretender; p. 98)." Even an insulation, her charade is only minimally successful; one sees her barely suppressing panic.

From elements dispersed throughout the early part of the text, the reader pieces together the motives of the heroine's unease. Outstanding among these is her anxiety about her femininity and reluctance to assume the adult female role. Previous critics have pointed out the sexual turbation she suffers, but the question of role in social interactions is also salient.[26] The heroine's rejection of role manifests itself in a minimalization of her potential for "feminine charm." Already a plain girl, she exaggerates her deviance from the ideal of young ladyhood. A stiff, pseudo-military gait, unkempt physical appearance and rough manners proclaim her refusal. In a well-known pattern (e.g., the so-called Bluestockings), disquietude over "womanliness" has as its concomitant a dedication to scholarly work. The classroom offers refuge from her confusion because it is the space "onde ela era tratada como um rapaz (where she was treated like a boy; p. 98)." Her ugly, noisy shoes emerge, through repeated mention, as the paradigmatic marks of her antifemininity.

XI

Clearly, the heroine cannot maintain her guarded "preciousness" indefinitely. It is too difficult a task to deny that she is a person in relation to other persons and, specifically, a woman in relation to men. Lispector's story here makes a point that is also key to Beauvoir's analysis of the female adolescent.[27] No matter how unappealing the young girl finds socially-defined womanhood, she cannot opt out of the web of social bonds. Explicitly or implicitly, she must confront conventional expectations about womanly comportment. The confrontation may result in a passive recreation of the circumscribed womanhood the girl has seen around her. The more aware adolescent, however, begins a struggle to reaccommodate women's role to her individual needs. She agrees to acquire certain attributes of womanhood, but feels torment upon doing so. Beauvoir cites literary, essay, and documentary sources that reveal this conflict. The necessity of becoming a woman generates fear of losing one's uniqueness and sense of life's rich texture. For Beauvoir, this terror is justified, since the current arrangement abruptly curtails the girl's freedom precisely at the moment when she assumes adult status.

The heroine of **"Preciosidade"** experiences such a confrontation during the course of the story. The event that triggers this confrontation is, in itself, trivial. Two youths, passing the girl on the street, reach out, touch her and flee.

Narrating in *tempo lento,* the third-person relator keeps the reader fully informed on the girl's mental processes. The information is conveyed through the narrator's summary and analysis, through indirect interior monologue and through quotations from her conscious formulations. What stands out here is not the sexuality expressed in the encounter. Rather, the heroine concentrates on the meeting as a social interaction. Her concerns are those of the young woman wondering how to behave in a social situation. As the two youths approach, she must structure her own behavior so as to maintain her dignity. Questions of posture, gait, where to cast her eyes and how to maintain

a composed face contribute to what sociologist Erving Goffman has called "the presentation of self in everyday life."[28] These quotidian preoccupations bring home the fact that the girl is, indeed, one of many human beings existing in interrelation. Forced to see herself through the eyes of others, she is suddenly aware of her poor performance in the female role. Her disheveled and unbathed person, her innate plainness and, above all, her clumping shoes make her a figure of social failure.

Following the encounter, the girl's voice disappears from the story temporarily. The narrator, in panoramic summary, informs us of her subsequent actions. The reason for not revealing her mental processes is explicitly given: "não tinha pensado em nada (she hadn't thought about anything; p. 106)." Dislodged from her strict life patterns, she avoids her school, shunning the one area in which she enjoys full mastery of the discourse situation. This anomalous renunciation suggests an incipient rejection of her stratagems for keeping discourse, and hence life, under close restraints.

The girl's voice resurfaces at the moment she attempts to reinsert herself into her old routine. In this scene and the following one, which takes place in the school rest room, the heroine has two opposing voices. The first to be heard is her old voice, with its devices for blocking out the problematic and disturbing. The signs of the girl's crisis are patent. Yet upon being questioned by a classmate, she denies that anything is amiss. This effort at denial is not only inefficacious but absurdly counter-productive. Unable to regulate her volume, the agitated heroine startles several schoolmates with a loud "Não (No; p. 106)."

The recognition of her loss of control drives the heroine to seek refuge in the restroom. Here, in solitude, another voice asserts itself for the first time. This new voice is radically unlike her evasive speech; it proclaims the truths the other voice labors to hide: "diante do grande silêncio dos ladrilhos, gritou aguda, supersônica: 'Estou sòzinha no mundo! Nunca ninguém vai me ajudar, nunca ninguém vai me amar! Estou sòzinha no mundo!' (before the great silence of the tiles, she cried out in a high shrill voice, 'I am all alone in the world! No one will ever help me, no one will ever love me! I am all alone in the world!'; p. 107)"

The new voice, with its disquieting assertions, cannot yet supplant the girl's old voice. Rather, the reader witnesses a dialectic between the two voices within the same young woman. As the accustomed voice resumes its evasive, dehumanizing tactics, the new voice contests the validity of such procedures. The result is an episode of literal self-questioning and self-confrontation. The narrator transcribes this debate as both uttered and unuttered statements in direct citation and as indirect interior monologue. The use of reflexive verbs in this reportage (interrompeu-se: she interrupted herself; retrucou-se: she retorted to herself) emphasizes that this is self-versus-self discourse.

In warring, the two voices lay bare the principal features of the girl's conflicted state. The old voice would turn away from her new existential insights, returning to quotidian routine before change and growth can take place. The new voice refuses to allow this banalization. Here they oppose one another within the space of one quotation. The girl is missing class because of her crisis, and begins with a trivial reaction to the situation: "Não faz mal, depois copio os pontos, peço emprestado os cadernos para copiar em casa—estou sòzinha no mundo! (It doesn't matter, I'll copy the notes later, I'll borrow someone's notes and copy them later at home—I am all alone in the world!; p. 107)" The issue being disputed is what Massaud Moisés calls "abandoning . . . the mental stagnation which maintains reality intact, in order to gain the condition of being a person."[29] The second focus of contention is the old voice's harshly dismissive attitude toward the human being. This deliberate denigration of self and others is intolerable to the new voice, who says in rebuke: "Não diga isso. . . . Uma pessoa é alguma coisa (Don't say that . . . a person is something; pp. 107-108)."

During this self-encounter, the girl takes preliminary steps toward reestablishing her neglected ties with her fellow beings. Her rather wild appearance, cultivated as a barrier between herself and others, now receives a critical review and remedial action. These measures point to two radical departures from the heroine's accustomed manner of life. On the levels of sex role and sexuality, she assumes the feminine responsibility for presenting herself as physically attractive—a definitive accommodation to her socially-defined part in life. On the level of her discourse problem, she moves toward opening up the lines of communication with others, toward signaling her human "approachability."

Implicit in the girl's changed behavior is the tenet Beauvoir discussed. To participate in society, the young girl must become not only a person, but also a woman, in some generally recognizable sense of womanliness. But does the heroine have an awareness of this principle? The following scene, in which she speaks out on behalf of her new sense of personhood, suggests that she is at least partially conscious of the problem she is resolving. Here are the girl's words to her family: "Preciso de sapatos novos! Os meus fazem muito barulho, uma mulher não pode andar com salto de madeira, chama muita atenção! (I need some new shoes! Mine make a lot of noise, a woman can't walk on wooden heels, it attracts too much attention!; p. 108)" All the elements that have come together in her transformation are there: the individual's right to self-esteem and visible self-care; the link between being a fully entitled person and being a woman; the need to accommodate oneself to role expectations of femininity. However, the girl's ability to articulate these ideas lags behind her perception of them. Unskilled in the labor of expressing existential concerns, she produces an utterance that strikes her listeners as illogical. Her family, moreover, has neither the experience nor the expectation of hearing their daughter speak out on such matters. They take her words at the most literal level possible, and answer her: "Você não é uma mulher e todo salto é de madeira (You are not a woman and all shoe heels are made of wood; p. 108)."

Despite this discouraging response, the girl's statement is not a failure. The reader can perceive the fundamentally valid notions that underlie her wild-sounding formulation. In terms of her new-found acceptance of role, she is a woman. Her preoccupation with footwear makes sense as a metonymic displacement of her desire to make a favorable presentation of herself. The girl, too, knows that she is right, as evidenced by her persistence in the face of her family's incomprehension. In sum, she is voicing her demand in terms that make sense to her, and that establish to her own satisfaction her ability to assert herself.

Even as pragmatic communication, her garbled demand has a measure of efficacy. While the girl's actual words baffle her family, the intensity of her need is unmistakable. Without quite following the processes at work, her listeners grasp the link between the sudden necessity for shoes and the young girl's most essential vital mechanisms. The story ends with the emergence of a woman who can make a claim for herself and be heard. The narrator's last report on the heroine is "E ela ganhou os sapatos novos (And she got her new shoes; p. 108)."

Notes

[1] Existential themes are discussed in Assis Brasil, *Clarice Lispector* (Rio de Janeiro: Editora Organização Simões, 1969); Benedito Nunes, *O mundo de Clarice Lispector* (Manaus: Edições, do Governo do Estado, 1966) and "O mundo imaginário de Clarice Lispector," in his *O dorso do tigre* (São Paulo: Editora Perspectiva, 1969), pp. 99-139; Rita Herman, "Existence in *Laços de familia*," *Luso-Brazilian Review,* 4, 1 (1967), 67-74; Alvaro Lins, discussion of Lispector in his *Os mortos de Sobrecasaca* (Rio de Janeiro Editora Civilização Brasileira, 1963). pp. 186-93; Massaud Moisés, "Clarice Lispector: Fiction and Cosmic Vision," trans. Sara McCabe, *Studies in Short Fiction,* 7, 1 (1971), 268-81; Wilson Martins, "O romance brasileiro contemporâneo," *Inti,* No. 3 (1976), 27-36; Giovanni Pontiero, "The Drama of Existence in *Laços de familia*," *Studies in Short Fiction,* 7, 1 (1971), 256-67, and "Testament of Experience: Some Reflections on Clarice Lispector's Last Narrative *A hora da estrela*," *Ibero-Amerikanisches Archiv,* 10, 1 (1984), 13-22; Edilberto Coutinho, "Uma mulher chamada Clarice Lispector," in his *Criaturas de papel* (Rio de Janeiro: Civilização Brasileira, 1980), pp. 165-70; and Haroldo Bruno, "Solilóquio de Clarice Lispector sobre o ser," in his *Novos estudos de literatura brasileira* (Rio de Janeiro: José Olympio/Instituto Nacional do Livro, 1980), pp. 12-20. These themes are studied together with formal aspects of the works in Teresinha Alves Pereira, *Estudo sôbre Clarice Lispector* (Coimbra: Edições Nova Era, 1975), and "Coincidencia de la técnica narrativa de Julio Cortázar y Clarice Lispector," *Nueva narrativa hispanoamericana,* 3, 1 (1973), 103-111; Earl E. Fitz, "The Leitmotif of Darkness in Seven Novels by Clarice Lispector," *Chasqui,* 8, 2 (1977), 18-27, and "Point of View in Clarice Lispector's *A hora da estrela*," *Luso-Brazilian Review* 19, 2 (1982), 195-208; Samira Youssef Campedelli and Benjamim Abdala, Jr., in their edition with commentary *Clarice Lispector, antologia comentada* (São Paulo: Abril, 1981); Olga de Sá, *Clarice Lispector* (Petrópolis: Vozes, 1979); Naomi Lindstrom, "Clarice Lispector: Articulating Women's Experience," *Chasqui,* 8, 1 (1978), 44-52, "A Discourse Analysis of 'Preciosidade' by Clarice Lispector," *Luso-Brazilian Review,* 19, 2 (1982), 187-94, and "A Feminist Discourse Analysis of Clarice Lispector's 'Daydreams of a Drunken Woman'," *Latin American Literary Review,* 9, 19 (1982), 7-16.

[2] Maria Luisa Nunes, "Narrative Modes in Clarice Lispector's *Laços de familia:* The Rendering of Consciousness," *Luso-Brazilian*

Review, 14, 12 (1977), 174-184. De Sá examines Lispector's varied narrative methods in "Clarice Lispector: processos criativos," *Revista Iberoamericana,* No. 126 (1984), 259-80.

[3] Silvio Castro, *A revolução da palavra* (Petrópolis: Vozes, 1976), p. 265; his Lispector commentary appears on pp. 263-67.

[4] Bella Jozef, "Clarice Lispector: la transgresión como acto de libertad," *Revista Iberoamericana,* Nos. 98-99 (1977), 22. See also her "Clarice Lispector: la recuperación de la palabra poética" and reviews of Lispector's posthumous fiction, *Revista Iberamericana,* No. 126 (1984), 239-57, 314-18, respectively.

[5] Owen Kellerman, *Estudios de la voz narrativa en el relato latinoamericano contemporáneo,* Diss. Arizona State University, 1975. See Lucia Helena, *"Aprendizagem* de Clarice Lispector," *Littera,* 5, 13 (1975), 99-104.

[6] Maria Ester Gilio, remark made to Lispector in an interview, "Mis libros son mis cachorros," *Crisis* [Buenos Aires], No. 39 (1976), 42. The issue of feminine writing is explored in Maria Luisa Nunes, "Clarice Lispector: artista andrógina ou escritora?," *Revista Iberoamericana,* No. 126 (1984), 281-89. The rendering of a female consciousness in the theme of Fitz, "Freedom and Self-Realization: Feminist Characterization in the Fiction of Clarice Lispector," *Modern Language Studies,* 10, 3 (1980), 51-61, and *Clarice Lispector* (Boston: Twayne, 1985).

[7] Dennis Seniff, "Self Doubt in Clarice Lispector's *Lacos de familia.*" *Luso-Brazilian Review,* 14, 2 (1977), 162.

[8] Rosario Castellanos, "Clarice Lispector: la memoria ancestral," in her *Muier que sabe latin . . .* (Mexico: SepSetentas, 1973), p. 129.

[9] Nancy T. Baden makes this point in "Clarice Lispector," in *A Dictionary of Contemporary Brazilian Authors* (Tempe: Center for Latin American Studies, 1981), p. 74.

[10] Jozef, 227.

[11] Jozef, 228.

[12] Note the many female protagonists in the existential novels of the Argentine Eduardo Mallea, especially Agata Cruz in *Todo verdor perecerá* (1941) and Gloria Bambil and Sra. de Cárdenas in *La bahía del silencio* (1940).

[13] Simone de Beauvoir, *The Second Sex,* trans. H. M. Parshley (New York: Knopf, 1953), p. 261; original 1949.

[14] Beauvoir, p. 142.

[15] Beauvoir, p. 34.

[16] Clarice Lispector, "Amor," in her *Laços de familia* (Rio: José Olympio Editora, 1974), p. 19. Further page numbers in the text refer to this edition. The English translations are from Giovanni Pontiero's excellent version of the work, published by the University of Texas Press, Austin, 1972.

[17] Maria Luisa Nunes, 177-78, 179.

[18] Maria Luisa Nunes gives this description of such passages: "Grammatically, the imperfect takes the place of the perfect, the conditional that of the future and the pluperfect that of the preterite in direct discourse. There is also a transferral of pronouns from the first to the third person," 174.

[19] Robin Lakoff, *Language and Woman's Place* (New York: Harper and Row, 1975).

[20] Jozef, 229.

[21] Especially illustrative of this concern is Kate Millett, *The Prostitution Papers* (New York: Basic Books, 1971). Millett describes prostitutes who worked together to develop a mode of presenting grievances. The women move from an inability to state their case to being relatively able spokeswomen. Like the third-person narrator in "Amor," Millett steps back and offers the *ipsissima verba* of the prostitutes (or at least her editing of their recorded statements) once the women have become sufficiently articulate.

[22] Maria Luisa Nunes, 177, comments: "The fact that she is a Portuguese woman living in Brazil is reflected by her unuttered speech and idioms, markedly Lusitanian as opposed to the colloquial speech of Brazil." For instance, one finds *cousa* rather than *coisa.* This Lusitanian speech also exerts a type of linguistic alienation effect on the story's Brazilian readers.

[23] Beauvoir, p. 478. Beauvoir's discussions of "The Married Woman," pp. 425-83, and "The Mother," pp. 484-527, present strong parallels to the representation of women characters in *Laços de familia.*

[24] Beauvoir, p. 518.

[25] Maria Luisa Nunes, 177.

[26] Pontiero, 260 of above-cited article, sees in this story a "dramatic and turbulent account of adolescence, with its penetrating analysis of the dark, tortured recesses of a girl's mind during the difficult time of puberty."

[27] See Beauvoir's chapters on "The Young Girl," pp. 328-70, and "Sexual Initiation," pp. 371-403.

[28] Erving Goffman, *The Presentation of Self in Everyday Life* (Garden City: Double-day, 1959).

[29] Moisés, above-cited article, 278.

Cristina Sáenz de Tejada (essay date 1994)

SOURCE: "The Eternal Non-Difference: Clarice Lispector's Concept of Androgyny," in *Luso-Brazilian Review,* Vol. XXXI, No. 1, Summer, 1994, pp. 39-56.

[*In the following excerpt, Sáenz de Tejada analyzes stories from Lispector's collections* A bela e a fera, A legião estrangeira, Felicidade clandestina, *and* Onde estivestes de noite? *and claims that even in her earliest work Lispector considers that androgyny is the natural state of the*

*human being, as her female and male characters resist
the gender roles expected of them by patriarchal society
and seek self-awareness and authenticity.*]

The idea of androgyny receives special consideration in
the context of contemporary feminist criticism[1] as a way to
question the veracity of sex differences, their immutability
and their ultimate power to affect the life of the human
being. It is a term generally used by feminist critics to
symbolize the desired socio-political equality between men
and women that women did not achieve in the patriarchal
society. Thus, the discovery of a truly androgynous human identity becomes the focus for these critics in their
studies of women writers and female characters.

However, Anglo-American and French feminist criticism
pose different criteria when it comes to defining the concept of androgyny. Anglo-American feminism considers
that masculinity and feminity are social constructs that
should be abandoned. Therefore, the starting point is the
psychological definition of androgyny, which refers "to
the state of a single individual, male or female, who possesses both traditionally masculine and traditionally feminine character traits."[2] Among these critics is the work of
Carolyn Heilbrun, who in *Toward a Recognition of Androgyny* (1973) proposes androgyny as the future solution
for sex differences:

> I believe that our future salvation lies in a movement
> away from sexual polarization and the prison of gender
> toward a world in which individual roles and the modes
> of personal behavior can be freely chosen. The ideal
> toward which I believe we should move is best described
> by the term "androgyny." This ancient Greek word—
> from *andro* (male) and *gyn* (female)—defines a condition
> under which the characteristics of the sexes, and the
> human impulses expressed by men and women, are not
> rigidly assigned. Androgyny seeks to liberate the
> individual from the confines of the appropriate.[3]

Androgyny is thus a psychological condition, but is not
to be confused with physical hermaphroditism, bisexuality
or homosexuality.[4]

A similar perspective can be found in Norma Grieve, who
refuses categorization based on social roles: "It is now
clear that psychological variation, both between and within men and women, cannot be represented by dichotomous, either/or categories, nor can it be based on a one
dimensional scale, with the end points being defined as
masculine and feminine."[5]

French feminist criticism has taken a different approach
towards women's concern from that posited by Heilbrun
and Grieve. Hélène Cixous, Julia Kristeva and Luce Irigaray, for example, argue that women's oppression is not
limited to the concrete organization of economic, political,
or social structures, but is embedded in the (male) Logos
and in the (male) linguistic and logical processes through
which meaning itself is produced.[6] They believe that language is a process of cultural artifice that both defines
and distances nature. Thus, only by exposing this (phallo)
logocentrism[7] and by its deconstruction do they hope to

transform the real through a language that, opposing the
male-centeredness of culture, defines women's writing and
sexuality. As Cixous says: "women must write through
their bodies, they must invent the impregnable language
that will wreck partitions, classes, rhetorics, regulations
and codes, they must submerge, cut through."[8] Therefore,
androgyny can be defined through a new language that
makes it possible to represent reality beyond the sexual
differences as they exist in a phallogocentric society.

However, in her reading of Hélène Cixous and Monique
Wittig, Susan Suleiman[9] fears that the French concept of
androgyny can also be a trap for women in the sense that
it tends to assimilate both sexes in a pseudo-wholeness as
exclusivist as phallogocentrism. She believes that neither
Cixous nor Wittig's feminization of language and history
succeeded in breaking the sex differences constructed by
phallogocentrism and, therefore, neither of them was able
to define an identity beyond the realm of opposites:

> Perhaps Wittig's *amantes*, whom I read as "female
> lovers," are not women, not female at all. Perhaps they
> represent a whole new species, neither man nor woman,
> the age of glory being precisely that age in which the
> boundaries of sex, as of class, will have been
> transcended. But if so, we are once again entrapped by
> language, which does not have a "third term"—a term
> that would not be neuter, genderless, but gender-
> undecidable (or better still, gender-multiple). Today, if
> I am reading French, I must read *amantes* as female,
> and Wittig's age of glory as single-sexed.[10]

In her efforts to find a meeting point between the Anglo-
American and the French feminist definition of androgyny,
or non-difference, Suleiman suggests fiction as the most
appropriate space for "equal rights" between man and
woman:

> Have we hit a dead end? Is there no alternative to
> "equal rights," in which all the old structures remain
> in place, only the roles are reversed—women on top—
> or to a celebration of difference that turns into the
> celebration of one sex, not two? From here on, we can
> only dream. But that is what stories, poems, have
> always invited us to do.[11]

Although the works of Clarice Lispector (1925-1977) has
rightly begun to be the subject of such critiques, it is
crucial to point out that her concept of androgyny reflects
a slightly different social perspective because some of her
male characters are also victims of phallogocentrism, a
term typically employed by feminist criticism to describe
women's oppression. This term applies to Clarice Lispector's writing as she combats the hierarchical oppositions
of phallogocentrism by creating characters, male and female, that question the authority and validity of their
culture and society by behaving as androgynous persons.
Some of the male characters incorporate feminine characteristics in their personalities, thus questioning the male
authority, while female characters think and act according
to the typical, social, and psychological category of the
masculine. On the other hand, Lispector confronts the
phallogocentrism in her own ambiguous narrative by us-

ing the oxymoron or blending of opposites and of nearopposites. I therefore believe that Clarice Lispector represents a literary example of the non-difference as defined by both Anglo-American and French feminists.

This article offers a close reading of some of Lispector's male and female characters in six short stories in order to show that, for this powerful Brazilian writer, the idea of androgyny cannot be limited to women. Moreover, Lispector's androgyny defines, ultimately, the union of opposites at all levels of human existence, an approach which brings her close to Jungian psychology.[12] Jungian androgyny defines an individual as one who

> knows the difference between masculinity and feminity, and chooses to incorporate an owned portion of the opposite gender into his or her dominant identity. An androgynous person does not pretend to be a member of the opposite sex. An androgynous male will not repress his feminine characteristics, however much he may, at times, decide to suppress them. He knows that they are a part of him, he has worked on his ego resistance to integrating them. He knows there will be times when he will choose to think and perhaps behave according to the "her" within him.[13]

This description of the androgyne accurately describes several of Lispector's male characters, exemplary among whom is the boy of **"A mensagem"**,[14] one of Lispector's most complex later stories. By creating this androgynous figure, Lispector foreshadows what feminists would later say about gender roles and psychological individuation not being defined by sex alone; indeed, not even chiefly. I believe, therefore, that Lispector's male characters should be (re)considered in the light of feminist criticism, which to date has been used to study female characters only from a very limited perspective.[15]

The Anglo-American and French feminist approach during the 1970s and 1980s had already been given literary form by Clarice Lispector in her first short stories in 1940. If we contrast the concept of "androgyny" adopted by feminist criticism today with the concept presented in Lispector's early work, we realize that Lispector's term does not really represent a model for radical feminists because she neither creates characters of ambiguous sexual orientation[16] nor limits social oppression to women. Men are also victims of their gender roles (though typically they don't realize it) and many of her male characters exemplify this. Therefore, androgyny in Lispector's work is best understood as a human being in conflict with the society that pushes her/him to divide her/his naturally androgynous identity in order to enter into the sociopolitical system of binary oppositions. Lispector's androgyny, however, resists this division; it acts or grows by blending opposite emotions (love and hate) or discourses (rational and irrational) and constantly seeks to recover the integrity that a person loses in contact with others. This is why Lispector's characters are phsychologically ambiguous and fluid, in flux, just as her language typically is.

Lispector's sense of androgyny can readily be found in her earliest characters, both male and female, who resist the gender role that the patriarchal society expects of them. The collection *A Bela e a Fera* (1979)[17] contains eight stories, six written by Lispector between 1940 and 1941, when the author was fourteen years old, and the last two written shortly before her death. I have selected **"História interrompida"** (1940) and **"Mais dois bêbedos"** (1941) for analysis because they typify her presentation of individuals (male and female) on their endless quest for self-awareness and authenticity of being.

"História interrompida" relates the abruptly truncated relationship between a woman and a man called W. Apparently, he has committed suicide, but this possibility, as well as his thoughts and feelings, remain ambiguous for the reader. Nor does Lispector ever mention the word "love" when describing their relationship, although the reader assumes it is a factor since the female character talks about their marriage. The story begins with a monologue of an undifferentiated voice because Lispector uses verbs with no subject indicated. However, it becomes differentiated when five paragraphs later it reveals itself as feminine through the use of a feminine adjective: "Voltei-me para dentro amolecida pela calma daqueles momentos" (16). This female voice is presented as being stronger and more independent than the male character and using a systematic, logical discourse that would be considered typical in a male. Lispector is then trying to prove that language and characterization, that of similar personality of the male and female characters, can decenter the reader's perception of what is masculine or feminine.

As in most of her fiction, Lispector's characters hardly ever behave according to sexual stereotypes; indeed, they prove, looking at their inner reality, that both men and women suffer from rigid gender expectations. In **"História interrompida,"** for example, the female voice describes W . . . as having the typical female reaction of silence as well as absence from reality:

> Eu lhe respondia que mesmo destruindo ele construía: pelo menos esse monte de cacos para onde olhar e de que falar. Perfeitamente absurdo. Ele, sem dúvida, também o achava, porque não respondia. Ficava muito triste, a olhar para o chão e a alisar seu gatinho morno. (15)

The silence and non-communication between them is accepted by the female character as less dangerous than the man's words, since the latter can destroy reality as well as her own identity: "Jamais falava comigo que não desse a entender que seu maior defeito consistia na sua tendência para a destruição. Foi então que pensei aquela coisa terrível: ou eu o destruo ou ele me destruirá" (15-16). By extending W's problem to men, the reader can surmise that Lispector is really talking about phallogocentrism:

> Com efeito, homens como W . . . passam a vida à procura da verdade, entram pelos labirintos mais estreitos, ceifam e destroem metade do mundo sob o pretexto de que cortam os erros, mas quando a verdade lhes surge diante dos olhos é sempre inopinadamente. (19)

Although she cannot find a reason to marry a man whose analytical perception of things could destroy her ambiguous identity, the female narrative nevertheless manifests her intentions to marry him. In order to protect herself from that mentality, however, her active and powerful personality will confront the male system. She decides, therefore, to act after first having planned exactly what to say and do: "Durante dois dias pensei sem cessar. Queria achar uma fórmula que mo desse pra mim" (18). As an androgynous character, her decision responds to a very intuitive impulse (feminine characteristic) that she rationalizes (masculine characteristic) and knowingly manipulates. When she therefore decides to ask him to marry her, she is departing from the stereotypical female figure, conceived of as passive and irrational.

The woman's masculine and feminine personality is presented in two other moments, using two different narratives to describe the process that precedes self-awareness. The first of them comes in a series of logically disconnected words that show her confused and unconscious feelings:

> Estava com preguiça de chegar em casa: invariavelmente o jantar, o longo serão vazio, um livro, o bordado e, enfim, a cama, o sono. Enveredei pelo atalho mais comprido. A relva crescida era penugenta e quando o vento soprava forte ele me acariciava as pernas. Mas eu estava inquieta. (17)

After pondering over her situation for two days, this female character finally comes to understand the source of her anxiety and becomes aware of what Jung defines as *animus,* that is, the masculine element in a woman's psyche that, when schooled and disciplined, provides her a power base. The development of this inner phallos-animus makes the woman independent as a person, especially in her relationships with men.[18] The narrative's form, consequently, changes into the oral dialogue reflective of logocentrism and, in so doing, highlights both her independence and her strong personality:

> Dir-lhe-ia (com o vestido azul que me fazia muito mais loura), a voz suave e firme, fixando-o nos olhos:
>
> —Tenho pensado muito a nosso respeito e resolvi que só nos resta . . .
>
> Não. Simplesmente.
>
> Não, não. Nada de perguntas.
>
> —W. . . ., nós vamos casar. (18)

In this paragraph, which serves as a good example of Lispector's handling of androgyny, the words show the conflict between the external and feminine appearance—"o vestido azul" and "a voz suave e firme"—with the internal functioning of the masculine principle—the strong, independent and active personality.

A similar situation develops when the female character is thinking about her wedding. She mixes her emotions and thoughts in a narrative that blends the masculine spoken language with the feminine written language of unconsciousness. Semantically, the content of her words are ambiguous because the reader eventually feels that she is talking about an intimate wedding between her and the world, one that, eventually, becomes a metaphor for androgyny's psychic wholeness:

> "W . . . vamos casar imediatamente, imediatamente." Peguei numa folha de papel e enchi-a de alto a baixo: "Eternidade. Vida. Mundo. Deus. Eternidade . . ." (20)

This marriage, consummated not so much through sex as through the spoken and written word, is followed by a feeling of real love, a condition that stands in contrast to the relationship between the female and the male characters: "A serenidade foi pouco a pouco voltando. E com ela, uma profunda e emocionante certeza de amor" (20). By blending different concepts, including the masculine and the feminine, Lispector has created a kind of androgyny that decenters the standard definition of the word itself. This then makes the reader deconstruct her texts in general in order to go beyond the meaning of the word and accept various interpretations.[19]

The characteristics of the narrative voice in **"Mais dois bêbedos"** (1941) are very similar to those of the first story. The primary difference between this story and **"História interrompida"** is that the main character is a male. Yet he is still presented as talking about similar problems; personal destruction, the isolation of human beings, self-consciousness and identity, all of which he is trying to recover through the other man and the wine he is drinking: "E embebedava-me não puramente, mas com um objetivo: Eu era alguém" (107). By using another male character as the Other that completes the protagonist, Lispector dissociates the masculine and feminine elements of the human psyche from the traditional sexual correlatives. This idea is shown through the isolation existing between the male character and his girlfriend in a type of relationship, man and woman, traditionally considered as the most satisfactory in order to achieve psychic wholeness. Woman, therefore, does not necessarily mean feminine:

> Ema tinha vaga ideia de que eu era diferente e debitava nessa conta tudo que de estranho eu pudesse fazer. De tal modo me aceitava, que eu ficava só quando estávamos juntos. E naquele momento evitava precisamente a solidão que seria uma bebida forte demais. (108)

The rational and logical narrative evolves into more poetic and disconnected outpourings, both private and directed at the other man, and finally it ends in silence. The wine, his anxiety, and his contact with the Other move the male narrative voice into the realm of the unconscious, into broken sentences, illogical thoughts and disconnected dialogue that, eventually, transform his initial position of superiority (which has isolated him) into a state of freedom and communication. The transformation of the main character is thus achieved through the androgynous personality of the other man, which, though jarring, compels him from the beginning: "Mas aquele homem que jamais sairia de seu estreito círculo, nem bastante feio, nem bastante bonito, o queixo fugitivo, tão importante como um cão trotando—que pretendia com seu arrogante silêncio? Não o interrogara várias vezes. Ele me ofendia" (108).

The ambiguous description of the other man, "nem bastante feio, nem bastante bonito," as well as the image of the circle symbolizing his wholeness, reflect the androgynous perspective of the narrative voice.[20] His melancholic anxiety yearns for an identity that, ironically, comes with wine, chaos and unconsciousness; he will eventually come to behave like a modern Dionysus, which, according to Heilbrun, best evokes the nature of androgyny.[21]

Both male personalities show an evident blending of aggressive, competent, controlling, unsentimental and violent masculine characteristics with sentimental, intuitive and uncontrolling feminine characteristics. Still, the function of language in the text, more than words themselves, helps the reader to understand the personalities of the characters. At the beginning of their temporary relationship, silence symbolizes the lack of communication that derives from the rigid linguistic system of the narrative voice that assigns fixed meanings to each word: "Sofro, em mim os sentimentos estão solidificados, diferenciados, ja nascem com rótulo, conscientes de si mesmos. Quanto ao senhor . . . Uma nebulosa de homem" (112).

The main character's struggle with words blurs his sense of what he is feeling and thinking, so much so that, eventually, the narrative voice has to escape the control of his system if he wants to communicate with the other male character. Embarking, then, on a search for a new language, one that will also give him a new identity, the protagonist invents a fantastic and exaggerated story about the other man's life in which he blends binarily based elements, like fiction and reality, as well as masculine and feminine positions. This external blending of opposite elements also reflects the combination of the internal *animus* and *anima*[22] of the human psyche. Significantly, this narration eventually connects the two men at the same time that the narrative voice enters into his personal chaos and confused emotions:

> A cena me pareceu tão cômica que me torci de rir. As lágrimas já me chegavam aos olhos e escorriam pelo meu rosto. Algumas pessoas voltaram a cabeça para meu lado. Já não tinha mais vontade de rir e no entanto ria sem parar. Estaquei de súbito. (111)

Thus, the protagonist's contact with the Other liberates him from his phallogocentrically induced suffering; his gradual transformation ends in an identification with the Other and, consequently, in a wholeness that, parallel to the female character of **"História interrompida,"** brings an androgynous harmony and pleasure to the narrative voice:

> Ele continuava com o palito na boca.
>
> Depois foi muito bom porque o vinho estava misturando-se. Peguei também um palito e segurei-o entre os dedos como se fosse fumá-lo. (114)

Although the narrative voice senses he can communicate with the other, once he is free from the trap in which his language and culture (that is, gender) has placed him, the reader never has the chance to listen to the two males talking because the narrative ends in silence:

> As palavras vagas, as frases arrastradas sem significado . . . Tão bom, tão suave . . . Ou era o sono?
>
> De repente, ele tirou o palito da boca, os olhos piscando, os lábios trêmulos como se fosse chorar, disse: (114)

This surprising and silent interruption is, however, structurally characteristic of Lispector's fiction and it has been considered as representative of her postmodernist way of writing:

> Literary postmodernism aspires to silence, to the kind of nonexpression and noncommunication that occurs when, living in a Babel of verbal noise, words come to lose the meanings we expect them to have . . . Yet Lispector's fiction is also built on a realization that while the silence that derives from a failure to communicate terrifies and intimidates people, it can also regenerate them, urging them toward the attainment of a more honest and personally satisfying existence.[23]

These two postmodernist meanings of silence, the failure of language and its ability to give birth to a new voice, are inscribed in Lispector's story in two parallel ways: on one hand, the lack of communication—despite, ironically, the use of language—is expressed by the word "silêncio": "No entanto ele persistia em seu mutismo, sem querer emocionar-se com a oportunidade de viver" (108). On the other hand, the communication between the two men is metaphorically described by the absence of words.

Androgyny, like silence, is a prime indicator of how Lispector reverses the binary combination of signified and signifier. By eliminating the word 'androgyny' itself (rendering it, as Derrida would say, both 'present' and 'absent'), Lispector also eliminates the sexual meaning that the word has evoked in Western culture since Plato mentioned it for the first time in his *Symposium*. Moreover, when Lispector describes a reality where emotions, individuals and words harmoniously combine opposite characteristics, the reader begins to think of androgyny as an accommodation of not merely opposite, but conflicting forces in general.

Clarice Lispector's narratives suggest that androgyny is the natural state of the human being, the state that society divides, via gender, in two definite halves. This explains the anxiety, lack of identity and quest for self-awareness that most of her characters present in the process of reconstructing his or her natural state. In the next three stories to be discussed—**"A mensagem"** (*A Legião Estrangeira,* 1964), **"As águas do mundo"** and **"O primeiro beijo"** (the latter two from *Felicidade Clandestina,* 1971)—Clarice Lispector describes both the social process of division and the individual process of reconstruction. The conflict that the characters suffer after the division in the first story contrasts with the sensual pleasure of unification in the stories from *Felicidade Clandestina.*[24]

"A mensagem" describes two teenagers, a male and a female, in the final steps of the human process toward adulthood, which is experienced by both of them with fear and uncertainty. According to the narrative voice, this uncertainty is caused by the schism that each individual suffers between her/his masculine and feminine part in relation to her/his sex when (s)he becomes an adult (the word's meaning being a moot point as well). As teenagers they are not totally aware of what is going to happen to them; they do not recognize the implications of the binary division of male/female and do not, therefore, believe in it. Their first intuitive reaction is anxiety, but it evolves into fear when the teenagers realize that eventually they will have to behave as adults. After being together and socially equal during their high school years, once they graduate they have to separate and face an uncertain future symbolized in their vision of an old house:

> O vago acontecimento em torno da casa velha só existiu porque eles estavam prontos para isso. Tratava-se apenas de uma casa velha e vazia. Mas eles tinham uma vida pobre e ansiosa como se nunca fossem envelhecer, como se nada jamais lhes fosse suceder— e então a casa tornou-se um acontecimento. Haviam voltado da última aula do período escolar. Tinham tomado o ônibus, saltado, e iam andando. Como sempre, andavam entre depressa e soltos, e de repente devagar, sem jamais acertar o passo, inquietos quanto à presença do outro. Era um dia ruim para ambos, véspera de férias. A última aula os deixava sem futuro e sem amarras, cada um desprezando o que na casa mútua de ambos as famílias lhes asseguravam como futuro e amor e incompreensão. Sem um dia seguinte e sem amarras, eles estavam pior que nunca, mudos, de olhos abertos. (36)

At the end of the story, the two young adults unconsciously have to assume their gendered roles: "Que é mas afinal o que me está acontecendo? assustou-se ele" (43).

The references to the psychological and physical transformations that the teenagers experience after they enter the realm of adulthood explicitly criticize the idea that gender roles are properly defined by sex and by "os outros" (43), in terms of male/masculine and female/feminine. The vision the two of them have at the same time of the mysterious house (in which they will have their tryst) reveals to the teenagers their new identity as woman and man. In the context of other works of Clarice Lispector, as well as in terms of the fearful reaction of the characters to what the future holds for them as "adultos," we can read the house as a metaphor of the patriarchal society that imprisons people in binary opposition:

> Mas, se antes else tinham sido forçados a olhá-lo, agora, mesmo que lhes avisassem que o caminho estava livre para fugirem, ali ficariam, presos pelo fascínio e pelo horror. Fixando aquela coisa erguida tão antes deles nascerem, aquela coisa secular e já esvaziada de sentido, aquela coisa vinda do passado. Mas e o futuro?!

> Oh Deus, dai-nos o nosso futuro! A casa sem olhos, com a potência de um cego. E se tinha olhos, eram redondos olhos vazios de estátua. Oh Deus, não nos deixeis ser filhos desse passado vazio, entregai-nos ao futuro. (39)

Their transformation into a man and a woman (and all the gender entrapment this entails) follows from the decodification of the mystery of the house. This is how the male perspective describes his new identity:

> Um corpo de homem era a solidez que o recuperava sempre. Volta e meia, quando precisava muito, ele se tornava um homem. Então, com mão incerta, acendeu sem naturalidade um cigarro, como se ele fosse *os outros,* socorrendo-se dos gestos que a maçonaria dos homens lhe dava como apoio e caminho. E ela? (40)

The girl described in a very feminine manner according to her new role, is presented thus:

> Mas a moça saiu de todo isso pintada com batom, com o ruge meio manchado, e enfeitada por um colar azul. Plumas que um momento antes haviam feito parte de uma situação e de um futuro, mas agora era como se ela não tivesse lavado o rosto antes de dormir e acordasse com as marcas impudicas de um orgia anterior. Pois ela, volta e meia, era uma mulher. (40-41)

From this point in the text, the characters start to act, think and behave responding to their adult gender roles, primary among which is the male's legitimized oppression of women. By now, both characters are trapped in their roles, no matter if they like it or not or if it destroys their ideal dream of becoming writers, that is, people who would use words in new ways to create new realities. The use of a male perspective in a third person narrative seemingly emphasizes Lispector's criticism of the phallogocentric structures that create and sustain these injurious identities: "Ignorante, inquieto, mal assumira a masculinidade, e uma nova fome, ávida nascia, uma coisa dolorosa como um homem que nunca chora" (42). At the end, the male describes his fear and anxiety as a result of the division of their original androgynous status, affirming that they need each other in order to preserve their authentic beings; otherwise, they will become like lower animals: "Ele precisava dela com fome para não esquecer que eram feitos da mesma carne, essa carne pobre da qual, ao subir no ônibus como um macaco, ela parecia ter feito um caminho fatal" (42-43).

In the first part of **"A mensagem,"** the male character describes his own status and that of his female friend (lover?) as being hybrid, authentic, sincere, rational and intuitive. Their language also fulfills a different function from that of the Others (the adults) because it is ambiguous and it constantly changes the meaning of the words. The characters consider the adults as the new sex they refuse to be because it is painful and limited. On the contrary, they would like to conserve what they intuitively understand in their androgynous identity because it helps them to communicate and because it unites their masculine and feminine elements:

> Estava porém suave e indeciso, como se qualquer dor só tornasse ainda mais moço, ao contrário dela, que estava agressiva. Informes como eram, tudo lhes era possível, inclusive às vezes permutavam as qualidades: ela se tornava como um homem, e ele como uma doçura quase ignóbil de mulher. (36)

Lispector's androgyny embraces sexual and social difference and yet accepts sex as a physical feature that can, nevertheless, trap and destroy anyone's psychic wholeness: "Sobretudo a moça já começara a não sentir prazer em ser condecorada como o título de homem ao menor sinal que apresentava de . . . de ser uma pessoa" (32). In order to conserve their state of harmonious androgyny, the characters realize that they have to be aware of others' lie—that is, that sex determines gender roles—and keep it under control: "Embora, se ambos não tomassem cuidado, o fato dela ser mulher poderia de súbito vir à tona. Eles tomavam cuidado" (33).

Although a reader could interpret this story as an example of an accusatory feminist position, it also suggests that even men (some men, at least) understand that they, too, are victims of the patriarchal society; clearly, they are not born with power over women, and many perceive the corruptive effect of this power. The male perspective of this story thus contributes to define Lispector's social consciousness beyond the limitations of much feminist criticism, which sometimes forgets that men, too, can be victims of gender oppression. Lispector suggests that in their common androgyny, male and female can be balanced, equal and aware of the false gender divisions that neither can easily (if at all) resist. At the end of the story, this humanizing androgyny has been undermined by the imposition of a rigidly held gendering of adulthood. As mentioned in the text, society does not allow individuals to choose their own identities, their own "rostos"; their identities are already defined in a certain way, that is, gendered, that women are mothers-to-be and men have to be dominating and oppressive: "Sou um homem, disse-lhe o sexo em obscura vitória" (41).

The final characteristic of Lispector's androgyny that I wish to point out is the function of language, which connects this story with the stories in *A Bela e a Fera.* While the female character of **"História interrompida"** achieves personal identity and pleasure through the written word—considered to be masculine—and the male character of **"Mais dois bêbedos"** does so through silence—considered to be feminine—the androgynous individuals of **"A mensagem"** use both silence and writing. They want to be writers because, presaging Derrida's "phonocentrism," "a linguagem falada mentia" (32) and when written language fails to communicate, they simply remain in silence: "Mesmo assim, jamais certas palavras era pronunciadas entre ambos. Dessa vez não porque a expressão fosse mais uma armadilha de que os *outros* dispõem para enganar os moços" (31). Once again, Lispector's texts end up presenting language as one of the main problems of society because, ultimately, it isolates the individual from the others, and from herself or himself.

In the next three stories to be discussed, Lispector's perspective is more positive in the sense that she describes the process of *recovering* the androgynous identity. In so doing, Clarice proves that the division between opposites is a temporary and basically false psychological state that can eventually be superseded through a transcendent experience, which she typically presents via images of water, birth, fountain, silence and body images, none of which is limited to female characters.

The androgynous state recovered by the woman of **"As águas do mundo"** and the man of **"O primeiro beijo"** ultimately becomes the main narrative focus in the story **"Onde estivestes de noite,"** which features a protagonist alternately named she/he and he/she. The first two stories come from the collection **Felicidade Clandestina,** while **"As águas do mundo"** is, verbatim, also a chapter from Lispector's novel *Uma Aprendizagem ou o Livro dos Prazeres* (1968),[25] in which she describes the moment of climax in Lori's individuation. The third text is included in the book with the same title, **Onde Estivestes de Noite** (1976),[26] where, for the first time, Lispector actually uses the word "androgyny" (with a different meaning, however) to define a person who, according to the female character of the story **"A procura de uma dignidade"**, is sexually ambiguous: the Brazilian pop singer Roberto Carlos.

"As águas do mundo," one of Lispector's most compelling pieces of writing, represents an example of what Monick calls New Consciousness's psyche or *unus mundus.*[27] Applying Jung's concept of psychoid unconscious, Monick points out a significant difference between the unitary world and the transgressive quality of both psyches. He believes that

> In the psychoid unconscious, unitary and transgressive characteristics of the psyche exist in a condition of primitive nondifferentiation. *Unus mundus,* however, is a state of awareness where division and cohesion in the cognitive process are no longer understood only as streams of energy moving in opposite directions, as in Jung's "first step," but are complementary, moving along the same path. *Unus mundus,* as individuation, does not happen without great struggle and contention with life and the unconscious on an intentional basis. As with phallus, inner urge and purpose initiate and support the work.[28]

According to this view, the new consciousness differs from Jung's psychoid unconscious in that while it is aware of the opposites, it nevertheless allows the androgynous male or female to decide to suppress or maintain them. Apropos of this, Lispector's characters integrate opposites in order to behave and think according to the her within him or the him within her. The technical device of the oxymoron (often paired with paradox) reflects this process of blending of opposites and of near-opposites that takes place in the story: "uma alegria fatal" (152). Besides, the individuation of the female character comes after her contact with the water where opposite elements finally blend into a new personality:

> Seu corpo se consola com sua própria exiguidade em relação à vastidão do mar porque é a exiguidade do corpo que o permite manter-se quente e é essa exiguidade que a torna pobre e livre gente, como sua parte de liberdade de cão nas areias. Esse corpo entrará no ilimitado frio que sem raiva ruge no silêncio das seis horas. A mulher é agora uma compacta e uma leve e uma aguda—e abre caminho na gelidez que, líquida, se opõe a ela, e no entanto a deixa entrar, como no amor em que a oposição pode ser um pedido. (151-152)

The technical device of the oxymoron supports Lispector's opinion that language can create differences as well as destroy them. The combination of female and male elements, and the act of penetrating the water, evoke very sensual images and, indeed, the sexual act itself: "O caminho lento aumenta sua coragem secreta. E de repente ela se deixa cobrir pela primeira onda. O sal, o iodo, tudo líquido, deixam-na por uns instantes cega, toda escorrendo—espantada de pé, fertilizada" (152). Overall, the union of the spirit and the body in this text describes an important integrating element of the New Consciousness androgyne:

> In the psychoid beginning and within the *unus mundus* at the end of Jung's mythology of the flesh, there is no ultimate separation of flesh and spirit. Each transgresses into the other. Invisible spirit, as archetypally masculine, manifests itself in flesh; visible flesh, as archetypally feminine, manifests phallus. Phallus, *membrum virile,* is flesh *and* spirit—in a word, psychoid.[29]

Therefore, in **"As águas do mundo,"** the water represents the spirit and the woman is the flesh that at the end of the story becomes phallus. The female character experiences an internal change that derives from the conscious development of her animus. She behaves according to the him within her, which Lispector presents as the fertilizing liquid of the water and as a metaphor of the semen: "Era isso o que lhe estava faltando: o mar por dentro como o líquido espesso de um homem" (153). The transformation that comes after this combination of opposites also reveals the development of the masculinity in the woman, in this case describing her with male attributes: "Às vezes o mar lhe opõe resistência puxando-a com força para trás, mas então a proa da mulher avança um pouco mais dura e áspera" (153).

Her decentering of the masculine element could be interpreted by a psychologist as the negative animus of the psyche of a woman that eventually can interrupt her process of individuation. The development of the female character's phallus-animus makes her more independent and silent, however, in a manner similar to the character in **"História interrompida"**: "Agora sabe o que quer. Quer ficar de pé parada no mar. Assim fica, pois. Como contra os costados de um navio, a água bate, volta, bate. A mulher não recebe transmissões. Não precisa de comuni-

cação" (153). Finally, she is aware of how her individuation will confront society because it has freed her, if only temporarily, from her gender role: "E sabe de algum modo obscuro que seus cabelos escorridos são de náufrago. Porque sabe—sabe que fez um perigo. Um perigo tão antigo quanto ser humano" (153).

"O primeiro beijo" describes a similar process, although the character is again a male whose age and fear is reminiscent of the male voice of **"A mensagem."**[30] The title suggests sensual and sexual connotations that, however, deconstruct themselves in the content of the text through the ambiguous use of the word "homem" in the last sentence in the same linguistic manner as in the other story.

The story takes place in two different times: from the present time (where he exists with his girlfriend) the man moves backward in time to his adolescence, where he describes, with a very poetic and sensual language, how he became androgynous. He remembers his psychological and physical transformation into a man, a gendered being. In referring to the changes that the passage to adulthood represents for a teenager, **"O primeiro beijo"** treats the same situation as that depicted in **"A mensagem,"** although in an inverse fashion. The positive flashback of this story, where the male character describes his individuation, contrasts with the gender role divisions perceived by the teenagers of **"A mensagem"** with regard to their future. In these two stories, as well as in other of Lispector's fictions, there is a common element: fear of society, and the changes, linguistically based and communicated, that it demands.

As in **"As águas do mundo,"** the individuation process is also associated with the image of water as a fertilizing agent: "mas não é de uma mulher que sai o líquido vivificador, o líquido germinador de vida . . . Olhou a estátua nua" (166). In this case, the water is clearly seen as feminine since it comes from a female statue. Yet the physical change suggested by the text is a metaphorical manifestation of the archetypal masculine inner phallic reality that every psyche experiences: "Deu um passo para trás ou para frente, nem sabia mais o que fazia. Perturbado, atônito, percebeu que uma parte de seu corpo, sempre antes relaxada, estava agora com uma tensão agressiva, e isso nunca lhe tinha acontecido" (166). The fear he feels after this transformation represents his perception of what being a man means, for better and for worse, in a patriarchal society. Once again, this feeling connects this man with the male character of **"A mensagem,"** who senses himself to be a victim of social oppression.

The five stories considered here present the progressive creation of the androgyne, who, it is interesting to note, lacks a name in each case. The absence of a name, however, does not imply that the character does not have an identity. Each could have received a name after the process of individuation, but the fact that this does not happen highlights even more the role of Lispector's androgyne as representing a new social identity, one in which words necessarily misrepresent reality, at the same time that they represent it.

If the stories of *A Bela e a Fera* and *A Legião estrangeira* describe the nature of Lispector's androgynous personality, the stories of *Felicidade Clandestina* and *Onde Estivestes de Noite* describe her sense of how the process of becoming androgynous itself works. **"Onde estivestes de noite"**, one of her most surrealistic pieces, moves a step further by getting into the unconscious realm to describe the androgyne and the process of individuation from the inside.

The world of the androgyne is here associated with night, darkness, dream and the unknown: "Na mesma hora estavam deitados na cama a dormir. Elas não sabiam de nada" (72). These terms describe how the conscious experiences and perceives the unconscious as a powerful force that attracts both men and women to it and which comes to intrude upon their consciousness: "Ele-ela pensava dentro deles" (61). The contact with the androgyne is necessary to preserve human identity, and the subsequent transformation takes place only in the psychoid unconscious. Without this, the people would experience only one aspect of the psyche as it is described in an unknown woman: "Estado de choque . . . Sua vida era uma constante subtração de si mesma. Tudo isso porque não atendeu ao chamado da sirene" (69-70). The fact that the androgyne itself describes the life of those who never initiate the process of individuation is significant: "acontecia que na cegueira da luz do dia a pessoa vivia na carne aberta e nos olhos ofuscados pelo pecado da luz—a pessoa vivia sem anestesia o terror de se estar vivo" (67).

This androgyne figure can be interpreted as the collective unconscious since it is experienced by a group of both males and females who share myth and religion as well as the physical characteristics of humankind.[31] An unknown narrator also presents the androgyne as a god-image who guides and regulates the personality of each individual: "Quando a Ela-ele parava um instante, homens e mulheres, entregues a eles próprios por um instante, diziam-se assustados: eu não sei pensar. Mas Ele-ela pensava dentro deles . . . Eles eram independentes e soberanos, apesar de guiados pelo Ele-ela" (62, 65). Moments after the contact with the androgyne, or beautiful monster (as it is described in the text), people feel the exhilarating freedom that comes from experiencing their own identities: "cada um deles começou a se sentir" (62).

Jungians define this androgyne and divine figure as the Self, or the "central ordering archetype of the psyche."[32] Crucial, in this regard, to Clarice Lispector's social consciousness is her description of this collective self because it explains her concept of the human being as a blending of the masculine and the feminine and, therefore, the nature of her ambiguous characters. The fusion and confusion of the masculine and feminine in the unconscious is literally expressed by the She-he/He-she character, described openly as an androgynous figure who shares balanced feminine and masculine attitudes which are alternately named "Ele-ela" or "Ela-ele". Therefore, in the unconscious realm of the androgynous figure there is no social difference between the feminine and the masculine

element: "ela estava personalizada no ele e o ele estava personalizado no ela" (60).

This combination of two opposites recalls the binary opposition typical of the logocentric and patriarchal society that Lispector is trying to subvert by continually reversing the position of the elements. She is clearly aware of the present power structure that always emphasizes the first element of the binary opposition and which is associated with masculine characteristics. Furthermore, by constantly alternating the position of He-she and She-he, Lispector makes it clear that none of those elements ever dominates the other. Thus, the androgyne (like Clarice Lispector's characters in general) is always in the process of transformation, moving from one element to the other in order to accomplish the necessary balance: "O Ele-ela só deixava mostrar o rosto de andrógina" (70). Therefore, if the unconscious is androgynous, the conscious should also be androgynous. However, the androgyne does not mean the physical blend of sexes, for these characters are not hermaphrodites. Although Lispector's characters are always aware of keeping their sexual differences, sexual physiology is not a criterion to consider when defining their common unconscious essence:

> Soprava no ar uma transparência como igual homem nenhum havia respirado antes. Mas eles espargiam pimenta em pó nos próprios órgãos genitais e se contorciam de ardor. E de repente o ódio. Elas não matavam uns aos outros mas sentiam tão implacável ódio que era como um dardo lançado num corpo. E se rejubilavam danados pelo que sentiam. O ódio era um vômito que os livrava de vômito maior, o vômito da alma. (65).

Sex, then, should not be a standard to separate individuals in the conscious realm; that is, the structured society of God and Logos. The last part of the story, which, with a significant shift in style and tone, takes place during the day, suggests the beginning of a new life symbolized in the substitution of the Christian god by the androgyne[33] as well as in the attitude of the parishioners towards the previous religion:

> Padre Jacinto ergueu com as duas mãos a taça de cristal que contém o sangue escarlate de Cristo. Eta, vinho bom. E uma flor nasceu. Uma flor leve, rósea, com perfume de Deus. Ele-ela há muito sumira no ar. A manhã estava límpida como coisa recém lavada. Os fiéis distraídos fizeram o sinal da Cruz (79).

"Onde estivestes de noite" thus epitomizes the concept of the androgyne that Lispector has used as a model to describe the psychological and, therefore, social equality of her characters. The androgynous constitution of the human being should be considered by each individual who wants to change preconceived ideas of how a person has to behave in society. If not, men and women will always be trapped in and by their gender roles. Although both feminist criticism and Clarice Lispector agree that social and psychological equality between men and women is a desirable goal, there are two basic differences between the feminist approach to androgyny and that of Clarice Lispector: first, androgyny is seen by the feminist as a socio-political way to give women the identity and power they deserve as human beings. For Lispector, androgyny is the ideal state of the human being (both male and female) and, therefore, it departs from sexual differences; second, for feminists androgyny is an ideal state that can be used to conquer and so it is basically limited to women, while for Clarice Lispector it is a primordial state to be recreated and then preserved not only by women but by men as well.

Lispector's androgyne, consequently, defines an individual—and the individual's transcendent experience—as being in constant oscillation between conflicting forces, a blending that, ultimately, will lead to social change via a new language and, through language, a new consciousness that, by analogy, will be androgynous as well. Linguistically, the androgyne figure represents the ambiguity which, at the textual level, engenders a totally androgynous text like *Água Viva*[34] that merges prose with poetry and that is as polysemic as reality is, reality being a linguistically based condition in which "É claro coisa alguma" (**"Mais dois bêbedos,"** 114). Lispector's androgyny, then, is as much a power ploy as it is a literary model for living the ambiguity that is life and places Lispector close to that idea of finding a "third term" that could go beyond the antagonisms, a dream that nowadays can only take place at the narrative level.[35]

Notes

[1] Mary Eagleton, ed., *Feminist Literary Theory* (New York & Oxford: Basil Blackwell, 1989); Rowena Fowler, "Feminist Criticism: The Common Pursuit" in *New Literary History* 19 (Autumn 1988): 61-62; Toril Moi, *Teoría Literaria Feminista* (Madrid: Cátedra, 1988); Elaine Showalter, ed., *The New Feminist Criticism, Essays on Women, Literature and Theory* (New York: Pantheon Books, 1985); Susan Suleiman, *Subversive Intent. Gender, Politics and the Avant-Garde* (Cambridge: Harvard University Press, 1990).

[2] Mary Ann Warren, *The Nature of Woman: An Encyclopedia and Guide to the Literature.* (Inverness, California: Edgepress, 1980), 17.

[3] Carolyn Heilbrun, *Toward a Recognition of Androgyny* (New York: Alfred A. Knopf, 1973), ix-x.

[4] Carolyn Heilbrun, "Androgyny and the Psychology of Sex Differences" in *The Future of Difference,* ed. Hester Eisenstein and Alice Jardine (Boston: Hall & Co., 1980), 258-266.

[5] Norma Grieve, "Beyond Sexual Stereotypes. Androgyny: A Model or An Ideal?" in *Australian Women: Feminist Perspectives* (Melbourne: Oxford University Press, 1981), Norma Grieve and Patricia Grimshaw, eds., 247.

[6] Domna C. Stanton, "Language and Revolution: The Franco-American DisConnection" in *The Future of Difference,* ed. Hester Eisenstein and Alice Jardine (Boston: G. K. Hall & Co., 1980), 73-87.

[7] Developed by Jacques Derrida in reference to Lacan's reading of Poe, phallogocentrism constitutes a signifying system organized

around gender, a binary concept of a relation that assumes such dichotomies as male presence/female absence, male word principle/female verbal object, male center/female margin, male signifier/female signified, where the first of these dual elements overpowers the other. This male-centeredness places the male-identified subject at the center of the intellect, perception, experience, values and language suggesting that the male represents the model of truth, identity, reason and logic: "Freud, like those who follow him here (maleness exists, but not femaleness), does nothing else but describe the necessity of phallogocentrism, explains its effects, which are as obvious as they are massive. Phallogocentrism is neither an accident nor a speculative mistake which may be imputed to this or that theoretician. It is an enormous and old root which must also be accounted for . . . It induces a practice, an ethic and an education hence a politics assuring the tradition of its truth. The ethico-educational purpose is declared by Lacan: the motif of authenticity, of the full word, of the pledged faith and of the "signifying convention" showed this sufficiently. It regulates itself systematically by a phallogocentric doctrine of the signifier. The entire phallogocentrism is articulated from the starting-point of a determinate *situation* in which the phallus *is* the mother's desire inasmuch as she does not have it. An (individual, perceptual, local, cultural, historical, etc.) situation on the basis of which is developed something called a "sexual theory": in it the phallus is not the organ, the penis or clitoris, which it symbolizes; but it does to a larger extent and in first place symbolize the penis. The sequel is familiar: phallogocentrism as androcentrism with the whole paradoxical logic and the reversals it engenders: for example that in the phallocentric dialectic, she [the woman] represents the absolute Other." Jacques Derrida, "The Purveyor of Truth" in *Yale French Studies* 52, (1975): 31-113. Also see Jacques Derrida, *Dissemination* (Chicago: The University of Chicago Press, 1981): 75-84.

[8] Hélèle Cixous. "The Laugh of the Medusa" in *New French Criticism.* Keith Cohen and Paula Cohen, translators, Elaine Marks and Isabelle de Courtivron, eds. (New York: Schocken, 1981): 256.

[9] Suleiman, *Subversive Intent,* 134.

[10] Suleiman, *Subversive Intent,* 134.

[11] Suleiman, *Subversive Intent,* 134

[12] James Hillman, *Anima. An Anatomy of a Personified Person* (Dallas: Spring Publications, Inc., 1985); Eugene Monick, *Phallos. Sacred Image of the Masculine* (Toronto: Inner City Books, 1987); Marion Woodman, *The Ravaged Bridegroom. Masculinity in Women* (Toronto: Inner City Books, 1990).

[13] Monik, *Phallos,* 70-71.

[14] Clarice Lispector, "A mensagem" in *A Legião Estrangeira.* (São Paulo: Editora Ática, 1987).

[15] Hélène Cixous, *Reading with Clarice Lispector* (Minneapolis: University of Minnesota Press, 1990); Naomi Lindstrom, "A Feminist Analysis of Clarice Lispector's *Daydreams of a Drunken Housewife,"* *Latin American Literary Review,* 10 (19) (1981): 7-16.

[16] *A Via Crucis do Corpo* is an exception where homosexuality, heterosexuality, group sex, sexuality and voyeurism receive Lispector's special attention. In the introduction of the book, however, Lispector admits that she wrote these short stories because her

editor asked her to write a text with sex as leitmotif, since this was a hot issue in the 70s. Lispector, however, refused to be labeled as a feminist like other women authors who wrote about sex in the same terms as men writers did.

[17] Clarice Lispector, *A Bela e a Fera* (Rio de Janeiro: Nova Fronteira, 1979).

[18] Monik, *Phallos,* 123.

[19] Earl Fitz, "The Passion of Logo(centrism), or, the Deconstructionist Universe of Clarice Lispector," *Luso-Brazilian Review,* XXV, 2, (1988): 33-44.

[20] Feminist criticism considers the circle as the way to break down "the fragmentation and linear thinking of patriarchy," creating a non-generic term, womon, in contrast to the generic term, woman, to describe the stronger sex. Cheris Kramarae and Paula A. Treichler, eds. *A Feminist Dictionary.* (London, Pandora, 1985), 94.

[21] Heilbrun, *Toward a Recognition of Androgyny,* xi.

[22] In opposition to animus, anima defines the feminine aspect in the male figure psyche: "The Latin *anima* in English means soul, which Jung described as the hidden, inferior, feeling inside of a man. Although theoretically it takes a decidedly second place to the masculine (let us say phallic) ego, its presence is felt in a man's moods and emotional reactions." Monik, *Phallos,* 121.

[23] Earl Fitz, "A Discourse of Silence: The Postmodernism of Clarice Lispector," *Contemporary Literature* 28 (4), (Winter 1987): 420-436.

[24] Clarice Lispector, *Felicidade Clandestina* (Rio de Janeiro: Nova Fronteira, 1987).

[25] Clarice Lispector, *Uma Aprendizagem ou o Livro dos Prazeres* (Rio de Janeiro: Francisco Alves Editora, 1990).

[26] Clarice Lispector, *Onde Estivestes de Noite* (Rio de Janeiro: Artenova, 1977).

[27] "New Consciousness designates the movement beyond patriarchy that no longer requires the diminishment of the feminine for phallic establishment. Masculinity finds its center as inner phallic reality. This, together with the anima, constitutes a restoration of wholeness in a male, made possible by the structural presence of phallos protos in the psychoid unconscious." Monik, *Phallos,* 68.

[28] Monik, *Phallos,* 66.

[29] Monik, *Phallos,* 68.

[30] This may explain why "A mensagem" was published again in *Felicidade Clandestina.*

[31] Woodman, *The Ravaged Bridegroom,* 69.

[32] Woodman, *The Ravaged Bridegroom,* 8.

[33] This identification between God and the androgyne is suggested as well in "As águas do mundo" and "O primeiro beijo," where the

sea and the female sculpture represent the mythical goddess of the mother that gives birth to a new identity.

[34] Clarice Lispector, *Água Viva* (Rio de Janeiro: Nova Fronteira, 1980).

[35] "The dream is to get beyond not only the number one—the number that determines unity, of body or of self—but also beyond the number two, which determines difference, antagonism, and exchange conceived of us as merely the coming together of opposites. That this dream is perhaps impossible is suggested. Its power remains, however, because the desire it embodies is a desire for both endless complication and creative movement." Suleiman, *Subversive Intent,* 136.

FURTHER READING

Anderson, Robert K. "Myth and Existentialism in Clarice Lispector's 'O crime do professor de matemática'." *Luso-Brazilian Review* 14, No. 2 (Winter 1977): 161-73.
> Interprets 'O crime do professor de matemática' as an archetypal "journey to the center" in which the protagonist takes responsibility for his existence.

Clark, María. "Facing the Other in Clarice Lispector's short story 'Amor'." *Letras femeninas* 16, Nos. 1-2 (Spring-Fall 1990): 13-20.
> Feminist reading analyzing the story "Amor" within the framework of Jacques Lacan's theory of subjectivity.

Cixous, Hélène. "'The Egg and the Chicken': Love Is Not Having." In *Reading with Clarice Lispector,* edited and translated by Verena Andermatt Conley. Minneapolis: University of Minnesota Press, 1990, pp. 98-122.
> Analyzes "The Egg and the Chicken" as a philosophical parody and a metaphor for the process of writing.

DiAntonio, Robert E. "Myth As a Unifying Force in 'O crime do professor de matemática'." *Luso-Brazilian Review* 22, No. 1 (Summer 1985): 27-32.
> Explores the story's existential themes and argues that myth is a unifying element in all of Lispector's work.

Douglas, Ellen. "Myth and Gender in Clarice Lispector: Quest as a Feminist Statement in 'A imitação da rosa'." *Luso-Brazilian Review* 25, No. 2 (Winter 1988): 15-31.
> Discusses the story 'A imitação da rosa' as a statement of feminism and humanism that challenges the traditional gender role of the quester in mythic narratives.

Fitz, Earl E. "Freedom and Self-Realization: Feminist Characterization in the Fiction of Clarice Lispector." *Modern Language Studies* 10 (1980): 51-61.
> Examines the female characters in Lispector's stories and novels, asserting that feminism is not an easily identified feature in her works since for Lispector feminism is not an "ideological cant."

————. *Clarice Lispector.* Boston: Twayne Publishers, 1985, 160 p.

Detailed and systematic analysis of all aspects of Lispector's work with some consideration of external factors influencing her career. Includes discussions of the short stories.

Gariglio, Maria Cristina de Aquino. "An Epiphany Inside an Epiphany? Clarice Lispector's 'A procura de uma dignidade'." *Romance Notes* 28, No. 2 (Winter 1987): 163-68.

Examines the use of literary epiphany to convey the protagonist's self-discovery.

Lastinger, Valerie C. "Humor in a New Reading of Clarice Lispector." *Hispania* 72, No. 1 (March 1989): 130-37.

Considers the role of humor in *Laços de família.*

Lindstrom, Naomi. "A Feminist Discourse Analysis of Clarice Lispector's 'Daydream of a Drunken Housewife'." *Latin American Literary Review* 9, No. 19 (Fall-Winter 1981): 7-16.

Interprets the story as a fictional critique of a woman's difficulty articulating her experience through verbal expression.

————. "A Discourse Analysis of 'Preciosidade'." *Luso-Brazilian Review* 19, No. 2 (Winter 1982): 187-94.

Examines the existentialism, narrative strategies, and feminine writing   prevalent in Lispector's story "Preciosidade."

Mathie, Barbara. "Feminism, Language or Existentialism: The Search for the Self in the Works of Clarice Lispector." In *Subjectivity and Literature from the Romantics to the Present Day,* edited by Philip Shaw and Peter Stockwell, pp. 121-34. London: Pinter Publications, 1991.

Shows how feminist, poststructuralist, and existential readings can be successfully applied to analyze *Laços de família* and *A via crucis do corpo.*

Muller, Ingrid R. "The Problematics of the Body in Clarice Lispector's *Family Ties.*" *Chasqui* 20, No. 1 (May 1990): 34-44.

Contends that the alienation of female characters in *Laços de família* is a result of the way they perceive their bodies.

Nunes, Maria Luisa. "Narrative Modes in Clarice Lispector's *Laços de família.*" *Luso-Brazilian Review* 14, No. 2 (Winter 1977): 174-84.

Discusses Lispector's use of narrative monologue, interior monologue, internal analysis, and direct discourse in rendering consciousness.

Peixota, Marta. "*Family Ties*: Female Development in Clarice Lispector." In *The Voyage In: Fictions of Female Development,* edited by Elizabeth Abel, Marianne Hirsch, and Elizabeth Langland, pp. 287-303. Hanover, NH: University of New England Press, 1983.

Feminist reading focuses on female life, from youth to old age, in *Laços de família.*

Rosenberg, Judith. "Taking Her Measurements: Clarice Lispector and 'The Smallest Woman in the World'." *Critique: Studies in Contemporary Fiction* 30, No. 2 (1989): 71-6.

Argues that the story "The Smallest Woman in the World" is about sexual politics and parodies the image of the great hunger.

Senna, Marta de. "'A Imitação da Rosa' by Clarice Lispector: An Interpretation." *Portugese Studies* 2 (1986): 159-65.

Presents a religious and symbolic reading of the story, examining the protagonist's quest for truth.

Wheeler, A. M. "Animal Imagery As Reflection of Gender Roles in Clarice Lispector's *Family Ties.*" *Critique: Studies in Modern Fiction* 28, No. 3 (Spring 1987): 125-34.

Contends that animal imagery in *Laços de família* represents Lispector's view of women's social roles.

Additional coverage of Lispector's life and career is contained in the following sources published by Gale Group: *Contemporary Authors,* **Vols. 116, 139;** *Contemporary Authors New Revision Series,* **Vol. 71;** *Contemporary Literature Criticism,* **Vol. 43; and** *Dictionary of Literary Biography,* **Vol. 113.**

"The Tell-Tale Heart"
Edgar Allan Poe

The following entry presents criticism of Poe's short story "The Tell-Tale Heart." For an overview of Poe's short fiction, see *Short Story Criticism,* Volume 1.

INTRODUCTION

This trademark horror tale shows Poe at the height of his imaginative and artistic powers, with its boldly original story line, exquisitely rendered form, and psychological complexity. The simple 2,200-word first-person narrative is the confession by a murderer to a grisly but apparently motiveless crime. The protagonist's madness is obvious from the beginning, but in his retelling of the story, the line between truth and hallucination is left blurred, disarming the reader and making the events in a madman's imagination seem chillingly real. In his discussions of the short story form, Poe insisted that each element of a story contribute to its total effect, and "The Tell-Tale Heart" is a perfect demonstration of this injunction. Every carefully crafted nuance of the tale contributes to its overall unity, from the narrator's protestations about his sanity in the opening lines to his confession in the last; the stylistic device of repeated phrases echoing the obsessiveness of the narrator's mind; and the interwoven symbolism creating a frighteningly charged effect.

The story's date of composition is uncertain, but there is evidence to believe it was written in mid-1842 shortly after Poe, then living in Philadelphia, suffered his third heart attack. In late 1842 Poe sent the tale off to the magazine *Boston Miscellany* for possible publication. It was rejected by editor Henry T. Tuckerman with the comment, "If Mr. Poe would condescend to furnish more quiet articles, he would be a most desirable correspondent." Poe turned the story over to his friend James Russell Lowell, who paid the financially strapped, unemployed author $10 and published it in the January 1843 issue of his monthly magazine, *The Pioneer.* The source of the story seems to have been Daniel Webster's description of an actual murder in Massachusetts in 1830, but, as critics have pointed out, Poe may also have found inspiration for the tale in horror stories by Charles Dickens and Edward Bulwer Lytton, William Shakespeare's *Macbeth,* and the circumstances of his own life.

Plot and Major Characters

The tale opens with the narrator insisting that he is not mad, avowing that his calm telling of the story that follows is confirmation of his sanity. He explains that he decided to take the life of an old man whom he loved and whose

house he shared. The only reason he had for doing so was that the man's pale blue eye, which was veiled by a thin white film and "resembled that of a vulture," tormented him, and he had to rid himself of the "Evil Eye" forever.

After again declaring his sanity, the narrator proceeds to recount the details of the crime. Every night for seven nights, he says, he had stolen into the old man's room at midnight holding a closed lantern. Each night he would very slowly unlatch the lantern slightly and shine a single ray of light onto the man's closed eye. As he enters the room on the eighth night, however, the old man stirs, then calls out, thinking he has heard a sound. The narrator shines the light on the old man's eye as usual, but this time finds it wide open. He begins to hear the beating of a heart and, fearing the sound might be heard by a neighbor, kills the old man by dragging him to the floor and pulling the heavy bed over him. He dismembers the corpse and hides it beneath the floorboards of the old man's room.

At four o'clock in the morning, the narrator continues, three policemen come asking to search the premises because a neighbor has reported a shriek coming from the house. The narrator invites the officers in, explaining that the noise came from himself as he dreamt. The old man, he tells them, is in the country. He brings chairs into the old man's room, placing his own seat on the very planks under which the victim lies buried. The officers are convinced there is no foul play, and sit around chatting amiably, but the narrator becomes increasingly agitated. He soon begins to hear a heart beating, much as he had just before he killed the old man. It grows louder and louder until he becomes convinced the policemen hear it too. They know of his crime, he thinks, and mock him. Unable to bear their derision and the sound of the beating heart, he springs up and, screaming, confesses his crime.

Major Themes

Most critics agree that there are two primary motifs in the story: the identification of the narrator with the man he kills and the psychological handling of time. The narrator says he understands his victim's terror just as he is about to murder him, and the beating heart he mistakes for the old man's may well be his own. Throughout the story the narrator is obsessed with time: the central image of the heart is associated with the ticking of a watch, the nightly visits take place precisely at midnight, and time seems to slow and almost stop as the murderer enters the old man's chamber. Another major theme is that of the eye, which some critics consider to have a double meaning, as the external "eye" of the old man is seen in contrast to the internal "I" of the narrator. Several commentators have pointed out that the symbolism in the work is highly structured and intertwined, so that the various themes—of death, time, nature, inner versus outer reality, the dream, the heart, and the eye—work together for accumulated effect. Other concerns by critics analyzing the story include Poe's influences in writing the story, the nature of the narrator's psychological disturbance, and the relationship between the narrator and the reader of the tale.

Critical Reception

Reaction to "The Tell-Tale Heart" upon its initial publication was mixed. The critic Horace Greeley commented in 1843 that the story was at once "strong and skillful" yet "overstrained and repulsive." Other reviewers found it "an article of thrilling interest" and "very wild and very readable." As a testament to its popularity, the sketch was reprinted in several magazines and newspapers in 1843 and 1845; however, it did not appear in a collection of stories during Poe's lifetime. It has been suggested that Poe's contemporary Nathaniel Hawthorne admired and was influenced by the tale, and a little over a decade after Poe's death Fyodor Dostoevsky, writing a preface to Russian translations of "The Black Cat," "Devil in Belfry," and "The Tell-Tale Heart," praised the American writer's

enormous talent and imagination. Over the next eighty years critics generally referred to the tale only in passing, sometimes admiringly and sometimes with distaste, when discussing Poe's other horror stories. Arthur Hobson Quinn's 1940 critical biography, however, which did much to bolster Poe's reputation as a serious writer, accorded the story slightly fuller treatment, asserting it to be "an almost perfect illustration of Poe's own theory of the short story, for every word contributes to the central effect." Later critics have agreed with that assessment, commenting on the story's unity of structure and economical yet powerful use of imagery. The tale has generated many different interpretations, from Marie Bonaparte's Freudian analysis, which sees the victim as a symbol of Poe's stepfather, to Gita Rajan's feminist reading, which views the protagonist as a woman. Perhaps because of its readability and the startling situation it describes, the tale has always enjoyed popular appeal, and ranks with "The Raven," "The Cask of Amontillado," and "The Fall of the House of Usher" not only as one of Poe's best-known works, but as one of the most familiar stories in American literature.

CRITICISM

Alfred C. Ward (essay date 1924)

SOURCE: "Edgar Allan Poe: 'Tales of Mystery and Imagination'," in *Aspects of the Modern Short Story: English and American,* University of London, 1924, pp. 32-44.

[*In the following excerpt, Ward points out that the lack of motive on the part of the narrator is a major flaw in "The Tell-Tale Heart."*]

"The Tell-Tale Heart" is one of the most effective parables ever conceived. Shorn of its fantastic details regarding the murdered man's vulture-like eye, and the long-drawn-out detail concerning the murderer's slow entrance into his victim's room, the story stands as an unforgettable record of the voice of a guilty conscience.

Despite its merit as a parable, **"The Tell-Tale Heart"** is marred by the insanity of the chief character. From the very first sentence his madness is apparent through his desperate insistence upon his sanity; and the preliminaries of his crime go to prove that madness. The vital weakness of Poe's stories in this kind is his repeated use of the motive of mental abnormality. Psychological fiction (and Poe was among its earliest practitioners) depends for its effect upon the study of the human mind in its *conscious* state—whereas insanity is, to all intents and purposes, a condition of unconsciousness.

Is it not possible to contemplate a re-writing of **"The Tell-Tale Heart"** in a manner which would preserve its unique character as a parable of the self-betrayal of a criminal by his conscience, while at the same time vastly increasing its interest as a story of human action? As Poe writes the story, we have the spectacle of a demented creature smothering his helpless old victim without reason or provocation, other than the instigation of his own mad obsession: "Object there was none. Passion there was none." This absence of motive robs the story of every vestige of dramatic interest, for it is an elementary axiom in criticism that what is motiveless is inadmissible in literary art. The provision of an adequate motive for the murder, and the subsequent commission of the murder by one who is otherwise sane, would bring the story on to the plane of credibility and dramatic interest. If the circumstances of the story were thus altered, the implacable workings of conscience and the portrayal of their cumulative influence upon the mind of the criminal, could scarcely fail to have a much more powerful effect upon the mind of the reader than is actually the case in the story as it stands.

Marie Bonaparte (essay date 1949)

SOURCE: "The Tell-Tale Heart," in *The Life and Works of Edgar Allan Poe: A Psycho-Analytic Interpretation,* Imago Publishing Company, 1949, pp. 491-504.

[*In the following excerpt, Bonaparte offers a Freudian reading of "The Tell-Tale Heart," asserting that the old man in the story resembles Poe's stepfather, on whom the author sought to enact his Oedipal revenge.*]

"True!—nervous—very, very dreadfully nervous I had been and am; but why *will* you say that I am mad?" begins the hero of **"The Tell-Tale Heart"**[1] who, like his fellows in **"The Black Cat"** and **"The Imp of the Perverse,"** writes from behind prison bars, where his crime has consigned him.

> "The disease had sharpened my senses—not destroyed—not dulled them. Above all was the sense of hearing acute. I heard all things in the heaven and in the earth. I heard many things in hell. How, then, am I mad? Hearken! and observe how healthily—how calmly I can tell you the whole story."

Thus the narrator—whom Poe evidently wishes to show as mad or, at least, the victim of the Imp of the Perverse—begins by denying his madness like the "logical" lunatic he is.

> "It is impossible to say how first the idea entered my brain; but once conceived, it haunted me day and night."

The nature of this obsessional thought will soon appear.

> "Object there was none. Passion there was none. I loved the old man. He had never wronged me. He had never given me insult. For his gold I had no desire."

This strangely resembles the representation, by its opposite, of Poe's own relation to his foster-father, John Allan! But let us see the *motive* our narrator assigns for his deed.

> "I think it was his eye! yes, it was this! One of his eyes resembled that of a vulture—a pale blue eye, with a film over it. Whenever it fell upon me, my blood ran cold; and so by degrees—very gradually—I made up my mind to take the life of the old man, and thus rid myself of the eye forever."

This eye, filmed over, if only in part, permitting of dim or oblique vision, corresponds to an excised eye and so brings us back to the main motif in **"The Black Cat."** All in all, the old man must be killed for the same reason as the cats. Here, however, the murder is premeditated, as in **"The Imp of the Perverse"** where, again, the victim is the father; there, it was for gold but, here, to annihilate the filmed eye.

> "You should have seen how wisely I proceeded—with what caution—with what foresight—with what dissimulation I went to work!"

For the father, indeed, is to be feared and needs a cautious approach!

> "I was never kinder to the old man than during the whole week before I killed him. And every night, about midnight, I turned the latch of his door and opened it—oh so gently! And then, when I had made an opening sufficient for my head, I put in a dark lantern, all closed, closed, so that no light shone out, and then I thrust in my head. . . . I moved it slowly—very, very slowly, so that I might not disturb the old man's sleep. It took me an hour to place my whole head within the opening so far that I could see him as he lay upon his bed. . . . And then, when my head was well in the room, I undid the lantern cautiously—oh, so cautiously—cautiously (for the hinges creaked)—I undid it just so much that a single thin ray fell upon the vulture eye. And this I did for seven long nights . . . but I found the eye always closed; and so it was impossible to do the work; for it was not the old man who vexed me, but his Evil Eye. And every morning, when the day broke, I went boldly into the chamber, and spoke courageously to him, calling him by name in a hearty tone, and inquiring how he had passed the night. So you see he would have been a very profound old man, indeed, to suspect that every night, just at twelve, I looked in upon him while he slept."

Here we see the son clearly outwitting the father in caution and astuteness! Even as we watch him enter the room, each morn, with friendly greeting, we seem to see the small Edgar as he visited his waking "Pa", calling him by "name" and asking had he "passed the night well?" For so children must often do, compelled as they are to be affectionate and behave, though recent punishments may inspire quite different feelings.

> "Upon the eighth night I was more than usually cautious in opening the door. A watch's minute hand moves more quickly than did mine. Never before that night, had I *felt* the extent of my own powers—of my sagacity. I could scarcely contain my feelings of triumph. To think that there I was, opening the door, little by little, and he not even to dream of my secret deeds or thoughts. I fairly chuckled at the idea; and

perhaps he heard me; for he moved on the bed suddenly, as if startled. Now you may think that I drew back— but no. His room was as black as pitch with the thick darkness, (for the shutters were close fastened, through fear of robbers,) and so I knew that he could not see the opening of the door, and I kept pushing it on steadily, steadily.

"I had my head in, and was about to open the lantern, when my thumb slipped upon the tin fastening, and the old man sprang up in bed, crying out—'Who's there?'."

Thus the adversaries are opposed; the eyes of the son, in the dark, being fixed on the menaced father.

"I kept quite still and said nothing. For a whole hour I did not move a muscle, and in the meantime I did not hear him lie down. He was still sitting up in the bed, listening;—just as I have done, night after night, hearkening to the death watches in the wall."

The old man's increasing terror is then described and the tale continues:

"When I had waited a long time, very patiently, without hearing him lie down, I resolved to open a little—a very, very little crevice in the lantern . . . until, at length, a simple dim ray, like the thread of the spider, shot from out the crevice and fell full upon the vulture eye".

"It was open—wide, wide open—and I grew furious as I gazed upon it. I saw it with perfect distinctness— all a dull blue, with a hideous veil over it that chilled the very marrow in my bones; but I could see nothing else of the old man's face or person: for I had directed the ray as if by instinct, precisely upon the damned spot."

We are not told whether it is with his good or clouded eye that the old man perceives the ray which shoots into the dark room, nor is it ever made clear exactly how much he sees with his "vulture eye". Whatever the case, the ray, thin as a spider's thread, striking the offending eye, is responsible for an amazing reaction:

". . . have I not told you that what you mistake for madness is but over acuteness of the senses?"

he says, almost as though a paranoiac justifying his auditory hallucinations—and, continuing;

". . . now, I say, there came to my ears a low, dull, quick sound, such as a watch makes when enveloped in cotton. I knew *that* sound well, too. It was the beating of the old man's heart. It increased my fury, as the beating of a drum stimulates the soldier into courage."

The murderer, however, restrains himself and remains motionless, his ray still fixed on that eye, while the "hellish tattoo" of the old man's heart goes on increasing. Meanwhile, his own terror rises to "uncontrollable" heights, as . . .

". . . the beating grew louder, louder! I thought the heart must burst. And now a new anxiety seized me— the sound would be heard by a neighbour! The old man's hour had come! With a loud yell, I threw open the lantern and leaped into the room. He shrieked once—once only. In an instant I dragged him to the floor, and pulled the heavy bed over him. I then smiled gaily, to find the deed so far done. But, for many minutes, the heart beat on with a muffled sound. This, however, did not vex me; it would not be heard through the wall. At length it ceased. The old man was dead. I removed the bed and examined the corpse. Yes, he was stone, stone dead. I placed my hand upon the heart and held it there many minutes. There was no pulsation. He was stone dead. His eye would trouble me no more."

The murderer then describes his "wise precautions" to conceal the body, as giving proof of his sound reason.

"The night waned, and I worked hastily, but in silence. First of all I dismembered the corpse. I cut off the head and the arms and the legs.

"I then took up three planks from the flooring of the chamber, and deposited all between the scantlings. I then replaced the boards so cleverly, so cunningly, that no human eye—not even *his*—could have detected anything wrong. There was nothing to wash out—no stain of any kind—no blood-spot whatever. I had been too wary for that. A tub had caught all—ha! ha!"

Now, however, it is four a.m., and knocks are heard at the street door. "A shriek had been heard by a neighbour" and the police have appeared, to investigate.

The murderer, nevertheless, is wholly at ease. "The shriek," he said, was his own in a dream. "The old man . . . was absent in the country . . ." And now, worthy precursor of the murderer in **"The Black Cat,"** (evidently written after **"The Tell-Tale Heart"**), he leads his visitors through the house and bids them search, and search well.

"I led them, at length, to *his* chamber. I showed them his treasures, secure, undisturbed. In the enthusiasm of my confidence, I brought chairs into the room, and desired them *here* to rest from their fatigues, while I myself, in the wild audacity of my perfect triumph, placed my own seat upon the very spot beneath which reposed the corpse of the victim."

This anticipates the murderer in **"The Black Cat,"** who raps on the cellar wall, both being reminiscent of those murderers who haunt the scene of their crime.

As might be expected, the victim, from the depths of his tomb, takes up the challenge. The statue on the Commander's tomb accepts the invitation of Don Juan and turns up at his feast. The walled-in cat shrieks out. And now the old man, whose heart beats so hellishly, *also* responds in his way.

> "The officers were satisfied . . . They sat, and while I answered cheerily, they chatted of familiar things. But, ere long, I felt myself getting pale and wished them gone. My head ached, and I fancied a ringing in my ears . . ."

The ringing increases "—until, at length, I found that the noise was *not* within my ears". The auditory hallucination is thus re-established.

> "No doubt I now grew *very* pale—but I talked more fluently, and with a heightened voice. Yet the sound increased—and what could I do? It was *a low, dull quick sound—much such a sound as a watch makes when enveloped in cotton.* I gasped for breath—and yet the officers heard it not. I talked more quickly—more vehemently; but the noise steadily increased. I arose . . ."

And now the poor wretch makes ever more desperate efforts to drown the increasing noise. In vain he paces heavily to and fro, or grates his chair on the boards: the sound

> "grew louder—louder—*louder!* And still the men chatted pleasantly, and smiled. Was it possible they heard not? Almighty God!—no, no! They heard!—they suspected!—they *knew!*—they were making a mockery of my horror!"

Whereupon, possessed by this illusion and no longer able to bear their derision, the murderer cries:

> "Villains! . . . dissemble no more! I admit the deed!—tear up the planks! here, here!—it is the beating of his hideous heart!"

Such is **"The Tell-Tale Heart,"** possibly the most shorn of trimmings of Poe's tales and thus, possibly, one that is nearest to our "modern" taste. Among Poe's works, it stands like a faint precursor of that great parricidal epic which is Dostoievsky's[2] opus.

It has been said[3] that the composition of **"The Tell-Tale Heart,"** to which Poe refers in a letter dated December 1842,[4] was doubtless stimulated by his severe heart attack, towards the summer of that year, after returning from Saratoga Springs. Possibly, it was this—according to Hervey Allen, Poe's third serious heart attack since the first, in 1834-35[5]—which furnished the adventitious cause for Poe's choice of just these anguished heart-beats to express the deep and buried complexes with which we shall now deal. The same device, also, was to serve him later, when his heart condition grew still worse, to express the weariness of living, in his poem "For Annie."[6] This explanation, however, far from exhausts all that **"The Tell-Tale Heart"** reveals.

Actually, we know, difficult as it may be for our conscious mental processes to grasp, that the functions of organs are not represented, in the unconscious, in a manner proportionate to the vital importance of each. The heart-beat, for instance, is so vitally important that, if it stops, death ensues. One might, therefore, imagine that the heart's activity would be extensively reflected in the psyche. This is not, however, the case; the beating of the heart no more disturbs the unconscious than do the rhythmic movements of the thorax. Both belong to those vegetative activities of organic functions which ordinarily do not concern the psychic unconscious.

Should, however, some organic disturbance suddenly disturb one or other of these important organs—or a conversion neurosis of hysterical or hypochondriac origin—we are likely to find them become a main source of anxiety. When this happens, however, it is never due to the organ as such and its function, but to the libidinal charge which invests it. Such organs then represent, apart from their proper function, that of the whole organism's libidinal function, now largely "displaced" upon them. In psychoneurotic disturbances less severe than the complete narcissistic regression that determines hypochondria, the libidinally hyper-cathected and disturbed organ may even serve to express the subjects' object relations to other beings.

So with Poe's story of **"The Tell-Tale Heart."** As already noted, the murdered old man resembles John Allan in several ways, even to the symptom of the thudding heart. Did not his first attack of dropsy occur in England, in 1820: which illness, worsening with age, in 1834, ended his life? . . . His fear of the pounding heart in the murdered old man's breast thus, doubtless, directly derives from the oppressed, labouring and dropsical heart of the Scotch merchant. With that heart, as a result of buried complexes we shall study—and by that identification with the father habitual with sons—Poe later, and unconsciously, identified his own neurotic, alcoholic heart.

Yet the mere fact that John Allan suffered from dropsy does not account for the whole content of this anxiety-fraught tale. To understand the deeper motives which inspire man to dream or artists to create, we must grasp, in their plenitude, all the primitive, vital instincts which throng the unconscious. . . .

[T]he child's sexual instincts awake much earlier than is deemed by adults. At an unbelievably early age, the child already possesses larval instinctual mechanisms which allow it to store up impressions of adult sex acts performed in its presence. That Poe, as a child, was present at such times, when sharing the room of his actress mother, the crime of the ape is almost certain testimony. For that very same crime, shrouded in London fog, those fogs among which Frances Allan acquired her mysterious illness, the **"Man of the Crowd"** is described as "type and genius of deep crime." For, to the child, at a time when coitus seems purely sadistic, the sex attack on the mother is the prototype of all crime.

Even though, when the child is small, adults do not always conceal themselves in the sex act, a time comes when they protect themselves from its eyes by what they imagine the impenetrable barrier of dark, so vividly described in **"The Tell-Tale Heart"** as, "pitch"-like. This darkness is indeed the preferred setting for the coitus of civilised man, as though it were something disapproved by society.

Nevertheless, alert as they are, the child's sex instincts continue to perceive and record, though in the dark. What it saw earlier may contribute to this but, even without sight, hearing would suffice. For, in effect, coitus has its own sounds, rhythmic movements and precipitate breath, combined with an accelerated heart beat. And even though these heart-beats may be imperceptible from a distance, the panting which accompanies them and characterises the sex-act, is strangely audible to infant ears, straining to every sound in the still darkness.

Thus, it need not surprise us to find, in **"The Tell-Tale Heart,"** reference to an almost supernatural acuteness of hearing. Doubtless, we have here the unconscious memory of nocturnal eavesdroppings when, in the night, "hellish" things were heard by the child:[7] in other words, the father's sex attack on the mother. Similar unconscious memories are found at the root of many auditory hallucinations of paranoia.

The old man's heart-beat, that "hellish tattoo" which grew "quicker and quicker, and louder and louder", would thus be the heart's fanfare for the sex act: its assault on the woman and supremest pleasure. Whence, doubtless, in the tale, the furious *crescendo* of the heart-beats, twice repeated, which culminate first in the old man's death and, next, in the murderer's seizure and eventual death also. Thus, the talion law is satisfied twice; first by punishment of the mother's *murderer* and, then, by punishment of the slayer of that murderer.

In the last analysis, therefore, it is the Man of the Crowd—in this tale lying in the old man's bed—who thus receives just punishment. In the same way that, in neurotic symptoms, the repressed material finally emerges from the repressing process itself so, here, the sign of the crime, the clamouring heart in the sex act, reappears in this retributive punishment of the heart that thuds with the anguish of death.

Also, it is under the *bed,* in which his crime—the sex attack—was enacted, that the old man is stifled to death. Thus, the instrument of his crime, becomes that of his destruction.

The darkness again, black as pitch, where the old man—or the beating heart—sleeps, into which the hero spies and which is pierced by his lantern beam must, evidently, be interpreted as an echo of the intensity with which the child once wished to see through the dark. I knew a young man, whose memories of spying on his parent's sex acts reappeared, in analysis, in the shape of a dream where he saw himself, as a child, observing them through the diaphragm of his camera lens instead of eyes. Photography was very young in Poe's time and here, in **"The Tell-Tale**

Heart," the lantern, instead, symbolises viewing. We know, in primitive concepts of vision, that it is not the illuminated object which sends rays to the eye, but the eye which projects its rays on the object. This primitive concept reappears here, implicit in this way of viewing through darkness by half-opening a lantern shutter as though an eyelid. Juxtaposing this element in the tale with its main motif, the heart-beat, we get some idea how much yearning, both visual and aural, must have remained in the child Poe, all through his life with the Allans, to go on responding to the sex-scene as he once knew it with his mother.

Nevertheless, our tale gives quite another reason why this father-figure must be destroyed by the son-figure. The narrator declares that he "loves the old man", who never had "wronged" him or "given him insult" while, as for his "gold", for that he had no desire: all which, in fact, represent the opposites, as we showed, of Edgar's relation to his "Pa", John Allan.[8] There is a certain hyprocrisy here and this tale, in which we might expect the son's ambivalence to the father to appear is, primarily, a tale of hate. The reason alleged, however, for this hate, is remarkable: the old man is hated for his eye.

> "I think it was his eye! yes, it was this! He had the eye of a vulture—a pale blue eye, with a film over it."

We shall not presume to affirm that, in this mention of the vulture, there is an incontestable allusion to the mother, though the vulture was a classic mother symbol of the Ancient Egyptians and though we find it, later, in the vulture phantasy of the child Leonardo da Vinci.[9] But, what cannot be denied, is that the old man's eye establishes a direct connection with the eyes of the mother totem cats in **"The Black Cat."** True, a film over the eye does not invariably imply a total loss of vision but, in general it does or, at least, suggests it. In other words, like Wotan in Germanic mythology, the father in **"The Tell-Tale Heart"** is represented as blind in one eye, which is equivalent to being castrated.[10]

Clearly also, castrated for his crimes! For, as regards the mother, the father was indeed the prototype of all crime, as to the son. Was it not he who kept the son from the mother by wielding the threat of castration? Here, however, lies the rub! For, if it is the mother who, by her body, manifests to the son that the dread possibility of deprivation of the penis exists, in the last analysis it is the father—by whom or in whose interests the Œdipal prohibitions were instituted—who, from remotest time and the depths of the unconscious, threatens to castrate the son for his guilty desires. It is because the father has committed this crime against the son, that the latter repays him by castration in retribution of the crime for which the son would have been castrated; that of possessing the mother. Thus Zeus, when grown, castrated his father Kronos who, himself, had castrated Uranos, *his* father.

These are the two great, eternally human themes which underlie Poe's tale and confer such sovereign power on it. The two prime complexes, through which all humanity and every child must pass, are its marrow and substance. Here, the son's Œdipus wish for his father's death becomes effective; the father is struck down for the crime of possessing the mother and for inventing the curse of castration, first as a threat to the son, but more for effecting it. For it is the father whom the son generally considers responsible for the woman's castration, when he discovers she lacks the penis. Secure in memories of the parents' coitus, the child imagines that though the mother did not succumb to the father's sadistic attacks, nevertheless it cost her a wound which, like Amfortas's hurt, would go on eternally *bleeding*. The menstruation, of which the child, sooner or later, becomes aware, is the proof. Thus, for the great crime of bringing castration into the world when, without it, all created beings would be whole and entire, each of the parents, in his or her way, is responsible; the mother for having undergone the castration and the father for having inflicted it. That is why both must be punished. The cats are hanged or immured and the old man is stifled under his mattress. Both flaunt the emblem of their common crime: the cats have a gouged-out eye and the old man's eye has a film over it.

Here it seems pertinent to ask whether the old man in **"The Tell-Tale Heart"** is, in fact, blind in that eye? Poe does not say: he even seems to imply that, in spite of its covering film, it still retains sight for, as he says at the start of the tale: "Whenever it fell upon me, my blood ran cold". Later, after the murder, when the dismembered body is buried under the floor, he once more tells us: "no human eye—not even *his*—could have detected any thing wrong". Thus, extreme acuity of vision is now attributed to that eye. There is some contradiction here for, if in Poe's unconscious the eye, though filmed, retained its vision, nevertheless it continued a *blind* eye, as in the Norse myth of Father Wotan.

We know, however, that contradictions in the manifest content of dreams or myths represent other, perfectly coherent thoughts, in the latent content. This contradiction then, as regards the eye, an eye that can see so well in spite of its blindness, must derive from the fact that, in this story, the father receives punishment for two distinct crimes; first, that of coitus with the mother and second, for its result, which led to castration, as the mother reveals. Yet, to effect castration, a weapon was needed and this was the penis, so that, to enact his deed, the father must still possess the penis, though he will later be punished by castration for it. The old man's eye that sees and is sightless would, thus, in this apparent contradiction, condense two successive aspects of the criminal father; first, when with his weapon the crime is committed and, then, when as punishment that weapon is cut off.[11]

There is a somewhat earlier tale by Poe where the father-castration motif appears far purer and death is not concomitant with castration. In **"The Man that was Used Up,"**[12] Brigadier John A. B. C. Smith, in full possession of his strength and faculties, while engaged in a more than epic campaign against the savage Kickapoos and Bugaboos, is captured and submitted to almost every kind of mutilation. The narrator, meeting the general at a social gathering, is at first dazzled by his fine presence, beautiful voice and

assured manner. The general, in particular, passes for a very lion with women. Nevertheless, it is whispered that some mystery surrounds him, the nature of which the narrator cannot discover. At his wits' ends, he seeks the truth at its source and, one fine morning, calls on our hero. Though the general is at his toilet, the visitor is shown in. As he enters, he stumbles over a nondescript bundle which emits the ghost of a voice. It is the general, in the state to which he is reduced when without the artificial limbs, organs and muscles, prodigies of modern invention, which remedy his many mutilations. The cardinal mutilation, however, is not mentioned, but we may well imagine it included, for the Kickapoos and Bugaboos who so generously relieved him of leg, arm, shoulders, pectoral muscles, scalp, teeth, eye, palate and seven-eights tongue, would surely not have left him the penis! The castration of prisoners, moreover, holds high place among tribes quite as savage as were the Kickapoos and Bugaboos!

Though the murderer in **"The Tell-Tale Heart"** also mutilated his victim by removing head, arms and legs before depositing him under the floor, what he "castrated" was but a corpse whereas the treatment to which General Smith is subjected is castration, in its pure symbolic form, and does not include death. For, though the castration motif (deprivation of the penis), is related to that of death (deprivation of existence), the two are not identical as this tale of **"The Man That Was Used Up"** shows.

Moreover, in this tale, we find echoes of Poe's army life and a time when his military superiors stood, for him, in the place of the Father he had left, in fleeing from John Allan.

Before we close this study of **"The Tell-Tale Heart,"** let us seek to discern those features of the murdered old man, which would relate him to the child Edgar's successive fathers.

Poe's unconscious memories, as we saw, of the parents' coitus, dated from the time when, as an infant, he shared his mother's room on her tours with Mr. Placide. At that time his father was David Poe whom, doubtless, a lover was soon to replace, . . . Probably it was this lover from whom, primarily, derived the motif of the increasingly violent heartbeats. And the fact that, at last, when the man with the lantern bursts into the old man's room, he reveals himself by yelling and opening his lantern—slips which imply the wish to be revealed—may well re-echo another frequent occurrence; namely when the childish, jealous eavesdropper, with his cries or need to urinate, sought to interrupt the parents' intercourse because of the excitement communicated, or for other reasons.

All these impressions however, so precociously stored up, after Edgar's adoption were transferred *en bloc* to John Allan, a far more imposing father whose harshness laid an indelible mark on the growing child. It was certainly in this respectable, middle-class household, that the repression of his precociously early sexuality was forced upon Poe. This was the time when he was scourged by the castration-complex, whence our morality derives. Thus, the old man's film-clouded, vulture-like eye belongs, in fact, to John Allan. It was on him that the full force of the child's Œdipal rage and resentment must have been concentrated, given the fact that, dour and forbidding, he stood in the father's position to Poe, in addition to owning and, martyrising, his new mother. To us, the old man's heart-beats appear, at least, triply determined. If, firstly they represent the panting of coitus, overheard in the dark of fortuitous lodgings during his mother's life, its cardiac transposition must be determined by memories of the heart attacks experienced by his dropsical father John Allan which again, in reality, were echoed by the neurotic, alcoholic, heart of the son Edgar. Yet, these hearts ail because they are guilty of one and the same sin; that of desiring the mother. Their disease, like their precipitate heartbeats, to Poe's unconscious, expresses both the crime and the punishment.

The compulsion of the man with the lantern to open the old man's door, night after night, that he may watch him asleep and alone, in bed, surely also re-echoes some precise reminiscence of Poe's, as a child. And indeed, it is unlikely that John Allan, who disliked his wife's love of the orphan, would have permitted him to sleep in their room, even if ill, to please her. Besides, the Allans had a large comfortable house and slaves. It was to one of these, his black "mammy", that Edgar would be entrusted and, with her, he would have slept.[13]

Perhaps through this negress, in "pitch"-black nights, nights as dark as her skin, the listening child may have re-experienced its responses to the parents' coitus,—which he could only hear in the dark—as the man with the lantern listens to the old man's heart. Nevertheless, the libido of this child, as Poe's life and tales both testify— for in neither do negresses play any part—was by then fixated on his foster mother, as white and pretty as his own, in accordance with the classic mechanism of the compulsion to repetition. It was on her room that, falling asleep, his childish desires must have converged at night, because he so loved and desired her, and because of his jealousy, too; all his yearning, in fact, to see what another was doing there.

That "other" was John Allan, whom the child would certainly suspect as guilty of similar attacks to those he remembered made on his mother. When the man with the lantern, night after night, feels urged to go and spy on the old man's bedroom, he doubtless only enacts what the child, kept by his nurse in his crib was, in his helplessness, prevented from doing. Though the image of the mother is here suppressed, as in **"The Man of the Crowd,"** it is nevertheless for her, that the father has one eye blinded and then is killed.

It is the old man's death that is at stake in this Œdipal battle, where the mother is the prize. But the mother is eliminated from the story, and the old man appears alone in bed, as the small Edgar would doubtless have wished John Allan always to be. Apparently, the old man's solitary sleep re-echoes one of the phantasy-wishes of the small Edgar.

Yet, though the old man sleeps alone, his heart beats in *crescendos*. Thus, he condenses in one being both the negation and affirmation of the father's coital activity, in the same way that his eye suggests both the presence and absence of the penis. Such modes of representation are natural to the unconscious, in which opposites exist side by side. Though conscious logic disapprove they, none the less, continue buried in our depths, as the dreams of the normal and the neurotic testify, as well as the myths to which humanity has given birth.

Notes

[1] "The Tell-Tale Heart": *The Pioneer,* January, 1843; *Broadway Journal,* II, 7.

[2] FREUD: *Dostoevsky and Parricide. International Journal of Psycho-Analysis,* 1945, 1-8: *Dostojewski und die Vatertötung,* 1928. *Ges. Werke,* Band XIV.

[3] Hervey Allen, *Israfel* (New York, 1927), p. 567.

[4] Lowell to Poe, Boston, December 17, 1842. (*Virginia Edition,* Vol. 17, p. 125.)

[5] *Israfel,* p. 540.

[6]
The moaning and groaning,
The sighing and sobbing,
Are quieted now,
With that horrible throbbing
At heart:—ah that horrible,
Horrible throbbing!

(Cf. pages 180-3.)

[7] Cf. Henri Barbusse, *L'Enfer,* (Paris, Librairie Mondiale, 1908) where sexuality in general is equated with "hell".

[8] Similarly, in "Thou Art the Man," (*Godey's Lady's Book,* November, 1844), the poor hack-writer, so appropriately named Mr. Pennifeather, is as innocent as the new-born babe of the murder of his rich uncle, Mr. Shuttleworthy, whose heir he is. Only a double of the latter, a rogue ironically called Old Charley Goodfellow, who likewise belongs to the series of "fathers", or hypocritical John Allans, could have been capable of so heinous a deed! Goodfellow succeeds in having the innocent nephew arrested and condemned to the gallows but, by a device typically Poe's, (the corpse of the victim rises to denounce his murderer from a case of wine), he is exposed and brought to justice. The murderer falls dead, while Pennifeather, released from prison, in all innocence enjoys the murdered man's fortune.

[9] FREUD: *Leonardo da Vinci: A Psycho-Sexual Study of an Infantile Reminiscence.* Op. cit. page 382, note 4.

[10] The *Encyclopædia Britannica,* article *Odin,* tells us that, among ancient peoples, prisoners taken in war were often sacrificed to the "one-eyed old man". "The commonest method of sacrifice was by hanging the victim on a tree; and in the poem, "Hávamál," the god himself is represented as sacrificed in this way." There must be something more than coincidence in the fact that Wotan, the castrated father, should be hanged or, in other words, have his penis mockingly restored, in the same way as the Black Cat, a one-eyed monster like Wotan.

[11] Yet another contradiction may be noted. The sound of the old man's heartbeats is likened to the ticking of a watch: a watch "enveloped in cotton", even. Now watches or the ticking of a watch (in contrast, as we shall see, with the imposing swing of a clock pendulum) are classic symbols, in the unconscious, for the female organ and the throbbings, in sexual excitement, of the tiny clitoris it conceals. Before the old man's heart-beats have swollen to the "hellish tattoo" of truly virile character, they thus begin to beat twice, muted as it were, and in *feminine* fashion. We therefore may have here another instance of a dualism similar to that of the film-covered eye which both sees and does not see or, in other words, which is at the same time ultra-virile and castrated.

[12] "The Man that was Used Up. A Tale of the Late Bugaboo and Kickapoo Campaign": Burton's Gentleman's Magazine, August 1839; 1840; 1843; Broadway Journal, II, 5.

[13] Cf. *Israfel*, p. 61, for a reference to this "mammy".

Patrick F. Quinn (essay date 1957)

SOURCE: "That Spectre in My Path," in *The French Face of Edgar Poe,* Southern Illinois University Press, 1957, pp. 216-56.

[*In the following excerpt, Quinn considers the details Poe uses to convey the particular type of madness exhibited by the narrator of "The Tell-Tale Heart."*]

To read **"The Man of the Crowd"** in conjunction with **"The Tell-Tale Heart"** is to become aware immediately of a number of resemblances between them. In the latter story, too, there is an old man; only this time it is not he who is "the type and the genius of deep crime," but rather the narrator himself. The narrator is the criminal; the story is an account of his crime and its discovery. If the pursuer of the man of the crowd had grasped the significance of what he had witnessed, and, in the insane hope of circumventing his destiny, had killed the man he was following, then all the essentials of **"The Tell-Tale Heart"** would be present. For this story is one more exploration of the psychology of the bipartite soul.

Living alone with an old man, the criminal-hero develops a profound hatred for him. This hatred he cannot explain, but it seems to him that the eye of the old man is somehow the cause of it. He resolves to murder him, and for a week he goes to the door of his room every night at midnight. At last the victim is awakened by a chance noise made by the madman, who then opens the shutter of his lantern so that a beam of light falls on the hateful eye. Believing he hears the sound of his victim's heart, and alarmed lest this become so loud as to rouse a neighbor, he enters the room and kills his enemy. After making sure that the heart has stopped, he hides the corpse under the boards of the floor. Soon after, the police arrive, and in the conviction that his deed cannot be found out, he leads them to the very room in which it was committed. But soon the murderer begins to hear a recurrence of the heart beats, and convinced finally that the police can hear them too, he shrieks his confession of guilt: "Villains! . . . dissemble no

more! I admit the deed!—tear up the planks!—here, here!—it is the beating of his hideous heart!"

What so brief a synopsis fails to clarify is the devices by which Poe makes this powerful story something more than a vivid melodrama. One device, although not of major importance, is the manner in which the insanity of the narrator is conveyed. When Baudelaire's translation of **"The Tell-Tale Heart"** first appeared in the French press he gave it a subtitle, "Plaidoyer d'un fou." He later suppressed the phrase, and rightly so, for the repeated and heated denials of insanity with which the story begins are wholly adequate indication of the mental state of the speaker. The cunning with which he went about his work was proof, for him, that he was not mad. But the cunning was far from perfect. Otherwise he would have had the foresight to oil the hinges of his dark lantern. That he should have neglected so essential a preparation refutes, on the level of his actions, what he too vehemently protests in his words.

But the engrossing interest this story has depends less on the general fact that the hero is mad than on the particular kind of madness that his case involves. What was the nature of his crime? He had no hatred for his victim. Quite the reverse: "I loved the old man." And so he casts about for a reason, a convincing motive: "I think it was his eye! yes, it was this! He had the eye of a vulture—a pale blue eye, with a film over it. Whenever it fell upon me, my blood ran cold; and so by degrees—very gradually—I made up my mind to take the life of the old man, and thus rid myself of the eye forever." A simpler solution, but one which the criminal apparently did not consider, would have been to leave the house, a house of which we are told that only the two men lived there. That this solution did not occur to the murderer is one more indication of his mental derangement; but, more than this, it carries a suggestion of the strange relationship in which the two characters were involved. Thus the feelings of the old man when he awoke to discover his executioner at the door were feelings that the executioner could identify himself with:

> He was still sitting up in the bed listening;—just as I have done night after night, hearkening to the death watches in the wall. Presently I heard a slight groan, and I knew it was the groan of mortal terror. It was not a groan of pain or of grief—oh no!—it was the low stifled sound that arises from the bottom of the soul when overcharged with awe. I knew the sound well. Many a night, just at midnight, when all the world slept, it has welled up from my own bosom, deepening, with its dreadful echo, the terrors that distracted me.

He carried a lantern but had no need of it. Without its aid he was able to see the old man as he lay on his bed, although the time was midnight and the room was "black as pitch with the thick darkness." He could see him well enough with the mind's eye, Poe is implying here; for the act of murder in this story took place on a psychological as well as a physical level, and the nature and meaning of the crime must be sought in the psychology of the hero rather than in the immediately visible external details of his actions.

The murderer identified himself with his victim: "I knew what the old man felt, and pitied him, although I chuckled at heart." But what he did not know was that through this crime he was unconsciously seeking his own death. The shuttered lantern in his hand chanced to symbolize the thing he hated, the pale blue eye of the old man, the eye with a film over it. Whenever that eye fell on him, his blood ran cold. Thus he used the lantern to project a beam of light that filled the old man with terror, and in this way executioner and victim exchanged experiences. But so closely had the madman identified himself with his adversary that the murder he committed also brought on his own death. With unwitting irony he later tells the police that the scream heard during the night was his own, "in a dream." Objectively, this is false, for the scream was uttered by the old man. But subjectively, in the unconscious merging of himself and his victim, that cry was his own. And then at the end of the story another sound is to be identified, the beating of the tell-tale heart. By an amazing stroke, Poe brings in a detail that makes the story, if taken on a literal, realistic plane, patently absurd; but which, if interpreted for its psychological significance, becomes a brilliant climax to the hidden drama that has been unfolding. The ever-louder heartbeats heard by the criminal, are they, as he says, the sound of the beating of the old man's heart, that old man whose corpse has been dismembered and concealed under the planking in the room? Certainly not—on the plane of realistic and objective fact. It is the "hideous heart" of the criminal himself which he hears. But if we remember that the criminal sought his own death in that of his victim, and that he had in effect become the man who now lies dead, then what he tells the police is true. His conscious purpose was to lie to them about the earlier scream, but then, unconsciously, he told the truth. Now, consciously, he attempts to tell the truth, and this time he is unconsciously in error. And inevitably so. For his consciousness, his very being, had become intrinsicate with that of the man he killed, and with the extinction of his victim the power to separate illusion from reality became extinct in him and his madness was complete.

E. Arthur Robinson (essay date 1965)

SOURCE: "Poe's 'The Tell-Tale Heart'," in *Nineteenth-Century Fiction,* Vol. 19, No. 4, March, 1965, pp. 369-78.

[*In the following essay, Robinson discusses the principles of thematic repetition and variation of incident in "The Tell-Tale Heart" and demonstrates how the story's two major themes—the psychological handling of time and the narrator's identification with his victim—are dramatized in Poe's other works.*]

Poe's **"The Tell-Tale Heart"** consists of a monologue in which an accused murderer protests his sanity rather than his innocence. The point of view is the criminal's, but the

tone is ironic in that his protestation of sanity produces an opposite effect upon the reader. From these two premises stem multiple levels of action in the story. The criminal, for example, appears obsessed with defending his psychic self at whatever cost, but actually his drive is self-destructive since successful defense upon either implied charge—of murder or of criminal insanity—automatically involves admission of guilt upon the other.

Specifically, the narrator bases his plea upon the assumption that madness is incompatible with systematic action, and as evidence of his capacity for the latter he relates how he has executed a horrible crime with rational precision. He reiterates this argument until it falls into a pattern: "If still you think me mad, you will think so no longer when I describe the wise precautions I took for concealment of the body."[1] At the same time he discloses a deep psychological confusion. Almost casually he admits lack of normal motivation: "Object there was none. Passion there was none. I loved the old man." Yet in spite of this affection he says that the idea of murder "haunted me day and night." Since such processes of reasoning tend to convict the speaker of madness, it does not seem out of keeping that he is driven to confession by "hearing" reverberations of the still-beating heart in the corpse he has dismembered, nor that he appears unaware of the irrationalities in his defense of rationality.

At first reading, the elements of **"The Tell-Tale Heart"** appear simple: the story itself is one of Poe's shortest; it contains only two main characters, both unnamed, and three indistinguishable police officers; even the setting of the narration is left unspecified. In the present study my object is to show that beneath its narrative flow the story illustrates the elaboration of design which Poe customarily sought, and also that it contains two of the major psychological themes dramatized in his longer works.

It is important to note that Poe's theory of art emphasizes development almost equally with unity of effect. There must be, he insists, "a repetition of purpose," a "dropping of the water upon the rock;"[2] thus he calls heavily upon the artist's craftsmanship to devise thematic modifications of the "preconceived effect." A favorite image in his stories is that of arabesque ornamentation with repetitive design. In **"The Tell-Tale Heart"** one can distinguish several such recurring devices filling out the "design" of the tale, the most evident being what the narrator calls his "over acuteness of the senses." He incorporates this physical keenness into his plea of sanity: ". . . why *will* you say that I am mad? The disease had sharpened my senses—not destroyed, not dulled them. Above all was the sense of hearing acute." He likens the sound of the old man's heart to the ticking of a watch "enveloped in cotton" and then fancies that its terrified beating may arouse the neighbors. His sensitivity to sight is equally disturbing, for it is the old man's eye, "a pale blue eye, with a film over it," which first vexed him and which he seeks to destroy. Similar though less extreme powers are ascribed to the old man. For example, the murderer congratulates himself that not even his victim could have detected anything wrong with the floor which has been replaced over the body, and earlier he imagines the old man, awakened by "the first slight noise," listening to determine whether the sound has come from an intruder or "the wind in the chimney." Variations such as these give the sensory details a thematic significance similar to that of the "morbid acuteness of the senses" of Roderick Usher in **"The Fall of the House of Usher"** or the intensity with which the victim of the Inquisition hears, sees, and smells his approaching doom in **"The Pit and the Pendulum."**

These sensory data provide the foundation for an interesting psychological phenomenon in the story. As the characters listen in the darkness, intervals of strained attention are prolonged until the effect resembles that of slow motion. Thus for seven nights the madman enters the room so "very, very slowly" that it takes him an hour to get his head through the doorway; as he says, "a watch's minute-hand moves more quickly than did mine." When on the eighth might the old man is alarmed, "for a whole hour I did not move a muscle." Later he is roused to fury by the man's terror, but "even yet," he declares, "I refrained and kept still. I scarcely breathed." On different nights both men sit paralyzed in bed, listening for terrors real or imagined. After the murder is completed, "I placed my hand upon the heart and held it there many minutes." In the end it seems to his overstrained nerves that the police officers linger inordinately in the house, chatting and smiling, until he is driven frantic by their cheerful persistence.

This psychological process is important to **"The Tell-Tale Heart"** in two ways. First, reduplication of the device gives the story structural power. Poe here repeats a dominating impression at least seven times in a brief story. Several of the instances mentioned pertain to plot, but others function to emphasize the former and to provide aesthetic satisfaction. To use Poe's words, "by such means, with such care and skill, a picture is at length painted which leaves in the mind of him who contemplates it with a kindred art, a sense of the fullest satisfaction. The idea of the tale, its thesis, has been presented unblemished. . . ."[3] Here Poe is speaking specifically of "skilfully-constructed tales," and the complementary aspects of technique described are first to omit extraneous material and second to combine incidents, tone, and style to develop the "pre-established design." In this manner, form and "idea" become one. The thematic repetition and variation of incident in **"The Tell-Tale Heart"** offer one of the clearest examples of this architectural principle of Poe's at work.

Second, this slow-motion technique intensifies the subjectivity of **"The Tell-Tale Heart"** beyond that attained by mere use of a narrator. In the psychological triad of stimulus, internal response, and action, the first and third elements are slighted and the middle stage is given exaggerated attention.[4] In **"The Tell-Tale Heart,"** stimulus in an objective sense scarcely exists at all. Only the man's eye motivates the murderer, and that almost wholly through his internal reaction to it. The action too, though decisive, is quickly over: "In an instant I dragged him to the floor, and pulled the heavy bed over him." In contrast, the intermediate, subjective experience is prolonged to a point

where psychologically it is beyond objective measurement. At first the intervals receive conventional description—an "hour," or "many minutes"—but eventually such designations become meaningless and duration can be presented only in terms of the experience itself. Thus, in the conclusion of the story, the ringing in the madman's ears first is "fancied," then later becomes "distinct," then is discovered to be so "definite" that it is erroneously accorded external actuality, and finally grows to such obsessive proportions that it drives the criminal into an emotional and physical frenzy. Of the objective duration of these stages no information is given; the experience simply "continued" until "at length" the narrator "found" that its quality had changed.

Through such psychological handling of time Poe achieves in several of his most effective stories, including **"The Tell-Tale Heart,"** two levels of chronological development which are at work simultaneously throughout the story. Typically, the action reaches its most intense point when the relation between the objective and subjective time sense falters or fails. At this point too the mental world of the subject is at its greatest danger of collapse. Thus we have the mental agony of the bound prisoner who loses all count of time as he alternately swoons and lives intensified existence while he observes the slowly descending pendulum. The narrator in **"The Pit and the Pendulum"** specifically refuses to accept responsibility for objective time-correlations: "There was another interval of insensibility; it was brief; for, upon again lapsing into life, there had been no perceptible descent in the pendulum. But it might have been long; for I knew there were demons who took note of my swoon, and who could have arrested the vibration at pleasure."[5] These demons are his Inquisitional persecutors, but more subjective "demons" are at work in the timeless terror and fascination of the mariner whirled around the abyss in **"The Descent into the Maelström,"** or the powerless waiting of Usher for days after he first hears his sister stirring within the tomb. In each instance the objective world has been reduced to the microcosm of an individual's experience; his time sense fades under the pressure of emotional stress and physical paralysis.

Even when not literally present, paralysis often may be regarded as symbolic in Poe's stories. In *The Narrative of Arthur Gordon Pym* (1838), Pym's terrifying dreams in the hold of the ship represent physical and mental paralysis: "Had a thousand lives hung upon the movement of a limb or the utterance of a syllable, I could have neither stirred nor spoken. . . . I felt that my powers of body and mind were fast leaving me."[6] Other examples are the "convolutions" of bonds about the narrator in **"The Pit and the Pendulum,"** the death-grasp on the ring-bolt in **"The Descent into the Maelström,"** the inaction of Roderick and (more literally) the catalepsy of Madeline Usher, and in part the supposed rationality of the madman in **"The Tell-Tale Heart,"** which turns out to be subservience of his mental to his emotional nature. In most applications of the slow-motion technique in **"The Tell-Tale Heart,"** three states of being are present concurrently: emotional tension, loss of mental grasp upon the actualities of the situation, and inability to act or to act deliberately. Often these conditions both invite and postpone catastrophe, with the effect of focusing attention upon the intervening experience.

In the two years following publication of **"The Tell-Tale Heart,"** Poe extended this timeless paralysis to fantasies of hypnosis lasting beyond death. **"Mesmeric Revelation"** (1844) contains speculations about the relation between sensory experience and eternity. In **"The Facts in the Case of M. Valdemar"** (1845) the hypnotized subject is maintained for nearly seven months in a state of suspended "death" and undergoes instant dissolution when revived. His pleading for either life or death suggests that his internal condition had included awareness and suffering. Similarly the narrator in **"The Tell-Tale Heart"** records: "Oh God! what *could* I do? I foamed—I raved—I swore!"—while all the time the police officers notice no foaming nor raving, for still they "chatted pleasantly, and smiled." His reaction is still essentially subjective, although he paces the room and grates his chair upon the boards above the beating heart. All these experiences move toward ultimate collapse, which is reached in **"The Tell-Tale Heart"** as it is for Usher and the hypnotized victims, while a last-moment reprieve is granted in **"The Pit and the Pendulum"** and **"The Descent into the Maelström."**

A second major theme in **"The Tell-Tale Heart"** is the murderer's psychological identification with the man he kills. Similar sensory details connect the two men. The vulture eye which the subject casts upon the narrator is duplicated in the "single dim ray" of the lantern that falls upon his own eye; like the unshuttered lantern, it is always one eye that is mentioned, never two. One man hears the creaking of the lantern hinge, the other the slipping of a finger upon the fastening. Both lie awake at midnight "hearkening to the death-watches in the wall." The loud yell of the murderer is echoed in the old man's shriek, which the narrator, as though with increasing clairvoyance, later tells the police was his own. Most of all the identity-is implied in the key psychological occurrence in the story—the madman's mistaking his own heartbeat for that of his victim, both before and after the murder.

These two psychological themes—the indefinite extension of subjective time and the psychic merging of killer and killed—are linked closely together in the story. This is illustrated in the narrator's commentary after he has awakened the old man by an incautious sound and each waits for the other to move:

> Presently I heard a slight groan, and I knew it was the groan of mortal terror. It was not a groan of pain or of grief—oh, no!—it was the low stifled sound that arises from the bottom of the soul when overcharged with awe. I knew the sound well. Many a night, just at midnight, when all the world slept, it has welled up from my own bosom, deepening, with its dreadful echo, the terrors that distracted me. I say I knew it well. I knew that he had been lying awake ever since the first slight noise, when he had turned in the bed. His fears had been ever since growing upon him. He had been trying to fancy them causeless, but could not.

He had been saying to himself—"It is nothing but the wind in the chimney—it is only a mouse crossing the floor," or "it is merely a cricket which has made a single chirp." Yes, he had been trying to comfort himself with these suppositions: but he had found all in vain.

Here the slow-motion technique is applied to both characters, with emphasis upon first their subjective experience and second the essential identity of that experience. The madman feels compelled to delay the murder until his subject is overcome by the same nameless fears that have possessed his own soul. The groan is an "echo" of these terrors within. The speaker has attempted a kind of catharsis by forcing his own inner horror to arise in his companion and then feeding his self-pity upon it. This pity cannot prevent the murder, which is a further attempt at exorcism. The final two sentences of the paragraph quoted explain why he believes that destruction is inevitable:

> *All in vain;* because Death, in approaching him, had stalked with his black shadow before him, and enveloped the victim. And it was the mournful influence of the unperceived shadow that caused him to feel—although he neither saw nor heard—to *feel* the presence of my head within the room.

The significance of these sentences becomes clearer when we consider how strikingly the over-all effect of time-extension in **"The Tell-Tale Heart"** resembles that produced in Poe's **"The Colloquy of Monos and Una,"** published two years earlier. In Monos's account of dying and passing into eternity, he prefaces his final experience with a sensory acuteness similar to that experienced by the narrator in **"The Tell-Tale Heart."** "The senses were unusually active," Monos reports, "though eccentrically so. . . ." As the five senses fade in death, they are not utterly lost but merge into a sixth—of simple duration:

> Motion in the animal frame had fully ceased. No muscle quivered; no nerve thrilled; no artery throbbed. But there seems to have sprung up in the brain . . . a mental pendulous pulsation. . . . By its aid I measured the irregularities of the clock upon the mantel, and of the watches of the attendants. . . . And this—this keen, perfect, self-existing sentiment of *duration* . . . this sixth sense, upspringing from the ashes of the rest, was the first obvious and certain step of the intemporal soul upon the threshold of the temporal Eternity.[7]

Likewise the old man in **"The Tell-Tale Heart"** listens as though paralyzed, unable either to move or to hear anything that will dissolve his fears. This resembles Monos' sensory intensity and the cessation of "motion in the animal frame." Also subjective time is prolonged, becomes partially divorced from objective measurement, and dominates it. The most significant similarity comes in the conclusion of the experience. The old man does not know it but he is undergoing the same dissolution as Monos. He waits in vain for his fear to subside because actually it is "Death" whose shadow is approaching him, and "it was the mournful influence of that shadow that caused him to feel" his destroyer within the room. Like Monos, beyond his normal senses he has arrived at a "sixth sense," which is at first duration and then death.

But if the old man is nearing death so too must be the narrator, who has felt the same "mortal terror" in his own bosom. This similarity serves to unify the story. In Poe's tales, extreme sensitivity of the senses usually signalizes approaching death, as in the case of Monos and of Roderick Usher. This "over acuteness" in **"The Tell-Tale Heart,"** however, pertains chiefly to the murderer, while death comes to the man with the "vulture eye." By making the narrator dramatize his feelings in the old man, Poe draws these two motifs together. We must remember, writes one commentator upon the story, "that the criminal sought his own death in that of his victim, and that he had in effect become the man who now lies dead."[8] Symbolically this is true. The resurgence of the beating heart shows that the horrors within himself, which the criminal attempted to identify with the old man and thus destroy, still live. In the death of the old man he sought to kill a part of himself, but his "demons" could not be exorcised through murder, for he himself is their destined victim.

From this point of view, the theme of **"The Tell-Tale Heart"** is self-destruction through extreme subjectivity marked paradoxically by both an excess of sensitivity and temporal solipsism. How seriously Poe could take this relativity of time and experience is evident in the poetic philosophy of his *Eureka* (1849). There time is extended almost infinitely into the life-cycle of the universe, but that cycle itself is only one heartbeat of God, who is the ultimate subjectivity. Romantically, indeed, Poe goes even further in the conclusion to *Eureka* and sees individual man becoming God, enclosing reality within himself, and acting as his own creative agent. In this state, distinction between subjective and objective fades: "the sense of individual identity will be gradually merged in the general consciousness."[9] Destruction then becomes self-destruction, the madman and his victim being aspects of the same universal identity. Death not only is self-willed but takes on some of the sanctity of creative and hence destructive Deity. The heartbeat of the red slayer and the slain merge in Poe's metaphysical speculations as well as in the denouement of a horror story.

This extreme subjectivity, moreover, leaves the ethical problem of **"The Tell-Tale Heart"** unresolved. In the opening paragraph of the story is foreshadowed an issue of good and evil connected with the speaker's madness: "I heard all things in the heaven and in the earth. I heard many things in hell. How, then, am I mad?" To be dramatically functional such an issue must be related to the murder. The only outward motivation for the murder is irritation at the "vulture eye." It is the evil of the eye, not the old man (whom he "loved"), that the murderer can no longer live with, and to make sure that it is destroyed he will not kill the man while he is sleeping. What the "Evil Eye" represents that it so arouses the madman we do not know, but since he sees himself in his companion the result is self-knowledge. Vision becomes insight, the "Evil Eye" an evil "I," and the murdered man a victim sacrificed to a self-constituted deity. In this story, we have undeveloped hints of the self-abhorrence uncovered in **"William Wilson"** and **"The Imp of the Perverse."**

Poe also has left unresolved the story's ultimate degree of subjectivity. No objective setting is provided; so completely subjective is the narration that few or no points of alignment with the external world remain. From internal evidence, we assume the speaker to be mad, but whether his words constitute a defense before some criminal tribunal or the complete fantasy of a madman there is no way of ascertaining.[10] The difference, however, is not material, for the subjective experience, however come by, *is* the story. Psychologically, the lengthening concentration upon internal states of being has divorced the murderer first from normal chronology and finally from relationship with the "actual" world. The result, in Beach's words, is "disintegration of the psychological complex." The victim images himself as another and recoils from the vision. Seeing and seen eye become identical and must be destroyed.

Notes

[1] "The Tell-Tale Heart," *Works,* ed. Clarence Edmund Stedman and George Edward Woodberry (New York, 1914), II, 70. Unless otherwise specified, all quotations from Poe are from this edition.

[2] "Hawthorne's 'Tales'," *Works,* VII, 37.

[3] "Twice-Told Tales," *Selected Writings of Edgar Allan Poe,* ed. Edward H. Davidson (Boston, 1956), p. 448.

[4] Joseph Warren Beach in *The Twentieth-Century Novel* (New York, 1932), p. 407, describes a similar effect in stream-of-consciousness writing: "The subjective element becomes noticeable in fiction, as in everyday psychology, when an interval occurs between the stimulus to action and the resulting act." In extreme application of this technique, he declares, "there is a tendency to exhaust the content of the moment presented, there is *an infinite expansion of the moment,*" and he adds that the danger is that "there may come to pass a disintegration of the psychological complex, a divorce between motive and conduct" (p. 409). This is close to the state of Poe's narrator and murderer.

[5] *Works,* I, 241-242.

[6] *Works,* V, 38.

[7] *Works,* I, 120-121.

[8] Patrick F. Quinn, *The French Face of Edgar Poe* (Carbondale, Illinois, 1957), p. 236. Quinn makes this identity the theme of the story, without describing the full sensory patterns upon which it is based.

[9] *Works,* IX, 164-169.

[10] Despite lack of objective evidence, "The Tell-Tale Heart" bears much resemblance to a dream. The narrator acknowledges that the murdered man's shriek was such as occurs in dreams, and his memory of approaching the old man's bed upon eight successive midnights has the quality of a recurring nightmare. Poe frequently couples madness and dreaming, often with the variant "opium dreams," as in "Ligeia" and "The Fall of the House of Usher." "The Black Cat," a companion piece published the same year as

"The Tell-Tale Heart" (1843), opens with an explicit denial of both madness and dreaming. The introductory paragraph of "Eleonora" (1842) runs the complete course of madness—dreams—death—good and evil: "Men have called me mad; but the question is not yet settled, whether madness is or is not the loftiest intelligence: whether much that is glorious, whether all that is profound, does not spring from disease of thought—from *moods* of mind exalted at the expense of the general intellect. They who dream by day are cognizant of many things which escape those who dream only by night. In their gray visions they obtain glimpses of eternity, and thrill, in awaking, to find that they have been upon the verge of the great secret. In snatches, they learn something of the wisdom which is of good, and more of the mere knowledge which is of evil" (*Works*, I, 96).

James W. Gargano (essay date 1968)

SOURCE: "The Theme of Time in 'The Tell-Tale Heart'," in *Studies in Short Fiction*, Vol. 5, No. 4, Summer, 1968, pp. 378-82.

[*In the following essay, Gargano analyzes the symbolism in "The Tell-Tale Heart" and contends that the images in the tale point to the fact that, unbeknownst to the narrator, his real foe is not Death, but Time.*]

The critic who wishes to read Edgar Allan Poe's **"The Tell-Tale Heart"** as a mere horror story may be content to accept its incidents as unmotivated and mysterious. How, the critic may argue, can the story be rationally explained when the narrator himself is at a loss to account for the frenzy inspired in him by his victim's "evil eye?" The critic may further maintain that Poe deliberately establishes and enhances the mystery of his tale by having the murderer eschew all explanations for his deed: "Object there was none. Passion there was none. I loved the old man." The critic may conclude that Poe waives logical and realistic considerations and simply sets out to make his reader feel the terror that comes from observing the unfolding of an inexplicable crime.[1]

Yet, there are two irresistible reasons for believing that Poe's purpose in **"The Tell-Tale Heart"** goes beyond the concoction of horror and mystification. First of all, he has artfully complicated his tale by making the narrator's description of himself and his actions appear unreliable. Ironically, the protagonist attempts to prove in language that is wild and disordered that he is methodical, calm, and sane. In addition, though he persuades himself that he felt no "passion" against the old man, he talks frequently of his "fury," "anxiety," and "uncontrollable terror." Secondly, Poe has built into his tale a set of internally consistent symbols that are charged with meaning. The structure of the story contains so much arrangement that it becomes almost impossible to view the pattern and accumulated force of the symbols as accidental.

If we approach **"The Tell-Tale Heart"** without traditional blinders, I am convinced that it will reveal itself to be a well-organized and thoughtful work of art with a striking economy of images and symbols. I believe, however, that

any serious analysis of the story must recognize a basic irony: that the narrator, though he does not understand his own character or actions, unconsciously provides all the clues necessary to a comprehension of them. Obviously, for all his acuteness and the "fine art" of his crime, Poe's protagonist increasingly demonstrates, with every vain denial, that he is mad. Moreover, in ascribing strangely revolting powers to someone outside himself, he reveals that his revulsion is a symptom of his own internal disorder. Finally, in focusing his violence against one man, he makes known that he is rebelling against the very terms on which life is granted to all men. In his rage against the nature of things, he resembles Prince Prospero, who immures himself in a castle fortified against death, and William Wilson, who tries one of the most amazing (and perhaps common) of all experiments—to repudiate a part of his own being.

An analysis of the symbolism of **"The Tell-Tale Heart"** will, I hope, identify the narrator's ultimate antagonist as the force that will inevitably cause him to resemble the old man with the appalling "eye of a vulture." His quarrel, then, is not with a ravaged individual but with Time, which on one level is symbolized by the omnipresent "watches" and on another by the "tell-tale" heart. The revelatory moments in the tale, thus, occur when both sets of symbols merge and when the old man, after death, becomes inseparable from his murderer.

As many of his works show, Poe was infatuated with puzzles, hoaxes, and ironies. It seems a bit incongruous, then, to insist that his horror tales be taken as straightforward and artless examples of American Gothicism. For Poe, human thought and motive were often the tricky means of leading men into self-created labyrinths. Such men devise their own confusions and intellectually refine them into a crooked but convincing rationale. But the unperceived logic of their well-thought-out schemes coerces them into self-exposure and destruction because fundamentally their inner turmoil cannot be resolved through the specious "organization" of their actions. Indeed, the planned actions themselves not only fail to be curative but betray the original delusions which inspired them. In a real sense, Poe's characters often trap themselves in the most elaborate of fine-spun hoaxes.

"The Tell-Tale Heart" is, technically speaking, a ruse perpetrated by the protagonist against himself. His ingenious concealment and ritualized rehearsal of his deed, apparently directed against the old man, are practiced upon himself. His cherished plot is an escape from self-knowledge into an absorbing and distracting action; yet, in his careful stalking of his enemy, he suggests the basis of his psychological insecurity. His "structured" violence draws him on to talk of his compulsive obsession with images and sounds that evoke the rhythm of time. Finally, he completes his own entrapment when his irrational preoccupation with these images and sounds breaks down the impressive order he has imposed upon his machinations.

Poe's major strategy in working out his design is to have the narrator attribute his own anguished feelings to his victim. Therefore, because of their "common" emotions, the murderer and the old man appear to be not only related but identical. The barrier between their individual beings begins to break down when the old man, hearing someone at his chamber door, springs up in bed and cries out. At that moment, the narrator offers a remarkably precise interpretation of his intended victim's state of mind: he declares that the old man "was still sitting up in bed listening—*just as I have done, night after night,* hearkening to the death watches in the wall." (My italics.) Poe effectively implies that the only emotions experienced by the old man are sensations that have afflicted the protagonist night after night. In short, the narrator may be said to feel for both men; he has, even before murdering the old man, entered into and completely preëmpted his life. What he does not see, however, is that in possessing another man's being, he is in turn assimilated and consumed by it.

Poe devotes a large part of his short tale to the narrator's analysis of the old man's agony as death approaches; ironically, however, the brilliant schemer unconsciously characterizes his own long-standing derangement: "Many a night, just at midnight, when all the world slept, it [a groan like the old man's] has welled up, from my own bosom, deepening, with its dreadful echo, the terrors that distracted me." Clearly, he can trace the gradual intensification of the old man's dread because he, too, has been subject to it. He, like the old man, has tried to dismiss this dread as "causeless," only to find it invading and filling his mind until he acknowledged all resistance to it as "vain." He knows, because he has already uttered them, the very words with which the suffering man tries to comfort himself in his extremity: "He had been saying to himself—'It is nothing but the wind in the chimney—it is only a mouse crossing the floor,' or 'it is merely a cricket which has made a single chirp.'"

It is significant, then, that the narrator sees the old man's responses to the menaces of the night as identical to his own. Indeed, the intended victim becomes a kind of surrogate for his persecutor, a projection of his most ingrained terrors. All his irrational hates and fears are embodied in the man he wishes to destroy. He wildly assumes that by ridding himself of the external symbol of his dementia he will be able to free himself from his psychic troubles.

But, as I have stated, the narrator's dream of freedom is illusory because the pervasive villain of **"The Tell-Tale Heart"** is Time itself. Heard from the "death watches" in the wall and seen in the waiting and expectant "eye of a vulture," it subtly undermines the narrator's self-assurance. Indeed, he has become so obsessed by the sound of time that he hears it everywhere and in all things. There is a great deal of psychological meaning to be found in his feverish declaration: "Above all was the sense of hearing acute. I heard all things in the heaven and in the earth. I heard many things in hell." Listening to the old man's groan, he even hears in it "the low stifled sound that arises from the bottom of the soul." For the narrator, all the sounds are interrelated and one; moreover, they have their source in a haunted and bewildered imagination.

Poe allows the main character's concern with the tyranny of time to betray itself through the nature and organization of his fictional details. First, the object of the narrator's crime is not so much an individual man, but an old man made revolting by time. In addition, the watches, which are obviously symbols of time, have become part of the narrator's consciousness and even lurk within the walls of his house. Climactically, the incessant beating of the old man's heart locates the cadence of time within the center of man's being. As if to leave no doubt about the primary connection between the heart and the watches, Poe has the protagonist speak of them as if they gave forth the same sounds: "there came to my ears a low, dull, quick sound, such as a watch makes when enveloped in cotton. I knew *that* sound well, too. It was the beating of the old man's heart." It requires no imaginative daring, then, to conclude that the "low stifled sound that arises from the bottom of the soul" is also intimately related to the low, muffled sound of the cotton-enveloped watch. In short, when the narrator is betrayed by the still-beating heart of his dead victim, he is really betrayed by the triumphant din of time, which is the sum of all sounds, within and outside of man.

Expertly as Poe manages the "sound images" in **"The Tell-Tale Heart,"** he displays equal skill in making the old man's "evil eye" the external counterpart of the hidden watches and the beating heart. To begin with, the eye's similarity to a vulture's suggests the predatoriness of "Father Time." Moreover, the relation of the eye to the theme of time is further shown by the sequence of events leading up to the murder. On the fateful night, the protagonist cannot go ahead with his crime until he has trained the rays of his lamp upon the eye; "Chilled [to] the very marrow in my bones" by the sight of "the damned spot," he becomes preternaturally sensitive to sound. In the still moment before he leaps upon and kills the old man, he tries to "maintain the ray upon the eye." It is then that the "hellish tattoo of the heart increased." The inextricable association of the eye and the heart (and by extension of the watches) is most effectively established once the old man is dead; the criminal now places his hand over the heart and, feeling no "pulsation," calmly asserts, "His eye would trouble me no more."

Of course, the narrator's intellectually flawless plot cannot overcome the subtle and radical forces that pursue him, for reason used for a foolish end is essentially unreasonable. Action, no matter how decisive and organized, dissipates into futility when it expends itself against eternal obstacles. The narrator naively persists in thinking that his foe is external and mortal when, in fact, he represents an immutable law of life. Consequently, no amount of intellectualized cunning will stop the old man's heart because, as the dénouement of the story proves, the old man's heart beats within the protagonist himself as well as in the walls and beneath the planks of the floor.

The major irony of **"The Tell-Tale Heart"** is that the narrator, like William Wilson, is crushed by, but never understands the meaning of, his experience. He does not know that his disgust at the old man's eye is merely a symptom of a more serious disease. Clearly revealed in his hallucinations, which are more "real" than his reasoning, this disease can be diagnosed as his refusal to accept himself as a creature caught in the temporal net. He cannot acknowledge the limitations that bind him to the earth and time, the limitations that wither, corrupt, and destroy. Like so many of his confrères in Poe's other tales, he wishes, essentially, to transcend his human limitations: one can almost imagine him echoing Ligeia's hope that "Man does not yield him to the angels, *nor unto death utterly, save only through the weakness of his feeble will.*" Yet, perversely, the only means he can employ to attain his ends inevitably act as agents of doom.

His misguided intellect and the ingenious schemes it hatches set him more firmly on the path he strives to avoid. For a brief interval after he has committed his crime, he mistakenly imagines that he has gained security and inward peace by the "wise precautions" he has taken in disposing of the old man's corpse. It is not long, however, before his solid assurance disintegrates. Once again, the fantastic sound to which all sounds attune themselves begins its heart-like, watch-like rhythm: "the sound increased—what could I do? It was *a low, dull, quick sound—much such a sound as a watch makes when enveloped in cotton.*" (Poe's italics.) The narrator's reliance on his spurious and concocted order collapses as he shrieks out his confession to the police and helplessly and ignorantly submits to the ceaseless and measured flow of time.

Notes

[1] There have been very few extended or illuminating critical analyses of "The Tell-Tale Heart." Most critics sum it up in a phrase or two, or, like William Bittner, *Poe: A Biography* (Boston, 1962) and Edward Wagenknecht, *Edgar Allan Poe: The Man Behind the Mask* (New York, 1963) seem to assume that the story is self-explanatory. One of Poe's best early critics, George Woodberry, formulistically refers to "The Tell-Tale Heart" as a "tale of conscience," *Edgar Allan Poe* (Boston, 1885), p. 186. In a fuller treatment of the story, Arthur Hobson Quinn mentions the "clock imagery" and the evil eye; he even declares that the effect of Poe's tale is heightened by the fact that the narrator "has himself suffered causeless terrors in the night," *Edgar Allan Poe: A Critical Biography* (New York, 1941), p. 394. Quinn, however, concerns himself with the "effect" rather than the meaning of Poe's work. Edward H. Davidson's insights into "The Tell-Tale Heart" are invariably interesting and perceptive. In *Poe: A Critical Study* (Cambridge, 1957), he sees the narrator as someone who "commits a crime because of the excess of emotion over intelligence; [someone who] is impelled to give himself up and pay the death penalty because he may thereby return to selfhood or primal being" (p. 203). I agree with Davidson that the narrator is deluded and invites his own destruction, but I feel, finally, that Davidson does not consider the nuances of Poe's story in arriving at his statement of the theme (pp. 188-189). By far the best intensive study of Poe's tale is E. Arthur Robinson's "Poe's 'The Tell-Tale Heart,'" *Nineteenth-Century Fiction*, XIX (March, 1965), 369-378. Although Robinson dwells on the "murderer's psychological identification with the man he kills," he does not significantly relate the Evil Eye and the omnipresent watches. Essentially, Robinson's brilliant essay is preoccupied with Poe's "slow-motion technique" and not with theme.

John E. Reilly (essay date 1969)

SOURCE: "The Lesser Death-Watch and 'The Tell-Tale Heart'," in *American Transcendental Quarterly*, Vol. 2, Second Quarter, 1969, pp. 3-9.

[*In the following essay, Reilly asserts that the narrator of "The Tell-Tale Heart" is a paranoid schizophrenic who really hears the rapping of the death-watch insect (a species of beetle or louse which makes a noise that is said to presage death), which he mistakes for the beating of the old man's heart.*]

Poe's **"The Tell-Tale Heart"** is a genuine mystery story, one which thus far has eluded satisfactory solution. The mystery surrounds the source of the sound which drove Poe's deranged narrator to murder an old man and subsequently to reveal both the crime and his own guilt to the police. The narrator himself believes the sound to have been the heart of his victim beating even after his dismembered body had been concealed beneath the floor boards of his bedchamber. Most commentators upon the tale identify the sound either as an hallucination or as the narrator's misapprehension of his own heart beat.[1] Only one commentator feels that the sound was indeed that of the old man's heart, first heard in fact and then "pounding in the murderer's ears after the man was dead."[2] Although any of these answers may seem to satisfy, they really only raise a still larger question, a crucial critical one involving the artistry of the tale itself. This larger question stems from the narrator's repeated insistence upon his acuteness of hearing. "The disease," he tells us of himself at the opening of the story, "had sharpened my senses—not destroyed—not dulled them. Above all was the sense of hearing acute."[3] "And have I not told you," he reiterates, "that what you mistake for madness is but over acuteness of the senses?" He describes what he heard or believes he heard, both before and after the murder, to have been "a low, dull, quick sound, such as a watch makes when enveloped in cotton."[4] Moreover, he insists that this sound originated outside of him. It "came to my ears," he says before murdering the old man; "the noise was *not* within my ears," he insists as he describes himself sitting over the dismembered body chatting with the police. If in fact he heard something other than his own heart, then what was it? If he really heard nothing, if it was only an hallucination, then why did Poe, who advocated economy in the short story, dwell in this, one of his shortest stories, upon the apparently inconsequential detail of his narrator's acuteness of hearing?

It is possible, of course, that the narrator's acuteness is as much a delusion as the sound may have been an hallucination. If this is true, then the question of artistry is forestalled. For if Poe left us with a narrator whose reliability cannot be measured against what really transpired on the night of the murder, much can be said about **"The Tell-Tale Heart,"** but little can be concluded.[5] The purpose of the present paper is to demonstrate that much can be concluded because the narrator is reliable at least to the extent that there was present in the old house where the murder took place a watch-like sound resembling the one the narrator describes, a sound he misapprehended to have been the heart beat of the old man. The presence of this sound establishes the extent of the narrator's reliability and helps to identify the nature of his malady. Furthermore, the source of the sound not only enhances our recognition of the ironic dimension of the narrative, but it renders **"The Tell-Tale Heart,"** as Arthur Hobson Quinn divined even in the absence of corroborative evidence, "an almost perfect illustration of Poe's own theory of the short story, for every word contributes to the central effect."[6]

I

Poe's narrator boasts that for seven nights preceding the murder, he had quietly edged into the old man's bedchamber just at midnight to peer at his sleeping victim with the aid of a lantern and that he had followed each surreptitious visit with a cheerful morning call. When he crept into the room on the eighth and fatal night, however, he fumbled with the tin fastening on his lantern. Startled by the sound, the old man sprang up and remained for an hour "sitting up in the bed listening," the narrator tells us, "just as I have done, night after night, hearkening to the death watches in the wall." It should be noted that it was not the old man who was listening to the death-watches, for he was trying to determine what made the noise produced by the tin fastening on the narrator's lantern, and the narrator imagines that the old man attributed the sound of the fastening to "a mouse crossing the floor" or "a cricket which has made a single chirp." It is the narrator, giving us a glimpse of himself alone in his own bedchamber, who has hearkened to the death-watches. Herein lies the source of the sound which the narrator believes to have been the heart beat of the old man.

Death-watches are insects which produce rapping sounds, sounds which superstition has held to presage the death of someone in the house where they are heard. There are two common varieties of the insect.[7] The "greater" death-watch, or *Xestobium rufovillosum*, is a wood boring beetle of the family *Anobiidae*. It has also been called *Anobium tesselatum* and *Scarabaeus galeatus pulsator*. The sound of the greater death-watch, presumably a mating call, is made by the rapping of its head upon whatever surface it is standing; and although it probably would go unnoticed against the background noise of waking hours, the rapping is sufficiently loud to be heard in the stillness of the night. The other insect, the "lesser" deathwatch, or *Liposcelis divinatorius*, is a louse-like *psocid* which thrives upon molds. It is commonly called *Atropos divinatoria*, but has also been called *Pediculus pulsatorius* and book louse. Much smaller than the bettle, the lesser death-watch emits a faint ticking sound believed to be produced by means of stridulatory organs.[8]

On the basis of the sound described by Poe's narrator, the insect in **"The Tell-Tale Heart"** is the lesser rather than the greater death-watch. The rapping of the greater death-watch bears little resemblance to the "low, dull, quick sound, such as a watch makes when enveloped in cotton." The rapping of the greater death-watch resembles instead the drumming of a pencil in irregularly occurring episodes

of six to eight beats. The sound of the lesser death-watch, on the other hand, is faint (and thereby appropriate to the narrator's acuteness of hearing), regular, and sustained over a period of hours. Most appropriately, however, it resembles the ticking of a watch, and it has often been described in precisely these terms. Among the "vulgar and common errors" which Sir Thomas Browne sought to dispel in his *Pseudodoxia Epidemica* (1646) is the melancholy superstition associated with "the noise of the Dead-watch, that is, the little clickling sound heard often in many rooms, somewhat resembling that of a Watch."[9] Several decades later (1668), John Wilkins, Dean of Ripon, identified the "lesser" death-watch as an insect "of a *long slender body*, frequent about houses, making a noise like the *minute* of a *Watch*, by striking the bottom of his *breast* against his *belly*."[10] Evidently unaware of the distinction between the "greater" and the "lesser," Benjamin Allen contributed an essay to the *Philosophical Transactions of the Royal Society* (1698) in which he described the death-watch as a "beetle" which "makes a Noise resembling exactly that of a Watch."[11] A more accurate observer than Allen, the Reverend William Derham, submitted two studies to the *Philosophical Transactions* (1701 and 1704) carefully distinguishing the sounds emitted by the "two sorts" of insect: "The [greater] *Death-Watch* beateth only about 7 or 8 strokes at a time, and quicker: but [the lesser] will beat some hours together, without intermission; and his strokes are more leisurely, and like the Beats of a Watch." They are "even as loud almost as the strongest Beats of a Pocket-Watch," Derham adds at the close of his first account; and in his second account, he alludes once more to their "regular clicking noises (like the Beats of a Pocket-Watch)."[12] In Poe's own time, the resemblance was noted in the kind of popular and semi-popular scientific literature with which he was familiar. William Kirby and William Spence, for example, devote several pages of their *Introduction to Entomology* (London, 1828) to the lesser death-watch, "so called, because it emits a sound resembling the ticking of a watch, supposed to predict the death of some one of the family in the house in which it is heard."[13] Similarly, two treatises by James Rennie, *Insect Architecture* and *Insect Miscellanies*, rehearse the superstition attached to the death-watch and describe its sound as "resembling the ticking of a watch."[14] Originally published in England, Rennie's books were republished in Boston in the early 1830's as a part of the popular Library of Entertaining Knowledge.

There are, then, a number of sources from which Poe could have become acquainted with the sound of the lesser death-watch. Similarly, there were a number of precedents for his use of the death-watch in literature. For **"The Tell-Tale Heart"** by no means marked its debut. In the *Spectator* for March 8, 1711, Joseph Addison alluded to the death-watch in the course of depicting "an extravagant Cast of Mind" which in some ways curiously anticipates the morbid narrator of Poe's tale:

> I know a Maiden Aunt, of a great Family, who is one of these Antiquated *Sybils*, that forebodes and prophesies from one end of the Year to the other. She is always seeing Apparitions, and hearing Death-Watches; and was the other Day almost frighted out

of her Wits by the great House-Dog, that howled in the Stable at a time when she lay ill of the Tooth-ach. Such an extravagant Cast of Mind engages Multitudes of People, not only in impertinent Terrors, but in supernumerary Duties of Life, and arises from that Fear and Ignorance which are natural to the Soul of Man. The Horrour with which we entertain the Thoughts of Death (or indeed of any future Evil) and the Uncertainty of its Approach, fill a melancholy Mind with innumerable Apprehensions and Suspicions, and consequently dispose it to the Observation of such groundless Prodigies and Predictions. For as it is the chief Concern of Wise-Men, to retrench the Evils of Life by the Reasonings of Philosophy; it is the Employment of Fools, to multiply them by the Sentiments of Supersision.[15]

Among Addison's "Fools" is the bumpkin Grubbinol in John Gay's *The Shepherd's Week* (1714) who associates the sound of the death-watch with the demise of the fair damsel Blouzelind: "When *Blouzelind* expir'd, the weather's bell / Before the drooping flock toll'd forth her knell; / The solemn death-watch click'd the hour she dy'd, / And shrilling crickets in the chimney cry'd."[16]

Jonathan Swift (1725) prescribed a decisive antidote for both the death-watch and the effects of its supersitition:

The Third is an Insect we call a *Wood*-Worm,
That lies in old *Wood* like a Hare in her Form:
With Teeth or with Claws it will bite or will
    scratch,
And Chambermaids christen this Worm a Death-
    Watch:
Because like a Watch it always cries *Click:*
Then Woe be to those in the House who are sick:
For, as sure as a Gun they will give up the Ghost
If the Maggot cries *Click* when it scratches the
    Post.
But a Kettle of scalding hot Water injected,
Infallibly cures the Timber affected;
The Omen is broke, the Danger is over;
The Maggot will dye, and the Sick will recover.[17]

Oliver Goldsmith's *Citizen of the World* (December 17, 1760) reported the conversation of a splenetic English acquaintance whose melancholy deepened at the sound of the death-watch:

"I sate silent for some minutes, and soon perceiving the ticking of my watch beginning to grow noisy and troublesome, I quickly placed it out of hearing; and strove to resume my serenity. But the watchman soon gave me a second alarm. I had scarcely recovered from this, when my peace was assaulted by the wind at my window; and when that ceased to blow, I listened for death-watches in the wainscot. I now found my whole system discomposed, I strove to find a resource in philosophy and reason; but what could I oppose, or where direct my blow, when I could see no enemy to combat. I saw no misery approaching, nor knew any I had to fear, yet still I was miserable."[18]

Similarly, and in Poe's own time, John Keats warned his reader against the influence of the death-watch ("the bee-

tle") upon melancholy: "Make not your rosary of yew-berries, / Nor let the beetle, nor the death-moth be / Your mournful Psyche" ("Ode on Melancholy"). And after Poe, Twain's Tom Sawyer lay in his darkened room hearkening to sinister sounds, among which was the mournful message of the death-watch:

Everything was dismally still. By and by, out of the stillness, little, scarcely perceptible noises began to emphasize themselves. The ticking of the clock began to bring itself into notice. Old beams began to crack mysteriously. The stairs creaked faintly. Evidently spirits were abroad. A measured, muffled snore issued from Aunt Polly's chamber. And now the tiresome chirping of a cricket that no human ingenuity could locate, began. Next the ghastly ticking of a death-watch in the wall at the bed's head made Tom shudder—it meant that somebody's days were numbered.

(Chapter IX)[19]

II

Although the sound described by Poe's narrator resembles the ticking of the lesser death-watch, there are discrepancies. Whereas the narrator heard the sound on two occasions during the night of the murder, the ticking of the lesser death-watch is said to continue for hours. Moreover, the narrator reports that the sound he heard increased in tempo just before the murder and grew in volume on both occasions, whereas the ticking of the lesser death-watch is uniformly faint. These discrepancies, however, are neither liberties nor lapses on the part of Poe. They are, instead, an expression and a measure of his narrator's derangement.

All the evidence in the story points to the likelihood that the narrator is a victim of paranoid schizophrenia He is "very, very dreadfully nervous," fearful, anxious, moody, suspicious, and, of course, homicidally violent in his effort to preserve his well-being against what he believes to have been the threat of the old man's eye. Even more significant, "the disease" had "sharpened" his "senses—not destroyed—not dulled them. Above all was the sense of hearing acute." One of the frequent symptoms of paranoid schizophrenia is perceptual disturbance, a disturbance often assuming the form of hyperesthesia, specifically the kind of hyperacusis suffered by Poe's narrator.[20] Although the term paranoid schizophrenia is of recent coinage, the phenomenon of perceptual disturbance accompanying insanity was noted in Poe's time. In his *Practical Observations on Insanity* (Philadelphia, 1811), for example, Joseph Mason Cox included among the signs of approaching insanity "listening to fancied whispers or obscure noises" (p. 13), and he noted that some insane persons "are a prey to fear and dread from the most ridiculous and imaginary sources" (p. 15). Similarly, John Conolly, *An Inquiry Concerning the Indications of Insanity* (London, 1830), observed that among the "plainly legible" indications, "impairment of some of the senses is not uncommon; or an increased acuteness of sense, which is made a subject of boasting with the patient" (p. 463).[21] A student of psychopathological disorders and perhaps even a sufferer himself at certain periods in his life, Poe did not need a formal introduction to the phenomenon of perceptual disturbance in order to invest his narrator with the symptoms of paranoid schizophrenia.

The presence and absence of the sound during the night of the murder was not, then, a function of its source, the faint ticking of the lesser death-watch, but a function of the narrator's frame of mind which gave rise to hyperacusis. Significantly, on the two occasions when he heard the sound, but at no other point in the tale, the narrator's condition was one of extreme agitation, an agitation conveyed in the very texture of the prose. The narrator was calm when he edged into the bedchamber, and he remained calm for an "hour" even when his fumbling with the tin fastening on his lantern startled the old man. But his calm vanished when he saw the "dull blue" eye: "It was open—wide, wide open—and I grew furious as I gazed upon it." In the grip of this fury he heard the sound: "And have I not told you that what you mistake for madness is but over acuteness of the senses?—now, I say, there came to my ears a low, dull, quick sound, such as a watch makes when enveloped in cotton." He then had to struggle to remain silent and to hold the ray of his lantern on the old man's eye:

> Meantime the hellish tattoo of the heart increased. It grew quicker and quicker, and louder and louder every instant. The old man's terror *must* have been extreme! It grew louder, I say, louder every moment!—do you mark me well? I have told you that I am nervous: so I am. And now at the dead hour of the night, amid the dreadful silence of that old house, so strange a noise as this excited me to uncontrollable terror. Yet, for some minutes longer I refrained and stood still. But the beating grew louder, louder! I thought the heart must burst. And now a new anxiety seized me—the sound would be heard by a neighbour! The old man's hour had come!

Having purged his fury by killing the old man, the narrator regained his composure, and he ceased to hear the sound. Calmly and deliberately, he set about dismembering and concealing the corpse. Even when he received the police officers sent to investigate the old man's scream, he "was singularly at ease." But his ease left him as the officers lingered to chat in the very room where the corpse was concealed: "I felt myself getting pale and wished them gone. My head ached, and I fancied a ringing in my ears: but still they sat and still they chatted. The ringing became more distinct:—it continued and became more distinct: I talked more freely to get rid of the feeling: but it continued and gained definiteness—until, at length, I found that the noise was *not* within my ears." The initial sound, the ringing, marked the onset of anxiety, and the ringing gave way to the ticking sound as hyperacusis once again developed. At that point the narrator's anxiety mounted to rage as he desperately tried to cope with the noise:

> No doubt I now grew *very* pale;—but I talked more fluently, and with a heightened voice. Yet the sound increased—and what could I do? It was *a low, dull, quick sound—much such a sound as a watch makes*

when enveloped in cotton. I gasped for breath—and yet the officers heard it not. I talked more quickly—more vehemently; but the noise steadily increased. I arose and argued about trifles, in a high key and with violent gesticulations; but the noise steadily increased. Why *would* they not be gone? I paced the floor to and fro with heavy strides, as if excited to fury by the observations of the men—but the noise steadily increased. Oh God! what *could* I do? I foamed—I raved—I swore! I swung the chair upon which I had been sitting, and grated it upon the boards, but the noise arose over all and continually increased. It grew louder—louder— *louder!* And still the men chatted pleasantly, and smiled. Was it possible they heard not? Almighty God!—no, no! They heard! they suspected! they knew! they were making a mockery of my horror!—this I thought, and this I think. But anything was better than this agony! Anything was more tolerable than this derision! I could bear those hypocritical smiles no longer! I felt that I must scream or die! and now—again!—hark! louder! louder! louder! *louder!*

Just as he had purged his fury by killing the old man, so the narrator purged his rage by exposing what he believed was the hypocrisy of the police. The result was self-incrimination.

The hyperacusis accompanying paranoid schizophrenia accounts for the apparent presence and absence of the ticking of the lesser death-watch, but it does not account for variations in the tempo and volume of the sound as the narrator perceived it. The sound "grew quicker" as the moment of the old man's death approached, whereas the tempo of the lesser death-watch is uniform. An explanation for this apparent discrepancy has already been suggested in an essay on **"The Tell-Tale Heart"** by E. Arthur Robinson.[22] He notes (1) "two levels of chronological development" in the story, objective time or duration and "subjective time sense" or the narrator's consciousness of time, and (2) "the psychic merging of killer and killed," or the identification of the narrator with his victim. Although Professor Robinson's interest is in "the slow-motion technique" of the narrator's subjective time sense, a rapid-motion technique is equally possible, *i.e.,* the narrator's subjective sense of time accelerated the regular ticking of the lesser death-watch. This acceleration occurred appropriately when, through identifying with his victim, the narrator imagined that terror had caused the old man's heart to beat faster: "Meantime the hellish tattoo of the heart increased. It grew quicker and quicker, and louder and louder every instant. The old man's terror *must* have been extreme!" And just as the narrator's deranged subjectivity controlled the apparent tempo of the sound, so it controlled the volume of what was, in fact, a uniformly faint ticking, amplifying the sound as his agitation increased. The sound seemed to become so loud on the first occasion that the narrator feared a neighbor would hear it, and on the second occasion he was convinced that the police officers only pretended not to be aware.

Briefly, then, the faint ticking of the lesser death-watch was present in the old man's bedchamber throughout the night of the murder, but the narrator's perception of it was governed by the hyperacusis which occurred during his moments of extreme agitation. On both occasions when he heard the sound, his deranged imagination altered its volume and tempo and attributed its origin not to the insect but to the heart of the old man beating even after he had been murdered, dismembered, and concealed.

III

The identity of the lesser death-watch as the source of the sound which the narrator heard sheds light upon the strategy of **"The Tell-Tale Heart"** and the extent of Poe's achievement. The strategy is a classic example of irony, of the dramatic collision of appearance and reality. The reality is an unusual but perfectly natural situation: an old house infested by a common insect and occupied by two men, one old and evidently partially blind, the other insane. The appearance is the illusion of the situation created by the disturbed perceptions and deranged imagination of the narrator. What brings the story to life and renders it a species of mystery is that Poe chose to limit his readers' knowledge of the total situation, of both the appearance and the reality, to the report of the disordered consciousness. Hence, just as the strategy of **"The Tell-Tale Heart"** is a classic example of irony, so it is also a classic example of the kind of unreliable narration through which the reader must penetrate to discover the truth.

One of Poe's achievements in **"The Tell-Tale Heart"** is the special use he made of the phenomenon of acute perception. Although they have been unable to identify what the narrator heard, several commentators upon **"The Tell-Tale Heart"** have noted similarities between his insistence upon his acuteness of hearing and the acute sensibilities of characters in other stories by Poe, especially **"The Fall of the House of Usher"** (1839) and **"The Colloquy of Monos and Una"** (1841), both of which appeared in print before **"The Tell-Tale Heart"** (1843). But there is a crucial difference. Roderick, we assume, heard and correctly identified the sound of Madeline struggling to escape from the vault "lying, at great depth," beneath the house of Usher. And there is no reason to doubt that Monos correctly apprehended the reports of his acute synesthetic sensibilities in the period immediately following his death. The narrator of **"The Tell-Tale Heart,"** however, heard the faint ticking of the death-watch but misinterpreted the sound, distorted its meaning into terms of his deranged image of the world. This more complex and dramatic use of perceptual anomaly represents an enlarging of the psychological dimension of Poe's fiction.

But an even greater achievement in **"The Tell-Tale Heart"** is the exquisite appropriateness of the lesser death-watch to what Poe would call the moral or allegorical dimension of his story. Much of Poe's fiction and poetry participates in the romantic complaint against Time, the lament that the spirit of man is the victim of corruption and death. In **"The Tell-Tale Heart,"** the innocuous sound of an insect becomes a measure of time under the aspect of death, a kind of metaphor binding together three tokens of man's mortality: the process of nature, the beating of the human heart, and the ticking of a watch. And it is the agony of Poe's deranged and superstitious narrator to have hear-

kened to the sound, to have been driven to homicidal frenzy by a metaphor.

Notes

[1] See, for example, Arthur Hobson Quinn, *Edgar Allan Poe* (New York, 1941), p. 394; N. Bryllion Fagin, *The Histrionic Mr. Poe* (Baltimore, 1949), pp. 204-205; Patrick F. Quinn, *The French Face of Edgar Poe* (Carbondale, Ill., 1957), pp. 232-236; Harry Levin, *The Power of Blackness* (New York, 1960), pp. 145-146; and E. Arthur Robinson, "Poe's 'The Tell-Tale Heart,'" *Nineteenth-Century Fiction,* XIX (March, 1965), 369-378.

[2] Edward H. Davidson, *Poe: A Critical Study* (Cambridge, Mass., 1957), pp. 189-190.

[3] Passages quoted from the story are taken from *The Complete Works of Edgar Allan Poe,* ed. James A. Harrison (New York, 1902), V, 88-94.

[4] This is the narrator's description of the sound, in the Harrison edition of *The Complete Works,* as he heard it just before the murder. The narrator uses slightly different wording, quoted later in this paper, to describe the sound as he heard it in the presence of the police. In the initial publication of "The Tell-Tale Heart," in James Russell Lowell's *The Pioneer,* I (January, 1843), 29-31, the narrator employs identical wording to describe the sound he heard on both occasions: *"a low, dull, quick sound—much such a sound as a watch makes when enveloped in cotton."* Italics here, as in other passages in this paper taken from the story, are Poe's.

[5] E. Arthur Robinson, for example, finds the narration "so completely subjective" there is "no way of ascertaining" whether the narrator's words "constitute a defense before some criminal tribunal or the complete fantasy of a madman" (pp. 377-378).

[6] A. H. Quinn, p. 394.

[7] I wish to acknowledge the assistance of Dr. Emmanuel I. Sillman, Professor of Biology, Duquesne University, on technical aspects of the entomology of the death-watch.

For recent accounts of the greater death-watch, see British Ministry of Technology, *The Death-Watch Beetle,* Forest Products Research Laboratory Leaflet No. 4 (revised April, 1963); and Norman E. Hickin, *The Insect Factor in Wood Decay* (London, 1963), p. 111. For recent literature on the lesser death-watch, see E. A. Back, "Psocids in Dwellings," *Journal of Economic Entomology,* XXXII (June, 1939), 419-423.

[8] Among modern accounts of the ticking of the lesser death-watch, the most detailed is recorded in a controversy over the sound: Claude Morley, "Notes and Observations," *The Entomologist,* XLIII (1910), 31-32; and C. J. Gahan, "The Taps of the 'Death-Watch Beetle,'" *The Entomologist,* XLIII (1910), 84-87. I am especially indebted, however, to M. G. White of the Forest Products Research Laboratory of the British Ministry of Technology. In a letter to this author, Mr. White described oscillographic studies of the sound of the greater death-watch, showing that "each 'tap' comprises 6 to 8 knocks of the frons delivered at intervals of about 105 milliseconds with a tendency to accelerate to a 90 millisecond interval toward the end." The sound of the lesser death-watch, Mr. White adds, "is a continuous ticking rather like a wrist watch and is said

to go on for hours without a stop. The noise is much softer than that of *Xestobium* and is believed to be made by stridulatory organs."

[9] *The Works of Sir Thomas Browne,* ed. Geoffrey Keynes (Chicago, 1964), II, 150-151.

[10] John Wilkins, *An Essay Towards a Real Character, And a Philosophical Language* (London, 1668), p. 127.

[11] Benjamin Allen, "An Account of the *Scarabaeus Galeatus Pulsator,* or the Death-Watch; taken *August.* 1695," *Philosophical Transactions,* XX (1698), 376-378.

[12] "A Letter from the Reverend Mr *William Derham* to the Publisher, concerning an Insect that is commonly called the *Death-Watch," Philosophical Transactions,* XXII (1701), 832-834; and William Derham, "A Supplement to the account of the *Pediculus Pulsatorius,* or *Death-Watch," Philosophical Transactions,* XXIV (1704), 1586-1594.

[13] William Kirby and William Spence, *An Introduction to Entomology* (London, 1828), pp. 381-383.

[14] James Rennie, *Insect Architecture,* in The Library of Entertaining Knowledge (Boston, 1830), IV, 304-305; and *Insect Miscellanies,* in The Library of Entertaining Knowledge (Boston, 1832), XII, 98-102.

[15] *The Spectator,* ed. Donald F. Bond (Oxford, 1965), I, 34.

[16] *The Poetical Works of John Gay,* ed. G. C. Faber (London, 1926), p. 49.

[17] *The Poems of Jonathan Swift,* ed. Harold Williams (Oxford, 1958), I, 351. The passage on the death-watch is taken from "*Wood,* an Insect," one of a series of Swift's poems attacking William Wood of "Wood's half-pence" fame.

[18] *Collected Works of Oliver Goldsmith,* ed. Arthur Friedman (Oxford, 1966), II, 367.

[19] Other allusions to the death-watch in literature include Coleridge's *Remorse* (IV.i.12) in 1812; the 1842 version of Tennyson's "The May Queen" (line 21 of the Conclusion); and Tennyson's "Forlorn" (line 24) in 1889.

[20] See, for example, Carney Landis, *Varieties of Psychopathological Experience,* ed. Fred A. Mettler (New York, 1964), especially pp. 90-96; The American Schizophrenia Foundation, *What You Should Know About Schizophrenia* (Ann Arbor, 1965), pp. 4-5; and Abram Hoffer and Humphry Osmond, "Some Psychological Consequences of Perceptual Disorder and Schizophrenia," *International Journal of Neuropsychiatry,* II (January-February, 1966), 1-19. In addition to presenting the results of their own research into the area of perceptual disturbance, Hoffer and Osmond cite a number of similar studies.

[21] A professor of the practice of medicine at University College, London, when his *Inquiry* was published, Conolly later achieved renown for his work with the insane at Hanwell Asylum.

[22] Robinson, *passim.*

John W. Canario (essay date 1970)

SOURCE: "The Dream in 'The Tell-Tale Heart'," in *English Language Notes,* Vol. 7, No. 3, March, 1970, pp. 194-97.

[*In the following essay, Canario argues that the narrator of "The Tell-Tale Heart" is the "deranged victim of a hallucinatory nightmare" about death.*]

Hervey Allen observed in a footnote to *Israfel* that the logic of Poe's stories is "the mad rationalization of a dream."[1] This observation is especially applicable to **"The Tell-Tale Heart,"** which becomes fully understandable only when the narrator is recognized as the deranged victim of an hallucinatory nightmare.

Most commentators on the story have praised it either for its powerful evocation of terror or its artistically skillful revelation by degrees of the narrator as a homicidal maniac. Arthur Hobson Quinn's description of the story as "a study of terror" and "a companion piece to **'The Pit and the Pendulum'**" exemplifies the first view.[2] E. Arthur Robinson's close analysis of Poe's handling of two psychological themes in the story—"the indefinite extension of subjective time" and "the murderer's psychological identification with the man he kills"—illustrates the second view.[3] Without denying the value of either of these widely held perspectives, I would like to suggest that Poe, on the most subtle level of his artistic aims, intended the tale of the narrator to be recognized finally as a madman's confession of a nightmare about death.

To understand the story as the relation of a dream, one must respond to suggestions of parallel situations and symbolic meanings in the action and imagery. That the narrator is reporting the events of a nightmare rather than actual happenings is not immediately discernible because the narrator himself is unable to separate fact from fancy. However, the hallucinatory nature of the events he relates becomes steadily clearer as he describes his victim and the circumstances of the supposed murder.

From the beginning of the story, the narrator's description of his relationship with the old man gradually gives rise to the suspicion that the old man is really an alter ego representing a side of the narrator toward which he feels ambivalent emotions of love and hate. This possibility is initially suggested by the narrator's statement that he loves the old man and by the fact that he lives in intimate association with him, but it is soon thereafter given more support by other developments. The narrator admits, for example, that he has experienced the same mortal terror as the old man, that he has groaned in the identical manner, and that he has undergone this experience again and again just at midnight, the time which he has chosen for his observations of the old man. Finally, the suspicion that the narrator and the old man are doubles becomes a certainty when the narrator complains of the loudness with which the old man's heart is beating. It is the increasing loudness of this beating heart, expressive of mounting emotion, that precipitates the narrator's leap upon his victim. Significantly, at this instant the murderer and the old man cry out simultaneously.

The discovery that the two characters are doubles raises the question as to what the narrator's desire to kill his alter ego means. The narrator announces very early in his confession that it is not the old man he wishes to do away with, but one of his eyes: "the eye of a vulture—a pale blue eye, with a film over it."[4] The narrator's obsession with this eye soon makes it apparent that he fears it not simply because it is ugly, but because he sees it as an emblem of his own mortality. That the eye is a symbol of death is suggested by its resemblance to the eyes of a corpse, by the fact that it belongs to an old man, and by the narrator's association of it with a vulture.

The identification of the narrator and the old man as doubles establishes that the narrator's account of the manner in which he killed the old man must be the report of a dream: "In an instant I dragged him to the floor, and pulled the heavy bed over him. I then smiled gaily, to find the deed so far done. But, for many minutes, the heart beat on with a muffled sound." In the symbolism of this dream, the old man can be seen to stand for the physical body of the dreamer, and the narrator to represent the mind and will of that body. Thus, the dream, which is hardly plausible as the description of a real murder, really objectifies the speaker's belief that he has destroyed his body and thereby escaped from death.

The narrator's elaborate preparations for the crime also establish that he is obsessed by a fear of death. His excessive concern with time ("it took me an hour," "seven long nights—every night just at midnight," "just at twelve," "a watch's minute hand moves more quickly than did mine," etc.) and his nightly visits to the room of the old man, during each of which he permitted only a single ray of light from his darkened lantern to shine upon his victim's face, are soon recognized as assisting in no practical way the accomplishment of the murder. On the other hand, these preparations, which are proudly held up by the narrator as evidences of his sanity, are really symbolic expressions of his insane conviction that he has indeed escaped from time and mortality through his own cunning.

The story ends with the narrator's anguished discovery that the old man's heart has resumed beating in thunderously loud pulsations, even after his body has been dismembered and stuffed under the floor. What is actually revealed is the narrator's sudden, horrified discovery, at the very moment when his exultation over his fantasy conquest of death is most intense, that he is still mortal. The narrator terminates his confession in mad ravings to three police officers who, having been attracted to the house by its occupant's scream in the night, are only waiting for conclusive evidence of the man's insanity before taking him into custody.

Notes

[1] Hervey Allen, *Israfel* (New York, 1927), II, 567.

[2] Arthur Hobson Quinn, *Edgar Allan Poe, a Critical Biography* (New York, 1941), p. 394.

[3] E. Arthur Robinson, "Poe's 'The Tell-Tale Heart,'" *Nineteenth-Century Fiction,* XIX (March, 1965), 374.

[4] Quotations from the story are from the text of the *Broadway Journal,* August 23, 1845, as reprinted in Eric W. Carlson, ed., *Introduction to Poe, A Thematic Reader* (Glenview, Ill., 1967).

Daniel Hoffman (essay date 1972)

SOURCE: "Madness!," in *Poe Poe Poe Poe Poe Poe Poe,* Doubleday and Company, 1972, pp. 226-32.

[*In the following essay, Hoffman examines the motif of the eye in "The Tell-Tale Heart" and explores the relationship of the deranged narrator and his victim.*]

There are no parents in the tales of Edgar Poe, nary a Mum nor a Dad. Instead all is symbol. And what does this total repression of both sonhood and parenthood signify but that to acknowledge such relationships is to venture into territory too dangerous, too terrifying, for specificity. Desire and hatred are alike insatiable and unallayed. But the terrible war of superego upon the id, the endless battle between conscience and impulse, the unsleeping enmity of the self and its Imp of the Perverse—these struggles are enacted and re-enacted in Poe's work, but always in disguise.

Take '**The Tell-Tale Heart,**' surely one of his nearly perfect tales. It's only four pages long, a triumph of the art of economy:

> How, then, am I mad? Hearken! and observe how healthily—how calmly I can tell you the whole story.

When a narrator commences in *this* vein, we know him to be mad already. But we also know his author to be sane. For with such precision to portray the methodicalness of a madman is the work not of a madman but of a man who truly understands what it is to be mad. Artistic control is the warrant of auctorial sanity. It is axiomatic in the psychiatric practice of our century that self-knowledge is a necessary condition for the therapeutic process. Never using the language of the modern diagnostician—which was unavailable to him in the first place, and which in any case he didn't need—Poe demonstrates the extent of his self-knowledge in his manipulation of symbolic objects and actions toward ends which his tales embody.

The events are few, the action brief. 'I' (in the story) believes himself sane because he is so calm, so methodical, so fully aware and in control of his purpose. Of course his knowledge of that purpose is limited, while his recital thereof endows the reader with a greater knowledge than his own. 'The disease,' he says right at the start, 'had sharpened my senses. . . . Above all was the sense of hearing acute. I heard all things in the heavens and in the earth. I heard many things in hell.' Now of whom can this be said but a delusional person? At the same time, mad as he is, this narrator is *the hero of sensibility.* His heightened senses bring close both heaven and hell.

His plot is motiveless. 'Object there was none. Passion there was none. I loved the old man. He had never wronged me. He had never given me insult. For his gold I had no desire.' The crime he is about to commit will be all the more terrible because apparently gratuitous. But let us not be lulled by this narrator's lack of admitted motive. He may have a motive—one which he cannot admit, even to himself.

> I think it was his eye! yes, it was this! One of his eyes resembled that of a vulture—a pale blue eye, with a film over it. Whenever it fell upon me, my blood ran cold; and so by degrees—very gradually—I made up my mind to take the life of the old man, and thus rid myself of the eye for ever.

And a paragraph later he reiterates, 'It was not the old man who vexed me, but his Evil Eye.'

Nowhere does this narrator explain what relationship, if any, exists between him and the possessor of the Evil Eye. We do, however, learn from his tale that he and the old man live under the same roof—apparently alone together, for there's no evidence of anyone else's being in the house. Is the young man the old man's servant? Odd that he would not say so. Perhaps the youth is the old man's son. Quite natural that he should not say so. 'I loved the old man. He had never wronged me. . . . I was never kinder to the old man than during the whole week before I killed him.' Such the aggressive revulsion caused by the old man's Evil Eye!

What can this be all about? The Evil Eye is a belief as old and as dire as any in man's superstitious memory, and it usually signifies the attribution to another of a power wished for by the self. In this particular case there are other vibrations emanating from the vulture-like eye of the benign old man. Insofar as we have warrant—which I think we do—to take him as a father-figure, his Eye becomes the all-seeing surveillance of the child by the father, even by The Father. This surveillance is of course the origin of the child's conscience, the inculcation into his soul of the paternal principles of right and wrong. As such, the old man's eye becomes a ray to be feared. For if the boy deviate ever so little from the strict paths of rectitude, *it will find him out.*

Poe, in other tales, seems to be obsessed with the eye to the point of fetishism. In **'Ligeia'** it is the lady's eyes which represent, to her husband, the total knowledge embodied in her person. By synecdoche the eyes become that which he worships. But the old man's eye is endowed with no such spiritual powers. Come to think of it, it is always referred to in the singular, as though he had but one. An old man with one all-seeing eye, an Evil Eye—from the plausible to the superstitious we pass in the text; perhaps further still to the mythical. One-eyed Odin, one-eyed because he sold his other *for knowledge.* Yet the

knowledge in a father's (or a father-figure's) eye which a child most likely fears is the suspicion that he has been seen in a forbidden act, especially masturbation, or some other exercise of the libido. That above all seems to the young child to be forbidden, and therefore what an all-seeing Eye would see. Yet this old man's ocular power is never so specified. What is specified, though, is the resemblance of his one eye to that of a vulture.

Vulture, vulture. Everywhere else in Poe's work, in Poe's mind, vulture is associated with TIME, and time is associated with our mortality, our confinement in a body. The vulture-like eye of an aged man is thus an insupportable reminder of the narrator's insufferable mortality. Could he but rid himself of its all-seeing scrutiny, he would then be free of his subjection to time.

All the more so if the father-figure in this tale be, in one of his aspects, a Father-Figure. As, to an infant, his own natural father doubtless is. As, to the baby Eddie, his foster-father may have been. Perhaps he had even a subliminal memory of his natural father, who so early deserted him, eye and all, to the hard knocks experience held in store. So, the evil in that Evil Eye is likely a mingling of the stern reproaches of conscience with the reminder of his own subjection to time, age, and death.

To murder the possessor of such an eye would be indeed to reverse their situations. In life, the old man seems to the narrator an absolute monarch, a personage whose power over him, however benignly exercised, is nonetheless immutable. Such exactly is the degree to which a murderer dominates his victim. And so it is that the narrator does not merely do the old man in. No, he stealthily approaches the sleeping old man, in the dead of night, and ever so craftily draws nearer, then plays upon his sleeping face a single ray from his lantern. A ray like the beam of an eye. This he does each night for a week—that very week in which he was never before so kind to him during the waking hours, when the old man had his eye working.

> Upon the eighth night I was more than usually cautious in opening the door. A watch's minute hand moves more quickly than did mine. Never before that night had I *felt* the extent of my powers—of my sagacity. I could scarcely contain my feelings of triumph. To think that there I was, opening the door, little by little, and he not even to dream of my secret deeds or thoughts.

This miscreant is full of the praise of his own sagacity, a terrible parody of the true sagacity of a Dupin or a Legrand. For what he takes to be ratiocination is in fact the irresistible operation of the principle of his own perversity, the urge to do secret deeds, have secret thoughts undetected by the otherwise ever-watchful eye of the old man. He is so pleased to have outwitted that eye that he chuckles—and the old man stirs, then cries 'Who's there?' The room is pitchy black, the shutters drawn for fear of robbers. Now the old man is sitting bolt upright in bed, 'listening;—just as I have done, night after night, hearkening to the death watches in the wall.'

The old man must have realized what was happening, what was about to happen, for

> Presently I heard a slight grown . . . not of pain or of grief—oh, no!—it was the low stifled sound that arises from the bottom of the soul when overcharged with awe. . . . I knew it well. I knew what the old man felt, and pitied him, although I chuckled at heart.

And then, breaking the darkness and the silence, he spots his ray directly 'upon the vulture eye.' 'Now, I say, there came to my ears a low, dull, quick sound, such as a watch makes when enveloped in cotton.' This is the sound, he says, of the old man's heartbeat.

Excited to a pitch of 'uncontrollable terror' by the drumbeat of his victim's heart, he gives a shout, flings wide the door of his lantern, and drags the old man to the floor. Then he suffocates him under the mattress. 'His eye would trouble me no more.'

Now, quickly, methodically, the murderer completes his work. 'First I dismembered the corpse. I cut off the head and the arms and the legs.' Then he places all between the beams under the floorboards. These he deftly replaces so that no eye could detect a thing. He had made care to catch all the blood in a tub. 'Ha! ha!'

Death by suffocation—this is a recrudescence of the favorite mode of dying everywhere else in Edgar Poe's tales of the dying, the dead, and the doomed. Illness is invariably phthisis; what character draws untroubled breath? Such sufferings seem inevitable to the imagination of a writer whose memory is blighted by the consumption which carried off the three women he most loved. But there is yet another reason for the young man's choosing to suffocate the eye which he could not abide. As is true of dreamwork, the vengeance is meted out thrice: he extinguishes the eye, he suffocates the old man, he dismembers him. I think these three terrible acts are disguises of each other.

In its aspect of getting rid of the Evil Eye, this murder is a more intense and violent form of blinding. And the symbolic content of blinding has been self-evident since Oedipus inflicted it upon himself as a partial remission for what the *lex talionis,* more strictly applied, would have required. In striking the Evil Eye of the old man, the young madman strikes, symbolically, at his sexual power. Nor does this contradict the other significations I have suggested for the ocular member. As the source of conscience, of surveillance of the boy's sexual misdemeanors, and as the reminder of his subjection to his own body, the eye derives some of its powers from its linkage, in imagination, with potency.

But what has suffocation to do with this? Only that the inability to breathe is an equivalent of impotence, of sexual impotence. By inflicting this form of death on the old man, the youth is denying his elder's sexual power.

And cutting off the head, the arms, the legs? These amputations, too, are symbolic castrations.

The 'I' is nothing if not methodical. He leaves nothing to chance.

No sooner has he replaced the floorboards—it is now four o'clock—but there is a rapping at his door. Neighbors, hearing a scream, had called the police. He explains that the scream was his own, *in a dream.* Then—why does he do this?—he invites the police into the house, to search and see for themselves, saying that the old man was away in the country.

> I led them, at length, to *his* chamber. I showed them his treasures, secure, undisturbed. In the enthusiasm of my confidence, I brought chairs into the room, and desired them *here* to rest from their fatigues, while I myself, in the wild audacity of my perfect triumph, placed my own seat upon the very spot beneath which reposed the corpse of the victim.

At first all is well, but as they sit, and chat, his head begins to ache, he hears a ringing in his ears. It grows in volume, *'a low, dull, quick sound . . . as a watch makes when enveloped in cotton. . . . hark! louder! louder! louder!'*

He could escape the Evil Eye, but not 'the beating of his hideous heart.'

Of course it was his own heart which the murderer heard beat. Would he have heard it, had not his Imp of the Perverse commanded that he lead the police to the very scene of the crime? Or was this Imp, whose impulse seems so inexplicable, his own conscience, inescapable as long as his own heart should beat, demanding punishment for the terrible crime he had wrought? Thus he is *never* free from the gaze of the old man's clear blue eye.

David Halliburton (essay date 1973)

SOURCE: "Tales: 'The Tell-Tale Heart'," in *Edgar Allan Poe: A Phenomenological View,* Princeton University Press, 1973, pp. 333-38.

[*In the following essay, Halliburton draws attention to Poe's use of sound and his depiction of the narrator as both victimizer and victim in "The Tell-Tale Heart."*]

The moon in "Irenë" watches the sleeper and worries about the harmful effects of an influence it does not recognize as its own. The first William Wilson watches *his* sleeper, the other Wilson, with full knowledge of the harm he intends, then fails to inflict it. The relation of the sleeper and the watcher in **"The Tell-Tale Heart"** is similar but more extreme. Here the watcher has no guardian role, as in the sleeper poems; unlike the first Wilson, he is not intimately involved with the sleeper, who means nothing to him. The defiant attitude of the second Wilson provides some slight justification for the behavior of the first; but even this is lacking in **"The Tell-Tale Heart."** The murderer's choice of victim is completely gratuitous. It is also completely conscious, for this first-person, to an even greater extent than Poe's other criminals, is a man who loves to wallow in his own mind. His theory about the old man's eye making his blood run cold satisfies that love. At the same time it provides a protection not unlike the one Egaeus provides for himself when he turns a big threatening object into a small manageable one. Drunk with his own shrewdness, the murderer expands verbally in all directions, as though by taking up all the space there is he could become the absolute of his own fiction, its center of motive and power. The murderer exists in a world of signs that he invents and that he wills himself to believe. This is not to say that he invents, for example, the old man's eye, which obviously exists independently of his perception of it. But it is the speaker who makes the eye exist as a sign. In contrast to other men who signify in order to connect and illuminate, this man signifies in order to separate and conceal. In explaining his behavior, he chooses points and details that protect him from dangerous confrontations with his inner self by making him appear not only sane but highly rational. His wall of rationality is, of course, transparent, for his arguments, proofs, and analyses are simply too "technical" to be believed: "Oh, you would have laughed to see how cunningly I thrust [my head] in! I moved it slowly—very, very slowly, so that I might not disturb the old man's sleep. It took me an hour to place my whole head within the opening so far that I could see him as he lay upon his bed. Ha!—would a madman have been so wise as this?" This is no ordinary mystification but a self-mystification, in which the creator himself believes and of which he is therefore the victim.

Unlike the normal, responsible communicator, this speaker underlines his argument at its weakest point. One thing that will never persuade anyone of his rationality is the mere deliberateness of his bodily movements; yet this is precisely what he chooses to emphasize: "And then, when my head was well in the room, I undid the lantern cautiously—oh, so cautiously—cautiously (for the hinges creaked)—I undid it just so much that a single thin ray fell upon the vulture eye." Unlike the responsible communicator, he dwells upon the obvious: "The old man was dead. I removed the bed and examined the corpse. Yes, he was stone, stone dead. I placed my hand upon the heart and held it there many minutes. There was no pulsation. He was stone dead." The rhythms of the narrator's speech express a peculiar will. It is not the will to certainty that we see in William Wilson, who is concerned to get things right, down to the last shade of meaning. The narrator in **"The Tell-Tale Heart"** exhibits a will to convince. If Wilson wants to know and be known, the murderer wants to believe and be believed. To convince his imaginary auditors is, of course, only part of the task; he must also convince himself. His insistence that the old man is dead is for his own benefit as much as for ours, and the same can be said of his insistence that he is sane. The rhythms of this man's speech are, in fact, doubly revealing, for while they show the strength of his will they also show (like the verbal repetitions in **"The Pit and the Pendulum"**) the depths of his terror. There is nothing contradictory about being willful and assertive on the one hand while being fearful and defensive on the other. A man

such as Poe describes asserts himself *because* of his fear. If he compels, it is because he is compulsive.

After so many "manuscript" stories, here is a story told by a voice. Despite the lack of a specific auditor, as in "Tamerlane," the narrator's phrasing, diction, and punctuation are those of a man who speaks, or thinks he speaks, in the hearing of another. His opening remark has the quality of a spontaneous vocal reply: "True!—nervous—very, very dreadfully nervous I had been and am; but why *will* you say that I am mad?" The repeated addressing of a second-person in the opening section adds to the effect. The tale becomes a kind of hysterical conversation-poem dominated by a speaker whose voice rises from a middle register of argument to a top register of shouted confession. Such a speaker lives in an intensely acoustic space: life hinges literally on sound, or on silence, which is the temporary absence of sound and its imminent return. By this acoustic space consciousness is surrounded and returned to itself as the echoes of a voice are returned to a speaker by an encompassing wall. In such a space I hear the other even as I hear myself. I share his silence and his sounds, his consciousness and his fears, and can therefore interpret the design of my own:

> Presently I heard a slight groan, and I knew it was the groan of mortal terror. It was not a groan of pain or of grief—oh, no!—it was the low stifled sound that arises from the bottom of the soul when overcharged with awe. I knew the sound well. Many a night, just at midnight, when all the world slept, it has welled up from my own bosom, deepening, with its dreadful echo, the terrors that distracted me. . . . I knew what the old man felt, and pitied him, although I chuckled at heart. I knew that he had been lying awake ever since the first slight noise, when he had turned in the bed. His fears had been ever since growing upon him. He had been trying to fancy them causeless, but could not. He had been saying to himself—"It is nothing but the wind in the chimney—it is only a mouse crossing the floor," or "it is merely a cricket which has made a single chirp."

Sound afflicts the victimizer both inwardly and outwardly, in the realm of his consciousness and in the public realm of everyday reality. What causes him to speak out at last, declaring his crime and offering himself as a victim, is the illusion that the one has crossed over into the other. As the narrative progresses, the sound of the rhythm that the speaker hears inwardly advances (so he feels) from inner space to outer. This rhythm is introduced analogically: "A watch's minute hand moves more quickly than did mine." As the victimizer contemplates his victim the rhythm begins to assert its autonomy: ". . . now, I say, there came to my ears a low, dull, quick sound, such as a watch makes when enveloped in cotton. I knew *that* sound well, too. It was the beating of the old man's heart. It increased my fury, as the beating of a drum stimulates the soldier into courage." The process is a kind of one-sided reciprocity in which the victimizer feeds upon the terror he arouses, turning the object of his torture into the object with which he tortures himself: "Meantime the hellish tattoo of the heart increased. It grew quicker and quicker, and louder and louder every instant. The old man's terror *must* have been extreme! It grew louder, I say, louder every moment!—do you mark me well? I have told you that I am nervous: so I am. And now at the dead hour of the night, amid the dreadful silence of that old house, so strange a noise as this excited me to uncontrollable terror." The circuit of terror thus ends where it begins, in the victimizer. The victim's terror, which also deserves to be recognized, is a natural response to a danger from the outside. But the victimizer is reacting to a danger in himself, the victim serving as a mediator whose duty it is to heighten the murderer's consciousness of his own sensations. The victimizer acts upon the victim, finally, so as to become himself a victim.

Throughout the process the victimizer enjoys the poise of upright posture while the sleeper is stretched out flat in the classic posture of the one-who-is-acted-upon. When the speaker places the body beneath that horizontal wall that he calls a floor he takes the victimization as far as it will go, the victim being at once recumbent, dead, and buried. By this burial the victimizer attempts to architecturalize his relationship to the victim, to demonstrate with the solidity of matter that victimizer and victim are separate, when in fact they are inseparable.[64] Each occupies a chamber he cannot leave. To the victim this chamber is a space of pure bondage. But the chamber confines the victimizer as much as it confines the victim. For the victim acts in the chamber so as to deprive himself of the power to act: by that same act which creates a chamber for his victim, the victimizer creates a chamber for himself. Victimization is a reciprocal state, and the chamber is its inevitable locale.

Having willed a separation between himself and his victim, the narrator must now, in order to become himself a victim, dissolve it. This is the function of the final emission of sound. Little by little the victimizer perceives that the sound which distresses him emanates from outside himself, unaware that it merely externalizes a desire in himself: "The ringing became more distinct:—it continued and became more distinct: I talked more freely to get rid of the feeling: but it continued and gained definiteness—until, at length, I found that the noise was *not* within my ears." The world of the victimizer-speaker has turned itself inside out. In the phase of temporary silence—of an acoustic space charged with withheld sound—he had been master, the proof of his mastery being his ability to extend time through his own slowness. As he loses control, the withheld sound releases itself and quickens: "It was *a low, dull, quick sound—much such a sound as a watch makes when enveloped in cotton.*" A rhythm growing steadily louder is the aural complement of velocity, which is complemented further by the staccato of the speaker's language: "I felt that I must scream or die! and now—again!—hark! louder! louder! louder! *louder!*"

Now the victimizer speaks for the first time so as to be heard by those in his presence: "'Villains!' I shrieked, 'dissemble no more! I admit the deed!—tear up the planks! here, here!—it is the beating of his hideous heart!'" In speaking, the murderer confesses and in confessing real-

izes his secret aim: to reveal himself as the victim he has always secretly been.

Note

[64] The close relationship of victim and victimizer is demonstrated by E. Arthur Robinson, "Poe's 'The Tell-Tale Heart,'" *Nineteenth-Century Fiction,* pp. 376-378.

Paul Witherington (essay date 1985)

SOURCE: "The Accomplice in 'The Tell-Tale Heart'," in *Studies in Short Fiction,* Vol. 22, No. 4, Fall, 1985, pp. 471-75.

[*In the following essay, Witherington argues that the reader of "The Tell-Tale Heart," seduced by the narrator into participating vicariously in his crime, is transformed into "an active voyeur" and "an accomplice after the fact" in the old man's murder.*]

"Poe's narrator tells a plain and simple story, which leaves no doubt that he is mad," T. O. Mabbott says in his preface to **"The Tell-Tale Heart."**[1] Most readers would agree, not only because the murder of an old man seems motiveless, but also because the narrator's confession comes across as calculated and heartless. Whereas **"The Cask of Amontillado"** offers witty dialogue and a romantic setting, inviting us into the story and thus eliciting our sympathy for the narrator in spite of our antipathy to the murder, **"The Tell-Tale Heart"** entombs us with the narrator's stark obsessions to which we react by shrouding ourselves with moral indignation and psychic detachment.

The story's plainness and simplicity, in fact, seem the means by which the narrator's madness is rendered transparent. Undistracted by context or extenuating circumstances, we focus our attention on his protestations of sanity, which of course fall apart with every "reason" he gives the listener, the "you" of the story who hears the confession. "Why *will* you say that I am mad?" the narrator asks (p. 792), explaining that his senses were not dulled but heightened during the horror; mania can't be madness, he argues unconvincingly. "Observe how healthily—how calmly I can tell you the whole story," he says, proceeding to undercut both calmness and wholeness by his agitated and incomplete rendition. And his emphasis on murder as a rational process only underscores the barbarity of the act itself. Faced with these attractive ironies, Poe critics have institutionalized the narrator's madness and gone on to concentrate on either the dynamics of that mental state (how the narrator becomes both murderer and victim)[2] or Poe's use of it to illustrate such ideas as passage to original Unity, or the frustrating of demon Time.[3]

This verdict of madness, however, comes less from the story itself than from our commonly held assumptions that all obsessive murderers are mad and that their madness is easily recognizable. If, on the other hand, we begin by assuming that anyone canny enough to carry out such a crime might be canny enough to disguise his own motives, and if we further assume that the narrator knows his listener's moral and rational position and thus makes his claims of mental health so absurd that they must fail to convince his audience, then we have a different story, though one quite faithful to Poe's other works where characters show no end to their duplicity, and where the lines between sanity and insanity blur in a nightmare atmosphere. To activate this reading, our attention must shift from the red herring of madness to the more subtle designs of the confession and the language by which the reader is induced, like one of M. Dupin's dupes, to select "odd" when he should have selected "even."

Pretending to share with the listener a universal concern for reason, the narrator seduces the listener by getting him to participate vicariously in the crime, an accomplice after the fact. He accomplishes this quickly and subtly in the third paragraph through the sense of sight: "You should have seen *me*," the narrator says and immediately repeats it: "You should have seen how wisely I proceeded—and with what caution—with what foresight—with what dis-simulation I went to work!" (p. 792). Later in that same paragraph, he takes further advantage of the listener by assuming his sympathetic reaction to the scene where the murderer pokes his head into the old man's room: "Oh, you would have laughed to see how cunningly I thrust it in!" (p. 793). By these suggestive nudges, the auditor is transformed into an active voyeur. The narrator concludes that long third paragraph with another subtlety: "So you see he would have been a very profound old man, indeed, to suspect that every night, just at twelve, I looked in upon him while he slept" (p. 793). In this sentence, "see" takes on the sense of understanding, though it does so without entirely relinquishing its primary meaning which is returned to by the narrator's claim to have "looked in." Meanwhile, the listener has been maneuvered from thoughts of missed opportunity ("You should have seen") to the thoughts that he and the narrator presumably share ("So you see").

After the third paragraph, the listener, now assumed to be a silent accomplice, comes across as being somewhat timid but anxious for the deed to be done: "Now you may think that I drew back—but no" (p. 793). He is put in the position not only of encouraging the narrator's story but also of egging on the murderer. The listener is also chided for his deficiency in imagination while the narrator exhibits his own powers of metaphor: "So I opened it [the lan-tern]—you cannot imagine how stealthily, stealthily—until, at length, a single dim ray, like the thread of the spider, shot from out the crevice and fell upon the vulture eye." (p. 794). This technique of attempting to limit the listener's access to the story and then tantalizing him with its details resembles in its psychological awareness and ultimate effect the game Montresor plays with Fortunato, enticing him to go more deeply into the wine cellar by telling him he should leave.

Final references to the listener return to the innocuous-ness of the opening remarks: "Have I not told you?" and "Do you mark me well? I have told you." (p. 795). The narrator may be chiding the "you" for his inattentiveness. But by this stage of the story his intent seems more gloating than goading, a kind of "I told you so," for we suspect that the listener is deeply and emotionally in-volved in the tale. The narrator has in fact assumed this involvement, for the "you" references disappear after paragraph thirteen (though the listener resurfaces at the end, as we shall see). The "you" of **"The Cask of Amon-tillado"** appears only once, in the first paragraph, perhaps to show that the narrator is speaking to a close friend. But Poe's narrator in **"The Tell-Tale Heart"** needs a continuing listener, somewhat less than a character but somewhat more than a device, to prove his point that if anyone can be seduced by narrative, then it becomes difficult to sepa-rate those who take pleasure in committing and confessing crime from those who take pleasure in hearing about it.

The motif of the listener becoming an accomplice comes directly from late eighteenth-century and early nineteenth-century Gothic literature. The confession of a villain often blasts the innocent listener out of composure and securi-ty, as in Coleridge's "The Rime of the Ancient Mariner" and William Godwin's *Caleb Williams*. Borrowed effec-tively for American literature by Brockden Brown and Hawthorne, this technique features a diabolical contract in which the two figures become collaborators moving away from the extremes of their original positions.

Poe himself uses demonic collaboration variously in earlier stories. The narrator's outfitting of a pentagonal room appropriate for Ligeia's return, and his attempt to invoke her by calling her name at Rowena's deathbed indicate that he may be in league with the occultish Ligeia who herself "used" him earlier to read the poem which seems to have precipitated her death. And the narrator in **"The Fall of the House of Usher"** reads to Roderick the very story most calculated to excite him to the imagination (or reality) of the bizarre ending. The influential opinion of Jungian critics that Ligeia dramatizes the narrator's anima and Roderick the narrator's shadow, in fact supports this collaboration theory, all being one in the psyche. But by making the listener in **"The Tell-Tale Heart"** a voiceless yet clear presence, Poe effects some last minute twists which are not typical of Gothic literature, and which point instead toward a much more sophisticated esthetic.

Toward the end of the story the police arrive and the narrator gives himself away to them while sitting over the dismembered body of his victim. Conscience wins out, or the "narrator's compulsion to unmask and destroy himself by finally admitting the crime," as Edward H. Davidson puts it.[4] In this mainstream interpretation, the police may be thought of as the murderer's super-ego, and the entire inner story a psychodrama of compulsions and counter compulsions.

Although the narrator may not have been in conscious control of the actual events, however, he seems to know exactly what he is doing in retelling them to the listener. By ignoring the listener toward the story's end, he en-courages the listener to become more actively involved in the ending and thus to identify with the police officers who listened to the murderer's original confession. This reaction seems reasonable for the listener because after becoming involved symbolically as accomplice, he must feel the need to shuck off guilt by identifying with the accusers rather than the accused. He can imagine himself sitting with the officers around the murderer, awaiting the final outburst with considerable pleasure since he is already familiar with the details. He has been allowed a margin of safety, to eat his cake and then have it returned to him whole.

Here of course the narrator springs another trap, telling the listener that at the climax of his confession to the police, he cried out, calling them "Villains!" (p. 797). Though this counterattack is anticipated a few lines earlier by his reference to the "hypocritical smiles" of the officers, its intensity (the narrator's accusation of the police is the only part of the story rendered in quotation marks) must come as a shock to the listener who has put himself in their shoes. What may well have been simple projection in the inner story now becomes a more calculated and loaded indictment of the listener, as he is made to feel the full guilt of his vicarious fantasies. He's a villain for wanting to listen to the recreation of a tale of horror, and he's a naive hypocrite for imagining that he can do so with impunity.

The cry of "Villains!" remains also to haunt the perceptive reader who has also presumably played the game of accomplice and accuser, whose desire for a good story has kept him reading and whose conscience has brought him up short—provided of course he is capable of this kind of response. Poe's contemporaries may not have been, we assume from our experience with reflexive literature and our cultivated self-consciousness as readers. In Alain Robbe-Grillet's "The Secret Room," for example, an implied narrator views a painting of the aftermath of a vicious murder and then, apparently by his curiosity, causes the scene to run backward as if it were movie film so that the murder itself is reenacted. Thus the reader, who shares this desire to know what has happened, becomes accomplice to both the viewer and the murderer. But Poe too envisioned this kind of reader response. In his 1847 review of Hawthorne's tales for *Godey's Lady's Book,* Poe speaks of the reader's engagement as co-creator: "He feels and intensely enjoys the seeming novelty of the thought, enjoys it as really novel, as absolutely original with the writer—*and himself.* They two, he fancies, have, alone of all men, thought thus. They two have, together, created this thing."[5]

Poe did not share Hawthorne's overly scrupulous concerns for the artist as one who observes life from a self-indulgent distance. But Poe certainly understood the demands audiences make on art: how the poet may be forced to write short stories in order to make a living, and how the gothic interests of readers often force writers to perversions of their craft. The relationship between murderer and victim is a two-way pull, as is the relationship between writer and reader. We are all accomplices, though some, by virtue of experience, are more aware of it.

Notes

[1] Thomas Olive Mabbott (ed.), *Collected Works of Edgar Allan Poe* (Cambridge, Mass.: Harvard University, Belknap Press, 1978), III, 789. All following quotations from this work will be indicated in the body of the text.

[2] See for example Edward H. Davidson, *Poe: A Critical Study* (Cambridge, Mass.: Harvard University, Belknap Press, 1966), pp. 189-190, and David Halliburton, *Edgar Allan Poe: A Phenomenological View* (Princeton, New Jersey: Princeton University Press, 1973), pp. 333-338.

[3] See for example Joseph J. Moldenhauer, "Murder as a Fine Art: Basic Connections Between Poe's Aesthetics, Psychology, and Moral Vision," *Publications of the Modern Language Association,* 83 (May 1968), 292-293, and E. Arthur Robinson, "Poe's 'The Tell-Tale Heart.'" *Nineteenth-Century Fiction,* 19 (March, 1965), 369-378.

[4] Davidson, p. 190.

[5] James T. Harrison (ed.), *The Complete Works of Edgar Allan Poe* (New York: AMS Press, 1965), XIII, 146.

Gita Rajan (essay date 1988)

SOURCE: "A Feminist Rereading of Poe's 'The Tell-Tale Heart'," in *Papers on Language and Literature,* Vol. 24, No. 3, Summer, 1988, pp. 283-300.

[*In the following essay, Rajan asserts that the narrator of "The Tell-Tale Heart" is female, and contends that a new, gender-marked rereading of the tale, as filtered through theories of narrativity inspired by Sigmund Freud, Jacques Lacan, and Hélène Cixous, reveals "the narrator's exploration of her female situation in a particular feminist discourse."*]

1

Some contemporary feminists and theorists argue that there is a difference between masculinist and feminist discourse in literary texts. French theorists like Julia Kristeva, Luce Irigaray, and Hélène Cixous follow Jacques Lacan and psychoanalytic theory and trace the unconscious drives exhibited in the discourse of the text as repressed male/female desires. Even though these desires may be contradictory and conflicting, they reveal the position of the speaking subject (male or female) within the discourse of the text. The French scholars, in seeking the overlapping or androgynous places of discourse in the text, assert that males and females engage in differently gendered readings. Kristeva and Cixous argue that sexual identity (male or female) is a metaphysical construct outside the boundaries of the text, while gender identity is based upon cultural notions of maleness and femaleness evidenced in the text. Gender identity is more fluid than the former and makes room for the crucial concept of androgyny that is central to feminist readings in demolishing the rigid patriarchal notion of what is male/female. Androgyny deconstructs crippling binary oppositions of masculinity and femininity by allowing the speaking subject to occupy either or both positions.

While sexual identity, and, consequently, discrimination, feature prominently in masculinist readings, French theorists are radically shifting the very nature of the struggle of the sexes by focusing on gender-governed identity. Hence, a feminist reinterpretation of a narrative typically could argue that an unmarked narrator can be seen as female. Such a reading would displace a whole series of masculinist assumptions. In accordance with this approach, I will focus on Poe's **"The Tell-Tale Heart,"** especially its narrator, and argue that the narrator is indeed female. Poe himself never indicates that the narrator is male; in fact, his text offers no gender markings. Readers have assumed that the narrator is male because a neutralized and unmarked term *is* generally granted to be male. This is a trap that the language of the tale innocuously lays before the reader. By positing a female narrator, I propose to dislodge the earlier, patriarchal notion of a male narrator for the story. I argue, instead, that a gender-marked *rereading* of this tale reveals the narrator's exploration of her female situation in a particular feminist discourse. My feminist reading of **"The Tell-Tale Heart"** profiles the identity of the narrator as filtered through Freud's, Lacan's, and Cixous's theories of narrativity.

2

Psychoanalysis partially bridges the gap between conscious and unconscious thought and language through dream theory. Freud argues that instinctual forces—eros and thanatos—manifest themselves through dreams, and that these forces coexist and continually contradict each other, being intertwined in pairs like love/hate, life/death, and passivity/aggression. However, Freud maintains that people manage to lead ordered lives because they sublimate these forces as desires in dreams through at least two specific mechanisms, "condensation" and "displacement." Freud builds his psychoanalytic theory on human sexuality and desire, seeing the male as superior, in possession of the phallus, i.e., power. A female is inferior for Freud because of her lack of the sexual organ to signify the phallus and the power it symbolizes. In short, Freud's definition of the male and female, locked into this privative power equation, automatically privileges the male and marginalizes the female.

Lacan, in his revision of Freudian theory, fastens upon three principles: desire (the phallus as power), condensation/displacement (the dream as a system of signs), and hierarchy (the male as superior, or possessing power through the penis: the female as inferior, or lacking power).[1] Relying on Roman Jakobson's structural linguistics, he combines these three principles to establish a relationship between language *per se* and conscious/unconscious thought. Jakobson uses language as a model of *signs* to explain human thought and consequent behavior. A sign, for Jakobson, is a representation through language of the relationship between signifier (the physical sound of speech or the written mark on the page) and the signified (the invisible concept that this sound or mark represents). Jakobson's linguistic formulations reveal the doubleness of the sign and the fragility of the signifier (word) and signified (concept) relationship. In effect, he sees meaning emerging in discourse not through the relationship between signifier and signified but through the interaction of one signifier with another.

Jakobson maintains that language is constructed along two axes—the vertical/metaphoric and the horizontal/metonymic. Lacan's matches Jakobson's theory of language with Freud's theory of dreams, positing that dreams are structured along metaphoric and metonymic lines.[2] Lacon claims that the "rhetoric of the unconscious" is constructed on two main tropes—metaphor and metonymy. He equates condensation with metaphor because it is a process of selection, substituting one signifier/word *for* another. Displacement he sees as metonymy because it combines one signifier/word *with* another. For Lacan, unconscious desire, like language, is structured as a system of signs, articulated metaphorically and metonymically in dreamwork and considered as discourse. While in Freudian analysis the focus is on the excavation of the subject's behavior, in Lacan it shifts to language, tracing the path of desire as a sequential power transaction in the discourse of the text. Thus, Lacan reconstructs Freud's behavioral model into a *seemingly* less prejudiced linguistic one by emphasizing the arbitrariness and precariousness of language itself.

Further, according to Lacan, the metaphoric register represents the masculine through the "transcendental phallus," embodying the ultimate power of the signifier as a linguistic mark whose meaning is forever repressed (in the unconscious or the "text") and never attainable. Hence, every subject must engage in a constant metaphoric game of substitution in the attempt to grasp this final desire. In contrast, the metonymic is temporal and sequential; it propels the signifier forward in an attempt to recover the (unconscious) signified through narration. Significantly, Lacan claims that this reaching forward to achieve completeness is a mark of femininity, a feminine marker in discourse. Finally, Lacan concludes that even though language itself is symbolic, the symptom that prompts discourse is metonymic. Thus, the metonymic, feminine, "imaginary" register is the force that propels narrative.[3]

It is at this point that Lacan differs radically from Freud. While Freud assumes that language can completely appropriate and express thought, granting closure in the text, Lacan posits an inherent gap in this relationship, arguing for never-ending narrativity. For Lacan, the sign can never be complete or made whole because a signifier can only point to another signifier, resulting in an unending chain of signifiers we *forever attempt* to bridge through language and thought. Lacan connects language to thought as expressions of patterns of desire, motivated and propelled towards possessing the ultimate sign of power— the "transcendental signified," or phallus. Thus, the transcendental signified belongs in the metaphoric register, and the desire to possess it creates narrativity, which belongs to the metonymic register. Lacan strategically argues that the desire to possess the "transcendental phallus" is universal, both in males and females, and *appears* to collapse sexual difference. But this apparent egalitarianism, I argue, does not in fact work.

A masculinist reading of Poe's tale using Lacan's theory still supports the Freudian notion of the Oedipal myth. However, the Lacanian approach emphasizes sexual difference less than the Freudian approach does. Robert Con Davis analyzes Poe's **"The Tell-Tale Heart"** using Lacanian principles in "Lacan, Poe and Narrative Repression." He focuses on the latent and repressed levels of the text as a method of locating the nexus of power. Davis argues the act of gazing, whether the old man's or the narrator's, is a metaphoric power transaction between the subject and the object of the gaze. Using Freud's "Instincts and Their Vicissitudes," with its traditional patriarchal dichotomies of "subject/object, active/passive," Davis matches Freud's theme of the "gaze" with Lacan's theory of voyeurism to interpret Poe's tale.[4] Davis highlights the "Evil Eye" as a predominant metaphor in Poe's tale that functions primarily through its power of the Gaze. Building on the theme of the gaze and voyeurism, Davis validates his masculinist reading by arguing that the old man and the narrator are indeed doubles, always already connected by the gaze. He sees both characters as having similar, almost paranoically sensitive hearing and sight, insomnia, and a preoccupation with death. The "eye" of the old man represents the Symbolic Law of the Father, or Lacan's version of Freud's Oedipal complex. Davis argues that in an attempt to escape paternal subjugation, the narrator engages in his own vindictive game of voyeurism. Davis sees the murder of the old man as a cruelly symbolic act of Oedipal mastery: "in choosing to heighten the old man's fear of death and kill him, the narrator controls—just as a voyeur sadistically controls—a situation *like his own,* as if the subject and object could be merged in a mirror phase of complete identification" (255). Davis even argues for a third voyeur in the figure of Death: "Death . . . had stalked with his black shadow . . . and enveloped the victim."[5] This allows him to posit a typical Lacanian triangle, consisting of the old man, the narrator, and Death, and create a constant shift in the power of the gaze through the triple itinerary of the signifier.

Because Davis places the narrator and the old man in the "double" positions connected by the gaze, he sees the gaps in the gaze between the subject and object *and* the gazer and voyeur as forces that produce the narrative, propel the tale forward, and alternately manifest and repress the text. Based on a primarily metaphoric interpretation—the eye as the Symbolic Gaze of the Father—Davis argues for a male narrator who acts as voyeur and exhibitionist alternately. Davis neatly sums up the final scene of Poe's tale as clearly metaphoric by saying: "His [the narrator's] resistance to being seen points to a desire to escape subjugation absolutely and to choose death rather than to become passive while alive" (254). Significantly, Lacan's suggestion that the metonymic dimension of the text is female is absent in Davis's reading. Thus, even though Lacanian readings *seem* to open the door to feminist perspectives, they ultimately only nudge the door ajar.

3

Cixous's feminist approach to psychoanalytic interpretation and her notion of feminine writing provide a fruitful way of sabotaging the masculinist-biased reading of texts. Hence a rereading of Poe's **"The Tell-Tale Heart"** with Cixous's paradigm offers an alternate gender-marked interpretation. She systematically interrogates existing critical presuppositions, deconstructs them, and advocates a three-step reinscription procedure.[6] First, according to Cixous, one must recognize a latent masculinist prejudice in society, a hidden privileging of the male and marginalizing of the female. Next, one must consciously undo the basic slanting in favor of the male term over the female term at the very nodes of these *seemingly logical* oppositions, such as male/female, reason/feeling, culture/nature, etc. Patriarchy, by creating these oppositions, privileges the first term and lowers the status of the second, forcing the textual subject to occupy either of these positions and accept the power (or lack thereof) that goes along with it. This logic divides each term against itself and makes the whole system of binary (Western) thought rigidly prescriptive. The male, according to this system of thought, can have an identity and value only in juxtaposition to an inferior female signifier and vice versa. Also, in privileging one term over another, the first term sets the norm for the second. More important, oppositional thinking, which is characteristic of patriarchy, forbids a wholeness or a shared existence for any term, focusing on maleness or on femaleness instead of the androgyny that Cixous and other French feminists advocate.

Consequently, Cixous's final step is to combat this problem of division by embracing these oppositions and erasing their differences. This is the "pretext," or background, for the process of *jouissance* that Cixous advocates. The strategy behind jouissance is to discredit the notion of difference by going beyond the idea of constraining divisions, to explore instead the freedom of excess, a utopian vision that subverts the male definition of desire. Patriarchy is based on a system of libidinal economy (a repression of desire both conscious and unconscious that creates meaning in a text). Cixous's jouissance demands a libidinal excess—additions of unconscious meanings through consciously constructed texts. The practical method behind this political feminist position is to create a multiplicity of meanings. In linguistic terms, jouissance creates an excess of signifiers, the freeplay of which will build several levels of meanings, all of which can be validated by the text. These meanings do not depend upon a series of repressed previous ones; they do not impoverish the meanings that come before them through a process of substitution but, instead, enhance each other through a process of addition. An example of this is the notion of androgyny which is central to some feminist readings. Instead of focusing on either male or female voice in the text, androgyny allows the same voice to be male and/or female in various parts of the text, allowing for numerous complementary interpretations.

Kristeva, in *Desire and Language,* and Cixous, in *La Juene Née,* argue that the concept of androgyny belongs to the realm of the "Imaginary," which, in Lacanian theory, is pre-Symbolic, or pre-Oedipal, and thus, is before the Law of the Father. While Cixous is explicit in calling this jouissance in the sense of the purely pleasurable state of excess, Kristeva connects jouissance to reproduction. However, they share this vision of utopia, with no boundaries or barriers of any kind, a vision that is based on unlimited joy.[7]

The inherent danger in Kristeva's and Cixous's vision of utopia is their marked privileging of the imaginative/poetic over the analytical/theoretical in feminist writing. Because of their emphasis on emotions rather than reason as the feminine mode, some patriarchal theorists do not treat feminist discourse seriously. Sentimentality is precisely the club that patriarchy holds over the woman to control and deem her inferior. However, there *is* a definite value in adopting Cixous's position of abundance in an effort to invalidate the rigid male parameters and explore the text with an expectation of plentitude and multiple meanings. It is essential to point out that Cixous's notion of jouissance as a pleasure principle is different from Lacan's notion of free space with an abundance of signifiers (or even Barthes's version of the "pleasures of the text"). The latter suggests a chasm with an abundance of repressed, free floating signifiers, while the former gathers up this abundance of signifiers to nourish and cherish separate multiple readings.

Cixous begins by questioning the validity of categories like male/female in both writing and reading texts. She sees these as gaps created by ideological differences propagated by a phallogocentric (phallus- and logos-oriented) interpretive community. Further, she argues that this kind of oppositional thinking is itself aggressive (very much like the male logic and body behind it), because one term in the couple comes into existence through the "death of the other." Cixous, in *La Jeune Née* asks, "Where is she?" (115) in a patriarchal binary thought system that creates divisions like "Activity/Passivity, Culture/Nature, Father/Mother, Head/Emotions, Logos/Pathos" (116) which is structured primarily on the male/female opposition. An effective way to allow both terms to exist is to ask for a gendered position that both males and females can occupy either jointly or individually within the texts, as speaking subjects. This is made possible through the notion of jouissance, which focuses on the speaking subject with a gendered (hence mobile) identity. Also, this deliberate exploration of multiple meanings would ceaselessly expose the hidden male agenda which is created to silence women.

4

I preface my rereading of Poe's tale with a Freudian analysis, much like that in Marie Bonaparte's *Life of Poe.*[8] However, while Bonaparte's emphasizes the element of primal-scene voyeurism, mine sees the male narrator's retelling of his story/dream as a narration of a rite of passage. **"The Tell-Tale Heart"** begins by describing the narrator's feelings about taking care of an old man. The old man's disturbing stare upsets the narrator, who decides on an impulse to kill him. The rest of the tale focuses on the narrator's elaborate plan to murder him, and ends with the narrator's confession of the crime. The story has Poe's typical macabre atmosphere and deliberately contradictory syntactical style. By killing the old man, the narrator symbolically castrates him, eliminating him from the text, and hopes to escape subjugation. This allows him to step into the old man's position of unchallenged power. The act of murder reveals the condensed expression of his desire to usurp the old man's place and authority. Similarly, his swing between neurotic and hysteric utterances, repeatedly assuring the reader of his sanity, is an effort to displace the sense of fear that is incumbent upon possessing such authority. At the beginning of the tale, the narrator shelters the old man (love), but ends up murdering him (hate). The narrator's contradictory actions, in an effort to possess ultimate power, are the result of the intertwining of eros and thanatos. The narrator's final confession to the policemen (the substitute father figures) is a combination and sublimation of his desire for power and fear of castration as a challenge to his new power.

The standard Oedipal interpretation is explicit in the climactic bedroom scene that graphically reveals the simultaneous condensed and displaced desires of the narrator. The bed serves to feed the contradictory instinctual urges of eros and thanatos, satisfying the young man's passion while smothering him to death, granting the young man power while nullifying it in the old man. The narrator's imbalanced emotional utterances about being "driven" by the old man's "eye" are symptoms of the condensed desire that make him conceive his elaborate plan of shutting the old man's "Evil eye forever" (303). It is his attempt to usurp that very authority of the old man's surveillance. And the narrator's own deafening "heartbeat" prods him on, leading him from one event to the next in the narrative, revealing his efforts to escape the displaced sense of fear in letting this desire get out of control. While the eye (condensation) represents the narrator's problem through a sense of abstract desire, the heartbeat (displacement) serves as the significant, concrete sense of fear in dealing with this problem. This enables the tale to maintain its ambivalence between myth and reality, dream and nightmare, due to a coexisting tension between metaphor/condensation and metonymy/displacement throughout the narration. In this traditional Freudian analysis, the identity of narrator remains fixedly male.

However, my rereading of the tale includes both a masculinist and feminist approach to the narrator. Using Lacanian principles, I profile the narrator as "speaking subject," presenting the narrator first as male, then as female. Unlike Davis's reading, my masculinist rereading focuses on both the metaphoric and metonymic aspects of the text, moving away from an exclusive "Gaze"-oriented interpretation of manifest and repressed levels of discourse. I treat the eye as a metaphor of patriarchal scrutiny and social control, and the heart as metonymic device to subvert such control. The narrator admits his obsession in saying, "when it [the eye] fell upon me, my blood ran cold; and so by degrees—very gradually—I made up my mind to take the life of the old man, and thus rid myself of the eye forever" (305). The narrator explicitly reveals his anger at the old man's symbolic method of subjugation and expresses his consequent desire to annihilate the old man, thereby negating and usurping his power. Davis too, points this out by showing how the narrator first isolates the gaze, then inverts it, so that he can gaze at and subjugate the old man. The narrator retaliates against the "Evil Eye" by voyeuristically gazing at the sleeping man. Thus, the gaze moves from the old man to the narrator, symbolizing the shift of power between them. Lacan calls this mobility the "itinerary of the signifier" (171) to indicate the constant substitution maneuvers that the metaphoric register undertakes in its attempt to possess the ultimate object of desire—the transcendental signifier.[9] Within Poe's tale, the "itinerary of the signifier" can be graphically traced along the "single thin ray" of light from the narrator's lantern that falls upon the "vulture eye . . . directed as if by instinct, precisely upon the damned spot" (306). Gaining new power through his reversal of the gaze makes the narrator heady, and he cries exultantly that the old man "was stone dead. His eye would trouble me no more" (306).

However, the "itinerary of the signifier," due to its constant process of substitution, does not allow power to rest with one gazer for a long period. The very nature of the gaze, as posited by both Freud and Lacan, is extremely volatile, temporary, and unpredictable. Consequently, in Poe's story the power of the gaze destabilizes the narrator, and it is for this reason that he breaks down and confesses to the mildly suspecting policemen. The police in Poe's tale are the literal representations of societal power, but they are also a metaphor for the Law of the Father in the unconscious. The policemen's gaze, thus, both literally and metaphorically represents the sanctioned authority that the narrator had just usurped from the old man. When they gaze at the narrator, they reverse the path of the gaze, once again throwing him back into the passive object position that is revealed by his hysterical and humiliating confession.

Equally crucial in a Lacanian analysis is the metonymic register, marked by the "heart" in Poe's tale. It exhibits a complicated displacement process working simultaneously on two manifest levels. At one level it represents the narrator's confused emotions, such that the narrator's passions and fears combine and clash, spurring the tale forward. The tale unfolds through the narrator's hysterical utterances, extreme passion (even though the narrator explicitly denies this at the beginning of his tale), obsessive desire, neurotic fears, and pathetic confession. At another level, it represents the physical pounding of the narrator's heart, giving him the energy to kill the old man. On the night of the assault, the narrator remarks: "Never, before that night, had I *felt* the extent of my own powers" (306). Notably, it is the narrator's fear of the imagined sound of the old man's heart, that overwhelming roar, that ultimately betrays him into confessing to the policemen. These two aspects of displacement embodied metonymically in the heart are fused in a strange manner, alternating

between hearing and feeling throughout the tale, such that they keep plummeting the narrative onwards. Thus, the sounds in the tale moves rapidly from heartbeat to creaking doors, to muffled smothering sounds, to loud ticking watches, and finally pounds as unbearable noise in the narrator's head till he articulates his fear through the confused discourse of a hysterical confession.

There is also a third kind of displacement at the repressed level of the text. This is evidenced in the metonymic shift not only between one aspect of the heart to the other, but in a total shift from sound to sight at crucial points in the text. Thus, the metonymic register displaces the narrator's feelings throughout the text in various ways. A good example is the elaborate precautions that the narrator takes to direct a single ray of light in a darkened room on the old man's eye (sight). When the narrative has been raised to a fever pitch on the night of the murder, the narrator suddenly fumbles with the catch on the lantern and goes into a detailed description of sounds of "death watches," and crickets in "chimneys," effectively displacing reader attention. The displacement and metonymic tactics repressed in the narrative itself act as a marker for signaling the manifest displacement of the narrator's fears regarding his uncontrolled and unsanctioned actions. It is here that Lacan's notion of the "itinerary of signifiers" in the metonymic register serves him well. Metonymy, as both agent and trope, by constantly shifting, mediates between thought and language, showing both the instability of this relationship, and its inability to bridge the gap. At the textual level, it highlights the constant forward movement in an attempt to narrate through the rapid and confusing chain of events. It reveals the obsessively fragmented discourse of the narrator, in a painful effort to make meaning, and to make whole this relationship between thought and language. Thus, in my masculinist reading, by using the Lacanian paradigm of a male speaking subject, I reveal the problematic nature of language itself. When the narrator fails, one glimpses—with a strange pathos—the failure of language, too.

In contrast, my Lacanian feminist rereading of Poe's tale, identifying a female narrator, yields an interpretation that is the reverse of the Oedipal myth. Instead of a young man desiring the power symbolized by the Father, *she* is the daughter desiring her father. I will show that Lacan's innovativeness lies in the way he volatilizes the metaphoric and metonymic registers through his theory of the "itinerary of the signifier." Lacan suggests that sex roles as represented by linguistic tropes can be made less rigid. Hence sexual difference can be erased by energizing and mobilizing these linguistic tropes. Metaphor as a trope represents a pattern of desiring and desired where the object of desire is the transcendental signified, or phallus. Metonymy would be the act of seeking and transacting this power through narrative. Thus, Lacan's strategy is to dislocate the fixity of sexual identity, or what he claims is gender identity, through the use of tropes as agents of desire. This would allow both men and women to possess the transcendental phallus, or its metaphoric power; but because of the temporary nature of this power, the very act of possession would be continually deferred and drawn out metonymically in narrative for both masculine and feminine subjects.

Within this framework, the narrator in Poe's tale can be posited as a female rather than a male who desires power. She stalks the old man and father figure for "seven long nights" and kills him in an attempt to escape the surveillance of his Evil Eye. The female narrator begins in the traditional feminine position of a *nurturer*. She takes him into her house and even remarks with dark irony after terrifying him with her nightly ritualistic voyeurism: "I went boldly into his chamber, and spoke courageously to him, calling him by his name in a hearty tone, and inquiring how he had passed the night" (306). But she deeply resents the scrutiny of his eye, feeling abused and objectified by his paternal surveillance. Angered and humiliated by his gaze, she goes through the same maneuver that the male narrator does in reversing the path of this gaze. Unlike the male narrator, her primary desire is to rid herself of the male gaze, or domination. However, in traveling through the gaze's path, she substitutes the first desire for her need physically to possess the old man. In this context, the climactic scene in the bedroom, with its implied sexual overtones, supports a Lacanian feminist reading better than a Oedipal one. In that one moment of possession, she becomes the aggressor; she even assumes a male sexual posture, forcing the old man to receive her, almost raping him, so that "he shrieked once— once only" (305). The scene culminates with her smirk: "There was nothing to wash out—no stain of any kind— no blood spot whatsoever. . . . A tub caught it all" (305). In this one act, the female narrator captures both the masculine gaze and masculine role. Thus, in appropriating the male posture, she even refers to herself in explicitly masculine terms, claiming repeatedly, that her actions are not those of a "madman."

Yet, ironically, the very authority of her newfound power makes her more vulnerable, more of an object of desire by others. Metaphorically, she moves from the position of actively desiring that Lacan allows to both the male and female to the position of being passively desired, one that is traditionally only the female's. It is here that the Lacanian "itinerary of the signifier" betrays her. The movement between male/female roles is ultimately restrictive to the female. Unlike the male narrator who confesses for fear of castration, the female narrator is denied this option. Acknowledging her femininity, she stands before the policemen, stripped of her power in her traditional posture as female, passive, subservient, and accountable to the male gaze—and exposed in the eyes of the Law through the return of the repressed (murdered) father. She begins and ends in a stereotypically feminine posture, the nurturer who has returned to her quintessentially repressed object position.

My feminist rereading with metonymy as focal point again reveals the confined position of the female narrator. The heart as an allegory of metonymy displaces the narrator's fears and desires, working on the two levels already examined, making her obey the dictates of her confused emotions. Further, Poe's text, if reread as narrated by a female

speaking subject, indicates that this desire and fear is more frequently associated with a female "voice" than it is with the male's. The female narrator of **"The Tell-Tale Heart"** focuses on evocations of space and emptiness, which are typical expressions of female consciousness. The narrator claims her fear was engulfing, making her feel as if "enveloped in cotton" (305), just like her "terrors" which "welled" up in her bosom, "deepening, with its dreadful echo" (304). Interestingly, Lacan's theory of metonymy as the motor of language supports the psychoanalytic view that links the female phobia of emptiness (as a primal corollary to lacking the phallus) with gaps in narrativity that make this tale seem discontinuous and disjointed.[10] Thus, the narrator's confused recounting of her tale is a method of compensating for this emptiness, from the initial display of desire in her heart to the culminating betrayal of that desire, resulting in her agonizing confession.

This feminist investigation into the speaking subject, both male and female, unmasks the hidden male agenda; it also shows that a feminist rereading using only the Lacanian principles of psychoanalysis is problematic. As already shown, the female narrator's voluntary confession to the mildly suspecting policemen reveals her restricted position. As woman, she reoccupies her traditional role as a submissive, victimized object, offering herself up to be scrutinized once more by the male gaze. She can, finally, never aspire to usurp this power or be outside/above the Law of the Father. Ironically, even though a feminist rereading grants the female narrator a temporary masculine, active, subject posture, it undercuts this interpretation in returning her to a traditionally female position by superimposing a judicial and patriarchal closure. Such a feminist reading shows how clearly the female is boxed into a role, making both her sexual and gender identity rigid. A feminist rereading must go beyond the unmasking of such oppression; it must seek alternate positions for the female speaking subject.

Although Lacanian psychoanalysis first creates a division between male/female and then erases it under the guise of gender equalization, it seems to suggest that certain codes of behavior and discourse are allowable *only* to a male. Should a female dare to transgress, she will be punished by the Law of the Father. Consequently, the female narrator is permitted to desire the "metaphoric" phallus as power, but she can never aspire to possess it. And if she chooses to disobey this basic patriarchal dictum, not only will she fail but she must bear the moral consequences. In a feminist rereading of the ending of the tale, the female narrator's marginalization becomes explicit. What was successfully interpreted as a dramatization of the Oedipal *myth* for the male narrator turns to the harsh *reality* of oppression for the female narrator.

A feminist theorist must suspect that this development reveals Lacan's bias in adapting Freud's notion of manifest and repressed texts. At the manifest level, Lacan explicitly advocates sexual egalitarianism, but at the repressed (more influential) level he implicitly subverts it. My feminist rereading of the manifest text is as presented in the above analyses. Yet if one were to reread the repressed text, the Lacanian prejudice against the female would become obvious. I submit that the unconscious, or repressed text, through the pressure it exerts on the conscious or manifest text, shows that patriarchal morality condemns a woman for being aggressive, for desiring power, and ultimately punishes her for achieving this power even temporarily. Both male and female readers of Poe's story have tended to accept the Law of the Father, together with all its arbitrary presuppositions, and grant power only to the male. Thus, the status of the male narrator in Poe's **"The Tell-Tale Heart"** has remained stable. But if one wishes to transcend this phallogocentric prejudice, one must look elsewhere than Freud and Lacan.

To experience what Cixous explains as jouissance within Poe's text, we must erase the rigidity of metaphor (eye) and metonymy (heart) as separate categories. Instead, a gendered reading of Poe's tale would make the "eye" and the "heart" serve as metaphors and metonymies simultaneously, intermingling and creating multiple meanings. Quite accurately, Cixous's use of tropes can be called gendered, as they have greater maneuverability than Lacan's sexual tropes, which are clearly marked as *metaphor/symbolic/male,* and *metonymy/imaginary/female.* This strategy is Cixous's way of combating Lacan's notion of gender dissemination, which is actually based on a sexual paradigm. Lacan's position is invested with patriarchal biases such that the female term is violated and abused either at the conscious (manifest text) or unconscious (repressed text) level. The "eye" as metaphor has yielded meaning to Poe's text, but reading it metonymically enriches the tale further. The "eye" is the virtual symptom of the female narrator's desire to gain power in a male dominated society. In this context, it energizes the sequence of events in the tale to climax in the narrator's confession. Since killing the old man does not grant her lasting power, she confesses to the policemen and, thus, recirculates her power. Paradoxically, in the confessional scene "she" adroitly forces the male gaze to expose the controlled violence of the patriarchy. Her aggression against the old man is an explicit assault on male domination. Her confession becomes her implicit critique of domination. For a feminist reader, this is gratifying, an expression of solidarity through her exposure of ideology. For a masculinist reader, it is one more reminder of rebellion against patriarchal oppression. Her confession reveals the latent fetters of bondage in a patriarchal ideology, and she *rer*everses the gaze of the policemen by letting it bounce off her objectified body by using the eye as a metonymic instrument. Here the gaze is just one more part in her plan to expose the system. She exchanges the virtual prison bars of the Father's Law for the actual ones of the penal system. Henceforth, she will covertly make her point on discrimination against women through the underlying irony of her tale.

Writhing under the policemen's scrutiny, she protests: "they were making a mockery of my horror! . . . But any thing was better than this agony . . . more tolerable than this derision" (306). This indicates that her first plan to usurp power from the old man had failed, and now she must adopt another, creating a new perspective for the final scene. Her confession, now read ironically and not as evidence of guilt, directs the gaze back into the metaphoric register. It activates her plan for the exposé. For a moment, between her first plan and the second one, the gaze falls on the metaphoric spectre of the Law. In this sense, the interweaving of metaphor and metonymy, as a slippage of tropes, allows for multiple readings that build on one another instead of repressing one meaning to manifest another. This is an example of the jouissance that Cixous advocates as a method of accretion.

Similarly, luxuriating in the jouissance of multiplicity, the "heart" can be moved from the metonymic to the metaphoric register. As a metaphor, it serves to foreground the tale as belonging to the romance genre, with all its associations of passion and fantasy. It also allows the tale to be read as wish fulfillment, a dream in which the narrator as melodramatic heroine becomes the cynosure in a male arena, the active speaking subject, instead of the fetishized object. She proudly declares: "I foamed—I raved—I swore" (307), as a way of explaining her frantic attempts to remain on center stage. This is an enactment of the stereotypical feminine posture. By obeying the dictates of her heart in committing the passionate crime (exaggerated, no doubt), she dramatizes her execrated position as woman. Now the female narrator emerges as the martyr through her confession, also a typical position for the female.

But when examining the text under the light of jouissance, the first step in reading is to expose such a patriarchal stereotyping. Yet the interweaving of the metaphoric and metonymic registers gives diverse readings. According to the metonymic register (eye), the female narrator is an active speaking subject who assumes a male gendered identity, but the metaphoric register (heart) forces her back into the archetypical female position of martyr. This slip between the metaphoric and metonymic registers is crucial to feminist writing because it reveals the androgyny created by jouissance. Moreover, gendered identity sheds a different light on the other characters in the tale, too. In the crucial, confessional scene, all the characters can be read androgynously. The literal keepers of the Law of the Father, the police*men* observe *passively* while the *female* narrator is explosively *active.* She is the speaking subject, frantically pacing, vigorously thumping the furniture, and energetically talking. She is catapulted into her final ironic, yet male and active posture by "the beating of *his* heart!" (307, italics added). It is the old man's heart, dramatized like a damsel in distress, that vocalizes the narrator's confession. In the ironic conclusion of the tale, both the policemen and the old man remain static, while the female narrator adopts the dynamic and aggressive role, deliberately calling attention to the subservient status of all women. What needs to be emphasized here is the active androgynous narrator who can be contrasted to the passive males; her actions should not be mistaken for the actions for a stereotypical "hysterical" female. This erroneous stereotyping will, no doubt, create a neat niche for the female, but leave the male position in the discourse vacant. Thus, Cixous's brand of androgyny and multiple readings cancel out stereotypical sexual markings of the text.

Poe's **"The Tell-Tale Heart"** can indeed be read as the female narrator's own cry from "the soul when overcharged with awe" (304), a tale of escape, but escape into deliberate captivity so that she can articulate a female discourse. She experiments and functions in both the active and passive registers as a speaking subject and passive object. In this venture, her discourse becomes a painful tool of signifying and defining herself within the confines of patriarchy. Through jouissance, interweaving metaphors and metonymies, constantly slipping between the tropes, defying libidinal economy, and creating an excess of signifiers, she inscribes an "other" discourse. This rewriting becomes possible through the complex pattern of gendered tropes that are occupied by both male and female characters in the tale. It is this embracing, this gathering together, not only of the tropes, but also of the characters occupying these gendered tropes, that makes this tale a revelation of feminist rewriting as well as rereading.

Notes

[1] Jacques Lacan, "L'Instance de la lettre dans l'inconscient," *Ecrits I,* trans. Alan Sheridan (New York: Norton, 1977). Lacan argues that metonymy is the "derailment of instinct . . . externally extended towards the desire of something else" (278).

[2] Roman Jakobson, "Two Aspects of Language and Two Types of Aphasic Disturbances," in *Fundamentals of Language* (The Hague: Mouton, 1956) 55-82. Lacan matches Saussure's linguistic model with Jakobson's to formulate the signifier/signified and metaphor/metonymy relationship (274).

[3] See Jerry Ann Flieger, "The Purloined Punchline: Joke as Textual Paradigm," *Contemporary Literary Criticism,* ed. Robert Con Davis (New York: Longman, 1986) 277-94, who claims that a text through its intersubjectivity acts as a feminine symptom of inexhaustible desire. Toril Moi, in her introduction to *Sexual/Textual Politics,* discusses Lacan's theory of the "symbolic/metaphoric" and male vector as always coexisting with the "imaginary/metonymic" and female vector in any discourse in an attempt to make meaning within the text. See Anthony Wilden, *The Language of the Self* (New York: Dell, 1975) 249-70, for a discussion of Lacan's symbolic/imaginary registers.

[4] Robert Con Davis, "Lacan, Poe, and Narrative Repression," in *Lacan and Narration: The Psychoanalytic Difference In Narrative Theory* (Baltimore: Johns Hopkins UP, 1984). Davis argues that, according to Freud, the act of gazing represents the gazer's status as subject actively engaged in a pleasurable power game with the receiver of the gaze. In the object position, the receiver passively submits to the painful humiliation of the gazer's oppressive surveillance. By incorporating Lacan into Freud's theory, Davis shows that the "Gaze" is composed of three shifting positions of the subject's desire for the Other. Beginning with the gazer in a voyeuristic subject position, scrutinizing an exhibitionist as object, we move to a second, mirror-like stage, where the subject/object of the gaze are replicas of each other. In the final moment, positions are reversed when the (former subject and current) object returns the gaze. Like the ever-shifting signifiers in language, the gaze is also a neverending game. Davis's Lacanian interpretation sees the gaze as a mark of desire for the Other that is revealed in the text through intersubjectivity and reciprocal looking. Thus the looker, by looking, loses some of his power through the gaze itself.

[5] Edgar Allan Poe, *The Complete Tales and Poems of Edgar Allan Poe* (New York: Modern Library, 1965) 303; cited hereafter in the text.

[6] Hélène Cixous, "An Imaginary Utopia," *Sexual/Textual Politics,* ed. Toril Moi (New York: Methuen, 1985) 102-27. Cixous's theoretical paradigm is based on Derrida's deconstructive poetics. This particular three-step reinscription is my synthesis of Cixous's position as expressed in "The Laugh of the Medusa," in *New French Feminisms,* ed. Elaine Marks and Isabelle de Courtivron (Amherst: U of Massachusetts P, 1980) 245-64, and in "Castration or Decapitation?" *Signs* 7 (1981): 41-55.

[7] For a more detailed discussion on the nature of patriarchal thought, the concept of sexual difference, and *écriture féminine* see Hélène Cixous and Catherine Clément, *La Jeune Née* (Paris: Union General d'Editions, 1975) 147; Julia Kristeva, *Desire in Language: A Semiotic Approach to Literature and Art,* ed. Leon S. Roudiez, trans. Thomas Gora, Alice Jardine, and Roudiez (New York: Columbia UP, 1980) 239-40; both cited hereafter in the text.

[8] Marie Bonaparte, *The Life and Works of Edgar Allan Poe* (1949; London: Hogarth P, 1971).

[9] Lacan, "L'Instance" 171.

[10] Jacques Lacan, "Seminar XX" in *Feminine Sexuality,* ed. Juliet Mitchell and Jaqueline Rose (New York: Norton, 1982). For Lacan's discussion of women, see 48.

Paige Matthey Bynum (essay date 1989)

SOURCE: "'Observe how healthily—how calmly I can tell you the whole story': Moral Insanity and Edgar Allan Poe's 'The Tell-Tale Heart'," in *Literature and Science as Modes of Expression,* edited by Frederick Amrine, Kluwer Academic Publishers, 1989, pp. 141-52.

[*In the following essay, Bynum asserts that Poe and his reading audience alike were familiar with the then-current debate about "moral insanity" and points out that while readers of "The Tell-Tale Heart" are drawn into the mind of a deranged killer, they still identify with the terror of his victim because of their frame of reference outside the text.*]

David R. Saliba has recently argued that Edgar Allan Poe's "structural omission of an objective viewpoint for the reader [in **'The Tell-Tale Heart'**] forces the reader to experience the tale with no point of reference outside the framework of the story". "The reader", says Saliba, "is led through the story by the narrator with no sense of reality other than what the narrator has to say". This narrative technique forces the reader to identify with the narrator and to take the narrator's values as his own (pp. 142-43n). What Saliba fails to realize is that no one can read a text without an external sense of reality; all audiences bring to a work of literature some frame of reference that exists outside the text. And for Poe's audience in the 1840s, that frame of reference would have included a knowledge of a controversial new disease called 'moral insanity' and of the legal and philosophical dilemmas that surrounded its discovery. Poe's narrator in **'The Tell-Tale Heart'** is a morally insane man, and Poe would have expected his readers to locate the symptoms of that condition in the language of his narration. Thus if we are to recover the meaning of the tale for Poe's audience, an audience that applauded **'The Tell-Tale Heart'** at the same time that it shunned tales like **'Ligeia'**, **'William Wilson'**, and **'The Fall of the House of Usher'**—indeed, if we are to assess the tale's significance for today's audience—we need to establish the medical history from which Poe drew.

We begin, then, with the 'father of American psychiatry', Benjamin Rush. In 1787, Rush was placed in charge of the insane at the Pennsylvania Hospital, and his work in this institution culminated in the first book on psychiatry by a native American, *Medical Inquiries and Observations upon the Diseases of the Mind* (1812). In his introduction to two of the essays Rush included in *Diseases of the Mind*,[1] E. T. Carlson explains how Rush developed a new theory of insanity based on associationism and faculty psychology. Following the Scottish school of mental philosophy, Rush posited nine basic capacities or "faculties" in the human mind, grouping these nine faculties into three categories: the "passions" included the passions *per se,* the will, and faith or "the believing faculty"; the "intellectual faculties" encompassed the reason or understanding, imagination, and memory; and the "moral faculties" included the moral faculty itself, conscience, and a sense of deity (Carlson, p. ix).[2] Insanity had long been recognized as a disease affecting what Rush called the intellectual faculties. Where Rush broke with traditional psychiatric theory was in declaring that insanity did not necessarily involve a disorder of the intellect, that the moral faculties alone were capable of succumbing to disease (Carlson, p. x). Like Philippe Pinel in France, he realized that a form of insanity might occur which perverted the sense of moral responsibility necessary to deter crime. Thus in a normal individual, an innate moral sense could stave off the passions while the intellect calmly concluded the proper conduct. But if this moral sense, this power to distinguish between good and evil, were momentarily suspended, the opportunity for calm inquiry would be denied, and the individual's will would become committed to a criminal act before his reason could repudiate it (Rush, 1972, p. 1). He would then become the victim of an "irresistible impulse" forced upon the will "through the instrumentality of the passions" (Rush, 1830, pp. 262; 355-57). In modern terminology, he would be emotionally disturbed.

Startling as it was, Rush's theory of "moral derangement" received little attention in America before the 1830s. Then, in 1835, James Cowles Prichard published his classic discussion of the problem in *Treatise on Insanity and Other Disorders Affecting the Mind.* This work popularized the study of what Prichard termed "moral insanity", making it, in the words of one historian, the "focus of psychological studies and polemical arguments until the end of the century" (Carlson, p. xi). Following the leads of Pinel and Rush, Prichard restated and developed the body of theory

which would eventually lead to the classification of psychopathic personalities. He posited a disease in which

> the intellectual faculties appear to have sustained little or no injury, while the disorder is manifested principally or alone, in the state of the feelings, temper, or habits. In cases of this description the moral and active principles of the mind are strangely perverted and depraved; the power of self-government is lost or greatly impaired; and the individual is found to be incapable, not of talking or reasoning upon any subject proposed to him, for this he will often do with great shrewdness and volubility, but of conducting himself with decency and propriety. . . . His wishes and inclinations, his attachments, his likings and dislikings have all undergone a morbid change, and this change appears to be the originating cause, or to lie at the foundations of any disturbance which the understanding itself may seem to have sustained, and even in some instances to form throughout the sole manifestation of the disease (pp. 4-5).

A disturbance of the emotions could be both the cause and the "sole manifestation" of mental illness. The morally insane man might be rational, might realize that those around him would condemn his behavior, but he himself would not.

In the decade following the appearance of Prichard's study, the concept of moral insanity became the topic of political, social, and theological debate both at home and abroad. As Rush himself foresaw, any new theories which emphasized the power of man's emotions to determine his actions occasioned intense hostility when they conflicted with other, presumably more agreeable, ideas about human nature. Such theories were opposed on the grounds that they degraded the quality of man's spiritual life, and for the more pragmatic reason that they reduced the incentives for good behavior. But nowhere were the new theories on moral insanity argued more strenuously that in the courts. Prior to the work of men like Rush and Prichard, if a person pleaded insanity in a court of law, he was presumed to be either an idiot or a raving maniac. A review of press releases concerning these trials, and of verbatim trial reports, shows that judges, counsel, witnesses, and observers tended to use three major criteria to establish insanity: the accused had to be unable to recognize right from wrong; he had to be illogical and virtually witless at all times; and he had to reveal a violent disposition before committing his offense ('Homicidal Insanity', p. 279; Wharton, I, 162-72). John Haslam's discussion of the jurisprudence of insanity in *Observations on Madness and Melancholy* (1810) reveals that madness was considered to be, in Haslam's words, as opposed to "reason and good sense as light is to darkness"; in order to exempt a man from criminal responsibility, the defense had to establish that he was "totally deprived of his understanding" and no more knew what he was doing "than an infant, than a brute, or a wild beast" (Haslam, 1975, p. 31; see also Coventry, p. 136). A man who, like Poe's narrator in **'The Black Cat'**, became unaccountably brutal, set fire to his home, and violently murdered his wife could not be judged insane if he appeared 'normal' to witnesses at the time of the trial.[3] And anyone who fled from the scene of a murder, or tried to hide the evidence, was legally sane because he was presumed to know right from wrong.

But the concept of moral insanity changed all this, and the legal dilemma posed by this new definition of madness was obvious. If God had so constituted men that their passions or impulses were not always governable by an intact reason, how could society punish them for indulging in these passions? As pleas of moral insanity became increasingly common, this question stymied a criminal court system established as an instrument of retribution rather than as an agency for determining mental health.[4] A reaction was inevitable and almost immediate. Judges found themselves asserting that moral insanity was, in Baron Rolfe's words, "an extreme moral depravity not only perfectly consistent with legal responsibility, but such as legal responsibility is expressly invented to restrain" ('Baron Rolfe's Charge to the Jury', p. 214). Some of America's leading pre-Civil War psychiatrists—men like Isaac Ray, Samuel B. Woodward, and Amariah Brigham—wrote numerous treatises and periodical articles delineating the characteristics and supporting the pleas of criminals claiming moral insanity, but they faced serious opposition within their own profession almost from the outset, and by the late 1840s even some distinguished asylum superintendents began denying the existence of a 'moral' insanity.

The views of these skeptical physicians were generally more in keeping with public sentiment, and those medical men who supported an accused murderer's claim of insanity came under increasingly sharp attacks in the periodical press. The average man tended to suspect deception in defense pleas of insanity, and newspapers often fanned these feelings. Thus by the time Poe wrote **'The Tell-Tale Heart'**, such trials were major events. When William Freeman was tried for the stabbing murders of the prominent Van Nest family in New York, the counsel included John Van Buren for the prosecution and ex-governor William H. Seward for the defense. Papers across the country kept track as seventy-two witnesses were called to testify as to his sanity, including a who's-who list of medical authorities, and Freeman himself, housed in a cage outside the courthouse, was the subject of "uncounted spectators" until he died of consumption in his cell almost eighteen months after his offense (*The Trial of William Freeman*, pp. 68-71, 79-80; Fosgate, pp. 409-14).[5]

Freeman and those like him were, to use the modern slang, "hot copy". The journals of the day devoted thousands of pages to analysis of them. Philosophical and literary societies debated the ethical and moral implications of decisions surrounding their cases. And writers like Poe—who was himself a trial reporter in the 1843 murder-by-reason-of-moral-insanity trial of James Wood ('The Trial of James Wood', pp. 105-106)[6]—used them as models for some of their most disturbing creations.

One of these creations came to life in **'The Tell-Tale Heart'**. Defendants in moral insanity trials were rarely allowed to speak in their own behalf, but Poe would let his character speak, and as he spoke, he would inadvertently let slip the very evidence which would establish him as morally insane.

The first thing we should notice about Poe's narrator is that his monologue is actually a long argument trying to establish not his innocence—he has already confessed to killing the old man—but rather his sanity. He builds this argument on the premise that insanity is irreconcilable with systematic action, and as evidence of his capacity for the latter, he explains how he has executed an atrocious crime with faultless precision. "This is the point", he tells us: "You fancy me mad. Madmen know nothing. But you should have seen *me*. You should have seen how wisely I proceeded—with what caution—with what foresight—with what dissimulation I went to work!" (Poe, 1978, p. 792). A madman, he implies, would be out of control, would be profoundly illogical and not even recognize the implications of his actions. His art in planning and coolness in executing his crime prove that he has the lucidity, control, and subtle reason which only a sane man could possess.

Poe's narrator is, of course, relying upon the old criteria used to establish insanity. But it would have been difficult for an audience reading his words in 1843 not to call to mind the medical publications and trial reports filling the popular press with a new theory of insanity. If they knew enough about this new theory, they might even have recognized Poe's narrator as a fair representation of Prichard's morally insane man. Like the patients in Prichard's study, he is capable of reasoning "with great shrewdness and volubility", but "his attachments . . . have undergone a morbid change" (Prichard, pp. 4-5).

This is not to say that Poe's narrator is always rational. He may be able to carry out his crime with a cool precision, but as he himself explains, his determination to murder his old friend stems from an irrational fear of his eye:

> Object, there was none. I loved the old man. He had never given me insult. For his gold I had no desire. I think it was his eye! yes it was this! One of his eyes resembled that of a vulture—a pale blue eye with a film over it. Whenever it fell upon me, my blood ran cold; and so by degrees—very gradually—I made up my mind to take the life of the old man, and thus rid myself of the eye forever.

Poe skillfully refrains from divulging exactly what the narrator fears, and his readers have consistently picked up the gauntlet and put forth their own theories. Robert Shulman believes that the filmed-over eye suggests that the old man is cut off from "insight into the ideal and the beautiful" and that the narrator's fear thus represents man's "psychological dread that existence is meaningless", or more specifically, is a reflection of Poe's feelings toward the stepfather who "called into question the meaning of [his] life" (pp. 259-60). Arthur Robinson argues that the feared "Evil Eye" is actually the "Evil I", that the narrator "images himself as another and recoils from the vision" (pp. 101-2). And in his introduction to **'The Tell-Tale Heart'**, T. O. Mabbott concludes that the tale is founded on the "popular superstition" of the Evil Eye and points out that Poe may even be suggesting that it really *is* the old man's eye which drives the otherwise sane narrator mad (Poe, 1978, p. 789). However we feel about these interpretations, we should perhaps realize that much of Poe's audience, and certainly Poe himself, would have been familiar with Rush's theory (1830, p. 173) that the insane were "for the most part easily terrified, or composed, by the eye of a man who possesses his reason". They would have surmised that Poe's narrator is terrified by, in Rush's words, "the mild and steady eye" of a sane man.[7]

But it is not the eye alone which brings about the final decision to take the old man's life. Rather, it is a *peculiar sound,* and to understand the medical significance of this sound, we must go back to the beginning of the tale. The narrator opens his defense by declaring that although he is "very, very dreadfully nervous", he is not mad (1978, p. 792). Poe's readers probably would have recognized his nervousness as one of the common predisposing causes of moral insanity. Certainly most physicians writing at the time of Poe's tale would have agreed with Samuel B. Woodward (p. 288) that moral insanity, unlike mere depravity, was always preceded or accompanied by "some diseased function of the organs, more or less intimately connected with the nerves". Rush had maintained that "all those states of the body . . . which are accompanied with preternatural irritability . . . dispose to vice" (1972, p. 20). But even if the audience was uncertain about the significance of the narrator's dreadful nervousness, they certainly would not have been uncertain about the significance of his next statement. This nervousness, or "disease", had "sharpened [his] senses", he tells us, "not destroyed—not dulled them", and "above all was [his] sense of hearing acute" (1978, p. 792).

It would be difficult to think of a worse argument for sanity in 1843 than what Poe's narrator calls his "over acuteness of the senses" (1978, p. 795). Medical opinion at home and abroad had long held that "there is scarcely any symptom more frequently attendant upon maniacal . . . disorders than a defect, excess, or some kind of derangement in the faculty of hearing" (Reid, p. 190), and that it is frequently "noises in the ear, such as sounds made during the night in the chimney", and in particular, "the noises of clocks and of bells" (Sigmond, p. 589; 'On Impulsive Insanity', p. 620) which haunt the minds of these men.[8] We should not be surprised then to learn that, as he stands over his intended victim, Poe's narrator hears "a low, dull, quick sound, such as a watch makes when enveloped in cotton" (1978, p. 795). His assertion that "he knew *that* sound well, too" reminds us that he has also been hearing another sound—that of the death-watches in the wall. "Night after night" he had listened to their ticking, telling himself that "it is nothing but the wind in the chimney", until the night when, "excited to uncontrollable terror" by the noise, he stalks his victim (1978, p. 796).

After the murder, the ticking sound returns, and the fear, outrage and paranoia it inspires increase until the seem-

ingly rational murderer must confess his crime to the unsuspecting police. Even this confession would have been considered strong evidence of moral insanity. In a typical case from 1832, a man on trial for the murder of his son was found insane because he had "slaughtered his unoffending son to whom he should have been attached", and then confessed. One reporter explains:

> The confession of the crime, I conceive, may be considered as an evidence of insanity of considerable weight. Not that every man who confesses a murder is to be considered insane, but, by this, taken along with other circumstances, as when the individual . . . attempts to give reasons for the propriety of his conduct, we have a strong indication . . . of the deranged condition of the intellect. . . . In short, it is so universal in such cases, that some very distinguished medical jurists consider this confession alone to be a significant test of insanity (Watson, 1832, p. 47).[9]

Observations such as this can be found throughout the trial reports of the 1830s and 40s, and while they may sound fairly obvious to today's readers, they contained new and fascinating information for Poe's. And this, of course, is the point. New medical theories were forcing upon Poe's audience questions of ethical moment and challenging their old ideas about the nature of man. It may even be that this audience, like most of the students I teach today, found the real terror in the story lay in identifying themselves not with the narrator, as Saliba suggests, but with the victim. It certainly would have been natural for Poe's 1843 readers to see themselves as the victims of the morally insane men discussed in the popular press, just as twentieth-century readers tend to associate themselves more with suffering families and felled presidents than with madmen who attack McDonald's and presidential assassins. In any case, Poe's narrator is maintaining a causal sequence—I can reason; therefore I am not insane—which Poe's audience had just discovered was false, so that it is not only the experiences the narrator reports that are unusual and problematic, but the report itself. "Observe how healthily—how calmly I can tell you the whole story", he begins (1978, p. 792). But "calmly" could no longer be equated with "healthily". The narrator's explanation fails to coincide with his audience's knowledge, and the implication is that Poe intends to display this disagreement in order that the audience might experience and evaluate it. Far from being trapped inside the story, the audience would stand outside the narrative and use its knowledge of the current medical controversy to replace the speaker's version of events with a better one, or even to question the moral implications of such an argument.

The narrator tells them that he has suffocated an old man because of his eye. But to make such an argument is finally to flaunt your lack of motive, and indeed he begins his explanation by admitting that "object there was none." (1978, p. 792). Those readers who insist upon positing an external motive on the narrator's part, or an unconscious motive on Poe's, deny the story some of its power. Like the murder of the Van Nest family, this murder is all the more terrifying because it is gratuitous. The narrator's obsessions have no logical object in the manifest text, and the tension produced by his explaining at length something for which there is no satisfactory explanation took Poe's story to the heart of the vexing question of moral responsibility as it dramatized the increasingly problematic nature of the human personality.

For Poe's 1843 audience, the new medical science had done more than just drag Diana from her car; it had questioned the integrity of even the 'rational' mind. But what about today's audience? Clearly the medical sources Poe drew from are now outdated, and we no longer recognize Poe's medical allusions. But the deep-seated and not always clearly verbalized anxiety generated by the knowledge that men like Prichard and Rush imparted is still with us. What Poe's 1843 audience had learned—what his present audience is still struggling with—was that a murderous rage could be present in any man, could begin to manifest itself without motivation, and once manifest, could exert complete control. The will to do wrong was internally derived; it could no longer be referred to poisonous miasmatas, solipsism, alcohol, or intellectual indulgence. Even reason could provide no check on these murderous rages, since the most careful plans and meticulous arguments could be made to support the most vicious actions. This was, and is, the real terror of Poe's tale: that there is in man the potential for an inexplicable moral short-circuit that makes it impossible to find protection from the dangers that lay within our neighbors—and ourselves. It is to Poe's credit as an artist that he has given this terror an imaginative representation which has remained valid long after Prichard's theories have disappeared.

Notes

[1] Rush originally published these essays in 1786. They were reprinted in *Medical Inquiries and Observations upon the Diseases of the Mind* in 1812, where they went through five editions and numerous translations. In 1972, Brunner/Mazel reprinted them again as a separate volume, introduced by E. T. Carlson, entitled *Two Essays on the Mind*.

[2] When combined with the notion that each faculty was connected to a particular area of the brain, Rush's theory gained widespread acceptance as phrenology. Poe was at one time an adherent to some of the ideas espoused by phrenology, but by the 1840s, his views were closer to the views of established medicine.

[3] A case fitting this description actually exists. See 'John Ball's Case' (pp. 85-6). See also 'Ancient Case of Homicidal Insanity' (pp. 283-4), which gives the case of a man convicted for murdering his wife despite the fact that he felt she was one of the witches and wizards haunting him.

[4] Thanks to the work of Pinel and the moral managers, public opinion regarding insanity was becoming more enlightened, and as public awareness increased, defense pleas of insanity became more common. There were only a few such cases before 1825, but by the late 1840s there were well over fifty.

[5] For a good example of how newspapers reported on these trials, see the reports of the Freeman trial in the [*New York*] *Evening*

Post, 19 March 1846, p. 1, col. 9, and the *New York Tribune,* 20 March 1846, p. 3, col. 1.

[6] It is clear, however, that Poe knew something about moral insanity as early as 1837. In the first chapter of *The Narrative of Arthur Gordon Pym* (1837), Pym compares Augustus's intoxication to that state of madness which "frequently enables the victim to imitate the outward demeanor of one in perfect possession of his senses" (Poe, 1975, p. 50).

[7] We should also remember that the fear-of-eyes theme runs throughout Poe's work of the 1830s and '40s and is not always associated with father-figures. Metzengerstein "turn[s] pale and [shrinks] away from the rapid and searching expression of his [horse's] earnest and human-looking eye" (Poe, 1978, p. 28). The narrator of 'Ligeia' is at first attracted to and then terrified by the black orbs of his first love. And of course, the narrator of 'The Black Cat' impulsively cuts out the searching eye of his pet.

[8] Both Sigmond and the author of 'On Impulsive Insanity' are quoting from an essay by "Dr. Baillarger" which won an award from the French Academy of Medicine for the best dissertation on psychological medicine in 1844 (Sigmond, p. 585). See also Rush's discussion of "uncommonly acute" hearing in *Diseases of the Mind* (1830, p. 143). John E. Reilly (pp. 5-6) has also noticed that the increased acuteness of the senses was thought to be a sign of insanity in Poe's time, but he fails to note that the ticking and, later, ringing sounds heard by Poe's narrator were singled out by Poe's contemporaries as common hallucinations among the insane. He believes the narrator actually hears the noise made by deathwatches in the wall, but resorts back to hallucination when he must explain why the ticking increases in tempo just before the murder.

[9] Gunnar Bjurman points out (pp. 220ff) that one source for Poe's plot might have been Daniel Webster's 1830 pamphlet on the trial of John Francis Knapp. Webster describes a self-possessed murderer who, like Poe's narrator, "feels [his crime] beating at his heart, rising into his throat, and demanding disclosure" (XI, 52-54). There is evidence that Poe knew about Webster's pamphlet, but it should be remembered that by 1843, Poe and his audience would have read many such pamphlets and reports. Between 1825 and 1838, the Philadelphia publishing house of Carey and Lea published almost twice as many medical books as those in any other category except fiction, and mental health was a staple concern in these works (Kaser, pp. 72, 119-23).

Works Cited

'Ancient Case of Homicidal Insanity', *Connecticut Courant,* 15 November 1785, reprinted in *American Journal of Insanity* 3 (1847) pp. 283-4.

'Baron Rolfe's Charge to the Jury, in the case of the Boy Allnutt, who was tried at the Central Criminal 'ourt, for the Murder of his Grandfather, on the 15th Dec., 1847', *Journal of Psychological Medicine and Mental Pathology* 1 (1848) pp. 193-216.

Bjurman, G.: *Edgar Allan Poe: En Litteraturhistorisk Studie,* Gleerup, Lund, 1916.

Carlson, E.: Introduction, B. Rush, *Two Essays on the Mind,* Brunner/Mazel, New York, 1972, pp. v-xii.

Coventry, C.: 'Medical Jurisprudence of Insanity', *American Journal of Insanity* 1 (1844) pp. 134-44.

Fosgate, B.: 'Case of William Freeman, the Murderer of the Van Nest Family', *American Journal of the Medical Sciences* 28 (1847) pp. 409-14.

Haslam, J.: 'The Nature of Madness', in *Madness and Morals: Ideas on Insanity in the Nineteenth Century* (ed. by V. Skultans), Routledge and Kegan Paul, Boston, 1975, p. 31. (Excerpted from J. Haslam, *Observations on Madness and Melancholy*, Callow, London, 1810.)

'Homicidal Insanity, Case of Hadfield', *American Journal of Insanity* 3 (1847) pp. 277-82.

'John Ball's Case', *New York City-Hall Recorder* 2 (1817) pp. 85-6.

Kaser, D.: *Messrs. Carey & Lea of Philadelphia: A Study in the History of the Booktrade*, Univ. of Pennsylvania Press, Philadelphia, 1957.

'On Impulsive Insanity', *Journal of Psychological Medicine and Mental Pathology* 1 (1848) pp. 609-22.

Poe, E.: 'Metzengerstein', in *The Collected Works of Edgar Allan Poe* (ed. by T. O. Mabbott), Harvard Univ. Press, Cambridge, 1978, Vol. 2, pp. 15-31.

Poe, E.: *The Narrative of Arthur Gordon Pym* (ed. by H. Beaver), Penguin, Baltimore, 1975.

Poe, E.: 'The Tell-Tale Heart', in *The Collected Works of Edgar Allan Poe* (ed. by T. O. Mabbott), Harvard Univ. Press, Cambridge, 1978, Vol. 3, pp. 789-99.

Prichard, J.: *A Treatise on Insanity and Other Disorders Affecting the Mind*, Sherwood, Gilbert, and Piper, London, 1835.

Reid, J.: *Essays on Hypochondriasis and Other Nervous Affections*, Longman, Hurst, Rees, Orme, and Brown, London, 1823.

Reilly, J.: 'The Lesser Death-Watch and "The Tell-Tale Heart"', *American Transcendental Quarterly* 2 (1969) pp. 3-9.

Robinson, A.: 'Poe's "The Tell-Tale Heart"', in *Twentieth Century Interpretations of Poe's Tales* (ed. by W. Howarth), Prentice-Hall, Englewood Cliffs, 1971, pp. 94-102.

Rush, B.: 'An Enquiry into The Influence of Physical Causes upon the Moral Faculty', in *Two Essays on the Mind*, Brunner/Mazel, New York, 1972, pp. 1-40.

Rush, B.: *Medical Inquiries and Observations upon Diseases of the Mind*, 4th edn., John Grigg, Philadelphia, 1830.

Saliba, D.: *A Psychology of Fear: The Nightmare Formula of Edgar Allan Poe*, Univ. Press of America, Lanham, 1980.

Shulman, R.: 'Poe and the Powers of the Mind', *ELH* 37 (1970) pp. 245-62.

Sigmond, G.: 'On Hallucinations', *Journal of Psychological Medicine and Mental Pathology* 1 (1848) pp. 585-608.

'The Trial of James Wood', *Proceedings of the American Antiquarian Society* 52 (1843) pp. 105-6.

The Trial of William Freeman, for the Murder of John G. Van Nest, including the Evidence and the Arguments of Counsel, with the Decision of the Supreme Court Granting a New Trial, and an Account of the Death of the Prisoner, and of the Post-Mortem Examination of His Body by Amariah Brigham, M.D., and Others (reported by B. Hall), Derby, Miller & Co., Auburn, 1848.

Watson, A.: 'Three Medico-legal Cases of Homicide, in which Insanity was pleaded in Exculpation', *Edinburgh Medical and Surgical Journal* 38 (1832) pp. 45-58.

Webster, D.: *Writings and Speeches*, National Edition, 18 vols., Little Brown and Co., Boston, 1903.

Wharton, F.: *A Treatise on Mental Unsoundness Embracing a General View of Psychological Law*, 2 vols., Kay & Brother, Philadelphia, 1873.

Woodward, S.: 'Moral Insanity', *Boston Medical and Surgical Journal* 30 (1844) pp. 323-36.

Brett Zimmerman (essay date 1992)

SOURCE: "'Moral Insanity' or Paranoid Schizophrenia: Poe's 'The Tell-Tale Heart'," in *Mosaic*, Vol. 25, No. 2, Spring, 1992, pp. 39-48.

[*In the following essay, Zimmerman demonstrates that Poe's narrator in "The Tell-Tale Heart" displays characteristic signs of what was in Poe's day classified broadly as "moral insanity" and today diagnosed as paranoid schizophrenia. Zimmerman also makes the case that Poe's sophisticated insight into his character's psychology suggests the author did considerable research into his protagonist's condition using scientific texts and journals in order to lend accuracy and verisimilitude to his tale.*]

In our time, creative writers are expected to do their "homework," and consequently to find "modern" scientific accuracy in a literary text comes as no surprise. To discover similar scientific accuracy in a text from an early period is a different matter—one which involves not only questions about the sophistication of the artist but also about the sophistication of the science of his/her time. A case in point is Poe's short story of 1843, **"The Tell-Tale Heart."** Narrated in retrospect, Poe's confessional tale features a "mad" protagonist who recalls his grisly murder of an old man, his living companion, and who tries to explain the reasons for both this abominable act and his ultimate confession. My purpose in the following essay is to demonstrate the extent to which Poe's characterization of this narrator corresponds with current psychoanalytic profiles of the "paranoid schizophrenic" personality. Subsequently, my purpose is to consider the "science" of Poe's time in order to show how it "anticipates" current thinking and so provides the context for Poe's own acute insights into the nature, cause and consequences of this kind of mental illness.

According to current psychological theory, the "active" phase of paranoid schizophrenia is preceded by a "prodromal" phase during which premonitory symptoms occur, one of which is "superstitiousness" (*DSM* 195).[1] In Poe's tale, what precipitated the narrator's insanity and the subsequent murder was his irrational obsession with the old man's so-called "Evil Eye." The narrator freely admits to his auditors that this was his *primum mobile:* "yes, it was this! He had the eye of a vulture—a pale blue eye, with a film over it. Whenever it fell upon me, my blood ran cold; and so by degrees—very gradually—I made up my mind to take the life of the old man, and thus rid myself of the eye forever" (88). Although it might be argued that the madman's comments about the "Evil Eye" constitute his rationalization about his decision to murder, the way he describes the object suggests that the "Eye" was indeed the thing which drove him to commit his atrocities. Although mad, he is not *entirely* an unreliable narrator, for what we should consider is the way his *idée fixe,* his superstition concerning the "Evil Eye," generated a kind of anxiety or "overwhelming stress" which, according to current theories, can lead to a full schizophrenic breakdown (Sue 441-42).

A major symptom of the active phase of schizophrenia involves hallucinations, and it is here that Poe critics have come closest to identifying the specific nature of the narrator's mental condition. For example, before she abandons herself to a Freudian interpretation, Marie Bonaparte refers to "auditory hallucinations of paranoia" (498). Similarly, in their anthology of short fiction, *The Abnormal Personality Through Literature,* Alan Stone and Sue Smart Stone include **"The Tell-Tale Heart"** in a chapter on psychotic symptoms—specifically, hallucinations. Closest to a more precise identification of the narrator's condition is John E. Reilly, who indeed describes the protagonist as a paranoid schizophrenic (5-6). To Reilly, the key index to the narrator's condition is his "hyperacusis," but it is at this point that his analysis falls short and the directions from current research become important.

According to modern researchers, paranoid schizophrenics often experience sensory perceptions that are not directly attributable to environmental stimuli. They also note that 74% of schizophrenics suffer from *auditory* hallucinations: they hear sounds that are not real to others (Sue 428). Usually these sensorial illusions involve voices which the victim perceives as originating outside his/her head, but occasionally "the auditory hallucinations are of sounds rather than voices" (*DSM* 189).

Poe's narrator insists that his "disease had sharpened [his] senses—not destroyed—not dulled them," and that "Above all was the sense of hearing acute." Yet when he goes on to add "I heard all things in the heaven and in the earth. I heard many things in hell" (88), his absurdly grandiose claim encourages us to suspect related claims he makes regarding his auditory capacity. He explains, for example, that "there came to my ears a low, dull, quick

sound, such as a watch makes when enveloped in cotton" (91). He interprets this sound as the beating of the old man's heart, but it would have been impossible for him to hear such a noise unless his ear were against the old man's chest. Some scholars argue, in turn, that the narrator was in fact hearing his *own* heart (Shelden 77; Hoffman 232; Howarth 11). While such an interpretation is possible, the narrator's claim to hear things in heaven, hell and the earth makes it more logical to conclude that the sound he heard was not the beating of his own heart, but rather was an auditory hallucination.

To Reilly, the cause of the sound was actually an insect called the "lesser death-watch," but he also admits that there are certain discrepancies in his theory: "Whereas the narrator heard the sound on two occasions during the night of the murder, the ticking of the lesser death-watch is said to continue for hours. Moreover, the narrator reports that the sound he heard increased in tempo just before the murder and grew in volume on both occasions, whereas the ticking of the lesser death-watch is uniformly faint" (5). Reilly then tries to account for the discrepancies by saying that the narrator's "subjective sense of time accelerated the regular ticking of the lesser deathwatch" and its volume (7). Such a convoluted explanation is, however, entirely unnecessary if we view the protagonist as a paranoid schizophrenic. If we see him as suffering from auditory hallucinations, then we do not need to suggest any material source, whether insect or heart, for the sounds he claims to have heard—they originated inside his head.

The narrator, of course, insists that "the noise was *not* within my ears" (94), but such a disclaimer simply highlights another, the most common, symptom of schizophrenia—a lack of insight: "during the active phase of their disorder, schizophrenics are unable to recognize that their thinking is disturbed" (Sue 426). Although Poe's narrator admits to having some kind of sensorial disease, he is obviously unaware that it is in fact a *mental* aberration: "why *will* you say that I am mad?"; "You fancy me mad. Madmen know nothing. But you should have seen *me*"; "have I not told you that what you mistake for madness is but over acuteness of the senses?"; "If still you think me mad, you will think so no longer when I describe the wise precautions I took for the concealment of the body" (88, 91, 92). One of the greatest sources of irony—and perhaps pathos—in the tale is the narrator's vehement insistence that he is sane, rather than insane.

The protagonist's inflated opinion of himself is also in keeping with the current view that a "common delusion among paranoid schizophrenics involves exaggerated grandiosity and self-importance" (Sue 439). Poe's narrator brags and boasts specifically of his brilliant circumspection in preparing to murder the old man: "You should have seen how wisely I proceeded—with what caution—with what foresight—with what dissimulation I went to work! . . . Never before that night, had I *felt* the extent of my own powers—of my sagacity. I could scarcely contain my feelings of triumph" (88-89). The narrator believes that he has engaged in what Thomas de Quincy thinks of as "the fine art of murder." He would agree with the facetious de Quincy that a murder can be a very meritorious performance—when committed by a man of superior powers.

Not only was the murder performed with circumspection and with finesse, but so was the disposal of the corpse; Poe's narrator believes that in hiding the evidence of his crime he had considered every possible contingency:

> If still you think me mad, you will think so no longer when I describe the wise precautions I took for the concealment of the body. . . .
>
> I then took up three planks from the flooring of the chamber, and deposited all between the scantlings. I then replaced the boards so cleverly, so cunningly, that no human eye—not even *his*—could have detected any thing wrong. There was nothing to wash out—no stain of any kind—no blood-spot whatever. I had been too wary for that. A tub had caught all—ha! ha! (92-93)

Then this narrator *gloriosus* boasts of the "enthusiasm of my confidence" and of "my perfect triumph."

Other symptoms of paranoid schizophrenia include shifts of mood (Sue 433-34), and Poe's madman exhibits these in a number of ways. When he begins his recall, he boasts of "how calmly I can tell you the whole story" (88), and indeed his recollection starts calmly enough. As soon as he begins to recall the alleged beating of the old man's heart, however, he becomes frenetic and he loses his composure: "The old man's terror *must* have been extreme! It grew louder, I say, louder every moment! . . . Yet, for some minutes longer I refrained and stood still. But the beating grew louder, louder! I thought the heart must burst. And now a new anxiety seized me—the sound would be heard by a neighbour! The old man's hour had come!" (92). As James W. Gargano has demonstrated, "there is often an aesthetic compatibility between [Poe's] narrators' hypertrophic language and their psychic derangement . . ." (166). In **"The Tell-Tale Heart"** Poe dramatizes the madman's shift from calmness to hysteria by the increased use of such rhetorical devices as repetition (diacope, epizeuxis, ploce), exclamations, emphatic utterances (italics), and the dash. After he confesses how he murdered the old man, Poe's narrator calms down again—until he relates how the police entered his house and the sound of the "heartbeat" recommenced, at which point he becomes one of the most hysterical, most frenzied narrators in all of Poe's fiction.

Associated with the narrator's mood alterations are other symptoms of schizophrenia, including the display of emotions that are at variance with the normal reaction to a given situation: "Schizophrenic patients may exhibit wild laughter or uncontrollable weeping that bears little relationship to current circumstances. . . . Schizophrenics may express the wrong emotions or may express them inappropriately" (Sue 433-34). Evidencing this trait, Poe's protagonist recalls with delight the artful way he performed the most hideous of crimes. He assumes, as well, that his audience shares similar emotions; relating his stealth and patience while putting his head into the old man's chamber, he explains: "Oh, you would have laughed to see how cunningly I thrust it in! . . . To think that there I was, opening the door, little by little, and he not even to dream of my secret deeds or thoughts. I fairly chuckled at the idea . . ." (89-90). Although he pitied his intended victim, he nevertheless "chuckled at heart." In addition, the care he displayed in avoiding blood stains is for him a great source of complacency and humor: "A tub had caught all—ha! ha!" (93).

Complications of schizophrenia include "violent acts" (*DSM* 191), and, of course, the murder of the old man is clearly the ultimate manifestation of such a tendency. Not all paranoid schizophrenics are homicidal maniacs, however; often if they are violent at all the violence is turned against themselves rather than others. Clearly, though, Poe's schizophrenic is the most dangerous kind: his violence is turned outward, and he originally had no intention of coming to harm himself.

Features of paranoid schizophrenia associated with violence include anxiety, anger and argumentativeness (*DSM* 197). The anxiety of Poe's narrator is something he admits to and, indeed, stresses at the outset: "True!—nervous—very, very dreadfully nervous I had been and am . . ." (88). Anger and argumentativeness are also evidenced in his response to the police: "I arose and argued about trifles, in a high key and with violent gesticulations. . . . I foamed—I raved—I swore!" (94). Such symptoms constitute what is currently labeled "dysphoric mood" (*DSM* 190).

Unfortunately for Poe's paranoid schizophrenic, what finally proved his undoing is yet another symptom of his disease—delusions of persecution. Psychologists note that "deluded individuals believe that others are plotting against them, are talking about them, or are out to harm them in some way. They are constantly suspicious, and their interpretations of the behavior and motives of others are distorted" (Sue 438-39). When Poe's narrator invited the three officers in, he was at first certain that they suspected nothing; then his auditory hallucination began again, and eventually he became convinced that they could not fail to hear the sound which was tormenting him:

> It grew louder—louder—*louder!* And still the men chatted pleasantly, and smiled. Was it possible they heard not? Almighty God!—no, no! They heard!—they suspected!—they *knew!*—they were making a mockery of my horror!—this I thought, and this I think. But anything was better than this agony! Anything was more tolerable than this derision! I could bear those hypocritical smiles no longer! I felt that I must scream or die! and now—again!—hark! louder! louder! louder! *louder!* (94)

Just as current researchers note the way paranoid schizophrenics might see a "friendly, smiling bus driver . . . as someone who is laughing at them derisively" (Sue 439), so the smiles of the police served only to convince Poe's narrator that they were conspiring against him—with the end result being his confession: "'Villains!' I shrieked, 'dissemble no more! I admit the deed!'"

What especially recommends a view of the narrator as a paranoid schizophrenic is that it uncovers the most plausible reason *why* he confessed. Contrary to the explanations usually given, I would argue that Poe's madman revealed his crime not because of a guilty conscience, not because some "imp of the perverse" goaded him into confessing, not because he hates himself and really wanted to be caught—not because he has self-destructive tendencies, in other words—but because he suffers from delusions of persecution. He believed that the officers had discovered his crime, and he could not bear the thought that they were mocking him. As Reilly notes, "the narrator purged his rage by exposing what be believed was the hypocrisy of the police," and thus "self-incrimination" was merely the byproduct (7).

The time span of **"The Tell-Tale Heart"**—from the time Poe's narrator began looking in on the old man every night at midnight, until the consummation of the murder, and even while he is confessing and insisting upon his sanity—corresponds nicely with the active phase of paranoid schizophrenia. According to psychiatrists, the active phase is of at least a week's duration and is characterized by the manifestation of psychotic symptoms (*DSM* 194). Poe's narrator had been suffering such symptoms for this same time period: he speaks of "the whole week before I killed him" (89), and when he mentions the "low, dull, quick sound" which he attributes to the old man's heart, he says that he "knew *that* sound well" (91). In other words, he had been experiencing his auditory hallucinations during the week before the murder, not just on the night of the crime.

It is one thing to apply twentieth-century psychology to Poe's tales, but it is quite another to account for the fact that Poe has given us a paranoid schizophrenic in the *absence* of twentieth-century psychology. In Poe's day the field of scientific psychology was relatively young, and schizophrenia did not even have a specific name; it was not until 1898 that Emil Kraepelin labeled the disease "Dementia Praecox," and it was given its modern name by Eugen Bleuler only in 1911. Thus, Poe portrayed a paranoid schizophrenic decades before nosologists labeled and separated that disease from other mental abnormalities.

Several explanations for this situation are possible. One is that Poe himself had experienced symptoms of paranoid schizophrenia, and used these as the basis for his narrator in **"The Tell-Tale Heart."** Another hypothesis is that Poe's portrait is purely a product of his imagination (and it is therefore a matter of coincidence that he portrayed what twentieth-century psychology calls a paranoid schizophrenic). The explanation I would like to advance and support, however, is that Poe acquired his knowledge of the symptoms by familiarizing himself with the scientific theories of his time.

The allusion to the phrenologist Spurzheim in **"The Imp of the Perverse"**; the references to the "moral treatment" of the insane in **"Dr. Tarr and Prof. Fether"**; the review of Mrs. L. Miles's *Phrenology* in the *Southern Literary Messenger*—these and other references to coeval theories of psychology in Poe's works show that he was very much a student of mental diseases. He may have learned a great deal from his discussions with medical men like his acquaintance Pliny Earle (a physician who dealt extensively with the insane at asylums in both Pennsylvania and New York), but probably he gleaned information from literary sources as well.

I.M. Walker is only one of several scholars (Elizabeth Phillips, Allan Gardner Smith, Robert D. Jacobs) who insist that Poe was familiar with the works of the psychologists of his day: "With his passion for scientific fact and his interest in abnormal mental states, Poe would have been likely to turn to systems of contemporary psychology in the same way that modern writers have turned to Freud and Jung. Moreover, in Poe's day . . . information regarding both mental and physical diseases was readily available to the intelligent layman, not only in the original works of the scientists, but also in popular journals and encyclopaedias" (588). A specialized publication, the *American Journal of Insanity,* began appearing in 1844 (only a matter of months before the final publication of **"The Tell-Tale Heart"** in the *Broadway Journal* on 23 August 1845). As for books, Paige Matthey Bynum notes that "Between 1825 and 1838, the Philadelphia publishing house of Carey and Lea published almost twice as many medical books as those in any other category except fiction, and mental health was a staple concern in these works" (150). In the bibliography to *The Analysis of Motives* Smith lists many works on psychology which were extant in Poe's America—books in English that describe the various symptoms which characterize the abnormal mental state of his narrator in **"The Tell-Tale Heart."**

Such descriptions are scattered, however. Because the science of psychology was in its infancy, there was much confusion and disagreement between medical men on how to classify and relate the symptoms of insanity. While twentieth-century students can find entire chapters devoted solely to schizophrenia in various manuals and textbooks, it is more difficult to find specific chapters which group *only* the features of this disease in the books by Poe's contemporaries—their categories were very broad and often vague.

Occasionally, however, we *can* find three or more of the symptoms listed together. One of the earlier texts available to Poe was John Haslam's *Observations on Madness and Melancholy* (1809). In a general chapter on insanity— "Symptoms of the Disease"—Haslam refers to suspiciousness (42) and later to auditory hallucinations and violence (69). In the next chapter he provides particular case studies. One of these, "Case XVI," concerns a man whose "temper was naturally violent, and he was easily provoked. . . . He would often appear to be holding conversations: but these conferences always terminated in a violent quarrel between the imaginary being and himself. He constantly supposed unfriendly people were placed in different parts of the house to torment and annoy him" (118-19). Here we have not only violence and argumentativeness, but also the two *essential* features of paranoid schizophrenia that modern psychologists have identified (*DSM* 197): delusions (of persecution) and the most common kind of auditory hallucination—that which involves voices.

Haslam's "Case XX" involves a woman who, like the male patient, evinced violent tendencies and delusions of persecution, in addition to mood shifts and optical and olfactory hallucinations: "At the first attack she was violent, but she soon became more calm. She conceived that the over-seers of the parish, to which she belonged, meditated her destruction. . . . She fancied that a young man, for whom she had formerly entertained a partiality, but who had been dead some years, appeared frequently at her bed-side, in a state of putrefaction, which left an abominable stench in her room" (126-27). Haslam also notes that the woman began to suffer her mental affliction "shortly after the death of her husband." The likelihood that the demise of her spouse created the extreme stress which triggered her breakdown corresponds with the current view that a "psychosocial stressor" may trigger the active phase of schizophrenia (*DSM* 190).

In his Introduction to a recent edition of Haslam's work, Roy Porter observes that "Historians of psychiatry have credited Haslam with giving the first precise clinical accounts of . . . schizophrenia" (xxvii). Prior to the publication of **"The Tell-Tale Heart,"** however, there were also other works which described the illness. In his *Treatise on Insanity and Other Disorders Affecting the Mind* (1837), for example, the American physician James Cowles Prichard records the case of a young man who suffered from what he calls "moral insanity":

> He frequently changed his residence, but soon began to fancy himself the object of dislike to every person in the house of which he became the inmate. . . . On being questioned narrowly as to the ground of the persuasion expressed by him, that he was disliked by the family with which he then resided, he replied that he heard whispers uttered in distant apartments of the house indicative of malevolence and abhorrence. An observation was made to him that it was impossible for sounds so uttered to be heard by him. He then asked if the sense of hearing could not, by some physical change in the organ, be occasionally so increased in intensity as to become capable of affording distinct perception at an unusual distance. . . . This was the only instance of what might be termed hallucination discovered in the case after a minute scrutiny [by physicians]. (38)

Apparent in this case are delusions of persecution and voice hallucinations. The young man's query about the possibility of hearing sounds at great distances, furthermore, certainly recalls Poe's insane narrator. Finally, the patient's hypothesis that his disorder is physiological rather than mental also indicates that he too lacks insight into his true psychical condition—another symptom of paranoid schizophrenia.

Other works on abnormal mental states written during Poe's day that describe symptoms of schizophrenia include Isaac Ray's *A Treatise on the Medical Jurisprudence of Insanity* (1838), in which he cites Joseph Mason Cox's *Practical Observations on Insanity* (1804). In a chapter on "General Moral Mania" Ray quotes Cox's report of a certain variety of "maniacs" who

> take violent antipathies, harbor unjust suspicions . . . are proud, conceited and ostentatious; easily excited . . . obstinately riveted to the most absurd opinions; prone to controversy . . . always the hero of their own tale, using . . . unnatural gesticulation, inordinate action. . . . On some occasions they suspect sinister intentions on the most trivial grounds; on others are a prey to fear and dread from the most ridiculous and imaginary sources. . . . If subjected to moral restraint, or a medical regimen, they yield with reluctance to the means proposed, and generally refuse and resist, on the ground that such means are unnecessary where no disease exists. . . . (172-73)

The symptoms Cox describes correspond very closely to those current psychologists associate with paranoid schizophrenia, just as they also closely match those evinced by the narrator of **"The Tell-Tale Heart"**: violence, delusions of persecution and of grandeur, mood shifts, nervousness, and a lack of insight into his own psychopathy.

Clearly, then, Poe and his contemporaries were describing paranoid schizophrenia, even if its symptoms were classified under the broad heading "Moral Insanity," which, as Norman Dain observes, "served as a catch-all for many forms of mental illness" in the early nineteenth century (73)—and which, as Bynum confirms, would indeed have been the way Poe's contemporaries would have diagnosed the condition of his narrator. Accordingly, although romanticists may like to see Poe as a tormented artist who wrote **"The Tell-Tale Heart"** to explore or to purge himself of his own psychotic or self-destructive tendencies, it seems better to regard him as a sophisticated writer who consulted scientific books and journals in an attempt to achieve accuracy and verisimilitude in his own works—the same Poe who familiarized himself with, for instance, the writings of Sir John Herschel, Thomas Dick and John P. Nichol for the astronomy in *Eureka*; and whose reviews of Washington Irving's *Astoria* and J.N. Reynolds's "South Sea Expedition" informed *Pym*. For Poe to consult psychology texts for the sake of scientific precision in **"The Tell-Tale Heart"** would have been typical of his standard practice.

In many ways, therefore, Poe is a precursor of modern artists who find in science not a threat but an ally, and the sophistication of his insights might encourage us to be more humble about our own sophistication. His insights might make us wonder whether the major contribution of twentieth-century psychology has taken the form of new knowledge or whether it consists instead in naming and classification, for it appears that Poe and his contemporaries knew a good deal about paranoid schizophrenia—even if they did not use this terminology.

Notes

[1] The abbreviation refers to the standard reference work in the field of psychology—*Diagnostic and Statistical Manual of Mental Disorders* (see my first entry in Works Cited).

Works Cited

American Psychiatric Association. "Schizophrenia." *Diagnostic and Statistical Manual of Mental Disorders*. 3rd ed, rev. Washington, D.C.: American Psychiatric Association, 1987. 187-98.

Bonaparte, Marie. "The Tell-Tale Heart." *The Life and Works of Edgar Allan Poe: A Psycho-Analytic Interpretation*. Trans. John Rodker. 1949. New York: Humanities, 1971. 491-504.

Bynum, Paige Matthey. "'Observe How Healthily—How Calmly I Can Tell You the Whole Story': Moral Insanity and Edgar Allan Poe's 'The Tell-Tale Heart'." *Literature and Science as Modes of Expression*. Ed. Frederick Amrine. Boston Studies in the Philosophy of Science 115. Boston: Kluwer, 1989. 141-52.

Dain, Norman. *Concepts of Insanity in the United States, 1789-1865*. New Brunswick, NJ: Rutgers UP, 1964.

Gargano, James W. "The Question of Poe's Narrators." *Poe: A Collection of Critical Essays*. Ed. Robert Regan. Englewood Cliffs: Prentice, 1967. 164-71.

Haslam, John. *Observations on Madness and Melancholy*. 2nd ed. London, 1809.

Hoffman, Daniel. "Grotesques and Arabesques." *Poe Poe Poe Poe Poe Poe Poe*. Garden City: Doubleday, 1972. 226-32.

Howarth, William L. Introduction. *Twentieth-Century Interpretations of Poe's Tales: A Collection of Critical Essays*. Englewood Cliffs: Prentice, 1971. 1-22.

Jacobs, Robert D. "The Matrix." *Poe: Journalist & Critic*. Baton Rouge: Louisiana State UP, 1969. 3-34.

Phillips, Elizabeth. "Mere Household Events: The Metaphysics of Mania." *Edgar Allan Poe: An American Imagination*. Port Washington: Kennikat, 1979. 97-137.

Poe, Edgar Allan. "The Tell-Tale Heart." In vol. 5 of *The Complete Works of Edgar Allan Poe*. Ed. James A. Harrison. 1902. New York: AMS, 1965. 88-94.

Porter, Roy. Introduction. *Illustrations of Madness*. By John Haslam. New York: Routledge, 1988. xi-lxiv.

Prichard, James Cowles. *A Treatise on Insanity and Other Disorders Affecting the Mind*. Philadelphia, 1837.

Ray, Isaac. *A Treatise on the Medical Jurisprudence of Insanity*. Boston, 1838.

Reilly, John E. "The Lesser Death-Watch and 'The Tell-Tale Heart'." *American Transcendental Quarterly* 2 (1969): 3-9.

Shelden, Pamela J. "'True Originality': Poe's Manipulation of the Gothic Tradition." *American Transcendental Quarterly* 29.1 (1976): 75-80.

Smith, Allan Gardner. "Chapter Two: Edgar Allan Poe." *The Analysis of Motives: Early American Psychology and Fiction*. Amsterdam: Rodopi, 1980. 38-75.

——. "The Psychological Context of Three Tales by Poe." *Journal of American Studies* 7.3 (1973): 279-92.

Stone, Alan A., and Sue Smart Stone. "Psychotic Symptoms." *The Abnormal Personality Through Literature*. Englewood Cliffs: Prentice, 1966. 126-31.

Sue, David, Derald Sue, and Stanley Sue. *Understanding Abnormal Behavior*. 2nd ed. Boston: Houghton, 1986. 425-45.

Walker, I. M. "The 'Legitimate Sources' of Terror in 'The Fall of the House of Usher'." *Modern Language Review* 61 (1966): 585-92.

Richard Kopley (essay date 1995)

SOURCE: "Hawthorne's Transplanting and Transforming 'The Tell-Tale Heart'," in *Studies in American Fiction*, Vol. 23, No. 2, Autumn, 1995, pp. 231-41.

[*In the following excerpt, Kopley offers insights into the critical reception, principal themes, and structure of "The Tell-Tale Heart" as he argues that that Nathaniel Hawthorne, Poe's contemporary, used elements of the story in his novel* The Scarlet Letter.]

Nathaniel Hawthorne's novel *The House of the Seven Gables* (1851) has long been recognized as having an affinity with Edgar Allan Poe's tale **"The Fall of the House of Usher"** (1839), especially with regard to setting and characters;[1] a reader may therefore wonder if Hawthorne's preceding novel, *The Scarlet Letter* (1850), also possesses an affinity with a Poe tale. In an early review of *The Scarlet Letter* (April 1, 1850), George Ripley noted several parallels between Hawthorne and Poe: "the same terrible excitement . . . the same minuteness of finish—the same slow and fatal accumulation of details, the same exquisite coolness of coloring, while everything creeps forward with irresistible certainty to a soul-harrowing climax." Then he qualified his observation, nothing Hawthorne's softening of the supernatural. But while he quoted amply from *The Scarlet Letter,* he did not go on to identify a specific related Poe tale.[2] Yet Ripley's general observation may be taken as encouragement for a search for a correspondence between *The Scarlet Letter* and a work of fiction by Poe. Such a search is rewarded, for evidence suggests that even as Hawthorne may have rebuilt the House of Usher for *The House of the Seven Gables,* he also transplanted **"The Tell-Tale Heart"** for *The Scarlet Letter.*

Hawthorne certainly would have read **"The Tell-Tale Heart"**—it appeared in the first issue (January 1843) of James Russell Lowell's literary magazine, *The Pioneer,* published in Boston. Lowell had visited Hawthorne in

Concord to solicit contributions for this magazine, and in the lead review in the first issue, Lowell favorably discussed Hawthorne's *Historical Tales for Youth*.[3] The high regard for Poe's creative work that Hawthorne would have brought to his reading of **"The Tell-Tale Heart"** is clear from "The Hall of Fantasy," written in the fall of 1842 and published in the second issue of *The Pioneer* (February 1843): Hawthorne includes Poe in a select company of poets and writers in the "Hall of Fantasy" "for the sake of his imagination" (though he threatens him with "ejectment" for his criticism).[4] Hawthorne would have been reminded of Poe's **"The Tell-Tale Heart"** as he read that second issue of Lowell's magazine, for comments on Poe's tale appeared there in three reprinted reviews of *The Pioneer's* first issue. These comments were striking. In his New York *Tribune* review, Horace Greeley wrote with a mixture of admiration and distaste that **"The Tell-Tale Heart"** was "a strong and skilful, but to our minds overstrained and repulsive analysis of the feelings and promptings of an insane homicide." In a Boston *Bay State Democrat* review, a critic asserted that the tale was "an article of thrilling interest." And in his *Brother Jonathan* review, N. P. Willis remarked with unmixed admiration for Poe's tale that "Mr. Poe's contribution is very wild and very readable, and that is the only thing in the number that most people would read and remember."[5] Hawthorne might later have been reminded of **"The Tell-Tale Heart"** by additional appearances of the work; the story was published in Philadelphia's *United States Gazette* and its *Dollar Newspaper* in 1843 and New York's *Broadway Journal* and Philadelphia's *Spirit of the Times* in 1845.[6]

In the years following the first publication of **"The Tell-Tale Heart,"** Hawthorne maintained his high opinion of Poe's fiction and a lower one of his criticism. In a June 17, 1846 letter to Poe, initially concerning *Mosses from an Old Manse* (a copy of which he had directed to Poe), Hawthorne wrote, "I admire you rather as a writer of Tales, than as a critic upon them," and he went on to apply to Poe's tales two terms that Poe had applied to Hawthorne's tales in a May 1842 review: "force" and "originality" (*CE* 16:168).[7] Hawthorne could well have had **"The Tell-Tale Heart"** in mind in late September 1849 as he "began work in earnest" on *The Scarlet Letter*,[8] in any case he would soon have had an unexpected but compelling reason to recall the Poe tales he admired: on October 7, 1849, Poe died. And then followed the broad press consideration of Poe's life and work.[9] Evidence for Hawthorne's use of Poe in his first novel is a pattern of parallels between **"The Tell-Tale Heart"** and *The Scarlet Letter*—parallels that suggest that in writing this classic novel, Hawthorne served as a **"Tell-Tale Heart"** surgeon, a literary Christiaan Barnard.

In Poe's story, for seven nights at "about midnight" a young man places his head inside the "chamber" of a sleeping "old man" with an "Evil Eye," and opens a lantern "cautiously (for the hinges creaked)" and shines it upon this "Evil Eye" (*M* 3:792-93). On the eighth night, the young man is "more than usually cautious in opening the door" of the room of the "old man," but the sound of the young man's chuckling startles his sleeping victim, who is therefore "lying awake" (*M* 3:793-94). The young

man opens his lantern "stealthily" and shines it upon the "Evil Eye," then jumps into the room and kills the "old man" because of his "Evil Eye" and his loudly beating heart (*M* 3:794-95). In Hawthorne's novel, an "old man"[10] with an "evil eye"—the physician Roger Chillingworth—seeks something "far worse than death" (*CE* 1:196): the violation of the guilty heart of the adulterous young minister, Arthur Dimmesdale. In the critical tenth chapter of *The Scarlet Letter*, "The Leech and His Patient," Poe's story is approximated by Hawthorne's presentation of a related figurative event and a similarly related literal one. Initially, Hawthorne writes that Chillingworth, as he probes for Dimmesdale's secret, "groped along as stealthily, with as cautious a tread, and as wary an outlook, as a thief entering a chamber where a man lies only half asleep,—or, it may be, broad awake" (*CE* 1:130). Hawthorne adds, "In spite of his premeditated carefulness, the floor would now and then creak." And just as Poe's "old man" sensed "the unperceived shadow" of "Death" (*M* 3:794), so too, does Dimmesdale "become vaguely aware" of "the shadow of [Chillingworth's] presence" (*CE* 1:130). The figurative becomes literal when Chillingworth, this "old man" with an "evil eye," actually enters "at noonday" the room of the sleeping young man, lays "his hand upon [the minister's] bosom," "thrust[s] aside the vestment," and discovers the scarlet letter on Dimmesdale's breast—the sign of the minister's secret guilt (*CE* 1:138). Chillingworth has trespassed, causing a spiritual exposure "far worse than death." Poe's intruder had taken a life; Hawthorne's intruder thinks he has taken a soul.

In **"The Tell-Tale Heart,"** after the murder of the old man, Poe's intruder "smiled gaily" (*M* 3:795), but soon thereafter, in great agony, confessed his deed (*M* 3:797). In *The Scarlet Letter*, after the violation of the minister, Hawthorne's intruder is in "ecstasy" (*CE* 1:138), and though Chillingworth does not acknowledge his guilt, Dimmesdale earlier asked the diabolical doctor a question that recalls the confession of the narrator in **"The Tell-Tale Heart"**: "Why should a wretched man, guilty, we will say, of murder, prefer to keep the dead corpse buried in his own heart, rather than fling it forth at once, and let the universe take care of it!" (*CE* 1:132). And Dimmesdale does eventually, after great agony, confess his deed (*CE* 1:254-55).

In both Poe's story and Hawthorne's novel, the heart is telltale. The imagined, perhaps projected beating of the buried heart of the murdered old man provokes Poe's narrator's confession of murder (*M* 3:797); and the evident stigma, the "A" upon Dimmesdale's chest, emerging from the minister's "inmost heart" (*CE* 1:258-59), indicates his sin of adultery. In both works, a heart reveals the heart's secret.[11]

George Ripley's general comment may be applied specifically: Poe's **"The Tell-Tale Heart"** and Hawthorne's *The Scarlet Letter* do both possess a "terrible excitement," a "minuteness of finish," a "slow and fatal accumulation of details," a "coolness of coloring," and a "soul-harrowing climax." But they share more than that. Poe's tale and Chapter 10 of Hawthorne's novel share language—"old man," "chamber," "creak," "shadow," "cautious," and "stealthily"—and the "old man" in both tale and novel possesses the "evil eye." Furthermore, **"The Tell-Tale Heart"** and the tenth chapter of *The Scarlet Letter* share a dramatic situation (anticipated figuratively, then rendered literally in that tenth chapter): at twelve o'clock, one man enters the room of another man, asleep or awakened, and assaults him, causing death or a violation thought worse than death. Also, tale and novel share the crucial theme of man's sinfulness, guilt, and need for confession. Significantly, Chapter 10 of *The Scarlet Letter* specifically mentions a tormented murderer's need to confess his crime. And in both **"The Tell-Tale Heart"** and *The Scarlet Letter,* a seemingly supernatural heart lays open man's sin. "For the sake of [Poe's] imagination"—and its sympathy with his own—Hawthorne evidently transplanted **"The Tell-Tale Heart"** to his greatest novel.

Yet, clearly, as Hawthorne transplanted Poe's great tale, he also transformed it. Again, Ripley's general comment may be applied specifically—Hawthorne did soften the supernatural of **"The Tell-Tale** Heart" in *The Scarlet Letter.* And he did much more. Hawthorne switched the young man and the old man—the former became the sleeper and the latter the intruder. He switched the time, as well—midnight became noon. He modified the motive of the intruder—the narrator's desire to alleviate his nameless terror became Chillingworth's desire to wreak vengeance on his wife's lover. And he modified the nature of the helpless victim—the terrified old man in **"The Tell-Tale Heart"** became the remorseful minister in *The Scarlet Letter.* Hawthorne also refashioned the heart in Poe's story—the provocative heart of the old man in **"The Tell-Tale Heart"** became the object of the scrutiny of the Faustian old man in *The Scarlet Letter.*[12] And Hawthorne adapted the murder in Poe's work to his own purpose, turning it into the violation of "the sanctity of a human heart" (*CE* 1:195)—a violation that he elsewhere considered the "Unpardonable Sin" ("Ethan Brand," *CE* 11:90, 94, 98-99). Unlike the sin of murder in Poe's story, this sin in Hawthorne's novel is never confessed.

Yet we see Dimmesdale confess his adultery and duplicity. And we see him triumphantly achieve salvation (*CE* 1:254-57), as we never do the tortured narrator of Poe's tale. Here is the essence of Hawthorne's transformation of **"The Tell-Tale Heart"**: Poe's work concerns damnation; Hawthorne's novel, salvation.

Clearly, there is a biblical tenor to language in **"The Tell-Tale Heart."** For example, the narrator's claim that "I heard all things in the heaven and in the earth" (*M* 3:792) seems to suggest both Psalms 113:6 ("Who humbleth himself to behold the things that are in heaven, and in the earth!") and Phillipians 2:10 ("at the name of Jesus every knee should bow, of things in heaven, and things in earth"). The narrator's description of the old man's room as "black as pitch with the thick darkness" (*M* 3:793) may recall verses in Exodus and Deuteronomy in which God abides in "thick darkness" (Exodus 20:21; Deuteronomy 4:11; 5:22). And the narrator's exclamation, "The old man's hour had come!" (*M* 3:795) seems to allude to John 13:1, "Jesus knew that his hour was come." However, Poe's use of these references is ironic, for the old man possesses the

"Evil Eye." The mad narrator seems damned at the beginning of the story, having "heard many things in hell" (*M* 3:792), and the "Evil Eye" apparently recognizes his damnation. After all, when the narrator buries the dismembered body of the old man, he says "no human eye—not even *his*—could have detected anything wrong" (*M* 3:796). The recognition by the "Evil Eye" of the narrator's guilt presumably led to his horror of it. Tellingly, the story is actually structured around the "Evil Eye."

The story comprises two halves, each of them featuring nine paragraphs, with the second half reversing the order of phrase in the first. Together, the halves yield chiasmus—the pattern ABCDEEDCBA. Thus the beginning's "You fancy me mad" (*M* 3:792), is answered by the ending's "If you still think me mad" (*M* 3:796); "For a whole hour" (*M* 3:794) by "for some minutes" (*M* 3:795), "mortal terror" (*M* 3:794) by "uncontrollable terror" (*M* 3:795), and so on into the heart of the story.[13] At the close of the ninth paragraph, at the center of the symmetrical phrasing, is the central phrase of the tale, "damned spot" (*M* 3:795)—Poe's allusion to the evidence of Lady Macbeth's guilt (*Macbeth* 5.1.35)—an allusion employed here to refer to the condemning "Evil Eye" itself.[14] The condemned narrator tries to relieve himself of his accuser by killing him, only to be further damned by the murder itself. His painful confession suggests momentary escape, but there is no evidence of redemption or salvation. The narrator is as damned at the tale's close as he had been as its beginning—indeed, if possible, even more so.

In contrast, Dimmesdale In *The Scarlet Letter* achieves salvation through his confession: "the minister stood with a flush of triumph in his face, as one who, in the crisis of acutest pain, had won a victory" (*CE* 1:255). He tells Hester Prynne that without his "agonies"—the torturing Chillingworth and the public confession—he would have been "lost forever" (*CE* 1:257). The sinful Dimmesdale has encountered the "evil eye" that used to intimidate him (*CE* 1:136), and he has defied it (*CE* 1:252-53), not by killing its possessor, but by acknowledging "God's eye" (*CE* 1:255). And in contrast to the "damned spot," the "Evil Eye" at the center of **"The Tell-Tale Heart,"** "God's eye" is at the center of *The Scarlet Letter.*

Notes

[1] Maurice Beebe, "The Fall of the House of Pyncheon," *NCF* 11 (1956), 1-17.

[2] [George Ripley], review of *The Scarlet Letter,* in *Hawthorne: The Critical Heritage,* ed. J. Donald Crowley (New York: Barnes & Noble, 1970), pp. 158-59. See also, for the quoted excerpts, Kenneth Walter Cameron, "Literary News in American Renaissance Newspapers (5)," *ATQ* 20 Supp. (1973): 18-19. For Ripley's mixed evaluation of Poe, see his January 19, 1850 review of *The Works of Edgar Allan Poe,* ed. Rufus Wilmot Griswold, in *Edgar Allan Poe: The Critical Heritage,* ed. I. M. Walker (London: Routledge & Kegan Paul, 1986), pp. 333-36.

[3] Lowell's visit to Hawthorne to obtain material for *The Pioneer* is mentioned in a letter from Maria White, Lowell's future wife, of

October 4, 1842. See Stephan Loewentheil and Thomas Edsall, comps., *The Poe Catalogue: A Descriptive Catalogue of the Stephan Loewentheil Collection of Edgar Allan Poe Material* (Baltimore: The 19th Century Shop, 1992), p. 56. The attribution to Lowell of the review of Hawthorne's book in *The Pioneer* has been noted by Sculley Bradley in his Introduction to *The Pioneer, A Literary Magazine* (New York: Scholars' Fascimiles and Reprints, 1947), xxvii.

[4] Nathaniel Hawthorne, *The Centenary Edition of the Works of Nathaniel Hawthorne*, ed. William Charvat *et al.*, 20 vols. to date (Columbus: Ohio State Univ. Press, 1962-), 10:636. Hereafter cited parenthetically as *CE*. The editors of the first *Centenary Edition* volume of Hawthorne's letters suggest that "The Hall of Fantasy" was "probably written in October or early November" of 1842 (*CE* 15:662n). Writing on January 4, 1843, about the imminent publication of "The Hall of Fantasy" in the second issue of *The Pioneer*, Hawthorne's wife Sophia acknowledged receipt of the first issue of that magazine (*CE* 15:667)—the issue that included "The Tell-Tale Heart."

[5] The second issue of *The Pioneer* also offered Poe's poem "Lenore"; the third featured Poe's essay "Notes upon English Verse" and Hawthorne's tale "The Birth-Mark." That Poe considered Lowell close to Hawthorne is evident from Poe's March 27, 1843 letter to Lowell requesting a piece by Hawthorne for the opening number of his planned journal, the *Stylus*. See Edgar Allan Poe, *The Letters of Edgar Allan Poe*, ed. John Ward Ostrom, 2 vols. (1948; repr. with a supplement, New York: Gordian Press, 1966), 1: 232. Hawthorne never provided the piece. See *CE* 15:684. For the Lowell-Willis relationship in January 1843, see Edward L. Tucker, "James Russell Lowell and Robert Carter: The *Pioneer* and Fifty Letters from Lowell to Carter," *Studies in the American Renaissance 1987*, ed. Joel Myerson (Charlottesville: Univ. Press of Virginia, 1987), pp. 201, 206, 208.

[6] Edgar Allan Poe, *Collected Works of Edgar Allan Poe*, ed. Thomas Ollive Mabbott, 3 vols. (Cambridge: Harvard Univ. Press, 1969-78), 3:791-92. Hereafter cited parenthetically as *M*. Also in 1845, Hawthorne published "P.'s Correspondence" (*CE* 10:361-80), a satire considered by Arlin Turner to suggest Poe (*Nathaniel Hawthorne: A Biography* [New York: Oxford, 1980], p. 159), but in which Poe apparently did not see himself. See Burton R. Pollin, ed., *Collected Writings of Edgar Allan Poe*, 4 vols. to date (Boston: Twayne, 1981; New York: Gordian Press, 1985-), 3:88-89.

[7] For Poe's use of "force" and "originality" in his May 1842 review of Hawthorne's *Twice-Told Tales*, see James A. Harrison, ed., *The Complete Works of Edgar Allan Poe*, 17 vols. (New York: AMS, 1979), 11:110-11. Hawthorne seems to have remembered Poe's November 1847 review of *Twice-Told Tales* and *Mosses from an Old Manse*. He wrote in his January 1851 "Preface" for *Twice-Told Tales* that "the book . . . if opened in the sunshine . . . is apt to look exceedingly like a volume of blank pages" (*CE* 9:5); Poe's review had recommended that Hawthorne "get a bottle of visible ink" (*Complete Works* 13:155). My thanks to Joseph J. Moldenhauer for this observation.

[8] For the dating of Hawthorne's beginning to write *The Scarlet Letter*, see Larry J. Reynolds, "The Scarlet Letter and Revolutions Abroad," *AL* 57 (1985), 57.

[9] For a compendium of four hundred press pieces on Poe after his death, see Burton R. Pollin, "A Posthumous Assessment: The

1849-1850 Periodical Press Response to Edgar Allan Poe," *American Periodicals* 2 (Fall 1992), 6-50. The journalistic treatments of Poe were sustained and encouraged by the publication of the first two volumes of *The Works of the Late Edgar Allan Poe*, which appeared "about January 10, 1850"; see Joy Bayless, *Rufus Wilmot Griswold: Poe's Literary Executor* (Nashville: Vanderbilt Univ. Press, 1943), p. 175. See also Bayless, "Edgar Allan Poe," *BAL* 7 (1983), 124. The first volume, *Tales*, included "The Tell-Tale Heart." According to a February 4, 1850 letter to Horatio Bridge, Hawthorne completed *The Scarlet Letter* on February 3, 1850 (*CE* 16:311). Hawthorne could have seen the two volumes before he completed his novel, but there is no conclusive evidence that he did. By mid-January 1850 he had doubtless already written the section of *The Scarlet Letter* most nearly related to "The Tell-Tale Heart," Chapter 10.

[10] Chillingworth is insistently so characterized; see *CE* 1:129, 131, 137, 139, 141, 167, 169, 172, 174, 175, 179, 194, 195, 224, 229, 252, 253, 256, 260.

[11] Another Poe work that might have reinforced for Hawthorne the idea of the revelatory heart is the "Marginalia" installment in the January 1848 issue of *Graham's Magazine*, which gave the title of the unwritable true autobiography as "My Heart Laid Bare" (*Collected Writings* 2:322-23). Poe writes that "The paper [of this autobiography] would shrivel and blaze at every touch of the fiery pen," Hawthorne that the falsely confessing Dimmesdale had expected his congregation to see "his wretched body shrivelled up before their eyes, by the burning wrath of the Almighty" (*CE* 1:143-44).

[12] The Faust motif in *The Scarlet Letter* is ably treated by William Bysshe Stein in *Hawthorne's Faust—A Study of the Devil Archetype* (Gainesville: Univ. of Florida Press, 1953), pp. 104-22, 163-64.

[13] For a consideration of chiasmus in Poe's "The Masque of the Red Death," *Eureka*, "The Fall of the House of Usher," and *The Narrative of Arthur Gordon Pym*, see Max Nänny, "Chiastic Structures in Literature: Some Forms and Functions," in *The Structure of Texts*, ed. Udo Fries (Tübingen: Gunter Narr, 1987), pp. 83, 91-96. Nänny makes use of Charles O'Donnell's important essay, "From Earth to Ether: Poe's Flight into Space," *PMLA* 77 (1962), 89-90. See also David Ketterer's earlier treatment of O'Donnell and of plot symmetry in *Pym* in *The Rationale of Deception in Poe* (Baton Rouge: Louisiana State Univ. Press, 1979), pp. 139-41, and my later discussion of verbal symmetry in *Pym* in "Poe's *Pym*-esque 'A Tale of the Ragged Mountains,'" *Poe and His Times: The Artist and His Milieu*, ed. Benjamin Franklin Fisher IV (Baltimore: The Edgar Allan Poe Society of Baltimore, 1990), pp. 170-71.

[14] Another analysis of the *Macbeth* allusion in "The Tell-Tale Heart" is offered by Richard Wilbur in "Poe and the Art of Suggestion," *University of Mississippi Studies in English* ns 3 (1982), 6-9.

FURTHER READING

Biography

Quinn, Arthur Hobson. *Edgar Allan Poe: A Critical Biography*. Baltimore: The Johns Hopkins University Press, 1998, 804 p.

Definitive biography of Poe, originally published in 1941. Includes background information and a brief analysis of "The Tell-Tale Heart."

Criticism

Davidson, Edward. *Poe: A Critical Study.* Cambridge: Bellknap Press of Harvard University, 1957, 296 p.

> Landmark study of Poe's place in American literature and the Romantic tradition that makes brief mention of "The Tell-Tale Heart."

Gargano, James W. "The Question of Poe's Narrators." *College English* XXV (1963): 178-80.

> Discussion of several stories, including brief remarks on "The Tell-Tale Heart" urging that Poe's style should not be confused with that of the narrator of the tale.

Krappe, Edith S. "A Possible Source for Poe's 'The Tell-Tale Heart' and 'The Black Cat." *American Literature* XII (March 1940): 84-8.

> Points out "striking parallels" between the two Poe stories and Charles Dickens's "The Clock Case: A Confession Found in Prison in the Time of Charles the Second."

May, Charles E. "The Short Fiction." In *Edgar Allan Poe: A Study of the Short Fiction.* Boston: Twayne, 1991, pp. 74-9.

> Overview of "The Tell-Tale Heart" that explores the major themes and narrative method.

Pillai, Johann. "Death and Its Moments: The End of the Reader in History." *Modern Language Notes,* No. 112 (1997): 836-75.

> Uses Poe's "Tell-Tale Heart" as an example to explore the relationship between the reader and the historically bound yet paradoxically "present" literary text.

Pollin, Burton R. "Bulwer Lytton and 'The Tell-Tale Heart'." *American Notes and Queries* IV (September 1965): 7-8.

> Argues that British writer Edward Bulwer Lytton's story "Monos and Daimonas" is a source of "The Tell-Tale Heart."

Robinson, E. Arthur. "Thoreau and the Deathwatch in Poe's 'The Tell-Tale Heart'." *Poe Studies* 4, No. 1 (June 1971): 14-16.

> Asserts that Poe's source for the deathwatch beetle in "The Tell-Tale Heart" may have been a journal entry, later published as an essay, by Henry David Thoreau.

Senelick, Laurence. "Charles Dickens and 'The Tell-Tale Heart'." *Poe Studies* 6, No. 1 (June 1973): 12-14.

> Suggests that Charles Dickens's "A Confession Found in a Prison" was inspiration for "The Tell-Tale Heart."

Strickland, Edward. "Dickens's 'A Madman's Manuscript' and 'The Tell-Tale Heart'." *Poe Studies* IX (1976): 22-3.

> Contends that there are noteworthy correspondences between "The Tell-Tale Heart" and Charles Dickens's story "A Madman's Manuscript."

Additional coverage of Poe's life and career is contained in the following sources published by Gale Group: *Authors and Artists for Young Adults,* Vol. 14; *Concise Dictionary of American Literary Biography, 1640-1865; Dictionary of Literary Biography,* Vols. 3, 59, 73, 74; *DISCovering Authors; DISCovering Authors: British; DISCovering Authors: Canadian; DISCovering Authors: Most-Studied Authors Module; DISCovering Authors: Poet's Module; Nineteenth-Century Literature Criticism,* Vols. 1, 16, 55; *Poetry Criticism,* Vol. 1; *Short Story Criticism,* Vols. 1, 22; *Something about the Author,* Vol. 23; and *World Literature Criticism.*

"The Celebrated Jumping Frog of Calaveras County"
Mark Twain

The following entry presents criticism of Twain's short story "The Celebrated Jumping Frog of Calaveras County." For an overview of Twain's short fiction, see *Short Story Criticism,* Volume 6.

INTRODUCTION

One of Twain's earliest literary successes and most accomplished early sketches, this 2,600-word narrative was written following a three-month stay at Jackass Hill and Angel's Camp in California's Calaveras County in late 1864 and early 1865. Twain first heard the tale of the jumping frog from Ben Coon, a fixture at the Angel's Camp Hotel bar. He liked the story, jotting down its details in a notebook, but was especially taken with Coon's masterful oral delivery of the anecdote: like other mining camp raconteurs, Coon recounted the episode with utter seriousness for dramatic and humorous effect. This particular brand of deadpan humor told in rich vernacular proved to be most influential on Twain's development as a writer and humorist.

Upon returning to San Francisco from Calaveras County, Twain received a letter from his friend and literary mentor, the writer Artemus Ward, requesting that he send a piece of writing to be included in a work Ward was editing about Nevada Territory travels. Twain thereupon began writing his own version of the frog story, but it took six months and several failed attempts to produce something to his satisfaction. In October 1865 he sent the manuscript of the sketch to New York for inclusion in the Ward collection, but it was turned down, probably because the book was about to go to press. The publisher sent the story to the *Saturday Press,* where it appeared in November, 1865 as "Jim Smiley and His Jumping Frog." The tale was an overnight sensation, and was reprinted in magazines and newspapers all over the country. In December 1865 Twain published a revised version of the story in the *Californian,* and a further revised version was used as the title story in his 1867 collection, *The Celebrated Jumping Frog of Calaveras Country, and Other Sketches.* The story has also been published under the title "The Notorious Jumping Frog of Calaveras County," and is often referred to by scholars simply as "the jumping frog story."

The tale is told using the structure of a traditional Southwestern frame story, wherein a genteel, educated narrator recounts a story he has heard from an unsophisticated teller, and gives a secondhand account of a career gambler who gets taken by a stranger passing through town. In the earliest published version of the story, Twain himself narrates the frame in the form of a letter to his friend Ward about a visit to the mining camp Noomerang where he

hears the story of Jim Greeley's frog. Later versions of the story drop the epistolary structure, use an anonymous narrator, change the name "Noomerang" to "Angel's Camp," and substitute the name "Smiley" for "Greeley."

Plot and Major Characters

The narrator, a mannered Easterner, describes his visit to a mining camp where, on behalf of a friend, he is searching for one Leonidas W. Smiley. He stops in an old tavern, where he meets "goodnatured, garrulous" old Simon Wheeler, who cannot recall a Leonidas Smiley, but does remember a Jim Smiley who lived in the camp around 1849 or 1850. Without prompting, Wheeler launches into an extended narrative about the gambler Smiley and his exploits. Smiley, he says, was "uncommon lucky," and had a reputation for betting on anything he could: horse races, dog fights, and even which of two birds sitting on a fence would fly first. His broken-down old nag somehow always managed to win races when Smiley bet on her. His bullpup, Andrew Jackson, also won all its fights. Smiley also owned rat terriers, chicken cocks, and tom-cats, and wagered on all of them—and won.

Smiley, Wheeler goes on, once caught a frog, which he named Dan'l Webster, and trained him to jump. And that frog was a remarkable jumper, beating out any frog brought from near and far to challenge him. One day a stranger came to the mining camp and, on seeing Smiley's frog, remarked he didn't see anything unusual about it. Smiley wagered $40 that his frog could outjump any other in Calaveras County. Since the stranger had no frog, Smiley went out to find him one. In Smiley's absence, the stranger pried open Dan'l Webster's mouth and filled it with quail-shot. When Smiley brought the new frog to challenge Dan'l, it hopped off, but Dan'l couldn't budge. The stranger took his $40 in winnings and remarked again that he really could not see any special points about Smiley's frog. When Smiley examined his frog and realized what had happened, he took off after the stranger, but never caught him.

At this point in the narrative, Wheeler is called outside. When he returns, he begins a new anecdote about Smiley's tail-less, one-eyed cow, but the narrator, sure he will not learn anything about Leonidas W. Smiley from another "interminable narrative," does not have the patience to listen to it, and departs.

Major Themes

With its complexity of characterization, sophisticated narrative structure, and controlled style, "Jim Smiley and His Jumping Frog" was the best work Twain had written to date, and marks a turning point in his development as an artist. While the sketch has its stylistic roots in the classical Southwestern frame story, there are touches in the tale that are purely Twain's, and which mark his later writing. Some major themes in the story that are found in other Southwestern folktales include that of shrewdness outwitted, as the wily old gambler finally meets his match in the person of the stranger; the confrontation between East and West, between the green Easterner and the slick Westerner, represented by the narrator and Wheeler; and the fantastic, as Wheeler's account of Smiley's assortment of animals and their talents becomes more and more improbable. However, as noted by several scholars, Twain overturns the traditional use of these themes as they are found in conventional Southwestern burlesques. Wheeler's innocence and self-absorbed frankness is a departure from the bragging style of the typical frontiersman. The genteel narrator's tale is not told at the expense of the yokel whose story he recounts, as is typical, but rather the joke is on himself, since his quest for the elusive Leonidas W. Smiley is in vain. Twain elevates the typical Southwestern humorous tale to new heights of sophistication with the creation of memorable characters and events and with his subtle use of shifting points of view and believ-

ably wrought narrative voices. The use of satire lurking beneath the surface of a supposedly simple, straightforward tale and the seriousness of voice betraying no recognition of the humor in the situations described are elements found in Twain's later works.

Critical Reception

The immediate response to Twain's story was almost entirely positive, and the story was reprinted more than ten times in the decade following its appearance in the *Saturday Press.* However, Twain was at first uncomfortable with the immediate reputation as a "western humorist" that the story conferred upon him, and dismissed it in an 1866 letter to his mother as a "villainous backwoods sketch." But his estimation of the story grew when he eventually cast off the bohemian sophistication he had hoped to achieve and recognized that public acceptance of this particular brand of writing and the persona of a "wild man of the West" could be a literary asset. Ten years after its initial publication, he wrote and published an elaboration of the story, called "The Jumping Frog in English, Then in French, Then Clawed Back into Civilized Language Once More by Patient, Unremunerated Toil," in response to a poor French translation of the tale and its accompanying unflattering assessment of his place in American letters. A further indication of the importance he attributed to the story is that almost twenty years later, Twain published "The Private History of the Jumping Frog Story," in which he considers a contemporary scholar's (unbeknownst to him, erroneous) claim that the frog story had a prototype in Greek literature.

Critical analysis of the story has focused on many issues, but all recognize that the story marks a transition in Twain's development as a writer, and agree that the seeds of his later genius are clearly found in the sketch. Early discussions tended to stress the story's origins in Southwestern folklore and its relationship to the work of other Westerners writing in the same genre. The first sustained critical commentary dealing with the content of the sketch was presented in 1950 by Edgar M. Branch, who pointed out the relationship between the storytellers Mark Twain and Simon Wheeler as representations of Eastern and Western sensibilities. Modern critics have taken up this point and have examined the related contrast between the narrative methods and structures of the two men's tales, which, they consider, tell us something about their attitudes. Some scholars have pointed out that there are actually several layers of stories within the framed story, and each successive tale in turn reveals the attitudes of characters toward each other: the genteel narrator's attitude toward Wheeler, Wheeler's attitude toward Smiley, Smiley's attitude toward the stranger, etc. Other critical analyses reveal the circumstances in Twain's life that occasioned the writing of the tale; examine Twain's use of satire; discuss humorous techniques found in the story that are developed in later works; understand the story as an assertion of true American values; and show how Twain's genius unfolds in this early work.

CRITICISM

Mark Twain (essay date 1894)

SOURCE: "Private History of the 'Jumping Frog' Story," in *How to Tell a Story and Other Essays,* Harper & Brothers, 1897, pp. 149-63.

[*In the following essay, originally published in the* North American Review *in 1894, Twain compares his story to a similar frog story that a scholar had claimed was of ancient Greek origins. In doing so, Twain reveals something of his attitude toward the narrator from whom he first heard the story. He then goes on to "retranslate" in humorous manner a bad French version of the story back into English.*]

Five or six years ago a lady from Finland asked me to tell her a story in our negro dialect, so that she could get an idea of what that variety of speech was like. I told her one of Hopkinson Smith's negro stories, and gave her a copy of *Harper's Monthly* containing it. She translated it for a Swedish newspaper, but by an oversight named me as the author of it instead of Smith. I was very sorry for that, because I got a good lashing in the Swedish press, which would have fallen to his share but for that mistake; for it was shown that Boccaccio had told that very story, in his curt and meagre fashion, five hundred years before Smith took hold of it and made a good and tellable thing out of it.

I have always been sorry for Smith. But my own turn has come now. A few weeks ago Professor Van Dyke, of Princeton, asked this question:

"Do you know how old your Jumping Frog story is?"

And I answered:

"Yes—forty-five years. The thing happened in Calaveras County in the spring of 1849."

"No; it happened earlier—a couple of thousand years earlier; it is a Greek story."

I was astonished—and hurt. I said:

"I am willing to be a literary thief if it has been so ordained; I am even willing to be caught robbing the ancient dead alongside of Hopkinson Smith, for he is my friend and a good fellow, and I think would be as honest as any one if he could do it without occasioning remark; but I am not willing to antedate his crimes by fifteen hundred years. I must ask you to knock off part of that."

But the professor was not chaffing; he was in earnest, and could not abate a century. He named the Greek author, and

offered to get the book and send it to me and the college text-book containing the English translation also. I thought I would like the translation best, because Greek makes me tired. January 30th he sent me the English version, and I will presently insert it in this article. It is my Jumping Frog tale in every essential. It is not strung out as I have strung it out, but it is all there.

To me this is very curious and interesting. Curious for several reasons. For instance:

I heard the story told by a man who was not telling it to his hearers as a thing new to them, but as a thing which *they had witnessed and would remember.* He was a dull person, and ignorant; he had no gift as a story-teller, and no invention; in his mouth this episode was merely history—history and statistics; and the gravest sort of history, too; he was entirely serious, for he was dealing with what to him were austere facts, and they interested him solely because they *were* facts; he was drawing on his memory, not his mind; he saw no humor in his tale, neither did his listeners; neither he nor they ever smiled or laughed; in my time I have not attended a more solemn conference. To him and to his fellow goldminers there were just two things in the story that were worth considering. One was the smartness of its hero, Jim Smiley, in taking the stranger in with a loaded frog; and the other was Smiley's deep knowledge of a frog's nature—for he knew (as the narrator asserted and the listeners conceded) that a frog *likes shot* and is always ready to eat it. Those men discussed those two points, and those only. They were hearty in their admiration of them, and none of the party was aware that a first-rate story had been told in a first-rate way, and that it was brimful of a quality whose presence they never suspected—humor.

Now, then, the interesting question is, *did* the frog episode happen in Angel's Camp in the spring of '49, as told in my hearing that day in the fall of 1865? I am perfectly sure that it did. I am also sure that its duplicate happened in Bœotia a couple of thousand years ago. I think it must be a case of history actually repeating itself, and not a case of a good story floating down the ages and surviving because too good to be allowed to perish.

I would now like to have the reader examine the Greek story and the story told by the dull and solemn Californian, and observe how exactly alike they are in essentials.

[*Translation.*]

THE ATHENIAN AND THE FROG.*

An Athenian once fell in with a Bœotian who was sitting by the road-side looking at a frog. Seeing the other approach, the Bœotian said his was a remarkable frog, and asked if he would agree to start a contest of frogs, on condition that he whose frog jumped farthest should receive a large sum of money. The Athenian replied that he would if the other would fetch him a frog, for the lake was near. To this he agreed, and when he was gone the Athenian took the frog, and, opening its mouth, poured some stones into its stomach, so that it did not indeed seem larger than before, but could not jump. The Bœotian soon returned with the other frog, and the contest began. The second frog first was pinched, and jumped moderately; then they pinched the Bœotian frog. And he gathered himself for a leap, and used the utmost effort, but he could not move his body the least. So the Athenian departed with the money. When he was gone the Bœotian, wondering what was the matter with the frog, lifted him up and examined him. And being turned upside down, he opened his mouth and vomited out the stones.

And here is the way it happened in California:

FROM "THE CELEBRATED JUMPING FROG OF CALAVERAS COUNTY."

Well, thish-yer Smiley had rat-tarriers, and chicken cocks, and tom-cats, and all them kind of things, till you couldn't rest, and you couldn't fetch nothing for him to bet on but he'd match you. He ketched a frog one day, and took him home, and said he cal'lated to educate him; and so he never done nothing for three months but set in his back yard and learn that frog to jump. And you bet you he *did* learn him, too. He'd give him a little punch behind, and the next minute you'd see that frog whirling in the air like a doughnut—see him turn one summerset, or maybe a couple if he got a good start, and come down flat-footed and all right, like a cat. He got him up so in the matter of ketching flies, and kep' him in practice so constant, that he'd nail a fly every time as fur as he could see him. Smiley said all a frog wanted was education, and he could do 'most anything—and I believe him. Why, I've seen him set Dan'l Webster down here on this floor—Dan'l Webster was the name of the frog—and sing out "Flies, Dan'l, flies!" and quicker'n you could wink he'd spring straight up and snake a fly off'n the counter there, and flop down on the floor ag'in as solid as a gob of mud, and fall to scratching the side of his head with his hind foot as indifferent as if he hadn't no idea he'd been doin' any more'n any frog might do. You never see a frog so modest and straightfor'ard as he was, for all he was so gifted. And when it come to fair and square jumping on a dead level, he could get over more ground at one straddle than any animal of his breed you ever see. Jumping on a dead level was his strong suit, you understand; and when it came to that, Smiley would ante up money on him as long as he had a red. Smiley was monstrous proud of his frog, and well he might be, for fellers that had travelled and been everywheres all said he laid over any frog that ever *they* see.

Well, Smiley kep' the beast in a little lattice box, and he used to fetch him down-town sometimes and lay for a bet. One day a feller—a stranger in the camp, he was—come acrost him with his box, and says:

"What might it be that you've got in the box?"

And Smiley says, sorter indifferent-like, "It might be a parrot, or it might be a canary, maybe, but it ain't— it's only just a frog."

And the feller took it, and looked at it careful, and turned it round this way and that, and says, "H'm— so 'tis. Well, what's *he* good for?"

"Well," Smiley says, easy and careless, "he's good enough for *one* thing, I should judge—he can outjump any frog in Calaveras County."

The feller took the box again and took another long, particular look, and give it back to Smiley and says, very deliberate, "Well," he says, "I don't see no p'ints about that frog that's any better'n any other frog."

"Maybe you don't," Smiley says. "Maybe you understand frogs and maybe you don't understand 'em; maybe you've had experience, and maybe you ain't only a amature, as it were. Anyways, I've got *my* opinion, and I'll resk forty dollars that he can outjump any frog in Calaveras County."

And the feller studies a minute, and then says, kinder sad like, "Well, I'm only a stranger here, and I ain't got no frog, but if I had a frog I'd bet you."

And then Smiley says: "That's all right—that's all right—if you'll hold my box a minute, I'll go and get you a frog." And so the feller took the box and put up his forty dollars along with Smiley's and set down to wait.

So he set there a good while thinking and thinking to hisself, and then he got the frog out and prized his mouth open and took a teaspoon and filled him full of quail shot—filled him pretty near up to his chin—and set him on the floor. Smiley he went to the swamp and slopped around in the mud for a long time, and finally he ketched a frog and fetched him in and give him to this feller, and says:

"Now, if you're ready, set him alongside of Dan'l, with his fore-paws just even with Dan'l's, and I'll give the word." Then he says, "One—two—three—*git!*" and him and the feller touched up the frogs from behind, and the new frog hopped off lively; but Dan'l give a heave, and hysted up his shoulders— so—like a Frenchman, but it warn't no use—he couldn't budge; he was planted as solid as a church, and he couldn't no more stir than if he was anchored out. Smiley was a good deal surprised, and he was disgusted, too, but he didn't have no idea what the matter was, of course.

The feller took the money and started away; and when he was going out at the door he sorter jerked his thumb over his shoulder—so—at Dan'l, and says again, very deliberate: "Well," he says, "*I* don't see no p'ints about that frog that's any better'n any other frog."

Smiley he stood scratching his head and looking down at Dan'l a long time, and at last he says, "I do wonder what in the nation that frog throw'd off for—I wonder if there ain't something the matter with him—he 'pears to look mighty baggy, somehow." And he ketched Dan'l by the nap of the neck, and hefted him, and says, "Why, blame my cats if he don't weigh five pound!" and turned him upside down, and he belched out a double handful of shot. And then he see how it was, and he was the maddest man—he set the frog down and took out after that feller, but he never ketched him.

The resemblances are deliciously exact. There you have the wily Bœotian and the wily Jim Smiley waiting—two thousand years apart—and waiting, each equipped with his frog and "laying" for the stranger. A contest is proposed—for money. The Athenian would take a chance "if the other would fetch him a frog"; the Yankee says: "I'm only a stranger here, and I ain't got no frog; but if I had a frog I'd bet you." The wily Bœotian and the wily Californian, with that vast gulf of two thousand years between, retire eagerly and go frogging in the marsh; the Athenian and the Yankee remain behind and work a base advantage, the one with pebbles, the other with shot. Presently the contest began. In the one case "they pinched the Bœotian frog"; in the other, "him and the feller touched up the frogs from behind." The Bœotian frog "gathered himself for a leap" (you can just *see* him!), but "could not move his body in the least"; the Californian frog "give a heave, but it warn't no use—he couldn't budge." In both the ancient and the modern cases the strangers departed with the money. The Bœotian and the Californian wonder what is the matter with their frogs; they lift them and examine; they turn them upside down and out spills the informing ballast.

Yes, the resemblances are curiously exact. I used to tell the story of the Jumping Frog in San Francisco, and presently Artemus Ward came along and wanted it to help fill out a little book which he was about to publish; so I wrote it out and sent it to his publisher, Carleton; but Carleton thought the book had enough matter in it, so he gave the story to Henry Clapp as a present, and Clapp put it in his *Saturday Press,* and it killed that paper with a suddenness that was beyond praise. At least the paper died with that issue, and none but envious people have ever tried to rob me of the honor and credit of killing it. The **"Jumping Frog"** was the first piece of writing of mine that spread itself through the newspapers and brought me into public notice. Consequently, the *Saturday Press* was a cocoon and I the worm in it; also, I was the gay-colored literary moth which its death set free. This simile has been used before.

Early in '66 the **"Jumping Frog"** was issued in book form, with other sketches of mine. A year or two later Madame Blanc translated it into French and published it in the *Revue des Deux Mondes,* but the result was not what should have been expected, for the *Revue* struggled along and pulled through, and is alive yet. I think the fault must have been in the translation. I ought to have translated it myself. I think so because I examined into the matter and finally retranslated the sketch from the French back into English, to see what the trouble was; that is, to see just what sort of a focus the French people got upon it. Then the mystery was explained. In French the story is too confused, and chaotic, and unreposeful, and ungrammatical, and insane; consequently it could only cause grief and sickness—it could not kill. A glance at my re-translation will show the reader that this must be true.

[*My Retranslation.*]

THE FROG JUMPING OF THE COUNTY OF CALAVERAS.

Eh bien! this Smiley nourished some terriers à rats, and some cocks of combat, and some cats, and all sort of things; and with his rage of betting one no had more of repose. He trapped one day a frog and him imported with him (et l'emporta chez lui) saying that he pretended to make his education. You me believe if you will, but during three months he not has nothing done but to him apprehend to jump (apprendre a sauter) in a court retired of her mansion (de sa maison). And I you respond that he have succeeded. He him gives a small blow by behind, and the instant after you shall see the frog turn in the air like a grease-biscuit, make one summersault, sometimes two, when she was well started, and re-fall upon his feet like a cat. He him had accomplished in the art of to gobble the flies (gober des mouches), and him there exercised continually—so well that a fly at the most far that she appeared was a fly lost. Smiley had custom to say that all which lacked to a frog it was the education, but with the education she could do nearly all—and I him believe. Tenez, I him have seen pose Daniel Webster there upon this plank—Daniel Webster was the name of the frog—and to him sing, "Some flies, Daniel, some flies!"—in a flash of the eye Daniel had bounded and seized a fly here upon the counter, then jumped anew at the earth, where he rested truly to himself scratch the head with his behind-foot, as if he no had not the least idea of his superiority. Never you not have seen frog as modest, as natural, sweet as she was. And when he himself agitated to jump purely and simply upon plain earth, she does more ground in one jump than any beast of his species than you can know.

To jump plain—this was his strong. When he himself agitated for that Smiley multiplied the bets upon her as long as there to him remained a red. It must to know, Smiley was monstrously proud of his frog, and he of it was right, for some men who were travelled, who had all seen, said that they to him would be injurious to him compare to another frog. Smiley guarded Daniel in a little box latticed which he carried bytimes to the village for some bet.

One day an individual stranger at the camp him arrested with his box and him said:

"What is this that you have then shut up there within?"

Smiley said, with an air indifferent:

"That could be a paroquet, or a syringe (*ou un serin*), but this no is nothing of such, it not is but a frog." The individual it took, it regarded with care, it turned from one side and from the other, then he said:

"*Tiens!* in effect!—At what is she good?"

"My God!" respond Smiley, always with an air disengaged, "she is good for one thing, to my notice (*à mon avis*), she can batter in jumping (*elle peut batter en sautant*) all frogs of the county of Calaveras."

The individual re-took the box, it examined of new longly, and it rendered to Smiley in saying with an air deliberate:

"*Eh bien!* I no saw not that that frog had nothing of better than each frog." (*Je ne vois pas que cette grenouille ait rien de mieux qu'aucune grenouille*). [If that isn't grammar gone to seed, then I count myself no judge.—M. T.]

"Possible that you not it saw not," said Smiley, "possible that you—you comprehend frogs; possible that you not you there comprehend nothing; possible that you had of the experience, and possible that you not be but an amateur. Of all manner (*De toute manière*) I bet forty dollars that she batter in jumping no matter which frog of the county of Calaveras."

The individual reflected a second, and said like sad:

"I not am but a stranger here, I no have not a frog; but if I of it had one, I would embrace the bet."

"Strong, well!" respond Smiley; "nothing of more facility. If you will hold my box a minute, I go you to search a frog (*j'irai vous chercher*)."

Behold, then, the individual, who guards the box, who puts his forty dollars upon those of Smiley, and who attends (*et qui attend*). He attended enough longtimes, reflecting all solely. And figure you that he takes Daniel, him opens the mouth by force and with a teaspoon him fills with shot of the hunt, even him fills just to the chin, then he him puts by the earth. Smiley during these times was at slopping in a swamp. Finally he trapped (*attrape*) a frog, him carried to that individual, and said:

"Now if you be ready, put him all against Daniel, with their before-feet upon the same line, and I give the signal"—then he added: "One, two, three—advance!"

Him and the individual touched their frogs by behind, and the frog new put to jump smartly, but Daniel himself lifted ponderously, exalted the shoulders thus, like a Frenchman—to what good? he could not budge, he is planted solid like a church, he not advance no more than if one him had put at the anchor.

Smiley was surprised and disgusted, but he not himself doubted not of the turn being intended (*mais il ne se doutait pas du tour bien entendu*). The individual empockted the silver, himself with it went, and of it himself in going is that he no gives not a jerk of thumb over the shoulder—like that—at the poor Daniel, in saying with his air deliberate—(*L'individu empoche l'argent s'en va et en s'en allant est ce qu'il ne donne pas un coup de pouce par-dessus l'épaule, comme ça, au pauvre Daniel, en disant de son air délibéré.*)

"Eh bien! *I no see not that that frog has nothing of better than another.*"

Smiley himself scratched longtimes the head, the eyes fixed upon Daniel, until that which at last he said:

"I me demand how the devil it makes itself that this beast has refused. Is it that she had something? One would believe that she is stuffed."

He grasped Daniel by the skin of the neck, him lifted and said:

"The wolf me bite if he no weigh not five pounds."

He him reversed and the unhappy belched two handfuls of shot (*et le malheureux,* etc.).—When Smiley recognized how it was, he was like mad. He deposited his frog by the earth and ran after that individual, but he not him caught never.

It may be that there are people who can translate better than I can, but I am not acquainted with them.

So ends the private and public history of the Jumping Frog of Calaveras County, an incident which has this unique feature about it—that it is both old and new, a "chestnut" and not a "chesnut"; for it was original when it happened two thousand years ago, and was again original when it happened in California in our own time.

Work Cited

* Sidgwick, *Greek Prose Composition,* page 116.

Frank R. Morrissey (essay date 1921)

SOURCE: "The Ancestor of the 'Jumping Frog'," in *The Bookman,* Vol. 53, No. 1, April, 1921, pp. 143-45.

[*In the following essay, Morrissey recounts a Virginia tale about a man and a trained grasshopper, claiming it to be a prototype of Twain's jumping frog story.*]

Occasionally it is given to lesser mortals not only to read the fiction of the gifted ones, but also to glimpse the skeleton of truth upon which the wordy flesh has been grown. For some such an experience holds no more of romance than watching a play from the wings; for other, more blessed, souls the insight serves to arouse further admiration at the deft touches that have made fancy far more pleasant than fact.

In those golden days in Virginia City of which Mark Twain writes so vividly in *Roughing It* there were four men whose names were linked like a Mexican puzzle ring—Mackay, Fair, Flood, and O'Brien, the euphony of the chain, by singular chance, following the order of their importance in "The Bonanza Four". Mackay was the dominating personality, by reason of his shrewdness, his prescience, his indomitable courage, and those other intangible qualities that make a man a leader. Yet for all this there was still something of the boy about him that drove him often to play, even when weighty affairs rested upon him.

Among the employees at the "Con. Virginia" mine was a man whose name is unimportant now, but whom Mackay rated as the best mine superintendent on the Comstock Lode. From him would Mackay tolerate familiarity, and between the two there existed a relationship that hinted not the least of master and man.

One day Mackay, coming unexpectedly into the office, found his superintendent and the paymaster on the floor measuring the distance between chalk marks. The superintendent explained that, coming down from the side of Mount Davidson, which looms tall above the Comstock, he had encountered a grasshopper of such remarkable agility that he had captured it in order to measure the length of its leap. The boy in Mackay swam to the surface and he instantly averred that, given time to search, he could find a dozen grasshoppers that would far outjump his superintendent's prodigy. The outcome of the challenge was a bet of proportions that made even blasé Virginia City gasp.

Mackay, with more pressing matters than hunting grasshoppers demanding his attention, dispatched two miners with a week's grub down California Gulch with instructions to bring back a choice selection of high and broad-jumping grasshoppers, promising a share of his winnings should they find him a champion. At the end of a week the men were back with a hundred grasshoppers of undoubted leg power. With the whole city interested in the wager, a chemist from the assay room, who had experimented, brought Mackay word that the least whiff of ammonia would inspire a grasshopper to outdo himself. Mackay tried the suggestion on a few of his "stable" and verified the assertion.

Having finally chosen his grasshopper Mackay notified his superintendent to bring on his jumper and prepare for defeat. The long office of the Consolidated Virginia mine was chosen as the field of contest. The superintendent placed his grasshopper on the chalk mark that marked the "take off" and touched it with a sharp stick. A cheer went up from his partisans as they viewed the length of the leap. With a grin of anticipated triumph Mackay placed his chosen challenger on the mark and, drawing a small bottle from his pocket, gave the "hopper" a whiff of the contents. The grasshopper seemed loggy and uncertain, so Mackay touched it with a match end. It hopped a few feeble inches and fell over on its side.

Amazement, chagrin, anger, flickered across Mackay's face, but like a true sport he ordered the bet paid. It was not until the superintendent had departed, gloating audibly, to celebrate at "The Crystal", that suspicion entered Mackay's mind. Calling for two other grasshoppers he tried to make them jump, with the same fatal results. Absently, to test the strength of his ammonia, Mackay placed the vial to his nostrils.

The odor of chloroform greeted him.

Substitute a country store for the Con. Virginia mine office, call John Mackay instead "this yere Smiley", and place his reliance in a frog named "Dan'l". Birdshot will produce the same effect on a frog as chloroform on a grasshopper, and is more picturesque. There you have the framework upon which a master sculptor of words can fashion **"The Jumping Frog of Calaveras County"**.

Edgar M. Branch (essay date 1950)

SOURCE: "The Californian: The Jumping Frog," in *The Literary Apprenticeship of Mark Twain, with Selections from His Apprentice Writing,* University of Illinois Press, 1950, pp. 120-29.

[*In the first important scholarly discussion of the jumping frog story, Branch examines Simon Wheeler's narrative method and asserts that there are three levels of reality in the story—the commonsense world, the realm of oddity, and the realm of the fantastic—as represented by the figures of the genteel narrator, Simon Wheeler, and Jim Smiley.*]

In the thirteen years between **"The Dandy Frightening the Squatter"** and **"Jim Smiley and His Jumping Frog"**[10] Mark Twain came full circle, for the major difference between these two tales is quality of workmanship. Each is a short narrative using a native theme. Each tells an anecdote in the tall tale tradition of the early Southwestern humorists.[11] Each is rooted in American folklore and came to written expression through oral transmission. But what **"The Dandy"** merely promised, **"The Jumping Frog"** completed. In reality of character, in humorous appeal, and in techniques of structure and dramatization, Simon Wheeler's yarn surpasses anything Mark Twain had written earlier.

The inevitability of **"The Jumping Frog"** is far from apparent. Nothing Mark Twain wrote for several years afterward equaled its excellence. Had he stopped writing upon coming East in 1867, he would be known today—like Thomas B. Thorpe—as the author of one outstanding tale. Nor do any of his western sketches written before **"The Jumping Frog"** foretell its creation. For years he had been under the spell of Far West newspaper humor. The journals of Nevada and California preferred, instead of indigenous tales, the kind of polite but extravagant comic journalism he practiced. His own critical taste was neither a strong nor accurate guide to composition. He called "Those Blasted Children" a "Pearl," and would have staked his reputation on its wide circulation. He thought he had written "many an article a man might be excused for thinking tolerably good," but considered **"The Jumping Frog"** to be merely a squib, a "villainous backwoods sketch."[12] Until he accepted the public's approval of it, he saw no reason to change that opinion.

At Angel's Camp and at Jackass Hill, conditions were ideal for the frog story to take shape in his mind. Perhaps not since those early days spent on his Uncle John Quarles' farm near Florida, Missouri, where he first learned to know the ways of animals, had he been so secluded from human commerce and town life. He left behind in San Francisco those urban experiences he habitually turned into comic copy. In the isolated hill region he felt no pressure to write for the *Californian* or the *Golden Era*. At Jackass Hill he joined a community undisturbed by "bloody affrays" or police corruption. The boom days were past, replaced by easygoing, individualistic pocket mining. Such a life left time for quiet interests and for talk with the old timers who lingered out their lives among the hills. Even the rain, which poured down steadily during his stay at Angel's Camp, seemed to conspire for his good. It kept him inside the tavern, sitting by the stove with Ben Coon. There, and in Jim Gillis' cabin, Mark Twain "at last found a value in being lazy."[13] There he rediscovered the value of leisurely talk.

Jim Gillis and Ben Coon were catalytic agents who brought about the transformation in his writing. Both loved the oral anecdote, although their deliveries were different. Jim, Mark Twain said, had "a bright and smart imagination . . . of the kind that turns out impromptu work and does it well . . . just builds a story as it goes along . . . enjoying each fresh fancy as it flashes from the brain. . . . Jim was born a humorist and a very competent one."[14] Standing before his big log fire, he would spin extravagant yarns about his partner, Dick Stoker, always soberly pretending that what he related was "veracious history." As Mark Twain said about the actor Fred Franks in 1864—a year before he wrote the frog story—Jim possessed the "first virtue of a comedian, which is to do humorous things with grave decorum and without seeming to know that they are funny."[15] Mark used more than one of Jim's tales: the story of **"The Burning Shame,"** and those about the jaybird and the acorns and Dick Baker's cat, Tom Quartz. Ben Coon's charm seemed even less artful. A former pilot on the Illinois River, he spent most of his time at Angel's Camp lounging in the barroom of the hotel. Paine has described him as a "solemn, fat-witted person, who dozed by the stove, or told slow, endless stories, without point or application."[16] Possibly he was a master of the deadpan style who convinced his listeners that he lacked a sense of humor. His story of the jumping frog prompted these notes in Mark's notebook:

> Coleman with his jumping frog—bet a stranger $50.— Stranger had no frog and C. got him one:—in the meantime stranger filled C's frog full of shot and he couldn't jump. The stranger's frog won.[17]

From these notes came Mark Twain's best writing in the West.

"The Jumping Frog" is a tale of shrewdness outwitted, of the sure thing defeated by cunning. Fortunately this theme is matched by an excellent structure. Mark Twain used the narrative technique developed by Thomas B. Thorpe, George W. Harris, and other writers of the Old Southwest. The technique was the framework structure—the written version of the oral tale enclosed within a frame supplied by the author speaking in his own person.[18] Thus Mark began **"The Jumping Frog"** with a few words to Artemus Ward:

> MR. A. WARD,
>
> DEAR SIR:—Well, I called on good-natured garrulous old Simon Wheeler, and I inquired after your friend Leonidas W. Smiley, as you requested me to do. . . .

He went on to tell how he found Simon dozing by the barroom stove in a dilapidated tavern in the mining camp of Noomerang. After introducing himself and inquiring about Leonidas W. Smiley, Mark was backed into a corner by Simon Wheeler, who began his long-winded tale:

> There was a feller here once by the name of *Jim* Smiley, in the winter of '49—or maybe it was the spring of '50—I don't recollect exactly, some how. . . .

Once started, Wheeler droned on. One by one he introduced Jim's pets, until he came to Dan'l Webster and the canny stranger. Leisurely he drawled out the yarn of the momentous wager. Mark then completed the frame by having Wheeler called out into the front yard. As Mark was leaving the tavern, he met Wheeler returning. The old man buttonholed him and began again:

> "Well, thish-yer Smiley had a yaller one-eyed cow that didn't have no tail only just a short stump like a bannanner, and—"
>
> "O, curse Smiley and his afflicted cow!" I muttered, good-naturedly, and bidding the old gentleman good-day, I departed.
>
> Yours, truly,
>
> Mark Twain.

With this slight touch that so cleverly links the worlds of Mark Twain, Simon Wheeler, and "thish-yer Smiley," Mark completed the structure that gave form and perspective to his tale.[19]

Within this general framework Simon Wheeler's tale is admirably constructed. The moment he starts to talk—and Mark never interrupts—a convincing monologue begins. We seem to hear real talk. Wheeler is garrulous, colloquial, and ungrammatical. His talk flows naturally and unpredictably in the rhythms of the accomplished storyteller. Yet, with all this, Mark skillfully directed the flow of Wheeler's words. The old codger first makes perfectly clear that Jim Smiley was "the curiosest man about always betting on anything that turned up you ever see. . . .":

> . . . if he even see a straddle-bug start to go any wheres, he would bet you how long it would take him to get wherever he was going to, and . . . he would foller that straddle-bug to Mexico but what he would find out . . . Why, it never made no difference to *him*— he would bet on *anything*—the dangdest feller.

We are soon perfectly satisfied that betting was Smiley's ungovernable passion: we learn that he wagered Parson Walker that the Parson's sick but convalescent wife would not recover! Having made his general point about Jim Smiley's character, Wheeler goes on to cite three extended instances to prove it. In length, complexity, surprise, and human interest, the three are arranged in ascending order, climaxing, of course, with the defeat of Dan'l Webster by the unknown frog from the local swamps.

Smiley's mare, the "fifteen-minute nag," is the animal-heroine of the first anecdote. She was a slow, asthmatic horse, always last to leave the post, but always a sure winner. At the fag end of the race, she would

> come cavorting and spraddling up, and scattering her legs around limber, sometimes in the air, and sometimes out to one side amongst the fences, and kicking up m-o-r-e dust, and raising m-o-r-e racket with her coughing and sneezing and blowing her nose—and always fetch up at the stand just about a neck ahead. . . .

To Smiley, of course, belonged the winnings. Her counterpart in the fight-ring was Andrew Jackson, Smiley's bull pup. It was Andrew Jackson's custom to just "set around and look ornery" until he smelled money. When matched with another dog, that dog "might tackle him, and bully-rag him, and bite him, and . . . Andrew Jackson would never let on but what he was satisfied," but at the end he, too, would win, hanging onto his opponent's hind leg with a vise-like grip. Andrew was a dog of genius, Wheeler says, for in fair fight he always came out on top, even though "he hadn't had no opportunities to speak of. . . ." But finally he died of a broken heart when Smiley matched him with a dog whose hind legs had been cut off. As Andrew "came to make a snatch for his pet holt, he saw in a minute how he'd been imposed on," and becoming discouraged he "got shucked out bad," gave Smiley a reproachful look, "laid down and died." The first anecdote is generalized, the second made more particular. Smiley's mare is not named, and we see her in no specific race. But we see Andrew Jackson as he fights his two-legged opponent. Both anecdotes depend upon the surprise finishes of Smiley's protégés. But only Andrew Jackson has the tables turned on him—a theme which anticipates the defeat of Dan'l Webster. Thus we feel that as Wheeler warms up to his subject, he becomes more detailed, more vivid, and more interested in his account. We expect that what follows should excel in all these and, perhaps, other ways.

What follows is, of course, the tale of Jim Smiley, his frog Dan'l, and the cunning stranger. Jim Smiley "ketched a frog one day and took him home and said that he cal'lated to educate him. . . ." Simon describes how Jim taught Dan'l to catch flies. He would jump up in the air, "snake a fly off'n the counter there, and flop down on the floor again as solid as a gob of mud," with no idea that "he'd done any more'n any frog might do." But "jumping on a dead level was his strong suit," and Jim Smiley was willing to

bet $40 with the reticent stranger who appeared one day, that Dan'l could "out-jump ary frog in Calaveras county." When the terms were arranged and Dan'l had been slyly filled with quail-shot, the stranger's frog "hopped off lively, but Dan'l give a heave, and hysted up his shoulders—so—like a Frenchman, but it wasn't no use—he couldn't budge. . . ." The stranger pocketed the money, and at the door he

> sorter jerked his thumb over his shoulder—this way— at Dan'l, and says again, very deliberate, "Well—*I* don't see no points about that frog that's any better'n any other frog."

Simon's tale then tapers off in Smiley's discovery of the trick and his fruitless pursuit of the stranger. In this anecdote there is development of interest and intensity. The climax comes with the stranger's last words, but Jim Smiley's reaction to the fraud supplies an additional tang and fulfills our expectations about the way this proud, shrewd animal fancier would act when duped.

The tale of the wager on Dan'l Webster, therefore, is a fitting climax to Simon Wheeler's entire narration. The two previous anecdotes lead up to it, both in type of action and in the emergent theme of the tables turned. Because of the clever selection of incidents portraying Dan'l's superior virtues, and because of our previous knowledge of Smiley as a proud and conscientious trainer, we can understand why Smiley was "monstrous proud of his frog," and why, his gullibility realized, he became "the maddest man." Dan'l, too, has a definite character. He was an educated frog and legitimately proud of his ability. Yet, as Wheeler says, "You never see a frog so modest and straightfor'ard . . . for all he was so gifted." The dose of quail-shot wounded his pride and outraged his decency. Such a frog, treated so cavalierly, adds a slight touch of comic pathos to the tale. We wonder if he, too, did not die of a broken heart.

The superior excellence of Simon's last anecdote is its dramatic presentation. Only in the story of Dan'l does interest in the human characters predominate over that in the animals. It is primarily Smiley himself, and not Dan'l, who is duped by the crafty stranger. In the anecdotes of the "fifteen-minute nag" and of Andrew Jackson, we are always aware of Simon Wheeler's dominant personality. But in the yarn about Dan'l, although Wheeler's personality and manner of narration are still evident, Jim Smiley and the stranger take over. Between them they act out the little drama in Noomerang, from the time the stranger noticed the box that Dan'l lived in:

> "What might it be that you've got in the box?"
>
> And Smiley says, sorter indifferent like, "It might be a parrot, or it might be a canary, maybe, but it ain't— it's only just a frog."
>
> And the feller took it, and looked at it careful, and turned it round this way and that, and says, "H'm— so 'tis. Well, what's *he* good for?"

"Well," Smiley says, easy and careless, "He's good enough for *one* thing I should judge—he can out-jump ary frog in Calaveras county."

Thus the intrinsic appeal of the yarn is increased by the dramatic presentation. We are interested in the human characters that talk and act before us. It makes no difference that we share a guilty knowledge of the stranger's trick. We do not need to be surprised at the outcome of the bet, for we are content to watch the stranger take his cool exit and to see Smiley come to a full realization of the truth.

The dramatization of the tale has an additional value. It creates a third level of reality in "The Jumping Frog." To the first belongs Mark Twain, who writes Artemus Ward about Simon Wheeler. This is the plane of common sense reality, the world of ordinary journalism familiar to Mark's readers. Simon Wheeler belongs to the second level, to a world of human oddity as seen through Mark Twain's eyes. But when Wheeler lets Jim Smiley and the stranger act out their sly battle of wits, a third and fantastic realm comes into view. These men with their interests and their actions are, for all their realism, creations of fantasy. Though Simon Wheeler speaks with his own voice and from his own observations, what he says is a genuine bit of American folklore portraying native manners—folklore which belongs with the exploits of Davy Crockett and Paul Bunyan.

In "The Jumping Frog" the Washoe comedian gets off the stage for Simon Wheeler and Jim Smiley. These characters are not hopelessly buried in horseplay and banter. Nor are they purposeless, unconvincing figures like John William Skae. The melodrama and the deliberately chaotic manner are gone. Convincing dialogue replaces Mark Twain's wagging tongue. The story is told with subtlety and objectivity, in a form that gives balance and perspective. A return to the methods and interests of the Old Southwestern humorists replaces the Washoe techniques that had produced neither competent narration nor humorous character.

The frog story is a development we might have hoped for, but hardly have expected, from Mark Twain's pre-Nevada writings. His interest in anecdote, beginning with **"The Dandy,"** continued throughout the Hannibal period and is found in the Thomas Jefferson Snodgrass letters, but is confined to a few short narrative squibs in Washoe. **"The Dandy,"** alone, is at all comparable to **"The Jumping Frog"** in structure, economy of development, and dramatization. With the interest in anecdote went an interest in character. But the dandy and the squatter were types. Abram Curts and Jim C——, Sam Clemens' Hannibal acquaintances, were not clearly conceived. Snodgrass had these faults and in addition was self-contradictory and grotesque. Yet the attempt at realism lay behind all these abortive characters. It is also seen in some of Mark Twain's letters and a few of his western sketches: old Boreas and a witness or two in **"Smith vs. Jones"** momentarily come to life.

The interest in animal character also recurred in the early writing, from the time he wrote to Annie Taylor about the bugs that pestered him at night in the print shop. In **"The Jumping Frog"** he first turned this interest to real account. The patient appreciation shown by Jim Smiley and Simon Wheeler for the emotions of Jim's pets is a major source of the humor. Their belief in the human qualities of animals is similar to the self-delusion that afflicted Isaiah Sellers, who comes closest, perhaps, to truly humorous character before Simon Wheeler begins to talk.

This "villainous backwoods sketch" is the first precipitation of Mark Twain's best artistry. It first gives convincing evidence of the change in his writing that took him beyond the western burlesque manner. Something in the voices of Jim Gillis and Ben Coon—the approach, the emphasis, the rhythms—entered into it, and continued to appear in his best humor. Once he had heard these old-timers talk, he knowingly or unknowingly had found a true vein. Listen to Ben Coon talking about the dictionary that the boys kept "sashaying around" from shanty to shanty for reading material. Ben appeared in the first sketch Mark published upon returning to San Francisco:

> Now Coddington had her a week, and she was too much for *him*—he couldn't spell the words; he tackled some of them regular busters, tow'rd the middle, you know, and they throwed him; next, Dyer, *he* tried her a jolt, but he couldn't *pronounce* 'em—Dyer can hunt quail or play seven-up as well as any man, understand me, but he can't *pronounce* worth a d—n; . . . and so, finally, Dick Stoker harnessed her, up there at his cabin, and sweated over her, and cussed over her, and rastled with her for as much as three weeks, night and day, till he got as far as R, and then passed her over to 'Lige Pickerell, and said she was the all-firedest dryest reading that ever *he* struck. . . .[20]

Now listen to Dick Baker in *Roughing It*—Jim Gillis in real life—talking about Tom Quartz:

> Gentlemen, I used to have a cat here, by the name of Tom Quartz, . . . and he was the remarkablest cat *I* ever see . . . he had more hard, natchral sense than any man in this camp—'n' a *power* of dignity. . . . He never ketched a rat in his life—'peared to be above it. He never cared for nothing but mining. He knowed more about mining, that cat did, than any man *I* ever see. . . . When we went to work, he'd scatter a glance around, 'n' if he didn't think much of the indications, he would give a look as much as to say, "Well, I'll have to get you to excuse *me*," 'n' without another word he'd hyste his nose into the air 'n' shove for home.[21]

The same tones appear in *A Tramp Abroad* as Jim Baker discourses on bluejays:

> There's more *to* a bluejay than any other creature. He has got more moods, and more different kinds of feelings than other creatures; and, mind you, whatever a bluejay feels, he can put into language. And no mere commonplace language, either, but rattling, out-and-out book-talk—and bristling with metaphor, too—just bristling! And as for command of language—why *you* never see a bluejay get stuck for a word. No man ever did. They just boil out of him! . . . Don't talk to *me*— I know too much about this thing.[22]

The same sort of fanciful gleams shoot through the mind of Huck Finn. The same positive assurance is found in Colonel Sellers. Huck talks at times in the same patiently explanatory, fantastic way. Similar accents fall from the lips of Jim, Tom Sawyer, the King, the Duke, Boggs, and a host of minor characters. The manner persists in most of Mark Twain's novels, and appears at intervals in the travel books. Many of his characters have the straight-faced manner of Jim Gillis and Ben Coon. With them, however, it is not put on, but is an indispensable part of their personalities. During his stay in the Tuolumne Hills, Mark Twain found one great clue to his interpretation of character, and in **"The Jumping Frog"** he first transformed it into literature.

As Mr. DeVoto has said, **"Jim Smiley and His Jumping Frog"** achieves "a blending of his inheritance with his individual gifts that for the first time expresses him."[23] The tale is typical of the short narratives that contain much of his best writing. It is an early example of the literature Mark Twain created out of the frontier humor that had been one of his favorite media ever since he wrote **"The Dandy Frightening the Squatter."**

Notes

[10] See p. 246. Mark Twain's frog story was first published in the New York *Saturday Press,* November 18, 1865, with the title "Jim Smiley and His Jumping Frog." It was written some time between March and October at the request of Artemus Ward, who wished to include a sketch of Mark Twain's in a collection of his tales to be published by George W. Carleton in New York. Either "The Jumping Frog" arrived too late or Carleton did not like it, for it was handed over to Henry Clapp, Jr., the publisher of the *Saturday Press.* On December 16, 1865, the *California* reprinted the tale with slight changes. "Jim Smiley" was changed to "Jim Greeley." In May, 1867, it served as the title sketch in Mark Twain's first book, *The Celebrated Jumping Frog of Calaveras County, and Other Sketches,* published by Charles Henry Webb, then in New York. Mark Twain later touched up the story still more for other reprintings. The original *Saturday Press* version has been accurately edited by Mr. Franklin Meine: *Jim Smiley and His Jumping Frog,* The Pocahantas Press, 1940.

[11] The frog story may have originated in the Midwest, possibly along the Mississippi River. Mr. Bernard DeVoto thinks it once may have existed as Negro folklore. He notices that the theme fits Indian and frontier folklore as well (*Mark Twain's America,* pp. 173-177). Mr. T. V. Bodine believes that the frog story was brought to Missouri from Tennessee by John Quarles, and that Clemens first heard it from him ("A Visit to Florida," *Kansas City Star,* May 19, 1912). Whoever brought the story west, several printed versions are now known. "A Toad Story" in the June 11, 1853, Sonora *Herald,* and a similar tale in the San Andreas *Independent* for December 11, 1858, are both reprinted in Mr. Oscar Lewis' *The Origin of the Celebrated Jumping Frog of Calaveras County,* The Book Club of California, 1931. A third version, Henry P. Leland's "Frogs Shot without Powder," first appeared in the *Spirit of the Times,* May 26, 1855, and is reprinted in Appendix B of DeVoto's *Mark Twain's America.*

[12] *Letters,* I, 101, dated January 20, 1866.

[13] Walker, *San Francisco's Literary Frontier,* p. 194.

[14] *Mark Twain in Eruption,* p. 359.

[15] "'Mark Twain' in the Metropolis," *Territorial Enterprise,* n. d. Extant in the *Golden Era,* June 26, 1864.

[16] Paine, I, 271.

[17] *Notebook,* p. 7.

[18] Cf. Blair, *Native American Humor,* p. 91 ff. for a discussion of the framework structure.

[19] Mark Twain used the framework structure to the best advantage for character portrayal. In a few short paragraphs at the beginning, Simon Wheeler is pictured dozing comfortably by the barroom stove. He is a fat, bald-headed, and friendly person, with "an expression of winning gentleness and simplicity. . . ." He begins his tale as a matter of course, irrelevant as it is to Mark Twain's inquiry. He is so earnest and sincere that obviously "far from imagining that there was anything ridiculous or funny about his story, he regarded it as a really important matter, and admired his two heroes as men of transcendent genius in finesse."

Mark Twain's place in the frame also is important for the story's effect. He pictures himself as a tolerant, good-natured listener, well aware of Wheeler's absurdity and the unconscious humor of his tale. He is also aware of the ridiculous position in which Artemus Ward has placed him, since Ward knew that if Wheeler were asked about Leonidas W. Smiley, he would begin an "infernal reminiscence" of Jim Smiley. The neutral tones of Mark Twain's personality and his correct and self-deprecatory speech from excellent contrasts with the language and personalities of Wheeler and Smiley.

Further economy in character depiction results from the interplay between the characters of Wheeler and Smiley. As Miss Brashear has noted (p. 44), the story "gets its peculiar quality from being the report of one oddity by another. The 'original,' Jim Smiley, is a highly interesting person to the 'original,' Simon Wheeler."

[20] "An Unbiased Criticism," *Californian,* March 18, 1865.

[21] II, 158-159.

[22] I, 16-17.

[23] *Mark Twain's America,* p. 176.

Roger Penn Cuff (essay date 1952)

SOURCE: "Mark Twain's Use of California Folklore in his Jumping Frog Story," in *Journal of American Folklore,* Vol. LXV, 1952, pp. 155-58.

[*In the following essay, Cuff discusses similarities between Twain's jumping frog story and earlier published versions with roots in California folklore, and asserts that while there are parallels in terms of content and phrasing among the various renditions, the imaginative, dramatic, and realistic detail in "Jim Smiley and His Jumping Frog" are clearly Twain's own contribution.*]

A few accounts of a jumping contest between frogs had appeared in print before Mark Twain wrote the story, **"Jim Smiley and His Jumping Frog,"**[1] later usually entitled, **"The Celebrated Jumping Frog of Calaveras County."** These earlier accounts may have served Twain as sources. His story echoes some of their phrases. The chief treasury from which he drew, however, must have been his own mind and personality—his stock of impressions of life and his ability to create original phrases.

The widely held idea that a Greek fable was one of his sources is erroneous. The mistaken notion probably sprang from Arthur Sidgwick's publishing in his textbook, *Greek Prose Composition,* a brief tale, "The Athenian and the Frog," containing in highly condensed form the leading details of Twain's **"Celebrated Jumping Frog."** Henry Van Dyke furnished Twain a copy of the Sidgwick book. Twain, supposing that Sidgwick's version was based on a Greek fable, wrote an essay, "Private History of the 'Jumping Frog' Story," giving a footnote reference to Sidgwick's textbook and expressing a theory that the two versions—one from Greece, the other from California—must have originated independently. The Sidgwick book and the Twain essay helped disseminate the belief that a Greek original existed. A few years later Twain learned that apparently Greece had produced no such story. No proof exists that Twain borrowed any of the details from Sidgwick. Sidgwick admitted that his version was based on Twain's story and explained why he had not acknowledged in his textbook an indebtedness to Twain.[2] There is clear evidence that Twain did not borrow from Sidgwick the essential details of the frog story. Neither did Twain have access to any prior Greek fable containing the essence of his frog-contest narrative. If Greece ever possessed a native anecdote of a contest between frogs, no one has yet submitted a copy to the attention of present-day students.

To the folklore of the Gold Rush era, to the stories that were current in California mining camps, Mark Twain was, however, in debt. One day during the winter of 1864-65, in a hotel barroom in Angel's Camp, Calaveras County, he heard Ben Coon, a former steamboat pilot, tell slowly and solemnly a narrative of a jumping contest between two frogs. Coon's manner showed that he did not suspect the humorous possibilities of the anecdote. Whether Twain had ever heard the story until told that day by Coon is not known. Albert Bigelow Paine has indicated that it was from Coon that Clemens first heard the tale.[3] But Bernard De Voto thinks that Twain may have been already acquainted with the story.[4]

Three toad stories, with striking similarities to Twain's version, were published prior to **"The Celebrated Jumping Frog."** Two of these earlier versions treat of a jumping contest; the other reveals a method of capturing a frog. Oscar Lewis has drawn attention to "A Toad Story"[5] as the earliest known published account of the jumping frog contest. De Voto has cited Henry P. Leland's "Frogs Shot Without Powder"[6] as containing some details that could have furnished Twain with suggestions for **"The Celebrated Jumping Frog."** And various writers have men-tioned that Twain may have borrowed from Samuel Seabough's article, "Tricks and Defeats of Sporting Genius,"[7] in which is embedded a story of Joe B— and jumping frogs.

Whether Twain had read any of these accounts when he wrote his version has not been established. Lewis believes that Twain probably had not read Seabough's article, because the *San Andreas Independent* expired in 1861, prior to the writing of **"The Celebrated Jumping Frog."** The same logic would hold that Twain had probably never seen "A Toad Story," because the *Sonora Herald* almost certainly ceased publication in 1857.[8] De Voto considers it likely that Twain had read "Frogs Shot Without Powder," and the possibility of such a reading must be granted; but the evidence that Twain had seen Leland's story is inconclusive. He may have read any or all of the three accounts mentioned or he may have seen none of them.

It is difficult, and may be beyond possibility, to know the extent to which Twain borrowed ideas and phrases from "A Toad Story," "Frogs Shot Without Powder," and "Tricks and Defeats of Sporting Genius," because no copy exists of the oral narrative that he heard from Coon. If it were possible to discover how many times Twain heard the story and the exact content of each of those oral narrations, one could more easily determine the indebtedness to the printed versions.

Twain's **"Celebrated Jumping Frog"** can, however, be compared to the known similar frog stories published earlier; and borrowed elements as well as new features can be found in Clemens's version. Both the added substance and the individual, imaginative, realistic, and dramatic manner of telling the story seem clearly to be contributions by Twain.

Comparison of Twain's story to the earlier versions reveals resemblances in content and phrasing. All these accounts, except "Frogs Shot Without Powder," which deals with frog-catching, focus attention upon competitive jumping; and even the excepted narrative resembles Twain's sketch in representing someone as filling the frog with shot. The Clemens story contains phrases similar to some that appeared in the earlier versions. It retains the saloon setting of "A Toad Story" but, instead of having the contest occur in the saloon, agrees with Leland in representing the narrative as being told in a barroom. It harmonizes with Seabough's version in naming Calaveras County as the locale of the jumping frog contest. In referring to bets as being "doubled and redoubled," it echoes Seabough's representation of Boniface as offering to "double" the bet of ten dollars that Joe B— had made. The bull-pup may have been suggested by the "Bull-paddy" in "Frogs Shot Without Powder" and by the cur that was blown to bits by a "dog battery" in "Tricks and Defeats of Sporting Genius." Smiley's training his frog to catch flies may be reminiscent of the statement in Seabough's story that Boniface fed Joe B—'s toad shot, which the creature mistook for flies. The swamp in which Jim found a frog for the stranger may have been suggested by the Seabough reference to Joe B— as obtaining a frog from a hole that contained water and mud. Smiley's fondness for betting may reflect Joe's willingness to bet on every game. Twain's word "quail-shot" closely resembles Seabough's "birdshot." Twain's phrase "a double handful of shot" may have been influenced by Leland's "a handfull of shot." Besides such possible borrowings of phrase, Twain's story is probably indebted for some of the traits that it attributes to Simon Wheeler. The monotone and the unvaryingly serious mood in which Wheeler presents his account of the frog contest were probably influenced by Ben Coon's manner of narration which Twain had observed in Angel's Camp. Wheeler's prototype was probably Ben Coon.

But after allowance is made for all possible borrowings from all known sources, Twain deserves credit for his contribution to the story. He gave to his version the imprint of individuality, surcharging the story with whimsical humor, verisimilitude, and dramatic power.

His frog sketch is more amusing than any earlier printed account. It employs humorous colloquial language, such as the statement that the dog "got shucked out bad" and that the frog "'pears to look mighty baggy, somehow." The situations on which Smiley places wagers are absurd, as are the extreme lengths to which he goes to win his bets. Humorous incongruity frequently appears in this story: the consumptive condition of Smiley's mare and her ability to win a race by an almost supernatural effort; the ornery appearance of the bullpup and its real shrewdness and skill in conquering opponents in fights; the inquiry about a minister named Smiley and then the reminder, which the question brings, of another Smiley who had been a mining-camp vagabond and gambler; and the assigning to the dog and to the frog the proper names of human beings who had achieved renown. The outwitting of a shrewd and usually successful gambler by the trick of feeding quail-shot to a frog is amusing; so is Wheeler's failure to recognize that the story he told contained laughable elements.

Twain imbued **"The Celebrated Jumping Frog"** with verisimilitude by using an abundance of concrete and specific detail. For example, Wheeler is described as fat, bald-headed, gentle. The racing of Smiley's mare and her winning of difficult victories are vividly described. Similes are rich in imagery: one compares the dog's jaw to the forecastle of a steamboat; another compares the savage appearance of the dog's teeth to that of furnaces. Distinct and realistic pictures are produced by similes that compare the frog's turning of a somerset to a doughnut's whirling in air, the frog's landing to a cat's alighting, and the frog's movement of his shoulders to that which a Frenchman might make.

And Twain imparted to his story an increased suspense, a dramatic quality heightened beyond what had appeared in the earlier versions. Under his touch, the horse race, the dog fight, the frog contest are all exciting. He raised the interest in the competition between the frogs by having Jim count to three and give the command, "Jump," and by saying that the two owners touched the frogs from behind. Less dramatically, the Seabough version had represented the frogs as jumping when the word was spoken. The *Sonora Herald* version, "A Toad Story," stopped short of remarking that either frog was punched and comparatively undramatically mentioned that some persons struck the boards back of the Yankee's toad. Twain also added drama to the story by stressing Smiley's surprise over the trained frog's failure to jump and this same gambler's anger on learning of having been outwitted. Furthermore, Twain heightened the drama by causing the stranger to insist that Smiley's frog was in no way superior to any common, untrained frog.

To California folklore Mark Twain was in debt for the frog story to which he gave world fame. He may have owed an obligation to the printed versions also. But, rising above all known published sources, he stamped his **"Celebrated Jumping Frog"** with striking originality. In this story his own powerful mind was the chief source of his materials; his genius refashioned, dramatized, and humanized what he borrowed.

Notes

[1] The first published version of Twain's jumping frog story appeared in the New York *Saturday Press* (Nov. 18, 1865), p. 248, cols. 2 and 3, and p. 249, cols. 1-3, and is obtainable from the Library of Congress.

[2] Mark Twain, *The Jumping Frog, in English, Then in French* (New York, 1903), pp. 65-66.

[3] *Mark Twain, a Biography* (New York, 1912), I, 271.

[4] *Mark Twain's America* (Boston, 1932), p. 172.

[5] This tale was published in the *Sonora Herald,* 3: 150 (June 11, 1853), p. 4, col. 1. A facsimile may be found in Lewis, *The Origin of the Celebrated Jumping Frog* (San Francisco, 1931), p. 49.

[6] Leland's version appeared in the New York *Spirit of the Times,* 25: 15 (May 26, 1855), 170; it may be obtained from the American Antiquarian Society.

[7] Published in the *San Andreas Independent,* 3: 12 (Dec. 11, 1858), p. 2, col. 3; obtainable from the California State Library.

[8] The issue of May 30, 1857, is the latest one known to the American Antiquarian Society.

Paul Schmidt (essay date 1956)

SOURCE: "The Deadpan on Simon Wheeler," in *Southwest Review,* Vol. 4, No. 3, Summer, 1956, pp. 270-77.

[*In the following essay, Schmidt investigates Twain's use of comic gravity in Simon Wheeler's narration of the frog story.*]

In the encounter between Mark Twain and Simon Wheeler which frames the story of **"The Notorious Jumping Frog** of Calaveras County" we are, apparently, expected to agree with the narrator, Mark Twain, that the "good natured, garrulous" miner is a comic butt. Wheeler tells his story, according to Mark Twain, like a simpleton:

> He never smiled, he never frowned, he never changed his voice from the gentle-flowing key to which he tuned his initial sentence, he never betrayed the slightest suspicion of enthusiasm; but all through the interminable narrative there ran a vein of impressive earnestness and sincerity . . .

His blank seriousness, his vernacular language, and the seeming naïveté with which his story personifies the frog, the asthmatic mare, and the bull pup would appear at first glance to be ample specification of provincial idiocy. Actually, of course, none of us is misled by this characterization, for we sense the play involved. The westerner, Wheeler, is engaged in his traditional role of taking in the pompous easterner. We are, indeed, so familiar with the devices of American humor that we are likely to underestimate how much Clemens accomplishes with them—deadpan, tall tale, and all the rest. To plunge below the innocently smiling surface of the story is to realize that we are engaged in a complex comic business and one which turns upon issues of great scope and vitality.

That business is traditionally described as burlesque, the reduction of the high to the low. The butt of this humor is the narrator himself, "Mark Twain," and what he represents. With his ostentatious formality, his pretentious language, and, above all, his preconceptions as to what this western miner is, he is obviously not to be identified with the author at all. He has been "commissioned," he says, to ask about a friend's "cherished companion," a companion who is a "minister of the Gospel," and if Wheeler will help him out he promises to be "under many obligations." Punctilio jealously guards the distance between this eastern visitor and his Calaveras County host; a jaundiced patronage is apparent in his mention of Wheeler's shabby surroundings—a "dilapidated tavern" in a "decayed mining camp." "Mark Twain" is, in short, the type genteel, ripe with overbearing sophistication. If Wheeler is a seedy dolt, he is so only from the point of view of the genteel "Mark Twain," the point of view which is Clemens' ultimate object of satire in this story.

This deliberate management of point of view is both an outgrowth of the traditions of southwestern humor in which Clemens worked and a sharp and distinctive departure from them. In earlier southwestern sketches and stories the frame and narration in the first person were standard equipment, but in the frame the author was, in contrast with Clemens here, fully identified with the narrator, and this author-narrator was serenely convinced of his refined superiority to the vernacular-speaking characters who appeared in the story proper. The narrator described the low life of the Crackers, Suckers, and Buckeyes with a condescension ranging from the amused tolerance of A. B. Longstreet's *Georgia Scenes* to the contempt of Johnson J. Hooper's stories of the rascal Simon Suggs.

The function of the frame, with its elegant diction and elevated taste, was to disinfect the author from contamination by the vernacular life he presented.

This narrative attitude derives in large outline from the Enlightenment celebration of the picturesque and its nineteenth-century heir, the local-color story, wherein the author is typically posed as an aristocrat edified by pastoral reflections on the lower classes, indulgent with rural antics, or, if the humble scene is pathetic, Olympian in pity. (Hawthorne's Town Pump sketches are conceived in this manner.) When such condescension is taken over into southwestern humorous sketches it collides head-on with the author's genuine admiration for the low characters in the story within the frame. Thus the sophistication which T. B. Thorpe adopts in the frame of "The Big Bear of Arkansas" is belied by the burlesque of sophistication in the story proper. Where the author moves into closer sympathy with vernacular speech and character, as George Washington Harris does in his Sut Lovingood sketches, the frame and the lofty narrator tend to disappear.

In **"The Jumping Frog"** Clemens hit upon a brilliant resolution of this confusion. Not only does he sharply dissever the point of view of his narrator, "Mark Twain," from his own; he goes even farther and takes on this sophisticated narrator with his local-colorist assumptions as an object of satire. This technical innovation with its accompanying insight accounts for much of the high distinction of this story and of Clemens' humor generally. It involves much more than the simple addition of another character to his satiric targets; when he takes on the moralizing narrator, what falls within the purview of his burlesque is nothing less than the entire point of view of the local-colorist. Clemens has moved his sights up from the simple dandy, or shyster, or circuit rider, who had figured in American humor from its beginnings, and leveled them on the genteel version of the Enlightened traveler and *belle esprit,* a representative nineteenth-century American rich in official and accepted attitudes.

In Clemens' earliest published sketch, **"The Dandy Frightening the Squatter,"** the genteel butt has only the crudest of pretensions—fancy dress and a few mannerisms; he is an oversimplified dude. **"The Jumping Frog"** gives us a more searching view. In the "Mark Twain" of this story a whole culture gone to seed in gentility is brought into the balance. With his unctuous formality of speech, his invidious amusement, and with the whole range of reference into which he proposes to fit Wheeler, he is consciously realized to his very fingertips and riddled with satire. He struts in front of Wheeler with an insufferably patronizing air and, perhaps as a consequence of this egotism, with an almost paranoiac distrust of others. He had, he says, a "lurking suspicion" that he must be on guard against the effronteries of the western vernacular. He is prepared to find Wheeler's story "interminable" and "ridiculous." ("Hostility," as Rilke says, "is our first response.") He sees Wheeler's manner and story as an "infamous" attempt which "blockades" him in the corner and bores him "to death."

This "Mark Twain" is more than a mere snob. The assumptions which govern his reception of Wheeler are those of an eastern traveler in the West, the assumptions which make up the complicated Enlightenment case of Civilization versus Nature, England and the Continent versus America, Boston versus the West. It is the paradoxical view of a refined (or jaded) culture pitted against a boorish (or naïvely noble) nature. As an inhabitant of the Wild West, Wheeler is viewed by "Mark Twain" as a reversion proper to the American frontier. In response to the pulls of this primitive environment the westerner is expected to become a rude, uncultivated barbarian. Hence Wheeler is presented as maundering through his idiotic tale, unable to hold his "simple" mind up to the refined level of his genteel visitor. Harriet Martineau had been shocked at the vulgarity of western table manners, Charles Dickens had been disgusted that the residents along the Mississippi River fought like bloodthirsty savages, and now "Mark Twain" is sure that Simon Wheeler is a fool.

Once we see the narrator and this genteel local-colorist view of the westerner as the target of Clemens' satire, the ostensible values of the story are reversed in characteristic burlesque fashion. Far from being a "good natured, garrulous old" idiot, as "Mark Twain" would lead us to suppose, Wheeler emerges as the initiator of the satire— the teller of the tall tale. He deliberately assumes the role of an unconscious barbarian as a play upon his visitor's preconceptions and with the intention of turning the tables on him. Contrary to "Mark Twain's" picture of him as "far from imagining that there was anything ridiculous or funny about his story," Wheeler is fully aware that his manner is comic and that he is clowning when he treats the frog in his story like a prima donna. He poses as stupid in order to ridicule what his genteel auditor, "Mark Twain," projects on the vernacular westerner, in order to show how ridiculously inappropriate the stereotype of the western barbarian is and how wrong the genteel values are which led to its imposition. The purpose of Wheeler's "impressive earnestness"—the traditional pokerface—becomes clear: it prevents his giving away his hand, his satire on the genteel "Mark Twain," and the role of outlandish stupidity he is assuming. His pose of "sincerity" and the story he tells are consciously designed, as both Clemens and Wheeler are aware, to take in his presumptuous listener. "Mark Twain" is the unconscious character in the frame, and he is the comic butt.

Clemens' additions to the simple story as it was told to him by a bartender in a California mining camp include not only this frame but also considerable elaboration of the characters and animals within the story proper. The rickety mare and the ornery-looking dog on whom Smiley has won so many bets parallel Wheeler in that they too are burlesquing stereotypes which flourish in the genteel mind; they play upon humanitarian sympathy for the Noble Animal. The mare is designed to poke fun at such specimens of romantic zoology as Black Beauty, or the donkey of Wordsworth's poem "Peter Bell." Like Wheeler, the mare is shabby and old. She was "slow and always had the asthma, or the distemper, or the consumption, or something of that kind." These points are designed to outrage

the genteel effort to view her as man's next best friend. Because of such handicaps her racing opponents gave her three hundred yards, and even then they would pass her under way. Yet she *always* wins.

> Always at the fag-end of the race she'd get excited and desperate-like, and come cavorting and straddling up, and scattering her legs around limber, sometimes in the air, and sometimes out to one side amongst the fences, and kicking up m-o-r-e dust and raising m-o-r-e racket with her coughing and sneezing and blowing her nose— and *always* fetch up at the stand just about a neck ahead, as near as you could cipher it down.

The distemper and consumption, the three-hundred-yard handicap add zest to her game; like Wheeler and his "simplicity" she parades these liabilities in order to take in the presumptuous. They certainly cannot be taken as evidence of modesty and a lack of interest in worldly goods, for in contrast to Black Beauty and heroes interested only in inner and spiritual victories, the mare wants a sensational and rackety finish, with as much pomp and circumstance as she can wring out of it. She is a coarse, vulgar, victorious western nag.

But this satire plows up attitudes more deeply rooted than the sentimentalities vested in the SPCA. It penetrates to a central doctrine of romantic individualism, the doctrine that the individual is free *by nature.* The animals are a burlesque of the assumption that the individual is by nature good, while society and its effect on the individual are by nature evil. The mare is by nature asthmatic. The central vision of Clemens' humor is his perception of this romantic illusion. The "scholarly savages" of James Fenimore Cooper arouse his satire in *Roughing It,* not because they were scholarly, but because Clemens is profoundly at variance with the romantic worship of "natural" virtue, whether in Noble Red Men, or frontiersmen, or animals.

Wheeler's story is designed to ridicule the romantic paradox that "natural" animal is more free and admirable than socially inhibited man. He tells us here about ordinary animals going through ordinary paces—a horse racing, a dog fighting, and a frog jumping—but he pretends to suppose these are noteworthy exploits, achievements sweated out in the teeth of adversity. The humor is developed by extending each side of the contradiction: he exaggerates the projection of value onto the animal—the "notorious" frog has "p'ints" which the expert Smiley understands even if the stranger doesn't—and on the other hand he slyly lets fall the crass details which shatter this projection (the mare's "coughing and sneezing and blowing her nose"). Long after the story had become famous Clemens tells of his and Joseph Twichell's helpless laughter over what was apparently for him the punch line of the story, the stranger's observation to Smiley, "Well—I don't see no p'ints about that frog that's any better'n any other frog."

At every turn the story satirizes romantic preconceptions. The mare's victories are, as noted above, the calculated opposite of romantic renunciations of the world. The world is her dish. She wins only after extracting the last ounce of dramatic and sociable value in the situation, wins with vulgar éclat while masquerading as a broken-down plug. Hers is Homeric skill and cunning played to the galleries, in deliberate contrast to Stoic inner victories wrung out in romantic solitude.

The dog, Andrew Jackson, develops further the play upon the inwardness of the romantic ideal. Wheeler's sentiments summing up his talents are a burlesque of the assumption that he possesses innate, inner worth.

> It was a good pup, was that Andrew Jackson, and would have made a name for hisself if he'd lived, for the stuff was in him, and he had genius—I know it, because he hadn't no opportunities to speak of, and it don't stand to reason that a dog could make such a fight as he could under them circumstances, if he hadn't no talent.

Wheeler soberly advances his ridiculous claims for these battered and sorry animals—"to look at the pup, you'd think he warn't worth a cent but to set around and look ornery and lay for a chance to steal something"—as a burlesque of romantic inner "genius." He is poking fun at the notion that the individual's value, his talent, is purely inherent, laughing off the cliché of the westerner with the heart of gold. Andrew Jackson is Gray's flower born to blush unseen, and Clemens is burlesquing the pastoral value of unappreciated native worth.

The frog, Daniel Webster, burlesques pastoral modesty.

> Quicker'n you could wink he'd spring straight up and snake a fly of'n the counter there, and flop down on the floor ag'in as solid as a gob of mud, and fall to scratching the side of his head with his hind foot as indifferent as if he hadn't no idea he'd been doin' any more'n any frog might do.

The point, of course, is that he has *not* done anything more. "You never see a frog," Wheeler adds, "so modest and straight-for'ard as he was, for all he was so gifted." Daniel Webster works so well for this satire because reading Natural Goodness into the animal, as the genteel projection would do, becomes immediately and obviously absurd when the animal is a cool-blooded amphibian frog. Dogs and horses may have a certain domesticated aptitude for the primitivist role as man's best friend, but not a frog. (Nor a pig. Clemens goes through the same burlesque routine elsewhere in his writing with a pig who eschews the glittering prospects of a stage career for a humble life in rural walks.)

The brilliant decorum of the animal characters for this story lies in their bearing on an important limitation of the doctrine of individualism—the doctrine which, watered down from its Protestant and transcendental origins, remained the mainstay of the genteel tradition. In extreme individualism human values tend to be redefined in terms of the solitary, solipsistic, and existential organism; that is,

in terms of physiological and animal values. A pig is, in fact, well fitted for a lonely life next to nature, and the individualist claim to innate value based on nature is on this showing absurd. Man's highest achievement is not communion with nature but, as Simon Wheeler also makes clear, with human nature. Wheeler's animals make the point that romantic primitivism, inherent and purely egocentric worth, is—if anything at all—physiology, the animal side of man. Thus we have a thoroughgoing counter-statement to the genteel claim that the vernacular westerner is an asocial and uncouth savage.

Wheeler's story, the story proper, bears on an associated theme, the relationship between community and the individual talent. Jim Smiley, the comic butt of the story, imposes on the mining town by his inveterate gambling. Superficially he seems to have none of the earmarks of the type gambler; he is neither money-mad, desperate, nor cynical. His gambling has a different rationale. He argues the "p'ints" of the frog with the proud conviction of one who invokes a pet theory. And herein lies his comic flaw. He has lost sight of the human community he belongs to (Angel's Camp) in the dazzling light of his own accomplishment. More specifically, he takes credit for the exploits of the animals on the grounds that he has educated them. He has devoted three months "to learn that frog to jump." For the eighteenth-century Natural Man, believing as he does in the *tabula rasa* and a mechanically intellectual reason, training was the decisive ingredient of career. Smiley has the same naïve faith. He says, "All a frog wanted was education, and he could do most anything." He is in the godlike position of Enlightening this mute inglorious creature. The delusion certifies him for the burlesque pratfall, and the comic peripeteia is brought about by the stranger's filling Daniel Webster with buckshot.

In this light Simon Wheeler emerges from the whole story as Clemens' answer to the eastern fear of the vernacular West as a threat to New England's leadership in the national culture, a threat to the eastern role of what in *Life on the Mississippi* he called "instructional torchbearing." Wheeler's poverty is a calculated affront to the genteel belief in property as a sign of election, his idleness and leisure in telling his tale are an affront to Benjamin Franklin's high interest rates on Time, his impenetrable simplicity (not only is he unaware but he is serene in his plight) is an affront to the worship of intensity in experience and the hard gemlike flame of consciousness which was the avatar of New England thinkers and writers from Jonathan Edwards to Henry James.

Indeed, challenging so much as it does, the story inevitably raises the question of cynicism. Is the humor here, the pleasure taken in Wheeler and his story, merely the weak and temporary satisfaction of getting rid of all spiritual uprightness, of reverting to the simple and childish? In any such final judgment as this question implies it is well to recall that the major purpose of comedy is not affirmation but rejection. **"The Jumping Frog"** is first of all an attack on the genteel tradition. But even this necessary qualification does not alter the larger fact that the strength of the comic rejection, the penetration of good comedy (in contrast to the licentiousness of, for example, a merely obscene story), is directly proportional to values perceived and affirmed. One cannot make a convincing case for ridiculing one position unless he stands on a better. Though values are not explicit in this story, they are nonetheless there. Their implicit presence is the purchase for the thrust of the humor.

If we are not to mangle the presentation of these values in the story it will be necessary to return to technique and to the perspective established by burlesque. If overtly burlesque brings the high down, it covertly elevates the low into the high. Clemens perceives high values in the western vernacular community which Wheeler represents. In the frame, for example, the narrator says that Wheeler is "good natured" and "tranquil," a person possessed of "winning gentleness and simplicity." In part this is, as we have seen, to be discounted as the comic deadpan, but it is also the poise and assurance of one who is fully aware, a serenity which rests on strength and maturity, not, as the genteel "Mark Twain" thinks, on stupidity. Wheeler braves out, as it were, "Mark Twain's" opinion of him, and finally demonstrates that his supposed liabilities are assets.

These values are most vividly apparent in Wheeler's general sensibility or style. He is relaxed and friendly, in contrast to the efforts of his visitor to be imposing and superior. He is leisurely. His sentences are extended and rounded periods with deliberately emphasized climaxes, and the windup for his story is as long as the story itself. With a background of physical work, mining, as against his visitor's leisure (or the pretense of it), his use of the vernacular makes apparent its roots in sensuous working relationships with objects and people. His talk throws up similes and terms growing out of the workaday world of steamboating, farming, carpentering, sawyering—a sensuously concrete lexicon whose value may be suggested by recalling that it was just such a texture which Hawthorne so patiently sought in keeping his notebook. Wheeler's language ignores official taste and has a syntax often not recognized by formal grammar. The frog, for example, goes whirling through the air "like a doughnut" to "nail" a fly on the counter of the barroom and then comes down "flat-footed and all right, like a cat."

The very attitude toward the world, the blooming buzzing confusion, is profoundly different from the traditional Stoic and Puritan distrust of color and outer shows in favor of the inner and inexpressible. The mare plays for the grandstand, not only in order to flout the genteel expectation, but also to affirm the value of doing as well as being, the value of gaudy colors and outer excitement. The dog Andrew Jackson has the same flair for the dramatic. He poses as shabby and unprepossessing, "but as soon as money was up on him he was a different dog; his under-jaw'd begin to stick out like the fo'castle of a steamboat, and his teeth would uncover and shine like the furnaces." The vernacular character delights in a full-panoplied parade of splendors; there is no need for him to hide his assets under a sober guise.

Wheeler's sanctions arise from his place in the mining community; the basis of his, and Clemens', values is community established in common work and play. His rejection of the pretensions of "Mark Twain," the competitive and hostile individualism of the genteel, is based on this relaxed and assured position. Wheeler polarizes the values generated by community, as against the inept and grotesque isolation of individualism. What the genteel "Mark Twain" carelessly dismisses in the last lines of this story is fraternity. He rudely walks out on Wheeler's invitation to hear the promising story of the "yaller one-eyed cow that didn't have no tail, only just a short stump like a bannanner." In terms of both the burlesque strategy and the style, then, Clemens' story ultimately asserts the superiority of vernacular brotherhood over the competitive individualism which animates genteel attitudes.

Kenneth S. Lynn (essay date 1959)

SOURCE: "An American Image," in *Mark Twain and Southwestern Humor,* Little, Brown and Company, 1959, pp. 140-73.

[*In the following excerpt, Lynn argues that in Twain's telling of the jumping frog story, the author stands the tradition of the conventional Southwestern folktale on its head. Lynn then goes on to discuss Twain's narrative technique and use of political humor.*]

In search of new forms to express a new idea of himself, Twain experimented in his Western period with a variety of humorous devices. Caricatures, puns, burlesques, hoaxes, and editorial bandinage were the stock-in-trade of Washoe journalism at the time, and Mark Twain of the *Enterprise* tried them all. In one of his most significant experiments, he produced a sort of literary ventriloquist's act, wherein the writer debated various questions with an uninhibited *alter ego* named "the Unreliable." By putting words in the mouth of this stooge, Twain was able to float out newly-thought-up opinions like so many trial balloons, without being held responsible for them. The fascination of a lifetime with the literary possibilities of twins may be said to date from these early pieces. (A couple of years later, in a series of travel letters to the *Alta California,* "the Unreliable" reappeared as Mark Twain's fictitious traveling companion, the antisocial Mr. Brown. Although these letters, with their distasteful joking about the fragrance of Negroes, reveal that on some social questions the young Missourian still had a lot to learn, the name Brown seems a curiously apt one for a character whom one Twain critic has likened to Caliban. Mr. Brown would have been outraged to know it, but he nevertheless foreshadows Twain's later use of a Negro *alter ego* as a way of commenting upon white society.)

Twain's most interesting literary experiment was **"The Celebrated Jumping Frog of Calaveras County,"** written the year after the author left Nevada. Possibly a Negro tale to begin with—the slyness with which the defeat of the champion is managed would seem to be the distinguishing mark of the slave upon it—the frog story was taken over by the rough-and-tumble society of the mining camps and incorporated in its democratic myth. Various versions of the story had been published in Western newspapers before Mark Twain ever reached California. In appropriating the story for his own purposes, he made numerous changes. First and foremost, he embellished the anecdote with a "frame," in which we are introduced to the narrator, "Mark Twain," who in turn tells us of his encounter with Simon Wheeler in the barroom at Angel's Camp. The narrator's casual reference to an Eastern friend, and his indulgently superior description of the "winning gentleness and simplicity" of Simon Wheeler's countenance, establish his affinity with the Self-controlled Gentleman of the Southwestern tradition . . . The similarities of structure and dramatic situation, however, are sufficient to make us expect the familiar puppet show. The story upsets all our calculations—and the narrator's as well. "Mark Twain," as things turn out, is not as clever as he thinks he is. Assuming himself to be more sophisticated than the man he meets, the encounter teaches him just the reverse—it is he, not Simon, who is simple. The innocence of Simon Wheeler's expression is in fact a mask, cunningly assumed to deceive the outsider by seeming to fulfill all his preconceived notions of Western simple-mindedness. Simon Wheeler's little joke, of course, is simply a California variation on the ancient con game of the trans-Allegheny frontiersman, but in literary terms the **"Jumping Frog"** marks a historic reversal. The narrator, it turns out, is telling a joke on himself, not on the Clown. In the **"Jumping Frog,"** it is the vernacular, not the polite style, which "teaches the lesson." The Southwestern tradition, in other words, has been stood on its head.

The "frame" is a drama of upset expectations, and so is the story proper. Simon launches his vernacular monologue about Jim Smiley (after having been asked for information concerning the Reverend Leonidas W. Smiley) with an anecdote about Jim Smiley's bulldog, who could whip any other dog by fastening his teeth on his opponent's hind leg and hanging on "till they throwed up the sponge, if it was a year," but who was finally defeated by a dog "that didn't have no hind legs, because they'd been sawed off in a circular saw. . . ." Doubtless Twain's Whig upbringing had something to do with the fact that the name of Smiley's bulldog is Andrew Jackson, for in making a dog of that name look ridiculous Twain in effect ridiculed a politician who he never ceased to believe had been a disastrous President. Simon Wheeler's ironic praise of the dog—"a good pup, was that Andrew Jackson, and would have made a name for hisself if he'd lived, for the stuff was in him and he had genius—I know it, because he hadn't no opportunities to speak of, and it don't stand to reason that a dog could make such a fight as he, could under them circumstances if he hadn't no talent"—would certainly have appealed to the Whiggish sense of humor of the earlier Southwestern writers. When we learn, however, as we do very shortly, that Jim Smiley's frog is named Daniel Webster, in honor of Whiggery's arch-hero, we begin to realize that this story is not playing political favorites in the old way at all, but is in fact saying a plague on both houses of a tragic era. Simon Wheeler's

tall tale does not take sides on past history, it rejects the past altogether, and turns toward the West and the future. It also endorses democracy by making fun of superior feelings, as the "frame" had done. Gazing at Daniel Webster, the stranger says, in one of the most famous remarks in the history of American humor, "I don't see no p'ints about that frog that's any better'n any other frog." The subsequent triumph of the anonymous underfrog over the vaunted Daniel Webster comically vindicates the stranger's radical democracy. As the author of the **"Jumping Frog"** had lately discovered, it didn't pay to be too proud in the West.

Catching the upturn of the national mood at the close of the Civil War, the **"Jumping Frog"** was an instantaneous success, James Russell Lowell hailing it as "the finest piece of humorous literature yet produced in America." If the story had any flaws, they resided in the character of the narrator. It was not quite certain who "Mark Twain" was. He seemed a more colloquial figure than the Self-controlled Gentleman, yet he continued to play the Gentleman's role, vis-à-vis the Clown. In the period following the publication of the **"Jumping Frog,"** Twain's major imaginative effort was devoted to solving the problem of his narrative persona.

Hennig Cohen (essay date 1963)

SOURCE: "Twain's Jumping Frog: Folktale to Literature to Folktale," in *Western Folklore,* Vol. 22, January, 1963, pp. 17-18.

[*In the following essay, Cohen claims that despite its clear origins in folklore, Twain's frog story achieved such a widespread reputation and was so clearly associated with his name that later folk versions of the tale were assumed to have used his tale as their source.*]

Sometime in February, 1865, when Mark Twain was at Angel's Camp, California, trying his luck at pocket mining, he made an entry in his notebook as follows:

> Coleman with his jumping frog—bet a stranger $50.—Stranger had no frog and C. got him one:—In the meantime stranger filled C's frog full of shot and he couldn't jump. The stranger's frog won.

He had heard the jumping frog story from Ben Coon, a solemn, old river pilot who spun yarns in a run-down tavern that Twain frequented.

The notebook entry suggests that Twain had been impressed by Coon's story and sensed its potential usefulness. As is well known, he worked it into **"Jim Smiley and His Jumping Frog,"** published in the New York *Saturday Press* of December 16, 1865, and thereafter widely reprinted. In 1867, as **"The Celebrated Jumping Frog of Calaveras County,"** it became the title story of Twain's first book (cover adorned with a sketch of a frog, its belly much distended). James Russell Lowell, an acknowledged authority in such matters, acclaimed it "the finest piece of humorous literature yet produced in America."

Although Twain's memorandum indicates that he had not heard Ben Coon's story before, it seems to have been current in oral tradition in both white and Negro versions, and it had appeared in various newspapers.[1] Oscar Lewis' *The Origins of the Celebrated Jumping Frog of Calaveras County* (San Francisco, 1931) has examples from the Sonora *Herald* of June 11, 1853, and the San Andreas *Independent* of December 11, 1858. Bernard DeVoto reprints a variant from the *Spirit of the Times* of May 26, 1855, in *Mark Twain's America* (Boston, 1932).

A progression from oral tradition to rather crude newspaper versions to more serious treatment is typical of the literary use of folk materials. Other examples can be found in Twain's writing, especially in his use of Southwestern frontier tales to which the jumping frog story is akin. Furthermore, it is not unusual for the reverse of this process to take place—the literary work of known authorship, having been widely disseminated through the agency of some mass medium, to enter oral tradition. This is true, for example, of English broadside ballads and nineteenth-century American sheet music. However, it is very rare to find a folk tale which has been given newspaper circulation and then literary treatment completing the circle by returning to the newspaper and thence, presumably, moving downward and back to the folk. The author of the newspaper article below, "A Match for the 'Jumping Frog'," suggests just this situation in the case of the gamecock that had been fed rifle balls (K17.4) in emulation, he felt, of Twain's jumping frog:

> There are few persons on the Pacific coast who have not read Mark Twain's story of the **"Jumping Frog of Calaveras."** Well, almost precisely the same sort of thing actually happened in this city a day or two since, a game chicken taking the place of the frog. A barber in this place had a game rooster which he had been "cultivating." He prided himself on the activity of his chicken. He (the rooster) was a high jumper—wonderful! Being perfectly satisfied as to the training of his chicken, he lingered about the cockpit in order to make a match. He finally got one to his mind. He posted all his friends in regard to the remarkable agility and celerity of his rooster, and got them to bet on him. For a time, the night the fight came off, his chicken was out of his sight—just while the gaffs were being strapped upon him, and he was having his feathers cut to a fighting trim. But that was all too long a time. When his pet chicken came to be put in the pit he was unable, do all the could, to rise more than two inches from the floor. There was no jump in him. The barber was astonished, and all his friends, backers of the chicken, began cursing. After a few passes that very active rooster was cleaned out, as were all who staked money on him. The barber took his rooster home wondering what could have come over him. While examining him to find out the seat of his disorder, for he concluded he must have been injured in some way, he heard something fall upon the floor. It was a Minic rifle ball. The next morning the chicken was found dead, and upon making a *post mortem* examination his whole inside was found to be packed with rifle balls.

No wonder he couldn't get off the ground! The fellow who played the trick most assuredly got the idea from having read Mark Twain's frog story.

The above article is copied from the San Francisco *Evening Bulletin* of December 11, 1867, where it is credited to the Virginia City *Territorial Enterprise,* the Nevada newspaper with which Twain had such important associations. The conjecture of the author of the article that the "fellow who played the trick got the idea from having read Mark Twain's frog story" seems possible and if true interesting indeed. But it is also possible that the story of the lead-packed gamecock (K17.4) existed independently as a folktale and the journalist, weighted down by his recognition of the parallel to Twain's frog, failed to jump to the right conclusion.

Notes

[1] The jumping frog folk tale may have entered American folklore by way of Latin America. Stith Thompson cites a Chilean collection of the tales of Pedro Urdemales, *Peter the Mischievous,* dated 1885, which contains a jumping frog story. See *Motif-Index of Folk-Literature* (Bloomington, Indiana, 1957), K17.4.

Paul Baender (essay date 1963)

SOURCE: "The 'Jumping Frog' as a Comedian's First Virtue," in *Modern Philology,* Vol. 40, No. 3, February, 1963, pp. 192-200.

[*In the following essay, Baender argues that although Twain's jumping frog story borrows conventions of the Southwestern frame story, the sketch is a creative departure from that traditional form. Baender points out that the tale includes many anecdotes that are clearly the author's own invention, and that it has national rather than regional appeal.*]

Mark Twain criticism is still violent and unsettled. Ever since the 1860's people have fought as to whether he was more than a humorist or only a humorist, civilized man or frontiersman, and more recently, conscious or unconscious artist. These issues have not been decided, and by the nature of their customary formulation they cannot be. No matter how refined the psychological, aesthetic, or ideological arguments, they have failed to produce their intended empirical settlement because they have been tied to terms which continuously require a contest with their opposites—civilization versus frontier, conscious versus unconscious—and thus the opposite terms keep just enough territory to carry on the war. The terms are gross, and their contests over so long a time must seem rather foolish to such outsiders as the sophisticated Jamesians, whose works by comparison amount to a smoothly developing organism. But Twain's career was also violent and unsettled; like his critics he contended with a lifelong maze of dichotomous identities, opinions, and purposes. And while his critics have wasted much enthusiasm and rage trying to decide the issues, they have compiled a body of studies whose general pattern roughly resembles their subject.

But with respect to particular works the critical tradition has sometimes gone astray. Such is the case with **"The Celebrated Jumping Frog of Calaveras County,"** which for years has been a basic text among those who consider Mark Twain a frontiersman. "The humor of the '**Jumping Frog**,'" wrote Archibald Henderson in 1912, ". . . is the savage and naive humor of the mining camp, not the sophisticated humor of civilization."[1] This merging of the sketch with a geographical area and a social group is typical, and even critics who defend Twain as a conscious artist do not question it. It follows from a principle well known to readers of Frederick Jackson Turner, that a man on the frontier enters into a relationship with the environment so close as to make him a symbol of its qualities, a realization of its latencies for politics and character. His works and acts contain cultural implications which may have nothing to do with his will or deliberative consciousness but which these cannot deny. Thus two recent critics, Paul Schmidt and Kenneth S. Lynn, regard the **"Jumping Frog"** as a parable illustrating cultural antagonisms between the East and the Frontier.[2] The frame narrator and Simon Wheeler engage in a contest of innuendo and insult, the narrator standing for eastern gentility and Simon Wheeler representing a western "vernacular community" (Schmidt, p. 276), like the author himself. "The basis of [Wheeler's] and Clemens's values," Schmidt says,

> is community established in common work and play. . . . Wheeler polarizes the values generated by community, as against the inept and grotesque isolation of individualism. . . . Clemens's story ultimately asserts the superiority of vernacular brotherhood over the competitive individualism which animates genteel attitudes (p. 277).

The frame narrator, on the other hand, stands for the "competitive and hostile individualism of the genteel" (p. 277). He holds the assumptions of "an eastern traveler in the West, the assumptions which make up the complicated Enlightenment case of Civilization versus Nature, England and the Continent versus America, Boston versus the West" (p. 272). Thus Simon Wheeler's tale about the defeat of Jim Smiley, whose assumptions are much the same as the narrator's, is a subtle rebuke by a cunning frontiersman only pretending to be fatuous, a rebuke so subtle as to make the narrator miss the point when he retells the story.

The chief support for such an interpretation is the southwestern frame-story tradition. During the thirty-five years before the **"Jumping Frog"** southwestern humorists commonly wrote sketches purporting to be travelers' accounts of their adventures among rustics and poor whites. One of the stereotypes they developed was the frame story. After giving necessary background information the traveler introduced the rustic, who would proceed to deliver a short and usually humorous narrative. Writers often capitalized on the juxtaposition of literate traveler and colloquial rustic, exaggerating their differences of manners and speech to suggest cultural absurdities in one or the other or both.

Some writers also contrived little contests between the traveler and the rustic in which the rustic deceived the traveler with a tall tale, thereby showing him up as a naïve gull.[3] At first sight the **"Jumping Frog"** seems to fit neatly in this tradition, and Lynn, who accepts Schmidt's interpretation for the most part, quite explicitly makes the connection.[4] A literate traveler has been asked by a "friend . . . in the East" to look up Simon Wheeler in Angel's Camp to discover the whereabouts of a certain Rev. Leonidas W. Smiley. He finds Simon Wheeler in a saloon, puts his question, and then stands by impatiently while Simon delivers a long series of anecdotes about a gambler named *Jim* Smiley. The traveler finally escapes by breaking off Simon Wheeler's tale with an interjection and suddenly walking away. Everything appears conventional so far as the summary goes. Speaking in dialect, a rustic tells a traveler a tall tale, and their differing attitudes toward it seem to indicate cultural divergences. Simon Wheeler talks with "impressive earnestness and sincerity," out of respect for Jim Smiley, while the traveler despises the old man's "monotonous narrative." The next step, one might think, is to infer a deliberate deadpan for Simon Wheeler and an effete gentility for the traveler-narrator. Thus eventually one might come out with an opposition between the East and the Frontier according to a common bias of southwestern humor and of local color sketches from the middle and far west.

But by the time Twain wrote the **"Jumping Frog"** the vogue of the southwestern frame story had declined, and his reason for using it in 1865 had more to do with his observation of literary comedians than with his southwestern heritage. In 1864, speaking of an inept tragic actor, Twain said ironically that he possessed "the first virtue of a comedian, which is to do funny things with grave decorum and without seeming to know that they are funny."[5] Years later he was to elaborate upon this criterion in his well-known manifesto, "How To Tell a Story." Stating once again that the "humorous story is told gravely" and that the teller should "conceal the fact that he even dimly suspects . . . there is anything funny," Twain would prize the manner still more: "The humorous story is strictly a work of art—high and delicate art—and only an artist can tell it."[6] Not long before this pronouncement he also described the man he heard tell the frog story at Angel's Camp early in 1865: "He was a dull person, and ignorant; he had no gift as a story-teller, and no invention . . . he was entirely serious, for he was dealing with what to him were austere facts . . . he saw no humor in his tale . . . none of the party was aware that a first-rate story had been told in a first-rate way."[7] Twain already knew in 1864 and 1865 how effective humorous gravity could be, for it was basic to Artemus Ward's expertise on the lecture platform, and it was precisely this oral effect that Twain tried to get through the southwestern frame story. Unfortunately he never fully explained his taste or said what cultural significance, if any, he associated with the deadpan manner. But we can tell from his silence in this regard what things not to look for, and one of them is deliberateness in Simon Wheeler and the narrator of the **"Jumping Frog,"** on the assumption that they possess the psychology or class consciousness of the more familiar sorts of characters in fiction.

The relevance of the southwestern frame story to Twain's interest is clear. It gave him, in the narrator, a conventional and unobtrusive means to emphasize at the outset Simon Wheeler's "impressive earnestness and sincerity," and thus to suggest the mode of delivery readers should imagine when Wheeler starts talking.[8] In 1865 Twain was in fact too eager to exploit this advantage. He had the narrator say, after mentioning Wheeler's gravity, that "the spectacle of a man drifting serenely along through such a queer yarn without ever smiling was exquisitely absurd."[9] This was to insist on the humorous criterion too explicitly, and Twain later deleted the statement, recognizing that it was more important to maintain the narrator's own seriousness and thereby to exploit another natural advantage of the frame story, the advantage of double deadpan. The only real problem in adapting the southwestern convention concerned Simon Wheeler's story of Jim Smiley. Twain could not have his narrator introduce the tale as "monotonous" and then proceed with something like the **"Blue-jay Yarn"**[10] or even **"Jim Blaine and His Grandfather's Old Ram,"** which take their hyperbolic courses at a comparative gallop. Nor on the other hand could he verge too close on actual monotony. His problem was to create an innocuous bore, so to speak, to devise a sketch that might seem the tedious talk of an old man, boring to the narrator yet amusing to us.

It will help show how Twain solved his problem to describe first the closest analogues of the **"Jumping Frog."** These were two brief sketches published in newspapers near Angel's Camp which Twain almost certainly never saw.[11] The first appeared in the Sonora *Herald,* south of Angel's Camp, in 1853. A Yankee bets on a toad against a gambler's frog, and the gambler wins. Next morning the Yankee is back, offering a larger bet. This time he wins twice in a row because for some reason the gambler's frog can't jump far. "'My frog is darn heavy this morning,' says the gambler. 'I reckoned it would be, stranger,' says the Yankee, 'for I rolled a pound of shot into him last night.'" The second sketch, longer but hardly more complicated, came out in the San Andreas *Independent,* north of Angel's Camp, in 1858. Its hero is a chronic but knuckleheaded gambler who is usually broke because he falls for con games like thimblerig and French monte. He catches a frog and bets him against an innkeeper's frog. He wins this bet but next morning, with the bet doubled, the innkeeper wins because the gambler's frog won't jump. The crowd is puzzled until a shrewd spectator called "Old Weasle-eye" picks up the frog and squeezes out a load of buckshot. The sketch ends with the roars and yells of the crowd as the gambler's coat tails disappear behind the next hill. These two sketches are what Twain would call comic stories.[12] They count upon the matter of the ironic frog race for their effect, not upon the manner of the telling. They pretend to no gravity, and the first sketch as well as the second stresses its comic point through a chorus of onlookers who roar and laugh. While the humorous story typically rambles on at some length,[13] these are quite short and would be shorter except that they must prepare for the buckshot trick. They are the barest embodiments of the reversal of fortune, a commonplace of folklore.

These sketches are important partly because they add to the evidence that most of Simon Wheeler's anecdotes about Jim Smiley were Twain's invention, from which we may infer a motive.[14] The analogues show that in the five years between them, over the thirty or so miles from Sonora through Angel's Camp to San Andreas, the frog story did not develop much and hardly became one example among others in an expanded career of the gambler. It does not seem likely, therefore, that the considerable expansion in Wheeler's yarn occurred before Twain arrived in the Sierra foothills six years after the San Andreas version. The analogues also point us to the special quality of the gambler's career in Twain's sketch. While they try for irony, Twain plays it down as far as possible. In addition to the frog episode he had Simon Wheeler mention cat fights, chicken fights, birds on a fence, Parson Walker's powers as a preacher, the wandering straddle-bug, the health of Parson Walker's wife, the asthmatic horse, the bull pup and the "yaller one-eyed cow that didn't have no tail, only just a short stump like a bannanner"—examples, like the frog, of Jim Smiley's gambling addiction. An obvious point of so many examples, all preceding the frog except the last, is to avoid ordinary narrative patterns of climax or of rise and fall. To this end Twain took the precaution of ordering Smiley's victories and defeats in a fairly hodgepodge way. His defeat in the frog episode follows a defeat which follows a victory, and we do not know the upshot of the "one-eyed cow" because the narrator leaves before Wheeler can do more than mention her.

The sequence implies Simon Wheeler's earnest strain, so tedious to the narrator. When Simon begins his irrelevant account in response to the question about Rev. Leonidas W. Smiley, it is only Jim Smiley's eccentric habit and his luck that interest him. But as he moves along, this interest matures into a respectful concern for Jim, his animals, and the circumstances of their contests. With each example the concern increases, consummating itself through the evocation of increasingly minute detail which in turn becomes the object for still further respect. When we reach the bull pup and the frog, Simon is bestowing heroism everywhere with homeric abandon. The animals are geniuses with elevating names, Andrew Jackson for the pup and Dan'l Webster for the frog, and their most poignant contests must be described not because they illustrate Smiley's habit but because they are dramatic and astonishing. These creatures even deserve simile: the pup's "underjaw'd begin to stick out like the fo'castle of a steamboat and his teeth would uncover and shine like the furnaces"; the frog whirled in the air "like a doughnut" and landed "like a cat" or "solid as a gob of mud"; and when weighted down with the buckshot, he heaves his shoulders "so—like a Frenchman." In his example of the frog Simon Wheeler recreates the dialogue between Smiley and the stranger—full of "he says" and then "Smiley says"—and at this point his account is like that of the "long, lanky man" in *Huckleberry Finn* who recreates Sherburn's killing of Boggs by going through the motions himself—aiming his cane like Sherburn aiming his pistol, shouting "Bang!" and falling backward the way Boggs did.

The sequence also imitates a sober and mindless infatuation. The end of each example is a natural pause, where
Simon might snap out of his indulgence and remember the
narrator's question about Rev. Smiley, yet each time he
moves up to a plateau of more systematic irrelevance. But
the pattern of his yarn does not devastate our interest as
the real thing would because the monologue is at the same
time a brilliant comic invention. Its structure is in fact a
condition of its brilliance as well as an image of tediousness. For though we recognize the kind of discourse and
can guess that example will follow example, we cannot
predict their nature or detail. Each example is wilder and
more exact than the previous, it turns out, and thus the
yarn amounts to a series of toppers. Meanwhile, according
to the narrator's opening statement, he is rigidly impatient
at Simon Wheeler, who has "never changed his voice from
the gentle-flowing key [and] never betrayed the slightest
suspicion of enthusiasm." We, however, are led only to
suppose his boredom. We may regard the serial structure
and Wheeler's manner as tedious under ordinary circumstances, and so far the narrator's response is understandable. But the circumstances are far from ordinary; what the
narrator claims to be dull turns out amusing, and the
discrepancy of responses is so thorough as to suggest an
opposition of tempers, not just of moods. The narrator
and Simon Wheeler represent the sober and the rigid, we
say (recalling our Bergson), while we are the volatile and
sensitive, for whom the humorous sketch is an exclusive
reward of perception. If any contest is to be associated
with the **"Jumping Frog,"** the winner is not frontier democracy or eastern gentility but the reader, not Wheeler
or the narrator but ourselves.

In this respect also the **"Jumping Frog"** reveals its artificiality with regard to the southwestern tradition. The
reader's superiority to characters had always been a common option of southwestern sketches, yet it was more
definitely a class superiority—or a superiority to classes—than is our response to the **"Jumping Frog."** Take
"The Big Bear of Arkansas" (1841), for example. Several
men from various regions are relaxing in the lounge of a
Mississippi steamboat when Jim Doggett, an Arkansas
frontiersman, suddenly enters, disarms the group with his
pleasant manner, and eases himself into a tall-tale account
of the tremendous flora and fauna of Arkansas. Some of
the men are doubters, particularly a "cynical-looking Hoo-
sier" and a "'live Sucker' from Illinois"; only a "gentlemanly foreigner . . . suspected to be an Englishman on
some hunting expedition" is credulous from the start. But
Doggett wins all of them over with his anecdote of the
"Big Bar" hunt, after which everyone sits in "grave silence," sharing a spooky uncertainty as to whether Doggett actually killed the bear or he *"'died when his time
come.'"* In this way Thorpe brings the conventional interplay of regional characters to a rather subtle conclusion.
At first, like so many other frame-story rustics, Doggett
exaggerates his matter and manner to confuse the outsiders and indulge in the regional brag their presence calls
for. Yet he loses himself in his own fantasy: his account
of the "Big Bar" is so agonistic and so successful among
the outsiders that, given a comic credulousness of his
own, he too becomes absorbed in its hyperbolic issue.

Thus regional and class lines have apparently been crossed
by the very style through which Doggett meant to stress
them. The irony is only apparent, however, for the common mood of gravity is a function of the regional differences, which are as strict at the end as at the beginning.
This *plus-ça-change* maneuver is part of Thorpe's humorous substance, and a full appreciation of his humor therefore requires us to rise above regional limitations and be
wise in their ways.

But the **"Jumping Frog"** lacks the regional concern that
leads to such a relation between reader and sketch. Twain's
adaptation of the southwestern frame story demanded at
least an appearance of this concern, and the appearance
is all he bothered to put forth, by giving the narrator and
Simon Wheeler different forms of speech and by placing
their meeting in Angel's Camp. The narrator does not
claim a cultural identity from his impatience, and we cannot claim it for him since his impatience is not a response
to an opposite claim or to a gambit like Jim Doggett's
invasion of the steamboat lounge. It is the response of a
vaguely middle-class figure to an old man's tediousness,
inspired also by the discovery that his "friend . . . from the
East" tricked him into the encounter. Simon Wheeler sees
no class or regional pretensions in the narrator and has
none of his own; he hears the name "Smiley" and the tale
follows of course, not as a regional outgrowth but as a
fabulous history even for the region. And though Twain
distinguished forms of speech, his distinction is the obvious one between dialect per se and standard speech. The
narrator is merely literate; Simon Wheeler uses the "Pike
County" speech Twain was already developing for the
comic urchins and rustics of various regions, San Francisco as well as Angel's Camp. Thus the sobriety of
Wheeler and the narrator has no foundation comparable to
Thorpe's. Posed at the beginning rather than developed in
Thorpe's manner, the narrator's boredom and Wheeler's
earnestness are syncopational failures of taste which direct us to the humor that follows. As such these attitudes
are rightly gratuitous, for their truly instrumental bearing
is toward the contest with our sense of humor, and it
might be blocked if they were allowed the implicit apology
of a sufficient cause. This bearing is all to the good.
Sobriety and deadpan are everywhere around us, and we
are more likely to attribute general and lasting relevance
to the sketch that presents them absolutely. This is one
reason why the **"Jumping Frog"** is still intelligible while
many frame stories not much older are as dense as the
cartoons in *Harper's Weekly.*

There remains the nagging conscience of Twain's famous
letter to his mother, dated January 20, 1866, two months
after the sketch was first published. After complaining
that his life is dull and that he wishes he were back
piloting on the Mississippi, he protests against the irony
that "after writing many an article a man might be excused
for thinking tolerably good, those New York people should
single out a villainous backwoods sketch to compliment
me on!—**'Jim Smiley and his Jumping Frog.'"** A few
lines later he pastes in a clipping from the San Francisco
Alta California, in which the paper's New York correspondent writes: "Mark Twain's story in the *Saturday*

Press of November 18th, called '**Jim Smiley and his Jumping Frog,**' has set all New York in a roar, and he may be said to have made his mark . . . the papers are copying it far and near. It is voted the best thing of the day."[15] The combination of high praise and Twain's disgust is of course remarkable, and it has attracted comment for many years. It suggests that he could not be consoled by the praise because he felt he had reverted to frontier type in spite of efforts to raise himself to a higher literary class. He had not merely imitated the southwestern convention but had fallen back to the real thing.

Yet his opinion is strange and questionable. He apparently wrote the sketch several months after his stay at Angel's Camp, and thus enough time passed for the deliberation which the text everywhere implies, deliberation of an extent and subtlety which seem odd in a man who is simply falling back to an unwanted heritage. Nor was this deliberation typical of Mark Twain in 1865; in no other work of that period did he take so much formal care or try so thoroughly to create what he already regarded as the highest form of humor. Moreover, his opinion of January, 1866, was not long in giving way to its opposite. By December, 1869, he could write to Livy that the "**Jumping Frog**" was the "best humorous sketch America has produced yet,"[16] and thereafter his opinion was consistently favorable. In the light of this change his use of "villainous" in January seems a clue to the instability of his first reaction. At least twice very near the day he wrote to his mother, Twain used the term "villainous" in published articles for an effect of comic elegance and pomposity,[17] an effect he often tried for in that period. Though he used the term seriously in his moment of rage, its serious use involved a reidentification too alien to be more than a fling. But he was angry enough not to mind a false haughtiness, whose very falsity gave him then as at other times room to burst in.[18]

I suggest that Twain's immediate reaction was a letdown, a genuine disappointment, while it lasted, concerning his sketch and his literary status. Beforehand he meant the work to be a step upward, and according to public as well as private criteria. He could no longer be content, as he had been in 1864, with a New York publication of the same rough stuff he wrote for Washoe and San Francisco. By late 1865, though his taste would always be fallible, he knew that genial humor would more likely succeed among the somewhat more literate audience he wanted to reach. Consequently he had his frame narrator describe Simon Wheeler at the outset as "good-natured," with "an expression of winning gentleness and simplicity upon his tranquil countenance." And in the first two versions of the sketch, before deciding that the consistency of the narrator's impatience was more important than geniality, Twain had him stop Simon's tale "good-naturedly, bidding the old gentleman good-day." The actual yarnspinner in Angel's Camp was "a dull person, and ignorant": we need only compare him with the fictional Simon Wheeler to see that Twain wanted the aura of geniality. He wanted it because it was characteristic of the amiable humorists, the good-natured eccentrics, who as Professor Tave has shown were the most widely popular kind of comic characters in

England by the mid-nineteenth century.[19] And it was just such characters as these that would soon make Bret Harte the rage of the United States, including Boston. To create such a character and to place him in such a proven form certainly did mean a step upward for Twain, whose favorite among his few previous New York publications was an extravaganza offering at its climax remedies for children's ailments, the remedy for stuttering being removal of the underjaw.[20]

But Twain was disappointed. Instead of recognizing the public success as a measure of his art and talent, he condemned the "**Jumping Frog**" by association with its earlier counterparts. The very report of his success may have touched him off. For though the news was good, he could hardly miss the allusion to Yorick or the correspondent's pun on his pseudonym: "[Twain] may be said to have made his mark." He was still Mark Twain the jester, in New York now as well as San Francisco, with whose name anyone might take liberties. And in a dark moment the nature of his sketch seemed sufficient reason for him to accuse not the public but his own work. What was the "**Jumping Frog**" but a southwestern frame story like so many other frame stories? How then could the readers of a sophisticated New York miscellany be blamed for failing to distinguish Mark Twain? This question must have been particularly insistent and galling in view of the fact that he had suppressed the zany first-person of his usual comic sketches to follow his strategy of the humorous tale. For the narrator of the "**Jumping Frog**" and the "Mark Twain" personality developed by that time had in common only the humorous solemnity; the "Mark Twain" personality already included much more than this. By insulting his own work on this occasion Twain tried out what later became his characteristic way of handling the question of his literary place: not to challenge the conventions which might slight him but to obviate their charges by calling himself a mere humorist. Later, writing for example to Howells, he applied this strategy unalloyed; in 1866, a youngish man writing to his mother, he could still eat his cake and have it too, claiming "many an article a man might be excused for thinking tolerably good" (by comparison, what were they?), at the same time he reduced his most successful work, a humorous sketch, to a past tradition. But as in later years he was not long in rebounding: in 1869 he writes Livy that the "**Jumping Frog**" is the "best humorous sketch America has produced yet."

The historical qualifications that apply to the "**Jumping Frog**" apply less strictly to Twain's humorous theory. Many years ago Constance Rourke wrote that it expressed the "tradition for the mask, and for the long procession of dull-looking, unlikely oracles [in the history of American humor]."[21] But though this statement is true, we must be careful once again not to confuse exploitation with simple derivation. Twain never defined the humorous tale as indigenous to a region, nor did he associate a cluster of regional motives with his principle that the humorous story should be told gravely. And when he developed his theory most elaborately in "How To Tell a Story," he said that the "humorous story is American"—not western or southwestern but American. His very abstraction of the principle, not to mention his silence as to its cultural significance, suggests that he had cut it free from wherever it may have been a customary mannerism and that he considered it important primarily in his professional dealings with a general American taste. This process is familiar, for Twain characteristically moved from the local to the national, from the old to the new, and he was always forced to adapt his heritage when it was relevant at all, answering the demands of the new sometimes by rejecting the past, yet also by saving it in the ways he could.

Notes

[1] *Mark Twain* (New York, 1912), p. 93.

[2] Paul Schmidt, "The Deadpan on Simon Wheeler," *Southwest Review*, XLI (Summer, 1956) 270-77; Kenneth S. Lynn, *Mark Twain and Southwestern Humor* (Boston, 1959), pp. 145-47.

[3] The bibliography on this subject is well known. Walter Blair, *Native American Humor* (San Francisco, 1960), pp. 62-101, and Norris W. Yates, *William T. Porter and "The Spirit of the Times"* (Baton Rouge, La., 1957), chap. vi, have been most useful to me.

[4] In turn, Frank Baldanza has accepted Lynn's adaptation of Schmidt (see Baldanza's *Mark Twain: An Introduction and Interpretation* [New York, 1961], pp. 32-33).

[5] [San Francisco] *Golden Era*, June 26, 1864, collected in *The Washoe Giant in San Francisco*, ed. Franklin Walker (San Francisco, 1938), p. 76.

[6] First published in *Youth's Companion* for October 3, 1895; collected, though not for the first time, in *How To Tell a Story and Other Essays* (New York, 1897). All the quotations are from this edition, p. 4.

[7] "Private History of the 'Jumping Frog' Story," first published in the *North American Review* for April, 1894; collected in *How To Tell a Story*, pp. 149-63. The quotation is from *ibid.*, pp. 151-52. Some doubt may be cast on MT's recollection of the original yarnspinner by two glaring lapses of memory: he speaks of the smartness of "Jim Smiley, in taking the stranger in with a loaded frog" and of hearing the frog story in the *fall* of 1865 (pp. 151-52). For the outcome of the frog contest as he really heard it, see *Mark Twain's Notebook*, ed. Albert Bigelow Paine (New York, 1935), p. 7. The errors may simply gauge MT's indifference to the particular facts, and the tone of his account shows that he was much more interested in the yarnspinner's character and manner than in the outcome of the frog contest (*pace* Schmidt). The outcome was not set straight until the various American Publishing Company editions—the "Autograph," "Underwood," etc.—of 1899 and later.

[8] MT may have doubted his success here. On December 14, 1869, in a letter to Livy, he writes "I must read [the **'Jumping Frog'**] in public some day, in order that people may know what there is in it." This suggests that he believed only oral delivery could have the full oral effect. Part of the letter, including the passage quoted here, is printed in *The Love Letters of Mark Twain*, ed. Dixon Wecter (New York, 1949), p. 41.

[9] Bret Harte and Mark Twain, *Sketches of the Sixties* (San Francisco, 1927), p. 195.

[10] Note that at the end of this sketch MT introduces the owl from Nova Scotia, who "couldn't see anything funny" about the acorn business. Here he saves his deadpan character for the important position of "snapper."

[11] They were collected by Oscar Lewis and published in *The Origin of the "Celebrated Jumping Frog of Calaveras County"* (San Francisco, 1931).

[12] *How To Tell a Story,* pp. 5-7.

[13] *Ibid.,* p. 3.

[14] In *Notebook,* p. 7, and in the "Private History" MT only mentions details connected with the frog story. In his account of MT's hearing the tale at Angel's Camp, Paine also discusses only them (see *Mark Twain: A Biography* [3 vols.; New York, 1912], I, 270-73).

[15] *Mark Twain's Letters,* ed. Albert Bigelow Paine (2 vols.; New York, 1917), I, 101-02.

[16] *Love Letters,* p. 41.

[17] Virginia City *Territorial Enterprise,* December 29, 1865, and February 6, 1866; in *Mark Twain: San Francisco Correspondent,* ed. Henry Nash Smith and Frederick Anderson (San Francisco, 1957), pp. 46, 93.

[18] In a letter to Orion dated October 19, 1865, MT writes: "But I *have* had a 'call' to literature, of a low order—*i.e.* humorous. It is nothing to be proud of, but it is my strongest suit." Yet note that his low estimate in October is not accompanied by the same pretension to higher status he would assume in January. Indeed he writes further: "I will drop all trifling, & sighing after vain impossibilities, & strive for a fame—unworthy & evanescent as it may be" (*My Dear Bro, A Letter from Samuel Clemens to his Brother Orion,* ed. Frederick Anderson [Berkeley, Calif., 1961], pp. 6, 8).

[19] Stuart M. Tave, *The Amiable Humorist* (Chicago, 1960), chap. xi.

[20] "Those Blasted Children," published in the New York *Sunday Mercury,* February 21, 1864; reprinted in *The Washoe Giant in San Francisco,* pp. 18-23 (see also *Mark Twain of the Enterprise,* ed. Henry Nash Smith [Berkeley, Calif., 1957], pp. 121-22).

[21] *American Humor* (New York, 1931), p. 212.

S. J. Krause (essay date 1964)

SOURCE: "The Art and Satire of Twain's 'Jumping Frog' Story," in *American Quarterly,* Vol. 16, No. 4, Winter, 1964, pp. 562-76.

[*In the following essay, Krause claims that Twain's jumping frog story combines Eastern political satire and traditional folk humor.*]

Recent analyses of Mark Twain's **"Notorious Jumping Frog of Calaveras County"** tend to stress its projection of the traditional conflict between eastern and western values—or, more precisely, between the values of a gentle, civilized class and those of the frontier.[1] Taking in its broadest potential reference, Paul Schmidt has seen the **"Jumping Frog"** as dramatizing those assumptions which, as he has it, "make up the complicated Enlightenment case of Civilization versus the West." Moreover, construing the tale as "an attack on the genteel tradition," Schmidt holds that it "ultimately asserts the superiority of vernacular brotherhood over the competitive individualism which animates genteel attitudes"; while in Wheeler's story, the tale within the tale, he sees an attack on Rousseau-esque romanticism.[2]

Schmidt's analysis seems to involve some high-powered assumptions for a fairly unsophisticated brand of fiction. Yet at least two reasons why the **"Jumping Frog"** rises above its genre are that its simplicity—like Simon Wheeler's—is ironic and its social symbolism—like Wheeler's story—implies more than it asserts. A major artistic consideration is, therefore, the matter of how the inward moving structure of the tale accommodates its outward moving symbolic reference. An aspect of the symbolism that has remained relatively untouched is the extensive satire suggested by Jim Smiley's naming his bull-pup "Andrew Jackson" and his frog "Dan'l Webster." With this in mind, I wish to consider three questions: the degree to which there is a complexity of form in the story to sustain its social implications; the degree to which there is a secondary satire in the story to justify the inclusion of those implications; and the degree to which the satire implies a judgment of the East and West. To explore these questions is to see what Twain accomplished in bringing together the cream of the humor that preceded him. For his **"Jumping Frog"** blends the political satire perfected in Down East humor with the framework and oral techniques perfected in Old Southwestern humor.[3]

Complex as the story is, the question of form—which has never been thoroughly described[4]—is rather easily handled. To begin with, Twain has more than just a tale within a tale. He has in fact at least eight levels of story interest, each of which has several sides to it, so that the design better resembles a nest of boxes than it does a frame. There is 1) the story of the narrator's spoken and unspoken attitudes toward a) the friend who wrote him from the East and lured him into a trap, toward b) Simon Wheeler whom he regards as a garrulous simpleton, toward c) Jim Smiley, the fabulous gambler, toward d) the animals that Wheeler personalizes, and toward e) the stranger who pulled a western trick on a Westerner and got away with it. Then there is 2) the story of Simon Wheeler's attitudes toward a) the narrator and through him and his friend, toward b) Easterners at large, toward c) Jim Smiley, toward d) the animals and toward e) the stranger. Wheeler, moreover, represents 3) the western community at large that is continuously entertained by Smiley's antics. Also there are the attitudes of 4) the stranger, and of 5) Sam Clemens toward the various parties in his tale. Finally, we have the more restricted attitudes of Jim Smiley himself, which are confined to his animals and such persons as he can get to bet on them; and not the least significant attitudes are

those of the animals themselves, particularly 7) the bull-pup and 8) the jumping frog.

At the level of story movement, the **"Jumping Frog"** has the same complexity as that of its multiple points of view. Twain employs an order of increasing detail and of ascending absurdity and fantasy. For example, after summary references to Smiley's willingness to bet "on anything that turned up"[5] (a horse-race, dog-fight, cat-fight or chicken-fight), Wheeler tosses in two eccentric types of wager, one on which of "two birds setting on a fence . . . would fly first" and the second on Parson Walker's being the "best exhorter." These are paired with two other situations, each of which is given in greater detail, and the first of which (number three in the sequence) is absurd and fantastic—Smiley's willingness to follow a straddle bug to Mexico, if necessary, to find out its goal. The last member of the group is crashingly absurd, figuratively fantastic and practically, insane, though, based on past performance, completely understandable as Smiley, on hearing that the Parson's sick wife seems to be recovering blurts out, "Well, I'll resk two-and-a-half she don't anyway."

In the grouping of mare, pup and frog, one proceeds from lesser to greater detail, complexity and surprise, but mainly from a lesser to a greater infusion of personality, one source of which is Smiley's hanging Jackson's name on the pup (which is connotatively apt) and Webster's on the frog (which is both connotatively *and* physically apt). Therein lies a considerable tale, for when such magisterial names are paired with the descriptions given these creatures, the reader has two of Twain's liveliest and most carefully developed burlesques. More of them in a moment. What should be noted here is the matter-of-factness of the impending satire, which deals with familiar history and can be called forth or not as the reader wishes, since, concurrently, there is so much else going on in the story.

The meshing of structure and satire in the interplay of eastern and western character traits may be seen not only in the sectional names given the animals, but, more obviously, in the various points of view, which polarize specifically eastern and western attitudes, in much the way that Webster and Jackson do. We rather guess that the stranger at the end is an Easterner, and this is borne out by Twain's subsequently having specifically labeled him a "Yankee."[6] He is therefore an Easterner who plays the game of the Westerner and is specifically induced to play it on Smiley's terms, those, as Twain described Smiley, of a "wily Californian."[7] Smiley is taken in by one of his own kind, and by a weakness—his avidity for gaming—induced by the wit which puts him into a class with the stranger. Moreover, as Twain recalled the original telling of the story (that is, original for him), he noted that the Westerners' major interest in it was in "the smartness of the stranger in taking in Smiley" and in his deep knowledge of a frog's nature for knowing that "a frog *likes* shot and is always ready to eat it."[8] The stranger whets Smiley's appetite first by his curiosity (What's in the box? What's the frog good for?), then by his smugness ("I don't see no p'ints about that frog that's any better'n any other frog"), and further by the helpless innocence of his appeal for western hospitality ("the feller . . . says, kinder sadlike, 'Well, I'm only a stranger here, and I ain't got no frog. . . .'"). At the moment when the stranger is filling the frog, Twain gives us a glimpse of Smiley, out in the swamp, where he "slogged around in the mud for a long time." Being a humor character in the Jonsonian sense, Smiley was duped by his own single-mindedness.

In essence, then, the structure of the Jim Smiley story is that of a moral satire in the classical mold: Smiley's gambling fever led him to relinquish the normal protective xenophobia that guilefully motivated Simon Wheeler in the instructive tales he told about the guile that strangers might practice on simple Westerners.

To this exposure of simplicity in Smiley, Wheeler was an excellent foil. Furthermore, the relation of Wheeler to our narrator, "Mark Twain," recapitulates the structure of moral satire given in the relation of Smiley to the stranger and, with an even subtler grade of irony and one that renders the Smiley story itself ironic. Again the mounting complexity is based on characterization. This in part may be observed from what Twain did with Ben Coon of Angel's Camp, who inspired his sphinx-like Wheeler. Coon, according to Twain, was

> a dull person, and ignorant; he had no gift as a storyteller, and no invention; in his mouth this episode was merely history . . . he was entirely serious, for he was dealing with what to him were austere facts and they interested him solely because they *were* facts; he was drawing on his memory, not his mind; he saw no humor in his tale, neither did his listeners; neither he nor they ever smiled or laughed; in my time I have not attended a more solemn conference.[9]

If the tiresome earnestness of Coon was what first made the story "amusing" for Twain, in his retelling it, his own storyteller's earnestness is all ironic and "Mark Twain's" comments upon that earnestness make him a butt of the irony. We see more than our outside narrator, Twain, does in the fact that Wheeler "backed" him into a corner and "blockaded" him there with his chair, and *then* reeled off "the monotonous narrative," Wheeler is always several steps ahead of the narrator and never so many as when the narrator thinks him oblivious to the importance of what he relates.

> He never smiled, he never frowned, he never changed his voice from the gentle-flowing key to which he tuned his initial sentence, he never betrayed the slightest suspicion of enthusiasm; but all through the interminable narrative there ran a vein of impressive earnestness and sincerity, which showed me plainly that, so far from his imagining that there was anything ridiculous or funny about his story, he regarded it as a really important matter, and admired its two heroes as men of transcendent genius in *finesse.*

Here is Ben Coon, but with a world of difference in the meaning attached to his seemingly obtuse incomprehension.

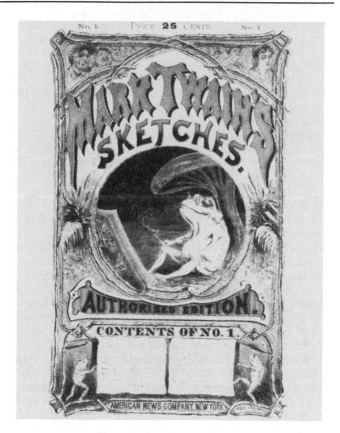

The moral satire comes clearly into focus when we see that Wheeler is to some extent the West getting its revenge for the trick of an Easterner as the same time that he plays an instructive joke on the fastidious Mark Twain, a Westerner trying to outgrow his background in exchange for eastern respectability. His pretensions can be immediately ascertained from his looking down upon Wheeler, from the difference between his language and Wheeler's,[10] and from his failure to see Wheeler's story as anything but long, tedious and useless. The fictive Twain thus stands somewhat in the relation to Wheeler that Smiley does to the stranger.[11]

Twain so completely maintains perspective on his characters that no single attitude can be strictly assigned to him as author. Yet that very condition reflects something of the final complexity of his own personal point of view on the interrelation of eastern and western attitudes. He had shown in the story that neither was morally sufficient unto itself, but that one could strengthen the other attitude, which was the view he would come to both in his life and subsequent writing. The fact that for several years after writing it he could, on and off, approve and disapprove of the **"Jumping Frog"** indicates that he was at first uncertain of where he really stood on the sectional aspects of his story. Not only had he been embarrassed that a "villainous backwoods sketch" should represent him in the East; he was also disturbed that his wife-to-be might judge him by "that Jumping Frog book," with its distinctively western contents. However, when oral readings began to bring out the richness of his story, Twain recanted and told Livy he thought it "the best humorous sketch in America." The national reference signifies a triumph over sectionalism in his own attitudes, and a recognition that his tale contains both a criticism and a union of eastern and western values. That Twain was fully aware of the complexities of structure and attitude in his story is intimated by his remark to Livy that "a man might tell that Jumping Frog story fifty times without knowing *how* to tell it." For this reason, he went on, "I must read it in public some day, in order that people may know what there is in it."[12]

The **"Jumping Frog"** assuredly does have a good deal more in it than usually meets the eye. Twain said that during one reading, "without altering a single word, it shortly [became] so absurd" that he had to laugh himself.[13] Capital instances of the absurd were the sizable caricatures he had drawn of Andrew Jackson and Daniel Webster.

Twain did not name irrelevantly. Simon Wheeler was a free-wheeling yarn-spinner. Smiley, who was "uncommon lucky," had the perennial optimism of the gambler, which was the optimism of the West itself, and which also accounts for the superstitious naming of the pup and frog. In the pairing of the two animals, we get a western name pitted against an eastern one, a frontier democrat (supposedly) and National Republican against a Whig and spokesman for eastern capital. Added to this is the free and easy irreverence of the West indulging in one of its favorite democratic sports. Thus, Smiley's naming assumes a composite sectional and structural reference. On the one hand, actual correspondences between the animals and well-known traits of Jackson and Webster open up a considerable range of secondary meanings which are related to the basic story by their development of the East-West motif. On the other hand the satire is functional. For while Twain seems to have been unacquainted with the earlier versions of his tale, he clearly had the imagination to recognize and exploit the vestigial ethos of its times, which Wheeler dates in the opening line of the internal story as "the winter of '49—or . . . spring of '50." In that context Smiley has the mood of a self-sufficient forty-niner; and as a means of dramatizing the assumptions of that mood Twain endowed Smiley with the "Territory's" compensatory indifference to the values of the "States," specifically to the exalted associations of two high-ranking names in national politics. Indeed, Jackson and Webster were household gods for Smiley's generation, and for "old" Simon Wheeler's too. What better way for the western Adam to declare his worth than by smashing a few idols?

The events of the tale bring to mind some of the leading facts associated with the names of Jackson and Webster.[14] Specifically, the bull-pup evokes the ironies of Jackson's reputation as a frontiersman, while the frog evokes the various flip-flops that characterized Webster's career. As the ironies surrounding Jackson are naturally different from those surrounding Webster, there are differences in the points Twain makes about them. However, with both men the central irony is that neither was what he seemed to have been.

Let us first consider Jackson and the bull-pup. For Wheeler to have had Jim Smiley casually compare his bull-pup with so stern a man as Jackson was to adopt the technique of insult used by the Whigs in Jackson's day when they associated him with the jackass. The technique was one of calculated insidiousness. Not only did the General not have the broad plebeian features of such animals as bulldogs and jackasses; he rather had the thinness, erect bearing and fine features of the true aristocat that he prided himself on being.[15] The nub of Twain's satire was that regardless of looks, it was how he acted and how he was thought of that counted; and Jackson, of course, had become identified with political democracy despite himself, and even with frontier ruffianism and the devious opportunism of Simon Suggs.[16]

In the pup's pugnacity, his combination of nonchalant confidence with tenacity in battle, his ferocity, his dependence on sheer will, his gambling spirit, his single-mindedness and iron nerve, as well as his having been "self-made," Twain's descriptions directly follow major aspects of Jackson's career. Like Smiley's dog, Old Hickory was the very image of toughness—to use the western idiom, he was just nothing but fight.[17] But much of his actual fighting record was somewhat at variance with the idolatrous view of it. For example, his pointless victory at New Orleans was more the result of British mistakes than of his own military genius; while, staunch friend that he was of Aaron Burr's, Jackson the duelist had gained himself a name for rashness, brutality and peremptoriness, which was corroborated by his campaigns against the Creek and Seminole Indians and his highhanded tactics in the Florida campaign of 1818, in which he had exceeded his orders. As for his famed truculence, outright brawling frontier style, as in a dog-fight, was something the aristocratic Jackson—quite unlike Lincoln, for example—would not stoop to. In fact, one of the ironies of Jackson's association with frontiersmen was that while they had made him a celebrated commander, and while there was mutual affection between him and them, in his personal dealings, Jackson disdained to fight anyone of lower station. Nor was Jackson's "indomitable perseverance"—so perfectly symbolized by the bulldog's grip—an unmixed blessing. His tenacity in battle was often in reality a euphemism for his equally well-known "inflexity of purpose," which netted him a hollow victory in his biggest political battle, that with Nicholas Biddle over the United States Bank.

Twain's description of the pup touches on several aspects of Jackson's relationship to the frontier. Take the opening statement about the pup: "And he had a little small bull-pup, that to look at him you'd think he warn't worth a cent but to set around and look ornery and lay for a chance to steal something." With such a look as that, this pup might be Simon Suggs, Sut Lovingood, Thomas Jefferson Snodgrass or even Davy Crockett. However, his look is also an analogue of the legendary flashes of temper with which Jackson was known to have frightened opponents into submission. At the same time, the broad descriptive touches make this dog a caricature of the Jackson whom Whig cartoonists had ominously portrayed as an embodiment of the western frontier—and that is just what the pup was meant to be.[18]

Twain's second sentence about the bull-pup neatly captures the images in which the East and entrenched Whiggery at large viewed the specific threat of Jacksonism: "But as soon as the money was up on him he was a different dog; his under-jaw'd begin to stick out like the fo'castle of a steamboat, and his teeth would uncover and shine like the furnaces." In addition to its suggesting the fearful union of savagery with avarice, the idea that Smiley's pup has caught the gambling fever also carries a lurking reference to the stories of Jackson's fabulous exploits in gaming.[19] Over and above other traits he shared with frontier gamblers, Jackson was exceedingly lucky, and in one well-known instance he helped his luck by adopting a special relationship with an animal he owned and bet on.[20]

Twain's most incisive reflection on Jackson involves the manner of his having become a self-made man—a legend Twain explicitly satirized several years after writing the **"Jumping Frog."**[21] Many of the eulogies on Jackson pictured him as a man who had been "born . . . of poor, but respectable parents" and had achieved greatness "by no other means than the energy of his character." *Character,* in Jackson's case, invariably meant "obduracy and vehemence of will."[22] In eulogizing the bull-pup, Wheeler gave a more meaningful account of character. He lamented that despite the inner quality of the dog ("it was a good pup"; "the stuff was in him"; he had "genius"), this Andrew Jackson had not had the chance to make a name for himself. In his last fight, seeing "how he'd been imposed on" by Smiley's mania for garish betting situations, the dog

> give Smiley a look, as much as to say his heart was broke, and it was *his* fault . . . and then he limped off a piece and laid down and died. It was a good pup, was that Andrew Jackson, and would have made a name for himself if he'd lived, for the stuff was in him and he had genius—I know it, because he hadn't no opportunities to speak of, and it don't stand to reason that a dog could make such a fight as he could under them circumstances if he hadn't no talent.

The crucial, and often repeated, question about Jackson's rise to eminence had been raised rather early in his career when Samuel Putnam Waldo inquired, "If he had not talents and virtues, would he not have remained in obscurity?"[23] Twain gave that question an ironic treatment, when, using the same terminology and reasoning, he had Wheeler emphasize opportunity as the instrument of success for persons naturally endowed with talent and goodness.

If ferocity and iron will had made a bulldog of Jackson, the political turnabouts, the desire for pacification and harmony, plus an overall jellylike softness were even more impressively the Websterian qualities suggested by Smiley's frog. While Jackson in no wise looked like the pup, Webster did resemble the frog. He had the protuberant belly,

the length of nose, the black eyes, the high cheek bones and downward sloping face;[24] and, of course, as a speaker, he had both the mouth and the wind of a frog as well as his deep intonation of voice. As politician, he could also display the frog's inscrutable placidity of mien. By such references as those to the frog's flopping down on the floor "solid as a gob of mud," to his being "solid as an anvil" (which in revision became a "church"), to his being "anchored out," and to his looking "mighty baggy" with the shot in him Twain underscored the staunch Whiggery and solidity of character that had gilded Webster's reputation, while each reference equally implies stodginess and like pejoratives. The frog's jumping was everything, though, for through it Twain illustrated the combination of lumpish conservatism with the hectic, often slippery, politicking that were in reality the alpha and omega of Webster's accomplishment.[25]

Closely allied to jumping are the matters of education and worth, which are its aims. On catching his frog, Smiley "cal'lated to educate him," and he did nothing for three months but "learn that frog to jump." This was more than a superfluous improvement on nature; for with the frog as much as with Webster, jumping was the triumph of an education that brought out what each was most gifted at. A ready learner, Webster developed the highest facility for moving from less to more convenient political positions. Still, for all his education, Webster was five times unsuccessful in capturing his party's presidential nomination, losing to some very ordinary, and, as he thought, unqualified candidates like Generals William Henry Harrison in 1840 and Winfield Scott in 1852. It was really as if the party had looked him over and found no points about Webster that made him any better than any other candidate.

But, fortunately for a man who had made a career of jumping, disappointments came as a challenge to his mobility. In fact, the politician's sense of numerous alternatives parallels the Westerner's sense of the vast opportunities afforded by the frontier. Since Webster's one unwavering motive had been to protect the New England business community, no small part of his role was to make the difficult jump or straddle, and, with froglike complacency, not let on that he had overly exerted himself. Additionally, Webster had an intense desire to enrich himself and to seem a man of moral worth.

Keeping in mind, then, the relevance to Webster of such matters as appearance, conservatism, education, jumping, complacency, cupidity and worth, one needs only to re-read the first paragraph about Smiley's frog to see how completely Twain had *done* Webster in almost every characterizing detail—as in the following:

> . . . He'd give him a little punch behind, and the next minute you'd see that frog whirling in the air like a doughnut—see him turn one summer-set, or maybe a couple, if he got a good start, and come down flat-footed and all right, like a cat. . . . Smiley said all a frog wanted was education, and he could do 'most anything—and I believe him. Why, I've seen him set

Dan'l Webster down here on this floor . . . and sing out, "Flies, Dan'l, flies!" and quicker'n you could wink he'd spring straight up and snake a fly off'n the counter there, and flop down on the floor ag'in as solid as a gob of mud, and fall to scratching the side of his head with his hind foot as indifferent as if he hadn't no idea he'd been doin' any more'n any frog might do. You never see a frog so modest and straightfor'ard as he was, for all he was so gifted. And when it come to fair and square jumping on a dead level, he could get over more ground at one straddle than any animal of his breed you ever see. . . . Smiley would ante up money on him as long as he had a red. Smiley was monstrous proud of his frog, . . . for fellers that had traveled and been everywheres all said he laid over any frog that ever *they* see.

To know the extent to which the frog's vaunted jumps—as well as his crucial failure to jump—form a compound satire on Webster's favorite maneuver, one need only refamiliarize oneself with the salient points in his record.

One gets a fairly good sample of his dexterity in a few of the jumps inspired by Jackson, whose name alone gave the arch Whig more than one punch from behind. For example, when he heard that Jackson had prepared to use force if necessary to prevent southern states from nullifying disagreeable aspects of the Tariff of 1828, Webster at first objected and then went over to Jackson's side. Just prior to this, Webster had bitterly opposed Jackson's veto of the bill for rechartering the United States Bank. But that position had not been completely firm, for when Jackson took action against the Bank, Webster was hesitant as to how he should react. He had every reason to support the Bank, but was reluctant to join Clay and Calhoun in its defense because he had been exposing them too recently as enemies of the Republic, and would have to condemn Executive interference with the Bank, after he had just approved Executive interference with the interests of South Carolina.

What was true of Webster's relationship to Jackson was true of his career as a whole. Richard C. Current probably understated his facility when he indicated that Webster "was to spend the better part of his long career in defending principles he had attacked and condemning others he had opposed during his apprentice years" (p. 23). The frequency of Webster's tergiversation placed him on both sides of every major issue of his time—free trade, protectionism, monopolies, nullification, states rights, the sale of public lands, executive authority, Unionism, the nonexpansion of slavery and the enforcement of the Fugitive Slave Law.[26] As with Smiley's frog, the very breadth of Webster's straddles gave promise of an ability that would be belied by his performance in crucial tests. When a combination of northern businessmen and southern planters envisioned the possibility of running him on a bipartisan Unionist ticket in 1852, Webster responded by refusing to jump when pressed by friends not to desert the Whigs, and then by jumping in his very refusal to do so by stating that he knew the people would not elect General Scott, and that be himself would vote for his New Hampshire neighbor Franklin Pierce.[27]

From all that one can tell, Twain's private opinions of Jackson and Webster were in some respects similar to those that emerge from the story and in others significantly different from them. He growled about Jackson's responsibility for the practice of using civil service for patronage, and he wished that the Battle of New Orleans had not been fought, so that the nation might have been spared the "harms" of Jackson's presidency.[28] On the other hand, Twain did not let his affinity for Whiggish ideas interfere with his dislike of Webster, whose love letters struck him is "diffuse, conceited, 'eloquent,' [and] bathotic" and who was identified in his mind with the moralizing and empty rhetoric he burlesqued in schoolgirl compositions.[29] With respect to the **"Jumping Frog,"** though Twain's political antipathy toward Jackson exceeded his literary antipathy toward Webster, the character and actions of the bull-pup have much more to recommend them than do the comparable aspects of the frog. Clearly, one reason why the story favors Jackson over Webster, despite the satire on *both* men, is the predominance of Simon Wheeler's point of view over others in the story. What happens, therefore, is that Wheeler's point of view permits Twain to eat his cake and have it: to vent his prejudices in the subsidiary satire and to maintain an artistic objectivity in the primary context of his story.

Twain's use of sectional values likewise reflects a coalescence of external comment (satire) with internal necessity (art). If he seems to favor the West over the East, sectional values are obviously mixed in the un-eastern credulity of the gentleman narrator and in the wryly un-western moral (beware of a stranger)[30] of the frog anecdote. Ultimately, the ideal suggested by Twain's modification of eastern and western attitudes, seems to require a blending of the Whiggish paragon of the self-made man with the realization of it achieved by an Andrew Jackson in the unfettered conditions of the frontier.

Notes

[1] See particularly Paul Schmidt, "The Deadpan on Simon Wheeler," *Southwest Review,* XLI (Summer 1956), 270-77; and Kenneth S. Lynn, *Mark Twain and Southwestern Humor* (Boston, 1960), pp. 145-47.

As part of the heritage from Old Southwestern humor, the juxtaposition of class (and/or sectional) values informs much of Twain's early writing. In his earliest printed sketch, "The Dandy Frightening the Squatter," which found its way into the *Carpet Bag* of Boston (May 1, 1852), we have a western item intended to amuse an eastern audience and in the Thomas Jefferson Snodgrass letters, written for the Keokuk *Post* in 1856, we have a low, rustic character who was intended to amuse a higher class, literate audience.

Examples of the traditional juxtaposition of classes appear in Augustus Baldwin Longstreet's *Georgia Scenes* (1835), Johnson J. Hooper's *Adventures of Simon Suggs* (1845), Joseph G. Baldwin's *The Flush Times of Alabama and Mississippi* (1853) and George Washington Harris' *Sut Lovingood* (1867). Examples of the juxtaposition of both classes and sections appear in such items as the

Davy Crockett literature (*e.g., An Account of Col. Crockett's Tour to the North and Down East,* 1835) and the second series of William Tappan Thompson's Major Joseph Jones series, *Major Jones's Sketches on Travel* (1848). Twain's Snodgrass letters closely resemble the last of these.

[2] *Southwest Review,* XLI, 272, 275, 277, 273.

[3] The best account of Twain's indebtedness to these schools of humor may be found, of course, in Walter Blair's *Native American Humor* (New York, 1937), pp. 150-58, *passim.* Also helpful is Bernard DeVoto's *Mark Twain's America* (Boston, 1932), chap. x. *Horse Sense In American Humor* (Chicago, 1942), Blair has neatly summarized the satire on Jackson and his "Kitchen Cabinet" drawn in the Jack Downing Letters of Bubba Smith and of Charles Augustus Davis (chap. iii).

[4] Paul Baender has analyzed the mounting detail and importance that Wheeler throws into his recitation of Smiley's exploits, but, as he is mainly concerned with the source of Twain's technique, Baender does nothing with the varied points of view and political satire ("The 'Jumping Frog' As a Comedian's First Virtue," *Modern Philology,* 40:3 [February 1963], 192-200). Gladys C. Bellamy has observed the "careful climactic arrangement" of the animals in *Mark Twain as a Literary Artist* (Norman, Okla., 1950), p. 148 Roger Penn Cuff has discussed the artistic and technical superiority of "Twain's Use of California Folklore in His Jumping Frog Story," *Journal of American Folklore,* LXV (April 1952), 155-59. The most comprehensive discussion of the story's structure has been given by Edgar M. Branch, *The Literary Apprenticeship of Mark Twain* (Urbana, Ill., 1950), pp. 120-29.

[5] All references to the "Jumping Frog" story are to the revised version of 1875 called "The Notorious Jumping Frog of Calaveras County" reprinted by Twain in an essay on his translating it back into English from a French translation. "The Jumping Frog," *Sketches New and Old* (Author's National Ed., New York, 1899), XIX, 25, 11 (All subsequent references to Twain's works are to the volumes of the Author's National Edition—hereafter designated as ANE.)

[6] That is, when he wrote an account of the "Private History of the 'Jumping Frog' Story," *How to Tell A Story and Other Essays,* ANE, XXII, 126.

[7] *Ibid.*

[8] *Ibid.,* p. 122.

[9] *Ibid.,* p. 121.

[10] Mark Twain's vocabulary is all the evidence Wheeler needs to know that he should be reformed. We can see this for ourselves in Twain's opening paragraph which contains such words as "compliance," "request," "garrulous," "personage," "conjectured" and "infamous," and such phrases as "I hereunto append the result," "lurking suspicion" and "exasperating reminiscence."

[11] It is possibly from noticing his unresponsiveness that Wheeler tries to enforce the lesson he has for would-be Easterners by calling Mark Twain "stranger" immediately after he finishes the frog story. But Mark misses even that innuendo, because he has been too busy *making* himself a stranger, patronizing "good natured, garrulous old Simon Wheeler," and Jim Smiley, "the enterprising vagabond."

The ironical part of Mark Twain's western orientation and his eastern aspirations is heightened by Twain's actual, personal attitude toward the acceptance of his Frog story by "those New York people." He was upset, he told his mother and sister, that "they should single out a villainous back-woods sketch" to compliment him on—a squib he apparently would not have written were it not that he wanted to please Artemus Ward. *Mark Twain's Letters,* ed. Albert B. Paine (New York, 1917), I, 101.

[12] *The Love Letters of Mark Twain,* ed. Dixon Wecter (New York, 1949), p. 41.

[13] *Ibid.*

[14] That Twain had an ulterior motive for giving the pup and frog their names we can gather from their being the only creatures to be named at all, and by his using the same oral formula in introducing each of them, which is to bypass the names and then bestow them in a familiar manner: "And Andrew Jackson—which was the names of the pup"; "I've seen him set Dan'l Webster down here on this floor—Dan'l Webster was the name of the frog."

Since there is no *source*—either comic or serious—which Twain may have draws upon for his satires on Jackson and Webster, I can say nothing definite about his prior intentions. All that I wish to suggest is the presence of secondary meanings that are based on common knowledge of the two men who were much involved (Jackson directly and insistently) in the sectional and class conflicts of traditional American humor.

[15] In fact, the master of Hermitage was a good deal like Twain's Colonel Grangerford in physique and temper (See *Adventures of Huckleberry Finn,* ANE, XIII, 146 ff.)—and Twain's portrait of the Colonel was fashioned somewhat after his father, who was alleged to have resembled Jackson (Dixon Wecter, *Sam Clemens of Hannibal* [Boston, 1952], p. 15).

[16] For the discussion of Jackson that follows I have culled my information from the following sources: *Monument to the Memory of General Andrew Jackson: Containing Twenty-five Eulogies and Sermons Delivered on the Occasion of his Death,* comp. B[enjamin] Dusenbery (Philadelphia, 1846); James Parton, *Life of Andrew Jackson* (2 vols.; New York, 1860); Marquis James, *The Life of Andrew Jackson* (2 vols.; Indianapolis & New York, 1938); Arthur M. Schlesinger Jr., *The Age of Jackson* (Boston, 1946); John William Ward, *Andrew Jackson: Symbol of an Age* (New York, 1955); and Richard Hofstadter, *The American Political Tradition* (New York, 1960), chap. iii. Since the facts I cite are rather commonly known, or are at least easily found in these books I make specific page references only where documentation seems to be clearly called for and identify individual works by the author's last name.

[17] Although he did not *look* like a bulldog, Jackson had fought like one. From boyhood on, as James points out, he "would fight at the drop of a hat." He had a strange habit of "slobbering" when fighting, and a schoolmate reported that as Jackson was too light to wrestle, he would easily "throw him three times out of four," though "he would never *stay throwed.*" (James, p. 17). With this one might compare the mock-heroic account of Smiley's pup: "A dog might tackle him and bully rag him, and bite him, and throw him over his shoulder two or three times, and Andrew Jackson

would never let on but what he was satisfied, and hadn't expected nothing else. . . ." The famed bulldog-like determination showed up in Jackson's later business and political dealings. Dr. Felix Robertson, son of James Robertson, the founder of Nashville, had said he was "a cool shrewd man of business . . . rarely wrong; but whether wrong or right hard to be shaken" (Parton, I. 249).

[18] Of course, the eastern impression of the frontier was no more like the real thing than Jackson was himself. However, while Jacksonism came to symbolize the unpredictable ruffian element on the frontier, Jackson's presidential campaign had naturally stressed the virtues of rusticity: he was the American Cincinnatus who preferred to remain on the farm rather than involve himself in politics. On his arrival in Washington, his headquarters at Gadsby's Hotel was called "The Wigwam." And, as Ward remarked, "his opponents expected to see a savage armed with a tomahawk and with a scalping knife in his teeth . . ."; whereas Jackson had just ordered French handpainted wallpaper for the hallway of the Hermitage and $1,500 worth of cut glass for her personal use (p. 43).

[19] Jackson once rolled the dice with his landlord for the rent, and on another occasion, being down on his luck, he entered a dice game in which he was offered 200 pounds against his horse—and won. During his young manhood, he was, according to Parton, "the most roaring, rollicking, game-cocking, horse-racing, card-playing, mischievous fellow that ever lived in Salisbury [South Carolina]" (I, 104).

[20] This was the horse, Truxton, whom Jackson worked to the limit of his endurance, implanting in him something of his own will to win. In his famous race with Captain Joseph Erwin's stallion, Plowboy, Truxton had the combined handicaps of Smiley's mare and pup; he ran as the underdog and with an injury. Disregarding the advice of friends who told him to pay the forfeit, Jackson was reported to have spoken to his horse, stroked his nose, and to have looked into his eyes as he would have into a man's; whereupon the horse responded by winning the first heat. Though Truxton limped on his bruised hind leg, though his front leg had gone lame and the plate had been sprung on one of his remaining good legs and lay across his foot, and thought it was raining hard, Jackson nonetheless raced him in the second heat (another two-mile race); and the horse won (James, I, III ff.).

[21] In May 1870, he had written a satire on the biographies of "Self-Made Men" for the Buffalo *Express*. In tracing the career of "Robert Kidd, Pirate," after noting that "the biography of self-made men is peculiarly edifying to the American youth to whom the adventitious aids of good birth, good breeding and hereditary wealth are generally denied," Twain gave the boy a father named "Andrew Jackson Kidd." *The Forgotten Writings of Mark Twain*, ed. Henry Duskis (New York, 1963), pp. 243 ff.

[22] Dusenbery, p. 199. Joseph G. Baldwin, "Representative Men," *Southern Literary Messenger*, XIX (September 1853), 523.

[23] *Memoirs of Andrew Jackson, Major-General of the United States, And Commander in Chief of the Division of the South* (Hartford, 1819), p. 35.

[24] J. A. J. Wilcox's often reproduced engraving of Webster "at Marshfield in his seventieth year"—used by Claude Moore Fuess as the frontispiece for the second volume of his biography and also

used in Vol. VI of the National Edition of Webster's *Writings* (both cited below)—brings out the froglike look of his face particularly well.

[25] For biographical data on Webster, I have consulted the following works: Peter Harvey, *Reminiscences and Anecdotes of Daniel Webster* (Boston, 1877); Claude Moore Fuess, *Daniel Webster* (2 vols.; Boston, 1930); and Richard N. Current, *Daniel Webster and The Rise of National Conservatism* (Boston, 1955). Since, as with Jackson, I deal for the most part with fairly well-known facts about Webster, I make only discretionary references to these sources and identify them by the author's last name. I have also consulted Webster's Congressional Speeches (*The Writings and Speeches of Daniel Webster* [Boston, 1903], V-X), but have had no occasion to cite any of them in particular.

[26] In the Dartmouth College Case, he had argued that corporation charters were inviolable contracts; in the Gibbons *v.* Ogden case he denied that they were. A free trader at first (for which he had invoked the principle of states' rights), he advocated "selective protectionism" after the War of 1812, while juggling the anti-protectionist demands of the India traders, and finally voted against the tariff when his proposed compromise failed. He began to oppose states' rights as he came more and more to be the spokesman of corporations engaged in interstate commerce, but that did not prevent him from deploring the spread of industry at the cost of agrarian values, which he professed to cherish. In 1819, prior to the Missouri Compromise, he warned that "a barrier" should be erected to prevent "the further [westward] progress of slavery." In 1850 he disapproved of the Wilmot Proviso which would have forbidden slavery in the new western territories and deplored the failure of Northerners to return escaped slaves to their masters.

[27] Webster declined to jump in a number of other important situations, when he was expected to. For example, once when Tyler refused to accept Clay's bill for the creation of a "fiscal corporation" comparable to a national bank, Clay retaliated by calling on all of his cabinet members to show their allegiance to the Whig cause and resign. All did so, except Tyler's Secretary of State, Webster, whose first experience in an administrative post had whetted his appetite for better things. Again, in 1844, when the Whigs were backing Clay against Tyler, it was hoped that Webster would at last jump off Tyler's cabinet as a sign of his supporting Clay, but he refused to be nudged.

[28] *Mark Twain-Howells Letters*, eds. Henry Nash Smith and William M. Gibson (Cambridge, 1960), II, 865. *Life On the Mississippi*, ANE, IX, 354. Twain's offhand remarks sound very much like those of a man who was born into his anti-Jackson Whiggery, and not without reason. For by Twain's own account, his father, a dyed-in-the-wool Whig, had had his fortunes damaged by "the great financial crash of '34," which John Clemens had laid to Jackson's attack on the Bank, whose southwestern branches, as Webster had predicted, were hardest hit by the subsequent drying up of credit. *Mark Twain's Autobiography*, ed. Albert B. Paine (New York, 1924), I, 15. Dixon Wecter, *Sam Clemens of Hannibal* (Boston, 1952), pp. 36 ff.

[29] *Mark Twain's Letters*, I, 384. *The Adventures of Tom Sawyer*, ANE, XII, 209.

[30] As part of a "Morals Lecture" he gave on his world tour of 1895-96, he used the "Jumping Frog" and "Mexican Plug" anec-

dotes to teach a person never to trust a stranger. Fred W. Lorch, "Mark Twain's 'Morals' Lecture During the American Phase of His World Tour in 1895-96," *American Literature,* XXVI (March 1954), 59.

Paul Smith (essay date 1964)

SOURCE: "The Infernal Reminiscence: Mythic Patterns in Mark Twain's 'The Celebrated Jumping Frog of Calaveras County'," in *Satire Newsletter,* Vol. 1, No. 2, Spring, 1964, pp. 41-4.

[*In the following essay, Smith offers a fantastic reading of Twain's jumping frog sketch in the poker-faced manner of Simon Wheeler, leading other critics to observe that Smith's article is in part a humorous jibe at the state of literary scholarship.*]

Much critical effort has been spent on fixing the original date of Mark Twain's darker view of humanity; and as the years have progressed, inevitably, the *terminus ad quem* of his pessimism has regressed, ineluctably: first it was placed in the early 1900's, later in the 1880's with *Adventures of Huckleberry Finn,* still later (or rather earlier) with *The Gilded Age* and the 1870's when the age was, indeed, gilded. However valid some of this critical work has been, to this writer's mind, it has overlooked the true turning point in Mark Twain's conception of man, one that rests in the hitherto misread and misunderstood tale, **"The Celebrated Jumping Frog of Calaveras County,"** first published in November of 1865.

In this dark and nearly tragic story, most frequently dismissed as a folk-tale with a dash of Western humor, Mark Twain seems to have first become aware of the archetypal and mythic, the deeply autochthonic qualities of his fictional material. In this tale Mark Twain first grasped the great theme of the tragic decline of American culture from its originally noble ideals, associated that theme with the great archetypes and myths of our culture, and reinvested it with a contemporary meaning, a social, political, religious, and ethnic habitation and name.

To read **"The Jumping Frog"** as a simple humorous tale is to ignore utterly the very subtle yet resonant clues which Mark Twain has scattered through his work to guide the perceptive reader to his theme—to say nothing of the very obvious date of this work, November 18, 1865, just seven short months after Appomattox. At the very outset of the story the narrator notes that he has "a lurking suspicion that *Leonidas W.* [author's italics] Smiley is a myth. . . ." And lest our suspicion be not aroused, the narrator tells us of his ineluctable impression, which simply will not down, that what we are about to experience is some "infernal reminiscence," some recorded memory, that is, of an experience in the underworld of punishment and damnation, which calls to mind that later infernal reminiscence of J. Alfred Prufrock (a character not altogether unlike what the Rev. Smiley must have been like) to which T. S. Eliot gave the epigraph:

S'io credesse che mia risposta fosse
A persona che mai tornasse al mondo . . . etc.

Finally, it is trenchantly consonant with Twain's penchant for the literary hoax that he should cloak a meaning of terrifying import in this seemingly guileless story of a garrulous raconteur.

The major events of the plot are familiar and need no summary. Briefly the narrator from the East, ostensibly at the request of a friend, is seeking the Reverend Leonidas W. Smiley by calling upon one Simon Wheeler at the tavern in Angel's Camp. The narrator is obliged to listen to a story obsessively narrated by the unsmiling Simon Wheeler which concerns one *Jim* [italics mine] Smiley. This "tale within a tale" begins with an exposition of the latter Smiley's habit of gambling on any thing or event, describes the titular symbol, the frog Dan[ie]l Webster, and concludes with the central incident in which a "stranger" challenges Smiley to a jumping contest, i.e., with frogs, fills Dan[ie]l Webster with quail-shot and wins the contest. In an abrupt return to the frame story, Wheeler is called away, then returns and offers to tell another story and is rebuked.

It is not long, however, before the perceptive reader becomes aware of elements in this tale which are evocative of deeper and deeper levels of meaning and archetypal associations, suggesting that beneath this simple folk-tale, as in most folk literature, there is a theme of tragic proportions. Indeed, even *before* we begin to read, we note the date (1865) which calls to mind now as it did then the issue of sectionalism, that traumatic split in the national consciousness. Later we will see that the issue of the North pitted against the South, often brother against brother, was sublimated in Mark Twain's subconscious; he could not, although strongly Unionist, put down his Secessionist heritage. The historical North-South struggle becomes in this tale a symbolic conflict between the East and the West (which, in fact, was a fact), reified in the struggle between the narrator in his quest for truth and Simon Wheeler in his attempts to conceal the truth from that narrator—the truth of the fate of Leonidas Smiley. One need not labor the point that beneath the contemporary social conflict lie deeper associations with a cultural and mythological conflict: the East, traditional cradle of civilization and fountainhead of Christianity, is here in conflict with the West, traditional direction and place of discovery, the source of mystery, the locus of giants and wizards, the very mystery of the Source, to mention but a few.

Read on this level, of course, we have re-enacted here the old legend of the innocent hero (the unidentified narrator who has yet to win his name and personal identity) on a quest which takes him from the known to the unknown, beyond the pale of civilization (the East) to the enchanted wilderness (the West). Using his wits he cleverly conceals his true mission by saying that he is looking for Leonidas Smiley as a favor to a friend. His quest takes him to the "old, dilapidated" (n.b., perilous) tavern of Angel's Camp (n.b., chapel), i.e., the Perilous Chapel (cf., Weston, *From Ritual to Romance*). Here he undergoes the spiritual trials conventional in the *pathos* of the quest-myth and necessary for the revivification of the Fisher-King figure, impotent, enthralled and lost. That figure is represented by the Reverend Leonidas W. Smiley. A "minister of the gospel," he is a revered Fisher of Men, and like Leonidas, the Spartan hero at Thermopylae, a King of men. His riant surname suggests that in him the hopes of the land are invested and in his rejuvenation rests the chance to turn the waste land into the smiling land it once was.

The climax of the quest comes at the Chapel Perilous when the narrator seeks information from that strangely suggestive figure, Simon Wheeler. Like the Ancient Mariner archetype, Simon Wheeler is compelled to narrate his strange story; but he is a more inimical figure than Coleridge's character. Like the folkloristic *eiron* character, Simple Simon, he feigns simplicity in his unsmiling narration of the tale; yet he is a "wheeler," a "turner," a "changer"; and we have in him the traditional enchanter who works evil through magic spells. It will be remembered that the Tenth Tarot (The *Wheel* of Fortune) pictures Anubis, the escort of the dead, and Typhon, the spirit of evil; who, other than Simon Wheeler, could more appropriately narrate this "infernal reminiscence"?

The tale that Wheeler tells, although apparently irrelevant to our quest theme, in fact indicates its denouement. For all its enigmatic elements, the story of *Jim* Smiley and his jumping frog Dan[ie]l Webster holds the answer to the riddle of *Leonidas* Smiley's disappearance and thus the end of the narrator's quest. The lost Fisher-King was overwhelmed by the all-powerful enchanter in the Waste Land of the West and, as in other folk-tales of fabulous metamorphoses, was changed into a frog. The evidence lies in the artfully chosen names of the two figures; for just as there was a physical transformation of the minister into a frog, so there is a similar anagramic transformation of the letters of their names:

"Daniel" is an anagram for "Leonidas" (veiled slightly by the incongruity of the O and the S) and the W (middle initial) of the minister's name undergoes an expansion into Webster. The surname is "lost" or, more tragically, usurped by the obsessive gambler, Jim.

Here Twain touched upon a responsive chord in American literature, for we have here a declension from the religious (Rev. Smiley) to the political (Daniel Webster) which reflects that great cultural declension in the American Experience from the 17th century to the 18th, a declension from the grail-like vision of the Puritans' "Citie Upon the Hill" to the comparatively bestial concerns of man as a political (Daniel Webster) animal (the frog). Nor can we ignore the irony of this tragic transformation. For the reverend man of God who once, no doubt, preached the doctrine of transformation that was witnessed in the As-

cension of Christ at Calvary, there is nothing left now but the cruel parody in *his* transformation and *de*-scension into the living hell of bestiality at *Calaveras,* with its diabolically mocking "ahh" sounds. That the questing narrator is aware of this irony is evident when, no longer able to bear the agony of the Reverend Smiley's degradation, he begs of Simon Wheeler to release his victim by affording him, at the very least, the dignity of a symbolic crucifixion (cf. the Hanged Man) and cries out, "Oh, hang Smiley. . . ." And lest we too easily grasp the burden of this tale, Mark Twain—humorist to the end—adds ". . . and his afflicted cow!"

Yet nevertheless however much a humorist Mark Twain was, he was aware of this tale's tragic significance and would have us share it with him. We need only note that he translated this tale into French and then retranslated it into English. Here then is a clear directive to the perceptive reader of this translation and retranslation of a physical "translation." Mark Twain could give us no more explicit instruction to suggest that we too translate this translation back into its original and mythic language.

J. Golden Taylor (essay date 1965)

SOURCE: Introduction to "The Celebrated Jumping Frog of Calaveras County," in *The American West,* No. 4, Fall, 1965, pp. 73-6.

[*In the following essay, Taylor contends that the significance of Twain's jumping frog story lies in the manner in which Twain elevates a humorous regional tale into a fable that provides insight into universal traits of human nature.*]

"The Celebrated Jumping Frog of Calaveras County" is one of the most widely acclaimed pieces of Western Americana, and it has now delighted millions of readers all over the world for exactly a century. Such fame is somewhat of a phenomenon considering that Mark Twain at first apparently had in mind no such life span for this humorous "squib," as he called it, which was written to please Artemus Ward. But the Jumping Frog is something more than a burst of superficial funniness. It has, what Mark Twain knew the best humorous writing so often has, an ironically scintillating surface story flowing with a deep undercurrent of some serious human concern. Twain's understanding of humor is borne out in practice in his masterpiece, *Huckleberry Finn,* as it is in his 1906 autobiographical dictation wherein he said: "Humor must not professedly teach, and it must not professedly preach, but it must do both if it would live forever. By forever, I mean thirty years."

The literary significance of the Jumping Frog lies in the authenticity and artistry with which a humorous incident in an early western mining camp is made to yield fable-like insights into certain universal traits in human nature, and it may still be what James Russell Lowell pronounced it when it first appeared, "the finest piece of humorous writing yet produced in America." Of considerable historic significance is the fact that through its publication Samuel Clemens found an audience—and himself—and thus became Mark Twain.

The amusing tale of a certain Coleman and his fiasco with his frog and a stranger at Angel's Camp, Calaveras County, California, on a spring day in 1849 had worked its way into the folklore of the region and had actually been published in several versions in newspapers between 1853 and 1858. But Mark Twain had apparently never heard the story until he went to stay with Jim Gillis at his cabin on Jackass Hill in the Mother Lode country. Gillis, with all his love of solitude, was an interesting companion, a keen observer of the human spectacle, and a fine storyteller. He told Mark Twain innumerable tales and, as a respite from weather and work, took him to Angel's Camp for refreshment and entertainment—and to hear Ben Coon, a former river pilot who at that time frequented the barrooms and regaled whoever would listen with tall tales. Twain recorded in his *Notebook* about February 1, 1865, the rudiments of Coon's story of the Jumping Frog: "Coleman with his jumping frog—bet a stranger $50.—Stranger had no frog and C. got him one.—In the meantime stranger filled C's frog full of shot and he couldn't jump. The stranger's frog won."

Returning to San Francisco on February 25, 1865, from his three-month interlude in the mountains, Twain resumed his writing for newspapers, physically refreshed and with an interesting stock of new literary materials. He recalled some forty years later:

> When Artemus Ward passed through California on a lecturing tour in 1865 or '66, I told him the "Jumping Frog" story in San Francisco and he asked me to write it out and send it to his publisher, Carleton, in New York, to be used in padding out a small book which Artemus had prepared for the press and which needed some more stuffing to make it big enough for the price which was to be charged for it.

In a letter at the time, Twain wrote to his mother that "it reached New York too late to appear in his book"; yet in his later years he remembered:

> It reached Carleton in time, but he didn't think much of it and was not willing to go to the typesetting expense of adding it to the book. He did not put it in the wastebasket, but made Henry Clapp a present of it, and Clapp used it to help out the funeral of his dying literary journal, *The Saturday Press.*

Elsewhere Twain noted in a similar vein that the Jumping Frog story "killed" it. In ink over the original *Notebook* entry of the plot, he wrote later: "Wrote this story for Artemus—his idiot publisher gave it to Clapp's *Saturday Press.*"

The Jumping Frog story is indeed the result of a favorable concatenation of incidents. Mark Twain would never have sought refuge on Jackass Hill and heard the tale in Angel's Camp if he had not gotten into trouble with the San Francisco Police and found it expedient to seek a safe retreat. In a series of newspaper articles for the *Territorial Enterprise,* Virginia City, Nevada, he had exposed and denounced in most outspoken language important San Francisco officials, especially the police department, for their corruption. Added impetus for Twain's leaving San Francisco arose from the fact that he was bailsman for his pugnacious friend, Steve Gillis, who after battering a burly bartender—a personal friend of the chief of police—had thought it best to leave Twain to assume the consequences and had secretly removed himself from the scene.

The publication of **"Jim Smiley and his Jumping Frog"** by the *Saturday Press* in New York City on November 18, 1865, must be accounted one of the happy accidents in American literary history. Up to this time Samuel Clemens had achieved only a local, western reputation for the audacity, descriptive power, and humor of his sketches in the various papers in San Francisco and what was essentially its eastern suburb, Virginia City, Nevada. At thirty years of age he had worked his way through several apprenticeships including printer, river pilot, frontier journalist, and prospector. Though he had been a "scribbler" of local items and sketches since he was sixteen for papers in Hannibal, Keokuk, and New Orleans, and though he could write in 1866 ". . . I am generally placed at the head of my breed of scribblers in this part of the country," there was no indication in anything he had written before the Jumping Frog that he was destined to be come a major writer or that "Mark Twain" was to become the most famous pen name in American literature.

The surprise and delight with which the Jumping Frog was received in the East is shown in his clipping from the San Francisco *Alta* submitted by its New York correspondent:

> Mark Twain's story in the *Saturday Press* of November 18th, called **"Jim Smiley and his Jumping Frog,"** has set all New York in a roar, and he may be said to have made his mark. I have been asked fifty times about it and its author, and the papers are copying it far and near. It is voted the best thing of the day. Cannot the *Californian* afford to keep Mark all to itself? It should not let him scintillate so widely without first being filtered through the California press.

One month later, December 16, 1865, the Frog was published in the *Californian,* under the editorship of Bret Harte. Of its first appearance Albert Bigelow Paine wrote:

> It brought the name of Mark Twain across the mountains, bore it up and down the Atlantic coast, and out over the prairies to the Middle West. . . . Now everyone who took a newspaper was treated to the tale of the wonderful Calaveras frog and received a mental impress of the author's signature. The name Mark Twain became hardly an institution, as yet, but it made a strong bid for national acceptance.

Within a year and a half Mark Twain's popularity had grown to such proportions that Charles Henry Webb, Mark Twain's enthusiastic western friend and founder of the *Californian,* arranged to bring out *The Celebrated Jumping Frog of Calaveras County, and Other Sketches* (May 1, 1867). This book, as Paine says, was "printed by John A. Gray & Green, the old firm for which the boy Sam Clemens had set type thirteen years before. The title page bore Webb's name as publisher, with the American News Company as selling agents." Webb, acting also as editor of the volume under the pseudonym of "John Paul," wrote in an introductory note: "Mark Twain is too well known to the public to require a formal introduction at my hands. By his story of the *Frog* he scaled the heights of popularity at a single jump and won for himself the *sobriquet* of The Wild Humorist of the Pacific Slope."

Although in writing his "Private History of the 'Jumping Frog' Story" in 1894 Mark Twain could look back almost thirty years and acknowledge that "the 'Jumping Frog' was the first piece of writing of mine that spread itself through the newspapers and brought me into public notice," there is evidence that from the first he had definite misgivings about the quality of the story and the kind of reputation it had given him. As soon as he received word that the story had been published, he wrote to his mother and sister in St. Louis: "To think that, after writing many an article a man might be excused for thinking tolerably good, those New York people should single out a villainous backwoods sketch to compliment me on!"

When the Jumping Frog appeared in book form, Twain revealed in a letter to his mother that he still had no very high opinion of it: "As for the Frog book, I don't believe it will ever pay anything worth a cent. I published it simply to advertise myself, and not with the hope of making anything out of it." He wrote also to Bret Harte about it at this time with more ambiguity than enthusiasm: "The book is out and it is handsome. It is full of damnable errors of grammar and deadly inconsistencies of spelling in the Frog sketch, because I was away and did not read the proofs; but be a friend and say nothing about these things. When my hurry is over, I will send you a copy to pisen the children with."

It is pretty hard for an author, no matter how high his literary attainments, to remain disdainful of an early work (whatever its faults, real or imaginary) which was the foundation on which he built his fame. Mark Twain, who was notoriously incapable of recognizing his best work, went through such a change toward the Jumping Frog. When in 1888 he chanced to meet George W. Carleton—who had *twice* refused to publish the Jumping Frog—he had had some time to upgrade the story while "in fancy" all these years he had devised "increasingly malignant ways" of taking Carleton's life. In this autobiographical passage of the 1906 dictation which DeVoto selected for inclusion in *Mark Twain in Eruption,* Twain gives convincing proof that he has finally accepted the Jumping Frog as a legitimate member of the family. After telling how he was superciliously dismissed by Carleton who had refused to publish the Jumping Frog book, he continues:

> Twenty-one years elapsed before I saw Carleton again.
> I was then sojourning with my family at the

Schweizerhof, in Lucerne. He called on me, shook hands cordially, and said at once without any preliminaries, "I am substantially an obscure person, but I have a couple of such colossal distinctions to my credit that I am entitled to immortality—to wit: I refused a book of yours and for this I stand without competitor as the prize ass of the nineteenth century."

Two amusing adventures Twain had with the Jumping Frog resulted from its being translated into French and Greek. Someone showed him an article dealing with American humorists in the *Revue des Deux Mondes* of July 15, 1872, which said "all manner of kind and complimentary things" about him. But then the author, Theodore Bentzon (who wrote under the pen name of Madame Blanc), went on to translate the Jumping Frog into French as **"La Grenouille Sauteuse du Comté de Calaveras."** Mark Twain was greatly pleased by all this but could not forego the amusement of pretending the translation had ruined his story for its French readers. So he wrote an article, **"The Jumping Frog"** (included in his *Sketches New and Old,* 1875), feigning the grave injury done him by this translation. To make his point he presented the Jumping Frog as it was originally published (but here entitled **"The Notorious Jumping Frog of Calaveras County"**), then the French translation, and finally the version, as he said, "clawed back into a civilized language once more by patient, unremunerated toil." The result is an astonishing tour de force in the literal translation of the French idiom.

Likely the most perplexing adventure Mark Twain had with the Jumping Frog was in being told by Professor Henry Van Dyke, of Princeton, in 1894, that **"The Celebrated Jumping Frog of Calaveras County"** was based on an early Greek tale at least two thousand years old. He presented as his authority a book by Professor Henry Sidgwick, *Greek Prose Composition,* which did actually contain a story entitled "The Athenian and his Frog," an exact duplicate of the plot Mark Twain had heard from Ben Coon and used in his own story. Twain was left in a state of consternation until he met, five years later, Professor Sidgwick, who explained that he had summarized and translated Mark Twain's story into Greek because it was so similar in form to the early Greek tales. Its appearance in a volume with genuine Greek prose gave the impression that it also was authentic, but Sidgwick explained to Mark Twain that he had not thought it necessary to give credit for a story so well known. What must have been Mark Twain's reaction upon discovering that his Ugly Frogling from the West had actually deceived the elect with the Greek beauty of its form!

The Jumping Frog is a notable artistic achievement primarily because of the skill with which Mark Twain devised the structure and developed important humorous techniques beyond the rudimentary *Notebook* entry of the folk tale he had heard. His most important innovation was the invention of the narrative framework for the frog episode in which an unnamed narrator (a sort of *persona* for Mark Twain himself) is used. The use of vernacular language (which is humorous in the disparity between its varied linguistic anomalies and standard American speech) is here believable and unusually effective because it does not depend on the mere malapropisms and bizarre misspellings characteristic of Harte, Artemus Ward, Josh Billings, or Lowell, who were considered among the best of the time. By the sustained use of a high-quality vernacular as the vehicle of his story, Mark Twain here anticipates by almost twenty years his preeminent achievement with this technique in *Huck Finn,* a work which virtually inaugurated modern American literature.

Besides functioning as a part of the frame, senile garrulity is well developed here as a separate humorous technique. The incoherent reminiscences of old Wheeler with his hopscotch mind are the ludicrous extreme from man's vaunted "god-like reason"; and Mark Twain also went on to use this technique in his later writing, notably in his tale of Jim Blaine and his grandfather's old ram in *Roughing It.* Finally the story is built upon the fundamentally humorous device of paradox: here the idea that pride, for example, does not actually reflect a strength—as its possessor supposes—but a weakness. Mark Twain employs it here to achieve a sort of parabolic enactment of the very ancient idea that "pride goeth before destruction and a haughty spirit before a fall."—(Proverbs 16:18). Mark Twain (who in his more pessimistic later years liked to make caustic commentaries on "the damned lousy human race") is here content to smile with only a mild cynicism at his country bumpkin's prideful self-assurance about frogs and to show how this pride blinds him to caution and even good sense.

There are those who might agree with DeVoto who wrote of the Jumping Frog in 1932:

> The story is an accomplished masterpiece, . . . but no one will ever laugh at it again as all America, in the actual presence of the life it wrought with, laughed at it in the closing weeks of 1865. . . . A quieter pleasure takes the place of that excitement.

But there is much in American life today that belies this strange assertion. Angel's Camp, for instance, a century after Mark Twain put it on the map with his story, has now become the home of an international frog-jumping contest—billed as "America's Truly Original Celebration"—complete with "frog-skin" money and a real one thousand-dollar prize for a jump that beats the world's record of seventeen feet, one and one-half inches. It looks as if Mark Twain's Jumping Frog is launched upon a brave new youth for a second hundred years—though he might well be surprised at the form the reincarnation has taken.

Having known the story for some forty years, I have to remind myself that there are individuals who have not read **"The Jumping Frog of Calaveras County"** at all, and many, no doubt, who have not read it well. I would suggest that it can be read and reread with much pleasure and perhaps with a perception of new dimensions of human insight such as only superior humor can convey.

Edgar M. Branch (essay date 1967)

SOURCE: "'My Voice is Still for Setchell': A Background Study of 'Jim Smiley and His Jumping Frog'," in *PMLA,* Vol. 82, No. 7, December, 1967, pp. 591-601.

[*Below, Branch discusses the influence of Twain's personal life on his composition of the jumping frog story.*]

I

For the past fifteen years scholars have examined many facets of Mark Twain's **"Jumping Frog"**: its narrative techniques and some of its textual history, its relation to folklore, American humor, and Clemens' theory of humorous gravity, and its political, regional, and cultural bearings.[1] This article, by focussing on the personal background to the tale, tries to cast light on the imagination that created the famous yarn. It first relates some of the tale's narrative elements—episodes, characters, names—to Clemens' prior experience, especially to some activities reflected in newly discovered examples of his San Francisco journalism of 1864 and 1865. Then it relates the tale to strong emotional currents in his life during the fall of 1865. Finally the article proposes a date of composition for the **"Jumping Frog"** and a reading of the tale that emphasizes the level of personal meaning.

Clemens left Nevada for San Francisco 29 May 1864, almost eighteen months before the first printing of the **"Jumping Frog"** on 18 November 1865, and for fifteen of those months he lived in the city. Soon after arriving he became the local reporter of the San Francisco *Call.* Probably he worked for the paper from 6 June to 10 October or possibly until a week later. During these four months he published hundreds of unsigned news items as well as feature articles and sketches in the *Call.* Growing dissatisfied with his job, he took an assistant in September and began working fewer hours for lower pay. Also he began to publish more ambitiously conceived sketches in C. H. Webb's *Californian,* nine in all between 1 October and 3 December. On 4 December he went to Jim Gillis' cabin at Jackass Hill. He remained there and at nearby Angel's Camp (from 22 January to 20 February) until his return to San Francisco 26 February 1865. From 18 March through October Clemens published twelve additional sketches in the *Californian* and placed a few elsewhere. At least by 20 June he had begun his correspondence for Joseph T. Goodman's Virginia City *Territorial Enterprise*—a working relationship he continued into 1866—although he may not have started his daily letter to that paper until the fall. The third major professional connection he made during 1865 was with the San Francisco *Dramatic Chronicle.* He appears to have worked as a *Chronicle* staff writer for about two months, beginning 16 October. He contributed a few sketches and some squibs, and at least part of the time he compiled the column "Amusements," which included the theater notices.

II

Clemens' experience of Angel's Camp was of course basic to the **"Jumping Frog."** The remote, primitive community, soggy with rain for days on end, gave him the setting for the frame and for the internal narrative, and it supplied the perfect environment to motivate nonstop indoor yarning like Simon Wheeler's. Ben Coon, whom Clemens met there, is usually regarded as the pattern for Wheeler, and Coon's yarn of Coleman and his frog is well recognized as the immediate source for the contest in which Jim Smiley's trained frog is frustrated in his specialty by "a double-handful of shot." Clemens' synopsis put down the main facts: "Coleman with his jumping frog—bet stranger $50—stranger had no frog, & C got him one—in the meantime stranger filled C's frog full of shot & he couldn't jump—the stranger's frog won."[2] Very likely Coon's deadpan manner and vernacular language made a strong impression on Clemens and helped him establish Wheeler's point of view. The frame narrator of the tale, the character Mark Twain, finds Wheeler's speech "monotonous" and "interminable" yet "exquisitely absurd" in its earnest, gravely serene progression: a mixture of feelings that may approximate Clemens' original reaction to Ben Coon.[3] But this characterization of Wheeler's narration may have been suggested to Clemens by other mining camp acquaintances as well. Before he recorded his meeting with Coon and before he summarized Coon's yarn, he wrote: "Mountaineers in habit telling same old experiences over & over again in these little back settlements. Like Dan's old Ram, while [sic] he always drivels about when drunk. And like J's [Jim Gillis'?] account of the finding of the Cardinel . . . & other great pockets, & the sums they produced in a few days or weeks (50 to 100 lbs gold a day)."[4] At least one other notebook observation made at Angel's Camp seems to reflect experience that supplied a narrative detail. Clemens developed Jim Smiley as a resourceful, dedicated gambler. Simon Wheeler says of him that "if he even see a straddle-bug start to go any wheres, he would bet you how long it would take him to get wherever he was going to, and if you took him up he would foller that straddlebug to Mexico but what he would find out where he was bound for." That passage may be compared to this notebook entry: "Louse betting by (sold) discharged soldiers coming through from Mexico to Cal in early days. The man whose louse got whipped had to get supper. Or place them on the bottom of a frying pan—draw chalk circle round them, heat the pan & the last louse over the line had to get supper."[5]

The appeal of the mining camp raconteur to Clemens' imagination is evident in **"An Unbiased Criticism,"** his first published sketch after his return to the city. Gladys C. Bellamy (*Mark Twain as a Literary Artist,* Norman, Okla., 1950, p. 146) has correctly recognized in this sketch a rehearsal for the **"Jumping Frog."** Its major figure, simply called Coon, almost immediately takes over from the Mark Twain persona, as though by force of character. Coon lacks some of Simon Wheeler's "winning gentleness" and ungrudging admiration of others, and his use of the comic *non sequitur,* a device Artemus Ward liked, perhaps adds an artificial touch. But essentially his vision and speech are Simon Wheeler's. Coon, who seems to know everything about everybody for miles around, discourses on his "mighty responsible old Webster-Unabridged, what there is left of it." The miners

started her sloshing around, and sloshing around, and sloshing around . . . , and I don't expect I'll ever see that book again; but what makes me mad, is that for all they're so handy about keeping her sashshaying around from shanty to shanty and from camp to camp, none of 'em's ever got a good word for her. Now Coddington had her a week, and she was too many for *him*—he couldn't spell the words; he tackled some of them regular busters, tow'rd the middle, you know, and they throwed him; next, Dyer, *he* tried her a jolt, but he couldn't *pronounce* 'em—Dyer can hunt quail or play seven-up as well as any man, understand me, but he can't *pronounce* worth a d—n; . . . and so, finally, Dick Stoker harnessed her, up there at his cabin, and sweated over her, and cussed over her, and rastled with her for as much as three weeks, night and day, till he got as far as R, and then passed her over to 'Lige Pickerell, and said she was the all-firedest dryest reading that ever *he* struck."[6]

Although Coon's voice is silenced before he can spin a tale, he speaks with Simon Wheeler's rambling omniscience and rhythms. His imagination like Simon's swarms with lively grotesques whom he observes with discriminating eyes. His dictionary takes on human outline too: something like an old hand-me-down prostitute who still is more than a match for her baffled and inadequate clients. The worthy book has some of the betrayed integrity of the dog Andrew Jackson, it goes through paces as frantic as those of Smiley's fifteen-minute nag, and it is "as likely a book as any in the State," just as Dan'l Webster "can out-jump any frog in Calaveras county." Both tale and sketch project a feeling of time hanging heavy. Their people are eccentrics preoccupied with oddities and committed to trivia. To a degree the two writings share an identical vocabulary to describe analogous details: a mouth (or door) "prized" open, a dog (or dictionary) "harnessed," a frog (or man) turning a double "summerset." Coon's monologue in **"An Unbiased Criticism"** permitted Clemens to test the mentality through which he later dramatized the statement: "Why, it never made no difference to *him*—he would bet on *anything*—the dangdest feller." It signals Clemens' discovery of the appropriate style to express Wheeler's consciousness in the tale.

III

The available evidence indicates that Ben Coon's narrative was restricted to the episode of the shot-laden frog and that it played up the idea of human trickery and not animal idiosyncrasy.[7] Also by 1865 Clemens was adept at creating humanized animals. Almost certainly, then, he alone—with no dependence on any mining camp raconteur—conceived the full range of Smiley's love for betting and his paternalistic exploitation of talented animals. Significantly Clemens kept the memory of Coon's yarn alive in his imagination by joking about it with Jim Gillis and Dick Stoker as all three panned for gold, and before writing the published version he may have sketched the tale in a letter to Artemus Ward and may have told it to Bret Harte and other San Franciscans.[8] The imaginative enlargement of Coon's anecdote that occurred in the long gestation is in fact partly traceable. In particular, when he composed the episodes of the fifteen-minute nag and the dog Andrew Jackson, it now appears that Clemens drew upon experience he gained as a San Francisco reporter.

Among the hundreds of local news items appearing in the *Call* during the time Clemens worked on the paper are several on the horse races held in the new and lavishly equipped Bay View Park, located on the bay shore west of Hunter's Point. Two of these turf reports are reprinted below. Although they are unsigned, in my opinion they are by Clemens and form part of the background out of which Jim Smiley's mare comes "cavorting" down the track.[9]

> THE HURDLE-RACE YESTERDAY.—The grand feature at the Bay View Park yesterday, was the hurdle race. There were three competitors, and the winner was Wilson's circus horse, "Sam." Sam has lain quiet through all the pacings and trottings and runnings, and consented to be counted out, but this hurdle business was just his strong suit, and he stepped forward promply when it was proposed. There was a much faster horse (Conflict) in the list, but what is natural talent to cultivation? Sam was educated in a circus, and understood his business; Conflict would pass him under way, trip and turn a double summerset over the next hurdle, and while he was picking himself up, the accomplished Sam would sail gracefully over the hurdle and slabber past his adversary with the easy indifference of conscious superiority. Conflict made the fastest time, but he fooled away too many summersets on the hurdles. The proverb saith that he that jumpeth fences with ye circus horse will aye come to grief.[10]

Six days later the *Call* published the lengthy "Race for the Occidental Hotel Premium." The first half of this report factually describes four heats in the trotting contest subsidized by the Occidental Hotel, where Clemens boarded. The horse Kentucky Hunter ran first in each race. The reporter then continues:

> Previous to the Occidental contest, a tandem race came off for a purse of one hundred and twenty-five dollars, mile heats, best 3 in 5. "Spot" and "Latham," driven by Mr. Covey, and "Rainbow" and "Sorrell Charley," driven by Mr. Ferguson, ran. Before the first half mile post was reached, Ferguson's team ran away, and Covey's trotted around leisurely and won the purse. The runaways flew around the race-track three or four times, at break neck speed, and fears were entertained that some of this break-neck would finally fall to Ferguson's share, as his strength soon ebbed away, and he no longer attempted to hold his fiery untamed Menkens, but only did what he could to make them stay on the track, and keep them from climbing the fence. Every time they dashed by the excited crowd at the stand, a few frantic attempts would be made to grab them, but with indifferent success; it is no use to snatch at a cannon ball—a man must stand before it if he wants to stop it. One man seized the lead horse, and was whisked under the wheels in an instant. His head was split open a little, but Dr. Woodward stitched the wound together, and the sufferer was able to report for duty in half an hour. Mr. Ferguson's horses should be taught to economize their speed; they wasted enough

> of it in that one dash, yesterday, to win every race this season, if judiciously distributed among them. The only Christian way to go out to Bay View, is to travel in one of the Occidental coaches, behind four Flora Temples, and with their master-spirit, Porter, on the box, and a crowd inside and out, consisting of moral young men and cocktails. Mr. Leland should be along, to keep the portable hotel.[11]

In the **"Jumping Frog"** Clemens writes of the mare whom the boys called

> the fifteen-minute nag, but that was only in fun, you know, because, of course, she was faster than that— and he used to win money on that horse, for all she was so slow and always had the asthma, or the distemper, or the consumption, or something of that kind. They used to give her two or three hundred yards' start, and then pass her under way; but always at the fag-end of the race she'd get excited and desperate- like, and come cavorting and spraddling up, and scattering her legs around limber, sometimes in the air, and sometimes out to one side amongst the fences, and kicking up m-o-r-e dust, and raising m-o-r-e racket with her coughing and sneezing and blowing her nose— and always fetch up at the stand just about a neck ahead, as near as you could cipher it down.

Like Kentucky Hunter, Smiley's mare is a consistent winner, capable of rousing herself and coming from behind to score. But clearly Sam's claim to be her sire is superior to Kentucky Hunter's. Competitors of both Sam and the mare "pass" each horse "under way," thus momentarily confirming to all observers the expected role of each underdog horse as an also-ran and adding that much more excitement to the eventual upset victories. Although Sam takes the hurdles gracefully, his slabbering form as a runner suggests the spraddling mare scattering her legs around, and suggests, too, that when the chips were really down, the easygoing Sam, like Smiley's nag, possibly would show up as a lathering slob. To be sure, Sam is as educated as Smiley's frog, and no doubt this training explains his casual confidence and his feeling of superiority, so different from the mare's female excitability and air of desperation. Sam's victory over the speedy Conflict, in fact, is a monument to "cultivation" in contrast to what must surely be an impressive "talent"—no less than that of the dog Andrew Jackson's—in the badly handicapped, snuffing nag. Yet these very differences help us to see that both the **"Jumping Frog"** and the *Call* report of the hurdle race humorously utilize, with varying emphases, the twin ideas of natural endowment and acquired training (facets of Clemens' more general speculations on necessity and freedom), ideas often linked in his thinking and writing.[12] The two unorthodox race horses are close kin in Clemens' large family of exceptional, strong-minded animals.[13]

IV

Smiley's mare was a consistent winner and so was the bull-pup Andrew Jackson until he "got shucked out bad" by the dog "that didn't have no hind legs, because they'd been sawed off in a circular saw." The disfigured hero who retired Andrew Jackson for good is a significant minor character. So far as we know, he was Jim Smiley's only nemesis before the tricky stranger walked into camp. His surprise triumph over Andrew Jackson resulted from a circumstance much less usual than the duplicity shown by the stranger. Presumably his victory might have suggested to Smiley more forcibly than it did that a sure thing, even a scrupulously educated and gifted frog, can never be taken for granted. It appears that the original of this unsung conqueror of Andrew Jackson claimed Clemens' attention during the third week of October 1865.

In a revealing letter dated 19 October 1865 and addressed to Orion and Mollie Clemens, but meant primarily for Orion, Clemens wrote: "I am also in debt. But I have gone to work in dead earnest to get out. Joe Goodman pays me $100 a month for a daily letter, and the *Dramatic Chronicle* pays me or rather *will* begin to pay me, next week— $40 a month for dramatic criticisms. Same wages I got on the *Call,* & more agreeable & less laborious work."[14] It seems clear that when Clemens wrote this letter he had begun his duties on the *Dramatic Chronicle* as a recently recruited staff member and was not, as an old hand, taking on a new assignment at an increase in pay.[15] Two days before, he had published his first sketch in the *Dramatic Chronicle,* **"Earthquake Almanac."** Two days later the column "Amusements," which customarily noticed the daily offerings at the theaters, museums, and resorts, included the following account of James White's Museum of freaks:

White's Museum

Meigg's wharf is the favorite resort of the little ones on Sunday. No one who goes to this part of the city should leave without paying a visit to White's Museum, where a most wonderful collection of curiosities, fully equal to anything which Barnum has, are on view. The three-quartered dog, a fine handsome fellow, and as intelligent and good-natured an animal as we have ever had the pleasure of being introduced to, is a most wonderful freak of nature. Poor fellow! Richard III was—

"Cheated of feature by dissembling nature, Deformed, unfinished,"

but this dog is actually cheated of a quarter by dissembling nature, who sent him into the world only three parts finished. However, he does not seem to mind it a bit; he is as strong and lively as any four-legged dog, and more intelligent than many two-legged puppies.[16]

This strong dog who accepts his defect is a fit model for the conqueror of a champion. Neither he nor Andrew Jackson's opponent is as vitally handicapped as Andrew Jackson, whose rigid habitual responses and tender-minded conviction that Smiley owed him a set-up prove to be a fatal combination. But Andrew Jackson is a more important character than his conqueror and in conceiving him Clemens dug more deeply into his past. Simon Wheeler

says that "to look at him you'd think he warn't worth a cent, but to set around and look ornery, and lay for a chance to steal something." Here Clemens may be remembering the orneriness and thievery of Curney and Tom, two dogs he wrote up in his Keokuk *Gate City* letter of 6 March 1862. But to describe Andrew Jackson's pugnacity when the "money was up on him" he reverted to sterner imagery from his piloting days: "his under-jaw'd begin to stick out like the for'castle [sic] of a steamboat, and his teeth would uncover, and shine savage like the furnaces." Andrew Jackson with his steam up was as lethal as the riverboat with its "long row of wide-open furnace doors shining like red-hot teeth" (*Writings,* XIII, 131) that smashed Huck's and Jim's raft.

Any San Franciscan writing of dogs at this time would almost automatically recall the famous friends Bummer and Lazarus, two dogs constantly publicized during the early 1860's in the San Francisco press. Clemens was aware of them and published an account of Bummer's death.[17] Andrew Jackson was not a vagrant like Bummer, but like Andrew Jackson, the valorous Bummer was a respected fighter. Clemens commented on his dignity, a quality similar to Andrew Jackson's pride that helped to undermine his will to live after "he saw in a minute how he'd been imposed on." Disillusioned, wounded to the heart, and mildly reproachful, Andrew Jackson "limped off a piece" to die alone, a defeated romantic. This comic sentimentality may be compared to the last moments of the more sociable Bummer, who "died with friends around him to smooth his pillow and wipe the death-damps from his brow, and receive his last words of love and resignation; because he died full of years, and honor, and disease, and fleas."

V

Clemens' experience as a San Francisco journalist may have influenced—consciously or not—his choice of names for some characters in the **"Jumping Frog,"** if only by making those names available for selection because of his recent awareness of them. His 1864 editorial "It Is the Daniel Webster" praises the Daniel Webster Mining Company for daring to make its records public at a time when most companies were not disclosing how they spent assessments. As a stockholder, Clemens suffered from the drain of assessments and had fretted about their misappropriation by secretaries and managers of mining companies.[18] The Daniel Webster Mining Company he now saw as a symbol of probity, "worthy of the name of Daniel Webster." Its policy eventually would force other companies to "adopt the system of published periodical statements." On that day, he exulted, stockholders would hear from Virginia City corporations that sport "costly and beautiful green chicken-cocks on the roof, which are able to tell how the wind blows, yet are savagely ignorant concerning dividends. So will other Companies come out and say what it cost to build their duck ponds; . . . another that we have in our eye will show what they did with an expensive lot of timbers, when they haven't got enough in their mine to shingle a chicken-coop with . . . and why they levy a forty-thousand-dollar assessment every six weeks to run a drift with. Secretaries, Superintendents, and Boards of Trustees, that don't like the prospect, had better resign."[19]

During the 1860's the name Daniel Webster still had considerable currency and Clemens had used it sparingly for many years. The physical resemblance of any frog to the famous politician is enough to have recalled the name once again to an imagination that often visualized animals as people, although Clemens' naming of Smiley's frog no doubt drew upon many interwoven associations, including the one deriving from his attack on the mining companies.

Through much of 1864 and 1865 in the *Call,* the *Dramatic Chronicle,* and the *Territorial Enterprise* Clemens repeatedly sniped at Albert S. Evans, the city editor of the San Francisco *Alta California* who was commonly known by his pen names Fitz Smythe and Amigo. Writing in the *Alta California* in mid-1864, Evans invented a stooge whom he named Armand Leonidas Stiggers, surely one of the dreariest comic characters of all time. Clemens ridiculed the labored jokes Evans constructed around Stiggers. His fondness for the name Leonidas is evident during late 1865 and 1866 in his continuing bouts with Evans, whom he rechristened Armand Leonidas Fitz Smythe Amigo Stiggers. Leonidas, an improbable name at best, in one sense suits the mythical friend who was not there, "the Rev. Leonidas W. Smiley" of the tale, whom Artemus Ward asked Mark Twain to look up. Yet to make a minister of God lion-like is almost as incongruous as the comic ennobling of Smiley's frog and bull-pup by naming them after great human leaders.

The name Smiley that supplanted Ben Coon's "Coleman" was Clemens' most brilliant choice. Paired with "Leonidas" it aptly describes the mocking phantom who lives only within the realm of Ward's practical joke on Mark Twain. Joined with "Jim" it admirably fits the wily gambler, adept and enduring in a man's world. Its source may be the case of the United States vs. Thomas J. L. Smiley publicized in the San Francisco papers during the summer of 1864 when Clemens was local reporter on the *Call.* In 1862 the ship *Golden Gate* out of San Francisco with almost $1,500,000 in treasure had sunk off the coast of Mexico near Manzanillo. The adventurer Smiley was indicted in the United States Circuit Court for salvaging and appropriating some of the treasure. But on 29 August 1864 Judge Ogden Hoffman ordered a *nolle prosequi,* and the *Call* reported that Smiley had compromised a second suit brought against him. The settlement left him "in the quiet possession of a large amount of the treasure-trove." The *Call* reporter, whether Clemens or another, gratuitously insinuated in a vein not foreign to Clemens' manner on occasion, that "Mr. Smiley, during his arrest, has moved about at his pleasure, attended by a Deputy of the Marshal, which courtesy will doubtless meet its due reward at the hands of the fortunate wrecker."[20]

Clemens characterized the appropriately named Simon Wheeler as a simple, earnest soul, gentle in character but an unswerving steamroller in his storytelling. The surname may have suggested itself to Clemens as a consequence

of his acquaintance with Reverend Osgood Church Wheeler. Wheeler lectured widely for the California Branch of the United States Sanitary Commission and served as its secretary. During September Clemens reported the Mechanics' Institute Industrial Fair in San Francisco. Various Fair exhibits collected money for the Sanitary Fund to aid the Civil War wounded, a cause Clemens helped to promote. In one of the Fair writeups the *Call* reporter credits Wheeler with supplying him statistics on public contributions to the Fund. But exactly one week earlier in the *Call* the local reporter had complained of a brush-off at Wheeler's office. He concluded: "We would like, in order to benefit the commission, to give publicity to the names of contributors to the Fund; but on applying for the list, recently, were all but peremptorily refused. The individual who attends to the business of receiving and recording the subscriptions is either too lazy or too disobliging for the position. He prefers his own case to the interests of the Commission."[21] Whether the offending individual was Wheeler or a clerk is not known, but by his complaint the reporter brought his man to account—following precisely the technique Clemens used more violently in **"A Small Piece of Spite"** (*Call,* 6 Sept. 1864, p. 1) three days later to flatten the Coroner's clerk in Atkins Massey's funeral establishment who had denied him information.

VI

Clemens' original version of his tale begins: "Mr. A. Ward, Dear Sir:—" A minor character not present in person, Ward serves to motivate he meeting between the frame narrator Mark Twain and the internal narrator Simon Wheeler. The reference to him was Clemens' indirect acknowledgment of Ward's invitation to contribute a sketch to his forthcoming book, *Artemus Ward: His Travels,* a request Clemens recorded in his 1865 notebook: "26th—Home again—home again at the Occidental Hotel, San Francisco—find letters from 'Artemus Ward' asking me to write a sketch for his new book of Nevada Territory travels which is soon to come out. Too late—ought to have got the letters 3 months ago. They are dated early in November."[22] Those letters of Ward's marked his second eruption in Clemens' life, the first having come in late December 1863 when Clemens heard his "Babes in the Woods" lecture in Virginia City and became personally acquainted with him. On both occasions Ward precipitated publications that helped Clemens' career. The opportunity that Clemens on 26 February believed he had missed opened up in succeeding months as Ward continued to press for a contribution.[23] Surely Ward, the generous friend, was alive in Clemens' thoughts during the incubation of the **"Jumping Frog."**

The less surprising, then, that Ward, the lecturer and writer, was alive in Clemens' literary imagination when he finally wrote the tale. One notes the letter form that begins the **"Jumping Frog,"** suggesting the way Ward began some of his sketches. Ward's "Babes in the Woods" was a series of digressions: anecdotes and pronouncements given coherence by Ward's platform presence. Similarly the main substance of Clemens' tale, the history of "thishyer Smiley," is a kind of self-perpetuating digression that unerringly expresses Simon Wheeler's personality. In both the lecture and the tale, as Clemens in effect demonstrates in "How to Tell a Story," the humor is founded on character that is displayed in the manner of telling. What counts is the wandering, bubbling, spun-out discourse, punctuated by studied pauses and afterthoughts, that is spoken by a narrator who is simple, innocent, earnestly sincere, unselfconscious—either naturally like Ben Coon or Simon Wheeler, or by calculated pretense like the platform artists Ward, Twain, Dan Setchell, or James Whitcomb Riley. The genius of the **"Jumping Frog"** dwarfs Ward's talent; in style, subtlety of organization, character creation, intellectual content, and imaginative power Clemens' tale transcends Wards influence. Yet Ward must be counted a pioneer of the broad literary approach Clemens followed in writing the tale that made such imaginative use of a personal experience including originals like Coon and Ward himself.

Beyond strictly literary influence, however, Ward probably played a crucial role in Clemens' psychology when the **"Jumping Frog"** was written. Years later Clemens affirmed that "Babes in the Woods" was the funniest thing he had ever listened to, and after hearing Ward lecture in 1863 he wrote: "There are perhaps fifty subjects treated in it, and there is a passable point in every one of them, and a hearty laugh also for any of God's creatures who have committed no crime, the ghastly memory of which debars him from smiling again while he lives. The man who is capable of listening to the Babes In The Woods from beginning to end without laughing, either inwardly or outwardly, must have done murder, or at least meditated it, at some time during his life."[24] Here Clemens contrasts the worthy result of Ward's humor—a life-giving laughter common to most of "God's creatures"—with murder, an act of violent and final separation. In his letter of 19 October he confides to Orion: "I *have* had a 'call' to literature, of a low order—*i.e.* humorous. It is nothing to be proud of, but it is my strongest suit" (*MDB,* p. 6). He then makes an important commitment. He asserts he will "strive for a fame—unworthy & evanescent though it must of necessity be" by turning his attention "to seriously scribbling to excite the *laughter* of God's creatures" (*MDB,* pp. 8, 6). The similar phrasing in letter and review inevitably suggests an imaginative identification of his commitment with Ward's accomplishment, the writing of humorous literature, and it reveals his concept of their identical purpose, the creation of beneficial laughter.

In "How to Tell a Story" Clemens associated Ward and the popular comedian Dan Setchell, Ward's good friend, as masters of humorous technique. His early piece from the mid-1860's, "A Voice for Setchell," further defines the value he finds in laughter. There he wrote that in "a long season of sensational, snuffling dramatic bosh, and tragedy bosh, and electioneering bosh" the people were "learning to wear the habit of unhappiness like a garment" until Setchell appeared as Captain Cuttle in John Brougham's extremely popular adaptation of *Dombey and Son* "and broke the deadly charm with a wave of his enchanted hook and the spell of his talismanic words, *'Awahst! awahst! awahst!'* And since that night all the powers of dreariness

combined have not been able to expel the spirit of cheerfulness he invoked. Therefore, my voice is still for Setchell. I have experienced more real pleasure, and more physical benefit, from laughing naturally and unconfinedly at his funny personations and extempore speeches than I have from all the operas and tragedies I have endured, and all the blue mass pills I have swallowed in six months."[25] Murder, Clemens seems to say, excludes laughter, but laughter buoys up the spirit and expels dreariness. As an antidote to misery, it ultimately offers escape from self-murder. His letter of 19 October closes: "I am utterly miserable . . . If I do not get out of debt in 3 months,—pistols or poison for one—exit *me.* There's a text for a sermon on Self-M[urder,]—proceed" (*MDB,* p. 9).

In 1865, then, Clemens undoubtedly valued laughter and consequently humorous writing for at least one important reason. Later he would appreciate more fully the social value of laughter and humor. On the other hand, in 1865 his implied reluctance to pursue literature "of a low order" that was "nothing to be proud of" is an early expression of later recurrent doubts about the fitness of a career in humor for a serious writer. In view of this conflict it may be supposed that the commitment expressed in his letter resulted less from a sudden dedication to literary values—after all, he had been writing and publishing since 1852—than from his need to get out of debt and keep that way, especially at a time when his mining stocks were proving worthless. In addition to its intrinsic but "low order" value, humorous writing that was more seriously pursued presumably offered him at least a chance for success—to make a name for himself if the stuff was in him.

Clemens' commitment also was supported by Orion's faith in him and, more significantly, by a favorable press in the East. Clemens continued in his letter: "*You* see in me a talent for humorous writing, & urge me to cultivate it. But I always regarded it as brotherly partiality on your part & attached no value to it. It is only now, when editors of standard literary papers in the distant east give me high praise, & who do not know me & cannot of course be blinded by the glamour of partiality, that I really begin to believe there must be something in it" (*MDB,* pp. 7-8). He was alluding to a recently published article on American humor in the New York *Round Table* ("American Humor and Humorists," 9 Sept. 1865, p. 2). The anonymous author, possibly one of the editors, H. E. Sweetser or C. H. Sweetser, broadly characterized American humor and surveyed native humorists. He placed Mark Twain "foremost among the merry gentlemen of the California press"; Twain's writing gave promise that "he may one day take rank among the brightest of our wits." On 18 October, the day before Clemens wrote to "My Dear Bro," the *Dramatic Chronicle,* whose staff he had just joined, reprinted ("Recognized," p. 3) the part of the article that praised him.

Three days later came Clemens' newspaper writeup of the three-quartered dog. If, as I believe, that dog was the model for Andrew Jackson's conqueror, thereby evoking him in Clemens' imagination, then Clemens' awareness of the museum freak at this precise time is a key piece fitting superbly into the puzzle of the date the **"Jumping Frog"** was composed. It seems probable that Clemens wrote **"Jim Smiley and His Jumping Frog"** during the week of 16-23 October. He had a new job in which he covered the city's amusements and plays. He was making every effort to clear away debt. A favorable press was waiting to be used. A clear-sighted self-examination arising from his unhappiness had called forth a commitment to write laughter-provoking humor, another name for "literature, of a low order"—"a villainous backwoods sketch" (*Letters,* I, 101) was what he called his laughter-provoking tale three months later. Nor is it likely that he undertook his commitment lightly. A proud man who four years earlier had come West with dreams of wealth, he still was in a subordinate position. He believed in his talent for humor, but still it was "nothing to be proud of." He had come to know already that success of any kind came hard and that a writer's life meant a continuing risk. Finally, if he made his commitment as the best immediate way to become and remain solvent, he must have seen it partly in terms of a life-risk: success or "exit *me.*"

The suggested time of writing is late, for it comes midway in the two-months period spanning the date Ward's book is said to have been published and the appearance of the tale.[26] Yet some evidence suggests that Clemens delayed excessively in writing the tale and that it arrived late in the East.[27] Also it should be observed that given Clemens' interest in freaks, he might have visited White's Museum in the summer or early fall, a supposition that supports an earlier dating of the Andrew Jackson episode assuming one grants the causal relationship between the two handicapped dogs suggested above. Yet, an earlier visit is purely speculative. So far as we know there was no specific motive for it and, if it was made, no visible consequence of it leading into the tale, other than possibly the Andrew Jackson episode itself. On the other hand, the requirement of covering the city's amusements for the *Dramatic Chronicle* was a strong motive for an October visit to White's Museum even if he had been there earlier. The newspaper writeup with its fresh impressions working actively in his imagination—the merging images of the deformed dog and Richard III—suggests both a recent visit and an available bridge to the tale.

VII

The **"Jumping Frog"** itself supports the date of composition proposed for it in this paper. When Clemens wrote his letter to "My Dear Bro" the uncertainties of his present and future were so troubling that he felt compelled to re-examine his past: "I never had but two *powerful* ambitions in my life. One was to be a pilot, & the other a preacher of the gospel. I accomplished the one & failed in the other, *because* I could not supply myself with the necessary stock in trade—*i.e.* religion. I have given it up forever. I never had a 'call' in that direction, anyhow, & my aspirations were the very ecstasy of presumption" (*MDB*, p. 6). The ministry, for Clemens a chimera of his distant boyhood, was for Orion, he believed, a real possibility founded on a "talent" for preaching. "You are honest, pious, virtuous," he wrote; "—what would you have more? *Go forth & preach"* (*MDB*, p. 7). Orion should become "a

minister of the gospel," not a "mud-cat of a *lawyer*" (*MDB*, pp. 8, 7). The general principle was simply "that to do the right you *must* multiply the one or the two or the three talents which the Almighty entrusts to your keeping" (*MDB*, p. 6). As a climax to his own sermon, he offered to strike a bargain with Orion: each would agree to develop his natural talent, "to do what his Creator intended him to do" (*MDB*, p. 7). This proposal, which links his own performance to Orion's, further qualifies the seriousness of Clemens' commitment to humorous literature. Moreover his letter was a perfect opportunity to over-dramatize his troubles before a sympathetic audience, and it is doubtful that any resolution, however seriously intended, could keep the pluralistic Clemens in a single path for very long. Yet after all allowances are made, we cannot miss the real unhappiness in the letter, or the latent bitterness: "I have a religion . . . It is that there is a God for the rich man but none for the poor" (*MDB*, p. 9). Nor can we miss the sense of loss as he touches on the old problem of natural endowment versus training ("the Almighty did His part by me—for the talent is a mighty engine when supplied with the steam of *education*—which I have not got" [*MDB*, p. 7]), the genuine uncertainty about his future, and his keen awareness of the element of risk that lay ahead in his life. The fact that these feelings were pressing for expression at that precise time—and perhaps were not so dominant a few days before or after—strengthens the probability that the tale was composed the week of 16-23 October. For those feelings fit the tale in a deeply personal way and help us to understand it in a new and intimate dimension.

Whatever else **"Jim Smiley and His Jumping Frog"** may be, it also is an unwittingly articulated parable of Clemens' complex state of mind, the pass he had come to, about the time he wrote his letter to Orion. The constructive imagination that built the tale seized on the conflicts and concepts, the forebodings and ambitions, that were at work within. In the tale the character Mark Twain (in life, the relatively unknown but promising humorist) is directed by the character Artemus Ward (in life, the nationally acclaimed maker of laughs) to find "a cherished companion" of Ward's boyhood, "Rev. Leonidas W. Smiley—a young minister of the gospel." The minister turns out to be a chimera, a shade, and for the character Mark Twain to have sought him was indeed a good joke, the "very ecstasy of presumption." Yet by this means Ward brings the seeker Mark Twain (who, in life, seeks to "multiply" his talent for humor) face to face with Simon Wheeler, and Mark Twain wakens the dozing humorist. With utmost seriousness, Wheeler awake seems to give over his entire being to his humorous narration. To his visitor's question about the minister Wheeler responds as though his long irrelevant answer were perfectly proper, as though, in fact, it were really relevant to another, unexpressed question in his listener's mind. His visitor sees that Wheeler accepts his own tale as "a really important matter," and Wheeler speaks with no condescension or irony or hint of trickery. As a storyteller Wheeler is a natural. Evidently of slight education, he performs, to God's own fulness, "what his Creator intended him to do," and he does it with an impressive objectivity. It is deeply appropriate that the character Mark Twain should sit silent before this man (as one might absorb a natural wonder), letting him "go on in his own way" without interrupting him once.

By means of his narrative Wheeler introduces Mark Twain, not to a pious, virtuous minister who knows the language of exhortation like Parson Walker of the tale, or like Orion, but to Jim Smiley, a resourceful adventurer who will slop around in the mud to get what he wants, a man who has done very well in a chancy world. Smiley works his talent for betting for all it is worth. He is enterprising and makes his own opportunities. He counts on the hopes of others and on the strengths of those he bets on. Although "he would bet on *anything*," "he was lucky—uncommon lucky"; and his luck is evidence that usually he knows what he is about. He knows the importance of persistent effort born of desperation (in the mare), of talent (in Andrew Jackson), and of talent combined with training (in Dan'l Webster). Knowing these things, he is equipped to win what victories he can by calculated means. From Andrew Jackson he presumably learns about the weakness of the sensitive romantic who expects too much from the world. From Dan'l's honest belch he learns once again that the unexpected can explode in his overconfident face, but when it does he responds vigorously. He has the courage to bet even when the outcome is totally unpredictable—which bird will fly first from a fence?—and he makes risk the condition of his existence. As Mrs. Wendy Stallard Flory has said, "he embraces chance itself as a way of life."[28] Jim Smiley is the hero of a fabulous world as "exquisitely absurd" as Wheeler's manner, but that world is very real too in the limitations and possibilities it holds for men.

Clemens made Wheeler and Smiley extreme individualists, as though already he were obscurely probing the implications of seriously making humor the business of his life. For Wheeler is the complete humorist. No mere trickster, he is absorbed like a true creator in the world he fashions through his patiently vivid imagination and his serene, rhythmic style. And Smiley, the mundane hero of that world, is the shrewd and determined man of action. He believes in rational effort but knows very well the full range of risk in life. His conduct implies courage and tough-minded hope. "Mr. A. Ward," Simon Wheeler and—through the lens of Wheeler's vision—Jim Smiley, his animals, and the fateful stranger are all meaningful configurations in Clemens' consciousness at a time of uncertainty and resolve, when he wanted to give a new but risky direction to his life.

Although the **"Jumping Frog"** was not soon equalled by Clemens, it was an important breakthrough in the long process of his development. Years of journalism still lay ahead, but by October 1865 he must have known that San Francisco journalism held little more for him. By 7 March of the next year he was more than ready to sail for the Sandwich Islands, an assignment that would offer fresh experience and the opportunity to cast off "the habit of unhappiness like a garment." But he was not yet ready to recognize fully the heights of humor he had reached in the **"Jumping Frog"** or to build upon them. His creation was more complex and profound than he knew. The tale is, in fact, a number of things: a blown-up frontier anecdote, a

teasing fable that suggests various social and political meanings—although these, I believe, were negligible in the creative impulse behind the tale—and, as Paul Baender has convincingly shown, a thoroughgoing illustration of Clemens' theory of humorous gravity. The voice that had spoken up for Setchell spoke for itself in the **"Jumping Frog,"** which above all else is a first-rate yarn taking extraordinary delight in humorous expression and character. As such, the tale appears to be also an intimately personal creation rising in shapely form from depths previously unsounded by Clemens, a consideration that helps to explain its compelling appeal and its poetic unity. For if the argument of this paper is correct, in writing **"Jim Smiley and His Jumping Frog"** Clemens utilized, consciously or not, two main areas of his personal background: past events experienced in San Francisco as well as in the mining camps, and certain tension-laden problems, closely connected with his need to find himself, that were pressing for immediate resolution.

Notes

[1] See Paul Baender, "The 'Jumping Frog' as a Comedian's First Virtue," *MP,* LX (1963), 192-200; Walter Blair, "Introduction," *Selected Shorter Writings of Mark Twain* (Boston, 1962), pp. xxii-xxiv; Hennig Cohen, "Twain's Jumping Frog: Folktale to Literature to Folktale," *WF,* XXII (1963), 17-18; Rufus A. Coleman, "Mark Twain's Jumping Frog: Another Version of the Famed Story," *Montana Magazine of History,* III (Summer 1953), 29-30; Pascal Covici, Jr., *Mark Twain's Humor* (Dallas, Tex., 1962), pp. 48-52; James M. Cox, *Mark Twain: The Fate of Humor* (Princeton, N. J., 1966), pp. 24-33; Roger Penn Cuff, "Mark Twain's Use of California Folklore in His Jumping Frog Story," *JAF,* LXV (1952), 155-158; John C. Gerber, "Mark Twain's Use of the Comic Pose," *PMLA,* LXXVII (1962), 297-304; Sydney J. Krause, "The Art and Satire of Twain's 'Jumping Frog' Story," *AQ,* XVI (1964), 562-576; Kenneth S. Lynn, *Mark Twain and Southwestern Humor* (Boston, 1959), pp. 145-147; Paul Schmidt, "The Deadpan on Simon Wheeler," *Southwest Review,* XLI (1956), 270-277; Henry Nash Smith, *Mark Twain: The Development of a Writer* (Cambridge, Mass., 1962), p. 11; J. Golden Taylor, introductory remarks to "The Celebrated Jumping Frog of Calaveras County," *American West,* II (Fall 1965), 73-76.

References to the "Jumping Frog" in this article are to the first printing, "Jim Smiley and His Jumping Frog," New York *Saturday Press,* 18 Nov. 1865, pp. 248-249.

[2] TS of Notebook 3, p. 8, Mark Twain Papers, Berkeley, Calif.—hereafter cited as MTP; reprinted with changes in *Mark Twain's Notebook,* ed. Albert Bigelow Paine (New York, 1935), p. 7.

[3] In his "Private History of the 'Jumping Frog' Story," *North American Review,* CLVIII (1894), 447, Clemens wrote of Coon and his audience of miners: "in his mouth this episode was . . . the gravest sort of history . . . ; he was entirely serious, for he was dealing with what to him were austere facts, and . . . he saw no humor in his tale . . . none of the party was aware . . . that it was brimful of a quality whose presence they never suspected—humor."

[4] TS of Notebook 3, p. 5, MTP. Copyright 196- by The Mark Twain Company.

[5] TS of Notebook 3, p. 8, MTP. Copyright 196- by The Mark Twain Company.

[6] *Californian,* 18 Mar. 1865, p. 8; reprinted with some changes in *Sketches of the Sixties,* ed. John Howell (San Francisco, 1927), pp. 158-165.

[7] See Clemens' emended version of "Private History . . . ," *How to Tell a Story and Other Essays* (Hartford, Conn., 1900), pp. 121-122; *Mark Twain's Letters* (New York, 1917), I, 170.

[8] *How to Tell a Story,* p. 126; T. Edgar Pemberton, *The Life of Bret Harte* (London, 1903), pp. 73-75; "'The Jumping Frog of Calaveras' by Mark Twain With an Introductory and Explanatory Note by J. G. H.," *Overland Monthly,* XL (Sept. 1902), 20-21; *Letters,* I, 170.

[9] As recently as Oct. 1863 Clemens had written up the races at the first annual fair of the Washoe Agricultural, Mining and Mechanical Society held in Carson City. See *Mark Twain of the Enterprise,* ed. Henry Nash Smith with the assistance of Frederick Anderson (Berkeley and Los Angeles, 1957), pp. 80-86. My article "Mark Twain Reports the Races in Sacramento," to appear in *HLQ,* shows that Clemens undertook a week's racetrack assignment at the 1866 California State Fair for James Anthony of the Sacramento *Union.*

[10] *Call,* 4 Sept. 1864, p. 1. Reports in other city papers name the winner as Strideover, nicknamed Sam. John Wilson was the proprietor of the circus at the Jackson Street Pavillion. Sam's "easy indifference of conscious superiority" is a phrase carrying almost the force of a signature. It marks the horse as one of Clemens' large class of self-assured characters who enjoy lording it over others because of superior skill or style or experience. For examples of Clemens' use of that phrase and its variants see: "San Francisco Correspondence," Napa County *Reporter,* 11 Nov. 1865, p. 2; *The Writings of Mark Twain,* Definitive Edition (New York, 1922), XII, 46, and XIV, 317. Hereafter this edition will be cited as *Writings.*

[11] *Call,* 10 Sept. 1864, p. 1. I have omitted the four concluding sentences that notice races to come. George N. Ferguson and Harris R. Covey were racetrack drivers. Wadsworth Porter owned a livery stable. Dr. George F. Woodward was the surgeon and physician of the United States Pension Bureau. Clemens' friend Lewis Leland was the proprietor of the Occidental Hotel and Clemens often joked him in print.

Clemens' comic use of "Christian" was routine, and he echoes his earlier review of "Mazeppa" in the phrase "fiery untamed Menkens" (Smith, *Enterprise,* pp. 78-80). Typical of his comic vision is the merging of discrete modes of being and the resulting implicit puns. Quality becomes commodity, as in the use of "break neck" and "break-neck." A burst of speed necessarily indivisible in time is coolly partitioned and distributed among several races (economizing speed for economic gain). Moral young men and cocktails combine (in two ways) to constitute a crowd (animate and animated). The bold, offhand formula for stopping a cannonball and the casually aloof phrasing of "His head was split open a little" familiarly echo the magisterial dispenser of advice and remedies and the Washoe reporter of gory prize fights.

[12] It is interesting that Conflict's awkward "double summerset" is a sign of a serious limitation by virtue of his lack of training in hurdle racing, whereas Dan'l Webster's graceful "one summerset, or maybe a couple," is a sign of his free mastery of conditions through training. The fated dog Curney in Clemens' letter in the Keokuk *Gate City,* 6 Mar. 1862, turns "somersets" as he races over the desert. In *Roughing It* "the rawest dog," probably modeled on the alkalied Curney, "threw double somersaults" in his frenzy (*Writings,* III, 260).

[13] For examples of Clemens' later use of turf imagery and terms relating to the *Call* pieces and to the "Jumping Frog" see: *Writings,* I, 32; IV, 99, 287; XII, 372; XIII, 206; XIV, 119; XXVII, 176; Walter F. Frear, *Mark Twain and Hawaii* (Chicago, 1947), p. 294.

[14] *My Dear Bro,* ed. Frederick Anderson (Berkeley, 1961) p. 8— hereafter cited as *MDB* and documented in text.

[15] See "Dictation of M. H. De Young," Bancroft Library, Berkeley. De Young helped establish the *Dramatic Chronicle* in 1865. His memory of Clemens' connection with the paper is faulty in some details.

[16] "Amusements," *Dramatic Chronicle,* 21 Oct. 1865, p. 3. The comparison with Richard III (whom Huck, the Duke, and the Dauphin knew all about), the punning, the easy slide from the factual into the fanciful, and above all the familiar delight in humanizing an animal suggest Clemens' comic imagination at this time.

[17] Extant as "Exit 'Bummer'," *Californian,* 11 Nov. 1865, p. 12, from the Virginia City *Territorial Enterprise,* 8 Nov. 1865. In "The Art and Satire . . ." (see n. 1) Sydney J. Krause argues that the bull-pup is Clemens' satirical portrait of the historical Andrew Jackson. He feels, e.g., that the pup's appearance of not being "worth a cent but to set around and look ornery and lay for a chance to steal something" is "an analogue of the legendary flashes of temper with which Jackson is known to have frightened opponents into submission" (p. 570). Referring to Mark Twain's sentence quoted in the text and comparing the pup's under-jaw to a steamboat's fo'castle, Krause writes: "In addition to its suggesting the fearful union of savagery with avarice, the idea that Smiley's pup has caught the gambling fever also carries a lurking reference to the stories of Jackson's fabulous exploits in gaming" (pp. 570-571). I feel that this view is overstated.

[18] See, e.g., "The Evidence in the Case of Smith vs. Jones," *Golden Era,* 26 June 1864, p. 4, collected in *The Washoe Giant in San Francisco,* ed. Franklin Walker (San Francisco, 1938), p. 82.

[19] *Call,* 21 Aug. 1864, p. 2. A clipping of the item is in Moffett Scrapbook 5, p. 58, MTP. In "The Art and Satire . . . ," p. 573, Krause argues that the portrait of Dan'l the frog is Clemens' political satire of Daniel Webster, showing "how completely Twain had *done* Webster in almost every characterizing detail." It should be noted that Webster died in 1852 and that Clemens' few references to him prior to 1865 are not politically hostile. See *Mark Twain's Letters in the Muscatine Journal,* ed. Edgar M. Branch (Chicago, 1942), p. 20; Franklin R. Rogers, *The Pattern for Mark Twain's Roughing It* (Berkeley and Los Angeles, 1961), p. 35. I feel that Krause is unduly hard on Dan'l's integrity and accomplishment because he reads into him unflattering characteristics attributed to Daniel Webster the politician.

[20] "A Wrecking Party in Luck," *Call,* 3 Sept. 1864, p. 2.

[21] "California Branch of the U. S. Sanitary Commission," *Call,* 3

Sept. 1864, p. 1. The later *Call* item is "A Philanthropic Nation," 10 Sept. 1864, p. 1.

[22] TS of Notebook 3, p. 10, MTP.

[23] *Mark Twain: A Biography,* ed. A. B. Paine (New York, 1912), I, 277. Paine's chronology here is vague, but his account suggests that considerable time passed before Ward renewed his invitation and that even then Clemens delayed his composition of the tale.

[24] "An Inapt Illustration," Virginia Evening *Bulletin,* 28 Dec. 1863, as preserved in Notebook 4, Carton 3, Grant H. Smith Papers, Bancroft Library, Berkeley. Courtesy of the Bancroft Library.

[25] "A Voice for Setchell," *Californian,* 27 May 1865, p. 9. The article is signed "X" but is unmistakably by Clemens. The editor of the *Californian* hints broadly at the authorship, and a clipping of the piece is in Clemens' *Scrapbook of Newspaper Clippings . . . ,* Beinecke Library, Yale Univ. Reviewers of Setchell's acting often compared his manner and humor to Ward's. In June 1865 Setchell played the part of Ward in *Artemus Ward, Showman,* a three act play written for him by Fred G. Maeder and Thomas B. Macdonough.

[26] Jacob Blanck, *Bibliography of American Literature* (New Haven, Conn., 1955), I, 314, No. 1527. Blanck notes that ten years after Ward's book appeared his publisher gave 23 Sept. as the publication date. The listing of Ward's book as received in the 14 Oct. issue of the New York *Saturday Press* may indicate a later publication date. West Coast periodicals noticed the book in late Nov. and early Dec. James M. Cox (*Mark Twain: The Fate of Humor,* p. 32) believes, as I do, that Clemens wrote the "Jumping Frog" and his letter of 19 Oct. 1865 about the same time. My article was accepted for publication in its present form several months before I read Cox's excellent book.

[27] See n. 23. Clemens usually claimed that the tale reached George W. Carleton too late for inclusion in *Artemus Ward: His Travels,* although he contradicts this in *Mark Twain in Eruption,* ed. Bernard DeVoto (New York, 1940), p. 144. See *Letters,* I, 102; Yale *Scrap Book,* opposite clipping of the "Jumping Frog"; *Notebook,* p. 7. Henry Clapp's admiring editorial preface to the "Jumping Frog" in the *Saturday Press* of 18 Nov. barely hints that the tale was inserted at the last moment.

[28] From "A Defense of 'Jim Smiley and His Jumping Frog' . . . ," an unpublished seminar paper. In my comments on Smiley I am indebted to Mrs. Flory.

Paul C. Rodgers, Jr. (essay date 1973)

SOURCE: "Artemus Ward and Mark Twain's 'Jumping Frog'," in *Nineteenth Century Fiction,* Vol. 28, December, 1973, pp. 273-86.

[*In the following essay, Rodgers surveys some of the notable scholarly interpretations of Twain's jumping frog story before arguing that the sketch can be best understood in the context of Twain's relationship to the man to whom it was addressed: Artemus Ward.*]

Over the last four decades, students of Twain's **"Jumping Frog"** sketch of 1865 have made their chief advances by working outward from the dramatic center of the tale, shifting their attention from Jim Smiley and his fateful frog to the ambiguous figure of Simon Wheeler, Smiley's garrulous memorialist, and finally to Mark Twain himself, the frame narrator, who introduces Wheeler's monologue.[1] As the purview broadened, wheels within wheels came to light: unsuspected structural complexity, "unreliable" narration, rhetorical finesse of the first order, paradox and irony, the possibility of parabolic authorial self-scrutiny, even satire. For better or worse, if we still get a chuckle out of this old story, we chuckle now for new reasons.

Back in the 1930's, Bernard De Voto and Walter Blair were content to cite the sketch as a superb latter-day example of the traditional Southwestern frame story. As Blair noted, "The technique—in its use of various types of incongruity, in its revelation—was in essentials exactly the technique of T. B. Thorpe's 'Big Bear of Arkansas,' of the Sut Lovingood yarns, of dozens of frontier masterpieces."[2] Other scholars of the day adopted similar or complementary attitudes: Smiley was an "original," marvelously well done, and Wheeler was too; the story's peculiar charm lay in its being "the report of one oddity by another."[3] A commonplace folk tale of a commonplace type had "become literature" because Twain had restated it "in terms of recognizable human personalities."[4]

This general view and judgment sufficed for the 1940's. Then in 1950, Edgar M. Branch undertook the first extended critical analysis of the tale. Acknowledging its Southwestern derivation and felicitous rendering of Smiley and Wheeler, Branch pushed on (in a pregnant footnote) to consider the effect of Mark Twain's presence in the frame: "He pictures himself as a tolerant, good-natured listener, well aware of Wheeler's absurdity and the unconscious humor of his tale. He is also aware of the ridiculous position in which Artemus Ward has placed him. . . . The neutral tones of Mark Twain's personality and his correct and self-deprecatory speech form excellent contrasts with the language and personalities of Wheeler and Smiley."[5]

This passage posed intriguing questions. If Twain is well aware of Wheeler's absurdity and unconscious humor, why does he insist he was utterly bored? Furthermore, can we be certain that Wheeler's humor is indeed unconscious? Branch elsewhere observes that Ben Coon (Wheeler's real-life prototype) may have been "a master of the deadpan style who convinced his listeners that he lacked a sense of humor" (p. 122). And finally, since Twain pictures himself as unamused by what is obviously amusing, must we not distinguish between Twain-the-character and Twain himself—and somehow account for the discrepancy?

Paul Schmidt, in 1956, addressed himself to these questions. Twain, he announced, was definitely not identifying himself with Twain-the-character: in fact, he intended to show up "this sophisticated narrator with his local-colorist assumptions as an object of satire."[6] Wheeler is a deadpan humorist who "deliberately assumes the role of an unconscious barbarian as a play upon his visitor's preconceptions and with the intention of turning the tables on him" (p. 272). Thus the tale exploits the traditional conflict of East and West and "ultimately asserts the superiority of vernacular brotherhood over the competitive individualism which animates genteel attitudes" (p. 277). This interpretation attracted considerable attention during the next decade. Kenneth S. Lynn embraced it enthusiastically in 1959: ". . . in literary terms the **'Jumping Frog'** marks a historic reversal. The narrator, it turns out, is telling a joke on himself, not on the Clown. . . . The Southwestern tradition, in other words, has been stood on its head."[7] Frank Baldanza followed Lynn's lead in 1961, as did Sidney J. Krause in 1964.[8]

In other commentaries of the 1960's, Schmidt's thesis was set aside by critics who seemed weary of ambiguities, unacknowledged cultural conflict, and so on. Is Wheeler unconsciously funny, or is he pulling Twain's leg? James Cox flatly declared the question unanswerable.[9] Robert Regan concluded that the text means precisely what it says, that neither Twain nor Wheeler finds any cause for amusement in their conversation, and that "the point" of the story is that Twain is taken in by Ward's practical joke.[10] In the same year (1966), William C. Spengemann, while agreeing essentially with Regan, remarked that Twain-the-character's obtuseness constituted a significant technical innovation: "Instead of explicitly describing reality, as frame-story authors did, [Twain] lets the two speakers unconsciously suggest the real situation which they cannot perceive. The reliable narrator of the old frame tale has removed himself from the scene. . . ."[11] Twain's sketch, in sum, perhaps had achieved "the most sophisticated use of the framework device in nineteenth-century American humor,"[12] but its comic appeal was as transparent as it was potent. Smiley and his earthbound frog were purely and simply funny; the unselfconscious Wheeler was funny, too; and ditto for the impercipient Twain. In fact, the tale was funny from beginning to end and very easy to understand.

Yet the questions suggested by Branch's footnote still had not been dealt with to the satisfaction of all, and two scholars meanwhile had touched briefly on the possibility of answering them by recognizing yet another level of irony. Playing down Twain's debt to Southwestern tradition, Paul Baender interpreted the sketch (in 1963) as an effort to secure an essentially oral effect, that of the platform comedian's "humorous gravity." According to this view, not only is Wheeler's earnestness an assumed posture, reflecting the guile of the practiced humorist, but Mark Twain himself is in on the act: his puzzling sobriety is a calculated put-on designed "to exploit another natural advantage of the frame story, the advantage of double deadpan." Both narrators, in short, are dissembling.[13] A variation of this rather startling idea had been broached the year before by Pascal Covici, Jr., who further complicated matters by combining it with Schmidt's claim of an East-West antagonism: "[Twain] presents himself as the innocent victim of Simon Wheeler's poker-faced nonsense," but this is only pretense. Pen in hand, he "offers up his innocent self as the Green Easterner imposed upon by the Old Westerner, thus perpetrating a double poker face."[14]

The prime apparent difficulty of the double-deadpan school of thought—to which I subscribe—is that it calls upon the reader to visualize two men, strangers to one another, sitting alone together, both fully aware of the humorous absurdity of the narrative one of them is unfolding and both determined to conceal this awareness, each from the other. What on earth, one may ask, is supposed to be going on? From the standpoint of social possibility, the situation is almost inconceivable. Wheeler's motive is clear enough. As a consummate practitioner of the art of sober-faced, tall-tale narration, he is playing upon Twain's seeming credulity, leading his victim through thickets of increasingly absurd circumstantial detail to the point where truth must dawn and Twain discover himself the butt of an undeniably excellent joke. But what is Twain's motive? Every dead pan requires an audience. Twain is Wheeler's, but who is Twain's?

In the present paper, I shall argue that this problem vanishes the moment we recall the circumstances under which the original version of the story was inspired and prepared for publication, and that Twain's imposition of epistolary form upon the traditional frame story, his hazardous gamble on deadpan narration both in the frame and in the tale it encloses, and quite possibly some of his most deeply felt private meanings (parabolically expressed) may best be accounted for by reviewing what we know of his relationship with the man to whom the sketch is addressed: Artemus Ward.

Twain's direct association with Artemus Ward took place in Virginia City, Nevada, and was limited to a period of about ten days late in December 1863.[15] Ward was on tour, at the peak of his fame as a platform humorist. After delivering his lectures, he happily postponed his departure from day to day in the riotous company of Mark Twain and a select group of fellow bon vivants from the staff of the *Territorial Enterprise*. The two men became fast friends, and Ward soon was urging Twain to leave "sage-brush obscurity" and share his fortunes on the journey east; there was even talk of a joint invasion of Europe in May or June.[16] Recognizing the literary promise of a brother humorist, Ward counseled Twain to seek Eastern outlets for his work and scribbled a note of introduction to the editors of the New York *Sunday Mercury,* who responded by printing at least two of Twain's pieces within the next eight weeks.[17]

For his own part, Twain no doubt was electrified by the sheer fact of Ward's success as a humorist and impressed by his astute handling of the practical details of his career, but there is no evidence that Ward exerted any noteworthy influence, either by precept or example, upon Twain's literary plans or narrative style. On the other hand, Ward's oral platform manner, which Twain had ample opportunity to observe during Ward's three appearances at the Virginia City Melodeon, clearly inspired Twain's own approach to audiences when he took to the platform a few years later. Current scholarly opinion on the subject unhesitatingly affirms that Ward's influence in this regard was direct and profound. As a lecturer, writes Paul Fatout, Twain obviously was "a close student of Ward," to whose example he "owed" his own lecture technique.[18] Fred Lorch believes that Twain "consciously attempted to adapt [Ward's devices, techniques, and manner] to his own platform personality, materials, and purposes."[19] James Austin concludes that Twain's performances were "noticeably modeled" on Ward's: "the rambling digression, the calculated pause, the premeditated afterthought, the sober expression, and the pose of worried innocence were characteristic of both."[20] Twain evidenced his admiration of Ward when he described him as "America's greatest humorist" and "one of the greatest humorists of his age" in a lecture delivered in 1871,[21] and again in 1894, in "How to Tell a Story," where he cited Ward as an arch-practitioner of the art of the "humorous" story, orally told.

The point to be emphasized here is that Twain's brief exposure to Ward's oral techniques, especially the famous pose of comic innocence, made a deep, permanent impression. Ward had brought the deadpan manner to the lecture platform. In time, Twain would adapt it in various ways to the written page—with revolutionary effect upon his literary development.[22]

This revolution began quietly in the Jumping Frog story of 1865, and Artemus Ward apparently played a significant, though quite unconscious role in bringing it about. By late 1864, Ward had made arrangements with his publisher, George W. Carleton, to issue a collection of his sketches under the title *Artemus Ward: His Travels.* With characteristic generosity he wrote Twain, who by then was established in San Francisco, inviting him to contribute a sketch to the book. Receipt of the letters was long delayed, for Twain left the city on 4 December 1864 for a three-month sojourn at his friend Jim Gillis' remote log cabin on Jackass Hill in Tuolumne County. He did not return till 26 February 1865, and by then assumed it was too late to accept the offer. But work on the book progressed slowly, Ward himself was still preparing material as late as June,[23] and the invitation was renewed, possibly several times. Still, Twain delayed. **"Jim Smiley and His Jumping Frog"** probably was not written until the week of 16-23 October,[24] and reached New York (according to George Carleton, who may have opposed publication for editorial reasons) too late to be used in the book. Carleton passed the manuscript on to Henry Clapp, editor of the *Saturday Press,* who published it on 18 November 1865.

Thus the absent Ward must have figured often in Twain's thoughts between February and October 1865, and Twain's memories of Ward's platform technique had no doubt been quickened and reinforced at Jackass Hill by his host, Jim Gillis, an accomplished deadpan humorist who entertained him on rainy days with absurd impromptu narratives invariably set forth as "veracious history" in the traditional tall-tale manner.[25] Ben Coon, the garrulous old-timer whom Twain heard tell the jumping frog anecdote at nearby Angel's Camp, seems not to have shared the gift of Gillis' sly dead pan; but here again, the effect must surely have been to recall Ward's artistry. Twain relished Coon's unselfconscious sobriety as much as the substance of his story and may very well have imitated Coon

when he repeated the anecdote for Bret Harte (and possibly others) upon his return to San Francisco.[26]

Lacking firm historical evidence of any sort regarding the frog story's metamorphosis, we can only work backward from the text of October 1865, viewing it as the product of a series of necessary (though not necessarily fully conscious) choices, noting options Twain may have considered, endeavoring to assign reasonable motives for judgments made. Of particular significance are his decisions (1) to employ the frame-story structure, (2) to endow his primary narrator with Ward's deadpan platform manner, (3) to identify himself by name as the frame narrator, (4) to assume the deadpan manner himself in his role as frame narrator, and (5) to present the sketch as a signed letter addressed to Ward. Since most of these decisions appear to have involved others, it would not be realistic to suggest he dealt with any particular question apart from the rest, or developed his overall conception in clear-cut stages over an extended period of time. All the same, the decisions originated as solutions to structural and rhetorical problems that Twain must have regarded as distinct. And as I hope to show in the sequel, Ward's influence very probably figured in each case as an active determinant.

For example, Twain took a momentous step when he decided to equip his central narrator with Ward's famous pose of comic innocence; that is, to convert Ben Coon (the story's Simon Wheeler) from the literal-minded dullard he unquestionably was, into a skillful, poker-faced humorist like Gillis or the actor Fred Franks, whom Twain had praised in 1864—shortly after witnessing Ward's Virginia City performances—for possessing the "first virtue of a comedian, which is to do humorous things with grave decorum and without seeming to know that they are funny."[27]

To effect this conversion, Twain of course had to expand and intensify the absurdity of the original material. All existing evidence suggests that the Coon donnée dealt only with a quondam citizen of Angel's Camp named Coleman, who lost a bet on a frog filled with bird shot. Coon had presented the anecdote as "the gravest sort of history," and Twain accepted it as such.[28] In developing and establishing a literary context for the story, while at the same time making Wheeler's tongue-in-cheek attitude clear beyond all possibility of doubt, Twain had to construct a narrative that would gradually take leave of the real and the probable, stretch plausibility to its furthest limits, and venture finally (and frankly) into the realm of the fabulously absurd. The method used, as James Cox has noted, was characteristic of Twain's approach to humor, early and late: his way was always to "enlarge upon" actual fact, in pursuit of "remarkable fictions whose whole intention is to evoke the reader's suspicion of their veracity."[29] Thus Coleman's solitary wager gave rise to Jim Smiley's unquenchable thirst for betting, which in turn happily summoned visions of exploits, not only of a frog, but of a whole menagerie of remarkable animals. Most of the tale's preliminary "stretchers" were based on incidents culled from Twain's recent reportorial experiences in San Francisco.[30]

The resulting story met Twain's narrative requirements admirably. The reader launches forth in good faith, accepting what he reads as sober truth, but by the end of the opening paragraph, he recognizes Wheeler's game and settles down to enjoy himself. Any vestige of doubt disappears as implausibility gives way to sheer impossibility. A habitual gambler may be willing to lay odds on which of two perching birds will fly first, but it is plainly preposterous to suggest that such a gambler will follow a straddle-bug from north-central California all the way to Mexico to find out "how long he was on the road." Asthmatic horses may conceivably win races through sheer determination, but two-legged dogs simply do not come out to fight, nor do their defeated canine opponents die of brokenhearted disillusionment. Furthermore (I humbly submit), no jumping frog from Calaveras County has ever weighed anything approaching the five pounds of Smiley's estimate, regardless of metallic content. The tale Wheeler builds is beautifully, exquisitely "tall," yet it maintains its magical "aura of outrageous plausibility"[31] all the way. Wheeler is no mere purblind literalist like Ben Coon, but a past master of the oral art form perfected by Artemus Ward.

To grant Wheeler such prominence was to pose the linked questions of style and method of presentation. Here Twain may have paused to weigh his options, but the choice surely could not have been difficult. On the one hand, if he told the story entirely or primarily in the language of a genteel narrator, he would have to sacrifice the charm of Wheeler's backwoods phraseology. Alternatively, if he rendered it entirely in Wheeler's Pike County vernacular, he would risk identifying "Mark Twain," in his first appearance before a nationwide audience, with a style he currently regarded as subliterary.[32] Neither of these possibilities being fully acceptable or even attractive to him, the obvious solution was to set up a narrative frame in which a cultivated speaker, socially distinct from and superior to Wheeler, would report Wheeler's dialect accurately and at the requisite length.

Commitment to a frame, however, did not obligate Twain to name himself as the frame narrator. It was his further commitment to an epistolary frame-around-the-frame that propelled him into his own story. And this decision can best be accounted for by recalling his need to adapt his sketch to the context of Ward's projected book. It is not unreasonable to suppose that Ward actually recommended the letter form, but even if Ward offered no guidance, Twain was well enough acquainted with Ward's famous "letters" to infer that the new book, like its predecessor,[33] would reprint a good many of them. He could easily have concluded, without direction from Ward, that a letter addressed to "Mr. A. Ward" and signed "Mark Twain" would consort well with Ward's own materials.

Whatever the case, **"Jim Smiley and His Jumping Frog"** would have fitted smoothly into Ward's *Travels.* Part I of the book, which carries the appropriate title of "Miscellany," comprises fifteen items reprinted from *Vanity Fair.* Eleven of these affect the epistolary style, and seven are signed. Part II, a hodgepodge of anecdotes and impressions which Ward had gathered during his recent transcontinental tour, offers a semblance of narrative unity. Twain's sketch would not have belonged among these pieces. But Carleton could have inserted it without difficulty, possibly with a word or two of introduction from Ward, at the close of Part I. Thus the choice of epistolary form proved a wise one, and this choice in itself virtually dictated use of frame-story structure. Indeed, it is hard to avoid the conclusion that if Twain had had no previous knowledge of the frame story, he would have invented it in 1865 as a consequence of Ward's proposal.

Ward's influence may even have helped determine the pose Twain adopted within the frame. Here again, there were several options, each with its own consequences to be considered. He could picture himself as fully aware of Wheeler's humor, but only at the cost of short-circuiting the reader's own adventure in perception. This was precisely what Ward had taught him not to do, and the blunder would have been all the more atrocious if he had opened the letter by announcing he had an amusing tale to tell. A second possibility was to characterize himself as extremely gullible, stupid enough to accept Wheeler's claims at face value. One insuperable objection ruled this out: Wheeler's delightful absurdity was simply too patent to go unrecognized by anyone. Such abysmal blindness, seriously insisted upon, would not be credible; it would merely perplex the reader. What, then, if he should grant himself normal powers of perception but deny himself the least trace of a sense of humor? Here at last, perhaps, was a viable option—a fully percipient, utterly humorless Mark Twain. But why should he attempt such an unlikely creation when he could assume Ward's own characteristic platform pose and confront the old showman with a deadpan tour de force: the spectacle of a deadpan humorist solemnly recalling how a second deadpan humorist recalled how one deadpan gambler was outwitted by a second?

In the event, Twain settled upon this fourth possibility despite the clear risk of being misunderstood. Ward, he could be certain, would not misunderstand; Ward would be delighted, even dazzled. Beyond Ward were the readers of the book, an audience that presumably included many persons whom Ward had taught to anticipate just such a performance. They, too, would understand and enjoy—or at least some of them would. In any case, the other options were all so unpromising that he had little real choice in the matter, and he could solace himself with the thought that if the humor of the frame failed to register, the loss would be minor. He could count on Simon Wheeler's extravaganza to carry the day.

And this of course is what happened. Encountering the story outside the context of Ward's *Travels,* readers saw no special significance in the salutation to "Mr. A. Ward," failed to recognize Twain's tongue-in-cheek posture within the three-paragraph opening segment of the frame, and soon forgot the frame as they passed under the spell of the saga of Jim Smiley. Clearly, Twain's claims that he was bored "nearly to death" by Wheeler's "long and tedious" narrative were no more meant to be taken seriously than were Wheeler's outrageous assertions about Smiley; but they were not *intrinsically* ridiculous and were separated from the material they referred to by a thought-arresting gap in the text.[34] It was only too easy to respond to the suggestion of the title and regard the frame merely as a flat, short bridge to a brilliant tale about a gambler and a frog; the curious fact that an ostensibly bored, unamused, unmotivated[35] Mark Twain had seen fit to report the telling of this tale verbatim and at full length went unappreciated. Even rereading failed to clarify Twain's intention. Those who pondered the paradox in the frame concluded that he must be seriously picturing himself—for reasons by no means evident—as humorless or ultra-naïve, the butt of Wheeler's joke. Ward's function as Twain's audience was ignored.

But if the gamble on the frame failed to pay off, Twain himself was partly to blame, for in his role as narrator he introduced contradictions that blurred his self-portrait. After soberly denying in the first two paragraphs that he was amused by Wheeler's maunderings about Smiley, he remarks near the end of the third paragraph that Wheeler saw nothing "ridiculous or funny" about his story and then comments: "To me, the spectacle of a man drifting serenely along through such a queer yarn without ever smiling was exquisitely absurd." This passage is hard to account for, except as a sudden, illogical reversion to memories of his hour with the real Ben Coon. Conceivably it is a remnant of an oral recounting of the actual episode at Angel's Camp. Even more puzzling is Twain's failure to note and correct this lapse when he revised the sketch two years later for his first book, *The Celebrated Jumping Frog and Other Sketches* (1867). Here the anachronistic epistolary apparatus was removed, but the material quoted above survived inspection. Not until 1875, when he put the sketch through a second revision for *Mark Twain's Sketches, New and Old,* did he cut the offending sentence. And even then, the phrase "ridiculous or funny," with its anomalous implication that Wheeler *was* ridiculous or funny, continued to stand.

Artemus Ward thus appears to have exerted a decisive, albeit indirect and quite unconscious influence upon Twain's determinations regarding characterization, point of view, style, pace, tone, structure, and so on. What is less apparent is the role Ward assumes *within* the story if we follow Edgar Branch's intriguing suggestion and view the sketch as "an unwittingly articulated parable of Clemens' complex state of mind" in mid-October 1865.[36] As Branch points out, Twain was in debt at the time, his investments in certain mining properties were proving worthless, his dreams of gaining wealth and prominence in the West had by no means materialized. His only negotiable personal asset appeared at the moment to be his knack for turning out literature "of a low order," "nothing to be proud of"—i.e., popular humor.[37] On 19 October, in a letter to his brother Orion, he announced that henceforth he intended to strive for fame, "unworthy & evanescent though it must of necessity be," as a literary humorist.[38] The very language of the announcement, as Branch demonstrates, hints strongly at an "imaginative identification"

both with Ward's accomplishment and with Ward's professional goal, "the creation of beneficial laughter."[39]

Accordingly, it was precisely at a moment of resolution, when he was embarking upon a hazardous new professional commitment, that he undertook the Jumping Frog sketch. Like Smiley, he well knew the worth of desperate, last-minute effort (illustrated by Smiley's twelve-minute nag), and the crucial importance of natural talent (like that of the bull-pup Andrew Jackson), and the supreme value of "education" that supplements and refines talent (as in the case of the redoubtable Dan'l Webster). Knowing all this, self-scanned and momentarily self-secure, he was ready to lay his money on the line; though he also knew, as his story so delightfully demonstrates, that even the surest of bets can pay off in sudden disaster.

Moreover, he was preparing to wager not merely once on a crude backwoods anecdote,[40] but repeatedly on his command of the techniques of humorous narration. Smiley's lessons he had long since learned from life itself; the art of humor could be learned only by sitting in silence before a master storyteller like Simon Wheeler—or Artemus Ward, whose friendly interest in a mythical Rev. Leonidas W. Smiley prompted Twain's inquiry in the barroom at Angel's Camp and precipitated Wheeler's unforgettable performance. That the lesson was indeed unforgettable—this lesson Ward had arranged—Twain's story amply attests.

Notes

[1] The original version of the sketch, which appeared on 18 November 1865, in the New York *Saturday Press,* opens as a letter addressed to "Mr. A. Ward" and closes with the signature "Mark Twain." Twain thus identifies himself by name as the frame narrator. In the present essay I shall cite Franklin J. Meine, ed., *Jim Smiley and His Jumping Frog,* by Mark Twain (n.p.: Pocahontas Press, 1940), which accurately reproduces the *Saturday Press* text.

[2] Walter Blair, *Native American Humor* (1937; rpt. San Francisco: Chandler, 1960), p. 156. De Voto's discussion appeared in *Mark Twain's America* (Boston: Little, Brown, 1932).

[3] Minnie Brashear, *Mark Twain, Son of Missouri* (Chapel Hill: Univ. of North Carolina Press, 1934), p. 44.

[4] DeLancey Ferguson, *Mark Twain: Man and Legend* (Indianapolis: Bobbs-Merrill, 1943), p. 104.

[5] *The Literary Apprenticeship of Mark Twain* (Urbana: Univ. of Illinois Press, 1950), p. 294, n. 19.

[6] "The Deadpan on Simon Wheeler," *Southwest Review,* 41 (1956), 271.

[7] *Mark Twain and Southwestern Humor* (Boston: Little, Brown, 1959), p. 146.

[8] Frank Baldanza, *Mark Twain: An Introduction and Interpretation,* American Authors and Critics Series (New York: Barnes & Noble, 1961), pp. 32-33; S. J. Krause, "The Art and Satire of Twain's

'Jumping Frog' Story," *AQ*, 16 (1964), 566. Schmidt's thesis has been ably criticized by Paul Baender, "The 'Jumping Frog' as a Comedian's First Virtue," *MP*, 60 (1963), 197, and by James M. Cox, *Mark Twain: The Fate of Humor* (Princeton, N.J.: Princeton Univ. Press, 1966), pp. 29-30.

[9] Cox, p. 30.

[10] *Unpromising Heroes: Mark Twain and His Characters* (Berkeley: Univ. of California Press, 1966), pp. 38-39.

[11] *Mark Twain and the Backwoods Angel: The Matter of Innocence in the Works of Samuel L. Clemens,* Kent Studies in English (Kent, Ohio: Kent State Univ. Press, 1966), p. 6.

[12] James C. Austin, *Artemus Ward,* United States Authors Series (New York: Twayne, 1964), p. 76.

[13] Baender, p. 194. I may not have stated Baender's position accurately. Elsewhere he appears to contradict or qualify the passage quoted above: ". . . what the narrator claims to be dull turns out amusing, and the discrepancy of responses is so through as to suggest an opposition of tempers, not just of moods. The narrator and Simon Wheeler represent the sober and the rigid, we say (recalling our Bergson), while we are the volatile and sensitive, for whom the humorous sketch is an exclusive reward of perception" (p. 196). In this statement Baender seems to align himself with Regan and Spengemann.

[14] *Mark Twain's Humor: The Image of a World* (Dallas: Southern Methodist Univ. Press, 1962), p. 51. Covici goes on to remark that "the reader must detect Twain-the-writer's unspoken contempt for Twain-the-character's inability to appreciate Simon Wheeler's yarn for what it is" (p. 51). Here he differs sharply from the position attributed to Baender above.

[15] Austin, pp. 112, 130, n. 14; Henry Nash Smith, ed., with the assistance of Frederick Anderson, *Mark Twain of the "Enterprise": Newspaper Articles & Other Documents 1862-1864* (Berkeley: Univ. of California Press, 1957), pp. 111, 127.

[16] Albert Bigelow Paine, *Mark Twain: A Biography* (New York: Harper, 1912), I, 244; Samuel Charles Webster, ed., *Mark Twain, Businessman* (Boston: Little, Brown, 1946), p. 80.

[17] "Doings in Nevada," 7 February 1864, and "Those Blasted *Children,*" 21 February 1864. See Fred W. Lorch, *The Trouble Begins at Eight: Mark Twain's Lecture Tours* (Ames: Iowa State Univ. Press, 1968), pp. 14, 334, n. 29. Paul Fatout mentions a third title, "For Sale or to Rent," also in the issue of 7 February (*Mark Twain in Virginia City* [Bloomington: Indiana Univ. Press, 1964], p. 131).

[18] *Mark Twain on the Lecture Circuit* (Bloomington: Indiana Univ. Press, 1960), pp. 199, 153. For specific borrowings, see pp. 47, 78, 85, 130.

[19] Lorch, p. 17.

[20] Austin, p. 114.

[21] Lorch, pp. 297, 298.

[22] Austin, p. 114.

[23] "Agriculture" (Ch. 15) in *Artemus Ward: His Travels* is dated 12 June 1865.

[24] Edgar M. Branch, "'My Voice Is Still for Setchell': A Background Study of 'Jim Smiley and His Jumping Frog,'" *PMLA*, 82 (1967), 599.

[25] Bernard De Voto, ed., *Mark Twain in Eruption: Hitherto Unpublished Pages about Men and Events by Mark Twain,* 3rd ed. (New York: Harper, 1940), p. 361.

[26] Margaret Duckett, *Mark Twain and Bret Harte* (Norman: Univ. of Oklahoma Press, 1964), pp. 8-9.

[27] Branch, *Apprenticeship,* p. 122.

[28] Mark Twain, "Private History of the 'Jumping Frog' Story," in *The Man That Corrupted Hadleyburg and Other Stories and Essays* (New York: Harper, 1901), pp. 376, 377.

[29] Cox, p. 22.

[30] Branch, "Background Study," pp. 591-97.

[31] Covici, p. 50.

[32] Franklin R. Rogers, *Mark Twain's Burlesque Patterns as Seen in the Novels and Narratives 1855-1885* (Dallas: Southern Methodist Univ. Press, 1960), p. 18.

[33] *Artemus Ward: His Book* (New York: Carleton, 1862) is made up almost entirely of letters-to-the-editor reprinted from the Cleveland *Plain Dealer* and *Vanity Fair* (see Austin, p. 70). In 1863, upon the eve of Ward's arrival in Virginia City, Twain prepared an item for the *Enterprise* in which he quoted a bogus letter from Ward. The letter demonstrates Twain's familiarity with Ward's work; it is typically Wardian both in conception and style. See Ivan Benson, *Mark Twain's Western Years* (1938; rpt. New York: Russell & Russell, 1966), p. 97.

[34] Twain intensified the effect of the extra space by inserting a long, centered horizontal line. Wheeler's monologue is thus set off as an independent block of narrative. It is not enclosed by quotation marks.

[35] Twain has no reason to supply Ward with information about *Jim* Smiley. Furthermore, since he suspects that the Rev. Leonidas W. Smiley is a "myth" and that Ward has played a trick on him by sending him to Simon Wheeler, he has good reason *not* to rehearse the details of Wheeler's story.

[36] Branch, "Background Study," p. 600. In this and the following paragraph, I have drawn heavily upon Branch's excellent article.

[37] Frederick Anderson, ed., *My Dear Bro: A Letter from Samuel Clemens to His Brother Orion* (Berkeley: Univ. of California Press, 1961), p. 6.

[38] Ibid., p. 8.

[39] Branch, "Background Study," p. 598.

[40] On 20 January 1866, in a letter to his mother, Twain contemptuously referred to the Jumping Frog story as a "villainous backwoods sketch" (Albert Bigelow Paine, ed., *Mark Twain's Letters* [New York: Harper, 1917], I, 101). Many explanations have been offered for this ironic outburst. To these I will add yet another: that he realized his experiment with deadpan narration in the frame had not succeeded and to his chagrin now found himself associated with purveyors of "low" frontier humor. Paul Baender takes a similar view: ". . . he felt he had reverted to frontier type in spite of efforts to raise himself to a higher literary class. He had not merely imitated the southwestern convention but had fallen back to the real thing" (p. 198).

Lawrence R. Smith (essay date 1978)

SOURCE: "Mark Twain's 'Jumping Frog': Toward an American Heroic Ideal," in *Mark Twain Journal,* Vol. XIX, No. 2, pp. 15-18.

[*In the following essay, Smith contends that Twain's purpose in the story is "to define and explore what is true and valuable about Simon Wheeler" and the particularly American qualities he represents.*]

Mark Twain's **"Jumping Frog"**[1] has been at the center of a critical controversy in recent years. This controversy focuses on one major question. Is the story satiric, with Simon Wheeler as a deadpan trickster making fun of the narrator, or is it simply a wild yarn told by a mindless yokel? Interpretations and claims for the story have varied widely. Some have argued that the **"Jumping Frog"** is the summation of Twain's faith in frontier democracy,[2] while others have held that it is no more than an amusing story, told in an "exquisitely absurd" manner.[3] A close examination of the structure and the component parts of the story itself, rather than argumentation in the abstract realms of cultural history and philosophy, indicates that the **"Jumping Frog"** is a great deal more than a yarn well told. Furthermore, it is more than a simple celebration of "vernacular" heroes and frontier democracy. Twain not only transcends the tradition of the Southwestern humorous frame story, from which the **"Jumping Frog"** is derived, he also passes beyond any narrow ideological statement. He has attempted to create a work that is broad and all-encompassing in its scope. In the encounter between the narrator and Simon Wheeler, Twain sets up a confrontation between the false and the true. As it happens, this is the classic confrontation between the "Whig gentleman" and the "vernacular" character. However, even this factor is not as vital to the meaning of the story as the larger conflict between the false and the true. It is Twain's main purpose to define and explore just what is true and valuable about Simon Wheeler and the qualities he represents. Relatively little time is spent in the deflation of the pretentious narrator; most of the story concerns Jim Smiley, his animals, and the stranger. It is here that Twain, through Simon Wheeler, creates an American heroic ideal. This ideal cannot be defined by such limiting terms as "vernacular," "frontier," "rural," or "western." The names of Smiley's two heroic animals, Andrew Jackson and Daniel Webster, reinforce the broadness and lack of regionality in Twain's vision. Yankee shrewdness and the East, conveyed by recalling the legendary Daniel Webster, are as much a part of the ideal Twain is defining as the frontier democracy represented by Andrew Jackson. Moreover, even the idealistic amalgam created by the Webster and Jackson images, and even the ideals represented by the optimistic gambler himself, are tempered by Smiley's deception at the hands of the stranger. What results from the whole tale is a synthesis of the best American traits: shrewdness, a spirit of enterprise and aspiration in Jim Smiley and his animals, and in the stranger the skeptical pragmatism necessary to keep the other characteristics within a useful and realistic framework. Simon Wheeler, as an American Homer, sings the praises of these heroes and the ideals they embody. Even if the narrator could never recognize these men or the traits for which they stand as heroic, Twain certainly does.

The **"Jumping Frog"** could be described as the ultimate example of a genre of Southwestern humor, both in its complexity and in its sophistication. The tradition of a rural character duping and deflating the pretentious, smug city gentleman has been multiplied into an ingenious system of layers: a trick within a trick within a trick. Simon Wheeler tells the story of Jim Smiley, a trickster himself, being tricked by a stranger, and at the same time Wheeler makes a fool of the frame narrator. Twain is ripening the narrative "I" for his deflation from the moment the story begins. The "gentleman" obviously considers himself wellbred and eloquent, but such elaborate constructions as "In compliance with the request of a friend of mine" and "I hereunto append the result" characterize the man as a prig. His attempts at stylistic flourish are pretentious; he is the stereotyped "genteel traveller" which Twain ridiculed throughout his career. It is noteworthy that the false quality of the narrator's style is immediately connected with the clergy, when we find that he is looking for a Rev. Leonidas W. Smiley. The fact that he has an inflated self-image is further reinforced by the two stilted phrases associated with the mention of the clergyman: "a cherished companion of his boyhood" and "a young minister of the Gospel."[4] Twain could have easily contrasted the genteel and the vernacular simply by stressing the difference between the names, "Leonidas" and "Jim," but he chose to exaggerate the disparity by making the fictitious "Leonidas" a clergyman. Twain's lifelong association of the clergy, Protestant or Catholic, with the most foolish pretense and hypocrisy hardly needs comment. The narrator's attitude is also conveyed by his obvious condescension for Simon Wheeler, whom he describes as "good-natured," "garrulous," full of "winning gentleness and simplicity," "tranquil," "fat and bald-headed." In other words, Wheeler is depicted as the stereotyped yokel as seen through the eyes of polite urban society: homely, lazy, mindless, and most important, harmless good fun. However, even before the tale begins, Twain hints that this superior attitude may not be justified. Old Wheeler's influence soon renders the narrator a helpless captive: "he backed me into a corner and blocked me there with a chair." The old timer is far from tranquil and passive. His irresistible presence is reminiscent of Coleridge's ancient mariner's hold over the unwary wedding guest.

The narrator further displays his lack of perception and his misapplied condescension in evaluating the yarn and Simon Wheeler's narrative manner. He calls the Jim Smiley story insignificant, "monstrous," "queer," and yet its implications, both for him and for American society as a whole, are monumental. He also finds the unemotional delivery of the old timer amusing, in fact, "exquisitely absurd." However, this only indicates that he has not recognized the traditional deadpan delivery of the rural character, and thus is properly ripe for being taken in. It should also be noticed that the narrator only thinks the manner of the telling "absurd," not the tale itself, and thus is unaware that Simon Wheeler is making fun of his ignorance of country life. The old miner's attribution of impossible characteristics to Daniel Webster the frog, and nevertheless convincing the narrator that they are normal, becomes his masterpiece of satirical one-up-manship.

Twain demonstrates Wheeler's awareness and his satirical nature at the beginning of the yarn. These qualities had to be established before the significance of the Jim Smiley story could be perceived. Simon Wheeler seems to fit the narrator's condescending characterization as he starts his tale with a digression, and continues with a long-winded list of examples of Jim Smiley's willingness to bet. However, he does not wait long before he launches his first barb. When we hear that Jim Smiley went to Parson Walker's "camp meetings" regularly in order to bet, we are puzzled. Does he bet on the length of the sermon, the number of conversions, or the number of furtive defections? Yet the ambiguity works well, because any interpretation is at the expense of Parson Walker and the clergy in general. It is only as Wheeler continues with the story of the straddlebug that we realize that Parson Walker has been included in a long list of animals, hierarchically arranged by size and importance, with the good parson only slightly above the bugs. Smiley's bet that Mrs. Walker will not recover from her grave illness, after the Parson's pious platitudes "thank the Lord for his inf'nit mercy" and "with the blessing of Prov'dence," only reinforces the mockery. At first glance this satiric jab at the clergy may seem gratuitous, but one has only to remember that the pretentious interloper, the narrator, is searching for a Rev. Leonidas W. Smiley. Furthermore, the narrator has been more than a little vain and pompous about his pious attitude toward the "young minister of the Gospel." The "simple" Simon Wheeler has already turned the tables on the man who had been so confident about his superiority. The old timer could hardly help being aware that jokes at the expense of the clergy, especially the sardonic joke about the death of the Parson's wife, would be highly unacceptable to the listener, who considers himself polite and well-bred. There should be no question as to whether this is Wheeler's humor or Twain's, because the mouthpiece for the author's satire is clearly aware of what he is doing.

After putting the narrator in his place,[5] Simon Wheeler continues his narrative with the stories of three of Jim Smiley's famous animals: the diseased mare, the bulldog pup, and the frog. All of these animals share one trait in common with their master: the ability to hustle suckers. Each one of his betting animals appears so unimposing,

even to the extent of feigning disadvantage in a contest, that it is easy for Jim to run up a large bet before winning and sweeping the board. Like the unimposing Simon Wheeler, Jim and his animals prefer to look harmless, hiding their wit and power until the proper moment. They forego a desire for, or a trust in, show and appearance for the superior benefits of strategy. It is important for us to realize that this trait characterizes Simon Wheeler as well as all of those whom he praises as heroes. Furthermore, it characterizes an entire segment of American society, the part which is diametrically opposed to the false concerns and values which the narrator represents. The "fifteen-minute" asthmatic nag looks so bad that the bettors offer Jim an absurdly large handicap, and consequently his horse always wins with her final burst of spirit and effort. Andrew Jackson, the pup with talent and genius, can feign utter helplessness and take a beating until the bets are high enough, and then win easily by sheer tenacity. Unfortunately, he and Jim meet their match (a portent of the stranger's quail shot in the frog trick) when someone puts up a dog with no hind legs, thus removing Andrew's "pet holt." Nonetheless, the story of the dog, even in its heartbroken defeat, is heavy with significance for Simon Wheeler. Andrew proves that even the humble can have genius, and given opportunity, anyone "can make a name for hisself." In other words, the dog is true to his name, an embodiment of the leveling ideals of Jacksonian democracy. Like the "enterprising vagabond" Jim Smiley, the bull pup finds his opportunity in the most mundane sources. This is a talent which his namesake, the legendary "Old Hickory," would certainly endorse. In an unpublished essay entitled "On Progress, Civilization, Monarchy, etc.", written by Twain a little over ten years after the **"Jumping Frog,"** he openly praises the American ideal the bull pup symbolizes:

> What I mean by Manhood . . . is a condition where all roads to betterment are public highways, not free to one and forbidden to another; where equal capacities have an equal chance . . . where a man's origin counts nothing for him and nothing against him; where a man is not a god because he was born in a church, nor a corpse because he was born in a graveyard, but is just a man in both instances—no more, no less.[6]

In this essay, Twain sees America as being far superior to the older, more traditional England. His vision of "Manhood" here points directly to the qualities for which Wheeler, Smiley, and his animals stand. Civilization is farther advanced by the values they represent than it is by all the pretensions to culture and refinement indicated by the narrator's stance.

The dog's anthropomorphic attributes are amusing, but Jim Smiley's theory of education, expounded in the story of Dan'l Webster the frog, is an even deeper exploration of this humorous vein. Here we are clearly in the realm of animal fable, where human characteristics are put into ironic perspective by applying them to common animals. However, Twain elaborates upon the tradition of the humorous animal fable by associating it with the tradition of the rural character's trick on the city gentleman. Twain applies human characteristics to Dan'l, but he multiplies the humor by also attributing the characteristics of other animals to the talented frog. Simon Wheeler's description of the frog could only be acceptable to a man who had never seen one, or at least had not looked at one very carefully. Thus, the ridiculous attributions are directed precisely at the ignorance of the narrator. Wheeler says that Dan'l sits "modestly . . . scratching the side of his head with his hind foot" after an amazing feat of fly-catching. Anyone who has ever watched a frog knows that it, unlike a cat or dog, cannot scratch its head with its hind foot. Evidently, though, the narrator is not aware of the discrepancy. Later we hear that the frog is filled with shot "up to his chin," but chins are difficult to find on frogs. Still later Wheeler mentions that Jim Smiley picked up the frog "by the nap of his neck." In case the humor of this statement escapes the reader, it is immediately reinforced by Smiley's exclamatory "blame my cats." The association is inevitable; we see the ridiculous image of a frog being picked up like a cat. The primary thrust of all these misattributions is to "impose on" the credulity and ignorance of the citified narrator. However, the amusing attribution of human and other traits to the bulldog pup and the frog has another important function. By making the ideal qualities which Dan'l and Andrew represent amusing, Twain subtly undercuts them. Jim Smiley's very name suggests his unbounded optimism about the opportunities of the common man in America. He and his animals represent shrewdness and self-reliance, but most of all they stand for the aspiration of the American. Using the humorous animal fable devices and the story about the stranger's trick, Twain warns his audience against being too sanguine about the validity of these ideals.

If the animal representation of admirable American qualities undermines them by causing us to laugh, it remains for the stranger to give our faith in them at least a temporary setback. Like other strangers in Twain's later works, such as the clever avenger in **"The Man Who Corrupted Hadleyburg"** and Satan in *The Mysterious Stranger,* this stranger is a dispenser of reality therapy. The stranger in the **"Jumping Frog"** does not destroy the ideals which have been established before his appearance in the story, but he necessitates a reevaluation, and perhaps a tempering of extravagant optimism. When the stranger asks Smiley what is in his box, the gambler replies with his usual device of understatement. Yet after implicitly comparing it to the exotic parrot and canary, Smiley clearly swells with pride as he announces that the box contains a homegrown product, "only" a humble American frog. Jim Smiley's faith in Dan'l and all that he represents is so great that he lowers his guard and leaves the box with the stranger, a mistake one would hardly expect from a horseracing expert. The stranger is not blinded by any such pride or idealism; as a backwoods pragmatist he seizes the opportunity and fixes the outcome of the match. In order to increase Smiley's humiliation, the stranger emphasizes the significance of Dan'l's defeat: "Well, I don't see no p'ints about that frog that's any better'n any other frog." The apparently infinite room for expansion and aspiration for the common American man, or frog, has been abruptly limited.

At the end of Simon Wheeler's tale, however, the victory is not at all one-sided. Even the narrator is able to perceive, in his introduction the yarn, that there are two heroes of "transcendant genius" in the **"Jumping Frog"** story: Jim Smiley as well as the stranger Smiley is similar to his talented bulldog pup; he is glorious in defeat. Never for a moment do we expect that this temporary setback will shake his optimism or put an end to his enterprising spirit. Nevertheless, the incident with the stranger has challenged the American ideal of the shrewd, aspiring common man, which Twain has presented through an amalgam of the images of Daniel Webster and Andrew Jackson. This challenge is so powerful that we can no longer be complacent about the total validity of the ideal. It is only functional and worthwhile as an ideal if it is combined with a healthy portion of the skepticism, realistic outlook, and prgamatism of the stranger. The synthesis, however, is not out of reach; the all-encompassing vision of the old miner indicates that. Simon Wheeler, as an American Homer, sings the praises of both Jim Smiley and the stranger in his illustration of a complex American heroic ideal. The synthesis is artistic; it is in Wheeler's clever narration that we see its culmination.

In spite of the multileveled significance of the yarn, it is clear that the narrator has not benefited at all from listening to the old timer, nor has he begun to understand the significance of the yarn as a parable for himself and the rest of America. On the contrary, his pretentious facade, and the continuing disparity between reality and his perception of it, is just as great at the end of the story as it was at the beginning. His lack of change is demonstrated when the narrator tells us that the parting angry curse "Oh! hang Smiley and his afflicted cow!" is only a "good-natured" adieu.[7] Far from understanding Simon Wheeler's depiction of the many faceted American ideal, the narrator has not even made the first step toward dropping his pretensions of polite good-breeding and gentility.

Notes

[1] The text used in this essay is "The Celebrated Jumping Frog of Calaveras County," from *The Celebrated Jumping Frog of Calaveras County and Other Sketches* (New York: C.H. Webb, 1867).

[2] See Paul Schmidt, "The Deadpan on Simon Wheeler," *Southwest Review,* XLI (Summer, 1956). Kenneth S. Lynn, in *Mark Twain and Southwestern Humor* (Boston, 1959), generally concurs with Schmidt's reading.

[3] Paul Baender, in "The 'Jumping Frog' as a Comedian's First Virtue," *Modern Philology,* LX, No. 3 (February, 1963) provides more evidence for this traditional reading than most of his predecessors.

[4] Henry Nash Smith explores the stylistic implications of false or assumed piety in *Mark Twain: the Development of a Writer* (Cambridge: Harvard Univ. Press, 1962). See especially "Two Ways of Viewing the World," the introductory chapter.

[5] Even though the narrator is never aware that he is the target of Wheeler's satire, or indeed that there is any satire at all, he is

clearly irritated by the old timer's lack of moral and artistic decorum. This serves just as well as an outright humiliation to put him at a disadvantage.

6 This passage is quoted from an unpublished manuscript in the Mark Twain Papers (Paine 102b, pp. 8, 23-6) by Roger B. Salomon in *Twain and the Image of History* (New Haven: Yale Univ. Press, 1961), p. 28. Salomon also includes a lengthy discussion of Twain's faith in America as the place where man could reach his ultimate perfection, and how this early belief was later modified.

7 This appears for the first time in the 1867 edition, as well as other comments of the narrator in his introduction to the tale.

John C. Gerber (essay date 1988)

SOURCE: "San Francisco: Literary Burlesques and 'The Celebrated Jumping Frog of Calaveras County'," in *Mark Twain,* Twayne, 1988, pp. 15-18.

[*In the following excerpt from a book-length critical study of Twain's work, Gerber outlines the frog story's circumstances of composition and remarks that the narrators, rather than the anecdote itself, are the central elements of the story.*]

Except for three months spent in the Tuolumne Hills, Mark Twain lived in San Francisco from May 1864 to March 1866. It was not one of the happiest periods of his life. Of necessity he took a job as local reporter with the *Morning Call,* the "washerwoman's paper." Most of what he wrote for the *Call* was routine reporting. But as daily contact with the sour underbelly of city life strengthened his impatience with cruelty and corruption, his treatment of such topics as street crime and police court procedures increasingly sharpened into satire.

As soon as he could, he left the *Call* and began to write for two literary journals, the *Californian* and the *Dramatic Chronicle.* These arrangements improved his income and provided a chance to write literary sketches and burlesques. Some twenty of the sketches he wrote for the *Californian* appeared while Bret Harte was editor. Twain later told T. B. Aldrich that Harte changed him from "an awkward utterer of coarse grotesquenesses to a writer of paragraphs and chapters that have found a certain favor in the eyes of even some of the very decentest people in the land."[19] Few have been able to detect such a splendid debt to Harte. In fact, Franklin R. Rogers argues that Twain owed more to Charles Henry Webb, another editor of the *Californian.* Rogers believes that Webb was especially helpful in getting Twain to drop what remained of his bumpkin style and to play more imaginatively with the sounds and rhythms of his words.[20]

Neither Harte nor Webb, however, cured Twain of his grotesqueries—if indeed they tried—for his sketches in the San Francisco weeklies were probably the silliest stuff he ever turned out: farces, burlesques, and, an old favorite, attacks on a rival editor. In one lampoon of advice to the lovelorn he recommended to a correspondent named Aurelia that she do the best she could under the circumstances though her lover had lost his smooth complexion, one leg, both arms, an eye, the other leg, and his scalp.[21]

By late 1865 Mark Twain was fed up with San Francisco. Once more Steve Gillis brought matters to a head. Arrested for taking part in a barroom brawl, he asked Twain to supply the bail bond. When Twain complied, Gillis skipped town. So did Twain, though it is not clear whether he feared the police or simply wanted fresh adventure. He left San Francisco with Jim Gillis, Steve's brother, for Jim's cabin on Jackass Hill in the Tuolomne Hills. They arrived there on 4 December, and Twain stayed until late February. Although he occasionally panned for gold with Gillis, Dick Stoker, and others, the stay on Jackass Hill was more important for him as a refresher course in Southwestern yarn-spinning. Gillis was a master storyteller,[22] and so were the locals with whom they swapped yarns in the tavern at Angel's Camp on rainy afternoons. One afternoon they heard a solemn duffer named Ben Coon tell a story about a frog that lost a jumping contest because his belly had been filled with shot by the owner of a competing frog.[23] Coon related the anecdote as though he were reciting statistics, offering no indication that he thought there was anything the least funny about it. Later, back on Jackass Hill, Twain and Gillis kept quoting from the yarn and laughing over it. What tickled them was not the yarn itself so much as Ben Coon's grave manner in telling it.

In late February Twain returned to San Francisco, where he found waiting for him a request from Artemus Ward, then in New York, for a sketch that Ward could include in a collection on travel in Nevada. Twain wrote back that he could not possibly meet Ward's deadline, but Ward persisted, and after still more delay Twain responded with **"Jim Smiley and His Jumping Frog,"** cast as a letter to Ward.[24] Although it arrived too late to be included in the collection, Ward liked it so well that he gave it to Henry Clapp, who published it in his *Saturday Press* for 18 November 1865. Immediately, with allowance for the hyperbole, it "set all New York in a roar,"[25] and did the same in San Francisco when Bret Harte reprinted it in the *Californian.* Soon, as it began appearing in other papers throughout the country, "Mark Twain" became a name known nationwide.

The **"Jumping Frog"** is probably Mark Twain's most firmly organized sketch. For its basic structure he borrowed the frame device that other Southwestern humorists commonly used to introduce and close stories told as oral tales. Thus in the introduction to his tale Mark Twain tells how he encountered a garrulous old fellow named Simon Wheeler in the decaying mining village of Angel's Camp, and in the conclusion he relates his difficulty in breaking away from Wheeler, who was set to talk for hours. Between these two parts of the "frame," Twain without interruption lets Wheeler spin a long yarn about a Jim Smiley. This overall organization is clear enough; less obvious is the tight control the author keeps on Wheeler's monologue, which on the surface seems wholly directionless. Actually, it is carefully molded for climax. After identifying

Smiley as a man who would bet on anything, Wheeler offers a series of examples, moving from the most common thing to bet on (horse racing) to something quite uncommon (the health of Parson Walker's wife). He repeats this climactic pattern in telling about the pets that Smiley kept for betting purposes, again moving from the ordinary (a nag) to the less ordinary (a bull pup) to the least ordinary (a frog he had trained to jump). To heighten the sense of progression Wheeler provides more details about the bull pup than he does about the nag, more about the frog than he does about the pup. The high spot comes when the frog, secretly filled with buckshot, can do no more than "hyst" his shoulders when commanded to jump. The sketch is three fifths over before the original frog story surfaces.

In centering his story on his narrators rather than on the jumping contest, Twain turns the old joke into a comic character study. He focuses, as he later said all humorists should do, on the manner of telling rather than on the matter of what is told.[26] In this instance, he focuses on two quite different manners. In the frame story he assumes the persona of an educated but stuffy visitor to Angel's Camp who at the request of a friend from the East is looking for the Reverend Leonidas W. Smiley. He is obviously miffed because he suspects that there is no Reverend Smiley there, and that his friend (Artemus Ward in the first version of the story) has deliberately sent him on a fool's errand so that he will be cornered by Simon Wheeler and have to listen to an interminable account of Jim Smiley. As narrator of the frame Mark Twain writes a stiff, literal, and bureaucratic style that serves dramatically as a foil for the richly figurative vernacular of the main story. As Simon Wheeler, narrator of the main story, Twain pretends to be an old loafer who in his simple and earnest way loves nothing more than regaling a new listener with his oft-repeated yarns. Basic to the fun, then, is the incongruity between the two points of view and the two styles that result. But an additional incongruity enhances the fun, and that is the contrast between the contents of Wheeler's yarn and his manner of telling it. Like Ben Coon, Wheeler is totally unconscious of anything ridiculous in the accomplishments of Jim Smiley. Wheeler thinks Smiley a person of transcendent genius, and tells about him with the gravity and earnestness ordinarily reserved for the relating of great events. Similarly, he views the frog with awe and wonderment. The persona of Simon Wheeler thus forces Mark Twain into doing what he would always do best, tell about ridiculous happenings gravely and in the vernacular. Twenty years later another earnest and humorless persona would result in *Adventures of Huckleberry Finn*.

In San Francisco, in the spring of 1866, though, Mark Twain was far from optimistic about his future. He wrote daily letters to the *Territorial Enterprise,* and started jabbing so vigorously at corruption in San Francisco that readers began viewing him as a reformer as well as a humorist. Yet he could not suppress the notion that he had committed himself to writing of a low order. In such a mood he could call even the **"Jumping Frog"** story a "villainous backwoods sketch." "Verily," he wrote his mother, "all is vanity and little worth—save piloting."[27]

Notes

[19] *Mark Twain's Letters* (New York, 1917), 1: 182-83.

[20] Franklin R. Rogers, *Mark Twain's Burlesque Patterns* (Dallas, 1960), 22-25.

[21] *Early Tales and Sketches,* 2:91-93.

[22] Mark Twain, for example, owed "Baker's Blue-jay Yarn" and "The Burning Shame" to Gillis.

[23] In different versions the anecdote had been a favorite for years among yarnspinners, and had even appeared in print in *The Spirit of the Times* and at least two California newspapers. See Walter Blair, *Native American Humor* (New York, 1937), 156. There is no reason to suppose, however, that Mark Twain knew the story before hearing Ben Coon tell it.

[24] Originally entitled "Jim Smiley and his Jumping Frog" (*Early Tales and Sketches,* 2:282-88), Mark Twain changed the title of the sketch to "The Celebrated Jumping Frog of Calaveras County" in the version included in his first book, *The Celebrated Jumping Frog of Calaveras County, and other Sketches* (New York, 1867). The title has also appeared as "The Notorious Jumping Frog of Calaveras County." After the initial publication Mark Twain dropped the salutation to Artemus Ward.

[25] Quoted from the *Alta California* in *Early Tales and Sketches,* 2:271.

[26] The statement occurs in "How to Tell a Story," first published in *Youth Companion,* 3 October 1895. For a detailed explanation of how this story exemplifies Mark Twain's theory of humorous storytelling, see Paul Baender, "The 'Jumping Frog' as a Comedian's First Virtue." *Modern Philology* 60 (February 1963): 192-200.

[27] *Mark Twain's Letters,* 1:101.

Bruce Michelson (essay date 1995)

SOURCE: "Mark Twain and the Escape from Sense," in *Mark Twain on the Loose: A Comic Writer and the American Self,* University of Massachusetts Press, 1995, pp. 1-38.

[*In the following excerpt, Michelson begins by discussing several traditional interpretations of the jumping frog sketch as greatly indebted to the humorous Southwestern frame story. He then asserts that Twain breaks from the conventional structure to create a complex, mischievous tale that calls into question reality and common sense and confounds interpretation.*]

"The Celebrated Jumping Frog," which Mark Twain also published as, among other things, **"The Notorious Jumping Frog of Calaveras County," "Jim Smiley and His Jumping Frog,"** and **"The Frog Jumping of the County of Calaveras"** (for in both name and substance this tale stayed appropriately restless in the retelling), indeed grew so "celebrated" that for years after its first appearance, an untitled frog-picture on handbills was advertisement enough for a Mark Twain stage show. Yet one can read long in the commentary without learning quite why the American public found this story so transcendently funny, such a frog-leap beyond Southwest humor of its own time. A pause over that mystery might help us turn as well to other Mark Twain works with renewed openness to their possibilities. This frog leads us into those narratives that helped make Twain a star, and that continue to be known around the world, no matter how hard it has been to describe the magic by which this particular sketch worked as comedy. If the secret lies in this tale's being just a little crazier and more deeply chaotic than we have wanted to believe, then that might be a secret worth remembering when Mark Twain's major works come into view.

Setting the frog in historical context is respectable, the "context" always being the humor of the Old Southwest. Without questioning Mark Twain's debt to that legacy, or our debt to scholars who have examined its workings, one can wonder about the tendency to romanticize Southwestern humor, to downplay its violence, its racism, its sexism, and its thematic instability. The best anthology of the mode seems wary about those problems,[33] and Kenneth Lynn's landmark study (still the best analytical book on this material) also presents patterns of sedate intentions that are seen as continuing through Mark Twain's best writing, not just in sketches but in the ambitious works that came years after. Lynn emphasizes continuity: the humor of the Southwest gains form, energy, and appeal thanks to the rise of Whig politics and the Jacksonian revolution; the comic tales sound rough fanfares for the common man, celebrate borderland cultures, and ease the terrors and dislocations inherent in such life.[34] Mark Twain, Josh Billings, Thomas Bangs Thorpe, Petroleum V. Nasby, and others were therefore comrades questing for a democratic literature and a true American vernacular, and Mark Twain owes much to the work of these others.

But Mark Twain was extraordinary as a Southwest humorist, and not just for his gifts in reconciling rustic dialects with readability, or for catching hilarious behavior and character in short narratives. If others pioneered and even perfected the Southwestern tale, it was Mark Twain who perfected the Southwestern *meta*-tale, the story of a story. He ventured to the frontiers of frontier humor early in his career. Frame-tale stories proliferate among Southwest humorists—but not frame-tale stories about being confounded by stories and storytellers, about stories not even getting told, tales and tellers derailing ordinary business, normal thinking, and basic assumptions about identity and real life. When a pratfall is taken by the tale itself, we leave rutted trails of conventional Wild West humor and plunge into Mark Twain's bewildering and trackless landscape. **"The Celebrated Jumping Frog"** is the best known of these breakouts, but there are others of note in the opening years of the career. **"A Touching Story of George Washington's Boyhood"** never comes close to talking about George Washington; it goes round and round about

aggravations of living near people who fancy themselves musicians. The suspense and the running gag of the sketch involve waiting for this counterfeit news article to start being what the title says it is. **"A Medieval Romance"** spends three thousand humid words maneuvering cliché lovers into "hopeless, helpless peril." Then it drops them with a shrug:

> The truth is, I have got my hero (or heroine) into such a particularly close place that I do not see how I am ever going to get him (or her) out of it again—and therefore I will wash my hands of the whole business and leave that person to get out the best way that offers or else stay there. I thought it was going to be easy enough to straighten out that little difficulty, but it looks different, now.[35]

In **"George Washington's Boyhood"** the reader is "sold" if he or she simply expects that an account will come around to its subject; **"Medieval Romance"** cons us into assuming that a published story that begins by emulating overwrought sentimental romance will arrive at some kind of ending, sentimental or not. In other words, a reader is "sold" in trusting to common sense—or rather in assuming that common sense extends to the cultural practice of writing and reading. The subversion is not of some particular modes of discourse, but of discourse itself. Mark Twain plays with the rarely questioned expectations that beginnings lead to endings, and that titles and texts have obligations to one another, and that sentences on a printed page will have discernible intentions other than laughter at intentionality. If egalitarian or realist ethics rattle in such tales as these, rejecting sentimentality and calling for stories of new times and new heroes, then such ethics coexist here with their own negation, with profound suspicion about all these nets of words earnestly published by nobody at nobody else. The reading experience grows complex and exciting; such tales delight, rather than wag an admonitory finger in a reader's face.

"Interpreting" a Mark Twain sketch, therefore, can amount to reading only half a sketch, unless possibilities are allowed that if the sketch be about anything it might also be about the idiocies of interpretation. The co-presence of contrary themes, of sense and refusal of sense, may be part of the comedy. It is worth testing such a premise on **"The Celebrated Jumping Frog,"** an international sensation in its time, and still perhaps the most famous light work in canonical American literature. But when **"Jumping Frog"** strikes students as less than side-splitting, when they wonder at its popularity in the late autumn of 1865, they seem unsatisfied by the standard explanations. Granted that the tale may have offered a flash of relief after four years of Civil War gloom. Granted too that **"Jumping Frog"** reflects patterns of the Southwest comic tradition and has *trompeur-trompé* archetypes in the foreground, of hustler Jim Smiley being hustled himself, and of a self-important narrator unwittingly revealing his own foolishness. The problem is that either line of talk about this story flattens it, for to categorize the tale either way, historically or aesthetically, reduces many possible dimensions to one surface or two. That is bad luck, especially if this tale could be about our own wrongful assumptions that knowing where we are, historically, aesthetically, or otherwise, means really knowing what in blazes is going on.

We can escape for a moment parameters of modern context-thinking and reawaken this story's possibilities. The trickster-tricked tale of Jim Smiley and Dan'l Webster is not the only situation farce in **"Jumping Frog,"** but one of several, nested within each other like matrioshka dolls. Dubious in several dimensions, a character named Jim Smiley is swindled not once but twice: one story-within-the-story is of his hind-leg-clamping bulldog losing a fight to a dog with no hind legs, which makes the frame-tale narrator the butt (again, only perhaps) of not one but two put-ons and possibly more. Drunk, or stupid, or pointlessly crafty, the unfathomably deadpan Simon Wheeler has blockaded him in a bar and "reeled off this monotonous narrative" about a stranger he does not care about, and who may be Wheeler's fantasy or even a way for Wheeler to tell about himself. As a mistake or a practical joke, the friend back East has sent the frame-tale narrator to Angel's Camp, California, looking for one Leonidas W. Smiley, which has set this narrator in Wheeler's grasp. "I have a lurking suspicion," says this narrator, "that your Leonidas W. Smiley is a myth—that you never knew such a personage, and that you only conjectured that if I asked old Wheeler about him it would remind him of his infamous *Jim* Smiley, and he would go to work to bore me nearly to death with some infernal reminiscence of him as long and tedious as it should be useless to me."[36] At the end of the frog-jumping, Jim Smiley at least knows he has been swindled; the frame-tale narrator stays perfectly uncertain about his own experience, for these are (perhaps, always perhaps!) blue-ribbon put-ons, with exquisite fake-outs and cop-outs. In what dimension (history, dream, drunken hallucination, satire, whatever) was there a frog, a bull-pup dog, an asthmatic horse, or even a stranger? In what dimension or was there a Jim Smiley, a Simon Wheeler, and a teller about them all? Who is it that believes in whom or dreams them up?

A moment ago I tried a nesting-doll analogy to catch this arrangement of stories within stories, each inner tale being as suspect as the tale that contains it. But that is just another gesture at *catching*; and part of the fun of this story of a story of a frog is its power to do whirls in the air and outleap its catchers. Arrangements, if they are here, are here to break down. The bulldog story and the asthmatic horse story do not frame or contain the story of the frog Dan'l Webster. They keep it company, certifying its uncertainty, its plausibility in a context that they make more implausible. If they mess up a tidy pattern of tale-within-tale, patterns are not the point.

Yet we cannot be sure even of interpretive chaos. For that certainty would give a species of dominion over this text, a key to these possibly compounded possible-put-ons, or at least an honorable escape. If there are tales within tales in **"Jumping Frog,"** and tales next to other tales, then those patterns and anti-patterns can collide and produce whatever comforting or comfortless Great Disorder they

will. Earlier, I mentioned the Big Bang theory of the universe as an analogy for a theory of humor, because it allows for vast possibilities. Let me go back to universes and big theories for a moment, to suggest that in a collision of models and thought-systems, a comic work can achieve liberation from everybody, including the model-happy interpreter. The great physicist Stephen Hawking retells the old story of an astronomer faced with a stolid English woman persuaded that the universe rides on an enormous turtle; when she was asked what this turtle stands on, she replied, "You're very clever, young man, very clever. But it's turtles all the way down!"[37] Preposterous and consoling at once, the idea puts literally everything into perspective. That perspective is mysterious and absurd—and perhaps no more unimaginable than the General Theory that Hawking has spent his imperiled life trying to get right.

If tales-within-tales do not quite work as a General Theory for **"Jumping Frog,"** then is it frogs all the way down? Such a pattern may be here if patterns we must have, either to nullify still other patterns or bolster an illusion that this text can be stabilized and fully understood. A clue beckons in one of the story's most famous lines, Simon Wheeler's moment of actual praise for the thinking of this lunatic Jim Smiley: "Smiley said all a frog wanted was education, and he could do 'most anything—and I believe him" (174). In a never-land where one such frog has become Daniel Webster, and a deceased bulldog has been Andrew Jackson, Wheeler's real or put-on conviction about the limitless powers of education can trigger some wondering. Jim Smiley may be an educated frog, having "never done nothing for three months but set in his back yard and learn that frog to jump," and succeeding at teaching a frog to do better what frogs already know much better than men. As Wheeler portrays him, Jim Smiley thinks froggy thoughts. The only thing on the creature's mind and coming out of his mouth is bet-talk, and if there are whiffs of the amphibian in Wheeler's representation of Smiley before he is actually heard, then he sounds just as peculiar in his own words:

> Maybe you understand frogs, and maybe you don't understand 'em; maybe you've had experience, and maybe you ain't only a amature, as it were. Anyways, I've got *my* opinion, and I'll resk forty dollars that he can outjump any frog in Calaveras County. (175)

Though this may be a comically right representation of a back-country drawl and dialect, it might also suggest the voice and mentality of something not entirely evolved from the swamp, something that understands frogs too well and human talk and thinking not quite well enough. A moment later, leaving the precious Dan'l Webster in the stranger's care, Smiley proves completely foolish about the betting he is obsessed with. As for the stranger, Mark Twain gives him the narrative's only repeated line, a line that whispers the craziness or frogginess of everybody in the region:

> "The feller took the box again, and took another long, particular look, and give it back to Smiley and says,

very deliberate, 'Well—I don't see no points about that frog that's any better'n any other frog.'" (175)

So Jim Smiley may not be the only perfect frog-nut or frog-man in the county. Someone else—or perhaps everyone else—may have spent too much time in the mud, understanding the "points" of frogs as if they were thorough-bred horses. In other words, Smiley may not be crazier than the norm, and the stranger's egging remark to him (thoroughly stupid, for as yet the stranger has no idea how to beat this frog, not even as Smiley leaves Dan'l Webster in his charge) fits the local *Gestalt*. But when Smiley heads for the swamp, the stranger has time to ponder, and the narrative does another whirl, jolting expectations that the story's teller, Simon Wheeler, is a fully certifiable human being:

> So he set there a good while thinking and thinking to hisself, and then he got the frog out and prized his mouth open and took a teaspoon and filled him full of quail-shot—filled him pretty near up to his chin—and set him on the floor. (175-176)

Now who saw this? Wheeler narrates as if *he* did—but if he did, why did he not warn Jim Smiley that Dan'l Webster had been sabotaged? There is no hint that Wheeler is in league with the stranger or bears Smiley any grudge; the hint, rather, is that Wheeler has sat and watched it all, like a man without discernible motives, just as he has no discernible motive for sitting and telling what might have become the never-ending story, had not the frame-tale narrator slipped away.

So the stranger is a fool for taking such a bet; Smiley is a fool for trusting his prized frog to the stranger he bets with; and "glassy-eyed, his voice never varying," Simon Wheeler is either a master put-on artist or—well, what? A man like these others, maybe an alcoholic, maybe a mad-man, maybe an educated frog? Whether or not he is frog-gy himself, the frame-tale narrator evidently does not know whom he has listened to, what he has heard, why the teller did the telling, or why or even *if* he has been sent to hear all this. Jim Smiley's frog problems seem a small farce, compared to the plight of his listener, this as-yet and perhaps-forever mysterious Mark Twain, who represents himself here as a trapped audience and a clueless story-teller at the same time.

But score-keeping of any kind only reenacts the earnestness that got this narrator into trouble in the first place. Worse, it evades reckoning with the master put-on of **"Jumping Frog,"** the biggest nesting-doll of the lot, involving ourselves as readers of this text, within a world in which everyone's "reality" is called into question. If the narrator is not sure about either of these Smileys, the frog, the stranger, the contest, or anything else he hears from Simon Wheeler, and is not sure even about Wheeler, and fails (apparently) to see a shred of humor in what Wheeler tells him, then where are *we,* if not likewise in an absurd predicament, hearing a deadpan narrator telling a tale about another deadpan narrator telling a suspect tale? The frame-tale narrative (the outermost one) does not

domesticate the Wild West story of Wheeler the storytell-er, or insert Jim Smiley as a gentle amusement into the real world of an Eastern American audience. The frame-tale conspires with Wheeler's account to mock such "reali-ties." If the narrator wonders what he is doing, in hearing and then retelling this evidently pointless tale, then the reader's situation is even odder, precisely because it is taken up voluntarily.

But no matter. These different interpretive pathways lead to the same predicament, the same funhouse where inter-pretive habits are confounded. A frog loses a contest because he is filled up with quail shot and "planted solid as a church." A nobody named Jim Smiley loses because he thinks this prize frog will stay the same when a man's back is turned for a few minutes, and that a frog weighs what it weighs; his dog loses because he is a complete, four-legged dog, with one dogged way of fighting, not half-a-dog like the dog that defeats him. The narrator has come looking for a somebody, not realizing that in the Angel's Camps of the world, one "Smiley," one name or grinning, vacuous face, may be the same as another. The frog loses because he is "settled"; a narrator loses be-cause in a place he cannot comprehend he hears a tale of idiotic obsessions, a tale he is not "shifty" enough to laugh at, not seeing that from some mysterious perspec-tive ministers of the Gospel and frog-trainers may be alike. *To become, to be "settled," is to lose.* The stone man of Nevada thumbs his nose again; the stone men of New England stare at nothing in that Boston banquet hall and listen to their epitaph. If **"The Jumping Frog"** tale has "themes," they may concern the virtues of emptiness, lightness, the evasion of routine, sobriety, normalcy, in-cluding normal discourse with purpose, and some equality among the individuals involved. To be alive and lucky in Angel's Camp is to "understand frogs," empty ones that can leap quick and far, as you must be able to yourself. Bad luck is not only immobility, being stuck at the jump-line with a crop full of bird-shot, or cornered in the back of a saloon by a glassy-eyed stranger with a dadaist monologue fifty years early. Mark Twain's comic West is a world where the self that is founded on psychological consistency, logic, decipherable speech and behavior, on faith, on education even loosely based in values of a too-civilized world, is a self jammed full of quail-shot, a self that cannot move.

"The Celebrated Jumping Frog," then, as Lettrist mani-festo *avant la lettre?* Of course not; this is humor, sub-version of seriousness, a plunge away from meaning and only a quick visit to the abyss. In light of that, is not any reading, any serious floor we think we see at the bottom, only another "meaning," another culture-inflected delu-sion to be vandalized on an escape-run into the dark? If "stop making sense!" is a theme of **"Jumping Frog,"** a source of its naughty pleasure for readers then and after, then even to say so is to scheme to make sense of it. Mark Twain knew that the compulsion to be sensible cannot be cured: human beings are too much like the blue jays of Jim Baker's yarn in *A Tramp Abroad,* a yarn that of all Mark Twain's sketches seems a perfect companion piece to the story of the frog (perfect, that is, to people compelled to think in terms of themes and symmetries). Dan'l Webster is undone because somebody has filled him up; Jim Baker's exasperated blue jay, described by Baker as human in his devious ways and dismal ethics, is laughed at by fellow birds because like them he is driven to fill things up, to keep putting acorns into holes even if the empty space on the other side of the hole is vast as a house. Human beings abhor vacuum, both in significance and in the self; they cannot leave empty things alone, though filling and meddling are mischief.

Notes

[33] *Humor of the Old Southwest,* ed. Hennig Cohen and William B. Dillingham (Athens: University of Georgia Press, 1975), offers this overview of the Southwestern humorist, an overview bearing down on solidarity and social high-seriousness:

> Often a devoted Whig, he was convinced that if the nation was to be saved from chaos and degradation, only the honor, reasonableness, and sense of responsibility of gentlemen—Whig gentlemen—could save it. Usually he was a lawyer and often also a judge, a state legislator, a congressman, or even a governor. . . . Frequently he was also a newspaper editor. For the South he felt a protective and defensive love, though he might have been born elsewhere. He was keenly angered by the North, which seemed to show little understanding of the South and its institutions. He defended slavery and, when the time came, secession, with passion. . . . This is a rigid mold, perhaps, but the Southwestern writers who do not fit into it are few. Seldom has a literary movement or school of writers of any time or place reflected more unanimity in background, temperament, literary productions, aims, and beliefs. (xv-xvi)

[34] Kenneth S. Lynn, *Mark Twain and Southwestern Humor* (Westport, Conn.: Greenwood, 1959), 23-31, 55-61.

[35] *Mark Twain: Collected Tales, Sketches, Speeches, and Essays, 1852-1890,* 339. Budd establishes the title as "An Awful —— Terrible Medieval Romance," though it appeared under the shortened title in the 1875 edition of *Sketches New and Old.*

[36] *Mark Twain: Collected Tales, Sketches, Speeches, and Essays, 1852-1890,* 171.

[37] Stephen W. Hawking, *A Brief History of Time* (New York: Bantam, 1988), 1.

FURTHER READING

Covici, Jr., Pascal. *Mark Twain's Humor: The Image of a World.* Dallas: Southern Methodist University Press, 1962, 266 p.

> Full-length study of Twain's humorous works, including a discussion of the frog story. Covici contends that Wheeler's deadpan style of narration, his inattention to his audience, and his inability to distinguish between the significant and trivial, and between the mundane and fantastic, are the main sources of humor in the tale.

Cox, James M. *Mark Twain: The Fate of Humor.* Princeton: Princeton University Press, 1966, 321 p.

> Freudian analysis of Twain's works, with a section on the frog sketch, assessing the significance of the tale's layered use of frames.

Lewis, Oscar. *The Origin of the Celebrated Jumping Frog.* San Francisco: The Book Club of California, 1931, 27 p.

> Traces the history of the story from its origins in the mining camps of California during the Gold Rush to its popularization in Twain's sketch.

Quirk, Tom. *Mark Twain: A Study of the Short Fiction.* Boston: Twayne, 1997, 232 p.

> General study of Twain's short stories containing a discussion of the frog story, arguing that in this early sketch we see evidence of Twain directing his previously unruly imagination and humorous bent into a tale that creates believable and sympathetic characters.

Rasmussen, R. Kent. *Mark Twain, A-Z: The Essential Reference to His Life and Writings.* New York: Facts on File, 1995, 552 p.

> General reference on Twain's work containing an entry on the jumping frog story that includes a brief overview, synopsis, and publication history.

Wilson, James. *A Reader's Guide to the Short Stories of Mark Twain.* Boston: G.K. Hall, 1987, 297 p.

> Critical evaluations of sixty-five stories, including the jumping frog sketch, with publication history; biographical and compositional information; thematic and stylistic analyses; critical synopsis; and bibliography.

Additional coverage of Twain's life and career is contained in the following sources published by Gale Group: *Authors and Artists for Young Adults,* Vol. 20; *Concise Dictionary of American Literary Biography, 1865-1917;* *Contemporary Authors,* Vols. 104, 135; *Dictionary of Literary Biography,* Vols. 11, 12, 23, 64, 74; *DISCovering Authors; DISCovering Authors: British; DISCovering Authors: Canadian; DISCovering Authors: Most-Studied Authors Module; DISCovering Authors: Novelists Module; Junior DISCovering Authors; Major Authors and Illustrators for Children and Young Adults; Short Story Criticism,* Vols. 6, 26; *Twentieth-Century Literary Criticism,* Vols. 6, 12, 19, 36, 48, 59; *World Literature Criticism;* and *Yesterday's Authors of Books for Children,* Vol. 2.

Hisaye Yamamoto (DeSoto)
1921–

American short story writer, non-fiction writer, and poet.

INTRODUCTION

One of the first Japanese-American writers to gain national attention in the United States after World War II, Yamamoto is concerned with issues ranging from the internment of Japanese-Americans during the Second World War to family tensions arising from a daughter's coming of age. A governing theme in her writing is the struggle of Japanese-American women, who often are isolated from society, caught between the traditional Japanese worlds of their husbands and the Western values and identities of their children. Frequently drawing upon places and events from her own life, Yamamoto creates complex characters; blends poignancy, compassion, and humor; employs irony and understatement; and constructs layered plots through the use of limited and shifting perspectives. Her best-known works are collected in the volume *Seventeen Syllables and Other Stories* (1988), and include the title story, "Yoneko's Earthquake," and "The Legend of Miss Sasagawara."

Biographical Information

Born in Redondo Beach, California, to first-generation immigrant parents, Yamamoto experienced the deeply divided realities of her Japanese heritage and life in the United States in the mid-twentieth century. The gulf between her Japanese ancestry and the dominant white American culture was made dramatically clear when she was forced to spend three years in the Poston Relocation Center in Arizona while she was in her early twenties. Poston was one of about ten Japanese internment camps in the Western United States that confined more than 110,000 Japanese-Americans—two-thirds of whom were American-born citizens—in the years immediately following the bombing of Pearl Harbor in December 1941. During that time, people of Japanese descent were considered potential enemies of the United States. They were removed from their homes, farms, and businesses and detained in relocation centers. Yamamoto's experiences in the camp significantly influenced her life and gave rise to several of her most highly acclaimed stories, notably "The Legend of Miss Sasagawara."

While at Poston, Yamamoto served as a reporter and columnist for the camp newspaper, the *Poston Chronicle.* After her release, she moved to Los Angeles, where she worked as a reporter for the *Los Angeles Tribune,* a small weekly newspaper intended for an African-American audi-ence. Her experiences there inspired the 1985 story "A Fire in Fontana." In 1948, Yamamoto's first story, "High-heeled Shoes," appeared in the *Partisan Review.*

In 1953, Yamamoto declined an opportunity to study at Stanford University with poet Ivor Winters, and instead headed East with her adopted son to volunteer at the Catholic Worker community farm on Staten Island. The community and its charismatic founder, Dorothy Day, impressed Yamamoto with their promotion of pacifist values and selfless ideals, as taught by Jesus Christ. Commentators have observed that Yamamoto's decision stands in interesting relation to her involuntary communal experience at Poston. Yamamoto wrote for the *Catholic Worker* newspaper, which she continued to do for years after leaving the community. Her story "Epithalamium" draws upon her experiences during this time. In 1955 Yamamoto married and returned to Los Angeles, where she became mother to four more children.

Major Works of Short Fiction

Most of Yamamoto's stories were published initially in small magazines and regional Japanese-American newspapers. Her first story, "High-heeled Shoes," delineates both the subtle and overt sexual abuse faced by women in American society. In "Seventeen Syllables," a *nisei* (second-generation Japanese-American) girl on the verge of womanhood witnesses conflict between her father, a farmer, and her mother, a poet. "The Wilshire Bus" tells the story of a Japanese-American woman, who, while taking a bus to visit her hospitalized husband, sees a drunken Caucasian man harass a Chinese couple. "The Brown House" describes the conflicts between an *issei* (first-generation Japanese immigrant) woman and her gambling husband. "Yoneko's Earthquake" is a tragic story about domestic turmoil in a Japanese-American family.

Several of Yamamoto's stories, such as "Seventeen Syllables," "Yoneko's Earthquake," and "The Legend of Miss Sasagawara," have appeared in numerous anthologies, including *The Best American Short Stories of 1952.* Yamamoto's first collection of stories was published in Japan in 1985 as *Seventeen Syllables: 5 Stories of Japanese American Life.* A collection of fifteen stories, *Seventeen Syllables and Other Stories,* appeared in the United States in 1988.

Critical Reception

Commentary has focused on Yamamoto's treatment of the Japanese experience in the United States. Critics have commented on the strength, courage, and honesty of her writing at a time when Japanese-Americans were openly disdained by much of American society. They have noted that Yamamoto draws on both Anglo-American and Japanese-American literary traditions to examine her themes and explore the complexity of human relationships. Her stories feature unreliable narrators, literary and historic references, imaginary dialogues, symbolism, and multiple plots. Several critics have noted compassion, understanding, wisdom, insight, and humor in Yamamoto's sympathetic portrayals of those on the periphery of American society.

PRINCIPAL WORKS

Seventeen Syllables: 5 Stories of Japanese American Life 1985
Seventeen Syllables and Other Stories 1988

CRITICISM

Dorothy Ritsuko McDonald and Katharine Newman (essay date 1980)

SOURCE: "Relocation and Dislocation: The Writings of Hisaye Yamamoto and Wakako Yamauchi," in *MELUS: The Journal of the Society for the Study of the Multi-Ethnic Literature of the United States,* Vol. 7, No. 3, Fall, 1980, pp. 21-38.

[*In the following excerpt, McDonald and Newman discuss several of Yamamoto's best-known stories in the context of what they identify as the "hallmarks" of Yamamoto's style and technique.*]

Yamamoto received her first rejection slip at the age of fourteen and persisted in her aspiration to be a writer until she received her first acceptance from a major periodical when she was twenty-six. In the years between, she completed the program at Compton Junior College, contributed to school, college, and small magazines, and wrote even while she was at Poston. After her release from camp she went to Los Angeles and obtained a reporter's job on the only newspaper that would hire a Japanese: the Negro *Los Angeles Tribune.* She worked there from 1945 to 1948. Her first story, **"High-heeled Shoes"** appeared in 1948.[6] The following year she was accorded a John Hay Whitney Opportunity Fellowship which enabled her to write without a worry for a year. During this time, in addition to more short stories, she translated the whole of Rene Boylesve's "L'Enfant à la Balustrade" from French into English.

While she was working at the *Tribune,* she had begun to collect copies of the *Catholic Worker,* and so, intrigued that there was a place where "non-violence, voluntary poverty, love for the land, and attempt to put into practice the precepts of the Sermon on the Mount" were the rules, she finally went East and spent the years 1953-1955 on the Catholic Worker farm on Staten Island. For years after she returned to California, she continued to write for the paper, the *Catholic Worker,* among her most important pieces being on Seabrook Farms, Iva Toguri ("God Sees the Truth but Waits"), and the United Farm Workers.

After the Catholic Worker experience she settled into a career as wife and housewife, then as mother of five kids, and now, also, the grandmother of two, all of whom live in or near the DeSoto home. In short, as she phrases it, she keeps busy "tending her own garden," which means family, flowers, friends, and writing.[7]

During all these years, there has never been a published collection of her work, but her reputation has been kept steadily alive by anthologists. Four of her short stories made Martha Foley's list of "distinctive" short stories for their particular years, with **"Yoneko's Earthquake"** reprinted as one of the *Best American Short Stories of 1952.* She has been represented in at least twenty anthologies, with favorites being **"Seventeen Syllables"** and **"The Legend of Miss Sasagawara."** Runners-up are **"Las Vegas Charley," "The Brown House,"** and **"Yoneko's Earthquake."**[8] It is noteworthy that between 1949 and 1952, when there was still some hostility and a great deal of apathy about the Japanese, Hisaye Yamamoto published five short stories that won national acclaim.

"High-heeled Shoes" is more essay than story, unlike those that followed, but it has the Yamamoto hallmarks:

1. References to literary materials outside the Japanese-American tradition. This shows her wide reading. In this story, Freud, Ellis, Stekel, Krafft-Ebbing, and Robert Browning are mentioned. In **"Epithalamium,"** she quotes extensively from Gerard Manley Hopkins as well as echoing the Miltonic poem. This strategy lifts her stories into the wider world of European-American culture and adds surprise and new angles of perspective.

2. References to actual events, place, or people. In this story she names Wakako Yamauchi as the friend who has given her the plants from which the narrator is picking pansies in the story.

3. Lists, particularly of foods, flowers, and oddments that give sensory appeal as well as substantiating the reality of the story. In **"High-heeled Shoes,"** she is irritated when the phone rings because she fantasizes that it is a salesman and she does not have money to buy from him. She lists what she would have bought by week's end if she only had money.

4. Soliloquies and imaginary dialogues. Here she has a talk with Gandhi about non-violent responses versus the suffering of women attacked by rapists. Gandhi does not come off well.

The keynote in all of Yamamoto's work is her use of her own mind: she is analytic, meditative, honest, compassionate, and ironic. Whether she uses the first person or a narrator, the final word is usually hers—and it is frequently so open-ended that the reader feels there are stories and meanings as yet unguessed implicit in each tale.

Yamamoto's pervasive love for humanity is found in **"The High-heeled Shoes."** The protagonist ("I") is confronted with sexual perversions: she receives an obscene telephone call at the story's beginning and this propels her mind into "unlovely, furtive things" about other encounters with men that she and her friends have had. The most startling was the time she caught sight of a pair of legs in black high-heeled shoes sticking out from the open door of a "dusty-blue, middle-aged sedan." As she approached and glanced in, she discovered that the shoes were worn by a naked man reclining on the front seat . . . and she was, "with frantic gestures, being enjoined to linger awhile."

The narrator calls on her reading for some understanding of this frightening experience but concludes: "Reading is reading, talking is talking, thinking is thinking, and living is different." However, she regards both incidents as caused by society and does not blame the men, believing that they were part of "a great dark sickness on the earth that no amount of pansies, pinks, or amaryllis, thriving joyously in what garden, however well-ordered and pointed to with pride, could even begin to assuage."

There is a final paragraph: her aunt calls, thus purifying the telephone from the contamination of the obscene caller, and she offers to come over for dinner, bringing food with her. This is the only "Japanese" touch in a story all too universal: "ricecakes with Indian bean frosting, as well as pickled fish on vinegared rice. She has also been able to get some yellowtail, to slice and eat raw." Yamamoto, as narrator, comments, "It is possible she wonders at my enthusiastic appreciation, which is all right, but all out of proportion."

What remains with the narrator is: "Whatever, whatever—I knew I had discovered yet another circle to put away with my collection of circles." A similar personal revelation of the sickness of humankind was revealed in **"The Wilshire Bus,"** a 1950 story, which deals with a Japanese-American woman's fear of being identified as Chinese by a drunken bigot. Shocked at finding this weakness in herself, she lost "her saving detachment . . . and she was filled once again in her life with the infuriatingly helpless, insidiously sickening sensation of there being in the world nothing solid she could put her finger on, nothing solid she could come to grips with, nothing solid she could sink her teeth into, nothing solid."[9]

She has written two stories about gamblers: **"The Brown House"** (1951), and **"Las Vegas Charley"** (1961). The former has a jocose tone: Mr. Hattori, weary of trying to make a living growing strawberries, seeks out a Chinese house where he can try his luck at gambling. The appearance of the house is whimsical: "recently painted brown and relieved with white window frames. . . . To the rear of the house was a ranshackle barn whose spacious blue roof advertised in great yellow letters a ubiquitous brand of physic."

During the travail, as the Hattoris come to argue and their marriage nearly expires, there are humorous incidents, such as a police raid and the semi-friendship between Mrs. Wu, wife of the manager of the brown house and Mrs. Hattori, who must wait, hour upon hour, in the car with the three little children. The children come to acquire a taste for the Chinese cookies that Mrs. Wu brings to the car and Mrs. Hattori becomes quite attached to the Chinese woman. But Mrs. Wu, looking at them, concludes "she had never before encountered a woman with such bleak eyes."[10] As the story ends, the reader goes back over it and sees that it never was humorous, that human interaction is "a collection of circles."

Las Vegas Charley began life as Kazuyuki Matsumoto, a prosperous young immigrant farmer until the death of his beloved wife in childbirth broke his spirit. Ultimately he has become a dishwasher in a restaurant in Las Vegas, spending his free time gambling. As he grows old, he becomes closer to his son and daughter-in-law in Los Angeles. Finally Charley dies, and the doctor who has attended him, complaining of his own frustrations at seeing his patients die, comments:

> "Well, at least your father had a good time—he drank, he gambled, he smoked; I don't do any of these things. All I do is work, work, work. At least he enjoyed himself while he was alive."

> And Noriyuki—who, without one sour word, had lived through a series of conflicting emotions about his father . . . finally, [reaching] something akin to compassion, when he came to understand that his father was not an evil man, but only an inadequate one with the most shining intentions, only one man among so many who lived from day to day as best they could, limited, restricted by the meager gifts Fate or God had doled out to them—could not quite agree.

Yamamoto's honesty also shows through in this story, because she sums up Kazuyuki Matsumoto's reaction, after one son is killed and the other leaves for Tule Lake:

> As for himself, he would be quite content to remain in the camp the rest of his life—free food, free housing, friends, flower cards; what more could life offer. It was true that he had partially lost his hearing in one ear, from standing by those hot stoves on days of unbearable heat, but that was a small complaint. The camp hospital had provided free treatment, free medicines, free cotton-balls to stuff in his bad ear.[11]

Obviously the future **"Las Vegas Charley"** was not of heroic mould, even so his adjustment to camp is, by contrarities, an indictment of it. A story like this in 1961, too, would have sufficient distance in time to arouse little disapproval. This was not the case in 1950 when Yamamoto's story, **"The Legend of Miss Sasagawara"** was accepted by the *Kenyon Review.*[12] This is probably her finest piece of writing and it is still one of the most evocative of all stories of the camp experience (as Wakako Yamauchi says, people did not want to talk about that experience). It is possible that the success of the story results from the way she controlled her own emotions as she wrote, for this time she used a filtered intelligence of a girl obviously herself to give the story through random glimpses of Miss Sasagawara. The rest of the other witnesses are unreliable: an ambulance driver, a teenaged boy, a hysterical woman, and people who love gossip for its own sake, not realizing the human anguish behind bizarre actions.

Miss Sasagawara, aged thirty-nine, has had no regrets that she has never married because she has traveled "all over the country a couple times, dancing in the ballet. . . . she's had her fun." But now, her mother having died, she is confined in a portion of a barracks with her father, a Buddhist priest. Yamamoto explains how adversely the pursuit of the Buddhist-Nirvana—"that saintly state of moral purity and universal wisdom"—can affect those close to the would-be saint. The daughter is the victim of a man who wished to "extinguish within himself all unworthy desire and consequently all evil, to concentrate on that serene, eight-fold path."

The relocation camp experience ironically freed the Reverend Sasagawara from worldly responsibilities, including those to his daughter. She, however, is filled with admiration of his superior being. But a full explanation comes to the narrator in later years when, in a college library, she finds an old poetry magazine which includes "the first published poem of a Japanese-American woman who is, at present, an evacuee from the West Coast making her home in a War Relocation Center in Arizona."

In other words, this is a poem which Miss Sasagawara wrote in the middle of the war, at the time of this story, before she was permanently committed to a mental institution. In an "erratically brilliant" poem, she questions: would not such a saint be "deaf and blind to the human passions" of another who does not wish to attain this sublime condition and wishes instead to respond to the "passions rising in anguished silence in the selfsame room?" The poet (who is Miss Sasagawara) regards the saint's intense idealism as madness, not seeing that she herself will only find freedom from this Buddhist idealism through her own madness.

The story operates on two levels. The news of the unhappy dancer comes to the reader in sporadic items, but the picture of life in the camp is sustained and highly informative. The young narrator sits on the front stoop with her best friend, using such phrases as "Oooh," and "Wow!" while watching the other people and slapping mosquitoes. We learn that two Army cots pushed together make a double bed for a husband and wife, that an apple crate makes a night table, that people eat in the mess hall by age classification. We have the complete program of the block Christmas entertainment. We can almost taste the boredom. But when the story ends, it is with Miss Sasagawara's own poem, her voice really heard at last,

and the details fall into the background of this tragic story of a woman beset jointly by the frustrations of her own culture and by the imprisonment imposed on her by her fellow-Americans.

In a pair of stories, **"Seventeen Syllables"**[13] and **"Yoneko's Earthquake,"**[14] Yamamoto depicts life on the little tenant farms before the War. So specific is she that the reader even learns about the two days' work and one night's discomfort that girls in Japan were glad to endure in order to have their fingernails "shining with a translucent red-orange color." Both of these stories are examinations of unhappy marriages; in one the wife seeks release through the writing of haiku, in the other, through intimacy with the Filipino farmhand after her husband is invalided in an earthquake. In the first, the wife begs the teenaged, blossoming daughter to promise never to marry. Yamamoto's realism hits its own low in the second story when the child, Yoneko, is annoyed by the invalid's threatening to pick his nose and wipe the snot on her and her friends' paper dolls.

Yamamoto selects as her main characters those who are hurt, who have deviated from the norm, who are grasping for some bits of beauty in their desperation: gamblers dreaming of the gifts they will heap on their loved ones when they make the big payoff, a ballet dancer being driven insane by confinement with a religious fanatic, a farmer's wife who writes haiku in the evenings, women who take lovers in order to find the love of which they have been cheated—all those who seek but lose are of interest to Yamamoto, and somehow she wins our understanding, largely through the accepting interpretations of the narrator.

In one late story, however, she goes even further; she makes the female narrator herself neurotic. In **"Epithalamium,"** the woman, Yuki Tsumagari, shows no apparent guilt in her tumultuous love afair with an Italian-American alcoholic seaman at a Catholic community for social rejects on Staten Island. Yuki herself is not a reject; up until now she has been supporting herself and now, at thirty-one, remains unmarried by choice. Though her mother, back in her earlier years, had urged marriage on her, her father had said, untraditionally, to leave her alone. Now an inexplicable love has come. As lovers, the Italian Marco and Japanese Yuki use all the secluded spots near the community, which neighbors a seminary. She even suffers a secret miscarriage; but though the narrator uses such words as "defile," "terrible," and "sordid" to describe their lovemaking, a love for all humanity hovers over the entire story, making it right for Yuki to marry the seaman while he is drunk. In **"Epithalamium,"** Yamamoto is not only forgiving sin; she has her persona, Yuki, embracing it. And in so doing, Yuki is acknowledging the inevitability of suffering and accepting the fact that this marriage will be as much a burden as a glory. On the way back to the Community after they are married, "with Marco slumped heavily against her, Yuki kept remembering Hopkins: 'The world is charged with the grandeur of God. . . .'"[15] She hopes that this is a sign from God that she has chosen the right way. But her thoughts then ramble on to the missal of the day which had told the story of St. Sabina, a Roman widow who, having become a Christian, was beheaded under the Emperor Hadrian, and secretly buried. . . . "However," the missal had added, "it was not certain whether such a woman had existed at all." Yamamoto thus enigmatically turns the story of a strong love and a sad wedding into a legend for the bride to ponder—what is God's reality after all?

Yamamoto's most recent publication, "what might be the second chapter of an autobiography," is **"Life among the Oilfields."**[16] Here are the familiar Yamamoto hallmarks: the contacts with non-Japanese children, the delights of the American candy store, the smells of her mother's kitchen, all the details that bring into near-camera realism the seasons of farming, the frequent moves, the constrictions of poverty—the life of the Nisei a generation ago. There is the self-deprecation (the teacher wonders what to do with "this deluded Oriental shrimp with second-grade pretensions").

But the realism of the story is set off by the epigraph from Fitzgerald and the conclusion. A speeding sports car, coming up the asphalt road in the oilfields, strikes her little brother, tosses him to the side of the road, and keeps on going. The child has not been killed, only badly bruised, to the relief of the sister, the child Hisaye. But the mature woman, keeping her detachment, muses:

> When I look back on that episode, the helpless anger of my father and my mother is my inheritance. But my anger is more intricate than theirs, warped by all that has transpired in between. For instance, I sometimes see the arrogant couple from down the road as young and beautiful, their speeding open roadster as definitely and stunningly red. They roar by; their tinkling laughter, like a long silken scarf, is borne back by the wind. I gaze after them from the side of the road, where I have darted to dodge the swirling dust and spitting gravel. And I know that their names are Scott and Zelda.

Another recent piece reinforces the continuing strand, from oilfields to the present, the determination to appreciate "just plain being alive at this time and in this place":

Survival

The freeway yonder, deferred
for a time, has at last come
through. At first the razed lots
reminded of war's aftermath but
gradually they merged under tree
and flower and weed to make an
impromptu park where children
stalked one another in hiding
games, where humming bird hovered
over nicotiana, where bumblebee
buzzed the wisteria and hollyhock,
where there was room for gopher,
field mouse, skunk, opossum,
golden garden spider, fat snail,
mating lizards, king snake skating
through the grass, and raccoon

sneaking over here to up-end the trash
in the dark of night.

They must have all gone
somewhere. The neighborhood
owl, giant, and white, has eaten
three kittens of our Manx,
leaving only bloody traces
of intestine smeared on the driveway
where he swooped to dine. Only
the runt of the litter, whom one
would have thought the easiest
prey, remains. It grows
by leaps and bounds, having
now all the milk
to itself.[17]

Notes

[6] *Partisan Review,* 15 (October 1948), 1079-85.

[7] Data supplied by Yamamoto in "a bibliography of sorts," April 24, 1980. For twenty-five years she has been a regular contributor of stories, essays, and poems to the Holiday Supplement of *Rafu Shimpo* and has reviews, reminiscences, and book introductions in various publications.

[8] "Seventeen Syllables," *Partisan Review,* November 1949; "Wilshire Bus," *Pacific Citizen,* December 1950; "Yoneko's Earthquake," *Furioso,* Winter 1951; "The Brown House," *Harper's Bazaar,* October 1951. A decade later she wrote "Epithalamium," *Carleton Miscellany,* Fall 1960, and "Las Vegas Charley," *Arizona Quarterly,* Winter 1961.

[9] Yamamoto read this story at the Asian-American Writers session at Beyond Baroque, Venice, California, 17 November 1979.

[10] "The Brown House," rpt. in *Asian-American Authors,* ed. Kai-yu Hsu and Helen Palubinskas (Boston: Houghton Mifflin, 1972). Also rpt. in *Yardbird Reader No. 3.*

[11] "Las Vegas Charley," rpt in *The Third Woman, Minority Women Writers of the United States,* ed. Dexter Fisher (Boston: Houghton Mifflin, 1980) and in *Asian-American Heritage,* ed. David Hsin-Fu Wand (New York: Washington Square Press, 1974).

[12] Rpt. in *Speaking for Ourselves,* ed. Lillian Faderman and Barbara Bradshaw (Glendale: Scott Foresman and Co., 1969, 1975). Also in *Amerasia Journal,* Vol. 3 No. 2 (1976) and *The Ethnic American Woman, Problems, Protests and Lifestyle,* ed. Edith Blicksilver (Dubuque: Kendall/Hunt, 1978).

[13] "Seventeen Syllables," rpt. in *The American Equation: Literature in a Multi-Ethnic Culture,* ed. Katharine D. Newman (Boston: Allyn and Bacon, 1971); *Ethnic American Short Stories,* ed. Katharine D. Newman (New York: Washington Square Press, 1975). Also in *Counterpoint,* ed. Emma Gee (UCLA Asian American Studies Center, 1976), and in school anthologies published by Harcourt Brace Jovanovitch; Ginn and Co.; Houghton Mifflin, and D. C. Heath.

[14] "Yoneko's Earthquake" was included in *Best American Short Stories of 1952,* ed. Martha Foley (Boston: Houghton Mifflin,

1952). Also in *Aiiieeeee!*, ed. Frank Chin, Jeffrey Paul Chan, Lawson Fusao Inada, Shawn Wong (Washington: Howard University Press, 1974; Doubleday Anchor, paper, 1974); *West Coast Fiction*, ed. James D. Houston (New York, Bantam Books, 1979).

¹⁵ "Epithalamium," *Carleton Miscellany*, 1 (Fall 1960), 56-67. Although the setting is reminiscent of the Catholic Worker refuge on Staten Island, Yamamoto says that the protagonist's religious deliberations are not autobiographical.

¹⁶ *Rafu Shimpo*, Holiday Supplement, 1979.

¹⁷ "Survival," *Bridge Magazine*, Part II of special double issue on Asian American Women, Vol. 7, No. 1 (Spring 1979).

Charles L. Crow (interview date 1987)

SOURCE: "A MELUS Interview: Hisaye Yamamoto," in *MELUS: The Journal of the Society for the Study of the Multi-Ethnic Literature of the United States*, Vol. 14, No. 1, Spring, 1987, pp. 73-84.

[*In the following interview, Yamamoto and Crow discuss the author's life and work, and in particular how Yamamoto's personal circumstances have influenced her writing.*]

Hisaye Yamamoto's reputation as a writer of fiction grows, despite the relatively small body of her work and its original publication in little magazines and in regional Japanese-American newspapers. By 1980, as Dorothy Ritsuko McDonald and Katharine Newman noted in *MELUS*, she had been reprinted in at least twenty anthologies (23). The best-known of her stories are **"Seventeen Syllables,"** **"Yoneko's Earthquake,"** **"The Legend of Miss Sasagawara,"** **"Las Vegas Charley,"** and **"The Brown House."** The first collection of her fiction, *Seventeen Syllables: 5 Stories of Japanese American Life,* was published in Tokyo in 1985; unfortunately, no such edition has yet appeared in the United States.

Yamamoto is known as "Si" to her many friends in MELUS, of which she was an early member. She had agreed to meet with me at the first MELUS convention (24-25 April 1987) and so, as the first day's meetings ended, we sat together on a sunny terrace at Heritage Center of the University of California at Irvine. There was a babble of nearby students and their radios which was distracting, and Yamamoto was doubtless frustrated by the failure of her one remaining match to light the cigarette she continued to hold throughout the interview. The impression she gave, nonetheless, was of great calm and patience. Her voice was soft and carefully modulated, easily spilling into self-deprecating laughter; it took on a certain edge only when speaking of her incarceration in the Poston relocation center during World War II.

Like many writers, Hisaye Yamamoto seems to dislike theoretical discussion of her fiction. She is, however, very forthcoming about her life and the sources of her work.

This interview provides some insight into the personal background of her stories, and of little-known but significant elements in her career: her two-year participation in the *Catholic Worker* community on Staten Island founded by Dorothy Day (1897-1980), and her friendship with Yvor Winters (1900-1968) and his wife Janet Lewis (b. 1899). *The Catholic Worker* episode, from 1953-55, was the result of sharp decision and commitment and stands in interesting symmetry with the other communal experience, her involuntary three years in the Poston Relocation Center.

This decision meant declining to attend Stanford and study under the strong-willed poet and critic Yvor Winters, author of *In Defense of Reason,* a manifesto of his principles of classical order and moral absolutism. While Yamamoto depicts the impact of Winters' thought upon her, and her willing discipleship, it should be remembered, again, that Winters first wrote to her after reading **"Yoneko's Earthquake"** (1951), so she already had achieved her mature voice. Yamamoto's correspondence with Winter's widow, Janet Lewis, suggests on artistic kinship between these two writers, who share a quiet authority and individualism, and who both excel in sensitive treatment of domestic tragedy (compare, for example, **"Seventeen Syllables"** and *The Wife of Martin Guerre.*)

The following interview is edited from the transcript of the meeting at Irvine, and from five handwritten pages of follow-up notes provided by Ms. Yamamoto.

[Crow]: *Did you once say that you had been writing and publishing since you were* fourteen?

[Yamamoto]: Well, for the Japanese newspapers. On weekends they would have a feature page, where people would send in all kinds of things. They'd print anything, so that's how I got started, and I haven't stopped yet! I'm still writing for those newspapers. The one person who has kept me writing all these years is Henry Mori, now retired but at one time the English section editor of the *Rafu Shimpo*. He kept asking me every year for a contribution to the holiday edition, even when I pleaded surgery, new baby, nervous breakdown, whatever, so I managed to send him something every year. I don't think I would have kept writing, if he hadn't been so insistent. We met in camp during the war and he also wrote for the *Poston Chronicle*. I will probably be writing from time to time when asked, as long as I can shuffle over to the typewriter.

I see. You must have always known you were a writer.

(Laughing) No, I still don't think of myself as a writer. I guess I wanted to be when I was young, because I liked to read, and, you know, writing seemed like an ideal thing to do. And then I wanted to be famous, a famous writer. But I had a fellowship one year where I tried to write every day because I was obligated, and I decided that I really wasn't a writer. A man from Japan came to interview me—last month, I think. They're putting out a special issue of a magazine on "the Japanese-American imagination," or something like that, so he thought I should be included.

And I told him I didn't have any imagination, I just *embroidered* on things that happened, or that people told me happened.

You're so modest about your fiction! Could this be a form of protective coloration, a smoke screen that you throw up when people ask you questions?

Oh . . . I don't know. Most of the time I am cleaning house, or cooking or doing yard work. Very little time is spent writing. But if somebody told me I couldn't write, it would probably grieve me very much.

I would like to ask you a little about your life in the relocation center. I've noticed that there are some Japanese-Americans—writers and others—who are interested in reliving that experience now and writing about it, or revisiting the camps, in some ways recreating that era.

Oh, yes, Lawson Inada wrote in one of his poems called "Japanese Geometry" that all these camps ought to be set aside as parklands or at least as a memorial, and one by one they've done that. Right now, this very weekend, they're having another pilgrimage to Manzanar, and they have a big ceremony every year.

Have you ever gone back to Poston, your camp in Arizona?

No. A friend went to the Grand Canyon once, and on the way back she and her husband and child visited Poston, where we were, and she said that the camp and grounds had all been taken back by the Indians, and they were growing alfafa on it, and they were living in the adobe school buildings that we all built *with our own hands,* and cooking in them, and about all that remains of us was the little plaque that dedicated the school, and told how it had been built.

You were in your teens when . . .

No, I was *twenty* when the evacuation order came, and I became 21 when I was in camp, so I think I was pretty bitter because—well, you know, people say "free, white, and 21." I wasn't white [laughing], but at 21 people are supposed to make their own decisions.

You were two or three years in the camp?

Yes, three years.

I know that many Issei families lost what they had worked for before the war—fishing boats and farms and so forth. Did your father suffer a great deal as a result of this?

Yes, well he was not a farmer on such a big scale, not like some of those that had huge farms, you know, but still he wasn't able to harvest the strawberries that he had planted himself. We lived on the land that is now Camp Pendleton, we farmed there, and there was a whole colony of Japanese there, growing strawberries mainly, and then the strawberries were bought up by a man from Montebello, Pearson I think, and then we all worked for him, picking the strawberries. And everybody used to pick strawberries together, before, but Pearson divided the Mexicans in one group, with a Mexican foreman, and the Japanese in another group, with a Japanese foreman, and that's the way we worked, until we got evacuated.

So he lost the crop.

Yes. Well, he got paid wages for picking it. And, I guess, his share of the price Pearson paid the farm cooperative. It wasn't much.

Did you father return to farming after the war?

No, first he went to a cannery in Utah, then he came back to L.A. and then he was a janitor for a while, and then started working in Chinese restaurants, washing dishes and busing.

Like the title character in **"Las Vegas Charley."**

Yes, it's based on my father, but not exactly, since I changed his background and the family structure. Yes, then he went to Las Vegas, where he worked for a Chinese restaurant. He worked for eight years, then got ill just like Charley in the story. That part is pretty factual. No, not *factual* but [laughing] . . .

It follows the outlines of his life in that "decline" period?

Yes.

That must be typical of many Japanese men of that generation who weren't able to get back their status or economic power.

Yes, well, the Issei started taking a back seat to the Nisei about that time. It started with the camps. Yes, I would say so.

Were you able to write while you were in Poston?

Yes, I did work for the camp newspaper, *The Poston Chronicle.* I remember that I wrote a mystery story, a serial, that the editor ordered [laughing], and later on I wrote a weekly column.

And do I understand that after the war you became a journalist for a Japanese-American newspaper in Los Angeles?

No, no, I worked for a *black* newspaper, the *Los Angeles Tribune,* which is no longer . . . it didn't last much longer after I left! [laughing]

I see: cause and effect?

No, no, it was a very good newspaper, and was considered the most creatively edited Negro newspaper in the county while it was alive.

What sort of journalism were you doing for the Tribune?

Everything. Writing stories, rewrite, and the longer I stayed the more I did: radio column, world news summary, man on the street, then I wrote a column, and I did book reviews, and about everything. There was just the editor, and me, and the secretary, and the publisher. Also the sports writer, who doubled as an ad salesman.

I had seen an ad in the *Pacific Citizen,* asking for a *man* to join the *Tribune* staff, and I think that the idea was that the *man* would go out into the Japanese community and get Japanese advertising, because while the Japanese were gone, Little Tokyo had become "Bronzeville," the blacks had moved into that area, and interracial friendship was the aim. They wanted an interracial paper, that was the ideal, but I wasn't the type to go out and get display advertising, so I don't think the paper got many Japanese subscribers on account of me. I was there from 1945 to 1948. I quit because I decided I wanted to go to school, but after I quit I didn't go back to school. I started writing. And there was something personal, too. There was a baby, Paul, born in the family, that nobody was in a position to care for, so I decided to take him, so I really couldn't go out to work any more.

And several years later you joined The Catholic Worker? *Could you tell me about this, and your relationship with Dorothy Day?*

The Catholic Worker came to the *Tribune* office as an exchange, and I got so addicted to it that I began taking it home instead of throwing it away with the rest of the exchanges. When I left the *Tribune* in 1948, I subscribed to *The Catholic Worker* and I had accumulated a seven-year file before I finally got up the nerve, in 1952, to write to the Workers to express my desire to join up. Dorothy Day didn't jump up and down for joy, but cautiously suggested I meet her later in the year when she was due in Los Angeles on a speaking engagement. I met her at a midnight mass at the Maryknoll Sisters in Boyle Heights, then later for lunch with a couple of others, one of whom was a priest she called a "fellow renegade." In September the following year, Paul (who was about five then) and I went to join *The Catholic Worker,* he as a Catholic and I as a worker.

Meanwhile, Yvor Winters had been encouraging me to accept one of the Stanford Writing Fellowships, but my heart chose *The Catholic Worker,* so when Richard Scowcroft contacted me to ask if I'd accept a fellowship *if* I were awarded one, I regretfully said no. I guess it was like the cliché about coming to the crossroads and choosing one road over the other.

Paul and I visited my brother and family in Springfield, Massachusetts, before going down to New York City. When the train was pulling into Grand Central Station— it was in the middle of a heat wave—we saw all these people leaning out of the windows of the endless brownstone tenements to get a breath of air. I thought, "What have I done?" And one of the first things we saw, on

arriving at the Catholic Worker house (St. Joseph's House) was a man lying in an alleyway. Paul was very curious, and I was again thinking, "What have I done?" And our first night was spent in Dorothy Day's own room upstairs, where cockroaches and bedbugs dismayed us through the night (Dorothy Day was elsewhere). The next day, after the ferry ride to Peter Maurin Farm, on Staten Island, someone at the farm asked, "What's that on your neck?" I looked in the mirror and found my neck covered with red welts—bedbug bites, I was told. So, again, I thought, "What have I done?"

Well, it was a pretty good two years at the farm, even though I found out Dorothy Day never wrote about the darker aspects of living in community in her column, which had so enchanted me. When I confronted her about a similar author who wrote only about the joys of Catholic family life, she said those aberrations were not the important thing, only incidentals. That was why she was able to continue the work for so long, I guess, even though there were many times, I gathered, that she felt like running away from it all. She's written her own autobiography[1] and several books have been written about the movement. I don't think any one of them really defined her—she was too complex for words, but a really charismatic personality. The work goes on without her, it seems, rippling out in wider and wider waves, Los Angeles has a really dynamic Catholic Worker Group, for instance, with new houses in Las Vegas and Orange County as the most recent offshoots. I believe Dorothy Day is the most important person this country has produced.

If I had chosen Stanford, would I be saying the same thing about Yvor Winters? The ironic thing is that when I was going to Compton Jr. College before the war my friend Emily and I had printed in large letters on our notebooks, "STANFORD OR BUST!"

Could you tell me more about your friendship with Winters and his wife, Janet Lewis? As you know, I am especially interested in her work. You have corresponded with her as well, haven't you?

Yvor Winters wrote me in 1952,[2] I believe, after he read **"Yoneko's Earthquake"** in *Furioso.* (Elizabeth Bishop also wrote—she was consultant in poetry at the Library of Congress at the time. She is my favorite contemporary poet.) So we corresponded pretty regularly until I left for the *Worker.* He sent me Janet Lewis' books and his own. Winters' *In Defense of Reason* staggered me. He was very kind about answering all the questions I asked and sent me his reading lists and I even attempted *The Rise of the Dutch Republic* because he recommended it. The thing in Motley that impressed me was the Catholicism in Holland. But when I told him of my decision to join *The Worker* (which he didn't really think much of), he gave me his blessing.

I began writing to Janet Lewis when I read about Yvor Winters' death, because I felt as though I hadn't really expressed my appreciation to him for tolerating all those questions and for encouraging me to go on writing. We've had a sporadic correspondence ever since. I met her (I never met Yvor Winters) when my friend Chizuko Omori let Wakako Yamauchi and her daughter and me and my daughter stay at her place in Palo Alto while we attended the first Asian-American Writers' Conference at the Oakland Museum. She came to breakfast one morning bearing a jar of guava jelly.

I met her at another seminar at the same place a couple of years later, a seminar on the "relocation camp" experience, but no one else seemed impressed that Janet Lewis was there, so I felt kind of angry about our "ethnocentricity"—here was a great writer and no one even recognized her name.

I went to her reading at Huntington Library here a few years ago, and that was the third time we met, I guess.

If I may turn back to your writing, one thing I've noticed in two or three of your stories is a very sympathetic picture of girls who seem to be incipient artists, like Yoneko in "Yoneko's Earthquake."

You know, you are the only one that has seen that. You picked up Yoneko's inventing songs when she wanted to put her brother's death out of her mind.[3] But I didn't particularly think of that as what she was going to be later . . . it was just a defense mechanism, so . . .

But Rosie does this too, doesn't she, in "Seventeen Syllables"?

She is more of a show-off who likes to perform for her friends. She's something of a mime.

Do you see yourself in either of those girls, and in their use of language?

Oh, yes! It's all based on me, and my friends, and what I've seen, and so I imagine there's quite a bit of me in there, but I wouldn't like to think I'm *them.*

Yes, I understand. But I am interested in the question of how writers find their voices, and it did seem to me that the issue is in "The Legend of Miss Sasagawara" too . . .

Oh, yes, that was based on a real woman, you know.

Whom you encountered in the relocation center?

Yes, and she later died at the age of 58 in a nursing home in Los Angeles. And I found out that she really was a writer, which I didn't know when I wrote the story, that she had written a lot of poetry when she was younger, for the same Japanese newspapers, but I had never seen the ones that she wrote . . . I guess she wrote a little before I started writing.

In the story the narrator discovers a poem by Miss Sasagawara in a magazine, so you had intuited that your model was a writer.

Yes . . . well, no, I *invented* that. I didn't know she was a writer.

Last summer I taught "Seventeen Syllables," and my class was particularly interested in the whole question of artists and audiences, and how the mother in "Seventeen Syllables" can't find an audience for what she wants to say, except for her haiku in the newspapers, and that's shut off for her when her husband essentially murders her voice. That's a powerful episode.

You seemed to think I treated the father viciously.

Most of my students thought that too. They saw the murdering of the mother's voice as the great crime of the story.

It is, it is, yes, I felt that too. But I didn't think I was being *vicious* toward the husband, because he was only acting the way he'd been brought up to act, the way men were supposed to be.

One of my students said about "Seventeen Syllables" that you were giving a voice to an inarticulate person, that is, the mother and the child can't communicate with each other, but you are communicating their story, and so you are giving a voice to the voiceless, to people who can't speak their own words.

Well, aren't most stories like that?

I suppose so, but these characters are so obviously frustrated, by the language barrier between them, and they can't communicate to each other the nature of their own personal tragedies or longings. And . . .

And then, aren't most relationships like that?

Yes, although the language barrier makes it so obvious. But all mothers and daughters are like that, aren't they?

The one's I've heard about, yes. Well, even with my own children, we speak the same language, we both speak English, but I know they don't tell me a lot that's going on . . . and then I think, if I know *this* much of what they won't tell me, I wonder what else is going on.

Or do you really want to know?

[laughing] No, I don't, not really. Don't tell me.

That same term I was teaching Maxine Hong Kingston's Woman Warrior, *and at one point she says that the difference between sane and insane people is that sane people can tell their stories, and insane people cannot.*

Maybe they can't put it in any kind of order. They can tell it but they haven't put it under their control. It's fragmented, and they haven't come to grips with it.

The dancer in "The Legend of Miss Sasagawara"—the title character—is an illustration of that, it seems to me, because she can't express whatever it is she's feeling, except in the poem that she writes which your narrator discovers later on.

Oh, I didn't see that. [Laughing] Because I didn't really consider her insane, I guess. I tried to say that if it weren't for being put in the camp, she might have gone on.

The camp is depriving her of her medium?

Yes, I would think so, yes. And the people that she knew outside, you know, who were her friends and co-performers.

One of the writers at the conference, Stephen Sumida, described you as an "aunt" figure to younger Asian-American writers. Are you impressed by the work of any such writer at the moment?

Well, a young writer named Cynthia Kadohata had a short story, "Charlie-O," in *The New Yorker* last year [10 October 1986] which Wakako Yamauchi sent me a photocopy of. I like her style very much deceptively simple. She must be a Sansei [third generation], and if she is any example of the way Sansei writers are going to be writing, there won't be any particular emphasis on the fact that the people in the story are Japanese.

In your short stories, what sort of audience were you seeking?

I don't know, I don't know if I had any *audience* in mind. I just wanted to be a writer, so I guess I was writing about the things that I knew. I don't think I envisioned any audience. I don't want anyone to see what I'm writing, until it's published, and then I don't care. It's over and done with. So I was really surprised when young people dug them all up And that's why I'm here today, I guess, [laughing] because in their research they found all these stories that I'd written.

But they were intended for the largest audience you could find, not just for the Japanese community in Los Angeles, presumably?

I don't even know that. I just wanted to write, and be published, that's all, you know. I wasn't very farsighted. [laughing]

Well, they finally did find a lot of people, obviously. By the way, I've tracked down only about 5 or 6 stories that you have written, so far, and there must be more that I haven't found yet . . .

I guess they were about all in the little magazines, and then the rest are in the Japanese newspapers. The *Rafu Shimpo* asked me every year for a contribution and I write short stories, poems . . . and then my nephew was until recently the acting editor of the *Pacific Citizen* (he's gone up to San Francisco now, and is the English section editor of the *Ho Kubei Mainichi*), so the last couple of years he has been asking for pieces, and then I used to write for *The Pacific Citizen* before, right after the war, and then there was a newspaper called *Crossroads* that would ask for contributions, and I wrote a few things for them, too.

Do you have any plans to collect any of the other pieces which have not been anthologized?

I don't, no.

Is there a scrapbook or file someplace where you have collected all these things you have written?

Oh yes, Emma Gee at UCLA xeroxed quite a few things for me—a whole big box full. They have the pieces that I wrote for the Japanese newspapers. They have the *Rafu Shimpo* on microfilm, at the Asian-American Studies Center, I believe.

I'm asking because there will be scholars who will want to learn more about your fiction, and it would be useful to know where materials can be found, aside from the anthologies. Of course the anthology published in Tokyo recently, **Seventeen Syllables and Other Stories,** *is a great help. There must be a growing interest in your work in Japan.*

Well, in all Japanese immigrant literature. It's been a fad for the past ten years or so. Joy Kogawa's novel *Obasan* was translated in Japan, also Toshio Mori's *Yokohama, California*. . . .

What is it, do you think, that interests the Japanese reader about the emigrant experience?

Well, more and more Japanese have gone abroad as tourists, too, and they've seen more of the world. And I'm curious too. I used to wonder, what if I'd been born in Japan, or what if my family had gone to Canada, or to Brazil, and it is just fascinating to hear about those other settlements, or . . . I don't know, I'm interested too. For example, a sansei writer named Karen Yamashita did her master's thesis, I believe, in Brazil, and she reported on the Japanese immigration there, and she said one of the things she heard about was a colony of Tolstoians from Japan which started a community in Brazil. I don't know what has become of it. It's interesting, because . . . it does give you alternatives . . . other things that could have happened. Possibilities.

Have you ever wanted to write a novel, or tried to?

Oh, I don't think I'm that serious a writer, that I could, you know, that I could do it.

But you are writing an autobiography, aren't you?

Yes, sort of, there have been three installments, in the *Rafu Shimpo*.[4] Whenever they ask me for something, I get an idea that maybe I could write a continuation of the autobiography. But probably it will never get finished.

If you can imagine yourself writing a complete autobiography, would there be certain key episodes which you would want to highlight?

Well, I guess that camp would be . . . one of the . . . not the high point, but, what is it? Low point.

A time of trial, of frustration?

Yes. And then working for the *Tribune*. And Paul coming. Then going to *The Catholic Worker*. Then getting married and having children . . . I don't think I'll ever get that far, though.

I notice that Gary Soto, who is here at the conference, is only 35 years old, and he's already written an autobiography. It seems to me that most autobiographies aren't the telling of a whole life—after all they can't be—but are the discovery of a pattern, a theme. What would be the theme of your autobiography? Would it be a success story?

Oh, no, no, no! A story of bumbling! Period!

Notes

[1] *The Long Loneliness*, 1952.

[2] In fact, 1951. The letter, dated January 24, 1951, was exhibited in a collection of Winters and Lewis memorabilia at Stanford in 1984. See the Brigitte Carnochan's exhibit catalogue, *The Strength of Art*, 36.

[3] Yamamoto had read my article "The *Issei* Father in the Fiction of Hisaye Yamamoto," a copy of which I had given her.

[4] Actually, several December essays in the *Rafu Shimpo* are autobiographical, at least in part. See list in Works Cited.

Works Cited

Carnochan, Brigitte Hoy. *The Strength of Art: Poets and Poetry in the Lives of Yvor Winters and Janet Lewis*. With an Introduction by N. Scott Momaday. Stanford, California: Stanford University Libraries, 1984.

Crow, Charles L. "The *Issei* Father in the Fiction of Hisaye Yamamoto." *Opening Up Literary Criticism*. Ed. Leo Truchlar. Salzburg, Austria: Wolfgang Neugebauer, 1986. 34-40.

Day, Dorothy. *The Long Loneliness*. New York: Doubleday, 1952.

McDonald, Dorothy Ritsuko, and Katharine Newman. "Relocation and Dislocation: The Writings of Hisaye Yamamoto and Wakako Yamauchi." *MELUS* 7:3 (Fall 1980): 21-38.

Winters, Yvor. *In Defense of Reason*. New York: The Swallow P and Morrow and Company, 1947.

Yamamoto, Hisaye. "Christmas Eve on South Boyle." *Rafu Shimpo* 20 December 1957: 9+.

———. "The Enormous Piano." *Rafu Shimpo* 20 Dec. 1977: 6+

———. "Having Babies." *Rafu Shimpo* 20 December 1962: 21.

———. "Life Among the Oil Fields." *Rafu Shimpo* 21 December 1979: 13+.

———. "The Losing of a Language." *Rafu Shimpo* 20 December 1963: 7+.

———. "The Nature of Things." *Rafu Shimpo* 20 Dec. 1965: 7+.

———. "The Other Cheek." *Rafu Shimpo* 19 Dec. 1959: 9.

———. *Seventeen Syllables: Five Stories of Japanese-American Life*. Ed. Robert Rolf and Norimitsu Ayuzawa. Tokyo: Kirihara Shoten, 1985.

———. "Sidney, The Flying Turtle." *Rafu Shimpo* 19 Dec. 1967: 15+.

———. "A Slight Case of Mistaken Identity." *Rafu Shimpo* 19 December 1964: 6.

———. "Writing." *Rafu Shimpo* 20 December 1968: 14+.

———. "Yellow Leaves." *Rafu Shimpo* 20 Dec. 1986: 36+.

King-Kok Cheung (essay date 1988)

SOURCE: Introduction to *Seventeen Syllables and Other Stories*, Kitchen Table: Women of Color Press, 1988, pp. xi-xxv.

[*In the following introduction to Yamamoto's collection of stories, Cheung provides an overview of Yamamoto's life and work, touching on the author's themes, styles, and techniques.*]

I first met Hisaye Yamamoto at a conference in Irvine, California in 1987. Long an admirer of her short stories, I asked which was her favorite. "None of them is any good," said the recipient of the Before Columbus Foundation's 1986 American Book Award for Lifetime Achievement, with a seemingly straight face. But her words, like her stories—often told by unreliable narrators and laden with irony—cannot be taken literally.

Born in 1921 in Redondo Beach, California, Yamamoto "had early contracted the disease of compulsive reading" and started writing as a teenager (for a time under the pseudonym Napoleon). She received her first rejection slip at fourteen and her first acceptance by a literary magazine at twenty-seven.[1] Much of her work is intimately connected with the places and the events of her own life; to borrow her own felicitous compliment about Toshio Mori's writing, she "shapes the raw dough of fact into the nicely-browned loaf of fiction." For instance, she reveals that **"Seventeen Syllables"** (her most widely anthologized piece) is her mother's story, though all the details are invented.[2] During World War II Yamamoto was interned in Poston, Arizona (the setting for **"The Legend of Miss Sasagawara"**). There she served as a reporter and a columnist for the *Poston Chronicle* (the camp newspaper) and published **"Death Rides the Rails To Poston,"** a serialized mystery. It was also in Poston that a lasting friendship between Yamamoto and Wakako Yamauchi began to develop. (A painter then, Yamauchi has since become an accomplished writer and playwright.) Like many of the Nisei[3] who left the camps to seek work or education in the

Midwest and the East, Yamamoto worked briefly as a cook in Springfield, Massachusetts, an experience recounted in **"The Pleasure of Plain Rice."** She went back to Poston upon receiving the news that one of her brothers had been killed in combat in Italy. After the war she worked for three years from 1945 to 1948 for the *Los Angeles Tribune,* a Black weekly; **"A Fire in Fontana"** is an artful memoir of her job as a reporter.

A John Hay Whitney Foundation Opportunity Fellowship (1950-1951) allowed Yamamoto to write full time for a while. Drawn to the pacifist and selfless ideals advocated in the *Catholic Worker,* she lived from 1953 to 1955 as a volunteer, with her adopted son Paul, in a Catholic Worker rehabilitation farm on Staten Island, where **"Epithalamium"** is set. She then married Anthony DeSoto, returned to Los Angeles and became mother to four more children. She confides that when she has to fill out a questionnaire, she must "in all honesty list [her] occupation as housewife."[4] Yet her best stories are equal to the masterpieces of Katherine Mansfield, Toshio Mori, Flannery O'Connor, Grace Paley, and Ann Petry.

Our appreciation of Yamamoto's fiction and achievement will be enhanced by knowledge of Japanese American history, of which only a glimpse can be given here.[5] Most Japanese immigrants came to the U.S. between 1885 (the year the Japanese government permitted the emigration of Japanese nationals) and 1924 (the year the Asian Exclusion Act was passed). The first waves of immigrants consisted mainly of single young men who saw North America as a land of opportunity. Only after establishing themselves in the new country did they contemplate starting a family. Some returned to Japan to seek wives; others arranged their marriages by means of an exchange of photographs across the Pacific. Hence a large number of Japanese "picture brides" came to this country after the turn of the century to meet bridegrooms they had never seen in person. By 1930 the American-born Nisei already outnumbered the Issei, and about half of the Japanese American population lived in rural areas in the western U.S. Japanese was the language generally spoken at home, so that many Nisei (including Toshio Mori and Yamamoto) spoke only Japanese until they entered kindergarten.

Interest in literature was strong among Japanese Americans. Despite the strenuousness of survival in the New World, a number of Issei maintained their interest in Japanese poetry. There were literary groups engaged in the traditional forms of haiku, tanka, and senryu, and numerous anthologies and magazines (e.g. *Tachibana* and *Remoncho*) devoted to Issei poetry. Nisei with a literary bent, on the other hand, mostly expressed themselves in the English sections of Japanese American newspapers such as *The New World, Kashu Mainichi,* and *Nichibei Shimbun* (Yamamoto contributed regularly to *Kashu Mainichi* as a teenager.) In the 1930s and 1940s, there were magazines such as *Reimei* and *Current Life* that published fiction and poetry by Nisei. *Yokohama, California,* a collection of short stories by Toshio Mori, probably the first Nisei writer read outside of the Japanese American community, was scheduled for publication by Caxton Print-

ers (Caldwell, Idaho) in spring, 1942, but did not appear until 1949 because of the war.

The life of just about every person of Japanese ancestry living in the U.S. was drastically altered by World War II. Within four months of the bombing of Pearl Harbor on December 7, 1941, over 110,000 Japanese Americans (two-thirds being American-born citizens) were forced to abandon homes, farms, and businesses throughout the West Coast and were detained in various internment camps as potential enemies despite overwhelming evidence to the contrary. Besides dislocating Japanese Americans physically, socially, and psychologically, the internment also disrupted their nascent literary tradition. The creative activities of most, if not all, Issei were arrested. Many destroyed all traces of their own writing in Japanese to avoid being suspected of disloyalty. But a few Nisei writers persisted in writing, even while in camp. Poems and short stories appeared in camp magazines such as the *Poston Chronicle, Trek* (Topaz, Utah), and *Tulean Dispatch Magazine* (Tule Lake). Almost every interned Nisei who wrote after the war—notably Miné Okubo, Monica Sone, John Okada, Yoshiko Uchida, Jeanne Wakatsuki Houston—sought to express the bewilderment of massive uprooting.[6] It is also significant that **"The Legend of Miss Sasagawara,"** Yamamoto's haunting story about derangement, is set in camp. Looking back on the internment, Yamamoto writes:

> Any extensive literary treatment of the Japanese in this country would be incomplete without some acknowledgement of the camp experience. . . . It is an episode in our collective life which wounded us more painfully than we realize. I didn't know myself what a lump it was in my subconscious until a few years ago when I watched one of the earlier television documentaries on the subject, narrated by the mellow voice of Walter Cronkite. To my surprise, I found the tears trickling down my cheeks and my voice squeaking out of control, as I tried to explain to my amazed husband and children why I was weeping.[7]

Yamamoto was one of the first Japanese American writers to gain national recognition after the war, when anti-Japanese sentiment was still rampant. Four of her short stories found their way to Martha Foley's yearly lists of "Distinctive Short Stories." (These lists are included in Foley's annual *Best American Short Stories* collections.) They are **"Seventeen Syllables"** (1949), **"The Brown House"** (1951), **"Yoneko's Earthquake"** (1951), and **"Epithalamium"** (1960); **"Yoneko's Earthquake"** was also chosen as one of the *Best American Short Stories: 1952.* Because of her extensive reading of American and European writers and her own cultural background, Yamamoto writes out of both an Anglo-American and a Japanese American literary tradition. But all her protagonists are Japanese Americans, and her sympathy is invariably with those who are on the fringes of American society.

All the same, her writing encompasses a wide range of subject matter, from vignettes of sexual harassment in **"The High-Heeled Shoes,"** her first major publication, to an Issei odyssey that spans Japanese American history in

"**Las Vegas Charley.**" Several themes, however, recur in her work: the interaction among various ethnic groups in the American West, the relationship between Japanese immigrants and their children, and the uneasy adjustment of the Issei in the New World, especially the constrictions experienced by Japanese American women. Intent on depicting human complexity, Yamamoto seldom casts her characters as heroes or villains, and rarely presents personal interaction in simple black and white terms. Discernible in her treatment of all three themes is a voice that is at once compassionate and ironic, gentle and probing, one that can elicit in rapid succession anger and pity, laughter and tears.

Having lived among both whites and non-whites, Yamamoto captures both the tension and the rapport among people from diverse ethnic backgrounds. Like Ann Petry, she can portray instances of racism in realistic and galling detail. Like Flannery O'Conner, she can do so without explicit accusations but with incisive irony. The white protagonist of "**Underground Lady,**" for example, betrays her own bigotry while complaining about her Japanese American neighbors to a Nisei listener. In "**Wilshire Bus,**" a story set in postwar Los Angeles, a drunk white man on a bus heaps racist slurs on a Chinese couple who are fellow passengers and demands that they return to where they came from. Soon the couple (one of whom is carrying a plant) get off at the veterans hospital—most likely to visit a son who is an American veteran injured in the war. "**Life among the Oilfields**" shows the insolence of a neighboring white couple who run over a Japanese American child in their car but who refuse to apologize or make compensation. By framing the incident with allusions to F. Scott Fitzgerald and his wife Zelda, and by linking this couple to the heartless one in the story, Yamamoto insinuates that the callous racism exposed in her story also characterizes the attitudes and work of some celebrated white writers.[8]

There are, however, touching instances of cross-cultural bonding as well. In "**The Eskimo Connection**" a friendship develops through the exchange of letters between a middle-aged Japanese American housewife and a young Eskimo prisoner. In "**Epithalamium**" we are privy to the thrills and heartaches of a Nisei woman who has fallen in love with an Italian alcoholic. "**A Fire in Fontana**" tracks the growing political consciousness of the narrator, whose inner self turns "Black" in empathy after reporting on a fire that has "accidentally" killed a Black family residing in a hostile white neighborhood. In each of these stories, a Nisei woman is drawn to persons who are marginalized as members of other ethnic groups.

Yamamoto's inter-ethnic encounters contain not just sober reflections but also funny touches. "The brown house"—the gambling establishment in the story of the same name—does not discriminate among races. During a police raid, its "windows and doors . . . began to spew out all kinds of people—white, yellow, brown, and black." A Black man seeks refuge and is granted shelter in the car of a Japanese woman, Mrs. Hattori, who with her five children is waiting for her husband. Before long Mr. Hat-

tori joins them and drives away without knowing that his car carries an extra passenger. When the Black man reveals his presence and asks to be let off, the driver receives a shock:

> Mrs. Hattori hastily explained, and the man, pausing on his way out, searched for words to emphasize his gratitude. He had always been, he said, a friend of the Japanese people; he knew no race so cleanly, so well-mannered, so downright nice. As he slammed the door shut, he put his hand on the arm of Mr. Hattori, who was still dumfounded, and promised never to forget this act of kindness. (page 42)

Once the fugitive is gone, Mr. Hattori reproaches his wife for offering sanctuary to a Black person, and Mrs. Hattori retorts that her husband has no misgivings about mixing with men of other colors when he is inside the brown house.

The episode is interwoven with humor, pathos, and irony. Besides presenting a comic sketch of "one minority stereotyping another,"[9] it plays on the discrepancy between appearance and reality. Mr. Hattori, whom the Black man thanks profusely, has performed an act of charity against his will. Assumed to be "well-mannered" and "downright nice," he refers to the thankful man derogatorily as *"kurombo,"* which is somewhere between "Blackie" and "Nigger" in its connotation. The ensuing argument about what Mrs. Hattori has done culminates in Mr. Hattori beating his wife later that night. Finally, one must reflect sadly on the irony that it is a gambling den that embraces people of various hues, and that it is only there that the inmates are above the iniquity of racism. Unlike overtly political statements that can be abstract and one-sided, Yamamoto presents race relations with an eye to nuances and resonances. The author, who identifies strongly with other people of color, satirizes both white and Asian prejudices. Yet her satire is ever so subtle. She exposes human narrowness not with the biting sarcasm of Joan Didion or the pungent rhetoric of John Okada, but with the acerbic wit of Grace Paley and the piquant understatement of Toshio Mori.

Another theme that Yamamoto explores repeatedly is the precarious relationship between Issei parents and Nisei children. While generational differences are by no means unique to Japanese Americans, in their case the gap between the old and the young is aggravated by language barriers and disparate cultural values. Rosie in "**Seventeen Syllables**" cannot appreciate her mother's haiku, though she pays lip service to its beauty:

> "Yes, yes, I understand. How utterly lovely," Rosie said, and her mother, either satisfied or seeing through the deception and resigned, went back to composing.

> The truth is that Rosie was lazy; English lay ready on the tongue but Japanese had to be searched for and examined and even then put forth tentatively (probably to meet with laughter). It was so much easier to say yes, yes, even when one meant no, no. (page 8)

The mother and daughter in **"Yoneko's Earthquake"** likewise talk at cross purposes. Out of guilt Mrs. Hosoume, who has undergone an abortion and then lost her younger son, envisions a causal link between the two premature deaths:

> "Never kill a person, Yoneko, because if you do, God will take from you someone you love."
>
> "Oh, that," said Yoneko quickly, "I don't believe in that, I don't believe in God." . . . She had believed for a moment that her mother was going to ask about the ring (which, alas, she had lost already, somewhere in the flumes along the cantaloupe patch). (page 56)

The mother's cryptic moral is entirely lost on Yoneko. Mrs. Hosoume is thinking of the abortion when she admonishes Yoneko against killing, but "someone you love" could refer either to the son who has recently died or to Marpo, her lover who has disappeared on the day of the abortion.[10] None of these possibilities occur to Yoneko, who merely balks at the very idea of God. She is more nervous about having lost the ring given to her by Mrs. Hosoume, who in turn has received it from Marpo. The daughter's loss of the ring symbolizes the mother's bereavement at the loss of her lover. A mere trinket in the eyes of the daughter, the ring is associated in the mother's mind with an inner tumult as intense as the earthquake that has unnerved Yoneko.

Despite difficulties and failures, these mothers at least attempt to impart their hard earned wisdom to their daughters, but the fathers, either preoccupied by material survival, or bent on spiritual enlightenment, or shackled by vice, communicate even less effectively, if at all, with their children. Mr. Hayashi in **"Seventeen Syllables"** and Mr. Hosoume in **"Yoneko's Earthquake"** are earthbound men oblivious to the artistic or romantic inclinations of their wives and daughters. On the other hand, the Buddhist father in **"The Legend of Miss Sasagawara"** is too absorbed in his spiritual pursuit to notice that his sensuous daughter is disintegrating mentally right under his saintly nose. Then there are Mr. Hattori and Charley (the title character of **"Las Vegas Charley"**), inveterate gamblers unfit to set examples for their children.[11] None of these men is evil, but each is severely limited. Noriyuki's mixed reaction to his deceased father at the end of **"Las Vegas Charley"** is illustrative. The doctor has just said of Charley, "At least he enjoyed himself while he was alive."

> And Noriyuki—who, without one sour word, had lived through a succession of emotions about his father— hate for rejecting him as a child; disgust and exasperation over that weak moral fiber, embarrassment when people asked what his father did for a living; and finally, something akin to compassion, when he came to understand that his father was not an evil man, but only an inadequate one with the most shining intentions, only one man among so many who lived from day to day as best as they could, limited, restricted, by the meager gifts Fate or God had doled out to them—could not quite agree.[12] (page 85)

Noriyuki's reflections on his Issei father can be connected to the third theme concerning the aspirations and difficulties of the Japanese immigrants, and the temptations and frustrations that await them in America. As Dorothy Ritsuko McDonald and Katharine Newman aptly observe, "all those who seek but lose are of interest to Yamamoto."[13] Ineffectual as the Issei fathers may be in her stories, they are never reduced simply to stereotypes. Perhaps it is because Yamamoto can understand so well the hardships that beset the newcomers to American soil that she can afford tender strokes even while painting incorrigible souls such as Charley and Mr. Hattori. Once a successful farmer, Charley turns to gambling in his lonely hours after the death of his beloved wife. Twice he tries to kick the habit, but renews his addiction when the monotony of camp life and his isolation in Las Vegas become unbearable. By delineating the circumstances that turn this well-meaning man into a compulsive gambler, Yamamoto gives us insights into a life that is otherwise all too easily condemned. Mr. Hattori, who gambles in the hope of making a quick fortune after losing money on his strawberry crop, has less claim on our sympathy. Yet even this gambler disarms us with his sincere though short-lived resolutions to reform.

But if Yamamoto portrays the failings of Mr. Hattori with tolerance, she extends the strongest sympathy to his long-suffering wife, who does not have the heart to leave her reckless husband permanently. At the end of the story, her family is mired in debt and she is pregnant again. Looking at Mrs. Hattori, Mrs. Wu (the Chinese proprietess of the brown house) "decided she had never before encountered a woman with such bleak eyes." (page 45) Whether or not one sees the author as a feminist ahead of her time, Yamamoto does reveal through her fiction the sorry plight of many female immigrants caught in unhappy marriages. What made the lives of these Issei women especially bleak was that unlike Black women, for example, who in similar situations often turned to other women for support, rural Issei women were not only separated by the Pacific from mothers and grandmothers, but often cut off from one another as well. Having to take care of children and to work alongside their husbands on isolated farms, they had little time and opportunity to cultivate friendships with other women. The only members of the same sex to whom they could unbosom their thoughts were their own daughters, who all too often had engrossing problems of their own.

Mrs. Hayashi in **"Seventeen Syllables"** is a haunting portrait of a repressed Issei who struggles to express herself through poetry. Notwithstanding her long hours of work at home and on the farm, she takes to writing haiku. But her husband, a farmer who is indifferent to her creative endeavors, expresses disapproval and resentment whenever she engages in long discussions of poetry with people who share her interests. The conflict comes to a head when she wins a haiku contest sponsored by a Japanese American newspaper. On the day the editor comes in person to deliver the award, a Hiroshige print, the family is busy packing tomatoes. Mr. Hayashi becomes increasingly impatient while his wife discusses poetry with the editor in the main house, and finally stalks inside in anger and emerges with the prize picture. What follows is the most wrenching passage in the story, told from the daughter's point of view:

> . . . he threw the picture on the ground and picked up the axe. Smashing the picture, glass and all (she heard the explosion faintly), he reached over for the kerosene that was used to encourage the bath fire and poured it over the wreckage. I am dreaming, Rosie said to herself, I am dreaming, but her father, having made sure that his act of cremation was irrevocable, was even then returning to the fields.

> Rosie ran past him and toward the house. What had become of her mother? She burst into the parlor and found her mother at the back window, watching the dying fire. They watched together until there remained only a feeble smoke under the blazing sun. Her mother was very calm. (page 18)

This haunting description attests to Yamamoto's genius at creating scenes that are powerful on both a literal and a symbolic level. The external calmness of the mother, almost frightening at this point, seems only to suggest the depth of her anguish. Although we are not immediately told of her inner reaction to her husband's outrage, the incinerated picture speaks for her: we feel that she too is consumed by seething rage and smoldering despair. More effective than registering a host of angry screams or plaintive wails, the tableau sears into our consciousness the husband's cruelty and the wife's desolation.[14]

Another striking use of a symbolic scene (analogous to a near epiphany) to convey repressed emotions occurs in **"Yoneko's Earthquake,"** when Mr. Hosoume drives his wife to the hospital to abort an illegitimate child. On the way the father hits a beautiful collie, but drives on as though nothing has happened. The unblinking killing of the animal enables us not only to perceive the father's intense anger and his total indifference to the life about to be destroyed but also to imagine the mother's contrasting psychological state. She must cringe inwardly as she witnesses the act that foreshadows the fate of her unborn child. The harrowing silence that accompanies the brutal burning in **"Seventeen Syllables"** and the unfeeling and unacknowledged killing in **"Yoneko's Earthquake"** heightens the horror of both episodes. We can almost feel the lifeblood slowly seeping from the two hurt women.

Two other narrative techniques contribute to the exquisite telling of **"Seventeen Syllables," "Yoneko's Earthquake,"** and **"The Legend of Miss Sasagawara"**: the use of limited point of view and the juxtaposition of a manifest and a latent plot.[15] These two strategies are interconnected: the limited point of view allows the author to suspend or conceal one of the plots of a given story.[16] Though narrated in third person, **"Seventeen Syllables"** is told from young Rosie's point of view. While we are informed of Mrs. Hayashi's poetic interest from the beginning and are reminded of it periodically, the first part of the story revolves around Rosie's adolescent concerns, especially her

secret rendezvous with Jesus, the son of the Mexican couple who work for her family. Only two thirds into the story does Yamamoto begin to unfold the submerged plot—the tragedy of the mother, whose artistic aspirations come to an abrupt halt in the wake of her jealous husband's fury. The burning of the award signals the end of Mrs. Hayashi's poetic career. As mother and daughter watch the dying fire together, their lives—separate strands at the outset—begin to intertwine. Rosie, who has newly experienced the thrills of her first romance, is made to look squarely at her mother's chastening marriage. Her "rosy" adolescent world must now be viewed through the darkening lens of Mrs. Hayashi's hindsight.

The counterpoint emotions of mother and daughter are deftly superimposed in the dramatic last paragraph of the story:

> Suddenly, her mother knelt on the floor and took her by the wrists. "Rosie," she said urgently, "Promise me you will never marry!" Shocked more by the request than the revelation, Rosie stared at her mother's face. Jesus, Jesus, she called silently, not certain whether she was invoking the help of the son of the Carrascos or of God, until there returned sweetly the memory of Jesus' hand, how it had touched her and where. Still her mother waited for an answer, holding her wrists so tightly that her hands were going numb. She tried to pull free. Promise, her mother whispered fiercely, promise. Yes, yes, I promise, Rosie said. But for an instant she turned away, and her mother, hearing the familiar glib agreement, released her. Oh, you, you, you, her eyes and twisted mouth said, you fool. Rosie, covering her face, began at last to cry, and the embrace and consoling hand came much later than she expected. (page 19)

As an expression of the mother's cynical wisdom, the shocking request reveals her thorough disillusionment with her past and present relationships with men. Deserted by her lover in Japan and stifled by her husband in America, Mrs. Hayashi has abandoned all hopes for herself; she can only try to prevent her daughter from repeating her mistakes. Her sudden kneeling and anxious clutching, however, oddly and ironically correspond to the posture and gesture of an ardent suitor proposing marriage. One suspects that the ironic correspondence flashes across Rosie's mind as well. Though not deaf to her mother's plea, Rosie drifts into a romantic reverie at the very moment Mrs. Hayashi implores her to remain single. Rosie's reaction to the entreaty is couched in words that recall her recent sexual awakening. "Jesus" is both a spontaneous exclamation and a conscious invocation of her beau, whose arousing grip contrasts with Mrs. Hayashi's tenacious clutch. "Yes, yes" recalls not only the double affirmative at the beginning of the story, when Rosie pretends to understand the workings of haiku, but also her first kiss with Jesus in the shed, when she can only think of "yes and no and oh. . . ." The affirmative answer also extends the proposal analogy: it is an answer many a suitor wishes to hear and many a woman in love longs to utter.[17] In the present context, however, it is a hollow acquiescence extorted by the mother and given grudgingly by the daughter. As a desperate plea against marriage and as a travesty of a proposal, the passage conflates the mother's disenchantment and the daughter's dampened but inextinguishable hopes.

The degree of Mrs. Hayashi's embitterment and the extent of Rosie's transformation are conveyed in the delicate understatement of the last sentence. Taking umbrage at Rosie's insincere reply, the disconsolate mother cannot bring herself to hug her sobbing daughter immediately. Although Rosie's "glib agreement" as well as Mrs. Hayashi's unspoken reprimand and temporary withdrawal hark back to the story's opening, when the mother treats Rosie as a child too young to grasp the intricacies of Japanese poetics, the last sentence also bespeaks Rosie's growth from a carefree child to a perplexed adult. As Stan Yogi observes, the image of delayed embrace "suggests the maturity that Mrs. Hayashi now expects of her daughter, who has been initiated into the excitement, pain, and disillusionment of adult life."[18]

Rosie's story and Mrs. Hayashi's story are inexorably enmeshed at the end. But in **"Yoneko's Earthquake,"** one of the plots remains hidden throughout. Also told from a daughter's point of view, the seemingly light-hearted tale ostensibly describes ten year old Yoneko's crush on Marpo, the twenty-seven year old Filipino farmhand who works for her family. Yoneko confides to us matters of utmost concern to *her* while reporting in passing the daily occurrences in her family, such as getting a ring from her mother one day and being driven by her father to a hospital another day. But her random digressions are in fact pregnant hints dropped by Yamamoto. These hints allow us to infer that Yoneko's mother is also in love with Marpo and that their liaison leads to an abortion. Just as we must unravel these secrets by piecing together Yoneko's haphazard observations, so must we gauge the emotional upheaval in the adult world by monitoring Yoneko's changing moods. Her passing crush on Marpo and fleeting sorrow after his departure at once parallel and contrast with the mother's passionate affair and unremitting sorrow at being deserted.

Because the story operates on multiple levels of consciousness—those of the young girl, the reader, and the author—there are unlimited occasions for dramatic irony. For instance, it is through Yoneko's separate admiration for Marpo and for the mother that we learn the likelihood of mutual attraction between the two adults. After Marpo's disappearance Yoneko only notes as a matter of fact that the new hired hand is "an old Japanese man who wore his gray hair in a military cut and who, unlike Marpo, had no particular intersts outside working, eating, sleeping, and playing an occasional game of *goh* with Mr. Hosoume." But the reader can appreciate the humor and the pathos behind the replacement: this time the father has taken precautions. The new worker is Marpo's antithesis in every way, devoid of youth, industry, and talents. Instead of being a constant companion for the mother, he is the father's playmate.

In **"The Legend of Miss Sasagawara,"** we are presented not so much with two plots as with shifting perspectives.

The word "legend" nicely calls into question the veracity of the information provided in the story, in which we are often misled into looking at a character or an event in a certain way, only to have our perceptions radically altered by the end. The title character is introduced to us through various secondhand reports, made up of gossip and rumors, the gist of them being that Miss Sasagawara is highly eccentric, if not downright crazy. As for her family, we know only that her mother is dead and that her father is a devout Buddhist priest. At the end of the story, however, the narrator discovers a poem written by Miss Sasagawara in which she intimates the torment of being tied to someone "whose lifelong aim had been to achieve Nirvana, that saintly state of moral purity and universal wisdom." The poet continues:

> But say that someone else, someone sensitive, someone admiring, someone who had not achieved this sublime condition and who did not wish to, were somehow called to companion such a man. Was it not likely that the saint, blissfully bent on cleansing from his already radiant soul the last imperceptible blemishes . . . would be deaf and blind to the human passions rising, subsiding, and again rising, perhaps in anguished silence, within the selfsame room? The poet could not speak for others, of course; she could only speak for herself. But she would describe this man's devotion as a sort of madness, the monstrous sort which, pure of itself, might possibly bring troublous, scented scenes to recur in the other's sleep. (page 33)

This revealing poem, the veiled record of a passionate daughter's anguished remonstration with an ascetic father, not only gives us new insight into Miss Sasagawara's tragedy but forces us to revise our earlier judgment of who is sane and who is not. The daughter, who feels circumscribed emotionally and aesthetically in the presence of her father, is also literally incarcerated. Because of the internment, father and daughter are condemned to live "within the selfsame room." Her mental illness seems an unconscious act of resistance against the chilling influence of her father and against the senseless decree of the U.S. government. By contrast, the other internees conduct their lives in camp as though they were at liberty. Miss Sasagawara's father, who "had felt free for the first time in his long life" during this confinement, offers the most bizarre example. The line between sanity and insanity is a hard one to draw in this story.

Though Yamamoto persistently confronts religious and moral issues, she is never dogmatic or moralistic in her judgment. Instead she can find fault with the seemingly divine and perceive redeeming grace among erring humanity. Her characters are often caught in circumstances that render unqualified approval or condemnation difficult. Thus Miss Sasagawara's father, so close to sainthood, is yet hopelessly oblivious and insensitive. By contrast, Charley the gambler and Mrs. Hosoume in **"Yoneko's Earthquake"** engage us not despite but because of their susceptibilities to vice and passion. Whether Yamamoto uses a Buddhist or a Christian frame of reference, her overriding tone is one of human questioning accompanied by understanding rather than of moral certainty coupled with religious complacency.

Not given to effusive rhetoric and militant statements, Yamamoto appeals to us in another way.[19] Reminiscent of the verbal economy of haiku, in which the poet "must pack all her meaning into seventeen syllables only," Yamamoto's stories exemplify precision and restraint. We must be attentive to all the words on the page to unbury covert plots, fathom the characters' repressed emotions, and detect the author's silent indictment and implicit sympathy. Many of her stories give added pleasure with each new reading, but some may actually have to be read at least twice to be fully appreciated. Then may we find ourselves echoing Rosie by saying, without glibness, "Yes, yes, I understand. How utterly lovely."

Notes

[1] Hisaye Yamamoto, "Writing," *Amerasia Journal* 3.2 (1976): 127, 128, 130. Yamamoto said that she hid under the pseudonym "as an apology for [her] little madness" (i.e. her immense zeal to write; 128).

[2] Yamamoto, "Introduction," *The Chauvinist and Other Stories* by Toshio Mori (Los Angeles: UCLA Asian American Studies Center, 1979), p. 12; Susan Koppelman, ed. *Between Mothers and Daughters: Stories Across a Generation* (Old Westbury, NY: Feminist Press, 1985), p. 162.

[3] Nisei are second generation Japanese Americans, children of the Issei, or Japanese immigrants. Sansei are the third generation.

[4] "Writing," 126.

[5] For a fuller discussion of the relationship between Japanese American history and literature, see Elaine H. Kim, *Asian American Literature: An Introduction to the Writings and their Social Context* (Philadelphia: Temple Univ. Press, 1982), 122-72. For a detailed study of Issei history, see Yuji Ichioka, *The Issei: The World of the First Generation Japanese Immigrants, 1885-1924* (New York: Free Press, 1988).

[6] Miné Okubo, *Citizen 13660* (New York: Columbia Univ. Press, 1946; Seattle: Univ. of Washington Press; 1983); Monica Sone, *Nisei Daughter* (Boston: Little Brown, 1953); John Okada, *No-No Boy* (Vermont: Tuttle, 1957; Seattle: Univ. of Washington Press, 1977); Yoshiko Uchida, *Desert Exile: The Uprooting of a Japanese American Family* (Seattle: Univ. of Washington Press, 1982); James Houston and Jeanne Wakatsuki Houston, *Farewell to Manzanar* (Boston: Houghton Mifflin, 1973).

[7] ". . . I Still Carry It Around," *RIKKA* 3.4 (1976): 11.

[8] I want to thank Barbara Smith for this suggestion.

[9] Robert Rolf, "The Short Stories of Hisaye Yamamoto, Japanese-American Writer," *Bulletin of Fukuoka University of Education* 30.1 (1982): 75.

[10] The ambiguous reference is noted by Charles Crow in "Home and Transcendence in Los Angeles Fiction," in *Los Angeles in Fiction:*

A Collection of Original Essays, ed. David Fine (Albuquerque: Univ. of New Mexico Press, 1984), p. 202.

[11] Not surprisingly, Charles Crow argues that Yamamoto's portrayals of Issei fathers are uniformly unflattering; see "The *Issei* Father in the Fiction of Hisaye Yamamoto," in *Opening Up Literary Criticism: Essays on American Prose and Poetry* (Salzburg: Verlag Wolfgang Neugebauer, 1986), pp. 34-40. Yet interestingly enough, unlike Maxine Hong Kingston and Alice Walker, who have been attacked by critics for reinforcing the negative stereotypes of respectively Chinese American men and Black men, Yamamoto has not had to answer similar charges. I believe this is due to Yamamoto's ability to soften her critical vision by rendering the vulnerabilities of Japanese American men sensitively, as in "Morning Rain" and "My Father Can Beat Muhammad Ali." Although the father figures in these stories are not of heroic mold, they are too human to be judged as caricatures.

[12] The poignancy of this ending recalls the ending of Hemingway's "My Old Man," but Yamamoto is closer to Steinbeck and Mansfield in her uncanny ability to shift imperceptibly from a comic to a tragic key. As in her presentation of interracial contact, her juxtaposition of Issei and Nisei can be funny as well as sad.

[13] "Relocation and Dislocation: The Writings of Hisaye Yamamoto and Wakako Yamauchi," *MELUS* 7.3 (1980): 28.

[14] The cremation scene reminds me of the many poignant accounts about Issei who burned everything associated with their country of origin after Pearl Harbor, so as to avoid being suspected by the War Relocation Authority. Yamamoto herself must have witnessed actual incidents whereby family heirlooms and literary manuscripts were turned into ashes, and the experience might have added to the graphic and heartrending quality of her description.

[15] For a detailed analysis of the technique of the double-plot, see Stan Yogi, "Legacies Revealed: Uncovering Buried Plots in the Stories of Hisaye Yamamoto and Wakako Yamauchi," MA thesis, Univ. of California, Berkeley, 1988. To Yogi I owe many insights; in particular, his thoughtful reading of "The Legend of Miss Sasagawara" (pp. 117-28) informs my own interpretation of the story.

[16] Although experimentation with limited as well as shifting points of view is common among both Modernist writers (e.g. James, Faulkner, Conrad, and Durrell) and women of color writers (e.g. Toni Morrison, Louise Erdrich, Leslie Silko), Yamamoto might have been inspired by the communication pattern characteristic of Nisei. According to Stanford Lyman, "conversations among *Nisei* almost always partake of the elements of an information game between persons maintaining decorum by seemingly mystifying one another. It is the duty of the listener to ascertain the context of the speech he hears and to glean from his knowledge of the speaker and the context just what is the important point" ("Generation and Character: The Case of the Japanese Americans," *Roots: An Asian American Reader* [Los Angeles: UCLA Asian American Studies Center, 1971], p. 53). Similarly, both "Yoneko's Earthquake" and "The Legend of Miss Sasagawara" engage the reader in information games.

[17] Perhaps the most famous literary example is Molly Bloom's reverie of her proposal that concludes Joyce's *Ulysses*: ". . . I asked him with my eyes to ask again yes and then he asked me would I yes to say yes my mountain flower and first I put my arms around him yes and drew him down to me so he could feel my

breasts all perfume yes and his heart was going like mad and yes I said yes I will Yes."

[18] "Legacies Revealed," p. 52.

[19] Yuri Kageyama considers Yamamoto's style (and that of Issei and Nisei writers in general) to be superior to the polemical style of some Sansei ("Hisaye Yamamoto—Nisei Writer," *Sunbury* 10:41). I tend to agree.

Valerie Matsumoto (review date 1989)

SOURCE: "Windows on a World," in *The Women's Review of Books,* Vol. VI, Nos. 10-11, July, 1989, p. 5.

[*In the following excerpt from a book review of* Seventeen Syllables, *Matsumoto discusses the scope and complexity of Yamamoto's stories, concluding that the stories "act on us, transforming our sense of ourselves and the world."*]

Hisaye Yamamoto's collection of short stories represents the work of 40 years, bringing together her most acclaimed pieces with several lesser known, all gleaned from an array of literary magazines, journals and newspapers ranging from the *Poston Chronicle* (the newspaper of the Poston concentration camp in Arizona where Yamamoto was interned) and the *Kashu Mainichi* (a Los Angeles Japanese-American newspaper) to the *Kenyon Review* and *Harper's Bazaar.* Yamamoto, one of the most widely recognized Japanese American authors, began to write as a teenager and published her first story in a literary magazine in 1948 at the age of 27. Four of her pieces were included in Martha Foley's annual lists of "Distinctive Short Stories" and **"Yoneko's Earthquake"** was one of *The Best American Short Stories of 1952.* In 1986 the Before Columbus Foundation recognized her literary contributions—including her own work and her nurturance of other writers—with the American Book Award for Lifetime Achievement. King-Kok Cheung's foreword to **Seventeen Syllables** provides an invaluable introduction to Yamamoto's career and fiction; the collection also includes a thorough annotated bibliography of her other works and secondary sources.

It is difficult to do justice to the scope and complexity of Yamamoto's writing. Her protagonists' struggles, limned with her distinctive blend of irony and compassion, defy stereotyping or indifference. Yamamoto carries us beyond the cardboard images of stoic Issei pioneers and introduces us to fully human artists, gamblers and dreamers like Mrs. Hayashi, composing haiku when the farm work and dinner dishes are done, and Las Vegas Charley, compulsively pursuing the jackpot that will enable him to transcend the losses in his life.

Yamamoto's writing is remarkable in its reflection of the spectrum of interracial relations, never clichéd or contrived, always complex. She reminds us that the early Japanese American communities were not completely isolated but sustained everyday contacts, whether in the form of a visiting Korean herbalist or in the arena of a gambling den run by Chinese Americans for men of many races. Whether or not it is a focus, such interaction is present in all of the stories, although it varies in intensity and impact, ranging from tragic collisions to camaraderie and love. "Yes," one thinks, "*this* is America."

These stories present not only Japanese American/Anglo relations but also the interchange among Asian Americans and between them and other ethnic minorities. Sometimes the meeting ground is love—a daring subject for the 1950s—as in the title story, in which young Rosie Hayashi has a crush on Jesus Carrasco, the son of the Mexican family hired to help with the tomato harvest, or in **"Epithalamium,"** which traces the marriage of an idealistic Nisei to an alcoholic Italian sailor. In **"Yoneko's Earthquake,"** a kind Philipino hired hand wins the hearts of both Yoneko and her mother.

In the interstices of these relations, Yamamoto makes us aware of the social tensions that pit ethnic groups against each other and suggests that even those often stereotyped are not immune from labeling others. Yoneko's father chastises her for wearing nail polish by saying, "'You look like a Filipino,' . . . for it was another irrefutable fact among Japanese in general that Filipinos in general were a gaudy lot." And the Issei gambler of **"The Brown House"** is horrified when he discovers that, in the course of a police raid on the gambling den, an African American has taken refuge in his car. The Black man, unaware of Mr. Hattori's reaction, draws on another kind of stereotype in a thank-you that leaves his unwitting benefactor dumbfounded and exhibits Yamamoto's characteristic mix of humor and irony: "He had always been . . . a friend of the Japanese people; he knew no race so cleanly, so well-mannered, so downright nice."

Besides probing the ties between Issei and Nisei, husbands and wives, Yamamoto's stories are time capsules that capture prewar life, making details of food, games and physical surroundings inextricable from the characters. For example, the catalog of mouthwatering dishes that once graced Kazuyuki Matsumoto's New Year's table serves to emphasize the emptiness of his later years. Such descriptions stitch together the patchwork quilt of the childhood of the Nisei we meet in **Seventeen Syllables**: the youngsters whose Japanese names metamorphose into the nicknames so many Nisei still have (like Chisato, whose classmates and brother call her "Cheese"), who pore over the exploits of the Katzenjammer Kids in the funnies and sing the Cream of Wheat song.

The pieces in this collection vary in power and effectiveness; some are more vignettes than stories. At their best they are haunting and catalytic. One comes away from them changed. They don't just fuse experience and imagination into "art": they act on us, transforming our sense of ourselves and the world.

Stan Yogi (essay date 1989)

SOURCE: "Legacies Revealed: Uncovering Buried Plots in the Stories of Hisaye Yamamoto," in *Studies in American Fiction,* Vol. 17, No. 2, Autumn, 1989, pp. 169-81.

[In the following essay, Yogi focuses on the stories "Seventeen Syllables" and "Yoneko's Earthquake," asserting that Yamamoto uses hidden plots and subtexts to explore the experiences of Japanese-American women caught within complex social environments hostile to their desires.]

Between 1949 and 1961 the Nisei woman Hisaye Yamamoto gained national attention as a short story writer.[1] Awarded a John Hay Whitney Foundation Opportunity Fellowship in 1949, Yamamoto's stories depicting the lives of Japanese immigrants and their children began appearing in national journals that same year.[2] That Yamamoto would be the subject of interest in 1949 is intriguing given the general lack of enthusiasm for women writers and the lingering hostility towards Japanese Americans in the aftermath of World War II. As a minority woman writer, Yamamoto had to contend with both sexual and racial barriers. She not only faced sexism from the general society, she also confronted it in her immediate community. Japanese immigrants brought with them cultural beliefs that discounted the importance of women. In an autobiographical story, Yamamoto succinctly captures these sentiments when she comments, "I gathered that my father didn't see any necessity of higher education for women."[3] Besides this devaluation of women, Yamamoto also had to deal with a mainstream culture that still viewed Japanese Americans negatively.[4] In 1949, when Yamamoto's stories were first published, World War II was still a fresh memory, and the antagonistic attitudes towards Japanese Americans that landed them in internment camps during the war still remained.

Although the sexism and racism Yamamoto encountered could have discouraged her literary efforts, a vibrant group of Nisei writers emerged in the 1930s and 1940s to spur the development of a literary voice. Building on the tradition of their parents, who wrote *haiku, tanka,* and *senryu* (Japanese poetic forms) for Japanese language papers in America,[5] young Nisei began a literary culture of their own. During the early 1930s, the English-language section editors of Japanese American papers in Los Angeles, San Francisco, and Seattle encouraged young writers to submit poems and stories.[6] As Elaine Kim notes,

> ironically, it was the segregation of the *nisei* that first encouraged their literary attempts. Among themselves, they did not need to fear being misconstrued according to some distorting stereotype or worry about having to preface each poem, story, or essay with an explanation of who they were, why they were writing in English, or how they differed from prevailing images of Japanese Americans. The existence of a small but concrete, palpable, and known audience of fellow *nisei* gave many writers a feeling of confidence.[7]

As Nisei writers became more organized, publishing such journals as *Reimei* in Salt Lake City and *Leaves* in Los Angeles, they received encouragement from progressive non-Japanese writers and artists, including Louis Adamic, Carey McWilliams, William Saroyan, and John Fante. In 1939 the League of Nisei Writers and Artists formed "for

the purpose of promoting individual and collaborative creative activity, of stimulating a critical outlook on matters of life, art and broad problems of society."[8]

A peripheral associate of the League of Nisei Writers and Artists, Yamamoto was nonetheless one of the few Nisei to gain recognition beyond the Japanese American community.[9] This recognition is well deserved, for Yamamoto's stories are not only powerful portraits of Japanese American life, they are also technically fascinating. Through the use of narrators with limited perspectives, Yamamoto develops "buried plots," veiled means of conveying stories that link her work with feminist critical theory as well as with Japanese American communication patterns.[10] Yamamoto crafts stories with surface meanings that hint at powerful undercurrents. In uncovering the buried plots of Yamamoto's stories, one can not only better understand the experiences of Japanese Americans but also explore the intersection of gender, culture, and language.[11]

Buried plots operate in different manners in Yamamoto's works. Two of her stories, **"Seventeen Syllables"** (1949) and **"Yoneko's Earthquake"** (1951), exemplify the varying ways that Yamamoto uses this device. **"Yoneko's Earthquake"** is deliciously ambiguous, containing hidden, often tragic, secrets. **"Seventeen Syllables"** begins with a focus on one plot but subtly shifts to disclose another that intertwines with the original action. The buried plots of each story reveal the experiences of Issei women and the troubling legacies they pass on to their daughters.

Ostensibly a story about the sexual awakening of an adolescent Nisei, **"Seventeen Syllables"** is as much a story about a young woman's mother as it is about her. Focused on a Japanese American farm family, the story deals with the initiation of a teen into the mysteries of adult life. Rosie Hayashi, the young central character, enters into a relationship with Jesus Carrasco, the teen-aged son of hired hands, and discovers the painful joy of sexual attraction. Through Rosie's perspective, Yamamoto reveals a plot concerning Rosie's mother. Mrs. Hayashi is deeply interested in writing haiku and spends increasing time pursuing this hobby, ultimately winning a haiku contest sponsored by a Japanese American newspaper. Her career as a poet, however, is aborted when her husband, who becomes increasingly intolerant of his wife's literary preoccupation, erupts in anger and violently destroys the prize she wins, a Hiroshige print.[12] After witnessing this incident, Rosie listens to her mother confess the disturbing events that led to her immigration to the U.S. Yamamoto crafts the story to demonstrate constant links between the two women, and the parallels she develops underscore the legacy of disruption and pain that mother passes on to daughter.

"Seventeen Syllables" operates on a series of deceptions and opens with an innocent hoax. After Mrs. Hayashi recites a haiku she has composed in Japanese, Rosie pretends "to understand it thoroughly and appreciate it no end."[13] Although Mrs. Hayashi seeks to convey the beauty of her hobby, an absence of genuine communication between the two women occurs because Rosie does not understand the Japanese her mother uses.[14] For Rosie, "it was so much easier to say, yes, yes even when one meant no, no" (p. 8), and she innocently attempts to deceive her mother by pretending to enjoy the poem.

Yamamoto links this initial and innocent deception to more calculated trickery. Jesus Carrasco, the son of seasonal workers, invites Rosie to meet him in a packing shed because, he tells Rosie, "I've got a secret I want to tell you." The two youths engage in adolescent teasing, and from this context it becomes apparent that Jesus' "secret" is a pretense to meet Rosie alone. Rosie, however, is blind to the import of Jesus' invitation. When she arrives at the shed at the appointed time she demands "now tell me the secret."

Jesus' claim of conveying a secret is not completely without merit, for he proceeds to disclose to Rosie what was, up to this point in her life, a secret: the complexity of sexual attraction. In her encounter with Jesus, Rosie echoes her earlier response to her mother:

> When he took hold of her empty hand, she could find no words to protest; her vocabulary had become distressingly constricted and she thought desperately that all that remained intact now was yes and no and oh, and even these few sounds would not easily out. Thus, kissed by Jesus, Rosie fell for the first time entirely victim to a helplessness delectable beyond speech (p. 14).

This image of Rosie, utterly dumfounded, strikingly resembles her struggle to hide her ignorance of the haiku's meaning. In her experience with Jesus, however, the limited vocabulary of "yes" and "no" reappears but cannot even be vocalized; Jesus has left her speechless. With the realization that "yes" and "no" are the basic words through which individuals express their will, one begins to recognize an important link between Rosie's encounter with Jesus and her earlier experience with her mother. For Mrs. Hayashi, writing haiku is a means of asserting herself and escaping the daily toil on the farm. Rosie's loss of will in this situation thus becomes an innocent analogue to the control Mrs. Hayashi lacks over her own life. Much like Rosie, who succumbs to Jesus' desires, Mrs. Hayashi is forced to cease writing by her husband.

Once establishing the plot concerning Rosie's relationship with Jesus, Yamamoto begins to develop the buried plot regarding Mrs. Hayashi. Jesus' deception of Rosie, resulting in her initiation into sexual knowledge, is in turn linked to the confession of deception that Rosie's mother makes. After serenely observing her husband chop up and burn the prize she won in a haiku contest, Mrs. Hayashi narrates the history behind her immigration to the U.S., a history hitherto kept secret:

> At eighteen she had been in love with the first son of one of the well-to-do families in her village. The two had met whenever and wherever they could, secretly, because it would not have done for his family to see him favor her—her father had no money; he was a

drunkard and a gambler besides. She had learned she was with child; an excellent match had already been arranged for her lover. Despised by her family, she had given premature birth to a stillborn son, who would be seventeen now (p. 18).

As an alternative to suicide, Mrs. Hayashi asks her sister in America to send for her. Her sister arranges a marriage with Rosie's father, who "was never told why his unseen betrothed was so eager to hasten the day of meeting" (p. 19).

Mrs. Hayashi's confession brings together many of the themes already introduced in the story. The constriction of communication explored in the opening has its more tragic parallel in the experiences of Rosie's mother: Mrs. Hayashi has no means of expressing her desires and feelings other than to kill herself or run away. She cannot, moreover, reveal her tarnished past to her husband. The theme of blossoming sexuality has its more dire consequences for Mrs. Hayashi. She consummates her affair but has no power to make it binding. Others dictate the termination of her relationship, and the stillborn child serves as a manifestation of her lost love.[15] Although Mrs. Hayashi's arranged marriage is not too far from common practice, her case is burdened with complicating circumstances: her family ships her off in shame, and she hides the secret of her affair and dead child from her husband. The options open to her are few. Having severed family ties, she cannot return to Japan. She is trapped in America, where she works like a machine in the fields and packing sheds. Writing, one of the few escapes from her demanding life, is denied her. Just as her love affair is cut off, just as her son is born too soon, so too is her career as a poet prematurely halted.

Only after learning of Mrs. Hayashi's history are the implications of the title **"Seventeen Syllables"** fleshed out. The haikus that Rosie's mother writes become metaphors of both freedom and constraint. Writing allows Mrs. Hayashi to transcend her mundane and harsh existence and ponder higher ideas. The haiku form, in which "she must pack all her meaning into seventeen syllables," also becomes a metaphor for the constraints that force Mrs. Hayashi to find meaning in small ways. The number seventeen, in addition, has special meaning for both Rosie and her mother. For Mrs. Hayashi, the number recalls a tragic loss; her stillborn son would at the time of the story be seventeen years old.[16] For Rosie, however, the number carries tremendous hope. Jesus, soon to be a senior in high school and her guide to budding sexuality, is probably seventeen years old.

After learning of her painful past, one can recognize the irony of the pen name Mrs. Hayashi adopts. "Ume Hanazono" literally translates as "Plum Flowergarden." (Yamamoto also links mother and daughter through their names. "Rosie" echoes the flower imagery of "Flowergarden.") The pen name is inappropriate, however, because Ume Hanazono's career as a poet never blossoms as the images of plums and flower gardens imply. On the contrary, Mrs. Hayashi's identity as a poet is ended before it fully develops.

After telling Rosie of her past, Mrs. Hayashi kneels on the floor and takes her by the wrists, insisting that her daughter capitulate to her demand: "Promise me you will never marry!" The image and the request dovetail with Rosie's encounter with Jesus. Her mother's grip reminds Rosie of "Jesus' hand, how it had touched her and where" (p. 19), creating a strong imagistic link between the two episodes and connecting Rosie's story with the buried plot concerning Mrs. Hayashi.[17] The "familiar glib agreement"— "Yes, yes, I promise"—which Rosie gives her mother recalls the constriction Rosie has vocalizing the words "yes" and "no" in her encounter with Jesus and her similar response in the beginning of the story. In this instance, however, the answer that Rosie gives her mother carries ominous weight. Her mother, as if seeing through this deception, looks at Rosie with "eyes and twisted mouth" that seem to say "you fool" (p. 19).

Rosie cannot understand, or perhaps does not want to recognize, the painful implications of her mother's story. She is about the same age her mother was when she had her affair. Before Mrs. Hayashi tells her story, Rosie, as if knowing the tale, thinks: "Don't tell me now . . . tell me tomorrow, tell me next week, don't tell me today" (p. 18). Rosie realizes, however, that her mother will continue regardless of protests. Rosie also feels that the "telling would combine with the other violence of the hot afternoon to level her life, her world to the very ground" (p. 18). Like an old weed strangling the stem of a supple flower, Mrs. Hayashi's history interweaves with and shadows Rosie's discovery of her sexuality. Rosie receives a complex legacy of subordination and thwarted pursuits, of resistance and containment. Mrs. Hayashi resists norms; she has an affair and writes poetry. These rebellions are squelched, and Mrs. Hayashi's warning not to marry is given out of concern that Rosie not follow in a path of disillusionment.

At the end of "Seventeen Syllables" it is unclear whether Rosie will accept the legacy of subordination her mother leaves her.[18] Although Rosie "glibly" agrees that she will not marry, the promise is not genuine; she agrees merely to please her mother. Rosie's exciting encounter with Jesus, however, is somewhat canceled out by the strife she witnesses between her parents and by her mother's confession of dashed love. As if a sign of her arrival into adulthood, Rosie receives an "embrace and consoling hand" from her mother much later than she expects. This image not only recalls the previous images of Jesus' embrace and Mrs. Hayashi's grip on Rosie's wrist, it also suggests the maturity that Mrs. Hayashi now expects of her daughter, who has been initiated into the excitement, pain, and disillusionment of adult life.

Included in *Best American Short Stories of 1952,* "Yoneko's Earthquake," like "Seventeen Syllables," focuses on a rural Japanese American family. The story chronicles the infatuation of a young Nisei girl, Yoneko Hosoume, with Marpo, a Filipino hired hand, in the context of emotional and psychological disturbances that occur within the family after an earthquake. "Yoneko's Earthquake" is spellbinding in its subtle conveyance of the buried story of Yoneko's mother. As the tale progresses, Yamamoto subtly suggests events unseen. Told through the prism of young Yoneko's eyes, the story seldom deals directly with the experiences of Mrs. Hosoume. Unlike Mrs. Hayashi's history, which is revealed explicitly, Mrs. Hosoume's actions are never directly conveyed. Her plot is buried within Yoneko's.

Yamamoto links the two plots, however, through Marpo, who is associated with the turbulent earthquake and, ironically, with Christ. Marpo and the fateful earthquake not only create physical havoc; much like Mrs. Hayashi's confession in "Seventeen Syllables," which threatens to level Rosie's life "to the very ground," they also serve as catalysts for domestic, generational, and ultimately spiritual upheavals.

As the story begins, Yamamoto introduces religion in conjunction with the idea of limited perspective. Yoneko is "impressed" by her cousins "the Christians." She joins them at a church service; when she does not know the words to a hymn, she "open[s] her mouth and grimace[s] nonchalantly to the rhythm."[19] This miming is paradigmatic of her actions throughout the story. Just as she mouths words without understanding their meaning, Yoneko observes and indeed participates in more ominous events without truly comprehending their significance.

Yoneko's cousins and the church service do not bring her closer to an understanding of God, so "it remained for Marpo to bring the word of God to Yoneko" (p. 47). After a "protracted discussion on religion" with Marpo, Yoneko unquestioningly accepts the tenets of Christianity and becomes "an ideal apostle, adoring Jesus, desiring Heaven, and fearing Hell" (p. 49). Marpo's evangelical role is important because he becomes a Christ figure to Yoneko. Not only does he bring her to a recognition of God, he takes on the proportions of a miracle worker, for to Yoneko "there seemed to be nothing Marpo could not do" (p. 47). To prove this, Yoneko catalogues Marpo's talents as an athlete, musician, artist, and radio technician. In her feelings towards Marpo, Yoneko mixes religious awe with childish love. Through Yoneko's infatuation, however, Yamamoto establishes an innocent foil which mirrors the more serious relationship the mother develops with Marpo.

Yamamoto not only links Marpo with Christ, she also associates him with the fateful earthquake. Among Marpo's many possessions is a "muscle-builder sent him by Charles Atlas which, despite his unassuming size, he could stretch the length of his outspread arms; his teeth gritted then and his whole body became temporarily victim to a jerky vibration" (p. 48). Not only are the grimace and body contortion an ironic mirror of the crucified Christ, the "jerky vibration" to which Marpo is subject associates him with the earthquake that sparks events that alter the psychic landscape of the characters. Yamamoto furthers Marpo's imagistic link with the disturbances caused by the earthquake. He sings, for example, with "professional quavers and rolled r's when he applie[s] a slight pressure to his Adam's apple with thumb and forefinger" (pp. 48-

49), and he sings songs with exaggerated "r's" such as "The Rose of Tralee" and the "Londonderry Air." He also builds a radio that brings in "equal proportions of static and entertainment." The trills and static become aural equivalents of physical shaking.

Yamamoto also employs quaking imagery with Mr. Hosoume and thus connects him with the upheavals that follow the earthquake. She ironically uses sexual references to describe Mr. Hosoume's experiences during and immediately after the earthquake. Mr. Hosoume is driving home when the earthquake hits, and his car is "kissed by a broken live wire dangling from a suddenly leaning pole" (p. 50). The word "kissed" is especially ironic because this experience will leave Mr. Hosoume impotent in almost all senses of the word. Yamamoto continues with more sexual imagery: to save himself from electrocution, Mr. Hosoume begins to "writhe and kick" away from the "sputtering wire." Upon returning home after the earthquake, he is "trembling." Through these images of shaking, Yamamoto not only bonds Mr. Hosoume with the alterations caused by the earthquake, she underscores his impotence through the orgasmic associations the images suggest.

Mr. Hosoume is incapacitated to such a degree that Marpo displaces him in almost every respect, and this displacement results in tragedy. Evidence of this displacement is seen as soon as the earth begins trembling. Yamamoto binds Marpo to Mrs. Hosoume through their respective reactions to the quake. As the earth rattles, Mrs. Hosoume screams *Jishin, Jishin!"* while gathering her children and running into an open field. As if a translated echo, "Marpo, stumbling in from the fields, join[s] them, saying, 'Earthquake, earthquake!'" (p. 50). The incident blossoms into a powerful image of Marpo taking Mr. Hosoume's place in the family. Marpo hugs Mrs. Hosoume and her children "as much to protect them as to support himself" (p. 50). This image visually symbolizes the "paternal" roles of supporter and comforter Marpo will take on in the family.

The displacement of Mr. Hosoume continues when Marpo takes over his employer's labor responsibilities. Mrs. Hosoume and Marpo now do all the field work. Marpo, in addition, does most of the driving, and he and Mrs. Hosoume go into town for weekly shopping trips. Mr. Hosoume, in contrast, stays "at home most of the time. Sometimes, if he had a relatively painless day, he would have supper on the stove when Mrs. Hosoume came in from the fields" (p. 51). This reversal of roles is significant when seen in context of Issei history. Issei families were usually strictly patriarchal. In addition to working beside their husbands in the fields, Issei women living on farms also had domestic duties. Issei divided daily activities and responsibilities along the lines of "inside" and "outside": "wives took care of things 'inside' the house, home or family, and men took care of 'everything else.'"[20] Cooking would be considered an "inside" responsibility, while interaction with merchants might be considered an "outside" activity. For Mr. Hosoume to perform domestic duties and for Mrs. Hosoume to take on traditionally masculine responsibilities is in itself a major upheaval.

After establishing Marpo as an integral part of the family, Yamamoto begins to develop more fully the buried plot. She provides a clue to this plot when Mrs. Hosoume, "breathless from the fields one day," presents Yoneko with a gold-colored ring with a glasslike stone. She tells Yoneko, "I'm going to give you this ring. If your father asks where you got it, say you found it on the street." Yoneko, oblivious to the origins of the ring, does not even question her mother. After Mrs. Hosoume returns to the fields, Yoneko puts "the pretty ring on her middle finger" (p. 52). This ambiguous incident initiates an investigation into the buried plot. Although it is never explicitly stated, one can gather from the events in the story that Mrs. Hosoume receives the ring from Marpo. The ring obviously is not from Mr. Hosoume, and Mrs. Hosoume interacts with Marpo on a daily basis, whether working in the fields or traveling into town. This constant contact blooms into a serious relationship.

The ring establishes a complex link between Yoneko and her mother. It not only symbolizes Marpo's feelings for Mrs. Hosoume, it also connects Mrs. Hosoume and Yoneko. The ring manifests the feelings they both share for Marpo. Mrs. Hosoume's acceptance of the ring and her subsequent relay of it to her daughter further illustrates upheaval in the family. Yoneko does not see the significance of the ring in the context of her mother's relationship with Marpo; she is too young to understand its importance. She participates, however, in deceiving her father of her mother's affair. Not only is Mrs. Hosoume's adultery a direct violation of patriarchal dominance in the family, Yoneko's unknowing compliance in hiding the affair suggests generational defiance of the patriarchy. Yoneko, who is already upset with her father for an annoying display in front of her friends, is delighted for the "chance to have some secret revenge on her father" (p. 52).

Further evidence of Mrs. Hosoume's affair and the erosion of Mr. Hosoume's power in the family is evident in a fight that erupts between Mr. and Mrs. Hosoume. After discussing with Mrs. Hosoume the merits of Yoneko's wearing nail polish, Mr. Hosoume, believing that his wife openly contradicts him, casts an insulting epithet at her. When Mrs. Hosoume resists this insult, her husband slaps her. That an Issei woman would stand up to her husband in this way would, indeed, be seen by an Issei male as insolent. The various reactions to the incident are also telling: "Mrs. Hosoume was immobile for an instant, although she glanced over at Marpo, who happened to be in the room reading a newspaper" (p. 53). That Marpo is present is important in itself because it demonstrates the extent to which he has displaced Mr. Hosoume. Although Mrs. Hosoume's glance can be interpreted as reflecting her concern that a family squabble take place in front of a hired hand, it can also represent silent communication between Mrs. Hosoume and Marpo. This interpretation gains credence when Marpo comes to Mrs. Hosoume's defense and stops Mr. Hosoume from slapping his wife again. This action is particularly powerful when one remembers that before the earthquake Marpo was "a rather shy young man meek to the point of speechlessness in the presence of Mr. and Mrs. Hosoume" (p. 49).

After this incident, Yamamoto fully develops the clues which hint at a buried plot. Marpo mysteriously leaves the family, and on the day of his disappearance the Hosoume family takes an enigmatic trip to the hospital. Yoneko and her brother, Seigo, do not comprehend why their parents make this trip. After her visit with the doctor, Mrs. Hosoume is obviously in pain, but when she responds to Yoneko's query as to the "source of her distress," she answers that "she was feeling a little under the weather and that the doctor had administered some necessarily astringent treatment" (p. 54). Only after the family returns home does Yamamoto offer evidence of untold actions.

This evidence, however, is not presented in a straightforward manner; it develops from a series of cryptic events, the most significant of which is the death of Yoneko's younger brother, Seigo. If Marpo is somehow linked to Christ, it is Seigo who is sacrificed, and his death subsequently instills Mrs. Hosoume's fervent faith in God. At the end, Mrs. Hosoume tells the innocent Yoneko, "never kill a person, Yoneko, because if you do, God will take from you someone you love" (p. 56). This statement becomes the key to uncovering previous events in the story. Through this warning, Yamamoto fleshes out Mrs. Hosoume's psychology. She feels that the death of Seigo is God's means of punishing her for killing another: it becomes apparent that the "killing" Mrs. Hosoume refers to is the abortion of a child.

This would explain the mysterious trip to the hospital. The purpose of the trip, of which Mr. Hosoume tells Yoneko and Seigo they must never speak, is to abort the unborn child of Marpo, the result of his affair with Mrs. Hosoume. Yamamoto offers a symbolic representation of the abortion through the images that frame the event. While driving to the hospital, Mr. Hosoume strikes "a beautiful collie which had dashed out barking from someone's yard. The car jerked with the impact, but Mr. Hosoume drove right on and Yoneko, wanting suddenly to vomit, looked back and saw the collie lying very still at the side of the road" (p. 54). Later, "on the way home they passed the place of the encounter with the collie, and Yoneko looked up and down the stretch of road but the dog was nowhere to be seen" (p. 54). Through this incident, Yamamoto hints at Mrs. Hosoume's "buried" action.[21]

After the abortion and the death of Seigo, the void once filled by Marpo is filled by God. Struck with guilt over the abortion and Seigo's death, Mrs. Hosoume finds comfort in Christianity. In a twisted sense, Marpo serves as an agent bringing Mrs. Hosoume to God. Her affair with Marpo results in events that ultimately lead her to God. Just as Christ initiated spiritual upheavals, Marpo is a catalyst who spiritually transforms characters in the story. He brings Yoneko to a recognition of God, although her faith is shattered during the earthquake. When she hears her mother talk of God, she is quick to respond, "I don't believe in that, I don't believe in God" (p. 56). Her rejection of God parallels her rejection of Marpo after he abruptly leaves the family. Yoneko lacks the faith in things unseen to which her mother now clings. Yoneko's experience with Marpo leaves her void of faith, while Mrs.

Hosoume's relationship with him ultimately results in her conversion.

Like "Seventeen Syllables," "Yoneko's Earthquake" ends ambiguously. It is unclear whether Yoneko will inherit the legacy of subjugation her mother offers. Yamamoto hints that his may not occur; Yoneko does not understand her mother's advice: "Never kill a person, Yoneko, because if you do, God will take from you someone you love." As Charles L. Crow notes, "Yoneko does not pause to ponder the ambiguities of this statement—was the person taken Seigo or Marpo?"[22] As if confirming that the daughter will not accept her mother's legacy, Yoneko loses the ring her mother gave her, a loss which symbolizes not only a lapse between Yoneko and Marpo but also a severed link between Yoneko and her mother.

Although both "Seventeen Syllables" and "Yoneko's Earthquake" end with Issei women surrendering to patriarchal systems, Yamamoto does not depict these choices as weak or simplistic. On the contrary, by layering her stories and developing buried plots, Yamamoto fully explores the tremendous psychological and emotional costs to Issei women who attempt to pursue their desires in a context hostile to their wishes. Unlike Rosie in "Seventeen Syllables," who can only feign understanding of her mother's haiku, readers who dig through to the buried plots of "Seventeen Syllables" and "Yoneko's Earthquake" will be rewarded with masterful storytelling by an author who has captured the complexities of Japanese American experiences.[23]

Notes

[1] The term "Nisei," a combination of the Japanese words for "two" and "generation," refers to second generation, American-born Japanese Americans. The term "Issei" refers to Japanese immigrants, parents of the Nisei.

[2] Yamamoto was also encouraged by Elizabeth Bishop and by Stanford professor and poet Yvor Winters, who had wanted her to accept a Stanford Writing Fellowship. Charles L. Crow, "A MELUS Interview: Hisaye Yamamoto," *MELUS,* 14, No. 2 (1987), 77-78.

[3] Hisaye Yamamoto, "Eju-kei-shung! Eju-kei-shung!" *Rafu Shimpo* (Dec. 20, 1980), p. 11. The Japanese American woman Mitsuye Yamada also captures the sexism of Issei when she recounts an argument she had with her father regarding her pacifist beliefs. She recalls, "My father reassured me that it was 'all right' for me to be a pacifist because as a . . . 'girl' *it didn't make any difference to anyone.*" Mitsuye Yamada, "Invisibility is an Unnatural Disaster: Reflections of an Asian American Woman," in *This Bridge Called My Back: Writings by Radical Women of Color,* ed. Cherríe Moraga and Gloria Anzaldua (New York: Kitchen Table: Women of Color Press, 1983), p. 38.

[4] G. M. Gilbert noted in 1951 that Japanese were still characterized as immature, sly, treacherous, and nationalistic. G. M. Gilbert, "Stereotype Persistence and Change among College Students," *Journal of Abnormal and Social Psychology,* 46 (1951), 245-54.

[5] Yamamoto's mother wrote *senryu* for these papers.

[6] Iwao Kawakami, English-language section editor of the San Francisco paper *The New World,* inaugurated a story and essay club on January 13, 1930.

[7] Elaine H. Kim, *Asian American Literature: An Introduction to the Writings and Their Social Context* (Philadelphia: Temple Univ. Press, 1982), p. 141.

[8] League of Nisei Writers and Artists, ts, 1939.

[9] Others who received national attention were Toyo Suyemoto, whose poetry was published in *Yale Review,* and the short sotry writer Toshio Mori, whose works appeared in national journals such as *New Directions in Poetry and Prose* and *Common Ground.* A collection of his stories, *Yokohama, California,* was slated for publication prior to the war. Because of wartime hostilities towards Japanese, it did not appear until 1949.

[10] "Buried plots" are related to the common literary idea of the "double plot." Whereas double plots involve an explicit presentation of a secondary, albeit related, plot in a story or play (for example, the Glouscester plot in *King Lear*), buried plots in Yamamoto's stories are not always clearly delineated. Often the reader must piece together a buried plot from clues garnered in the "main" or "surface plot." Buried plots are also related to the feminist literary theories of Elaine Showalter and Annette Kolodny. Showalter has developed the idea of "muted stories" and asserts that "in the purest feminist literary criticism we are . . . presented with a radical alteration of our vision, a demand that we see meaning in what has previously been empty space. The orthodox plot recedes, and another plot, hitherto submerged in the anonymity of the background stands out in bold relief like a thumbprint." See Elaine Showalter, "Feminist Criticism in the Wilderness," in *The New Feminist Criticism: Essays on Women, Literature and Theory,* ed. Elaine Showalter (New York: Pantheon, 1985), p. 266. Showalter suggests a stylistic interpretation or reinterpretation of explicit actions or events in a surface plot to uncover the muted rebellion of women. Although related to Showalter's muted stories, the concept of buried plots is somewhat different. Often in Yamamoto's works, we need not reinterpret the "surface" plot but rather look to what is only alluded to, what remains unstated. In addition, the term "buried" is flexible; in some cases, a plot is buried in the sense that it does not appear, or is not fully developed, until well into the story. These buried plots often focus on a character who is defined through the actions of others. This elliptical character development in Yamamoto's stories relates to Annette Kolodny's identification of "reflexive perception" in works by women writers. Kolodny argues that reflexive perception is a typical stylistic feature of female fiction and occurs when a character "discover[s] herself or find[s] some part of herself in activities she had not planned or in situations she cannot fully comprehend." See Annette Kolodny, "Some Notes on Defining a 'Feminist Literary Criticism,'" *Critical Inquiry,* 2 (1975), 79. Yamamoto employs variations of this device. Although characters in her stories are often involved in situations they cannot fully understand, this does not always result in self-discovery.

[11] Buried plots have forceful analogues in Japanese American culture. The behavior associated with the idea of *enryo* among Japanese Americans provides a cogent parallel. *Enryo* is difficult to define since it involves several different types of behavior including the denial of something proffered even though that item is wanted, the acceptance of a less desired object even if given a choice, and the hesitancy to ask questions or to make demands. The actions associated with *enryo* originated with norms in Japan that governed the ways in which "inferiors" were to behave to-

wards "superiors." Transferred to and altered in America, *enryo* now encompasses a whole range of behaviors from "what to do in ambiguous situations, to how to cover moments of confusion, embarrassment, and anxiety." See Harry H. L. Kitano, *Japanese Americans: The Evolution of a Subculture* (Englewood Cliffs: Prentice-Hall, 1976), p. 24. Linking the diverse behaviors associated with *enryo* is the idea that manifest actions do not always accurately reflect inner feelings. Those unfamiliar with Japanese American culture might not be sensitive to the subtleties underlying behavior and consequently misinterpret actions associated with *enryo.* The *enryo* dynamic is a potential cultural equivalent to a literary buried plot.

[12] Japanese artist, 1797-1858.

[13] Hisaye Yamamoto, "Seventeen Syllables," in *"Seventeen Syllables" and Other Stories* (Latham: Kitchen Table: Women of Color Press, 1988), p. 8. Hereafter page references will appear in parentheses within the text.

[14] Robert Rolf argues that the haiku form "functions as a symbol of the incomplete communication between Issei parent and Nisei child." Robert Rolf, "The Short Stories of Hisaye Yamamoto, Japanese-American Writer," *Bulletin of Fukuoka University of Education,* 31 (1982), 81.

[15] That Rosie's mother would immigrate to the U.S. under these circumstances may strike readers unfamiliar with Japanese American history as odd. In fact, the type of marriage in which Mrs. Hayashi is involved was not too deviant from the prevalent practice of "picture marriages" among Issei. Arranged marriages were traditional in Japan. As Yuji Ichioka explains:

> Heads of household selected marriage partners for family members through intermediaries or go-betweens. An exchange of photographs. sometimes occurred in the screening process, with family genealogy, wealth, education, and health figuring heavily in the selection criteria. Go-betweens arranged parleys between families at which proposed unions were discussed and negotiated. Although at such meetings prospective spouses normally met each other for the first time, it would be unusual for them to talk to each other. After all, the meetings were for the benefit of heads of family, and not designed for future couples to become acquainted with each other. If the families mutually consented, engagement and marriage ensued. See Yuji Ichioka, *The Issei: The World of the First Generation Japanese Immigrants, 1885-1924* (New York: Free Press, 1988), p. 164.

When Japanese men in the U.S. sought to marry, this traditional practice was altered to suit the needs of Issei. Men forwarded their relatives photographs of themselves along with information about their situation in America. Relatives would then negotiate a marriage, and an Issei man would in turn receive a picture of his new spouse. Women would be sent off to America where they would meet their husbands for the first time. Anti-Japanese forces cited picture-marriages as proof of Japanese unassimilability. Although the exact number of picture-brides is unknown, "the majority of wives who entered [Japanese] immigrant society between 1910 and 1920 came as picture-brides." Ichioka, p. 165.

[16] Charles L. Crow also notes this in his essay, "The *Issei* Father in the Fiction of Hisaye Yamamoto," in *Opening Up Literary*

Criticism: Essays on American Prose and Poetry, ed. Leo Truchlar (Salzburg: Verlag Wolfgang Neugebauer, 1986), p. 35. Crow considers Yamamoto's portrayal of the father in "Seventeen Syllables" as unflattering. Yamamoto has responded that Mr. Hayashi "was only acting in the way he'd been brought up to act, the way men were supposed to be." Crow, "A MELUS Interview," p. 80.

[17] Yamamoto suggests the patriarchy of Christianity when Rosie, after her mother demands, that she never marry, calls out silently to Jesus, "not certain whether she was invoking the help of the son of the Carrascos or of God" (p. 19). Rosie is searching for a male savior to help her escape the troubling request her mother makes. The mixture of romantic and religious associations is intriguing and is repeated in "Yoneko's Earthquake." Jesus, the son of the Carrascos, could "save" Rosie by proving to her that romance is not always doomed as it was in Mrs. Hayashi's experience. Jesus, the son of God, on the other hand, could "save" Rosie by healing the psychological and emotional wounds from which the family suffers.

[18] Elaine Kim suggests that Rosie will learn from her mother's experience. Kim, p. 163.

[19] Hisaye Yamamoto, "Yoneko's Earthquake," in *"Seventeen Syllables" and Other Stories,* p. 47. Hereafter page references will appear in parentheses within the text.

[20] Sylvia Junko Yanagisako, *Transforming the Past: Tradition and Kinship Among Japanese Americans* (Stanford: Stanford Univ. Press, 1985), p. 101. Yanagisako's study deals with urban Issei. Since no comparable study focuses on rural Issei, I generalize her findings to rural Issei.

[21] Yuri Kageyama also notes the symbolic nature of the collie's death. Yuri Kageyama, "Hisaye Yamamoto—Nisei Writer," *Sunbury 10,* p. 36. King-Kok Cheung observes, "the unblinking killing of the animal enables us not only to perceive the father's intense anger and his total indifference to the life about to be destroyed but also to imagine the mother's contrasting psychological state. She must cringe inwardly as she witnesses the act that foreshadows the fate of her unborn child." King-Kok Cheung, "Introduction," *"Seventeen Syllables" and Other Stories,* p. xix.

[22] Charles L. Crow, "Home and Transcendence in Los Angeles Fiction," in *Los Angeles Fiction,* ed. David Fine (Albuquerque: Univ. of New Mexico Press, 1984), p. 202.

[23] The author thanks Susan Schweik, King-Kok Cheung, Eric Sundquist, Genaro Padilla, and Gayle Fujita-Sato for their helpful comments on earlier versions of this essay.

Zenobia Baxter Mistri (essay date 1990)

SOURCE: "'Seventeen Syllables': A Symbolic Haiku," in *Studies in Short Fiction,* Vol. 27, No. 2, Spring, 1990, pp. 197-202.

[*In the following essay, Mistri examines Yamamoto's use of haiku as a metaphor for the themes explored in her story "Seventeen Syllables."*]

In 1942, the Japanese Relocation Act incarcerated 110,000 Japanese in Poston, Arizona. Born in 1921 of Japanese immigrant parents, Hisaye Yamamoto is a Nisei[1] and one of those who watched closely the effects of that tragic internment. Although there are books, taped reminiscences bound into collections, and a slender handful of films, there is little criticism available that examines the experience of fiction writers who may have been marked by concentration camps like Manzanar, which was the first of ten such camps. The saga of the people who suffered this indignity has been documented by writers. Michi Weglyn, for example, gives a detailed account of this experience in *Years of Infamy: The Untold Story of America's Concentration Camps.*

In the brief biographical information on Hisaye Yamamoto that she provides in *Between Mothers and Daughters* preceeding Yamamoto's short story **"Seventeen Syllables,"** Susan Koppleman writes: "she, along with 110,000 other Japanese Americans, was subjected to relocation and imprisonment. . . . During the war, she moved to Massachusetts for a summer, but returned to camp, and then to California in 1945 where she was employed by the *Los Angeles Tribune*" (161). Confinement seems to have sensitized Yamamoto to the devastating results of a loss of control. In almost all her short stories, her central characters battle overwhelming odds. In "Relocation and Dislocation: The Writings of Hisaye Yamamoto and Wakako Yamauchi" McDonald and Newman accurately assess that she selects characters who are "hurt, who have deviated from the norm, who are grasping for some bits of beauty in their desperation. . . . All who seek but lose are of interest to Yamamoto" (28). This assessment also applies to Yamamoto's much anthologized **"Seventeen Syllables."** However, despite its popularity, the artistic levels in the tale, as in the others, remain unexplored. Koppleman draws attention to the fact that Yamamoto's stories[2] have been reprinted at least twenty times in one or more of twelve anthologies since 1969. Yet Yamamoto still has not received the critical attention she merits.

Typical of a Yamamoto story, **"Seventeen Syllables"** offers multiple perspectives which need to be peeled back layer upon layer, for this tale simultaneously records a daughter's—Rosie's—awakening sexuality, and depicts a mother's—Tome Hayashi's—devastating annihilation. The tale's power lies in the vortex created by the mother's stepping outside her traditional Japanese Issei role of farm worker, cook, housekeeper, and wife. The narrative tensions arise out of a seemingly simple interest that Tome develops, haiku. At one level, the story depicts the cultural barrier that haiku creates and reveals among Tome, her husband, and her daughter; at another level, the tale unravels the destruction of a woman who creates independently.

To neglect Yamamoto's artistic achievement in using haiku is to bypass the deeper metaphor for separation which it suggests. To understand the subtle symbolism of haiku, one must understand the complexity of this art form: its simplicity is deceptive in depth of content and in origin. In the Introduction to the first of his four volumes entitled *Haiku,* R. H. Blyth explains that this type of poetry needs to be understood from the Zen point of view. He describes haiku as "a spiritual state of mind in which individuals are not separated from other things, instead remain identical with them while yet retaining their individuality and defining peculiarities" (iii). Obviously, neither Rosie nor Mr. Hayashi is able to understand haiku or the meaning it has for Tome. Both father and daughter lack the undiluted, intuitive understanding necessary, for haiku represents the Eastern world of religious and poetic experience. Japanese traditional roles and the American world seem to have stripped Mr. Hayashi and Rosie of the innate ability to be one and yet separate. Blyth compares the haiku experience to a kind of enlightenment in which the reader sees into the life of things.

During the three months that Tome contributes haiku to *Mainichi Shinbun,* "The Daily Newspaper," she takes the "blossoming name" of Ume Hanazono. In Japanese, the name *Ume* stands for an exquisite flowering tree which blossoms in early spring and bears fruit by the end of spring—that is, in three months. *Hanazono* means "a flower garden." Both names enfold one of the central experiences described in the story: Tome Hayashi's brief awakening into a creative independence which does not include her Japanese husband of "simple mind" or her Nisei daughter who pretends to understand Japanese because she doesn't want to disillusion her mother about the "quantity and quality" (163) of the Japanese she knows. On the other hand, *Tome* ironically signifies "good fortune," or "luck," while *Hayashi* means "woods." In the names, one sees some of the subtle shades of meaning implied in this Nisei, second generation Japanese-American, story.

The number three plays a subtle role in **"Seventeen Syllables."** Tome's/Ume's brief awakening lasts for *"perhaps three months"* (164; italics mine)—a *season*—as does her namesake tree, Ume, which blossoms and bears fruit in *three* months. The brief three months are echoed by the *three* line scheme—five, seven, and five syllables—used for haiku when it is translated or written in English. Haiku becomes the metaphor for Tome's separateness. After she works in the fields, keeps house, cooks, washes, and serves dinner, she becomes a significant other person; she transforms into Ume Hanazone—a poetess.

The creative pull Ume feels assumes threatening dimensions as she discusses haiku with other males. Tome steps outside her role as an insignificant other and strives for intellectual stimulation and challenges in the process of composing poetry. Essentially, haiku transforms her from a quiet wife into one who becomes in a sense a true Japanese, an "earnest muttering stranger, who often neglected speaking when spoken to and stayed busy at the parlor table as late as midnight scribbling with pencil on scratch paper . . ." (164). Mr. Hayashi now must play solitaire. The gulf between the Hayashis widens each time the family goes visiting. Her haiku makes her forget her traditional role—the submissive, passive working person—for Tome engages in comparing ecstatic notes with visiting poets while her husband entertains "the nonliterary members" (164) or looks at *Life* magazine instead of intuiting *life* through his wife's poetry as would a true lover of haiku or ukiyo-e.

Rosie's emerging womanhood parallels the three months of Tome's poetry writing. Rosie secretly meets with Jesus Carrasco, the son of the Mexican family hired for the harvest. With the first stolen kiss, he awakens her sensuality: "Once he had made her screech hideously by crossing over, while her back was turned, to place atop the tomatoes in her green-stained basket a truly monstrous, pale green worm (it had looked more like an infant snake)" (168). The phallic innuendo is hard to ignore.

Rosie is so wrapped in herself that she fails to see her mother's need for identity, creativity, and approval. Each time Ume reads a poem for approval, Rosie's response is a refrain: "It was so much easier to say yes, yes, even when one meant no, no" (163). The "yes, yes" she says to placate her mother reflects the cultural vacuum that exists between the mother and daughter as it reflects Rosie's inability to become one with the haiku that Ume writes. However, the language barrier between the mother and daughter pales besides the growing haiku barrier between the parents.

One hot afternoon, "the hottest day of the year," when the creative pull seems to have reached breaking point, the haiku editor of the *Mainichi Shinbun* personally delivers the first-prize award that Ume wins. The Hiroshiges Mr. Kuroda brings subtly echoes the spiritual chasm between the Hayashis, as it affirms the deep relationship of oriental art to haiku. Blyth explains:

> a haiku poet may express his understanding pictorially as well as verbally. . . . It is indirect, in that the pictures he sees teach him how to look at and feel and listen to the world of nature. . . . They show him where the value and meaning of things [are], so he may say in words what the pictures say in lines, concerning that mysterious interplay of the simple and the complicated, the general and the particular. . . . The ukiyo-e of Hiroshige would have no significance, were the scenery of Japan as plain and clear in outline as they. (86)

Like haiku, Hiroshige's famous landscapes evoke emersion and must be intuited. The viewer must feel her feet in the pink clouds he paints and become one of the individuals in the sampans that float near the pines. The gap in understanding is reflected in Rosie's cold, literal description of the Horoshiges:

> Rosie thought it was a pleasant picture, which looked to have been sketched with delicate quickness. There were pink clouds, containing some graceful caligraphy, and a sea that was a pale blue except at the edges, containing four sampans with indications of people in them. (173)

The entire description reflects the failure to see the mysterious interplay among life, the painting and the self. Rosie's inability to imagine the floating world of ukiyo-e or to intuit what the picture suggests reaffirms the barriers between her mother and herself as well as between the Japanese culture and herself.

In the excitement of receiving the prize, Ume takes over from Tome—the subservient tomato packer—and entertains the illustrious Japanese visitor at tea. Once more cut out from a true understanding, Mr. Hayashi storms in, seizes the prize, takes it outside, and proceeds to smash and burn it.

After the mother and daughter watch the fire die, Tome tells her story to her daughter. "It was like a story out of the magazines. . . . Her mother, at nineteen, had come to America and married her father as an alternative to suicide" (175). At this point, the title **"Seventeen Syllables"** becomes meaningful. It seems to stand not only for the number of syllables in a haiku but also for the stillborn illegitimate child Tome bore *seventeen years* ago in Japan, a syllable for each silent year she lives in America. The reader then recalls the patience with which Ume had explained haiku: "See Rosie, . . . it was a *haiku,* a poem in which she must pack all her meaning into seventeen syllables only . . ." (163).

The power of this seemingly simple Nisei tale comes from several interwoven themes. The primary one reveals a cultural straitjacket in which a male dominates and destroys a gentle woman who is consumed by an urgent need to create and express herself. Moreover, the narrative suggests another possible female tragedy in Rosie's future. Rosie and Jesus' relationship harbors a potential intercultural conflict, for Jesus is not of her ethnic group or station. Rosie's romance recalls her mother's unfortunate love affair with the young Japanese who was above her social position.

The conclusion of the story echoes the cultural chasm between the mother and daughter also, for Tome asks Rosie, "Promise me you will never marry." Tome receives the same glib agreement Rosie used for haiku—the old lie—"Yes, yes, I promise" (176). Ironically, just as Tome barely understands English, Rosie scarcely understands the mother's suffocating plea. Each is a prisoner, isolated in solitary confinement. Tragically, Tome loses her second child also, this time to an alien culture which does not have an artistic spiritual intuitiveness or the same gender restrictions as the Japanese. Rejected by both husband and daughter, Ume Hanazone is destroyed, no more to be a flowering garden.

Tome's fate is played in counterpoint, as it were, in the story of Mrs. Hayano, who we are told bore four lovely daughters, each named after *one season* (again, *three months*) of the year. Haru, *spring,* is her first-born. The reader is told "something had been wrong with Mrs. Hayano ever since the birth of her first child" (164). Mrs. Hayano, who was reputed to have been the belle of her native village, moves stooped and shuffling, violently trembling, always. Mr. Hayano, we are told, is "handsome, tall, and strong" (168). So Mrs. Hayano has her brief spring like Ume/Tome and is destroyed.

What is the reader to intuit about the female role in this culture? These women blossom/create and pay the price—intense personal jeopardy or annihilation. The duration of their flowering shrinks to the length of almost a season; confined and compressed, their existences recall a sparse seventeen-syllable ephermal haiku.

"Seventeen Syllables" remains irrevocably a woman's story. The flavor and anguish which lace it and make it powerful come from the collision of Eastern and Western values. Tome steps outside her place as child bearer, housekeeper, and farmworker when she attempts to gain control and carve an independent artistic territory for herself, and she is smothered. Rosie identifies with her American background and culture. Ironically, even in Japanese class, she entertains her friend by mimicking a series of British and American movie stars. Rosie doesn't understand Tome, nor does she understand her own roots or the Japanese language and culture.

Both the Japanese and American cultures make demands which by themselves can create intense disequilibrium. In close juxtaposition, they seem to destroy the occupants or at best leave them in the middle of the *woods* (Hayashi). Perhaps a letter written by Yamamoto, which Koppleman quotes in her introduction to this story, throws additional light on the power of this tale; Yamamoto speaks of the pain she feels when she thinks of her mother, who could have used a more understanding daughter (162). Yamamoto goes on to say that **"Seventeen Syllables"** is her mother's story, even though the details are not true. Although the Japanese and American cultures do not fuse in this tale, art and the artist do, for **"Seventeen Syllables"** becomes the daughter's symbolic haiku for the mother—the "yes, yes" said finally, packed with all the intuitive meaning and understanding in Zen fashion.

Notes

[1] Weglyn explains that the Japanese were usually lumped together into one derogatory group—"Japs"—during the war years, but needed to be seen as four groups, for they had experienced different formative backgrounds. (1) The Issei were first generation Japanese who had an entire Japanese cultural background. (2) The Nisei were second generation Japanese who had received their entire education in the United States. (3) The Kibei were Nisei who were divided into two groups. The Japanese used this term to refer to those American-born Japanese who received their education in Japan till they were seventeen, and also to those who received their early formative education in America and then went to Japan for four or five years of education (41).

[2] Hisaye Yamamoto shares some private thoughts on the nature of the Nisei and their yearnings as writers in "Writing." *Amerasia Journal* 3.2 (1976): 126-33 (rpt. from *Rafu Shimpo*). Importantly, she mentions some of the journals in which her stories have been published: *Partisan Review, Kenyon Review, Harper's Bazaar, Furioso, Frontier, The Carlton Micellany, Arizona Quarterly, Pacific Citizen, Crossroads, Rafu Shimpo*. As she herself notes, many of her stories have made Martha Foley's list of "distinctive" short stories for their particular year.

Works Cited

Blyth, R. H. *Haiku.* 4 vols. Japan: Hokuseido, 1966. Vol. 1.

McDonald Ritsuko, Dorothy, and Katherine Newman. "Relocation and Dislocation: The Writings of Hisaye Yamamoto and Wakako Yamauchi." *Melus* 7 (1980): 21-38.

Weglyn, Michi. *Years of Infamy: The Untold Story of America's Concentration Camps.* New York: Morrow Quill, 1976.

Yamamoto, Hisaye. "Seventeen Syllables." *Partisan Review,* November 1949. Rpt. in *Between Mothers and Daughters: Stories Across a Generation* Ed. Susan Koppleman. New York: Feminist Press, City U of New York, 1985, 161-176.

———. "Writing." *Amerasia Journal* 3.2 (1976): 126-133.

Ming L. Cheng (essay date 1994)

SOURCE: "The Unrepentant Fire: Tragic Limitations in Hisaye Yamamoto's 'Seventeen Syllables'," in *MELUS: The Journal of the Society for the Study of the Multi-Ethnic Literature of the United States,* Vol. 19, No. 4, Winter, 1994, pp. 91-107.

[*In the following essay, Cheng emphasizes the social, cultural, economic, and gender conditions that influence the actions of the* issei *father in "Seventeen Syllables."*]

"Seventeen Syllables," perhaps the most anthologized, acclaimed and analyzed short story by Hisaye Yamamoto, epitomizes the complex rendering of characters within an intricately drawn plot characteristic of her larger body of works. Yamamoto masks a secondary, deeper plot concerning the relationship between Mr. and Mrs. Hayashi in an ostensibly larger, primary plot relating a stage in the maturation of their daughter Rosie, narrated from her limited point of view.[1] In analyzing the dynamics of the husband-wife relationship within this "subplot," critical commentary is aligned on the discussion of the role of the male. McDonald and Newman state that "the wife [Mrs. Hayashi] seeks release [from an unhappy marriage] through the writing of haiku," and as a result begs her daughter never to marry (28). The cause of her unhappiness is revealed by Stan Yogi in his description of the actions of the male, "who becomes increasingly intolerant of his wife's literary preoccupation, erupts in anger and violently destroys the prize she wins, a Hiroshiges print" (170). The negative assessment of the male's role in the tragic end of **"Seventeen Syllables"** is further developed in King-Kok Cheung's introduction to the 1982 volume entitled *Seventeen Syllables and Other Stories*: "But her husband, a farmer who is indifferent to her creative endeavors, expresses disapproval and resentment whenever she engages in long discussions of poetry with people who share her interests. Mr. Hayashi becomes increasingly impatient while his wife discusses poetry with the editor in the main house, and finally stalks inside in anger and emerges with the prize picture" (xviii). Cheung describes the father's final act as "cruelty," an "outrage," and "a jealous husband's fury" while remarking upon the wife's "anguish" as a direct result (xix). Charles Crow clearly perceives the female as the victim, murdered by "the ineptitude and

brutality of the men she has known" ("Issei Father" 35). In an unusually accusatory critique of the author, he blames Yamamoto for his perception of her negative depiction of the male—a portrayal, similarly drawn by most critics, depicting Mr. Hayashi as an angry chauvinist who aggrieves a disillusioned, victimized mother.

Critical analyses to date lack examination and emphasis of the male perspective, without which comprehension of the limitations of both characters remains incomplete. While critics seem content with faulting Mr. Hayashi for the tragic victimization of the female, this viewpoint is too often symptomatic of and assessed with an incomplete understanding of the ulterior causation of the actions criticized.[2] Yamamoto herself, in defense of Rosie's father and in response to Crow's accusation, explains that Mr. Hayashi is only doing what is expected in accordance with tradition; although she does not justify his actions, she indicates that they nevertheless must be examined within a defined, traditional context.[3] Cheung's criticism of the male character is surprising in the wake of her accurate, insightful analysis of the author: "Intent on depicting human complexity, Yamamoto seldom casts her characters as heroes or villains, and rarely presents personal interaction in simple black and white terms" (xiv). In a later passage, she further elaborates, "Though Yamamoto persistently confronts religious and moral issues, she is never dogmatic or moralistic in her judgement. Instead she can find fault with the seemingly divine and perceive redeeming grace among erring humanity. Her characters are often caught in circumstances that render unqualified approval or condemnation difficult" (xxii-xxiii). Yet she, like her counterparts, does render an unqualified condemnation of the actions of Mr. Hayashi. The seeming interpretive impasse of present criticism imparts a responsibility to Yamamoto and a challenge to her readers to go beyond simplistic answers—to emphasize gender, economic, and social limitations both male and female face, and to explore respective responsibilities, including complicity in one's own oppression, in the analysis of this powerful, disturbing treatise on the tragedy of limitations. Examination of **"Seventeen Syllables"**—perhaps Yamamoto's artistry at its highest and most complex—from an alternative perspective, in the context of the external and internal limitations of the male and the female, will shed more light upon the singular brilliance of a woman's unique perception.[4]

Necessity and extravagance, harvest and destruction—these contrasting elements form the basis of an unassuming theme woven into the fabric of Yamamoto's **"Seventeen Syllables."**[5] It sinks beneath the layers Yamamoto creates, barely visible from our societal vantage within the mist of the illusory American ideals of equality and unlimited opportunity, in a tale seen through Rosie's denying eyes. But the view lies in the perspective. From below this misty haze, critically armed with the realization that right and wrong are dependent upon the cultural and social context which define one's actions, examination of the Hayashis and the events leading to the story's climax reveals a compelling theme: Rosie's father, an ordinary man of simple means, is driven by a non-traditional wife's extravagance to commit an act of violence to regain a necessary measure of control, economic and social, within the limitations inherent in the struggle of first-generation immigrant life.

The requirements of survival in the harsh environment of the immigrant Nisei heightens the claim necessity makes against the lives of the Hayashis. Necessity is the single-minded direction of resources towards livelihood; it is "the linear image of the riverbank, which suggests purposefulness, direction, containment, control" (Wong 6). However, "[a] line turned in upon itself is a circle . . . signifying a traditional way of life which has become mindlessly self-perpetuating; if a symbol of perfection and self-sufficiency, a circle also represents confinement" (6). If "the dehumanizing demands of Necessity" (6) drive the actions of the husband, to an ever increasing extent an extravagance born of the desire to escape confinement motivates the actions of the wife. Extravagance is that done "just for the sake of doing it" (6), or, "doing something not because one has to but because one wants to" (7) without considering the limitations imposed by the macrocosm. Against the external limitations of the macrocosm, signified by the impending harvest, the increasing extravagance of the wife builds as a powerful counter-force, deeply affecting the fabric of the Hayashis's existence. As Rosie's narrative unfolds, this extravagant challenge cannot go unmet; indeed, **"Seventeen Syllables"** is Rosie's narration of this conflict and the resulting tensions which rise, continuously and inexorably, towards an eventual climax. Tragically, necessity, which through its confinement motivates the extravagant desire to break free, eventually forces its inevitable destruction. As the livelihood of the Hayashis, symbolized by the harvest, regains its preeminence through the destruction of the Hiroshiges, the circle turns in upon itself and is once again complete.

Mr. Hayashi is, as Aunt Taka describes, "a young man of whom she [Taka] knew, but lately arrived from Japan, a young man of simple mind, it was said, but of kindly heart" (19). He is a first-generation Japanese-American who views the necessities of life through the lens of traditional values. He and his wife have lived a rural life of hard work and limited means, and have successfully supported a family, raising a teenage daughter. The Hayashis are far from rich, and Mr. Hayashi's greatest concerns are the necessary tasks which allow them to eke a living from their small tomato farm, which, according to McDonald and Newman, belongs in the category of small pre-war tenant farms tended by immigrant Japanese farmers (28). Yamamoto's descriptions of the tomato farm, the house, and the old green Ford, in any case, attest to the privation of the Hayashis. Constrained by economic considerations, Mr. Hayashi cannot afford the luxury of concerns unrelated to his livelihood, and thus has no apparent inclination to become more than the simple farmer he is. His simplicity is his family's simplicity, born of a pragmatic assessment of the limitations imposed by societal and economic concerns and the necessities of farm life.

Tome Hayashi, by contrast, is a woman with passions which consume, who ignores the limits imposed by societal mores and the norms of behavior indicated by tradi-tional gender roles. In her youth, she is consumed by an affair with a lover from a higher social class. The fire of her passion is fueled by ambition; her liaison seems to be chosen with an eye towards advancement of her social position. Tome disregards the impossibility of marriage due to class differences and the matrimonial arrangement of her lover to another. From this indiscretion, out of wedlock, she comes to be with child—an event so disparate with the norms of her society that it almost leads to her suicide. In this interplay between necessity and extravagance, tradition clashes with the unyielding passions of a youthful Tome, superseding and nearly destroying her. And for the first time, her disregard of limits set forth by tradition and society leads to her downfall.

Fifteen years hence, after escaping her death from extravagance through the traditional institution of marriage, Tome Hayashi is again consumed, this time by a passion for writing haiku. Haiku, an art of the Japanese leisure class, is a passion fueled by a renewed ambition to rise in social position. The resulting disruption of the Hayashis's rural family life is considerable. The rebirth of the passionate Tome is symbolized by the appearance of Ume Hanazono, who ignores her disturbance of family routine, the disapproval of her husband, and the economic considerations of the necessities of harvest as the youthful Tome disregarded the incongruities of her affair years past. Rosie, in a rare moment of enlightenment, notes that "the new interest had some repercussions on the household routine" (9). In a rural lifestyle of early to bed and early to rise, Ume's departure in daily routine causes the marital relations of the Hayashis to suffer.

The disruption increases when the Hayashis's routine in entertaining their guests is also altered. Social occasions become polarized as the wife engages in discussion with male haiku writers, relegating her husband to socializing with the remaining, more likely female, members of their social guests. Here, the division of husband and wife is more problematic. It separates them into members of two separate classes—the literary and the non-literary—against the grain of traditional gender roles; social peers now see the Hayashis as Mrs. Hayashi-the-poet and Mr. Hayashi-the-farmer. Through her separation and her association with male literary figures, Mrs. Hayashi acquires, to the indirect detriment of her husband, the status of the literary class and the connotations of power and authority. Unlike the previous "private" separation within the microcosm of the family, this "public" separation is an explicit threat to traditional gender roles: it is damaging and unacceptable to a traditional Japanese, to whom public appearance often transcends private realities in importance.

As the tension of the disruption of lifestyle and gender role rises, Rosie's father finally makes his displeasure and disapproval overt during a visit to the Hayanos. Unable to control the macrocosm which places social and economic limitations upon his household, he cannot afford to lose control of the microcosm of his family's simple rural existence necessitated by these limitations. Mrs. Hayashi's public disruption of the status quo, in contrast with the acceptable, unthreatening domestic madness and silence of Mrs. Hayano, for the first time forces him to exercise actual power in an attempt to regain control.[6] With the pretext of necessity for farmwork, he forces his family to cut short their visit (11). The abruptness of his actions, in a culture where even the smallest gestures are of great consequence, sends a clear signal. It induces an atmosphere so intense that Rosie "[feels] a rush of hate for both—for her mother for begging, [and] for her father for denying her mother" (12). Rosie, unwilling to confront what she subconsciously understands, leaves unexplained what her mother is begging for—and what her father is denying her mother. As an Issei woman married for fifteen years, Mrs. Hayashi, unlike her daughter, fully realizes the proper interpretation of her husband's actions and the disruption her passion for haiku has caused. Although she apologetically states, "I'm sorry, . . . you must be tired," she knows that the cause of her husband's anger is not fatigue, and correspondingly her apology, which Rosie termed "begging," is for forgiveness of her disruption (11). With his actions, his silence, and his demeanor, Rosie's father draws a line. His position is clear: he denies Tome Hayashi his forgiveness and by inference his previously tacit acceptance of her passion for haiku. By her apology she accepts this denial in accordance with the dictates of Japanese society and tradition.

But Mrs. Hayashi soon disregards her husband's position, and her previous acceptance of it is revealed as a pretense of respect. She dangerously continues her passionate affair with haiku because she lacks an outside avenue to ascend in social status; in America, where she can barely speak English, she has few choices. She must rise socially from within the private sphere, the microcosm of her family, for she, like her husband, is limited by the economic and social constraints of the macrocosm. During a subsequent social call by Aunt Taka, she engages in conversation concerning haiku, the same public activity which brought about her husband's initial exercise of power at the Hayanos. The resulting disruption is ever more distinct as Mr. Hayashi, on this occasion, has no one with whom he can carry an intercourse on his "level." His sullen and conspicuous absence during Taka's visit reaffirms his position, and once again, while Rosie does not consciously comprehend the implications of her father's anger and absence, her mother surely does.[7] Mrs. Hayashi also reveals her resourcefulness in defying her husband's stand, gingerly and cleverly crossing the line he drew at the Hayanos during a social occasion in which her husband is powerless to enforce his position: during the visit of Aunt Taka, before whom her husband must defer great respect due to her age and her matrimonial role with the Hayashis.[8]

Taka's visit marks the first explicit evidence of a parallel in the behavior of mother and daughter. This occasion, for Rosie as for her mother, marks a "signal of permission, of grace, and [Rosie] had definitely made up her mind to" embark on her illicit rendezvous (13). Rosie's desire for Jesus and her mother's desire for social advancement are dual passions running on parallel tracks of extravagance. The scene immediately preceding Taka's visit tells of a death that does not occur; the significance of Rosie's

unfulfilled death wish becomes apparent when, in the end, mother relates to daughter her own previously unfulfilled wish to commit suicide. Rosie's break from tradition, foreshadowed by this scene, parallels the extravagance of her mother during a period of dangerous freedom granted by Taka's exceptional status. Yamamoto utilizes the accurate, accessible, apparently unrelated actions and feelings of Rosie within the overlying plot to suggest her mother's concurrent motivations within the subplot, which otherwise would go undescribed by an unreliable narrator. Rosie's romantic wants are tantalizingly suggestive of the social ambitions of her mother in a manner most aptly expressed by Sau-ling Wong: "Sexual desire, 'primitive' in origin, profoundly pleasurable, and intensely private, is an apt metaphor for the basic human drive to seek individual fulfillment" (7). Yamamoto's utilization of this metaphor precedes Wong's description by a few decades, yet the power of the metaphor, in statement as in use, is evident in the length of the passage Yamamoto devotes to Rosie's affair with Jesus, accounting for one-third of the length of **"Seventeen Syllables."**

Aunt Taka's visit marks the critical watershed in the plot of **"Seventeen Syllables."** During its course, the seduction of mother and daughter by extravagance becomes inevitable and irreversible. For Rosie, tradition is parental control, and Jesus introduces the possibility of meeting "outside the range of both their parents' dubious eyes" (12). Rosie is torn by ambivalence, for she does not know if a break from tradition is feasible; she fears retribution, and "cautiously answered maybe" (13). Her feelings reflect those of her mother, who is yet unsure and apologetic of her actions. For both, these feelings disappear with the visit of Taka, a seemingly God-given signal for a pursuit of extravagance. Rosie lies to escape the eyes of parental control; although she says she is going to the "benjo," she does not (13).[9] Rosie's disregard of her verbal contract mirrors Mrs. Hayashi's disregard of her husband's tacit but clear position; her decision to leave "as she was bowing [her elders] welcome" reflects her mother's self-contradiction and pretense of respect for tradition.[10] Through Rosie's feelings, Yamamoto also relates Mrs. Hayashi's unnarrated headiness from the anticipation of the breaking of constraints, for "now that [Rosie, thus by inference Mrs. Hayashi] was actually on her way, her heart pumped in such an undisciplined way that she could hear it with her ears" (13). Yet, "the shed was up ahead, one more patch away, in the middle of the fields. Its bulk, looming in the dimness, took on a sinisterness that was funny when Rosie reminded herself that it was only a wooden frame with a canvas roof and three canvas walls that made a slapping sound in breezy days." Both the shed, the location of Rosie's rendezvous, and the mother's eventual prize, the Hiroshiges print, are canvas with a wood frame; their similar construction is symbolic of the equivalent nature of their seduction by extravagance. Somberly, Rosie's perception of a sinisterness connected with canvas and wood bodes a bleak end to her mother's passion for haiku.

Yamamoto's metaphorical suggestion continues as Rosie arrives at the shed. The canvas-and-wood symbolism connects Rosie's actions to the impending actions of her mother; as Rosie reaches the shed, she reaches into the future, and her subsequent actions foreshadow the climactic eventual outcome. The shed contains tomatoes, and she takes one, "bit into it and began sucking out the pulp and the seeds" (13). The palpable sustenance the ripe tomato provides embodies the real, physical sustenance the tomato gives to the Hayashis, whose economic survival depends completely upon its harvest. Paralleling the future role of the haiku editor, Jesus, the tool of Rosie's extravagance, "took the hollow tomato from her hand and dropped it back into the stall." He interrupts the sustenance the tomato yields and becomes the fulfillment of extravagance.[11] Rosie experiences a brief flash of superiority, as she "fleetingly felt the older of the two, realizing a brand-new power which vanishes without category under her recognition," foretelling the unnarrated, brief sensation of power her mother experiences over her father (13). Rosie reverses the order of age with Jesus in much the same manner as Mrs. Hayashi reverses traditional gender roles with her husband by her later actions in the midst of the impending harvest. Through his role in the premonitory motivations and actions of Rosie, Jesus emerges as a complex, pivotal figure in Yamamoto's symbolism.

Similar to Rosie's parallel with her mother, Jesus symbolizes the two critical functions of Mr. Hayashi and Mr. Kuroda—the traditional male gender role that mother and daughter need to overcome, and the fulfillment of extravagance that both desire. Jesus, like the haiku editor, gives the female a brief taste of the attainment of extravagance, and Rosie "could find no words to protest; her vocabulary had become distressingly constricted and she thought desperately that all that remained intact now was yes and no and oh" (14). Like her mother, Rosie has at this point crossed so far into the realm of extravagance that options are limited; now is the time for choosing, and there is, for mother and daughter, a dearth of possible choices.[12] "Thus, kissed by Jesus, Rosie fell for the first time entirely victim to a helplessness delectable beyond speech. But the terrible, beautiful sensation lasted no more than a second" (14). This description of Rosie's seduction is startlingly similar to her mother's seduction, as Mrs. Hayashi is similarly "rapt" in the company of the haiku editor; both are correspondingly removed and distracted from the reality of their earthbound existence for the briefest of moments.[13] Yamamoto gives equal weight to necessity and extravagance in her description: Rosie's youthful seduction is at once terrible, yet beautiful—terrible in the context of tradition and necessity, but beautiful in the realm of the lyrical and the romantic, in the extravagance of haiku.

For Rosie, tradition in the form of parental control is something she cannot cross yet must somehow avoid in the pursuit of her desires. This ambivalent position, in which there is an accession to the dictates of tradition even in the attempt to break free from its implications, is what Rosie sees and refuses to confront in the increasing tension between her parents on the previous trip home from the Hayanos. In the context of the parallel analysis, we can better understand Rosie's wish to die; she would rather die than confront these same mixed feelings, for

they are feelings of her own which foreshadow her choices in the initiation of her relationship with Jesus. Ambivalence is the reason she, as the narrator of **"Seventeen Syllables,"** registers the situation and does not analyze it,[14] for admission of her mother's conflicts would force her to admit her own, and it is so much easier to disregard all: upon returning from her rendezvous, she engages in a ritualized cleansing of her body in the form of a hot bath, loudly singing because, "she was possessed by the notion that any attempt now to analyze would result in spoilage and she believed that the larger the volume [of her singing] the less she would be able to hear herself think" (15). The unwillingness to confront is symptomatic of her denial, yet by denying the ambivalence, Rosie acknowledges its existence; although she feigns not to understand, her pretense is revealed in her song.

The necessity of harvest dramatically coincides with the ultimate extravagance of the big-city magazine editor, on one of the hottest days of the year. Since the timely accomplishment of this necessary task is momentarily the most important aspect of the Hayashis's economic existence, the editor's arrival disrupts the Hayashi household on two different levels: it interrupts the completion of the harvest, and it is an extremely visible intrusion of urban extravagance exacerbating the division created by Mrs. Hayashi's passion for haiku. Yet the extravagance of the editor, manifest in the prestige of his high class speech and elegant black car, does not lead to Mr. Hayashi's act of violence. With the editor's arrival and the presentation of the prize, Mr. Hayashi is still very much a civil, even polite person (16-17). It is the subsequent publicly prejudicial and disloyal actions of his wife which force him to commit his act of violence.

In inviting the editor to tea, Mrs. Hayashi disregards the necessity of the harvest. By having tea with the editor for a period of time beyond the norms of civility, she irreparably crosses the line drawn by her husband, a line she has previously acknowledged. At this point, Rosie's mother, with her upper class speech, slips into the world of the editor, marking the truest emergence of Ume Hanazono, who, through her daughter, tells her lower class husband that the harvest will wait (17). On this occasion, the economic effect of the disruption of the harvest promises to be of much greater consequence than her previous nightly disruptions of the family's routine. Similarly, her public separation as the higher class Mrs. Hanazono-the-poet socializing with the urbane haiku editor versus Mr. Hayashi-the-farmer harvesting tomatoes in the hot sun is much more brazen and polarizing than her previous separation at the Hayanos, which had already sufficed to induce her husband's previous exercise of power. It is this blatant, almost condescending disregard for her husband's position which compels him to act.

The burning of the prize, Mr. Hayashi's second, final exercise of authority to regain control within the microcosm of his family's existence, is thus consistent with his position, clear since the Hayano visit and defined by his gender role in the context of traditional Japanese society and the limitations imposed upon his family by the macrocosm. Tome Hayashi, in acting with the full knowledge of the implications of her actions, drives her husband to commit his act of violence. The results of the burning of the prize are symbolic: once again, only the economic necessities of the Hayashi's livelihood—the farm, the house, the tomatoes, and the chores and daily routine attached to them—remain; in this manner the primacy of the self-contained, simple rural lifestyle and its necessary tasks is regained against the extravagant centrifugal tendencies of Rosie's mother (Wong 9).[15] Mr. Hayashi's subsequent return to the fields is also symbolic: he is returning to the necessity of the harvest, asserting that necessity in the form of the farm and its harvest supersedes the extravagant ambitions of his wife. Once again, necessity and tradition clash with the unyielding passions of Tome Hayashi, and for the second time her disregard of limits set forth by tradition and society leads to her downfall—to the fiery death of Ume Hanazono.

For the dying Ume Hanazono, and perhaps for Rosie as well, the flame of the burning of the Hiroshiges is the age-old flame of the class and gender struggle for advancement.[16] This advancement is denied to the first-generation Japanese-American Tome by economic and social limitations; in the light of tradition, her flame is the symbol of extravagance. A stillborn child, a symbol of fruitlessness, is the result of Ume's first foray into extravagance which concludes with her capitulation to tradition in the form of marriage. Her capitulation to tradition reveals an ambivalence identical to that of her daughter: an accession to the dictates of tradition even in the attempt to break free from its implications. Tome Hayashi marks Ume's passing with the silent realization that concession would again prove fruitless, and the knowledge that Ume's death was necessary: she chooses to die instead of living a compromise, realizing that to concede again would only delay her eventual reckoning.[17] Her silence is also the silence of complicity, an acknowledgement of partial guilt in her own death. Ume's living daughter is symbolic of her non-capitulation; although Ume dies from her ambivalence, this time her extravagance is not fruitless. The living Rosie, however, is more than a symbolic representation of non-capitulation. The shock of Ume's death and her mother's resulting revelations, threatening "to level her life, her world [of denial] to the very ground," force Rosie to accept the reality of what she denies, and effectively returns her to a conscious life in the real world (18). Ironically, extravagance can survive only through Ume Hanazono's death. The aware Rosie is the fruit of Ume's death, the product of an extravagance which burned without concession.[18] As the fire of the Hiroshiges still burns, Tome attempts to pass the flame to her daughter—to a future generation for whom the hold of tradition can be less tenuous, social and economic reality more broad, and the realization of class and gender advancement more possible—by asking her child not to marry, for marriage is the symbol of her own misguided pact with tradition. By utilizing marriage to escape a death from extravagance, Mrs. Hayashi agreed to conform to an institution in which inequality, in the form of class and gender biases, is inherent. Tome could never break the circle of necessity in the form of tradition: her birth within it engendered her attempt to escape; by her

attempt to escape, she was forced to return, and finally, tragically, although her return gave her life, it also consigned her to her death. Rosie's mother ultimately could not live a life devoid of what is defined by tradition as extravagant. Yet, even in her extravagance, she could not avoid her ambivalence; her complicity with tradition is the result, not only of external limitations, but also of an internalized traditional value system she could never escape. This internalization is evidenced by her plea—"Rosie, promise me you will never marry"—imparting the urgency not to accede to limitations present in the macrocosm, through her traditional kneeling and clutching (19).[19] Mrs. Hayashi's actions are symbolic of her attempt to make a pact with her daughter, as inescapable as her own matrimonial pact with tradition—as binding as a proposal for marriage. From Jesus, the fulfillment of her extravagance, Rosie draws the strength to answer her mother's troubling request; thus she evokes his name in facing the ambivalence of her mother, who, unable to escape her internalized conception of tradition even in her extravagant plea not to accede to it, supplicates her daughter in a manner reminiscent of a traditional proposal of marriage. As Rosie, "shocked more by the request than the revelation," calls upon her savior Jesus to help her, she draws strength by reliving the ethereal detachment of Jesus's extravagance, and finds the will to answer her mother's desperate plea (19). Yamamoto, in alluding that Rosie is not really shocked by the revelation, quietly reveals Rosie's knowledge and understanding of her mother's position despite her apparent, consistent denial. Rosie, however, is shocked by her mother's request to bear the flame of extravagance, the source of her mother's present sorrow, even as both mother and daughter are immersed in its numbing aftermath.

In Rosie's reply, however, the final intensely ironic parallel, revealing the hidden tragedy of the final scene, is drawn: as ambivalence is evident in the supplication of the mother, so is it evident in the slow, tortured agreement of the daughter. Rosie's need to call upon a male figure, a combination of "the son of the Carrascos [and] of God" for aid is an affirmation of her continued ambivalence, for an extravagance dependent upon the support of a more powerful male is still an accession to tradition, reminiscent of her previous ambivalence (19).[20] Even as she agrees to resist, her words indicate its continued presence, revealing that the internalization of limitations, previously noted in Rosie's mother, is also agonizingly present in Rosie. Within the context of the struggle against class and gender inequalities, this parallel takes on a disturbingly painful, tragic quality: as mother attempts to pass the struggle to daughter in her brief, dying moments, society has already ingrained its social limitations, deeply and imperceptibly, in the daughter.[21]

The death of the passionate Tome is quite real, evident upon Rosie's initial, unusually keen observation, "Ume Hanazono's life span, even for a poet's, was very brief" (9). Rosie, relating the story with an understanding of what has occurred, is mindful of the reality of her mother's death for she does not relate its passage as a simple passing of interest in haiku. Unlike the rest of **"Seventeen

Syllables," the complexity with which she recounts the dramatic end, replete with the nuances and innuendos necessary for the reader to grasp its significance, is evidence that she truly comprehends her mother's message. In the end, it is revealed that although the daughter surprisingly understands the mother, it is perhaps the mother who, in losing faith, shows that she does not quite grasp the depth of her own daughter. Kim recognizes that "there is still the chance that the daughter might come to comprehend the meaning of her mother's experience in time to benefit from it" (163). In **"Seventeen Syllables,"** Yamamoto refuses to make the death of the extravagant, an otherwise clear, recurrent theme in Asian American literature, complete. She leaves a flicker, an ember of potential possibilities. Her unwillingness to sacrifice the "extravagant" is more than justified; the beauty of Yamamoto's works belies the notion that extravagance, as defined by traditional, male-dominated culture, must eventually die.

Examination of **"Seventeen Syllables"** in the context of gender, economic, and social limitations yields a more complete understanding of the complexities of Yamamoto's characters. In the analysis of human actions bound by external limitations, there are those actions motivated by necessity, and the counterbalancing actions motivated by extravagance. In Yamamoto's works, more often necessity is the domain of the male, while extravagance is the realm of the female. But the importance which should not be lost is that all characters, male or female, are subject to the social and economic limitations of the macrocosm, and the traditional and gender limitations of the microcosm. It is through examination of these limitations that we can come to a more complete understanding of the ulterior causation of a character's thoughts and actions.

This form of analysis is by no means limited to **"Seventeen Syllables."** The thwarting of extravagance by necessity is a common thread binding **"Seventeen Syllables"** to two of Yamamoto's other works, **"Yoneko's Earthquake"** and **"Miss Sasagawara."** **"Yoneko's Earthquake,"** published two years later, contains much of the same plot dynamics and symbolism. There is the initial exercise of authority by the male when Mr. Hosoume, in disciplining his wife, draws a line justified by necessity. Similarly, as Yoneko's mother delves deeper into extravagance, Yoneko follows. Mrs. Hosoume subsequently engages in an extravagant, an illicit affair—clearly crossing the line, forcing the second, violent act of authority: the abortion and the departure of Marpo, the hired hand and Mrs. Hosoume's lover. Unlike **"Seventeen Syllables,"** Mrs. Hosoume's extravagance, embodied in her aborted fetus, is fruitless, as Yoneko, devastated and emotionally drained by Marpo's departure, rejects extravagance.[22] **"The Legend of Miss Sasagawara"** is narrated by Kiku, whose internment in an Arizona camp is punctuated by the intrigue surrounding a female camp member. Camp crowding blurs personal and public life, creating a pressure to conform or risk ridicule. Into this setting is thrust the dancer Mari and her father Rev. Sasagawara, an ascetic with whom she must share living quarters. While her father epitomizes the extremes of necessity required for sainthood, the incompatibility of his devotion with Mari's extravagance, "passions rising, sub-

siding, and again rising, perhaps in anguished silence, within the selfsame room," leads her to describe her father's saintly devotion as madness—yet it is her extravagance which is derided by the camp as madness (33). For Miss Sasagawara, an artist previously free to dance unshackled by necessity, the limitations imposed by her macrocosm are severe. In Mari's realm, the realm of the lyrical and the romantic, of the extravagance of ballet, it is not extravagance but ascetic necessity which is "madness, the monstrous sort which, pure of itself, might possibly bring troublous, scented scenes to recur in the other's sleep" (33).

In the context of external and internal limitations, limited points of view and secondary plots are revealed to be not mere literary devices but artful brushstrokes upon a much larger canvas. If a singer imparts by the arch in her back and the strain in her neck more than what her words themselves can say, then Yamamoto conveys through her unreliable narrators the painful effects of human limitations to greater effect than her plots do tell. Mrs. Hosoume's affair is more passionate than Ume Hanazono's flirtation with haiku, and the death of collie and unborn child is more violent and repulsive than the destruction of the Hiroshiges.[23] The resulting psychological trauma borne by Yoneko, and the limitations of her narration, is correspondingly much greater than that of Rosie—even the title is suggestive of the greater depth of anguish Yoneko has experienced. Similarly, while the internees in Kuki's camp experience dehumanization, their denial and concomitant rejection of Miss Sasagawara's extravagance are balms which soothe their pain. In **"Seventeen Syllables,"** as in **"Yoneko's Earthquake"** and **"Miss Sasagawara,"** the narrative is composed by a reluctant witness whose life has been leveled, in Rosie's own words, "to the very ground" (18). In recounting a deep wound in her psyche, it is at once inevitable and revealing that Rosie is unreliable—for what is not told is often as meaningful as what is. Denial and a limited point of view allow Rosie, and Yoneko and Kuki as well, to cope with childhoods scarred by the violent effects of external limitations. Despite the pain, however, for Rosie, the least scarred of these three children, there is yet hope. Although Rosie's mother laments her daughter's inability to understand her message, it is not evident that Rosie does not. Rosie, the seed of her mother, may yet burst forth in the passionate flame of vindication.

Notes

[1] "Seventeen Syllables" is narrated from the limited point of view of Rosie. Yamamoto chooses Rosie's voice to facilitate her "plot within a plot" technique. For an in-depth discussion concerning limited perspectives and "buried plots," see Yogi.

[2] Those who declare Mr. Hayashi the relentless oppressor without examination of the how and why are limited in their analytical scope. In the view of some social historians, this form of blame does not address the social limitations of their subjects. Examination of actions from the "bottom-up" often reveal character insights unavailable from analyses from the "top-down." See Levine.

[3] The exact quote reads, "Yamamoto [to Crow]: You seem to think I treated the father viciously. . . . He was only acting the way he'd

been brought up to act, the way men were supposed to be" (Crow *MELUS* 80).

[4] "External" and "internal" limitations refer, respectively, to constraints imposed by the macrocosm, such as those of tradition, economy and class, and the manifestations of these constraints in the microcosm of the family.

[5] "Necessity vs. extravagance" is a comparison and contrast first described by Sau-ling Wong in "Necessity and Extravagance in Maxine Hong Kingston's *The Woman Warrior*"; her insightful categorization, as an analytical tool, is here applied to the works of Yamamoto.

[6] The role tradition plays in the dynamics of the relationship between the Hayashis is evident by contrast: to a non-traditional family, the spouse of Mrs. Hayano would be much more likely to be publicly embarrassed.

[7] What Rosie does not admit, Rosie does not relate—the obvious effect of a limited point of view.

[8] The marriage of the Hayashis was arranged by Aunt Taka.

[9] The toilet facility of the Hayashis is located outside of the house.

[10] Mother and daughter reveal their pretense of respect through the deliberateness of their actions in defiance of tradition. Their pretense, in the context of their struggle against tradition, is a form of trickery necessary to garner a degree of agency otherwise difficult to obtain through direct confrontation in the face of a more powerful foe; it does not suggest that mother and daughter are not torn between necessity and extravagance. Their ambivalence is quite real, as evidenced in subsequent analysis.

[11] Yogi places much emphasis upon Jesus's deception of Rosie. Although Jesus does attempt to deceive Rosie, it is evident that she is not fooled. During the entire episode, Rosie realizes why she is keeping her appointment; her apparent lack of knowledge is only a denial designed primarily to persuade herself of the innocence of the affair prior to its occurrence, and perhaps also to fool Jesus; it is similar to her self-denial and pretense of unawareness regarding the interplay between her parents. Jesus's ineffectual deception of Rosie is thus relegated by her clear perception of his trickery to unimportance; this perception is evident by her trepidation and excitement prior to the rendezvous. Her deception of her parents, and its parallel with her mother's deception of her father, however, is much more worthy of analysis.

[12] The constriction of choices occurs three times: in Mrs. Hayashi's affair in Japan, and during Aunt Taka's fateful visit for both mother and daughter. In all three instances, the precipitating factor is the great depth to which the characters had entered extravagance.

[13] In comparison to the length of her marriage, Tome Hayashi's interlude with haiku is indeed brief, and thus comparable to the terrible, beautiful sensation of her daughter. The seduction of Rosie and her mother is, as previously discussed, by extravagance, not by Jesus or Kuroda, the magazine editor.

[14] Rosie's limited point of view is the result of her denial, not merely the product of a difference in cultural orientation or a language/ generation gap proposed by some critics. For a discussion of the role language/ generation/ culture differences play between mother and daughter, see Kim.

[15] Wong uses "centrifugal tendencies" to refer to actions which challenge tradition, in obvious reference to a force directed outward against the circular path of necessity.

[16] In contrast, Yogi (170) believes that the mother is passing on to her daughter "a legacy of disruption and pain," in agreement with Cheung (xx), who believes that having lost all hope, Mrs. Hayashi "can only try to prevent her daughter from repeating her mistakes."

[17] This interpretation is contrasted with Cheung's (xviii-xix): "The external calmness of the mother, almost frightening at this, seems only to suggest the depth of her anguish. . . . More effective than registering a host of angry screams or plaintive wails, the tableau sears into our consciousness the husband's cruelty and the wife's desolation." While the contrast Cheung notes is striking, the present interpretation is more accurate in the context of the psychological development of Mrs. Hayashi—an understanding, mournful Tome seems more capable of silence.

[18] Rosie's intelligence also reveals an aspect of Yamamoto's plot-within-a-plot technique undiscussed by previous workers. Yamamoto utilizes the lack of understanding of haiku, something which reflects a language or generation gap, and the professed innate laziness of Rosie, both related craftily to her readers in the beginning of "Seventeen Syllables," to mask Rosie's subsequent understanding and denial of the situation between her parents.

[19] The request not to marry may seem enigmatic. Previous critics have indicated that it is a warning not to follow in the path of "disillusionment" (Cheung xx), not to "accept the legacy of subordination" (Yogi 173). In the context of the current analysis, the request is seen as a plea for her daughter not to capitulate to tradition.

[20] The symbolism of the accession to a more powerful male is important in the context of an accession to tradition. Without the linkage of the protagonist Jesus to Jesus, the powerful son of God, it is doubtful that readers would appreciate his parallel to Mr. Hayashi, who exerts authority on two occasions. Yamamoto's name choice thus reveals the importance of this symbolism.

[21] Although Tome is not physically dying, the death of Ume and the feel of finality given by Yamamoto to the passage indicates that this will be the only occasion Rosie's mother will breach the subject. We sense that Mrs. Hayashi will become a shell of her former self, similar to Mrs. Hayano, now that her passion has been extinguished.

[22] Yoneko's rejection of extravagance is clear, symbolized by the loss of her mother's ring, a symbol of extravagance her mother attempted to pass on to her.

[23] Note that the dog struck by the Hosoumes's car, symbolic of the unborn child and a product of extravagance, is described as a beautiful collie by Yamamoto. She could just as easily have chosen an ugly mongrel. Yamamoto adds to the pathos of the scene by suggesting that necessity invariably kills that which is beautiful, passionate, lyrical or romantic within us. Throughout her works,

Yamamoto is unremittingly sympathetic with the extravagant, and treats its death with a sadness often reminiscent of Shakespearean tragedies.

Works Cited

Cheung, King-Kok. Introduction. *Seventeen Syllables and Other Stories.* Latham, NY: Kitchen Table P, 1986. xi-xxv.

Crow, Charles. "The Issei Father in the Fiction of Hisaye Yamamoto." *Opening Up Literary Criticism: Essays on American Prose and Poetry.* Ed. Leo Truchlar. Salzburg, Austria: Verlag Wolfgang Neugbauer, 1986. 34-40.

————. "A *MELUS* Interview: Hisaye Yamamoto." *MELUS* 14.1 (1987): 77-78.

Kim, Elaine H. *Asian American Literature: An Introduction to the Writings and Their Social Context.* Philadelphia: Temple U P, 1982.

Levine, Lawrence W. *Black Culture and Black Consciousness: Afro-American Folk Thought from Slavery to Freedom.* New York: Oxford U P, 1977.

McDonald, Ritsuko, and Katharine Newman. "Relocation and Dislocation: The Writings of Hisaye Yamamoto and Wakako Yamauchi." *MELUS* 7.3 (1980): 21-38.

Wong, Sau-ling. "Necessity and Extravagance in Maxine Hong Kingston's *The Woman Warrior:* Art and the Ethnic Experience." *MELUS* 15.1 (1988): 3-26.

Yamamoto, Hisaye. "The Legend of Miss Sasagawara." *Seventeen Syllables and Other Stories.* Latham, NY: Kitchen Table P, 1986. 46-56.

————. "Seventeen Syllables." *Seventeen Syllables and Other Stories.* Latham, NY: Kitchen Table P, 1986. 8-19.

————. "Yoneko's Earthquake." *Seventeen Syllables and Other Stories.* Latham, NY: Kitchen Table P, 1986. 46-56.

Yogi, Stan. "Legacies Revealed: Uncovering Buried Plots in the Stories of Hisaye Yamamoto and Wakako Yamauchi." *Studies in American Fiction* 17.2 (1989): 169-81.

King-Kok Cheung (essay date 1995)

SOURCE: "The Dream in Flames: Hisaye Yamamoto, Multiculturalism, and the Los Angeles Uprising," in *Bucknell Review: A Scholarly Journal of Letters, Arts, and Sciences,* Special Issue—Having Our Way: Women Rewriting Tradition in Twentieth-Century America, edited by Harriet Pollack, Vol. XXXIX, No. 1, 1995, pp. 118-30.

[In the following essay, Cheung relates the subject matter and themes of Yamamoto's 1985 story "A Fire in Fontana" to the 1992 Los Angeles riots that followed the acquittal of four police officers accused of using exces-sive force in the arrest and beating of African-American motorist Rodney King.]

The 1992 Los Angeles riot broke out three months before I was to give a paper in a panel entitled "The American Dream" at the Japanese American National Museum in Los Angeles. I chose to speak on Hisaye Yamamoto's **"A Fire in Fontana,"** not only because this memoir casts sobering reflections on the American Dream, but also because it speaks directly to current events. As in so many of Yamamoto's short stories, **"Fire"** has a double structure. The external plot, which juxtaposes the ruthless killing of a black family and the 1965 Watts rebellion, yields provocative parallels with the incidents surround-ing the acquittal of four police officers accused of brutally beating Rodney King. The internal plot, which traces the narrator's evolving racial consciousness and her deepen-ing black allegiance, offers insights into the meaning and possibility of what is now called "multiculturalism"—a challenge faced today by teachers and community leaders alike.[1]

Yamamoto, author of **Seventeen Syllables and Other Stories** (1988), is a *nisei* (second-generation Japanese Amer-ican) born in 1921 in Redondo Beach, California. During World War II she was interned in a detention camp in Poston, Arizona. After the war she worked from 1945 to 1948 as a columnist and rewrite person for the *Los Angeles Tribune,* a black weekly. She volunteered in 1953 to work for a Catholic Worker community farm on Staten Island, and returned to Los Angeles after her marriage in 1955. In 1986 she received the American Book Award for Lifetime Achievement from the Before Columbus Foundation. Yama-moto was one of the first Japanese American writers to gain national recognition after the war—a time when anti-Japanese sentiment was still rampant. Several of her sto-ries appeared in Martha Foley's lists of "Distinctive Short Stories" and one was included in *Best American Short Stories.* Her reputation has been especially strong in Asian American literary circles. The editors of *Aiiieeeee! An Anthology of Asian-American Writers* consider her to be "Asian-America's most accomplished short story writer"; Elaine H. Kim describes her fiction as "consummately women's stories."[2] What distinguishes Yamamoto's writ-ing is not merely her craft of storytelling and her feminist consciousness, which are justly celebrated, but also her ability to include, empathize with, and give voice to people of different racial backgrounds long before the civil rights movement.

"Fire" is an autobiographical essay about Yamamoto's experience as a staffwriter with the *Los Angeles Tribune,* a job that "colored the rest of [her] life."[3] The narrator was reminded of that experience, and specifically of an incident that she had to "report" for the *Tribune* shortly after World War II, when she watched the Watts riot on tele-vision. She begins her recollection by describing the mi-lieu of the newspaper office, which was on the mezzanine of the Dunbar Hotel.[4] People who stayed in the hotel included celebrities like Billy Eckstine, Ossie Davis, and Ruby Dee. Those who visited the newspaper office were less spectacular, though one character seemed timeless:

"A tall young police lieutenant, later to become mayor of the city, came by to protest the newspaper's editorial on police brutality" ("F," 369).

The episode that gives the memoir its title concerns a young black man named Short, who showed up in the editorial office one day and informed the staff that ever since he had bought a house in a white neighborhood in Fontana he had been getting threatening notes from his neighbors asking him to "get-out-or-else" ("F," 370). He hoped to enlist the help of three black newspapers, the *Los Angeles Tribune* included, to publicize his situation and to muster support for his right to live in Fontana. Later that week his house went up in flames. Short, his wife, and his two children were killed in the blaze.

Though the fire "appeared to have started with gasoline poured all around the house and outbuildings," the police's "official conclusion was that probably the man had set the gasoline fire himself, and the case was closed" ("F," 370). Among those who doubted this conclusion was a white priest who wrote a play called *Trial by Fire*; after it was presented on the stage the priest was "suddenly transferred to a parish somewhere in the boondocks of Arizona" ("F," 370).

The television coverage of the Watts riot brought back to the narrator the memory of the fire, which had left her with "something like an itch [she] couldn't locate, or like food not being cooked enough, or something undone which should have been done, or something forgotten which should have been remembered" ("F," 370). The scenes she saw on television, horrible as they were, also offered her a sense of resolution:

> Appalled, inwardly cowering, I watched the burning and looting on the screen and heard the reports of the dead and wounded. But beneath all my distress, I felt something else. . . . To me, the tumult in the city was the long-awaited, gratifying next chapter of an old movie that had flickered about in the back of my mind for years. In the film . . . there was this modest house out in the country. Suddenly the house was in flames. . . . Then there could be heard the voices of a man and woman screaming, and the voices of two small children as well. ("F," 373)

It appears that another family of four—just like the black family in Fontana—was burned to death during the Watts riot. But this time the skin color of the perpetrators and the victims might have been reversed.

I will discuss the implications of this chilling ending later. For now I would like to show how this external or surface plot of the memoir—through its juxtaposition of individual abuse and civil disorder, its revelation of the elusiveness of the American Dream, and its interrogation of the police and the media—resonates with the events surrounding the Rodney King beating. With King, the connection between the first "not guilty" verdict given the four officers and the subsequent L.A. riot in 1992 was hard to miss, though the media played down the connection.[5] In **"Fire,"** the connection between the fire in Fontana and the burn-

ing that occurred during the Watts riot is made in the narrator's mind. The juxtaposition of the two fires suggests that mass insurrection has roots in the quotidian violation of individual rights. Short and King were both victims of violence who had allegedly brought injury on themselves (though King admittedly was not guiltless). These cycles of individual abuse and group rebellion support Robert Gooding-Williams's contention that the beating of King, the verdict and its aftermath should not be treated simply as news, "as transient curiosities that have accidently supervened on the circumstances of day-to-day life."[6]

Anger at injustice can spawn further injustice, however. Like Short and King, the victims of the Watts riot and the L.A. riot got what they did not deserve. Just as the fire in Fontana destroyed Short's "American Dream," the dreams of many immigrants who had believed in succeeding in America through hard work were also reduced to ashes during the 1992 fire. Apparently the American Dream is not equally accessible to all Americans; even individual lives seem to differ in value. Short's right to own a house in Fontana was violently revoked; the murder of his family was whitewashed as suicide. Elaine H. Kim has noted how many Americans of color cried in vain for help during the 1992 upheaval:

> When the Korean Americans in South Central and Koreatown dialed 911, nothing happened. When their stores and homes were being looted and burned to the ground, they were left completely alone for three horrifying days. How betrayed they must have felt by what they believed was a democratic system that protects its people from violence. . . . What they had to learn was that . . . protection in the U. S. is by and large for the rich and powerful. If there were a choice between Westwood and Koreatown, it is clear that Koreatown would have to be sacrificed.[7]

Unlike the fire in Fontana and the Watts riot, in which the conflict was largely between blacks and whites, the recent uprising revealed friction between racial minorities as well. Yamamoto, uncovering interethnic cleavages in **"Fire,"** is ahead of her time. She shows how people of color may discriminate against one another, either out of ethnocentrism or because they have internalized the attitudes of the dominant culture. The narrator recalls a Korean real estate agent who put her children into Catholic schools because the public schools were "integrated." Yet this same woman did not hesitate to urge local real estate onto her black clients because the resulting profits made possible "her upward mobility into less integrated areas" ("F," 373). Mutual disdain and stereotyping between African Americans and Korean Americans loomed large in the 1992 riot. As Sumi K. Cho points out, "many Korean shopowners had accepted widespread stereotypes about African Americans as lazy, complaining criminals. . . . On the other hand, many African Americans also internalize stereotypes of Korean Americans [as] callous unfair competitors."[8] Cho argues that this mode of thinking is often reinforced by the media: "the media [were] eager to sensationalize the events by excluding Korean perspectives from coverage and stereotyping the immigrant community. . . . Stereotypic media portrayals of Koreans as smiling, gun-toting vigilantes and African Americans as vandals and hoodlums trivialize complex social and economic problems."[9]

The media also played a problematic role in **"Fire."** The brutal murder of Short's family was presented by both the police and the press as suicide. The narrator, a reporter herself, though sickened by the event, was unable to vent her outrage through divulging the bigotry of Short's white neighbors: "Given the responsibility by the busy editor, I had written up from my notes a calm, impartial story, using 'alleged' and 'claimed' and other cautious journalese" ("F," 371). She deplores the journalistic ethics that forced her to present a partial story in the guise of impartiality, that obliged her to cite dubious "official" sources, and that prevented her from offering her own analysis of the fire in Fontana. The media coverage of the recent L. A. riot, in zeroing in on the conflict among racial minorities, similarly deflected blame from the dominant culture. Kim compares the coverage to the Chinese film *Raise the Red Lantern,* in which three concubines and wife plot endlessly against each other while the husband who controls and exploits them all remains very much out of the picture and outside the fray: "We only hear his mellifluous voice as he benignly admonishes his four wives not to fight among themselves."[10]

My intention in reading Yamamoto's memoir against the recent upheaval is not, however, simply to furnish parallels but also to draw instructive examples from the internal plot about the narrator's political evolution. The civic awareness and interracial empathy exemplified by the narrator run counter to the group-oriented politics that threaten to splinter our multicultural society today. While I welcome the present curricular emphasis on ethnic history and cultural knowledge, I believe a more interactive approach is needed to discourage insularity and to promote understanding among different groups. As scholars and teachers we must do more than simply focus on the history and concerns of a particular ethnic group. Merely adopting what Ronald Takaki calls the "add-on" approach is not enough: "[Educators] . . . add a week on African-Americans and another on Hispanics. . . . Meanwhile, inter-group relationships remain invisible, and the big picture is missing."[11]

Such an approach cannot remedy the social fragmentation demonstrated in the 1992 upheaval. To me one of the most troubling revelations emerging from the occurrences that preceded and followed the "not guilty" verdict was the seeming inability of people to relate to and stand up for those of another race. Such an inability, as Cho argues, was responsible in part for allowing the hostility between African Americans and Korean Americans that had been building up long before the Rodney King beating to go unchecked: "Because Korean- and Asian-American academics failed to speak up and condemn the light sentence that Judge Karlin rendered in the Du [the female shopkeeper who killed a black teenager suspected of shoplifting] case *before* the riots forced this reckoning, we were complicit in the sentencing as well. Likewise, African-American scholars could have taken a position on the

blatant promotion of hate violence against Korean Americans in Ice Cube's lyrics but failed to do so."[12]

While it is understandable that people identify most readily with and therefore are more defensive or protective of those of the same extraction, it would promote the search for justice by all concerned, juries included, if more Caucasians and Asians could speak with moral indignation about the double standard of justice in America that is often stacked against African Americans, and if more African Americans could unequivocally condemn actions such as the battering of Reginald Denny and the burning of Korean stores. The media was perhaps again to blame in often selecting black spokespersons to defend blacks, white spokespersons to denounce them, and so forth (as in the coverage of the Denny trial). Yet this kind of media coverage can well turn into a self-fulfilling prophecy, reinforcing in the public mind that only people of the same color could and should stick together.

The alternative attitude of the narrator in **"Fire"** offers an effective antidote to colorfast ideology. She not only crosses racial barriers but also combats prejudice without resorting to the rhetoric of opposition, and addresses interracial conflict rationally and feelingly. Her memoir opens as follows:

> Something weird happened to me not long after the end of the Second World War. I wouldn't go so far as to say that I, a Japanese American, became Black. . . . But some kind of transformation did take place. . . . Sometimes I see it as my inward self being burnt black in a certain fire. ("F," 366-67)

The narrator felt so incensed by the fire in Fontana that she began to identify viscerally with African Americans, grappling with both white and Asian prejudice against blacks. The "blackening" of her inward self occurred, however, even before that fire. Interned for being a Japanese American during World War II, she could readily connect the injustices she herself had encountered with the discrimination against blacks she witnessed in the fifties and sixties. On her way back to the internment camp in Arizona during World War II, she was sitting next to a blond woman on a bus out of Chicago who, upon seeing an African American man being denied a drink at a restaurant south of Springfield, "was filled with glee." The narrator instinctively linked her "seatmate's joy and [her] having been put in that hot and windblown place of barracks" ("F," 367).

Recognizing common oppression and forging alliances with other marginalized groups can prevent people of color from being caught in the "Red Lantern" trap Kim describes. Yet, like the polarization of black and white spokespersons by the media, a rhetoric of opposition based on skin color—specifically the generic whites versus non-whites—may exacerbate divisions along racial lines and homogenize important differences within each group. The narrator indicates that "more than once [she] was easily put down with a casual, 'That's mightly White of you,' the connotations of which were devastating" ("F," 369).

But outward pigmentation cannot encode political sensibility, as the narrator's black allegiance attests.

Her gravitation toward African Americans notwithstanding, the narrator refrains from writing all white people off. While she gives ample glaring examples of white prejudice, she also furnishes counterexamples. Unlike Miss Moten, the African American secretary at the *Tribune* office who, upon hearing Short's story, "spat out the words 'I hate White people! They're all the same!'" ("F," 370), she begins her memoir with exceptions to this rule:

> I remember reading a book . . . based on the life of Bix Beiderbecke, in which the narrator early wonders if his musician friend would have come to the same tragic end if he hadn't become involved with Negroes. . . . In real life, there happened to be a young White musician in an otherwise Black band. . . . His name was Johnny Otis. . . . In more recent years he has become the pastor of a church in Watts. I suppose he, too, arrived at a place in his life from which there was no turning back. But his life, as I see it, represents a triumph. ("F," 366-67)

The narrator, as indicated earlier, also makes a point of remembering the white priest who was relocated after his play cast doubts on the police theory about the fire in Fontana. These anecdotes suggest that regardless of one's skin color it is possible to reach out to people of a different race.

To conclude on this sanguine note alone, however, is to ignore Yamamoto's trenchant testimony, implicit in her account of the narrator's inner transformation, about the depth and magnitude of racism (often aggravated by the reluctance of the dominant culture to confront or even admit the problem) and its profound emotional impact on the afflicted minorities. Isolated cases of whites who ally with blacks socially or politically are insufficient, Yamamoto implies, to allay the anger of those subject to persistent abuse or to prevent them from seeing all white people as the enemy.

The narrator demonstrates the cumulative and erosive effects of racism by tracking her own mounting indignation and diminishing self-assurance. During the early stages of her apprenticeship with the *Tribune,* she was puzzled by her co-workers' preoccupation with race: "The inexhaustible topic was Race, always Race. . . . Sometimes I got to wondering whether Negroes talked about anything else" ("F," 369). However, after protracted exposure to hate crimes in the course of doing her job, which included "[toting] up the number of alleged lynchings across the country and [combining] them into one story" ("F," 368), she found herself becoming more and more like her black colleagues, to the extent of losing several correspondents because of her own obsession with race: "When one fellow dared to imply that I was really unreasonable on the subject of race relations, saying that he believed it sufficient to make one's stand known only when the subject happened to come up, the exchange of letters did not continue much longer" ("F," 371). Her initiation at the newspaper office was compounded by lessons on the

street, as when she heard a white drive insult the driver of her bus, "Why, you Black bastard!" The black driver kept going, but the narrator "was sick, cringing from the blow of those words." She who had been shocked earlier by Miss Moten's wholesale denunciation of whites at this point "knew Miss Moten's fury for [her] very own" ("F," 372).

The most telling indication of the narrator's transformation appears at the end of the memoir, quoted earlier, when she describes the rampage she saw on the screen during the Watts riot as "the long-awaited, *gratifying* next chapter of an old movie that had flickered about in the back of my mind for years" (my emphasis). Throughout the memoir, the narrator, while revealing her growing affiliation with black Americans, has shown unusual sensitivity in chronicling race relations and remarkable restraint in expressing her own sentiment. Her use of the adjective "gratifying" (albeit qualified by mention of her "cowering" and "distress" at the spectacle) to describe the destruction on the screen stands out as a grim reminder of the pernicious effect of racism on the afflicted psyche. In admitting to feeling "a tiny trickle of warmth which [she] finally recognized as an undercurrent of exultation" while watching the burning of another family of four (who were likely to be as innocent as the Short family), the narrator makes us aware that those who constantly suffer from racist abuse or bear witness to it cannot be expected to always think and feel rationally, that no amount of reasoning and individual good will can check the anger and hatred of those incapable of obtaining justice from law enforcement officials (who may, in the event, actually persecute the victims or turn a deaf ear to their grievances), that inequity will provoke retaliation, if only vicariously and even at the expense of other innocent people.

While this haunting ending concludes the external plot, the internal plot of the narrative offers a different form of vengeance and provides a resolution which I believe is more promising and gratifying to the writer and reader alike. At the beginning of the memoir, the narrator, after judging the life of Johnny Otis to be a "triumph" because of his commitment to blacks, wonders: "But I don't know whether mine is or not" ("F," 367). She doubts whether her life amounts to a similar triumph (despite her own unquestionable loyalty to blacks) presumably because the "burning" of her inward self has left considerable scars. She has suffered the impotent rage and gnawing frustration of being unable to speak up on behalf of African Americans. Empathy alone cannot take away her sense of guilt for what she has *not* done.

The narrator repeatedly evokes this feeling of paralysis and futility. She regrets her inability to articulate the true cause of the fire in Fontana. She reflects on the way she could have reported and the way she actually reported the news by recalling two characters often seen in Little Tokyo. One was a Japanese evangelist who, before the war, "used to shout on the northeast corner of First and San Pedro in Little Tokyo" ("F," 370). His call to salvation could be heard from a distance and, closer up, one could see "his face awry and purple with the passion of his message" ("F," 371). The other was a boy in a wheelchair, pushed by a little girl or another boy. Dependent as a baby, this boy, who appeared regularly on the sidewalks, "always wore a clean white handkerchief round his neck to catch the bit of saliva which occasionally trickled from a corner of his mouth" ("F," 371). The narrator sees herself mirrored in the disabled boy rather than in the ardent evangelist, though she wishes it were otherwise:

> It seems to me that my kinship . . . was with the large boy in the wheelchair, not with the admirable evangelist. . . . For, what had I gone and done? . . . I should have been an evangelist . . . shouting out the name of the Short family and their predicament in Fontana. But I had been as handicapped as the boy in the wheelchair, as helpless. ("F," 371)

She felt similarly choked after hearing the racial slurs against the black driver: "I wanted to yell out the window at the other driver, but what could I have said? I thought of reporting him to management, but what could I have said?" ("F," 372). On another occasion, she objected to some guests' obnoxious remarks about "edgeacated niggers," but she "knew nothing had been accomplished" ("F," 372).

The narrator's recurrent failure to defend black people through speech or writing had been so debilitating and demoralizing that she quit her job with the *Tribune*:

> Not long after [the incident on the bus], going to work one morning, I found myself wishing that the streetcar would rattle on and on and never stop. I'd felt the sensation before, on the way to my mother's funeral. If I could somehow manage to stay on the automobile forever, I thought, I would never have to face the fact of my mother's death. A few weeks [later] I mumbled some excuse about planning to go back to school and left the paper.

> I didn't go back to school, but . . . I got on trains and buses that carried me several thousand miles across the country and back. . . . I was realizing my dream of travelling forever (escaping responsibility forever) . . . and most of the time I didn't argue with anyone. ("F," 372)

The passage, particularly the analogy to the mother's funeral, intimates the narrator's anguish at her lack of agency and, more specifically, her loss of faith in the efficacy of her own words. Yet stopping writing altogether and escaping responsibility forever can hardly assuage the curdling inside.

It is in the context of the narrator's deepening silence that the memoir represents, knowingly or not, her ultimate triumph. In the very act of writing it, the narrator has effectively exposed a long-forgotten crime. Like the play of the white priest (and like the video of the Rodney King beating), this memoir disputes the police version of what happened and opens the audience's eyes to a flagrant violation of civil rights. Though the criminals remain unidenti-

fied, the readers decidedly can tell that the black family in Fontana was murdered, can perhaps even know Miss Moten's fury as their very own. One is reminded of an analogy in Maxine Hong Kingston's *The Woman Warrior*: "The [Chinese] idioms for *revenge* are "report a crime."[13] Yamamoto, through her memoir, has figuratively avenged the Short family by reporting the hate crime, writing/righting the wrong. She has implicated the white neighbor(s), the conniving police and, to some extent, the press and journalism, as she finds she can only articulate truth and voice her protest in another medium. She has written the story that may make up for the "lame" report she wrote earlier for the *Tribune*; she has vindicated and reclaimed her own voice. Finally, by committing the fire in Fontana to an eponymous memoir, she has ensured that this disturbing event will never be forgotten as mere "news."

The American Dream seems to have narrowed with time, from a dream—albeit never realized—of freedom and democracy for all to one of personal and often material success. Because this nation celebrates individualism almost without reservation, the American Dream has become increasingly self-centered. Individuals no longer look beyond their own welfare, and an oppressed group cannot look beyond its own oppression. Worse still, people may fulfill their dreams at others' expense. Without the bigger dream, however, individual prosperity may come to naught. Short's dream of living in a house of his own was snuffed out along with his life. The Korean real estate agent realized her dream of upward mobility by exploiting her black clients. The dreams of many new immigrants went up in the flames of the 1992 L.A. riot. To prevent the American Dream from turning into a national nightmare, we need a multicultural education that will not only provide us with knowledge about different ethnic groups but will also foster a sense of accountability across racial lines.

Yamamoto's memoir, through its double structure, offers two scenarios of what can happen in our multiracial society. The external plot forewarns that injustices such as the live incineration of the Short family (or, more recently the police brutality again Rodney King) seed civil unrest that can lead to irreparable breach among peoples, that can culminate in uncontrollable social explosions not unlike the one we experienced in 1992. The internal plot, by contrast, evinces the possibility of reciprocal solicitude and personal agency. It suggests that we can take someone else's dream and grievance as our own, that even though we cannot alter the color of our skins, our inner selves can take on different shades.

Notes

[1] Hisaye Yamamoto, "A Fire in Fontana," in *Rereading America: Cultural Contexts for Critical Thinking and Writing,* ed. Gary Columbo et al., 2d ed. (Boston: Bedford Books, 1992), 366-73. Hereafter "Fire," cited in the text. An earlier version of the present essay was presented at the Japanese American National Museum and was excerpted in *Humanities Network* 15 (1993):2-3, 10. I have also discussed Yamamoto's technique of "double-telling" at length in my book *Articulate Silences: Hisaye Yamamoto, Maxine Hong Kingston, Joy Kogawa* (Ithaca: Cornell University Press, 1993), 27-73.

Opinions differ on whether to characterize the post-verdict upheaval in Los Angeles as a riot or a rebellion. I believe elements of both were present and hence use terms such as "riot," "civil disorder," "rebellion," "uprising," and "insurrection" interchangeably.

[2] *Aiiieeeee! An Anthology of Asian-American Writers,* ed. Frank Chin et al. (1974; reprint, Washington, D. C.: Howard University Press, 1983), xxxiv. Elaine H. Kim, *Asian-American Literature: An Introduction to the Writings and Their Social Context* (Philadelphia: Temple University Press, 1982), 160.

[3] Hisaye Yamamoto, "Writing," in *"Seventeen Syllables"/Hisaye Yamamoto,* ed. King-Kok Cheung (New Brunswick, N.J.: Rutgers University Press, 1994), 64.

[4] The Dunbar Hotel, located at 4225 S. Central Avenue, was the first hotel in America built specifically for blacks in 1928 "because prejudice made it impossible for blacks to find adequate lodging while traveling. During its heyday in the 1930s, almost every prominent black who visited Los Angeles stayed at the Dunbar." See Richard Saul Wurman, *LA/Access* (Los Angeles: Access Press, 1982), 90.

[5] Robert Gooding-Williams observes that views presented on television after the L. A. riot suggested that the commotion had little to do with the verdict: "the conservative view saw the 'rioters' [as] embodying an uncivilized chaos. . . . The liberal view . . . emphasized the social causes of the 'riots'. . . . It strains credulity to deny . . . that the uprising in Los Angeles was not for many an act of political protest." See "Look, A Negro!" in *Reading Rodney King: Reading Urban Uprising,* ed. Robert Gooding-Williams (New York: Routledge, 1993), 169, 170.

[6] Gooding-Williams, "Introduction: On Being Stuck," *Reading Rodney King,* 1. Gooding-Williams states that his book on Rodney King deliberately "contests the representation of the Rodney King incidents as *news,* viz., as new and dramatic news events, no less than it contests the remembrance of these incidents as old news. By stripping these incidents of the aura of the extraordinary, this book attempts to recover and to explicate their connections to the uneventful and ordinary realities which, while ignored by the news, persistently affect life in urban America" (2).

[7] Elain H. Kim, "Home Is Where the *Han* Is: A Korean-American Perspective on the Los Angeles Upheavals," *Reading Rodney King,* 219.

[8] Sumi K. Cho, "Korean Americans vs. African Americans: Conflict and Construction," *Reading Rodney King,* 199.

[9] Ibid., 197, 203.

[10] Kim, "Home is Where the *Han* Is," 217.

[11] Ronald Takaki, "Are the Multicultural Experiments Working?" *Washington Post,* 1 August 1993, 36. See also Ronald Takaki, *A Different Mirror: A History of Multicultural America* (Boston: Little, Brown, 1993).

[12] Cho, "Korean Americans vs. African Americans," 209.

[13] Maxine Hong Kingston, *The Woman Warrior: Memoirs of a Girlhood among Ghosts* (1976; reprint, New York: Vintage Books, 189), 53.

Naoko Sugiyama (essay date 1996)

SOURCE: "*Issei* Mothers' Silence, *Nisei* Daughters' Stories: The Short Fiction of Yamamoto," in *Comparative Literature Studies,* Vol. 33, No. 1, 1996, pp. 1-14.

[*In the following essay, Sugiyama describes the use of silence in Yamamoto's stories both as a stylistic technique and as a key element in the lives of her characters.*]

Silence is often seen as evidence of women's oppressed position in society. Tillie Olsen, in her book *Silences,* describes how the creative talents of women have been forced into "unnatural" silences by the constant demands of daily life, which allow them no existence other than that of mothers, wives, daughters, and nurturers. Minority women, in particular, have often been "doubly muted," as Roberta Rubenstein points out in *Boundaries of the Self.*[1] Alice Walker—along with other African-American women authors—argues in her essay, "In Search of Our Mothers' Gardens," that black women have been doubly silenced because of their gender and their race. Lamenting the distorted and short life of Phillis Wheatley, Walker argues that African-American women with creative talents have been driven to silent insanity by the harsh reality of slavery, racism, and sexism.[2]

Moreover, women have been particularly silenced on certain issues. As Adrienne Rich points out in *Of Woman Born,* it is difficult to articulate one's feelings as a mother within a patriarchal family structure. Rich argues that motherhood, "as defined and restricted under patriarchy," is deeply rooted in our society and internalized by many women, and forbids women to express their feelings as mothers, especially when the feelings are negative.[3] Women are taught to express only self-effacing affection toward their children. As Rich explains, "Mother-love is supposed to be continuous, unconditional. Love and anger cannot coexist" (46). Unwanted pregnancies and abortions have been among the greatest of tabooed topics and practices.

Many women have difficulty expressing their thoughts and feelings, especially in a mother-daughter relationship. Mothers and daughters feel ambivalent toward each other because of women's powerlessness in society; a mother "identifies intensely with her daughter, but through weakness, not through strength" (Rich 244). Daughters, in their psychological development as individuals, feel a need to distance themselves from their mothers, while at the same time, keeping strong attachment to them, a struggle wrought with tensions.

Silence, however, is not always caused by oppression; it does not always mean a lack of opportunity to speak, nor the lack of self-assertion that is necessary for self-expression. It may, instead, be a paradoxical mode of expression. Silence can have different meanings in different contexts. For example, in the often-quoted short story by Susan Glaspell, "A Jury of Her Peers," two women express their understanding and support of a woman accused of murdering her husband by keeping quiet about the evidence they have found. Their silence subverts the judicial system, represented by men, and saves the accused woman from being prosecuted as a murderer. The women, by being silent, function as a women's jury which declares the accused not guilty.[4] Also as Patricia Wetzel argues in her essay, "Are 'Powerless' Communication Strategies the Japanese Norm?," silence may have different cultural meanings according to one's gender and ethnicity. In a Japanese and Japanese-American context, silence can be a highly esteemed sign of modesty, fortitude, and self-control. Moreover, Japanese literature has a tradition of poetry written in short forms, namely *haiku* and *tanka*. These forms express deep feelings and philosophies or describe landscapes, in just seventeen and thirty one syllables, respectively. This stoically minimalist aesthetic has existed throughout Japanese literary history, influencing not only Japanese-American artists but also American modernist poets of the early twentieth century.[5]

Yet we should be careful not to overestimate the power of silence in discourse; it is often a form of passive resistance or resentment rather than positive self-assertion, especially in the case of women. Various works, such as *Onna To Kotoba*—Akiko Jugaku's linguistic study—as well as *Issei, Nisei, War Bride*—Evelyn Nakano Glenn's historical research on Japanese-American women—show that women's silence can serve and has served as evidence of male domination in Japanese and Japanese-American settings.[6] However, we should be aware of the complex and multilayered nature of silence, especially in multicultural contexts.

Hisaye Yamamoto, a *nisei* (second generation) Japanese-American woman writer, uses multilayered silences in her short stories, drawing from both her Japanese-American heritage and broader, American cultural experiences. As King-Kok Cheung emphasizes in *Articulate Silences: Hisaye Yamamoto, Maxine Hong Kingston, Joy Kogawa,* silence plays an important part in Yamamoto's multicultural stories. Yamamoto's stories, most of which are written from a young *nisei* daughter's point of view, often show *issei* (first generation) mothers pathetically silenced into a life of drudgery and isolation. Yamamoto, while being sympathetic to the fate of mothers, expresses the emotional complexity that exists between mothers and daughters, and at the same time, pays tribute to her own Japanese-American cultural tradition by skillfully making silences tell stories. In two of her stories, which focus on *issei* mother/*nisei* daughter relationships—**"Seventeen Syllables"** and **"Yoneko's Earthquake"**—Yamamoto achieves this seemingly paradoxical task. She describes the silence of women as a form of oppression in the patriarchal social context of pre-World War II, Japanese-American society, and also in the psychological context of mothers, in general, and of mother/daughter relationships, in particular. In addition, Yamamoto's careful description of silence, as well as her minimalist technique, which charges these two short stories with hidden meanings, proves that silence, usually a negative sign of powerlessness and oppression, can be used in a subversive way, as a means for Japanese-American women to find their voices and to pass on their stories.

In **"Seventeen Syllables"** and **"Yoneko's Earthquake,"** *issei* mothers are forced into silence by their difficult living situations as first-generation immigrants. Mothers in both stories are portrayed as isolated figures. The hard daily toil on the farm, as well as at home, and their rural location prevent the *issei* women from having any substantial relationship with other women. While the Hayashi family in **"Seventeen Syllables"** has occasional visitors, the Hosoumes in **"Yoneko's Earthquake"** are "the only Japanese thereabouts."[7] They are, of course, cut off from their own families by the Pacific Ocean. Their difficulty in understanding English also prevents them from communicating, even with their own daughters—let alone women of other ethnic backgrounds. In the beginning episode of **"Seventeen Syllables,"** the mother and the teenage daughter try to communicate with each other about *haiku,* demonstrating how limited language skills and cultural differences block mothers from communicating with their American-born daughters, who are fluent in English but know "formal Japanese by fits and starts" only (8).

Patriarchal social norms also silence *issei* women in Japanese-American society. Although male dominance is not explicitly described in these stories, we can see how it forces women into silence in their relations with their husbands. In **"Seventeen Syllables,"** Mr. Hayashi is irritated by his wife Tome's absorption in writing and discussing poetry, which distracts her from working on the farm and from keeping him company. Finally, he terminates her career as a poet by smashing and burning a woodprint she has won at a *haiku* contest. Tome does not protest, or even lament, verbally; she stands "at the back window watching the dying fire" (18).

Her silence is not enforced by her husband alone, but by Japanese and Japanese-American social norms. While Tome and her daughter, Rosie, watch as the fire burns Tome's prize woodprint, Tome tells Rosie the secret story of forbidden love between herself and "the first son of one of the well-to-do families in her village" (18). Her pregnancy and the birth of a stillborn son disgrace her, as well as her family, and she escapes to the United States and marries her husband "as an alternative to suicide" (18). The flawlessness of her story makes Rosie realize that her mother has been repeating this story to herself over and over again without being able to tell anyone else, let alone her husband. She tells her secret life story to Rosie as an explanation of why she tolerates her husband's dominance over her. Thus, Tome has accepted the social norms that punish her for premarital sexual behavior and shame her into silence. She cannot articulate her anger toward the social institution that shames her into silence, nor can she express her anger toward the husband who kills the poet inside her. Her rage at Rosie—who is becoming romantically involved with a young Mexican man and, apparently, ready to repeat Tome's foolish mistakes—is in fact her anger at herself in thin disguise. But even this anger, however fierce, is never put into words but only expressed by "her eyes and her twisted mouth" and the tightness of her grip on Rosie's wrists (19).

This silence, enforced by male control, is underlined also by Rosie's observation of the silence of Mrs. Hayano, another *issei* woman who "sat all evening in the rocker, as motionless and unobtrusive as it was possible for her to be" (Yamamoto 10). Mrs. Hayano's feeble condition, caused by her first childbirth, makes her mentally, as well as physically, disturbed, while her husband remains "handsome, tall, and strong" (10). The grim picture of Mrs. Hayano's fate, under a patriarchal system which reduces her to a child-bearing machine, is ironically stated: "this woman, in this same condition, had carried and given issue to three babies" (10).

Even Tome's attempt to discover her own creative voice as a *haiku* poet had a limit. Although Tome achieves a certain degree of autonomy as "Ume Hanazono," her poetic pseudonym, *haiku* poetry, itself, confines her within Japanese-American cultural norms. We should bear in mind that the brief *haiku* is probably the only form of art allowed to Tome, since she can compose only after "the dinner dishes [are] done" (9).[8] *Haiku*'s Japanese language limits her audience, and its brevity and rigid form prevents Ume/Tome from expressing herself freely. The number seventeen, which signifies the number of syllables in *haiku,* corresponds to the seventeen years since she gave birth to a stillborn son, the years in which Tome has been silenced, and which symbolize her rigid confinement by the Japanese cultural tradition.

Mrs. Hosoume is also silenced by her husband's physical brutality in **"Yoneko's Earthquake."** Because of an accident during the Long Beach earthquake of 1933, Mr. Hosoume is, physically, too weak to do the farm work and is probably also sexually impotent, while his wife and the young Filipino farmhand, Marpo, practically run the farm together.[9] Frustrated by his own powerlessness, he complains that his wife, Marpo, and the children are disrespectful and impudent toward him. When Mr. Hosoume criticizes Yoneko for wearing nail polish and Mrs. Hosoume defends her, Mr. Hosoume calls his wife "nama-iki" ("which is a shade more revolting than being merely insolent") and then slaps her in the face (53). When Mrs. Hosoume has an affair with Marpo and becomes pregnant, Mr. Hosoume drives her to a Japanese hospital for an abortion and Marpo disappears from the farm on the same day. Although we are not explicitly told, we can assume that both the abortion and Marpo's discharge take place under Mr. Hosoume's command. Mrs. Hosoume, overwhelmed by the abortion and the sudden death of her five-year-old son Seigo, retreats into the Christian faith and "[does] not seem interested in discussing anything but God and Seigo" (55).

Her affair with Marpo, like Tome's *haiku,* is limited in itself. While it is a deviation from the conventional norms that sustain the patriarchal family structure, Mrs. Hosoume is, in fact, only replacing one dominant male figure with another. Stan Yogi points out in "Legacies Revealed: Uncovering Plots in the Stories of Hisaye Yamamoto," that after the earthquake, which makes Mr. Hosoume an invalid and stimulates the affair, Marpo practically replaces Mr. Hosoume.[10] We are told that Marpo "happened to be in the

room reading a newspaper" while Mrs. Hosoume stands ironing (53). When Mr. Hosoume hits his wife, Marpo, responding to Mrs. Hosoume's glance toward him, behaves as a protective patriarch, holding back Mr. Hosoume and saying, "The children are here" (53). This, as Yogi points out, is a startling change in a character who used to be shy and meek in front of Mr. and Mrs. Hosoume (177). After the abortion, Mrs. Hosoume totally surrenders to the Japanese social order, symbolized by the Japanese-American church that she now frequents. Her feebleness resurrects Mr. Hosoume's authoritative position, and he can now afford to be "very gentle" toward his wife (55). Mrs. Hosoume never expresses her feelings nor explains to ten-year-old Yoneko what actually has happened.

Finally, at the core of their silence, Tome and Mrs. Hosoume share the forbidden topic—the unwanted pregnancy and lost babies, stillborn in Tome's case and aborted in Mrs. Hosoume's. As Judith Wilt points out in *Abortion, Choice, and Contemporary Fiction,* abortion is, historically, a topic on which women have been especially silenced.[11] Barbara Johnson, in her essay "Apostrophe, Animation, and Abortion," examines the indistinguishability of abortion and other forms of the loss of a child in women's consciousness, arguing that "any death of a child is perceived as a crime committed by the mother."[12] Going further, Johnson cites Jacques Lacan, explaining how difficult it is for a woman to speak as a subject from a mother's viewpoint, especially when her child is lost, since "the verbal development of an infant . . . begins as a demand addressed to the mother, and out of which, the entire verbal universe is spun." Therefore, "the mother" is "a personification . . . of Otherness itself" (641). Thus, doubly silenced by guilt and psycholinguistic otherness, Tome can speak of her stillborn son, but only in a tightly condensed manner, not unlike her *haiku.* Tome's telling of the story, which is perceived by Rosie as a form of "violence," is, in fact, the violent act of breaking a taboo, and therefore is expressed in a very restricted way. As Johnson points out, "when a woman speaks about the death of children in any sense other than that of pure loss, a powerful taboo is being violated" (641). Mrs. Hosoume remains even more silent than Tome. Her only outlet is her "peculiarly intent eyes" gazing at Yoneko, and her short and enigmatic comment "Never kill a person, Yoneko, because if you do, God will take from you someone you love" (56). As the comment suggests, Mrs. Hosoume regards abortion as the killing of "a person," and is therefore overwhelmed by guilt, surrendering to silence without a word of protest or anger.

Thus, Yamamoto's *issei* women exemplify the silencing of the mothers who went through marriage, pregnancy, and child rearing in pre-World War II, Japanese and Japanese-American communities. Along with the Japanese cultural traditions that honor silence—in both women and men—as a sign of fortitude and selflessness, and the *issei* women's silence—forced by male dominance—both Tome and Mrs. Hosoume are further silenced, as mother, by what Rich calls "motherhood as institution." Yamamoto's technique describes the moments in which *issei* mothers' repressed feelings emerge through their silence, charging the silences with meaning.

As I have already stated, Yamamoto uses *nisei* daughters' point of view in these stories. Their immature ages and their preoccupation with themselves, which is typical of their developmental stages, prevent them from understanding, much less articulating, what is really happening to their mothers. Therefore, much of the important part of their mothers' stories has to be guessed at because it is not explicitly told. Apart from her conscious use of the limited point of view (as well as the influence of Japanese tradition which values subtlety and silence, rather than eloquence), why does Yamamoto choose the immature daughters' perspective?[13] This question leads us to another silence in the stories, the untold story of mother-daughter relationships, buried even more deeply than the secret stories of *issei* mothers.

In **"Seventeen Syllables"** and **"Yoneko's Earthquake,"** the daughters have ambivalent feelings toward their mothers. Both Rosie and Yoneko admire and sympathize with their mothers and resent their fathers' oppressive behavior. At the same time, however, they resent and distance themselves from their mothers, though with a sense of guilt. Recent feminist psychoanalytic studies, such as Nancy Chodorow's *The Reproduction of Mothering,* argue that while a daughter has strong attachment to, and identification with, her mother, she also feels a strong need to distance herself from the mother, in order to have a sense of separate individuality. Also, as Rich suggests, daughters feel anger toward their mothers who, as role models, as well as socializing agents, are complicit in the perpetuation of male dominance in the family structure, passing on to their daughters powerlessness and a sense of inferiority.[14] The daughters in these stories are forced to confront this ambivalence when its tension is most heightened. Yamamoto captures the intense moments of the daughters' ambivalence in the economy of minimalist language, illustrating the sense of powerlessness experienced by the daughters in expressing this ambivalence—especially the anger and the need to separate themselves psychologically from their own mothers.

In **"Seventeen Syllables,"** we see Rosie's ambivalence when she responds to her mother on the subject of *haiku.* When Tome first talks to Rosie about the *haiku,* which she has just composed, we sense Rosie's respect for her mother as a poet who can express, in just seventeen syllables, "the charm of a kitten, as well as comment on the superstition that owning a cat of three colors meant good luck" (8). Moreover, we see her desire to communicate with her mother, imagining herself talking to her about her own version of *haiku* which she found in her mother's magazine:

> . . . This was what was in [Rosie's] mind to say: I was looking through one of your magazines from Japan last night, Mother, and toward the back I found some *haiku* in English that delighted me . . .

> It is morning, and lo!
> I lie awake, comme il faut,
> Sighing for some dough. (8)

However, this nonsensical *haiku* parody, which is a hybrid of English, French, and a Japanese form—with one excessive syllable—can be seen as both respect for her mother's literary tradition and an effort to break away from it. By bringing up this *haiku* parody, Rosie is distancing herself from her mother by critiquing the rigid form of "seventeen syllables only which [are] divided into three lines of five, seven, and five syllables" (8), and from her mother's seriousness toward the subject of *haiku.* She is searching for her own voice, apart from her mother's, preferring English which is "ready on the tongue" to Japanese "which [has] to be searched for and examined, and even then put forth tentatively (probably to meet with laughter)" (8). This effort for separation is accompanied by a sense of guilt, which, in Rosie's case, is guilt for not being fluent in her "mother tongue." Rosie, unable to express her feelings toward her mother because of their psychological complexity, as well as her sense of guilt, retreats into a glib "yes, yes, I understand" (8).

When Tome apologizes to her husband about her absorption in *haiku* and he only grunts, Rosie hates her father for "denying her mother" but, at the same time, she hates her mother as well "for begging" (12). We can see here the moment in which, as Rich explains, a daughter's anger at her mother "dissolves into grief and anger *for* her" (224). This anger at her mother, coupled with anger *for* her, is both Rosie's identification with her mother as well as her distancing herself from her, leading Rosie not only to imagine both parents dead, but also to imagine a self-destructive image of "three contorted, bleeding bodies, one of them hers" (12). When Mr. Kuroda, the *haiku* editor of the Japanese newspaper, visits Tome to distribute the first prize woodprint and Tome invites him into the house for a cup of tea, her husband becomes impatient because of the time lost from the farm work. We see that Rosie sympathizes with her mother, rather than her father, because when he tells her to go and remind her mother of the tomatoes, she goes "slowly," which can be interpreted as a passive support for her mother's involvement with *haiku* and a silent protest against her father's intolerance (17). But when she finds her mother listening to Mr. Kuroda's *haiku* theory, we sense that she also feels alienated from her mother, who pushes her away while "speaking in the language of Mr. Kuroda" (17).

During their last confrontation, Rosie feels strong ambivalence about her mother's life story. Rosie's first reaction is to shy away from the shocking story; she secretly wishes, "Don't tell me now . . . tell me tomorrow, tell me next week, don't tell me today" (18). After listening to her mother's love story, which resulted in the birth of a stillborn son, Rosie shows her understanding and sympathy, though in a clumsy way, by saying "I would have liked a brother" (19). At the same time, this comment can be seen as Rosie's effort to deny her mother's totally negative attitude toward heterosexual relationships and to "[push] back the illumination which [threatens] all that darkness that had hitherto been merely mysterious or even glamorous" (19). Her mother's command never to marry, a desperate attempt to save Rosie from the tragedy of female sexuality, does not reach Rosie, who is too preoccupied with her own new-found sexuality, awakened by Jesús, a young Mexican who works for the Hayashi farm. She tries to break away from her mother's grip on her wrists, and answers her, again, with only "the familiar glib agreement" (19).

In **"Yoneko's Earthquake,"** Yoneko's feelings for her mother are, because of her younger age, more of a pure admiration and close attachment than are Rosie's. Yoneko cherishes the memory of her mother when she was younger: "She had at times been so struck with her mother's appearance that she had dropped to her knees and mutely clasped her mother's legs in her arms" (53). However, this memory is accompanied with the memory of rejection. She "learned to control her feelings because at such times her mother had usually walked away, saying 'My, what a clinging child you are. You've got to learn to be a little more independent'" (53). She still admires her mother's beauty, and when her mother talks about the elaborate process she used to go through to dye her nails with ground flower petals when she was a child in Japan, Yoneko is fascinated and imagines that her mother must have been a beautiful child. Though Yoneko does not know what happened, she is totally sympathetic when her mother is in pain and in sorrow. She accompanies her mother to the Japanese church after Seigo's death, even though she herself does not believe in God. However, the various questions that Yoneko asks about God's character imply her distancing from Mrs. Hosoume's passive acceptance of Japanese-American values, in which she is silently confined, and which are symbolized by the Japanese-language version of "Let Us Gather at the River," which they sing at the Japanese-Christian church.

Yoneko's moment of detachment from her mother comes, when, toward the end of the story, her mother tells her, "Never kill a person, Yoneko, because if you do, God will take from you someone you love," to which Yoneko quickly responds "I don't believe in that, I don't believe in God" (56). Although Yoneko is never told of her mother's secret relationship with Marpo, she somehow senses that there is a connection between her mother's comment and the ring that Marpo gave Mrs. Hosoume. Her reaction is to shy away from the subject. Thus Yoneko is unconsciously rejecting both her mother's negative representation of heterosexual relationships in separation, death, and guilt, and the male-centered social order, represented by "God," to which her mother surrenders. As in Rosie's case, this distancing is accompanied with guilt on Yoneko's part, symbolized by her guilt over the secret ring, which she already lost.

In both stories, the daughters verbally express neither their desire to identify with, nor their detachment from, the mothers. As Rich explains, it is difficult for a daughter to articulate her feelings towards her mother in a patriarchal society (221).[15] Yamamoto, by making the daughters adolescent, captures the heightened tensions and dramatizes the silent, though intense, ambivalence on the part of daughters.

While the silences of these stories show women's oppressed status in Japanese-American culture, there are other kinds of silences, which are modes of expression rather than the result of female oppression. In **"Seventeen Syllables,"** Mr. Hayashi's silence shows his irritation and anger rather than oppression. When the Hayashis visit the Hayano family, Mr. Hayashi reads a *Life* magazine while his wife and Mr. Hayano discuss *haiku,* and then abruptly leaves the house "saying nothing" (11). When Tome apologizes to her husband by saying "You know how I get when it's *haiku* . . . I forget what time it is," he only "grunts," and Rosie aptly senses that her father is "denying her mother" (12). Likewise, Tome's calm silence, while watching her prize woodprint burning, expresses her deep despair and loneliness—though in a passive way.

In **"Yoneko's Earthquake,"** the story of Mrs. Hosoume, hidden behind the seemingly sporadic episodes, is told not explicitly by words, but by silences. We start suspecting Mrs. Hosoume of having an affair with Marpo when she gives a ring to Yoneko and tells her, "If your father asks where you got it, say you found it on the street"—without explaining to her where it is actually from (52). Obviously, someone other than her husband gave her the ring, and she has to keep it secret from him. When the Hosoume family takes a trip on a weekday afternoon to a Japanese hospital in the city—a "most unusual" thing to do—the parents do not explain the nature of the trip to the children, and the father demands that the children tell no one about the visit (54). Besides the brief description of Mrs. Hosoume's state of pain when she comes out of the hospital, and the vague explanation that "she was feeling a little under the weather and that the doctor had administered some necessarily astringent treatment," we, as well as Yoneko, are given no details (54). Because of this silence of the parents and the silence forced on the children, we assume that Mrs. Hosoume had an abortion. Also the silence of Marpo, when he disappears from the farm without even saying good-bye to Yoneko and Seigo, confirms our suspicion. His silence strikes us as strange because Yoneko and Seigo were quite attached to him and he has become indispensable to the family. Thus, these two stories not only illustrate the oppression of silenced women but go further and tell their life stories by the use of different kinds of silences.

As Charles Crow points out in "The *Issei* Father in the Fiction of Hisaye Yamamoto," the stories show possibilities for the daughters to break through the multilayered silences and obtain their own artistic voices.[16] Rosie, who obviously inherits her mother's sensitivity toward language, reads *haiku* magazines and cherishes the *haiku* parody written in English. She also skillfully imitates various movie stars to entertain her friends at school. Yoneko also shows the will to search for her own voice. When she is converted to Christianity, she tries to create her own version of God's image by asking Marpo questions: Who did Marpo suppose was God's favorite movie star? Or, what sound did Jesus' laughter have (it must be like music, she added, nodding sagely, answering herself to her own satisfaction), and did Marpo suppose that God's sense of humor would have appreciated the delicious chant she had learned from friends at school today:

There ain't no bugs on us,
There ain't no bugs on us,
There may be bugs on the rest of you mugs,
But there ain't no bugs on us? (49-50)

She enjoys word play and composes songs as a means of survival, as well as for fun. After Siego dies, "Whenever the thought of Seigo crossed her mind, she instantly began composing a new song, and this worked very well" (56). By having access to various forms of expression, as well as skills in English, the daughters have more freedom to tell stories—and a potentially bigger audience. They learn their mothers' stories, in spite of, and by way of, their silences, and tell the stories articulately to larger audiences. I would push Crow's point further and argue that Yamamoto's daughters gain creativity, not only by breaking through the silences, but also by making use of the silences. It is important, therefore, that these stories be written in the form of the daughters' retrospection, told with a grown-up consciousness. Yamamoto, by using young *nisei* daughters' viewpoints, suggests the future possibility of daughters, finally able to tell their mothers' stories. Indeed, these stories themselves are Yamamoto's own achievement as a *nisei* daughter giving voice to her mother's silences, though in a fictional form.[17] By using young daughters' points of view, Yamamoto succeeds in representing mothers without appropriating their voices and expresses the reality of the *nisei* daughters—their irritation, detachment, anger, and identification with *issei* mothers.

Rich argues "women are made taboo to women—not just sexually, but as comrades, cocreators, coinspiritors. In breaking this taboo, we are reuniting with our mothers; in reuniting with our mothers, we are breaking this taboo" (255). Yamamoto recaptures *issei* mothers' experiences as well as *nisei* daughters' visions. By using minimalist technique, and making use of silences, she not only succeeds in telling daughters' stories but also in making the mothers' silence tell their own stories. While mothers and daughters can never openly talk to each other about their experiences and feelings, recognition of these feelings, acknowledgement of the very existence of "this cathexis between mother and daughter," as Rich describes it, is a way to articulate women's reality (225). By recovering *issei* mothers stories, giving them voice through silence, Yamamoto recreates a usable past for *nisei* daughters and for every one of us willing to share it.

Notes

[1] Roberta Rubenstein, *Boundaries of the Self: Gender, Culture, Fiction* (Urbana: U of Illinois P, 1987) 8.

[2] On interpretation and evaluation of women's silences, see the introduction of King-Kok Cheung's *Articulate Silences: Hisaye Yamamoto, Maxine Hong Kingston, Joy Kogawa* (Ithaca: Cornell UP, 1993) 1-26. While owing much to Cheung's study of multicultural silences, my article focuses on the meanings of silences in mother-daughter relationships.

[3] Adrienne Rich, *Of Woman Born: Motherhood as Experience and Institution* (New York: Norton, 1976) 13.

[4] Susan Glaspell, "A Jury of Her Peers," *Lifted Masks and Other Stories* (Ann Arbor: U of Michigan P, 1993) 279-306.

[5] Patricia J. Wetzel, "Are 'Powerless' Communication Strategies the Japanese Norm?" *Language in Society* 17.4 (1988): 555-64. Also see Masao Miyoshi's *Accomplices of Silence: The Modern Japanese Novel* (Berkeley: U of California P, 1974), in which he explains the characteristics of modern Japanese literature:

> Perhaps more important than any other factor in this whole problem of language and style [of modern Japanese fiction] is the typical Japanese dislike of the verbal. It might be said that the culture is primarily visual, that reticence, not eloquence, is rewarded. Similarly, in art it is not articulation but the subtle art of silence that is valued. *Haiku* is the most perfect embodiment of this spirit but it is visible elsewhere as well . . . this passion for silence is in evidence in the narrator's attitude toward the story. Often, the scene of the *Japanese* novel is set by suggestion and evocation rather than description. (xv)

[6] Akiko Jugaku, *Onna to Kotoba (Women and Language)* (Tokyo: Iwanami Shoten, 1989) 38-39, and Evelyn Nakano, *Issei, Nisei, War Bride: Three Generations of Japanese American Women in Domestic Service* (Philadelphia: Temple UP, 1986) 207.

[7] Hisaye Yamamoto, *Seventeen Syllables and Other Stories* (Catham NY: Kitchen Table, 1988) 46.

[8] Also it might be relevant that *haiku* is often considered to be respectable and therefore a suitable form for women. Mitsuye Yamada, in "A MELUS Interview: Mitsuye Yamada," *MELUS* 15.1 (1988): 97-107, recollects her mother making the distinction that "Senryu ["A lower type of poetry than haiku" and "a grass roots form" according to Yamada] is alright for men, but women should be writing haiku" (99-100).

[9] Although there is no explicit reference to the matter, I would argue that we can assume that he is sexually impotent because Mrs. Hosoume's abortion shows that both Mr. and Mrs. Housome believe that she became pregnant by Marpo.

[10] Stan Yogi, "Legacies Revealed: Uncovering Buried Plots in the Stories of Hisaye Yamamoto," *Studies in American Fiction* 17.2 (1989): 175.

[11] Judith Wilt, *Abortion, Choice, and Contemporary Fiction* (Chicago: U of Chicago P, 1990) 10.

[12] Barbara Johnson, "Apostrophe, Animation, and Abortion," *Feminisms: An Anthology of Literary Theory and Criticism*, eds. Robyn R. Warhol and Diane Price Herndl (New Brunswick: Rutgers UP, 1991) 641.

[13] Many critics who discuss Yamamoto's short fiction, such as King-Kok Cheung, refer to the influence of modernist technique of limited point of view (278). Charles L. Crow more specifically mentions Henry James' *What Maisie Knew* in "Home and Transcendence in Los Angeles Fiction," *Los Angeles in Fiction: A Collection of Original Essays*, ed. David Fine (Albuquerque: U of New Mexico P, 1984) 189-205, and "The Issei Father in the Fiction of Hisaye Yamamoto," *Opening Up Literary Criticism: Essays on American Prose and Poetry*. ed. Lo Truchlar (Salzburg: Verlag Wolfgang Nugebauer, 1986) 34-40.

[14] Nancy Chodorow. *The Reproduction of Mothering: Psychoanalysis and the Sociology of Gender* (Berkeley: U of California P, 1978) 243-44.

[15] Yamamoto, in "A MELUS Interview," acknowledges the difficulty in mother-daughter communication in general (80),

[16] Crow, "Issei" 36.

[17] Yamamoto, in her letter quoted by Susan Koppelman, writes that "Seventeen Syllables" is her mother's story, though the details are not true.

FURTHER READING

Cheung, King-Kok. "Rhetorical Silence: 'Seventeen Syllables,' 'Yoneko's Earthquake,' and 'The Legend of Miss Sasagawara.'" In *Articulate Silences: Hisaye Yamamoto, Maxine Hong Kingston, Joy Kogawa*, pp. 27-73. Ithaca, N.Y.: Cornell University Press, 1993.

> Explores the multiple levels and forms of silence employed in Yamamoto's stories, focusing on "Seventeen Syllables," "Yoneko's Earthquake," and "The Legend of Miss Sasagawara."

———. "Reading between the Syllables: Hisaye Yamamoto's *Seventeen Syllables and Other Stories*." In *Teaching American Ethnic Literatures: Nineteen Essays*, edited by John R. Maitino and David R. Peck, pp. 313-25. Albuquerque: University of New Mexico Press, 1996.

> Broad overview of Yamamoto's themes, styles, and techniques; includes suggestions for group activities, discussion questions, and a bibliography of related works and criticism.

Crow, Charles L. "The *Issei* Father in the Fiction of Hisaye Yamamoto." In *Opening Up Literary Criticism: Essays on American Prose and Poetry*, edited by Leo Truchlar, pp. 34-40. Salzburg: Neugebauer, 1986.

> Considers Yamamoto's stories in terms of her first-generation immigrant Japanese male characters.

Miner, Valerie. A review of *Seventeen Syllables and Other Stories*. *The Nation* 248, No. 16 (1989): 566-68.

> Brief discussion, commenting on Yamamoto's realism and culturally diverse characters.

Osborne, William P., and Sylvia A. Watanabe. "A Conversation with Hisaye Yamamoto." *Chicago Review* 39, Nos. 3-4 (1993): 34-8.

> Interview focusing on ethnic and cultural issues surrounding Yamamoto and her work.

Payne, Robert M. "Adapting (to) the Margins: *Hot Summer Winds* and the Stories of Hisaye Yamamoto." *East-West Film Journal* 7, No. 2 (July 1993): 39-53.

> Analyzes the television film *Hot Summer Winds* in terms of its "striking differences" from the Yamamoto stories "Seventeen Syllables" and "Yoneko's Earthquake" on which it is based.

Wheeler, Elizabeth A. "A Concrete Island: Hisaye Yamamoto's Postwar Los Angeles." *Southern California Quarterly* LXXVIII, No. 1 (Spring 1996): 19-50.

> Examines Yamamoto as "an urban writer, a chronicler of postwar Los Angeles," focusing on the story "The Wilshire Bus."

Yogi, Stan. "Rebels and Heroines: Subversive Narratives in the Stories of Wakako Yamauchi and Hisaye Yamamoto." In *Reading the Literatures of Asian America*, edited by Shirley Geok-lin Lim and Amy Ling, pp. 131-50. Philadelphia: Temple University Press, 1992.

> Treats Yamamoto's stories "Seventeen Syllables" and "Yoneko's Earthquake" as subversive to the strict cultural codes of female behavior within the *issei* family.

Additional coverage of Yamamoto's life and career is contained in the following source published by Gale Group: *Asian American Literature.*

Appendix:

Select Bibliography of General Sources on Short Fiction

BOOKS OF CRITICISM

Allen, Walter. *The Short Story in English*. New York: Oxford University Press, 1981, 413 p.

Aycock, Wendell M., ed. *The Teller and the Tale: Aspects of the Short Story* (Proceedings of the Comparative Literature Symposium, Texas Tech University, Volume XIII). Lubbock: Texas Tech Press, 1982, 156 p.

Averill, Deborah. *The Irish Short Story from George Moore to Frank O'Connor*. Washington, D.C.: University Press of America, 1982, 329 p.

Bates, H. E. *The Modern Short Story: A Critical Survey*. Boston: Writer, 1941, 231 p.

Bayley, John. *The Short Story: Henry James to Elizabeth Bowen*. Great Britain: The Harvester Press Limited, 1988, 197 p.

Bennett, E. K. *A History of the German Novelle: From Goethe to Thomas Mann*. Cambridge: At the University Press, 1934, 296 p.

Bone, Robert. *Down Home: A History of Afro-American Short Fiction from Its Beginning to the End of the Harlem Renaissance*. Rev. ed. New York: Columbia University Press, 1988, 350 p.

Bruck, Peter. *The Black American Short Story in the Twentieth Century: A Collection of Critical Essays*. Amsterdam: B. R. Grüner Publishing Co., 1977, 209 p.

Burnett, Whit, and Burnett, Hallie. *The Modern Short Story in the Making*. New York: Hawthorn Books, 1964, 405 p.

Canby, Henry Seidel. *The Short Story in English*. New York: Henry Holt and Co., 1909, 386 p.

Current-García, Eugene. *The American Short Story before 1850: A Critical History*. Twayne's Critical History of the Short Story, edited by William Peden. Boston: Twayne Publishers, 1985, 168 p.

Flora, Joseph M., ed. *The English Short Story, 1880-1945: A Critical History*. Twayne's Critical History of the Short Story, edited by William Peden. Boston: Twayne Publishers, 1985, 215 p.

Foster, David William. *Studies in the Contemporary Spanish-American Short Story*. Columbia, Mo.: University of Missouri Press, 1979, 126 p.

George, Albert J. *Short Fiction in France, 1800-1850*. Syracuse, N.Y.: Syracuse University Press, 1964, 245 p.

Gerlach, John. *Toward an End: Closure and Structure in the American Short Story*. University, Ala.: The University of Alabama Press, 1985, 193 p.

Hankin, Cherry, ed. *Critical Essays on the New Zealand Short Story*. Auckland: Heinemann Publishers, 1982, 186 p.

Hanson, Clare, ed. *Re-Reading the Short Story*. London: MacMillan Press, 1989, 137 p.

Harris, Wendell V. *British Short Fiction in the Nineteenth Century*. Detroit: Wayne State University Press, 1979, 209 p.

Huntington, John. *Rationalizing Genius: Ideological Strategies in the Classic American Science Fiction Short Story*. New Brunswick: Rutgers University Press, 1989, 216 p.

Kilroy, James F., ed. *The Irish Short Story: A Critical History*. Twayne's Critical History of the Short Story, edited by William Peden. Boston: Twayne Publishers, 1984, 251 p.

Lee, A. Robert. *The Nineteenth-Century American Short Story*. Totowa, N. J.: Vision / Barnes & Noble, 1986, 196 p.

Leibowitz, Judith. *Narrative Purpose in the Novella*. The Hague: Mouton, 1974, 137 p.

Lohafer, Susan. *Coming to Terms with the Short Story*. Baton Rouge: Louisiana State University Press, 1983, 171 p.

Lohafer, Susan, and Clarey, Jo Ellyn. *Short Story Theory at a Crossroads*. Baton Rouge: Louisiana State University Press, 1989, 352 p.

Mann, Susan Garland. *The Short Story Cycle: A Genre Companion and Reference Guide*. New York: Greenwood Press, 1989, 228 p.

Matthews, Brander. *The Philosophy of the Short Story*. New York, N.Y.: Longmans, Green and Co., 1901, 83 p.

May, Charles E., ed. *Short Story Theories*. Athens, Oh.: Ohio University Press, 1976, 251 p.

McClave, Heather, ed. *Women Writers of the Short Story: A Collection of Critical Essays*. Englewood Cliffs, N. J.: Prentice-Hall, 1980, 171 p.

Moser, Charles, ed. *The Russian Short Story: A Critical History*. Twayne's Critical History of the Short Story, edited by William Peden. Boston: Twayne Publishers, 1986, 232 p.

New, W. H. *Dreams of Speech and Violence: The Art of the Short Story in Canada and New Zealand*. Toronto: The University of Toronto Press, 1987, 302 p.

Newman, Frances. *The Short Story's Mutations: From Petronius to Paul Morand*. New York: B. W. Huebsch, 1925, 332 p.

O'Connor, Frank. *The Lonely Voice: A Study of the Short Story*. Cleveland: World Publishing Co., 1963, 220 p.

O'Faolain, Sean. *The Short Story*. New York: Devin-Adair Co., 1951, 370 p.

Orel, Harold. *The Victorian Short Story: Development and Triumph of a Literary Genre*. Cambridge: Cambridge University Press, 1986, 213 p.

O'Toole, L. Michael. *Structure, Style and Interpretation in the Russian Short Story*. New Haven: Yale University Press, 1982, 272 p.

Pattee, Fred Lewis. *The Development of the American Short Story: An Historical Survey*. New York: Harper and Brothers Publishers, 1923, 388 p.

Peden, Margaret Sayers, ed. *The Latin American Short Story: A Critical History*. Twayne's Critical History of the Short Story, edited by William Peden. Boston: Twayne Publishers, 1983, 160 p.

Peden, William. *The American Short Story: Continuity and Change, 1940-1975*. Rev. ed. Boston: Houghton Mifflin Co., 1975, 215 p.

Reid, Ian. *The Short Story*. The Critical Idiom, edited by John D. Jump. London: Methuen and Co., 1977, 76 p.

Rhode, Robert D. *Setting in the American Short Story of Local Color, 1865-1900*. The Hague: Mouton, 1975, 189 p.

Rohrberger, Mary. *Hawthorne and the Modern Short Story: A Study in Genre*. The Hague: Mouton and Co., 1966, 148 p.

Shaw, Valerie. *The Short Story: A Critical Introduction*. London: Longman, 1983, 294 p.

Stephens, Michael. *The Dramaturgy of Style: Voice in Short Fiction*. Carbondale, Ill.: Southern Illinois University Press, 1986, 281 p.

Stevick, Philip, ed. *The American Short Story, 1900-1945: A Critical History*. Twayne's Critical History of the Short Story, edited by William Peden. Boston: Twayne Publishers, 1984, 209 p.

Summers, Hollis, ed. *Discussion of the Short Story*. Boston: D. C. Heath and Co., 1963, 118 p.

Vannatta, Dennis, ed. *The English Short Story, 1945-1980: A Critical History*. Twayne's Critical History of the Short Story, edited by William Peden. Boston: Twayne Publishers, 1985, 206 p.

Voss, Arthur. *The American Short Story: A Critical Survey*. Norman, Okla.: University of Oklahoma Press, 1973, 399 p.

Walker, Warren S. *Twentieth-Century Short Story Explication: New Series, Vol. 1: 1989-1990*. Hamden, Conn.: Shoe String, 1993, 366 p.

Ward, Alfred C. *Aspects of the Modern Short Story: English and American*. London: University of London Press, 1924, 307 p.

Weaver, Gordon, ed. *The American Short Story, 1945-1980: A Critical History*. Twayne's Critical History of the Short Story, edited by William Peden. Boston: Twayne Publishers, 1983, 150 p.

West, Ray B., Jr. *The Short Story in America, 1900-1950*. Chicago: Henry Regnery Co., 1952, 147 p.

Williams, Blanche Colton. *Our Short Story Writers*. New York: Moffat, Yard and Co., 1920, 357 p.

Wright, Austin McGiffert. *The American Short Story in the Twenties*. Chicago: University of Chicago Press, 1961, 425 p.

CRITICAL ANTHOLOGIES

Atkinson, W. Patterson, ed. *The Short-Story*. Boston: Allyn and Bacon, 1923, 317 p.

Baldwin, Charles Sears, ed. *American Short Stories*. New York, N.Y.: Longmans, Green and Co., 1904, 333 p.

Charters, Ann, ed. *The Story and Its Writer: An Introduction to Short Fiction*. New York: St. Martin's Press, 1983, 1239 p.

Current-García, Eugene, and Patrick, Walton R., eds. *American Short Stories: 1820 to the Present*. Key Editions, edited by John C. Gerber. Chicago: Scott, Foresman and Co., 1952, 633 p.

Fagin, N. Bryllion, ed. *America through the Short Story*. Boston: Little, Brown, and Co., 1936, 508 p.

Frakes, James R., and Traschen, Isadore, eds. *Short Fiction: A Critical Collection*. Prentice-Hall English Literature Series, edited by Maynard Mack. Englewood Cliffs, N.J.: Prentice-Hall, 1959, 459 p.

Gifford, Douglas, ed. *Scottish Short Stories, 1800-1900*. The Scottish Library, edited by Alexander Scott. London: Calder and Boyars, 1971, 350 p.

Gordon, Caroline, and Tate, Allen, eds. *The House of Fiction: An Anthology of the Short Story withCommentary*. Rev. ed. New York: Charles Scribner's Sons, 1960, 469 p.

Greet, T. Y., et. al. *The Worlds of Fiction: Stories in Context*. Boston, Mass.: Houghton Mifflin Co., 1964, 429 p.

Gullason, Thomas A., and Caspar, Leonard, eds. *The World of Short Fiction: An International Collection*. New York: Harper and Row, 1962, 548 p.

Havighurst, Walter, ed. *Masters of the Modern Short Story*. New York: Harcourt, Brace and Co., 1945, 538 p.

Litz, A. Walton, ed. *Major American Short Stories*. New York: Oxford University Press, 1975, 823 p.

Matthews, Brander, ed. *The Short-Story: Specimens Illustrating Its Development*. New York: American Book Co., 1907, 399 p.

Menton, Seymour, ed. *The Spanish American Short Story: A Critical Anthology*. Berkeley and Los Angeles: University of California Press, 1980, 496 p.

Mzamane, Mbulelo Vizikhungo, ed. *Hungry Flames, and Other Black South African Short Stories*. Longman African Classics. Essex: Longman, 1986, 162 p.

Schorer, Mark, ed. *The Short Story: A Critical Anthology*. Rev. ed. Prentice-Hall English Literature Series, edited by Maynard Mack. Englewood Cliffs, N. J.: Prentice-Hall, 1967, 459 p.

Simpson, Claude M., ed. *The Local Colorists: American Short Stories, 1857-1900*. New York: Harper and Brothers Publishers, 1960, 340 p.

Stanton, Robert, ed. *The Short Story and the Reader*. New York: Henry Holt and Co., 1960, 557 p.

West, Ray B., Jr., ed. *American Short Stories*. New York: Thomas Y. Crowell Co., 1959, 267 p.

Short Story Criticism Indexes

Literary Criticism Series
Cumulative Author Index

SSC Cumulative Nationality Index
SSC Cumulative Title Index

How to Use This Index

The main references

Calvino, Italo
  1923–1985 .... CLC 5, 8, 11, 22, 33, 39,
                                          73; SSC 3

list all author entries in the following Gale Literary Criticism series:

BLC = *Black Literature Criticism*
CLC = *Contemporary Literary Criticism*
CLR = *Children's Literature Review*
CMLC = *Classical and Medieval Literature Criticism*
DA = *DISCovering Authors*
DAB = *DISCovering Authors: British*
DAC = *DISCovering Authors: Canadian*
DAM **=** *DISCovering Authors: Modules*
        DRAM: *Dramatists Module;* *MST*: *Most-Studied Authors Module;*
        MULT: *Multicultural Authors Module;* *NOV*: *Novelists Module;*
        POET: *Poets Module;* *POP*: *Popular Fiction and Genre Authors Module*
DC = *Drama Criticism*
HLC = *Hispanic Literature Criticism*
LC = *Literature Criticism from 1400 to 1800*
NCLC = *Nineteenth-Century Literature Criticism*
PC = *Poetry Criticism*
SSC = *Short Story Criticism*
TCLC = *Twentieth-Century Literary Criticism*
WLC = *World Literature Criticism, 1500 to the Present*

The cross-references

See also CANR 23; CA 85-88;
    obituary CA116

list all author entries in the following Gale biographical and literary sources:

AAYA = *Authors & Artists for Young Adults*
AITN = *Authors in the News*
BEST = *Bestsellers*
BW = *Black Writers*
CA = *Contemporary Authors*
CAAS = *Contemporary Authors Autobiography Series*
CABS = *Contemporary Authors Bibliographical Series*
CANR = *Contemporary Authors New Revision Series*
CAP = *Contemporary Authors Permanent Series*
CDALB = *Concise Dictionary of American Literary Biography*
CDBLB = *Concise Dictionary of British Literary Biography*
DLB = *Dictionary of Literary Biography*
DLBD = *Dictionary of Literary Biography Documentary Series*
DLBY = *Dictionary of Literary Biography Yearbook*
HW = *Hispanic Writers*
JRDA = *Junior DISCovering Authors*
MAICYA = *Major Authors and Illustrators for Children and Young Adults*
MTCW = *Major 20th-Century Writers*
NNAL = *Native North American Literature*
SAAS = *Something about the Author Autobiography Series*
SATA = *Something about the Author*
YABC = *Yesterday's Authors of Books for Children*

Literary Criticism Series
Cumulative Author Index

Andress, Lesley
See Sanders, Lawrence
Andrewes, Lancelot 1555-1626 .... **LC 5**
See also DLB 151, 172
Andrews, Cicily Fairfield
See West, Rebecca
Andrews, Elton V.
See Pohl, Frederik
Andreyev, Leonid (Nikolaevich) 1871-1919
TCLC 3
See also CA 104
Andric, Ivo 1892-1975 .... **CLC 8**
See also CA 81-84; 57-60; CANR 43, 60; DLB
147; MTCW 1
Androvar
See Prado (Calvo), Pedro
Angelique, Pierre
See Bataille, Georges
Angell, Roger 1920- .... **CLC 26**
See also CA 57-60; CANR 13, 44, 70; DLB 171,
185
Angelou, Maya 1928-**CLC 12, 35, 64, 77; BLC
1; DA; DAB; DAC; DAM MST, MULT,
POET, POP; WLCS**
See also AAYA 7, 20; BW 2; CA 65-68; CANR
19, 42, 65; CLR 53; DLB 38; MTCW 1, 2;
SATA 49
Anna Comnena 1083-1153 .... **CMLC 25**
Annensky, Innokenty (Fyodorovich) 1856-1909
TCLC 14
<indexSee also CA 110; 155
Annunzio, Gabriele d'
See D'Annunzio, Gabriele
Anodos
See Coleridge, Mary E(lizabeth)
Anon, Charles Robert
See Pessoa, Fernando (Antonio Nogueira)
Anouilh, Jean (Marie Lucien Pierre) 1910-1987
CLC 1, 3, 8, 13, 40, 50; DAM DRAM; DC 8
See also CA 17-20R; 123; CANR 32; MTCW 1,
2
Anthony, Florence
See Ai
Anthony, John
See Ciardi, John (Anthony)
Anthony, Peter
See Shaffer, Anthony (Joshua); Shaffer, Peter
(Levin)
Anthony, Piers 1934- ...... **CLC 35; DAM POP**
See also AAYA 11; CA 21-24R; CANR 28, 56,
73; DLB 8; MTCW 1, 2; SAAS 22; SATA 84
Anthony, Susan B(rownell) 1916-1991 . **T C L C
84**
See also CA 89-92; 134
Antoine, Marc
See Proust, (Valentin-Louis-George-Eugene-)
Marcel
Antoninus, Brother
See Everson, William (Oliver)
Antonioni, Michelangelo 1912- .... **CLC 20**
See also CA 73-76; CANR 45, 77
Antschel, Paul 1920-1970
See Celan, Paul
See also CA 85-88; CANR 33, 61; MTCW 1
Anwar, Chairil 1922-1949 .... **TCLC 22**
See also CA 121
Apess, William 1798-1839(?) **NCLC 73; DAM
MULT**
See also DLB 175; NNAL
Apollinaire, Guillaume 1880-1918 **TCLC 3, 8,
51; DAM POET; PC 7**
See also Kostrowitzki, Wilhelm Apollinaris de
See also CA 152; MTCW 1

Appelfeld, Aharon 1932- .... **CLC 23, 47**
See also CA 112; 133
Apple, Max (Isaac) 1941- .... **CLC 9, 33**
See also CA 81-84; CANR 19, 54, DLB 130
Appleman, Philip (Dean) 1926- .... **CLC 51**
See also CA 13-16R; CAAS 18; CANR 6, 29, 56
Appleton, Lawrence
See Lovecraft, H(oward) P(hillips)
Apteryx
See Eliot, T(homas) S(tearns)
Apuleius, (Lucius Madaurensis) 125(?)-175(?)
CMLC 1
See also DLB 211
Aquin, Hubert 1929-1977 .... **CLC 15**
See also CA 105; DLB 53
Aquinas, Thomas 1224(?)-1274 ...... **CMLC 33**
See also DLB 115
Aragon, Louis 1897-1982 ... **CLC 3, 22; DAM
NOV, POET**
See also CA 69-72; 108; CANR 28, 71; DLB 72;
MTCW 1, 2
Arany, Janos 1817-1882 .... **NCLC 34**
Aranyos, Kakay
See Mikszath, Kalman
Arbuthnot, John 1667-1735 .... **LC 1**
See also DLB 101
Archer, Herbert Winslow
See Mencken, H(enry) L(ouis)
Archer, Jeffrey (Howard) 1940-**CLC 28; DAM
POP**
See also AAYA 16; BEST 89:3; CA 77-80;
CANR 22, 52; INT CANR-22
Archer, Jules 1915- .... **CLC 12**
See also CA 9-12R; CANR 6, 69; SAAS 5; SATA
4, 85
Archer, Lee
See Ellison, Harlan (Jay)
Arden, John 1930-**CLC 6, 13, 15; DAM DRAM**
See also CA 13-16R; CAAS 4; CANR 31, 65,
67; DLB 13; MTCW 1
Arenas, Reinaldo 1943-1990 .. **CLC 41; DAM
MULT; HLC**
See also CA 124; 128; 133; CANR 73; DLB 145;
HW; MTCW 1
Arendt, Hannah 1906-1975 .... **CLC 66, 98**
See also CA 17-20R; 61-64; CANR 26, 60;
MTCW 1, 2
Aretino, Pietro 1492-1556 .... **LC 12**
Arghezi, Tudor 1880-1967 .... **CLC 80**
See also Theodorescu, Ion N.
See also CA 167
Arguedas, Jose Maria 1911-1969. **CLC 10, 18**
See also CA 89-92; CANR 73; DLB 113; HW
Argueta, Manlio 1936- .... **CLC 31**
See also CA 131; CANR 73; DLB 145; HW
Ariosto, Ludovico 1474-1533 .... **LC 6**
Aristides
See Epstein, Joseph
Aristophanes 450B.C.-385B.C. **CMLC 4; DA;
DAB; DAC; DAM DRAM, MST; DC 2;
WLCS**
See also DLB 176
Aristotle 384B.C.-322B.C. ...... **CMLC 31; DA;
DAB; DAC; DAM MST; WLCS**
See also DLB 176
Arlt, Roberto (Godofredo Christophersen)
1900-1942 **TCLC 29; DAM MULT; HLC**
See also CA 123; 131; CANR 67; HW
Armah, Ayi Kwei 1939- .... **CLC 5, 33; BLC 1;
DAM MULT; POET**
See also BW 1; CA 61-64; CANR 21, 64; DLB
117; MTCW 1

Armatrading, Joan 1950- .... **CLC 17**
See also CA 114
Arnette, Robert
See Silverberg, Robert
Arnim, Achim von (Ludwig Joachim von Arnim)
1781-1831 .... **NCLC 5; SSC 29**
See also DLB 90
Arnim, Bettina von 1785-1859 .... **NCLC 38**
See also DLB 90
Arnold, Matthew 1822-1888**NCLC 6, 29; DA;
DAB; DAC; DAM MST, POET; PC 5;
WLC**
See also CDBLB 1832-1890; DLB 32, 57
Arnold, Thomas 1795-1842 .... **NCLC 18**
See also DLB 55
Arnow, Harriette (Louisa) Simpson 1908-1986
CLC 2, 7, 18
See also CA 9-12R; 118; CANR 14; DLB 6;
MTCW 1, 2; SATA 42; SATA-Obit 47
Arouet, Francois-Marie
See Voltaire
Arp, Hans
See Arp, Jean
Arp, Jean 1887-1966 .... **CLC 5**
See also CA 81-84; 25-28R; CANR 42, 77
Arrabal
See Arrabal, Fernando
Arrabal, Fernando 1932- ...... **CLC 2, 9, 18, 58**
See also CA 9-12R; CANR 15
Arrick, Fran .... **CLC 30**
See also Gaberman, Judie Angell
Artaud, Antonin (Marie Joseph) 1896-1948
TCLC 3, 36; DAM DRAM
See also CA 104; 149; MTCW 1
Arthur, Ruth M(abel) 1905-1979 .... **CLC 12**
See also CA 9-12R; 85-88; CANR 4; SATA 7,
26
Artsybashev, Mikhail (Petrovich) 1878-1927
TCLC 31
See also CA 170
Arundel, Honor (Morfydd) 1919-1973**CLC 17**
See also CA 21-22; 41-44R; CAP 2; CLR 35;
SATA 4; SATA-Obit 24
Arzner, Dorothy 1897-1979 .... **CLC 98**
Asch, Sholem 1880-1957 .... **TCLC 3**
See also CA 105
Ash, Shalom
See Asch, Sholem
Ashbery, John (Lawrence) 1927-**CLC 2, 3, 4, 6,
9, 13, 15, 25, 41, 77; DAM POET; PC 26**
See also CA 5-8R; CANR 9, 37, 66; DLB 5, 165;
DLBY 81; INT CANR-9; MTCW 1, 2
Ashdown, Clifford
See Freeman, R(ichard) Austin
Ashe, Gordon
See Creasey, John
Ashton-Warner, Sylvia (Constance) 1908-1984
CLC 19
See also CA 69-72; 112; CANR 29; MTCW 1, 2
Asimov, Isaac 1920-1992**CLC 1, 3, 9, 19, 26, 76,
92; DAM POP**
See also AAYA 13; BEST 90:2; CA 1-4R; 137;
CANR 2, 19, 36, 60; CLR 12; DLB 8; DLBY
92; INT CANR-19; JRDA; MAICYA; MTCW
1, 2; SATA 1, 26, 74
Assis, Joaquim Maria Machado de
See Machado de Assis, Joaquim Maria
Astley, Thea (Beatrice May) 1925- .... **CLC 41**
See also CA 65-68; CANR 11, 43, 78
Aston, James
See White, T(erence) H(anbury)

Banks, Iain M(enzies) 1954- .... **CLC 34**
See also CA 123; 128; CANR 61; DLB 194; INT 128

Banks, Lynne Reid .... **CLC 23**
See also Reid Banks, Lynne
See also AAYA 6

Banks, Russell 1940- .... **CLC 37, 72**
See also CA 65-68; CAAS 15; CANR 19, 52, 73; DLB 130

Banville, John 1945- .... **CLC 46, 118**
See also CA 117; 128; DLB 14; INT 128

Banville, Theodore (Faullain) de 1832-1891 **NCLC 9**

Baraka, Amiri 1934-**CLC 1, 2, 3, 5, 10, 14, 33, 115; BLC 1; DA; DAC; DAM MST, MULT, POET, POP; DC 6; PC 4; WLCS**
See also Jones, LeRoi
See also BW 2; CA 21-24R; CABS 3; CANR 27, 38, 61; CDALB 1941-1968; DLB 5, 7, 16, 38; DLBD 8; MTCW 1, 2

Barbauld, Anna Laetitia 1743-1825 **NCLC 50**
See also DLB 107, 109, 142, 158

Barbellion, W. N. P. .... **TCLC 24**
See also Cummings, Bruce F(rederick)

Barbera, Jack (Vincent) 1945- .... **CLC 44**
See also CA 110; CANR 45

Barbey d'Aurevilly, Jules Amedee 1808-1889 **NCLC 1; SSC 17**
See also DLB 119

Barbour, John c. 1316-1395 .... **CMLC 33**
See also DLB 146

Barbusse, Henri 1873-1935 .... **TCLC 5**
See also CA 105; 154; DLB 65

Barclay, Bill
See Moorcock, Michael (John)

Barclay, William Ewert
See Moorcock, Michael (John)

Barea, Arturo 1897-1957 .... **TCLC 14**
See also CA 111

Barfoot, Joan 1946- .... **CLC 18**
See also CA 105

Baring, Maurice 1874-1945 .... **TCLC 8**
See also CA 105; 168; DLB 34

Baring-Gould, Sabine 1834-1924 .... **TCLC 88**
See also DLB 156, 190

Barker, Clive 1952- .... **CLC 52; DAM POP**
See also AAYA 10; BEST 90:3; CA 121; 129; CANR 71; INT 129; MTCW 1, 2

Barker, George Granville 1913-1991 . **CLC 8, 48; DAM POET**
See also CA 9-12R; 135; CANR 7, 38; DLB 20; MTCW 1

Barker, Harley Granville
See Granville-Barker, Harley
See also DLB 10

Barker, Howard 1946- .... **CLC 37**
See also CA 102; DLB 13

Barker, Jane 1652-1732 .... **LC 42**

Barker, Pat(ricia) 1943- .... **CLC 32, 94**
See also CA 117; 122; CANR 50; INT 122

Barlach, Ernst 1870-1938 .... **TCLC 84**
See also DLB 56, 118

Barlow, Joel 1754-1812 .... **NCLC 23**
See also DLB 37

Barnard, Mary (Ethel) 1909- .... **CLC 48**
See also CA 21-22; CAP 2

Barnes, Djuna 1892-1982 **CLC 3, 4, 8, 11, 29; SSC 3**
See also CA 9-12R; 107; CANR 16, 55; DLB 4, 9, 45; MTCW 1, 2

Barnes, Julian (Patrick) 1946- **CLC 42; DAB**
See also CA 102; CANR 19, 54; DLB 194; DLBY 93; MTCW 1

Barnes, Peter 1931- .... **CLC 5, 56**
See also CA 65-68; CAAS 12; CANR 33, 34, 64; DLB 13; MTCW 1

Barnes, William 1801-1886 .... **NCLC 75**
See also DLB 32

Baroja (y Nessi), Pio 1872-1956**TCLC 8; HLC**
See also CA 104

Baron, David
See Pinter, Harold

Baron Corvo
See Rolfe, Frederick (William Serafino Austin Lewis Mary)

Barondess, Sue K(aufman) 1926-1977 **CLC 8**
See also Kaufman, Sue
See also CA 1-4R; 69-72; CANR 1

Baron de Teive
See Pessoa, Fernando (Antonio Nogueira)

Baroness Von S.
See Zangwill, Israel

Barres, (Auguste-) Maurice 1862-1923 **T C L C 47**
See also CA 164; DLB 123

Barreto, Afonso Henrique de Lima
See Lima Barreto, Afonso Henrique de

Barrett, (Roger) Syd 1946- .... **CLC 35**

Barrett, William (Christopher) 1913-1992 **CLC 27**
See also CA 13-16R; 139; CANR 11, 67; INT CANR-11

Barrie, J(ames) M(atthew) 1860-1937**TCLC 2; DAB; DAM DRAM**
See also CA 104; 136; CANR 77; CDBLB 1890-1914; CLR 16; DLB 10, 141, 156; MAICYA; MTCW 1; SATA 100; YABC 1

Barrington, Michael
See Moorcock, Michael (John)

Barrol, Grady
See Bograd, Larry

Barry, Mike
See Malzberg, Barry N(athaniel)

Barry, Philip 1896-1949 .... **TCLC 11**
See also CA 109; DLB 7

Bart, Andre Schwarz
See Schwarz-Bart, Andre

Barth, John (Simmons) 1930-**CLC 1, 2, 3, 5, 7, 9, 10, 14, 27, 51, 89; DAM NOV; SSC 10**
See also AITN 1, 2; CA 1-4R; CABS 1; CANR 5, 23, 49, 64; DLB 2; MTCW 1

Barthelme, Donald 1931-1989**CLC 1, 2, 3, 5, 6, 8, 13, 23, 46, 59, 115; DAM NOV; SSC 2**
See also CA 21-24R; 129; CANR 20, 58; DLB 2; DLBY 80, 89; MTCW 1, 2; SATA 7; SATA-Obit 62

Barthelme, Frederick 1943- .... **CLC 36, 117**
See also CA 114; 122; CANR 77; DLBY 85; INT 122

Barthes, Roland (Gerard) 1915-1980 **CLC 24, 83**
See also CA 130; 97-100; CANR 66; MTCW 1, 2

Barzun, Jacques (Martin) 1907- .... **CLC 51**
See also CA 61-64; CANR 22

Bashevis, Isaac
See Singer, Isaac Bashevis

Bashkirtseff, Marie 1859-1884 .... **NCLC 27**

Basho
See Matsuo Basho

Bass, Kingsley B., Jr.
See Bullins, Ed

Bass, Rick 1958- .... **CLC 79**
See also CA 126; CANR 53; DLB 212

Bassani, Giorgio 1916- .... **CLC 9**
See also CA 65-68; CANR 33; DLB 128, 177; MTCW 1

Bastos, Augusto (Antonio) Roa
See Roa Bastos, Augusto (Antonio)

Bataille, Georges 1897-1962 .... **CLC 29**
See also CA 101; 89-92

Bates, H(erbert) E(rnest) 1905-1974 **CLC 46; DAB; DAM POP; SSC 10**
See also CA 93-96; 45-48; CANR 34; DLB 162, 191; MTCW 1, 2

Bauchart
See Camus, Albert

Baudelaire, Charles 1821-1867**NCLC 6, 29, 55; DA; DAB; DAC; DAM MST, POET; PC 1; SSC 18; WLC**

Baudrillard, Jean 1929- .... **CLC 60**

Baum, L(yman) Frank 1856-1919 ..... **TCLC 7**
See also CA 108; 133; CLR 15; DLB 22; JRDA; MAICYA; MTCW 1, 2; SATA 18, 100

Baum, Louis F.
See Baum, L(yman) Frank

Baumbach, Jonathan 1933- .... **CLC 6, 23**
See also CA 13-16R; CAAS 5; CANR 12, 66; DLBY 80; INT CANR-12; MTCW 1

Bausch, Richard (Carl) 1945- .... **CLC 51**
See also CA 101; CAAS 14; CANR 43, 61; DLB 130

Baxter, Charles (Morley) 1947- . **CLC 45, 78; DAM POP**
See also CA 57-60; CANR 40, 64; DLB 130; MTCW 2

Baxter, George Owen
See Faust, Frederick (Schiller)

Baxter, James K(eir) 1926-1972 .... **CLC 14**
See also CA 77-80

Baxter, John
See Hunt, E(verette) Howard, (Jr.)

Bayer, Sylvia
See Glassco, John

Baynton, Barbara 1857-1929 .... **TCLC 57**

Beagle, Peter S(oyer) 1939- .... **CLC 7, 104**
See also CA 9-12R; CANR 4, 51, 73; DLBY 80; INT CANR-4; MTCW 1; SATA 60

Bean, Normal
See Burroughs, Edgar Rice

Beard, Charles A(ustin) 1874-1948 **TCLC 15**
See also CA 115; DLB 17; SATA 18

Beardsley, Aubrey 1872-1898 .... **NCLC 6**

Beattie, Ann 1947-**CLC 8, 13, 18, 40, 63; DAM NOV, POP; SSC 11**
See also BEST 90:2; CA 81-84; CANR 53, 73; DLBY 82; MTCW 1, 2

Beattie, James 1735-1803 .... **NCLC 25**
See also DLB 109

Beauchamp, Kathleen Mansfield 1888-1923
See Mansfield, Katherine
See also CA 104; 134; DA; DAC; DAM MST; MTCW 2

Beaumarchais, Pierre-Augustin Caron de 1732-1799 .... **DC 4**
See also DAM DRAM

Beaumont, Francis 1584(?)-1616**LC 33; DC 6**
See also CDBLB Before 1660; DLB 58, 121

Beauvoir, Simone (Lucie Ernestine Marie Bertrand) de 1908-1986**CLC 1, 2, 4, 8, 14, 31, 44, 50, 71; DA; DAB; DAC; DAM MST, NOV; WLC**
See also CA 9-12R; 118; CANR 28, 61; DLB 72; DLBY 86; MTCW 1, 2

Becker, Carl (Lotus) 1873-1945 ...... **TCLC 63**
See also CA 157; DLB 17

Berger, Melvin H. 1927- .... **CLC 12**
　　See also CA 5-8R; CANR 4; CLR 32; SAAS 2;
　　SATA 5, 88
Berger, Thomas (Louis) 1924-**CLC 3, 5, 8, 11,
　　18, 38; DAM NOV**
　　See also CA 1-4R; CANR 5, 28, 51; DLB 2;
　　DLBY 80; INT CANR-28; MTCW 1, 2
Bergman, (Ernst) Ingmar 1918- ..**CLC 16, 72**
　　See also CA 81-84; CANR 33, 70; MTCW 2
Bergson, Henri(-Louis) 1859-1941 . **TCLC 32**
　　See also CA 164
Bergstein, Eleanor 1938- .... **CLC 4**
　　See also CA 53-56; CANR 5
Berkoff, Steven 1937- .... **CLC 56**
　　See also CA 104; CANR 72
Bermant, Chaim (Icyk) 1929- .... **CLC 40**
　　See also CA 57-60; CANR 6, 31, 57
Bern, Victoria
　　See Fisher, M(ary) F(rances) K(ennedy)
Bernanos, (Paul Louis) Georges 1888-1948
　　TCLC 3
　　See also CA 104; 130; DLB 72
Bernard, April 1956- .... **CLC 59**
　　See also CA 131
Berne, Victoria
　　See Fisher, M(ary) F(rances) K(ennedy)
Bernhard, Thomas 1931-1989 ..**CLC 3, 32, 61**
　　See also CA 85-88; 127; CANR 32, 57; DLB 85,
　　124; MTCW 1
Bernhardt, Sarah (Henriette Rosine) 1844-1923
　　TCLC 75
　　See also CA 157
Berriault, Gina 1926- ... **CLC 54, 109; SSC 30**
　　See also CA 116; 129; CANR 66; DLB 130
Berrigan, Daniel 1921- .... **CLC 4**
　　See also CA 33-36R; CAAS 1; CANR 11, 43,
　　78; DLB 5
Berrigan, Edmund Joseph Michael, Jr.
　　1934-1983
　　See Berrigan, Ted
　　See also CA 61-64; 110; CANR 14
Berrigan, Ted .... **CLC 37**
　　See also Berrigan, Edmund Joseph Michael, Jr.
　　See also DLB 5, 169
Berry, Charles Edward Anderson 1931-
　　See Berry, Chuck
　　See also CA 115
Berry, Chuck .... **CLC 17**
　　See also Berry, Charles Edward Anderson
Berry, Jonas
　　See Ashbery, John (Lawrence)
Berry, Wendell (Erdman) 1934-**CLC 4, 6, 8, 27,
　　46; DAM POET**
　　See also AITN 1; CA 73-76; CANR 50, 73; DLB
　　5, 6; MTCW 1
Berryman, John 1914-1972**CLC 1, 2, 3, 4, 6, 8,
　　10, 13, 25, 62; DAM POET**
　　See also CA 13-16; 33-36R; CABS 2; CANR 35;
　　CAP 1; CDALB 1941-1968; DLB 48; MTCW
　　1, 2
Bertolucci, Bernardo 1940- .... **CLC 16**
　　See also CA 106
Berton, Pierre (Francis Demarigny) 1920-
　　CLC 104
　　See also CA 1-4R; CANR 2, 56; DLB 68; SATA
　　99
Bertrand, Aloysius 1807-1841 .... **NCLC 31**
Bertran de Born c. 1140-1215 .... **CMLC 5**
Besant, Annie (Wood) 1847-1933 ...... **TCLC 9**
　　See also CA 105
Bessie, Alvah 1904-1985 .... **CLC 23**
　　See also CA 5-8R; 116; CANR 2; DLB 26

Bethlen, T. D.
　　See Silverberg, Robert
Beti, Mongo .... **CLC 27; BLC 1; DAM MULT**
　　See also Biyidi, Alexandre
Betjeman, John 1906-1984**CLC 2, 6, 10, 34, 43;
　　DAB; DAM MST, POET**
　　See also CA 9-12R; 112; CANR 33, 56; CDBLB
　　1945-1960; DLB 20; DLBY 84; MTCW 1, 2
Bettelheim, Bruno 1903-1990 .... **CLC 79**
　　See also CA 81-84; 131; CANR 23, 61; MTCW
　　1, 2
Betti, Ugo 1892-1953 .... **TCLC 5**
　　See also CA 104; 155
Betts, Doris (Waugh) 1932- .... **CLC 3, 6, 28**
　　See also CA 13-16R; CANR 9, 66, 77; DLBY
　　82; INT CANR-9
Bevan, Alistair
　　See Roberts, Keith (John Kingston)
Bey, Pilaff
　　See Douglas, (George) Norman
Bialik, Chaim Nachman 1873-1934 **TCLC 25**
　　See also CA 170
Bickerstaff, Isaac
　　See Swift, Jonathan
Bidart, Frank 1939- .... **CLC 33**
　　See also CA 140
Bienek, Horst 1930- .... **CLC 7, 11**
　　See also CA 73-76; DLB 75
Bierce, Ambrose (Gwinett) 1842-1914(?)
　　**TCLC 1, 7, 44; DA; DAC; DAM MST; SSC
　　9; WLC**
　　See also CA 104; 139; CANR 78; CDALB
　　1865-1917; DLB 11, 12, 23, 71, 74, 186
Biggers, Earl Derr 1884-1933 .... **TCLC 65**
　　See also CA 108; 153
Billings, Josh
　　See Shaw, Henry Wheeler
　　<indexbody>**Billington, (Lady) Rachel (Mary)**
　　1942- **CLC 43**
　　See also AITN 2; CA 33-36R; CANR 44
Binyon, T(imothy) J(ohn) 1936- .... **CLC 34**
　　See also CA 111; CANR 28
Bioy Casares, Adolfo 1914-1984 **CLC 4, 8, 13,
　　88; DAM MULT; HLC; SSC 17**
　　See also CA 29-32R; CANR 19, 43, 66; DLB
　　113; HW; MTCW 1, 2
Bird, Cordwainer
　　See Ellison, Harlan (Jay)
Bird, Robert Montgomery 1806-1854**NCLC 1**
　　See also DLB 202
Birkerts, Sven 1951- .... **CLC 116**
　　See also CA 128; 133; CAAS 29; INT 133
Birney, (Alfred) Earle 1904-1995 **CLC 1, 4, 6,
　　11; DAC; DAM MST, POET**
　　See also CA 1-4R; CANR 5, 20; DLB 88; MTCW
　　1
Biruni, al 973-1048(?) .... **CMLC 28**
Bishop, Elizabeth 1911-1979**CLC 1, 4, 9, 13, 15,
　　32; DA; DAC; DAM MST, POET; PC 3**
　　See also CA 5-8R; 89-92; CABS 2; CANR 26,
　　61; CDALB 1968-1988; DLB 5, 169; MTCW
　　1, 2; SATA-Obit 24
Bishop, John 1935- .... **CLC 10**
　　See also CA 105
Bissett, Bill 1939- .... **CLC 18; PC 14**
　　See also CA 69-72; CAAS 19; CANR 15; DLB
　　53; MTCW 1
Bitov, Andrei (Georgievich) 1937- ..... **CLC 57**
　　See also CA 142
Biyidi, Alexandre 1932-
　　See Beti, Mongo
　　See also BW 1; CA 114; 124; MTCW 1, 2

Bjarme, Brynjolf
　　See Ibsen, Henrik (Johan)
Bjoernson, Bjoernstjerne (Martinius)
　　1832-1910 .... **TCLC 7, 37**
　　See also CA 104
Black, Robert
　　See Holdstock, Robert P.
Blackburn, Paul 1926-1971 .... **CLC 9, 43**
　　See also CA 81-84; 33-36R; CANR 34; DLB 16;
　　DLBY 81
Black Elk 1863-1950 **TCLC 33; DAM MULT**
　　See also CA 144; MTCW 1; NNAL
Black Hobart
　　See Sanders, (James) Ed(ward)
Blacklin, Malcolm
　　See Chambers, Aidan
Blackmore, R(ichard) D(oddridge) 1825-1900
　　TCLC 27
　　See also CA 120; DLB 18
Blackmur, R(ichard) P(almer) 1904-1965**C L C
　　2, 24**
　　See also CA 11-12; 25-28R; CANR 71; CAP 1;
　　DLB 63
Black Tarantula
　　See Acker, Kathy
Blackwood, Algernon (Henry) 1869-1951
　　TCLC 5
　　See also CA 105; 150; DLB 153, 156, 178
Blackwood, Caroline 1931-1996**CLC 6, 9, 100**
　　See also CA 85-88; 151; CANR 32, 61, 65; DLB
　　14, 207; MTCW 1
Blade, Alexander
　　See Hamilton, Edmond; Silverberg, Robert
Blaga, Lucian 1895-1961 .... **CLC 75**
　　See also CA 157
Blair, Eric (Arthur) 1903-1950
　　See Orwell, George
　　See also CA 104; 132; DA; DAB; DAC; DAM
　　MST, NOV; MTCW 1, 2; SATA 29
Blair, Hugh 1718-1800 .... **NCLC 75**
Blais, Marie-Claire 1939- **CLC 2, 4, 6, 13, 22;
　　DAC; DAM MST**
　　See also CA 21-24R; CAAS 4; CANR 38, 75;
　　DLB 53; MTCW 1, 2
Blaise, Clark 1940- .... **CLC 29**
　　See also AITN 2; CA 53-56; CAAS 3; CANR 5,
　　66; DLB 53
Blake, Fairley
　　See De Voto, Bernard (Augustine)
Blake, Nicholas
　　See Day Lewis, C(ecil)
　　See also DLB 77
Blake, William 1757-1827 .. **NCLC 13, 37, 57;
　　DA; DAB; DAC; DAM MST, POET; PC 12;
　　WLC**
　　See also CDBLB 1789-1832; CLR 52; DLB 93,
　　163; MAICYA; SATA 30
Blasco Ibanez, Vicente 1867-1928 ..**TCLC 12;
　　DAM NOV**
　　See also CA 110; 131; HW; MTCW 1
Blatty, William Peter 1928-**CLC 2; DAM POP**
　　See also CA 5-8R; CANR 9
Bleeck, Oliver
　　See Thomas, Ross (Elmore)
Blessing, Lee 1949- .... **CLC 54**
Blish, James (Benjamin) 1921-1975 ..**CLC 14**
　　See also CA 1-4R; 57-60; CANR 3; DLB 8;
　　MTCW 1; SATA 66
Bliss, Reginald
　　See Wells, H(erbert) G(eorge)
Blixen, Karen (Christentze Dinesen) 1885-1962
　　See Dinesen, Isak

Butler, Samuel 1612-1680 .... **LC 16, 43**
See also DLB 101, 126
Butler, Samuel 1835-1902 ... **TCLC 1, 33; DA; DAB; DAC; DAM MST, NOV; WLC**
See also CA 143; CDBLB 1890-1914; DLB 18, 57, 174
Butler, Walter C.
See Faust, Frederick (Schiller)
Butor, Michel (Marie Francois) 1926- **CLC 1, 3, 8, 11, 15**
See also CA 9-12R; CANR 33, 66; DLB 83; MTCW 1, 2
Butts, Mary 1892(?)-1937 .... **TCLC 77**
See also CA 148
Buzo, Alexander (John) 1944- .... **CLC 61**
See also CA 97-100; CANR 17, 39, 69
Buzzati, Dino 1906-1972 .... **CLC 36**
See also CA 160; 33-36R; DLB 177
Byars, Betsy (Cromer) 1928- .... **CLC 35**
See also AAYA 19; CA 33-36R; CANR 18, 36, 57; CLR 1, 16; DLB 52; INT CANR-18; JRDA; MAICYA; MTCW 1; SAAS 1; SATA 4, 46, 80
Byatt, A(ntonia) S(usan Drabble) 1936- . **C L C 19, 65; DAM NOV, POP**
See also CA 13-16R; CANR 13, 33, 50, 75; DLB 14, 194; MTCW 1, 2
Byrne, David 1952- .... **CLC 26**
See also CA 127
Byrne, John Keyes 1926-
See Leonard, Hugh
See also CA 102; CANR 78; INT 102
Byron, George Gordon (Noel) 1788-1824 **NCLC 2, 12; DA; DAB; DAC; DAM MST, POET; PC 16; WLC**
See also CDBLB 1789-1832; DLB 96, 110
Byron, Robert 1905-1941 .... **TCLC 67**
See also CA 160; DLB 195
C. 3. 3.
See Wilde, Oscar
Caballero, Fernan 1796-1877 .... **NCLC 10**
Cabell, Branch
See Cabell, James Branch
Cabell, James Branch 1879-1958 ...... **TCLC 6**
See also CA 105; 152; DLB 9, 78; MTCW 1
Cable, George Washington 1844-1925 **TCLC 4; SSC 4**
See also CA 104; 155; DLB 12, 74; DLBD 13
Cabral de Melo Neto, Joao 1920- .... **CLC 76; DAM MULT**
See also CA 151
Cabrera Infante, G(uillermo) 1929- **CLC 5, 25, 45; DAM MULT; HLC**
See also CA 85-88; CANR 29, 65; DLB 113; HW; MTCW 1, 2
Cade, Toni
See Bambara, Toni Cade
Cadmus and Harmonia
See Buchan, John
Caedmon fl. 658-680 .... **CMLC 7**
See also DLB 146
Caeiro, Alberto
See Pessoa, Fernando (Antonio Nogueira)
Cage, John (Milton, Jr.) 1912-1992 ... **CLC 41**
See also CA 13-16R; 169; CANR 9, 78; DLB 193; INT CANR-9
Cahan, Abraham 1860-1951 .... **TCLC 71**
See also CA 108; 154; DLB 9, 25, 28
Cain, G.
See Cabrera Infante, G(uillermo)
Cain, Guillermo
See Cabrera Infante, G(uillermo)

Cain, James M(allahan) 1892-1977 **CLC 3, 11, 28**
See also AITN 1; CA 17-20R; 73-76; CANR 8, 34, 61; MTCW 1
Caine, Mark
See Raphael, Frederic (Michael)
Calasso, Roberto 1941- .... **CLC 81**
See also CA 143
Calderon de la Barca, Pedro 1600-1681 **LC 23; DC 3**
Caldwell, Erskine (Preston) 1903-1987 **CLC 1, 8, 14, 50, 60; DAM NOV; SSC 19**
See also AITN 1; CA 1-4R; 121; CAAS 1; CANR 2, 33; DLB 9, 86; MTCW 1, 2
Caldwell, (Janet Miriam) Taylor (Holland) 1900-1985 **CLC 2, 28, 39; DAM NOV, POP**
See also CA 5-8R; 116; CANR 5; DLBD 17
Calhoun, John Caldwell 1782-1850 **NCLC 15**
See also DLB 3
Calisher, Hortense 1911- **CLC 2, 4, 8, 38; DAM NOV; SSC 15**
See also CA 1-4R; CANR 1, 22, 67; DLB 2; INT CANR-22; MTCW 1, 2
Callaghan, Morley Edward 1903-1990 **CLC 3, 14, 41, 65; DAC; DAM MST**
See also CA 9-12R; 132; CANR 33, 73; DLB 68; MTCW 1, 2
Callimachus c. 305B.C.-c. 240B.C. . **CMLC 18**
See also DLB 176
Calvin, John 1509-1564 .... **LC 37**
Calvino, Italo 1923-1985 **CLC 5, 8, 11, 22, 33, 39, 73; DAM NOV; SSC 3**
See also CA 85-88; 116; CANR 23, 61; DLB 196; MTCW 1, 2
Cameron, Carey 1952- .... **CLC 59**
See also CA 135
Cameron, Peter 1959- .... **CLC 44**
See also CA 125; CANR 50
Campana, Dino 1885-1932 .... **TCLC 20**
See also CA 117; DLB 114
Campanella, Tommaso 1568-1639 .... **LC 32**
Campbell, John W(ood, Jr.) 1910-1971 **CLC 32**
See also CA 21-22; 29-32R; CANR 34; CAP 2; DLB 8; MTCW 1
Campbell, Joseph 1904-1987 .... **CLC 69**
See also AAYA 3; BEST 89:2; CA 1-4R; 124; CANR 3, 28, 61; MTCW 1, 2
Campbell, Maria 1940- .... **CLC 85; DAC**
See also CA 102; CANR 54; NNAL
Campbell, (John) Ramsey 1946- **CLC 42; SSC 19**
See also CA 57-60; CANR 7; INT CANR-7
Campbell, (Ignatius) Roy (Dunnachie) 1901-1957 .... **TCLC 5**
See also CA 104; 155; DLB 20; MTCW 2
Campbell, Thomas 1777-1844 .... **NCLC 19**
See also DLB 93; 144
Campbell, Wilfred .... **TCLC 9**
See also Campbell, William
Campbell, William 1858(?)-1918
See Campbell, Wilfred
See also CA 106; DLB 92
Campion, Jane .... **CLC 95**
See also CA 138
Campos, Alvaro de
See Pessoa, Fernando (Antonio Nogueira)
Camus, Albert 1913-1960 **CLC 1, 2, 4, 9, 11, 14, 32, 63, 69; DA; DAB; DAC; DAM DRAM, MST, NOV; DC 2; SSC 9; WLC**
See also CA 89-92; DLB 72; MTCW 1, 2
Canby, Vincent 1924- .... **CLC 13**
See also CA 81-84

Cancale
See Desnos, Robert
Canetti, Elias 1905-1994 **CLC 3, 14, 25, 75, 86**
See also CA 21-24R; 146; CANR 23, 61; DLB 85, 124; MTCW 1, 2
Canfield, Dorothea F.
See Fisher, Dorothy (Frances) Canfield
Canfield, Dorothea Frances
See Fisher, Dorothy (Frances) Canfield
Canfield, Dorothy
See Fisher, Dorothy (Frances) Canfield
Canin, Ethan 1960- .... **CLC 55**
See also CA 131; 135
Cannon, Curt
See Hunter, Evan
Cao, Lan 1961- .... **CLC 109**
See also CA 165
Cape, Judith
See Page, P(atricia) K(athleen)
Capek, Karel 1890-1938 **TCLC 6, 37; DA; DAB; DAC; DAM DRAM, MST, NOV; DC 1; WLC**
See also CA 104; 140; MTCW 1
Capote, Truman 1924-1984 **CLC 1, 3, 8, 13, 19, 34, 38, 58; DA; DAB; DAC; DAM MST, NOV, POP; SSC 2; WLC**
See also CA 5-8R; 113; CANR 18, 62; CDALB 1941-1968; DLB 2, 185; DLBY 80, 84; MTCW 1, 2; SATA 91
Capra, Frank 1897-1991 .... **CLC 16**
See also CA 61-64; 135
Caputo, Philip 1941- .... **CLC 32**
See also CA 73-76; CANR 40
Caragiale, Ion Luca 1852-1912 .... **TCLC 76**
See also CA 157
Card, Orson Scott 1951- **CLC 44, 47, 50; DAM POP**
See also AAYA 11; CA 102; CANR 27, 47, 73; INT CANR-27; MTCW 1, 2; SATA 83
Cardenal, Ernesto 1925- **CLC 31; DAM MULT, POET; HLC; PC 22**
See also CA 49-52; CANR 2, 32, 66; HW; MTCW 1, 2
Cardozo, Benjamin N(athan) 1870-1938 **TCLC 65**
See also CA 117; 164
Carducci, Giosue (Alessandro Giuseppe) 1835-1907 .... **TCLC 32**
See also CA 163
Carew, Thomas 1595(?)-1640 .... **LC 13**
See also DLB 126
Carey, Ernestine Gilbreth 1908- .... **CLC 17**
See also CA 5-8R; CANR 71; SATA 2
Carey, Peter 1943- .... **CLC 40, 55, 96**
See also CA 123; 127; CANR 53, 76; INT 127; MTCW 1, 2; SATA 94
Carleton, William 1794-1869 .... **NCLC 3**
See also DLB 159
Carlisle, Henry (Coffin) 1926- .... **CLC 33**
See also CA 13-16R; CANR 15
Carlsen, Chris
See Holdstock, Robert P.
Carlson, Ron(ald F.) 1947- .... **CLC 54**
See also CA 105; CANR 27
Carlyle, Thomas 1795-1881 ... **NCLC 70; DA; DAB; DAC; DAM MST**
See also CDBLB 1789-1832; DLB 55; 144
Carman, (William) Bliss 1861-1929 . **TCLC 7; DAC**
See also CA 104; 152; DLB 92
Carnegie, Dale 1888-1955 .... **TCLC 53**
Carossa, Hans 1878-1956 .... **TCLC 48**
See also CA 170; DLB 66

Chapman, George 1559(?)-1634 **LC 22; DAM DRAM**
See also DLB 62, 121
Chapman, Graham 1941-1989 .... **CLC 21**
See also Monty Python
See also CA 116; 129; CANR 35
Chapman, John Jay 1862-1933 .... **TCLC 7**
See also CA 104
Chapman, Lee
See Bradley, Marion Zimmer
Chapman, Walker
See Silverberg, Robert
Chappell, Fred (Davis) 1936- .... **CLC 40, 78**
See also CA 5-8R; CAAS 4; CANR 8, 33, 67;
DLB 6, 105
Char, Rene(-Emile) 1907-1988 **CLC 9, 11, 14, 55; DAM POET**
See also CA 13-16R; 124; CANR 32; MTCW 1,
2
Charby, Jay
See Ellison, Harlan (Jay)
Chardin, Pierre Teilhard de
See Teilhard de Chardin, (Marie Joseph) Pierre
Charles I 1600-1649 .... **LC 13**
Charriere, Isabelle de 1740-1805 .... **NCLC 66**
Charyn, Jerome 1937- .... **CLC 5, 8, 18**
See also CA 5-8R; CAAS 1; CANR 7, 61; DLBY
83; MTCW 1
Chase, Mary (Coyle) 1907-1981 .... **DC 1**
See also CA 77-80; 105; SATA 17; SATA-Obit
29
Chase, Mary Ellen 1887-1973 .... **CLC 2**
See also CA 13-16; 41-44R; CAP 1; SATA 10
Chase, Nicholas
See Hyde, Anthony
Chateaubriand, Francois Rene de 1768-1848 **NCLC 3**
See also DLB 119
Chatterje, Sarat Chandra 1876-1936(?)
See Chatterji, Saratchandra
See also CA 109
Chatterji, Bankim Chandra 1838-1894 **NCLC 19**
Chatterji, Saratchandra .... **TCLC 13**
See also Chatterje, Sarat Chandra
Chatterton, Thomas 1752-1770 .. **LC 3; DAM POET**
See also DLB 109
Chatwin, (Charles) Bruce 1940-1989 **CLC 28, 57, 59; DAM POP**
See also AAYA 4; BEST 90:1; CA 85-88; 127;
DLB 194, 204
Chaucer, Daniel
See Ford, Ford Madox
Chaucer, Geoffrey 1340(?)-1400 . **LC 17; DA; DAB; DAC; DAM MST, POET; PC 19; WLCS**
See also CDBLB Before 1660; DLB 146
Chaviaras, Strates 1935-
See Haviaras, Stratis
See also CA 105
Chayefsky, Paddy .... **CLC 23**
See Chayefsky, Sidney
See also DLB 7, 44; DLBY 81
Chayefsky, Sidney 1923-1981
See Chayefsky, Paddy
See also CA 9-12R; 104; CANR 18; DAM
DRAM
Chedid, Andree 1920- .... **CLC 47**
See also CA 145

Cheever, John 1912-1982 **CLC 3, 7, 8, 11, 15, 25, 64; DA; DAB; DAC; DAM MST, NOV, POP; SSC 1; WLC**
See also CA 5-8R; 106; CABS 1; CANR 5, 27,
76; CDALB 1941-1968; DLB 2, 102; DLBY
80, 82; INT CANR-5; MTCW 1, 2
Cheever, Susan 1943- .... **CLC 18, 48**
See also CA 103; CANR 27, 51; DLBY 82; INT
CANR-27
Chekhonte, Antosha
See Chekhov, Anton (Pavlovich)
Chekhov, Anton (Pavlovich) 1860-1904 **T C L C 3, 10, 31, 55; DA; DAB; DAC; DAM DRAM, MST; DC 9; SSC 2, 28; WLC**
See also CA 104; 124; SATA 90
Chernyshevsky, Nikolay Gavrilovich 1828-1889 **NCLC 1**
Cherry, Carolyn Janice 1942-
See Cherryh, C. J.
See also CA 65-68; CANR 10
Cherryh, C. J. .... **CLC 35**
See also Cherry, Carolyn Janice
See also AAYA 24; DLBY 80; SATA 93
Chesnutt, Charles W(addell) 1858-1932 **T C L C 5, 39; BLC 1; DAM MULT; SSC 7**
See also BW 1; CA 106; 125; CANR 76; DLB
12, 50, 78; MTCW 1, 2
Chester, Alfred 1929(?)-1971 .... **CLC 49**
See also CA 33-36R; DLB 130
Chesterton, G(ilbert) K(eith) 1874-1936 **TCLC 1, 6, 64; DAM NOV, POET; SSC 1**
See also CA 104; 132; CANR 73; CDBLB
1914-1945; DLB 10, 19, 34, 70, 98, 149, 178;
MTCW 1, 2; SATA 27
Chiang, Pin-chin 1904-1986
See Ding Ling
See also CA 118
Ch'ien Chung-shu 1910- .... **CLC 22**
See also CA 130; CANR 73; MTCW 1, 2
Child, L. Maria
See Child, Lydia Maria
Child, Lydia Maria 1802-1880 .... **NCLC 6, 73**
See also DLB 1, 74; SATA 67
Child, Mrs.
See Child, Lydia Maria
Child, Philip 1898-1978 .... **CLC 19, 68**
See also CA 13-14; CAP 1; SATA 47
Childers, (Robert) Erskine 1870-1922 **T C L C 65**
See also CA 113; 153; DLB 70
Childress, Alice 1920-1994 **CLC 12, 15, 86, 96; BLC 1; DAM DRAM, MULT, NOV; DC 4**
See also AAYA 8; BW 2; CA 45-48; 146; CANR
3, 27, 50, 74; CLR 14; DLB 7, 38; JRDA;
MAICYA; MTCW 1, 2; SATA 7, 48, 81
Chin, Frank (Chew, Jr.) 1940- .... **DC 7**
See also CA 33-36R; CANR 71; DAM MULT;
DLB 206
Chislett, (Margaret) Anne 1943- .... **CLC 34**
See also CA 151
Chitty, Thomas Willes 1926- .... **CLC 11**
See also Hinde, Thomas
See also CA 5-8R
Chivers, Thomas Holley 1809-1858 **NCLC 49**
See also DLB 3
Choi, Susan .... **CLC 119**
Chomette, Rene Lucien 1898-1981
See Clair, Rene
See also CA 103
Chopin, Kate . **TCLC 5, 14; DA; DAB; SSC 8; WLCS**
See also Chopin, Katherine
See also CDALB 1865-1917; DLB 12, 78

Chopin, Katherine 1851-1904
See Chopin, Kate
See also CA 104; 122; DAC; DAM MST, NOV
Chretien de Troyes c. 12th cent. - .... **CMLC 10**
See also DLB 208
Christie
See Ichikawa, Kon
Christie, Agatha (Mary Clarissa) 1890-1976
CLC 1, 6, 8, 12, 39, 48, 110; DAB; DAC; DAM NOV
See also AAYA 9; AITN 1, 2; CA 17-20R; 61-64;
CANR 10, 37; CDBLB 1914-1945; DLB 13,
77; MTCW 1, 2; SATA 36
Christie, (Ann) Philippa
See Pearce, Philippa
See also CA 5-8R; CANR 4
Christine de Pizan 1365(?)-1431(?) .... **LC 9**
See also DLB 208
Chubb, Elmer
See Masters, Edgar Lee
Chulkov, Mikhail Dmitrievich 1743-1792 **LC 2**
See also DLB 150
Churchill, Caryl 1938- .... **CLC 31, 55; DC 5**
See also CA 102; CANR 22, 46; DLB 13; MTCW
1
Churchill, Charles 1731-1764 .... **LC 3**
See also DLB 109
Chute, Carolyn 1947- .... **CLC 39**
See also CA 123
Ciardi, John (Anthony) 1916-1986 **CLC 10, 40, 44; DAM POET**
See also CA 5-8R; 118; CAAS 2; CANR 5, 33;
CLR 19; DLB 5; DLBY 86; INT CANR-5;
MAICYA; MTCW 1, 2; SAAS 26; SATA 1,
65; SATA-Obit 46
Cicero, Marcus Tullius 106B.C.-43B.C. **C M L C 3**
See also DLB 211
Cimino, Michael 1943- .... **CLC 16**
See also CA 105
Cioran, E(mil) M. 1911-1995 .... **CLC 64**
See also CA 25-28R; 149
Cisneros, Sandra 1954- ... **CLC 69, 118; DAM MULT; HLC; SSC 32**
See also AAYA 9; CA 131; CANR 64; DLB 122,
152; HW; MTCW 2
Cixous, Helene 1937- .... **CLC 92**
See also CA 126; CANR 55; DLB 83; MTCW 1,
2
Clair, Rene .... **CLC 20**
See also Chomette, Rene Lucien
Clampitt, Amy 1920-1994 ...... **CLC 32; PC 19**
See also CA 110; 146; CANR 29; DLB 105
Clancy, Thomas L., Jr. 1947-
See Clancy, Tom
See also CA 125; 131; CANR 62; INT 131;
MTCW 1, 2
Clancy, Tom ... **CLC 45, 112; DAM NOV, POP**
See also Clancy, Thomas L., Jr.
See also AAYA 9; BEST 89:1, 90:1; MTCW 2
Clare, John 1793-1864 . **NCLC 9; DAB; DAM POET; PC 23**
See also DLB 55, 96
Clarin
See Alas (y Urena), Leopoldo (Enrique Garcia)
Clark, Al C.
See Goines, Donald
Clark, (Robert) Brian 1932- .... **CLC 29**
See also CA 41-44R; CANR 67
Clark, Curt
See Westlake, Donald E(dwin)
Clark, Eleanor 1913-1996 .... **CLC 5, 19**
See also CA 9-12R; 151; CANR 41; DLB 6

Condillac, Etienne Bonnot de 1714-1780LC 26

Condon, Richard (Thomas) 1915-1996CLC 4, 6, 8, 10, 45, 100; DAM NOV
Scc also BEST 90:3; CA 1-4R; 151; CAAS 1; CANR 2, 23; INT CANR-23; MTCW 1, 2

Confucius 551B.C.-479B.C. ...CMLC 19; DA; DAB; DAC; DAM MST; WLCS

Congreve, William 1670-1729. LC 5, 21; DA; DAB; DAC; DAM DRAM, MST, POET; DC 2; WLC
See also CDBLB 1660-1789; DLB 39, 84

Connell, Evan S(helby), Jr. 1924-CLC 4, 6, 45; DAM NOV
See also AAYA 7; CA 1-4R; CAAS 2; CANR 2, 39, 76; DLB 2; DLBY 81; MTCW 1, 2

Connelly, Marc(us Cook) 1890-1980 ... CLC 7
See also CA 85-88; 102; CANR 30; DLB 7; DLBY 80; SATA-Obit 25

Connor, Ralph .... TCLC 31
See also Gordon, Charles William
See also DLB 92

Conrad, Joseph 1857-1924 TCLC 1, 6, 13, 25, 43, 57; DA; DAB; DAC; DAM MST, NOV; SSC 9; WLC
See also AAYA 26; CA 104; 131; CANR 60; CDBLB 1890-1914; DLB 10, 34, 98, 156; MTCW 1, 2; SATA 27

Conrad, Robert Arnold
See Hart, Moss

Conroy, Pat
See Conroy, (Donald) Pat(rick)
See also MTCW 2

Conroy, (Donald) Pat(rick) 1945-CLC 30, 74; DAM NOV, POP
See also Conroy, Pat
See also AAYA 8; AITN 1; CA 85-88; CANR 24, 53; DLB 6; MTCW 1

Constant (de Rebecque), (Henri) Benjamin 1767-1830 .... NCLC 6
See also DLB 119

Conybeare, Charles Augustus
See Eliot, T(homas) S(tearns)

Cook, Michael 1933- .... CLC 58
See also CA 93-96; CANR 68; DLB 53

Cook, Robin 1940- .... CLC 14; DAM POP
See also BEST 90:2; CA 108; 111; CANR 41; INT 111

Cook, Roy
See Silverberg, Robert

Cooke, Elizabeth 1948- .... CLC 55
See also CA 129

Cooke, John Esten 1830-1886 .... NCLC 5
See also DLB 3

Cooke, John Estes
See Baum, L(yman) Frank

Cooke, M. E.
See Creasey, John

Cooke, Margaret
See Creasey, John

Cook-Lynn, Elizabeth 1930- ... CLC 93; DAM MULT
See also CA 133; DLB 175; NNAL

Cooney, Ray .... CLC 62

Cooper, Douglas 1960- .... CLC 86

Cooper, Henry St. John
See Creasey, John

Cooper, J(oan) California (?)- CLC 56; DAM MULT
See also AAYA 12; BW 1; CA 125; CANR 55; DLB 212

Cooper, James Fenimore 1789-1851 NCLC 1, 27, 54
See also AAYA 22; CDALB 1640-1865; DLB 3; SATA 19

Coover, Robert (Lowell) 1932-CLC 3, 7, 15, 32, 46, 87; DAM NOV; SSC 15
See also CA 45-48; CANR 3, 37, 58; DLB 2; DLBY 81; MTCW 1, 2

Copeland, Stewart (Armstrong) 1952-CLC 26

Copernicus, Nicolaus 1473-1543 .... LC 45

Coppard, A(lfred) E(dgar) 1878-1957TCLC 5; SSC 21
See also CA 114; 167; DLB 162; YABC 1

Coppee, Francois 1842-1908 .... TCLC 25
See also CA 170

Coppola, Francis Ford 1939- .... CLC 16
See also CA 77-80; CANR 40, 78; DLB 44

Corbiere, Tristan 1845-1875 .... NCLC 43

Corcoran, Barbara 1911- .... CLC 17
See also AAYA 14; CA 21-24R; CAAS 2; CANR 11, 28, 48; CLR 50; DLB 52; JRDA; SAAS 20; SATA 3, 77

Cordelier, Maurice
See Giraudoux, (Hippolyte) Jean

Corelli, Marie 1855-1924 .... TCLC 51
See also Mackay, Mary
See also DLB 34, 156

Corman, Cid 1924- .... CLC 9
See also Corman, Sidney
See also CAAS 2; DLB 5, 193

Corman, Sidney 1924-
See Corman, Cid
See also CA 85-88; CANR 44; DAM POET

Cormier, Robert (Edmund) 1925-CLC 12, 30; DA; DAB; DAC; DAM MST, NOV
See also AAYA 3, 19; CA 1-4R; CANR 5, 23, 76; CDALB 1968-1988; CLR 12, 55; DLB 52; INT CANR-23; JRDA; MAICYA; MTCW 1, 2; SATA 10, 45, 83

Corn, Alfred (DeWitt III) 1943- .... CLC 33
See also CA 104; CAAS 25; CANR 44; DLB 120; DLBY 80

Corneille, Pierre 1606-1684LC 28; DAB; DAM MST

Cornwell, David (John Moore) 1931- . CLC 9, 15; DAM POP
See also le Carre, John
See also CA 5-8R; CANR 13, 33, 59; MTCW 1, 2

Corso, (Nunzio) Gregory 1930- ..... CLC 1, 11
See also CA 5-8R; CANR 41, 76; DLB 5, 16; MTCW 1, 2

Cortazar, Julio 1914-1984 CLC 2, 3, 5, 10, 13, 15, 33, 34, 92; DAM MULT, NOV; HLC; SSC 7
See also CA 21-24R; CANR 12, 32; DLB 113; HW; MTCW 1, 2

CORTES, HERNAN 1484-1547 .... LC 31

Corvinus, Jakob
See Raabe, Wilhelm (Karl)

Corwin, Cecil
See Kornbluth, C(yril) M.

Cosic, Dobrica 1921- .... CLC 14
See also CA 122; 138; DLB 181

Costain, Thomas B(ertram) 1885-1965CLC 30
See also CA 5-8R; 25-28R; DLB 9

Costantini, Humberto 1924(?)-1987 .. CLC 49
See also CA 131; 122; HW

Costello, Elvis 1955- .... CLC 21

Costenoble, Philostene
See Ghelderode, Michel de

Cotes, Cecil V.
See Duncan, Sara Jeannette

Cotter, Joseph Seamon Sr. 1861-1949 . T C L C 28; BLC 1; DAM MULT
See also BW 1; CA 124; DLB 50

Couch, Arthur Thomas Quiller
See Quiller-Couch, SirArthur (Thomas)

Coulton, James
See Hansen, Joseph

Couperus, Louis (Marie Anne) 1863-1923 TCLC 15
See also CA 115

Coupland, Douglas 1961-CLC 85; DAC; DAM POP
See also CA 142; CANR 57

Court, Wesli
See Turco, Lewis (Putnam)

Courtenay, Bryce 1933- .... CLC 59
See also CA 138

Courtney, Robert
See Ellison, Harlan (Jay)

Cousteau, Jacques-Yves 1910-1997 ... CLC 30
See also CA 65-68; 159; CANR 15, 67; MTCW 1; SATA 38, 98

Coventry, Francis 1725-1754 .... LC 46

Cowan, Peter (Walkinshaw) 1914- ...... SSC 28
See also CA 21-24R; CANR 9, 25, 50

Coward, Noel (Peirce) 1899-1973CLC 1, 9, 29, 51; DAM DRAM
See also AITN 1; CA 17-18; 41-44R; CANR 35; CAP 2; CDBLB 1914-1945; DLB 10; MTCW 1, 2

Cowley, Abraham 1618-1667 .... LC 43
See also DLB 131, 151

Cowley, Malcolm 1898-1989 .... CLC 39
See also CA 5-8R; 128; CANR 3, 55; DLB 4, 48; DLBY 81, 89; MTCW 1, 2

Cowper, William 1731-1800 .. NCLC 8; DAM POET
See also DLB 104, 109

Cox, William Trevor 1928-CLC 9, 14, 71; DAM NOV
See also Trevor, William
See also CA 9-12R; CANR 4, 37, 55, 76; DLB 14; INT CANR-37; MTCW 1, 2

Coyne, P. J.
See Masters, Hilary

Cozzens, James Gould 1903-1978CLC 1, 4, 11, 92
See also CA 9-12R; 81-84; CANR 19; CDALB 1941-1968; DLB 9; DLBD 2; DLBY 84, 97; MTCW 1, 2

Crabbe, George 1754-1832 .... NCLC 26
See also DLB 93

Craddock, Charles Egbert
See Murfree, Mary Noailles

Craig, A. A.
See Anderson, Poul (William)

Craik, Dinah Maria (Mulock) 1826-1887 NCLC 38
See also DLB 35, 163; MAICYA; SATA 34

Cram, Ralph Adams 1863-1942 ...... TCLC 45
See also CA 160

Crane, (Harold) Hart 1899-1932TCLC 2, 5, 80; DA; DAB; DAC; DAM MST, POET; PC 3; WLC
See also CA 104; 127; CDALB 1917-1929; DLB 4, 48; MTCW 1, 2

Crane, R(onald) S(almon) 1886-1967 CLC 27
See also CA 85-88; DLB 63

Crane, Stephen (Townley) 1871-1900TCLC 11, 17, 32; DA; DAB; DAC; DAM MST, NOV, POET; SSC 7; WLC
See also AAYA 21; CA 109; 140; CDALB 1865-1917; DLB 12, 54, 78; YABC 2

Dashwood, Edmee Elizabeth Monica de la Pasture 1890-1943
See Delafield, E. M.
See also CA 119; 154

Daudet, (Louis Marie) Alphonse 1840-1897
NCLC 1
See also DLB 123

Daumal, Rene 1908-1944 .... **TCLC 14**
See also CA 114

Davenant, William 1606-1668 .... **LC 13**
See also DLB 58, 126

Davenport, Guy (Mattison, Jr.) 1927- **CLC 6, 14, 38; SSC 16**
See also CA 33-36R; CANR 23, 73; DLB 130

Davidson, Avram (James) 1923-1993
See Queen, Ellery
See also CA 101; 171; CANR 26; DLB 8

Davidson, Donald (Grady) 1893-1968 **CLC 2, 13, 19**
See also CA 5-8R; 25-28R; CANR 4; DLB 45

Davidson, Hugh
See Hamilton, Edmond

Davidson, John 1857-1909 .... **TCLC 24**
See also CA 118; DLB 19

Davidson, Sara 1943- .... **CLC 9**
See also CA 81-84; CANR 44, 68; DLB 185

Davie, Donald (Alfred) 1922-1995 **CLC 5, 8, 10, 31**
See also CA 1-4R; 149; CAAS 3; CANR 1, 44; DLB 27; MTCW 1

Davies, Ray(mond Douglas) 1944- ..... **CLC 21**
See also CA 116; 146

Davies, Rhys 1901-1978 .... **CLC 23**
See also CA 9-12R; 81-84; CANR 4; DLB 139, 191

Davies, (William) Robertson 1913-1995 **CLC 2, 7, 13, 25, 42, 75, 91; DA; DAB; DAC; DAM MST, NOV, POP; WLC**
See also BEST 89:2; CA 33-36R; 150; CANR 17, 42; DLB 68; INT CANR-17; MTCW 1, 2

Davies, W(illiam) H(enry) 1871-1940 **TCLC 5**
See also CA 104; DLB 19, 174

Davies, Walter C.
See Kornbluth, C(yril) M.

Davis, Angela (Yvonne) 1944- **CLC 77; DAM MULT**
See also BW 2; CA 57-60; CANR 10

Davis, B. Lynch
See Bioy Casares, Adolfo; Borges, Jorge Luis

Davis, Harold Lenoir 1894-1960 .... **CLC 49**
See also CA 89-92; DLB 9, 206

Davis, Rebecca (Blaine) Harding 1831-1910 **TCLC 6**
See also CA 104; DLB 74

Davis, Richard Harding 1864-1916 **TCLC 24**
See also CA 114; DLB 12, 23, 78, 79, 189; DLBD 13

Davison, Frank Dalby 1893-1970 .... **CLC 15**
See also CA 116

Davison, Lawrence H.
See Lawrence, D(avid) H(erbert Richards)

Davison, Peter (Hubert) 1928- .... **CLC 28**
See also CA 9-12R; CAAS 4; CANR 3, 43; DLB 5

Davys, Mary 1674-1732 .... **LC 1, 46**
See also DLB 39

Dawson, Fielding 1930- .... **CLC 6**
See also CA 85-88; DLB 130

Dawson, Peter
See Faust, Frederick (Schiller)

Day, Clarence (Shepard, Jr.) 1874-1935 **TCLC 25**
See also CA 108; DLB 11

Day, Thomas 1748-1789 .... **LC 1**
See also DLB 39; YABC 1

Day Lewis, C(ecil) 1904-1972 ... **CLC 1, 6, 10; DAM POET; PC 11**
See also Blake, Nicholas
See also CA 13-16; 33-36R; CANR 34; CAP 1; DLB 15, 20; MTCW 1, 2

Dazai Osamu 1909-1948 .... **TCLC 11**
See also Tsushima, Shuji
See also CA 164; DLB 182

de Andrade, Carlos Drummond
See Drummond de Andrade, Carlos

Deane, Norman
See Creasey, John

de Beauvoir, Simone (Lucie Ernestine Marie Bertrand)
See Beauvoir, Simone (Lucie Ernestine Marie Bertrand) de

de Beer, P.
See Bosman, Herman Charles

de Brissac, Malcolm
See Dickinson, Peter (Malcolm)

de Chardin, Pierre Teilhard
See Teilhard de Chardin, (Marie Joseph) Pierre

Dee, John 1527-1608 .... **LC 20**

Deer, Sandra 1940- .... **CLC 45**

De Ferrari, Gabriella 1941- .... **CLC 65**
See also CA 146

Defoe, Daniel 1660(?)-1731 **LC 1, 42; DA; DAB; DAC; DAM MST, NOV; WLC**
See also AAYA 27; CDBLB 1660-1789; DLB 39, 95, 101; JRDA; MAICYA; SATA 22

de Gourmont, Remy(-Marie-Charles)
See Gourmont, Remy (-Marie-Charles) de

de Hartog, Jan 1914- .... **CLC 19**
See also CA 1-4R; CANR 1

de Hostos, E. M.
See Hostos (y Bonilla), Eugenio Maria de

de Hostos, Eugenio M.
See Hostos (y Bonilla), Eugenio Maria de

Deighton, Len .... **CLC 4, 7, 22, 46**
See also Deighton, Leonard Cyril
See also AAYA 6; BEST 89:2; CDBLB 1960 to Present; DLB 87

Deighton, Leonard Cyril 1929-
See Deighton, Len
See also CA 9-12R; CANR 19, 33, 68; DAM NOV, POP; MTCW 1, 2

Dekker, Thomas 1572(?)-1632 ... **LC 22; DAM DRAM**
See also CDBLB Before 1660; DLB 62, 172

Delafield, E. M. 1890-1943 .... **TCLC 61**
See also Dashwood, Edmee Elizabeth Monica de la Pasture
See also DLB 34

de la Mare, Walter (John) 1873-1956 **TCLC 4, 53; DAB; DAC; DAM MST, POET; SSC 14; WLC**
See also CA 163; CDBLB 1914-1945; CLR 23; DLB 162; MTCW 1; SATA 16

Delaney, Franey
See O'Hara, John (Henry)

Delaney, Shelagh 1939- **CLC 29; DAM DRAM**
See also CA 17-20R; CANR 30, 67; CDBLB 1960 to Present; DLB 13; MTCW 1

Delany, Mary (Granville Pendarves) 1700-1788 **LC 12**

Delany, Samuel R(ay, Jr.) 1942- **CLC 8, 14, 38; BLC 1; DAM MULT**
See also AAYA 24; BW 2; CA 81-84; CANR 27, 43; DLB 8, 33; MTCW 1, 2

De La Ramee, (Marie) Louise 1839-1908
See Ouida

See also SATA 20

de la Roche, Mazo 1879-1961 .... **CLC 14**
See also CA 85-88; CANR 30; DLB 68; SATA 64

De La Salle, Innocent
See Hartmann, Sadakichi

Delbanco, Nicholas (Franklin) 1942- **CLC 6, 13**
See also CA 17-20R; CAAS 2; CANR 29, 55; DLB 6

del Castillo, Michel 1933- .... **CLC 38**
See also CA 109; CANR 77

Deledda, Grazia (Cosima) 1875(?)-1936 **TCLC 23**
See also CA 123

Delibes, Miguel .... **CLC 8, 18**
See also Delibes Setien, Miguel

Delibes Setien, Miguel 1920-
See Delibes, Miguel
See also CA 45-48; CANR 1, 32; HW; MTCW 1

DeLillo, Don 1936- **CLC 8, 10, 13, 27, 39, 54, 76; DAM NOV, POP**
See also BEST 89:1; CA 81-84; CANR 21, 76; DLB 6, 173; MTCW 1, 2

de Lisser, H. G.
See De Lisser, H(erbert) G(eorge)
See also DLB 117

De Lisser, H(erbert) G(eorge) 1878-1944 **TCLC 12**
See also de Lisser, H. G.
See also BW 2; CA 109; 152

Deloney, Thomas 1560(?)-1600 .... **LC 41**
See also DLB 167

Deloria, Vine (Victor), Jr. 1933- **CLC 21; DAM MULT**
See also CA 53-56; CANR 5, 20, 48; DLB 175; MTCW 1; NNAL; SATA 21

Del Vecchio, John M(ichael) 1947- .... **CLC 29**
See also CA 110; DLBD 9

de Man, Paul (Adolph Michel) 1919-1983 **CLC 55**
See also CA 128; 111; CANR 61; DLB 67; MTCW 1, 2

De Marinis, Rick 1934- .... **CLC 54**
See also CA 57-60; CAAS 24; CANR 9, 25, 50

Dembry, R. Emmet
See Murfree, Mary Noailles

Demby, William 1922- **CLC 53; BLC 1; DAM MULT**
See also BW 1; CA 81-84; DLB 33

de Menton, Francisco
See Chin, Frank (Chew, Jr.)

Demijohn, Thom
See Disch, Thomas M(ichael)

de Montherlant, Henry (Milon)
See Montherlant, Henry (Milon) de

Demosthenes 384B.C.-322B.C. .... **CMLC 13**
See also DLB 176

de Natale, Francine
See Malzberg, Barry N(athaniel)

Denby, Edwin (Orr) 1903-1983 .... **CLC 48**
See also CA 138; 110

Denis, Julio
See Cortazar, Julio

Denmark, Harrison
See Zelazny, Roger (Joseph)

Dennis, John 1658-1734 .... **LC 11**
See also DLB 101

Dennis, Nigel (Forbes) 1912-1989 .... **CLC 8**
See also CA 25-28R; 129; DLB 13, 15; MTCW 1

Dent, Lester 1904(?)-1959 .... **TCLC 72**
See also CA 112; 161

Dorfman, Ariel 1942- .... **CLC 48, 77; DAM MULT; HLC**
See also CA 124; 130; CANR 67, 70; HW; INT 130

Dorn, Edward (Merton) 1929- ..... **CLC 10, 18**
See also CA 93-96; CANR 42; DLB 5; INT 93-96

Dorris, Michael (Anthony) 1945-1997 .... **C L C 109; DAM MULT, NOV**
See also AAYA 20; BEST 90:1; CA 102; 157; CANR 19, 46, 75; DLB 175; MTCW 2; NNAL; SATA 75; SATA-Obit 94

Dorris, Michael A.
See Dorris, Michael (Anthony)

Dorsan, Luc
See Simenon, Georges (Jacques Christian)

Dorsange, Jean
See Simenon, Georges (Jacques Christian)

Dos Passos, John (Roderigo) 1896-1970 **CLC 1, 4, 8, 11, 15, 25, 34, 82; DA; DAB; DAC; DAM MST, NOV; WLC**
See also CA 1-4R; 29-32R; CANR 3; CDALB 1929-1941; DLB 4, 9; DLBD 1, 15; DLBY 96; MTCW 1, 2

Dossage, Jean
See Simenon, Georges (Jacques Christian)

Dostoevsky, Fedor Mikhailovich 1821-1881 **NCLC 2, 7, 21, 33, 43; DA; DAB; DAC; DAM MST, NOV; SSC 2, 33; WLC**

Doughty, Charles M(ontagu) 1843-1926 **TCLC 27**
See also CA 115; DLB 19, 57, 174

Douglas, Ellen .... **CLC 73**
See also Haxton, Josephine Ayres; Williamson, Ellen Douglas

Douglas, Gavin 1475(?)-1522 .... **LC 20**
See also DLB 132

Douglas, George
See Brown, George Douglas

Douglas, Keith (Castellain) 1920-1944 **T C L C 40**
See also CA 160; DLB 27

Douglas, Leonard
See Bradbury, Ray (Douglas)

Douglas, Michael
See Crichton, (John) Michael

Douglas, (George) Norman 1868-1952 **T C L C 68**
See also CA 119; 157; DLB 34, 195

Douglas, William
See Brown, George Douglas

Douglass, Frederick 1817(?)-1895 **NCLC 7, 55; BLC 1; DA; DAC; DAM MST, MULT; WLC**
See also CDALB 1640-1865; DLB 1, 43, 50, 79; SATA 29

Dourado, (Waldomiro Freitas) Autran 1926- **CLC 23, 60**
See also CA 25-28R; CANR 34; DLB 145

Dourado, Waldomiro Autran
See Dourado, (Waldomiro Freitas) Autran

Dove, Rita (Frances) 1952- **CLC 50, 81; BLCS; DAM MULT, POET; PC 6**
See also BW 2; CA 109; CAAS 19; CANR 27, 42, 68, 76; DLB 120; MTCW 1

Doveglion
See Villa, Jose Garcia

Dowell, Coleman 1925-1985 .... **CLC 60**
See also CA 25-28R; 117; CANR 10; DLB 130

Dowson, Ernest (Christopher) 1867-1900 **TCLC 4**
See also CA 105; 150; DLB 19, 135

Doyle, A. Conan
See Doyle, Arthur Conan

Doyle, Arthur Conan 1859-1930 **TCLC 7; DA; DAB; DAC; DAM MST, NOV; SSC 12; WLC**
See also AAYA 14; CA 104, 122, CDBLB 1890-1914; DLB 18, 70, 156, 178; MTCW 1, 2; SATA 24

Doyle, Conan
See Doyle, Arthur Conan

Doyle, John
See Graves, Robert (von Ranke)

Doyle, Roddy 1958(?)- .... **CLC 81**
See also AAYA 14; CA 143; CANR 73; DLB 194

Doyle, Sir A. Conan
See Doyle, Arthur Conan

Doyle, Sir Arthur Conan
See Doyle, Arthur Conan

Dr. A
See Asimov, Isaac; Silverstein, Alvin

Drabble, Margaret 1939- **CLC 2, 3, 5, 8, 10, 22, 53; DAB; DAC; DAM MST, NOV, POP**
See also CA 13-16R; CANR 18, 35, 63; CDBLB 1960 to Present; DLB 14, 155; MTCW 1, 2; SATA 48

Drapier, M. B.
See Swift, Jonathan

Drayham, James
See Mencken, H(enry) L(ouis)

Drayton, Michael 1563-1631 **LC 8; DAM POET**
See also DLB 121

Dreadstone, Carl
See Campbell, (John) Ramsey

Dreiser, Theodore (Herman Albert) 1871-1945 **TCLC 10, 18, 35, 83; DA; DAC; DAM MST, NOV; SSC 30; WLC**
See also CA 106; 132; CDALB 1865-1917; DLB 9, 12, 102, 137; DLBD 1; MTCW 1, 2

Drexler, Rosalyn 1926- .... **CLC 2, 6**
See also CA 81-84; CANR 68

Dreyer, Carl Theodor 1889-1968 .... **CLC 16**
See also CA 116

Drieu la Rochelle, Pierre(-Eugene) 1893-1945 **TCLC 21**
See also CA 117; DLB 72

Drinkwater, John 1882-1937 .... **TCLC 57**
See also CA 109; 149; DLB 10, 19, 149

Drop Shot
See Cable, George Washington

Droste-Hulshoff, Annette Freiin von 1797-1848 **NCLC 3**
See also DLB 133

Drummond, Walter
See Silverberg, Robert

Drummond, William Henry 1854-1907 **T C L C 25**
See also CA 160; DLB 92

Drummond de Andrade, Carlos 1902-1987 **CLC 18**
See also Andrade, Carlos Drummond de
See also CA 132; 123

Drury, Allen (Stuart) 1918-1998 .... **CLC 37**
See also CA 57-60; 170; CANR 18, 52; INT CANR-18

Dryden, John 1631-1700 **LC 3, 21; DA; DAB; DAC; DAM DRAM, MST, POET; DC 3; PC 25; WLC**
See also CDBLB 1660-1789; DLB 80, 101, 131

Duberman, Martin (Bauml) 1930- .... **CLC 8**
See also CA 1-4R; CANR 2, 63

Dubie, Norman (Evans) 1945- .... **CLC 36**
See also CA 69-72; CANR 12; DLB 120

Du Bois, W(illiam) E(dward) B(urghardt) 1868-1963 **CLC 1, 2, 13, 64, 96; BLC 1; DA; DAC; DAM MST, MULT, NOV; WLC**
See also BW 1, CA 85-88, CANR 34, CDALB 1865-1917; DLB 47, 50, 91; MTCW 1, 2; SATA 42

Dubus, Andre 1936- . **CLC 13, 36, 97; SSC 15**
See also CA 21-24R; CANR 17; DLB 130; INT CANR-17

Duca Minimo
See D'Annunzio, Gabriele

Ducharme, Rejean 1941- .... **CLC 74**
See also CA 165; DLB 60

Duclos, Charles Pinot 1704-1772 .... **LC 1**

Dudek, Louis 1918- .... **CLC 11, 19**
See also CA 45-48; CAAS 14; CANR 1; DLB 88

Duerrenmatt, Friedrich 1921-1990 **CLC 1, 4, 8, 11, 15, 43, 102; DAM DRAM**
See also CA 17-20R; CANR 33; DLB 69, 124; MTCW 1, 2

Duffy, Bruce 1953(?)- .... **CLC 50**
See also CA 172

Duffy, Maureen 1933- .... **CLC 37**
See also CA 25-28R; CANR 33, 68; DLB 14; MTCW 1

Dugan, Alan 1923- .... **CLC 2, 6**
See also CA 81-84; DLB 5

du Gard, Roger Martin
See Martin du Gard, Roger

Duhamel, Georges 1884-1966 .... **CLC 8**
See also CA 81-84; 25-28R; CANR 35; DLB 65; MTCW 1

Dujardin, Edouard (Emile Louis) 1861-1949 **TCLC 13**
See also CA 109; DLB 123

Dulles, John Foster 1888-1959 .... **TCLC 72**
See also CA 115; 149

Dumas, Alexandre (pere)
See Dumas, Alexandre (Davy de la Pailleterie)

Dumas, Alexandre (Davy de la Pailleterie) 1802-1870 ... **NCLC 11; DA; DAB; DAC; DAM MST, NOV; WLC**
See also DLB 119, 192; SATA 18

Dumas, Alexandre (fils) 1824-1895 **NCLC 71; DC 1**
See also AAYA 22; DLB 192

Dumas, Claudine
See Malzberg, Barry N(athaniel)

Dumas, Henry L. 1934-1968 .... **CLC 6, 62**
See also BW 1; CA 85-88; DLB 41

du Maurier, Daphne 1907-1989 **CLC 6, 11, 59; DAB; DAC; DAM MST, POP; SSC 18**
See also CA 5-8R; 128; CANR 6, 55; DLB 191; MTCW 1, 2; SATA 27; SATA-Obit 60

Dunbar, Paul Laurence 1872-1906 **TCLC 2, 12; BLC 1; DA; DAC; DAM MST, MULT, POET; PC 5; SSC 8; WLC**
See also BW 1; CA 104; 124; CDALB 1865-1917; DLB 50, 54, 78; SATA 34

Dunbar, William 1460(?)-1530(?) .... **LC 20**
See also DLB 132, 146

Duncan, Dora Angela
See Duncan, Isadora

Duncan, Isadora 1877(?)-1927 .... **TCLC 68**
See also CA 118; 149

Duncan, Lois 1934- .... **CLC 26**
See also AAYA 4; CA 1-4R; CANR 2, 23, 36; CLR 29; JRDA; MAICYA; SAAS 2; SATA 1, 36, 75

Fairbairn, Roger
See Carr, John Dickson
Fairbairns, Zoe (Ann) 1948- .... CLC 32
See also CA 103; CANR 21
Falco, Gian
See Papini, Giovanni
Falconer, James
See Kirkup, James
Falconer, Kenneth
See Kornbluth, C(yril) M.
Falkland, Samuel
See Heijermans, Herman
Fallaci, Oriana 1930- .... CLC 11, 110
See also CA 77-80; CANR 15, 58; MTCW 1
Faludy, George 1913- .... CLC 42
See also CA 21-24R
Faludy, Gyoergy
See Faludy, George
Fanon, Frantz 1925-1961 ..... CLC 74; BLC 2;
DAM MULT
See also BW 1; CA 116; 89-92
Fanshawe, Ann 1625-1680 .... LC 11
Fante, John (Thomas) 1911-1983 .... CLC 60
See also CA 69-72; 109; CANR 23; DLB 130;
DLBY 83
Farah, Nuruddin 1945-CLC 53; BLC 2; DAM
MULT
See also BW 2; CA 106; DLB 125
Fargue, Leon-Paul 1876(?)-1947 .... TCLC 11
See also CA 109
Farigoule, Louis
See Romains, Jules
Farina, Richard 1936(?)-1966 .... CLC 9
See also CA 81-84; 25-28R
Farley, Walter (Lorimer) 1915-1989 . CLC 17
See also CA 17-20R; CANR 8, 29; DLB 22;
JRDA; MAICYA; SATA 2, 43
Farmer, Philip Jose 1918- .... CLC 1, 19
See also AAYA 28; CA 1-4R; CANR 4, 35; DLB
8; MTCW 1; SATA 93
Farquhar, George 1677-1707 .... LC 21; DAM
DRAM
See also DLB 84
Farrell, J(ames) G(ordon) 1935-1979 .. CLC 6
See also CA 73-76; 89-92; CANR 36; DLB 14;
MTCW 1
Farrell, James T(homas) 1904-1979 CLC 1, 4,
8, 11, 66; SSC 28
See also CA 5-8R; 89-92; CANR 9, 61; DLB 4,
9, 86; DLBD 2; MTCW 1, 2
Farren, Richard J.
See Betjeman, John
Farren, Richard M.
See Betjeman, John
Fassbinder, Rainer Werner 1946-1982CLC 20
See also CA 93-96; 106; CANR 31
Fast, Howard (Melvin) 1914- . CLC 23; DAM
NOV
See also AAYA 16; CA 1-4R; CAAS 18; CANR
1, 33, 54, 75; DLB 9; INT CANR-33; MTCW
1; SATA 7; SATA-Essay 107
Faulcon, Robert
See Holdstock, Robert P.
Faulkner, William (Cuthbert) 1897-1962 C L C
1, 3, 6, 8, 9, 11, 14, 18, 28, 52, 68; DA; DAB;
DAC; DAM MST, NOV; SSC 1; WLC
See also AAYA 7; CA 81-84; CANR 33; CDALB
1929-1941; DLB 9, 11, 44, 102; DLBD 2;
DLBY 86, 97; MTCW 1, 2
Fauset, Jessie Redmon 1884(?)-1961 CLC 19,
54; BLC 2; DAM MULT
See also BW 1; CA 109; DLB 51

Faust, Frederick (Schiller) 1892-1944(?)TCLC
49; DAM POP
See also CA 108; 152
Faust, Irvin 1924- .... CLC 8
See also CA 33-36R; CANR 28, 67; DLB 2, 28;
DLBY 80
Fawkes, Guy
See Benchley, Robert (Charles)
Fearing, Kenneth (Flexner) 1902-1961CLC 51
See also CA 93-96; CANR 59; DLB 9
Fecamps, Elise
See Creasey, John
Federman, Raymond 1928- .... CLC 6, 47
See also CA 17-20R; CAAS 8; CANR 10, 43;
DLBY 80
Federspiel, J(uerg) F. 1931- .... CLC 42
See also CA 146
Feiffer, Jules (Ralph) 1929-CLC 2, 8, 64; DAM
DRAM
See also AAYA 3; CA 17-20R; CANR 30, 59;
DLB 7, 44; INT CANR-30; MTCW 1; SATA
8, 61
Feige, Hermann Albert Otto Maximilian
See Traven, B.
Feinberg, David B. 1956-1994 .... CLC 59
See also CA 135; 147
Feinstein, Elaine 1930- .... CLC 36
See also CA 69-72; CAAS 1; CANR 31, 68; DLB
14, 40; MTCW 1
Feldman, Irving (Mordecai) 1928- ...... CLC 7
See also CA 1-4R; CANR 1; DLB 169
Felix-Tchicaya, Gerald
See Tchicaya, Gerald Felix
Fellini, Federico 1920-1993 .... CLC 16, 85
See also CA 65-68; 143; CANR 33
Felsen, Henry Gregor 1916- .... CLC 17
See also CA 1-4R; CANR 1; SAAS 2; SATA 1
Fenno, Jack
See Calisher, Hortense
Fenollosa, Ernest (Francisco) 1853-1908
TCLC 91
Fenton, James Martin 1949- .... CLC 32
See also CA 102; DLB 40
Ferber, Edna 1887-1968 .... CLC 18, 93
See also AITN 1; CA 5-8R; 25-28R; CANR 68;
DLB 9, 28, 86; MTCW 1, 2; SATA 7
Ferguson, Helen
See Kavan, Anna
Ferguson, Samuel 1810-1886 .... NCLC 33
See also DLB 32
Fergusson, Robert 1750-1774 .... LC 29
See also DLB 109
Ferling, Lawrence
See Ferlinghetti, Lawrence (Monsanto)
Ferlinghetti, Lawrence (Monsanto) 1919(?)-
CLC 2, 6, 10, 27, 111; DAM POET; PC 1
See also CA 5-8R; CANR 3, 41, 73; CDALB
1941-1968; DLB 5, 16; MTCW 1, 2
Fernandez, Vicente Garcia Huidobro
See Huidobro Fernandez, Vicente Garcia
Ferrer, Gabriel (Francisco Victor) Miro
See Miro (Ferrer), Gabriel (Francisco Victor)
Ferrier, Susan (Edmonstone) 1782-1854NCLC
8
See also DLB 116
Ferrigno, Robert 1948(?)- .... CLC 65
See also CA 140
Ferron, Jacques 1921-1985 ..... CLC 94; DAC
See also CA 117; 129; DLB 60
Feuchtwanger, Lion 1884-1958 .... TCLC 3
See also CA 104; DLB 66
Feuillet, Octave 1821-1890 .... NCLC 45
See also DLB 192

Feydeau, Georges (Leon Jules Marie) 1862-1921
TCLC 22; DAM DRAM
See also CA 113; 152; DLB 192
Fichte, Johann Gottlieb 1762-1814 . NCLC 62
See also DLB 90
Ficino, Marsilio 1433-1499 .... LC 12
Fiedeler, Hans
See Doeblin, Alfred
Fiedler, Leslie A(aron) 1917- .... CLC 4, 13, 24
See also CA 9-12R; CANR 7, 63; DLB 28, 67;
MTCW 1, 2
Field, Andrew 1938- .... CLC 44
See also CA 97-100; CANR 25
Field, Eugene 1850-1895 .... NCLC 3
See also DLB 23, 42, 140; DLBD 13; MAICYA;
SATA 16
Field, Gans T.
See Wellman, Manly Wade
Field, Michael 1915-1971 .... TCLC 43
See also CA 29-32R
Field, Peter
See Hobson, Laura Z(ametkin)
Fielding, Henry 1707-1754LC 1, 46; DA; DAB;
DAC; DAM DRAM, MST, NOV; WLC
See also CDBLB 1660-1789; DLB 39, 84, 101
Fielding, Sarah 1710-1768 .... LC 1, 44
See also DLB 39
Fields, W. C. 1880-1946 .... TCLC 80
See also DLB 44
Fierstein, Harvey (Forbes) 1954- ..... CLC 33;
DAM DRAM, POP
See also CA 123; 129
Figes, Eva 1932- .... CLC 31
See also CA 53-56; CANR 4, 44; DLB 14
Finch, Anne 1661-1720 .... LC 3; PC 21
See also DLB 95
Finch, Robert (Duer Claydon) 1900- . CLC 18
See also CA 57-60; CANR 9, 24, 49; DLB 88
Findley, Timothy 1930- .. CLC 27, 102; DAC;
DAM MST
See also CA 25-28R; CANR 12, 42, 69; DLB 53
Fink, William
See Mencken, H(enry) L(ouis)
Firbank, Louis 1942-
See Reed, Lou
See also CA 117
Firbank, (Arthur Annesley) Ronald 1886-1926
TCLC 1
See also CA 104; DLB 36
Fisher, Dorothy (Frances) Canfield 1879-1958
TCLC 87
See also CA 114; 136; DLB 9, 102; MAICYA;
YABC 1
Fisher, M(ary) F(rances) K(ennedy) 1908-1992
CLC 76, 87
See also CA 77-80; 138; CANR 44; MTCW 1
Fisher, Roy 1930- .... CLC 25
See also CA 81-84; CAAS 10; CANR 16; DLB
40
Fisher, Rudolph 1897-1934 TCLC 11; BLC 2;
DAM MULT; SSC 25
See also BW 1; CA 107; 124; DLB 51, 102
Fisher, Vardis (Alvero) 1895-1968 .... CLC 7
See also CA 5-8R; 25-28R; CANR 68; DLB 9,
206
Fiske, Tarleton
See Bloch, Robert (Albert)
Fitch, Clarke
See Sinclair, Upton (Beall)
Fitch, John IV
See Cormier, Robert (Edmund)
Fitzgerald, Captain Hugh
See Baum, L(yman) Frank

FitzGerald, Edward 1809-1883 .... **NCLC 9**
See also DLB 32

Fitzgerald, F(rancis) Scott (Key) 1896-1940
TCLC 1, 6, 14, 28, 55; DA; DAB; DAC;
DAM MST, NOV; SSC 6, 31; WLC
See also AAYA 24; AITN 1; CA 110; 123;
CDALB 1917-1929; DLB 4, 9, 86; DLBD 1,
15, 16; DLBY 81, 96; MTCW 1, 2

Fitzgerald, Penelope 1916- ..... **CLC 19, 51, 61**
See also CA 85-88; CAAS 10; CANR 56; DLB
14, 194; MTCW 2

Fitzgerald, Robert (Stuart) 1910-1985**CLC 39**
See also CA 1-4R; 114; CANR 1; DLBY 80

FitzGerald, Robert D(avid) 1902-1987**CLC 19**
See also CA 17-20R

Fitzgerald, Zelda (Sayre) 1900-1948**TCLC 52**
See also CA 117; 126; DLBY 84

Flanagan, Thomas (James Bonner) 1923-**C L C
25, 52**
See also CA 108; CANR 55; DLBY 80; INT 108;
MTCW 1

Flaubert, Gustave 1821-1880 **NCLC 2, 10, 19,
62, 66; DA; DAB; DAC; DAM MST, NOV;
SSC 11; WLC**
See also DLB 119

Flecker, Herman Elroy
See Flecker, (Herman) James Elroy

Flecker, (Herman) James Elroy 1884-1915
TCLC 43
See also CA 109; 150; DLB 10, 19

Fleming, Ian (Lancaster) 1908-1964**CLC 3, 30;
DAM POP**
See also AAYA 26; CA 5-8R; CANR 59; CDBLB
1945-1960; DLB 87, 201; MTCW 1, 2; SATA
9

Fleming, Thomas (James) 1927- .... **CLC 37**
See also CA 5-8R; CANR 10; INT CANR-10;
SATA 8

Fletcher, John 1579-1625 .... **LC 33; DC 6**
See also CDBLB Before 1660; DLB 58

Fletcher, John Gould 1886-1950 ..... **TCLC 35**
See also CA 107; 167; DLB 4, 45

Fleur, Paul
See Pohl, Frederik

Flooglebuckle, Al
See Spiegelman, Art

Flying Officer X
See Bates, H(erbert) E(rnest)

Fo, Dario 1926-**CLC 32, 109; DAM DRAM; DC
10**
See also CA 116; 128; CANR 68; DLBY 97;
MTCW 1, 2

Fogarty, Jonathan Titulescu Esq.
See Farrell, James T(homas)

Folke, Will
See Bloch, Robert (Albert)

Follett, Ken(neth Martin) 1949-**CLC 18; DAM
NOV, POP**
See also AAYA 6; BEST 89:4; CA 81-84; CANR
13, 33, 54; DLB 87; DLBY 81; INT
CANR-33; MTCW 1

Fontane, Theodor 1819-1898 .... **NCLC 26**
See also DLB 129

Foote, Horton 1916-**CLC 51, 91; DAM DRAM**
See also CA 73-76; CANR 34, 51; DLB 26; INT
CANR-34

Foote, Shelby 1916-**CLC 75; DAM NOV, POP**
See also CA 5-8R; CANR 3, 45, 74; DLB 2, 17;
MTCW 2

Forbes, Esther 1891-1967 .... **CLC 12**
See also AAYA 17; CA 13-14; 25-28R; CAP 1;
CLR 27; DLB 22; JRDA; MAICYA; SATA 2,
100

Forche, Carolyn (Louise) 1950-**CLC 25, 83, 86;
DAM POET; PC 10**
See also CA 109; 117; CANR 50, 74; DLB 5,
193; INT 117; MTCW 1

Ford, Elbur
See Hibbert, Eleanor Alice Burford

Ford, Ford Madox 1873-1939**TCLC 1, 15, 39,
57; DAM NOV**
See also CA 104; 132; CANR 74; CDBLB
1914-1945; DLB 162; MTCW 1, 2

Ford, Henry 1863-1947 .... **TCLC 73**
See also CA 115; 148

Ford, John 1586-(?) .... **DC 8**
See also CDBLB Before 1660; DAM DRAM;
DLB 58

Ford, John 1895-1973 .... **CLC 16**
See also CA 45-48

Ford, Richard 1944-...................... **CLC 46, 99**
See also CA 69-72; CANR 11, 47; MTCW 1

Ford, Webster
See Masters, Edgar Lee

Foreman, Richard 1937-..................... **CLC 50**
See also CA 65-68; CANR 32, 63

Forester, C(ecil) S(cott) 1899-1966 .... **CLC 35**
See also CA 73-76; 25-28R; DLB 191; SATA 13

Forez
See Mauriac, Francois (Charles)

Forman, James Douglas 1932- .... **CLC 21**
See also AAYA 17; CA 9-12R; CANR 4, 19, 42;
JRDA; MAICYA; SATA 8, 70

Fornes, Maria Irene 1930-**CLC 39, 61; DC 10**
See also CA 25-28R; CANR 28; DLB 7; HW;
INT CANR-28; MTCW 1

Forrest, Leon (Richard) 1937-1997 ... **CLC 4;
BLCS**
See also BW 2; CA 89-92; 162; CAAS 7; CANR
25, 52; DLB 33

Forster, E(dward) M(organ) 1879-1970**CLC 1,
2, 3, 4, 9, 10, 13, 15, 22, 45, 77; DA; DAB;
DAC; DAM MST, NOV; SSC 27; WLC**
See also AAYA 2; CA 13-14; 25-28R; CANR 45;
CAP 1; CDBLB 1914-1945; DLB 34, 98, 162,
178, 195; DLBD 10; MTCW 1, 2; SATA 57

Forster, John 1812-1876 .... **NCLC 11**
See also DLB 144, 184

Forsyth, Frederick 1938- **CLC 2, 5, 36; DAM
NOV, POP**
See also BEST 89:4; CA 85-88; CANR 38, 62;
DLB 87; MTCW 1, 2

Forten, Charlotte L. .... **TCLC 16; BLC 2**
See also Grimke, Charlotte L(ottie) Forten
See also DLB 50

Foscolo, Ugo 1778-1827 .... **NCLC 8**

Fosse, Bob .... **CLC 20**
See also Fosse, Robert Louis

Fosse, Robert Louis 1927-1987
See Fosse, Bob
See also CA 110; 123

Foster, Stephen Collins 1826-1864 .. **NCLC 26**

Foucault, Michel 1926-1984 ... **CLC 31, 34, 69**
See also CA 105; 113; CANR 34; MTCW 1, 2

Fouque, Friedrich (Heinrich Karl) de la Motte
1777-1843 .... **NCLC 2**
See also DLB 90

Fourier, Charles 1772-1837 .... **NCLC 51**

Fournier, Henri Alban 1886-1914
See Alain-Fournier
See also CA 104

Fournier, Pierre 1916- .... **CLC 11**
See also Gascar, Pierre
See also CA 89-92; CANR 16, 40

Fowles, John (Philip) 1926-**CLC 1, 2, 3, 4, 6, 9,
10, 15, 33, 87; DAB; DAC; DAM MST; SSC**

33
See also CA 5-8R; CANR 25, 71; CDBLB 1960
to Present; DLB 14, 139, 207; MTCW 1, 2;
SATA 22

Fox, Paula 1923- .... **CLC 2, 8**
See also AAYA 3; CA 73-76; CANR 20, 36, 62;
CLR 1, 44; DLB 52; JRDA; MAICYA;
MTCW 1; SATA 17, 60

Fox, William Price (Jr.) 1926- .... **CLC 22**
See also CA 17-20R; CAAS 19; CANR 11; DLB
2; DLBY 81

Foxe, John 1516(?)-1587 .... **LC 14**
See also DLB 132

Frame, Janet 1924-**CLC 2, 3, 6, 22, 66, 96; SSC
29**
See also Clutha, Janet Paterson Frame

France, Anatole .... **TCLC 9**
See also Thibault, Jacques Anatole Francois
See also DLB 123; MTCW 1

Francis, Claude 19(?)- .... **CLC 50**

Francis, Dick 1920- **CLC 2, 22, 42, 102; DAM
POP**
See also AAYA 5, 21; BEST 89:3; CA 5-8R;
CANR 9, 42, 68; CDBLB 1960 to Present;
DLB 87; INT CANR-9; MTCW 1, 2

Francis, Robert (Churchill) 1901-1987**CLC 15**
See also CA 1-4R; 123; CANR 1

Frank, Anne(lies Marie) 1929-1945**TCLC 17;
DA; DAB; DAC; DAM MST; WLC**
See also AAYA 12; CA 113; 133; CANR 68;
MTCW 1, 2; SATA 87; SATA-Brief 42

Frank, Bruno 1887-1945 .... **TCLC 81**
See also DLB 118

Frank, Elizabeth 1945-........................ **CLC 39**
See also CA 121; 126; CANR 78; INT 126

Frankl, Viktor E(mil) 1905-1997 .... **CLC 93**
See also CA 65-68; 161

Franklin, Benjamin
See Hasek, Jaroslav (Matej Frantisek)

Franklin, Benjamin 1706-1790 .... **LC 25; DA;
DAB; DAC; DAM MST; WLCS**
See also CDALB 1640-1865; DLB 24, 43, 73

Franklin, (Stella Maria Sarah) Miles (Lampe)
1879-1954 .... **TCLC 7**
See also CA 104; 164

Fraser, (Lady) Antonia (Pakenham) 1932-**CLC
32, 107**
See also CA 85-88; CANR 44, 65; MTCW 1, 2;
SATA-Brief 32

Fraser, George MacDonald 1925-........ **CLC 7**
See also CA 45-48; CANR 2, 48, 74; MTCW 1

Fraser, Sylvia 1935-............................ **CLC 64**
See also CA 45-48; CANR 1, 16, 60

Frayn, Michael 1933- **CLC 3, 7, 31, 47; DAM
DRAM, NOV**
See also CA 5-8R; CANR 30, 69; DLB 13, 14,
194; MTCW 1, 2

Fraze, Candida (Merrill) 1945- .... **CLC 50**
See also CA 126

Frazer, J(ames) G(eorge) 1854-1941**TCLC 32**
See also CA 118

Frazer, Robert Caine
See Creasey, John

Frazer, Sir James George
See Frazer, J(ames) G(eorge)

Frazier, Charles 1950- .... **CLC 109**
See also CA 161

Frazier, Ian 1951- .... **CLC 46**
See also CA 130; CANR 54

Frederic, Harold 1856-1898 .... **NCLC 10**
See also DLB 12, 23; DLBD 13

Frederick, John
See Faust, Frederick (Schiller)

Frederick the Great 1712-1786 .... **LC 14**
Fredro, Aleksander 1793-1876 .... **NCLC 8**
Freeling, Nicolas 1927- .... **CLC 38**
See also CA 49-52; CAAS 12; CANR 1, 17, 50;
DLB 87
Freeman, Douglas Southall 1886-1953 **T C L C 11**
See also CA 109; DLB 17; DLBD 17
Freeman, Judith 1946- .... **CLC 55**
See also CA 148
Freeman, Mary Eleanor Wilkins 1852-1930
TCLC 9; SSC 1
See also CA 106; DLB 12, 78
Freeman, R(ichard) Austin 1862-1943 **T C L C 21**
See also CA 113; DLB 70
French, Albert 1943- .... **CLC 86**
See also CA 167
French, Marilyn 1929- **CLC 10, 18, 60; DAM DRAM, NOV, POP**
See also CA 69-72; CANR 3, 31; INT CANR-31;
MTCW 1, 2
French, Paul
See Asimov, Isaac
Freneau, Philip Morin 1752-1832 ..... **NCLC 1**
See also DLB 37, 43
Freud, Sigmund 1856-1939 .... **TCLC 52**
See also CA 115; 133; CANR 69; MTCW 1, 2
Friedan, Betty (Naomi) 1921- .... **CLC 74**
See also CA 65-68; CANR 18, 45, 74; MTCW
1, 2
Friedlander, Saul 1932- .... **CLC 90**
See also CA 117; 130; CANR 72
Friedman, B(ernard) H(arper) 1926- .. **CLC 7**
See also CA 1-4R; CANR 3, 48
Friedman, Bruce Jay 1930- .... **CLC 3, 5, 56**
See also CA 9-12R; CANR 25, 52; DLB 2, 28;
INT CANR-25
Friel, Brian 1929- ... **CLC 5, 42, 59, 115; DC 8**
See also CA 21-24R; CANR 33, 69; DLB 13;
MTCW 1
Friis-Baastad, Babbis Ellinor 1921-1970 **C L C 12**
See also CA 17-20R; 134; SATA 7
Frisch, Max (Rudolf) 1911-1991 **CLC 3, 9, 14, 18, 32, 44; DAM DRAM, NOV**
See also CA 85-88; 134; CANR 32, 74; DLB 69,
124; MTCW 1, 2
Fromentin, Eugene (Samuel Auguste) 1820-1876
NCLC 10
See also DLB 123
Frost, Frederick
See Faust, Frederick (Schiller)
Frost, Robert (Lee) 1874-1963 **CLC 1, 3, 4, 9, 10, 13, 15, 26, 34, 44; DA; DAB; DAC; DAM MST, POET; PC 1; WLC**
See also AAYA 21; CA 89-92; CANR 33;
CDALB 1917-1929; DLB 54; DLBD 7;
MTCW 1, 2; SATA 14
Froude, James Anthony 1818-1894 **NCLC 43**
See also DLB 18, 57, 144
Froy, Herald
See Waterhouse, Keith (Spencer)
Fry, Christopher 1907- . **CLC 2, 10, 14; DAM DRAM**
See also CA 17-20R; CAAS 23; CANR 9, 30,
74; DLB 13; MTCW 1, 2; SATA 66
Frye, (Herman) Northrop 1912-1991 **CLC 24, 70**
See also CA 5-8R; 133; CANR 8, 37; DLB 67,
68; MTCW 1, 2

Fuchs, Daniel 1909-1993 .... **CLC 8, 22**
See also CA 81-84; 142; CAAS 5; CANR 40;
DLB 9, 26, 28; DLBY 93
Fuchs, Daniel 1934- .... **CLC 34**
See also CA 37-40R; CANR 14, 48
Fuentes, Carlos 1928- **CLC 3, 8, 10, 13, 22, 41, 60, 113; DA; DAB; DAC; DAM MST, MULT, NOV; HLC; SSC 24; WLC**
See also AAYA 4; AITN 2; CA 69-72; CANR
10, 32, 68; DLB 113; HW; MTCW 1, 2
Fuentes, Gregorio Lopez y
See Lopez y Fuentes, Gregorio
Fugard, (Harold) Athol 1932- **CLC 5, 9, 14, 25, 40, 80; DAM DRAM; DC 3**
See also AAYA 17; CA 85-88; CANR 32, 54;
MTCW 1
Fugard, Sheila 1932- .... **CLC 48**
See also CA 125
Fuller, Charles (H., Jr.) 1939- **CLC 25; BLC 2; DAM DRAM, MULT; DC 1**
See also BW 2; CA 108; 112; DLB 38; INT 112;
MTCW 1
Fuller, John (Leopold) 1937- .... **CLC 62**
See also CA 21-24R; CANR 9, 44; DLB 40
Fuller, Margaret .... **NCLC 5, 50**
See also Ossoli, Sarah Margaret (Fuller marchesa
d')
Fuller, Roy (Broadbent) 1912-1991 **CLC 4, 28**
See also CA 5-8R; 135; CAAS 10; CANR 53;
DLB 15, 20; SATA 87
Fulton, Alice 1952- .... **CLC 52**
See also CA 116; CANR 57; DLB 193
Furphy, Joseph 1843-1912 .... **TCLC 25**
See also CA 163
Fussell, Paul 1924- .... **CLC 74**
See also BEST 90:1; CA 17-20R; CANR 8, 21,
35, 69; INT CANR-21; MTCW 1, 2
Futabatei, Shimei 1864-1909 .... **TCLC 44**
See also CA 162; DLB 180
Futrelle, Jacques 1875-1912 .... **TCLC 19**
See also CA 113; 155
Gaboriau, Emile 1835-1873 .... **NCLC 14**
Gadda, Carlo Emilio 1893-1973 .... **CLC 11**
See also CA 89-92; DLB 177
Gaddis, William 1922-1998 **CLC 1, 3, 6, 8, 10, 19, 43, 86**
See also CA 17-20R; 172; CANR 21, 48; DLB
2; MTCW 1, 2
Gage, Walter
See Inge, William (Motter)
Gaines, Ernest J(ames) 1933- **CLC 3, 11, 18, 86; BLC 2; DAM MULT**
See also AAYA 18; AITN 1; BW 2; CA 9-12R;
CANR 6, 24, 42, 75; CDALB 1968-1988;
DLB 2, 33, 152; DLBY 80; MTCW 1, 2;
SATA 86
Gaitskill, Mary 1954- .... **CLC 69**
See also CA 128; CANR 61
Galdos, Benito Perez
See Perez Galdos, Benito
Gale, Zona 1874-1938 **TCLC 7; DAM DRAM**
See also CA 105; 153; DLB 9, 78
Galeano, Eduardo (Hughes) 1940- .... **CLC 72**
See also CA 29-32R; CANR 13, 32; HW
Galiano, Juan Valera y Alcala
See Valera y Alcala-Galiano, Juan
Galilei, Galileo 1546-1642 .... **LC 45**
Gallagher, Tess 1943- **CLC 18, 63; DAM POET; PC 9**
See also CA 106; DLB 212

Gallant, Mavis 1922- **CLC 7, 18, 38; DAC; DAM MST; SSC 5**
See also CA 69-72; CANR 29, 69; DLB 53;
MTCW 1, 2
Gallant, Roy A(rthur) 1924- .... **CLC 17**
See also CA 5-8R; CANR 4, 29, 54; CLR 30;
MAICYA; SATA 4, 68
Gallico, Paul (William) 1897-1976 .... **CLC 2**
See also AITN 1; CA 5-8R; 69-72; CANR 23;
DLB 9, 171; MAICYA; SATA 13
Gallo, Max Louis 1932- .... **CLC 95**
See also CA 85-88
Gallois, Lucien
See Desnos, Robert
Gallup, Ralph
See Whitemore, Hugh (John)
Galsworthy, John 1867-1933 **TCLC 1, 45; DA; DAB; DAC; DAM DRAM, MST, NOV; SSC 22; WLC**
See also CA 104; 141; CANR 75; CDBLB
1890-1914; DLB 10, 34, 98, 162; DLBD 16;
MTCW 1
Galt, John 1779-1839 .... **NCLC 1**
See also DLB 99, 116, 159
Galvin, James 1951- .... **CLC 38**
See also CA 108; CANR 26
Gamboa, Federico 1864-1939 .... **TCLC 36**
See also CA 167
Gandhi, M. K.
See Gandhi, Mohandas Karamchand
Gandhi, Mahatma
See Gandhi, Mohandas Karamchand
Gandhi, Mohandas Karamchand 1869-1948
TCLC 59; DAM MULT
See also CA 121; 132; MTCW 1, 2
Gann, Ernest Kellogg 1910-1991 .... **CLC 23**
See also AITN 1; CA 1-4R; 136; CANR 1
Garcia, Cristina 1958- .... **CLC 76**
See also CA 141; CANR 73
Garcia Lorca, Federico 1898-1936 **TCLC 1, 7, 49; DA; DAB; DAC; DAM DRAM, MST, MULT, POET; DC 2; HLC; PC 3; WLC**
See also CA 104; 131; DLB 108; HW; MTCW
1, 2
Garcia Marquez, Gabriel (Jose) 1928- **CLC 2, 3, 8, 10, 15, 27, 47, 55, 68; DA; DAB; DAC; DAM MST, MULT, NOV, POP; HLC; SSC 8; WLC**
See also AAYA 3; BEST 89:1, 90:4; CA 33-36R;
CANR 10, 28, 50, 75; DLB 113; HW; MTCW
1, 2
Gard, Janice
See Latham, Jean Lee
Gard, Roger Martin du
See Martin du Gard, Roger
Gardam, Jane 1928- .... **CLC 43**
See also CA 49-52; CANR 2, 18, 33, 54; CLR
12; DLB 14, 161; MAICYA; MTCW 1; SAAS
9; SATA 39, 76; SATA-Brief 28
Gardner, Herb(ert) 1934- .... **CLC 44**
See also CA 149
Gardner, John (Champlin), Jr. 1933-1982 **C L C 2, 3, 5, 7, 8, 10, 18, 28, 34; DAM NOV, POP; SSC 7**
See also AITN 1; CA 65-68; 107; CANR 33, 73;
DLB 2; DLBY 82; MTCW 1; SATA 40;
SATA-Obit 31
Gardner, John (Edmund) 1926- **CLC 30; DAM POP**
See also CA 103; CANR 15, 69; MTCW 1
Gardner, Miriam
See Bradley, Marion Zimmer

Gardner, Noel
    See Kuttner, Henry
Gardons, S. S.
    See Snodgrass, W(illiam) D(e Witt)
Garfield, Leon 1921-1996 .... **CLC 12**
    See also AAYA 8; CA 17-20R; 152; CANR 38,
        41, 78; CLR 21; DLB 161; JRDA; MAICYA;
        SATA 1, 32, 76; SATA-Obit 90
Garland, (Hannibal) Hamlin 1860-1940**T C L C
    3; SSC 18**
    See also CA 104; DLB 12, 71, 78, 186
Garneau, (Hector de) Saint-Denys 1912-1943
    TCLC 13
    See also CA 111; DLB 88
Garner, Alan 1934-**CLC 17; DAB; DAM POP**
    See also AAYA 18; CA 73-76; CANR 15, 64;
        CLR 20, DLB 161, MAICYA, MTCW 1, 2;
        SATA 18, 69
Garner, Hugh 1913-1979 .... **CLC 13**
    <indexSee also CA 69-72; CANR 31; DLB 68
Garnett, David 1892-1981 .... **CLC 3**
    See also CA 5-8R; 103; CANR 17; DLB 34;
        MTCW 2
Garos, Stephanie
    See Katz, Steve
Garrett, George (Palmer) 1929-**CLC 3, 11, 51;
    SSC 30**
    See also CA 1-4R; CAAS 5; CANR 1, 42, 67;
        DLB 2, 5, 130, 152; DLBY 83
Garrick, David 1717-1779**LC 15; DAM DRAM**
    See also DLB 84
Garrigue, Jean 1914-1972 .... **CLC 2, 8**
    See also CA 5-8R; 37-40R; CANR 20
Garrison, Frederick
    See Sinclair, Upton (Beall)
Garth, Will
    See Hamilton, Edmond; Kuttner, Henry
Garvey, Marcus (Moziah, Jr.) 1887-1940
    TCLC 41; BLC 2; DAM MULT
    See also BW 1; CA 120; 124
Gary, Romain .... **CLC 25**
    See also Kacew, Romain
    See also DLB 83
Gascar, Pierre .... **CLC 11**
    See also Fournier, Pierre
Gascoyne, David (Emery) 1916- .... **CLC 45**
    See also CA 65-68; CANR 10, 28, 54; DLB 20;
        MTCW 1
Gaskell, Elizabeth Cleghorn 1810-1865**N C L C
    70; DAB; DAM MST; SSC 25**
    See also CDBLB 1832-1890; DLB 21, 144, 159
Gass, William H(oward) 1924-**CLC 1, 2, 8, 11,
    15, 39; SSC 12**
    See also CA 17-20R; CANR 30, 71; DLB 2;
        MTCW 1, 2
Gasset, Jose Ortega y
    See Ortega y Gasset, Jose
Gates, Henry Louis, Jr. 1950-**CLC 65; BLCS;
    DAM MULT**
    See also BW 2; CA 109; CANR 25, 53, 75; DLB
        67; MTCW 1
Gautier, Theophile 1811-1872 ... **NCLC 1, 59;
    DAM POET; PC 18; SSC 20**
    See also DLB 119
Gawsworth, John
    See Bates, H(erbert) E(rnest)
Gay, John 1685-1732 ..... **LC 49; DAM DRAM**
    See also DLB 84, 95
Gay, Oliver
    See Gogarty, Oliver St. John
Gaye, Marvin (Penze) 1939-1984 .... **CLC 26**
    See also CA 112

Gebler, Carlo (Ernest) 1954- .... **CLC 39**
    See also CA 119; 133
Gee, Maggie (Mary) 1948- .... **CLC 57**
    Scc also CA 130; DLB 207
Gee, Maurice (Gough) 1931- .... **CLC 29**
    See also CA 97-100; CANR 67; CLR 56; SATA
        46, 101
Gelbart, Larry (Simon) 1923- ...... **CLC 21, 61**
    See also CA 73-76; CANR 45
Gelber, Jack 1932- .... **CLC 1, 6, 14, 79**
    See also CA 1-4R; CANR 2; DLB 7
Gellhorn, Martha (Ellis) 1908-1998**CLC 14, 60**
    See also CA 77-80; 164; CANR 44; DLBY 82,
        98
Genet, Jean 1910-1986**CLC 1, 2, 5, 10, 14, 44,
    46; DAM DRAM**
    See also CA 13-16R; CANR 18; DLB 72; DLBY
        86; MTCW 1, 2
Gent, Peter 1942- .... **CLC 29**
    See also AITN 1; CA 89-92; DLBY 82
Gentlewoman in New England, A
    See Bradstreet, Anne
Gentlewoman in Those Parts, A
    See Bradstreet, Anne
George, Jean Craighead 1919- .... **CLC 35**
    See also AAYA 8; CA 5-8R; CANR 25; CLR 1;
        DLB 52; JRDA; MAICYA; SATA 2, 68
George, Stefan (Anton) 1868-1933**TCLC 2, 14**
    See also CA 104
Georges, Georges Martin
    See Simenon, Georges (Jacques Christian)
Gerhardi, William Alexander
    See Gerhardie, William Alexander
Gerhardie, William Alexander 1895-1977**C L C
    5**
    See also CA 25-28R; 73-76; CANR 18; DLB 36
Gerstler, Amy 1956- .... **CLC 70**
    See also CA 146
Gertler, T. .... **CLC 34**
    See also CA 116; 121; INT 121
Ghalib .... **NCLC 39**
    See also Ghalib, Hsadullah Khan
Ghalib, Hsadullah Khan 1797-1869
    See Ghalib
    See also DAM POET
Ghelderode, Michel de 1898-1962 **CLC 6, 11;
    DAM DRAM**
    See also CA 85-88; CANR 40, 77
Ghiselin, Brewster 1903- .... **CLC 23**
    See also CA 13-16R; CAAS 10; CANR 13
Ghose, Aurabinda 1872-1950 .... **TCLC 63**
    See also CA 163
Ghose, Zulfikar 1935- .... **CLC 42**
    See also CA 65-68; CANR 67
Ghosh, Amitav 1956- .... **CLC 44**
    See also CA 147
Giacosa, Giuseppe 1847-1906 .... **TCLC 7**
    See also CA 104
Gibb, Lee
    See Waterhouse, Keith (Spencer)
Gibbon, Lewis Grassic .... **TCLC 4**
    See also Mitchell, James Leslie
Gibbons, Kaye 1960- **CLC 50, 88; DAM POP**
    See also CA 151; CANR 75; MTCW 1
Gibran, Kahlil 1883-1931 .. **TCLC 1, 9; DAM
    POET, POP; PC 9**
    See also CA 104; 150; MTCW 2
Gibran, Khalil
    See Gibran, Kahlil
Gibson, William 1914- .... **CLC 23; DA; DAB;
    DAC; DAM DRAM, MST**
    See also CA 9-12R; CANR 9, 42, 75; DLB 7;
        MTCW 1; SATA 66

Gibson, William (Ford) 1948- .... **CLC 39, 63;
    DAM POP**
    See also AAYA 12; CA 126; 133; CANR 52;
        MTCW 1
Gide, Andre (Paul Guillaume) 1869-1951
    **TCLC 5, 12, 36; DA; DAB; DAC; DAM
    MST, NOV; SSC 13; WLC**
    See also CA 104; 124; DLB 65; MTCW 1, 2
Gifford, Barry (Colby) 1946- .... **CLC 34**
    See also CA 65-68; CANR 9, 30, 40
Gilbert, Frank
    See De Voto, Bernard (Augustine)
Gilbert, W(illiam) S(chwenck) 1836-1911
    TCLC 3; DAM DRAM, POET
    See also CA 104; 173; SATA 36
Gilbreth, Frank B., Jr. 1911- .... **CLC 17**
    See also CA 9-12R; SATA 2
Gilchrist, Ellen 1935-**CLC 34, 48; DAM POP;
    SSC 14**
    See also CA 113; 116; CANR 41, 61; DLB 130;
        MTCW 1, 2
Giles, Molly 1942- .... **CLC 39**
    See also CA 126
Gill, Eric 1882-1940 .... **TCLC 85**
Gill, Patrick
    See Creasey, John
Gilliam, Terry (Vance) 1940- .... **CLC 21**
    See also Monty Python
    See also AAYA 19; CA 108; 113; CANR 35; INT
        113
Gillian, Jerry
    See Gilliam, Terry (Vance)
Gilliatt, Penelope (Ann Douglass) 1932-1993
    CLC 2, 10, 13, 53
    See also AITN 2; CA 13-16R; 141; CANR 49;
        DLB 14
Gilman, Charlotte (Anna) Perkins (Stetson)
    1860-1935 .... **TCLC 9, 37; SSC 13**
    See also CA 106; 150; MTCW 1
Gilmour, David 1949- .... **CLC 35**
    See also CA 138, 147
Gilpin, William 1724-1804 .... **NCLC 30**
Gilray, J. D.
    See Mencken, H(enry) L(ouis)
    <indexGilroy, Frank D(aniel) 1925-   C L C
    2
    See also CA 81-84; CANR 32, 64; DLB 7
Gilstrap, John 1957(?)- .... **CLC 99**
    See also CA 160
Ginsberg, Allen 1926-1997**CLC 1, 2, 3, 4, 6, 13,
    36, 69, 109; DA; DAB; DAC; DAM MST,
    POET; PC 4; WLC**
    See also AITN 1; CA 1-4R; 157; CANR 2, 41,
        63; CDALB 1941-1968; DLB 5, 16, 169;
        MTCW 1, 2
Ginzburg, Natalia 1916-1991**CLC 5, 11, 54, 70**
    See also CA 85-88; 135; CANR 33; DLB 177;
        MTCW 1, 2
Giono, Jean 1895-1970 .... **CLC 4, 11**
    See also CA 45-48; 29-32R; CANR 2, 35; DLB
        72; MTCW 1
Giovanni, Nikki 1943- . **CLC 2, 4, 19, 64, 117;
    BLC 2; DA; DAB; DAC; DAM MST,
    MULT, POET; PC 19; WLCS**
    See also AAYA 22; AITN 1; BW 2; CA 29-32R;
        CAAS 6; CANR 18, 41, 60; CLR 6; DLB 5,
        41; INT CANR-18; MAICYA; MTCW 1, 2;
        SATA 24, 107
Giovene, Andrea 1904- .... **CLC 7**
    See also CA 85-88
Gippius, Zinaida (Nikolayevna) 1869-1945
    See Hippius, Zinaida
    See also CA 106

Graham, Tom
  See Lewis, (Harry) Sinclair
Graham, W(illiam) S(ydney) 1918-1986 . **C L C
  29**
  See also CA 73-76; 118; DLB 20
Graham, Winston (Mawdsley) 1910- . **CLC 23**
  See also CA 49-52; CANR 2, 22, 45, 66; DLB
  77
Grahame, Kenneth 1859-1932 **TCLC 64; DAB**
  See also CA 108; 136; CLR 5; DLB 34, 141, 178;
  MAICYA; MTCW 2; SATA 100; YABC 1
Granovsky, Timofei Nikolaevich 1813-1855
  NCLC 75
  See also DLB 198
Grant, Skeeter
  See Spiegelman, Art
Granville-Barker, Harley 1877-1946 **TCLC 2;
  DAM DRAM**
  See also Barker, Harley Granville
  See also CA 104
Grass, Guenter (Wilhelm) 1927-**CLC 1, 2, 4, 6,
  11, 15, 22, 32, 49, 88; DA; DAB; DAC; DAM
  MST, NOV; WLC**
  See also CA 13-16R; CANR 20, 75; DLB 75,
  124; MTCW 1, 2
Gratton, Thomas
  See Hulme, T(homas) E(rnest)
Grau, Shirley Ann 1929- .... **CLC 4, 9; SSC 15**
  See also CA 89-92; CANR 22, 69; DLB 2; INT
  CANR-22; MTCW 1
Gravel, Fern
  See Hall, James Norman
Graver, Elizabeth 1964- .... **CLC 70**
  See also CA 135; CANR 71
Graves, Richard Perceval 1945- .... **CLC 44**
  See also CA 65-68; CANR 9, 26, 51
Graves, Robert (von Ranke) 1895-1985**CLC 1,
  2, 6, 11, 39, 44, 45; DAB; DAC; DAM MST,
  POET; PC 6**
  See also CA 5-8R; 117; CANR 5, 36; CDBLB
  1914-1945; DLB 20, 100, 191; DLBD 18;
  DLBY 85; MTCW 1, 2; SATA 45
Graves, Valerie
  See Bradley, Marion Zimmer
Gray, Alasdair (James) 1934- .... **CLC 41**
  See also CA 126; CANR 47, 69; DLB 194; INT
  126; MTCW 1, 2
Gray, Amlin 1946- .... **CLC 29**
  See also CA 138
Gray, Francine du Plessix 1930-**CLC 22; DAM
  NOV**
  See also BEST 90:3; CA 61-64; CAAS 2; CANR
  11, 33, 75; INT CANR-11; MTCW 1, 2
Gray, John (Henry) 1866-1934 .... **TCLC 19**
  See also CA 119; 162
Gray, Simon (James Holliday) 1936-**CLC 9, 14,
  36**
  See also AITN 1; CA 21-24R; CAAS 3; CANR
  32, 69; DLB 13; MTCW 1
Gray, Spalding 1941-**CLC 49, 112; DAM POP;
  DC 7**
  See also CA 128; CANR 74; MTCW 2
Gray, Thomas 1716-1771**LC 4, 40; DA; DAB;
  DAC; DAM MST; PC 2; WLC**
  See also CDBLB 1660-1789; DLB 109
Grayson, David
  See Baker, Ray Stannard
Grayson, Richard (A.) 1951- .... **CLC 38**
  See also CA 85-88; CANR 14, 31, 57
Greeley, Andrew M(oran) 1928-**CLC 28; DAM
  POP**
  See also CA 5-8R; CAAS 7; CANR 7, 43, 69;
  MTCW 1, 2

Green, Anna Katharine 1846-1935 . **TCLC 63**
  See also CA 112; 159; DLB 202
Green, Brian
  See Card, Orson Scott
Green, Hannah
  See Greenberg, Joanne (Goldenberg)
Green, Hannah 1927(?)-1996 .... **CLC 3**
  See also CA 73-76; CANR 59
Green, Henry 1905-1973 .... **CLC 2, 13, 97**
  See also Yorke, Henry Vincent
  See also DLB 15
Green, Julian (Hartridge) 1900-1998
  See Green, Julien
  See also CA 21-24R; 169; CANR 33; DLB 4,
  72; MTCW 1
Green, Julien .... **CLC 3, 11, 77**
  See also Green, Julian (Hartridge)
  See also MTCW 2
Green, Paul (Eliot) 1894-1981 **CLC 25; DAM
  DRAM**
  See also AITN 1; CA 5-8R; 103; CANR 3; DLB
  7, 9; DLBY 81
Greenberg, Ivan 1908-1973
  See Rahv, Philip
  See also CA 85-88
Greenberg, Joanne (Goldenberg) 1932-**CLC 7,
  30**
  See also AAYA 12; CA 5-8R; CANR 14, 32, 69;
  SATA 25
Greenberg, Richard 1959(?)- .... **CLC 57**
  See also CA 138
Greene, Bette 1934-............................. **CLC 30**
  See also AAYA 7; CA 53-56; CANR 4; CLR 2;
  JRDA; MAICYA; SAAS 16; SATA 8, 102
Greene, Gael .... **CLC 8**
  See also CA 13-16R; CANR 10
Greene, Graham (Henry) 1904-1991**CLC 1, 3,
  6, 9, 14, 18, 27, 37, 70, 72; DA; DAB; DAC;
  DAM MST, NOV; SSC 29; WLC**
  See also AITN 2; CA 13-16R; 133; CANR 35,
  61; CDBLB 1945-1960; DLB 13, 15, 77, 100,
  162, 201, 204; DLBY 91; MTCW 1, 2; SATA
  20
Greene, Robert 1558-1592 .... **LC 41**
  See also DLB 62, 167
Greer, Richard
  See Silverberg, Robert
Gregor, Arthur 1923- .... **CLC 9**
  See also CA 25-28R; CAAS 10; CANR 11; SATA
  36
Gregor, Lee
  See Pohl, Frederik
Gregory, Isabella Augusta (Persse) 1852-1932
  TCLC 1
  See also CA 104; DLB 10
Gregory, J. Dennis
  See Williams, John A(lfred)
Grendon, Stephen
  See Derleth, August (William)
Grenville, Kate 1950- .... **CLC 61**
  See also CA 118; CANR 53
Grenville, Pelham
  See Wodehouse, P(elham) G(renville)
Greve, Felix Paul (Berthold Friedrich)
  1879-1948
  See Grove, Frederick Philip
  See also CA 104; 141; DAC; DAM MST
Grey, Zane 1872-1939 ... **TCLC 6; DAM POP**
  See also CA 104; 132; DLB 212; MTCW 1, 2
Grieg, (Johan) Nordahl (Brun) 1902-1943
  TCLC 10
  See also CA 107

Grieve, C(hristopher) M(urray) 1892-1978
  CLC 11, 19; DAM POET
  See also MacDiarmid, Hugh; Pteleon
  See also CA 5-8R; 85-88; CANR 33; MTCW 1
Griffin, Gerald 1803-1840 .... **NCLC 7**
  See also DLB 159
Griffin, John Howard 1920-1980 .... **CLC 68**
  See also AITN 1; CA 1-4R; 101; CANR 2
Griffin, Peter 1942-............................. **CLC 39**
  See also CA 136
Griffith, D(avid Lewelyn) W(ark) 1875(?)-1948
  TCLC 68
  See also CA 119; 150
Griffith, Lawrence
  See Griffith, D(avid Lewelyn) W(ark)
Griffiths, Trevor 1935- ....**CLC 13, 52**
  See also CA 97-100; CANR 45; DLB 13
Griggs, Sutton Elbert 1872-1930(?) **TCLC 77**
  See also CA 123; DLB 50
Grigson, Geoffrey (Edward Harvey) 1905-1985
  CLC 7, 39
  See also CA 25-28R; 118; CANR 20, 33; DLB
  27; MTCW 1, 2
Grillparzer, Franz 1791-1872 .... **NCLC 1**
  See also DLB 133
Grimble, Reverend Charles James
  See Eliot, T(homas) S(tearns)
Grimke, Charlotte L(ottie) Forten 1837(?)-1914
  See Forten, Charlotte L.
  See also BW 1; CA 117; 124; DAM MULT,
  POET
Grimm, Jacob Ludwig Karl 1785-1863 **N C L C
  3**
  See also DLB 90; MAICYA; SATA 22
Grimm, Wilhelm Karl 1786-1859 ..... **NCLC 3**
  See also DLB 90; MAICYA; SATA 22
Grimmelshausen, Johann Jakob Christoffel von
  1621-1676 .... **LC 6**
  See also DLB 168
Grindel, Eugene 1895-1952
  See Eluard, Paul
  See also CA 104
Grisham, John 1955-...... **CLC 84; DAM POP**
  See also AAYA 14; CA 138; CANR 47, 69;
  MTCW 2
Grossman, David 1954- .... **CLC 67**
  See also CA 138
Grossman, Vasily (Semenovich) 1905-1964
  CLC 41
  See also CA 124; 130; MTCW 1
Grove, Frederick Philip .... **TCLC 4**
  See also Greve, Felix Paul (Berthold Friedrich)
  See also DLB 92
Grubb
  See Crumb, R(obert)
Grumbach, Doris (Isaac) 1918-**CLC 13, 22, 64**
  See also CA 5-8R; CAAS 2; CANR 9, 42, 70;
  INT CANR-9; MTCW 2
Grundtvig, Nicolai Frederik Severin 1783-1872
  NCLC 1
Grunge
  See Crumb, R(obert)
Grunwald, Lisa 1959-......................... **CLC 44**
  See also CA 120
Guare, John 1938- ... **CLC 8, 14, 29, 67; DAM
  DRAM**
  See also CA 73-76; CANR 21, 69; DLB 7;
  MTCW 1, 2
Gudjonsson, Halldor Kiljan 1902-1998
  See Laxness, Halldor
  See also CA 103; 164
Guenter, Erich
  See Eich, Guenter

Hanley, James 1901-1985 .... **CLC 3, 5, 8, 13**
See also CA 73-76; 117; CANR 36; DLB 191; MTCW 1

Hannah, Barry 1942- .... **CLC 23, 38, 90**
See also CA 108; 110; CANR 43, 68; DLB 6; INT 110; MTCW 1

Hannon, Ezra
See Hunter, Evan

Hansberry, Lorraine (Vivian) 1930-1965 **C L C 17, 62; BLC 2; DA; DAB; DAC; DAM DRAM, MST, MULT; DC 2**
See also AAYA 25; BW 1; CA 109; 25-28R; CABS 3; CANR 58; CDALB 1941-1968; DLB 7, 38; MTCW 1, 2

Hansen, Joseph 1923- .... **CLC 38**
See also CA 29-32R; CAAS 17; CANR 16, 44, 66; INT CANR-16

Hansen, Martin A(lfred) 1909-1955 **TCLC 32**
See also CA 167

Hanson, Kenneth O(stlin) 1922- .... **CLC 13**
See also CA 53-56; CANR 7

Hardwick, Elizabeth (Bruce) 1916- . **CLC 13; DAM NOV**
See also CA 5-8R; CANR 3, 32, 70; DLB 6; MTCW 1, 2

Hardy, Thomas 1840-1928 **TCLC 4, 10, 18, 32, 48, 53, 72; DA; DAB; DAC; DAM MST, NOV, POET; PC 8; SSC 2; WLC**
See also CA 104; 123; CDBLB 1890-1914; DLB 18, 19, 135; MTCW 1, 2

Hare, David 1947- .... **CLC 29, 58**
See also CA 97-100; CANR 39; DLB 13; MTCW 1

Harewood, John
See Van Druten, John (William)

Harford, Henry
See Hudson, W(illiam) H(enry)

Hargrave, Leonie
See Disch, Thomas M(ichael)

Harjo, Joy 1951- .... **CLC 83; DAM MULT**
See also CA 114; CANR 35, 67; DLB 120, 175; MTCW 2; NNAL

Harlan, Louis R(udolph) 1922- .... **CLC 34**
See also CA 21-24R; CANR 25, 55

Harling, Robert 1951(?)- .... **CLC 53**
See also CA 147

Harmon, William (Ruth) 1938- .... **CLC 38**
See also CA 33-36R; CANR 14, 32, 35; SATA 65

Harper, F. E. W.
See Harper, Frances Ellen Watkins

Harper, Frances E. W.
See Harper, Frances Ellen Watkins

Harper, Frances E. Watkins
See Harper, Frances Ellen Watkins

Harper, Frances Ellen
See Harper, Frances Ellen Watkins

Harper, Frances Ellen Watkins 1825-1911 **TCLC 14; BLC 2; DAM MULT, POET; PC 21**
See also BW 1; CA 111; 125; DLB 50

Harper, Michael S(teven) 1938- ..... **CLC 7, 22**
See also BW 1; CA 33-36R; CANR 24; DLB 41

Harper, Mrs. F. E. W.
See Harper, Frances Ellen Watkins

Harris, Christie (Lucy) Irwin 1907- .. **CLC 12**
See also CA 5-8R; CANR 6; CLR 47; DLB 88; JRDA; MAICYA; SAAS 10; SATA 6, 74

Harris, Frank 1856-1931 .... **TCLC 24**
See also CA 109; 150; DLB 156, 197

Harris, George Washington 1814-1869 **N C L C 23**
See also DLB 3, 11

Harris, Joel Chandler 1848-1908 **TCLC 2; SSC 19**
See also CA 104; 137; CLR 49; DLB 11, 23, 42, 78, 91; MAICYA; SATA 100; YABC 1

Harris, John (Wyndham Parkes Lucas) Beynon 1903-1969
See Wyndham, John
See also CA 102; 89-92

Harris, MacDonald .... **CLC 9**
See also Heiney, Donald (William)

Harris, Mark 1922- .... **CLC 19**
See also CA 5-8R; CAAS 3; CANR 2, 55; DLB 2; DLBY 80

Harris, (Theodore) Wilson 1921- .... **CLC 25**
See also BW 2; CA 65-68; CAAS 16; CANR 11, 27, 69; DLB 117; MTCW 1

Harrison, Elizabeth Cavanna 1909-
See Cavanna, Betty
See also CA 9-12R; CANR 6, 27

Harrison, Harry (Max) 1925- .... **CLC 42**
See also CA 1-4R; CANR 5, 21; DLB 8; SATA 4

Harrison, James (Thomas) 1937- **CLC 6, 14, 33, 66; SSC 19**
See also CA 13-16R; CANR 8, 51; DLBY 82; INT CANR-8

Harrison, Jim
See Harrison, James (Thomas)

Harrison, Kathryn 1961- .... **CLC 70**
See also CA 144; CANR 68

Harrison, Tony 1937- .... **CLC 43**
See also CA 65-68; CANR 44; DLB 40; MTCW 1

Harriss, Will(ard Irvin) 1922- .... **CLC 34**
See also CA 111

Harson, Sley
See Ellison, Harlan (Jay)

Hart, Ellis
See Ellison, Harlan (Jay)

Hart, Josephine 1942(?)- **CLC 70; DAM POP**
See also CA 138; CANR 70

Hart, Moss 1904-1961 **CLC 66; DAM DRAM**
See also CA 109; 89-92; DLB 7

Harte, (Francis) Bret(t) 1836(?)-1902 **TCLC 1, 25; DA; DAC; DAM MST; SSC 8; WLC**
See also CA 104; 140; CDALB 1865-1917; DLB 12, 64, 74, 79, 186; SATA 26

Hartley, L(eslie) P(oles) 1895-1972 **CLC 2, 22**
See also CA 45-48; 37-40R; CANR 33; DLB 15, 139; MTCW 1, 2

Hartman, Geoffrey H. 1929- .... **CLC 27**
See also CA 117; 125; DLB 67

Hartmann, Sadakichi 1867-1944 ..... **TCLC 73**
See also CA 157; DLB 54

Hartmann von Aue c. 1160-c. 1205 **CMLC 15**
See also DLB 138

Hartmann von Aue 1170-1210 .... **CMLC 15**

Haruf, Kent 1943- .... **CLC 34**
See also CA 149

Harwood, Ronald 1934- **CLC 32; DAM DRAM, MST**
See also CA 1-4R; CANR 4, 55; DLB 13

Hasegawa Tatsunosuke
See Futabatei, Shimei

Hasek, Jaroslav (Matej Frantisek) 1883-1923 **TCLC 4**
See also CA 104; 129; MTCW 1, 2

Hass, Robert 1941- ..... **CLC 18, 39, 99; PC 16**
See also CA 111; CANR 30, 50, 71; DLB 105, 206; SATA 94

Hastings, Hudson
See Kuttner, Henry

Hastings, Selina .... **CLC 44**

Hathorne, John 1641-1717 .... **LC 38**

Hatteras, Amelia
See Mencken, H(enry) L(ouis)

Hatteras, Owen .... **TCLC 18**
See also Mencken, H(enry) L(ouis); Nathan, George Jean

Hauptmann, Gerhart (Johann Robert) 1862-1946 .... **TCLC 4; DAM DRAM**
See also CA 104; 153; DLB 66, 118

Havel, Vaclav 1936- ..... **CLC 25, 58, 65; DAM DRAM; DC 6**
See also CA 104; CANR 36, 63; MTCW 1, 2

Haviaras, Stratis .... **CLC 33**
See also Chaviaras, Strates

Hawes, Stephen 1475(?)-1523(?) **LC 17**
See also DLB 132

Hawkes, John (Clendennin Burne, Jr.) 1925-1998 **CLC 1, 2, 3, 4, 7, 9, 14, 15, 27, 49**
See also CA 1-4R; 167; CANR 2, 47, 64; DLB 2, 7; DLBY 80, 98; MTCW 1, 2

Hawking, S. W.
See Hawking, Stephen W(illiam)

Hawking, Stephen W(illiam) 1942- **CLC 63, 105**
See also AAYA 13; BEST 89:1; CA 126; 129; CANR 48; MTCW 2

Hawkins, Anthony Hope
See Hope, Anthony

Hawthorne, Julian 1846-1934 .... **TCLC 25**
See also CA 165

Hawthorne, Nathaniel 1804-1864 . **NCLC 39; DA; DAB; DAC; DAM MST, NOV; SSC 3, 29; WLC**
See also AAYA 18; CDALB 1640-1865; DLB 1, 74; YABC 2

Haxton, Josephine Ayres 1921-
See Douglas, Ellen
See also CA 115; CANR 41

Hayaseca y Eizaguirre, Jorge
See Echegaray (y Eizaguirre), Jose (Maria Waldo)

Hayashi, Fumiko 1904-1951 .... **TCLC 27**
See also CA 161; DLB 180

Haycraft, Anna
See Ellis, Alice Thomas
See also CA 122; MTCW 2

Hayden, Robert E(arl) 1913-1980 **CLC 5, 9, 14, 37; BLC 2; DA; DAC; DAM MST, MULT, POET; PC 6**
See also BW 1; CA 69-72; 97-100; CABS 2; CANR 24, 75; CDALB 1941-1968; DLB 5, 76; MTCW 1, 2; SATA 19; SATA-Obit 26

Hayford, J(oseph) E(phraim) Casely
See Casely-Hayford, J(oseph) E(phraim)

Hayman, Ronald 1932- .... **CLC 44**
See also CA 25-28R; CANR 18, 50; DLB 155

Haywood, Eliza (Fowler) 1693(?)-1756 **LC 1, 44**
See also DLB 39

Hazlitt, William 1778-1830 .... **NCLC 29**
See also DLB 110, 158

Hazzard, Shirley 1931- .... **CLC 18**
See also CA 9-12R; CANR 4, 70; DLBY 82; MTCW 1

Head, Bessie 1937-1986 . **CLC 25, 67; BLC 2; DAM MULT**
See also BW 2; CA 29-32R; 119; CANR 25; DLB 117; MTCW 1, 2

Headon, (Nicky) Topper 1956(?)- ...... **CLC 30**

Heaney, Seamus (Justin) 1939- **CLC 5, 7, 14, 25, 37, 74, 91; DAB; DAM POET; PC 18; WLCS**
See also CA 85-88; CANR 25, 48, 75; CDBLB 1960 to Present; DLB 40; DLBY 95; MTCW 1, 2

MAICYA; MTCW 1, 2; SATA 7

Jarry, Alfred 1873-1907 .. **TCLC 2, 14; DAM DRAM; SSC 20**
See also CA 104; 153; DLB 192

Jarvis, E. K.
See Bloch, Robert (Albert); Ellison, Harlan (Jay); Silverberg, Robert

Jeake, Samuel, Jr.
See Aiken, Conrad (Potter)

Jean Paul 1763-1825 .... **NCLC 7**

Jefferies, (John) Richard 1848-1887**NCLC 47**
See also DLB 98, 141; SATA 16

Jeffers, (John) Robinson 1887-1962**CLC 2, 3, 11, 15, 54; DA; DAC; DAM MST, POET; PC 17; WLC**
See also CA 85-88; CANR 35; CDALB 1917-1929; DLB 45, 212; MTCW 1, 2

Jefferson, Janet
See Mencken, H(enry) L(ouis)

Jefferson, Thomas 1743-1826 .... **NCLC 11**
See also CDALB 1640-1865; DLB 31

Jeffrey, Francis 1773-1850 .... **NCLC 33**
See also DLB 107

Jelakowitch, Ivan
See Heijermans, Herman

Jellicoe, (Patricia) Ann 1927- .... **CLC 27**
See also CA 85-88; DLB 13

Jen, Gish ....**CLC 70**
See also Jen, Lillian

Jen, Lillian 1956(?)-
See Jen, Gish
See also CA 135

Jenkins, (John) Robin 1912-...............**CLC 52**
See also CA 1-4R; CANR 1; DLB 14

Jennings, Elizabeth (Joan) 1926- ....**CLC 5, 14**
See also CA 61-64; CAAS 5; CANR 8, 39, 66; DLB 27; MTCW 1; SATA 66

Jennings, Waylon 1937- ....**CLC 21**

Jensen, Johannes V. 1873-1950 ....**TCLC 41**
See also CA 170

Jensen, Laura (Linnea) 1948- ....**CLC 37**
See also CA 103

Jerome, Jerome K(lapka) 1859-1927**TCLC 23**
See also CA 119; DLB 10, 34, 135

Jerrold, Douglas William 1803-1857 **NCLC 2**
See also DLB 158, 159

Jewett, (Theodora) Sarah Orne 1849-1909 **TCLC 1, 22; SSC 6**
See also CA 108; 127; CANR 71; DLB 12, 74; SATA 15

Jewsbury, Geraldine (Endsor) 1812-1880 **NCLC 22**
See also DLB 21

Jhabvala, Ruth Prawer 1927-**CLC 4, 8, 29, 94; DAB; DAM NOV**
See also CA 1-4R; CANR 2, 29, 51, 74; DLB 139, 194; INT CANR-29; MTCW 1, 2

Jibran, Kahlil
See Gibran, Kahlil

Jibran, Khalil
See Gibran, Kahlil

Jiles, Paulette 1943- ....**CLC 13, 58**
See also CA 101; CANR 70

Jimenez (Mantecon), Juan Ramon 1881-1958 **TCLC 4; DAM MULT, POET; HLC; PC 7**
See also CA 104; 131; CANR 74; DLB 134; HW; MTCW 1, 2

Jimenez, Ramon
See Jimenez (Mantecon), Juan Ramon

Jimenez Mantecon, Juan
See Jimenez (Mantecon), Juan Ramon

Jin, Ha 1956- ....**CLC 109**
See also CA 152

Joel, Billy .... **CLC 26**
See also Joel, William Martin

Joel, William Martin 1949-
See Joel, Billy
See also CA 108

John, Saint 7th cent. - .... **CMLC 27**

John of the Cross, St. 1542-1591 .... **LC 18**

Johnson, B(ryan) S(tanley William) 1933-1973 **CLC 6, 9**
See also CA 9-12R; 53-56; CANR 9; DLB 14, 40

Johnson, Benj. F. of Boo
See Riley, James Whitcomb

Johnson, Benjamin F. of Boo
See Riley, James Whitcomb

Johnson, Charles (Richard) 1948- **CLC 7, 51, 65; BLC 2; DAM MULT**
See also BW 2; CA 116; CAAS 18; CANR 42, 66; DLB 33; MTCW 2

Johnson, Denis 1949- ....**CLC 52**
See also CA 117; 121; CANR 71; DLB 120

Johnson, Diane 1934-...................**CLC 5, 13, 48**
See also CA 41-44R; CANR 17, 40, 62; DLBY 80; INT CANR-17; MTCW 1

Johnson, Eyvind (Olof Verner) 1900-1976**CLC 14**
See also CA 73-76; 69-72; CANR 34

Johnson, J. R.
See James, C(yril) L(ionel) R(obert)

Johnson, James Weldon 1871-1938 . **TCLC 3, 19; BLC 2; DAM MULT, POET; PC 24**
See also BW 1; CA 104; 125; CDALB 1917-1929; CLR 32; DLB 51; MTCW 1, 2; SATA 31

Johnson, Joyce 1935- ....**CLC 58**
See also CA 125; 129

Johnson, Judith (Emlyn) 1936- ......**CLC 7, 15**
See also CA 25-28R; 153; CANR 34

Johnson, Lionel (Pigot) 1867-1902 . **TCLC 19**
See also CA 117; DLB 19

Johnson, Marguerite (Annie)
See Angelou, Maya

Johnson, Mel
See Malzberg, Barry N(athaniel)

Johnson, Pamela Hansford 1912-1981 **CLC 1, 7, 27**
See also CA 1-4R; 104; CANR 2, 28; DLB 15; MTCW 1, 2

Johnson, Robert 1911(?)-1938 .... **TCLC 69**

Johnson, Samuel 1709-1784**LC 15; DA; DAB; DAC; DAM MST; WLC**
See also CDBLB 1660-1789; DLB 39, 95, 104, 142

Johnson, Uwe 1934-1984 ....**CLC 5, 10, 15, 40**
See also CA 1-4R; 112; CANR 1, 39; DLB 75; MTCW 1

Johnston, George (Benson) 1913- ...... **CLC 51**
See also CA 1-4R; CANR 5, 20; DLB 88

Johnston, Jennifer 1930- ....**CLC 7**
See also CA 85-88; DLB 14

Jolley, (Monica) Elizabeth 1923-**CLC 46; SSC 19**
See also CA 127; CAAS 13; CANR 59

Jones, Arthur Llewellyn 1863-1947
See Machen, Arthur
See also CA 104

Jones, D(ouglas) G(ordon) 1929- ....**CLC 10**
See also CA 29-32R; CANR 13; DLB 53

Jones, David (Michael) 1895-1974**CLC 2, 4, 7, 13, 42**
See also CA 9-12R; 53-56; CANR 28; CDBLB 1945-1960; DLB 20, 100; MTCW 1

Jones, David Robert 1947-
See Bowie, David
See also CA 103

Jones, Diana Wynne 1934-..................**CLC 26**
See also AAYA 12; CA 49-52; CANR 4, 26, 56; CLR 23; DLB 161; JRDA; MAICYA; SAAS 7; SATA 9, 70

Jones, Edward P. 1950- ....**CLC 76**
See also BW 2; CA 142

Jones, Gayl 1949- .....**CLC 6, 9; BLC 2; DAM MULT**
See also BW 2; CA 77-80; CANR 27, 66; DLB 33; MTCW 1, 2

Jones, James 1921-1977 ....**CLC 1, 3, 10, 39**
See also AITN 1, 2; CA 1-4R; 69-72; CANR 6; DLB 2, 143; DLBD 17; DLBY 98; MTCW 1

Jones, John J.
See Lovecraft, H(oward) P(hillips)

Jones, LeRoi ....**CLC 1, 2, 3, 5, 10, 14**
See also Baraka, Amiri
See also MTCW 2

Jones, Louis B. 1953- ....**CLC 65**
See also CA 141; CANR 73

Jones, Madison (Percy, Jr.) 1925- ....**CLC 4**
See also CA 13-16R; CAAS 11; CANR 7, 54; DLB 152

Jones, Mervyn 1922-.....................**CLC 10, 52**
See also CA 45-48; CAAS 5; CANR 1; MTCW 1

Jones, Mick 1956(?)-...........................**CLC 30**

Jones, Nettie (Pearl) 1941- ....**CLC 34**
See also BW 2; CA 137; CAAS 20

Jones, Preston 1936-1979 ....**CLC 10**
See also CA 73-76; 89-92; DLB 7

Jones, Robert F(rancis) 1934- ....**CLC 7**
See also CA 49-52; CANR 2, 61

Jones, Rod 1953- ....**CLC 50**
See also CA 128

Jones, Terence Graham Parry 1942- . **CLC 21**
See also Jones, Terry; Monty Python
See also CA 112; 116; CANR 35; INT 116

Jones, Terry
See Jones, Terence Graham Parry
See also SATA 67; SATA-Brief 51

Jones, Thom 1945(?)-...........................**CLC 81**
See also CA 157

Jong, Erica 1942- .. **CLC 4, 6, 8, 18, 83; DAM NOV, POP**
See also AITN 1; BEST 90:2; CA 73-76; CANR 26, 52, 75; DLB 2, 5, 28, 152; INT CANR-26; MTCW 1, 2

Jonson, Ben(jamin) 1572(?)-1637**LC 6, 33; DA; DAB; DAC; DAM DRAM, MST, POET; DC 4; PC 17; WLC**
See also CDBLB Before 1660; DLB 62, 121

Jordan, June 1936-**CLC 5, 11, 23, 114; BLCS; DAM MULT, POET**
See also AAYA 2; BW 2; CA 33-36R; CANR 25, 70; CLR 10; DLB 38; MAICYA; MTCW 1; SATA 4

Jordan, Neil (Patrick) 1950- ....**CLC 110**
See also CA 124; 130; CANR 54; INT 130

Jordan, Pat(rick M.) 1941- ....**CLC 37**
See also CA 33-36R

Jorgensen, Ivar
See Ellison, Harlan (Jay)

Jorgenson, Ivar
See Silverberg, Robert

Josephus, Flavius c. 37-100 .... **CMLC 13**

Josipovici, Gabriel 1940- ....**CLC 6, 43**
See also CA 37-40R; CAAS 8; CANR 47; DLB 14

Levon, O. U.
See Kesey, Ken (Elton)
Levy, Amy 1861-1889 .... NCLC 59
See also DLB 156
Lewes, George Henry 1817-1878 .... NCLC 25
See also DLB 55, 144
Lewis, Alun 1915-1944 .... TCLC 3
See also CA 104; DLB 20, 162
Lewis, C. Day
See Day Lewis, C(ecil)
Lewis, C(live) S(taples) 1898-1963 CLC 1, 3, 6,
14, 27; DA; DAB; DAC; DAM MST, NOV,
POP; WLC
See also AAYA 3; CA 81-84; CANR 33, 71;
CDBLB 1945-1960; CLR 3, 27; DLB 15, 100,
160; JRDA; MAICYA; MTCW 1, 2; SATA 13,
100
Lewis, Janet 1899-1998 .... CLC 41
See also Winters, Janet Lewis
See also CA 9-12R; 172; CANR 29, 63; CAP 1;
DLBY 87
Lewis, Matthew Gregory 1775-1818 NCLC 11,
62
See also DLB 39, 158, 178
Lewis, (Harry) Sinclair 1885-1951 TCLC 4, 13,
23, 39; DA; DAB; DAC; DAM MST, NOV;
WLC
See also CA 104; 133; CDALB 1917-1929; DLB
9, 102; DLBD 1; MTCW 1, 2
Lewis, (Percy) Wyndham 1882(?)-1957 T C L C
2, 9; SSC 34
See also CA 104; 157; DLB 15; MTCW 2
Lewisohn, Ludwig 1883-1955 .... TCLC 19
See also CA 107; DLB 4, 9, 28, 102
Lewton, Val 1904-1951 .... TCLC 76
Leyner, Mark 1956- .... CLC 92
See also CA 110; CANR 28, 53; MTCW 2
Lezama Lima, Jose 1910-1976 CLC 4, 10, 101;
DAM MULT
See also CA 77-80; CANR 71; DLB 113; HW
L'Heureux, John (Clarke) 1934- .... CLC 52
See also CA 13-16R; CANR 23, 45
Liddell, C. H.
See Kuttner, Henry
Lie, Jonas (Lauritz Idemil) 1833-1908(?)
TCLC 5
See also CA 115
Lieber, Joel 1937-1971 .... CLC 6
See also CA 73-76; 29-32R
Lieber, Stanley Martin
See Lee, Stan
Lieberman, Laurence (James) 1935- CLC 4, 36
See also CA 17-20R; CANR 8, 36
Lieh Tzu fl. 7th cent. B.C.-5th cent. B.C. C M L C
27
Lieksman, Anders
See Haavikko, Paavo Juhani
Li Fei-kan 1904-
See Pa Chin
See also CA 105
Lifton, Robert Jay 1926- .... CLC 67
See also CA 17-20R; CANR 27, 78; INT
CANR-27; SATA 66
Lightfoot, Gordon 1938- .... CLC 26
See also CA 109
Lightman, Alan P(aige) 1948- .... CLC 81
See also CA 141; CANR 63
Ligotti, Thomas (Robert) 1953- CLC 44; SSC
16
See also CA 123; CANR 49

Li Ho 791-817 .... PC 13
Liliencron, (Friedrich Adolf Axel) Detlev von
1844-1909 .... TCLC 18
See also CA 117
Lilly, William 1602-1681 .... LC 27
Lima, Jose Lezama
See Lezama Lima, Jose
Lima Barreto, Afonso Henrique de 1881-1922
TCLC 23
See also CA 117
Limonov, Edward 1944- .... CLC 67
See also CA 137
Lin, Frank
See Atherton, Gertrude (Franklin Horn)
Lincoln, Abraham 1809-1865 .... NCLC 18
Lind, Jakov .... CLC 1, 2, 4, 27, 82
See also Landwirth, Heinz
See also CAAS 4
Lindbergh, Anne (Spencer) Morrow 1906-
CLC 82; DAM NOV
See also CA 17-20R; CANR 16, 73; MTCW 1,
2; SATA 33
Lindsay, David 1878-1945 .... TCLC 15
See also CA 113
Lindsay, (Nicholas) Vachel 1879-1931 . T C L C
17; DA; DAC; DAM MST, POET; PC 23;
WLC
See also CA 114; 135; CDALB 1865-1917; DLB
54; SATA 40
Linke-Poot
See Doeblin, Alfred
Linney, Romulus 1930- .... CLC 51
See also CA 1-4R; CANR 40, 44
Linton, Eliza Lynn 1822-1898 .... NCLC 41
See also DLB 18
Li Po 701-763 .... CMLC 2
Lipsius, Justus 1547-1606 .... LC 16
Lipsyte, Robert (Michael) 1938- CLC 21; DA;
DAC; DAM MST, NOV
See also CA 17-20R; CANR 8, 57; CLR
23; JRDA; MAICYA; SATA 5, 68
Lish, Gordon (Jay) 1934- ..... CLC 45; SSC 18
See also CA 113; 117; DLB 130; INT 117
Lispector, Clarice 1925(?)-1977 CLC 43; SSC
34
See also CA 139; 116; CANR 71; DLB 113
Littell, Robert 1935(?)- .... CLC 42
See also CA 109; 112; CANR 64
Little, Malcolm 1925-1965
See Malcolm X
See also BW 1; CA 125; 111; DA; DAB; DAC;
DAM MST, MULT; MTCW 1, 2
Littlewit, Humphrey Gent.
See Lovecraft, H(oward) P(hillips)
Litwos
See Sienkiewicz, Henryk (Adam Alexander Pius)
Liu, E 1857-1909 .... TCLC 15
See also CA 115
Lively, Penelope (Margaret) 1933- CLC 32, 50;
DAM NOV
See also CA 41-44R; CANR 29, 67; CLR 7; DLB
14, 161, 207; JRDA; MAICYA; MTCW 1, 2;
SATA 7, 60, 101
Livesay, Dorothy (Kathleen) 1909- CLC 4, 15,
79; DAC; DAM MST, POET
See also AITN 2; CA 25-28R; CAAS 8; CANR
36, 67; DLB 68; MTCW 1
Livy c. 59B.C.-c. 17 .... CMLC 11
See also DLB 211
Lizardi, Jose Joaquin Fernandez de 1776-1827
NCLC 30
Llewellyn, Richard
See Llewellyn Lloyd, Richard Dafydd Vivian

See also DLB 15
Llewellyn Lloyd, Richard Dafydd Vivian
1906-1983 .... CLC 7, 80
See also Llewellyn, Richard
See also CA 53-56; 111; CANR 7, 71; SATA 11;
SATA-Obit 37
Llosa, (Jorge) Mario (Pedro) Vargas
See Vargas Llosa, (Jorge) Mario (Pedro)
Lloyd, Manda
See Mander, (Mary) Jane
Lloyd Webber, Andrew 1948-
See Webber, Andrew Lloyd
See also AAYA 1; CA 116; 149; DAM DRAM;
SATA 56
Llull, Ramon c. 1235-c. 1316 .... CMLC 12
Lobb, Ebenezer
See Upward, Allen
Locke, Alain (Le Roy) 1886-1954 .. TCLC 43;
BLCS
See also BW 1; CA 106; 124; DLB 51
Locke, John 1632-1704 .... LC 7, 35
See also DLB 101
Locke-Elliott, Sumner
See Elliott, Sumner Locke
Lockhart, John Gibson 1794-1854 ... NCLC 6
See also DLB 110, 116, 144
Lodge, David (John) 1935- CLC 36; DAM POP
See also BEST 90:1; CA 17-20R; CANR 19, 53;
DLB 14, 194; INT CANR-19; MTCW 1, 2
Lodge, Thomas 1558-1625 .... LC 41
Lodge, Thomas 1558-1625 .... LC 41
See also DLB 172
Loennbohm, Armas Eino Leopold 1878-1926
See Leino, Eino
See also CA 123
Loewinsohn, Ron(ald William) 1937- CLC 52
See also CA 25-28R; CANR 71
Logan, Jake
See Smith, Martin Cruz
Logan, John (Burton) 1923-1987 .... CLC 5
See also CA 77-80; 124; CANR 45; DLB 5
Lo Kuan-chung 1330(?)-1400(?) .... LC 12
Lombard, Nap
See Johnson, Pamela Hansford
London, Jack ... TCLC 9, 15, 39; SSC 4; WLC
See also London, John Griffith
See also AAYA 13; AITN 2; CDALB 1865-1917;
DLB 8, 12, 78, 212; SATA 18
London, John Griffith 1876-1916
See London, Jack
See also CA 110; 119; CANR 73; DA; DAB;
DAC; DAM MST, NOV; JRDA; MAICYA;
MTCW 1, 2
Long, Emmett
See Leonard, Elmore (John, Jr.)
Longbaugh, Harry
See Goldman, William (W.)
Longfellow, Henry Wadsworth 1807-1882
NCLC 2, 45; DA; DAB; DAC; DAM MST,
POET; WLCS
See also CDALB 1640-1865; DLB 1, 59; SATA
19
Longinus c. 1st cent. - .... CMLC 27
See also DLB 176
Longley, Michael 1939- .... CLC 29
See also CA 102; DLB 40
Longus fl. c. 2nd cent. - .... CMLC 7
Longway, A. Hugh
See Lang, Andrew
Lonnrot, Elias 1802-1884 .... NCLC 53
Lopate, Phillip 1943- .... CLC 29
See also CA 97-100; DLBY 80; INT 97-100

Medoff, Mark (Howard) 1940- .... **CLC 6, 23;
  DAM DRAM**
    See also AITN 1; CA 53-56; CANR 5; DLB 7;
    INT CANR-5
Medvedev, P. N.
    See Bakhtin, Mikhail Mikhailovich
Meged, Aharon
    See Megged, Aharon
Meged, Aron
    See Megged, Aharon
Megged, Aharon 1920- .... **CLC 9**
    See also CA 49-52; CAAS 13; CANR 1
Mehta, Ved (Parkash) 1934- .... **CLC 37**
    See also CA 1-4R; CANR 2, 23, 69; MTCW 1
Melanter
    See Blackmore, R(ichard) D(oddridge)
Melies, Georges 1861-1938 .... **TCLC 81**
Melikow, Loris
    See Hofmannsthal, Hugo von
Melmoth, Sebastian
    See Wilde, Oscar
Meltzer, Milton 1915- .... **CLC 26**
    See also AAYA 8; CA 13-16R; CANR 38; CLR
    13; DLB 61; JRDA; MAICYA; SAAS 1;
    SATA 1, 50, 80
Melville, Herman 1819-1891 **NCLC 3, 12, 29,
  45, 49; DA; DAB; DAC; DAM MST, NOV;
  SSC 1, 17; WLC**
    See also AAYA 25; CDALB 1640-1865; DLB 3,
    74; SATA 59
Menander c. 342B.C.-c. 292B.C. ..... **CMLC 9;
  DAM DRAM; DC 3**
    See also DLB 176
Mencken, H(enry) L(ouis) 1880-1956**TCLC 13**
    See also CA 105; 125; CDALB 1917-1929; DLB
    11, 29, 63, 137; MTCW 1, 2
Mendelsohn, Jane 1965(?)- .... **CLC 99**
    See also CA 154
Mercer, David 1928-1980**CLC 5; DAM DRAM**
    See also CA 9-12R; 102; CANR 23; DLB 13;
    MTCW 1
Merchant, Paul
    See Ellison, Harlan (Jay)
Meredith, George 1828-1909 ... **TCLC 17, 43;
  DAM POET**
    See also CA 117; 153; CDBLB 1832-1890; DLB
    18, 35, 57, 159
Meredith, William (Morris) 1919- **CLC 4, 13,
  22, 55; DAM POET**
    See also CA 9-12R; CAAS 14; CANR 6, 40; DLB
    5
Merezhkovsky, Dmitry Sergeyevich 1865-1941
    TCLC 29
    See also CA 169
Merimee, Prosper 1803-1870**NCLC 6, 65; SSC
  7**
    See also DLB 119, 192
Merkin, Daphne 1954- .... **CLC 44**
    See also CA 123
Merlin, Arthur
    See Blish, James (Benjamin)
Merrill, James (Ingram) 1926-1995 **CLC 2, 3,
  6, 8, 13, 18, 34, 91; DAM POET**
    See also CA 13-16R; 147; CANR 10, 49, 63;
    DLB 5, 165; DLBY 85; INT CANR-10;
    MTCW 1, 2
Merriman, Alex
    See Silverberg, Robert
Merriman, Brian 1747-1805 .... **NCLC 70**
Merritt, E. B.
    See Waddington, Miriam

Merton, Thomas 1915-1968 **CLC 1, 3, 11, 34,
  83; PC 10**
    See also CA 5-8R; 25-28R; CANR 22, 53; DLB
    48; DLBY 81; MTCW 1, 2
Merwin, W(illiam) S(tanley) 1927-**CLC 1, 2, 3,
  5, 8, 13, 18, 45, 88; DAM POET**
    See also CA 13-16R; CANR 15, 51; DLB 5, 169;
    INT CANR-15; MTCW 1, 2
Metcalf, John 1938- .... **CLC 37**
    See also CA 113; DLB 60
Metcalf, Suzanne
    See Baum, L(yman) Frank
Mew, Charlotte (Mary) 1870-1928 ... **TCLC 8**
    See also CA 105; DLB 19, 135
Mewshaw, Michael 1943- .... **CLC 9**
    See also CA 53-56; CANR 7, 47; DLBY 80
Meyer, June
    See Jordan, June
Meyer, Lynn
    See Slavitt, David R(ytman)
Meyer-Meyrink, Gustav 1868-1932
    See Meyrink, Gustav
    See also CA 117
Meyers, Jeffrey 1939- .... **CLC 39**
    See also CA 73-76; CANR 54; DLB 111
Meynell, Alice (Christina Gertrude Thompson)
  1847-1922 .... **TCLC 6**
    See also CA 104; DLB 19, 98
Meyrink, Gustav .... **TCLC 21**
    See also Meyer-Meyrink, Gustav
    See also DLB 81
Michaels, Leonard 1933- . **CLC 6, 25; SSC 16**
    See also CA 61-64; CANR 21, 62; DLB 130;
    MTCW 1
Michaux, Henri 1899-1984 .... **CLC 8, 19**
    See also CA 85-88; 114
Micheaux, Oscar 1884-1951 .... **TCLC 76**
    See also DLB 50
Michelangelo 1475-1564 .... **LC 12**
Michelet, Jules 1798-1874 .... **NCLC 31**
Michels, Robert 1876-1936 .... **TCLC 88**
Michener, James A(lbert) 1907(?)-1997**CLC 1,
  5, 11, 29, 60, 109; DAM NOV, POP**
    See also AAYA 27; AITN 1; BEST 90:1; CA
    5-8R; 161; CANR 21, 45, 68; DLB 6; MTCW
    1, 2
Mickiewicz, Adam 1798-1855 .... **NCLC 3**
Middleton, Christopher 1926- .... **CLC 13**
    See also CA 13-16R; CANR 29, 54; DLB 40
Middleton, Richard (Barham) 1882-1911
    TCLC 56
    See also DLB 156
Middleton, Stanley 1919- .... **CLC 7, 38**
    See also CA 25-28R; CAAS 23; CANR 21, 46;
    DLB 14
Middleton, Thomas 1580-1627 . **LC 33; DAM
  DRAM, MST; DC 5**
    See also DLB 58
Migueis, Jose Rodrigues 1901- .... **CLC 10**
Mikszath, Kalman 1847-1910 .... **TCLC 31**
    See also CA 170
Miles, Jack .... **CLC 100**
Miles, Josephine (Louise) 1911-1985**CLC 1, 2,
  14, 34, 39; DAM POET**
    See also CA 1-4R; 116; CANR 2, 55; DLB 48
Militant
    See Sandburg, Carl (August)
Mill, John Stuart 1806-1873 ..... **NCLC 11, 58**
    See also CDBLB 1832-1890; DLB 55, 190
Millar, Kenneth 1915-1983**CLC 14; DAM POP**
    See also Macdonald, Ross
    See also CA 9-12R; 110; CANR 16, 63; DLB 2;
    DLBD 6; DLBY 83; MTCW 1, 2

Millay, E. Vincent
    See Millay, Edna St. Vincent
Millay, Edna St. Vincent 1892-1950 . **TCLC 4,
  49; DA; DAB; DAC; DAM MST, POET; PC
  6; WLCS**
    See also CA 104; 130; CDALB 1917-1929; DLB
    45; MTCW 1, 2
Miller, Arthur 1915-**CLC 1, 2, 6, 10, 15, 26, 47,
  78; DA; DAB; DAC; DAM DRAM, MST;
  DC 1; WLC**
    See also AAYA 15; AITN 1; CA 1-4R; CABS 3;
    CANR 2, 30, 54, 76; CDALB 1941-1968;
    DLB 7; MTCW 1, 2
Miller, Henry (Valentine) 1891-1980**CLC 1, 2,
  4, 9, 14, 43, 84; DA; DAB; DAC; DAM
  MST, NOV; WLC**
    See also CA 9-12R; 97-100; CANR 33, 64;
    CDALB 1929-1941; DLB 4, 9; DLBY 80;
    MTCW 1, 2
Miller, Jason 1939(?)- .... **CLC 2**
    See also AITN 1; CA 73-76; DLB 7
Miller, Sue 1943- .... **CLC 44; DAM POP**
    See also BEST 90:3; CA 139; CANR 59; DLB
    143
Miller, Walter M(ichael, Jr.) 1923- **CLC 4, 30**
    See also CA 85-88; DLB 8
Millett, Kate 1934- .... **CLC 67**
    See also AITN 1; CA 73-76; CANR 32, 53, 76;
    MTCW 1, 2
Millhauser, Steven (Lewis) 1943- **CLC 21, 54,
  109**
    See also CA 110; 111; CANR 63; DLB 2; INT
    111; MTCW 2
Millin, Sarah Gertrude 1889-1968 .... **CLC 49**
    See also CA 102; 93-96
Milne, A(lan) A(lexander) 1882-1956**TCLC 6,
  88; DAB; DAC; DAM MST**
    See also CA 104; 133; CLR 1, 26; DLB 10, 77,
    100, 160; MAICYA; MTCW 1, 2; SATA 100;
    YABC 1
Milner, Ron(ald) 1938-**CLC 56; BLC 3; DAM
  MULT**
    See also AITN 1; BW 1; CA 73-76; CANR 24;
    DLB 38; MTCW 1
Milnes, Richard Monckton 1809-1885 **N C L C
  61**
    See also DLB 32, 184
Milosz, Czeslaw 1911-**CLC 5, 11, 22, 31, 56, 82;
  DAM MST, POET; PC 8; WLCS**
    See also CA 81-84; CANR 23, 51; MTCW 1, 2
Milton, John 1608-1674 . **LC 9, 43; DA; DAB;
  DAC; DAM MST, POET; PC 19; WLC**
    See also CDBLB 1660-1789; DLB 131, 151
Min, Anchee 1957- .... **CLC 86**
    See also CA 146
Minehaha, Cornelius
    See Wedekind, (Benjamin) Frank(lin)
Miner, Valerie 1947- .... **CLC 40**
    See also CA 97-100; CANR 59
Minimo, Duca
    See D'Annunzio, Gabriele
Minot, Susan 1956- .... **CLC 44**
    See also CA 134
Minus, Ed 1938- .... **CLC 39**
Miranda, Javier
    See Bioy Casares, Adolfo
Mirbeau, Octave 1848-1917 .... **TCLC 55**
    See also DLB 123, 192
Miro (Ferrer), Gabriel (Francisco Victor)
  1879-1930 .... **TCLC 5**
    See also CA 104

See also CA 111

Morris, William 1834-1896 .... **NCLC 4**
See also CDBLB 1832-1890; DLB 18, 35, 57, 156, 178, 184

Morris, Wright 1910-1998 **CLC 1, 3, 7, 18, 37**
See also CA 9-12R; 167; CANR 21; DLB 2, 206; DLBY 81; MTCW 1, 2

Morrison, Arthur 1863-1945 .... **TCLC 72**
See also CA 120; 157; DLB 70, 135, 197

Morrison, Chloe Anthony Wofford
See Morrison, Toni

Morrison, James Douglas 1943-1971
See Morrison, Jim
See also CA 73-76; CANR 40

Morrison, Jim .... **CLC 17**
See also Morrison, James Douglas

Morrison, Toni 1931- **CLC 4, 10, 22, 55, 81, 87; BLC 3; DA; DAB; DAC; DAM MST, MULT, NOV, POP**
See also AAYA 1, 22; BW 2; CA 29-32R; CANR 27, 42, 67; CDALB 1968-1988; DLB 6, 33, 143; DLBY 81; MTCW 1, 2; SATA 57

Morrison, Van 1945- .... **CLC 21**
See also CA 116; 168

Morrissy, Mary 1958- .... **CLC 99**

Mortimer, John (Clifford) 1923- **CLC 28, 43; DAM DRAM, POP**
See also CA 13-16R; CANR 21, 69; CDBLB 1960 to Present; DLB 13; INT CANR-21; MTCW 1, 2

Mortimer, Penelope (Ruth) 1918- .... **CLC 5**
See also CA 57-60; CANR 45

Morton, Anthony
See Creasey, John

Mosca, Gaetano 1858-1941 .... **TCLC 75**

Mosher, Howard Frank 1943- .... **CLC 62**
See also CA 139; CANR 65

Mosley, Nicholas 1923- .... **CLC 43, 70**
See also CA 69-72; CANR 41, 60; DLB 14, 207

Mosley, Walter 1952- . **CLC 97; BLCS; DAM MULT, POP**
See also AAYA 17; BW 2; CA 142; CANR 57; MTCW 2

Moss, Howard 1922-1987 . **CLC 7, 14, 45, 50; DAM POET**
See also CA 1-4R; 123; CANR 1, 44; DLB 5

Mossgiel, Rab
See Burns, Robert

Motion, Andrew (Peter) 1952- .... **CLC 47**
See also CA 146; DLB 40

Motley, Willard (Francis) 1909-1965 **CLC 18**
See also BW 1; CA 117; 106; DLB 76, 143

Motoori, Norinaga 1730-1801 .... **NCLC 45**

Mott, Michael (Charles Alston) 1930- **CLC 15, 34**
See also CA 5-8R; CAAS 7; CANR 7, 29

Mountain Wolf Woman 1884-1960 .... **CLC 92**
See also CA 144; NNAL

Moure, Erin 1955- .... **CLC 88**
See also CA 113; DLB 60

Mowat, Farley (McGill) 1921- **CLC 26; DAC; DAM MST**
See also AAYA 1; CA 1-4R; CANR 4, 24, 42, 68; CLR 20; DLB 68; INT CANR-24; JRDA; MAICYA; MTCW 1, 2; SATA 3, 55

Mowatt, Anna Cora 1819-1870 .... **NCLC 74**

Moyers, Bill 1934- .... **CLC 74**
See also AITN 2; CA 61-64; CANR 31, 52

Mphahlele, Es'kia
See Mphahlele, Ezekiel
See also DLB 125

Mphahlele, Ezekiel 1919-1983 **CLC 25; BLC 3; DAM MULT**
See also Mphahlele, Es'kia
See also BW 2; CA 81-84; CANR 26, 76; MTCW 2

Mqhayi, S(amuel) E(dward) K(rune Loliwe) 1875-1945 **TCLC 25; BLC 3; DAM MULT**
See also CA 153

Mrozek, Slawomir 1930- .... **CLC 3, 13**
See also CA 13-16R; CAAS 10; CANR 29; MTCW 1

Mrs. Belloc-Lowndes
See Lowndes, Marie Adelaide (Belloc)

Mtwa, Percy (?)- .... **CLC 47**

Mueller, Lisel 1924- .... **CLC 13, 51**
See also CA 93-96; DLB 105

Muir, Edwin 1887-1959 .... **TCLC 2, 87**
See also CA 104; DLB 20, 100, 191

Muir, John 1838-1914 .... **TCLC 28**
See also CA 165; DLB 186

Mujica Lainez, Manuel 1910-1984 .... **CLC 31**
See also Lainez, Manuel Mujica
See also CA 81-84; 112; CANR 32; HW

Mukherjee, Bharati 1940- **CLC 53, 115; DAM NOV**
See also BEST 89:2; CA 107; CANR 45, 72; DLB 60; MTCW 1, 2

Muldoon, Paul 1951- **CLC 32, 72; DAM POET**
See also CA 113; 129; CANR 52; DLB 40; INT 129

Mulisch, Harry 1927- .... **CLC 42**
See also CA 9-12R; CANR 6, 26, 56

Mull, Martin 1943- .... **CLC 17**
See also CA 105

Muller, Wilhelm .... **NCLC 73**

Mulock, Dinah Maria
See Craik, Dinah Maria (Mulock)

Munford, Robert 1737(?)-1783 .... **LC 5**
See also DLB 31

Mungo, Raymond 1946- .... **CLC 72**
See also CA 49-52; CANR 2

Munro, Alice 1931- **CLC 6, 10, 19, 50, 95; DAC; DAM MST, NOV; SSC 3; WLCS**
See also AITN 2; CA 33-36R; CANR 33, 53, 75; DLB 53; MTCW 1, 2; SATA 29

Munro, H(ector) H(ugh) 1870-1916
See Saki
See also CA 104; 130; CDBLB 1890-1914; DA; DAB; DAC; DAM MST, NOV; DLB 34, 162; MTCW 1, 2; WLC

Murdoch, (Jean) Iris 1919- **CLC 1, 2, 3, 4, 6, 8, 11, 15, 22, 31, 51; DAB; DAC; DAM MST, NOV**
See also CA 13-16R; CANR 8, 43, 68; CDBLB 1960 to Present; DLB 14, 194; INT CANR-8; MTCW 1, 2

Murfree, Mary Noailles 1850-1922 .... **SSC 22**
See also CA 122; DLB 12, 74

Murnau, Friedrich Wilhelm
See Plumpe, Friedrich Wilhelm

Murphy, Richard 1927- .... **CLC 41**
See also CA 29-32R; DLB 40

Murphy, Sylvia 1937- .... **CLC 34**
See also CA 121

Murphy, Thomas (Bernard) 1935- .... **CLC 51**
See also CA 101

Murray, Albert L. 1916- .... **CLC 73**
See also BW 2; CA 49-52; CANR 26, 52, 78; DLB 38

Murray, Judith Sargent 1751-1820 **NCLC 63**
See also DLB 37, 200

Murray, Les(lie) A(llan) 1938- **CLC 40; DAM POET**
See also CA 21-24R; CANR 11, 27, 56

Murry, J. Middleton
See Murry, John Middleton

Murry, John Middleton 1889-1957 **TCLC 16**
See also CA 118; DLB 149

Musgrave, Susan 1951- .... **CLC 13, 54**
See also CA 69-72; CANR 45

Musil, Robert (Edler von) 1880-1942 . **TCLC 12, 68; SSC 18**
See also CA 109; CANR 55; DLB 81, 124; MTCW 2

Muske, Carol 1945- .... **CLC 90**
See also Muske-Dukes, Carol (Anne)

Muske-Dukes, Carol (Anne) 1945-
See Muske, Carol
See also CA 65-68; CANR 32, 70

Musset, (Louis Charles) Alfred de 1810-1857 **NCLC 7**
See also DLB 192

My Brother's Brother
See Chekhov, Anton (Pavlovich)

Myers, L(eopold) H(amilton) 1881-1944 **TCLC 59**
See also CA 157; DLB 15

Myers, Walter Dean 1937- ... **CLC 35; BLC 3; DAM MULT, NOV**
See also AAYA 4, 23; BW 2; CA 33-36R; CANR 20, 42, 67; CLR 4, 16, 35; DLB 33; INT CANR-20; JRDA; MAICYA; MTCW 2; SAAS 2; SATA 41, 71; SATA-Brief 27

Myers, Walter M.
See Myers, Walter Dean

Myles, Symon
See Follett, Ken(neth Martin)

Nabokov, Vladimir (Vladimirovich) 1899-1977 **CLC 1, 2, 3, 6, 8, 11, 15, 23, 44, 46, 64; DA; DAB; DAC; DAM MST, NOV; SSC 11; WLC**
See also CA 5-8R; 69-72; CANR 20; CDALB 1941-1968; DLB 2; DLBD 3; DLBY 80, 91; MTCW 1, 2

Nagai Kafu 1879-1959 .... **TCLC 51**
See also Nagai Sokichi
See also DLB 180

Nagai Sokichi 1879-1959
See Nagai Kafu
See also CA 117

Nagy, Laszlo 1925-1978 .... **CLC 7**
See also CA 129; 112

Naidu, Sarojini 1879-1943 .... **TCLC 80**

Naipaul, Shiva(dhar Srinivasa) 1945-1985 **CLC 32, 39; DAM NOV**
See also CA 110; 112; 116; CANR 33; DLB 157; DLBY 85; MTCW 1, 2

Naipaul, V(idiadhar) S(urajprasad) 1932- **CLC 4, 7, 9, 13, 18, 37, 105; DAB; DAC; DAM MST, NOV**
See also CA 1-4R; CANR 1, 33, 51; CDBLB 1960 to Present; DLB 125, 204, 206; DLBY 85; MTCW 1, 2

Nakos, Lilika 1899(?)- .... **CLC 29**

Narayan, R(asipuram) K(rishnaswami) 1906- **CLC 7, 28, 47; DAM NOV; SSC 25**
See also CA 81-84; CANR 33, 61; MTCW 1, 2; SATA 62

Nash, (Frediric) Ogden 1902-1971 .. **CLC 23; DAM POET; PC 21**
See also CA 13-14; 29-32R; CANR 34, 61; CAP 1; DLB 11; MAICYA; MTCW 1, 2; SATA 2, 46

Ostrovsky, Alexander 1823-1886 NCLC **30, 57**
Otero, Blas de 1916-1979 .... **CLC 11**
　See also CA 89-92; DLB 134
Otto, Rudolf 1869-1937 .... **TCLC 85**
Otto, Whitney 1955- .... **CLC 70**
　See also CA 140
Ouida .... **TCLC 43**
　See also De La Ramee, (Marie) Louise
　See also DLB 18, 156
Ousmane, Sembene 1923- ..... **CLC 66; BLC 3**
　See also BW 1; CA 117; 125; MTCW 1
Ovid 43B.C.-17 **CMLC 7; DAM POET; PC 2**
　See also DLB 211
Owen, Hugh
　See Faust, Frederick (Schiller)
Owen, Wilfred (Edward Salter) 1893-1918
　　TCLC 5, 27; DA; DAB; DAC; DAM MST,
　　POET; PC 19; WLC
　See also CA 104; 141; CDBLB 1914-1945; DLB
　　20; MTCW 2
Owens, Rochelle 1936- .... **CLC 8**
　See also CA 17-20R; CAAS 2; CANR 39
Oz, Amos 1939- **CLC 5, 8, 11, 27, 33, 54; DAM**
　　NOV
　See also CA 53-56; CANR 27, 47, 65; MTCW
　　1, 2
Ozick, Cynthia 1928- . **CLC 3, 7, 28, 62; DAM**
　　NOV, POP; SSC 15
　See also BEST 90:1; CA 17-20R; CANR 23, 58;
　　DLB 28, 152; DLBY 82; INT CANR-23;
　　MTCW 1, 2
Ozu, Yasujiro 1903-1963 .... **CLC 16**
　See also CA 112
Pacheco, C.
　See Pessoa, Fernando (Antonio Nogueira)
Pa Chin .... **CLC 18**
　See also Li Fei-kan
Pack, Robert 1929- .... **CLC 13**
　See also CA 1-4R; CANR 3, 44; DLB 5
Padgett, Lewis
　See Kuttner, Henry
Padilla (Lorenzo), Heberto 1932- ...... **CLC 38**
　See also AITN 1; CA 123; 131; HW
Page, Jimmy 1944- .... **CLC 12**
Page, Louise 1955- .... **CLC 40**
　See also CA 140; CANR 76
Page, P(atricia) K(athleen) 1916- . **CLC 7, 18;**
　　DAC; DAM MST; PC 12
　See also CA 53-56; CANR 4, 22, 65; DLB 68;
　　MTCW 1
Page, Thomas Nelson 1853-1922 .... **SSC 23**
　See also CA 118; DLB 12, 78; DLBD 13
Pagels, Elaine Hiesey 1943- .... **CLC 104**
　See also CA 45-48; CANR 2, 24, 51
Paget, Violet 1856-1935
　See Lee, Vernon
　See also CA 104; 166
Paget-Lowe, Henry
　See Lovecraft, H(oward) P(hillips)
Paglia, Camille (Anna) 1947- .... **CLC 68**
　See also CA 140; CANR 72; MTCW 2
Paige, Richard
　See Koontz, Dean R(ay)
Paine, Thomas 1737-1809 .... **NCLC 62**
　See also CDALB 1640-1865; DLB 31, 43, 73,
　　158
Pakenham, Antonia
　See Fraser, (Lady) Antonia (Pakenham)
Palamas, Kostes 1859-1943 .... **TCLC 5**
　See also CA 105
Palazzeschi, Aldo 1885-1974 .... **CLC 11**
　See also CA 89-92; 53-56; DLB 114

Paley, Grace 1922- **CLC 4, 6, 37; DAM POP;**
　　SSC 8
　See also CA 25-28R; CANR 13, 46, 74; DLB
　　28; INT CANR-13; MTCW 1, 2
Palin, Michael (Edward) 1943- .... **CLC 21**
　See also Monty Python
　See also CA 107; CANR 35; SATA 67
Palliser, Charles 1947- .... **CLC 65**
　See also CA 136; CANR 76
Palma, Ricardo 1833-1919 .... **TCLC 29**
　See also CA 168
Pancake, Breece Dexter 1952-1979
　See Pancake, Breece D'J
　<indexSee also CA 123; 109
Pancake, Breece D'J .... **CLC 29**
　See also Pancake, Breece Dexter
　See also DLB 130
Panko, Rudy
　See Gogol, Nikolai (Vasilyevich)
Papadiamantis, Alexandros 1851-1911 **T C L C**
　29
　See also CA 168
Papadiamantopoulos, Johannes 1856-1910
　See Moreas, Jean
　See also CA 117
Papini, Giovanni 1881-1956 .... **TCLC 22**
　See also CA 121
Paracelsus 1493-1541 .... **LC 14**
　See also DLB 179
Parasol, Peter
　See Stevens, Wallace
Pardo Bazan, Emilia 1851-1921 .... **SSC 30**
Pareto, Vilfredo 1848-1923 .... **TCLC 69**
Parfenie, Maria
　See Codrescu, Andrei
Parini, Jay (Lee) 1948- .... **CLC 54**
　See also CA 97-100; CAAS 16; CANR 32
Park, Jordan
　See Kornbluth, C(yril) M.; Pohl, Frederik
Park, Robert E(zra) 1864-1944 .... **TCLC 73**
　See also CA 122; 165
Parker, Bert
　See Ellison, Harlan (Jay)
Parker, Dorothy (Rothschild) 1893-1967 **C L C**
　　15, 68; DAM POET; SSC 2
　See also CA 19-20; 25-28R; CAP 2; DLB 11,
　　45, 86; MTCW 1, 2
Parker, Robert B(rown) 1932- **CLC 27; DAM**
　　NOV, POP
　See also AAYA 28; BEST 89:4; CA 49-52;
　　CANR 1, 26, 52; INT CANR-26; MTCW 1
Parkin, Frank 1940- .... **CLC 43**
　See also CA 147
Parkman, Francis, Jr. 1823-1893 .... **NCLC 12**
　See also DLB 1, 30, 186
Parks, Gordon (Alexander Buchanan) 1912-
　　CLC 1, 16; BLC 3; DAM MULT
　See also AITN 2; BW 2; CA 41-44R; CANR 26,
　　66; DLB 33; MTCW 2; SATA 8
Parmenides c. 515B.C.-c. 450B.C. .. **CMLC 22**
　See also DLB 176
Parnell, Thomas 1679-1718 .... **LC 3**
　See also DLB 94
Parra, Nicanor 1914- **CLC 2, 102; DAM MULT;**
　　HLC
　See also CA 85-88; CANR 32; HW; MTCW 1
Parrish, Mary Frances
　See Fisher, M(ary) F(rances) K(ennedy)
Parson
　See Coleridge, Samuel Taylor
Parson Lot
　See Kingsley, Charles

Partridge, Anthony
　See Oppenheim, E(dward) Phillips
Pascal, Blaise 1623-1662 .... **LC 35**
Pascoli, Giovanni 1855-1912 .... **TCLC 45**
　See also CA 170
Pasolini, Pier Paolo 1922-1975 **CLC 20, 37, 106;**
　　PC 17
　See also CA 93-96; 61-64; CANR 63; DLB 128,
　　177; MTCW 1
Pasquini
　See Silone, Ignazio
Pastan, Linda (Olenik) 1932- .. **CLC 27; DAM**
　　POET
　See also CA 61-64; CANR 18, 40, 61; DLB 5
Pasternak, Boris (Leonidovich) 1890-1960
　　CLC 7, 10, 18, 63; DA; DAB; DAC; DAM
　　MST, NOV, POET; PC 6; SSC 31; WLC
　See also CA 127; 116; MTCW 1, 2
Patchen, Kenneth 1911-1972 .... **CLC 1, 2, 18;**
　　DAM POET
　See also CA 1-4R; 33-36R; CANR 3, 35; DLB
　　16, 48; MTCW 1
Pater, Walter (Horatio) 1839-1894 ... **NCLC 7**
　See also CDBLB 1832-1890; DLB 57, 156
Paterson, A(ndrew) B(arton) 1864-1941 **TCLC**
　　32
　See also CA 155; SATA 97
Paterson, Katherine (Womeldorf) 1932- **C L C**
　　12, 30
　See also AAYA 1; CA 21-24R; CANR 28, 59;
　　CLR 7, 50; DLB 52; JRDA; MAICYA;
　　MTCW 1; SATA 13, 53, 92
Patmore, Coventry Kersey Dighton 1823-1896
　　NCLC 9
　See also DLB 35, 98
Paton, Alan (Stewart) 1903-1988 **CLC 4, 10, 25,**
　　55, 106; DA; DAB; DAC; DAM MST, NOV;
　　WLC
　See also AAYA 26; CA 13-16; 125; CANR 22;
　　CAP 1; DLBD 17; MTCW 1, 2; SATA 11;
　　SATA-Obit 56
Paton Walsh, Gillian 1937-
　See Walsh, Jill Paton
　See also CANR 38; JRDA; MAICYA; SAAS 3;
　　SATA 4, 72
Patton, George S. 1885-1945 .... **TCLC 79**
Paulding, James Kirke 1778-1860 .... **NCLC 2**
　See also DLB 3, 59, 74
Paulin, Thomas Neilson 1949-
　See Paulin, Tom
　See also CA 123; 128
Paulin, Tom .... **CLC 37**
　See also Paulin, Thomas Neilson
　See also DLB 40
Paustovsky, Konstantin (Georgievich)
　　1892-1968 .... **CLC 40**
　See also CA 93-96; 25-28R
Pavese, Cesare 1908-1950 **TCLC 3; PC 13; SSC**
　　19
　See also CA 104; 169; DLB 128, 177
Pavic, Milorad 1929- .... **CLC 60**
　See also CA 136; DLB 181
Pavlov, Ivan Petrovich 1849-1936 .. **TCLC 91**
　See also CA 118
Payne, Alan
　See Jakes, John (William)
Paz, Gil
　See Lugones, Leopoldo
Paz, Octavio 1914-1998 **CLC 3, 4, 6, 10, 19, 51,**
　　65, 119; DA; DAB; DAC; DAM MST,
　　MULT, POET; HLC; PC 1; WLC
　See also CA 73-76; 165; CANR 32, 65; DLBY
　　90, 98; HW; MTCW 1, 2

p'Bitek, Okot 1931-1982 **CLC 96; BLC 3; DAM MULT**
See also BW 2; CA 124; 107; DLB 125; MTCW 1, 2

Peacock, Molly 1947- .... **CLC 60**
See also CA 103; CAAS 21; CANR 52; DLB 120

Peacock, Thomas Love 1785-1866 .. **NCLC 22**
See also DLB 96, 116

Peake, Mervyn 1911-1968 .... **CLC 7, 54**
See also CA 5-8R; 25-28R; CANR 3; DLB 15, 160; MTCW 1; SATA 23

Pearce, Philippa .... **CLC 21**
See also Christie, (Ann) Philippa
See also CLR 9; DLB 161; MAICYA; SATA 1, 67

Pearl, Eric
See Elman, Richard (Martin)

Pearson, T(homas) R(eid) 1956- .... **CLC 39**
See also CA 120; 130; INT 130

Peck, Dale 1967- .... **CLC 81**
See also CA 146; CANR 72

Peck, John 1941- .... **CLC 3**
See also CA 49-52; CANR 3

Peck, Richard (Wayne) 1934- .... **CLC 21**
See also AAYA 1, 24; CA 85-88; CANR 19, 38; CLR 15; INT CANR-19; JRDA; MAICYA; SAAS 2; SATA 18, 55, 97

Peck, Robert Newton 1928- **CLC 17; DA; DAC; DAM MST**
See also AAYA 3; CA 81-84; CANR 31, 63; CLR 45; JRDA; MAICYA; SAAS 1; SATA 21, 62

Peckinpah, (David) Sam(uel) 1925-1984 **CLC 20**
See also CA 109; 114

Pedersen, Knut 1859-1952
See Hamsun, Knut
See also CA 104; 119; CANR 63; MTCW 1, 2

Peeslake, Gaffer
See Durrell, Lawrence (George)

Peguy, Charles Pierre 1873-1914 .... **TCLC 10**
See also CA 107

Peirce, Charles Sanders 1839-1914 **TCLC 81**

Pena, Ramon del Valle y
<indSee Valle-Inclan, Ramon (Maria) del

Pendennis, Arthur Esquir
See Thackeray, William Makepeace

Penn, William 1644-1718 .... **LC 25**
See also DLB 24

PEPECE
See Prado (Calvo), Pedro

Pepys, Samuel 1633-1703 .. **LC 11; DA; DAB; DAC; DAM MST; WLC**
See also CDBLB 1660-1789; DLB 101

Percy, Walker 1916-1990 **CLC 2, 3, 6, 8, 14, 18, 47, 65; DAM NOV, POP**
See also CA 1-4R; 131; CANR 1, 23, 64; DLB 2; DLBY 80, 90; MTCW 1, 2

Percy, William Alexander 1885-1942 **TCLC 84**
See also CA 163; MTCW 2

Perec, Georges 1936-1982 .... **CLC 56, 116**
See also CA 141; DLB 83

Pereda (y Sanchez de Porrua), Jose Maria de 1833-1906 .... **TCLC 16**
See also CA 117

Pereda y Porrua, Jose Maria de
See Pereda (y Sanchez de Porrua), Jose Maria de

Peregoy, George Weems
See Mencken, H(enry) L(ouis)

Perelman, S(idney) J(oseph) 1904-1979 **CLC 3, 5, 9, 15, 23, 44, 49; DAM DRAM; SSC 32**
See also AITN 1, 2; CA 73-76; 89-92; CANR 18; DLB 11, 44; MTCW 1, 2

Peret, Benjamin 1899-1959 .... **TCLC 20**
See also CA 117

Peretz, Isaac Loeb 1851(?)-1915 **TCLC 16; SSC 26**
See also CA 109

Peretz, Yitzkhok Leibush
See Peretz, Isaac Loeb

Perez Galdos, Benito 1843-1920 ..... **TCLC 27**
See also CA 125; 153; HW

Perrault, Charles 1628-1703 .... **LC 2**
See also MAICYA; SATA 25

Perry, Brighton
See Sherwood, Robert E(mmet)

Perse, St.-John
See Leger, (Marie-Rene Auguste) Alexis Saint-Leger

Perutz, Leo(pold) 1882-1957 .... **TCLC 60**
See also CA 147; DLB 81

Peseenz, Tulio F.
See Lopez y Fuentes, Gregorio

Pesetsky, Bette 1932- .... **CLC 28**
See also CA 133; DLB 130

Peshkov, Alexei Maximovich 1868-1936
See Gorky, Maxim
See also CA 105; 141; DA; DAC; DAM DRAM, MST, NOV; MTCW 2

Pessoa, Fernando (Antonio Nogueira) 1888-1935 **TCLC 27; DAM MULT; HLC; PC 20**
See also CA 125

Peterkin, Julia Mood 1880-1961 .... **CLC 31**
See also CA 102; DLB 9

Peters, Joan K(aren) 1945- .... **CLC 39**
See also CA 158

Peters, Robert L(ouis) 1924- .... **CLC 7**
See also CA 13-16R; CAAS 8; DLB 105

Petofi, Sandor 1823-1849 .... **NCLC 21**

Petrakis, Harry Mark 1923- .... **CLC 3**
See also CA 9-12R; CANR 4, 30

Petrarch 1304-1374 **CMLC 20; DAM POET; PC 8**

Petrov, Evgeny .... **TCLC 21**
See also Kataev, Evgeny Petrovich

Petry, Ann (Lane) 1908-1997 ..... **CLC 1, 7, 18**
See also BW 1; CA 5-8R; 157; CAAS 6; CANR 4, 46; CLR 12; DLB 76; JRDA; MAICYA; MTCW 1; SATA 5; SATA-Obit 94

Petursson, Halligrimur 1614-1674 .... **LC 8**

Peychinovich
See Vazov, Ivan (Minchov)

Phaedrus c. 18B.C.-c. 50 .... **CMLC 25**
See also DLB 211

Philips, Katherine 1632-1664 .... **LC 30**
See also DLB 131

Philipson, Morris H. 1926- .... **CLC 53**
See also CA 1-4R; CANR 4

Phillips, Caryl 1958- .. **CLC 96; BLCS; DAM MULT**
See also BW 2; CA 141; CANR 63; DLB 157; MTCW 2

Phillips, David Graham 1867-1911 . **TCLC 44**
See also CA 108; DLB 9, 12

Phillips, Jack
See Sandburg, Carl (August)

Phillips, Jayne Anne 1952- **CLC 15, 33; SSC 16**
See also CA 101; CANR 24, 50; DLBY 80; INT CANR-24; MTCW 1, 2

Phillips, Richard
See Dick, Philip K(indred)

Phillips, Robert (Schaeffer) 1938- ..... **CLC 28**
See also CA 17-20R; CAAS 13; CANR 8; DLB 105

Phillips, Ward
See Lovecraft, H(oward) P(hillips)

Piccolo, Lucio 1901-1969 .... **CLC 13**
See also CA 97-100; DLB 114

Pickthall, Marjorie L(owry) C(hristie) 1883-1922 .... **TCLC 21**
See also CA 107; DLB 92

Pico della Mirandola, Giovanni 1463-1494 **LC 15**

Piercy, Marge 1936- .. **CLC 3, 6, 14, 18, 27, 62**
See also CA 21-24R; CAAS 1; CANR 13, 43, 66; DLB 120; MTCW 1, 2

Piers, Robert
See Anthony, Piers

Pieyre de Mandiargues, Andre 1909-1991
See Mandiargues, Andre Pieyre de
See also CA 103; 136; CANR 22

Pilnyak, Boris .... **TCLC 23**
See also Vogau, Boris Andreyevich

Pincherle, Alberto 1907-1990 .... **CLC 11, 18; DAM NOV**
See also Moravia, Alberto
See also CA 25-28R; 132; CANR 33, 63; MTCW 1

Pinckney, Darryl 1953- .... **CLC 76**
See also BW 2; CA 143

Pindar 518B.C.-446B.C. ...... **CMLC 12; PC 19**
See also DLB 176

Pineda, Cecile 1942- .... **CLC 39**
See also CA 118

Pinero, Arthur Wing 1855-1934 .... **TCLC 32; DAM DRAM**
See also CA 110; 153; DLB 10

Pinero, Miguel (Antonio Gomez) 1946-1988 **CLC 4, 55**
See also CA 61-64; 125; CANR 29; HW

Pinget, Robert 1919-1997 .... **CLC 7, 13, 37**
See also CA 85-88; 160; DLB 83

Pink Floyd
See Barrett, (Roger) Syd; Gilmour, David; Mason, Nick; Waters, Roger; Wright, Rick

Pinkney, Edward 1802-1828 .... **NCLC 31**

Pinkwater, Daniel Manus 1941- .... **CLC 35**
See also Pinkwater, Manus
See also AAYA 1; CA 29-32R; CANR 12, 38; CLR 4; JRDA; MAICYA; SAAS 3; SATA 46, 76

Pinkwater, Manus
See Pinkwater, Daniel Manus
See also SATA 8

Pinsky, Robert 1940- **CLC 9, 19, 38, 94; DAM POET**
See also CA 29-32R; CAAS 4; CANR 58; DLBY 82, 98; MTCW 2

Pinta, Harold
See Pinter, Harold

Pinter, Harold 1930- **CLC 1, 3, 6, 9, 11, 15, 27, 58, 73; DA; DAB; DAC; DAM DRAM, MST; WLC**
See also CA 5-8R; CANR 33, 65; CDBLB 1960 to Present; DLB 13; MTCW 1, 2

Piozzi, Hester Lynch (Thrale) 1741-1821 **NCLC 57**
See also DLB 104, 142

Pirandello, Luigi 1867-1936 **TCLC 4, 29; DA; DAB; DAC; DAM DRAM, MST; DC 5; SSC 22; WLC**
See also CA 104; 153; MTCW 2

Pirsig, Robert M(aynard) 1928- **CLC 4, 6, 73; DAM POP**
See also CA 53-56; CANR 42, 74; MTCW 1, 2; SATA 39

Pisarev, Dmitry Ivanovich 1840-1868 **NCLC 25**

Pix, Mary (Griffith) 1666-1709 .... **LC 8**
See also DLB 80

Riding, Laura .... CLC 3, 7
  See also Jackson, Laura (Riding)
Riefenstahl, Berta Helene Amalia 1902-
  See Riefenstahl, Leni
  See also CA 108
Riefenstahl, Leni .... CLC 16
  See also Riefenstahl, Berta Helene Amalia
Riffe, Ernest
  See Bergman, (Ernst) Ingmar
Riggs, (Rolla) Lynn 1899-1954TCLC 56; DAM
  MULT
  See also CA 144; DLB 175; NNAL
Riis, Jacob A(ugust) 1849-1914 ...... TCLC 80
  See also CA 113; 168; DLB 23
Riley, James Whitcomb 1849-1916 TCLC 51;
  DAM POET
  See also CA 118; 137; MAICYA; SATA 17
Riley, Tex
  See Creasey, John
Rilke, Rainer Maria 1875-1926TCLC 1, 6, 19;
  DAM POET; PC 2
  See also CA 104; 132; CANR 62; DLB 81;
  MTCW 1, 2
Rimbaud, (Jean Nicolas) Arthur 1854-1891
  NCLC 4, 35; DA; DAB; DAC; DAM MST,
  POET; PC 3; WLC
Rinehart, Mary Roberts 1876-1958 TCLC 52
  See also CA 108; 166
Ringmaster, The
  See Mencken, H(enry) L(ouis)
Ringwood, Gwen(dolyn Margaret) Pharis
  1910-1984 .... CLC 48
  See also CA 148; 112; DLB 88
Rio, Michel 19(?)- .... CLC 43
Ritsos, Giannes
  See Ritsos, Yannis
Ritsos, Yannis 1909-1990 .... CLC 6, 13, 31
  See also CA 77-80; 133; CANR 39, 61; MTCW
  1
Ritter, Erika 1948(?)- .... CLC 52
Rivera, Jose Eustasio 1889-1928 .... TCLC 35
  See also CA 162; HW
Rivers, Conrad Kent 1933-1968 .... CLC 1
  See also BW 1; CA 85-88; DLB 41
Rivers, Elfrida
  See Bradley, Marion Zimmer
Riverside, John
  See Heinlein, Robert A(nson)
Rizal, Jose 1861-1896 .... NCLC 27
Roa Bastos, Augusto (Antonio) 1917-CLC 45;
  DAM MULT; HLC
  See also CA 131; DLB 113; HW
Robbe-Grillet, Alain 1922-CLC 1, 2, 4, 6, 8, 10,
  14, 43
  See also CA 9-12R; CANR 33, 65; DLB 83;
  MTCW 1, 2
Robbins, Harold 1916-1997CLC 5; DAM NOV
  See also CA 73-76; 162; CANR 26, 54; MTCW
  1, 2
Robbins, Thomas Eugene 1936-
  See Robbins, Tom
  See also CA 81-84; CANR 29, 59; DAM NOV,
  POP; MTCW 1, 2
Robbins, Tom .... CLC 9, 32, 64
  See also Robbins, Thomas Eugene
  See also BEST 90:3; DLBY 80; MTCW 2
Robbins, Trina 1938- .... CLC 21
  See also CA 128
Roberts, Charles G(eorge) D(ouglas) 1860-1943
  TCLC 8
  See also CA 105; CLR 33; DLB 92; SATA 88;
  SATA-Brief 29

Roberts, Elizabeth Madox 1886-1941TCLC 68
  See also CA 111; 166; DLB 9, 54, 102; SATA
  33; SATA-Brief 27
Roberts, Kate 1891-1985 .... CLC 15
  See also CA 107; 116
Roberts, Keith (John Kingston) 1935-CLC 14
  See also CA 25-28R; CANR 46
Roberts, Kenneth (Lewis) 1885-1957TCLC 23
  See also CA 109; DLB 9
Roberts, Michele (B.) 1949- .... CLC 48
  See also CA 115; CANR 58
Robertson, Ellis
  See Ellison, Harlan (Jay); Silverberg, Robert
Robertson, Thomas William 1829-1871N C L C
  35; DAM DRAM
Robeson, Kenneth
  See Dent, Lester
Robinson, Edwin Arlington 1869-1935 T C L C
  5; DA; DAC; DAM MST, POET; PC 1
  See also CA 104; 133; CDALB 1865-1917; DLB
  54; MTCW 1, 2
Robinson, Henry Crabb 1775-1867 NCLC 15
  See also DLB 107
Robinson, Jill 1936- .... CLC 10
  See also CA 102; INT 102
Robinson, Kim Stanley 1952- .... CLC 34
  See also AAYA 26; CA 126
Robinson, Lloyd
  See Silverberg, Robert
Robinson, Marilynne 1944- .... CLC 25
  See also CA 116; DLB 206
Robinson, Smokey .... CLC 21
  See also Robinson, William, Jr.
Robinson, William, Jr. 1940-
  See Robinson, Smokey
  See also CA 116
Robison, Mary 1949- CLC 42, 98
  See also CA 113; 116; DLB 130; INT 116
Rod, Edouard 1857-1910 .... TCLC 52
Roddenberry, Eugene Wesley 1921-1991
  See Roddenberry, Gene
  See also CA 110; 135; CANR 37; SATA 45;
  SATA-Obit 69
Roddenberry, Gene .... CLC 17
  See also Roddenberry, Eugene Wesley
  See also AAYA 5; SATA-Obit 69
Rodgers, Mary 1931- .... CLC 12
  See also CA 49-52; CANR 8, 55; CLR 20; INT
  CANR-8; JRDA; MAICYA; SATA 8
Rodgers, W(illiam) R(obert) 1909-1969CLC 7
  See also CA 85-88; DLB 20
Rodman, Eric
  See Silverberg, Robert
Rodman, Howard 1920(?)-1985 .... CLC 65
  See also CA 118
Rodman, Maia
  See Wojciechowska, Maia (Teresa)
Rodriguez, Claudio 1934- .... CLC 10
  See also DLB 134
Roelvaag, O(le) E(dvart) 1876-1931 TCLC 17
  See also CA 117; 171; DLB 9
Roethke, Theodore (Huebner) 1908-1963C L C
  1, 3, 8, 11, 19, 46, 101; DAM POET; PC 15
  See also CA 81-84; CABS 2; CDALB
  1941-1968; DLB 5, 206; MTCW 1, 2
Rogers, Samuel 1763-1855 .... NCLC 69
  See also DLB 93
Rogers, Thomas Hunton 1927- .... CLC 57
  See also CA 89-92; INT 89-92
Rogers, Will(iam Penn Adair) 1879-1935
  TCLC 8, 71; DAM MULT
  See also CA 105; 144; DLB 11; MTCW 2; NNAL

Rogin, Gilbert 1929- .... CLC 18
  See also CA 65-68; CANR 15
Rohan, Koda .... TCLC 22
  See also Koda Shigeyuki
Rohlfs, Anna Katharine Green
  See Green, Anna Katharine
Rohmer, Eric .... CLC 16
  See also Scherer, Jean-Marie Maurice
Rohmer, Sax .... TCLC 28
  See also Ward, Arthur Henry Sarsfield
  See also DLB 70
Roiphe, Anne (Richardson) 1935-.... CLC 3, 9
  See also CA 89-92; CANR 45, 73; DLBY 80;
  INT 89-92
Rojas, Fernando de 1465-1541 .... LC 23
Rolfe, Frederick (William Serafino Austin Lewis
  Mary) 1860-1913 .... TCLC 12
  See also CA 107; DLB 34, 156
Rolland, Romain 1866-1944 .... TCLC 23
  See also CA 118; DLB 65
Rolle, Richard c. 1300-c. 1349 .... CMLC 21
  See also DLB 146
Rolvaag, O(le) E(dvart)
  See Roelvaag, O(le) E(dvart)
Romain Arnaud, Saint
  See Aragon, Louis
Romains, Jules 1885-1972 .... CLC 7
  See also CA 85-88; CANR 34; DLB 65; MTCW
  1
Romero, Jose Ruben 1890-1952 ..... TCLC 14
  See also CA 114; 131; HW
Ronsard, Pierre de 1524-1585 ... LC 6; PC 11
Rooke, Leon 1934- ... CLC 25, 34; DAM POP
  See also CA 25-28R; CANR 23, 53
Roosevelt, Theodore 1858-1919...... TCLC 69
  See also CA 115; 170; DLB 47, 186
Roper, William 1498-1578 .... LC 10
Roquelaure, A. N.
  See Rice, Anne
Rosa, Joao Guimaraes 1908-1967 ...... CLC 23
  See also CA 89-92; DLB 113
Rose, Wendy 1948-CLC 85; DAM MULT; PC
  13
  See also CA 53-56; CANR 5, 51; DLB 175;
  NNAL; SATA 12
Rosen, R. D.
  See Rosen, Richard (Dean)
Rosen, Richard (Dean) 1949- .... CLC 39
  See also CA 77-80; CANR 62; INT CANR-30
Rosenberg, Isaac 1890-1918........... TCLC 12
  See also CA 107; DLB 20
Rosenblatt, Joe .... CLC 15
  See also Rosenblatt, Joseph
Rosenblatt, Joseph 1933-
  See Rosenblatt, Joe
  See also CA 89-92; INT 89-92
Rosenfeld, Samuel
  See Tzara, Tristan
Rosenstock, Sami
  See Tzara, Tristan
Rosenstock, Samuel
  See Tzara, Tristan
Rosenthal, M(acha) L(ouis) 1917-1996CLC 28
  See also CA 1-4R; 152; CAAS 6; CANR 4, 51;
  DLB 5; SATA 59
Ross, Barnaby
  See Dannay, Frederic
Ross, Bernard L.
  See Follett, Ken(neth Martin)
Ross, J. H.
  See Lawrence, T(homas) E(dward)
Ross, John Hume
  See Lawrence, T(homas) E(dward)

Ross, Martin
See Martin, Violet Florence
See also DLB 135

Ross, (James) Sinclair 1908- ..**CLC 13; DAC;
DAM MST; SSC 24**
See also CA 73-76; DLB 88

Rossetti, Christina (Georgina) 1830-1894
**NCLC 2, 50, 66; DA; DAB; DAC; DAM
MST, POET; PC 7; WLC**
See also DLB 35, 163; MAICYA; SATA 20

Rossetti, Dante Gabriel 1828-1882 . **NCLC 4;
DA; DAB; DAC; DAM MST, POET; WLC**
See also CDBLB 1832-1890; DLB 35

Rossner, Judith (Perelman) 1935-**CLC 6, 9, 29**
See also AITN 2; BEST 90:3; CA 17-20R;
CANR 18, 51, 73; DLB 6; INT CANR-18;
MTCW 1, 2

Rostand, Edmond (Eugene Alexis) 1868-1918
**TCLC 6, 37; DA; DAB; DAC; DAM
DRAM, MST; DC 10**
See also CA 104; 126; DLB 192; MTCW 1

Roth, Henry 1906-1995 ...... **CLC 2, 6, 11, 104**
See also CA 11-12; 149; CANR 38, 63; CAP 1;
DLB 28; MTCW 1, 2

Roth, Philip (Milton) 1933-**CLC 1, 2, 3, 4, 6, 9,
15, 22, 31, 47, 66, 86, 119; DA; DAB; DAC;
DAM MST, NOV, POP; SSC 26; WLC**
See also BEST 90:3; CA 1-4R; CANR 1, 22, 36,
55; CDALB 1968-1988; DLB 2, 28, 173;
DLBY 82; MTCW 1, 2

Rothenberg, Jerome 1931- .... **CLC 6, 57**
See also CA 45-48; CANR 1; DLB 5, 193

Roumain, Jacques (Jean Baptiste) 1907-1944
TCLC 19; BLC 3; DAM MULT
See also BW 1; CA 117; 125

Rourke, Constance (Mayfield) 1885-1941
TCLC 12
See also CA 107; YABC 1

Rousseau, Jean-Baptiste 1671-1741 ....**LC 9**
Rousseau, Jean-Jacques 1712-1778**LC 14, 36;
DA; DAB; DAC; DAM MST; WLC**
Roussel, Raymond 1877-1933 .... **TCLC 20**
See also CA 117

Rovit, Earl (Herbert) 1927- .... **CLC 7**
See also CA 5-8R; CANR 12

Rowe, Elizabeth Singer 1674-1737 ...... **LC 44**
See also DLB 39, 95

Rowe, Nicholas 1674-1718 ....**LC 8**
See also DLB 84

Rowley, Ames Dorrance
See Lovecraft, H(oward) P(hillips)

Rowson, Susanna Haswell 1762(?)-1824**N C L C
5, 69**
See also DLB 37, 200

Roy, Arundhati 1960(?)- .... **CLC 109**
See also CA 163; DLBY 97

Roy, Gabrielle 1909-1983 . **CLC 10, 14; DAB;
DAC; DAM MST**
See also CA 53-56; 110; CANR 5, 61; DLB 68;
MTCW 1; SATA 104

Royko, Mike 1932-1997 .... **CLC 109**
See also CA 89-92; 157; CANR 26

Rozewicz, Tadeusz 1921-..... **CLC 9, 23; DAM
POET**
See also CA 108; CANR 36, 66; MTCW 1, 2

Ruark, Gibbons 1941- .... **CLC 3**
See also CA 33-36R; CAAS 23; CANR 14, 31,
57; DLB 120

Rubens, Bernice (Ruth) 1923- ...... **CLC 19, 31**
See also CA 25-28R; CANR 33, 65; DLB 14,
207; MTCW 1

Rubin, Harold
See Robbins, Harold

Rudkin, (James) David 1936- .... **CLC 14**
See also CA 89-92; DLB 13

Rudnik, Raphael 1933- .... **CLC 7**
See also CA 29-32R

Ruffian, M.
See Hasek, Jaroslav (Matej Frantisek)

Ruiz, Jose Martinez .... **CLC 11**
See also Martinez Ruiz, Jose

Rukeyser, Muriel 1913-1980**CLC 6, 10, 15, 27;
DAM POET; PC 12**
See also CA 5-8R; 93-96; CANR 26, 60; DLB
48; MTCW 1, 2; SATA-Obit 22

Rule, Jane (Vance) 1931- .... **CLC 27**
See also CA 25-28R; CAAS 18; CANR 12; DLB
60

Rulfo, Juan 1918-1986 .... **CLC 8, 80; DAM
MULT; HLC; SSC 25**
See also CA 85-88; 118; CANR 26; DLB 113;
HW; MTCW 1, 2

Rumi, Jalal al-Din 1297-1373 .... **CMLC 20**

Runeberg, Johan 1804-1877 .... **NCLC 41**

Runyon, (Alfred) Damon 1884(?)-1946 **T C L C
10**
See also CA 107; 165; DLB 11, 86, 171; MTCW
2

Rush, Norman 1933- .... **CLC 44**
See also CA 121; 126; INT 126

Rushdie, (Ahmed) Salman 1947-. **CLC 23, 31,
55, 100; DAB; DAC; DAM MST, NOV,
POP; WLCS**
See also BEST 89:3; CA 108; 111; CANR 33,
56; DLB 194; INT 111; MTCW 1, 2

Rushforth, Peter (Scott) 1945- .... **CLC 19**
See also CA 101

Ruskin, John 1819-1900 .... **TCLC 63**
See also CA 114; 129; CDBLB 1832-1890; DLB
55, 163, 190; SATA 24

Russ, Joanna 1937- .... **CLC 15**
See also CANR 11, 31, 65; DLB 8; MTCW 1

Russell, George William 1867-1935
See Baker, Jean H.
See also CA 104; 153; CDBLB 1890-1914;
DAM POET

Russell, (Henry) Ken(neth Alfred) 1927- **C L C
16**
See also CA 105

Russell, William Martin 1947- .... **CLC 60**
See also CA 164

Rutherford, Mark .... **TCLC 25**
See also White, William Hale
See also DLB 18

Ruyslinck, Ward 1929-........................ **CLC 14**
See also Belser, Reimond Karel Maria de

Ryan, Cornelius (John) 1920-1974 ...... **CLC 7**
See also CA 69-72; 53-56; CANR 38

Ryan, Michael 1946- .... **CLC 65**
See also CA 49-52; DLBY 82

Ryan, Tim
See Dent, Lester

Rybakov, Anatoli (Naumovich) 1911-1998**CLC
23, 53**
See also CA 126; 135; 172; SATA 79

Ryder, Jonathan
See Ludlum, Robert

Ryga, George 1932-1987**CLC 14; DAC; DAM
MST**
See also CA 101; 124; CANR 43; DLB 60

S. H.
See Hartmann, Sadakichi

S. S.
See Sassoon, Siegfried (Lorraine)

Saba, Umberto 1883-1957 .... **TCLC 33**
See also CA 144; DLB 114

Sabatini, Rafael 1875-1950 .... **TCLC 47**
See also CA 162

Sabato, Ernesto (R.) 1911- **CLC 10, 23; DAM
MULT; HLC**
See also CA 97-100; CANR 32, 65; DLB 145;
HW; MTCW 1, 2

Sa-Carniero, Mario de 1890-1916 .. **TCLC 83**

Sacastru, Martin
See Bioy Casares, Adolfo

Sacher-Masoch, Leopold von 1836(?)-1895
NCLC 31

Sachs, Marilyn (Stickle) 1927- .... **CLC 35**
See also AAYA 2; CA 17-20R; CANR 13, 47;
CLR 2; JRDA; MAICYA; SAAS 2; SATA 3,
68

Sachs, Nelly 1891-1970 .... **CLC 14, 98**
See also CA 17-18; 25-28R; CAP 2; MTCW 2

Sackler, Howard (Oliver) 1929-1982 . **CLC 14**
See also CA 61-64; 108; CANR 30; DLB 7

Sacks, Oliver (Wolf) 1933-.................. **CLC 67**
See also CA 53-56; CANR 28, 50, 76; INT
CANR-28; MTCW 1, 2

Sadakichi
See Hartmann, Sadakichi

Sade, Donatien Alphonse Francois, Comte de
1740-1814 .... **NCLC 47**

Sadoff, Ira 1945- .... **CLC 9**
See also CA 53-56; CANR 5, 21; DLB 120

Saetone
See Camus, Albert

Safire, William 1929- .... **CLC 10**
See also CA 17-20R; CANR 31, 54

Sagan, Carl (Edward) 1934-1996**CLC 30, 112**
See also AAYA 2; CA 25-28R; 155; CANR 11,
36, 74; MTCW 1, 2; SATA 58; SATA-Obit 94

Sagan, Francoise .... **CLC 3, 6, 9, 17, 36**
See also Quoirez, Francoise
See also DLB 83; MTCW 2

Sahgal, Nayantara (Pandit) 1927- ...... **CLC 41**
See also CA 9-12R; CANR 11

Saint, H(arry) F. 1941- .... **CLC 50**
See also CA 127

St. Aubin de Teran, Lisa 1953-
See Teran, Lisa St. Aubin de
See also CA 118; 126; INT 126

Saint Birgitta of Sweden c. 1303-1373 **C M L C
24**

Sainte-Beuve, Charles Augustin 1804-1869
NCLC 5

**Saint-Exupery, Antoine (Jean Baptiste Marie
Roger) de** 1900-1944 **TCLC 2, 56; DAM
NOV; WLC**
See also CA 108; 132; CLR 10; DLB 72;
MAICYA; MTCW 1, 2; SATA 20

St. John, David
See Hunt, E(verette) Howard, (Jr.)

Saint-John Perse
See Leger, (Marie-Rene Auguste) Alexis
Saint-Leger

Saintsbury, George (Edward Bateman)
1845-1933 .... **TCLC 31**
See also CA 160; DLB 57, 149

Sait Faik .... **TCLC 23**
See also Abasiyanik, Sait Faik

Saki .... **TCLC 3; SSC 12**
See also Munro, H(ector) H(ugh)
See also MTCW 2

Sala, George Augustus .... **NCLC 46**

Salama, Hannu 1936- .... **CLC 18**

Salamanca, J(ack) R(ichard) 1922- **CLC 4, 15**
See also CA 25-28R

Sale, J. Kirkpatrick
See Sale, Kirkpatrick

Sale, Kirkpatrick 1937-...................... **CLC 68**
  See also CA 13-16R; CANR 10
Salinas, Luis Omar 1937- .... **CLC 90; DAM MULT; HLC**
  See also CA 131; DLB 82; HW
Salinas (y Serrano), Pedro 1891(?)-1951**TCLC 17**
  See also CA 117; DLB 134
Salinger, J(erome) D(avid) 1919- **CLC 1, 3, 8, 12, 55, 56; DA; DAB; DAC; DAM MST, NOV, POP; SSC 2, 28; WLC**
  See also AAYA 2; CA 5-8R; CANR 39; CDALB 1941-1968; CLR 18; DLB 2, 102, 173; MAICYA; MTCW 1, 2; SATA 67
Salisbury, John
  See Caute, (John) David
Salter, James 1923- .... **CLC 7, 52, 59**
  See also CA 73-76; DLB 130
Saltus, Edgar (Everton) 1855-1921 .. **TCLC 8**
  See also CA 105; DLB 202
Saltykov, Mikhail Evgrafovich 1826-1889 **NCLC 16**
Samarakis, Antonis 1919- .... **CLC 5**
  See also CA 25-28R; CAAS 16; CANR 36
Sanchez, Florencio 1875-1910 .... **TCLC 37**
  See also CA 153; HW
Sanchez, Luis Rafael 1936-.................. **CLC 23**
  See also CA 128; DLB 145; HW
Sanchez, Sonia 1934-**CLC 5, 116; BLC 3; DAM MULT; PC 9**
  See also BW 2; CA 33-36R; CANR 24, 49, 74; CLR 18; DLB 41; DLBD 8; MAICYA; MTCW 1, 2; SATA 22
Sand, George 1804-1876**NCLC 2, 42, 57; DA; DAB; DAC; DAM MST, NOV; WLC**
  See also DLB 119, 192
Sandburg, Carl (August) 1878-1967**CLC 1, 4, 10, 15, 35; DA; DAB; DAC; DAM MST, POET; PC 2; WLC**
  See also AAYA 24; CA 5-8R; 25-28R; CANR 35; CDALB 1865-1917; DLB 17, 54; MAICYA; MTCW 1, 2; SATA 8
Sandburg, Charles
  See Sandburg, Carl (August)
Sandburg, Charles A.
  See Sandburg, Carl (August)
Sanders, (James) Ed(ward) 1939- .... **CLC 53; DAM POET**
  See also CA 13-16R; CAAS 21; CANR 13, 44, 78; DLB 16
Sanders, Lawrence 1920-1998 **CLC 41; DAM POP**
  See also BEST 89:4; CA 81-84; 165; CANR 33, 62; MTCW 1
Sanders, Noah
  See Blount, Roy (Alton), Jr.
Sanders, Winston P.
  See Anderson, Poul (William)
Sandoz, Mari(e Susette) 1896-1966 ... **CLC 28**
  See also CA 1-4R; 25-28R; CANR 17, 64; DLB 9, 212; MTCW 1, 2; SATA 5
Saner, Reg(inald Anthony) 1931- .... **CLC 9**
  See also CA 65-68
Sankara 788-820 .... **CMLC 32**
Sannazaro, Jacopo 1456(?)-1530 .... **LC 8**
Sansom, William 1912-1976 . **CLC 2, 6; DAM NOV; SSC 21**
  See also CA 5-8R; 65-68; CANR 42; DLB 139; MTCW 1
Santayana, George 1863-1952 .... **TCLC 40**
  See also CA 115; DLB 54, 71; DLBD 13
Santiago, Danny .... **CLC 33**
  See also James, Daniel (Lewis)

  See also DLB 122
Santmyer, Helen Hoover 1895-1986 ..**CLC 33**
  See also CA 1-4R; 118; CANR 15, 33; DLBY 84; MTCW 1
Santoka, Taneda 1882-1940 .... **TCLC 72**
Santos, Bienvenido N(uqui) ·1911-1996**CLC 22; DAM MULT**
  See also CA 101; 151; CANR 19, 46
Sapper .... **TCLC 44**
  See also McNeile, Herman Cyril
Sapphire
  See Sapphire, Brenda
Sapphire, Brenda 1950- .... **CLC 99**
Sappho fl. 6th cent. B.C.-**CMLC 3; DAM POET; PC 5**
  See also DLB 176
Saramago, Jose 1922- .... **CLC 119**
  See also CA 153
Sarduy, Severo 1937-1993 .... **CLC 6, 97**
  See also CA 89-92; 142; CANR 58; DLB 113; HW
Sargeson, Frank 1903-1982 .... **CLC 31**
  See also CA 25-28R; 106; CANR 38
Sarmiento, Felix Ruben Garcia
  See Dario, Ruben
Saro-Wiwa, Ken(ule Beeson) 1941-1995 **C L C 114**
  See also BW 2; CA 142; 150; CANR 60; DLB 157
Saroyan, William 1908-1981 **CLC 1, 8, 10, 29, 34, 56; DA; DAB; DAC; DAM DRAM, MST, NOV; SSC 21; WLC**
  See also CA 5-8R; 103; CANR 30; DLB 7, 9, 86; DLBY 81; MTCW 1, 2; SATA 23; SATA-Obit 24
Sarraute, Nathalie 1900-**CLC 1, 2, 4, 8, 10, 31, 80**
  See also CA 9-12R; CANR 23, 66; DLB 83; MTCW 1, 2
Sarton, (Eleanor) May 1912-1995 **CLC 4, 14, 49, 91; DAM POET**
  See also CA 1-4R; 149; CANR 1, 34, 55; DLB 48; DLBY 81; INT CANR-34; MTCW 1, 2; SATA 36; SATA-Obit 86
Sartre, Jean-Paul 1905-1980**CLC 1, 4, 7, 9, 13, 18, 24, 44, 50, 52; DA; DAB; DAC; DAM DRAM, MST, NOV; DC 3; SSC 32; WLC**
  See also CA 9-12R; 97-100; CANR 21; DLB 72; MTCW 1, 2
Sassoon, Siegfried (Lorraine) 1886-1967 **C L C 36; DAB; DAM MST, NOV, POET; PC 12**
  See also CA 104; 25-28R; CANR 36; DLB 20, 191; DLBD 18; MTCW 1, 2
Satterfield, Charles
  See Pohl, Frederik
Saul, John (W. III) 1942-**CLC 46; DAM NOV, POP**
  See also AAYA 10; BEST 90:4; CA 81-84; CANR 16, 40; SATA 98
Saunders, Caleb
  See Heinlein, Robert A(nson)
Saura (Atares), Carlos 1932- .... **CLC 20**
  See also CA 114; 131; HW
Sauser-Hall, Frederic 1887-1961 .... **CLC 18**
  See also Cendrars, Blaise
  See also CA 102; 93-96; CANR 36, 62; MTCW 1
Saussure, Ferdinand de 1857-1913 . **TCLC 49**
Savage, Catharine
  See Brosman, Catharine Savage
Savage, Thomas 1915- .... **CLC 40**
  See also CA 126; 132; CAAS 15; INT 132

Savan, Glenn 19(?)- .... **CLC 50**
Sayers, Dorothy L(eigh) 1893-1957 . **TCLC 2, 15; DAM POP**
  See also CA 104; 119, CANR 60, CDBLB 1914-1945; DLB 10, 36, 77, 100; MTCW 1, 2
Sayers, Valerie 1952- .... **CLC 50**
  See also CA 134; CANR 61
Sayles, John (Thomas) 1950- .... **CLC 7, 10, 14**
  See also CA 57-60; CANR 41; DLB 44
Scammell, Michael 1935- .... **CLC 34**
  See also CA 156
Scannell, Vernon 1922- .... **CLC 49**
  See also CA 5-8R; CANR 8, 24, 57; DLB 27; SATA 59
Scarlett, Susan
  See Streatfeild, (Mary) Noel
Scarron
  See Mikszath, Kalman
Schaeffer, Susan Fromberg 1941-**CLC 6, 11, 22**
  See also CA 49-52; CANR 18, 65; DLB 28; MTCW 1, 2; SATA 22
Schary, Jill
  See Robinson, Jill
Schell, Jonathan 1943- .... **CLC 35**
  See also CA 73-76; CANR 12
Schelling, Friedrich Wilhelm Joseph von 1775-1854 .... **NCLC 30**
  See also DLB 90
Schendel, Arthur van 1874-1946 .... **TCLC 56**
Scherer, Jean-Marie Maurice 1920-
  See Rohmer, Eric
  See also CA 110
Schevill, James (Erwin) 1920- .... **CLC 7**
  See also CA 5-8R; CAAS 12
Schiller, Friedrich 1759-1805 .. **NCLC 39, 69; DAM DRAM**
  See also DLB 94
Schisgal, Murray (Joseph) 1926- .... **CLC 6**
  See also CA 21-24R; CANR 48
Schlee, Ann 1934- .... **CLC 35**
  See also CA 101; CANR 29; SATA 44; SATA-Brief 36
Schlegel, August Wilhelm von 1767-1845 **NCLC 15**
  See also DLB 94
Schlegel, Friedrich 1772-1829 .... **NCLC 45**
  See also DLB 90
Schlegel, Johann Elias (von) 1719(?)-1749**LC 5**
Schlesinger, Arthur M(eier), Jr. 1917-**CLC 84**
  See also AITN 1; CA 1-4R; CANR 1, 28, 58; DLB 17; INT CANR-28; MTCW 1, 2; SATA 61
Schmidt, Arno (Otto) 1914-1979 .... **CLC 56**
  See also CA 128; 109; DLB 69
Schmitz, Aron Hector 1861-1928
  See Svevo, Italo
  See also CA 104; 122; MTCW 1
Schnackenberg, Gjertrud 1953-......... **CLC 40**
  See also CA 116; DLB 120
Schneider, Leonard Alfred 1925-1966
  See Bruce, Lenny
  See also CA 89-92
Schnitzler, Arthur 1862-1931**TCLC 4; SSC 15**
  See also CA 104; DLB 81, 118
Schoenberg, Arnold 1874-1951 .... **TCLC 75**
  See also CA 109
Schonberg, Arnold
  See Schoenberg, Arnold
Schopenhauer, Arthur 1788-1860 ... **NCLC 51**
  See also DLB 90
Schor, Sandra (M.) 1932(?)-1990 .... **CLC 65**
  See also CA 132

Shamlu, Ahmad 1925- .... **CLC 10**

Shammas, Anton 1951- .... **CLC 55**

Shange, Ntozake 1948-**CLC 8, 25, 38, 74; BLC 3; DAM DRAM, MULT; DC 3**
See also AAYA 9; BW 2; CA 85-88; CABS 3; CANR 27, 48, 74; DLB 38; MTCW 1, 2

Shanley, John Patrick 1950- .... **CLC 75**
See also CA 128; 133

Shapcott, Thomas W(illiam) 1935- .... **CLC 38**
See also CA 69-72; CANR 49

Shapiro, Jane .... **CLC 76**

Shapiro, Karl (Jay) 1913-**CLC 4, 8, 15, 53; PC 25**
See also CA 1-4R; CAAS 6; CANR 1, 36, 66; DLB 48; MTCW 1, 2

Sharp, William 1855-1905 .... **TCLC 39**
See also CA 160; DLB 156

Sharpe, Thomas Ridley 1928-
See Sharpe, Tom
See also CA 114; 122; INT 122

Sharpe, Tom .... **CLC 36**
See also Sharpe, Thomas Ridley
See also DLB 14

Shaw, Bernard .... **TCLC 45**
See also Shaw, George Bernard
See also BW 1; MTCW 2

Shaw, G. Bernard
See Shaw, George Bernard

Shaw, George Bernard 1856-1950 **TCLC 3, 9, 21; DA; DAB; DAC; DAM DRAM, MST; WLC**
Scc also Shaw, Bernard
See also CA 104; 128; CDBLB 1914-1945; DLB 10, 57, 190; MTCW 1, 2

Shaw, Henry Wheeler 1818-1885 .... **NCLC 15**
See also DLB 11

Shaw, Irwin 1913-1984 .. **CLC 7, 23, 34; DAM DRAM, POP**
See also AITN 1; CA 13-16R; 112; CANR 21; CDALB 1941-1968; DLB 6, 102; DLBY 84; MTCW 1, 21

Shaw, Robert 1927-1978 .... **CLC 5**
See also AITN 1; CA 1-4R; 81-84; CANR 4; DLB 13, 14

Shaw, T. E.
See Lawrence, T(homas) E(dward)

Shawn, Wallace 1943- .... **CLC 41**
See also CA 112

Shea, Lisa 1953- .... **CLC 86**
See also CA 147

Sheed, Wilfrid (John Joseph) 1930- **CLC 2, 4, 10, 53**
See also CA 65-68; CANR 30, 66; DLB 6; MTCW 1, 2

Sheldon, Alice Hastings Bradley 1915(?)-1987
See Tiptree, James, Jr.
See also CA 108; 122; CANR 34; INT 108; MTCW 1

Sheldon, John
See Bloch, Robert (Albert)

Shelley, Mary Wollstonecraft (Godwin) 1797-1851**NCLC 14, 59; DA; DAB; DAC; DAM MST, NOV; WLC**
See also AAYA 20; CDBLB 1789-1832; DLB 110, 116, 159, 178; SATA 29

Shelley, Percy Bysshe 1792-1822 .. **NCLC 18; DA; DAB; DAC; DAM MST, POET; PC 14; WLC**
See also CDBLB 1789-1832; DLB 96, 110, 158

Shepard, Jim 1956- .... **CLC 36**
See also CA 137; CANR 59; SATA 90

Shepard, Lucius 1947- .... **CLC 34**
See also CA 128; 141

Shepard, Sam 1943- **CLC 4, 6, 17, 34, 41, 44; DAM DRAM; DC 5**
See also AAYA 1; CA 69-72; CABS 3; CANR 22; DLB 7, 212; MTCW 1, 2

Shepherd, Michael
See Ludlum, Robert

Sherburne, Zoa (Morin) 1912- .... **CLC 30**
See also AAYA 13; CA 1-4R; CANR 3, 37; MAICYA; SAAS 18; SATA 3

Sheridan, Frances 1724-1766 .... **LC 7**
See also DLB 39, 84

Sheridan, Richard Brinsley 1751-1816 **NCLC 5; DA; DAB; DAC; DAM DRAM, MST; DC 1; WLC**
See also CDBLB 1660-1789; DLB 89

Sherman, Jonathan Marc .... **CLC 55**

Sherman, Martin 1941(?)- .... **CLC 19**
See also CA 116; 123

Sherwin, Judith Johnson
See Johnson, Judith (Emlyn)

Sherwood, Frances 1940- .... **CLC 81**
See also CA 146

Sherwood, Robert E(mmet) 1896-1955 **TCLC 3; DAM DRAM**
See also CA 104; 153; DLB 7, 26

Shestov, Lev 1866-1938 .... **TCLC 56**

Shevchenko, Taras 1814-1861 .... **NCLC 54**

Shiel, M(atthew) P(hipps) 1865-1947 **TCLC 8**
See also Holmes, Gordon
See also CA 106; 160; DLB 153; MTCW 2

Shields, Carol 1935- .... **CLC 91, 113; DAC**
See also CA 81-84; CANR 51, 74; MTCW 2

Shields, David 1956- .... **CLC 97**
See also CA 124; CANR 48

Shiga, Naoya 1883-1971 ...... **CLC 33; SSC 23**
See also CA 101; 33-36R; DLB 180

Shikibu, Murasaki c. 978-c. 1014 ..... **CMLC 1**

Shilts, Randy 1951-1994 .... **CLC 85**
See also AAYA 19; CA 115; 127; 144; CANR 45; INT 127; MTCW 2

Shimazaki, Haruki 1872-1943
See Shimazaki Toson
See also CA 105; 134

Shimazaki Toson 1872-1943 .... **TCLC 5**
See also Shimazaki, Haruki
See also DLB 180

Sholokhov, Mikhail (Aleksandrovich) 1905-1984 **CLC 7, 15**
See also CA 101; 112; MTCW 1, 2; SATA-Obit 36

Shone, Patric
See Hanley, James

Shreve, Susan Richards 1939- .... **CLC 23**
See also CA 49-52; CAAS 5; CANR 5, 38, 69; MAICYA; SATA 46, 95; SATA-Brief 41

Shue, Larry 1946-1985**CLC 52; DAM DRAM**
See also CA 145; 117

Shu-Jen, Chou 1881-1936
See Lu Hsun
See also CA 104

Shulman, Alix Kates 1932- .... **CLC 2, 10**
See also CA 29-32R; CANR 43; SATA 7

Shuster, Joe 1914- .... **CLC 21**

Shute, Nevil .... **CLC 30**
See also Norway, Nevil Shute
See also MTCW 2

Shuttle, Penelope (Diane) 1947- .... **CLC 7**
See also CA 93-96; CANR 39; DLB 14, 40

Sidney, Mary 1561-1621 .... **LC 19, 39**

Sidney, Sir Philip 1554-1586 . **LC 19, 39; DA; DAB; DAC; DAM MST, POET**
See also CDBLB Before 1660; DLB 167

Siegel, Jerome 1914-1996 .... **CLC 21**
See also CA 116; 169; 151

Siegel, Jerry
See Siegel, Jerome

Sienkiewicz, Henryk (Adam Alexander Pius) 1846-1916 .... **TCLC 3**
See also CA 104; 134

Sierra, Gregorio Martinez
See Martinez Sierra, Gregorio

Sierra, Maria (de la O'LeJarraga) Martinez
See Martinez Sierra, Maria (de la O'LeJarraga)

Sigal, Clancy 1926- .... **CLC 7**
See also CA 1-4R

Sigourney, Lydia Howard (Huntley) 1791-1865 **NCLC 21**
See also DLB 1, 42, 73

Siguenza y Gongora, Carlos de 1645-1700**LC 8**

Sigurjonsson, Johann 1880-1919 .... **TCLC 27**
See also CA 170

Sikelianos, Angelos 1884-1951 .... **TCLC 39**

Silkin, Jon 1930- .... **CLC 2, 6, 43**
See also CA 5-8R; CAAS 5; DLB 27

Silko, Leslie (Marmon) 1948-**CLC 23, 74, 114; DA; DAC; DAM MST, MULT, POP; WLCS**
See also AAYA 14; CA 115; 122; CANR 45, 65; DLB 143, 175; MTCW 2; NNAL

Sillanpaa, Frans Eemil 1888-1964 ..... **CLC 19**
See also CA 129; 93-96; MTCW 1

Sillitoe, Alan 1928- ...... **CLC 1, 3, 6, 10, 19, 57**
See also AITN 1; CA 9-12R; CAAS 2; CANR 8, 26, 55; CDBLB 1960 to Present; DLB 14, 139; MTCW 1, 2; SATA 61

Silone, Ignazio 1900-1978 .... **CLC 4**
See also CA 25-28; 81-84; CANR 34; CAP 2; MTCW 1

Silver, Joan Micklin 1935- .... **CLC 20**
See also CA 114; 121; INT 121

Silver, Nicholas
See Faust, Frederick (Schiller)

Silverberg, Robert 1935- . **CLC 7; DAM POP**
See also AAYA 24; CA 1-4R; CAAS 3; CANR 1, 20, 36; DLB 8; INT CANR-20; MAICYA; MTCW 1, 2; SATA 13, 91; SATA-Essay 104

Silverstein, Alvin 1933- .... **CLC 17**
See also CA 49-52; CANR 2; CLR 25; JRDA; MAICYA; SATA 8, 69

Silverstein, Virginia B(arbara Opshelor) 1937- **CLC 17**
See also CA 49-52; CANR 2; CLR 25; JRDA; MAICYA; SATA 8, 69

Sim, Georges
See Simenon, Georges (Jacques Christian)

Simak, Clifford D(onald) 1904-1988**CLC 1, 55**
See also CA 1-4R; 125; CANR 1, 35; DLB 8; MTCW 1; SATA-Obit 56

Simenon, Georges (Jacques Christian) 1903-1989**CLC 1, 2, 3, 8, 18, 47; DAM POP**
See also CA 85-88; 129; CANR 35; DLB 72; DLBY 89; MTCW 1, 2

Simic, Charles 1938-**CLC 6, 9, 22, 49, 68; DAM POET**
See also CA 29-32R; CAAS 4; CANR 12, 33, 52, 61; DLB 105; MTCW 2

Simmel, Georg 1858-1918 .... **TCLC 64**
See also CA 157

Simmons, Charles (Paul) 1924- .... **CLC 57**
See also CA 89-92; INT 89-92

Simmons, Dan 1948- ...... **CLC 44; DAM POP**
See also AAYA 16; CA 138; CANR 53

Simmons, James (Stewart Alexander) 1933- **CLC 43**
See also CA 105; CAAS 21; DLB 40

Soedergran, Edith (Irene) 1892-1923 **TCLC 31**
Softly, Edgar
  See Lovecraft, H(oward) P(hillips)
Softly, Edward
  See Lovecraft, H(oward) P(hillips)
Sokolov, Raymond 1941- .... **CLC 7**
  See also CA 85-88
Solo, Jay
  See Ellison, Harlan (Jay)
Sologub, Fyodor .... **TCLC 9**
  See also Teternikov, Fyodor Kuzmich
Solomons, Ikey Esquir
  See Thackeray, William Makepeace
Solomos, Dionysios 1798-1857 .... **NCLC 15**
Solwoska, Mara
  See French, Marilyn
Solzhenitsyn, Aleksandr I(sayevich) 1918- **CLC**
  1, 2, 4, 7, 9, 10, 18, 26, 34, 78; DA; DAB;
  DAC; DAM MST, NOV; SSC 32; WLC
  See also AITN 1; CA 69-72; CANR 40, 65;
  MTCW 1, 2
Somers, Jane
  See Lessing, Doris (May)
Somerville, Edith 1858-1949 .... **TCLC 51**
  See also DLB 135
Somerville & Ross
  See Martin, Violet Florence; Somerville, Edith
Sommer, Scott 1951- .... **CLC 25**
  See also CA 106
Sondheim, Stephen (Joshua) 1930- **CLC 30, 39;**
  DAM DRAM
  See also AAYA 11; CA 103; CANR 47, 68
Song, Cathy 1955- .... **PC 21**
  See also CA 154; DLB 169
Sontag, Susan 1933- **CLC 1, 2, 10, 13, 31, 105;**
  DAM POP
  See also CA 17-20R; CANR 25, 51, 74; DLB 2,
  67; MTCW 1, 2
Sophocles 496(?)B.C.-406(?)B.C. **CMLC 2; DA;**
  DAB; DAC; DAM DRAM, MST; DC 1;
  WLCS
  See also DLB 176
Sordello 1189-1269 .... **CMLC 15**
Sorel, Georges 1847-1922 .... **TCLC 91**
  See also CA 118
Sorel, Julia
  See Drexler, Rosalyn
Sorrentino, Gilbert 1929- **CLC 3, 7, 14, 22, 40**
  See also CA 77-80; CANR 14, 33; DLB 5, 173;
  DLBY 80; INT CANR-14
Soto, Gary 1952- .. **CLC 32, 80; DAM MULT;**
  HLC
  See also AAYA 10; CA 119; 125; CANR 50, 74;
  CLR 38; DLB 82; HW; INT 125; JRDA;
  MTCW 2; SATA 80
Soupault, Philippe 1897-1990 .... **CLC 68**
  See also CA 116; 147; 131
Souster, (Holmes) Raymond 1921- **CLC 5, 14;**
  DAC; DAM POET
  See also CA 13-16R; CAAS 14; CANR 13, 29,
  53; DLB 88; SATA 63
Southern, Terry 1924(?)-1995 .... **CLC 7**
  See also CA 1-4R; 150; CANR 1, 55; DLB 2
Southey, Robert 1774-1843 .... **NCLC 8**
  See also DLB 93, 107, 142; SATA 54
Southworth, Emma Dorothy Eliza Nevitte
  1819-1899 .... **NCLC 26**
Souza, Ernest
  See Scott, Evelyn

Soyinka, Wole 1934- **CLC 3, 5, 14, 36, 44; BLC**
  3; DA; DAB; DAC; DAM DRAM, MST,
  MULT; DC 2; WLC
  See also BW 2; CA 13-16R; CANR 27, 39; DLB
  125; MTCW 1, 2
Spackman, W(illiam) M(ode) 1905-1990 **C L C**
  46
  See also CA 81-84; 132
Spacks, Barry (Bernard) 1931- .... **CLC 14**
  See also CA 154; CANR 33; DLB 105
Spanidou, Irini 1946- .... **CLC 44**
Spark, Muriel (Sarah) 1918- **CLC 2, 3, 5, 8, 13,**
  18, 40, 94; DAB; DAC; DAM MST, NOV;
  SSC 10
  See also CA 5-8R; CANR 12, 36, 76; CDBLB
  1945-1960; DLB 15, 139; INT CANR-12;
  MTCW 1, 2
Spaulding, Douglas
  See Bradbury, Ray (Douglas)
Spaulding, Leonard
  See Bradbury, Ray (Douglas)
Spence, J. A. D.
  See Eliot, T(homas) S(tearns)
Spencer, Elizabeth 1921- .... **CLC 22**
  See also CA 13-16R; CANR 32, 65; DLB 6;
  MTCW 1; SATA 14
Spencer, Leonard G.
  See Silverberg, Robert
Spencer, Scott 1945- .... **CLC 30**
  See also CA 113; CANR 51; DLBY 86
Spender, Stephen (Harold) 1909-1995 **CLC 1, 2,**
  5, 10, 41, 91; DAM POET
  See also CA 9-12R; 149; CANR 31, 54; CDBLB
  1945-1960; DLB 20; MTCW 1, 2
Spengler, Oswald (Arnold Gottfried) 1880-1936
  TCLC 25
  See also CA 118
Spenser, Edmund 1552(?)-1599 **LC 5, 39; DA;**
  DAB; DAC; DAM MST, POET; PC 8;
  WLC
  See also CDBLB Before 1660; DLB 167
Spicer, Jack 1925-1965 . **CLC 8, 18, 72; DAM**
  POET
  See also CA 85-88; DLB 5, 16, 193
Spiegelman, Art 1948- .... **CLC 76**
  See also AAYA 10; CA 125; CANR 41, 55, 74;
  MTCW 2
Spielberg, Peter 1929- .... **CLC 6**
  See also CA 5-8R; CANR 4, 48; DLBY 81
Spielberg, Steven 1947- .... **CLC 20**
  See also AAYA 8, 24; CA 77-80; CANR 32;
  SATA 32
Spillane, Frank Morrison 1918-
  See Spillane, Mickey
  See also CA 25-28R; CANR 28, 63; MTCW 1,
  2; SATA 66
Spillane, Mickey .... **CLC 3, 13**
  See also Spillane, Frank Morrison
  See also MTCW 2
Spinoza, Benedictus de 1632-1677 .... **LC 9**
Spinrad, Norman (Richard) 1940- ..... **CLC 46**
  See also CA 37-40R; CAAS 19; CANR 20; DLB
  8; INT CANR-20
Spitteler, Carl (Friedrich Georg) 1845-1924
  TCLC 12
  See also CA 109; DLB 129
Spivack, Kathleen (Romola Drucker) 1938-
  CLC 6
  See also CA 49-52
Spoto, Donald 1941- .... **CLC 39**
  See also CA 65-68; CANR 11, 57
Springsteen, Bruce (F.) 1949- .... **CLC 17**
  See also CA 111

Spurling, Hilary 1940- .... **CLC 34**
  See also CA 104; CANR 25, 52
Spyker, John Howland
  See Elman, Richard (Martin)
Squires, (James) Radcliffe 1917-1993 **CLC 51**
  See also CA 1-4R; 140; CANR 6, 21
Srivastava, Dhanpat Rai 1880(?)-1936
  See Premchand
  See also CA 118
Stacy, Donald
  See Pohl, Frederik
Stael, Germaine de 1766-1817
  See Stael-Holstein, Anne Louise Germaine
  Necker Baronn
  See also DLB 119
Stael-Holstein, Anne Louise Germaine Necker
  Baronn 1766-1817 .... **NCLC 3**
  See also Stael, Germaine de
  See also DLB 192
Stafford, Jean 1915-1979 **CLC 4, 7, 19, 68; SSC**
  26
  See also CA 1-4R; 85-88; CANR 3, 65; DLB 2,
  173; MTCW 1, 2; SATA-Obit 22
Stafford, William (Edgar) 1914-1993 **CLC 4, 7,**
  29; DAM POET
  See also CA 5-8R; 142; CAAS 3; CANR 5, 22;
  DLB 5, 206; INT CANR-22
Stagnelius, Eric Johan 1793-1823 ... **NCLC 61**
Staines, Trevor
  See Brunner, John (Kilian Houston)
Stairs, Gordon
  See Austin, Mary (Hunter)
Stalin, Joseph 1879-1953 .... **TCLC 92**
Stannard, Martin 1947- .... **CLC 44**
  See also CA 142; DLB 155
Stanton, Elizabeth Cady 1815-1902 **TCLC 73**
  See also CA 171; DLB 79
Stanton, Maura 1946- .... **CLC 9**
  See also CA 89-92; CANR 15; DLB 120
Stanton, Schuyler
  See Baum, L(yman) Frank
Stapledon, (William) Olaf 1886-1950 **TCLC 22**
  See also CA 111; 162; DLB 15
Starbuck, George (Edwin) 1931-1996 **CLC 53;**
  DAM POET
  See also CA 21-24R; 153; CANR 23
Stark, Richard
  See Westlake, Donald E(dwin)
Staunton, Schuyler
  See Baum, L(yman) Frank
Stead, Christina (Ellen) 1902-1983 **CLC 2, 5, 8,**
  32, 80
  See also CA 13-16R; 109; CANR 33, 40; MTCW
  1, 2
Stead, William Thomas 1849-1912 . **TCLC 48**
  See also CA 167
Steele, Richard 1672-1729 .... **LC 18**
  See also CDBLB 1660-1789; DLB 84, 101
Steele, Timothy (Reid) 1948- .... **CLC 45**
  See also CA 93-96; CANR 16, 50; DLB 120
Steffens, (Joseph) Lincoln 1866-1936 **TCLC 20**
  See also CA 117
Stegner, Wallace (Earle) 1909-1993 **CLC 9, 49,**
  81; DAM NOV; SSC 27
  See also AITN 1; BEST 90:3; CA 1-4R; 141;
  CAAS 9; CANR 1, 21, 46; DLB 9, 206; DLBY
  93; MTCW 1, 2
Stein, Gertrude 1874-1946 **TCLC 1, 6, 28, 48;**
  DA; DAB; DAC; DAM MST, NOV, POET;
  PC 18; WLC
  See also CA 104; 132; CDALB 1917-1929; DLB
  4, 54, 86; DLBD 15; MTCW 1, 2

Torsvan, Berwick Traven
See Traven, B.
Torsvan, Bruno Traven
See Traven, B.
Torsvan, Traven
See Traven, B.
Tournier, Michel (Edouard) 1924- **CLC 6, 23, 36, 95**
See also CA 49-52; CANR 3, 36, 74; DLB 83; MTCW 1, 2; SATA 23
Tournimparte, Alessandra
See Ginzburg, Natalia
Towers, Ivar
See Kornbluth, C(yril) M.
Towne, Robert (Burton) 1936(?)- .... **CLC 87**
See also CA 108; DLB 44
Townsend, Sue .... **CLC 61**
See also Townsend, Susan Elaine
See also AAYA 28; SATA 55, 93; SATA-Brief 48
Townsend, Susan Elaine 1946-
See Townsend, Sue
See also CA 119; 127; CANR 65; DAB; DAC; DAM MST
Townshend, Peter (Dennis Blandford) 1945-
CLC 17, 42
See also CA 107
Tozzi, Federigo 1883-1920 .... **TCLC 31**
See also CA 160
Traill, Catharine Parr 1802-1899 ... **NCLC 31**
See also DLB 99
Trakl, Georg 1887-1914 .... **TCLC 5; PC 20**
See also CA 104; 165; MTCW 2
Transtroemer, Tomas (Goesta) 1931- **CLC 52, 65; DAM POET**
See also CA 117; 129; CAAS 17
Transtromer, Tomas Gosta
See Transtroemer, Tomas (Goesta)
Traven, B. (?)-1969 .... **CLC 8, 11**
See also CA 19-20; 25-28R; CAP 2; DLB 9, 56; MTCW 1
Treitel, Jonathan 1959- .... **CLC 70**
Tremain, Rose 1943- .... **CLC 42**
See also CA 97-100; CANR 44; DLB 14
Tremblay, Michel 1942- . **CLC 29, 102; DAC; DAM MST**
See also CA 116; 128; DLB 60; MTCW 1, 2
Trevanian .... **CLC 29**
See also Whitaker, Rod(ney)
Trevor, Glen
See Hilton, James
Trevor, William 1928- **CLC 7, 9, 14, 25, 71, 116; SSC 21**
See also Cox, William Trevor
See also DLB 14, 139; MTCW 2
Trifonov, Yuri (Valentinovich) 1925-1981 **C L C 45**
See also CA 126; 103; MTCW 1
Trilling, Lionel 1905-1975 .... **CLC 9, 11, 24**
See also CA 9-12R; 61-64; CANR 10; DLB 28, 63; INT CANR-10; MTCW 1, 2
Trimball, W. H.
See Mencken, H(enry) L(ouis)
Tristan
See Gomez de la Serna, Ramon
Tristram
See Housman, A(lfred) E(dward)
Trogdon, William (Lewis) 1939-
See Heat-Moon, William Least
See also CA 115; 119; CANR 47; INT 119

Trollope, Anthony 1815-1882 **NCLC 6, 33; DA; DAB; DAC; DAM MST, NOV; SSC 28; WLC**
See also CDBLB 1832-1890; DLB 21, 57, 159; SATA 22
Trollope, Frances 1779-1863 .... **NCLC 30**
See also DLB 21, 166
Trotsky, Leon 1879-1940 .... **TCLC 22**
See also CA 118; 167
Trotter (Cockburn), Catharine 1679-1749 **LC 8**
See also DLB 84
Trout, Kilgore
See Farmer, Philip Jose
Trow, George W. S. 1943- .... **CLC 52**
See also CA 126
Troyat, Henri 1911- .... **CLC 23**
See also CA 45-48; CANR 2, 33, 67; MTCW 1
Trudeau, G(arretson) B(eekman) 1948-
See Trudeau, Garry B.
See also CA 81-84; CANR 31; SATA 35
Trudeau, Garry B. .... **CLC 12**
See also Trudeau, G(arretson) B(eekman)
See also AAYA 10; AITN 2
Truffaut, Francois 1932-1984 .... **CLC 20, 101**
See also CA 81-84; 113; CANR 34
Trumbo, Dalton 1905-1976 .... **CLC 19**
See also CA 21-24R; 69-72; CANR 10; DLB 26
Trumbull, John 1750-1831 .... **NCLC 30**
See also DLB 31
Trundlett, Helen B.
See Eliot, T(homas) S(tearns)
Tryon, Thomas 1926-1991 .. **CLC 3, 11; DAM POP**
See also AITN 1; CA 29-32R; 135; CANR 32, 77; MTCW 1
Tryon, Tom
See Tryon, Thomas
Ts'ao Hsueh-ch'in 1715(?)-1763 .... **LC 1**
Tsushima, Shuji 1909-1948
See Dazai Osamu
See also CA 107
Tsvetaeva (Efron), Marina (Ivanovna) 1892-1941 .... **TCLC 7, 35; PC 14**
See also CA 104; 128; CANR 73; MTCW 1, 2
Tuck, Lily 1938- .... **CLC 70**
See also CA 139
Tu Fu 712-770 .... **PC 9**
See also DAM MULT
Tunis, John R(oberts) 1889-1975 .... **CLC 12**
See also CA 61-64; CANR 62; DLB 22, 171; JRDA; MAICYA; SATA 37; SATA-Brief 30
Tuohy, Frank .... **CLC 37**
See also Tuohy, John Francis
See also DLB 14, 139
Tuohy, John Francis 1925-
See Tuohy, Frank
See also CA 5-8R; CANR 3, 47
Turco, Lewis (Putnam) 1934- .... **CLC 11, 63**
See also CA 13-16R; CAAS 22; CANR 24, 51; DLBY 84
Turgenev, Ivan 1818-1883 **NCLC 21; DA; DAB; DAC; DAM MST, NOV; DC 7; SSC 7; WLC**
Turgot, Anne-Robert-Jacques 1727-1781 . **L C 26**
Turner, Frederick 1943- .... **CLC 48**
See also CA 73-76; CAAS 10; CANR 12, 30, 56; DLB 40
Tutu, Desmond M(pilo) 1931- **CLC 80; BLC 3; DAM MULT**
See also BW 1; CA 125; CANR 67

Tutuola, Amos 1920-1997 **CLC 5, 14, 29; BLC 3; DAM MULT**
See also BW 2; CA 9-12R; 159; CANR 27, 66; DLB 125; MTCW 1, 2
Twain, Mark **TCLC 6, 12, 19, 36, 48, 59; SSC 34; WLC**
See also Clemens, Samuel Langhorne
See also AAYA 20; DLB 11, 12, 23, 64, 74
Tyler, Anne 1941- **CLC 7, 11, 18, 28, 44, 59, 103; DAM NOV, POP**
See also AAYA 18; BEST 89:1; CA 9-12R; CANR 11, 33, 53; DLB 6, 143; DLBY 82; MTCW 1, 2; SATA 7, 90
Tyler, Royall 1757-1826 .... **NCLC 3**
See also DLB 37
Tynan, Katharine 1861-1931 .... **TCLC 3**
See also CA 104; 167; DLB 153
Tyutchev, Fyodor 1803-1873 .... **NCLC 34**
Tzara, Tristan 1896-1963 **CLC 47; DAM POET**
See also CA 153; 89-92; MTCW 2
Uhry, Alfred 1936- **CLC 55; DAM DRAM, POP**
See also CA 127; 133; INT 133
Ulf, Haerved
See Strindberg, (Johan) August
Ulf, Harved
See Strindberg, (Johan) August
Ulibarri, Sabine R(eyes) 1919- **CLC 83; DAM MULT**
See also CA 131; DLB 82; HW
Unamuno (y Jugo), Miguel de 1864-1936 **TCLC 2, 9; DAM MULT, NOV; HLC; SSC 11**
See also CA 104; 131; DLB 108; HW; MTCW 1, 2
Undercliffe, Errol
See Campbell, (John) Ramsey
Underwood, Miles
See Glassco, John
Undset, Sigrid 1882-1949 **TCLC 3; DA; DAB; DAC; DAM MST, NOV; WLC**
See also CA 104; 129; MTCW 1, 2
Ungaretti, Giuseppe 1888-1970 **CLC 7, 11, 15**
See also CA 19-20; 25-28R; CAP 2; DLB 114
Unger, Douglas 1952- .... **CLC 34**
See also CA 130
Unsworth, Barry (Forster) 1930- .... **CLC 76**
See also CA 25-28R; CANR 30, 54; DLB 194
Updike, John (Hoyer) 1932- **CLC 1, 2, 3, 5, 7, 9, 13, 15, 23, 34, 43, 70; DA; DAB; DAC; DAM MST, NOV, POET, POP; SSC 13, 27; WLC**
See also CA 1-4R; CABS 1; CANR 4, 33, 51; CDALB 1968-1988; DLB 2, 5, 143; DLBD 3; DLBY 80, 82, 97; MTCW 1, 2
Upshaw, Margaret Mitchell
See Mitchell, Margaret (Munnerlyn)
Upton, Mark
See Sanders, Lawrence
Upward, Allen 1863-1926 .... **TCLC 85**
See also CA 117; DLB 36
Urdang, Constance (Henriette) 1922- **CLC 47**
See also CA 21-24R; CANR 9, 24
Uriel, Henry
See Faust, Frederick (Schiller)
Uris, Leon (Marcus) 1924- . **CLC 7, 32; DAM NOV, POP**
See also AITN 1, 2; BEST 89:2; CA 1-4R; CANR 1, 40, 65; MTCW 1, 2; SATA 49
Urmuz
See Codrescu, Andrei
Urquhart, Jane 1949- .... **CLC 90; DAC**
See also CA 113; CANR 32, 68

Wyndham, John .... **CLC 19**
 See also Harris, John (Wyndham Parkes Lucas)
 Beynon
Wyss, Johann David Von 1743-1818 **NCLC 10**
 See also JRDA; MAICYA; SATA 29; SATA-Brief
 27
Xenophon c. 430B.C.-c. 354B.C. ..... **CMLC 17**
 See also DLB 176
Yakumo Koizumi
 See Hearn, (Patricio) Lafcadio (Tessima Carlos)
Yamamoto, Hisaye 1921- **SSC 34; DAM MULT**
Yanez, Jose Donoso
 See Donoso (Yanez), Jose
Yanovsky, Basile S.
 See Yanovsky, V(assily) S(emenovich)
Yanovsky, V(assily) S(emenovich) 1906-1989
 CLC 2, 18
 See also CA 97-100; 129
Yates, Richard 1926-1992 .... **CLC 7, 8, 23**
 See also CA 5-8R; 139; CANR 10, 43; DLB 2;
 DLBY 81, 92; INT CANR-10
Yeats, W. B.
 See Yeats, William Butler
Yeats, William Butler 1865-1939 **TCLC 1, 11,**
 18, 31; DA; DAB; DAC; DAM DRAM,
 MST, POET; PC 20; WLC
 See also CA 104; 127; CANR 45; CDBLB
 1890-1914; DLB 10, 19, 98, 156; MTCW 1,
 2
Yehoshua, A(braham) B. 1936- .... **CLC 13, 31**
 See also CA 33-36R; CANR 43
Yep, Laurence Michael 1948- .... **CLC 35**
 See also AAYA 5; CA 49-52; CANR 1, 46; CLR
 3, 17, 54; DLB 52; JRDA; MAICYA; SATA
 7, 69
Yerby, Frank G(arvin) 1916-1991 **CLC 1, 7, 22;**
 BLC 3; DAM MULT
 See also BW 1; CA 9-12R; 136; CANR 16, 52;
 DLB 76; INT CANR-16; MTCW 1
Yesenin, Sergei Alexandrovich
 See Esenin, Sergei (Alexandrovich)
Yevtushenko, Yevgeny (Alexandrovich) 1933-
 CLC 1, 3, 13, 26, 51; DAM POET
 See also CA 81-84; CANR 33, 54; MTCW 1
Yezierska, Anzia 1885(?)-1970 .... **CLC 46**
 See also CA 126; 89-92; DLB 28; MTCW 1
Yglesias, Helen 1915- .... **CLC 7, 22**
 See also CA 37-40R; CAAS 20; CANR 15, 65;
 INT CANR-15; MTCW 1
Yokomitsu Riichi 1898-1947 .... **TCLC 47**
 See also CA 170
Yonge, Charlotte (Mary) 1823-1901 **TCLC 48**
 See also CA 109; 163; DLB 18, 163; SATA 17
York, Jeremy
 See Creasey, John
York, Simon
 See Heinlein, Robert A(nson)
Yorke, Henry Vincent 1905-1974 .... **CLC 13**
 See also Green, Henry
 See also CA 85-88; 49-52
Yosano Akiko 1878-1942 ..... **TCLC 59; PC 11**
 See also CA 161
Yoshimoto, Banana .... **CLC 84**
 See also Yoshimoto, Mahoko
Yoshimoto, Mahoko 1964-
 See Yoshimoto, Banana
 See also CA 144
Young, Al(bert James) 1939- **CLC 19; BLC 3;**
 DAM MULT
 See also BW 2; CA 29-32R; CANR 26, 65; DLB
 33
Young, Andrew (John) 1885-1971 .... **CLC 5**
 See also CA 5-8R; CANR 7, 29

Young, Collier
 See Bloch, Robert (Albert)
Young, Edward 1683-1765 .... **LC 3, 40**
 See also DLB 95
Young, Marguerite (Vivian) 1909-1995 **CLC 82**
 See also CA 13-16; 150; CAP 1
Young, Neil 1945- .... **CLC 17**
 See also CA 110
Young Bear, Ray A. 1950- .... **CLC 94; DAM**
 MULT
 See also CA 146; DLB 175; NNAL
Yourcenar, Marguerite 1903-1987 **CLC 19, 38,**
 50, 87; DAM NOV
 See also CA 69-72; CANR 23, 60; DLB 72;
 DLBY 88; MTCW 1, 2
Yurick, Sol 1925- .... **CLC 6**
 See also CA 13-16R; CANR 25
Zabolotsky, Nikolai Alekseevich 1903-1958
 TCLC 52
 See also CA 116; 164
Zamiatin, Yevgenii
 See Zamyatin, Evgeny Ivanovich
Zamora, Bernice (B. Ortiz) 1938- .... **CLC 89;**
 DAM MULT; HLC
 See also CA 151; DLB 82; HW
Zamyatin, Evgeny Ivanovich 1884-1937 **TCLC**
 8, 37
 See also CA 105; 166
Zangwill, Israel 1864-1926 .... **TCLC 16**
 See also CA 109; 167; DLB 10, 135, 197
Zappa, Francis Vincent, Jr. 1940-1993
 See Zappa, Frank
 See also CA 108; 143; CANR 57
Zappa, Frank .... **CLC 17**
 See also Zappa, Francis Vincent, Jr.
Zaturenska, Marya 1902-1982 .... **CLC 6, 11**
 See also CA 13-16R; 105; CANR 22
Zeami 1363-1443 .... **DC 7**
Zelazny, Roger (Joseph) 1937-1995 ... **CLC 21**
 See also AAYA 7; CA 21-24R; 148; CANR 26,
 60; DLB 8; MTCW 1, 2; SATA 57;
 SATA-Brief 39
Zhdanov, Andrei Alexandrovich 1896-1948
 TCLC 18
 See also CA 117; 167
Zhukovsky, Vasily (Andreevich) 1783-1852
 NCLC 35
 See also DLB 205
Ziegenhagen, Eric .... **CLC 55**
Zimmer, Jill Schary
 See Robinson, Jill
Zimmerman, Robert
 See Dylan, Bob
Zindel, Paul 1936- **CLC 6, 26; DA; DAB; DAC;**
 DAM DRAM, MST, NOV; DC 5
 See also AAYA 2; CA 73-76; CANR 31, 65; CLR
 3, 45; DLB 7, 52; JRDA; MAICYA; MTCW
 1, 2; SATA 16, 58, 102
Zinov'Ev, A. A.
 See Zinoviev, Alexander (Aleksandrovich)
Zinoviev, Alexander (Aleksandrovich) 1922-
 CLC 19
 See also CA 116; 133; CAAS 10
Zoilus
 See Lovecraft, H(oward) P(hillips)
Zola, Emile (Edouard Charles Antoine)
 1840-1902 **TCLC 1, 6, 21, 41; DA; DAB;**
 DAC; DAM MST, NOV; WLC
 See also CA 104; 138; DLB 123
Zoline, Pamela 1941- .... **CLC 62**
 See also CA 161

Zorrilla y Moral, Jose 1817-1893 ..... **NCLC 6**
Zoshchenko, Mikhail (Mikhailovich) 1895-1958
 TCLC 15; SSC 15
 See also CA 115; 160
Zuckmayer, Carl 1896-1977 .... **CLC 18**
 See also CA 69-72; DLB 56, 124
Zuk, Georges
 See Skelton, Robin
Zukofsky, Louis 1904-1978 **CLC 1, 2, 4, 7, 11,**
 18; DAM POET; PC 11
 See also CA 9-12R; 77-80; CANR 39; DLB 5,
 165; MTCW 1
Zweig, Paul 1935-1984 .... **CLC 34, 42**
 See also CA 85-88; 113
Zweig, Stefan 1881-1942 .... **TCLC 17**
 See also CA 112; 170; DLB 81, 118
Zwingli, Huldreich 1484-1531 .... **LC 37**
 See also DLB 179

Short Story Criticism
Cumulative Nationality Index

ALGERIAN
Camus, Albert **9**

AMERICAN
Adams, Alice (Boyd) **24**
Aiken, Conrad (Potter) **9**
Alcott, Louisa May **27**
Algren, Nelson **33**
Anderson, Sherwood **1**
Auchincloss, Louis (Stanton) **22**
Baldwin, James (Arthur) **10, 33**
Barnes, Djuna **3**
Barth, John (Simmons) **10**
Barthelme, Donald **2**
Beattie, Ann **11**
Bellow, Saul **14**
Benet, Stephen Vincent **10**
Berriault, Gina **30**
Bierce, Ambrose (Gwinett) **9**
Bowles, Paul (Frederick) **3**
Boyle, Kay **5**
Boyle, T(homas) Coraghessan **16**
Bradbury, Ray (Douglas) **29**
Cable, George Washington **4**
Caldwell, Erskine (Preston) **19**
Calisher, Hortense **15**
Capote, Truman **2**
Carver, Raymond **8**
Cather, Willa Sibert **2**
Chandler, Raymond (Thornton) **23**
Cheever, John **1**
Chesnutt, Charles W(addell) **7**
Chopin, Kate **8**
Cisneros, Sandra **32**
Coover, Robert (Lowell) **15**
Cowan, Peter (Walkinshaw) **28**
Crane, Stephen (Townley) **7**
Davenport, Guy (Mattison Jr.) **16**
Dixon, Stephen **16**
Dreiser, Theodore (Herman Albert) **30**
Dubus, Andre **15**
Dunbar, Paul Laurence **8**
Elkin, Stanley L(awrence) **12**
Ellison, Harlan (Jay) **14**
Ellison, Ralph (Waldo) **26**
Farrell, James T(homas) **28**
Faulkner, William (Cuthbert) **1**
Fisher, Rudolph **25**
Fitzgerald, F(rancis) Scott (Key) **6, 31**
Freeman, Mary Eleanor Wilkins **1**
Gardner, John (Champlin) Jr. **7**
Garland, (Hannibal) Hamlin **18**
Garrett, George (Palmer) **30**
Gass, William H(oward) **12**
Gilchrist, Ellen **14**
Gilman, Charlotte (Anna) Perkins (Stetson) **13**
Glasgow, Ellen (Anderson Gholson) **34**
Gordon, Caroline **15**
Grau, Shirley Ann **15**
Hammett, (Samuel) Dashiell **17**
Harris, Joel Chandler **19**
Harrison, James (Thomas) **19**
Harte, (Francis) Bret(t) **8**

Hawthorne, Nathaniel **3, 29**
Hemingway, Ernest (Miller) **1, 25**
Henderson, Zenna (Chlarson) **29**
Henry, O. **5**
Hughes, (James) Langston **6**
Hurston, Zora Neale **4**
Irving, Washington **2**
Jackson, Shirley **9**
James, Henry **8, 32**
Jewett, (Theodora) Sarah Orne **6**
<indKing, Stephen (Edwin) **17**
Lardner, Ring(gold) W(ilmer) **32**
Le Guin, Ursula K(roeber) **12**
Ligotti, Thomas (Robert) **16**
Lish, Gordon (Jay) **18**
London, Jack **4**
Lovecraft, H(oward) P(hillips) **3**
Maclean, Norman (Fitzroy) **13**
Malamud, Bernard **15**
Marshall, Paule **3**
Mason, Bobbie Ann **4**
McCarthy, Mary (Therese) **24**
McCullers, (Lula) Carson (Smith) **9, 24**
Melville, Herman **1, 17**
Michaels, Leonard **16**
Murfree, Mary Noailles **22**
Nabokov, Vladimir (Vladimirovich) **11**
Nin, Anais **10**
Norris, Frank **28**
Oates, Joyce Carol **6**
O'Connor, (Mary) Flannery **1, 23**
O'Hara, John (Henry) **15**
Olsen, Tillie **11**
Ozick, Cynthia **15**
Page, Thomas Nelson **23**
Paley, Grace **8**
Parker, Dorothy (Rothschild) **2**
Perelman, S(idney) J(oseph) **32**
Phillips, Jayne Anne **16**
Poe, Edgar Allan **1, 22**
Pohl, Frederik **25**
Porter, Katherine Anne **4, 31**
Powers, J(ames) F(arl) **4**
Price, (Edward) Reynolds **22**
Pynchon, Thomas (Ruggles Jr.) **14**
Roth, Philip (Milton) **26**
Salinger, J(erome) D(avid) **2, 28**
Saroyan, William **21**
Selby, Hubert Jr. **20**
Singer, Isaac Bashevis **3**
Stafford, Jean **26**
Stegner, Wallace (Earle) **27**
Steinbeck, John (Ernst) **11**
Stuart, Jesse (Hilton) **31**
Styron, William **25**
Suckow, Ruth **18**
Taylor, Peter (Hillsman) **10**
Thomas, Audrey (Callahan) **20**
Thurber, James (Grover) **1**
Toomer, Jean **1**
Twain, Mark **6, 26**
Updike, John (Hoyer) **13, 27**
Vinge, Joan (Carol) D(ennison) **24**

Vonnegut, Kurt Jr. **8**
Walker, Alice (Malsenior) **5**
Warren, Robert Penn **4**
Welty, Eudora **1, 27**
West, Nathanael **16**
Wharton, Edith (Newbold Jones) **6**
Williams, William Carlos **31**
Wodehouse, P(elham) G(renville) **2**
Wolfe, Thomas (Clayton) **33**
Wright, Richard (Nathaniel) **2**

ARGENTINIAN
Bioy Casares, Adolfo **17**
Borges, Jorge Luis **4**
Cortazar, Julio **7**
Valenzuela, Luisa **14**

AUSTRALIAN
Jolley, (Monica) Elizabeth **19**
Lawson, Henry (Archibald Hertzberg) **18**

AUSTRIAN
Kafka, Franz **5, 29**
Musil, Robert (Edler von) **18**
Schnitzler, Arthur **15**
Stifter, Adalbert **28**

BRAZILIAN
Lispector, Clarice **34**
Machado de Assis, Joaquim Maria **24**

CANADIAN
Atwood, Margaret (Eleanor) **2**
Bellow, Saul **14**
Gallant, Mavis **5**
Laurence, (Jean) Margaret (Wemyss) **7**
Munro, Alice **3**
Ross, (James) Sinclair **24**
Thomas, Audrey (Callahan) **20**

CHILEAN
Donoso (Yanez), Jose **34**

CHINESE
Chang, Eileen **28**
Lu Hsun **20**
P'u Sung-ling **31**

COLOMBIAN
Garcia Marquez, Gabriel (Jose) **8**

CUBAN
Calvino, Italo **3**

CZECH
Kafka, Franz **5, 29**
Kundera, Milan **24**

DANISH
Andersen, Hans Christian **6**
Dinesen, Isak **7**

ENGLISH
Ballard, J(ames) G(raham) **1**

SSC Cumulative Title Index

Title Index

Title Index

Title Index

Title Index

Title Index

Title Index

ISBN 0-7876-3080-2

9 780787 630805

90000

HAY LIBRARY
WESTERN WYOMING COMMUNITY COLLEGE